Fundamentals of
PSYCHOPATHOLOGY

Milestones in Psychopathology

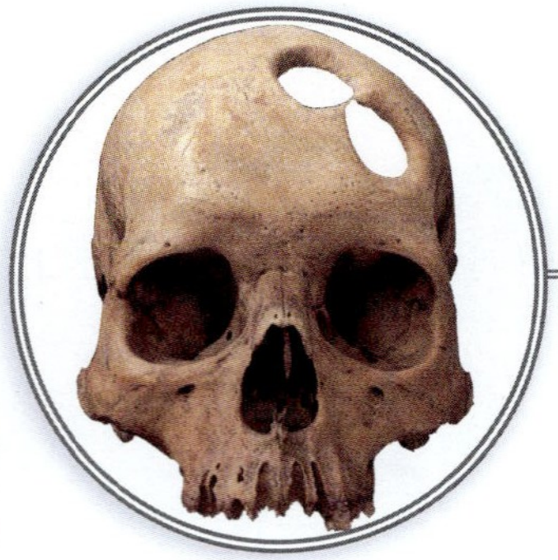
Professor John Verano

Library of Congress/Science Source

Jim Davis/The Boston Globe via Getty Images

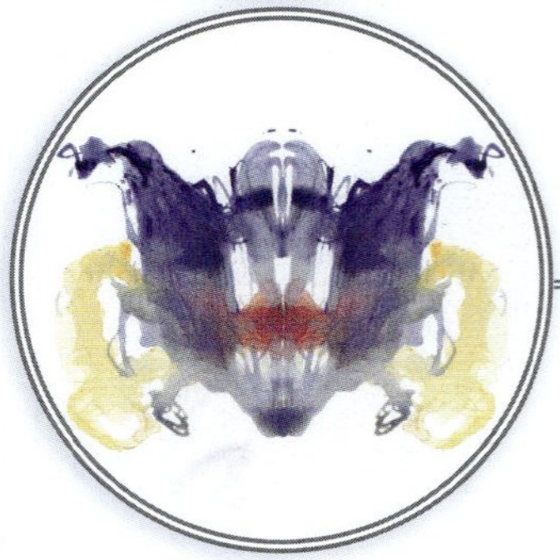
Spencer Sutton/Science Source

Stone Age	Mental disorders treated by trephination. p. 11
430–377 B.C.E.	Hippocrates cites brain as source of mental disorders. p. 11
500–1450	Middle Ages adopts demonological explanations and treatments. p. 12
1547	Bethlehem Hospital in London converted into asylum. p. 13
1693	Witch-hunting trials peak in Salem, Massachusetts. p. 12
1773	First American mental hospital opens in Williamsburg, Virginia. p. 14
1793	Philippe Pinel frees asylum patients at La Bicêtre in Paris. p. 14
1812	Benjamin Rush writes first American textbook on psychiatry. p. 14
1842	Dorothea Dix begins campaign to reform mental hospitals in the United States. p. 14
1865	Gregor Mendel publishes theories of genetics. p. 45
1879	Wilhelm Wundt establishes first laboratory for experimental study of psychology. p. 26
1883	Emil Kraepelin develops first modern system for classifying mental disorders. p. 15
1892	American Psychological Association founded. p. 23
1893	Sigmund Freud, with Josef Breuer, publishes first chapters of *On the Psychical Mechanisms of Hysterical Phenomena,* launching psychoanalysis. p. 49
1896	Lightner Witmer coins term "clinical psychology" and establishes first outpatient psychological clinic in the United States at the University of Pennsylvania. p. 23
1897	General paresis linked to physical cause, syphilis. p. 15
1900	Freud publishes *The Interpretation of Dreams.* p. 52
1900	Morton Prince uses hypnosis to treat multiple personality disorder. p. 176
1901	Ivan Pavlov demonstrates classical conditioning. p. 55
1905	First intelligence test published. p. 91
1907	Alzheimer's disease identified by Dr. Alois Alzheimer. p. 528
1909	Freud makes his only visit to America and lectures at Clark University. p. 17
1913	Behaviorist John Watson argues that psychology should abandon study of consciousness. p. 55
1917	The U.S. Congress declares all nonmedical opioids illegal. p. 339
1921	Rorschach test published. p. 84
1929	EEG developed. p. 88
1935	Alcoholics Anonymous founded. pp. 368–369
1935	First use of lobotomy for mental disorders. p. 411
1937	Marijuana made illegal throughout the entire United States. p. 355
1938	Electroconvulsive therapy introduced in Rome. p. 192
1938	B. F. Skinner proposes operant conditioning. p. 55
1939	The Wechsler–Bellevue Intelligence Scale published. p. 91
1943	LSD's hallucinogenic effect discovered. p. 349
1943	Minnesota Multiphasic Personality Inventory (MMPI) published. p. 86
1943	Jean-Paul Sartre's existential book *Being and Nothingness* published. p. 62
1949	Lithium salts first used for bipolar disorder. p. 213
1951	Chlorpromazine, first antipsychotic drug, tested. p. 413
1951	Carl Rogers publishes *Client-Centered Therapy.* p. 60
1952	First edition of DSM published by the American Psychiatric Association. p. 94
1955	The Los Angeles Suicide Prevention Center founded. p. 241

LHB Photo/Alamy

Sergio Flores/AFP via Getty Images

Ben Nelms/Reuters/Alamy Stock Photo

Hesther Ng/SOPA Images/Sipa USA via AP Images

1956 Family systems theory and therapy launched. p. 66
1958 Joseph Wolpe develops desensitization. p. 124
1961 Thomas Szasz publishes *The Myth of Mental Illness*. p. 7
1962 Albert Ellis proposes rational-emotive therapy. p. 115
1963 The Community Mental Health Act helps trigger deinstitutionalization in the United States. pp. 18, 419
1963 Antianxiety drug Valium introduced in the United States. p. 118
1964 U.S. Surgeon General warns that smoking can be dangerous to human health. pp. 342–343
1967 Aaron Beck publishes cognitive theory and therapy for depression. pp. 197, 201
1967 Methadone maintenance treatment begins. p. 367
1970 Masters and Johnson publish *Human Sexual Inadequacy* and launch sex therapy. pp. 365–366
1972 CAT scan introduced. p. 90
1973 DSM stops listing homosexuality as a mental disorder. p. 99
1975 Endorphins—natural opioids—discovered in human brain. p. 339
1975 U.S. Supreme Court declares that patients in institutions have right to adequate treatment. pp. 555–556
1981 MRI first used as diagnostic tool. p. 90
1982 John Hinckley found not guilty by reason of insanity for the attempted murder of President Reagan. p. 545
1987 Antidepressant Prozac approved in the United States. p. 190
1988 Association for Psychological Science founded. p. 26
1990 FDA approves clozapine, first of the second-generation antipsychotic drugs. p. 415
1995 APA task force begins search to identify empirically supported (evidence-based) treatments. p. 101
1997 PTSD patients are treated with virtual reality programs first time. pp. 164–165
1998 Viagra goes on sale in the United States, followed later by Cialis, Levitra, and Stendra. p. 370
1999 Killing rampage at Columbine High School stirs public concern about dangerousness in children. p. 554
2000 Scientists finish mapping (i.e., sequencing) the human genome. p. 45
2002 New Mexico grants prescription privileges to specially trained psychologists. pp. 558–559
2004 FDA orders black box warnings on all antidepressant drug containers. p. 482
2006 U.S. Supreme Court upholds Oregon's Death with Dignity Act. p. 239
2008 Canadian government apologizes for its role in the Canadian Indian residential school system, which had forcibly separated 150,000 Indigenous children from their families and cultures. p. 72
2011 The American Psychological Association declares its support for the legalization of same-sex marriages. pp. 99, 374
2012 Marijuana use (for any purpose) made legal in Colorado and Washington. p. 356
2013 DSM-5 published. p. 94
2014 The Affordable Care Act goes into effect, requiring all insurance plans to offer equal ("parity") coverage for mental and physical problems. p. 21
2016 CDC publishes physician guidelines for prescribing pain relievers to help address opioid crisis. p. 341
2017 APA Code of Ethics declares that psychologists must not "participate in, facilitate, assist, or otherwise engage in torture." pp. 562–563
2018 The World Health Organization announces plans to remove transgender functioning as a mental disorder in ICD-11, the newest edition of its classification system. pp. 99, 196
2020 In response to the COVID-19 pandemic, federal and state policy makers mandate that all insurance plans provide coverage for telemental health services. p. 24
2020 The president of the American Psychological Association states, "We are living in a racism pandemic, which is taking a heavy psychological toll on our African American citizens." pp. 71–72
2021 The American Psychological Association declares that sexual orientation change efforts (SOCE) and gender identity change efforts (GICE) are harmful and should not be conducted. pp. 224, 225, 374
2022 DSM-5-TR published. p. 94

Achieve for Psychology

Engaging Every Student. Supporting Every Instructor. Setting the New Standard for Teaching and Learning.

Overview

Co-designed with instructors and students to foster engagement, Macmillan Learning's Achieve complements instructors' unique teaching styles and course needs with effective **assessment, activities,** and **analytics**. Developed through years of research and continuous improvement, Achieve leads the market in the breadth and quality of its content library for psychology, giving instructors an unparalleled array of teaching tools and the ability to customize them for any course.

- **Assessment** Assessment is fundamental to Achieve. This course includes a variety of ***formative and summative assessment tools***, including our popular adaptive quizzing system ***LearningCurve***, and ***Practice Quizzes*** and ***Test Bank*** questions—all written for this specific title.
- **Activities** In addition to the full ***e-book***, this title features an extensive ***video library***, ***immersive learning activities*** to help students build their critical and scientific thinking, ***skill-building activities*** to increase student success and retention (syllabus reading, time management, etc.), and more.
- **Analytics** The ***Reports and Insights*** area of Achieve tracks students' engagement and performance against course learning objectives. Keep track of your students' activity and monitor their progress on key learning objectives in real time!

All of this exists in a **mobile-friendly interface**, ready for **deep platform integration with your campus LMS**, and built to industry-leading standards of **accessibility** to meet the needs of ALL learners!

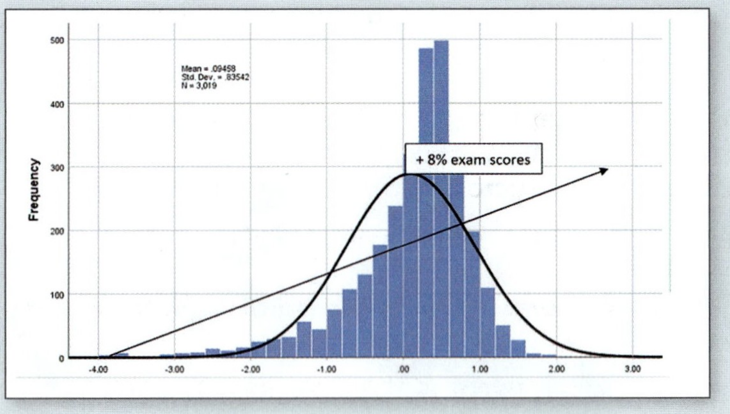

Achieve supports exam success! In a recent study of 3,000 students, increased usage of Achieve was associated with an eight percent increase in exam scores.

Macmillan Learning makes Achieve easy to access and implement for your course.

- **Customer Support** Our Achieve Client Success Team—dedicated platform experts—provides collaboration, software expertise, and consulting to tailor each course to fit your instructional goals and student needs. Start with a demo at a time that works for you to learn more about how to set up your customized course. Sign up for a demo or training at go.oncehub.com/AchieveTraining.
- **LMS Integration** Macmillan Learning offers ***deep platform integration*** of Achieve with all LMS providers, including Canvas, Blackboard, Brightspace, and Moodle. With integration, students can access course content and their grades through one sign-in. And you can pair Achieve with course tools from your LMS, such as discussion boards, chat, and gradebook functionality. LMS integration is also available with ***Inclusive Access***. For more information, visit MacmillanLearning.com/college/us/solutions/LMS-Integration, or talk to your local sales representative.
- **Affordability** Macmillan Learning's Achieve was developed with affordability in mind, in order to *inspire what's possible for every learner!* Pricing and bundling options are available at Store.MacmillanLearning.com.
- **Accessibility** Macmillan Learning builds all of our online products to WCAG 2.1 AA compliance standards and has been recognized as Global Certified Accessible by the nonprofit Benetech for providing "born accessible" products. For more information, visit MacmillanLearning.com/college/us/Our-Story/Accessibility.
- **Inclusion** Macmillan Learning is committed to taking steps that ensure our textbooks and digital courseware consider the backgrounds and needs of our community of learners, with the knowledge that diversity, equity, and inclusion (DEI) landscapes are constantly evolving. That's why we dedicate so much of our content and product development processes to critical self-reflection, listening, planning, innovation, and collaboration. From the art and photo program, to the presentation of research and perspectives, to the language used in the narrative and assessment, to the accessibility of Achieve, DEI in learning materials matters at Macmillan. For more information, visit MacmillanLearning.com/college/us/Our-Story/Diversity-and-Inclusion.

Assessment

LearningCurve Adaptive Quizzing

Based on extensive learning and memory research, and proven effective for millions of students, LearningCurve adaptive quizzing helps students practice core concepts and gives them instant feedback on their responses. After identifying the student's level of understanding, the system adapts to each student—choosing questions that will challenge them based on their performance. Each question is tied to a learning objective and linked to the appropriate section of the e-book to encourage students to discover the right answer—with no penalty to their grade. LearningCurve has consistently been rated the #1 resource in our collection by instructors and students alike.

- LearningCurve's game-like quizzing promotes retrieval practice through its unique delivery of questions and its point system.
- Students with a firm grasp on the material get plenty of practice but proceed through the activity relatively quickly.
- Students who make incorrect guesses are given more questions, so that they get the practice they need.

- Instructors can adjust the quiz topics and the Target Score, so students have to answer more (or fewer) questions to complete the quiz.
- Instructors can monitor results for each student and the class as a whole to identify areas that may need more coverage in lectures and assignments.

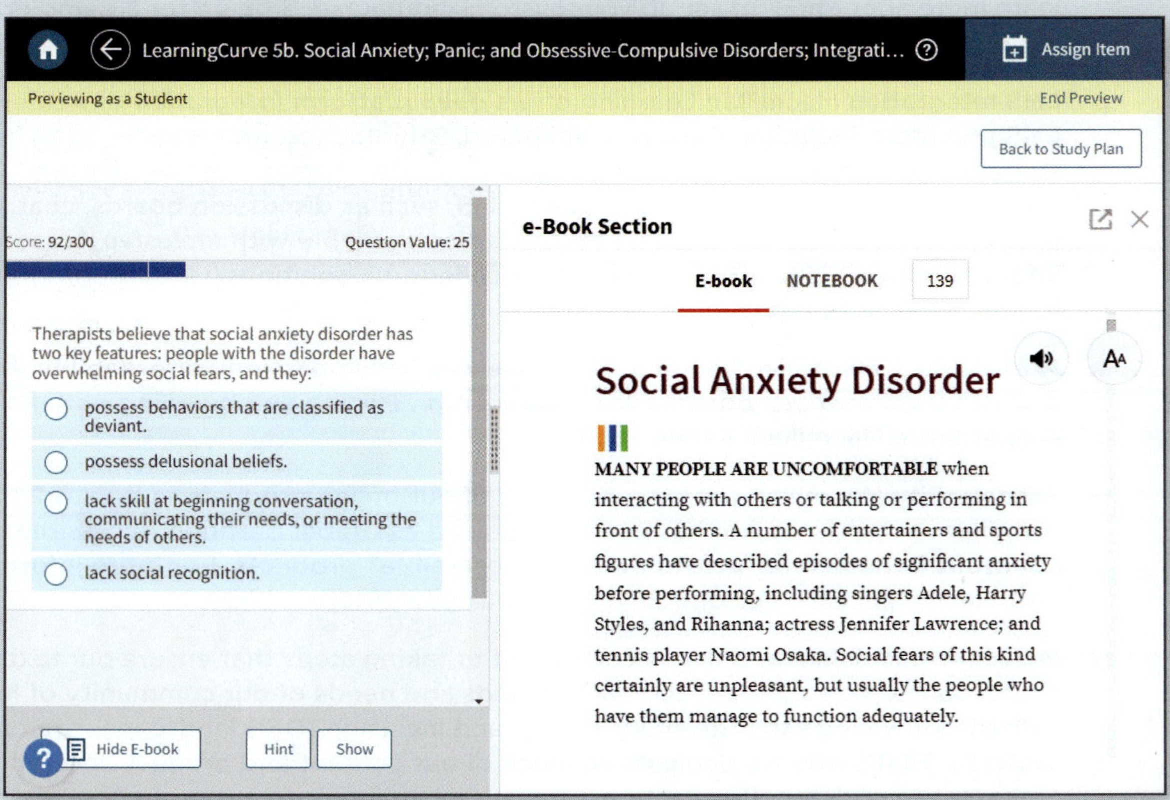

Test Bank

The Test Bank includes thousands of multiple choice and essay questions meticulously checked against the updated content of the text, and tagged to content learning objectives. All questions are written and edited according to Macmillan Learning's guidelines for clarity and accuracy, and third-party checked to ensure they meet Macmillan's DEI standards. You can assign out-of-the-box exams or create your own by:

- choosing from thousands of multiple-choice questions (plus additional essay questions) in our database.
- filtering questions by type, topic, difficulty, and Bloom's level.
- customizing questions from the test bank.
- integrating your own questions into the exam.

Exam and quiz results report to a Gradebook that lets you monitor student progress individually and classwide.

Practice Quizzes

Practice Quizzes mirror the experience of a test, with questions that are similar but distinct from those in the Test Bank. Each quiz includes a pool of multiple-choice questions for each of the major sections of the chapter. The system randomly selects multiple questions from each pool, so each student receives a unique set of questions, covering all of the major sections in the chapter. The Practice Quizzes are fully customizable and can be assigned for practice or for credit.

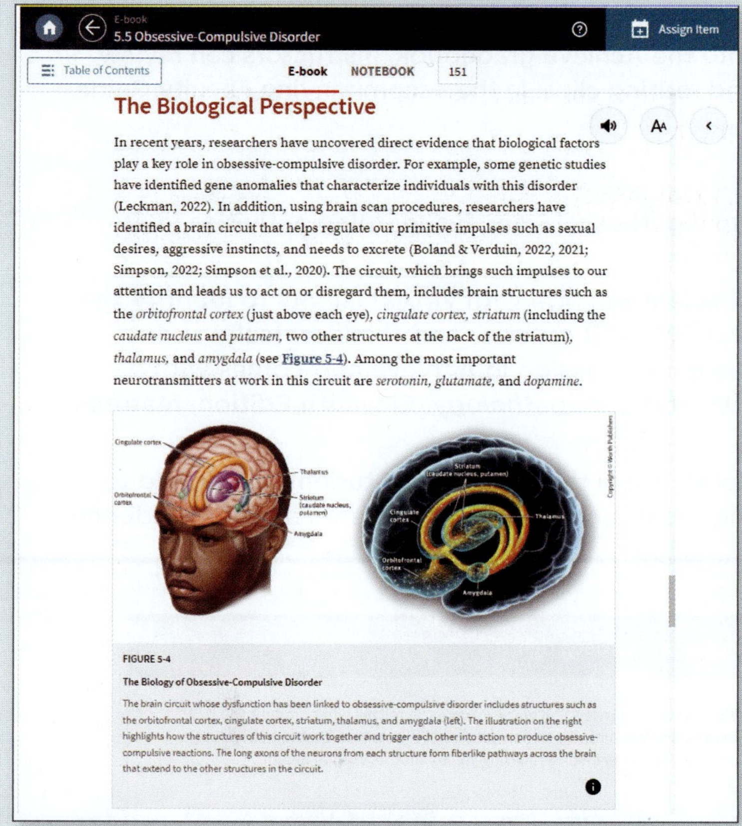

E-book

Macmillan Learning's e-book is an interactive version of the textbook built to industry-leading standards of web accessibility. In addition to highlighting, bookmarking, and note-taking capabilities, students can also test themselves with built-in, low-stakes self-assessments. The font resizing options include *OpenDyslexic*, a typeface to help mitigate some of the common reading errors caused by dyslexia. And all of the photos and figures come with alt text that is compatible with screen readers and other assistive technologies. Students can download the e-book to read offline, or have it read aloud to them.

Activities

Achieve is designed to support and encourage active learning in and out of the classroom!

Video Collection for Psychopathology

This extraordinary collection features over 250 clips from high-quality sources—classic and contemporary—as well as engaging original content, all selected by authors Ronald Comer and Jonathan Comer. It's a remarkably diverse and versatile resource, perfect for illustrating key concepts, stimulating in-class discussion, and bringing online coursework to life.

Newsy/BoClips

The collection includes 68 new clips on captivating topics such as:

- The lived experience of people with disorders such as PTSD and Autism Spectrum Disorder
- Neurodiversity and neurodivergence
- Gender diversity
- Postpartum depression and psychosis
- Culturally responsive therapies
- ADHD in female and adult populations
- Race and mental health
- Clinician-police partnerships to reduce arrests of people with mental disorders

Videos are fully accessible and closed-captioned, and each clip is available as a Video Activity, which includes assessment questions with results reporting into the Achieve gradebook. Instructors can review detailed video descriptions, and information on new and retiring clips, in the accompanying Faculty Guide.

Immersive Learning Activities

With a focus on student engagement and critical thinking, these immersive learning activities invite students to explore the work of clinicians and researchers.

- In **Clinical Choices**, students experience how clinicians engage with virtual clients to identify the symptoms of psychological disorders (based on DSM-5-TR criteria) and think critically about diagnosis and treatment options. Each activity is easy to assign in Achieve and comes with a separate quiz for easy assessment. *Fundamentals of Psychopathology*, Eleventh Edition, features two new and two completely revised scenarios.
- **Research Exercises** in each chapter help stimulate critical thinking skills. Students are asked to consider real research, make connections among ideas, and analyze arguments and the evidence on which they are based.

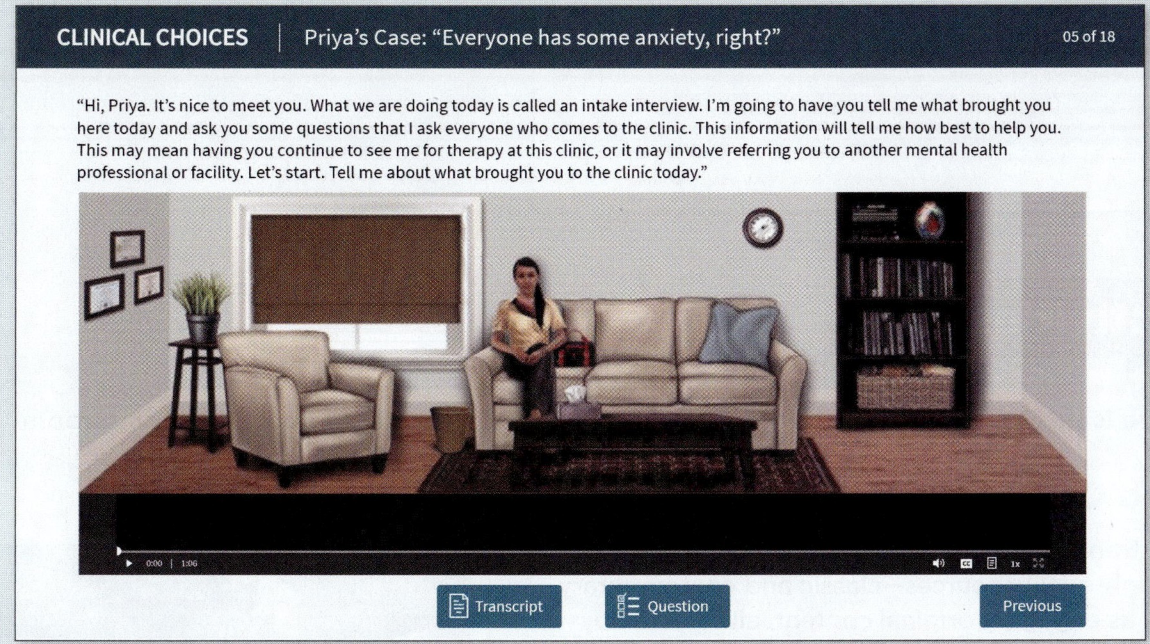

NEW Skills for Success Activities

We worked with instructors to build a collection of interactive Skills for Success activities to help ***increase student success and retention***, based on survey feedback about the essential skills needed for psychology students. Topics include How to Read a Syllabus, Time Management, Note Taking, APA Style, and How to Read a Research Paper. These engaging activities guide students through the key elements and include assessment to test student understanding and allow for assignability, so that you don't need to spend precious class time on student preparedness.

Instructor Activity Guides

Instructor Activity Guides provide you with a structured plan for using Achieve's active learning opportunities in both face-to-face and online courses. Each guide offers step-by-step instructions—from pre-class reflection to in-class engagement to post-class follow-up. The guides include suggestions for discussion questions, group work, presentations, and simulations, with estimated class time, implementation effort, and Bloom's taxonomy level for each activity.

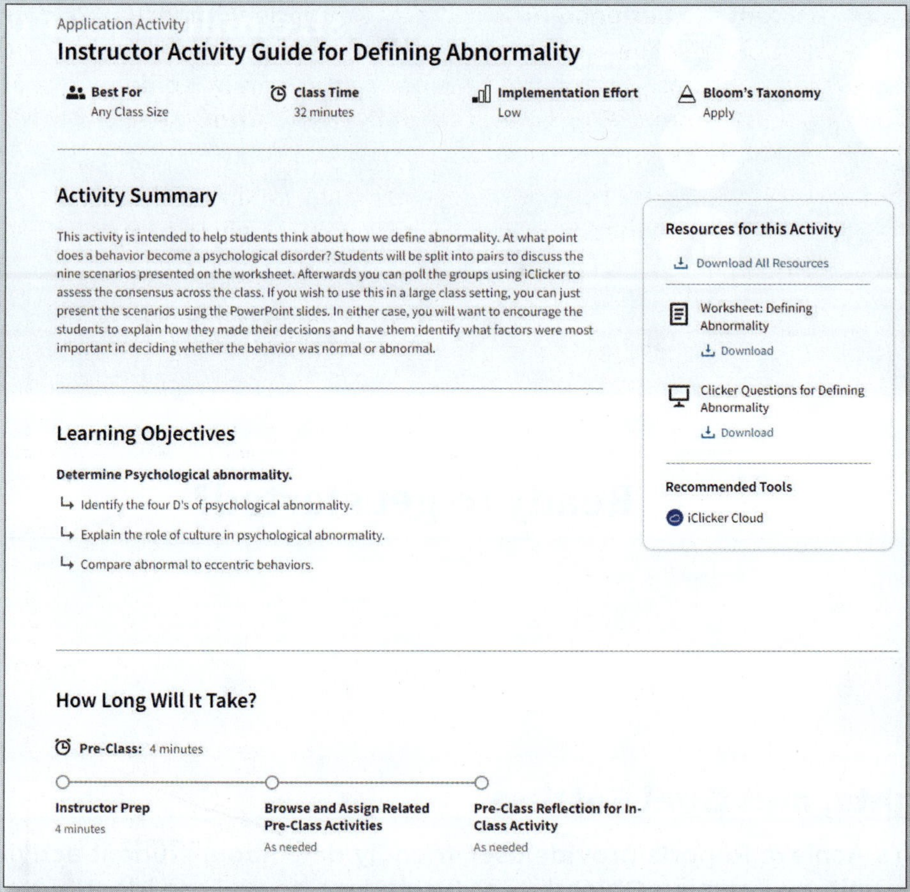

iClicker Classroom Response System

Achieve seamlessly integrates iClicker, Macmillan Learning's highly acclaimed classroom response system. Free with Achieve, iClicker helps you engage, assess, and guide learning.

- iClicker's attendance feature helps you make sure students are actually attending in-person classes.
- Use flexible polling and quizzing options to engage students, check their understanding, and get their feedback in real time.
- iClicker allows students to participate using laptops, mobile devices, or in-class remotes.
- You can easily integrate your existing slides and polling questions without re-entering them.
- Take advantage of the available chapter-specific questions, as well as the questions in our Instructor Activity Guides, to improve opportunities for all students to be active in class.

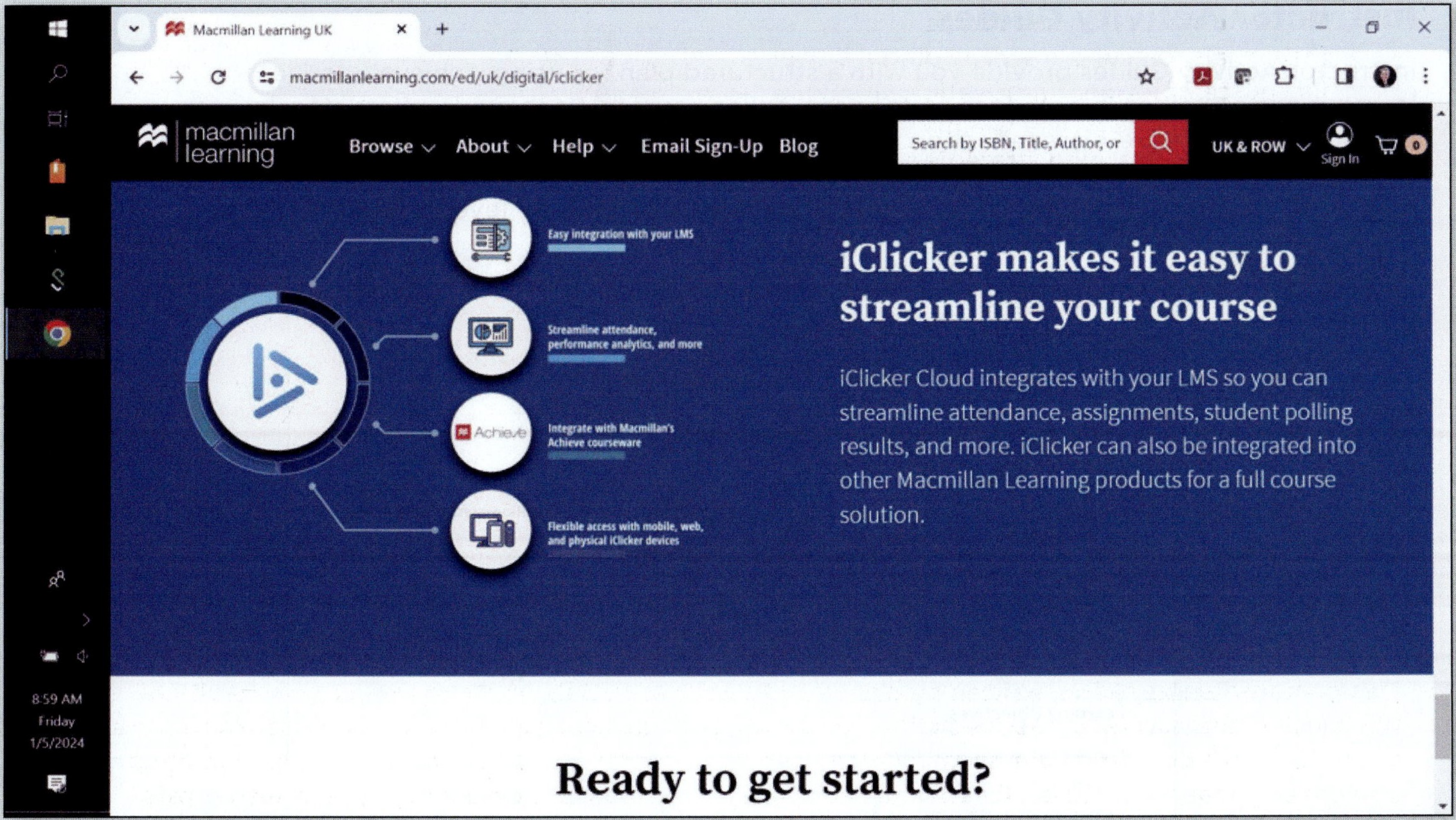

Analytics

Reports, Insights, and Goal Setting

Macmillan Learning's Achieve Reports provide user-friendly data about student activities, assignments, and assessments by unit, by Learning Objective, or by student, so you can identify trouble spots and adjust your efforts accordingly. The Achieve Insights allow you to answer such questions as:

- What Learning Objectives and assignments should I review in this unit?
- What is the range of performance on a particular assignment?
- How many students aren't logging in?

Goal-Setting and Reflection surveys help students plan and direct their learning, and provide instructors with an unprecedented view into students' metacognition. These tools help students develop control over their learning and foster a growth mindset to build long-lasting academic success.

- The **Intro Survey** asks students to consider their goals for the class, providing a powerful source of intrinsic motivation. Students then consider how they will manage their time and use learning strategies to achieve their plan.
- **Checkpoint Surveys** ask students to monitor and assess their progress, and prompt them to make changes as needed.
- **Each completed survey generates a report** for the instructor that reveals how the class is progressing—going well beyond the course grades.

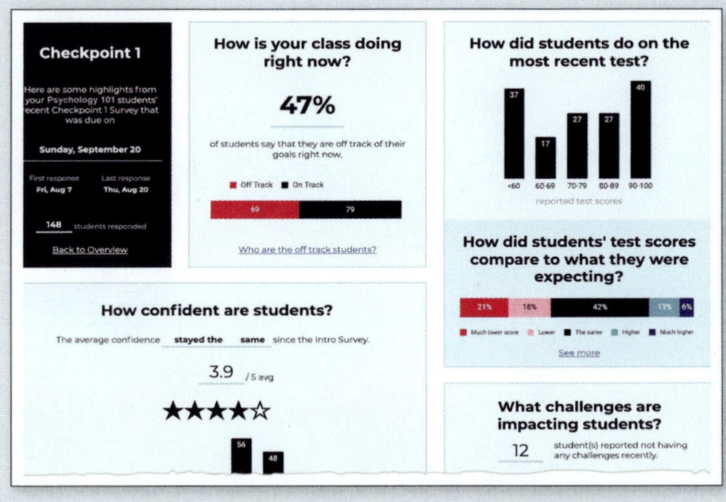

Additional Instructor Resources

Instructor's Resource Manual

This comprehensive guide, written by experienced instructor Jeffrey B. Henriques (University of Wisconsin-Madison) and seasoned clinician Laurie Frost, ties together the resource package for users of the Eleventh Edition. The manual includes detailed chapter outlines, lists of principal learning objectives, ideas for lectures, classroom activities, extra credit projects, and more. It also offers strategies for using the accompanying videos and media, as well as materials from outside sources such as feature films, documentaries, and more.

Image Slides and Tables

Accessible, downloadable Image Slides contain chapter illustrations, photos, and tables, and can be customized to fit your needs. All images come with alt text embedded for learners using assistive software.

Lecture Slides

Accessible, downloadable Lecture Slides include the chapter illustrations, photos, tables, and embedded alt text, but also provide lecture outlines to support key concepts and themes from the text. Lecture slides can also be customized to fit your needs.

iClicker Questions

Take active learning and student engagement to another level with our iClicker classroom response system, which is fully integrated and free with Achieve. Engaging iClicker **questions** are available for each chapter.

Macmillan Learning's Achieve Read & Practice

Seamlessly integrating with any LMS, Achieve Read & Practice marries Macmillan Learning's mobile-accessible e-book with the acclaimed LearningCurve adaptive quizzing. It is an easy-to-use yet exceptionally powerful teaching and learning option that streamlines the process of increasing student engagement and understanding, and reduces cost. If students struggle with a particular topic, they are encouraged to re-read the material and answer a few short additional questions. Achieve Read & Practice makes it easy to integrate the e-book with assignments in your campus LMS. See MacmillanLearning.com/ReadandPractice for more information.

Fundamentals of PSYCHOPATHOLOGY

ELEVENTH EDITION

RONALD J. COMER • **JONATHAN S. COMER**
Princeton University
Florida International University

worth publishers
Macmillan Learning
New York

Program Director, Editorial Development, Psychology: Suzanne Jeans
Executive Manager, Development, Psychology: Christine Brune
Senior Executive Program Manager: Daniel DeBonis
Associate Development Editor: Nick Rizzuti
Assistant Editor: Emily Kelly
Director of Media Editorial: Adam Whitehurst
Media Editors: Clarah Grossman, Andrew Sylvester
Executive Manager, Marketing: Katherine Nurre
Senior Director, Content Management Enhancement: Tracey Kuehn
Executive Managing Editor: Michael Granger
Senior Manager of Publishing Services: Gregory Erb
Lead Content Project Manager: Pamela Lawson
Workflow Project Manager: Lisa McDowell
Production Supervisor: Jose Olivera
Director of Design, Content Management: Diana Blume
Senior Design Services Manager: Natasha A. S. Wolfe
Interior Design: Dirk Kaufman
Cover Design: John Callahan
Art Manager: Matthew McAdams
Illustrations: Charles Yuen
Senior Director, Rights and Permissions: Hilary Newman
Text Permissions Researcher: Elaine Kosta, Lumina Datamatics, Inc.
Executive Manager, Permissions: Christine Buese
Photo Editor: Jennifer Atkins
Senior Director of Digital Production: Keri deManigold
Advanced Media Project Manager: Eve Conte
Editorial Services: Lumina Datamatics, Inc.
Copyeditor: Bruce Owens
Composition: Lumina Datamatics, Inc.
Printing and Binding: Lakeside Book Company

Library of Congress Control Number: 2024932682

ISBN 978-1-319-47251-1 (paperback)
ISBN 978-1-319-54228-3 (Loose-leaf Edition)
ISBN 978-1-319-58980-6 (International Edition)

Printed in the United States of America.

1 2 3 4 5 6 29 28 27 26 25 24

Acknowledgments

Text acknowledgments and copyrights appear at the back of the book on page C-1, which constitutes an extension of the copyright page. Art acknowledgments and copyrights appear on the same page as the art selections they cover.

Worth Publishers
120 Broadway
New York, NY 10271
www.macmillanlearning.com

With great appreciation, to Dan DeBonis, who oversees our books with boundless wisdom, vision, and verve.

About the Authors

Denise Applewhite, Princeton University

Courtesy Jon Comer

RONALD J. COMER has been a professor in Princeton University's Department of Psychology for the past 50 years, also serving for many years as director of Clinical Psychology Studies and as chair of the university's Institutional Review Board. In 2016 he transitioned to emeritus status at the university. He has received the President's Award for Distinguished Teaching at Princeton, where his various courses in psychopathology were among the university's most popular.

Professor Comer is also Clinical Associate Professor of Family Medicine and Community Health at Rutgers Robert Wood Johnson Medical School. He has also been a practicing clinical psychologist and served as a consultant to numerous hospitals, family practice residency programs, and autism programs.

In addition to writing the textbooks *Fundamentals of Psychopathology* (eleventh edition), *Psychopathology: Science and Practice* (twelfth edition), *Psychology Around Us* (fourth edition), and *Case Studies in Abnormal Psychology* (third edition), Professor Comer has published a range of journal articles and produced numerous widely used educational video programs, including *The Higher Education Video Library Series, The Video Anthology for Psychopathology, The Worth Video Collection for Psychopathology, Video Segments in Neuroscience, Introduction to Psychology Video Clipboard,* and *Developmental Psychology Video Clipboard.*

Professor Comer was an undergraduate at the University of Pennsylvania and a graduate student at Clark University. He currently lives in Florida with his wife, Marlene.

JONATHAN S. COMER is a professor of psychology at Florida International University, where he also directs the Mental Health Interventions and Novel Therapeutics (MINT) Program and the Network for Enhancing Wellness in Disaster-Affected Youth (NEW DAY). He is Past President of the Society of Clinical Psychology (Division 12 of the American Psychological Association) and a leader in the field of child mental health. The author of over 250 scientific papers and chapters, he has received career awards from the American Psychological Association, the Association for Psychological Science, and the Association for Behavioral and Cognitive Therapies for his research on innovative treatment methods, child anxiety and behavioral challenges, the intergenerational transmission of psychopathology, and the impact of traumatic stress, disasters, and public health crises on children.

In addition to *Fundamentals of Psychopathology* (eleventh edition) and *Psychopathology: Science and Practice* (twelfth edition), Professor Comer has authored *Childhood Disorders* (second edition) and edited *The Oxford Handbook of Research Strategies for Clinical Psychology*. He serves as Editor of the journal *Behavior Therapy* and is a Fellow of the American Psychological Association. He is also a practicing clinical psychologist.

Professor Comer was an undergraduate at the University of Rochester and a graduate student at Temple University. He currently lives in South Florida with his wife, Jami, and their children Delia and Emmett. He loves being dazzled by his daughter's stunning artwork and his son's electrifying basketball skills. He also enjoys playing and listening to music, painting rocks with his family, and keeping an eye on the often-frustrating Philadelphia sports teams that his father taught him to love/hate.

Brief Contents

Psychopathology: Science and Clinical Practice

Problems of Anxiety and Mood

Problems of the Mind and Body

Problems of Psychosis

Life-Span Problems

Conclusion

Contents

CHAPTER 15

CHAPTER 16

Preface

So what's happened since we wrote our previous edition of this textbook three years ago? As usual, quite a bit. When we published that edition, Covid-19 was spreading across the world and, to one degree or another, affecting the daily activities, emotions, decision-making, family life, social relationships, work and school routines, economic security, and well-being of everyone on earth. Correspondingly, much of that edition focused on the unfolding psychological impact of the pandemic. Today, while Covid-19 is still very much around us, the worst of the pandemic is considered largely over. Given the passage of time and the virus's current status, our new edition is able to look at the past psychological impact of the pandemic with research-based observations and to also consider the continuing effects of the pandemic on psychological functioning today.

At the same time, the evolution of the pandemic is not the only momentous occurrence since the writing of our previous edition. In particular, many people in our society have experienced a dramatic growth in their appreciation of the moral importance of inclusion and the far-reaching benefits to society of diversity. Such growth has featured a heightened commitment to respecting people of all backgrounds, to welcoming multiple perspectives and viewpoints when solving complex problems, to ensuring everyone's fair access to opportunities and resources, to avoiding the marginalization or exclusion of individuals, and to eliminating discrimination and intolerance.

The growing recognition has permeated almost every realm of life, from the arts and the workplace to social relationships and discourse. It has likewise affected the study and treatment of psychopathology. In turn, in ways that we will discuss in detail shortly, this new edition of our textbook strives for sincere and pervasive inclusivity in its coverage, presentations, language, terminology, case material, art program, and more. Of course, this is not a new goal for us, but we, like so many others, have come to appreciate the limitations of our (and the clinical field's) past efforts.

Beyond the new dimensions and features hinted at in the previous paragraphs, this new edition adds important perspectives and features that broaden our presentation of psychopathology. For example, as you will also read shortly, we more prominently include in our coverage the viewpoints and efforts of people with *lived experience* (for example, those with mental health challenges), as well as the therapists who work with them and the researchers who study them. Such coverage includes discussions of the neurodiversity perspective, community-based participatory research, social activism by people with psychological challenges and their families, and therapist efforts at cultural humility.

Of course, the past three years have also witnessed other important developments in society and in the study and treatment of psychopathology, developments that have produced a broader array of clinical research strategies, a better understanding of various forms of psychopathology, novel biological and psychological treatments, changes in mental health-related laws, technological innovations, and more. Needless to say, these developments also receive in-depth coverage in the current edition of our textbook. Indeed, altogether, we have added an enormous amount of new material and important new features for this edition of *Fundamentals of Psychopathology*—while at the same time retaining the successful themes, material, and techniques that have been embraced enthusiastically by past students and instructors.

Between our two textbooks, *Fundamentals of Psychopathology* and *Psychopathology: Science and Practice,* the current textbook represents the twenty-fourth edition of one or the other. As we noted in previous editions, this textbook journey has been joyful and stimulating. Our goal has always been to make each edition fresh and relevant by approaching our coverage and pedagogical offerings as if we were writing a completely new book. As a result, each edition includes cutting-edge content reflecting new developments in the field, as well as in the world around us, delivered to readers via innovative and enlightening pedagogical techniques. We believe that the current edition once again meets these important criteria.

New and Expanded Features

This edition of *Fundamentals of Psychopathology* reflects the many changes that have occurred over the past several years in the fields of psychopathology, education, and publishing, and, as we noted earlier, in the world. Accordingly, we have introduced a number of new features and changes to the current edition.

New Book Title For those of you who have read our previous editions, the first thing you may notice is the change of title for our textbook, from the previous *Fundamentals of Abnormal Psychology* to the current *Fundamentals of Psychopathology*. There has been a growing unrest in the psychology field with the use of terms such as “abnormal” and “abnormality,” partly because the terms have become quite stigmatizing; and, indeed, many psychologists and scientific journals no longer feature those terms in their speech and writings. For example, in 2022 the prestigious *Journal of Abnormal Psychology* changed its long-standing name to the *Journal of Psychopathology and Clinical Science*. Similarly, we have changed the title of this textbook to refer to *psychopathology,* and in our discussions we largely use terms such as “psychopathology,” “psychological difficulties,” and “mental challenges.” At the same time, it is important to recognize that these terms are themselves less than perfect.

Al Bello/Getty Images

Stress and depression Correlational studies find that stressors produced by natural disasters, medical catastrophes, and the like are often accompanied by depression and other psychological symptoms. In the first year of the Covid-19 pandemic, for example, the stress of social distancing and extended separations resulted in severe levels of depression, loneliness, and other painful emotions for many people. Here, a woman hugs her granddaughter through a protective plastic drop sheet after the two had not seen each other for many months. (see page 28)

Newly Informed Pandemic-Related Discussions Although the worst of the worldwide pandemic appears to be largely behind us, its lingering psychological impact continues. In this edition, we discuss—now with the benefit of three years' worth of additional research—the impact that the pandemic had on psychological functioning and clinical treatment at its peak and the continuing effects that it has on many people and treatment programs. We have added a large body of pandemic-related material and findings throughout the book, covering ties between the pandemic and anxiety disorders, PTSD, job stress, depression, feelings of loneliness, suicide, immune system functioning, substance abuse, sexual functioning, domestic violence, eating disorders, feelings of distrust, and schizophrenia as well as the ties between the pandemic and the emergence of telemental health in the clinical field. (see, for example, pages 151, 237, 419, 473–476)

Heightened Emphasis on Inclusion and Diversity As discussed earlier, the clinical field has come to more comprehensively appreciate the importance of inclusion and the benefits of diversity in the understanding and treatment of people with psychological challenges. Correspondingly, these themes are woven into the fabric of this edition of *Fundamentals of Psychopathology*. Even a quick look through the pages of the book readily reveals the heterogeneity of our society and of the field of psychopathology—for example, in the book's use of wide-ranging case studies, rich contextual material, inclusive terminology and language, and diverse photography and art; in its many discussions of the research findings, risk factors, and cultural strengths found among people of various ethnicities, races, economic circumstances, genders, sexual orientations, immigration backgrounds, and abilities; and in its coverage of developments such as culturally responsive treatments, therapist cultural humility, community-based participatory research undertakings, cultural health disparities, intersectionality, historical trauma, cultural bereavement, affirmative therapy, diagnostic bias, the negative impacts of efforts to change sexual orientation or gender identity, and the psychological effects of discrimination and prejudice. (see, for example, pages 182–183, 204–206, 296–299)

Adam Scotti/Prime Minister's Office/Handout via Reuters/Redux

Historical trauma *Historical trauma* refers to the cumulative psychological wounds carried across generations by the members of a cultural group that was subjected to extraordinary past oppression such as slavery, genocide, forced migration, or violent colonialization. According to research, a variety of actions can help promote individual healing, reconciliation, and social change, including participation in community gatherings and peaceful demonstrations. Here, an Indigenous woman in Canada protests the generations of oppression experienced by her cultural group. (see page 157)

Additional Focus: The Lived Experience As we noted earlier, this edition of *Fundamentals of Psychopathology* includes the perspectives and efforts of people with *lived experience*—the individuals who experience mental health challenges—as well as their therapists and the researchers who study their difficulties. By including this frame of reference, the clinical field has enhanced its understanding of psychological challenges, widened its research undertakings, and improved its treatment approaches. The lived experience is on display, for example, in our book's discussions of the *neurodiversity* perspective (the view that the functioning and brains of autistic people and those with certain other challenges are simply different, not disordered), community-based participatory research undertakings, social activism by people with psychological difficulties and their families, and therapist efforts at cultural humility. (see, for example, pages 35, 72–73, 497–498, 502)

Additional Topics Over the past several years, many topics in psychopathology have received new or special attention, and in this edition we have added those important developments. In addition to the new material mentioned elsewhere in this preface, some of the other topics new to this edition are *generosity and mental health* (page 59); *prolonged grief disorder* (page 160); *climate change anxiety* (page 112); *overcrowding and stress* (page 269); *ACEs* (page 158); *written exposure therapy* (page 165); *988 Suicide and Crisis Lifeline* (page 242); *compulsive sexual behavior* (page 372); *sexual orientation change efforts, or SOCEs* (pages 224, 225, 374); *chatbots, sexbots, and sexual*

"Embracing neurodiversity" Today, many autistic people embrace the perspective of neurodiversity. Like the person in this photo, they do not view their autism as a disorder but rather a reflection of neurodivergent brain development and operation—alternative brain functioning that can, in fact, produce certain strengths and advantages if accommodated by the person's surrounding environment. (see page 498)

behavior (page 376); *supported employment* (page 422); *teenage heartache, depression, and angst* (pages 479, 481, 482); *joint police-counselor intervention programs for mental health crises* (page 553); *AI and mental health* (pages 376, 568); *changing health care laws* (pages 21, 24–25); *ketamine treatment for depression* (pages 190–191); *telemental health* (pages 24–25, 56); *mass shootings and mental health* (page 440); *social media employment screening* (page 80); *body shaming* (page 294); *athletes and eating disorders* (pages 293, 301); *the fentanyl crisis* (pages 319–320, 335, 346); *changing cannabis laws* (pages 331–332); *the normalization of sexting* (page 375); *mental health courts* (page 420); *mentalization* (pages 447, 449); *parenting interventions* (pages 486, 493, 504); *school lockdown drills and child anxiety* (pages 473, 476); and *outpatient civil commitment* (pages 548, 550, 553, 555).

More than a little off the top Louisville, Kentucky, barber Alex Daniel trims a man's hair as part of The Confess Project — a national *barbershop- based intervention* started by Lorenzo Lewis to train barbers and stylists in Black neighborhoods to become mental health advocates for their communities. Barbers in The Confess Project are taught how to comfortably discuss mental health issues with their customers and talk openly about emotions. (see page 35)

Additional Boxes In this edition we continue to offer a wide variety of boxes, including such new boxes as *A New Disorder: Prolonged Grief Disorder* (page 160) and *Gender Dysphoria: A Legitimate Category?* (pages 196–197).

Expanded Coverage of Modern Research Designs In this edition we offer a still broader array of the research designs and strategies used by today's clinical investigators. For example, we have added new and enhanced sections on *qualitative methods, mixed-methods designs*, and *community-based participatory research*; and we have discussed how such methods are transforming the reach and relevance of clinical programs—as exemplified by the research-based screening and support programs now conducted in barbershops and hair salons in underserved neighborhoods throughout the United States. (see, for example, pages 34, 35)

DSM-5-TR and Alternative Classification Systems In 2022, the American Psychiatric Association replaced DSM-5 with an amended version called DSM-5-TR (DSM-5 Text Revision). Our new edition of *Fundamentals of Psychopathology* examines the changes found in DSM-5-TR in depth, and discussions of DSM-5-TR are included throughout the book, highlighting the classification system's flaws as well as its utility. In addition to weaving DSM-5-TR material into the narrative of each chapter, we regularly provide a reader-friendly pedagogical feature called *Dx Checklist* to help students fully grasp DSM-5-TR and related diagnostic tools. At the same time, our new edition offers in-depth discussions of alternative diagnostic and classification systems such as the *Hierarchical Taxonomy of Psychopathology* (*HiTOP*), *Research Domain Criteria* (*RDoC*), and the *International Classification of Diseases* (*ICD*). (see, for example, pages 96–99, 109, 185, 464–467)

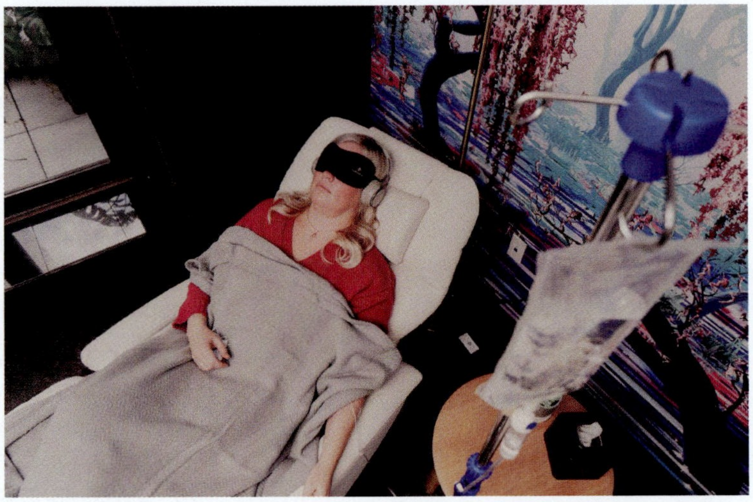

Victor Llo rente/The New York Times/Redux

Ketamine for severe depression This patient is receiving an intravenous infusion of ketamine under medical supervision. In an alternative ketamine-based approach, some patients with severe depression take a recently approved drug called esketamine, which is available as a nasal spray. (see page 190)

Relocating the Discussion of Transgender and Nonbinary Functioning Past editions of the DSM asserted that transgender and nonbinary people qualified for a diagnosis called *gender identity disorder,* a formal designation that inadvertently added to the clinical, societal, and legal mistreatment of these populations. That diagnostic category was finally dropped from the DSM and the ICD, but most textbooks continued to locate discussions of transgender functioning and nonbinary functioning as if they were forms of psychopathology. In our current edition, these gender variations are discussed instead in a section on the dangers of diagnosis and labeling, as an example of how past editions of the DSM sometimes incorrectly listed healthy but less common patterns of functioning as forms of psychopathology (page 99). In addition, we have moved the discussion of *gender dysphoria,* a current DSM category that connotes significant distress or impairment due to one's gender identity, to a box called *Gender Dysphoria: A Legitimate Category?* (pages 196–197). In that box and elsewhere we clarify that this DSM category is controversial, that ICD has now dropped *gender dysphoria* as a category of pathology, and that the category may also be dropped from future editions of the DSM.

Additional Focus on Technology In this edition we have further expanded the previous edition's focus on the psychological impact of technology and the use of new technology in treatment and research. Throughout the book — in numerous text discussions, *MindTech* boxes, photographs, and figures — we examine technology topics such as *telemental health* (pages 24–25, 56), *the growth of mental health apps* (pages 67, 103), *interventions that use smartwatches and other "wearables"* (page 67), *the normalization of sexting* (page 375), *online research strategies* (page 36), *social media and emotions* (page 128), *online bullying* (pages 472–474), *pro-Ana sites* (page 290), *live streaming of suicides* (page 223), *social media and older adults* (page 526), *AI and mental health* (pages 376, 568), and *chatbots, sexbots, and sexual behavior* (page 376).

Thorough Update In this edition we present the most current theories, research, and events, and we include more than 2,500 new references from the years 2022–2024, as well as numerous new photos, tables, and figures.

Continuing Strengths

As we noted earlier, in this edition we have also retained the themes, material, and techniques that have worked successfully for and been embraced enthusiastically by past readers.

Breadth and Balance The field's many theories, studies, disorders, and treatments are presented completely and accurately. All major models — psychological, biological, sociocultural, and integrative — receive objective, balanced, up-to-date coverage, without bias toward any single approach.

Integration of Models Discussions throughout the text help students better understand where and how the various models work together and how they differ.

Coverage of Brain Circuitry In this edition, *brain circuits* continue to be at the center of the textbook's biological discussions of the various psychological disorders, revealing how sets of particular neurons, brain structures, and brain chemicals communicate and work together to produce typical and atypical functioning. To bring greater clarity and relevance to readers, we have featured many stunning drawings of the circuits in action, indicating how their parts interconnect and bringing the biological explanations to life. (see, for example, pages 44–45, 138–139, 401–402)

Enhanced Coverage of the Developmental Psychopathology Perspective We have continued and expanded our coverage of the *developmental psychopathology perspective,* the cutting-edge viewpoint that helps integrate the explanations and treatments offered by the various models of psychopathology, using a developmental framework. In particular, throughout our discussions we offer stimulating pedagogical drawings and artwork that brings the principles of this perspective to life and help readers better understand its explanations. (see, for example, pages 75–77, 161–162)

Infographic Data Our previous editions introduced a feature called **InfoCentrals**—numerous full-page infographics on important topics in the field. Given the very positive reader response to the InfoCentrals, we have included them again in this edition—updating all of them and adding brand-new elements to several of them. (see, for example, pages 22, 153, 321, 465)

Rich Case Material Over the years, one of the hallmarks of the *Fundamentals of Psychopathology* textbook has been hundreds of rich clinical examples that bring theoretical and clinical issues to life. In our continuing quest for relevance to the reader and to today's world, we have replaced or revised many of the clinical examples and cases in this edition, and, as noted earlier, we have brought enhanced diversity to our clinical material. (see, for example, pages 145, 219–220, 251, 257, 317–318, 387–388, 471–472)

Critical Thought Questions *Critical thought questions* have long been a stimulating feature of our textbook. These questions, which propel readers to think critically about the topic at hand, pop up within the text narrative, asking students to pause at precisely the right moment and think critically about the material they have just read. We have added a number of new such questions throughout this edition. (see, for example, pages 191, 206, 280, 285, 373)

The "of Note . . ." Feature This edition retains a fun and thought-provoking feature that has been very popular among students and professors over the years: the reader-friendly *of Note* . . . feature, which consists of surprising facts, current events, historical notes, interesting trends, lists, and quotes that are strategically placed in the book's margins. Numerous new *of Notes* . . . have been added to this edition. (see, for example, pages 113, 148, 233, 285, 519)

Expanded Coverage of Prevention and Mental Health Promotion In accord with the clinical field's growing emphasis on prevention, positive psychology, and psychological wellness, we have increased the textbook's attention to these important approaches. (see, for example, pages 19–20, 241–245, 306, 540)

Empathy The subject of psychopathology is people—very often, people in great pain. We have tried therefore to always write with empathy and to impart this awareness to students.

Integrated Coverage of Treatment Numerous discussions of treatment are presented and integrated throughout the book. In addition to a complete overview of treatment in the opening chapters, each of the pathology chapters includes a full discussion of relevant treatment approaches.

Margin Glossary Hundreds of key words are defined in the margins of pages on which the words appear. In addition, a traditional glossary is featured at the back of the book.

Striking Photos and Stimulating Illustrations Concepts, disorders, treatments, and applications are brought to life for the reader with stunning photographs, diagrams, graphs, and anatomical figures. All of the figures, graphs, and tables, many new to this edition, reflect the most up-to-date data available. The photos range from historical to today's world to pop culture, and, as mentioned earlier, they fully reflect our diverse society. The photos do more than just illustrate topics: they touch, move, and inform readers.

Adaptability Chapters are self-contained, so they can be assigned in any order that makes sense to the professor.

Resources for Teaching and Learning

We are delighted by the enthusiastic responses of both professors and students to the resources that have accompanied *Fundamentals of Psychopathology* over the years. This edition offers those resources once again, revised and enhanced.

For Professors

Worth Video Collection for Psychopathology (New Edition) *Produced and edited by Ronald Comer, Princeton University, and Gregory Comer, Princeton Academic Resources. Faculty Guide included.* This incomparable video package offers more than 250 contemporary video clips on different kinds of clinical events, psychopathologies, research undertakings, and treatments, including brand-new videos on such current topics as the psychological impact of Covid-19, telemental health approaches, neurodiversity, climate anxiety, barbershop interventions, culturally responsive therapies, Indigenous boarding schools, athletes and eating disorders, traumatization by online predators, the mass shooting in Buffalo, the "988" Suicide and Crisis Lifeline, sexting, vaping, mental health apps and wearables, mental health interventions by police, body shaming, the stress of overcrowding, mindfulness-based interventions, cell phone addiction, gaming addiction, and more. These cutting-edge videos are available in Macmillan Learning's **Achieve.** The series is accompanied by a guide that fully describes and discusses each video clip, so that professors can make informed decisions about the use of the segments in lectures.

Instructor's Resource Manual *by Jeffrey B. Henriques, University of Wisconsin–Madison and Laurie A. Frost.* This comprehensive guide, revised by experienced instructors and clinicians, ties together the ancillary package for professors and teaching assistants. The manual includes detailed chapter outlines, lists of principal learning objectives, ideas for lectures, discussion launchers, classroom activities, extra credit projects, and diagnostic criteria for each of the disorders discussed in the text. It also offers strategies for using the accompanying media, including the video collection. Finally, it includes a comprehensive set of valuable materials that can be obtained from outside sources—items such as relevant feature films, documentaries, teaching references, and Internet sites related to psychopathology.

Lecture Slides and Handout Slides Each chapter comes with a ready-to-use set of lecture slides and handouts for easy lecture preparation. These slides focus on key concepts and themes from the text and can be used as is or customized to fit a professor's needs. Also included are image slides for all of the chapter photos, illustrations, and tables.

iClicker Classroom Response System This is a versatile polling system, developed by educators for educators, that makes class time more efficient and interactive. iClicker allows you to ask questions and instantly record your students' responses, take attendance, and gauge students' understanding and opinions. A set of iClicker Questions for each chapter is available online and in Macmillan Learning's **Achieve**.

Assessment Tools

The **Macmillan Learning Test Bank** includes a full assortment of test items. Each chapter features over 200 questions to test students at several levels of Bloom's taxonomy. All the questions are tagged to the outcomes recommended in the *APA Guidelines for the Undergraduate Psychology Major,* Bloom's level, the book page, the chapter section, and the learning objective from the *Instructor's Resource Manual.*

For Students

***Case Studies in Abnormal Psychology,* Third Edition,** *by Ethan E. Gorenstein, Behavioral Medicine Program, Columbia University Medical Center, and Ronald J. Comer, Princeton University.* This third edition of our popular case study book provides 20 case histories, each going beyond diagnoses to describe the individual's history and symptoms, a theoretical discussion of treatment, a specific treatment plan, and the actual treatment conducted. Every page features *margin notes* that further engage, enlighten, and stimulate the reader. The casebook also provides three cases without diagnoses or treatment so that readers can identify disorders and suggest appropriate therapies. Across the third edition, wonderful case material has been added by Zachary Rosenthal of Duke University.

Acknowledgments

We are very grateful to the many people who have contributed to writing and producing this book. We particularly thank Gregory Comer of Princeton Academic Resources for his outstanding work on a range of text, case, and digital materials; Anthony Dick and Matthew Sutherland, each of Florida International University, for their invaluable feedback on this edition's expanded coverage of brain circuits; and Jami Furr of Florida International University, Donna Pincus of Boston University, and Amanda Sanchez of George Mason University for their superb scholarly and creative input throughout the writing of this edition. In addition, we are indebted to Marlene Glissmann and Bruce Owens for their fast, furious, and skillful work on the references.

We are indebted greatly to those outstanding academicians and clinicians who have provided exceptional feedback on this new edition of *Fundamentals of Psychopathology,* along with that of its partner, *Psychopathology: Science and Practice,* and have commented with great insight and wisdom on its clarity, accuracy, and completeness. Their collective knowledge has in large part shaped the current edition: Patricia Adams, Pitt Community College; Kacie Posuniak, Eastern Maine Community College; Bettina Viereck, University of Hartford; Janelle McDaniel, University of Louisiana Monroe; Jessamy Comer, Rochester Institute of Technology; Kevin Antshel, Syracuse University; David Wasieleski, Valdosta State University; Paige Williams, Indiana University Southeast; Tracy Robinson-Wood, Northeastern University; Michael Poulakis, University of Indianapolis; Kary Fukunaga, Cerritos College; Linda Muckey, South Dakota State University; Jessica Fede, Johnson & Wales University; Lisa Smith, Sacred Heart University; Jacobose Ammons, Kansas City Kansas Community College; Christine Greco-Covington, Brookdale Community College; Jenni Teeters, Western Kentucky University; Jessica Houser, West Shore Community College.

We would also like to thank the following professionals who gave us expert feedback about our coverage of BIPOC, LGBTQ+ individuals, people with disabilities, and other marginalized persons, and the impact of mental health issues on them and their communities: Alex Andrade, California State University; Andrea Holman, Huston-Tillotson University; Jerry Mize, George Mason University; Carmen-Ochoa-Galindo, University of Illinois Chicago; Amanda L. Sanchez, George Mason University; and Elizabeth Yeater, University of New Mexico.

Earlier we also received valuable feedback from academicians and clinicians who reviewed portions of the previous editions of *Fundamentals of Psychopathology* and *Psychopathology: Science and Practice*. Certainly their collective knowledge has also helped shape this new edition, and we gratefully acknowledge their important contributions: Christopher Adams, Fitchburg State University; Dave W. Alfano, Community College of Rhode Island; Jeffrey Armstrong, Northampton Community College; Alisa Aston, University of North Florida; Kathryn Alves-Labore, Forsyth Technical Community College; Kent G. Bailey, Virginia Commonwealth University; Stephanie Baralecki, Chestnut Hill College; Sonja Barcus, Rochester College; Wendy Bartkus, Albright College; Marna S. Barnett, Indiana University of Pennsylvania; Jennifer Bennett, University of New Mexico; Jillian Bennett, University of Massachusetts Boston; Otto A. Berliner, Alfred State College; Allan Berman, University of Rhode Island; Douglas Bernstein, University of Toronto, Mississauga; Sarah Bing, University of Maryland Eastern Shore; Greg Bolich, Cleveland Community College; Stephen Brasel, Moody Bible Institute; Conrad Brombach, Christian Brothers University; Barbara Brown, Georgia Perimeter College; Seth A. Brown, University of Northern Iowa; Christine Browning, Victory University; Gregory M. Buchanan, Beloit College; Jeffrey A. Buchanan, Minnesota State University, Mankato; Laura Burlingame-Lee, Colorado State University; Loretta Butehorn, Boston College; Glenn M. Callaghan, San José State University; E. Allen Campbell, University of St. Francis; Robin Campbell, Eastern Florida State College; Julie Carboni, San Jose Christian College and National University; David N. Carpenter, Southwest Texas University; Andrea Cartwright, Jefferson Community & Technical College; Marc Celentana, The College of New Jersey; Edward Chang, University of Michigan; Daniel Chazin, Rutgers University; Sarah Cirese, College of Marin; June Madsen Clausen, University of San Francisco; Victor B. Cline, University of Utah; E. M. Coles, Simon Fraser University; Michael Connor, California State University, Long Beach; Frederick L. Coolidge, University of Colorado, Colorado Springs; Patrick J. Courtney, Central Ohio Technical College; Charles Cummings, Asheville Buncombe Technical Community College; Dennis Curtis, Metropolitan Community College; Lauren Dattilo, University of South Carolina; Timothy K. Daugherty, Missouri State University; Lisa Davies, Nashville State Community College; Megan Davies, NOVA, Woodbridge Campus; Pernella Deams, Grambling State University; Lauren Doninger, Gateway Community College; Mary Dosier, University of Delaware; S. Wayne Duncan, University of Washington, Seattle;

Anne Duran, California State University, Bakersfield; Morris N. Eagle, York University; Miriam Ehrenberg, John Jay College of Criminal Justice; Jon Elhai, University of Toledo; Frederick Ernst, University of Texas, Pan American; Daniella K. C. Errett, Pennsylvania Highlands Community College; Carlos A. Escoto, Eastern Connecticut State University; William Everist, Pima Community College; Jennifer Fiebig, Loyola University Chicago; David M. Fresco, Kent State University; Anne Fisher, University of Southern Florida; William E. Flack Jr., Bucknell University; John Forsyth, State University of New York, Albany; Alan Fridlund, University of California, Santa Barbara; Stan Friedman, Southwest Texas State University; Dale Fryxell, Chaminade University; Lawrence L. Galant, Gaston College; Kathryn E. Gallagher, Georgia State University; Rosemarie B. Gilbert, Brevard Community College; Karla Gingerich, Colorado State University; Andrea Glenn, University of Alabama; Jessica Goodwin Jolly, Gloucester County College; Nicholas Greco, College of Lake County; Nancy Gup, Georgia State University Perimeter College; Amanda Haliburton, Virginia Polytechnic Institute and State University; Jane Halonen, James Madison University; Bonnie Hamm, Virginia Western Community College; James Hansell, University of Michigan; Hansjörg Neth, Rensselaer Polytechnic Institute; David Harder, Tufts University; Morton G. Harmatz, University of Massachusetts; Jinni A. Harrigan, California State University, Fullerton; Jumi Hayaki, College of the Holy Cross; RaNae Healy, GateWay Community College; Brett Heintz, Delgado Community College; Jacqueline Heath, Ohio State University; Anthony Hermann, Kalamazoo College; Paul Hewitt, University of British Columbia; Abby Hill, Trinity International University; David A. Hoffinan, University of California, Santa Cruz; Tony Hoffman, University of California, Santa Cruz; Art Hohmuth, The College of New Jersey; Art Houser, Fort Scott Community College; Lenze Holliman, Georgia State University Perimeter College; Rebecca Howell, Forsyth Technical Community College; Danae Hudson, Missouri State University; William G. Iacono, University of Minnesota; Rick Ingram, The University of Kentucky; Ashleigh E. Jones, University of Illinois at Urbana-Champaign; Ricki E. Kantrowitz, Westfield State University; Barbara Kennedy, Brevard Community College; Lynn M. Kernen, Hunter College; Audrey Kim, University of California, Santa Cruz; Julia Kim-Cohen, University of Illinois–Chicago; Guadalupe Vasquez King, Milwaukee Area Technical College; Tricia Z. King, Georgia State University; Bernard Kleinman, University of Missouri, Kansas City; Futoshi Kobayashi, Northern State University; Alan G. Krasnoff, University of Missouri, St. Louis; Robert D. Langston, University of Texas, Austin; Kimberlyn Leary, University of Michigan; Craig Knapp, College of St. Joseph; Sally Kuhlenschmidt, Western Kentucky University; Harvey R. Lerner, Kaiser-Permanente Medical Group; Arnold D. LeUnes, Texas A&M University; Michael P. Levin, Kenyon College; Barbara Lewis, University of West Florida; Paul Lewis, Bethel College; Mary Margaret Livingston, Louisiana Technical University; Karsten Look, Columbus State Community College; Joseph LoPiccolo, University of Missouri, Columbia; L. E. Lowenstein, Southern England Psychological Services; Gregory Mallis, University of Indianapolis; Rajesh Malik, Dawson College; Jerald J. Marshall, University of Central Florida; Toby Marx, Union County College; Janet R. Matthews, Loyola University; Robert J. McCaffrey, State University of New York, Albany; Rosemary McCullough, Ave Maria University; F. Dudley McGlynn, Auburn University; Tara McKee, Hamilton College; Lily D. McNair, University of Georgia; Mary W. Meagher, Texas A&M University; Dorothy Mercer, Eastern Kentucky University; Michele Metcalf, Coconino Community College; Joni L. Mihura, University of Toledo; Andrea Miller, Georgia Southwestern State University; Antoinette Miller, Clayton State University; Regina Miranda, Hunter College; John Mitchell, Lycoming College; Robin Mogul, Queens University; Linda M. Montgomery, University of Texas, Permian Basin; Jeri Morris, Roosevelt University; Karen Mottarella, University of Central Florida; Maria Moya, College of Southern Nevada; Karla Klein Murdock, University of Massachusetts, Boston; Taryn Myers, Virginia Wesleyan University; Sandy Naumann, Delaware Technical Community

College; David Nelson, Sam Houston State University; Paul Neunuebel, Sam Houston State University; Ryan Newell, Oklahoma Christian University; Katherine M. Nicolai, Rockhurst University; Susan A. Nolan, Seton Hall University; Fabian Novello, Purdue University; Edward O'Brien, Marywood University; Ryan O'Loughlin, Nazareth College; Mary Ann M. Pagaduan, American Osteopathic Association; Crystal Park, University of Connecticut; Dominic J. Parrott, Georgia State University; Daniel Paulson, Carthage College; Paul A. Payne, University of Cincinnati; Justin Peer, University of Michigan–Dearborn; Mary Pelton-Cooper, Northern Michigan University; David V. Perkins, Ball State University; Julie C. Piercy, Central Virginia Community College; Lloyd R. Pilkington, Midlands Technical College; Harold A. Pincus, chair, DSM-IV, University of Pittsburgh, Western Psychiatric Institute and Clinic; Chris Piotrowski, University of West Florida; Debbie Podwika, Kankakee Community College; Ginger Pope, South Piedmont Community College; Norman Poppel, Middlesex County College; David E. Powley, University of Mobile; Laura A. Rabin, Brooklyn College; Max W. Rardin, University of Wyoming, Laramie; Lynn P. Rehm, University of Houston; Leslie A. Rescorla, Bryn Mawr College; R. W. Rieber, John Jay College, CUNY; Lisa Riley, Southwest Wisconsin Technical College; Esther Rothblum, University of Vermont; Vic Ryan, University of Colorado, Boulder; Randall Salekin, Florida International University; Edie Sample, Metropolitan Community College; Jackie Sample, Central Ohio Technical College; A. A. Sappington, University of Alabama, Birmingham; Martha Sauter, McLennan Community College; Laura Scaletta, Niagara County Community College; Ty Schepis, Texas State University; Larry Schor, University of West Georgia; Elizabeth Seebach, Saint Mary's University of Minnesota; George W. Shardlow, City College of San Francisco; Shalini Sharma, Manchester Community College; Roberta S. Sherman, Bloomington Center for Counseling and Human Development; Wendy E. Shields, University of Montana; Jerome Short, George Mason University; Sandra T. Sigmon, University of Maine, Orono; Susan J. Simonian, College of Charleston; Janet A. Simons, Central Iowa Psychological Services; Jay R. Skidmore, Utah State University; Rachel Sligar, James Madison University; Katrina Smith, Polk Community College; LaTishia Smith, Ivy Tech Community College of Indiana; Robert Sommer, University of California, Davis; Jason S. Spiegelman, Community College of Baltimore County; John M. Spores, Purdue University, South Central; Jeannine Stamatakis, Diablo Valley College; Caroline Stanley, Wilmington College; Wayne Stein, Brevard Community College; Arnit Steinberg, Tel Aviv University; David Steitz, Nazareth College; B. D. Stillion, Clayton College & State University; Deborah Stipp, Ivy Tech Community College; Joanne H. Stohs, California State University, Fullerton; Jaine Strauss, Macalester College; Mitchell Sudolsky, University of Texas, Austin; John Suler, Rider University; Sandra Todaro, Bossier Parish Community College; Terry Trepper, Purdue University Calumet; Thomas A. Tutko, San José State University; Arthur D. VanDeventer, Thomas Nelson Community College; Maggie VandeVelde, Grand Rapids Community College; Lora Vasiliauskas, Virginia Western Community College; Jennifer Vaughn, Metropolitan Community College; Norris D. Vestre, Arizona State University; Jamie Walter, Roosevelt University; Steve Wampler, Southwestern Community College; Eleanor M. Webber, Johnson State College; Lance L. Weinmann, Canyon College; Doug Wessel, Black Hills State University; Laura Westen, Emory University; Brook Whisenhunt, Missouri State University; Joseph L. White, University of California, Irvine; Justin Williams, Georgia State University; Amy C. Willis, Veterans Administration Medical Center, Washington, DC; Sandra Wills, Nashville State Community College; James M. Wood, University of Texas, El Paso; Lisa Wood, University of Puget Sound; Lucinda E. Woodward, Indiana University Southeast; Kim Wright, Trine University; Thomas Wrobel, University of Michigan; Dong Xie, University of Central Arkansas; David Yells, Utah Valley State College; Jessica Yokely, University of Pittsburgh; Carlos Zalaquett, University of South Florida; and Anthony M. Zoccolillo, Rutgers University.

We would also like to thank a group of talented professors who provided valuable feedback that shaped the development of our exciting immersive learning activities, *Clinical Choices:* Cassandra Bailey, Metropolitan State University of Denver; David Berg, Community College of Philadelphia; Seth Brown, University of Northern Iowa; Ty Brumback, Northern Kentucky University; Julia Buckner, Louisiana State University; Robin Campbell, Eastern Florida State University; Paul Deal, Missouri State University; Douglas Dinero, Onondaga Community College; Christopher J. Dyszelski, Madison Area Technical College; Jessica Fede, Johnson and Wales University; Seth I. Finkle, Moravian University; Urminda Firlan, Kalamazoo Valley Community College; Roy Fish, Zane State College; Julie Hanauer, Suffolk County Community College; Erin Jane Henshaw, Denison University; Stephanie Brooke Hindman, Greenville Technical College; Sally Kuhlenschmidt, Western Kentucky University; Angela Mar, University of Texas Rio Grande Valley; Matthew A. McGuire, Northern Kentucky University; Alejandro Morales, California State Polytechnic University, Pomona; Erica Musser, Florida International University; Garth Neufeld, Highline Community College; John Ordiway, Casper College; Leighann Ostrowsky-Leonard, Eastern Florida State Titusville; Lauren A. Otrimski, Edgecombe Community College; Kruti Patel, Ohio University; Jeremy Pettit, Florida International University; Michael Poulakis, Ivy Tech Community College Indianapolis.

A special thank you to the authors of the book's supplements package for doing splendid jobs with their respective supplements: Jeffrey B. Henriques, University of Wisconsin, Madison, and Laurie A. Frost (*Instructor's Resource Manual*); Taryn Myers, Virginia Wesleyan University (*Clinical Choices*); and Bittner Development Group (*Practice Quizzes*). And thank you to the contributors from previous editions: Ann Brandt-Williams, Glendale Community College; Elaine Cassel, Marymount University and Lord Fairfax Community College; Danae L. Hudson, Missouri State University; John Schulte, Cape Fear Community College and University of North Carolina; Kathleen Stellmach, Pasco-Hernando State College; and Brooke L. Whisenhunt, Missouri State University (additional website materials).

We also extend our deep appreciation to the core team of professionals at Macmillan Learning who worked with us almost every day for the past year to produce this edition: Nick Rizzuti, the book's development editor; Dan DeBonis, executive program manager for Psychology; Pamela Lawson, lead content project manager; and Jennifer Atkins, photo researcher. It is accurate to say that these members of the core team were our co-authors and co-teachers in this enterprise, and we are in their debt.

We also thank the following individuals, each of whom made significant contributions to the writing and production of this textbook: Shani Fisher, vice president, social sciences; Paul Rohloff, workflow project manager; Suzanne Jeans, program director, social sciences; Tracey Kuehn, director of content management enhancement; Diana Blume, director of design; Natasha Wolfe, design services manager; Matthew McAdams, art manager; Chuck Yuen, book and InfoCentral designer; Gary Hespenheide, book designer; Matt Manley, Susan Aldworth, Graam Dean, Emma Prempeh, and Charlotte Orr, chapter-opener artists; Simon Prades, cover artist; Clarah Grossman, media editor; Lindsay Sanders, director of media editorial, social sciences; Hilary Newman, senior director, rights and permissions; Christine Buese, executive manager, permissions; Elaine Kosta, text permissions researcher; and Bruce Owens, copyeditor.

And, of course, not to be overlooked are the outstanding professionals at Worth Publishers who continuously work with great passion, skill, and judgment to bring our books to the attention of professors across the world: Katherine Nurre, executive marketing manager; Greg David, vice president, academic sales; and the company's wonderful sales representatives. Thank you so much.

A few remaining notes: We are both very aware of just how fortunate we are. We are privileged to be able to work with so many interesting and stimulating students during this important and exciting stage of their lives. Similarly, we are deeply grateful for our dear family members and friends. Of course, on the other side of our gratitude for what we have is our recognition that a great many people in the world do not have our good fortune—a point driven home by the stressful times we live in and the emotional, medical, safety, social, cultural, family, and economic hardships experienced by so many. With this in mind, we'll conclude this preface with the same hope that we have stated in previous editions: that with help from the health sciences, the outreach of others, and improvements in our society and our world, all such individuals will come to experience a better day, be afforded lives without fear or loss or injustice, and attain emotional harmony and peace of mind.

Ronald J. Comer   Jonathan S. Comer

Psychopathology: Past and Present

CHAPTER 1

TOPIC OVERVIEW

Amira *cries herself to sleep every night. Each day, she becomes more certain that the future holds nothing but misery. "I'm going to suffer, and my daughters will suffer as well. We're doomed. The world is so ugly. I hate my life." She has great trouble sleeping. She is afraid to close her eyes. When she does, the hopelessness of her life—and the terrible future that awaits her family—becomes all the clearer to her. When she drifts off to sleep, her dreams are nightmares filled with terrible images—sickness, bodies, death.*

Some mornings Amira has trouble getting out of bed. The thought of facing another day weighs her down. She wishes she were dead—"if not for the girls." She knows that they need her, and she loves them so much. She feels overwhelmed by loneliness, depression, and anxiety—flooded by fears of becoming ill, too tired to try anymore. On such mornings, she huddles her daughters close to her, trying to enjoy them as she used to, to remember past joys, and to believe that such happiness will eventually revisit her. But these efforts often fall short, and before long, she feels dispirited again, convinced that life has betrayed her. She is furious at life and afraid of it at the same time.

For the first 26 years of his life, **Finn** *was, by all appearances, a happy, friendly, and family-oriented person. He had always been very close to his parents, and upon entering college, he had chosen to go by Finn instead of Freddie in tribute to his family's Irish ancestry. After college, he received training as a radiology technician, gained employment, and fell in love with his coworker Joshua. Finn and Joshua eventually married and bought a house in Flagstaff, Arizona. They seemed happy together, developed a circle of caring friends, and enjoyed visiting Finn's parents weekly.*

Then, in his 27th year, Finn started hearing mysterious voices that told him to quit his job, prepare for an upcoming invasion, and cut off all contact with his parents, his friends, and Joshua. These voices brought tremendous confusion and emotional turmoil to Finn's life. He believed the voices were coming from beings in distant parts of the universe who were somehow wired to him. Although it gave him a sense of purpose and specialness to be the chosen target of their communications, the voices also made him tense and anxious. He did all he could to warn others of the coming apocalypse. Following instructions from the voices, he identified online articles that seemed filled with foreboding signs, and he posted comments urging readers to recognize the articles' underlying messages. Similarly, he posted long, rambling YouTube videos in which he described the invasion to come. The online feedback he received typically mocked him. But whenever he tried to reject the voices' instructions and stop his commentaries and videos, the voices would insult and threaten him and turn his days into a waking nightmare.

Finn put himself on a sparse diet as protection against the possibility that his enemies might be contaminating his food. He moved out of the house he shared with Joshua and relocated to a small apartment far from his old haunts, where he started collecting a good stock of knives and other blades. Upon witnessing the troubling changes in Finn's behavior and watching his ranting videos, Finn's parents and Joshua kept trying to reach out to him, understand his deterioration, and dissuade him from the disturbing course he was taking. Every day, however, he retreated further into a world of mysterious voices and imagined dangers.

Most of us would probably consider Amira's and Finn's emotions, thoughts, and behaviors unusual, perhaps even strange—the result of a state sometimes called *psychopathology, abnormal functioning, maladjustment, psychological dysfunction, emotional disturbance*, or *mental illness*. These terms have been applied interchangeably to the many challenges that seem closely tied to the human brain or mind. The various terms can be stigmatizing, and there is currently much debate about their acceptability; however, at present, they continue to be widely used by professionals and the public alike. Psychological difficulties can bring emotional pain, but they can also be the source of inspiration and energy.

Because they are so common and so personal, these challenges capture the interest of us all. Countless novels, plays, films, and television programs have explored what many people see as the dark side of human nature, and psychology self-help books flood the market. Mental health experts appear regularly on television, radio, social media, and the Internet.

Dan Reynolds/CartoonStock Ltd.

For the past century, the field devoted to the scientific study of mental health problems was usually called *abnormal psychology*, and, correspondingly, the previous 10 editions of this textbook were titled *Fundamentals of Abnormal Psychology*. In recent years, however, psychologists have grown concerned about the professional and scientific appropriateness of this term. One concern is that the words "abnormal" and "abnormality" have taken on a degrading connotation when used in public discourse. Moreover, rather than seeing certain behaviors as clearly *normal* and all other behaviors as *abnormal*, the clinical field is increasingly viewing behaviors, even ones that cause significant personal and social difficulties, as reflecting human differences that vary with regard to functionality, painfulness, dangerousness, and the like.

In recognition of these important issues, many psychologists and scientific journals no longer feature the terms "abnormal" and "abnormality" in their speech and writings. Correspondingly, we have changed the title of this textbook to refer to *psychopathology*, and in our discussions we largely use terms such as "psychopathology," "psychological challenges," and "mental stress." At the same time, these terms are themselves less than perfect, and they too are currently under scrutiny. ■

What Are the Key Features of Psychopathology?

OUR JOURNEY THROUGH THIS CHAPTER—and indeed the entire textbook—should begin with a precise definition of **psychopathology.** According to the American Psychological Association, the field of psychopathology is the scientific study of mental difficulties or disorders, including their explanations, causes, progression, symptoms, assessment, diagnosis, and treatment (APA, 2022). Beyond referring to this field of study, the word "psychopathology" is also used as a synonym for the broad range of mental disorders (or symptoms) themselves—that is, an individual with significant and disabling problems of mood, thought, or behavior is said to be experiencing psychopathology.

As in any science, workers in this field, called *clinical scientists*, gather information systematically so that they can describe, predict, and explain the phenomena they study. The knowledge that they acquire is then used by *clinical practitioners*, whose role is to detect, assess, and treat patterns of psychopathology.

Although their general goals are similar to those of other scientific professionals, clinical scientists and practitioners face problems that make their work especially

psychopathology The scientific study of mental difficulties or disorders, including their explanations, causes, progression, symptoms, assessment, diagnosis, and treatment. The word also is used as a synonym for the disorders (or symptoms) themselves.

difficult. One of the most troubling is that the defining features of psychopathology are hard to pinpoint. Consider once again Amira and Finn. Why are we so ready to describe their experiences in terms of psychopathology?

While many defining features of psychopathology have been proposed over the years, none has won total acceptance (APA, 2022). Four of the most commonly cited features, often called the "four Ds," are deviance, distress, dysfunction, and danger. That is, patterns of psychopathology are typically *deviant* (different, extreme, or unusual), *distressing* (unpleasant and upsetting to the person), *dysfunctional* (interfering with the person's ability to conduct daily activities in a constructive way), and possibly *dangerous*. These defining features offer a useful starting point from which to explore the phenomena of psychopathology. As you will read, however, they each have key limitations.

of NOTE ...

Verbal Debuts

According to the *Oxford English Dictionary*, the word "insanity" made its debut in the late 1500s, "abnormality" and "psychopathology" in the mid-1800s, "mental illness" in the late 1800s, and "dysfunction" in the mid-1900s.

Deviance

Mental and behavioral disturbances are often *deviant*, but deviant from what? Amira's and Finn's behaviors, thoughts, and emotions appear to be different from those that we tend to consider typical in our place and time. We do not expect people to cry themselves to sleep each night, hate the world, wish themselves dead, or obey voices that no one else hears.

However, judgments of deviance and of psychopathology must take *specific circumstances* into consideration. What if, for example, we were to learn that Amira was living with her partner, Jayden, and their two young children in a cramped New York City apartment during the early months of the Covid-19 pandemic? As the pandemic brought the city to a standstill, Amira and Jayden had been furloughed from their jobs, their daughters' school had been closed, and the state had ordered them all to stay at home indefinitely. After a few weeks, the full impact of the shutdown and social isolation began to wear down Amira, who had previously been a happy and optimistic person. Their savings were gone; she hadn't seen her mother, sisters, or friends in person for ages; and the stress between the children, Jayden, and her was mounting. Moreover, Amira was terrified that she, Jayden, or the children might contract Covid-19, particularly given that they are Black and Covid-19 mortality rates in the United States were significantly higher among Black people than among White people (Asch et al., 2021).

Then, a month later, the unthinkable happened. Jayden, always so strong and energetic, came down with Covid-19—first he had a harmless cough, then a rising temperature, and eventually trouble breathing. In critical condition, he landed in an overcrowded and understaffed hospital fighting the virus without Amira and the daughters he adored. Amira was devastated. She felt overwhelmed and horribly alone—unable to make everything work. Increasingly, she wondered whether her family would survive this ordeal intact.

In this light, Amira's emotions and thoughts do not seem as strange. One clearly disturbed thing here was her situation—a pandemic, social isolation, extended unemployment, severe family illness, and more. Many human experiences produce intense reactions—financial ruin, large-scale catastrophes and disasters, rape, child abuse, war, terminal illness, and chronic pain. Is there an "appropriate" way to react to such things? Should we ever call reactions to such experiences pathological?

Daniel Zuchnik/Getty Images

Context is key A couple dressed as Supergirl and Superman stop and point upward as they cross a street in New York City. Their appearance and behavior might suggest psychological dysfunction were it not for the fact that they are attendees at a recent Comic-Con, one of the many popular conventions held across the country to showcase pop culture entertainment.

Distress

A person's behavior or emotions may be assessed as deviant, even after their difficult situation is taken into consideration, but that alone does not mean their experiences are

Hinterhaus Productions/Getty Images

Changing times for ink Here a woman congratulates her best friend as she gets ready for her wedding. Just decades ago, the elaborate body art on her arms and neck would have been considered outrageous and strange, perhaps even pathological. Today, however, tattoos—even extensive ones—are relatively common. As many as 40 percent of adults in the United States have at least one tattoo; 25 percent have multiple tattoos.

necessarily pathological. According to many clinical theorists, behavior, ideas, or emotions typically must cause *distress* before they can be regarded as signs of psychopathology. Consider the Ice Breakers, a group of people in Michigan who go swimming in lakes throughout the state every weekend from November through February. The colder the weather, the better they like it. One man, a member of the group for 17 years, says he loves the challenge of human against nature. A 37-year-old lawyer believes that the weekly shock is good for her health. "It cleanses me," she says. "It perks me up and gives me strength." Certainly these people are different from most of us, but should their behavior be considered pathological? Far from experiencing distress from the cold, they feel energized and challenged. Their positive feelings must cause us to hesitate before we decide that they are functioning in a manner that reflects psychopathology.

Should we conclude, then, that feelings of distress must *always* be present before a person's functioning can be considered to reflect psychopathology? Not necessarily. Some people experiencing psychopathology maintain a positive frame of mind. Consider once again Finn, the young man who hears mysterious voices. What if he enjoyed listening to the voices, felt honored to be chosen, loved sending out warnings on the Internet, and looked forward to saving the world? Despite such upbeat feelings, his functioning might still be viewed as pathological.

Dysfunction

Psychopathology tends to be *dysfunctional;* that is, it interferes with daily functioning. It so upsets, distracts, or confuses people that they cannot care for themselves properly, participate in ordinary social interactions, or work productively. Finn, for example, quit his job; left his partner, parents, and friends; and prepared to withdraw from the productive life he once led. Because our society holds that it is important to carry out daily activities in an effective manner, Finn's behavior is likely to be regarded as dysfunctional and undesirable and, in turn, an indication of psychopathology. In contrast, the behavior of the Ice Breakers, who continue to perform well in their jobs and enjoy fulfilling relationships, would probably be considered simply unusual.

Danger

Perhaps the ultimate psychological dysfunction is behavior that becomes *dangerous* to oneself or others. Individuals whose behavior is consistently careless, hostile, desperate, or confused may be placing themselves or those around them at risk. Finn, for example, seemed to be endangering both himself, with his diet, and others, with his buildup of bladed weapons.

Although danger is often cited as a feature of psychopathology, research suggests that it is actually the exception rather than the rule (Battaglia, Mamak, & Goldberg, 2022). Most people experiencing overwhelming anxiety, depression, and even highly distorted thinking pose no immediate danger to themselves or to anyone else (Ghiasi, Azhar, & Singh, 2023).

The Roles of Society and Culture

An essential question has been implied throughout our discussion of the defining features of psychopathology, namely, how to judge whether a given behavior is, in fact, too deviant, distressing, dysfunctional, and/or dangerous. As you will read later in this chapter, specific assessments of psychopathology are made by clinical practitioners. But their determinations are ultimately influenced by two broad factors: *societal norms* and *cultural differences*.

Societal Norms

Each society establishes its own set of **norms**—stated and unstated rules for proper conduct. Behavior that breaks legal norms is considered to be criminal. Behavior, thoughts, and emotions that break norms of psychological functioning may be labeled pathological.

Judgments about what constitutes psychopathology vary from society to society. A society's norms grow from its particular **culture**—its history, values, institutions, habits, skills, technology, and arts. A society that values competition and assertiveness may accept aggressive behavior, whereas one that emphasizes cooperation and gentleness may consider aggressive behavior unacceptable and even pathological. A society's values may also change over time, causing its views of what is psychopathology to change as well. In Western society, for example, for a woman to seek the power of running a major corporation or leading a country would have been considered inappropriate and even delusional a hundred years ago. Today, the same behavior is valued.

Buena Vista Images/Getty Images

Different but not psychopathology
This woman, like others from the Padaung tribe in Myanmar (Burma), is preoccupied with the length of her neck and wears heavy stacks of brass rings to try to extend it—seeking to achieve what her culture teaches her is the perfect neck size. In Western society, the same behavior and goals would break behavioral norms and might well be considered pathological.

Thus, ultimately, a society selects general standards for defining psychopathology and then clinical practitioners apply those standards to particular cases. One influential theorist, Thomas Szasz, placed such emphasis on society's role that he found the whole concept of mental illness to be invalid, a *myth* of sorts (Szasz, 2011, 1963, 1960). According to Szasz, the deviations that society calls psychopathology are simply "problems in living," not signs of something wrong within the person. As you will learn in the chapter on models of psychopathology, a number of today's clinical theorists similarly de-emphasize the role of "illness" or "disorder" when seeking to understand psychopathology and instead look at broader societal factors.

It is worth noting that the powerful impact of societal norms can sometimes lead clinicians and the public to inadvertently minimize or overlook significant psychological problems. If a behavior—excessive use of alcohol among college students, say—is familiar enough, the society may fail to recognize that it is deviant, distressful, dysfunctional, and dangerous. Thousands of college students throughout the United States are so dependent on alcohol that it interferes with their personal and academic lives, causes them great discomfort, jeopardizes their health, and often endangers them and the people around them (NIAAA, 2023). Yet their problem often goes unnoticed and undiagnosed. Alcohol is so much a part of the college subculture that it is easy to overlook drinking behavior that has become pathological.

What behaviors fit the criteria of deviant, distressful, dysfunctional, or dangerous but would not be considered by most people to reflect psychopathology?

In a related vein, overattention to a society's norms may lead clinicians and the public to confuse *eccentricities*—unusual patterns with which others have no right to interfere—with mental disturbances—patterns that may require intervention. From time to time, we see or hear about people who behave in ways we consider strange, such as an individual who lives alone with dozens of cats and rarely talks to other people. The behavior of such people may not fit a society's behavioral norms, and it may well be dysfunctional, yet many professionals think of it as eccentric rather than reflecting psychopathology (see **PsychWatch**).

Cultural Differences: The Importance of "Cultural Humility"

Discussions sometimes make it sound like a society is composed of a homogeneous population living in a single geographical area, with a fully shared history and set of values. But, in fact, a society consists of multiple subsocieties, each of which may have somewhat different norms, histories, and values than the society at large. In turn, the norms of psychological functioning and behavior can vary within a given society, particularly in societies characterized by people of varying races, ethnicities, nationalities, and languages.

Thus, when determining whether an individual is displaying psychopathology, it is important that clinicians (and the public in general) look at the behavior in question

norms A society's stated and unstated rules for proper conduct.

culture A people's common history, values, institutions, habits, skills, technology, and arts.

PSYCHWATCH

Marching to a Different Drummer: Eccentrics

- **Benjamin Franklin** took "air baths" for his health, sitting naked in front of an open window.
- To save money, financier **Hetty Green**—arguably the richest woman in America during the late 1800s—wore the same dress each day and never changed her underwear until they wore out.
- **Alexander Graham Bell** covered the windows of his house to keep out the rays of the full moon. He also tried to teach his dog how to talk.
- Wealthy heiress **Sarah Lockwood Winchester** spent much of her fortune on decades of uninterrupted, around-the-clock reconstruction of her home. She believed that continuous modifications, including several staircases to nowhere, were needed to ward off evil spirits.
- Writer **D. H. Lawrence** enjoyed removing his clothes and climbing mulberry trees.
- As long as she kept winning, tennis legend **Serena Williams** would always wear the same pair of unwashed socks throughout each tournament.
- Facebook cofounder **Mark Zuckerberg's** closet is full of multiple versions of the exact same outfit—a gray T-shirt and blue jeans. He claims that wearing the same outfit every day, rather than deciding each morning what to wear, helps conserve his energy and creativity for more important decisions throughout the day.

These famous persons have been called eccentrics. The dictionary defines an *eccentric* as a person who deviates from common behavior patterns or displays odd or whimsical behavior. But how can we separate a psychologically healthy person who has unusual habits from a person whose oddness is a symptom of psychopathology? Little research has been done on eccentrics, but a few pieces of work offer some insights (Kaeley, 2021; Gencarella, 2018; Sinclair, 2017; Weeks & James, 1995).

For example, researcher David Weeks (2015) studied 1,000 eccentrics and estimated that as many as 1 in every 5,000 persons may be a "classic, full-time eccentric." Weeks pinpointed 15 characteristics common to the eccentrics in his study: *nonconformity, creativity, strong curiosity, idealism, extreme interests and hobbies, lifelong awareness of being different, high intelligence, outspokenness, noncompetitiveness, unusual eating and living habits, disinterest in others' opinions or company, mischievous sense of humor, nonmarriage, eldest or only child,* and *poor spelling skills.*

Weeks suggests that eccentrics do not typically manifest psychopathology. Whereas the unusual behavior of persons with mental disorders is thrust upon them and usually causes them considerable upset, eccentricity is chosen freely and provides pleasure (Grover, 2023). In short, "Eccentrics know they're different and glory in it" (Weeks & James, 1995, p. 14). Similarly, the thought processes of eccentrics are not severely disrupted and do not leave these persons dysfunctional. In fact, Weeks found that eccentrics in his study actually had fewer emotional problems than individuals in the general population. Perhaps being an "original" is good for mental health.

AP Photo/Thanh Nien

Eccentric, but not pathological Tran Van Hay holds his hair—more than 20 feet in length—around his body, as if it were a cobra. By the time of his death in 2010, he had not had a haircut for 50 years. The married Vietnamese man otherwise lived and worked as a highly respected and productive herbalist. He just liked his hair on the long side—longer than any other person on Earth.

through the lens of the individual's cultural norms and values, not exclusively through that of the clinician's own culture, personal outlook, or notions of appropriate functioning. More generally, in their clinical work and research investigations, clinical practitioners and scientists must adopt a stance of **cultural humility,** a process of ongoing discovery and self-reflection in which professionals continuously examine their own beliefs and cultural identities, explore client cultures and historical realities that differ from their own, seek to understand the cultural context of each person's mental health challenges, and respond accordingly (Loue, 2022; Akerele, McCall, & Aragam, 2021).

When scientists and practitioners do not conduct their work in this way, they run a serious risk of mislabeling culturally appropriate behavior as pathological or, conversely, of failing to recognize pathological behavior and treatment needs in some people.

The call for cultural humility by clinicians and researchers has grown stronger over the past decade, as the clinical field has come to recognize the enormous impact of cultural influences in the determination, understanding, and treatment of mental health matters. You will see this growing recognition in our many discussions of multicultural issues and influences throughout the textbook.

cultural humility A process in which clinical scientists or practitioners continuously examine their own beliefs and cultural identities, explore individuals' cultures and historical realities that differ from their own, seek to understand the cultural context of each person's mental health challenges, and respond accordingly.

treatment A systematic procedure designed to change dysfunctional behavior into more functional behavior. Also called *therapy*.

SUMMING UP

What Are the Key Features of Psychopathology?

Psychopathology is generally considered to be deviant, distressful, dysfunctional, and sometimes dangerous. However, behavior must also be considered in the context in which it occurs. Defining "psychopathology" depends on the norms of the society in question. Moreover, professionals must consider cultural context and differences when they are assessing, treating, or researching psychopathology.

What Is Treatment?

ONCE CLINICIANS DECIDE that a person is indeed displaying some form of psychopathology, they seek to treat it. **Treatment**, or **therapy**, is a procedure designed to change pathological behavior into less disturbed, more functional behavior; it, too, requires careful definition. For clinical scientists, the problem is closely related to defining psychopathology. Consider the case of Bodhi:

FEBRUARY: *He cannot leave his apartment; Bodhi knows this for a fact. The apartment is the only place where he feels safe—safe from humiliation, danger, even ruin. If he were to go to work, his coworkers would certainly find him lacking. A pointed remark, a quizzical look—that's all it would take for Bodhi to get the message. Bodhi's state of mind has changed so much in recent months. Three months ago, he started a new job—an incredible opportunity as an associate city planner. But in quick order, everything went to pot. For this new job, he had to move away from his beloved San Francisco, where he had many friends and where there was a large population of people who, like him, grew up in India and shared many of the same customs and traditions. Bodhi now found himself with no friends, plagued with self-doubt, faced with work projects that he felt were above his head, and consumed with unrelenting feelings of anxiety and depression. Thus, a week ago, he asked for a leave of absence from his job.*

Since then, he has been at home, unable to push himself out of the apartment or even to get out of bed. He believes that if he were to go out shopping, everyone would wind up staring at him before long. Surely other people would see his dark mood and thoughts; he wouldn't be able to hide them. He doesn't dare to even go for a walk in a quiet park—his heart would probably start racing again, bringing him to his knees and leaving him breathless and unable to get home. No, he's better off staying in his room, trying to get through another painful evening. Thank goodness for social media. Were it not for that, he would, he knows, be cut off from the world altogether.

SEPTEMBER: *Bodhi's social life revolves around a growing number of friends, including Joseph and Makayla, colleagues from the city planning office, and Cruz and Tim, whom he met at a watercolor painting class, of all places. Yes, he, Bodhi, actually joined a painting class not far from his apartment. Beyond the painting class and other organized activities, he frequently goes out with his friends for dinner, drinks, or a get-together at someone's house to chat about life, their jobs, current events, or whatever. Particularly*

(continued on the next page)

special in Bodhi's life is Priya, whom he met at an Indian cooking class he discovered a couple of towns over. They go to clubs, sporting events, and concerts together. They also run together a lot and enjoy exploring restaurants in the area. They even found an authentic Indian restaurant less than 30 minutes away that reminded Bodhi of his grandmother's delicious cooking. Priya thinks Bodhi is just terrific, and Bodhi finds himself beaming whenever she's around. As far as work goes, Bodhi actually looks forward every day to the demands and surprises of his job and to his dealings with colleagues, associates, and community and political leaders. He is now a happy, active, and socially engaged person, enjoying both the pleasures and the challenges that life offers.

Carla Carniel/Reuters/Alamy Stock Photo

All the rage A woman relieves her stress by smashing bottles in a Brazilian "rage room." Such popular spaces offer people opportunities to vent their anger by safely destroying objects and wreaking havoc. Rage room sessions may be therapeutic for some, but they are not considered therapy. The sessions lack, for example, systematic contacts with a "trained healer."

In February, Bodhi's thoughts, feelings, and behavior interfered with all aspects of his life. Yet by September, most of his symptoms had disappeared. All sorts of factors may have contributed to Bodhi's improvement—conversations with family members, advice from a lifelong friend, fun adventures with new friends, visits back to his old city, a relaxing vacation, fortuitous events, or perhaps a big change in his diet. Any or all of these things may have been useful to Bodhi, but they could not be considered treatment or therapy. Those terms are usually reserved for special, systematic procedures for helping people overcome their psychological difficulties. According to pioneering clinical theorist Jerome Frank, all forms of therapy have three essential features:

> 1. A *sufferer* who seeks relief from the healer.
> 2. A trained, socially accepted *healer*, whose expertise is accepted by the sufferer and the sufferer's social group.
> 3. A *series of contacts* between the healer and the sufferer, through which the healer . . . tries to produce certain changes in the sufferer's emotional state, attitudes, and behavior.
>
> (Frank, 1973, pp. 2–3)

Most parts of Frank's criteria are still embraced by today's clinical theorists. Despite his seemingly straightforward definition, clinical treatment is surrounded by conflict and, at times, confusion. Like Frank, some clinicians view psychopathology as an illness, and so they consider therapy a procedure that helps *cure* the illness and relieve suffering. Others see psychopathology as a problem in living that may or may not involve suffering, and they see therapists as *teachers* or *coaches* of more functional behavior and thought. Clinicians even differ on what to call the person who receives therapy: those who see psychopathology as an illness speak of the "patient," while those who view it as a problem in living refer to the "client." Because both terms are so common, this book will use them interchangeably.

Despite their differences, most clinicians do agree that large numbers of people can benefit from therapy of one kind or another. Later you will encounter evidence that therapy is indeed often helpful.

SUMMING UP

What Is Treatment?

Therapy is a systematic process for helping people overcome their psychological difficulties. It typically requires a patient or client, a therapist, and a series of therapeutic contacts.

How Was Psychopathology Viewed and Treated in the Past?

IN ANY GIVEN YEAR, as many as 30 percent of the adults and 17 percent of the children and adolescents in the United States display significant psychological disturbances and are in need of clinical treatment (MHA, 2023; NAMI, 2023). The rates in many other countries are similarly high. It is tempting to conclude that something about the modern world is responsible for these many emotional problems—perhaps rapid technological change; the Covid-19 pandemic; deep political and social divides; the rising number of hate crimes; increasing threats of terrorism, mass shootings, and natural disasters; or a decline in religious, family, or other support systems. But, as we shall learn in the following sections, every society, past and present, has witnessed psychopathology.

Ancient Views and Treatments

Historians who have examined the unearthed bones, artwork, and other remnants of ancient societies have concluded that these societies probably regarded psychopathology as the work of evil spirits. People in prehistoric societies apparently believed that all events around and within them resulted from the actions of magical, sometimes sinister, beings who controlled the world. In particular, they viewed the human body and mind as a battleground between external forces of good and evil. Disturbed behavior was typically interpreted as a victory by evil spirits, and the cure for such behavior was to force the demons from a victim's body.

This supernatural view of psychopathology may have begun as far back as the Stone Age, a half-million years ago. Some skulls from that period recovered in Europe and South America show evidence of an operation called **trephination,** in which a stone instrument, or *trephine,* was used to cut away a circular section of the skull (Farreras, 2023). Some historians have concluded that this early operation was performed as a treatment for severe psychopathology—either *hallucinations,* in which people saw or heard things not actually present, or *melancholia,* characterized by extreme sadness and immobility. The purpose of opening the skull was to release the evil spirits that were supposedly causing the problem (Selling, 1940).

The treatment for problematic thoughts and behaviors in these early societies was often *exorcism.* The idea was to coax the evil spirits to leave or to make the person's body an uncomfortable place in which to live. A *shaman,* or priest, might recite prayers, plead with the evil spirits, insult the spirits, perform magic, make loud noises, or have the person drink bitter potions. If these techniques failed, the shaman performed a more extreme form of exorcism, such as whipping or starving the person.

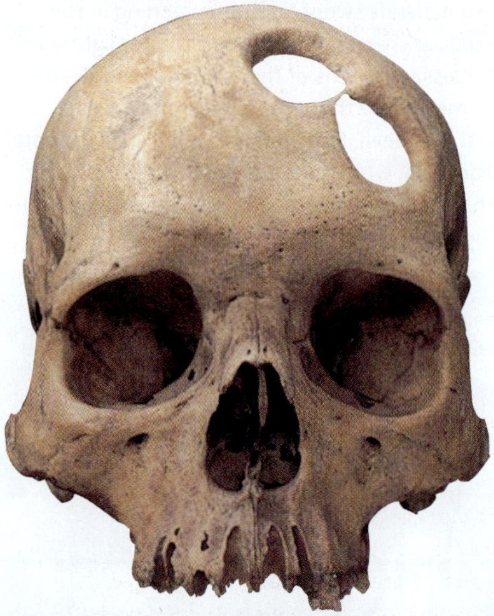

Professor John Verano

Expelling evil spirits The two holes in this skull recovered from ancient times indicate that the person underwent trephination, possibly for the purpose of releasing evil spirits and curing mental dysfunction.

Early European and Asian Views and Treatments

In the years from roughly 500 B.C.E. to 500 C.E., when the Greek and Roman civilizations thrived in Europe, philosophers and physicians often offered different explanations and treatments for disturbed mood and behavior. Hippocrates (460–377 B.C.E.), commonly called the father of modern medicine, taught that illnesses had *natural* causes. He saw pathological behavior as a disease arising from internal physical problems. Specifically, he believed that some form of brain pathology was the culprit and that it resulted—like all other forms of disease, in his view—from an imbalance of four fluids, or **humors,** that flowed through the body: *yellow bile, black bile, blood,* and *phlegm* (Chrysopoulos, 2022). An excess of yellow bile, for example, caused *mania,* a state of frenzied activity; an excess of black bile was the source of *melancholia,* a condition marked by unshakable sadness.

trephination An ancient operation in which a stone instrument was used to cut away a circular section of the skull to treat severe psychopathology.

humors According to the Greeks and Romans, bodily chemicals that influence mental and physical functioning.

To treat psychological dysfunction, Hippocrates sought to correct the underlying physical pathology. He believed, for instance, that the excess of black bile underlying melancholia could be reduced by a quiet life, a diet of vegetables, temperance, exercise, celibacy, and even bleeding. Hippocrates' focus on internal causes for psychopathology was shared by the great Greek philosophers Plato (427–347 B.C.E.) and Aristotle (384–322 B.C.E.) and by influential Greek and Roman physicians.

Around this same time, early medical writings in China were also moving away from supernatural explanations of psychopathology. Much like the early Greek and Roman views, Chinese medical texts characterized disturbed mood and behavior as arising, in part, from physical pathology as well as from disharmony with nature and one's surroundings. Early Chinese writings further saw the mind–body connection as a two-way street such that an overabundance of emotion could lead to a range of bodily ailments. To treat mental disturbances, emphasis was placed on achieving greater balance in life, avoiding emotional extremes, and treating the mind and body as a whole.

Europe in the Middle Ages: Demonology Returns

The enlightened views of Greek, Roman, and Chinese healers and scholars were not enough to shake ordinary people's belief in demons throughout Europe. With the decline of Rome, for example, demonological views and practices became popular once again in the region. A growing distrust of science spread throughout Europe.

From 500 to 1350 C.E., the period known as the Middle Ages, the power of the clergy increased greatly throughout Europe. In those days, the church, which controlled all education, rejected scientific forms of investigation. Religious beliefs of the time, which were highly superstitious and demonological, came to dominate all aspects of life. Deviant behavior, particularly behavior reflecting psychopathology, was seen as evidence of the devil's influence.

Bewitched or bewildered? A great fear of witchcraft swept Europe beginning in the 1300s and extending through the "enlightened" Renaissance. Tens of thousands of people, mostly women, were thought to have made a pact with the devil. Some appear to have had mental disorders, which caused them to act strangely. This woman is being "dunked" repeatedly until she confesses to witchery.

Bettmann/Getty Images

The Middle Ages were a time of great stress and anxiety—of war, urban uprisings, and plagues. People blamed the devil for these troubles and feared being possessed (Katajala-Peltomaa, 2020). Psychopathology apparently increased greatly during this period. In addition, there were outbreaks of *mass madness,* in which large numbers of people apparently shared hallucinations and also *delusions,* or absurd false beliefs. In one such disorder, *tarantism* (also known as *Saint Vitus' dance*), groups of people would suddenly start to jump, dance, and go into convulsions (Fischer, 2022). All were convinced that they had been bitten and possessed by a wolf spider, now called a tarantula, and they sought to cure their disorder by performing a dance called a tarantella. In another form of mass madness, *lycanthropy,* people thought they were possessed by wolves or other animals. They acted wolflike and imagined that fur was growing all over their bodies.

Not surprisingly, some of the earlier demonological treatments for psychopathology reemerged during the Middle Ages. Once again, the key to the cure was to rid the person's body of the devil that possessed it. Exorcisms were revived, and clergy, who generally were in charge of treatment during this period, would plead, chant, or pray to the devil or evil spirit (Farreras, 2023). If these techniques did not work, they had other approaches to try, some amounting to torture.

How might social media facilitate current forms of mass madness?

It was not until the Middle Ages drew to a close that demonology and its methods began to lose favor. Towns throughout Europe grew into cities, and government officials gained more power and took over nonreligious activities. Among their responsibilities, they began to run hospitals and direct the care of people experiencing mental disorders. Medical views of psychopathology gained favor once again, and many people with psychological disturbances received treatment in medical hospitals, such as the Trinity Hospital in England (Allderidge, 1979).

The Renaissance and the Rise of Asylums

During the early part of the Renaissance, a period of flourishing cultural and scientific activity from about 1400 to 1700, demonological views of psychopathology continued to decline. Dutch physician Johann Weyer (1515–1588), the first physician to specialize in mental illness, believed that the mind was as susceptible to sickness as the body. He is now considered the founder of the modern study of psychopathology.

The care of people with mental disorders continued to improve in this atmosphere. In England, such people might be kept at home while their families were aided financially by the local parish. Across Europe, religious shrines were devoted to the humane and loving treatment of people with mental disorders. Perhaps the best known of these shrines was at Gheel in Belgium. (The city name is now spelled "Geel.") Beginning in the fifteenth century, people came to Gheel from all over the world for psychic healing. Local residents welcomed these pilgrims into their homes, and many stayed on to form the world's first "colony" of mental patients. Gheel was the forerunner of today's *community mental health programs,* and it continues to demonstrate that people with psychological disorders can respond to loving care and respectful treatment (Geppert, 2022). Many patients still live in foster homes there, interacting with other residents, until they recover.

Bettmann/Getty Images

Asylum care As patient care increasingly gave way to patient restraint, the "crib" and other unthinkable devices were developed for use in some asylums.

Unfortunately, these improvements in care began to fade by the mid-sixteenth century. Government officials discovered that private homes and community residences could house only a small percentage of those with severe mental disorders and that medical hospitals were too few and too small. More and more, they converted hospitals and monasteries into **asylums,** institutions whose primary purpose was to care for people with mental illness. These institutions were begun with the intention that they would provide good care (Pichot & Goodwin, 2020). Once the asylums started to overflow, however, they became virtual prisons where patients were held in filthy conditions and treated with unspeakable cruelty.

In 1547, for example, Bethlehem Hospital was given to the city of London by Henry VIII for the sole purpose of confining the mentally ill. In this asylum, patients bound in chains cried out for all to hear. The hospital even became a popular tourist attraction; people were eager to pay to look at the howling and gibbering inmates. The hospital's name, pronounced "Bedlam" by the local people, has come to mean a chaotic uproar (Farreras, 2023).

The Nineteenth Century: Reform and Moral Treatment

As the year 1800 approached, the treatment of people with mental disorders began to improve once again. Historians usually point to La Bicêtre, an asylum in Paris for male patients, as the first site of asylum reform. In 1793, during the French Revolution, Philippe Pinel (1745–1826) was named the chief physician there. He argued that the patients were sick people whose illnesses should be treated with sympathy and kindness rather than chains and beatings (Farreras, 2023; Pearce, 2020). He allowed

asylum A type of institution that first became popular in the sixteenth century to provide care for persons with mental disorders. Most asylums became virtual prisons.

them to move freely about the hospital grounds; replaced the dark dungeons with sunny, well-ventilated rooms; and offered support and advice. Pinel's approach proved remarkably successful. Many patients who had been shut away for decades improved greatly over a short period of time and were released. Pinel later brought similar reforms to a mental hospital in Paris for female patients, La Salpêtrière.

Meanwhile, an English Quaker named William Tuke (1732–1819) was bringing similar reforms to northern England. In 1796, he founded the York Retreat, a rural estate where about 30 mental patients lived as guests in quiet country houses and were treated with a combination of rest, talk, prayer, and manual work (Farreras, 2023; Pearce, 2020).

The Spread of Moral Treatment

The methods of Pinel and Tuke, called **moral treatment** because they emphasized moral guidance and humane and respectful techniques, caught on throughout Europe and the United States. Patients with psychological problems were increasingly perceived as potentially productive human beings who deserve individual care, including discussions of their problems, useful activities, work, companionship, and quiet.

Bettmann/Getty Images

A moral imperative As head of La Bicêtre in Paris, Philippe Pinel helped usher in an era of moral treatment, characterized by sympathetic care and more humane conditions. In this painting, Pinel is depicted ordering the removal of chains from a patient at the asylum.

The person most responsible for the early spread of moral treatment in the United States was Benjamin Rush (1745–1813), an eminent physician at Pennsylvania Hospital who is now considered the father of American psychiatry. Limiting his practice to mental illness, Rush developed humane approaches to treatment (Kittle, 2020). For example, he required that the hospital hire intelligent and sensitive attendants to work closely with patients, reading and talking to them and taking them on regular walks. He also suggested that it would be therapeutic for doctors to give small gifts to their patients now and then.

Rush's work was influential, but it was a Boston schoolteacher named Dorothea Dix (1802–1887) who made humane care a public and political concern in the United States. From 1841 to 1881, Dix went from state legislature to state legislature and to Congress, speaking of the horrors she had observed at asylums and calling for reform. Dix's campaign led to new laws and greater government funding to improve the treatment of people with mental disorders (Farreras, 2023; Markel, 2020). Each state was made responsible for developing effective public mental hospitals, or **state hospitals,** all of which were intended to offer moral treatment. Similar hospitals were established throughout Europe.

The Decline of Moral Treatment

By the 1850s, a number of mental hospitals throughout Europe and America reported success using moral approaches. By the end of that century, however, several factors led to a reversal of the moral treatment movement (Lindeque, 2022; Bloom, 2020). One factor was the speed with which the movement had spread. As mental hospitals multiplied, severe money and staffing shortages developed, recovery rates declined, and overcrowding in the hospitals became a major problem. Another factor was the assumption behind moral treatment that all patients could be cured if treated with just humanity and dignity. For some, this was indeed sufficient. Others, however, needed more effective treatments than any that had yet been developed. An additional factor contributing to the decline of moral treatment was the emergence of a new wave of prejudice against people with mental disorders. The public came to view them as strange and dangerous. Moreover, many of the patients entering public mental hospitals in the United States in the late nineteenth century were immigrants with limited resources whom the public had little interest in helping.

By the early years of the twentieth century, the moral treatment movement had ground to a halt in both the United States and Europe. Public mental hospitals were providing only custodial care and ineffective medical treatments and were becoming more overcrowded every year. Long-term hospitalization became the rule once again.

The Early Twentieth Century: The Somatogenic and Psychogenic Perspectives

As the moral movement was declining in the late 1800s, two opposing perspectives emerged and began to compete for the attention of clinicians: the **somatogenic perspective,** the view that psychopathology has physical causes, and the **psychogenic perspective,** the view that the chief causes of psychopathology are psychological factors. These perspectives came into full bloom during the twentieth century.

Massoud Hossaini/AFP via Getty Images

The more things change . . . Unfortunately, in some parts of the world today, horrific "treatments" are still applied to people with severe mental disorders. Here a man is chained to a wall at a holy shrine in a local village of Afghanistan, the primary intervention for his psychological disorder.

The Somatogenic Perspective

The somatogenic perspective has at least a 2,400-year history—remember Hippocrates' view that psychopathology resulted from brain disease and an imbalance of humors? Not until the late nineteenth century, however, did this perspective make a triumphant return and begin to gain wide acceptance.

Two factors were responsible for this rebirth. One was the work of a German researcher, Emil Kraepelin (1856–1926). In 1883, Kraepelin published a textbook arguing that physical factors, such as fatigue, are responsible for mental dysfunction. In addition, as you will learn later in the textbook, he developed the first modern system for classifying different kinds of psychopathology, listing their physical causes and discussing their expected course (Farreras, 2023; Heckers, Engstrom, & Kendler, 2022). As you will read in a later chapter, some of Kraepelin's writings on mental illness, race, and society have received criticism in recent years, and their contribution to the mistreatment and even persecution of people from certain racial and ethnic groups have come to light, but his nineteenth-century textbook and classification system did open the door to the somatogenic perspective.

New biological discoveries also triggered the rise of the somatogenic perspective. One of the most important discoveries was that an organic disease, *syphilis,* led to *general paresis,* an irreversible disorder with both mental symptoms, such as delusions of grandeur, and physical ones, such as paralysis (Ha, Tadi, & Dubensky, 2023). In 1897, the German neurologist Richard von Krafft-Ebing (1840–1902) injected matter from syphilis sores into patients with general paresis and found that none of the patients developed symptoms of syphilis. Their immunity could have been caused only by an earlier case of syphilis. Since all of his patients with general paresis were now immune to syphilis, Krafft-Ebing theorized that syphilis had been the cause of their general paresis. The work of Kraepelin and the new understanding of general paresis led many researchers and practitioners to suspect that physical factors were responsible for many mental disorders, perhaps all of them.

Despite the general optimism, biological approaches yielded mostly disappointing results throughout the first half of the twentieth century. Although many medical treatments were developed for patients in mental hospitals during that time, most of the techniques failed to work. Physicians tried tooth extraction, tonsillectomy, hydrotherapy (alternating hot and cold baths), and lobotomy, a surgical cutting of certain nerve fibers in the brain. Even worse, biological views and claims led, in some circles, to proposals for immoral solutions such as *eugenic sterilization,* the elimination (through medical or other means) of a person's ability to reproduce (see **Table 1-1**). Not until the 1950s, when a number of effective medications were finally discovered, did the somatogenic perspective truly begin to pay off for patients.

moral treatment A nineteenth-century approach to treating people with mental dysfunction that emphasized moral guidance and humane and respectful treatment.

state hospitals State-run public mental institutions in the United States.

somatogenic perspective The view that psychopathology has physical causes.

psychogenic perspective The view that the chief causes of psychopathology are psychological factors.

TABLE 1-1

Eugenics and Mental Disorders

Year	Event
1896	Connecticut became the first state in the United States to prohibit persons with mental disorders from marrying.
1896–1933	Every state in the United States passed a law prohibiting marriage by persons with mental disorders.
1907	Indiana became the first state to pass a bill calling for people with mental disorders, as well as criminals and other people who were termed "defectives," to undergo sterilization.
1927	The U.S. Supreme Court ruled that eugenic sterilization was constitutional.
1907–1945	Approximately 45,000 Americans were sterilized under eugenic sterilization laws; 21,000 of them were patients in state mental hospitals.
1929–1932	Denmark, Norway, Sweden, Finland, and Iceland passed eugenic sterilization laws.
1933	Germany passed a eugenic sterilization law, under which 375,000 people were sterilized by 1940.
1940	Nazi Germany began to use "proper gases" to kill people with mental disorders; 70,000 or more such people were killed in less than two years.
1945–1999	An estimated 30,000 nonconsensual sterilizations were performed in the United States, mostly on people of color, prisoners, and those receiving public assistance.
2014	The state of California, which once accounted for 80 percent of forced sterilizations in the United States, passes law banning sterilization procedures in correctional facilities, unless such a procedure is needed to save a prisoner's life.

Information from: Liscum & Garcia, 2022; McConnell & Phelan, 2022; Villarosa, 2022; Markfield, 2019; Lombardo, 2017; Stern, 2016; Fischer, 2012; Whitaker, 2002.

The Psychogenic Perspective The late 1800s also saw the emergence of the psychogenic perspective, the view that the chief causes of psychopathology are often psychological factors. This view, too, had a long history, but it did not gain much of a following until studies of *hypnotism* demonstrated its potential.

Hypnotism is a procedure in which a person is placed in a trancelike mental state during which they become extremely suggestible. It was used to help treat psychological disorders as far back as 1778, when an Austrian physician named Friedrich Anton Mesmer (1734–1815) established a clinic in Paris. His patients exhibited *hysterical disorders,* mysterious bodily ailments that had no apparent physical basis. Mesmer had his patients sit in a darkened room filled with music; then he appeared, dressed in a colorful costume, and touched the troubled area of each patient's body with a special rod. A surprising number of patients seemed to be helped by this treatment, called *mesmerism* (Spilde, 2020). Their pain, numbness, or paralysis disappeared. Several scientists believed that Mesmer was inducing a trancelike state in his patients and that this state was causing their symptoms to disappear. The treatment was so controversial, however, that eventually Mesmer was banished from Paris.

It was not until years after Mesmer died that many researchers had the courage to investigate his procedure, later called *hypnotism* (from *hypnos,* the Greek word for "sleep"), and its effects on hysterical disorders. The experiments of two physicians practicing in the city of Nancy in France, Hippolyte-Marie Bernheim (1840–1919) and Ambroise-Auguste Liébeault (1823–1904), showed that hysterical disorders could actually be induced in otherwise healthy people while they were under the influence

of NOTE ...

Myth Buster

Although it is popularly believed that a full moon is accompanied by significant increases in crime, strange and unusual behaviors, and admissions to mental hospitals, decades of research have failed to support this notion.

(Kaufmann, 2023; Launer, 2021)

of hypnosis. That is, the physicians could make healthy people experience deafness, paralysis, blindness, or numbness by means of hypnotic suggestion—and they could remove these artificial symptoms by the same means. Thus, they established that a *mental* process—hypnotic suggestion—could both cause and cure even a physical dysfunction. Leading scientists concluded that hysterical disorders were largely psychological in origin, and the psychogenic perspective rose in popularity.

Among those who studied the effects of hypnotism on hysterical disorders was Josef Breuer (1842–1925) of Vienna. Breuer, a physician, discovered that his patients sometimes awoke free of hysterical symptoms after speaking candidly under hypnosis about past upsetting events. During the 1890s, Breuer was joined in his work by another Viennese physician, Sigmund Freud (1856–1939). As you will learn in the chapter on models of psychopathology, Freud's work eventually led him to develop the theory of **psychoanalysis,** which holds that many forms of psychological functioning—both pathological and nonpathological—are psychogenic. In particular, Freud believed that *unconscious* psychological processes are at the root of such functioning.

Freud also developed the *technique* of psychoanalysis, a form of discussion in which clinicians help troubled people gain insight into their unconscious psychological processes. He believed that such insight, even without hypnotic procedures, would help the patients overcome their psychological problems. Freud and his followers offered psychoanalytic treatment to patients in their offices for sessions of approximately an hour—a format of treatment now known as *outpatient therapy.* By the early twentieth century, psychoanalytic theory and treatment were widely accepted throughout the Western world.

Phanie/Alamy Stock Photo

"Sometimes your words just hypnotize me" Here, a young client is hypnotized by a clinician. Hypnotism opened the door for the psychogenic perspective, and, as illustrated by the above words from a Notorious B.I.G. song, it continues to influence many areas of modern life.

SUMMING UP

III How Was Psychopathology Viewed and Treated in the Past?

The history of psychological disorders stretches back to ancient times. Prehistoric societies apparently viewed psychological dysfunction as the work of evil spirits. There is evidence that Stone Age cultures used trephination to treat such dysfunction. People of early societies also sought to drive out evil spirits by exorcism.

Physicians of the Greek and Roman empires offered more enlightened explanations of mental disorders. Hippocrates, for example, believed that psychopathology was caused by an imbalance of the four bodily fluids, or humors. Early Chinese medical writings also saw disturbed mood and behavior as arising from physical pathology as well as from disharmony with the natural world and one's surroundings.

In the Middle Ages, Europeans returned to demonological explanations of psychopathology. The clergy, who were very influential, held that mental disorders were the work of the devil. As the Middle Ages drew to a close, such explanations and treatments began to decline, and people with psychopathology were increasingly treated in hospitals instead of by the clergy.

Care of people with mental disorders continued to improve during the early part of the Renaissance. Certain religious shrines became dedicated to the humane treatment of such people. By the middle of the sixteenth century, however, persons with mental disorders were being warehoused in asylums.

Care of those with psychopathology started to improve again in the nineteenth century. In Paris, Philippe Pinel started the movement toward moral treatment. In the United States, Dorothea Dix spearheaded a movement to ensure legal rights and protection for people with mental disorders and to establish state hospitals for their care. By the late nineteenth century, however, the moral treatment movement disintegrated, and mental hospitals again became warehouses where inmates received minimal care.

The turn of the twentieth century saw the return of the somatogenic perspective and the rise of the psychogenic perspective. Sigmund Freud's psychogenic approach, psychoanalysis, eventually gained wide acceptance.

psychoanalysis Either the theory or the treatment of psychopathology that emphasizes unconscious psychological forces as the cause of psychological dysfunction.

From Juilliard to the streets Nathaniel Ayers, subject of the book and movie *The Soloist*, plays his violin on the streets of Los Angeles while living as an unhoused person in 2005. Once a promising musical student at the Juilliard School in New York, Ayers developed schizophrenia and eventually found himself without treatment and without a residence.

Recent Decades and Current Trends

IT WOULD HARDLY BE ACCURATE to say that we now live in a period of great enlightenment about mental disorders or dependable treatment of these disorders. In fact, surveys have found that 31 percent of those surveyed consider such disorders to be a sign of personal weakness, 17 percent believe that seeking treatment reflects weakness, and 47 percent say they would feel uncomfortable living next door to someone with a significant psychological disorder (Roper Center, 2022). Nevertheless, there have been major changes over the past 75 years in the ways clinicians understand and treat psychopathology. There are more theories and types of treatment, more research studies, more information, and—perhaps because of those increases—more disagreements about psychopathology today than at any time in the past.

How Are People with Severe Challenges Cared For?

In the 1950s, researchers discovered a number of new **psychotropic medications**—drugs that primarily affect the brain and reduce many symptoms of psychological dysfunction. They included the first *antipsychotic drugs,* which help reduce extremely confused and distorted thinking; *antidepressant drugs,* which lift the mood of depressed people; and *antianxiety drugs,* which reduce tension and worry.

When given these drugs, many patients who had spent years in mental hospitals began to show signs of improvement. Hospital administrators, encouraged by these results and pressured by a growing public outcry over the terrible conditions in public mental hospitals, began to discharge patients almost immediately.

Since the discovery of these medications, mental health professionals in most of the developed nations of the world have followed a policy of **deinstitutionalization,** releasing hundreds of thousands of patients from public mental hospitals. On any given day in 1955, close to 600,000 people were confined in public mental institutions across the United States (see **Figure 1-1**). Today, the daily patient population in the same kinds of hospitals is between 38,000 and 75,000, although most clinical experts believe this relatively low number is partly due to a shortage of available beds in public mental hospitals throughout the country (AHA, 2022, 2019; BH, 2022, 2020; Hudson, 2021). In addition, thousands of people receive treatment in *private* psychiatric hospitals, care that is paid for by the patients themselves and/or their insurance companies. On average, the private facilities offer more pleasant surroundings and more favorable staff–patient ratios than the public ones.

Without question, outpatient care has now become the primary mode of treatment for people with severe psychological challenges as well as for those with more moderate problems. When severely disturbed people do need institutionalization these days, they are usually hospitalized for a short period of time. Ideally, they are then provided with outpatient psychotherapy and medication in community programs and residences.

In later chapters, you will read much more about this relatively recent emphasis on community care for people with severe psychological disturbances—a philosophy called the *community mental health approach*. The approach has been helpful for many patients, but too few community programs are available to address current needs in the United States. As a result, hundreds of thousands of persons with severe disturbances do not have lasting recoveries, and they shuttle back and forth between the mental hospital and the community. After release from the hospital, they at best receive minimal care and often wind up living in substandard rooming houses or on the streets. More than 140,000 people with such disturbances are unhoused on any given day; at least another 440,000 are incarcerated (NAMI, 2023; MIPO, 2022). Their abandonment is truly a national disgrace.

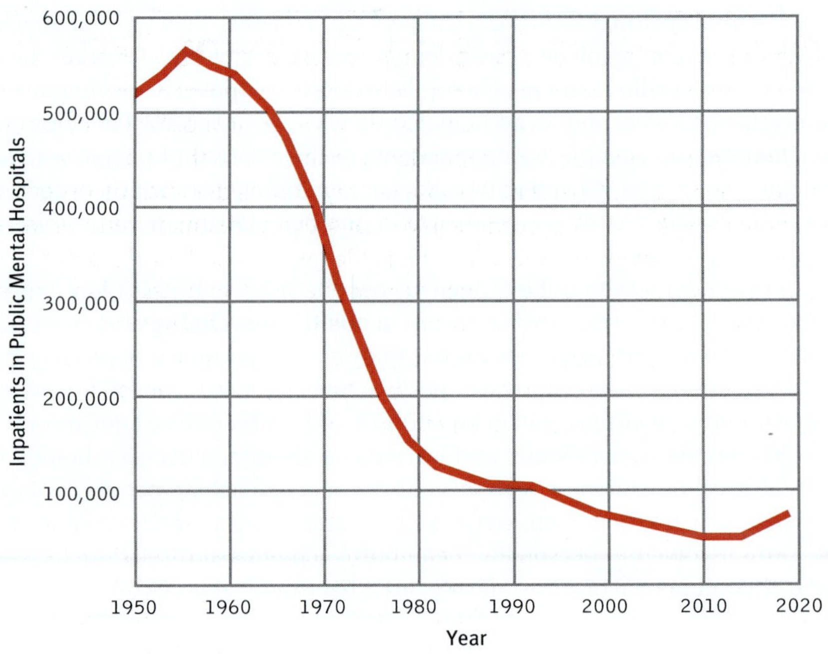

FIGURE 1-1

The Impact of Deinstitutionalization

The daily number of patients now hospitalized in public mental hospitals in the United States (between 38,000 and 75,000) is a small fraction of the daily number hospitalized in 1955. (Information from: AHA, 2022, 2019; BH, 2022, 2020; Hudson, 2021; O'Reilly, Allison, & Bastiampiallai, 2019; Amadeo, 2017)

How Are People with Less Severe Challenges Treated?

The treatment picture for people with moderate psychological challenges has been more positive than that for people with severe disorders. Since the 1950s, outpatient care has continued to be the preferred mode of treatment for people who experience moderate difficulties, and the number and types of facilities that offer such care have expanded to meet the need.

Before the 1950s, almost all outpatient care took the form of **private psychotherapy,** in which individuals meet with a self-employed therapist for counseling services. Since the 1950s, most health insurance plans have expanded coverage to include private psychotherapy, so that it is now more widely available to people of all incomes. Today, outpatient therapy is also offered in a number of less expensive settings, such as community mental health centers, crisis intervention centers, family service centers, and other social service agencies. Surveys suggest that in the United States, around 43 percent of people with psychological disorders receive treatment in the course of a year (MHA, 2023).

Outpatient treatments are also becoming available for more and more kinds of conditions. When Freud and his colleagues first began to practice, most of their patients were experiencing anxiety or depression. Almost half of today's clients experience those same conditions, but people with other kinds of disorders are also receiving therapy. In addition, at least 20 percent of clients enter therapy because of milder disruptions in living—difficulties with marital, family, job, peer, school, or community relationships (APA, 2023).

Yet another change in outpatient care since the 1950s has been the development of programs devoted exclusively to specific psychological conditions. We now have, for example, suicide prevention centers, substance use programs, eating disorder programs, phobia clinics, and sexual dysfunction programs. Clinicians in these programs have the kind of expertise that can be acquired only by concentration in a single area.

psychotropic medications Drugs that mainly affect the brain and reduce many symptoms of mental dysfunction.

deinstitutionalization The practice, begun in the 1960s, of releasing hundreds of thousands of patients from public mental hospitals.

private psychotherapy An arrangement in which a person directly pays a therapist for counseling services.

A Growing Emphasis on Preventing Disorders and Promoting Mental Health

Although the community mental health approach has often failed to address the needs of people with severe disorders, it has given rise to an important principle of mental health care—**prevention** (MHA, 2023; Cuijpers, 2022). Rather than wait for psychological disorders to occur, many of today's community programs try to correct the social conditions that underlie many psychological conditions (poverty or violence in the community, for example) and try to help people who are at risk for developing emotional challenges (for example, teenage parents or the children of people with severe psychological disorders). As you will read later, community prevention programs are not always successful, but they have grown in number, offering great promise as the ultimate form of intervention.

Why do you think it has taken psychologists so long to start studying positive behaviors?

Prevention programs have been further energized in the past few decades by the clinical field's ever-growing interest in **positive psychology** (Smith et al., 2023; Ryff, 2022). Positive psychology is the study and enhancement of positive feelings such as optimism and happiness, positive traits like hard work and wisdom, and group-directed virtues, including altruism and tolerance (see ***InfoCentral***).

While researchers study and learn more about positive psychology in the laboratory, clinical practitioners with this orientation are teaching people coping skills that may help protect them from stress and adversity and are encouraging them to become more involved in personally meaningful activities and relationships—thus helping to prevent mental disorders (Pan et al., 2022; Comer et al., 2020).

AP Photo/Matthew S. Gunby

Positive psychology in action Often, positive psychology and multicultural psychology work together. Here, two young girls come together as one at the end of a "slavery reconciliation" walk by 400 people in Maryland. The walk was intended to promote racial understanding and to help Americans overcome the lasting psychological effects of slavery.

Multicultural Psychology

We are, without question, a society of multiple cultures, ethnicities, and languages. People of color in the United States collectively make up 40 percent of the population, a percentage that is expected to grow to 52 percent by 2055 (USAFacts, 2023). This change is due in part to shifts in age structure, birth rates, and migration patterns (Frey, 2023, 2021). The Asian American and Hispanic populations in the United States, for example, have grown by over 80 and 70 percent, respectively, during the past two decades, and the number of Americans belonging to multiple racial or ethnic groups has more than doubled during the past decade, with over 33 million Americans now identifying as multiracial or multiethnic (Budiman & Ruiz, 2021; Jones et al., 2021).

In response to this growing diversity, an area of study called **multicultural psychology** has emerged and surged in popularity. Multicultural psychologists seek to understand how race, ethnicity, gender, sexual orientation, religion, disability, language, socioeconomic class, and other such factors affect behavior, emotion, and thought. As noted earlier, people from across various backgrounds, traditions, and experiences are shaped by their unique histories, opportunities, and barriers and thus may differ psychologically (Blume, 2022; Vasquez & Johnson, 2022). Multicultural theorists are particularly interested in the experiences and psychological effects that result when multiple factors of this kind *intersect* in a given person, a concept referred to as **intersectionality.** As you read earlier, the field of multicultural psychology has also begun to have a powerful effect on our understanding and treatment of psychopathology.

The Increasing Influence of Insurance Coverage

Around 67 percent of Americans have *private* health insurance, most often purchased directly or through an employer, while the remainder are either uninsured (almost 9 percent of Americans) or enrolled in a *public-supplemented* insurance program such as Medicare, Medicaid, the Children's Health Insurance Program (CHIP), or military insurance (U.S. Census Bureau, 2023). So many people now seek mental health services that most private and public insurance programs have changed their coverage for these services in recent decades. The dominant form of insurance now consists of **managed care programs**—programs in which the insurance company determines such key issues as which therapists its clients may choose, the cost of sessions, and the number of sessions for which a client may be reimbursed (Hughes, 2023; McCarthy, 2022).

Managed care coverage for mental health treatment follows the same basic principles as coverage for medical treatment, including a limited pool of practitioners from which patients can choose, preapproval of treatment by the insurance company, strict standards for judging whether conditions and treatments qualify for reimbursement, and ongoing reviews. In the mental health realm, both therapists and clients typically dislike managed care programs (Goldman, 2022; Smith et al., 2022). They fear that the programs inevitably shorten therapy (often for the worse), unfairly favor treatments whose results are not always lasting (for example, drug therapy), pose a special hardship for those with severe mental disorders, and result in treatments determined by insurance companies rather than by therapists.

A key problem with insurance coverage—both managed care and other kinds of insurance programs—is that reimbursements for mental disorders tend to be lower than those for physical disorders. This places persons with psychological difficulties at a distinct disadvantage. Thus, in 2008, the U.S. Congress passed a federal *parity* law that directed insurance companies to provide equal coverage for mental and physical conditions, and in 2014, the mental health provisions of the Affordable Care Act (ACA) went into effect and extended the reach of the earlier parity law. Moreover, the ACA designated mental health care as 1 of 10 types of "essential health benefits" that *must* be provided by all insurers.

The parity laws have brought about some important improvements in mental health insurance coverage. However, many insurance companies still manage to shortchange the mental health claims of their members (MHA, 2023; SAMHSA, 2022). Thus, in 2021, Congress passed yet another law calling for stricter government regulation of each insurance company's parity coverage. It remains to be seen whether this law will indeed produce full parity.

prevention Interventions aimed at deterring mental disorders before they can develop.

positive psychology The study and enhancement of positive feelings, traits, and abilities.

multicultural psychology The field that seeks to understand how the varied histories, opportunities, and barriers experienced by people of different races, ethnicities, genders, sexual orientations, disabilities, languages, and other such factors affect behavior, emotion, and thought.

intersectionality The cumulative experiences and psychological effects that result from interactions and intersections between *multiple* factors, such as race, sexual orientation, gender, discrimination, and socioeconomic class, for a given person.

managed care program Health care coverage in which the insurance company largely controls the nature, scope, and cost of medical or psychological services.

What Are Today's Leading Theories and Professions?

One of the most important developments in the clinical field has been the growth of numerous theoretical perspectives that now coexist. Before the 1950s, the *psychoanalytic* perspective, with its emphasis on unconscious psychological conditions as the cause of psychopathology, was dominant. Since then, additional influential perspectives have emerged, particularly the *biological, cognitive-behavioral, humanistic-existential, sociocultural,* and *developmental psychopathology* schools of thought. At present, no single viewpoint dominates the clinical field as the psychoanalytic perspective once did. In fact, the perspectives often conflict and compete with one another.

In addition, a variety of professionals now offer help to people with psychological disorders (see **Table 1-2**). Before the 1950s, psychotherapy was offered only by *psychiatrists,* physicians who complete three to four additional years of training after medical

TABLE 1-2

Profiles of Mental Health Professionals in the United States

	Degree	Began to Practice	Current Number	Average Annual Salary	Percent Female	Percent Persons of Color	Percent LGBTQ+	Percent Over 40-yrs old
Psychiatrists	MD, DO	1840s	26,000	$250,000	55%	36%	10%	73%
Psychologists	PhD, PsyD, EdD	Late 1940s	179,000	$ 81,000	65%	21%	21%	66%
Social Workers	MSW, DSW	Early 1950s	716,000	$ 50,000	81%	33%	20%	66%
Counselors	Various	Early 1950s	328,000	$ 49,000	62%	32%	13%	56%

Information from: BLS, 2022; Zippia, 2022.

HAPPINESS

Positive psychology is the study of positive feelings, traits, and abilities. A better understanding of constructive functioning enables clinicians to better promote psychological wellness. **Happiness** is the positive psychology topic currently receiving the most attention. Many, but far from all, people are happy. In fact, only **one-third** of adults declare themselves "very happy." Let's take a look at some of today's leading facts, figures, and notions about happiness.

WHO Is "Very Happy?"

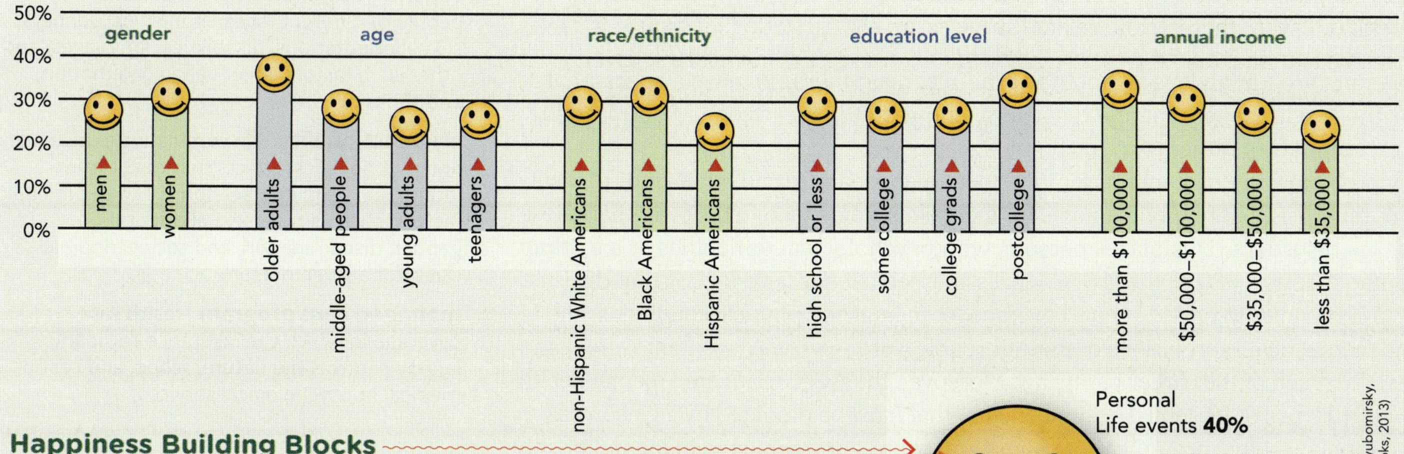

(Ellwood, 2022; Twenge & Cooper, 2022; Assari, 2019; Harris Poll, 2016, 2015, 2013)

Happiness Building Blocks

Are people born with a happy disposition? Or do their surroundings and life circumstances make them more or less happy? Researchers of this **nature-versus-nurture** question have learned that both sets of factors **interact** to determine one's degree of happiness. But the factors have different degrees of impact.

(Cherry, 2022; Lyubomirsky, 2019, 2008; Brooks, 2013)

Who Tends to Be *Happier*?

Unashamed people	Guilt-ridden people
Peaceful people	Angry people
Extroverts	Introverts
Regular church attenders	Church nonattenders

(Brooks, 2021; Margolis & Lyubomirsky, 2019; Harris Poll, 2016, 2015; Brooks, 2013; *The Economist*, 2010)

The Pursuit of Happiness

People tend to pursue a happy life. For some, that means pursuit of a **pleasant life**—filled with as many pleasures as possible. Others pursue an **engaging life**, characterized by satisfaction in work, parenting, love, and leisure. Still others pursue a **meaningful life**—recognizing and using their strengths in the service of others.

(Cherry, 2022; Diener et al., 2018; Seligman, 2012, 2002)

WHAT Do Happy People Do?

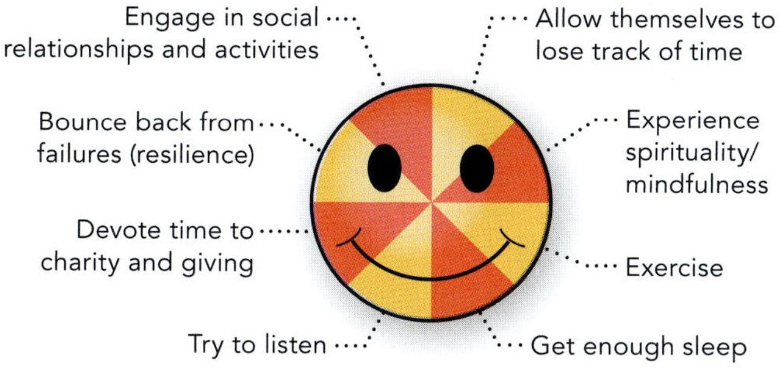

(Cherry, 2022; Aknin et al., 2019; Twenge, 2019; Bratskeir, 2013)

Happiest Professions

Percentage of employees who are happy

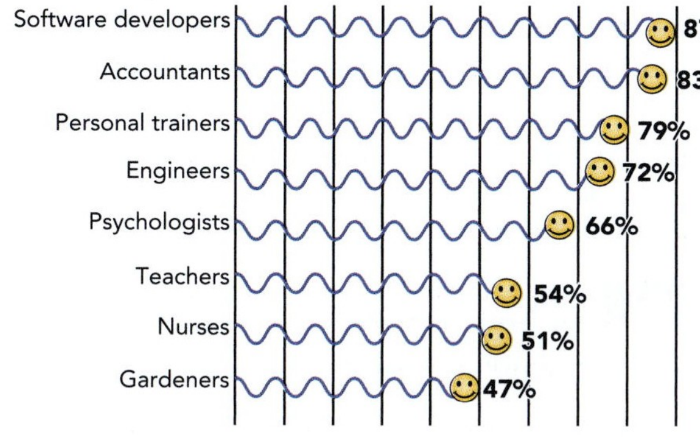

(Shor, 2022; Lin, 2021)

Non-online Social Contact and Happiness

The more social contact, the happier we are—up to a point!

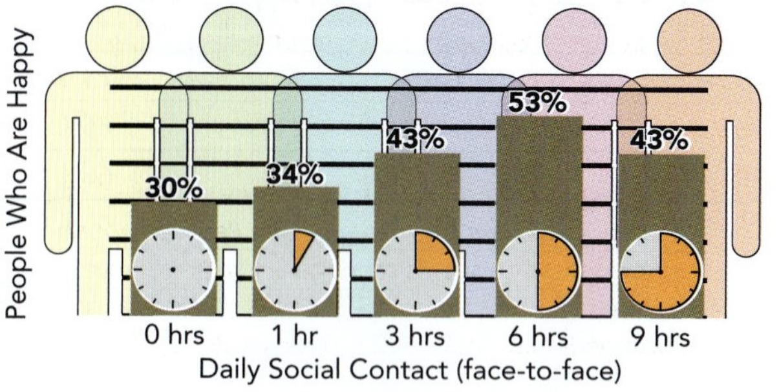

(Twenge, 2023, 2019; WC, 2022; Rahim, 2017; Crabtree, 2011)

Marriage and Happiness

Married people are, on average, a bit happier than people with a different marital status.

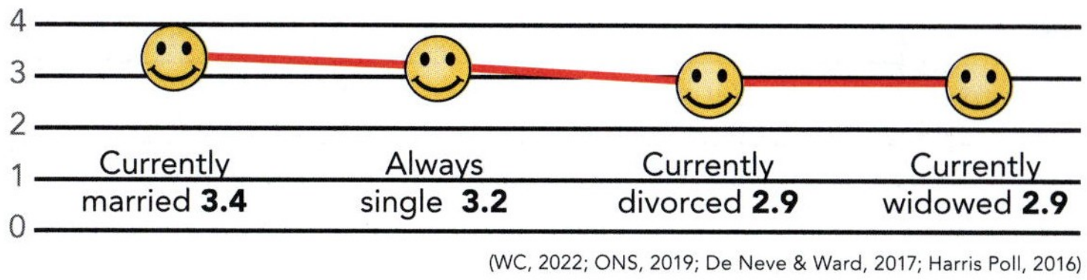

(WC, 2022; ONS, 2019; De Neve & Ward, 2017; Harris Poll, 2016)

school (a *residency*) in the treatment of mental difficulties. After World War II, however, with millions of soldiers returning home to countries throughout North America and Europe, the demand for mental health services expanded so rapidly that other professional groups had to step in to fill the need.

Among those other groups are *clinical psychologists*—professionals who earn a doctorate in clinical psychology by completing four to five years of graduate training in psychopathology and its treatment as well as a one-year internship in a mental health setting. Psychotherapy and related services are also provided by *counseling psychologists, educational and school psychologists, mental health counselors, psychiatric nurses, marriage therapists, family therapists, faith-based therapists,* and—the largest group—*clinical social workers*. Each of these specialties has its own graduate training program. Theoretically, each conducts therapy in a distinctive way, but in reality, clinicians from the various specialties often use similar techniques.

A related development in the study and treatment of mental disorders since World War II has been the growth of effective research. *Clinical researchers* have worked to determine which concepts best explain and predict psychopathology, which treatments are most effective, what factors enhance the effectiveness of given treatments, and what kinds of changes may be required. Well-trained clinical researchers conduct studies in universities, medical schools, laboratories, mental hospitals, mental health centers, and other clinical settings throughout the world. Their work has produced important discoveries and has changed many of our ideas about psychopathology.

Technology and Mental Health

The breathtaking rate of technological change that characterizes today's world has had significant effects—both positive and negative—on the mental health field, and it will undoubtedly affect the field even more in the coming years.

Our digital world provides new sources for psychological dysfunction (Ali et al., 2022). As you will learn in a later chapter, for example, many people who grapple with gambling disorder have found the ready availability of Internet gambling to be all too inviting. Similarly, social media, the Internet, and texting have become convenient tools for those who wish to stalk or bully others, express sexual exhibitionism, or pursue pedophilic desires. Likewise, some clinicians believe that violent video games may contribute to the development of antisocial behavior. And, in the opinion of many clinicians, constant texting, social media use, and Internet browsing may become an addictive behavior or may lead to shorter attention spans.

A number of clinicians also worry that social networking can contribute to psychological dysfunction in certain cases (see **Figure 1-2**). On the positive side, research

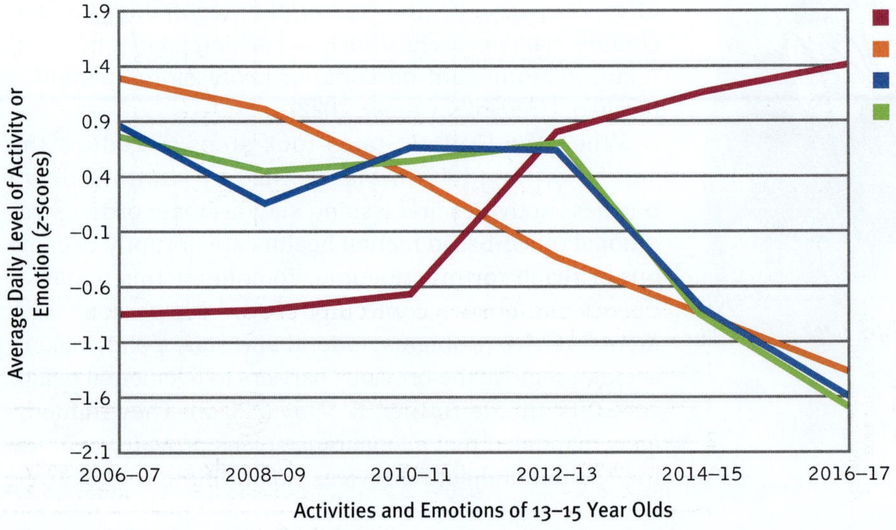

FIGURE 1-2

The Digital Explosion

Over the past 15 years, online behavior has increased while other key activities have dropped off. By converting results from various surveys into scores on a common scale (known as *z-scores*), researchers have learned that today's teens spend fewer hours each day sleeping and socializing in face-to-face interactions than adolescents did 15 years ago. Perhaps not so coincidentally, today's teenagers also have lower levels of happiness. (Information from: Shawcroft et al., 2022; Twenge & Hamilton, 2022; Twenge, 2019) indicates that, on average, social media users are particularly likely to maintain close relationships, receive social support, be trusting, and lead active lives. But, on the negative side, there is research suggesting that social media platforms may increase peer pressure and social anxiety in some adolescents (Popat & Tarrant, 2022). Such platforms may, for example, cause some people to develop fears that others in their network will exclude them socially (so-called *fear of missing out*, or *FOMO*). Similarly, the platforms may facilitate shy or socially anxious people's withdrawal from valuable face-to-face relationships.

In addition, our digital world has greatly expanded the amount of mental health information available to the public. Indeed, countless websites offer such information. When accurate, material of this kind can be very useful to people in search of mental health answers, help, and guidance. Unfortunately, along with this wealth of online information comes an enormous amount of misinformation about psychological conditions and their treatments.

What kinds of problems might result from the growing availability and use of mental health apps in today's world?

The face of clinical treatment is also changing in our fast-moving digital world. For example, computerized intervention programs and Internet-based support groups are now widely available. Moreover, there are hundreds of smartphone apps devoted to relaxing people, cheering them up, giving them feel-good advice, helping them track their shifting moods and thoughts, or otherwise improving their psychological states (Carl et al., 2022; Hong, Sanchez, & Comer, 2020). Increasingly, therapists are even including *wearable technologies* in their treatment (for example, "smart" watches/bands and "smart" glasses) to help monitor key psychophysiological processes that unfold throughout individuals' lives, such as sleep quality, physical activity, respiration, and heart rate (Andrews et al., 2022).

Finally, **telemental health,** the use of remote technologies (such as long-distance videoconferencing) to provide real-time therapy sessions without the therapist being physically present, has grown by leaps and bounds (Comer, 2021; Comer et al., 2021). Enthusiasm for telemental health services had been gaining momentum among clinicians and clients for over a decade, but it was the Covid-19 pandemic and related social distancing that truly propelled such services into the clinical mainstream. Prior to the pandemic, certain barriers were preventing telemental health from being practiced on a large scale. For example, a number of insurance providers were refusing to reimburse this form of treatment, rendering it unaffordable for many people. Moreover, in the years prior to the pandemic, many clinicians were reluctant to offer telemental health, fearing that technology-related confidentiality breaches, such as hacking incidents, could result in significant personal or professional penalties (Freitag, Urcuyo, & Comer, 2022).

When the United States took steps to reduce the spread of Covid-19 in March 2020 by shutting down business activities and issuing stay-at-home orders, traditional office-based mental health care abruptly became out of reach for most people. To counter this negative impact and ensure continuity of care for persons with mental health problems, federal and state policymakers acted to remove the previous barriers to telemental health care (Sistani, de Bittner, & Shaya, 2022). They immediately mandated that all insurance plans provide coverage for telemental health services. In addition, they waived

Hartley Lin/CartoonStock Ltd.

"I do think it would speed things up if you followed my social media"

penalties against clinicians for unintended confidentiality violations that might arise from the use of remote communication technologies. These policy changes empowered therapists to practice telemental health without concern for personal or professional consequences.

Within weeks of these mandates, the vast majority of mental health services in the United States were being conducted online. Indeed, during the peak of the pandemic, 78 percent of mental health practitioners reported that they were integrating telemental health services into their practice (Sistani et al., 2022). Moreover, during the post-peak period of the pandemic, 50 percent of practitioners continued to use a telemental health format with at least some of their outpatients, and, indeed, 36 percent of all outpatient visits continue to be conducted via telemental health (Clay, 2022). As the advantages of online mental health services have unfolded over the past several years—greater affordability, accessibility, convenience, and outreach—it has become clear that telemental health will, to one degree or another, remain a permanent part of the clinical field, extending well beyond the Covid-19 pandemic.

telemental health The use of remote technologies, such as long-distance videoconferencing, to deliver mental health services without the therapist being physically present.

SUMMING UP

Recent Decades and Current Trends

Over the past 75 years, there have been major changes in the understanding and treatment of psychopathology. In the 1950s, researchers discovered a number of new psychotropic medications. Their success contributed to a policy of deinstitutionalization, under which hundreds of thousands of patients were released from public mental hospitals. In addition, outpatient treatment has become the primary approach for most people with mental disorders, both mild and severe; prevention programs are growing in number and influence; the field of multicultural psychology has increasingly influenced how clinicians view and treat psychopathology; and insurance coverage is having a significant impact on the way treatment is conducted.

It is also the case that a variety of perspectives and professionals have come to operate in the field of psychopathology, and many well-trained clinical researchers now investigate the field's theories and treatments. And finally, the technological advances of recent times, including the proliferation of mental health apps and telemental health services, have greatly affected the mental health field.

What Do Clinical Researchers Do?

RESEARCH IS THE KEY TO ACCURACY in all fields of study; it is particularly important with regard to psychopathology because a wrong belief in this field can lead to great suffering. At the same time, clinical researchers, also called *clinical scientists,* face certain challenges that make their work particularly difficult. For example, clinical researchers must always ensure that the rights of their research participants, both human and animal, are not violated (Kazdin, 2021). They must also figure out how to measure such elusive concepts as unconscious motives, private thoughts, mood changes, and human potential. They must consider the different cultural backgrounds, races, sexual orientations, and genders of the people they choose to study, and they must work to understand how such factors shape the personal meaning and impact of various life experiences.

Clinical researchers try to discover broad laws, or principles, of mental dysfunction and challenges. They search for a general, or *nomothetic,* understanding of the nature,

of NOTE ...

Their Words

"The temptation to form premature theories upon insufficient data is the bane of our profession."

Sherlock Holmes in *The Valley of Fear,* 1914

Scott Legato/Getty Images

Flawed research, gigantic impact Dan Reynolds, the lead singer for the rock group Imagine Dragons, drapes himself in a pride flag as he speaks out against so-called *conversion therapy* and the psychological harm it has inflicted on the LGBTQ+ community. This practice, which is now widely discredited, purports to help gay and transgender people change their sexual orientation or gender identity, respectively. In 2012, Robert Spitzer, one of the world's most respected psychiatric researchers, offered an extraordinary public apology to the LGBTQ+ community for his influential and supportive 2003 study on this practice. Spitzer called his earlier study both fatally flawed and morally wrong.

causes, and treatments of psychopathology across individuals. Except for research purposes, they do not assess, diagnose, or treat individual clients; that is the job of clinical practitioners, who seek an *idiographic,* or individualistic, understanding of psychopathology. You will read about the work of practitioners in later chapters.

To gain nomothetic insights, clinical researchers, like scientists in other fields, use the **scientific method**—that is, they collect and evaluate information through careful observations. These observations in turn enable them to pinpoint and explain relationships between variables. Simply stated, a *variable* is any characteristic or event that can vary, whether from time to time, from place to place, or from person to person. Age, gender, and ethnicity, for example, are human variables. So are eye color, occupation, and social status. Clinical researchers are interested in variables such as childhood upsets, present life experiences, moods, social functioning, cultural identity, and responses to treatment. They try to determine whether two or more such variables change together and whether a change in one variable causes a change in another. Will the death of a parent cause a child to become depressed? If so, will a given treatment reduce that depression?

Such questions cannot be answered by logic and reflection alone because scientists, like all human beings, frequently make errors in thinking. Thus, clinical researchers depend mainly on three methods of investigation: the *case study,* which typically focuses on one individual, and the *correlational method* and *experimental method,* approaches that are usually used to gather information about many individuals. Each is best suited to certain kinds of circumstances and questions. As a group, these methods enable scientists to form and test **hypotheses**—hunches or predictions that certain variables are related in certain ways—and to draw broad conclusions as to why. More properly, a hypothesis is a tentative explanation offered to provide a basis for an investigation.

The Case Study

A **case study** is a detailed description of a person's life and psychological problems. It describes the person's history, present circumstances, and symptoms. It may also include speculation about why the problems developed, and it may describe the person's treatment (Cherry, 2022). As you will learn later in the textbook, one of the field's best-known case studies, called *The Three Faces of Eve,* describes a woman with three alternating personalities, each having a distinct set of memories, preferences, and personal habits.

Most clinicians take notes and keep records in the course of treating their patients, and some further organize such notes into a formal case study to be shared with other professionals. The clues offered by a case study may help a clinician better understand or treat the person under discussion. In addition, case studies may play nomothetic roles that go far beyond the individual clinical case.

How Are Case Studies Helpful?

Case studies are useful to researchers in many ways (Cherry, 2022; Mohan, 2021). They can, for example, be a source of *new ideas* about behavior, setting the stage for new lines of research and discovery. Sigmund Freud's theory of psychoanalysis was based mainly on the patients he saw in private practice. He pored over their case studies to find what he believed to be broad psychological processes and principles of development. In addition, a case study may offer *tentative support* for a theory. Freud used case studies in this way as well, regarding them as evidence for the accuracy of his ideas. Conversely, case studies may serve to *challenge a theory's assumptions.*

Why do case studies and other anecdotal offerings influence people so much, often more than systematic research does?

Case studies may also show the value of *new therapeutic techniques.* And finally, case studies may offer opportunities to study *unusual problems* that do not occur often enough to permit a large number of observations. Investigators of relatively uncommon disorders, such as *dissociative identity disorder* (previously called multiple personality disorder), the pattern on display in *The Three Faces of Eve,* once relied entirely on case studies for information.

Suzanne Tenner/©HBO/courtesy Everett Collection

Case studies and the arts Case studies often find their way into the arts or media and capture the public's attention. The HBO series *In Treatment*, for example, presents various fictitious cases, highlighted by provocative therapy sessions, including this session, in which therapist Dr. Brooke Taylor offers insights to her client.

What Are the Limitations of Case Studies?

Case studies also have limitations (Cherry, 2022; Passer, 2021). First, they are reported by *biased observers,* that is, by therapists who have a personal stake in seeing their treatments succeed. These therapists must choose what to include in a case study, and their choices may at times be self-serving. Second, case studies rely on *subjective evidence.* Is a client's difficulty really caused by the events that the therapist or client says are responsible? After all, those are only a fraction of the events that may be contributing to the situation. Finally, case studies provide little basis for generalization. Events or treatments that seem important in one case may be of no help at all in efforts to understand or treat other cases.

The limitations of the case study are largely addressed by two other leading methods of investigation: the *correlational method* and the *experimental method.* These methods do not offer the rich detail and depth that make case studies so interesting, but they do help investigators draw broad conclusions about psychopathology in the population at large. Thus, most clinical investigators prefer these methods over the case study.

Three features of the correlational and experimental methods enable clinical investigators to gain general, or nomothetic, insights: (1) The researchers typically observe many individuals. (2) The researchers apply procedures uniformly. Other researchers can thus repeat, or *replicate,* a particular study to see whether it consistently gives the same findings. (3) The researchers use *statistical tests* to analyze the results of a study and determine whether broad conclusions are justified.

The Correlational Method

Correlation is the degree to which events or characteristics vary along with each other. The **correlational method** is a research procedure used to determine this "co-relationship" between variables (Cherry, 2022). This method can be used, for example, to answer the question "Is there a correlation between the amount of stress in people's lives and the degree of depression they experience?" That is, as people keep experiencing stressful events, are they increasingly likely to become depressed?

To test this question, researchers have collected life stress scores (for example, the number of threatening events experienced during a certain period of time) and depression scores (for example, scores on a depression survey) from individuals and have correlated these scores. The people who are chosen for a study are its subjects, or *participants,* the term preferred by today's investigators. The participants in a given study are collectively called its *sample.* Typically, investigators have found that life stress and depression do indeed increase or decrease together (Lauche et al., 2023; Clarke et al., 2022). That is, the greater someone's life stress score, the higher their score on a depression scale. When variables change the same way, the correlation of those variables is said to have a positive *direction* and is referred to as a *positive correlation* (Cherry, 2022; Passer, 2021). Alternatively, correlations can have a negative direction rather than a positive one. In a *negative correlation,* the value of one variable increases as the value of the other variable decreases (Cherry, 2022). Researchers have found, for example, a negative correlation between depression and activity level. The greater one's depression, the lower the number of one's activities.

scientific method The process of systematically gathering and evaluating information, through careful observations, to understand a phenomenon.

hypothesis A hunch or prediction that certain variables are related in certain ways.

case study A detailed account of a person's life and psychological problems.

correlation The degree to which events or characteristics vary along with each other.

correlational method A research procedure used to determine how much events or characteristics vary along with each other.

Stress and depression Correlational studies find that stressors produced by natural disasters, medical catastrophes, and the like are often accompanied by depression and other psychological symptoms. In the first year of the Covid-19 pandemic, for example, the stress of social distancing and extended separations resulted in severe levels of depression, loneliness, and other painful emotions for many people. Here, a woman hugs her granddaughter through a protective plastic drop sheet after the two had not seen each other for many months.

There is yet a third possible outcome for a correlational study. The variables under study may be *unrelated,* meaning that there is no consistent relationship between them (Cherry, 2022). As the measures of one variable increase, those of the other variable sometimes increase, sometimes decrease, and sometimes stay the same. Studies have found, for example, that depression and intelligence are unrelated. That is, knowing someone's depression score provides no useful information for predicting their intelligence score.

In addition to knowing the direction of a correlation, researchers need to know its *magnitude,* or strength. That is, how closely do the two variables correspond? Does an increase in one correspond to a large increase in the other, or does an increase in one correspond to a smaller increase in the other? When changes in one variable correspond to large changes in the other variable in person after person, the correlation is said to be high, or strong (Cherry, 2022).

The direction and magnitude of a correlation are often calculated numerically and expressed by a statistical term called the *correlation coefficient* (Frey, 2022). The correlation coefficient can vary from +1.00, which indicates a perfect positive correlation between two variables, down to –1.00, which represents a perfect negative correlation. The *sign* of the coefficient (+ or –) signifies the direction of the correlation; the *number* represents its magnitude. A correlation coefficient of .00 reflects a zero correlation, or no relationship between variables. The closer the correlation is to .00, the weaker, or lower in magnitude, it is. Thus, correlations of +.75 and –.75 are of equal magnitude and equally strong (just in opposite directions), whereas a correlation of +.25 is weaker than either.

Everyone's behavior is changeable, and many human responses can be measured only approximately. Most correlations found in psychological research, therefore, fall short of a perfect positive or negative correlation. For example, hundreds of studies of life stress and depression, conducted over the past half-century, have found correlations as high as +.53 (Krishnan, 2022; Miller, Ingham, & Davidson, 1976). Although hardly perfect, a correlation of this magnitude is considered large in psychological research.

When Can Correlations Be Trusted?

Scientists must decide whether the correlation they find in a given sample of participants accurately reflects a real correlation in the general population. Could the observed correlation have occurred by mere chance? Scientists can never know for certain, but they can test their conclusions with a *statistical analysis* of their data, using principles of probability (Dane & Carhart, 2022). In essence, they ask how likely it is that the study's particular findings have occurred by chance. If the statistical analysis indicates that chance is unlikely to account for the correlation they found, researchers may conclude that their findings reflect a real correlation in the general population. A cutoff point helps researchers make this decision. By convention, if there is less than a 5 percent probability that a study's findings are due to chance (signified as $p < .05$), the findings are said to be *statistically significant* and are thought to likely reflect a true correlation in the larger population.

What Are the Merits of the Correlational Method?

The correlational method has certain advantages over the case study (see **Table 1-3**). Because correlation researchers measure their variables, observe many participants, and apply statistical analyses, they are in a better position to generalize their conclusions to people beyond the ones they have studied. Furthermore, researchers can easily repeat correlational studies using new samples of participants to check the results of earlier studies.

On the other hand, although correlations allow researchers to describe the relationship between two variables, they do not *explain* the relationship (Steiner, Shadish, & Sullivan, 2023). When we look at the positive correlation found in many life stress

TABLE 1-3

Relative Strengths and Weaknesses of Research Methods

	Provides Individual Information	Provides General Information	Provides Causal Information	Statistical Analysis Possible	Replicable
Case Study	Yes	No	No	No	No
Correlational Method	No	Yes	No	Yes	Yes
Experimental Method	No	Yes	Yes	Yes	Yes

studies, we may be tempted to conclude that increases in recent life stress cause people to feel more depressed. In fact, however, the two variables may be correlated for any one of three reasons: (1) Life stress may cause depression. (2) Depression may cause people to experience more life stress (for example, symptoms of depression may cause people to perform poorly at work or may interfere with social relationships). (3) Depression and life stress may each be caused by a third variable, such as financial problems.

Can you think of other correlations in life that are interpreted mistakenly as causal?

Although correlations say nothing about causation, they can still be of great use to clinicians. Clinicians know, for example, that suicide attempts increase as people become more depressed. Thus, when working with severely depressed clients, clinicians stay on the lookout for signs of suicidal thinking. Perhaps depression directly causes suicidal behavior, or perhaps a third variable, such as a sense of hopelessness, causes both depression and suicidal thoughts. Whatever the cause, just knowing that there is a correlation may enable clinicians to take measures (such as hospitalization) to help save lives.

Of course, in other instances, clinicians do need to know whether one variable causes another. Do parents' conflicts with each other cause their children to be more anxious? Does job dissatisfaction lead to feelings of depression? Will a given treatment help people to cope more effectively in life? Questions about causality call for the experimental method.

The Experimental Method

An **experiment** is a research procedure in which a variable is manipulated and the manipulation's effect on another variable is observed (Dane & Carhart, 2022; Frey, 2022). The variable that the researcher manipulates is called the **independent variable,** and the variable being observed for change is called the **dependent variable.**

To examine the experimental method more fully, let's consider a question that is often asked by clinicians (Chambless & Hollon, 2023; Rush, 2023): "Does a particular therapy relieve the symptoms of a particular disorder?" Because this question is about a causal relationship, researchers may use an experiment to answer it. They may give the therapy in question to people with a particular disorder and then observe whether those people improve. In this experiment, the therapy is the independent variable, and psychological improvement is the dependent variable.

If the true cause of changes in the dependent variable cannot be separated from other possible causes, then an experiment gives very little information. Thus, in their studies, experimenters must try to eliminate all **confounds**—variables other than the independent variable that may also be affecting the dependent variable. When there are confounds in an experiment, those confounds, rather than the independent variable, may be causing the observed changes.

For example, situational variables, such as the location of the therapy office (say, a quiet country setting) or soothing background music in the office, may have

experiment A research procedure in which a variable is manipulated and the effect of that manipulation on another variable is observed.

independent variable The variable in an experiment that is manipulated to determine whether it has an effect on another variable.

dependent variable The variable in an experiment that is expected to change as the independent variable is manipulated.

confound In an experiment, a variable other than the independent variable that is also acting on the dependent variable.

a therapeutic effect on participants in a therapy study. Or perhaps the participants are unusually motivated or have high expectations that the therapy will work, factors that thus account for their improvement. To guard against confounds, researchers should include three important features in their experiments—a *control group, random assignment,* and a *masked design* (Ariel, Bland, & Sutherland, 2022).

Patrick Hardin/CartoonStock Ltd

"It would never work, Nichole; I'm in the experimental group and you're in the control."

The Control Group

A **control group** is a group of research participants who are not exposed to the independent variable under investigation but whose experience is otherwise similar to that of the **experimental group**, the participants who are exposed to the independent variable. By comparing the two groups, an experimenter can better determine the effect of the independent variable.

To study the effectiveness of a particular therapy, for example, experimenters commonly divide participants into two groups after obtaining their consent to participate in the study. The experimental group may come into an office and receive the therapy for an hour, while the control group may simply come into the office for an hour. If the experimenters find later that the people in the experimental group improve more than the people in the control group, they may conclude that the therapy was effective, above and beyond the effects of time, the office setting, and any other confounds. To guard against confounds, experimenters try to provide all participants, both control and experimental, with experiences that are identical in every way—except for the independent variable.

Of course, it is possible that the differences observed between an experimental group and a control group have occurred simply by chance. Thus, as with correlational studies, investigators who conduct experiments must do a statistical analysis on their data and find out how likely it is that the observed differences are due to chance. If the likelihood is very low—less than 5 percent ($p < .05$)—the differences between the two groups are considered to be statistically significant, and the experimenter may conclude with some confidence that the differences are due to the independent variable.

An additional point is worth noting with regard to clinical treatment experiments. It is always important to distinguish between *statistical significance* and a notion called *clinical significance*. As you have just read, *statistical significance* indicates whether a participant's improvement in functioning—large or small—occurred because of treatment. *Clinical significance* indicates whether the amount of improvement is meaningful in the individual's life. Even if the moods of depressed participants improve because of treatment, the individuals may still be too unhappy to enjoy life.

Random Assignment

Researchers must also watch out for differences in the *makeup* of the experimental and control groups since those differences may also confound a study's results. In a therapy study, for example, the experimenter may unintentionally put wealthier participants in the experimental group and participants of more limited economic means in the control group. This difference, rather than their therapy, may be the cause of the greater improvement later found among the experimental participants. To reduce the effects of preexisting differences between groups, experimenters typically use **random assignment.** This is the general term for any selection procedure that ensures that every participant in the experiment is as likely to be placed in one group as in the other (Christensen, Turner, & Johnson, 2023), as though group assignments are being determined by flipping a coin or picking names out of a hat. In practice, researchers typically use a computer program that assigns participants to groups randomly.

of NOTE ...

Research Demographics

In the United States, around 79 percent of the human participants in medical and mental health studies are non-Hispanic White people, and 21 percent are people of color.

(Information from: Blakemore, 2022; Turner et al., 2022)

Masked Design

A final confound problem is *bias*. Participants may bias an experiment's results by trying to please or help the experimenter. In a therapy experiment, for example, if those participants who receive the treatment know the purpose of the study and know which group they are in, they might actually work harder to feel better or to fulfill the experimenter's expectations. If so, *participant bias* rather than therapy could be causing their improvement.

To avoid this bias, experimenters can prevent participants from finding out which group they are in. This experimental strategy is called a **masked design** because the individuals are kept unaware of their assigned group (Frey, 2022). In a therapy study, for example, control participants could be given a *placebo* (Latin for "I shall please"), something that looks or tastes like real therapy but has none of its key ingredients. For example, control participants might receive an "imitation" therapy, called **placebo therapy,** such as attending weekly "sessions" to discuss life events with a therapist but not being taught the same coping skills as those being taught to participants in the true therapy condition (Bai et al., 2023; Passer, 2021). If the experimental (true therapy) participants then improve more than the control (placebo therapy) participants, experimenters have more confidence that the true therapy has caused their improvement.

An experiment may also be confounded by *experimenter bias*—that is, experimenters may have expectations that they unintentionally transmit to the participants in their studies. In a drug therapy study, for example, the experimenter might smile and act confident while providing real medications to the experimental participants but frown slightly and appear hesitant while offering placebo drugs to the control participants. This kind of bias is sometimes referred to as the *Rosenthal effect,* after the psychologist who first identified it (Rosenthal, 1966). Experimenters can eliminate their own bias by arranging to be unaware themselves. In a drug therapy study, for example, an aide could make sure that the real medication and the placebo drug look identical. The experimenter could then administer treatment without knowing which participants were receiving true medications and which were receiving false medications, leaving no chance that the experimenter might unintentionally reveal which medication each participant is actually getting. While either the participants or the experimenter may be kept unaware in an experiment, it is best that both be unaware—a research strategy called a *double-masked design* (Frey, 2022). In fact, most medication experiments now use double-masked designs to test promising drugs.

Alternative Research Designs

Designing an informative and proper study presents many hurdles. It is not easy, for example, to devise an experiment that is fully controlled, randomly assigns participants to groups, prevents every possible confound, and avoids ethical problems. To work around such limitations, clinical scientists often must use procedures and designs that vary somewhat from those discussed above. Some of today's leading alternative research designs are the *matched design, natural experiment, analogue experiment, single-case experiment, longitudinal study, epidemiological study, qualitative study,* and *mixed-methods design.*

In **matched designs**, investigators make use of groups that already exist in the world. Consider, for example, research into the effects of child abuse. Because it would be unethical for investigators to create an experimental group by actually abusing a randomly chosen group of children, they must instead compare children who already have a history of abuse with children who do not. To make this comparison as valid as possible, the researchers match the experimental participants (abused children) with control participants (non-abused children) who are similar in age, gender, cultural backgrounds, family size, socioeconomic status, type of neighborhood, or other characteristics. When the data from studies using this kind of design show that abused children are typically sadder and have lower self-esteem than matched control participants who have not been abused, the investigators can conclude with some confidence that abuse, not these other variables, is causing the differences (Cavanaugh & Nelson, 2022; Wang et al., 2022).

In **natural experiments,** nature itself manipulates the independent variable, while the experimenter observes the effects. That is, the participants in these studies are

control group In an experiment, a group of participants who are not exposed to the independent variable.

experimental group In an experiment, the participants who are exposed to the independent variable under investigation.

random assignment A selection procedure in an experiment that ensures that participants are randomly placed either in the control group or in the experimental group.

masked design A feature of an experiment in which participants do not know whether they are in the experimental condition or the control condition.

placebo therapy A pretend treatment that the participant in an experiment believes to be genuine.

matched design A research design that matches the experimental participants with control participants who are similar on key characteristics.

natural experiment An experiment in which nature rather than an experimenter manipulates an independent variable.

of NOTE ...

Animal Studies

- Estimates vary widely. Between 12 million and 111 million animals are used as subjects in research studies in the United States each year.
- Around 95 percent of these animals are mice and rats. Fewer that 1 percent are monkeys, dogs, and cats.

(Information from: SR, 2022; Grimm, 2021)

selected by an accident of fate rather than by the investigator's design. Natural experiments must be used for studying the psychological effects of unusual and unpredictable events, such as floods, earthquakes, and fires.

On December 26, 2004, an earthquake occurred beneath the Indian Ocean off the coast of Sumatra, Indonesia. The earthquake triggered a series of massive tsunamis that flooded the ocean's coastal communities, killed more than 228,000 people, and injured and left millions of survivors unhoused, particularly in Indonesia, Sri Lanka, India, and Thailand. Within months of this disaster, researchers conducted natural experiments in which they collected data from hundreds of survivors and from control groups of people who lived in areas not directly affected by the tsunamis. The disaster survivors scored significantly higher on anxiety and depression measures (dependent variables) than the control groups did. The survivors also experienced more sleep problems, feelings of detachment, arousal, difficulties concentrating, startle responses, and guilt feelings (Ranasinghe et al., 2023; Jang, Ekyalongo, & Kim, 2021). Over the past decade, other natural experiments have focused on survivors of natural disasters around the world and have revealed lingering psychological symptoms among those survivors as well (Hong et al., 2022; Ide-Okochi et al., 2022; Dick et al., 2021).

Raveendran/AFP/Getty Images

Making a point The rights of animal subjects must also be considered in research studies. Here, with his body painted as a monkey, an activist from the organization PETA (People for the Ethical Treatment of Animals) sits in a cage to protest the use of animals in research at a medical science institute in India.

Researchers often run **analogue experiments.** Here they induce laboratory participants to behave in ways that seem to resemble real-life psychopathology and then conduct experiments on the participants in the hope of shedding light on the real-life psychopathology. Analogue studies often (but not always) use animals as participants (Parise et al., 2022).

As you will read in the chapter on depressive disorders, investigator Martin Seligman, in a classic body of work, has used analogue studies to investigate the causes of human depression. Seligman has produced depression-like symptoms in laboratory participants—both animals and humans—by repeatedly exposing them to negative events (shocks, loud noises, task failures) over which they have no control. In these "learned helplessness" analogue studies, the participants seem to give up, lose their initiative, and become sad—suggesting to some clinicians that human depression itself may indeed be caused by loss of control over the unpleasant events in one's life.

Scientists often use a **single-case experimental design,** also called a **single-subject experimental design,** when they do not have the luxury of experimenting on many participants (Ferron, Kirby, & Lipien, 2023). Here a single participant is observed both before and after the manipulation of an independent variable. For example, to determine whether a particular clinical treatment is helpful, a researcher might employ the kind of single-case experimental design called an *ABA*, or *reversal, design*. The researcher could first observe a client's behavior for a month while the person is not receiving any treatment (condition A), next apply treatment for a month and observe the treatment's impact on the client's behavior (condition B), and, finally, withdraw treatment for a month (condition A again) to observe whether the gains from treatment now disappear. If the treatment effects do indeed cease, the experimenter may surmise that the client's gains had been the result of treatment.

Obviously, single-case experiments are similar to individual case studies in their focus on one participant. In single-case experiments, however, the independent variable is manipulated systematically so that the investigator can, with some degree of confidence, draw conclusions about the cause of an observed effect. At the same time, because only one person is investigated in a single-case experiment, the researcher cannot be sure that the participant's reaction to the independent variable is typical of people in general.

Yet another alternative research design is the **longitudinal study**, in which investigators observe the same individuals on many occasions over a long period of time (Littlefield, 2023; Frey, 2022). In several such studies, investigators have observed the progress over the years of typically developing children whose parents have schizophrenia (Knudsen et al., 2022; Yung et al., 2021). The researchers have found, among other things, that the children of the parents with the most severe cases of schizophrenia were particularly likely to develop a psychological disorder, display certain cognitive impairments, and be charged with crimes at later points in their development.

As with some of the other alternative research designs, in a longitudinal study researchers do not directly manipulate the independent variable or randomly assign participants to conditions, and so they cannot definitively pinpoint causes. However, because longitudinal studies report the *order* of events, they do provide compelling clues about which events are more likely to be causes and which events are more likely to be consequences. Certainly, in the above example, the children's problems did not cause their parents' schizophrenia.

Life is a longitudinal study These similarly posed photos of the same individuals at different points in their lives underscore the logic behind longitudinal studies. Just as the individuals' eyes, noses, and smiles in childhood predict similar facial features in adulthood, so too might a person's early temperament, sociability, or other psychological features sometimes predict adult characteristics or difficulties.

Another research design is the **epidemiological study,** a study that reveals how often a problem, such as a particular psychological disorder, occurs in a particular population (Price & Tastet, 2023). More specifically, it determines the incidence and prevalence of the problem. **Incidence** is the number of new cases that emerge in a population during a given period of time. **Prevalence** is the total number of cases in the population during a given period; prevalence includes both existing cases and new cases.

Over the past 50 years, clinical researchers throughout the United States have worked on one of the largest epidemiological studies of mental disorders ever conducted, called the Epidemiologic Catchment Area Study. They have interviewed more than 20,000 people in five cities to determine the prevalence of many psychological disorders in the United States and the treatment programs used. Three other large-scale epidemiological studies in the United States—the National Comorbidity Survey, the National Comorbidity Survey Replication, and the National Epidemiologic Survey on Alcohol and Related Conditions—have collectively questioned almost 60,000 individuals. Findings from these broad-population studies have been further compared with epidemiological studies of specific subpopulations, such as Asian Americans, or with epidemiological studies conducted in other countries to see how rates of mental disorders and treatment programs vary from population to population and from country to country.

Such epidemiological studies have helped researchers identify groups at risk for particular disorders. Women, it turns out, have a relatively high rate of anxiety disorders and depression, and men have a relatively high rate of alcohol use disorder. Older adults have a higher rate of suicide than young people. Black, Hispanic, and Indigenous people experience posttraumatic stress disorder more than non-Hispanic White people in the United States. Depression is more prevalent among LGBTQ+ people than people outside of LGBTQ+ communities. And people in Western countries have higher rates of eating disorders than people in non-Western countries. These trends may lead researchers to suspect that something unique about certain populations or the pressures they are subjected to is helping to cause particular disorders. However, epidemiological studies alone cannot confirm such suspicions of causation.

analogue experiment A research method in which the experimenter produces psychopathology-like behavior in laboratory participants and then conducts experiments on the participants.

single-case experimental design A research method in which a single participant is observed and measured both before and after the manipulation of an independent variable. Also called *single-subject experimental design*.

longitudinal study A study that observes the same participants on many occasions over a long period of time.

epidemiological study A study that measures the incidence and prevalence of a problem, such as a disorder, in a given population.

incidence The number of new cases that emerge in a population during a given period of time.

prevalence The total number of cases in the population during a given period; prevalence includes both existing cases and new cases.

qualitative methods Natural and unfiltered research methods intended to seek out each participant's direct perspective—gathering information that is offered in the participant's own words.

mixed-methods research A research tradition that combines, or *mixes*, both quantitative and qualitative approaches within the same research project.

community-based participatory research A research tradition that has members of an affected community work collaboratively with academically trained researchers at *all* stages of the research process.

Qualitative Studies and Mixed-Methods Designs

As you have read, clinical researchers are typically interested in using findings from a study to test hypotheses and draw conclusions. The researchers measure, or *quantify*, relationships between variables and then use statistical analyses to make predictions about broader populations. Such *quantitative methods*, as they are often known, have been the dominant tradition in the study of psychopathology for over a century.

Quantitative methods work well when assessing objective and straightforward information across participants—such as the number of depression symptoms participants have been dealing with or the number of nights per week they have had trouble sleeping. But clinical researchers are also often interested in learning about inner experiences that may not lend themselves so easily to standard measurement and analysis. What does it *feel* like to have depression? How do depressed participants *describe* their symptoms? And what *meaning* do participants make of their experiences with depression?

To study such subjective experiences, many clinical investigators are now turning to **qualitative methods** (Riley & LaMarre, 2023). Qualitative researchers use natural and *unfiltered* methods to seek out each participant's direct perspective—gathering information that is offered in the participant's own words as opposed to information that has been filtered through forced-choice questions and through the researcher's expectations. They use techniques such as open-ended questions—techniques that position participants as the true experts on their own experiences and that may generate rich, in-depth descriptive accounts.

At the same time, it is hard to group together qualitative information that has been gathered across participants and to draw broad conclusions and predictions about wider populations. Thus, qualitative findings are not well suited for testing hypotheses or drawing conclusions beyond the sample under study.

Many researchers appreciate the *depth* of information that qualitative methods can offer yet also value the *breadth* of information that quantitative methods can provide across participants. That is, they are interested both in collecting rich descriptive accounts of participants' inner experiences *and* in making predictions, testing hypotheses, and drawing broad conclusions from their findings. These investigators may conduct **mixed-methods research,** a design that combines, or *mixes,* both qualitative and quantitative approaches within the same research project (Guetterman & Perez, 2023).

Consider, for example, a researcher studying the effectiveness of Alcoholics Anonymous (AA), a self-help organization for people with alcohol-related problems. Using an experimental design, the researcher might randomly assign participants with alcohol-related problems to either three months of attending AA group meetings (experimental group) or three months of regularly reading about alcohol-related health hazards (control group). To then determine whether attending AA meetings was indeed more helpful than simply reading about alcohol-related health hazards, the experimenter might quantify the amount of alcohol that participants are consuming after the three-month period by, for example, conducting a series of random breathalyzer tests on all participants. If the results show that the AA participants have lower blood alcohol levels after treatment than the control participants do, the researcher might conclude that AA attendance was indeed an effective intervention. But this quantitative result alone would not provide clues as to *why* those in the AA condition displayed greater improvement.

Thus, a mixed-methods researcher might additionally conduct open-ended interviews and focus groups to collect rich qualitative information from the participants in their own voice—information that could help explain the quantitative findings. The researcher might, for example, ask participants what they believe were the most helpful aspects of their treatment. If the open-ended answers of the various AA participants repeatedly center on themes of social connectedness and social support, the researcher

of NOTE ...

Their Words

"All life is an experiment."

Ralph Waldo Emerson

might further speculate that the positive effects of the AA condition were due, at least in part, to the special opportunities for connectedness and support in AA groups. Clearly, findings from mixed-methods research often provide fuller and more revealing information than either quantitative or qualitative studies alone.

Community-Based Participatory Research

Research on psychopathology has traditionally been designed, carried out, and analyzed by investigators with academic training in mental health research. The individuals who stand to benefit most from research on psychopathology—that is, those with psychological challenges, their loved ones, and the professionals who work with them—are involved only as research participants to be observed and studied.

In contrast, in the **community-based participatory research** (CBPR) approach, members of an affected community work collaboratively with academically trained scientists on *all* stages of the research process (Leavy, 2022; McFarlane et al., 2022). The members of the community and the researchers share equal responsibility for shaping the research questions, conducting the research, analyzing the results, and applying the study's findings in the community. By directly collaborating with affected community members to develop the research agenda and make sense of a study's findings, the CBPR approach recognizes the respective strengths and wisdom that researchers and community members can each offer.

The CBPR approach has, for example, brought about some important insights and changes in the realm of *health disparity*. As you will read throughout the textbook, in our society people of color often have elevated health risks, substandard professional detection of health problems, and more restricted access to health care in both the psychological sphere and the medical sphere. Among Black people, in particular, such disparities have been linked to economic disadvantage, inadequate living conditions, deficient health care services, and distrust of health care providers—distrust that can be traced to a history of shameful medical practices and research undertakings that specifically harmed Black populations (CISCRP, 2023; Rogers et al., 2022).

To help reduce the current health disadvantages for Black people, Black community leaders and organizations have partnered with university researchers to develop creative barbershop-based and hair salon–based interventions in Black neighborhoods throughout the United States (Dill et al., 2020). In these CBPR undertakings, the community members have helped the researchers to appreciate that in Black neighborhoods, barbershops and hair salons are among the most trusted spaces outside of the home—places where individuals often socialize for hours, discuss personal and family matters, and participate in recreational activities (Palmer et al., 2021). Similarly, the community members have helped the researchers recognize that there could be great benefit in bringing health information and health screenings to these settings.

Thus, drawing on the wisdom and local knowledge of affected communities, academic researchers have designed barbershop and hair salon outreach, assessment, and intervention programs in which barbers and hairstylists are trained to provide health-related advice, information, support, and referral services to their patrons. Extensive research indicates that such programs often make a significant difference in the patrons' acquisition of medical and mental health information, quality of self-care, health care pursuits, and health outcomes. And, indeed, such barbershop and hair salon health programs are now used with great success in neighborhoods across the United States—promoting health checkups, awareness, conversation, and behaviors among Black people for problems extending from hypertension and diabetes to depression (Coy et al., 2023; Nadison et al., 2022).

of NOTE ...

Distrusting Pharmaceutical Company Research

75% Black Americans who distrust research conducted by pharmaceutical companies

47% Black Americans who cite past mistreatment of research participants as the reason for their distrust of pharmaceutical companies

(Information from: CISCRP, 2023)

More than a little off the top Louisville, Kentucky, barber Alex Daniel trims a man's hair as part of The Confess Project—a national *barbershop-based intervention* started by Lorenzo Lewis to train barbers and stylists in Black neighborhoods to become mental health advocates for their communities. Barbers in The Confess Project are taught how to comfortably discuss mental health issues with their customers and talk openly about emotions.

Institutional Review Board An ethics committee in a research facility that is empowered to protect the rights and safety of human research participants.

Protecting Human Participants

Human research participants have needs and rights that must be respected (see ***MindTech***). In fact, every researcher's primary obligation is to avoid harming the human participants in their studies—physically or psychologically.

The vast majority of researchers are conscientious about fulfilling this obligation. They try to conduct studies that test their hypotheses and that advance scientific knowledge in a safe and respectful way. But there have been some notable exceptions to this over the years—in particular, several infamous studies conducted in the mid-twentieth century. Partly because of such exceptions, the U.S. government and the institutions in which research is conducted now take careful measures to ensure that the safety and rights of human research participants are properly protected.

Who, beyond researchers themselves, might directly watch over the rights and safety of human participants? For the past 50 years, that responsibility has been given to **Institutional Review Boards** (IRBs). Each research facility has

MINDTECH

The Use and Misuse of Social Media

More and more of today's researchers are turning to social networks for their studies. In one study, for example, 58,000 Facebook subscribers allowed researchers access to their list of "likes," and the subscribers further filled out online personality tests. The study found that information about a subscriber's likes could predict with some accuracy their personality traits, level of happiness, use of addictive substances, and level of intelligence, among other variables. Similarly, other studies have predicted individuals' traits, attitudes, feelings, and other responses based on information from their social media posts and tweets (Di Cara et al., 2023; Matz, 2023; Phillips, 2022).

What a great resource, right? Not so fast. This study did ask subscribers whether they were willing to participate. However, in a number of other such studies, social media users do not know that their posted data are being examined and tested, perhaps violating one of research's most important principles—obtaining *informed consent* from participants.

Another area of ethical concern involves the direct and secret *manipulation* of social media users by investigators—an approach illustrated in a study conducted by a team of researchers from Facebook and academia several years ago (Kramer, Guillory, & Hancock, 2014). The investigators wanted to determine whether the content of Facebook news feeds influences its users' moods. Without informing users, the researchers reduced the number of positive news feed posts seen by around 350,000 users and reduced the number of negative posts seen by another 350,000 users over a one-week period. As a result, the moods of the former users became slightly (but significantly) more negative than those of the latter users.

One key concern raised by this study was that, by inducing negative moods, the researchers in this study might have been feeding into the clinical depressions of some negative news feed users (McDermott & Hatemi, 2020).

The potential for misconduct in social media research came under special scrutiny when a political consulting firm named Cambridge Analytica acknowledged that while working for a presidential campaign in 2016, its researchers misled 300,000 Facebook users into believing they were participating in a personality study and releasing their user data for academic purposes. Actually, when the users downloaded an app in the study, it opened up both their own data and those of their friends, revealing the private user data of around 50 million Facebook members. The

Dominic Lipinski/Press Association via AP Images

consulting firm then derived psychological profiles of those members and sent them personalized advertisements favoring the candidate for whom the firm was consulting: ads that appealed to the users' emotions, attitudes, and needs—a strategy called *psychological targeting* (Matz, 2023).

Social media users and services, professional associations, and government regulators alike are currently trying to sort out and address the concerns and possible misuses that accompany social media research. In the meantime, while the technology-driven questions of what's public, what's private, and what's a proper use of data are under debate, it is probably best that social media users follow an increasingly sacred rule of our digital world: "poster beware."

an IRB—a committee of five or more members who review and monitor every study conducted at that institution, starting when the studies are first proposed (Fried & Jansen, 2023; APA, 2022). The institution may be a university, medical school, psychiatric or medical hospital, private research facility, mental health center, or the like. If research is conducted there, the institution must have an IRB, and that IRB has the responsibility and power to require changes in a proposed study as a condition of approval. These powers are granted to IRBs (or similar ethics committees) by nations around the world. In the United States, for example, IRBs are empowered by two agencies of the federal government—the Office for Human Research Protections and the Food and Drug Administration.

It turns out that protecting the rights and safety of human research participants is a complex undertaking. Thus, IRBs often are forced to conduct a kind of risk–benefit analysis in their reviews. They may, for example, approve a study that poses minimal or slight risks to participants if that "acceptable" level of risk is offset by the study's potential benefits to society. In general, IRBs try to ensure that each study grants the following rights to its participants:

Stephen Jaffe/AFP/Getty Images

A national disgrace In a 1997 White House ceremony, President Bill Clinton offers an official apology to 94-year-old Herman Shaw and other Black American men whose syphilis was purposefully left untreated by government doctors and researchers in the Tuskegee Syphilis Study, a research undertaking conducted from 1932 to 1972, prior to the emergence of Institutional Review Boards. In this infamous study on the natural course of untreated syphilis, 399 participants were not informed that they had the disease, and they continued to go untreated even after it was discovered that penicillin is an effective intervention. More than 100 of the men died from syphilis-related complications.

- The participants enlist voluntarily.
- Before the participants enlist, they are adequately informed about what the study entails ("informed consent").
- The participants can end their participation in the study at any time.
- The benefits of the study outweigh its costs/risks to participants.
- The participants are protected from physical and psychological harm.
- The participants have access to information about the study.
- The participants' privacy is protected by principles such as confidentiality or anonymity.

Unfortunately, even with IRBs on the job, these rights can be in jeopardy. Consider, for example, the right of informed consent (HHS, 2023). To help ensure that participants understand what they are getting into when they enlist for a study, IRBs typically require that the individuals read and sign an "informed consent" document that spells out everything they need to know. But how clear are such documents? Not very, according to some investigations (Shah et al., 2023; Fischer et al., 2021; O'Sullivan et al., 2020).

It turns out that most such forms—the very forms deemed acceptable by IRBs—are too long and/or are written above the reading level of a large percentage of participants. In fact, fewer than half of all participants may fully understand the informed consent documents they are signing. Still other investigations indicate that relatively few human participants ask questions of researchers during the informed consent phase of a study, and fewer still carefully read the informed consent forms before signing them.

In short, the IRB system is flawed, much like the research undertakings that it oversees. One reason for this is that ethical principles are subtle notions that do not always translate into simple guidelines. Another reason is that ethical decisions—whether by IRB members or by researchers—are subject to differences in perspective, interpretation, and decision-making style. Despite such problems, most observers agree that the creation and work of IRBs have helped improve the rights and safety of human research participants over the years.

SUMMING UP

What Do Clinical Researchers Do?

Researchers use the scientific method to uncover nomothetic, or general, principles of psychopathology. They attempt to identify and examine relationships between variables, and they depend primarily on three methods of investigation: the case study, the correlational method, and the experimental method.

A case study is a detailed account of a person's life, psychological problems, and, in some instances, treatment. Correlational studies are used to systematically observe the degree to which events or characteristics vary along with each other. This method allows researchers to draw broad conclusions about psychopathology in the population at large.

In experiments, researchers manipulate suspected causes to see whether expected effects will result. This method enables researchers to determine the causes of various conditions or events. The findings of experiments, like those of correlational studies, are analyzed statistically.

Clinical scientists must often implement alternative research designs. These include the matched design, natural experiment, analogue experiment, single-case experiment, longitudinal study, epidemiological study, qualitative study, and mixed-method design.

Community-based participatory research has members of an affected community work collaboratively with trained researchers at all stages of the research process. This approach ensures that the work is directly informed and shaped by persons with firsthand knowledge and who stand to benefit most from the findings.

Each research facility has an Institutional Review Board (IRB) that has the power and responsibility to protect the rights and safety of human participants in all studies conducted at that facility. Members of the IRB review each study before participant recruitment and can require changes in the study before granting approval for the undertaking.

of NOTE ...

WEIRD Participants

More than 70 percent of psychology studies use college students as participants. These participants are often described by the acronym WEIRD because they are overwhelmingly from societies that are Western, Educated, Industrialized, Rich, and Democratic.

Moving Forward

SINCE ANCIENT TIMES, people have tried to explain, treat, and study psychopathology. By examining the responses of past societies to pathological behaviors, we can better understand the roots of our present views and treatments and the impressive progress that the clinical field has made. At the same time, we must recognize the many problems in the clinical field today. Without question, our current understanding of psychopathology represents a work in progress. The field's most important insights, investigations, and changes are yet to come.

How, then, should you proceed in your study of psychopathology? To begin with, you need to learn about the basic perspectives and tools used by today's scientists and practitioners. This chapter's focus on widely used research designs has helped achieve that goal. So too will the next two chapters on today's leading models of psychopathology and prominent tools of clinical assessment and diagnosis. Later chapters will then help you to appreciate in depth the major categories of psychopathology as well as the leading explanations and treatments for each of them. In the final chapter, you will read about how mental health science and practice interact with legal, social, and other institutions in our world.

Quick Quiz

1. What features are common to psychopathological functioning? pp. 4–7
2. Why is cultural humility important in the work of clinical researchers and practitioners? pp. 7–9
3. Name two forms of past treatments that reflect a demonological view of psychopathology. pp. 11–15
4. Give examples of the somatogenic view of psychopathology from Hippocrates, the Renaissance, the nineteenth century, and the twentieth century. Describe the role of hypnotism and hysterical disorders in the development of the psychogenic view. pp. 11–17
5. Describe the major changes that have occurred since the 1950s in the understanding and treatment of psychopathology. pp. 18–23
6. How have recent technological developments affected the mental health field? What impact has the Covid-19 pandemic had on telemental health? pp. 23–25
7. What are the advantages and disadvantages of the case study, correlational method, and experimental method? What techniques do researchers include in experiments to guard against the influence of confounds? pp. 26–31
8. Describe the various alternative research designs often used by investigators. pp. 31–35
9. What are the advantages of community-based participatory research? p. 35
10. What are Institutional Review Boards, and what are their responsibilities and goals? pp. 35–37

Models of Psychopathology

CHAPTER 2

Jorge, *a 23-year-old of Mexican American descent, arrived at the emergency room after his sister Bella had called 911 when he told her he was thinking of ending his life. He had not left his apartment for nearly a week. Everything outside seemed too scary to face. Jorge appeared gaunt, with unkempt hair and several days of beard growth.*

Jorge told the psychiatrist on duty that he had recently lost his bookstore job because he called in sick too often. When pressed, he clarified that he actually had quit because "they were sick of me and about to fire me. Then, when I quit, the boss turned around and asked me to reconsider. What kind of mind games was he playing?"

Jorge told the psychiatrist he was constantly worried about money. He ate only once or twice a day so he wouldn't run out of money, although he never did run out. A year earlier, he experienced what he thought was a heart attack—he became dizzy, started sweating, could not stop his hands from shaking, and more. However, he did not see a doctor at that time because he was afraid of what he'd hear.

These episodes happened several more times, and although he tried to ignore them, he came to fear leaving his apartment and increasingly made excuses to cancel plans to see his girlfriend, Ivy. He told the psychiatrist, "Ivy dumped me right after that, saying that I neglected her and that she was tired of my saying she was too good for me and should find someone better. I was upset, but her actions proved my suspicions about her had been right. She probably already had another man lined up. In short order, I found myself making accusations about her and telling her that in fact I was better off without her if she wasn't committed to me." During that time, Jorge also kept avoiding his friends. Eventually, they stopped calling, which led him to conclude that they would rather be with people who were more fun than him. And then he began to miss work a lot until he barely went out. At this point, he told the psychiatrist that he had remained mostly homebound for the past three months.

When the psychiatrist asked Jorge if he had spoken to his family during this time, Jorge said he hadn't spoken to his parents in two years. His father, Jorge Sr., owned a chain of department stores that had made the family wealthy. "The controlling old man planned my whole future from the time I was 5," Jorge said. "He insisted that I would eventually go to business school and someday run our business. Pop was affectionate but obsessed with my grades. If I ever got a B during my childhood, he would sit me down to discuss what I'd done wrong. As for my mother, I barely remember even seeing her after I was 8, once my sister Bella was born. She did nothing but fuss over Bella—Bella's dance lessons, horseback riding, swimming. I was always an afterthought."

Later, in business school, Jorge always felt out of place, largely due to his Mexican heritage. He told the psychiatrist that one of his classmates, a hateful guy named Philip, assumed Jorge had gotten into the school and received financial aid simply because he had "filled a quota," and so Philip resented him. Philip repeatedly told Jorge that he didn't know what he was doing and would never graduate. Jorge said that when he got average grades his first semester, his father overreacted, yelled at him, and ordered him to take his life seriously for a change.

Jorge eventually became convinced he was failing at business school, and he dropped out "before the school could kick me out." He claimed that on the phone, his father had asked, "What did I ever do to you that would make you hurt me like this?" His mother's reaction was even worse: "¡Eres vago! You're lazy," she said. "You're wasting your life. I'm ashamed. You'll never be anything. You're nothing."

(continued on the next page)

TOPIC OVERVIEW

His relationship with his parents continued to deteriorate. Jorge said his father gave him some money but told him he was cut off from that point on, unless he returned to business school. Jorge told the psychiatrist, "A week later, Pop called and left a message: 'Why don't we all talk things through, a little calmer this time?' But I knew this was a sinister trap. I knew they'd just insult me again. So I e-mailed them, saying, 'From now on, Bella will tell you how I'm doing.' They've been calling ever since. I've been very scared about money, but I won't stoop to returning their calls. In fact, last year Bella became very depressed and had to be hospitalized in a psychiatric ward, but as much as I love her, I never even visited her in the hospital because I was afraid I might run into my parents. So, in that way, they even denied me seeing my sister during her time of need!"

Overall, Jorge told the psychiatrist, he felt terrified and embarrassed by his problems and his shortcomings. His real passion was writing, and he would love to be a writer, but he assumed he would be no good at that either. He wanted to believe that God loved him as his Catholic faith had taught him, but he suspected that he had let God down and that God was as disappointed in him as his parents were. "I just don't see anything good to look forward to," he added. "Still, I don't want to go back on those anxiety pills that I was put on for a while in college. I never remembered to take them anyway."

Given his suicidal thoughts and desperate state of mind, the psychiatrist decided to hospitalize Jorge for several days. While in the hospital, his deeply concerned parents came to see him for the first time in years. After their visit, Jorge Sr. told the psychiatrist, "In the past I said some things to my son—out of concern—that I later regretted, but I never insisted he pursue a career in business, and we certainly planned to continue to support him regardless. Yes, we were often hard on him, perhaps too hard, because he was a boy and much would be expected of him in life. My own father had been hard on me, too. But we truly love Jorge. He just totally cut us off." Jorge's mother, Petra, added, "I was angry, but I called to apologize to Jorge the next day. He never answered the phone, neither then nor afterwards. We've gone out of our minds with worry over him for the past two years."

Jorge remained under observation in the hospital for the following week.

of NOTE ...

Their Words

"Help! I'm being held prisoner by my heredity and environment."

Dennis Allen

Jorge, the subject of this case study, is clearly a person with troubles, but how did he come to be that way? How do we explain and address his many challenges? To answer these questions, we must first look at the wide range of difficulties we are trying to understand: Jorge's profound feelings of depression, anxiety, and anger; self-defeating life decisions; social withdrawal; distrust of those around him; and dysfunction within his family. Then we must sort through all kinds of potential causes—internal and external, biological and interpersonal, past and present.

Although we may not realize it, we all use theoretical frameworks as we read about Jorge. Over the course of our lives, each of us has developed a perspective that helps us make sense of the things other people say and do. In science, the perspectives used to explain events are known as **models,** or **paradigms.** Each model spells out the scientist's basic assumptions, gives order to the field under study, and sets guidelines for its investigation (Kuhn, 1962). It influences what the investigators observe as well as the questions they ask, the information they seek, and how they interpret this information. To understand how a clinician explains or treats a specific set of symptoms, such as Jorge's, we must know that clinician's preferred model of psychopathology.

Until relatively recently, clinical scientists of a given place and time tended to agree on a single model of psychopathology—a model greatly influenced by the beliefs of their culture. The *demonological model* that was used to explain psychological dysfunction during the Middle Ages, for example, borrowed heavily from medieval society's concerns with religion, superstition, and warfare. Medieval practitioners would have seen the devil's guiding hand in Jorge's suicidal thoughts and his feelings of depression, anxiety, and rage. Similarly, their treatments for him—from exorcisms to whippings—would have sought to drive foreign spirits from his body.

Today, several models are used to explain and treat psychopathology. At one end of the spectrum is the *biological model*, which sees physical processes in the body as key to human behavior. In the middle are three models that focus on more psychological and personal aspects of human functioning: the *psychodynamic model* looks at people's unconscious internal processes and conflicts; the *cognitive-behavioral model* emphasizes behavior, the ways in which it is learned, and the thinking that underlies behavior and emotions; and the *humanistic-existential model* stresses the role of values and choices. At the far end of the spectrum is the *sociocultural model*, which looks to familial, social, and cultural forces as the keys to human functioning.

None of these models is complete in itself. Each focuses mainly on one aspect of human functioning, and none can explain all aspects of psychopathology. As a result, several additional perspectives have emerged that seek to *integrate* the explanations and techniques of the various models of psychopathology. A leading one is the *developmental psychopathology perspective*, which uses a developmental framework to understand how principles from the various models may collectively account for human functioning. ■

model A set of assumptions and concepts that help scientists explain and interpret observations. Also called a *paradigm*.

neuron A nerve cell.

The Biological Model

JORGE IS a biological being. His thoughts and feelings are the results of biochemical and bioelectrical processes throughout his brain and body. Proponents of the *biological model* believe that a full understanding of Jorge's thoughts, emotions, and behavior must therefore include an understanding of their biological basis. In turn, proponents of this model believe that the most effective treatments for his difficulties will be biological ones.

How Do Biological Theorists Explain Psychopathology?

Adopting a medical perspective, biological theorists view psychopathology as an illness brought about by malfunctioning parts of the organism. Typically, they point to irregularities in the brain as the cause of such behavior.

Brain Chemistry and Psychopathology

The brain is made up of approximately 86 billion nerve cells, called **neurons**, and thousands of billions of support cells, called *glia* (from the Greek word for "glue") (Caire, Reddy, & Varacallo, 2023). Information is communicated throughout the brain in the form of electrical impulses that travel from one neuron to one or more others. An impulse is first received by a neuron's *dendrites*, antenna-like extensions located at one end of the neuron. From there, it travels down the neuron's *axon*, a long fiber extending from the neuron's body. Finally, it is transmitted through the *nerve ending* at the end of the axon to the dendrites of other neurons (see **Figure 2-1**). Each neuron has multiple dendrites and a single axon. But that axon can be very long indeed, often extending from one area of the brain to another.

How do messages get from the nerve ending of one neuron to the dendrites of another? After all, the neurons do not actually touch each other. A tiny space, called the

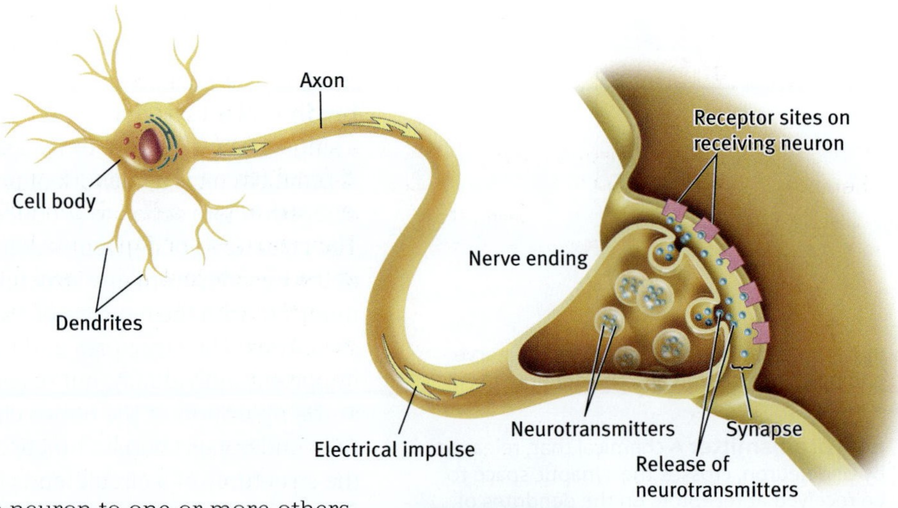

FIGURE 2-1

A Neuron Communicating Information

A message in the form of an electrical impulse travels down the sending neuron's axon to its nerve ending, where neurotransmitters are released and carry the message across the synaptic space to the dendrites of a receiving neuron.

synapse, separates one neuron from the next, and the message must somehow move across that space. When an electrical impulse reaches a neuron's ending, the nerve ending is stimulated to release a chemical, called a **neurotransmitter,** that travels across the synaptic space to **receptors** on the dendrites of the neighboring neurons. After binding to the receiving neuron's receptors, some neurotransmitters give a message to receiving neurons to "fire," that is, to trigger their own electrical impulse. Other neurotransmitters carry an inhibitory message; they tell receiving neurons to stop all firing. Researchers have identified dozens of neurotransmitters in the brain, and they have learned that each neuron uses only certain kinds.

What might the popularity of biological explanations and treatments for psychological challenges suggest about coping styles and problem-solving skills in our society?

Studies indicate that irregular activity by certain neurotransmitters is sometimes tied to mental disorders. Depression, for example, has been linked in part to low or irregular activity of the neurotransmitters *serotonin, norepinephrine,* and *glutamate.* Perhaps disrupted serotonin activity is at play in Jorge's feelings of severe depression and rage.

In addition to neurotransmitters, researchers have learned that mental disorders are sometimes related to irregular chemical activity in the body's *endocrine system.* Endocrine glands, located throughout the body, work along with neurons to control such vital activities as growth, reproduction, sexual activity, heart rate, body temperature, and responses to stress. The glands release chemicals called **hormones** into the bloodstream, and these chemicals then propel body organs into action. During times of stress, for example, the *adrenal glands,* located on top of the kidneys, secrete the hormone *cortisol* to help the body deal with the stress. Atypical secretions of this chemical have been tied to anxiety and depression.

Brain Anatomy, Circuitry, and Psychopathology

Within the brain, large groups of neurons form distinct regions, or *brain structures.* The neurons in each of these brain structures help control important functions. Clinical researchers have sometimes linked particular psychological disorders to problems in specific structures of the brain. For example, *Huntington's disease*—a disorder marked by involuntary body movements, violent emotional outbursts, memory loss, suicidal thinking, and highly distorted beliefs—has been linked in part to a loss of neurons in two brain structures: the basal ganglia and the cerebral cortex.

Over the past two decades, biological researchers have increasingly focused on **brain circuits** as the key to psychological disorders rather than on dysfunction within a single brain structure or by a single brain chemical (Schirmer, Arichi, & Chung, 2023). A brain circuit is a network of particular brain structures that work together, triggering each other into action to produce a distinct behavioral, cognitive, or emotional reaction. The structures of a given circuit work together through their neurons. The long axons of the neurons from one structure bundle together and extend across the brain to communicate with the neurons of another structure, setting up a fiber pathway between the structures. The structures and neurotransmitters that make up a given brain circuit are important individually, but research indicates that it is usually most informative to look at the operation of the entire circuit, including its interconnecting fiber pathways, to fully understand human functioning. Proper *interconnectivity* (communication) among the structures of a circuit tends to result in healthy psychological functioning, whereas flawed interconnectivity may lead to psychological dysfunction.

One of the most important circuits is the "fear circuit" (see **Figure 2-2**). As you will read in the chapter on anxiety disorders, this circuit consists of a number of specific structures (including the *prefrontal cortex, anterior cingulate cortex, insula,* and *amygdala*) whose interconnecting fiber pathways enable the structures to trigger each other into action and to produce our everyday fear reactions. The neurons in this circuit further use particular neurotransmitters to communicate with each other. Studies suggest that this circuit functions improperly (that is, displays flawed interconnectivity) in people who are experiencing certain anxiety disorders

synapse The tiny space between the nerve ending of one neuron and the dendrite of another.

neurotransmitter A chemical that, released by one neuron, crosses the synaptic space to be received at receptors on the dendrites of neighboring neurons.

receptor A site on a neuron that receives a neurotransmitter.

hormones The chemicals released by endocrine glands into the bloodstream.

brain circuit A network of particular brain structures that work together, triggering each other into action to produce a distinct kind of behavioral, cognitive, or emotional reaction.

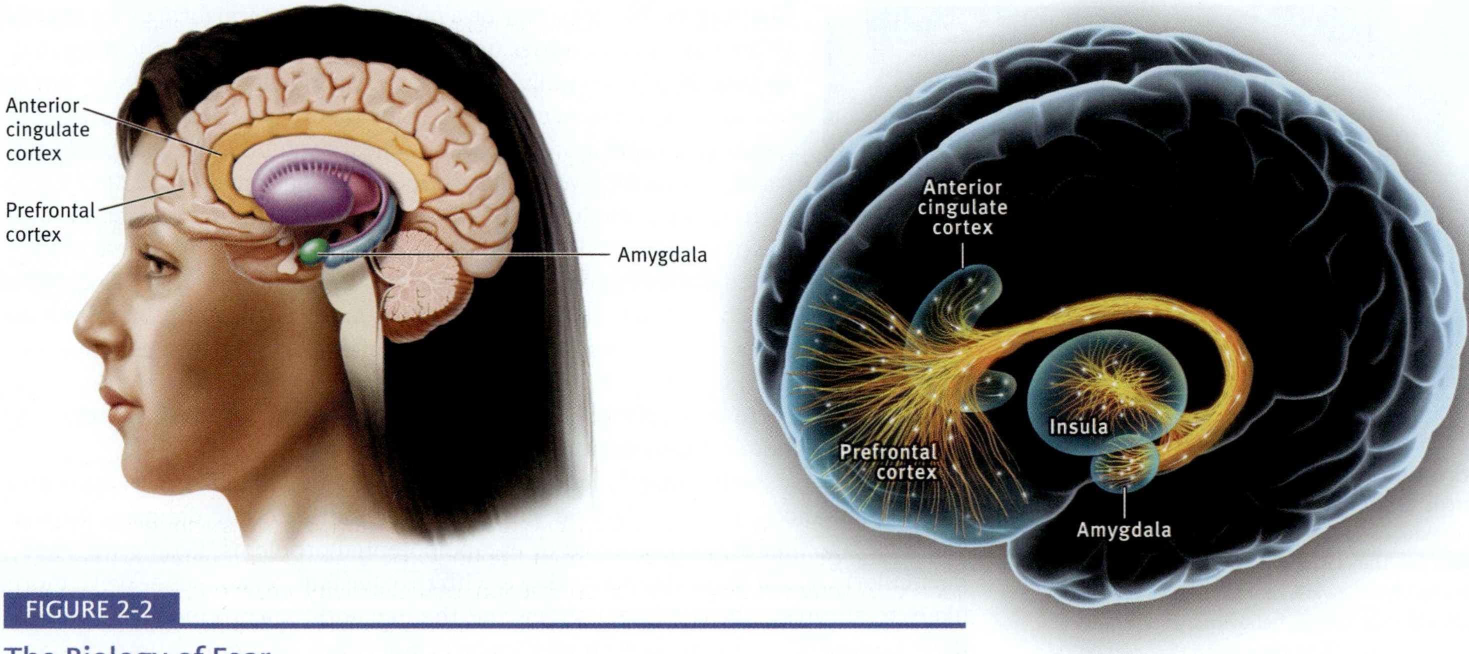

FIGURE 2-2

The Biology of Fear

The "fear circuit"—the brain circuit that helps produce fear reactions—includes structures such as the prefrontal cortex, anterior cingulate cortex, insula, and amygdala. The illustration on the left shows where these structures are located throughout the brain (the insula is not visible from this particular view of the brain). The illustration on the right highlights how the structures of this circuit actually work together and trigger each other into action to produce fear reactions. The long axons of the neurons from each structure form fiberlike pathways that extend to the other structures in the circuit.

(Penninx et al., 2021). Perhaps dysfunction by Jorge's fear circuit is contributing to his repeated concerns that things will go badly, his fears of leaving his apartment, his excessive worries about money, and his concerns that other people will have low opinions and negative motives toward him, fears that help trigger his feelings of depression and anger.

Sources of Biological Irregularities

Why might the neurotransmitters, brain structures, or brain circuits of some people function in an atypical manner? As you will learn throughout this book, a wide range of factors can play a role—from prenatal events to brain injuries, viral infections, environmental experiences, and stress. Two factors that have received particular attention in the biological model are *genetics* and *evolution*.

GENETICS AND PSYCHOPATHOLOGY Each cell in the typical human brain and body contains 23 pairs of *chromosomes,* with each chromosome in a pair inherited from one of the person's parents. Every chromosome contains numerous **genes**—segments that control the characteristics and traits a person inherits. Altogether, each cell contains at least 20,000 genes (Howes, 2022). Scientists have known for years that genes help determine such physical characteristics as hair color, height, and eyesight. Genes can make people more prone to heart disease, cancer, or diabetes and perhaps to possessing artistic or musical skill. Studies suggest that inheritance also can play a part in certain mental disorders (Giangrande, Weber, & Turkheimer, 2022). In most instances, several or more genes combine to help produce our actions and reactions, both functional and dysfunctional.

EVOLUTION AND PSYCHOPATHOLOGY Genes that contribute to mental disorders are typically viewed as unfortunate occurrences—almost mistakes of inheritance.

genes Chromosome segments that control the characteristics and traits we inherit.

Brian Rothmuller/Icon Sportswire via AP Images

More than coincidence? Identical twins Marcus and Markieff Morris have both enjoyed successful careers playing the position of power forward in the National Basketball Association. Like the Morris twins, many identical twins display similar tastes, behaviors, and career choices—supporting the notion that certain aspects of behavior and personality are influenced, in part, by genetic factors.

The responsible gene may be a *mutation,* an atypical form of the appropriate gene that emerges unexpectedly. Or the problematic gene may be inherited by an individual after it has initially entered their family line as a mutation. According to some theorists, however, many of the genes that contribute to psychological dysfunction are actually the result of ordinary *evolutionary* principles (Constant et al., 2022).

In general, evolutionary theorists argue that human reactions and the genes responsible for them have survived over the course of time because they have helped individuals to thrive and adapt. Ancestors who had the ability to run fast, for example, or the craftiness to hide were most able to escape their enemies and to reproduce. Thus, the genes responsible for effective walking, running, or problem-solving were particularly likely to be passed on from generation to generation to the present day.

Similarly, say evolutionary theorists, the capacity to experience fear was—and in many instances still is—adaptive. Fear alerted our ancestors to dangers, threats, and losses so that they could avoid or escape potential problems. People who were particularly sensitive to danger—those with greater fear responses—were more likely to survive catastrophes, battles, and the like and to reproduce and pass on their fear genes. Of course, in today's world, pressures are more numerous and often more subtle than they were in the past, condemning many individuals with such genes to a near-endless stream of fear and arousal. That is, the very genes that helped their ancestors to survive and reproduce might now leave these individuals particularly prone to fear reactions, anxiety disorders, or related psychological patterns.

The evolutionary perspective is controversial in the clinical field and has been rejected by many theorists. Scientists often find evolution-based explanations imprecise and at times impossible to research and thus unacceptable.

Biological Treatments

When they treat people who are behaving atypically, biological practitioners look for certain kinds of clues. Does the person's family have a history of that behavior and hence a possible genetic predisposition to it? (Jorge's case history mentions that his sister had been hospitalized for depression.) Is the behavior produced by events that could have had a physiological effect? (Jorge had significantly reduced his food intake and stopped taking care of his bodily needs.) Does the behavior include somatic symptoms? (Jorge's anxiety is accompanied and sometimes triggered by episodes of dizziness, sweating, and shaking.) Once the clinicians have pinpointed physical sources of dysfunction, they are in a better position to choose a biological course of treatment. The three leading kinds of biological treatments used today are *drug therapy, brain stimulation,* and *psychosurgery.* Drug therapy is by far the most common of these approaches.

In the 1950s, researchers discovered several effective **psychotropic medications,** drugs that mainly affect emotions and thought processes. These drugs have greatly changed the outlook for a number of mental disorders and today are used widely, either alone or with other forms of therapy (Healy, 2022) (see **Trending**). Moreover, in a recent poll of highly esteemed treatment experts, most of the respondents predicted that the use of psychotropic medications will grow still more in the coming decade (Norcross, Pfund, & Cook, 2022). However, the psychotropic drug revolution has also produced some major problems. Many people believe, for example, that the drugs are overused. Moreover, while drugs are effective in many cases, they do not help everyone.

Four major psychotropic drug groups are used in therapy. *Antianxiety drugs,* also called *anxiolytics,* help reduce tension and anxiety. *Antidepressant drugs* help improve the functioning of people with depression and certain other disorders. *Antibipolar*

of NOTE ...

Slow Passage

Psychotropic drugs, like all medications, reach the marketplace only after an extended period of systematic research and government review. It takes an average of 12 to 15 years and hundreds of millions of dollars for a pharmaceutical company in the United States to bring a newly identified chemical compound to market.

...TRENDING

TV Drug Ads Come Under Attack

"Ask your doctor about Abilify." "There is no need to suffer any longer." Anyone who watches television or browses the Internet is familiar with phrases such as these. They are at the heart of *direct-to-consumer* (*DTC*) drug advertising—advertisements in which pharmaceutical companies appeal directly to consumers, coaxing them to ask their physicians to prescribe particular drugs for them. Around 80 percent of U.S. adults have seen these ads, and at least 30 percent ask their doctors about the specific medications they see advertised (Llamas, 2021; Sullivan et al., 2020). *Psychotropic drugs,* such as antibipolar and antidepressant drugs, are among the leading DTC-advertised medications (Liu et al., 2022).

DTC ads have flooded the airwaves since 1997, when the U.S. Food and Drug Administration (FDA) relaxed its restrictions for drug advertising on television, requiring simply that DTC ads recommend that consumers speak with a doctor about the drug, mention the drug's important risks, and indicate where consumers can get further information about it—often a website or phone number (So & Kim, 2022). Such ads have received considerable criticism in recent years, with numerous consumer groups, government leaders, and even the American Medical Association calling for a ban on them and saying the ads often contribute to economic hardships, patient misinformation, and less-than-optimal treatment.

First, the economic concerns. Altogether, pharmaceutical companies now spend more than $6.6 billion a year on American television and some online advertising, an amount that keeps growing (GAO, 2023, 2021). This leads to higher drug prices at a time when prescription drug costs and insurance premiums are already skyrocketing (Khokhar, Weathers, & Mattingly, 2022). Moreover, the DTC ads typically promote newer and more expensive drugs, inflating the demand for such drugs even when older, generic, and cheaper drugs or lifestyle changes such as exercise or better nutrition might be equally or more appropriate (Avery et al., 2022).

DTC ads also may adversely affect patient awareness and clinical treatment (Liu et al., 2022; Roberts, 2021). Three-quarters of surveyed doctors believe that most of the ads overemphasize a drug's benefits while leaving out key negative information. Nevertheless, doctors often feel pressured to prescribe DTC-advertised drugs, even in cases in which the drugs are not appropriate for patients (So & Kim, 2022; WHO, 2020). Over half of patient requests for such drugs are granted by doctors.

So why do DTC ads continue to rise in number? One reason is that this form of advertising has its supporters. The FDA, for example, believes that the ads may indeed provide a public service, protecting consumers—although imperfectly—by directly educating them about drugs that are available in the marketplace (Roberts, 2021). Many doctors also believe that DTC ads get patients more involved in their mental and physical health care, and a number report that they now have better discussions with their patients about treatment options as a result of DTC advertising (So & Kim, 2022; Sullivan et al., 2020). Finally, not to be overlooked are the profits that DTC advertising helps generate for pharmaceutical companies.

drugs, also called *mood stabilizers,* help steady the moods of those with a bipolar disorder, a condition marked by mood swings from mania to depression. And *antipsychotic drugs* help reduce the confusion, hallucinations, and delusions that often accompany *psychosis,* a loss of contact with reality found in schizophrenia and other disorders.

As the name implies, a second form of biological treatment, **brain stimulation,** refers to interventions that directly or indirectly stimulate certain areas of the brain. The oldest (and most controversial) such approach, used primarily on severely depressed people, is **electroconvulsive therapy (ECT).** Two electrodes are attached to a patient's forehead, and an electrical current of 65 to 140 volts is passed briefly through the brain. The current causes a brain seizure that lasts up to a few minutes. After seven to nine ECT sessions, each spaced two or three days apart, many patients feel considerably less depressed. This treatment is used on tens of thousands of people annually, particularly those whose depression fails to respond to other treatments (MHA, 2023).

psychotropic medications Drugs that primarily affect the brain and reduce many symptoms of mental dysfunction.

brain stimulation Interventions that directly or indirectly stimulate the brain in order to bring about psychological improvement.

electroconvulsive therapy (ECT) A treatment in which a brain seizure is triggered when an electric current passes through electrodes attached to the patient's forehead.

As you will read in the chapter on depressive disorders, several other brain stimulation techniques have increasingly been used over the past decade, particularly in cases of depression (Chen, Fitzgerald, & Blumberger, 2022). In one, *transcranial magnetic stimulation* (*TMS*), an electromagnetic coil is placed on or above a person's head, sending a current into certain areas of the brain. In another such technique, *vagus nerve stimulation* (*VNS*), a pulse generator is implanted in a person's neck, helping to stimulate their vagus nerve, a long nerve that extends from the brain down through the neck and on to the abdomen. The stimulated vagus nerve then delivers electrical signals to the brain. Research suggests that, like ECT, each of these newer brain stimulation techniques is able to improve the psychological functioning of many people whose depressive or related disorders have been unresponsive to other forms of treatment (Holtzheimer, 2023, 2022).

of NOTE ...

Dubious Accolade

António Egas Moniz, who developed the lobotomy, was awarded the Nobel Prize in 1949 for his work.

A third kind of biological treatment is **psychosurgery,** brain surgery for mental disorders. It has roots as far back as *trephining,* the prehistoric practice of chipping a hole in the skull of a person whose behavior was perceived to be highly strange. Modern procedures are derived from a notorious technique developed in the late 1930s by a Portuguese neuropsychiatrist, António Egas Moniz. In that procedure, known as a *lobotomy,* a surgeon would cut the connections between the brain's frontal lobes and the brain's lower regions. Today's psychosurgery procedures are much more precise and much safer than the lobotomies of the past. Even so, they are typically used only after certain severe disorders have continued for years without responding to any other treatment. In one current form of psychosurgery, called *deep brain stimulation,* electrodes are surgically implanted in specific areas of a person's brain and connected to a battery ("pacemaker") in the chest. The pacemaker proceeds to power the electrodes, sending a steady stream of low-voltage electricity to the targeted brain areas. This procedure, actually a combination of psychosurgical and brain stimulation techniques, has proved quite helpful for many individuals with severe, hard-to-treat depression (Holtzheimer, 2022).

Assessing the Biological Model

Today, the biological model enjoys considerable respect. Biological research constantly produces valuable new information, and biological treatments often bring great relief when other approaches have failed. At the same time, this model has its shortcomings. Some of its proponents seem to expect that all human behavior can be explained in biological terms and treated with biological methods. This view can limit rather than enhance our understanding of psychopathology. Our mental life is an interplay of biological and nonbiological factors, and it is important to understand that interplay rather than to focus on biological variables alone.

Another shortcoming is that several of today's biological treatments are capable of producing significant undesirable effects. Certain antipsychotic drugs, for example, may produce movement problems, such as severe shaking, alarming contractions of the face and body, and extreme restlessness, and others can cause serious metabolic and cerebrovascular problems. Clearly, such costs must be addressed and weighed against the drug's benefits.

SUMMING UP

The Biological Model

Biological theorists look at biological processes to explain psychopathology, pointing, for example, to irregularities in brain chemistry, structures, or circuitry. Such irregularities are sometimes the result of genetic inheritance of atypical gene structures or ordinary evolution. Biological therapists use physical and chemical methods to help people overcome their psychological difficulties. The leading methods are drug therapy, brain stimulation, and psychosurgery.

psychosurgery Brain surgery for mental disorders.

The Psychodynamic Model

THE PSYCHODYNAMIC MODEL is the oldest and most famous of the modern psychological models. Psychodynamic theorists believe that all behaviors are determined largely by underlying psychological forces of which individuals are not consciously aware. These internal forces are described as *dynamic*—that is, they interact with one another—and their interaction gives rise to a person's behavior, thoughts, and emotions. Psychopathological symptoms are viewed as the result of conflicts between these forces.

Psychodynamic theorists would view Jorge as a person in inner conflict. They would want to explore his past experiences because, in their view, psychological conflicts are tied to early relationships and to traumatic experiences that occurred during childhood. Psychodynamic theories rest on the *deterministic* assumption that no symptom or behavior is "accidental": all behavior is determined by past experiences. Thus, Jorge's relationship with his demanding father, the hurtful rejections by his mother, his mother's seeming preoccupation with his sister throughout his childhood, and the frequent scorn and derogation from other students in school may all be relevant to the inner conflicts that underlie his current problems.

The psychodynamic model was first formulated by Viennese neurologist Sigmund Freud (1856–1939) at the turn of the twentieth century. After studying hypnosis, Freud developed the theory of *psychoanalysis* to explain psychological functioning as well as a conversational method of treatment (also called psychoanalysis) for people with mental problems. During the early 1900s, Freud and several of his colleagues in the Vienna Psychoanalytic Society—including Carl Gustav Jung (1875–1961)—became the most influential clinical theorists in the Western world.

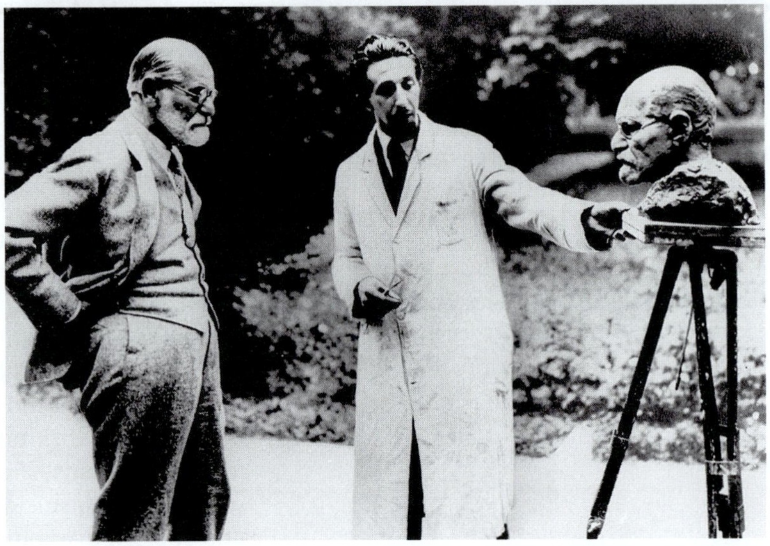

AP Photo

Freud takes a closer look at Freud
Sigmund Freud, founder of psychoanalytic theory and therapy, contemplates a sculptured bust of himself in 1931 at his village home in Potzlein, near Vienna. As Freud and the bust go eyeball to eyeball, one can only imagine what conclusions each is drawing about the other.

How Did Freud Explain Psychological Functioning?

Freud believed that three central forces shape the personality: instinctual needs, rational thinking, and moral standards. All of these forces, he believed, operate at the *unconscious level,* unavailable to immediate awareness; he further believed these forces to be dynamic, or interactive. Freud called the forces the *id*, the *ego,* and the *superego*.

The Id

Freud used the term **id** to denote instinctual needs, drives, and impulses. The id operates in accordance with the *pleasure principle;* that is, it always seeks gratification. Freud also believed that all id instincts tend to be sexual, noting that from the very earliest stages of life, a child's pleasure is obtained from nursing, defecating, masturbating, or engaging in other activities that he considered to have sexual ties. He further suggested that a person's *libido,* or sexual energy, fuels the id.

The Ego

During our early years, we come to recognize that our environment will not meet every instinctual need. Our parents, for example, are not always available to do our bidding. A part of the id separates off and becomes the **ego.** Like the id, the ego unconsciously seeks gratification, but it does so in accordance with the *reality principle,* the knowledge we acquire through experience that it can be unacceptable to express

id According to Freud, the psychological force that produces instinctual needs, drives, and impulses.

ego According to Freud, the psychological force that employs reason and operates in accordance with the reality principle.

Lucasfilm Ltd./20th Century Fox/Photofest

"Luke . . . I am your father." This lightsaber fight between Luke Skywalker and Darth Vader highlights the most famous, and contentious, father–son relationship in movie history. According to Sigmund Freud, however, all fathers and sons have significant tensions and conflicts that they must work through, even in the absence of the special pressures faced by Luke and his father in the *Star Wars* series.

our id impulses outright. The ego, employing reason, guides us to know when we can and cannot express those impulses.

The ego develops basic strategies, called **ego defense mechanisms,** to control unacceptable id impulses and avoid or reduce the anxiety they arouse. The notion of defense mechanisms was actually stated most clearly by Freud's daughter Anna Freud, a prolific and highly influential psychoanalyst in her own right. There are many ego defense mechanisms, and each of us tends to favor some over others (see **Table 2-1**).

The Superego

The **superego** is the personality force that operates by the *morality principle,* a sense of what is right and what is wrong. As we learn from our parents that many of our id impulses are unacceptable, we unconsciously adopt our parents' values. Judging ourselves by their standards, we feel good when we uphold their values; conversely, when we go against them, we feel guilty. In short, we develop a *conscience.*

According to Freud, these three parts of the personality—the id, the ego, and the superego—are often in some degree of conflict with each other. A healthy personality is one in which an effective working relationship, an acceptable compromise, has formed among the three inner forces. If the id, ego, and superego are in excessive conflict, the person's behavior may show signs of dysfunction.

Freudians would therefore view Jorge as someone whose personality forces have a poor working relationship. His ego and superego are unable to control his id. His id impulses lead him repeatedly to act in self-defeating and often dangerous ways—having suicidal thoughts, picking fights with others, withdrawing from family and society, dropping out of business school and later his job, and responding with outbursts of anger.

Developmental Stages

Freud proposed that at each stage of development, from infancy to maturity, new events challenge individuals and require adjustments in their id, ego, and superego. The adjustments, if they are successful, lead to personal growth. If they are not, the person may become **fixated,** or stuck, at an early stage of development. Then all subsequent development suffers, and the individual may well be headed for maladaptation and psychopathology in the future. Because parents are the key figures during the early years of life, they are often seen as the cause of improper development.

Freud named each stage of development after the body area that he considered most important to the child at that time. For example, he referred to the first 18 months of life as the *oral stage.* Freud believed that during this stage, children fear that the mother who feeds and comforts them will disappear. Children whose mothers consistently fail to gratify their *oral* needs may become fixated at the oral stage and display an "oral character" throughout their lives, one marked by extreme dependence or extreme mistrust. According to Freud, such persons are particularly prone to develop depression. As you will learn in later chapters, Freud linked fixations at the other stages of development—*anal* (18 months to 3 years of age), *phallic* (3 to 5 years), *latency* (5 to 12 years), and *genital* (12 years to adulthood)—to yet other kinds of psychological dysfunction.

of NOTE ...

Freud Facts

- For almost 40 years, Freud treated patients 10 hours per day, 5 or 6 days per week.
- Freud reportedly spoke 8 languages.
- To increase the comfort of patients, Freud often had his dog Jofi sit in during therapy sessions.
- Freud was nominated for the Nobel Prize in 12 different years, but never won.

(Information from: Facts.net, 2023; Cherry, 2022; Lal, 2020; Gay, 2006, 1999)

TABLE 2-1

The Defense Never Rests

Defense Mechanism	Operation	Example
Repression	Person avoids anxiety by simply not allowing painful or dangerous thoughts to become conscious.	An executive desires to run amok and to attack a colleague at a board meeting, but the executive does not allow this scary wish to enter into conscious awareness.
Denial	Person simply refuses to acknowledge the existence of an external source of anxiety.	You are not prepared for tomorrow's final exam, but you tell yourself that it's not actually an important exam and that there's no good reason not to go to a movie tonight.
Projection	Person attributes their own unacceptable impulses, motives, or desires to other individuals.	The executive who repressed destructive desires to attack a colleague may project this anger onto the colleague and claim that it is actually the colleague who is hostile.
Rationalization	Person creates a socially acceptable reason for an action that actually reflects unacceptable motives.	A student explains away poor grades by citing the importance of the "total experience" of going to college and claiming that too much emphasis on grades would actually interfere with a well-rounded education.
Displacement	Person displaces hostility away from a dangerous object and onto a safer substitute.	After a perfect parking spot is taken by a person who cuts in front of your car, you release your pent-up anger by starting an argument with your roommate.
Intellectualization	Person represses emotional reactions in favor of overly logical responses to a problem.	A person who has been beaten and raped gives a detached, methodical description of the effects that such attacks may have on victims.
Regression	Person retreats from an upsetting conflict to an early developmental stage in which no one is expected to behave maturely or responsibly.	A child who cannot cope with the anger they feel toward a rejecting parent regresses to infantile behavior, soiling their clothes and no longer taking care of basic needs.

How Do Other Psychodynamic Explanations Differ from Freud's?

Personal and professional differences between Freud and his colleagues led to a split in the Vienna Psychoanalytic Society early in the twentieth century. Carl Jung and others developed new theories. Although the new theories departed from Freud's ideas in important ways, each held on to Freud's belief that human functioning is shaped by dynamic (interacting) psychological forces. Thus, all such theories, including Freud's, are referred to as *psychodynamic*.

Two of today's most influential psychodynamic theories are self theory and object relations theory (Sharma & Spiro, 2023; Kernberg, 2022, 2021; Kohut, 2014). **Self theorists** emphasize the role of the *self*—the unified personality. They believe that the basic human motive is to strengthen the wholeness of the self. **Object relations theorists,** on the other hand, propose that people are motivated mainly by a need to have relationships with others and that severe problems in the relationships between children and their caregivers may lead to dysfunctional development.

Psychodynamic Therapies

Psychodynamic therapies range from Freudian psychoanalysis to modern therapies based on self theory or object relations theory. Psychodynamic therapists seek to uncover past traumas and the inner conflicts that have resulted from them (APsA, 2023). They try to help clients resolve, or settle, those conflicts and to resume personal development.

According to most psychodynamic therapists, therapists must subtly guide therapy discussions so that the patients discover their underlying problems for themselves. To aid in the process, the therapists rely on such techniques as *free association, therapist interpretation, catharsis,* and *working through.*

ego defense mechanisms According to psychoanalytic theory, strategies developed by the ego to control unacceptable id impulses and to avoid or reduce the anxiety they arouse.

superego According to Freud, the psychological force that represents a person's values and ideals.

fixation According to Freud, a condition in which the id, ego, or superego do not mature properly and are frozen at an early stage of development.

self theory The psychodynamic theory that emphasizes the role of the self—our unified personality.

object relations theory The psychodynamic theory that views the desire for relationships as the key motivating force in human behavior.

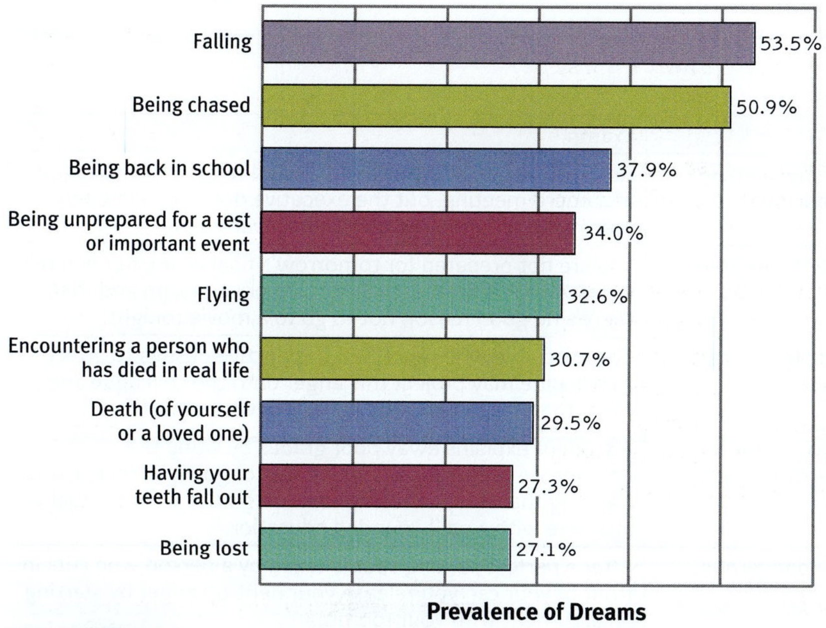

FIGURE 2-3

Top Dreams

Some dream themes are particularly common among people. According to surveys, more than half of adults in the United States have recurrent dreams of "falling" and of "being chased." (Information from: Hyde, 2023)

Free Association

In psychodynamic therapies, the therapist tells the client to describe any thought, feeling, or image that comes to mind, even if it seems unimportant. This practice is known as **free association.** The therapist expects that the client's associations will eventually uncover important unconscious events.

Therapist Interpretation

Psychodynamic therapists listen carefully as clients talk, looking for clues, drawing tentative conclusions, and sharing interpretations when they think the client is ready to hear them. Throughout treatment, the therapists interpret three phenomena in particular—resistance, transference, and dreams.

Clients are showing *resistance,* an unconscious refusal to participate fully in therapy, when they suddenly cannot free associate or when they change a subject to avoid a painful discussion. They are demonstrating *transference* when they act and feel toward the therapist as they did or do toward important persons in their lives, especially their parents, siblings, and partners. Finally, because defense mechanisms are thought to operate less completely during sleep, the *dreams* of clients are considered a rich source of information about unconscious instincts, needs, and wishes (Summer & Rehman, 2023; Erdelyi, 2022) (see **Figure 2-3**).

A therapist's interpretations of these phenomena are typically gentle and subtle in psychodynamic therapy, often offered in the form of a question rather than a statement, as shown in this discussion of a client's resistance and transference issues:

Patient: *I get so excited by what is happening here. I feel I'm being held back by needing to be nice. . . . The worst thing would be that you wouldn't like me. You wouldn't speak to me friendly . . . you'd feel you can't treat me and discharge me from treatment. . . .*

Therapist: *Where do you think these attitudes come from?*

Patient: *When I was nine years old, . . . Mother would scold me. Don't frown, don't talk so much. Sit on your hands, over and over again. I did all kinds of things. I was a naughty child. She told me I'd be hurt.*

(Wolberg, 2005, 1967)

Catharsis

Insight must be an emotional process as well as an intellectual one. Psychodynamic therapists believe that clients must experience *catharsis,* a reliving of past repressed feelings, if they are to settle internal conflicts and overcome their problems.

Working Through

A single episode of interpretation and catharsis will not change the way a person functions. The client and therapist must examine the same issues over and over in the course of many sessions, each time with greater clarity. This process, called *working through,* usually takes a long time, often years.

Current Trends in Psychodynamic Therapy

The past 45 years have witnessed significant changes in the way many psychodynamic therapists conduct sessions. An increased demand for focused, time-limited psychotherapies has resulted in efforts to make psychodynamic therapy more direct, efficient, and affordable. Two current psychodynamic approaches that illustrate this trend are *short-term psychodynamic therapies* and *relational psychoanalytic therapy.*

free association A psychodynamic technique in which the client describes any thought, feeling, or image that comes to mind, even if it seems unimportant.

SHORT-TERM PSYCHODYNAMIC THERAPIES In several short versions of psychodynamic therapy, clients choose a single problem—a *dynamic focus*—to work on, such as difficulty getting along with other people. The therapist and client focus on this problem throughout the treatment and work only on the psychodynamic issues that relate to it (such as unresolved oral needs). Findings suggest that these more focused approaches are sometimes quite helpful to clients (Sharma & Spiro, 2023; Olano & Rosenbaum, 2022).

RELATIONAL PSYCHOANALYTIC THERAPY Whereas Freud believed that psychodynamic therapists should take on the role of a neutral, distant expert during a treatment session, a contemporary school of psychodynamic therapy referred to as *relational psychoanalytic therapy* argues that therapists are key figures in the lives of clients—figures whose reactions and beliefs should be included in the therapy process (Mitchell, 2023). Thus, a key principle of relational therapy is that therapists should also disclose things about themselves, particularly their own reactions to clients, and try to establish more equal relationships with clients.

Assessing the Psychodynamic Model

Freud and his followers have helped change the way psychopathology is understood. Largely because of their work, a wide range of theorists today look for answers outside of biological processes. Psychodynamic theorists have also helped us to understand that dysfunctional behavior may be rooted in the same processes as functional behavior. Psychological conflict is a common experience; it leads to dysfunction only if the conflict becomes excessive.

Freud and his many followers have also had a monumental impact on treatment. They were the first to apply theory systematically to treatment. They were also the first to demonstrate the potential of psychological, as opposed to biological, treatment, and their ideas have served as starting points for many other psychological treatments.

At the same time, the psychodynamic model has its shortcomings (Cherry, 2023; Sharma & Spiro, 2023). In particular, its concepts are hard to research. Because processes such as id drives, ego defenses, and fixation are abstract and supposedly operate at an unconscious level, there is no way of knowing for certain if they are occurring. Not surprisingly, then, *classical*—or long-term—psychoanalytic explanations and treatments have received relatively limited research support over the years, although short-term and relational psychodynamic therapies have gathered more support. In turn, according to recent surveys, only 3 percent of today's clinical psychologists identify themselves as classical psychoanalytic therapists, a number that treatment experts expect to fall still further in the coming years, while 15 percent identify themselves as short-term or relational psychodynamic therapists, a number that is expected to keep rising over the next decade (Norcross et al., 2022; Prochaska & Norcross, 2018).

"But if I say I'm in denial then, by definition, I'm not in denial."

SUMMING UP

The Psychodynamic Model

Psychodynamic theorists believe that an individual's behavior, whether functional or dysfunctional, is determined by underlying psychological forces. They consider psychological conflicts to be rooted in early parent–child relationships and traumatic experiences. The psychodynamic model was formulated by Sigmund Freud, who said that three dynamic forces—the id, ego, and superego—interact to produce thought, feeling, and behavior. Other psychodynamic theories are self theory and object relations theory.

Psychodynamic therapists help people uncover past traumas and the inner conflicts that have resulted from them. They use a number of techniques, including free association and interpretations of psychological phenomena such as resistance, transference, and dreams. Leading contemporary psychodynamic approaches include short-term psychodynamic therapies and relational psychoanalytic therapy.

The Cognitive-Behavioral Model

THE COGNITIVE-BEHAVIORAL MODEL of psychopathology focuses on the behaviors people display and the thoughts they have. The model is also interested in the interplay between behaviors and thoughts—how behavior affects thinking and how thinking affects behavior. In addition, the model is concerned with the impact the behavior–cognition interplay often has on feelings and emotions.

Whereas the psychodynamic model had its beginnings in the clinical work of physicians, the cognitive-behavioral model began in laboratories where psychology researchers had been studying *behaviors,* the responses an organism makes to its environment, since the late 1800s. Such researchers believed that behaviors can be external (going to work, say) or internal (having a feeling), and they ran experiments on **conditioning,** simple forms of learning, in order to better understand how behaviors are acquired. In these experiments, researchers would manipulate *stimuli* and *rewards,* then observe how such manipulations affect the behaviors of animal and human subjects.

During the 1950s, a number of clinicians, frustrated with what they viewed as the vagueness and slowness of the psychodynamic model, began to explain and treat psychopathology by applying principles derived from those laboratory conditioning studies. The clinicians viewed severe human anxiety, depression, and the like as maladaptive behaviors, and they focused their work on how such behaviors might be learned and changed.

A decade or so later, more clinicians came to believe that a focus on behaviors alone, while moving in the right direction, was too simplistic, that behavioral conditioning principles failed to account fully for the complexity of human functioning and dysfunction. They recognized that human beings also engage in *cognitive processes,* such as anticipating or interpreting—ways of thinking that until then had been largely ignored in the behavior-focused explanations and therapies. These clinicians developed cognitive-behavioral theories of psychopathology that took both behaviors and cognitive processes into account and cognitive-behavioral therapies that sought to change both counterproductive behaviors and dysfunctional ways of thinking (Bieling, McCabe, & Antony, 2022).

of NOTE ...

Their Words

"The greatest discovery of my generation is that human beings can alter their lives by altering their attitudes of mind."

William James (1842–1910)

Although some of today's cognitive-behavioral theorists and therapists still focus exclusively on the behavioral aspects of psychopathological functioning and others focus only on cognitive processes, most of them include *both* behavioral and cognitive principles in their work. To best appreciate this model, let us look first at its behavioral dimension and then at its cognitive dimension.

The Behavioral Dimension

Many learned behaviors help people cope with daily challenges and lead productive lives. However, dysfunctional behaviors also can be learned. Jorge, for example, might be viewed as a person who has received improper training: he has learned behaviors that keep leading him to disappointing outcomes, unpleasant social interactions, occupational difficulties, and personal pain.

Theorists have identified several forms of conditioning, and each may produce functional behavior as well as dysfunctional behavior. In **classical conditioning,** for example, people learn to respond to one stimulus the same way they respond to another as a result of the two stimuli repeatedly occurring together close in time. If, say, a physician wears a white lab coat whenever giving painful allergy shots to a little boy, the child may learn to fear not only injection needles but also white lab coats. Many phobias are acquired by classical conditioning, as you will learn in the chapter on anxiety disorders (Beckers et al., 2023; Krause & Askew, 2022). In **modeling,** another form of conditioning, individuals learn responses simply by observing other individuals and then repeating their behaviors. Phobias can also be acquired by modeling. If a little girl observes her father becoming frightened whenever a dog crosses his path, she herself may develop a phobic fear of dogs.

In a third form of conditioning, **operant conditioning,** individuals learn to behave in certain ways as a result of experiencing consequences of one kind or another—*reinforcements* (for example, *rewards*) or *punishments*—whenever they perform the behavior (Skinner, 1958, 1957). Research suggests that a number of problematic behaviors may be acquired by operant conditioning (Edelson, 2022). Some children, for example, learn to display extremely aggressive behaviors when their parents or peers consistently surrender to their demands or shower them with extra attention when they act out. In addition, a number of people learn to abuse alcohol because initially such behaviors bring feelings of calm, comfort, or pleasure.

The Washington Post/Getty Images

The ethics of conditioning animals
Animals can be taught many tricks by using the principles of conditioning—but at what cost? Here an Asian elephant performs one called "the living statue" as she acknowledges the crowd at a circus in Virginia. In recent years, the public has become alarmed at the training procedures used on circus animals, contributing to the closing of several circuses, including the famous Ringling Brothers and Barnum & Bailey Circus.

In treatment, behavior-focused therapists seek to replace such types of behaviors with more appropriate ones, applying the principles of operant conditioning, classical conditioning, or modeling (Krause & Askew, 2022). When treating extremely aggressive children, for example, the therapists may guide parents to change the reinforcements they have been unintentionally providing for their children's problematic behaviors. The parents may be taught to systematically reinforce the polite and appropriate behaviors of their children by providing them with extra attention or special privileges. In addition, the parents may be taught to systematically punish highly aggressive behaviors by withdrawing attention and withholding privileges in the aftermath of such behaviors.

The Cognitive Dimension

Jorge, like the rest of us, has *cognitive* abilities—special intellectual capacities to think, remember, and anticipate. These abilities can help him accomplish a great deal in life. Yet they can also work against him. As he thinks about his experiences, Jorge may misinterpret them in ways that lead to poor decisions, maladaptive responses, and painful emotions.

In the 1960s, two clinicians, Albert Ellis (1962) and Aaron Beck (1967), proposed that we can best explain and treat psychopathology not only by looking at behaviors but also by focusing on cognitions. Ellis and Beck claimed that clinicians must ask questions about the assumptions and attitudes that color a client's perceptions, the thoughts running through that person's mind, and the conclusions to which the assumptions and thoughts are leading.

According to these and other cognition-focused theorists, psychopathological functioning can result from several kinds of cognitive problems. Some people may make *assumptions* and adopt *attitudes* that are disturbing and inaccurate (Doyle, Hickey, & DiGiuseppe, 2022). Jorge, for example, often seems to assume that his past history has locked him into his present situation. He believes, for example, that he was victimized

conditioning A simple form of learning.

classical conditioning A process of learning by temporal association in which two events that repeatedly occur close together in time become fused in a person's mind and produce the same response.

modeling A process of learning in which an individual acquires responses by observing and imitating others.

operant conditioning A process of learning in which individuals come to behave in certain ways as a result of experiencing consequences of one kind or another whenever they perform the behavior.

Su Arslanoglu/Getty Images

Meeting at your place . . . and mine A client (on the computer screen) sits at home while working with a therapist in an online therapy session. Telemental health treatment of this kind has increased greatly in recent years, a rise triggered initially by the Covid-19 outbreak and accompanying early concerns about the health risks of in-person contacts.

by his parents and negative business school experiences and that he is now doomed by his past. He approaches all new experiences and relationships with expectations of failure and disaster. Moreover, such attitudes and expectations contribute to repeated misinterpretations throughout his personal, social, and occupational life.

Illogical thinking processes are another source of psychopathological functioning, according to cognition-focused theorists. Beck found that people with depression consistently think in illogical ways and keep arriving at self-defeating conclusions (Mcleod, 2023; Beck, 2020). They may, for example, *overgeneralize*—draw broad negative conclusions on the basis of single insignificant events. While in history class, one student with depression couldn't remember the date on which the Declaration of Independence was adopted. Overgeneralizing, the student spent the rest of the day in despair over their wide-ranging ignorance.

In treatment, cognition-focused therapists use several strategies to help people with psychological disorders adopt new, more functional ways of thinking (Leahy, 2022). In an influential approach developed by Beck, the therapists guide clients with depression to identify and challenge any negative thoughts, biased interpretations, and errors in logic that dominate their thinking and contribute to their disorder. The therapists also guide the clients to try out new ways of thinking in their daily lives. As you will read in the chapter on depressive disorders, people with depression treated with Beck's approach improve much more than those who receive no treatment (MHN, 2023; Rogiers et al., 2022).

In the case excerpt that follows, a therapist using Beck's approach works with Sofia, an Italian American woman with depression living in Chicago who feels she is a general failure—a belief that emerged in full force after a recent setback at work:

Therapist: *You just called yourself "an utter loser." What does that mean to you?*

Sofia: *Tony got the promotion instead of me. That shows that I'm a loser.*

Therapist: *That was understandably disappointing, but do you really feel that your company decided to promote someone else simply because you are, as you say, "a loser"?*

Sofia: *I know that if I wasn't such an embarrassing failure, they would have promoted me.*

Therapist: *By that logic, anyone who does not receive a particular promotion would be considered an "embarrassing failure." Do you agree with that notion?*

Sofia: *Well, maybe not everyone, but . . .*

Therapist: *I think you would agree that your definition of a "loser" is out of step with most people's definition of a "loser." People who maintain a good job for years, with excellent performance reviews, as you have, are not generally considered "losers" simply because they weren't promoted on one occasion. . . . How do you think people define "winners," or successful people?*

Sofia: *I think they'd call someone a winner when they are well-liked, achieve success in things they set out to do, and make the lives of the people close to them better. . . .*

Therapist: *Now, could you say any of that about yourself? Have you done some of the things you set out to do? Are you well-liked by any people close to you, and have you ever made their lives better?*

Sofia: *Yes, I guess I have.*

Therapist: *Doesn't your thinking seem somewhat illogical, then? You say you're a "loser," and yet you acknowledge that you meet your own criteria for a "winner."*

Sofia: *Yes, I guess that is illogical . . .*

The Cognitive-Behavioral Interplay

As you read earlier, most of today's cognitive-behavioral theorists and therapists interweave both behavioral and cognitive elements in their explanations and treatments. Let's look, for example, at the cognitive-behavioral approach to social anxiety disorder, a condition that you will read more about later in the textbook.

People with *social anxiety disorder* have severe anxiety about social situations in which they may face scrutiny by other people. They worry that they will function poorly in front of others and will wind up feeling humiliated. Thus, they may avoid speaking in public, reject social opportunities, and limit their lives in numerous ways.

Cognitive-behavioral theorists contend that people with this disorder hold a group of social beliefs and expectations that consistently work against them (Schneier, 2023). These include the following:

- Holding unrealistically high social standards and so believing that they must perform perfectly in social situations.
- Viewing themselves as unattractive social beings.
- Viewing themselves as socially unskilled and inadequate.
- Believing they are always in danger of behaving incompetently in social situations.
- Believing that inept behaviors in social situations will inevitably lead to terrible consequences.

Overrun by such beliefs and expectations, people with social anxiety disorder find that their anxiety levels increase as soon as they enter into a social situation. In turn, say cognitive-behavioral theorists, the individuals learn to regularly perform "avoidance" and "safety" behaviors (Stentz & Cougle, 2022). Avoidance behaviors include, for example, talking only to people they already know well at gatherings or parties or avoiding social gatherings altogether. Safety behaviors include wearing gloves in public so no one can see if their hands shake. Such behaviors are reinforced by eliminating or reducing the individuals' feelings of anxiety and the number of unpleasant events they encounter.

To undo this cycle, cognitive-behavioral therapists combine several techniques, including **exposure therapy,** a behavior-focused intervention in which fearful people are repeatedly exposed to the objects or situations they dread. In cases of social anxiety disorder, the therapists encourage clients to immerse themselves in various dreaded social situations and to remain there until their fears subside (Hildebrand et al., 2022). Usually, the exposure is gradual. Then, using a cognitive-focused intervention, the clinicians and clients reexamine and challenge the individuals' maladaptive beliefs and expectations in light of the recent social encounters. In cognitive-behavioral approaches of this kind, clients often come to adopt more accurate social beliefs, engage in more social situations, and experience less fear during, and in anticipation of, social encounters (Caletti et al., 2022).

exposure therapy A behavior-focused intervention in which fearful people are repeatedly exposed to the objects or situations they dread.

Third Wave Cognitive-Behavioral Therapies

As it turns out, clients are not always able to rid themselves fully of their negative thoughts and biased interpretations (Bieling et al., 2022). In light of this, a more recent group of therapies, sometimes called *third wave cognitive-behavioral therapies,* has emerged in recent years. (The cognitive-behavioral model's initial focus on behaviors alone is called the *first wave,* and its subsequent focus on challenging and changing maladaptive cognitions is considered the *second wave.*) These third wave approaches, including the frequently used *acceptance and commitment therapy (ACT),* help clients to *accept* many of their troubling thoughts rather than judge them, act on them, or try fruitlessly to change them (Hayes et al., 2023; Perkins et al., 2023; Hayes, Hofmann, & Ciarrochi, 2022). The hope is that by recognizing

of NOTE ...

Their Words

"We cannot solve our problems with the same thinking we used when we created them."

Albert Einstein

such thoughts for what they are—just thoughts—clients will eventually be able to let them pass through their awareness without being particularly troubled by them.

As you will read in the chapter on anxiety disorders, ACT and similar therapies often employ *mindfulness-based* techniques to help clients achieve such acceptance. These techniques are rooted in Eastern healing traditions and borrow heavily from a form of meditation called *mindfulness meditation,* which teaches individuals to pay attention to the thoughts and feelings that are flowing through their minds during meditation and to accept such thoughts in a nonjudgmental way.

of NOTE ...

Wandering Thoughts

It is estimated that your mind wanders between one-third and one-half of the time (Weimer, 2022).

Assessing the Cognitive-Behavioral Model

The cognitive-behavioral model has become a powerful force in the clinical field. Various cognitive and behavioral theories have been proposed over the years, and many treatment techniques have been developed. As shown in **Figure 2-4**, according to recent surveys, nearly half of today's clinical psychologists report that their approach is cognitive and/or behavioral; moreover, treatment experts expect the number of such practitioners to rise still further over the coming decade (Norcross et al., 2022; Prochaska & Norcross, 2018).

One reason for the appeal of the cognitive-behavioral model is that it can be tested in the laboratory, whereas psychodynamic theories generally cannot. Many of the model's basic concepts—stimulus, response, reward, attitude, and interpretation—can be observed or at least measured. Moreover, investigators have found that people with psychological disorders often display the kinds of reactions, assumptions, and errors in thinking that cognitive-behavioral theorists would predict (Bieling et al., 2022).

Yet another reason for the popularity of this model is the impressive research performance of cognitive-behavioral therapies. Both in the laboratory and in real life, cognitive-behavioral therapies have proved very helpful to many people with anxiety disorders, depression, sexual dysfunction, intellectual disability, and other conditions (Bieling et al., 2022; Twohig, Levin, & Petersen, 2022).

At the same time, the cognitive-behavioral model has drawbacks. First, although maladaptive behaviors and disturbed cognitive processes are found in many forms of psychopathology, their precise role has yet to be determined. The problematic behaviors and cognitions seen in people with psychological conditions could well be a result rather than a cause of their difficulties. Second, although cognitive-behavioral therapies are clearly of help to many people, they do not help everyone. Third, by focusing primarily on clients' current experiences and functioning, cognitive-behavioral therapists may be paying too little attention to the influence of early life experiences and relationships on a client's current difficulties.

FIGURE 2-4

Theoretical Orientations of Today's Clinical Psychologists

In recent surveys, 22 percent of clinical psychologists labeled their approach as "eclectic," 46 percent considered their model "cognitive" and/or "behavioral," and 18 percent called their orientation "psychodynamic." Experts predict that the number of therapists who use cognitive-behavioral, existential, interpersonal, or multicultural therapy will continue to increase in the coming decade. (Information from: Norcross et al., 2022; Prochaska & Norcross, 2018)

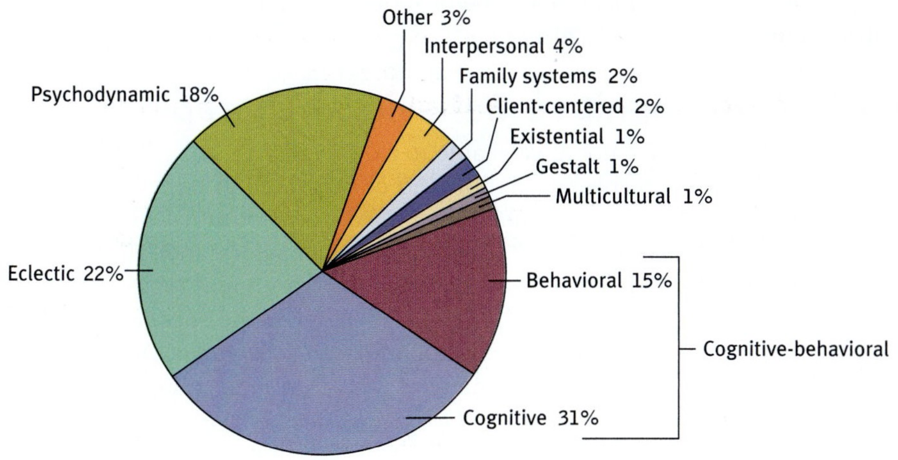

A final drawback of the cognitive-behavioral model is that it is narrow in certain ways. Although behavior and cognition obviously are key dimensions in life, they are still only two aspects of human functioning. Shouldn't explanations of human functioning also consider broader issues, such as how people approach life, what value they extract from it, and how they deal with the question of life's meaning? This is the position of the humanistic-existential model.

SUMMING UP

The Cognitive-Behavioral Model

Proponents of the cognitive-behavioral model focus on maladaptive behaviors and cognitions to explain and treat psychological disorders. Most such proponents now include *both* the behavioral and cognitive dimensions in their work.

On the behavioral dimension, the theorists hold that three types of conditioning—classical conditioning, modeling, and operant conditioning—account for behavior, whether functional or dysfunctional. Therapists try to replace problematic behaviors with more appropriate ones, using techniques based on one or more of the principles of learning. On the cognitive dimension, the model's proponents point to cognitive challenges, like maladaptive assumptions and illogical thinking processes, to help explain psychological dysfunction. In treatment, therapists may try to help clients recognize, challenge, and change their problematic ways of thinking.

In addition to the traditional cognitive-behavioral approaches, third wave cognitive-behavioral therapies, such as acceptance and commitment therapy, draw on Eastern healing traditions and mindfulness-based meditation to help clients become more mindful of and accept many of their troubling thoughts.

The Humanistic-Existential Model

JORGE IS MORE than the sum of his psychological conflicts, learned behaviors, or cognitions. Being human, he also has the ability to pursue philosophical goals such as self-awareness, strong values, a sense of meaning in life, and freedom of choice. According to humanistic and existential theorists, Jorge's challenges can be understood only in the light of such complex goals. Humanistic and existential theorists are often grouped together—in an approach known as the *humanistic-existential model*—because of their common focus on these broader dimensions of human existence. At the same time, there are important differences between them.

Humanists, the more optimistic of the two groups, believe that human beings are born with a natural tendency to be friendly, cooperative, and constructive. People, these theorists propose, are driven to **self-actualize**—that is, to fulfill their potential for goodness and growth. They can do so, however, only if they honestly recognize and accept their weaknesses as well as their strengths and establish satisfying personal values to live by. Humanists further suggest that self-actualization leads naturally to a concern for the welfare of others and to behavior that is loving, courageous, spontaneous, and independent (Carvalho et al., 2022; Maslow, 1970).

Existentialists agree that human beings must have an accurate awareness of themselves and live meaningful—they say "authentic"—lives in order to be psychologically well-adjusted. These theorists do not believe, however, that people are naturally inclined to live positively. They believe that from birth, we have total freedom, either to face up to our existence and give meaning to our lives or to shrink from that

of NOTE ...

Self-Actualization Through Giving

70%	Percentage of U.S. adults who make charitable contributions each year
25%	Percentage of U.S. adults who do volunteer work each year

(Information from: Appel, 2022)

self-actualization The humanistic process by which people fulfill their potential for goodness and growth.

responsibility. Those who choose to "hide" from responsibility and choice will view themselves as helpless and may live empty, inauthentic, and dysfunctional lives as a result (Lebow, 2022).

The humanistic and existential theories were extremely popular during the 1960s and 1970s, years of considerable soul-searching and social upheaval in Western society. They have since lost some of their popularity, but they continue to influence the ideas and work of many clinicians. In particular, humanistic principles are apparent throughout *positive psychology* (the study and enhancement of positive feelings, traits, abilities, and selfless virtues), an area of psychology that has gained much momentum in recent years, as you read earlier in the textbook.

Rogers' Humanistic Theory and Therapy

According to Carl Rogers, the road to dysfunction begins in infancy (Farber, Suzuki, & Ort, 2022; Rogers, 1987, 1951). We all have a basic need to receive *positive regard* from the important people in our lives (primarily our parents). Those who receive *unconditional* (nonjudgmental) *positive regard* early in life are likely to develop *unconditional self-regard*. That is, they come to recognize their worth as persons, even while recognizing that they are not perfect. Such people are in a good position to actualize their positive potential.

Unfortunately, some children repeatedly are made to feel that they are not worthy of positive regard. As a result, they acquire *conditions of worth,* standards that tell them they are lovable and acceptable only when they conform to certain guidelines. To maintain positive self-regard, these people have to look at themselves very selectively, denying or distorting thoughts and actions that do not measure up to their conditions of worth. Thus, they acquire an inauthentic view of themselves and their experiences. They do not know what they are truly feeling, what they genuinely need, or what values and goals would be meaningful for them. Difficulties in functioning are then inevitable.

Khadejeh Nikouyeh/The Charlotte Observer via AP

Unconditional positive regard Carl Rogers argued that clients must receive unconditional positive regard in order to overcome their problems. In this spirit, a number of clinicians recommend that clients form close relationships with gentle and nonjudgmental dogs, often called *emotional support dogs*. Here, an Air Force veteran is reunited with his former emotional support dog, whose physical closeness and reassuring presence had helped him reduce feelings of depression.

Rogers might view Jorge as a person who has gone astray. Rather than striving to fulfill his positive human potential, he is drifting—neither seeking nor attaining meaningful and pleasurable relationships and experiences in his family, social, and occupational spheres. In every interaction, he is defending himself, trying to interpret events in ways he can live with, usually blaming his challenges on other people. Nevertheless, his basic negative self-image continually reveals itself. Rogers would probably link this problem to the critical ways Jorge was treated by his father and mother throughout his childhood.

Consistent with his views about human functioning, Rogers developed **client-centered therapy,** a warm and supportive treatment approach. Here clinicians try to create an accepting climate in which clients feel able to look at themselves honestly and acceptingly (Farber et al., 2022). The therapist must display three important qualities throughout the therapy—*unconditional positive regard* (full and warm acceptance for the client), *accurate empathy* (skillful listening and restating), and *genuineness* (sincere communication). In the following case, the client-centered therapist uses these qualities to move the client toward greater self-awareness:

Client: *No one else would be as cruel to me as I am.*
Therapist: *And make such harsh judgments, you're pretty tough on yourself.*
Client: *Yes, I wouldn't judge my friends the way I judge myself. . . .*
Therapist: *Maybe because you can see what is lovable in them, but not in yourself. To you, you're unlovable.*

Client: *Maybe there are small pieces of me that are lovable.*
Therapist: *(Pause) So there are parts of you that you see as OK, as worthy of being loved.*
Client: *Yes, I guess. The child in me. . . . She, I, can still be playful and fun and warm.*
Therapist: *Those are very wonderful qualities. . . . She's a part of you that you can hold on to.*
Client: *Yes.*
Therapist: *Do you think she'd judge you so harshly?*
Client: *No, she loves me.*
Therapist: *To this special child part of you, none of you is unforgivable.*
Client: *No, she loves all of me.*

(Farber, Suzuki, & Lynch, 2019)

In such an atmosphere, clients are expected to feel accepted and understood by their therapists. They then may be able to look at themselves with honesty and acceptance. They begin to value their own emotions, thoughts, and behaviors, and so they are freed from the insecurities and doubts that prevent self-actualization.

Client-centered therapy has not fared very well in research (Duffy et al., 2023; Yao & Kabir, 2023). All the same, Rogers' therapy has had a positive influence on clinical practice (Farber et al., 2022). It was one of the first major alternatives to psychodynamic therapy, and it helped open up the clinical field to new approaches. Rogers also helped pave the way for *psychologists* to practice psychotherapy, which had previously been considered the exclusive territory of psychiatrists. And his commitment to clinical research helped promote the systematic study of treatment. Recent surveys suggest that approximately 2 percent of today's clinical psychologists, 1 percent of social workers, and 3 percent of counseling psychologists employ the client-centered approach; these numbers are expected to hold steady in the coming years (Norcross et al., 2022; Prochaska & Norcross, 2018).

of NOTE ...

Their Words

"I've learned that people will forget what you said, people will forget what you did, but people will never forget how you made them feel."

Maya Angelou

Gestalt Theory and Therapy

Gestalt therapy, another humanistic approach, was developed in the 1950s by a charismatic clinician named Frederick (Fritz) Perls (1893–1970). Gestalt therapists, like client-centered therapists, guide their clients toward self-recognition and self-acceptance (Lobb & Cavaleri, 2023; Farnsworth, 2022). But unlike client-centered therapists, they try to achieve this goal by challenging and even frustrating the clients, demanding that they stay in the *here and now* during therapy discussions, and pushing them to embrace their real emotions.

For example, gestalt therapists often use the technique of *role-playing,* instructing clients to act out various roles. A person may be told to be another person, an object, an alternative self, or even a part of the body. The gestalt version of role-playing can become intense, as individuals are encouraged to express emotions fully. Many cry out, scream, kick, or pound. Through this experience, they may come to "own" (accept) feelings that previously made them uncomfortable.

According to recent surveys, approximately 1 percent of today's clinical psychologists and other kinds of clinicians describe themselves as gestalt therapists, a total that has been falling over the past few decades and is expected to drop still further in the coming years (Norcross et al., 2022; Prochaska & Norcross, 2018). Because they believe that subjective experiences and self-awareness cannot be measured objectively, proponents of gestalt therapy have not often performed controlled research on this approach (Lindsay, 2022).

client-centered therapy The humanistic therapy developed by Carl Rogers in which clinicians try to help clients by conveying acceptance, accurate empathy, and genuineness.

gestalt therapy The humanistic therapy developed by Fritz Perls in which clinicians actively move clients toward self-recognition and self-acceptance by using techniques such as role playing and self-discovery exercises.

Spiritual Views and Interventions

For most of the nineteenth and twentieth centuries, clinicians viewed religion as a negative—or at best neutral—factor in mental health. Indeed, "religious insanity" was a common diagnosis assigned to patients admitted to mental hospitals in the 1800s, reflecting the clinical notion that religious beliefs and practices often caused mental disorders (Hood, 2022; Richards, Allen, & Judd, 2022). This negative view of religion now seems to be ending, however. During the past 15 years, many articles and books linking spiritual issues to clinical treatment have been published, and the ethical codes of psychologists, psychiatrists, and counselors have each concluded that religion is an important aspect of diversity that mental health professionals must respect (Richards et al., 2022; Sperry, 2022).

Researchers have learned that spirituality does, in fact, often correlate with psychological health. In particular, studies have examined the mental health of people who are devout and who view God as warm, caring, helpful, and dependable. Repeatedly, these individuals are found to be less stressed, lonely, pessimistic, depressed, or anxious than people without any religious beliefs or those who view God as cold and unresponsive (Plante, 2022; Richards et al., 2022). Do such correlations indicate that spirituality helps *produce* greater mental health? Not necessarily. As you read in the previous chapter, correlations do not indicate causation. It may be, for example, that a sense of optimism leads to more spirituality and that, independently, optimism contributes to greater mental health. Whatever the proper interpretation, many therapists now make a point of including spiritual issues when they treat religious clients, and some further encourage clients to use their spiritual resources to help them cope with current stressors (Norcross et al., 2022; Sperry, 2022).

What various explanations might account for the correlation between spirituality and mental health?

Existential Theories and Therapy

Like humanists, existentialists believe that psychological dysfunction is caused by self-deception; existentialists, however, are talking about a kind of self-deception in which people hide from life's responsibilities and fail to recognize that it is up to them to give meaning to their lives. According to existentialists, many people become overwhelmed by the pressures of present-day society and so look to others for explanations, guidance, and authority. They overlook their personal freedom of choice and avoid responsibility for their lives and decisions (Lebow, 2022). Such people are left with empty, inauthentic lives. Their dominant emotions are anxiety, frustration, boredom, alienation, and depression.

Existentialists might view Jorge as a man who feels overwhelmed by the forces of society. He sees his father as controlling, both of his parents as calculating, his girlfriend as manipulative, and his business school classmate as oppressive. In general, he fails to appreciate his choices in life and his own capacity for finding meaning and direction. Quitting becomes a habit with him—he flees all difficult situations, leaves his family, ends his romantic and social relationships, quits his job, and surrenders all positive aspirations.

In **existential therapy,** people are encouraged to accept responsibility for their lives and for their difficulties. Therapists try to help clients recognize their freedom so that they may choose a different course and live with greater meaning (Webster, 2023). The precise techniques used in existential therapy vary from clinician to clinician. At the same time, most existential therapists place great emphasis on the *relationship* between therapist and client and try to create an atmosphere of honesty, hard work, and shared learning and growth.

existential therapy A therapy that encourages clients to accept responsibility for their lives and to live with greater meaning and value.

Client: *I turn[ed] to a person I thought was a close friend, and even she, apparently, can't stand the sight of me, and I just don't get it—don't know where to turn. . . .*

Therapist: *Boy, you have a lot of energy all of a sudden, James.*

Client: *Yeah, I do—but what the hell good is it? I can get mad from now until doomsday, and it won't change the fact that women think I'm a pervert, men think I'm a weakling, and my boss thinks I'm incompetent!*

Therapist: *And what do you think of you? What do you feel towards yourself?*

Client: *I feel like a jerk—what do you think!?*

Therapist: *I don't know, James, I can't speak for you, but I hear you. . . .*

Client: (Eyes moistening) *I'm stuck, I'm screwed. . . . Yeah, sometimes I feel like my life is a big wall—and I'm the bug that constantly gets squashed.*

Therapist: *Is that where you are now?*

Client: *Not exactly.*

Therapist: *Take a moment and be with where you are, James.*

Client: *I'm hurting. . . . How could I have done that? How could I have taken a perfectly decent relationship . . . and push it off the cliff? There's just no way around it, I'm doomed to be a shit. . . .*

Therapist: *. . . Is that acceptable to you?*

Client: *No, but there's nothing I can do about it.*

Therapist: *What are you willing to do about it? . . .*

Client: *Well, I am sick and tired of it.*

Therapist: *I hear you. What else is here, James?*

Client: *That maybe I wasn't as much the shit as I made myself out to be—that I always make myself out to be. That I slipped up—I made a stupid comment, am I gonna condemn myself for life?*

Therapist: *Stay with it, James, what else is present for you?*

Client: *A hint of pride, fight . . .*

(Schneider, 2007)

Existential therapists do not believe that experimental methods can adequately test the effectiveness of their treatments. To them, research dehumanizes individuals by reducing them to test measures. Not surprisingly, then, little controlled research has been devoted to the effectiveness of this approach (Webster, 2023; Heidenreich et al., 2021). Nevertheless, recent surveys reveal that around 1 percent of today's clinical psychologists, 7 percent of counseling psychologists, and 4 percent of social workers use an approach that is primarily existential, and these figures are expected to increase in the coming years (Norcross et al., 2022; Prochaska & Norcross, 2018).

Assessing the Humanistic-Existential Model

The humanistic-existential model appeals to many people in and out of the clinical field. In recognizing the special challenges of human existence, humanistic and existential theorists tap into an aspect of psychological life that typically is missing from the other models (Farber et al., 2022; Bohart & Watson, 2020). Moreover, the factors that they say are essential to effective functioning—self-acceptance, personal values, personal meaning, and personal choice—are certainly lacking in many people with psychological disturbances.

The optimistic tone of the humanistic-existential model is also an attraction. Such optimism meshes quite well with the goals and principles of *positive psychology*

Jonny Hawkins/CartoonStock Ltd.

"Do you promise to love me warts and all?"

AP Photo/The Daily Telegram, Lad Strayer

Beating the blues Gestalt therapists often guide clients to express their needs and feelings in their full intensity by banging on pillows, crying out, kicking, or pounding things. Building on these techniques, an approach called *drum therapy* teaches clients, such as this woman, how to beat drums in order to help release traumatic memories, change beliefs, and feel more liberated.

(Snyder et al., 2021). Theorists who follow the principles of the humanistic-existential model offer great hope when they assert that, despite past and present events, we can make our own choices, determine our own destiny, and accomplish much. Still another attractive feature of the model is its emphasis on health. Unlike clinicians from some of the other models who see individuals as clients with psychological illnesses, humanists and existentialists view them simply as people who have yet to fulfill their potential.

At the same time, the humanistic-existential focus on abstract issues of human fulfillment gives rise to a major problem from a scientific point of view: these issues are difficult to research. In fact, with the notable exception of Rogers, who tried to investigate his clinical methods carefully, humanists and existentialists have traditionally rejected the use of empirical research. This antiresearch position is now beginning to change among some humanistic and existential researchers—a change that may lead to important insights about the humanistic-existential model (Farber et al., 2022).

SUMMING UP

The Humanistic-Existential Model

The humanistic-existential model focuses on the human need to successfully deal with philosophical issues such as self-awareness, values, meaning, and choice.

Humanists believe that people are driven to self-actualize. When this drive is interfered with, psychopathology may result. One group of humanistic therapists, client-centered therapists, tries to create a very supportive therapy climate in which people can look at themselves honestly and acceptingly, thus opening the door to self-actualization. Another group, gestalt therapists, uses more active techniques to help people recognize and accept their needs. Recently, the role of spirituality as an important factor in mental health and in psychotherapy has caught the attention of researchers and clinicians.

According to existentialists, psychopathology results from hiding from life's responsibilities. Existential therapists encourage people to accept responsibility for their lives, recognize their freedom to choose a different course, and choose to live with greater meaning.

The Sociocultural Model: Family-Social and Multicultural Perspectives

JORGE IS ALSO a social and cultural being. He is surrounded by people and by institutions, he is a member of a family and a cultural group, he participates in social relationships, and he holds cultural values. Such forces are always operating upon Jorge, setting rules and expectations that guide or pressure him, and helping to shape his behaviors, thoughts, and emotions.

According to the *sociocultural model,* psychopathology is best understood in light of the broad forces that influence an individual. What are the norms of the individual's society and culture? What roles does the person play in the social environment? What kind of family structure or cultural background is the person a part of? And how do other people view and react to the individual? In fact, the sociocultural model is composed of two major perspectives—the *family-social perspective* and the *multicultural perspective.*

How Do Family-Social Theorists Explain Psychopathology?

Proponents of the family-social perspective argue that clinical theorists should concentrate on those broad forces that operate *directly* on individuals as they move through life—that is, family relationships, social interactions, and community events. The proponents believe that such forces help account for both functional and dysfunctional behavior, and they pay particular attention to three kinds of factors: *social labels and roles, social connections and supports,* and *family structure and communication.*

Social Labels and Roles

The behavior of people with psychological problems can be influenced greatly by the labels and roles assigned to them by others (Balakrishnan & Akshaya, 2023; Tillory, 2021). When people stray from the norms of their society, the society calls them deviant and, in many cases, "mentally ill." Such labels tend to stick. Moreover, when people are viewed in particular ways, reacted to as "crazy," and perhaps even encouraged to act sick, they gradually learn to accept and play the assigned social role. Ultimately, the label seems appropriate.

The potential impact—both positive and negative—of pathology labels is noted by journalist Jeannette Cooperman, who writes this:

> *Today, people [often] announce that they are "stressed out" or "socially awkward," admit to anxiety and depression, make TikTok "diagnosis videos" about symptoms and their label. This is great, in that it dissolves stigma and encourages community, awareness, and the seeking of help. This is lousy, though, in that those lists of symptoms can make anybody feel like they have anything, and soon everyday behaviors and feelings are pathologized.*
>
> (Cooperman, 2022)

Isolation A man in Paris, France, looks out of his balcony in 2020 after the French government ordered him and all citizens to stay home for an extended period due to the Covid-19 pandemic. Given the relationship between social isolation and mental disorders such as depression, clinical theorists have been concerned about the psychological effects—immediate, ongoing, and long-term—brought about by the strategies of social distancing, isolation, and confinement initially used to help contain the virus.

Chesnot/Getty Images

Social Connections and Supports

Family-social theorists are also concerned with the direct social environments in which people operate, including their social and professional relationships. How well do they communicate with others? What kind of signals do they send to others or receive from others? Researchers have often found ties between deficient social connections and psychological dysfunction (Rustamov et al., 2023; Vella et al., 2023). They have observed, for example, that people who are isolated and lack social support or intimacy in their lives are more likely to become depressed when under stress and to remain depressed longer than are people with supportive partners or warm friendships.

Some clinical theorists believe that people who are unwilling or unable to communicate and develop relationships in their everyday lives will, alternatively, find adequate social contacts online, using social networking platforms like Facebook or Instagram. Although this may be true for some such individuals, research suggests that people's online relationships tend to parallel their offline relationships. Several studies of college students, for example, have found that students who are self-disclosing and have many friends on social media also are particularly social offline, while those who reveal less about themselves and initiate fewer relationships on social media are less willing to communicate with other people offline (Yang, Dongdong, & Yu, 2021; Lieberman & Schroeder, 2020).

Family Structure and Communication Of course, one of the most important social networks for an individual is the family. According to **family systems theory,** the family is a system of interacting parts—the family members—who interact with one another in consistent ways and follow unwritten rules unique to each family (Suppes, 2022). Family systems theorists believe that the *structure* and *communication* patterns of some families actually force individual members to behave in a way that otherwise seems peculiar. If the members were to behave conventionally, they would severely strain the family's usual manner of operation and would actually increase their own and their family's turmoil.

Family systems theory holds that certain family systems and interaction patterns are particularly likely to produce psychological dysfunction in individual members (Stern, King, & Diamond, 2022). Some families, for example, have an *enmeshed* structure in which the members are grossly overinvolved in one another's activities, thoughts, and feelings. Children from this kind of family may have great difficulty becoming independent in life. Some families display *disengagement,* which is marked by very rigid boundaries between the members. Children from these families may find it hard to function in a group or to give or request support.

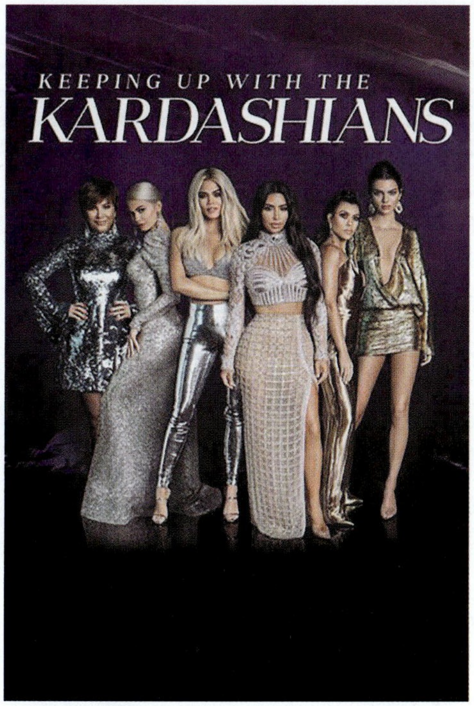

Today's TV families Unlike television viewers during the twentieth century, when problem-free families ruled the airwaves, today's viewers prefer more complex and occasionally dysfunctional families, like the Kardashians, whose trials and tribulations and relationship issues have been on display since 2007 in the hugely popular reality series *Keeping Up with the Kardashians* and its spinoffs.

Jorge's angry and anxious personal style might be seen as the product of a disturbed family structure. According to family systems theorists, the whole family—Jorge's father, mother, and sister and Jorge himself—has related over the years in such a way as to maintain Jorge's behavior. Thus, family systems theorists would seek to clarify the precise nature of Jorge's relationship with each parent. For example, is there evidence of enmeshment in his relationship with his father and/or evidence of disengagement in his relationship with his mother? And is his behavior the result or the cause of his parents' demanding style? Just as importantly, such theorists would examine the relationship between Jorge's mother and father, including possible miscommunications between them and imbalances in their power regarding family decisions. The theorists would look, too, at the unwritten rules governing the sibling relationship in the family, the relationship between Jorge's parents and his sister, and the nature of parent–child relationships in previous generations of the family. Recall, for example, how Jorge's mother gave disproportionate attention to his sister throughout his childhood and how Jorge's grandfather had been very demanding of Jorge's father.

Family-Social Treatments

The family-social perspective has helped spur the growth of several treatment approaches, including *interpersonal psychotherapy; group, family,* and *couple therapy;* and *community treatment.* The clinicians who use these various approaches believe that psychological problems emerge in social settings, and so these clinicians hold that strategies focusing on relationships and interactions must be featured prominently in treatment (see **MindTech**).

family systems theory A theory that views the family as a system of interacting parts whose interactions exhibit consistent patterns and unstated rules.

MINDTECH

Therapy, Now Ready-to-Wear?

Modern mobile computing has also opened new doors in mental health care. Text message–based interventions are on the rise, and mental health apps offering digital self-help have flooded the marketplace, especially since the onset of Covid-19 in 2020 (Litke et al., 2023; Carl et al., 2022; Comer, 2021).

With the ever-growing production of small and low-profile computer devices that can be worn, such as "smart" watches/wristbands and "smart" glasses, forward-thinking clinicians have increasingly used these wearable devices to help manage the emotional and behavioral challenges of their clients (Griffiths et al., 2022; Matcham et al., 2022). Wearable devices are able to continuously monitor key physiological and behavioral processes—including heart rate, respiration, sleep quality, physical activity, and tone of voice—in clients' everyday lives and to instantly identify problematic areas of functioning (Paganini et al., 2023; Timmons et al., 2022).

One form of wearable therapy—known as the "Just-in-Time Adaptive Intervention" (or JITAI)—aims to deliver just the right types and doses of support to clients (known as "micro-interventions"), at the most appropriate times and in the most relevant settings, in direct response to the clients' shifting states (Coppersmith et al., 2022; Dowling et al., 2022). For example, a JITAI seeking to increase a client's level of physical activity might use a smartwatch to continuously detect instances when the individual is too sedentary. When such an instance is identified, the JITAI would provide an in-the-moment micro-intervention—perhaps a smartwatch text instructing the person to get up and do 10 jumping jacks or simply a tone to remind them to do so (Mair et al., 2022).

Critics of mental health JITAIs argue that although wearable technologies may accurately detect activities and psychophysiological states, they cannot reliably detect the more subjective emotional states that typically bring clients into treatment, such as anger, sadness, and stress. Critics further worry that relying exclusively on computer algorithms to determine interventions will eliminate critical human elements from mental health care, such as a therapist's clinical judgments or the therapeutic bond between the client and the therapist.

Proponents of mental health JITAIs, on the other hand, are very optimistic about

PeopleImages/Getty Images

the usefulness of wearable technologies to help guide clinical interventions and believe that the technology's potential benefits far outweigh its drawbacks. They argue that delivering automated micro-interventions to clients in specific moments of need can add up and eventually result in greater behavioral change (for example, increased physical activity) than typically results from traditional therapist-led care that focuses on broader and longer-term goals (such as going to the gym more often). To these proponents, the "around-the-clock" availability of wearable technologies will one day help to identify the subjective psychological states that are most relevant to mental health care.

Interpersonal Psychotherapy

Developed several decades ago, **interpersonal psychotherapy (IPT)** holds that any of four interpersonal problem areas may help lead to psychopathology and must be addressed in treatment: interpersonal losses, interpersonal role disputes, interpersonal role transitions, and interpersonal deficits (Swartz et al., 2023; Mattos et al., 2022). Over the course of around 20 sessions, IPT therapists address these areas.

First, IPT therapists encourage clients who have experienced recent *interpersonal losses* to explore their relationship with the lost persons, develop new ways of remembering them, and also look for new relationships. Second, IPT therapists help clients examine and resolve *interpersonal role disputes* they may be involved in. Role disputes occur when two people have different expectations of their relationship and of the role each should play. Third, IPT therapists help clients who are going through *interpersonal role transitions* develop the social supports and skills their new roles require. Role transitions are typically the result of major life changes, such as divorce or the birth of a child. And fourth, IPT therapists help clients who may display significant *interpersonal deficits*—such as extreme shyness or social awkwardness—to recognize their deficits, appreciate the disruptive impact that these deficits can have on intimate relationships, and develop more effective social skills and assertiveness.

interpersonal psychotherapy A therapy that addresses four interpersonal problem areas that may be leading to psychopathology: interpersonal losses, interpersonal role disputes, interpersonal role transitions, and interpersonal deficits.

group therapy A therapy format in which people with similar problems meet together with a therapist to work on those problems.

support group A group made up of people with similar problems who help and support one another without the direct leadership of a clinician. Also called a *self-help group, peer group,* or *mutual-help group.*

family therapy A treatment in which a therapist meets with all members of a family and helps them change in therapeutic ways.

Numerous studies suggest that IPT and related interpersonal treatments are often very helpful for clients, especially those with depression (Swartz et al., 2023; Law et al., 2022). According to recent surveys, approximately 4 percent of today's clinical psychologists identify their primary therapy orientation as interpersonal, a figure that treatment experts expect will keep increasing in the coming years (Norcross et al., 2022; Prochaska & Norcross, 2018).

Group Therapy

Thousands of therapists specialize in **group therapy,** a format in which a therapist meets with a group of clients who have similar problems. Typically, members of a therapy group meet together with a therapist and discuss the problems of one or more of the people in the group. Together they develop important insights, build social skills, strengthen feelings of self-worth, and share useful information or advice. Many groups are created with particular client populations in mind; for example, there are groups for people with addictions, for those with physical disabilities, and for people who have experienced divorce, abuse, or bereavement. Research suggests that group therapy is of help to many clients, often as helpful as individual therapy (Bieling et al., 2022).

Why might group therapy actually be more helpful than individual therapy for some people with psychological problems?

A format similar to group therapy is the **support group** (also called **self-help group, peer group,** or **mutual-help group**). Here people who have similar difficulties or challenges (for example, bereavement, substance use disorder, illness, unemployment, or divorce) come together to help and support one another without the direct leadership of a professional clinician (Anderson et al., 2022; Hybholt et al., 2022). In such groups, members may join together in person, or they may connect online. It is estimated that there are millions of support groups across the world, and treatment experts expect this number to continue to rise in the coming years (Norcross et al., 2022).

Family Therapy

In **family therapy,** first introduced in the 1950s, a therapist meets with all members of a family, identifies problem behaviors and interactions, and helps the whole family to change its ways (Suppes, 2022). Here, the entire family is viewed as the unit under treatment, even if only one of the members receives a clinical diagnosis. In the following case, for example, Jake, a 17-year-old, has recently been arrested on drug charges; however, the therapist works with the boy's whole family, helping them identify and correct problems in family functioning—problems that may be contributing to Jake's behavioral difficulties:

Hispanolistic/E+/Getty Images

Support from those who know A leading kind of group intervention is the *support group*, in which people with similar problems or experiences come together to help one another, typically without direct professional leadership. Here, college students in one such group meet to share their experiences of stress, empathize, and offer each other support, information, and advice.

Sarah, 8 years old:	(Cuddles into her mom. Mom puts her arm around Sarah, kissing her on the head.)
Therapist:	(to Dad) *What's it like to see Sarah like this?*
Dad:	*I hate it. I hate how she (Mom) babies her.*
Therapist:	*It seems like Mom does the comforting in the family and you draw the hard line. It must be tough sometimes, playing the bad guy.*
Dad:	*Somebody's got to do it. . . .*
Therapist:	(To Sarah) *It looks like you might be feeling afraid.*
Sarah:	(Shakes her head)
Therapist:	*Dad, what do you think Sarah might need right now, while she's cuddled into Mom, holding up her shield?*
Dad:	*She wants her mom.*
Therapist:	*I'm thinking you might be able to do something for her too. Why don't you move over to this couch and sit next to Sarah. Sarah, would that be okay?*
Sarah:	(Nods her head)
Dad:	(Moves next to Sarah, puts his arm around her)
Therapist:	*So Jake, what would you add . . . ?*
Jake, 17 years old:	*No one here used to give a shit about me. I was never taken care of like Sarah is now.*
Therapist:	*. . . Talk to your mom about this. Tell her about your anger and your hurt.*
Jake:	*Mom, you weren't there for me. I took care of these kids most of the time. I'm sick of cleaning up your messes.*
Mom:	(Tears up, looks down)
Therapist:	*Mom, let's let Dad sit with Sarah, so you can focus on Jake. Move over here so you can face him.*
Mom:	(Moves over, avoids looking at Jake)
Therapist:	*It's even hard to look at him. You're feeling a lot of guilt. Tell Jake about your tears.*
Mom:	*I'm just really sorry.*
Jake:	*You being sorry don't take it away. It doesn't fix everything.*
Sarah:	(Moves toward Mom, climbs into her lap.)
Therapist:	*Sarah, I wonder if you could be brave and try something new for me. Let's let Mom feel what she needs to feel and talk to Jake. This is going to be a little scary, being so new. Who would you like to sit with while Mom and Jake tell each other about their hurt and sorrow?*
Anna, 14 years old:	(Opens her arms for Sarah. Sarah walks over and is held next to her. An authentic conversation between Mom and Jake continues. . . .)

(Sommers-Flanagan & Sommers-Flanagan, 2018, pp. 332–333)

Family therapists may follow any of the major theoretical models, but many of them adopt the principles of *family systems theory*. As illustrated in the case above, they may try to change the family's power structure and implicit rules, the roles each person plays, and the relationships between members. The therapists may also try to help members recognize and change harmful patterns of communication (Suppes, 2022; Hogue et al., 2021). Recent surveys suggest that 2 percent of today's

of NOTE ...

Changing Families

23% Percentage of U.S. children currently living with a single caregiver, compared to 9% a half-century ago

(Information from: U.S. Census Bureau, 2023)

couple therapy A treatment in which the therapist works with two people who share a long-term relationship. Also called *marital therapy.*

community mental health treatment A treatment approach that emphasizes community care.

clinical psychologists, 4 percent of counseling psychologists, and 14 percent of social workers identify themselves mainly as *family systems therapists,* numbers that are expected to hold steady over the next decade (Norcross et al., 2022; Prochaska & Norcross, 2018).

Family therapy is often helpful, although research has not yet clarified how helpful. Some studies have found significant improvements in as many as 65 percent of family therapy cases, while other studies suggest much lower success rates. Nor has any one type of family therapy emerged as consistently more helpful than the others (Berry et al., 2023; Morales-Brown, 2023).

Couple Therapy

In **couple therapy,** or **marital therapy,** the therapist works with two individuals who are in a long-term relationship. Often, they are married, but the couple need not be married or even living together. Like family therapy, couple therapy often focuses on the structure and communication patterns in the relationship (Lebow & Snyder, 2022). A couple approach may also be used when a child's psychological problems are traced to problems in the parents' relationship.

Although some degree of conflict exists in any long-term relationship, many couples in our society experience serious discord. The divorce rate in Canada, the United States, and Europe is now close to 50 percent of the marriage rate (CDC, 2023). Many unmarried couples who live together apparently have similar levels of difficulty.

Couple therapy, like family therapy and group therapy, may follow the principles of any of the major therapy orientations. *Cognitive-behavioral couple therapy,* for example, uses many techniques from the cognitive and behavioral perspectives. Therapists help partners recognize and change problem behaviors largely by teaching specific problem-solving and communication skills. A broader version, called *integrative behavioral couple therapy,* further helps partners *accept* behaviors that they cannot change and embrace the whole relationship nevertheless. Partners are asked to see such behaviors as an understandable result of basic differences between them (Christensen et al., 2022). Couples treated by couple therapy seem to show greater improvement in their relationships than couples with similar problems who do not receive treatment, but no one form of couple therapy stands out as superior to others (Lebow & Snyder, 2022).

Silvia Izquierdo/AP Photo

Community mental health: Brazilian style Different countries and cultures each have their own way of reaching out to people with psychological disorders. Here patients and members of the community come together and dance during the annual Carnival parade and street party in front of the Psychiatric Institute in Rio de Janeiro, Brazil. The goal of the event is to promote community awareness, acceptance, and outreach by blurring the lines between patients and nonpatients.

Community Treatment

In **community mental health treatment** programs, clients, particularly those with severe psychological difficulties, receive treatment in familiar social surroundings as they try to recover. Such community-based treatments, including *community day programs* and *residential services,* seem to be of special value to people with severe mental disorders (Trane et al., 2022). A number of countries have launched such programs over the past several decades.

As you read in the opening chapter of the textbook, a key principle of community treatment is *prevention.* This involves clinicians actively reaching out to at-risk individuals rather than waiting for them to seek treatment. Research suggests that such efforts are often very successful (Trane et al., 2022). Community workers recognize three types of prevention, which they call *primary, secondary,* and *tertiary.*

Primary prevention consists of efforts to improve community attitudes and policies and overall wellness. Its goal is to offer information and supports for everyone, regardless of individual risk factors or functioning, and so it is often called "universal prevention." Community workers may, for example, consult with a local school board, offer public workshops on stress reduction, or construct websites for the public on how to cope effectively.

Secondary prevention consists of identifying and treating psychological conditions in the early stages, before they become serious. Community workers may work with teachers, ministers, or police to help them recognize the early signs of psychological dysfunction and teach them how to help people find treatment. Similarly, hundreds of websites provide this same kind of information to family members, teachers, and the like.

The goal of *tertiary prevention* is to provide effective treatment to specific persons who have already developed moderate or severe disorders so that these disorders do not become long-term problems. Although community agencies across the United States successfully offer tertiary care for millions of people with moderate psychological problems, they often fail to provide the services needed by hundreds of thousands with severe disturbances. One of the reasons for this failure is lack of funding, an issue that you will read about in later chapters.

How Do Multicultural Theorists Explain Psychopathology?

Culture refers to the set of values, attitudes, beliefs, history, and behaviors shared by a group of people and communicated from one generation to the next. We are, without question, a society of multiple backgrounds, ethnicities, languages, abilities, customs, and so on. In response to this growing diversity, the **multicultural perspective** has emerged.

As you read in opening chapter, multicultural theorists seek to understand how race, ethnicity, gender, sexual orientation, religion, abilities, socioeconomic class, and other such factors affect behavior, emotion, and thought and how people of diverse backgrounds may differ psychologically (Vasquez & Johnson, 2022). The groups in the United States who have received the most attention from multicultural researchers are **people of color** (the general term for people who are Black, Hispanic, Indigenous, and/or Asian American) and other **marginalized people,** such as women, LGBTQ+ people, individuals with low income, and people with disabilities. Members of each of these groups are subjected to unique, often profound, pressures in American society that may contribute to feelings of stress and, in some cases, to psychological dysfunction (González, Carvacho, & Jiménez-Moya, 2022).

In order to derive a fuller understanding of Jorge, multicultural theorists would be interested in his Mexican American upbringing and the consequent values, beliefs, and perspective he has come to embrace, as well as the related discomforts, stressors, and discrimination he experienced throughout his life due to his heritage. They might pay particular attention, for example, to the nature and impact of his business school years, where he was subjected to ongoing accusations, bullying, negative predictions, and derogation largely due to his background.

Researchers have learned that psychopathology, especially severe psychopathology, is more common among people with limited resources and lower incomes than among people with housing security and higher incomes (Lemon, 2023; Marbin et al., 2022). Perhaps the pressures of poverty explain this relationship. Similarly, multicultural researchers have found that the prejudice and discrimination faced by many people of color and other marginalized groups may contribute to various forms of psychopathology (MHA, 2023). Black, Hispanic, and Indigenous people in the United States are more likely than non-Hispanic White persons to experience serious psychological distress (ADAA, 2022). Moreover, Indigenous groups have exceptionally high alcohol use and suicide rates (OMH, 2023; González et al., 2022; Stone et al., 2022). And LGBTQ+ people have particularly high rates of depression, eating disorders, substance use disorder, and suicidal thinking and behavior (ADAA, 2022). Although many factors may combine to produce these differences, prejudice and inequities can contribute to underlying patterns of tension, unhappiness, and low self-esteem.

Today's multicultural view is different from past—less enlightened—cultural perspectives in several ways. First, when multicultural theorists now explore differences *between* cultural groups, they are careful to not imply that marginalized groups are in some way inferior or less adequate than a country's **dominant population**—the societal group that holds, on average, greater power, privilege, and social status (Sagiv & Schwartz,

multicultural perspective The view that each culture in a society has particular values, beliefs, and pressures that influence the behavior and functioning of its members.

people of color The general term for people who are Black, Hispanic, Indigenous, and/or Asian American.

marginalized people People whose communities experience discrimination, as well as social, political, and economic exclusion, due to unequal power relationships across a society.

dominant population The societal group that holds, on average, the greatest power, privilege, and social status.

of NOTE ...

"Hispanic" is a *gender-free* term that refers specifically to people who descend from Spanish-speaking countries, regardless of geography. The terms "Latina" and "Latino" are *gender-based* terms that refer specifically to people who descend from Latin American and Caribbean countries, regardless of language. Although all such terms have limitations and none is all-encompassing, "Hispanic" is often used interchangeably with the others, and our textbook is using "Hispanic" as an all-inclusive term in its discussions.

Lasting effects Years of marginalization and severe oppression have contributed to exceptionally high rates of psychological disorders in Indigenous groups. Here, Patricia Tucknaow pays tribute to her fellow survivors of the Canadian Indian residential school system—a network of boarding schools set up from the 1840s to the 1990s to "assimilate" Indigenous children by separating them from their families, communities, customs, and ancestral language. Abuse was common in these schools, thousands of children died (mostly from disease), and thousands more have gone on to develop depression, substance use disorders, and other such problems.

2022). Second, today's multicultural theorists focus as much on differences *within* cultural groups as on differences between cultural groups (Sanchez et al., 2022). That is, each member of a given cultural group embraces the broad attitudes, values, and customs of that group to a different degree. This makes the task of determining an individual's cultural identity and experiences far more complex than simply knowing the cultural groups to which they belong.

Third, today's multicultural theorists take into consideration that an individual is often a member of multiple diverse groups. Many people of color, for example, also have low income. In turn, the higher rates of incarceration, unemployment, overcrowding, and housing insecurity; the inferior medical care; and the limited educational opportunities common among less affluent people are disproportionately experienced by people of color (Snowden, Cordell, & Bui, 2022). Thus, as you read in the opening chapter, today's multicultural theorists try to understand people through the lens of **intersectionality:** they examine how an individual's memberships in multiple diverse groups and exposure to multiple stressors combine to shape the person's experiences, outlook, and functioning.

Multicultural Treatments: Culturally Responsive Therapies

As we noted in the previous chapter, studies conducted throughout the world have found that people of color and other marginalized groups tend to show less improvement in clinical treatment, make less use of mental health services, and stop therapy sooner than members of dominant groups (APA, 2023; Miller, 2022).

A number of studies suggest that two features of treatment can increase a therapist's effectiveness with clients from the full spectrum of cultural backgrounds: (1) greater sensitivity to cultural issues and (2) inclusion of cultural morals and models in treatment, for adult, adolescent, and child clients (Sanchez et al., 2022; Vasquez & Johnson, 2022). Given such findings, clinicians have developed **culturally responsive therapies,** approaches designed to help address the unique cultural issues faced by clients, especially marginalized individuals (Harkness & Pachankis, 2022; Williams & La Torre, 2022). Recent surveys indicate that around 1 percent of today's clinical psychologists identify their primary orientation as culturally responsive, but this figure has been rising and is expected to increase substantially over the next decade (Norcross et al., 2022; Prochaska & Norcross, 2018).

Culturally responsive approaches embrace a therapist posture of *cultural humility,* a crucial therapy process discussed in the opening chapter, and typically include many of the following elements:

1. Special cultural instruction for therapists in their formal and ongoing training.
2. Therapist efforts to reflect on their own cultural identities and values and to explore cultures and historical realities that differ from their own.
3. Therapist efforts to understand and respect the client's cultural values, attitudes, and beliefs and the cultural context of the client's challenges.
4. Therapist awareness of the stress, prejudices, and stereotypes to which people of color and other marginalized clients are exposed.
5. Helping clients recognize the impact of both their own culture and the dominant culture on their self-views and behaviors.
6. Helping clients identify and express anger and pain.
7. Helping clients achieve a cultural balance that feels right for them.
8. Helping clients raise their self-esteem—a sense of self-worth that has often been damaged by generations of negative messages.

Therapists who offer *affirmative therapy,* one kind of culturally responsive treatment, follow these principles to validate and advocate for the needs of LGBTQ+ clients; guide the clients to achieve greater self-acceptance regarding their sexual orientation or gender identity; and, correspondingly, help the clients achieve a better state of mental health (APA, 2022). Affirmative therapy is illustrated in the following excerpt from the case of Luke, a 27-year-old gay man with depression and anxiety.

> *Throughout the treatment, Luke identified numerous situations contributing to his current distress, including disconnectedness from the gay community, anticipation of rejection from desired romantic partners, and . . . social competition related to body image among his gay peers. . . . Luke's early and ongoing symptoms of anxiety and shame were understood and validated as normative responses to minority stress . . . , [and] education was provided to further contextualize his symptoms as specific to living within a . . . society [that sees homosexuality as pathological]. . . .*
>
> *Luke's intentions were to be involved in the gay community—socially and romantically—while feeling at ease in his surroundings and comfortable with his body. Additionally, he hoped to engage with peers and potential partners without fears of rejection. . . .*
>
> *. . . [His]therapist was able to build Luke's motivation to employ [positive self-appraisals] in place of negative self-talk and to improve his distress tolerance. . . . [Luke came to develop a] more hopeful and balanced self-evaluation as treatment progressed.*
>
> *. . . [The therapist also focused] on building genuine relationships. . . . These supportive relationships were eventually able to provide crucial scaffolding for Luke's new attempts to enact empowered, assertive behavior for which he could be proud. . . . [He became increasingly] able to respond to challenging situations with new assertive stances guided by thoughts such as "It's okay for me to prioritize my needs" and "I can allow someone else to see me . . . and not feel like I have to retreat.". . .*
>
> *(Pachankis et al., 2022)*

Assessing the Sociocultural Model

The family-social and multicultural perspectives have added greatly to the understanding and treatment of psychopathology. Today, most clinicians take family, cultural, social, and societal issues into account, factors that were overlooked just 40 years ago. In addition, clinicians have become more aware of the impact of clinical and social roles. Finally, the treatment formats offered by the sociocultural model sometimes succeed where traditional approaches have failed.

At the same time, the sociocultural model has certain problems. To begin with, sociocultural research findings are often difficult to interpret. Indeed, research may reveal a relationship between certain family or cultural factors and a particular disorder yet fail to establish that they are its *cause*. Studies show a link between family conflict and schizophrenia, for example, but that finding does not necessarily mean that family dysfunction causes schizophrenia. It is equally possible that family functioning is disrupted by the tension and conflict created by the psychosis of a family member.

Another limitation of the sociocultural model is its inability to predict psychological dysfunction in specific individuals. If, for example, social conditions such as prejudice and discrimination are key causes of anxiety and depression, why do only some of the people subjected to such forces experience psychological disorders? Are still other factors necessary for the development of the disorders?

Given these limitations, most clinicians view the family-social and multicultural explanations as operating in conjunction with the biological or psychological explanations.

of NOTE ...

Experiencing Discrimination

76% Percentage of Black Americans who report being regularly or occasionally treated unfairly because of their race

58% Percentage of Hispanic Americans who report being regularly or occasionally treated unfairly because of their ethnicity

(Information from: Jones & Lloyd, 2021; KFF, 2020; Horowitz, Brown, & Cox, 2019)

intersectionality The interconnections among multiple factors such as race, ethnicity, sexual orientation, gender, religion, ability, socioeconomic class, and discrimination that interact in a given person to help produce particular experiences and psychological effects.

culturally responsive therapies Approaches that are designed to help address the unique issues faced by members of different cultural groups.

of NOTE ...

Social Enhancement

57% Percentage of teenagers who have made one or more new friends online

29% Percentage of teenagers who have made five or more new friends online

33% Percentage of marriages in the United States that began online

(Information from: Lieberman & Schroeder, 2020)

They agree that family, social, and cultural factors may create a climate favorable to the development of certain disorders. They believe, however, that biological or psychological conditions—or both—must also be present for the disorders to evolve.

SUMMING UP

The Sociocultural Model

One sociocultural perspective, the *family-social perspective*, looks outward to three kinds of factors: social labels and roles, social connections and supports, and the family system. Practitioners from the family-social model may practice interpersonal psychotherapy, group therapy, family therapy, couple therapy, or community treatment.

The multicultural perspective, another sociocultural perspective, holds that an individual's behavior, whether functional or dysfunctional, is best understood when examined in the light of the person's unique cultural context, including the values of that culture and the special external pressures faced by members of that culture. Practitioners of this perspective may practice culturally responsive therapies, including affirmative therapy. Increasingly, multicultural theorists are emphasizing the principle of intersectionality to understand how multiple factors such as race, ethnicity, gender, sexual orientation, religion, ability, socioeconomic class, and discrimination intersect in a given person to help produce particular experiences and psychological effects.

Integrating the Models: The Developmental Psychopathology Perspective

TODAY'S LEADING MODELS vary widely, and none of the models has proved consistently superior (see **Table 2-2**). Each helps us appreciate a key aspect of human functioning, and each has important strengths as well as serious limitations.

Despite all their differences, the conclusions and techniques of the various models are often compatible. Indeed, many clinicians now favor explanations of psychopathology that consider more than one kind of cause at a time. Such integrative explanations,

TABLE 2-2

Comparing the Models

	Biological	Psychodynamic	Cognitive-Behavioral	Humanistic	Existential	Family-Social	Multicultural
Cause of dysfunction	Biological malfunction	Underlying conflicts	Maladaptive thinking and learning	Self-deceit	Avoidance of responsibility	Family or social stress	External pressures or cultural conflicts
Research support	Strong	Modest	Strong	Weak	Weak	Moderate	Moderate
Therapist role	Doctor	Interpreter	Collaborator/teacher	Observer	Collaborator	Family/social facilitator	Cultural advocate/teacher
Key therapy technique	Biological intervention	Free association and interpretation	Reasoning and conditioning	Reflection	Varied	Family/social intervention	Culturally responsive intervention
Therapy goal	Biological repair	Broad psychological change	Functional thoughts and behaviors	Self-actualization	Authentic life	Effective family or social system	Cultural awareness and comfort

sometimes referred to as *biopsychosocial theories,* state that psychopathology results from the interaction of genetic, biological, emotional, behavioral, cognitive, social, cultural, and societal influences (Nunes et al., 2022). In a similar quest for integration, many therapists now combine treatment techniques from several models (Behan, 2022). In fact, 22 percent of today's clinical psychologists, 31 percent of counseling psychologists, and 26 percent of social workers describe their approach as "eclectic" or "integrative," a trend that is expected to continue in the coming years (Norcross et al., 2022; Prochaska & Norcross, 2018). Studies confirm that clinical conditions often respond better to combined approaches than to any one therapy alone.

One of today's most influential integrative views is the **developmental psychopathology** perspective. As its name implies, this perspective uses a *developmental* framework to understand how variables and principles from the various models may collectively account for human functioning—both adaptive and maladaptive functioning (Cicchetti, 2023, 2018, 2016; Fonagy, Campbell, & Luyten, 2023). As such, the perspective pays particular attention to the *timing* of influential variables. The emergence of particular events, experiences, or biological factors—from neurons to neighborhoods—can continue to have an enormous impact on later functioning if they occur at vulnerable points in a person's life. Moreover, the critical question for developmental psychopathologists is not *which* single factor is the cause of an individual's current psychological challenges but rather when, how, in what context, and to what degree the multiple factors in their life interact with one another. In Jorge's case, for example, when did his sister's birth occur, what was going on in Jorge's life at that point in time, how did his father's ambitiousness and his mother's passivity affect their parenting skills, did his childhood experiences teach him how to cope effectively with stress, and were his sociocultural systems during childhood, adolescence, and early adulthood supportive, or did they intensify his difficulties?

What factors do developmental psychopathologists look at collectively when seeking to understand a person's psychological difficulties? As noted above, they draw from each of the clinical field's major models. They draw from the biological model, for example, by determining how certain genetic and brain factors have set the stage for the individual's important environmental experiences. They extract from the psychodynamic model by considering how earlier events in a person's life—including parent–child relationships—have stifled subsequent development. They employ principles from the cognitive-behavioral model by determining how the individual's maladaptive behaviors have been reinforced over the years and how the person has interpreted and processed life experiences. In addition, developmental psychopathologists draw from the humanistic-existential model by considering the person's competencies, uniqueness, and resilience, even in the face of overwhelming life stress. And finally, they embrace the sociocultural model's emphasis on the influence of social context and culture—both present and past—on the individual's functioning.

The developmental psychopathology perspective contends that various developmental routes can lead to dysfunction. In fact, two key principles—*equifinality* and *multifinality*—are at the center of the perspective. According to the principle of **equifinality,** a number of different developmental routes can lead to the same psychological disorder. Consider, for example, two teenage boys with *conduct disorder,* a disorder that you will read about in the chapter on disorders of childhood and adolescence. Both boys may come to display the same characteristic symptoms of this disorder, such as stealing, skipping school, lying, and breaking into cars. However, as illustrated in **Figure 2-5**, for one of the boys, factors such as unfavorable genes, a difficult temperament, and neglectful parenting may have interacted to foster the development of conduct disorder. In contrast, the other boy with the disorder may have had favorable genes, been born with a positive temperament, and been raised by highly attentive parents. His serious conduct problems may have resulted instead from an interaction of low self-esteem, strong needs for peer approval, and affiliations with peers who typically engage in delinquent activities.

of NOTE ...

Their Words

"You may be done with the past, but the past may not be done with you."

Jennifer Dwight, *The Tolling of Mercedes Bell*

developmental psychopathology A perspective that uses a developmental framework to understand how variables and principles from the various models may collectively account for human functioning.

equifinality The principle that a number of different developmental routes can lead to the same psychological disorder.

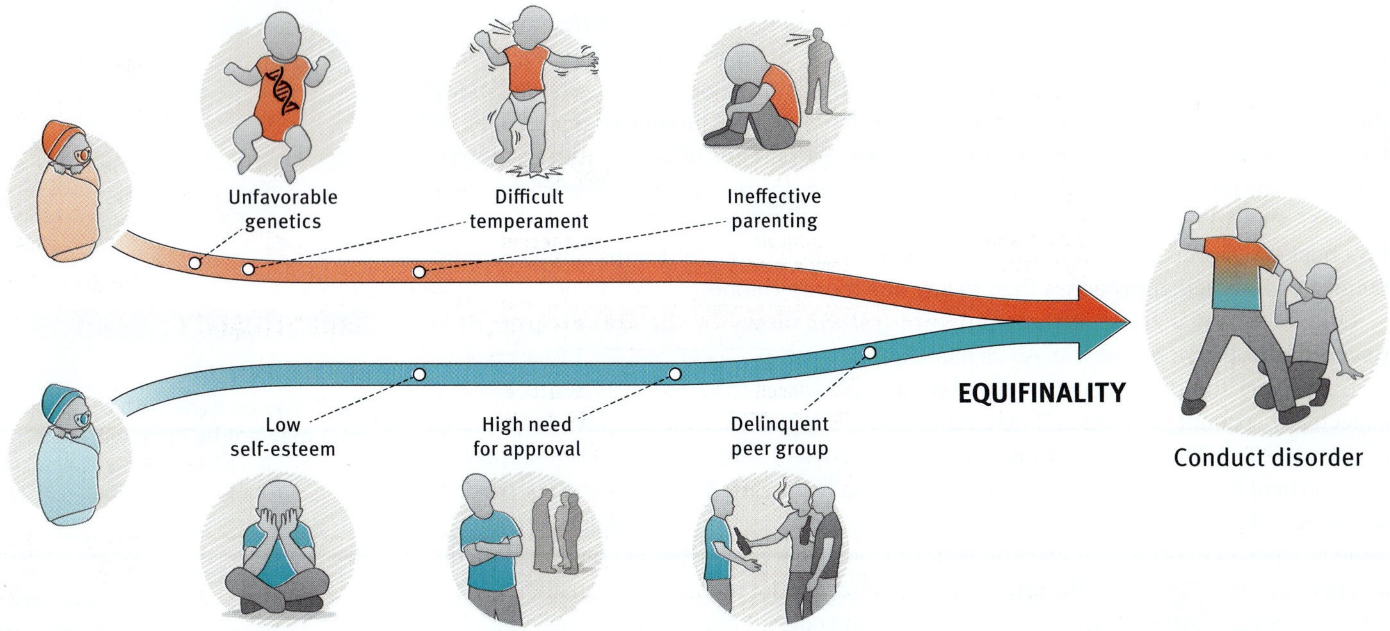

FIGURE 2-5

Equifinality in Action

Equifinality, one of the key principles of the developmental psychopathology perspective, is on display in this illustration. Two boys who experience different negative variables throughout their development each wind up manifesting the same problem—conduct disorder—as teenagers.

According to the other principle of developmental psychopathology, the principle of **multifinality,** people who have experienced a number of similar developmental variables (for example, comparable biological predispositions, family structures, schools, and neighborhoods) may nevertheless have different clinical outcomes. Consider two boys who are each challenged by unfavorable genes and a difficult temperament as they are growing up, along with other negative variables like poverty, traumatic events, and community violence. As illustrated in **Figure 2-6**, despite their very similar backgrounds, one boy may develop conduct disorder as a teenager, while the other may be well-adjusted. Why this enormous difference in outcome? Perhaps other aspects of their developmental histories differ in key ways. The former boy may, for example, have experienced less effective parenting throughout his childhood, while the latter may have been raised by effective parents who helped him develop a strong sense of resilience. When a positive developmental variable such as effective parenting helps to offset the impact of negative variables such as unfavorable genes or a difficult temperament, it is often referred to as a **protective factor.**

Given the developmental psychopathology perspective's emphasis on timing and development to help explain psychological disorders, it is not surprising that its practitioners focus more on the timing of treatment than on specific treatment techniques. For example, they tend to prioritize prevention, the introduction of protective factors, and early intervention for vulnerable people (Cicchetti, 2023, 2018, 2016; Hawes & Allen, 2023). Furthermore, consistent with the perspective's special emphasis on context and sociocultural influences, developmental psychopathologists echo the call of community mental health advocates for community-wide interventions, commonly targeting entire schools or neighborhoods, as opposed to individual treatment formats. Indeed, developmental psychopathologists often play prominent roles in social policy, seeking changes in societal factors that negatively influence development, such as poverty, community violence, and social inequalities.

Given the rise of integrative perspectives and combination treatments, our examinations of psychopathology throughout this book will take two directions. As various disorders are presented, we will look at how today's models explain and treat each disorder and how well those explanations and treatments are supported by research. Just as important, however, we will also be observing how the explanations and treatments may build upon one another, and we will examine current efforts toward integration of the models, including the efforts of developmental psychopathologists.

multifinality The principle that persons with similar developmental histories may nevertheless have different clinical outcomes or react to comparable current situations in different ways.

protective factor A positive developmental variable such as effective parenting that helps to offset the impact of negative variables such as unfavorable genes or a difficult temperament.

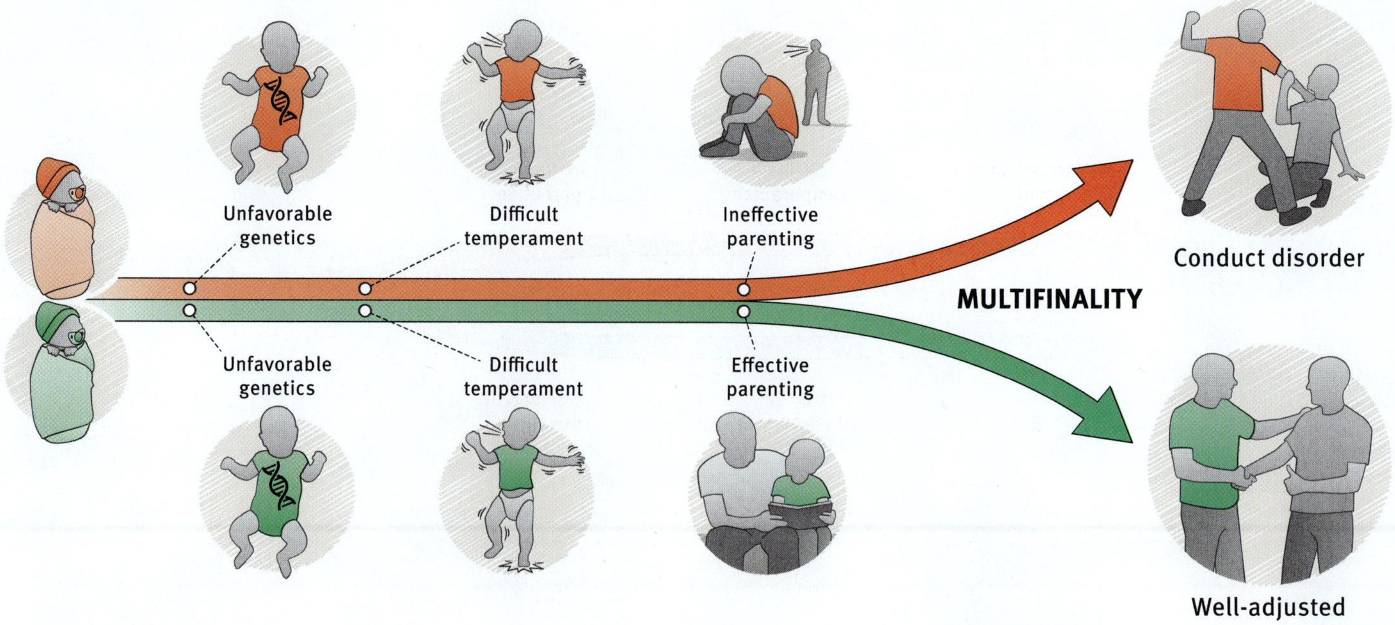

FIGURE 2-6

Multifinality in Action

Multifinality is displayed in this drawing. Two boys who are challenged by several similar negative variables in their childhoods, such as unfavorable genes and a difficult temperament, wind up with very different teenage outcomes (conduct disorder for one, good adjustment for the other). This is largely because one boy had the additional disadvantage of ineffective parents, while the other boy had the good fortune of effective parents.

SUMMING UP

Integrating the Models

Many theorists now favor explanations for psychopathology that consider more than one kind of cause at a time, and many therapists combine treatment techniques from several models. An influential integrative view, the developmental psychopathology perspective, uses a developmental framework to understand how variables and principles from the various models may collectively account for human functioning—both adaptive and maladaptive functioning. Two principles at the center of this perspective are equifinality and multifinality.

Quick Quiz

1. What are neurotransmitters, brain structures, and brain circuits? Describe the biological treatments for psychological disorders. pp. 43–48
2. Identify the models associated with learned responses (p. 54), values (p. 59), responsibility (p. 59), spirituality (p. 62), underlying conflicts (p. 49), and maladaptive assumptions (p. 55).
3. Identify the treatments that use unconditional positive regard (p. 60), free association (p. 52), exposure (p. 57), mindfulness meditation (p. 58), and dream interpretation (p. 52).
4. What are the key principles of the psychodynamic (pp. 49–51), cognitive-behavioral (pp. 54–57), humanistic-existential (pp. 59–63), and sociocultural models (pp. 64–66, 71–72)?
5. According to psychodynamic theorists, what roles do the id, ego, and superego play in the development of both functional and dysfunctional behavior? What are the key techniques used by psychodynamic therapists? pp. 49–53
6. What principles and treatments do cognitive-behavioral practitioners focus on in their explanations and treatments of psychopathology? pp. 54–58
7. How do humanistic theories and therapies differ from existential ones? pp. 59–63
8. How might social labels and roles, social connections and supports, family factors, and culture relate to psychological functioning? pp. 64–66
9. What are the key features of culturally responsive therapies, interpersonal psychotherapy, group therapy, family therapy, couple therapy, and community treatment? pp. 66–73
10. What are the key principles of the developmental psychopathology perspective? How does this perspective integrate the principles found in the various models of psychopathology? pp. 74–77

Clinical Assessment, Diagnosis, and Treatment

CHAPTER 3

TOPIC OVERVIEW

Sung-Hoon, known as Sam to his friends and coworkers, started seeing a therapist at the urging of his friend Jesse. It had been almost four months since Sam broke up with his girlfriend Taylor, and he still seemed unable to pull himself together.

Although Jesse and some other friends took him out several times to cheer him up right after his breakup, Sam soon started claiming he was much too busy to go out. And within weeks, Sam eventually stopped playing sports and attending trivia nights, things he normally enjoyed greatly and did with his friends on a regular basis. More recently, Sam stopped returning any of Jesse's calls, and none of his other friends heard from him either. Eventually, Sam did call Jesse back, but his tone and behavior during the call alarmed Jesse. Sam sounded flat, not even attempting any of his famous bad jokes during the conversation. He just repeated, with a heavy sigh, "I'm fine, really," over and over.

During that call, Sam mentioned in passing several serious and avoidable mistakes that he had recently made at the bank where he worked, but he barely seemed to care. He also confided that he felt very tired and was unable to eat more than a little food each day, as though that were perfectly normal. Sam said he doubted he'd ever find someone who could make him happy as Taylor had, at least not one who would have anything to do with him. He noted, bitterly, that his mother, who was always uncomfortable that Taylor was not Korean, was delighted by his split. "My mom says, 'Now, maybe you can find yourself a nice Korean girl,'" Sam told Jesse. "What year does she think this is? Does she think it's the 1950s? She's in total denial. She thinks she can turn me into the son she wishes she had and never lets me forget her shame at the person I turned out to be. If she only realized I'm twice as disappointed in myself as she could ever be."

Jesse suspected that Sam was clinically depressed, but, then again, he was not a therapist.

Feelings of despondency led Sam to make an appointment with a therapist at a local counseling center. His clinician's first step was to learn as much as possible about Sam and his disturbance: Who is he, what is his life like, and what are his symptoms? The answers to these questions might help to reveal the causes and probable course of his present challenges and suggest what kinds of strategies would be most likely to help him. Treatment could then be tailored to Sam's needs and particular pattern of dysfunction.

In the previous two chapters, you read about how researchers who study psychopathology build a general understanding of mental disturbances. Clinical practitioners apply this broad information in their work, but their main focus when faced with new clients is to gather **idiographic**, or individual, information about them. To help a client overcome problems, clinicians must fully understand the client and the client's particular difficulties. To gather such individual information, clinicians use the procedures of *assessment* and *diagnosis*. Then they are in a position to offer *treatment*. ■

Matt Manley

Clinical Assessment: How and Why Is the Client Showing Psychopathology?

ASSESSMENT IS SIMPLY the collecting of relevant information in an effort to reach a conclusion. It goes on in every realm of life. We make assessments when we decide what cereal to buy or which presidential candidate to vote for. College admissions officers, who have to select the "best" of the students applying to their college, often depend on academic records, recommendations, achievement test scores, essays, interviews, and application forms to help them decide. Employers, who have to predict which applicants are most likely to be effective workers, collect information from résumés, interviews, references, and perhaps on-the-job observations.

Clinical assessment is used to determine whether, how, and why a person is behaving in a dysfunctional manner and how that person may be helped. It also enables clinicians to evaluate people's progress after they have been in treatment for a while and decide whether the treatment should be changed. The hundreds of clinical assessment techniques and tools that have been developed fall into three categories: *clinical interviews, tests,* and *observations*. To be useful, these tools must be *standardized* and must have clear *reliability* and *validity*.

of NOTE ...

Employment Screening

As many as 70 percent of companies use social media to help screen job candidates. Why? To determine whether candidates present themselves accurately and professionally, are good fits for the company's culture, and/or are well rounded (CareerBuilder, 2023).

Characteristics of Assessment Tools

All clinicians must follow the same procedures when they use a particular type of **assessment** tool. To **standardize** such a tool is to set up common steps to be followed whenever the tool is administered. Similarly, clinicians must standardize the way they interpret the results of an assessment tool in order to be able to understand what a particular score means. They may standardize the scores of a test, for example, by first administering it to a group of research participants whose performance will then serve as a common standard, or norm, against which later individual scores can be measured. The group that initially takes the test must be typical of the larger population for whom the test is intended. If an aggressiveness test meant for the public at large were standardized on a group of professional rugby players, for example, the resulting "norm" might turn out to be misleadingly high.

Reliability refers to the *consistency* of assessment measures. A good assessment tool will always yield similar results in the same situation (Lane, Aslinger, & Shrout, 2023; Cohen, Schneider, & Tobin, 2022). An assessment tool has high *test–retest reliability,* one kind of reliability, if it yields similar results every time it is given to the same people. If a person's responses on a particular test indicate that they are generally a heavy drinker, the test should produce a similar result when they take it again a week later. To measure test–retest reliability, participants are tested on two occasions, and the two scores are correlated. The higher the correlation, the greater the test's reliability.

An assessment tool shows high *interrater* (or *interjudge*) *reliability,* another kind of reliability, if different judges independently agree on how to score and interpret it. True–false and multiple-choice tests yield consistent scores no matter who evaluates them, but other tests require that the evaluator make a judgment. Consider a test that requires the person to draw a copy of a picture that a judge then rates for accuracy. If the rules for interpretation are not spelled out and applied consistently, different judges may give different ratings to the same drawing.

Finally, an assessment tool must have **validity;** that is, it must *accurately* measure what it is supposed to measure (Grimm & Widaman, 2023). Suppose a weight scale

idiographic information Information about a particular individual, as opposed to a larger population.

assessment The process of collecting and interpreting relevant information about a client or research participant.

standardization The process in which a test is administered to a large group of people whose performance then serves as a standard or norm against which any individual's score can be measured.

reliability A measure of the consistency of test or research results.

validity A measure of the accuracy of a test's or study's results.

Joe Murphy/Getty Images

Reliable assessment? Former National Basketball Association stars Magic Johnson, Shaquille O'Neal, Tracy McGrady, Dikembe Mutombo, and George Gervin served as judges at an All-Star slam dunk contest. Assigning a relatively wide range of scores after each dunk, they displayed low interrater reliability.

reads 12 pounds every time a 10-pound bag of sugar is placed on it. Although the scale is reliable because its readings are consistent, those readings are not valid, or accurate.

A given assessment tool may appear to be valid simply because it makes sense and seems reasonable. However, this sort of validity, called *face validity,* does not by itself mean that the instrument is trustworthy. A test for depression, for example, might include questions about how often a person cries. Because it makes sense that depressed people would cry, these test questions have face validity. It turns out, however, that many people cry a great deal for reasons other than depression, and some people with severe depression do not cry at all. Thus, an assessment tool should not be used unless it has high *predictive validity* or *concurrent validity.*

Predictive validity is a tool's ability to predict future characteristics or behavior. Let's say that a test has been developed to identify elementary schoolchildren who are likely to take up cigarette smoking in high school. The test gathers information about the children's parents—their personal characteristics, smoking habits, and attitudes toward smoking—and on that basis identifies high-risk children. To establish the test's predictive validity, investigators could administer it to a group of elementary school students, wait until they are in high school, and then check to see which children actually did become smokers.

Concurrent validity is the degree to which the measures gathered from one tool agree with the measures gathered from other assessment techniques. Participants' scores on a new test designed to measure anxiety, for example, should correlate highly with their scores on other anxiety tests (Freitag et al., 2023; Comer et al., 2022) or with their behavior during clinical interviews.

How reliable and valid are the tests you take for school? What about tests you take online for fun?

Before any assessment technique can be fully useful, it must meet the requirements of standardization, reliability, and validity. No matter how insightful or clever a technique may be, clinicians cannot profitably use its results if those results are uninterpretable, inconsistent, or inaccurate. Unfortunately, more than a few clinical assessment tools fall short, and clinicians who use such tools may come to incorrect conclusions about their clients. In the following sections, we will discuss several kinds of assessment techniques and their strengths and weaknesses.

of NOTE ...

Famous Clinicians in Cinema

Dr. Stoner (*Joker*, 2019)
Matilda (*The Angry Birds Movie*, 2016)
Dr. Aurelius (*Hunger Games*, 2015)
Dr. Cliff Patel (*Silver Linings Playbook*, 2012)
Dr. Swanson (*Office Space*, 1999)
Dr. Malcolm Crowe (*The Sixth Sense*, 1999)
Dr. Sean Maguire (*Good Will Hunting*, 1997)

Clinical Interviews

Most of us feel instinctively that the best way to get to know people is to meet with them person-to-person. Under these circumstances, we can take note of their reactions to what we do and say, we can observe as well as listen as they answer, and we can generally get a sense of who they are. A *clinical interview* is just such a person-to-person encounter (Slade & Sergent, 2023). If during a clinical interview a man looks as happy as can be while describing his sadness over the recent death of his mother, the clinician may suspect that the man actually has conflicting emotions about this loss. Traditionally, most clinical interviews have been conducted in person, but since the start of the Covid-19 pandemic in 2020 and the increase of social-distancing measures, the use of telemental health interviewing and assessment formats has increased significantly (Bagner et al., 2022; Maye et al., 2022; Comer, 2021).

Conducting the Interview

The interview is often the first contact between client and clinician. Clinicians use it to collect detailed information about the person's difficulties and feelings, lifestyle and relationships, and other personal history. They may also ask about the person's expectations of therapy and motives for seeking it. The clinician who worked with Sam began with a face-to-face interview:

Sam arrived for his appointment in gray sweatpants and a T-shirt. His stubble suggested that he had not shaved, and his shirt had many food stains on it. Sam spoke without emotion and slouched into the chair, sending clear signals that he did not want to be there.

When pressed, he talked about his two-year relationship with Taylor, who, at 25, was 13 years younger than he was. Sam had believed she would eventually be his wife, but Taylor's domineering mother was unhappy about their age difference. She would always speak glowingly about Taylor's ex—Peter—and Sam believed she wanted Taylor to reunite with Peter. Given that they were in an exclusive relationship, Sam wanted Taylor to move in with him, but Taylor said she needed her own living space for a while longer. Sam took this as a total rebuff and permanent lack of commitment and stormed out during one of their fights, saying he was leaving for good and didn't have time for someone who couldn't even stand up to her mother. He soon regretted this, but Taylor refused to take him back.

When asked by the therapist about his childhood, Sam described his father's death in a car crash on his way to pick up 12-year-old Sam from soccer practice. Initially, his father had told Sam that he could not pick him up, but Sam "threw a tantrum," and his father rearranged his schedule. Sam believed himself responsible for his father's death.

He stated that his mother had actually encouraged this self-blame, complaining that she had been forced to "give up her life" to raise Sam alone. She often berated Sam, and he felt this only got worse when he began dating people who were not Korean. She was cold to his various partners. No matter how many times Sam tried to explain that he was simply being true to himself, his mother would urge him to "date Korean girls—you'll be happier." More than once, she predicted he would "die alone."

Sam described being very unhappy throughout his school years. He hated school and felt stupid compared with other kids. A teacher's critique—meant as encouragement—could leave him unable to do homework for days, and his grades suffered. His low self-image continued throughout childhood and into adulthood. When, for example, he was promoted to bank manager at the young age of 27, he attributed this accomplishment exclusively to hard work rather than ability. "I know I'm not as smart as the others there."

Sam explained that since the breakup with Taylor, he had experienced more unhappiness than ever before. He often spent all night watching television, though he barely paid attention to what was happening on the screen. He said that some days he'd forget to eat. He had no wish to see his friends. At work, days blurred into one another, characterized by a growing number of mistakes and reprimands. He believed his supervisors had finally figured out that he had not been good enough for the job all along.

Beyond gathering basic background data of this kind, clinical interviewers give special attention to those topics they consider most important (Henry, 2023; Brown & Barlow, 2021). Psychodynamic interviewers try to learn about the person's needs and memories of past events and relationships. Cognitive-behavioral interviewers try to identify information about the stimuli that trigger responses, consequences of the responses, and/or assumptions and interpretations that influence the person. Humanistic clinicians ask about the person's self-evaluation, self-concept, and values. Biological clinicians look for signs of biochemical or brain dysfunction. And sociocultural interviewers ask about the family, social, and cultural environments (Urcuyo et al., 2023; Sanchez et al., 2022).

Interviews can be either unstructured or structured. In an *unstructured interview,* the clinician asks mostly open-ended questions, perhaps as simple as "Would you tell me about yourself?" The lack of structure allows the interviewer to follow leads and explore relevant topics that could not have been anticipated before the interview (Slade & Sergent, 2023).

In a *structured interview,* clinicians ask prepared—mostly specific—questions. Sometimes they use a published *interview schedule*—a standard set of questions designed for all interviews (Albano & Silverman, 2023; Madill, 2023). Many structured interviews include a **mental status exam,** a set of questions and observations that systematically evaluate the client's awareness, orientation with regard to time and place, attention span, memory, judgment and insight, thought content and processes, mood, and appearance (Morrison, 2023). A structured format ensures that clinicians will cover the same kinds of important issues in all of their interviews and enables them to compare the responses of different individuals.

Although most clinical interviews have both unstructured and structured portions, many clinicians favor one kind over the other (Madill, 2023). Unstructured interviews typically appeal to psychodynamic and humanistic clinicians, while structured formats are widely used by cognitive-behavioral clinicians, who need to pinpoint behaviors or thinking processes that may underlie psychological dysfunction.

Pandemic-related social distancing triggered an increased reliance on telemental health clinical interviewing. Might such interviewing be less informative than in-person interviewing?

What Are the Limitations of Clinical Interviews?

Although interviews often produce valuable information about people, there are limits to what they can accomplish. One problem is that they sometimes lack validity, or accuracy. Clients may downplay their symptoms in order to present themselves in a positive light or to avoid discussing embarrassing topics. Or people may be unable to give an accurate report in their interviews. Individuals with depression, for example, take a negative view of themselves and may describe themselves as "poor workers" or "inadequate parents" when that isn't the case at all.

Interviewers too may make mistakes in judgment that slant the information they gather (Slade & Sergent, 2023). They usually rely too heavily on first impressions, for example, and give too much weight to unfavorable information about a client. Interviewer biases, including gender, race, and age biases, may also influence an interviewer's interpretation of what a client says.

Interviews, particularly unstructured ones, may also lack reliability (McConaughy & Whitcomb, 2022). People respond differently to different interviewers, providing, for example, less information to a cold interviewer than to a warm and supportive one (Slade & Sergent, 2023). Similarly, a clinician's race, gender, age, and appearance may influence a client's responses.

Because different clinicians can obtain different answers and draw different conclusions even when they ask the same questions of the same person, some researchers believe that interviewing, particularly unstructured interviewing, should be discarded as a tool of clinical assessment. As you'll see, however, the two other methods of clinical assessment also have serious limitations.

mental status exam A set of interview questions and observations designed to reveal the degree and nature of a client's psychopathology.

clinical test A device for gathering information about a few aspects of a person's psychological functioning from which broader information about the person can be inferred.

projective test A test consisting of ambiguous material that people interpret or respond to.

Clinical Tests

Clinical tests are devices for gathering information about a few aspects of a person's psychological functioning from which broader information about the person can be inferred. On the surface, it may look easy to design an effective test. Websites, for example, regularly present new tests that supposedly tell us about our personalities, relationships, sex lives, reactions to stress, or ability to succeed. Such tests might sound convincing, but most of them lack reliability, validity, and standardization. That is, they do not yield consistent, accurate information or reveal where we stand in comparison with others.

More than 1,000 clinical tests are currently in use around the world (EBSCO, 2023). Clinicians use six kinds most often: *projective tests, personality inventories, response inventories, psychophysiological tests, neuroimaging and neuropsychological tests,* and *intelligence tests.*

Projective Tests

Projective tests require that clients interpret vague stimuli, such as inkblots or ambiguous pictures, or follow open-ended instructions, such as "Draw a person." Theoretically, when clues and instructions are so general, people will "project" aspects of their personality onto the task. Projective tests are used primarily by psychodynamic clinicians to help assess the unconscious drives and conflicts they believe to be at the root of pathological functioning (Cohen et al., 2022). The most widely used projective tests are the *Rorschach test,* the *Thematic Apperception Test, sentence-completion tests,* and *drawings* (McGrath, Twibell, & Carroll, 2023).

RORSCHACH TEST In 1911, Hermann Rorschach, a Swiss psychiatrist, experimented with the use of inkblots in his clinical work. He made thousands of blots by dropping ink on paper and then folding the paper in half to create a symmetrical but wholly accidental design, such as the one shown in **Figure 3-1**. Rorschach found that everyone saw images in these blots. In addition, the images a viewer saw seemed to correspond in important ways with their psychological condition. People diagnosed with schizophrenia, for example, tended to see images that differed from those described by people experiencing depression.

Rorschach selected 10 inkblots and published them in 1921 with instructions for their use in assessment. This set was called the Rorschach Psychodynamic Inkblot Test. Rorschach died just eight months later, at the age of 37, but his work was continued by others, and his inkblots took their place among the most widely used projective tests of the twentieth century.

FIGURE 3-1

An Inkblot Similar to Those Used in the Rorschach Test

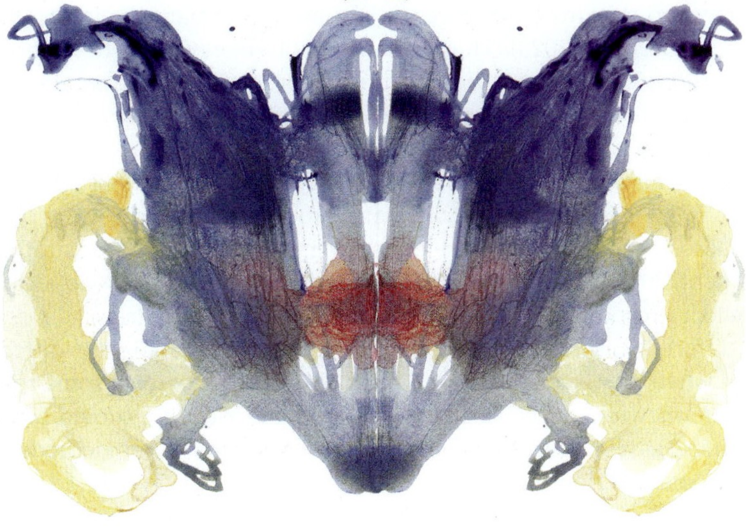

Spencer Sutton/Science Source

Clinicians administer the "Rorschach," as it is commonly called, by presenting one inkblot card at a time and asking respondents what they see, what the inkblot seems to be, or what it reminds them of. In the early years, Rorschach testers paid special attention to the themes and images that the inkblots brought to mind (McGrath et al., 2023; Mihura et al., 2022). Testers now also pay attention to the style of the responses: Do the clients view the design as a whole or see specific details? Do they focus on the blots or on the white spaces between them?

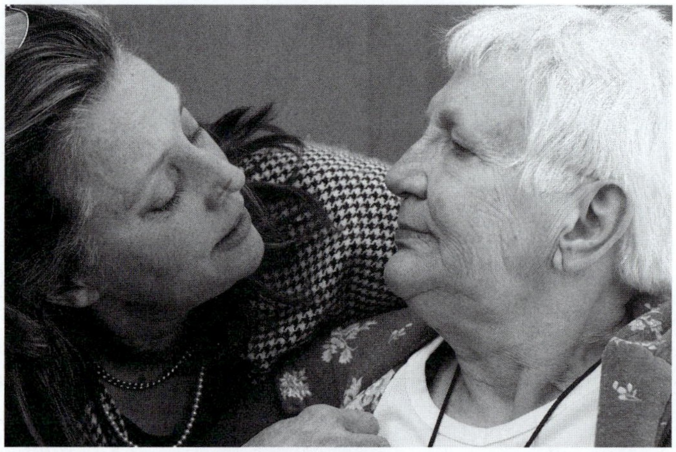

ManoAfrica/Getty Images

FIGURE 3-2

A Picture Similar to One Used in the Thematic Apperception Test

THEMATIC APPERCEPTION TEST The Thematic Apperception Test (TAT) is a pictorial projective test (Jenkins, 2023). People who take the TAT are commonly shown 30 cards with black-and-white pictures of individuals in vague situations and are asked to make up a dramatic story about each card. They must tell what is happening in the picture, what led up to it, what the characters are feeling and thinking, and what the outcome of the situation will be.

Clinicians who use the TAT believe that people always identify with one of the characters on each card. The stories are thought to reflect the individuals' own circumstances, needs, and emotions. For example, a female client seems to be revealing her own feelings when telling this story about a TAT picture similar to the image shown in **Figure 3-2:**

> *"This is a woman who has been quite troubled by memories of a mother she was resentful toward. She has feelings of sorrow for the way she treated her mother; her memories of her mother plague her. These feelings seem to be increasing as she grows older and sees her children treating her the same way that she treated her mother."*
>
> *(Aiken, 1985, p. 372)*

SENTENCE-COMPLETION TEST In the sentence-completion test, first developed in the 1920s (Payne, 1928), the test-taker completes a series of unfinished sentences, such as "I wish . . ." or "My father . . ." The test is considered a good springboard for discussion and a quick and easy way to pinpoint topics to explore (APA, 2023).

DRAWINGS On the assumption that a drawing tells us something about its creator, clinicians often ask clients to draw human figures and talk about them (McGrath et al., 2023). Evaluations of these drawings are based on the details and shape of the drawing, the solidity of the pencil line, the location of the drawing on the paper, the size of the figures, the features of the figures, the use of background, and the comments made by the respondent during the drawing task. In the *Draw-a-Person (DAP) test,* the most popular of the drawing tests, individuals are first told to draw "a person" and then to draw a person whose gender is different from the first drawing.

Drawing test As part of a UNICEF therapy program, this young Nigerian refugee draws an attack scene. The program is provided in Baga Sola, a town in western Chad that welcomes people who have fled extremist groups in northeastern Nigeria.

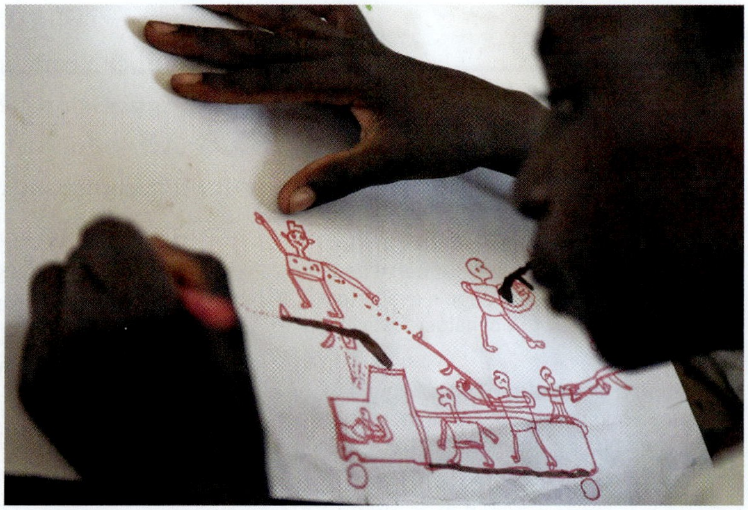

Philippe Desmazes/Getty Images

WHAT ARE THE MERITS OF PROJECTIVE TESTS? Until the 1950s, projective tests were the most commonly used method for assessing personality. In recent years, however, clinicians and researchers have relied on them largely to gain "supplementary" insights (McGrath et al., 2023). One reason for this shift is that practitioners who follow the newer models have less use for the tests than psychodynamic clinicians do. Even more important, the tests have not consistently shown much reliability or validity.

Kim Wark/CartoonStock Ltd.

"Hey, this isn't a QR code."

In reliability studies, different clinicians have tended to score the same person's projective test quite differently. Similarly, in validity studies, when clinicians try to describe a client's personality and feelings on the basis of responses to projective tests, their conclusions often fail to match the self-report of the client, the view of the psychotherapist, or the picture gathered from an extensive case history (McGrath et al., 2023; Rosso & Camoirano, 2022).

Another validity problem is that projective tests are sometimes biased against people of color and other marginalized persons (Leong, Bernal, & Buchanan, 2024) (see **Table 3-1**). For example, people are supposed to identify with the characters in the TAT when they make up stories about them, yet no persons of color are represented in the TAT pictures. In response to this problem, some clinicians have developed other TAT-like tests with Black or Hispanic figures (Costantino, Dana, & Malgady, 2020; Costantino, 2014; Costantino, Dana, & Malgady, 2007).

Personality Inventories

An alternative way to collect information about individuals is to ask them to assess themselves. Respondents to a **personality inventory** answer a wide range of questions about their behavior, beliefs, and feelings. In the typical personality inventory, individuals indicate whether each of a long list of statements applies to them. Clinicians then use the responses to draw conclusions about the person's personality and psychological functioning (Spores, 2022).

By far the most widely used personality inventory is the *Minnesota Multiphasic Personality Inventory* (*MMPI*). Several adult versions are available—the original test, published in 1945; the *MMPI-2,* a 1989 revision that was itself revised in 2001; the *MMPI-2 Restructured Form,* a shorter version of the inventory, developed in 2008; and the *MMPI-3,* a 2020 revision that added a number of new items and scales—changes based on the responses of standardization groups that more accurately reflected population diversity across the United States. Still another version, *MMPI-A,* offers a special version of the test for adolescents.

The MMPI-3 consists of 335 self-statements, to be labeled "true," "false," or "cannot say" by the test-taker. The statements cover issues ranging from physical concerns to mood, sexual behaviors, and social activities. Altogether, the statements make up over 50 scales, on each of which an individual can score from 0 to 120. When people score above 70 on a scale, their functioning on that scale is considered "deviant." When the scale scores are considered side by side, a pattern called a *profile* takes shape, indicating the person's general personality. The many scales on the MMPI-3 include the following:

- **Self-Doubt** Items suggesting that the person has feelings of uselessness and low self-confidence.
- **Worry** Items showing an excessive preoccupation with possible negative outcomes.
- **Anger Proneness** Items that characterize hostility and impatience with others.
- **Aggression** Items that suggest a pattern of hostile actions and violent behavior.
- **Activation** Items that suggest elevated energy and excitement levels.
- **Psychoticism** Items that suggest the person is disconnected from reality.

The MMPI-3 and other personality inventories have several advantages over projective tests (Cohen et al., 2022; Frick, Barry, & Kamphaus, 2020). Because they are computerized or paper-and-pencil tests, they do not take much time to administer, and they are objectively scored. Most of them are standardized, so one person's scores can be compared with those of many others. Moreover, they often display greater test–retest reliability than projective tests. For example, people who take the MMPI-3 a second time after a period of less than two weeks receive approximately the same scores (Floyd & Gupta, 2023).

personality inventory A test, designed to measure broad personality characteristics, consisting of statements about behaviors, beliefs, and feelings that people evaluate as either characteristic or uncharacteristic of them.

response inventories Tests designed to measure a person's responses in one specific area of functioning, such as affect, social skills, or cognitive processes.

Personality inventories also appear to have more validity, or accuracy, than projective tests (Cohen et al., 2022; Frick et al., 2020). However, they can hardly be considered *highly* valid. When clinicians have used these tests alone, they have not regularly been able to judge a respondent's personality accurately. One problem is that the personality traits that the tests seek to measure cannot be examined directly. How can we fully know a person's character, emotions, and needs from self-reports alone? Another problem is that despite the fact that the MMPI-3 designers have used more diverse standardization groups, this and other personality tests continue to have certain cultural limitations. Responses that indicate a psychological disorder in one culture may be appropriate responses in another.

Despite such criticisms of the personality inventories, they continue to be popular. Research indicates that they can help clinicians learn about people's personal styles and disorders as long as they are used in combination with interviews or other assessment tools (Floyd & Gupta, 2023).

Response Inventories

Like personality inventories, **response inventories** ask people to provide detailed information about themselves, but these tests focus on one specific area of functioning. For example, one such test may measure affect (emotion), another social skills, and still another cognitive processes. Clinicians can use the inventories to determine the role that such factors play in a person's disorder.

Affective inventories measure the severity and management of such emotions as anxiety, depression, and anger (Freitag et al., 2023). In one of the most widely used affective inventories, the Beck Depression Inventory, people rate their level of sadness and its effect on their functioning. For *social skills inventories,* used particularly by

TABLE 3-1

Multicultural Hot Spots in Assessment and Diagnosis

Cultural Hot Spot	Effect on Assessment or Diagnosis
Immigrant Client	**Dominant-Culture Assessor**
Homeland culture may differ from current country's dominant culture	May misread culture-bound reactions as pathology
May have left homeland to escape war or oppression	May overlook client's vulnerability to posttraumatic stress disorder
May have weak support systems in this country	May overlook client's heightened vulnerability to stressors
Lifestyle (wealth and occupation) in this country may fall below lifestyle in homeland	May overlook client's sense of loss and frustration
May not speak dominant language	May misunderstand client's assessment responses, or may overlook or misdiagnose client's symptoms
Client from Marginalized Cultural Group	**Dominant-Culture Assessor**
May reject or distrust members of dominant culture, including assessor	May experience little rapport with client, or may misinterpret client's distrust as pathology
May be uncomfortable with dominant culture's values (e.g., assertiveness, confrontation) and so find it difficult to apply clinician's recommendations	May incorrectly view client as unmotivated
May manifest stress in culture-bound ways (e.g., somatic symptoms such as stomachaches)	May misinterpret symptom patterns
May hold cultural beliefs that seem strange to dominant culture (e.g., belief in communication with the dead)	May misinterpret cultural responses as pathology (e.g., a delusion)
May be uncomfortable during assessment	May overlook and feed into client's discomfort
Mere cultural differences may be interpreted as pathological symptoms	May be unknowledgeable or biased about client's culture
May become tense and anxious	May nonverbally convey own discomfort to client

Information from: Leong et al., 2024; Sue et al., 2022; Leong, Lui, & Kalibatseva, 2020; Reynolds, Altmann, & Allen, 2020; Dana, 2015; Westermeyer, 2004, 2001, 1993; Kirmayer, 2003, 2002, 2001.

psychophysiological test A test that measures physical responses (such as heart rate and muscle tension) as possible indicators of psychological conditions.

neuroimaging techniques Neurological tests that provide images of brain structure or activity, such as CT scans, PET scans, and MRIs. Also called *brain scanning*.

behavioral and family-social clinicians, respondents indicate how they would react in a variety of social situations. *Cognitive inventories* reveal a person's typical thoughts and assumptions and can help uncover counterproductive patterns of thinking.

Both the number of response inventories and the number of clinicians who use them have increased steadily in the past 35 years. At the same time, however, these inventories have major limitations. With the notable exception of the Beck Depression Inventory and some others, few of the tests have been subjected to careful standardization, reliability, and validity procedures (Lee & Park, 2021). Often they are created as a need arises, without being tested for accuracy and consistency.

Psychophysiological Tests

Clinicians may also use **psychophysiological tests,** which measure physiological responses as possible indicators of psychological problems. This practice began three decades ago, after several studies suggested that states of anxiety are regularly accompanied by physiological changes, particularly increases in heart rate, body temperature, blood pressure, skin reactions (*galvanic skin response*), and muscle contractions. The measuring of physiological changes has since played a key role in the assessment of certain psychological disorders (Tassinary et al., 2023). Low-profile, wearable mobile devices with sensors are increasingly being used to remotely monitor clients' psychophysiological activity throughout their day-to-day lives.

One psychophysiological test is the *polygraph,* popularly known as a *lie detector* (Kaminsky, 2022). Electrodes attached to various parts of a person's body detect changes in breathing, perspiration, and heart rate while the person answers questions. The clinician observes these functions while the person answers "yes" to *control questions*—questions whose answers are known to be yes, such as "Are both your parents alive?" Then the clinician observes the same physiological functions while the person answers *test questions,* such as "Did you commit this robbery?" If breathing, perspiration, and heart rate suddenly increase, the person is suspected of lying.

Like other kinds of clinical tests, psychophysiological tests have their drawbacks (Tassinary et al., 2023; Kaminsky, 2022). Many require expensive equipment that must be carefully tuned and maintained. In addition, psychophysiological measurements can be inaccurate and unreliable (see ***Trending***). The laboratory equipment itself—elaborate and sometimes frightening—may arouse a participant's nervous system and thus change their physical responses. Physiological responses may also change when they are measured repeatedly in a single session. Galvanic skin responses, for example, often decrease during repeated testing.

Making waves As part of a study conducted at York University in Toronto, a mother and her 5-year-old autistic child play, socialize, and share tasks while wearing nets containing EEG sensors. The electrodes attached to their scalps help measure their brain waves, and these measurements are later compared to those derived from other mothers and their non-autistic children during similar interactions.

Peter Sibbald/Redux

Neuroimaging and Neuropsychological Tests

Some difficulties in personality or behavior are caused primarily by damage to the brain or by changes in brain activity. Head injuries, brain tumors, brain malfunctions, alcohol use disorder, infections, and other disorders can all cause such impairment. If a psychological dysfunction is to be treated effectively, it is important to know whether the primary cause of the dysfunction is a physical irregularity in the brain.

A number of techniques may help pinpoint brain irregularities. Some procedures, such as brain surgery, biopsy, and X-ray, have been used for many years. More recently, scientists have developed a number of **neuroimaging techniques,** or **brain-scanning,** which are designed to measure brain structure and activity directly (deBettencourt, Bainbridge, & Rosenberg, 2023; Harmon-Jones et al., 2023). One neuroimaging

...TRENDING

The Truth, the Whole Truth, and Nothing but the Truth

In movies, lawbreakers being grilled by the police reveal their guilt by sweating, shaking, cursing, or twitching. When they are hooked up to a *polygraph* (a lie detector), the needles on the machine bounce all over the paper. This image has been with us since World War I, when some clinicians developed the theory that people who are telling lies display systemic changes in their breathing, perspiration, and heart rate (Kaminsky, 2022).

The danger of relying on polygraph tests is that they do not work as well as we would like (Brennen & Magnussen, 2023). Research indicates that at least 1 out of 10 truths, or as many as 1 out of 4 truths, are, on average, called lies in polygraph testing (NITV, 2022). Imagine how many innocent people might be convicted of crimes if polygraph findings were taken as valid evidence in criminal trials. The tests may be particularly likely to yield inaccurate readings if test-takers have conditions that significantly affect their autonomic nervous system, such as alcohol use disorder or arthritis.

Given such findings, polygraphs are less trusted and less popular today than they once were. For example, few courts now admit results from such tests as evidence of criminal guilt (Bell, 2023; Kaminsky, 2022). Nevertheless, the U.S. Department of Defense, the FBI, and other law enforcement agencies use them extensively in criminal investigations, interrogations, and security screenings; parole boards and probation offices routinely administer them to help decide whether to release individuals convicted of offenses; and their use may actually be on the increase in public-sector hiring, such as for police officers and government employees (Kyzer, 2023; Wilcoxson & Turley, 2023).

Given the polygraph's flawed performance, over the past 20 years, researchers have been looking for other ways to detect lies (Brennen & Magnussen, 2023). In one alternative, a computer detects a person's eye activity as a possible indicator of lying. In other alternatives, computers detect stress-produced changes in individuals' voice frequencies or facial expressions. Yet another new approach uses *brain scanning*. Some fMRI studies, for example, have found that when participants deny clear truths, certain parts of their brains become more active than when they are confirming such truths. Although such alternative approaches have sometimes yielded better lie-detection rates than polygraphs do, these procedures can themselves produce *false positives*. That is, the measures targeted by these techniques may become heightened not only by lying but also by intense anxiety or related emotions.

Despite the less-than-stellar performance of both the traditional and newer techniques, many researchers believe that a new frontier in lie detection may be on the horizon (Lisbona, 2022). This is because some studies have begun to suggest that the *combined* use of these techniques, along with yet other tools, yields more accurate lie detection than any one of them alone. As such, it may just be that scientific and clinical efforts to find out "the whole truth and nothing but the truth" will soon be taking a serious step forward.

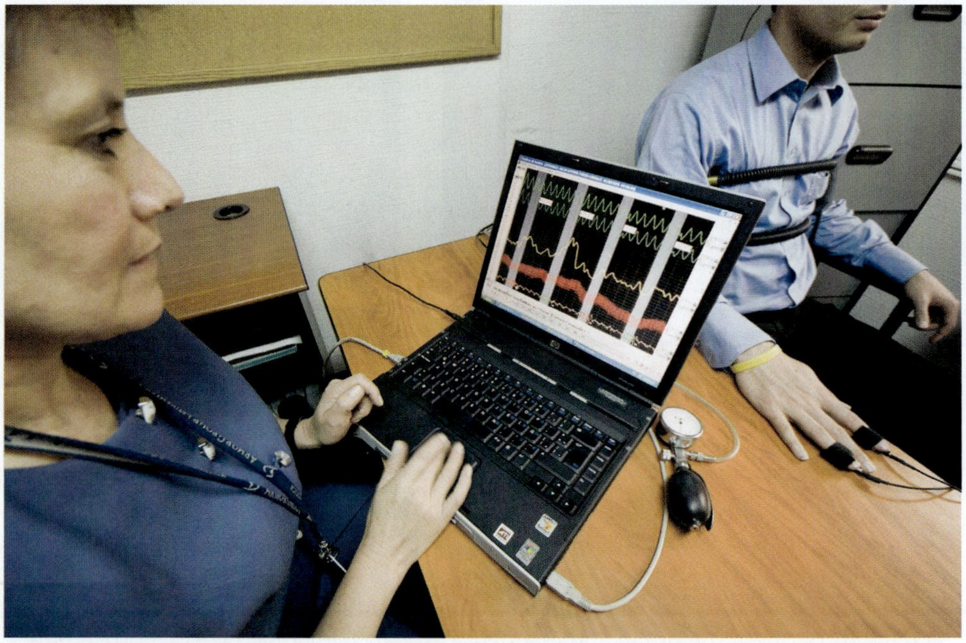

Guy Bell/Alamy

Checking on employees A security administrator conducts a polygraph exam in Bogotá, Colombia. Despite evidence that these tests are often invalid, they are widely used by businesses in Colombia, where deception by employees has become a major problem.

technique is the *electroencephalogram* (*EEG*), which records *brain waves*, the electrical activity that takes place within the brain as a result of neurons firing. In an EEG, electrodes placed on the scalp send brain-wave impulses to a machine that records them. Although an EEG is helpful in identifying the presence of electrical activity across different regions of the brain, it does not offer enough resolution to pinpoint precisely where in the brain this activity is occurring.

Variations in scanning (a) A doctor prepares a patient for an MRI procedure. Today's most widely used neuroimaging techniques each produce pictures of the living brain. Here, (b) an MRI scan shows the image of a typical functioning brain, (c) a CAT scan reveals a mass of blood within the brain, and (d) a PET scan shows which areas of the brain are active (those colored in red, orange, and yellow) when an individual is being stimulated.

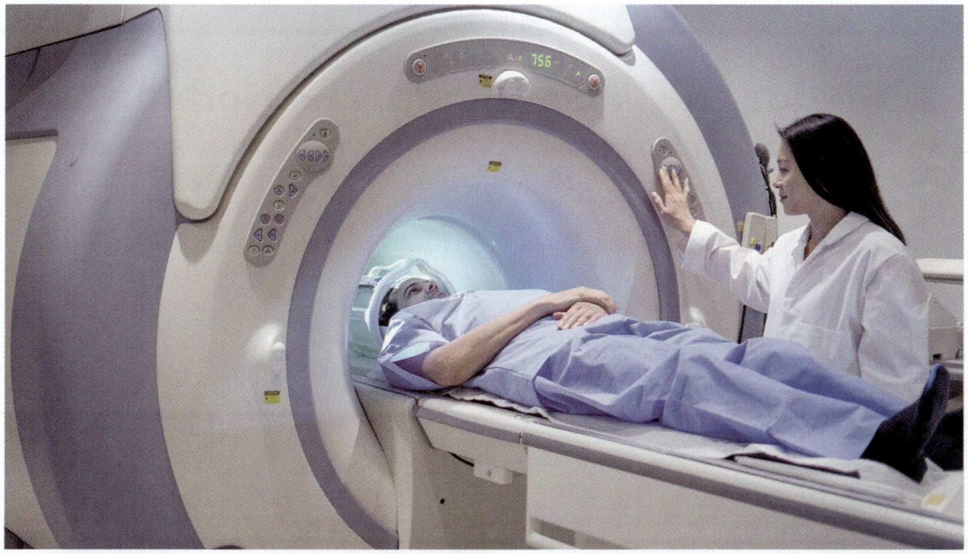

(a) MRI machine

Monty Rakusen/Getty Images

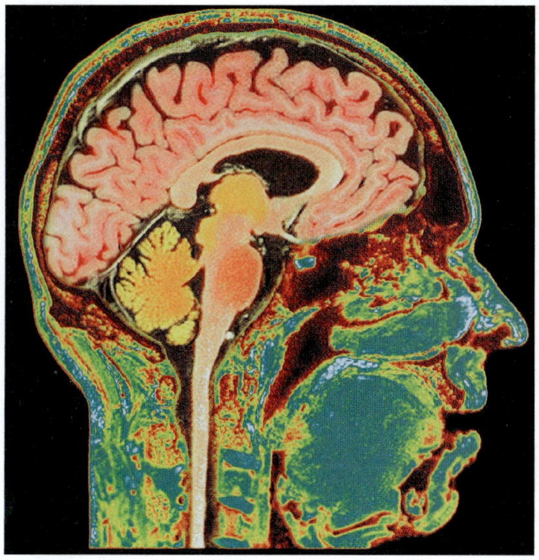

Du Cane Medical Imaging LTD. Science Photo Library/Getty Images

(b) MRI scan

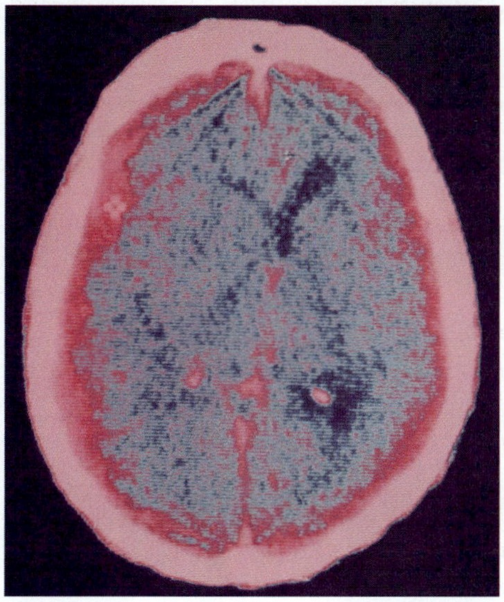

Lester V. Bergman/Getty Images

(c) CAT scan

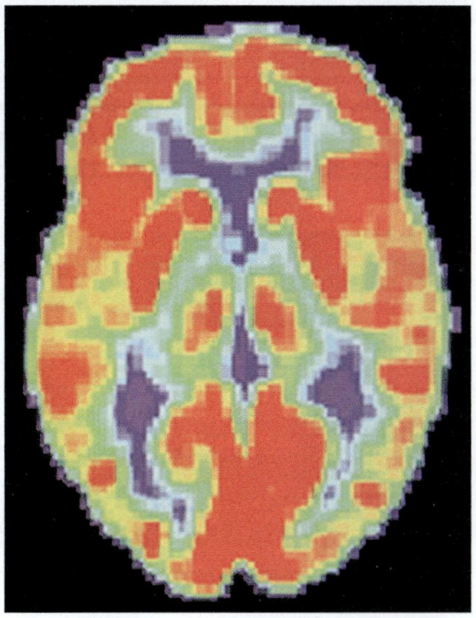

National Institute on Aging/NIH/Science Source

(d) PET scan

Other neuroimaging techniques offer higher-resolution "pictures" of brain structure or brain activity that provide for more precise pinpointing of activity in the brain. These techniques include *computerized axial tomography* (*CT scan* or *CAT scan*), in which X-rays of the brain's structure are taken at different angles and combined; *positron emission tomography* (*PET scan*), a computer-produced motion picture of chemical activity throughout the brain; and *magnetic resonance imaging* (*MRI*), a procedure that uses the magnetic property of certain hydrogen atoms in the brain to create a detailed picture of the brain's structure.

One version of the MRI, *functional magnetic resonance imaging* (*fMRI*), converts MRI pictures of brain structures into detailed pictures of neuron activity, thus offering a picture of the *functioning* brain. Partly because fMRI-produced images of brain functioning are so much clearer than PET scan images, the fMRI has generated enormous enthusiasm among brain researchers since it was first developed in 1990.

Though widely used, these techniques are sometimes unable to detect subtle brain pathology. Clinicians have therefore developed less direct but sometimes more revealing **neuropsychological tests** that measure cognitive, perceptual, and motor performances on certain tasks; clinicians interpret significantly atypical performances as an indicator of underlying brain irregularities (Parsons & Braun, 2024). Brain damage is especially likely to affect visual perception, memory, and visual-motor coordination, so neuropsychological tests focus particularly on these areas. The famous *Bender Visual-Motor Gestalt Test,* for example, consists of nine cards, each displaying a simple geometrical design. Patients look at the designs one at a time and copy each one onto a piece of paper. Later they try to redraw the designs from memory. Notable errors in accuracy by individuals older than 12 are thought to reflect organic brain impairment. Clinicians often use a *battery,* or series, of neuropsychological tests, each targeting a specific skill area (Parsons & Braun, 2024).

neuropsychological test A test that detects brain impairment by measuring a person's cognitive, perceptual, and motor performances.

intelligence test A test designed to measure a person's intellectual ability.

intelligence quotient (IQ) An overall score derived from intelligence tests.

Intelligence Tests

An early definition of the term *intelligence* described it as "the capacity to judge well, to reason well, and to comprehend well" (Binet & Simon, 1916, p. 192). Because intelligence is an *inferred* quality rather than a specific physical process, it can be measured only indirectly. In 1905, French psychologist Alfred Binet and his associate Théodore Simon produced an **intelligence test** consisting of a series of tasks requiring people to use various verbal and nonverbal skills. The general score derived from this and later intelligence tests is termed an **intelligence quotient (IQ).** There are now more than 100 different intelligence tests available. As you will read in a later chapter, intelligence tests play a key role in the diagnosis of intellectual disability, and they can also help clinicians identify other difficulties.

Intelligence tests are among the most carefully produced of all clinical tests (Spores, 2022; Colom, 2020). Because the tests have been standardized on large groups of people, clinicians have a good idea how each individual's score compares with the performance of the population at large. These tests have also shown very high reliability: people who repeat the same IQ test years later receive approximately the same score. Finally, the major IQ tests appear to have fairly high validity: for example, children's IQ scores often correlate with their performance in school.

Nevertheless, intelligence tests have some key shortcomings (Holden & Tanenbaum, 2023). Factors that have nothing to do with intelligence, such as low motivation or high anxiety, can greatly influence test performance. In addition, IQ tests may contain cultural biases in their language or tasks that place people of one background at an advantage over those of another background. Similarly, some individuals from marginalized populations may have little experience with this kind of test. Or members of a marginalized cultural group may be uncomfortable when they are tested by a member of the dominant cultural group. At the same time, test examiners may hold biases about various groups that can have a negative impact on test administration or scoring. Any or all of these variables can lead to IQ scores that are inaccurately low for members of certain racial, ethnic, and other marginalized groups.

How might IQ scores be misused by school officials, parents, or other individuals? Why is society preoccupied with these scores?

Clinical Observations

In addition to interviewing and testing people, clinicians may systematically observe their behavior. In one technique, called *naturalistic observation,* clinicians observe clients in their everyday environments. In another, *analogue observation,* they observe them in an artificial setting, such as a clinical office or laboratory. Finally, in *self-monitoring,* clients are instructed to observe themselves.

Naturalistic and Analogue Observations

Naturalistic clinical observations usually take place in homes, schools, institutions such as hospitals and prisons, or community settings. In the treatment of children and families, most naturalistic clinical observations focus on parent–child, parent–parent, sibling–sibling, peer–peer, or teacher–child interactions and on fearful, aggressive, or disruptive behavior. Such observations can be made by trained clinical staff or by *participant observers*—key people in the client's environment—and reported to the clinician.

of NOTE ...

Their Words

"You can observe a lot just by watching."

Yogi Berra, baseball great

When naturalistic observations are not practical, clinicians may resort to analogue observations, often aided by special equipment such as a video camera or one-way mirror. For such observations, clinicians may set up a specific type of situation to observe during the session rather than waiting for the situation to occur naturally. For example, clinicians interested in observing family conflicts might instruct a parent to work in session with their child on an academic task or have a married couple discuss and try to settle a recent disagreement. Similarly, those interested in observing the fear responses of phobic clients may have a client approach the feared object during a session. Or clinicians may have a client who struggles with perfectionism spend the session handwriting a letter to their boss while using their nondominant hand only.

Although clinicians can learn much from actually witnessing behavior, clinical observations have certain disadvantages (Bakeman & Quera, 2023; Cherry, 2022). For one thing, they are not always reliable. It is possible for various clinicians who observe the same person to focus on different aspects of behavior, assess the person differently, and arrive at different conclusions. Careful training of observers and the use of observer checklists can help reduce this problem.

Orbon Alija/Getty Images

Singing in the shower Like this man, many of us bust out a tune in the privacy of our own shower from time to time. But put us in front of a crowd or just one other person, and we clam up and struggle to squeak out a single note. Similarly, the mere presence of a clinical observer can dramatically alter a client's natural behavior—a phenomenon known as client *reactivity*.

Similarly, observers may make errors that affect the validity, or accuracy, of their observations. The observer may experience *overload* and be unable to keep track of or record all of the important behaviors and events. Or the observer may experience *observer drift*, a steady decline in accuracy as a result of fatigue or of a gradual unintentional change in the standards used when an observation continues for a long period of time. Another possible problem is *observer bias*—the observer's judgments may be influenced by information and expectations they already have about the person.

A client's *reactivity* may also limit the validity of clinical observations; that is, their behavior may be affected by the very presence of the observer. If schoolchildren are aware that someone special is watching them, for example, they may change their usual classroom behavior, perhaps in the hope of creating a good impression.

Finally, clinical observations may lack *cross-situational validity*. A child who behaves aggressively in school is not necessarily aggressive at home or with friends after school. Because behavior is often specific to particular situations, observations in one setting cannot always be applied to other settings (De Los Reyes et al., 2023; De Los Reyes & Asmundson, 2022).

Self-Monitoring

As you read earlier, personality and response inventories are tests in which individuals report their own behaviors, feelings, or cognitions. In a related assessment procedure, *self-monitoring*, people observe themselves in an ongoing manner and carefully record the frequency of certain behaviors, feelings, or thoughts as they occur over time (Faulhaber, Lee, & Gentile, 2023; Li et al., 2023). How frequently, for instance, does a person with a substance use disorder have an urge for drugs or a person with chronic headaches have a migraine? Self-monitoring is especially useful in assessing behavior that occurs so infrequently that it is unlikely to appear in session or during other kinds of observations. It is also useful for observing behaviors that occur so frequently that any other method of observing them in detail would be impossible—for example, smoking, drinking, or other drug use. Finally, self-monitoring may be the only way to observe and measure private thoughts or perceptions. More and more people in treatment are recording such private experiences on smartphone apps as the experiences are occurring—observations that can be sent immediately to their therapists or collectively reported in their treatment sessions (Hawker et al., 2021; Hong, Sanchez, & Comer, 2020).

Like all other clinical assessment procedures, however, self-monitoring has drawbacks (Cherry, 2022; Schumacher et al., 2021). Here too, validity is often a problem. People do not always manage or try to record their observations accurately. Furthermore, when people monitor themselves, they may change their behaviors unintentionally. For example, people begin to make healthier food choices when they are monitoring themselves, those who smoke often smoke fewer cigarettes than usual, and teachers give their students more positive comments and fewer negative ones.

SUMMING UP

Clinical Assessment

Clinical practitioners are interested primarily in gathering *idiographic* information about their clients. Through clinical assessment and diagnosis, they seek an understanding of the specific nature and origins of a client's difficulties.

To be useful, assessment tools must be standardized, reliable, and valid. Most clinical assessment methods fall into three general categories: clinical interviews, tests, and observations, each of which has both merits and limitations. A clinical interview may be either unstructured or structured. Types of clinical tests include projective, personality, response, psychophysiological, neuroimaging, neuropsychological, and intelligence tests. Types of observation include naturalistic observation, analog observation, and self-monitoring.

Diagnosis: Does the Client's Syndrome Match a Known Disorder?

CLINICIANS USE THE INFORMATION from interviews, tests, and observations to construct an integrated picture of the factors that are causing and maintaining a client's disturbance, a construction sometimes known as a *clinical picture*, or *case formulation* (Reed, Ritchie, & Maercker, 2024; Eells, 2022). The clinical picture also may be influenced to a degree by the clinician's theoretical orientation. The psychologist who worked with Sam held a cognitive-behavioral view of psychopathology and so produced the following clinical picture, which emphasized modeling and reinforcement principles and Sam's expectations, assumptions, and interpretations:

Sam's mother had reinforced his feelings of insecurity and his belief that he was unintelligent and inferior. When teachers tried to encourage and push Sam, his mother would often call him "an idiot." Although he was the only one in his family to attend college and did well there, she told him he was probably too inadequate to succeed in the world. When he received a B in a college algebra course, his mother told him, "You'll never have money." She once even said, "You're just like your father, dumb as a post," and railed against "the dumb men I got stuck with."

As a child, Sam had watched his parents argue. Between his mother's self-serving complaints and his father's rants about his backbreaking work to provide for his family, Sam had decided that life would inevitably be unpleasant. He believed it was natural for couples to argue and blame each other. Using his parents as models, Sam believed that when he was displeased with a partner—Taylor or a prior partner—he should yell at them. At the same time, Sam was mystified that Taylor had complained about his temper.

He took the termination of his relationship with Taylor as proof that he was indeed inadequate and "stupid." He felt foolish to have broken up with Taylor. Sam interpreted his behavior and the breakup as proof that he would never be loved and would never find happiness. In his mind, all he had to look forward to was a lifetime of troubled relationships, fights, and getting fired from lesser and lesser jobs. This hopelessness fed his feelings of depression and made it hard for him to try to make himself feel better.

of NOTE ...

Their Words

"You're driving me normal."

Dexter Morgan, in *Dearly Devoted Dexter*

diagnosis A determination that a person's difficulties reflect a particular disorder.

syndrome A cluster of particular symptoms that usually occur together.

classification system A list of disorders, along with descriptions of symptoms and guidelines for making appropriate diagnoses.

DSM-5-TR (*Diagnostic and Statistical Manual of Mental Disorders*, 5th Edition, Text Revision) The newest edition of the DSM, published in 2022.

With the assessment data and clinical picture in hand, clinicians are ready to make a **diagnosis**—that is, a determination that a person's psychological conditions constitute a particular disorder. When clinicians decide, through diagnosis, that a client's pattern of dysfunction reflects a particular disorder, they are saying that the pattern is basically the same as one that has been displayed by many other people, has been investigated in a variety of studies, and perhaps has responded to particular forms of treatment. They can then apply what is generally known about the disorder to the particular individual they are trying to help. They can, for example, better predict the future course of the person's condition and the treatments that are likely to be helpful.

Classification Systems

The principle behind diagnosis is straightforward. When a cluster of particular symptoms—also called a **syndrome**—occur together regularly and follow a certain course, clinicians agree that those symptoms make up a particular mental disorder. If people display this particular pattern of symptoms, diagnosticians assign them to that diagnostic category. A list of such categories, or disorders, with descriptions of the symptoms and guidelines for assigning individuals to the categories, is known as a **classification system.**

The *Diagnostic and Statistical Manual of Mental Disorders* (*DSM*) is the classification system currently written by the American Psychiatric Association. The DSM is the most widely used classification system in North America. Its content has been changed significantly over time. The current edition, called **DSM-5-TR,** was published in 2022 (APA, 2022). It is an update of *DSM-5,* a version of the DSM that was published in 2013. Most other countries rely primarily on a system called the *International Classification of Diseases* (*ICD*), developed by the World Health Organization, which lists both medical and psychological disorders (Reed et al., 2024). The newest edition of this system, ICD-11, went into operation in 2022.

Although there are some differences between the disorders listed in the DSM and those in the ICD, as well as differences in their descriptions of criteria for various disorders (the DSM's descriptions are more detailed), the numerical codes used by the DSM for most disorders match those used by the ICD, a matching that produces uniformity when clinicians fill out insurance reimbursement forms.

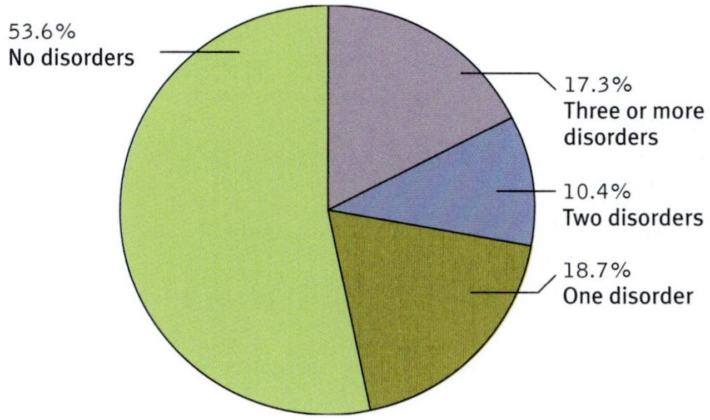

FIGURE 3-3

How Many People in the United States Qualify for a DSM Diagnosis During Their Lives?

Almost half, according to some surveys. Some people even experience two or more different disorders, which is known as comorbidity. (Information from: Marshall, 2022; Cuncic, 2021; Kapil, 2019; Kessler et al., 2005.)

DSM-5 and DSM-5-TR

As noted earlier, DSM-5 was published in 2013. It listed more than 500 mental disorders (see **Figure 3-3**). Each entry described the criteria for diagnosing the disorder and the key clinical features of the disorder. The system also described features that are often but not always related to the disorder. The classification system was further accompanied by background text information such as relevant research findings; age, culture, or gender trends; and each disorder's prevalence, risk, course, complications, predisposing factors, and family patterns.

In 2022, the American Psychiatric Association published the DSM-5 Text Revision (DSM-5-TR), an amended version of DSM-5 that primarily updated DSM-5's background text information; added a new mental disorder, *prolonged grief disorder* (see the chapter on trauma and stress disorders); and provided deeper discussions regarding the impact of racism and other kinds of discrimination on mental disorders. Given that DSM-5-TR retained all the DSM-5 disorders while at the same time introducing a new disorder and offering other enhancements, DSM-5-TR is the version of DSM now cited in most diagnostic discussions, including those throughout this textbook.

Providing Categorical and Dimensional Information

DSM-5-TR requires clinicians to provide both categorical and dimensional information as part of a proper diagnosis. *Categorical information* refers to the name of the distinct category (disorder) indicated by the client's symptoms. *Dimensional information* is a rating of how severe a client's symptoms are and how dysfunctional the client is across various dimensions of personality and behavior.

Regarding categorical information, the clinician must decide whether the person is displaying one of the hundreds of psychological disorders listed in DSM-5-TR. Some of the most frequently diagnosed disorders are the anxiety disorders and depressive disorders.

"TWO BLACK EYES. SOLITARY. LETHARGIC. DEFINITELY IN THE DSM-V."

- **Anxiety disorders** People with anxiety disorders may experience general feelings of anxiety and worry (*generalized anxiety disorder*); fears of specific situations, objects, or activities (*phobias*); anxiety about social situations (*social anxiety disorder*); repeated outbreaks of panic (*panic disorder*); or anxiety about being separated from one's parents or from other key individuals (*separation anxiety disorder*).
- **Depressive disorders** People with depressive disorders may experience an episode of extreme sadness and related symptoms (*major depressive disorder*), persistent and chronic sadness (*persistent depressive disorder*), or severe premenstrual sadness and related symptoms (*premenstrual dysphoric disorder*).

Although people may receive just one diagnosis from the DSM-5-TR list, they often receive more than one (Morrison, 2023). Sam would likely receive a diagnosis of *major depressive disorder*. In addition, recall that Sam described many fears in his life: fear that he would perform poorly at work and school, that others were forming negative opinions about him, and that his future was doomed to be one failure after another. Suppose that Sam's therapist concluded that such fears were in fact examples of a much broader, persistent pattern of excessive worry, concern, and avoidance. Sam might then receive an additional diagnosis of *generalized anxiety disorder*. When an individual receives two or more separate diagnoses, the person is said to have *comorbid* disorders. Alternatively, if Sam's anxiety symptoms did not rise to the level of generalized anxiety disorder, his diagnosis of major depressive disorder might simply specify that he is experiencing some features of anxiety (*major depressive disorder with anxious distress*).

In addition to deciding which disorder (or disorders) a client is displaying (categorical information), diagnosticians using DSM-5-TR must provide dimensional information. That is, as noted above, they must assess the current severity of the client's disorder—how extensive are the symptoms, and how much do they impair the client's functioning? For each disorder, DSM-5-TR suggests various rating scales for evaluating the severity of the disorder (Morrison, 2023; APA, 2022). Using a depression rating scale, for example, Sam's therapist might assign a severity rating of *moderate* to the young man's depression, meaning his symptoms are quite frequent and disabling but not as extreme and incapacitating as those found in the most severe cases of depression. Unlike earlier versions of the DSM, DSM-5-TR consistently seeks both categorical and dimensional information as equally important parts of the diagnosis rather than categorical information alone.

Why do you think clinicians prefer the label "person with a depressive disorder" over "a depressive person"?

Additional Information

Clinicians also may include other useful information when making a diagnosis. They may, for example, indicate particular psychosocial conditions the client has. Sam's recent breakup with his girlfriend might be noted as *relationship distress*. Altogether, Sam might receive the following diagnosis:

Diagnosis: Major depressive disorder with anxious distress
Severity: Moderate
Additional information: Relationship distress

Each diagnosis also has a numerical code that clinicians must state—a code listed in the ICD, the international classification system mentioned earlier. Thus, if Sam were assigned the DSM-5-TR diagnosis indicated above, his clinician would also state a numerical code of *F32.1*—the ICD code corresponding to *major depressive disorder, moderate severity.*

Is DSM-5-TR an Effective Classification System?

A classification system, like an assessment method, is judged by its reliability and validity. Here *reliability* means that different clinicians are likely to agree on the diagnosis when they use the system to diagnose the same client. Early versions of the DSM were, at best, moderately reliable. In the early 1960s, for example, four clinicians, each relying on DSM-I, the first edition of the DSM, independently interviewed 153 patients (Beck et al., 1962). Only 54 percent of their diagnoses were in agreement. Because all four clinicians were experienced diagnosticians, their failure to agree suggested deficiencies in the classification system.

In 2013, the developers of DSM-5 followed certain procedures to help ensure that the new DSM would have greater reliability than the previous DSMs. For example, they conducted extensive reviews of research to pinpoint which categories in past DSMs had been too vague and unreliable. They then developed a number of new diagnostic criteria and categories, expecting that the new criteria and categories would be reliable. Although some studies did indeed find enhanced reliability in the new criteria and categories, others did not (Brown & Barlow, 2021; Pape et al., 2021). In short, DSM-5's reliability remained at least somewhat limited. And, of course, such limited reliability findings also apply to DSM-5-TR, which has retained all of the DSM-5 criteria and categories.

of NOTE ...

What Is a Nervous Breakdown?

The term "nervous breakdown" is used by laypersons, not clinicians. Most people use it to refer to a sudden psychological disturbance that incapacitates a person, perhaps requiring hospitalization. Some people use the term simply to connote the onset of any psychological disorder (Abrams, 2023; Washington & Scaccia, 2022).

The *validity* of a classification system is the accuracy of the information that its diagnostic categories provide. Categories are of most use to clinicians when they demonstrate *predictive validity*—that is, when they help predict future symptoms or events. A common symptom of major depressive disorder is either insomnia or excessive sleep. When clinicians give Sam a diagnosis of *major depressive disorder,* they expect that he may eventually develop sleep difficulties, even if none are present now. In addition, they expect him to respond to treatments that are effective for other people with depression. The more often such predictions are accurate, the greater a category's predictive validity.

DSM-5's framers tried to also ensure the validity of the manual by conducting extensive reviews and consulting with numerous clinical advisers. Although some subsequent studies did indeed find DSM-5's new criteria and categories to have stronger validity than those of the earlier DSMs, other research indicated that the manual's validity was still less than desirable (Di Vincenzo, 2023; Hayes & Hofmann, 2020). Among other validity issues, some of DSM-5's criteria and categories (and, likewise, DSM-5-TR's criteria and categories) reflect gender or racial bias.

Why are medical diagnoses usually valued while the use of psychological diagnoses is often criticized?

One very important organization has concluded that the validity of the DSM is lacking, and the organization is acting accordingly. The National Institute of Mental Health (NIMH), the world's largest funding agency for mental health research, no longer gives financial support to clinical studies that rely exclusively on DSM criteria. And, more generally, the agency has developed its own neuroscience-focused classification tool, called the *Research Domain Criteria* (*RDoC*), which many researchers now use as a primary guide (NIMH, 2023). Proceeding from the basic premise that mental disorders are best understood as a biological phenomenon, RDoC guides researchers to identify disorders as clusters of underlying biological variables rather than as syndromes of specific clinical symptoms (Morris et al., 2022). Critics of RDoC worry that it minimizes environmental and psychological factors at the expense of a primary focus on genetics, brain scans, and related areas of study.

Yet another attempt to improve upon the DSM is the *Hierarchical Taxonomy of Psychopathology* (*HiTOP*), a system for classifying psychopathology developed by an influential group of assessment researchers (Conway, Forbes, & the HiTOP Consortium, 2022; Kotov et al., 2021). Proponents of the HiTOP model believe that the DSM's prominent focus on distinct psychopathology *categories* (mental disorders) does not sufficiently capture the *dimensional* nature of psychopathology (degrees of severity and frequency) that is so often observed in clinical practice and research. Thus, whereas DSM-5-TR describes psychopathology in both categorical and dimensional manners, the HiTOP model describes psychopathology in dimensional terms only.

The HiTOP model's focus on dimensionality allows diagnosticians to further detect "lower levels" of pathology that are often neglected by the DSM—such as modest but potentially problematic levels of distress, risk taking, or eating pathology. After all, many people without a DSM depressive disorder still experience problematic sadness from time to time, many without an anxiety disorder still experience some degree of fear on an ongoing basis, and many without a substance use disorder may drink alcohol excessively, and, according to the HiTOP model, these lower-level patterns should also be recognized as part of a proper assessment. According to HiTOP proponents, there are rarely natural cutoff points for distinguishing people with psychopathology from those without; people simply vary in the frequency and severity of various maladaptive traits and behaviors. The HiTOP model offers a hierarchical organization that enables assessors to note, at one end, narrow dimensions of psychopathology—such as worry, avoidance, insomnia, hopelessness, and low well-being—and, at the other end, broader dimensions of psychopathology in which the narrow dimensions cluster together to produce more severe psychological difficulties. Those who prefer the HiTOP model over DSM believe that this hierarchical organization better captures the many shared features found across the disorders listed in the DSM.

Clearly, DSM-5 (and, in turn, DSM-5-TR) has raised concerns among many clinical practitioners and researchers (see ***InfoCentral***). In addition to noting the reliability and validity limitations described above, critics argue that some of the current DSM criteria and categories are ill-advised and can, on occasion, lead to problems for clients. For example, the DSM includes a category of *premenstrual dysphoric disorder* that many consider unfounded and sexist (refer to the chapter on depressive disorders) and a category of *mild neurocognitive disorder* that may, in some cases, be misapplied to ordinary age-related forgetfulness (refer to the chapter on disorders of aging and cognition).

of NOTE ...

Bands with Psychological Names

- Rage Against the Machine
- Jane's Addiction
- 10,000 Maniacs
- Insane Clown Posse
- Suicidal Tendencies

The power of labeling When looking at this late-nineteenth-century photograph of a baseball team at the State Homeopathic Asylum for the Insane in Middletown, New York, most observers assume that the players were patients. As a result, they tend to "see" depression or confusion in the players' faces and posture. In fact, the players were members of the asylum staff, some of whom even sought their jobs for the express purpose of playing for the hospital team.

Elizabeth Eckert, Middletown, NY. Courtesy Tracy DeMichiel

Can Diagnosis and Labeling Cause Harm?

Even with trustworthy assessment data and reliable and valid classification categories, clinicians will sometimes arrive at a wrong conclusion (Chao et al., 2022). Like all human beings, clinicians are flawed information processors. Studies show that they are overly influenced by information gathered early in the assessment process. In addition, they may pay too much attention to certain sources of information, such as a parent's report about a child, and too little to others, such as the child's point of view. Finally, their judgments can be distorted by any number of personal biases—gender, age, race, ethnicity, and socioeconomic status, to

DSM: THE BIGGER PICTURE

The Diagnostic and Statistical Manual of Mental Disorders (DSM) is the most widely used classification system in North America. It is actually a work in progress. DSM-5-TR, the 1,120-page current edition, is but the latest version of this system, which has undergone many changes over the past seven decades. The DSM also faces competition from other diagnostic systems around the world.

Competitors

Both within North America and around the world, the **DSM** faces competition from three other diagnostic systems—the **International Classification of Disorders (ICD)**, **Research Domain Criteria (RDoC)**, and **Hierarchical Taxonomy of Psychopathology (HiTOP)**.

	DSM	ICD	RDoC	HiTop
Producer	APA	WHO*	NIMH**	Researcher Consortium
Disorders	Psychological	Psychological/ medical	Psychological	Psychological
Criteria	Detailed	Brief	Neuro/ biological	Dimensional/ Hierarchical
Application	Practice/ research	Practice/ research	Research	Research/ Practice
Area of use	North America	Worldwide	United States	Worldwide

* World Health Organization ** National Institute of Mental Health

Just a Generation Ago . . .

Many of the disorders listed in the DSM are very familiar, giving the impression that they have been recognized forever. But many of the disorders and/or their labels are relatively new.

Just a generation ago, the DSM did not include:

- Bulimia nervosa
- Autistic disorder
- PTSD
- Panic disorder
- Narcissistic personality disorder
- Borderline personality disorder

Just a generation ago, the DSM had different names for certain disorders:

Past	Present
Mental retardation	Intellectual disability
Manic-depressive disorder	Bipolar disorder
Multiple personality disorder	Dissociative identity disorder
Dementia	Neurocognitive disorder
Hypochondriasis	Illness anxiety disorder

Top DSM-5-TR Concerns

Many of the recent DSM changes have raised concerns. Several have been particularly controversial in some clinical circles.

People with a **serious medical disease**, such as cancer, may also receive a psychiatric diagnosis if they are "excessively" distressed.

People experiencing **common grief reactions** may receive a psychiatric diagnosis of depression or prolonged grief disorder if they are "excessively" distressed.

Many **behaviors pursued excessively**, such as sex, Internet use, and shopping, may eventually be considered behavioral addictions.

People with **typical age-related forgetfulness** may receive a psychiatric diagnosis of mild neurocognitive disorder.

The DSM Timeline

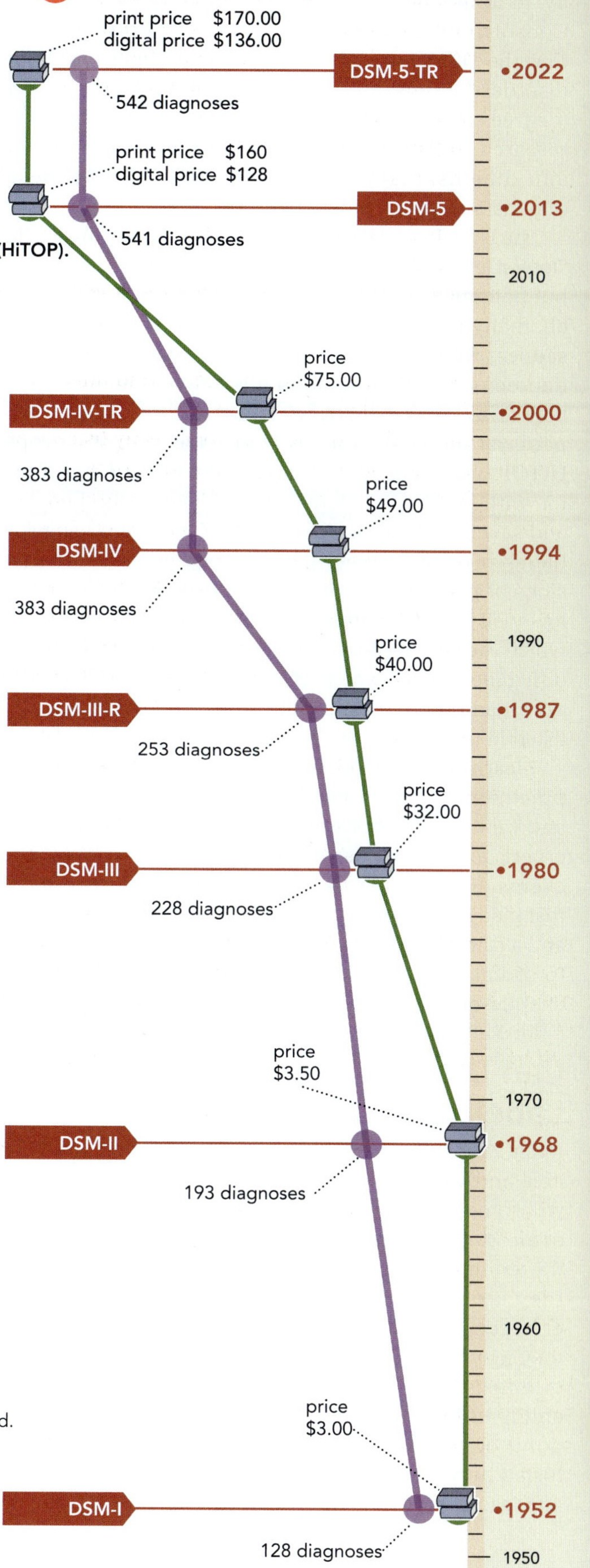

(APA, 2022, 2020; First et al., 2022; Blashfield et al., 2014; Gorenstein, 2013)

name just a few. Given the limitations of assessment tools, assessors, and classification systems, it is small wonder that studies sometimes uncover shocking errors in diagnosis, especially in hospitals (Ayano et al., 2021).

Beyond the potential for misdiagnosis, the very act of classifying people can lead to unintended results. As you read in the previous chapter, for example, many sociocultural theorists believe that diagnostic labels can become self-fulfilling prophecies. When people are diagnosed as mentally disturbed, they may be perceived that way and reacted to correspondingly. If others expect them to take on a sick role, they may begin to consider themselves sick as well and act that way. Furthermore, our society attaches a stigma to psychopathology (Corrigan, 2022; Mayer et al., 2022). People who are labeled mentally ill may find it difficult to get a job, especially a position of responsibility, or to be welcomed into social relationships. Once a label has been applied, it may stick for a long time.

Taylor Hill/Getty Images

Fighting "Thee" stigma One strategy to help reduce the stigma of mental disorders is for well-known and successful people to publicly affirm their own psychological challenges. Rapper Megan Thee Stallion, shown here at a Forbes 30 Under 30 Summit, has been open about her emotional struggles and treatment experiences. To pay it forward, she launched an online mental health resource that helps people in need locate therapists, crisis hotlines, and more—including specialized mental health resources for people of color and in LGBTQ+ communities.

In a similar vein, there are some very unfortunate instances in which certain editions of the DSM incorrectly listed a particular pattern of functioning or behaving as a form of psychopathology, thus contributing to the misdiagnosis, stigmatization, and mistreatment of many millions of individuals as well as leading to laws and even police actions against them. For example, in the first two editions of the DSM, *homosexuality* was listed as a mental disorder. A growing body of compelling research and protests by gay activist groups and clinicians eventually led to the DSM's elimination of this sexual orientation as a mental disorder in 1973, but the DSM did, at that time, still retain a category called *ego dystonic homosexuality*—the experience of extreme distress over one's homosexual orientation. Ultimately, this latter category too was dropped from the DSM in 1987. In the meantime, the clinical field had added to the persecution, anxiety, and humiliation of millions of people whose sexual orientation differed from the norms of their society at that time (Comer et al., 2024).

Another regrettable case in point is the DSM's past assertion that *transgender* functioning is a form of psychopathology. Transgender people are individuals whose actual gender identity (that is, their own internal sense of their gender) is different from their assigned gender at birth. In contrast, *cisgender* people are individuals whose gender identity is consistent with their assigned gender at birth. In DSM editions prior to 2013, transgender people (as well as nonbinary people) qualified for a DSM diagnosis called *gender identity disorder,* thus adding to the clinical, societal, and legal mistreatment of this population. This diagnostic category was finally dropped from the DSM when DSM-5 was published in 2013, a change rooted once again in growing research, clinical insights, and societal change as well as the hard work of transgender advocates and their allies.

It is worth noting that DSM-5-TR (like DSM-5) still retains a transgender-related mental disorder called *gender dysphoria,* which you will read more about in the chapter on depressive disorders. A diagnosis of *gender dysphoria* is assigned to persons who persistently experience significant distress or impairment due to their gender identity and its contradiction to their assigned gender. However, as you will read, this category is controversial and may be dropped from future editions of the DSM, just as the category *ego dystonic homosexuality* was eventually eliminated. Many clinicians argue that since a transgender pattern reflects an alternative—not pathological—way of experiencing and expressing one's gender identity, it should never be considered a psychological disorder, even when accompanied by significant unhappiness. And, in fact, ICD-11, the new edition of the international classification system, does not include transgender functioning *or* gender dysphoria as mental disorders.

of NOTE ...

Stigma Continues

22%	Percentage of Americans who say they would not seek counseling because of the stigma attached to mental disorders
33%	Percentage of Americans who would not seek counseling for fear of being labeled "mentally ill"
51%	Percentage of Americans who would hesitate to see a psychotherapist if a diagnosis were required

(Roper Center for Public Opinion, 2022, 2017; Nietzel, 2021)

SUMMING UP

Diagnosis

After collecting assessment information, clinicians form a clinical picture and decide on a diagnosis. The diagnosis is chosen from a classification system. The system used most widely in North America is the DSM. Most other countries rely primarily on a system called the ICD. Alternatively, many researchers use a more neuroscience-focused classification model called RDoC or a more dimension-focused model called HiTOP.

The most recent version of the DSM, known as DSM-5-TR, which primarily updates the background text information found in DSM-5, lists more than 500 disorders. The reliability and validity of the DSM been receiving considerable clinical review and, in some circles, criticism.

Even with trustworthy assessment data and reliable and valid classification categories, clinicians will not always arrive at the correct conclusion. They are human and so fall prey to various biases, misconceptions, and expectations. Another problem related to diagnosis is the prejudice that labels arouse, which may be damaging to the person who is diagnosed. In a similar vein, over the years, various editions of the DSM have incorrectly listed certain alternative patterns of functioning as being pathological.

of NOTE ...

In-Person vs. Digital Therapy

Surveys of people seeking outpatient psychotherapy indicate that, medical considerations aside, 46% prefer in-person visits and 54% prefer telemental health visits (Berman, 2021; Severe et al., 2020; Renn et al., 2019).

Treatment: How Might the Client Be Helped?

OVER THE COURSE of 10 months, Sam was treated for depression and related symptoms. He improved considerably during that time, as the following case report describes:

During therapy, Sam's debilitating depression relented. Increasingly, he came to appreciate that his mother's accusations against him—and his self-accusations—were not accurate. He also was able to consider the possibility that Taylor's reluctance to commit to him had been more about where Taylor was in her life than about a profound inadequacy in Sam. Eventually, Sam and Taylor talked again, although they did not renew their relationship. To a large extent, Sam felt better just realizing that Taylor did not hate him. Taylor even said that her mother had said some kind things about Sam after their breakup.

Over the course of therapy, Sam also explained some of his difficulties to his immediate supervisor at the bank and committed himself to improving his performance. The supervisor, with whom Sam had been friendly before his struggles, said she was glad that he was communicating openly and was happy to give him the opportunity to improve his performance. Sam was surprised to hear how highly he had been regarded at the bank over the years, although as his supervisor put it, "Why would you have been promoted otherwise?"

With the help of his therapist, Sam also forced himself to spend more time having fun with his friends. He found his mood on the upswing as a result. One night, Jesse brought his coworker Laurie out to dinner with them, and Sam and Laurie really hit it off. Not long after, they began dating. Jesse denied planning to set up Sam and Laurie that first night, but he always had a twinkle in his eye when asked about it. Sam often considered the lessons he learned in treatment, trying to handle himself and this new relationship in ways different from the destructive patterns of his past.

Clearly, treatment helped Sam, and by its conclusion, he was a happier, more functional person than the individual who had first sought help 10 months earlier. But how did his therapist decide on the treatment program that proved to be so helpful?

Treatment Decisions

Like all therapists, Sam's therapist began with assessment information and diagnostic decisions. Knowing the specific details and background of Sam's condition (*idiographic data*) and combining this individual information with broad information about the nature and treatment of depression, the clinician arrived at a treatment plan for him.

Yet therapists also may be influenced by additional factors when they make treatment decisions. Their treatment plans typically reflect their theoretical orientations and how they have learned to conduct therapy (Henry, 2023). As therapists apply a favored model in case after case, they become more and more familiar with its principles and treatment techniques and tend to use them in work with still other clients.

Rob Schoenbaum/Polaris

It's the taxi driver who gives tips There are hundreds of different kinds of therapy available around the world. In one unusual format, psychologist Mia Fahlén rides the streets of Stockholm, Sweden, providing psychotherapy, at no extra charge, to her taxi passengers. Because many Stockholmers experience depression during the long, dark Nordic winter months, the cab company Taxi Stockholm decided it should offer such counseling during taxi rides.

Current research may also play a role. Most clinicians say that they value research as a guide to practice (Barkham, Lutz, & Castonguay, 2021; Tasca, 2020). However, not all of them actually read research articles, so they cannot be directly influenced by them. In fact, according to surveys, therapists gather much of their information about the latest developments in the field from colleagues, professional newsletters, workshops, conferences, websites, books, and the like (Barkham et al., 2021). Unfortunately, the accuracy and usefulness of these sources vary widely.

To help clinicians become more familiar with research findings and apply those findings, there is an influential movement in North America, the United Kingdom, and elsewhere toward **evidence-based treatment** (Todd & Branch, 2022). Proponents of this movement have formed task forces that seek to identify which therapies have received clear research support for each disorder, to propose corresponding treatment guidelines, and to spread such information to clinicians. The movement has gained considerable momentum over the past few decades.

The Effectiveness of Treatment

Altogether, hundreds of forms of therapy are currently practiced in the clinical field (NAMI, 2023; Spilde & Jakobsen, 2023). Naturally, the most important question to ask about each of these therapies is whether it does what it is supposed to do (Chambless & Hollon, 2023). Does a particular treatment really help people overcome their psychological difficulties? On the surface, the question may seem simple. In fact, it is one of the most difficult questions for clinical researchers to answer.

The first problem is how to *define* "success." If Sam still has much progress to make at the conclusion of therapy, should his recovery be considered successful? The second problem is how to *measure* improvement. Should researchers give equal weight to the reports of clients, friends, relatives, therapists, and teachers? Should they use rating scales, inventories, therapy insights, observations, or some other measure?

Perhaps the biggest problem in determining the effectiveness of treatment is the *variety* and *complexity* of the treatments currently in use. People differ in their challenges, personal styles, and motivations for therapy. Therapists differ in skill, experience, orientation, and personality. And therapies differ in theory, format, and

evidence-based treatment Therapy that has received clear research support for a particular disorder and has corresponding treatment guidelines.

FIGURE 3-4

What Factors Contribute to Therapy Outcomes?

According to research, a client's progress in therapy relates only partly to the specific strategies used by their therapist. In fact, factors such as the client's expectations, the client–therapist relationship, and current events in the client's life may collectively have the most influence on the outcome of treatment. (Information from: Bailey & Ogles, 2023; Costantino et al., 2021; Crits-Christoph & Gibbons, 2021; Wampold & Owen, 2021; Cuijpers, Reijnders, & Huibers, 2019; Norcross & Lambert, 2011; Cooper, 2008.)

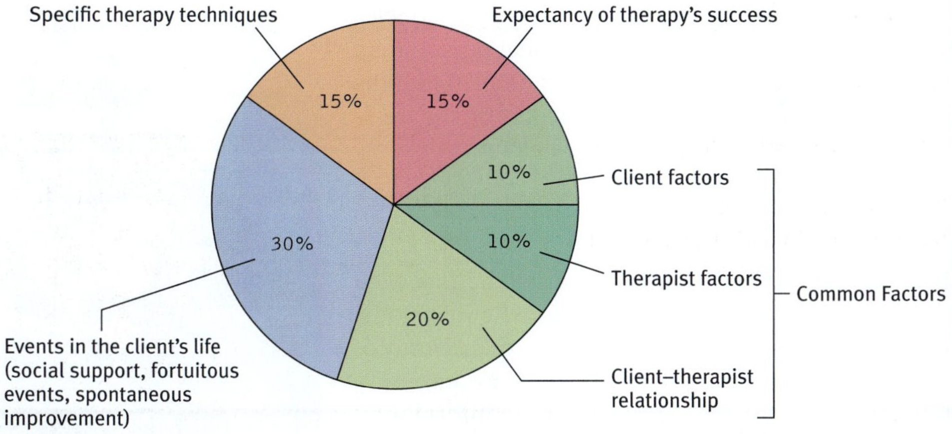

setting. Because an individual's progress is influenced by all these factors and more, the findings of a particular study will not always apply to other clients and therapists (see **Figure 3-4**).

Proper research procedures address some of these problems. By using control groups, random assignment, matched research participants, and the like, clinicians can draw certain conclusions about various therapies. Even in studies that are well designed, however, the variety and complexity of treatment limit the conclusions that can be reached (Chambless & Hollon, 2023; Kazdin, 2021).

Despite these issues and difficulties, the job of evaluating therapies must be done, and clinical researchers have plowed ahead with it. Investigators have, in fact, conducted thousands of *therapy outcome studies,* studies that measure and compare the effects of various treatments (see **MindTech**). The studies typically ask one of three questions: (1) Is therapy *generally* effective? (2) Are *particular* therapies *generally* effective? (3) Are *particular* therapies effective for *particular* conditions?

Is Therapy Generally Effective?

Studies suggest that therapy often is more helpful than no treatment or more helpful than placebos. A pioneering review examined 375 controlled studies, covering a total of almost 25,000 clients from a wide assortment of therapies (Smith, Glass, & Miller, 1980; Smith & Glass, 1977). The reviewers combined the findings of these studies by using a special statistical technique called *meta-analysis* (Valentine, Pigott, & Morris, 2023). According to this analysis, the average person who received treatment was better off than 75 percent of the untreated persons. Other meta-analyses have found similar relationships between treatment and improvement (APA, 2023).

Coaching the coach In the hit television series *Ted Lasso*, the inspiring soccer coach typically serves as a calm, optimistic, and supportive role model for his players. But behind the upbeat exterior, Coach Lasso himself struggles with deep emotional wounds, causing him to seek help from the team's sports psychologist, Dr. Sharon Fieldstone.

Colin Hutton/©Apple TV+/Courtesy Everett Collection

Some clinicians have concerned themselves with an important related question: Can therapy be harmful? A number of studies suggest that 3 to 15 percent of patients actually seem to get worse because of therapy (Botanov, Williams, & Sakaluk, 2022; McKay & Jensen-Doss, 2021). Their symptoms may become more intense, or they may develop new ones, such as a sense of failure, guilt, reduced self-concept, or hopelessness, because of their inability to profit from therapy.

Are Particular Therapies Generally Effective?

The studies you have read about so far have lumped all therapies together to consider their general effectiveness. Many researchers, however, consider it wrong to treat all therapies alike. Some critics suggest that these studies are operating under a *uniformity*

MINDTECH

There's an App for That . . . But Does It Work?

Westend61/Getty Images

As you read in the previous chapter, many therapists now include apps with *wearable* technologies in their treatment programs, including "smart" watches and glasses to monitor their clients' psychophysiological reactions throughout their daily lives. However, wearable apps are but a small fraction of the thousands of mental health apps currently flooding the marketplace—apps targeted for the treatment of conditions extending from depression and anxiety to eating disorders, addictions, and attention-deficit/hyperactivity disorder (Hsu et al., 2022; Lu et al., 2022). This ever-expanding mobile mental health movement represents a large portion of the entire digital health industry.

In certain respects, this is a positive trend, but there are major problems attached to it (Agarwal et al., 2022; Singh & Sagar, 2022). First, the vast majority of mental health apps are sold directly to consumers, without any input or guidance from experienced mental health professionals. In most cases, individuals are on their own in their selection and use of the apps, without a clue about which apps are more effective and which ones might even be harmful. Second, relatively few of the mobile mental health apps have been properly investigated or sufficiently supported by research, and, in fact, many of them fail to include well-established features of successful treatment (Carl et al., 2022). For example, only 20 percent of mobile apps for the treatment of child anxiety encourage children to directly and repeatedly confront their feared situations or objects, even though exposure exercises of this kind are among the most effective strategies for treating child anxiety, as you'll learn in the next chapter.

Still another problem is that, according to research, shortly after consumers download mental health apps, their use of the apps begins to slow down or stop altogether, unless they are further receiving professional guidance. That is, engagement and adherence rates typically drop off sharply when an app is not combined with some degree of "supportive accountability," namely, a professional who remotely monitors the app usage and provides empathic coaching and motivation, perhaps in the form of brief phone calls or text messages (Alfaro et al., 2022; Meyer, Wisniewski, & Torous, 2022).

So how can the pitfalls of mental health apps be minimized and their enormous potential achieved? Enter new approaches to digital health apps and software, collectively known as "digital therapeutics" (Carl et al., 2022; Nwosu et al., 2022). Digital therapeutics follow two key criteria: (1) *prior* to marketing, digital therapeutic apps must demonstrate clear effectiveness and safety in rigorous research studies, and (2) such apps must be *prescribed* by a professional who will monitor user engagement and provide supportive accountability rather than being marketed directly to consumers. With such essential standards in place, clinicians hope that apps offered under the digital therapeutics umbrella will continue to grow in number and receive increased approval from the U.S. Food and Drug Administration, steps that will significantly increase the outreach and efficacy of the mental health field (Rahaman, 2023).

myth—a false belief that all therapies are equivalent despite differences in the therapists' training, experience, theoretical orientations, and personalities (APA, 2023).

Thus, an alternative approach examines the effectiveness of *particular* therapies. Most research of this kind shows each of the major forms of therapy to be superior to no treatment or to placebo treatment (APA, 2023). A number of other studies have compared particular therapies with one another and found that no one form of therapy generally stands out over all others across the full spectrum of mental health conditions (Barkham & Lambert, 2021).

If different kinds of therapy have similar successes, might they have something in common? People in the **rapprochement movement** have tried to identify a set of *common factors,* or *common strategies,* that may run through all effective therapies,

rapprochement movement A movement to identify a set of common factors, or common strategies, that run through all successful therapies.

Brian Lawless – PA Images/Getty Images

An artistic recommendation Irish street artist Joe Caslin created this mural in Dublin to normalize psychotherapy for men under the age of 35 and encourage them to consider psychological treatment when they are struggling. Research finds that men between the ages of 20 and 35 are among the least likely to seek professional help.

regardless of the clinicians' particular orientations (Bailey & Ogles, 2023; Costantino, Boswell, & Coyne, 2021; Wampold & Owen, 2021). Surveys of highly successful therapists suggest, for example, that most such therapists give feedback to clients, help clients focus on their own thoughts and behavior, pay attention to the way they and their clients are interacting, try to promote self-control and proficiency in their clients, and develop skill at working with clients from a range of cultural backgrounds. In short, effective therapists of any type may practice more similarly than they preach.

Are Particular Therapies Effective for Particular Conditions?

People with different disorders may respond differently to the various forms of therapy (Barkham & Lambert, 2021). In an oft-quoted statement, influential clinical theorist Gordon Paul said over a half-century ago that the most appropriate question regarding the effectiveness of therapy may be "*What* specific treatment, by *whom,* is most effective for *this* individual with *that* specific condition, and under *which* set of circumstances?" (Paul, 1967, p. 111). Researchers have investigated how effective particular therapies are at treating particular disorders, and they often have found sizable differences among the various therapies. Cognitive-behavioral therapies, for example, appear to be the most effective of all in treating phobias and other anxiety-related conditions, whereas drug therapy seems to be the single most effective treatment for schizophrenia (Stroup & Marder, 2023).

How can people make wise decisions about therapists and treatment approaches when they are seeking treatment?

As you read previously, studies also show that some clinical disorders may respond better to *combined* approaches (Sanborn, Ali, & Creedon, 2023). Drug therapy is sometimes combined with certain forms of psychotherapy, for example, to treat depression or anxiety. In fact, it is now common for clients to be seen by two therapists—one of them a **psychopharmacologist,** a psychiatrist who primarily prescribes medications, and the other a psychologist, social worker, or other therapist who conducts psychotherapy. Obviously, knowledge of how particular therapies fare with particular disorders can help therapists and clients alike make better decisions about treatment. We will keep returning to this issue as we examine the various disorders throughout the book.

SUMMING UP

III Treatment

The treatment decisions of therapists may be influenced by assessment information, the diagnosis, the clinician's theoretical orientation and familiarity with research, and the state of knowledge in the field. Therapy outcome studies have led to three general conclusions: (1) people in therapy are usually better off than people with similar difficulties who receive no treatment, (2) the various therapies do not appear to differ dramatically in their general effectiveness, and (3) certain therapies or combinations of therapies do appear to be more effective than other therapies for certain disorders. Some therapists advocate evidence-based treatment—the active identification, promotion, and teaching of those interventions that have received clear research support.

psychopharmacologist A psychiatrist who primarily prescribes medications.

What Lies Ahead?

IT IS CLEAR from this chapter that proper diagnoses and effective treatments rest on the shoulders of accurate clinical assessment. Correspondingly, before the 1950s, assessment tools were a highly regarded part of clinical practice. However, as research in the 1960s and 1970s began to reveal that a number of the tools were inaccurate or inconsistent, many clinicians abandoned systematic assessment. Today, respect for assessment is on the rise once again, and assessment is increasingly being used through the full course of treatment, as opposed to only at the outset of treatment (McLeod et al., 2022). One reason for this renewal of interest is the drive by researchers for more rigorous tests to help them select appropriate participants for clinical studies. Still another factor is the growing belief in the field that brain-scanning techniques may soon offer assessment information about a wide range of psychological disorders. Along with heightened respect for assessment has come increased research in this area.

Ironically, just as clinicians and researchers are rediscovering systematic assessment, rising costs and economic factors may be conspiring to discourage the use of assessment tools. As you read in the opening chapter, insurance parity and treatment coverage, including assessment coverage, for people with psychological conditions had been improving during the twenty-first century as a result of federal parity laws and the Affordable Care Act. However, with different health care priorities now unfolding in Congress and in some states, many experts fear that clinical assessment will receive only limited insurance support in the future. Which forces will ultimately have a stronger influence on clinical assessment—promising research or economic pressure? Only time will tell.

James D. Smith via AP

Raising public awareness As part of a National Football League campaign called My Cause My Cleats, cornerback Anthony Brown played an entire game in these custom-designed cleats, which featured important messages. Public gestures such as this seek to raise mental health awareness, increase community compassion, and encourage people in emotional pain to seek out mental health services.

Quick Quiz

1. What forms of reliability and validity should clinical assessment tools display? pp. 80–81
2. What are the strengths and weaknesses of structured and unstructured interviews? pp. 82–83
3. List and describe today's leading projective tests. pp. 84–86
4. What are the key features of the MMPI? pp. 86–87
5. What are the strengths and weaknesses of projective tests (pp. 85–86), personality inventories (p. 87), and other kinds of clinical tests (pp. 88–91)?
6. How do clinicians determine whether psychological problems are linked to brain dysfunction? pp. 88–91
7. Describe the ways in which clinicians may make observations of clients' behaviors. pp. 91–93
8. What is the purpose of clinical diagnoses? pp. 93–94
9. Describe DSM-5-TR. What problems may accompany the use of classification systems and the process of clinical diagnosis? pp. 94–100
10. According to therapy outcome studies, how effective is therapy? pp. 101–104

Anxiety, Obsessive-Compulsive, and Related Disorders

Within her family, Jale, age 29, was thought of as the success story, the culmination of three generations of struggle. Her maternal grandparents had emigrated from Turkey to the United States in 1971, one step ahead of a dangerous coup in their country. They spoke little English and barely eked out a living. Their daughter (Jale's mother) had a less difficult life, but her professional potential was never fulfilled, as she was not able to attend college and never rose above the level of secretary at work. Jale, on the other hand, earned a master's degree, developed a thriving web design business, and made a very comfortable (some would say lucrative) living. There was one problem, however. Jale was afraid that she was "losing her mind."

She had always been a worrier. She worried about her health, her husband, her work, her social life, her future, her finances, and so on. Would her best friend get angry at her? Was her husband, Peter, tiring of her? Were she and Peter investing their money wisely? Were her clients pleased with her work? But, lately, those worries had increased to an unbearable level. She was consumed with the notion that something terrible was about to happen to her. Within an hour's time, she might have intense concerns about going broke, developing cancer, losing one of her parents, offending her friends, her rheumatoid arthritis becoming worse, and more. She was certain that crisis awaited her at every turn. No amount of reassurance, from herself or from others, brought relief for very long.

She started therapy with Dr. Adena Morven, a clinical psychologist. Dr. Morven immediately noticed how unsettled Jale was. She looked tense, pale, and frightened and could not sit comfortably in her chair; she kept tapping her feet and jumped when she heard traffic noise from outside the office building. She kept sighing throughout the visit, fidgeting with her long blond hair and shifting her position, and she appeared breathless while telling Dr. Morven about her difficulties.

Jale described her frequent inability to concentrate. When designing client websites, she would lose her train of thought. Less than five minutes into a project, she would forget much of her overall strategy. During conversations, she would begin a sentence and then forget the point she was about to make. Watching TV had become impossible. She found it difficult to focus on anything for more than a few minutes. When she and Peter recently trimmed their Christmas tree, she had felt unable to make decisions about ornaments, and Peter wound up handling all of the decorating.

To say the least, she was worried about all of this. "I'm worried about being so worried," she told Dr. Morven, almost laughing at her own remark. Jale said that she expected the worst whenever she began a conversation, task, or outing. If an event or interaction started to go awry, she would quickly feel overwhelmed, with uncomfortable physical effects—her heart would beat faster, her breathing rate would increase, and she'd sweat profusely. On some occasions, she thought she was having a heart attack—at the ripe old age of 29.

Typically, such physical reactions lasted less than a minute. However, those seconds felt like an eternity to Jale. She acknowledged coming back down to earth after the feelings subsided—but "back down to earth" meant back to worrying and then worrying some more.

(continued on the next page)

CHAPTER 4

TOPIC OVERVIEW

Dr. Morven empathized with Jale about how upsetting this all must be. She asked why Jale had decided to come into therapy now—as opposed to last year, last month, or last week. Jale pinpointed several things. First, all the worrying and anxiety seemed to be on the increase. Second, she was finding it hard to sleep. Her nights were filled with tossing and turning—and, of course, more worrying. Third, she suspected that her constant worrying, physical symptoms, and lack of sleep were bad for her health. Wouldn't they eventually lead to a major medical problem? And finally, her anxiety had begun to interfere with her life. She found herself turning down social invitations and work opportunities more and more. She had even quit her once-beloved political action group. Not that staying home helped in any real way. She wondered how much longer she could go on like this.

You don't need to be as troubled as Jale to experience fear and anxiety. Think about a time when your breathing quickened, your muscles tensed, and your heart pounded with a sudden sense of dread. Was it when your car almost skidded off the road in the rain? When your professor announced a pop quiz? What about when the person you were in love with went out with someone else or when your boss suggested that your job performance ought to improve? Any time you face what seems to be a serious threat to your well-being, you may react with the state of immediate alarm known as **fear.** Sometimes you cannot pinpoint a specific cause for your alarm, but still you feel tense and edgy, as if you expect something unpleasant to happen. This vague sense of being in danger is usually called **anxiety,** and it has the same features—the same increases in breathing, muscular tension, perspiration, and so forth—as fear.

of NOTE ...

Their Words

"My anxieties have anxieties."

Charlie Brown

Although everyday experiences of fear and anxiety are not pleasant, they often are useful. They prepare us for action—for "fight or flight"—when danger threatens. They may lead us to drive more cautiously in a storm, keep up with our reading assignments, treat our friends more sensitively, and work harder at our jobs. However, some people experience such disabling fear and anxiety that their lives are profoundly disrupted. Their discomfort is too severe or too frequent, lasts too long, or is activated too easily. These people are said to have an *anxiety disorder* or a related kind of disorder.

Anxiety disorders are the most common mental disorders in the United States. In any given year, around 19 percent of the adult population display one or another of the anxiety disorders listed in DSM-5-TR, while close to 31 percent of all people develop one of the disorders at some point in their lives (NAMI, 2023; NIMH, 2023). Around 37 percent of these individuals receive treatment (ADAA, 2022).

As you will learn in this chapter, the most prominent anxiety disorders are *generalized anxiety disorder, specific phobias, agoraphobia, social anxiety disorder,* and *panic disorder.* People with one anxiety disorder often experience a second one as well (Roy-Byrne, 2022). Jale, for example, has the excessive worry found in generalized anxiety disorder and the repeated attacks of terror that mark panic disorder. In addition, many people with an anxiety disorder also experience depression (Baldwin, 2023).

Anxiety also plays a major role in a different group of problems, called *obsessive-compulsive and related disorders.* People with these disorders feel overrun by recurrent thoughts that cause anxiety or by the need to perform certain repetitive actions to reduce anxiety. Because anxiety is so prominent in these disorders, they will be examined in this chapter along with the anxiety disorders. ■

fear The central nervous system's physiological and emotional response to a serious threat to one's well-being.

anxiety The central nervous system's physiological and emotional response to a vague sense of threat or danger.

generalized anxiety disorder A disorder marked by persistent and excessive feelings of anxiety and worry about numerous events and activities.

Michael Owens/Getty Images

Quinn Rooney/Getty Images

Throughout the sports world A growing number of today's professional and amateur athletes are revealing that they have mental health challenges. Several have recently talked about their battles with debilitating anxiety and depression, including NFL Pro Bowl quarterback Dak Prescott (left) and Grand Slam tennis champion Naomi Osaka (right).

Generalized Anxiety Disorder

PEOPLE WITH GENERALIZED ANXIETY DISORDER experience excessive anxiety under most circumstances and worry about practically anything. In fact, their problem is sometimes described as *free-floating anxiety*. Like the young web designer Jale, they typically feel restless, keyed up, or on edge; tire easily; have difficulty concentrating; suffer from muscle tension; and have sleep problems (see **Table 4-1**). The symptoms last at least six months (APA, 2022) and lead to a reduced quality of life. Nevertheless, many people with the disorder are able, although with some difficulty, to carry on social relationships and job activities.

Generalized anxiety disorder is common in Western nations. Surveys suggest that at least 3 percent of the population in the United States have the symptoms of this disorder in any given year, a rate that holds across Canada, Britain, and other Western countries (APA, 2023; NIMH, 2023). Altogether, around 6 percent of all people develop generalized anxiety disorder sometime during their lives. It may emerge at any age (see ***Trending***). There is some evidence that transgender people and nonbinary people are more likely than cisgender people to develop the disorder (Hajek et al., 2023; Wittlin, Kuper, & Olson, 2023; Pinna et al., 2022). Research conducted with mostly cisgender populations finds that women are twice as likely as men to experience this disorder. Generalized anxiety disorder is more prevalent among lesbian, gay, and bisexual people than among heterosexual people (Gmelin et al., 2022). And non-Hispanic White Americans are more likely than people of color to develop the disorder, although the rates for various racial and ethnic groups are becoming more similar (MHA, 2023; NAMI, 2023). Around 43 percent of people who have generalized anxiety disorder receive treatment for it (ADAA, 2022).

A variety of explanations and treatments have been proposed for this disorder. Let's look at the views and approaches offered by the sociocultural, psychodynamic, humanistic, cognitive-behavioral, and biological models.

TABLE 4-1

Dx Checklist

Generalized Anxiety Disorder
1. For 6 months or more, person experiences disproportionate, uncontrollable, and ongoing anxiety and worry about multiple matters.
2. The symptoms include at least three of the following: edginess, fatigue, poor concentration, irritability, muscle tension, sleep problems.
3. Significant distress or impairment.

Information from: APA, 2022.

The Sociocultural Perspective: Societal and Multicultural Factors

According to sociocultural theorists, generalized anxiety disorder is most likely to develop in people who are faced with ongoing societal conditions that are dangerous. Studies have found that people in highly threatening environments are indeed more

...TRENDING

Separation Anxiety Disorder: Not Just for Kids Anymore

Individuals with *separation anxiety disorder* feel extreme anxiety, often panic, whenever they are separated from home or from key people in their lives.

As attorneys at the NAACP Legal Defense and Educational Fund in New York City, Reggie's parents successfully handled a wide range of challenging situations. But they were at a loss when it came to Reggie's separation anxiety disorder. The symptoms of the disorder began a little over a year ago, when Reggie was 4 years old. In an early "meltdown," he began crying as soon as his parents tried to place him in the car for the 30-minute trip to his grandparents' house for an overnight weekend there. He screamed, "I only want to be here with you! If you make me go, I'll never see you again! What if you like it better without me? What if you die?" He cried all the way to his grandparents' house. At their door, Reggie hugged his mother as though he would never let her go. During the next several months, Reggie became hysterical every time his parents tried to get him to leave the house for a play date or a journey elsewhere.

Five months later, Reggie began kindergarten. His parents were concerned about how it would go, given Reggie's recent behavior and the fact that he would be one of only three Black children in his class, but it went far worse than they had feared. That first day lasted all of two hours. The principal called, asking the parents to come get the child. Though sympathetic, the principal explained that Reggie's nonstop crying was affecting all the other children. "Perhaps tomorrow Reggie will have a better day," he said. But the next day, Reggie's reaction was the same. And the next day. And the next day.

SDI Productions/Getty Images

Like Reggie, children with separation anxiety disorder have great trouble traveling away from their family, and they often refuse to visit friends' houses, go on errands, or attend camp or school. Many cannot stay alone in a room, and they cling to their parents around the house. Some also have temper tantrums, cry, or plead to keep their parents from leaving them. The children may fear that they will get lost when separated from their parents or that the parents will meet with an accident or illness. As long as the children are near their parents, they may function quite typically. At the first hint of separation, however, the dramatic pattern of symptoms may be set in motion.

For years, clinicians believed that separation anxiety disorder is developed *only* by children or adolescents. But today, DSM-5-TR maintains that the disorder can also occur in adulthood, particularly after adults have experienced traumas such as the death of a child or intimate partner, a relationship breakup, separation caused by military service, or the like (Feriante, Torrico, & Bernstein, 2023; APA, 2022). Such individuals may become consumed with concern about the health, safety, or well-being of a significant other—their partner, a surviving child, or another important person in their life. They may constantly and excessively try to be with the other person, check on their whereabouts, protect the other person, and restrict the other person's activities and travels. Their extreme anxiety and invasive demands cause them severe distress and can greatly damage their social and occupational lives (Feriante et al., 2023).

Given this relatively new perspective, DSM-5-TR categorizes separation anxiety disorder as one kind of anxiety disorder rather than as a unique childhood disorder. It states that symptoms must persist for at least six months for adults to receive a diagnosis, compared to four weeks for children. Applying DSM-5-TR's criteria, studies find that as many as 2 percent of all adults have the disorder in addition to 4 percent of all children (APA, 2023; Bennett & Walkup, 2022). Although most clinicians agree with DSM-5-TR that certain adults do indeed manifest the loss-triggered symptoms described above, many of them believe that the adult syndrome may be qualitatively different from the one displayed by Reggie and other such children (Feriante et al., 2023).

likely to develop the general feelings of tension, anxiety, and fatigue and the sleep disturbances found in this disorder. For example, there are higher rates of generalized anxiety disorder and similar syndromes among people who live in neighborhoods where crime and violence are prevalent (APA, 2023; MHF, 2023).

One of the most powerful forms of societal stress is poverty. People with low incomes are particularly likely to live in underserved communities with high crime rates, have fewer educational and job opportunities, experience housing and food insecurity, run a greater risk for health problems, and receive inadequate health care. As sociocultural theorists would predict, such people also have a higher rate of generalized anxiety disorder (Marbin et al., 2022). Across North America, the rate is almost twice as high among people with low incomes as among those with higher incomes. As wages decrease, the rate of generalized anxiety disorder steadily increases.

Societal danger and stress may also come in the form of widespread contagious diseases. Dating back to the bubonic plague in medieval Europe, studies have found increases in the prevalence of anxiety disorders in communities and nations overrun by epidemics (KFF, 2022). Thus, it was not surprising to clinical investigators that, less than one year into the Covid-19 pandemic, almost 30 percent of surveyed people had developed moderate to severe symptoms of generalized anxiety—symptoms that extended well beyond the specific health, economic, and family fears triggered directly by the spread of the virus (Cénat et al., 2021; Fountoulakis et al., 2021).

Will Dickey/The Florida Times-Union via AP

The role of society Leonel Rivas and Beatriz Villanueva De Rivas attend a vigil for their 7-year-old daughter Heidy, who was killed in 2018 by a stray bullet near their home in Jacksonville, Florida. People who live in dangerous environments experience greater anxiety and have a higher rate of generalized anxiety disorder than those who live in other settings.

Although poverty, widespread illness, and other societal pressures may help create a climate in which generalized anxiety disorder is more likely to develop, these sociocultural variables are not the only factors at work. After all, most people in such environments do not develop this disorder. Even if sociocultural factors play a broad role, theorists still must explain why some people develop the disorder and others do not. The psychodynamic, humanistic, cognitive-behavioral, and biological schools of thought have all tried to explain why and have offered corresponding treatments.

The Psychodynamic Perspective

As you read earlier in the textbook, Sigmund Freud (1933, 1917) believed that all children experience some degree of anxiety as part of growing up and that all use ego defense mechanisms to help control such anxiety. However, according to Freud, some children have particularly high levels of anxiety, or their defense mechanisms are particularly inadequate, and these individuals may develop generalized anxiety disorder.

Psychodynamic Explanations: When Childhood Anxiety Goes Unresolved

According to Freud, early developmental experiences may produce an unusually high level of anxiety in certain children. Say that children are spanked every time they cry to be fed during infancy, mess their pants as 2-year-olds, and explore their genitals as toddlers. They may eventually come to believe that their various id impulses are very dangerous, and they may feel overwhelming anxiety whenever they have such impulses, setting the stage for generalized anxiety disorder.

Alternatively, a child's ego defense mechanisms may be too weak to cope with even mild levels of anxiety. Overprotected children, shielded by their parents from all

of NOTE ...

Their Words

"Unexpressed emotions will never die."

Sigmund Freud

client-centered therapy The humanistic therapy developed by Carl Rogers in which clinicians try to help clients by being accepting, empathizing accurately, and conveying genuineness. Also known as *person-centered therapy.*

basic irrational assumptions The inaccurate and inappropriate beliefs held by people with various psychological disorders, according to Albert Ellis.

frustrations and threats, have little opportunity to develop effective defense mechanisms. When they face the pressures of adult life, their defense mechanisms may be too weak to cope with the resulting anxieties.

Today's psychodynamic theorists often disagree with specific aspects of Freud's explanation for generalized anxiety disorder. Most continue to believe, however, that the disorder can be traced to difficulties in the early relationships between children and their parents (Kidd et al., 2022). Researchers have tested the psychodynamic explanations in various ways. In one strategy, they have tried to show that people with generalized anxiety disorder are particularly likely to use defense mechanisms. For example, a classic investigation examined the early therapy transcripts of patients with this diagnosis and found that the patients often reacted defensively. When asked by therapists to discuss upsetting experiences, they would quickly forget (*repress*) what they had just been talking about, change the direction of the discussion, or deny having negative feelings (Luborsky, 1973).

In another line of research, investigators have studied people who as children experienced harsh punishment for id impulses. As psychodynamic theorists would predict, these people have higher levels of anxiety later in life (Liu et al., 2022). In addition, several studies have supported the psychodynamic position that extreme protectiveness by parents may often lead to high levels of anxiety in their children (Bennett & Walkup, 2022).

Although these studies are consistent with psychodynamic explanations, some scientists question whether they show what they claim to show. When people have difficulty talking about upsetting events early in therapy, for example, they are not necessarily repressing those events. They may be focusing purposely on the positive aspects of their lives, or they may be too embarrassed to share personal negative events until they develop trust in the therapist.

Psychodynamic Therapies

Psychodynamic therapists use the same general techniques to treat all psychological problems: *free association* and the therapist's interpretations of *transference, resistance,* and *dreams*. *Freudian psychodynamic therapists* use these methods to help clients with generalized anxiety disorder become less afraid of their id impulses and more successful in controlling them. Other psychodynamic therapists, particularly *object relations therapists,* use them to help anxious clients identify and settle the childhood relationship problems that continue to produce anxiety in adulthood (Black, 2022; Broudy, 2022).

Controlled studies have typically found long-term psychodynamic therapy to be of only modest help to persons with generalized anxiety disorder (Craske, 2023). On the other hand, *short-term psychodynamic therapy,* the approach you read about in the chapter on models of psychopathology, has in some cases significantly reduced the levels of anxiety, worry, and social difficulty of clients with this disorder (Leichsenring et al., 2023; Barber et al., 2021).

Climate change anxiety More and more studies are linking climate change to negative mental health and physical consequences (Clayton & Swim, 2024), prompting these protesting health care workers to speak out about the impact such change is having on their patients. Many individuals, for example, now experience *climate change anxiety*—symptoms of persistent worry, stress, and fear over the existential threats posed by higher temperatures, rising sea levels, and extreme weather events.

Vuk Valcic/Alamy Stock Photo

The Humanistic Perspective

Humanistic theorists propose that generalized anxiety disorder, like other psychological disorders, arises when people stop looking at themselves honestly and acceptingly. Repeated denials of their true thoughts, emotions, and behavior make these people extremely anxious and unable to fulfill their potential as human beings.

The humanistic view of why people develop this disorder is best explained by Carl Rogers. As you learned earlier in the textbook, Rogers believed that children who fail to receive *unconditional positive regard* from others may become overly critical of themselves and develop harsh self-standards, what Rogers called *conditions of worth*. They try to meet these standards by repeatedly distorting and denying their true thoughts and experiences. Despite such efforts, however, threatening self-judgments keep breaking through and causing them intense anxiety. This onslaught of anxiety sets the stage for generalized anxiety disorder or some other form of psychological dysfunction.

Practitioners of Rogers' treatment approach, **client-centered therapy** (also called *person-centered therapy*), try to show unconditional positive regard for their clients and to empathize with them (Cooper & Di Malta, 2023; Farber, Suzuki, & Ort, 2022). The therapists hope that an atmosphere of genuine acceptance and caring will help clients feel secure enough to recognize their true needs, thoughts, and emotions. When clients eventually are honest and comfortable with themselves, their anxiety or other symptoms will subside.

Controlled studies have failed to offer strong support for this approach. Although research does suggest that client-centered therapy is usually more helpful to anxious clients than no treatment, the approach is only sometimes superior to placebo therapy or to other kinds of therapy (Yao & Kabir, 2023; Elliot et al., 2021). In addition, researchers have found, at best, only limited support for Rogers' explanation of broad and excessive anxiety. Nor have other humanistic theories and treatment received much research support.

of NOTE ...

Need to Blame

Throughout history, people have sought to assign blame to specific groups for large-scale disease outbreaks, partly to reestablish feelings of certainty, clarity, and control during the unpredictable ordeals—thus reducing their levels of anxiety (White, 2022). This phenomenon was at work, for example, during the fourteenth-century bubonic plague (Jewish people were targeted), the 2009 swine flu epidemic (Hispanic Americans), the 2014 Ebola outbreak (people of African descent), and the 2020 Covid-19 pandemic (people of Asian descent).

The Cognitive-Behavioral Perspective

As you read earlier in the textbook, followers of the cognitive-behavioral model suggest that psychological disorders are often caused by problematic behaviors and dysfunctional ways of thinking. With regard to generalized anxiety disorder, the model's theorists and therapists focus largely on the cognitive dimension of the disorder.

Maladaptive Assumptions

Initially, cognitive-behavioral theorists suggested that generalized anxiety disorder is caused primarily by *maladaptive assumptions*, a notion that continues to be influential. Albert Ellis, for example, proposed that many people are guided by irrational beliefs that lead them to act and react in inappropriate ways (Terjesen et al., 2023). Ellis called these **basic irrational assumptions,** and he claimed that people with generalized anxiety disorder often hold the following ones:

> *"It is a dire necessity for an adult human being to be loved or approved of by virtually every significant other person in his community."*
>
> *"It is awful and catastrophic when things are not the way one would very much like them to be."*
>
> *"If something is or may be dangerous or fearsome, one should be terribly concerned about it and should keep dwelling on the possibility of its occurring."*
>
> *"One should be thoroughly competent, adequate, and achieving in all possible respects if one is to consider oneself worthwhile."*
>
> *(Ellis, 1962)*

When people who make these assumptions are faced with a stressful event, such as an exam or a first date, they are likely to interpret it as dangerous, to overreact, and to feel fear. As they apply the assumptions to more and more events, they may begin to develop generalized anxiety disorder.

"Upside Down" delights Many people enjoy the feeling of fear as long as it occurs under controlled circumstances, as when they are safely watching the tension grow in the hugely popular television series *Stranger Things*. The spine-tingling show follows young friends as they unravel supernatural and paranormal mysteries in their small town of Hawkins, Indiana.

PA Images/Alamy Stock Photo

Similarly, theorist Aaron Beck argued that people with generalized anxiety disorder constantly hold silent assumptions (for example, "A situation or a person is unsafe until proven to be safe" or "It is always best to assume the worst") that imply they are in imminent danger (Chand, Kuckel, & Huecker, 2023; Clark & Beck, 2023). Since the time of Ellis' and Beck's initial proposals, researchers have repeatedly found that people with generalized anxiety disorder do indeed hold maladaptive assumptions, particularly about dangerousness, and are, in turn, overattentive to potentially threatening stimuli (Baldwin, 2023).

Other Cognitive-Behavioral Explanations

Over the past two decades, several additional cognitive-behavioral explanations for generalized anxiety disorder have emerged. Each of them builds on the work of Ellis and Beck and their emphasis on danger.

The *metacognitive theory*, developed by the researcher Adrian Wells, suggests that people with generalized anxiety disorder implicitly hold both positive and negative beliefs about worrying (Wells et al., 2023; Wells, 2021, 2019, 2005). On the positive side, they believe that worrying is a useful way of appraising and coping with threats in life. And so they look for and examine all possible signs of danger—that is, they worry constantly (see **Figure 4-1**).

Why might many people believe, at least implicitly, that worrying is useful—even necessary—for problems to work out?

At the same time, Wells argues, people with generalized anxiety disorder also hold negative beliefs about worrying, and these negative attitudes are the ones that open the door to the disorder. Because society teaches them that worrying is a bad thing, they come to believe that their repeated worrying is in fact harmful (mentally and physically) and uncontrollable. Now they further worry about the fact that they always seem to be worrying (so-called *meta-worries*). Their meta-worries may include concerns that they are "going crazy" with worry, making themselves ill with worry, or losing out in life because of worrying. The net effect of all this worrying: generalized anxiety disorder.

This explanation has received considerable research support. Studies indicate, for example, that people who generally hold both positive and negative beliefs about worrying are particularly prone to developing generalized anxiety disorder and that repeated meta-worrying is a powerful predictor of developing the disorder (Baldwin, 2023; Dunkley & Robichaud, 2022).

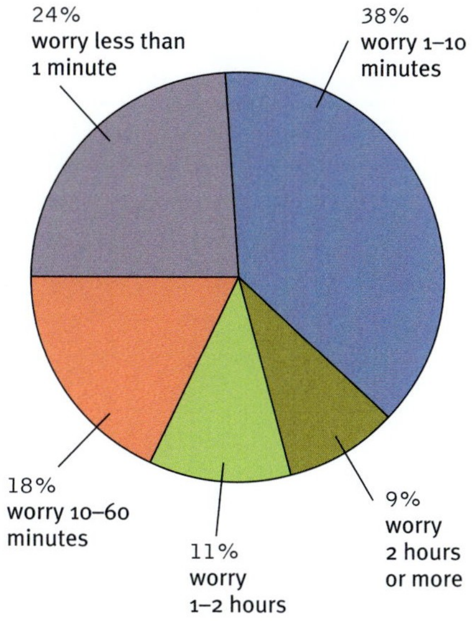

FIGURE 4-1

How Long Do Your Worries Last?

In one survey, 62 percent of college students said they spend less than 10 minutes at a time worrying about something. In contrast, 20 percent worry for more than an hour. (Information from: Tallis, 2019, 2015, 2014; Tallis, Davey, & Capuzzo, 1994.)

According to another modern explanation for generalized anxiety disorder, the *intolerance of uncertainty theory,* some people cannot tolerate the knowledge that negative events *may* occur, even if the possibility of occurrence is very small. Inasmuch as life is filled with uncertain events, these people worry constantly that such events are about to occur. Such intolerance and worrying leave them highly vulnerable to the development of generalized anxiety disorder (Laposa et al., 2022; Zemestani et al., 2022). Think of when you meet someone you're attracted to and how you then feel prior to texting or calling this person for the first time—or how you feel while you're waiting for the individual to contact you for the first time. The worry that you experience in such instances—the sense of unbearable uncertainty over the possibility of an unacceptable negative outcome—is, according to this theory, how people with generalized anxiety disorder feel all the time.

Proponents of this theory believe that people with generalized anxiety disorder continually worry as they try to find "correct" solutions for and restore certainty to various situations in their lives. However, because it is never certain that a given solution is a correct one, they are always left to grapple with intolerable levels of uncertainty, triggering new rounds of worrying. As with the metacognitive theory of worry, considerable research supports this theory. Studies have found, for example, that people with generalized anxiety disorder display higher levels of intolerance of uncertainty than people with more typical degrees of anxiety (Baldwin, 2023; Hunt et al., 2022). Research also suggests that intolerance of uncertainty is biologically based, develops in early childhood, and can be passed on from parents to children (Bennett & Walkup, 2022).

Finally, a third relatively modern cognitive-behavioral explanation for generalized anxiety disorder, the *avoidance theory,* developed by researcher Thomas Borkovec, suggests that people with this disorder have greater bodily arousal (higher heart rate, perspiration, and respiration) than other people and that worrying actually serves to *reduce* this arousal, perhaps by distracting the individuals from their unpleasant physical feelings (Dunkley & Robichaud, 2022). In short, the avoidance theory holds that people with generalized anxiety disorder worry repeatedly in order to reduce or avoid uncomfortable states of bodily arousal. For example, when they find themselves in an uncomfortable job situation or social relationship, they implicitly choose to worry about losing their job or losing a friend rather than having to stew in a state of intense negative arousal.

Borkovec's explanation has been supported by numerous studies as well. Research reveals that people with generalized anxiety disorder experience particularly fast and intense bodily reactions, find such reactions overwhelming, worry more than other people upon becoming aroused, and successfully reduce their arousal whenever they worry (Baldwin, 2023; Kim & Newman, 2022).

of NOTE ...

Actual Odds of Feared Calamities

1 in 366	You will be in a car accident (per 1,000 miles driven).
1 in 1,000	Your home will be burglarized this year.
1 in 20,000	You will be murdered this year.
1 in 1,200,000	You will be struck by lightning this year.
1 in 5,000,000	You will be attacked by a shark this year.

(Information from: NWS, 2023; Berk, 2022; CheckVideo, 2022; Levine, 2022; Knudson, 2021)

Cognitive-Behavioral Therapies

Two kinds of cognitive-behavioral approaches are used in cases of generalized anxiety disorder. In one, therapists help clients change the maladaptive assumptions that characterize their disorder. In the other, therapists help clients understand the special role that worrying may play in their disorder, modify their views about worrying, and change their behavioral reactions to such unnerving concerns.

CHANGING MALADAPTIVE ASSUMPTIONS Therapists using Ellis' technique of **rational-emotive therapy** point out the irrational assumptions held by clients, suggest more appropriate assumptions, and assign homework that gives the clients practice at challenging old assumptions and applying new ones (Terjesen et al., 2023). Studies suggest that this and similar approaches bring at least modest relief to those experiencing generalized anxiety (Clark & Beck, 2023; Newman et al., 2022).

rational-emotive therapy A cognitive therapy developed by Albert Ellis that helps clients identify and change the irrational assumptions and thinking that help cause their psychological disorder.

Ellis' approach is illustrated in the following discussion between a therapist and a generally anxious client, a station chef at a high-end restaurant who currently fears failure and disapproval at work, especially over a party he is throwing for his supervisor:

Client: *I can't stop worrying about the party I'm hosting for Giada to honor her promotion to head chef. I keep thinking, "What if things are not ready on time? What if the food is overcooked?" Then Giada's opinion of me would crater. Everyone would lose respect for me. I might even be fired.*

Therapist: *Be aware that you are creating these worries—you're reacting to your own baseless thoughts. Actually, you've planned meticulously, and your previous parties and work have gone well. But you've convinced yourself of something illogical—that any missteps with the party will cause your boss and coworkers to turn against you, even get you fired—yet you've always had a warm relationship with Giada, served effectively as her go-to person, and been respected by her and your coworkers.*

Client: *I know, but my life goal is to be a good chef, and if I can't even get this promotion party right, I'm really a poor chef . . . in fact, a pretty pathetic person.*

Therapist: *Only if you tell yourself that. Five years of successful work as a station chef would suggest you're a good chef. If something goes wrong with the party, that would be a disappointment. But would that mean you're not a quality chef, that your years of work have been a failure? Moreover, even if there are hiccups in your work, as in every pressured position, does that erase your value as a person?*

BREAKING DOWN WORRYING Alternatively, many of today's third wave cognitive-behavioral therapists specifically guide clients with generalized anxiety disorder to recognize and change their dysfunctional use of worrying (Dunkley & Robichaud, 2022; Newman et al., 2022). They begin by educating the clients about the role of worrying in their disorder and have them observe their bodily arousal and cognitive responses across various life situations. In turn, the clients come to appreciate the triggers of their worrying, their misconceptions about worrying, and their misguided efforts to control their lives by worrying. As their insights grow, they try out more constructive ways of dealing with arousal and worry less about the fact that they worry so much. Research indicates that a concentrated focus on worrying is indeed helpful for people with generalized anxiety disorder.

Treating individuals with generalized anxiety disorder by helping them to recognize their inclination to worry is similar to another third wave cognitive-behavioral approach that you read about earlier in the textbook, *mindfulness-based cognitive-behavioral therapy,* the approach brought into the mainstream by psychologist Steven Hayes and his colleagues as part of their broader treatment approach called *acceptance and commitment therapy* (Hayes, Hofmann, & Ciarrochi, 2023; Hayes et al., 2022). Here therapists help clients to become aware of their streams of thoughts, including their worries, as those thoughts are occurring and to *accept* such thoughts as mere events of the mind. By observing and accepting their worries rather than trying to eliminate them, the clients are expected to be less upset by them and less influenced by them in their behaviors and life decisions. This is indeed what happens for many clients with generalized anxiety disorder when they receive this and related forms of treatment (Smith, Smith, & Bluett, 2022). Mindfulness-based therapy has also been applied to a range of other psychological conditions (Twohig, Levin, & Petersen, 2022) (see ***InfoCentral***).

Meditation G.O.A.T. All-time NBA scoring champion LeBron James routinely uses mindfulness and other forms of meditation to help him remain calm in tense game moments and deal with the pressures of being a celebrity. Similarly, research finds that regular meditation practice and mindfulness-based therapy can help reduce the numerous worries and ongoing tensions of people with generalized anxiety disorder.

AP Photo/Brandon Dill

MINDFULNESS

Over the past decade, **mindfulness** has become one of the most common terms in psychology. Mindfulness involves being in the present moment, intentionally and nonjudgmentally. **Mindfulness training programs** use mindfulness **meditation** techniques to help treat people suffering from pain, anxiety disorders, and depressive disorders, as well as a variety of other psychological disorders.

MINDFULNESS TRAINING PROGRAMS

- Have the goal of achieving a state of intentional, nonjudgmental attention on the present.

attention to **body** sensations

attention to **breathing** sensations

attention to **wandering** and busy **thoughts**

simple **yoga**

homework **assignments** (practice and **journal** keeping)

8 weeks of instruction

(Fischer et al., 2022; Lycke et al., 2022; Miller, 2019)

- Help reduce the anxiety found in . . .

generalized **anxiety** disorder

social **anxiety** disorder

panic disorder

test **anxiety**

illness **anxiety**

depressive disorder with **anxious** distress

(Coulter, 2022; Stahl, 2022; Carlton et al., 2020; B. Zhou et al., 2020)

- Help treat other disorders, including:

pain conditions

PTSD and other **stress** disorders

depressive disorders

insomnia

substance use disorders

borderline personality disorder

(NCCIH, 2022; J. Wang et al., 2022)

Number of mindfulness apps
2,500

Number of medical schools in North America that teach mindfulness
>140

Why Do People Seek Mindfulness?

Reason	Percentage
Better health	76%
More energy	60%
Better memory and attention	50%
Reduce stress	35%
Reduce anxiety	29%
Alleviate depression	18%

(Arsenovic, 2021; Upchurch & Johnson, 2019; Cramer et al., 2016)

Estimated amount that U.S. adults spend on mindfulness programs and apps each year
$2 billion

Percentage of the U.S. population that practice mindfulness meditation techniques
14%

Percentage of employers who offer mindfulness training
35% – 52%

(Gulens, 2022; Hassed, 2022; NCCIH, 2022; Singh, 2022; Smith, 2022; Korn, 2018; ABMP, 2016)

MINDFUL LIFE STRATEGIES

(Boyce et al., 2022; Gant, 2022; Ledesma et al., 2022; Adams, 2020; Decker, 2020)

Employ conscious awareness each morning—notice how you feel before starting the day. • Slow yourself down throughout the day. • Do nothing for at least 5 minutes each day. • Practice mindful breathing for 5 to 30 minutes throughout the day, especially before important tasks. • Inhale and exhale deeply and focus on your breath. • Take regular breaks from sitting at your desk. • Unplug from technology periodically throughout the day. • Eat lunch slowly, savoring every bite and body sensation. • Choose an object in your environment and observe it carefully for 60 seconds. • Take a slow 10-minute walk, synchronizing your breathing with your steps. • At the end of the day, reflect about the day, without judgment.

RESEARCH-SUPPORTED EFFECTS OF MINDFULNESS

Mindfulness appears to

- improve control over anxiety and related emotions
- promote more peaceful sleep
- improve functioning of the autonomic nervous system
- decrease rumination and other negative thinking
- improve occupational functioning
- lower stress
- improve decision making under stress
- heighten attention
- improve working memory and verbal reasoning
- improve functioning of the immune system
- increase enjoyment and experience of music
- decrease feelings of loneliness among older adults

(Bazzano et al., 2022; Gerszberg, 2022; Mirabito & Verhaeghen, 2022; Peters et al., 2022; Jha, 2021; Zhov et al., 2020)

family pedigree study A research design in which investigators determine how many and which relatives of a person with a disorder have the same disorder.

benzodiazepines The most common group of antianxiety drugs, which includes Valium and Xanax.

gamma-aminobutyric acid (GABA) A neurotransmitter whose low activity in the brain's fear circuit has been linked to anxiety.

brain circuits Networks of brain structures that work together, triggering each other into action.

The Biological Perspective

Biological theorists believe that generalized anxiety disorder is caused chiefly by biological factors. For years, this claim was supported primarily by **family pedigree studies,** in which researchers determine how many and which relatives of a person with a disorder have the same disorder. If biological tendencies toward generalized anxiety disorder are inherited, people who are biologically related should have similar probabilities of developing this disorder. Studies have in fact found that biological relatives of persons with generalized anxiety disorder are more likely than nonrelatives to have the disorder (Baldwin, 2023). And the closer the relative (an identical twin, for example), the greater the likelihood that the relative will also have the disorder.

Biological Explanations

In recent decades, important discoveries by brain researchers have offered clearer evidence that generalized anxiety disorder is related to biological factors. One of the first such discoveries was made in the 1950s, when investigators determined that **benzodiazepines,** the family of drugs that includes *alprazolam* (Xanax), *lorazepam* (Ativan), and *diazepam* (Valium), provide relief from anxiety. At first, no one understood why benzodiazepines reduce anxiety. Eventually, however, researchers were able to pinpoint the exact neurons in the brain to which benzodiazepines travel (Mohler & Okada, 1977). Apparently, certain neurons have receptors that receive the benzodiazepines, just as a lock receives a key.

Investigators then discovered that these benzodiazepine receptors ordinarily receive **gamma-aminobutyric acid (GABA),** a common neurotransmitter in the brain (Foitzick et al., 2020). As you read earlier in the textbook, neurotransmitters are chemicals that carry messages from one neuron to another. GABA carries *inhibitory* messages: when GABA is received at a receptor, it causes the neuron to stop firing (and, in turn, helps anxiety to subside). Thus, many researchers believe that GABA activity throughout the brain may be deficient in people with generalized anxiety disorder.

Although low GABA activity seems to play an important role in generalized anxiety disorder, a growing body of research on brain circuits indicates that the biological basis of this disorder is more complicated than the disturbed activity of this single neurotransmitter. As you read in the chapter on models of psychopathology, investigators now know that our everyday fear reactions—like most other emotional, behavioral, and cognitive reactions—are tied to **brain circuits,** networks of brain structures that work together, triggering each other into action. In a given brain circuit, the long axons of the neurons from one structure bundle together, extend across the brain, and use neurotransmitters to communicate with the neurons of another structure—thus setting up interconnecting fiber pathways between the structures. As you also read in that earlier chapter, the particular circuit that produces and manages fear reactions, often called the "fear circuit," includes such brain structures as the *prefrontal cortex, anterior cingulate cortex, insula,* and *amygdala,* a small almond-shaped brain structure that usually starts the emotional chain of events (Baldwin, 2023).

Studies reveal that the fear circuit is excessively active (that is, *hyperactive*) in people with generalized anxiety disorder, producing experiences of fear and worry that are excessive in number and duration. In turn, many theorists have concluded that such fear circuit hyperactivity is responsible for the development of the disorder (Bennett & Walkup, 2022; Ressler, 2020). GABA is one of the important neurotransmitters at work in this circuit, so low GABA activity could indeed help produce excessive communications between the structures in the brain circuit and so contribute to the development of generalized anxiety disorder (Sabihi et al., 2021). At the same time, improper functioning by various neurons, structures, interconnections, or other neurotransmitters throughout the fear circuit can also lead to broad circuit hyperactivity and contribute to the development of generalized anxiety disorder.

of NOTE ...

What is a Generic Drug?

Drug authorities choose a generic name for a psychotropic drug when it is first developed. Upon approval, the drug's manufacturer then has an exclusive right to sell it for a period of years under a trade (brand) name that it creates. When that right expires, competing companies may sell the drug either under its generic name or under trade names that they create.

Drug Therapies After they were discovered in the 1950s, benzodiazepines were marketed as **sedative-hypnotic drugs**—drugs that calm people in low doses and help them fall asleep in higher doses. The benzodiazepines seemed less addictive than previous sedative-hypnotic medications, such as *barbiturates*, and they appeared to produce less tiredness. Thus, these newly discovered drugs were quickly embraced by both doctors and patients, and many new ones were developed to help alleviate anxiety (see **Table 4-2**).

As you have read, researchers eventually learned that benzodiazepines reduce anxiety by traveling to neuron receptor sites in the brain circuit that ordinarily receive the neurotransmitter GABA. Apparently, when benzodiazepines bind to these receptor sites, they increase the ability of GABA itself to bind to the sites and to stop neurons from firing, thus helping to improve the overall functioning of the fear circuit and, in turn, reducing an individual's excessive levels of anxiety (Engin, 2023).

Studies indicate that as many as 60 percent of people with generalized anxiety disorder experience at least some improvement when they take benzodiazepines compared to 40 percent of similar individuals who take placebo drugs (Craske & Bystritsky, 2023; Healy, 2022). However, clinicians have come to realize that these drugs pose significant problems. First, the effects of the medications are short-lived. When they are stopped, anxiety returns as strong as ever. Second, people who take benzodiazepines in large doses for an extended time can become physically dependent on them. Third, the drugs can produce undesirable effects, such as drowsiness, lack of coordination, memory loss, depression, and aggressive behavior. Finally, the drugs mix badly with certain other drugs or substances. For example, if people on benzodiazepines drink even small amounts of alcohol, their breathing can slow down dangerously.

Thus, over the past two decades, other kinds of drugs have become more widely prescribed for people with generalized anxiety disorder (Craske & Bystritsky, 2023). The treatment of choice is now *antidepressant* medications, drugs that have been used for decades to lift the moods of people with depression. Like benzodiazepines, these drugs bring at least some relief to 60 percent of the people with generalized anxiety disorder who take them. As you will read in the chapter on depression, antidepressant drugs often increase the activity of the neurotransmitters *serotonin* and *norepinephrine*. These two neurotransmitters are prominent in certain parts of the fear circuit. The antidepressant drugs may help relieve anxiety by improving the functioning of the fear circuit in these areas. Finally, *antipsychotic* medications, drugs commonly given to people with schizophrenia and other forms of psychosis, are also helpful to some individuals with more severe and treatment-resistant generalized anxiety disorder.

Why are antianxiety drugs so popular in today's world? Does their popularity say something about our society?

TABLE 4-2

Common Benzodiazepine Drugs

Generic Name	Trade Name
Alprazolam	Xanax
Chlordiazepoxide	Librium
Clonazepam	Klonopin
Clorazepate	Tranxene
Diazepam	Valium
Estazolam	ProSom
Lorazepam	Ativan
Midazolam	Versed
Oxazepam	Serax

SUMMING UP

Generalized Anxiety Disorder

People with *generalized anxiety disorder* experience excessive anxiety and worry about a wide range of events and activities. According to the sociocultural view, societal dangers, economic stress, or related racial and cultural pressures may create a climate in which cases of generalized anxiety disorder are more likely to develop.

In the original psychodynamic explanation, Freud said that generalized anxiety may develop when anxiety is excessive and defense mechanisms break down and function poorly. Psychodynamic therapists use free association, interpretation, and related psychodynamic techniques to help people overcome this problem. The leading humanistic theorist, Carl Rogers, believed that people with generalized anxiety fail to

sedative-hypnotic drugs Drugs that calm people at lower doses and help them fall asleep at higher doses.

receive unconditional positive regard from significant others during their childhood and so become overly critical of themselves. He treated such individuals with client-centered therapy.

Cognitive-behavioral theorists believe that generalized anxiety disorder is caused by various maladaptive assumptions and/or inaccurate beliefs about the power and value of worrying. Cognitive-behavioral therapists help their clients to change their maladaptive thinking and/or dysfunctional uses of worrying.

Biological theorists hold that generalized anxiety disorder results from a hyperactive fear circuit in the brain. Common biological treatments are antidepressant drugs, benzodiazepines, and antipsychotic drugs.

Phobias

A PHOBIA IS a persistent and unreasonable fear of a particular object, activity, or situation. People with a phobia (from the Greek word for "fear") become fearful if they even think about the object or situation they dread, but they usually remain comfortable as long as they avoid it or thoughts about it. DSM-5-TR indicates that a phobia is more intense and persistent than other kinds of fears, and the desire to avoid the feared object or situation is stronger (APA, 2022). People with phobias often feel so much distress that their fears may interfere dramatically with their lives.

Most phobias technically fall under the category of *specific phobias,* DSM-5-TR's label for an intense and persistent fear of a specific object or situation. In addition, there is a broader kind of phobia called *agoraphobia,* a fear of venturing into public places or situations in which escape might be difficult if one were to become panicky or incapacitated.

TABLE 4-3

Dx Checklist

Specific Phobia
1. Marked, persistent, and disproportionate fear of a particular object or situation; usually lasting at least 6 months.
2. Exposure to the object produces immediate fear.
3. Avoidance of the feared situation.
4. Significant distress or impairment.

Information from: APA, 2022.

Specific Phobias

A **specific phobia** is a persistent fear of a specific object or situation (see **Table 4-3**). When people with a phobia are exposed to the feared object or situation, they typically experience immediate fear. Common specific phobias are intense fears of specific animals or insects, heights, enclosed spaces, thunderstorms, and blood. Here a clinician describes Waya, a 35-year-old client who had grappled with a phobia of dogs for the past 20 years:

> *Waya considered it ironic that his parents had named him after the Cherokee word for "wolf," given his terror of dogs. Whenever he'd hear barking, which was common in his neighborhood in Tahlequah, Oklahoma, his heart pounded and he had to stop what he was doing until the barking stopped, even if he was actually safe inside his home. He would practically run to and from his car to minimize the time spent outside, certain that a dog would attack him. He refused to participate in any outdoor activities. He never entered the houses of persons who owned a dog, and he had become estranged from several formerly close friends after those friends acquired pet dogs.*

phobia A persistent and unreasonable fear of a particular object, activity, or situation.

specific phobia A severe and persistent fear of a specific object or situation.

agoraphobia An anxiety disorder in which a person is afraid to be in public situations from which escape might be difficult or help unavailable if panic-like or embarrassing symptoms were to occur.

Each year, as many as 9 percent of all people in the United States have the symptoms of a specific phobia (APA, 2023; NIMH, 2023). Almost 13 percent of individuals develop such phobias at some point during their lives, and many people have more than one at a time. According to research conducted with mostly cisgender populations, women

Barcroft Media/Getty Images

Don't look down Although these young women cling tightly to each other, frozen with fear as they try to walk across a bridge, they are *not* displaying a phobia. A closer look reveals that the bridge, which stands 600 feet high and spans 1,000 feet, has a glass floor. Almost all visitors to this tourist destination in China initially experience the same emotional reaction—near-immobilizing fear.

with the disorder outnumber men by at least 2 to 1. Researchers have not yet determined the rate of the disorder for transgender people and nonbinary people.

The impact of a specific phobia on a person's life depends on what arouses the fear. People whose phobias center on dogs, insects, or water will keep encountering the objects they dread. Their efforts to avoid them must be elaborate and may greatly restrict their activities. Urban residents with snake phobias have a much easier time. At most, 32 percent of people with a specific phobia seek treatment (McCabe & Bui, 2023). Most individuals with the disorder try instead to avoid the objects they fear.

Agoraphobia

People with **agoraphobia** are afraid of being in public places or situations in which escape might be difficult or help unavailable if they experience panic or become incapacitated (APA, 2022) (see **Table 4-4**). This is a pervasive and complex phobia. Around 1 percent of the population experience agoraphobia in any given year; around 1.3 percent display it at some point in their lives (APA, 2023; NIMH, 2023). Research conducted with predominantly cisgender populations finds that women are twice as likely as men to develop the disorder. Its rate among transgender people and nonbinary people is not yet known. Around 46 percent of those with agoraphobia receive treatment for it (NIMH, 2023, 2017).

It is typical of people with agoraphobia to avoid entering crowded streets or stores, driving in parking lots or on bridges, and traveling on public transportation or in airplanes. If they venture out of the house at all, it is usually only in the company of close relatives or friends. Some insist that family members or friends stay with them at home, but even at home and in the company of others, they may continue to feel anxious.

In many cases, the intensity of the agoraphobia fluctuates. In severe cases, people become virtual prisoners in their own homes. Their social life dwindles, and they cannot hold a job. Many people with agoraphobia have extreme and sudden explosions of fear, called *panic attacks,* when they enter public places, attacks that may have first set the stage for their development of agoraphobia. Such individuals may receive two diagnoses—agoraphobia and *panic disorder,* an anxiety disorder that you will read about later in this chapter—because their difficulties extend considerably beyond an excessive fear of venturing away from home into public places (APA, 2022).

TABLE 4-4

Dx Checklist

Agoraphobia
1. Pronounced, disproportionate, or repeated fear about being in at least two of the following situations: • Public transportation (e.g., auto or plane travel) • Parking lots, bridges, or other open spaces • Shops, theaters, or other confined places • Lines or crowds • Away from home unaccompanied
2. Fear of such agoraphobic situations derives from a concern that it would be hard to escape or get help if panic, embarrassment, or disabling symptoms were to occur.
3. Avoidance of the agoraphobic situations.
4. Symptoms usually continue for at least 6 months.
5. Significant distress or impairment.

Information from: APA, 2022.

Dan Reynolds/CartoonStock Ltd.

What Causes Phobias?

Each of the models offers explanations for phobias. Those offered by *cognitive-behavioral* theorists have received the most research support. Focusing primarily on the behavioral dimension of this disorder, these theorists believe that people with phobias first learn to fear certain objects, situations, or events through conditioning. Once the fears are acquired, the individuals avoid the dreaded object or situation, permitting the fears to become all the more entrenched.

How Are Fears Learned?

Many cognitive-behavioral theorists propose that phobic reactions are commonly acquired through **classical conditioning** (Brewer et al., 2024). Here, two events that occur close together in time become strongly associated with each other in a person's mind, and the person then reacts similarly to both of them. If one event triggers a fear response, the other may trigger such a response as well.

In the 1920s, a clinician described the case of a young woman who apparently acquired a specific phobia of running water through classical conditioning (Bagby, 1922). At age 7, she went on a picnic with her mother and aunt and ran off by herself into the woods after lunch. While she was climbing over some large rocks, her feet became caught between two rocks. The harder she tried to free herself, the more trapped she became. No one heard her screams, and she grew more and more terrified. In the language of behaviorists, the entrapment was eliciting a fear response.

Entrapment → Fear response

As she struggled to free her feet, the girl heard a waterfall nearby. The sound of the running water became linked in her mind to her terrifying battle with the rocks, and she developed a fear of running water as well.

Running water → Fear response

Eventually, the aunt found the screaming child, freed her from the rocks, and comforted her, but the psychological damage had been done. From that day forward, the girl was terrified of running water. For years, family members had to hold her down to bathe her. When she traveled on a train, friends had to cover the windows so that she would not have to look at any streams. The young woman had apparently acquired a specific phobia through classical conditioning.

In conditioning terms, the entrapment was an *unconditioned stimulus* (*US*) that understandably elicited an *unconditioned response* (*UR*) of fear. The running water represented a *conditioned stimulus* (*CS*), a formerly neutral stimulus that became associated with entrapment in the child's mind and came also to elicit a fear reaction. The newly acquired fear was a *conditioned response* (*CR*).

US: Entrapment → UR: Fear

CS: Running water → CR: Fear

Another way of acquiring a fear reaction is through **modeling,** that is, through observation and imitation (Brewer et al., 2024; Bandura & Rosenthal, 1966). A person may observe that others are afraid of certain objects or events and develop fears of the same things. Consider a young child whose parent is afraid of illness, doctors, and hospitals. If the parent frequently expresses those fears, before long, the child may come to also fear illness, doctors, and hospitals.

Why should one or a few upsetting experiences or observations develop into a long-term phobia? Shouldn't the child recognize later that illnesses are temporary and doctors and hospitals are helpful? Cognitive-behavioral theorists believe that after acquiring a fear response, people try to *avoid* what they fear. They do not get close to the dreaded objects often enough to learn that the objects are really quite harmless.

classical conditioning A process of learning in which two events that repeatedly occur close together in time become tied together in a person's mind and so produce the same response.

modeling A process of learning in which a person observes and then imitates others. Also, a therapy approach based on the same principle.

preparedness A predisposition to develop certain fears.

How Have Cognitive-Behavioral Explanations Fared in Research? Some laboratory studies have found that animals and humans can indeed be taught to fear objects through classical conditioning (Brewer et al., 2024; Beckers et al., 2023). In one famous report, psychologists John B. Watson and Rosalie Rayner (1920) described how they taught a baby called Little Albert to fear white rats. For weeks, Albert was allowed to play with a white rat and appeared to enjoy doing so. One time when Albert reached for the rat, however, the experimenter struck a steel bar with a hammer, making a very loud noise that frightened Albert. The next several times that Albert reached for the rat, the experimenter again made the loud noise. Albert acquired a fear-and-avoidance response to the rat.

What concerns might today's human-participant research review boards raise about the study on Little Albert?

Research has also supported the cognitive-behavioral position that fears can be acquired through modeling. In a pioneering study, for example, psychologists Albert Bandura and Theodore Rosenthal (1966) had human research participants observe a person apparently being shocked by electricity whenever a buzzer sounded. The victim was actually the experimenter's accomplice—in research terminology, a *confederate*—who pretended to feel pain by twitching and yelling whenever the buzzer was turned on. After the unsuspecting participants had observed several such episodes, they themselves had a fear reaction whenever they heard the buzzer. Similarly, some studies on children with real-life fears and phobias have found that modeling played a key role in the acquisition of such problems (Bilodeau-Houle et al., 2023).

Although these studies support cognitive-behavioral explanations of phobias, other research has called those explanations into question (McCabe & Bui, 2023). Several laboratory studies with children and adults have failed to condition fear reactions. In addition, although many case studies have traced phobias to incidents of classical conditioning or modeling, quite a few fail to do so. So, although it appears that a phobia *can* be acquired by classical conditioning or modeling, researchers have not established that the disorder is *ordinarily* acquired in this way.

A Behavioral-Evolutionary Explanation Some phobias are much more common than others. Phobic reactions to animals, heights, and darkness are more common than phobic reactions to meat, grass, and houses. Theorists often account for these differences by proposing that human beings, as a species, have a predisposition to develop certain fears (McCabe & Bui, 2023; Coelho et al., 2021). This idea is referred to as **preparedness** because human beings, theoretically, are *prepared* to acquire some phobias and not others. The following case makes the point:

> *A 4-year-old girl was playing in the park. Thinking that she saw a snake, she ran to her parents' car and jumped inside, slamming the door behind her. Unfortunately, the girl's hand was caught by the closing car door, the results of which were severe pain and several visits to the doctor. Before this, she may have been afraid of snakes, but not phobic. After this experience, a phobia developed, not of cars or car doors, but of snakes. The snake phobia persisted into adulthood, at which time she sought treatment from me.*
>
> *(Marks, 1977, p. 192)*

Where might such predispositions to fear come from? According to some theorists, the predispositions have been transmitted genetically through an evolutionary process. Among our ancestors, the ones who more readily acquired fears of animals, darkness, heights, and the like were more likely to survive long enough to reproduce and to pass on their fear inclinations to their offspring (Koskinen & Hovatta, 2023; Coelho et al., 2021).

Courtesy Ko Kobayakawa

New best friends? Is a mouse's fear of cats a conditioned reaction or genetically hardwired? Scientists at Tokyo University used genetic engineering to switch off this rodent's instinct to cower at the smell or presence of cats. But mouse beware! The cat has not been genetically engineered correspondingly.

How Are Phobias Treated?

Every theoretical model has its own approach to treating phobias, but the cognitive-behavioral approach is more widely used and, according to research, more successful than the rest, particularly for specific phobias. Here again, practitioners of the model focus primarily on the behavioral dimension of phobias.

Treatments for Specific Phobias

Specific phobias were among the first anxiety disorders to be treated successfully. The major cognitive-behavioral approach to treating them is **exposure treatment,** an approach in which people are exposed to the objects or situations they dread (Banducci et al., 2023; McCabe & Bui, 2023). There are actually a number of different exposure techniques. Three of the oldest and best known are *systematic desensitization, flooding,* and *modeling.*

Ocean/Corbis

Recovering lost revenues Several amusement parks offer behavioral programs to help prospective customers overcome their fears of roller coasters and other horror rides. After "treatment," some clients are able to ride the rails with the best of them. For others, it's back to the relative calm of the merry-go-round.

People treated by **systematic desensitization,** an exposure technique developed by Joseph Wolpe (1987, 1969), learn to relax while gradually facing the objects or situations they fear. Since relaxation and fear are incompatible, the new relaxation response is thought to substitute for the fear response. Desensitization therapists first offer *relaxation training* to clients, teaching them how to bring on a state of deep muscle relaxation at will. In addition, the therapists help clients create a *fear hierarchy,* a list of feared objects or situations, ordered from mildly to extremely upsetting (Gega & Wright, 2022).

Then clients learn how to pair relaxation with the objects or situations they fear. While the client is in a state of relaxation, the therapist has the client face the event at the bottom of the hierarchy. This may be an actual confrontation, a process called *in vivo desensitization.* A person who fears heights, for example, may stand on a chair or climb a stepladder. Or the confrontation may be imagined, a process called *covert desensitization.* In this case, the person imagines the frightening event while the therapist describes it. The client moves through the entire list, pairing relaxation responses with each feared item. Because the first item is only mildly frightening, it is usually only a short while before the person is able to relax totally in its presence. Over the course of several sessions, clients move up the ladder of their fears until they reach and overcome the one that frightens them most of all.

Another exposure treatment for specific phobias is **flooding** (Samra & Abdijadid, 2023; Gega & Wright, 2022). Therapists who use flooding believe that people will stop fearing things when they are exposed to them repeatedly and made to see that they are actually quite harmless. Clients are forced to face their feared objects or situations without relaxation training and without a gradual buildup. The flooding procedure, like desensitization, can be either in vivo or covert.

When flooding therapists guide clients in imagining feared objects or situations, they often exaggerate the description so that the clients experience intense emotional arousal. In the case of a client with a snake phobia, the therapist had her imagine the following scene, among others:

> *Close your eyes again. Picture the snake out in front of you, now make yourself pick it up. Reach down, pick it up . . . and feel it wiggling around. Kind of explore its body with your fingers and hand. You don't like to do it, make yourself do it. Make yourself do it. Really grab onto the snake. Squeeze it a little bit, feel it. Feel it kind of start to wind around your hand. Let it. Leave your hand there, feel it touching your hand and winding around it, curling around your wrist.*
>
> *(Hogan, 1968, p. 423)*

exposure treatment Treatment in which clients are exposed to the objects or situations they dread.

systematic desensitization An exposure treatment that uses relaxation training and a fear hierarchy to help clients with phobias react calmly to the objects or situations they dread.

flooding An exposure treatment for phobias in which clients are exposed repeatedly and intensively to a feared object and made to recognize that it is actually harmless.

In another exposure technique, *modeling,* it is the therapist who confronts the feared object or situation while the fearful person observes (Krause & Askew, 2022). The therapist acts as a model to demonstrate that the person's fear is groundless. After several sessions, many clients are able to approach the objects or situations calmly. In one version of modeling, *participant modeling,* the client is actively encouraged to join in with the therapist.

Clinical researchers have repeatedly found that these and other exposure treatments help people with specific phobias. Around 70 percent of phobic patients show significant improvement after receiving exposure treatment (McCabe & Bui, 2023). The key to greater success in all forms of exposure treatment appears to be *actual* contact with the feared object or situation. That is, in vivo exposure tends to be more effective than covert exposure. It is also worth noting that a growing number of cognitive-behavioral therapists are using *virtual reality*—3D computer graphics that simulate real-world objects and situations—as an exposure tool and are having considerable success with this approach (Hawajri, Lindberg, & Suominem, 2023). You'll read more about this tool in the next chapter.

Debbie Egan-Chin/NY Daily News Archive via Getty Images

Slithering support Exposure techniques play varying roles in the clinical field. For example, exposure therapy helps people confront and overcome their fears in phobic, social anxiety, panic, and obsessive-compulsive disorders. Alternatively, in animal-assisted interventions, guided exposure produces positive feelings for people in need. Here, Beverly (right) derives pleasure and joy from handling and caressing a snake in a program designed to lift the spirits of residents at her senior living facility.

Treatments for Agoraphobia

Cognitive-behavioral therapists have also developed a variety of exposure approaches to help people overcome agoraphobia (Barnhill, 2023). These approaches are not always as beneficial to clients as the highly successful treatments for specific phobias, but they do offer considerable relief to many people. The therapists typically help clients to venture farther and farther from their homes and to gradually enter outside places, one step at a time. Sometimes the clinicians use support, reasoning, and coaxing to get clients to confront the outside world.

Exposure therapy for people with agoraphobia often includes supplementary features—particularly the use of *support groups* and *home-based self-help programs* (Manicavasagar & Silove, 2022). In the support group approach, a small number of people with agoraphobia go out together for exposure sessions that last for several hours. The group members support and encourage one another, and they eventually coax one another to move away from the safety of the group and perform exposure tasks on their own. In the home-based self-help programs, clinicians give clients and their families detailed instructions for carrying out exposure treatments themselves.

Around 70 percent of clients with agoraphobia who receive exposure treatment find it easier to enter public places, and the improvement persists for years (Craske, 2022; Manicavasagar & Silove, 2022). Unfortunately, these improvements are often partial rather than complete, and as many as half of successfully treated clients have relapses, although they readily recapture previous gains if they are treated again. Those whose agoraphobia is accompanied by a panic disorder seem to benefit less than others from exposure therapy alone. We will take a closer look at this group when we investigate treatments for panic disorder.

SUMMING UP

Phobias

A phobia is a severe, persistent, and unreasonable fear of a particular object, activity, or situation. The two main categories of phobias are specific phobias and agoraphobia. Cognitive-behavioral theorists believe that phobias are often learned from the environment through classical conditioning or modeling and maintained by avoidance behaviors.

Specific phobias have been treated most successfully with exposure techniques. The exposures may be gradual and relaxed (desensitization), intense (flooding), or observed (modeling). Agoraphobia is also treated effectively by exposure therapy.

Social Anxiety Disorder

Kevin Winter/Getty Images

Behind the scenes Actress and singer Zendaya accepts an Emmy award in 2022 for her role on the series *Euphoria*. Although she exudes an air of steady confidence and composure in her many undertakings, the celebrated star has struggled with significant anxiety and self-doubt throughout her career, especially when performing live. In posts and interviews, she talks openly about her condition and treatment and encourages others with similar difficulties to also seek therapy.

MANY PEOPLE ARE UNCOMFORTABLE when interacting with others or talking or performing in front of others. A number of entertainers and sports figures have described episodes of significant anxiety before performing, including singers Adele, Harry Styles, and Rihanna; actress Jennifer Lawrence; and tennis player Naomi Osaka. Social fears of this kind certainly are unpleasant, but usually the people who have them manage to function adequately.

People with **social anxiety disorder,** by contrast, have severe, persistent, and irrational anxiety about social or performance situations in which they may face scrutiny by others and possibly feel embarrassment (APA, 2022) (see **Table 4-5**). The social anxiety may be narrow, such as a fear of talking in public or eating in front of others, or it may be broad, such as a general fear of functioning poorly in front of others. In both forms, people repeatedly judge themselves as performing less competently than they actually do (see ***MindTech***). The disorder tends to begin in late childhood or adolescence and may continue into adulthood (Schneier, 2023).

Social anxiety disorder can interfere greatly with one's life (Schneier, 2023). A person who cannot interact with others or speak in public may fail to carry out important responsibilities. One who cannot eat in public may reject meal invitations and other social offerings. Since many people with this disorder keep their fears secret, their social reluctance is often misinterpreted as snobbery, lack of interest, or hostility.

Surveys reveal that 7 percent of people in the United States and other Western countries experience social anxiety disorder in any given year, and 12 percent develop it at some point in their lives (APA, 2023; NIMH, 2023) (see **Table 4-6**). According to research conducted with mostly cisgender populations, women diagnosed with this disorder outnumber men 3 to 2 (APA, 2022). Clinicians suspect that the rate of the disorder is higher for transgender people and nonbinary people than for cisgender people, but there have been few studies on this belief (Morandini et al., 2023; Pinciotti et al., 2022). People with lower incomes are more likely than people with higher incomes to have social anxiety disorder. Non-Hispanic White Americans are more likely to experience the problem than people of color (APA, 2022; Cuncic, 2020). Around 40 percent of people with the disorder are currently in treatment (NIMH, 2023, 2017).

What Causes Social Anxiety Disorder?

The leading explanation for social anxiety disorder has been proposed by cognitive-behavioral theorists (Hofmann, 2023). The explanation features an interplay of both cognitive and behavioral factors. As you read in the chapter on models of

TABLE 4-5

Dx Checklist

Social Anxiety Disorder
1. Pronounced, disproportionate, and repeated anxiety about social situation(s) in which the individual could be exposed to possible scrutiny by others; typically lasting six months or more.
2. Fear of being negatively evaluated by or offensive to others.
3. Exposure to the social situation almost always produces anxiety.
4. Avoidance of feared situations.
5. Significant distress or impairment.

Information from: APA, 2022.

social anxiety disorder A severe and persistent fear of social or performance situations in which embarrassment may occur.

psychopathology, cognitive-behavioral theorists start with the contention that people with this disorder hold a group of dysfunctional beliefs and expectations regarding the social realm. These can include the following:

- Holding unrealistically high social standards and so believing that they must perform perfectly in social situations.
- Believing that they are unattractive social beings.
- Believing that they are socially unskilled and inadequate.
- Believing that they are always in danger of behaving incompetently in social situations.
- Believing that inept behaviors in social situations will inevitably lead to terrible consequences.
- Believing that they have no control over the feelings of anxiety that emerge in social situations.

Cognitive-behavioral theorists hold that, because of these beliefs, people with social anxiety disorder keep anticipating that social disasters will occur, overestimate how poorly things go in their social interactions, and dread most social situations (Hofmann, 2023; Nordhal & Wells, 2022). Moreover, they learn to perform "avoidance" and "safety" behaviors to help prevent or reduce such disasters (Swee, Wilmer, & Heimberg, 2022). Avoidance behaviors include, for example, avoiding parties or avoiding interactions with new coworkers or acquaintances. Safety behaviors include wearing makeup to cover up blushing or gloves to hide shaking hands. Behaviors of this kind are reinforced by reducing feelings of anxiety and the number of awkward encounters.

Mike Gruhn/CartoonStock Ltd.

Researchers have found that people with social anxiety disorder do indeed manifest the beliefs, expectations, interpretations, feelings, and behaviors listed above (Swee et al., 2022). These dysfunctional cognitions and behaviors have been tied to factors such as genetic predispositions, trait tendencies, biological irregularities, traumatic childhood experiences, and overprotective parent–child interactions (Schneier, 2023).

Treatments for Social Anxiety Disorder

Effective treatment for social anxiety disorder has been made possible by a growing recognition that the disorder has two distinct features that may feed upon each other: (1) people with the disorder have overwhelming social fears, and (2) they often lack skill at starting conversations, communicating their needs, or meeting the needs of others.

TABLE 4-6

Profile of Anxiety Disorders and Obsessive-Compulsive Disorder

	One-Year Prevalence	Typical Age at Onset	Prevalence Among Close Relatives	Percentage Receiving Clinical Treatment Currently
Generalized anxiety disorder	3.0%	0–35 years	Elevated	43%
Specific phobia	9.0%	Variable	Elevated	32%
Agoraphobia	1.0%	15–35 years	Elevated	46%
Social anxiety disorder	7.0%	10–20 years	Elevated	40%
Panic disorder	3.1%	15–35 years	Elevated	59%
Obsessive-compulsive disorder	1.0%–2.0%	4–25 years	Elevated	40%

Information from: APA, 2023; Baldwin, 2023; McCabe & Bui, 2023; NAMI, 2023; NIMH, 2023, 2017; Schneier, 2023; Simpson, 2023; ADAA, 2022; Roy-Byrne, 2022; Wang et al., 2005.

MINDTECH

Social Media Jitters

Researchers have learned that the use of computers and mobile devices can unintentionally produce various forms of anxiety, including social and generalized anxiety. The biggest culprit here seems to be spending too much time on social media such as TikTok, Instagram, Snapchat, X, or Facebook. On the positive side, frequenting social network sites helps many people feel supported and included, but for others, it seems to produce significant insecurities and fears (Anto et al., 2023; Ren & Yan, 2022). Surveys suggest, for example, that more than one-third of social networkers develop a fear that others will post or use information or photos of them without their permission. In addition, one-fourth of all users feel a constant pressure to disclose too much personal information to their social networks, and a number feel intense pressure to post material that will be popular and get numerous comments and "likes." More than a few users also worry that they will discover posts about social activities from which they were excluded.

Geoff Smith/Alamy

Studies indicate that one-third of users may feel distinctly worse immediately after visiting their social network—more anxious, more envious, and more dissatisfied with their lives (Anto et al., 2023; Abi-Jaoude, Naylor, & Pignatiello, 2020). These feelings are particularly triggered when users observe vacation photos of other users, read birthday greetings received by other users, and see how many "likes" or comments others receive for their postings or photos. Such experiences seem to lead some users to worry that they are less desirable, less interesting, or less capable than most other social media users (Barsova et al., 2022; Chen & Xiao, 2022).

Of course, many of today's users do feel more positive about their social network visits. But even these people may have some social network–induced anxiety and tension. Around two-thirds, for example, are truly afraid that they will miss something if they don't check their social networks constantly—the phenomenon known as FOMO ("fear of missing out") (Anto et al., 2023; Li et al., 2022).

Social media is not the only digital source of anxiety. Studies show that excessive screen time and smartphone use often results in high levels of anxiety and tension (Barsova et al., 2022; ProCon, 2022). Why? Some theorists speculate that frequent phone users feel obligated to stay in touch with friends, another version of FOMO. Others believe that the rise in anxiety among heavy phone users is really the result of other smartphone-related effects, such as academic difficulties, loss of sleep, or a reduction in positive time spent alone and self-reflecting (Azhari et al., 2022). Whatever the explanation, two-thirds of smartphone users report feeling "panicked" when they misplace or lose their phones, even for a few minutes. Many experience *nomophobia* (no-mobile-phone-phobia), or the rush of fear that people have when they realize that they are disconnected from the world, friends, and family (Abdoli et al., 2023).

Armed with this insight, clinicians treat social anxiety disorder by trying to reduce social fears, by providing training in social skills, or both.

How Can Social Fears Be Reduced?

Medication often helps alleviate social fears (Healy, 2022; Stein, 2022). Such fears are reduced to some degree in 55 percent of those who take either benzodiazepines or antidepressant drugs, compared to 24 percent who take placebo drugs. It appears that these medications bring about relief by improving functioning in the brain's fear circuit, which tends to be hyperactive for people with social anxiety disorder, just as it is in cases of generalized anxiety disorder (Stein, 2022; Lai, 2020).

At the same time, cognitive-behavioral therapy has proved to be at least as effective as medication at reducing social fears, and people helped by this approach seem less likely to relapse than those treated with medications alone (Hofmann, 2023; Stein & Taylor, 2022). This finding suggests to some clinicians that this form of therapy should always be featured in the treatment of social fears, either alone or in combination with medication.

To undo the cycle of problematic social beliefs and behaviors described earlier, cognitive-behavioral therapists combine both behavioral and cognitive techniques (Nordhal & Wells, 2022; Swee et al., 2022). On the behavioral side, they conduct *exposure therapy,* the intervention so effective with phobias. The therapists encourage clients to expose themselves to their dreaded social situations and to remain in these situations as their fears subside. Usually the exposure is gradual, and it often includes homework assignments. On the cognitive side, the clinicians and clients have systematic therapy discussions in which the clients are guided to reexamine and challenge their maladaptive beliefs and expectations, given the less-than-dire outcomes of their social exposures.

How Can Social Skills Be Improved?

In **social skills training,** also conducted by cognitive-behavioral therapists, several techniques are combined. The therapists usually *model* appropriate social behaviors for clients and encourage the individuals to try them out. The clients then *role-play* with the therapists, *rehearsing* their new behaviors until they become more effective. Throughout the process, therapists provide frank *feedback* and *reinforce* (praise) the clients for effective performances.

Reinforcement from other people with similar social difficulties is often more powerful than reinforcement from a therapist alone. Thus, in *social skills training groups* and *assertiveness training groups,* members try out and rehearse new social behaviors with other group members. Such groups also provide guidance on what is socially appropriate. According to research, social skills training, in both individual and group formats, has helped many people perform better in social situations (Cuncic, 2023; Moore, 2023).

of NOTE ...

Their Words

"There are two types of speakers. Those who get nervous and those who are liars."

Mark Twain

SUMMING UP

Social Anxiety Disorder

People with social anxiety disorder experience severe and persistent anxiety about social or performance situations in which they may be scrutinized by others or be embarrassed. Cognitive-behavioral theorists believe that the disorder is particularly likely to develop among people who hold certain dysfunctional social beliefs and expectations and learn to perform corresponding avoidance and safety behaviors. Therapists who treat this disorder try to reduce social fears by drug therapy and/or cognitive-behavioral therapy (including exposure techniques). They may try to improve social skills by social skills training.

Panic Disorder

SOMETIMES AN ANXIETY REACTION takes the form of a smothering, nightmarish panic in which people lose control of their behavior and, in fact, are practically unaware of what they are doing. Anyone can react with panic when a real threat looms up suddenly. Some people, however, experience **panic attacks**—periodic, short bouts of panic that occur suddenly, reach a peak within minutes, and gradually pass (APA, 2022). The attacks feature at least four of the following symptoms of panic: palpitations of the heart, tingling in the hands or feet, shortness of breath, sweating, hot and cold flashes, trembling, chest pains, choking sensations, faintness, dizziness, and a feeling

social skills training A therapy approach that helps people learn or improve social skills and assertiveness through role-playing and rehearsing of desirable behaviors.

panic attacks Periodic, short bouts of panic that occur suddenly, reach a peak within minutes, and gradually pass.

AP Photo/Hendra Permana

Panic's aftermath A pair of trampled shoes sits in the stands of Kanjuruhan Stadium in Malang, Indonesia, following a deadly stampede by soccer fans in 2022. The tragedy began when police fired tear gas to disperse agitated fans. In turn, panic ensued, and thousands bolted frantically for the exits. At least 135 fans were killed and hundreds more seriously injured as a result of stampeding and crushing. Such catastrophes remind us that people with panic disorder are not the only ones to experience panic.

of unreality. Small wonder that during a panic attack, many people fear they will die, "go crazy," or lose control. Val, a 32-year-old woman who has been having panic attacks for six years, describes her first episode:

> *It was so weird because the first panic attack hit at a time in my life when I was finally feeling comfortable with myself and free. I'd finished my gender confirmation treatments and was, for the first time ever, living as who I really am; my mom had been nothing but supportive; and earlier that night I'd been on a great first date with someone I really liked. I came home from the date, and as I was about to call my sister to talk about it, I suddenly started sweating, like a lot, and my hands began to shake. I could feel my heart racing, and I couldn't catch my breath. I thought I was about to die, and I felt a wave of terror that just grew and grew. My body, my mind, my everything felt totally out of control. For some reason, I thought a glass of water might save my life, but when I stood up to get it, I felt dizzy and numb all over and knew I had to sit back down immediately. As I sat there, praying this would pass, I felt hot everywhere and caught myself thinking, "At least I'll leave this life as me." That sounds silly to me now, thinking back on it. Eventually, I was able to take a couple of deep breaths and steady my hands enough to call an ambulance.*

TABLE 4-7

Dx Checklist

Panic Disorder
1. Unforeseen panic attacks occur repeatedly.
2. One or more of the attacks precede either of the following symptoms: (a) At least a month of continual concern about having additional attacks. (b) At least a month of dysfunctional behavior changes associated with the attacks (for example, avoiding new experiences).

Information from: APA, 2022.

Approximately one-third of all people have one or more panic attacks at some point in their lives (Roy-Byrne, 2022). Some people, however, have such attacks repeatedly and unexpectedly and for no apparent reason. They may be experiencing **panic disorder.** In addition to the panic attacks, people who are diagnosed with panic disorder experience dysfunctional changes in their thinking or behavior as a result of the attacks (see **Table 4-7**). They may, for example, worry persistently about having additional attacks, have concerns about what such attacks mean ("Am I losing my mind?"), or plan their lives around the possibility of future attacks (APA, 2022).

Around 3 percent of all people in the United States experience panic disorder in a given year; 5 percent develop it at some point in their lives (APA, 2023; ADAA, 2022). The disorder tends to develop in late adolescence or early adulthood. Clinical observations suggest that the rate of the disorder is higher for transgender people and nonbinary people than for cisgender people, but systematic research on these observations is lacking (Morandini et al., 2023; Nicdao et al., 2023; Pinna et al., 2022). According to studies conducted with predominantly cisgender populations, the disorder is at least twice as common among women as among men. Non-Hispanic White Americans are more likely to experience panic disorder than people of color (APA, 2022). And people with lower incomes are more likely to experience the disorder than are those of greater affluence (APA, 2022). Surveys indicate that 59 percent of people with this disorder in the United States are currently in treatment (NIMH, 2023, 2017).

As you read earlier, panic disorder is often accompanied by agoraphobia, the broad phobia in which people are afraid to travel to public places where escape might be difficult if they have panic symptoms or become incapacitated. In such cases, the panic disorder typically sets the stage for the development of agoraphobia. That is, after experiencing multiple unpredictable panic attacks, a person becomes increasingly fearful of having new attacks in public places.

panic disorder An anxiety disorder marked by recurrent and unpredictable panic attacks.

locus coeruleus A small area of the brain that seems to be active in the regulation of emotions. Many of its neurons use norepinephrine.

The Biological Perspective

Over the past 60 years, researchers have learned that panic disorder has biological underpinnings and can respond to biological treatments. Researchers began their journey in the 1960s, when they discovered that the symptoms of this disorder were sometimes alleviated by *antidepressant drugs,* specifically those antidepressant drugs that increase the activity of the neurotransmitter *norepinephrine* throughout the brain (Klein & Fink, 1962).

What Biological Factors Contribute to Panic Disorder?

Given that norepinephrine-enhancing drugs were so helpful in eliminating panic attacks, the researchers initially suspected that panic disorder might be caused by atypical activity of norepinephrine, particularly in a brain structure called the **locus coeruleus**—an area rich in neurons that use norepinephrine. However, research eventually clarified that the root of panic attacks is more complicated than a single neurotransmitter or a single brain structure. It turns out that panic reactions are produced by a brain circuit—often called the "panic circuit"—consisting of structures such as the *amygdala, hippocampus, ventromedial nucleus of the hypothalamus, central gray matter,* and *locus coeruleus* (Kyriakoulis & Kyrios, 2023) (see **Figure 4-2**). When a person confronts a frightening object or situation, the amygdala is stimulated. In turn,

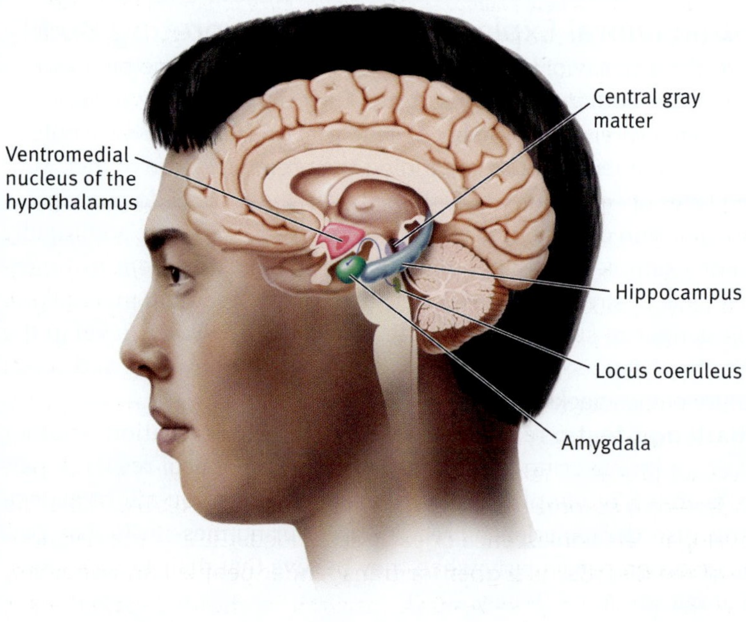

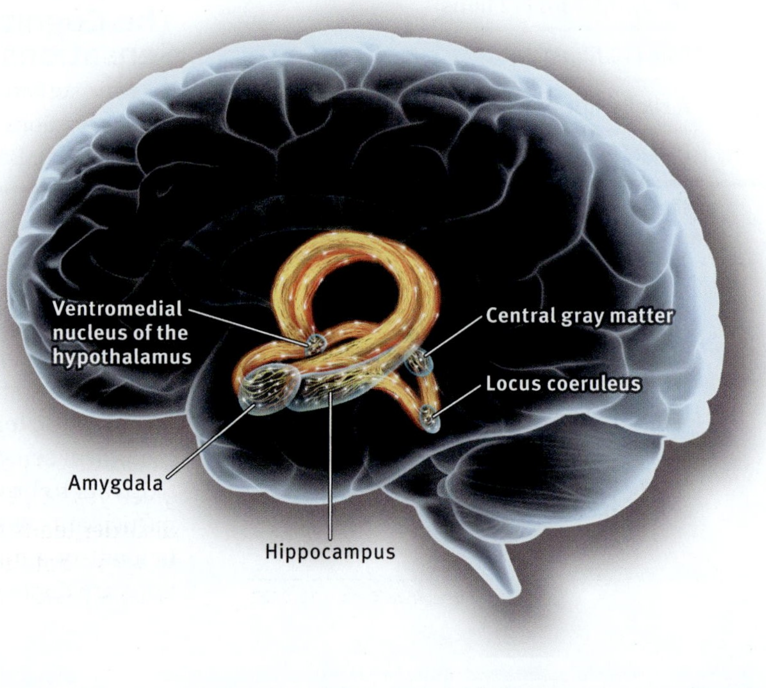

FIGURE 4-2

The Biology of Panic

The brain circuit that helps produce panic reactions includes structures such as the amygdala, hippocampus, ventromedial nucleus of the hypothalamus, central gray matter, and locus coeruleus (left). The illustration on the right highlights how the structures of this circuit work together and trigger each other into action to produce panic reactions. The long axons of the neurons from each structure form fiberlike pathways across the brain that extend to the other structures in the circuit.

the amygdala stimulates the other structures in the brain circuit, temporarily setting into motion an "alarm and escape" response (increased heart rate, respiration, blood pressure, and the like) that is very similar to a panic reaction. Most of today's researchers believe that this brain circuit is hyperactive in people who display panic disorder (Roy-Byrne, 2022).

Why might some people have hyperactive panic circuits and be prone to the development of panic disorder? One possibility is that a predisposition to develop such irregularities is inherited. Once again, if a genetic factor is at work, close relatives should have higher rates of panic disorder than more distant relatives. Studies do find that among identical twins (twins who share all their genes), if one twin has panic disorder, the other twin has the same disorder in 31 percent of cases (Kyriakoulis & Kyrios, 2023). Among fraternal twins (who share only some of their genes), if one twin has panic disorder, the other twin has the same disorder in, at most, only 11 percent of cases.

Drug Therapies

Ever since researchers discovered in 1962 that certain antidepressant drugs could prevent or reduce panic attacks, studies across the world have repeatedly confirmed this initial observation. Various antidepressant drugs bring at least some improvement to more than two-thirds of people who have panic disorder, and the improvement can last indefinitely, as long as the drugs are continued (Healy, 2022; Roy-Byrne & Craske, 2022). These antidepressant drugs appear to prevent or reduce panic attacks by increasing the activity of the neurotransmitters *serotonin* and *norepinephrine* in the locus coeruleus and other parts of the panic circuit, thus helping to correct the brain circuit's tendency to be hyperactive. Researchers have also discovered that certain benzodiazepine drugs can be effective in many cases of panic disorder, although they are used less often than antidepressants because of their potential for producing physical dependence and other risks (Healy, 2022). These various antidepressant drugs and benzodiazepines also seem to be helpful in cases of panic disorder accompanied by agoraphobia.

of NOTE ...

Top Fear Film Franchises

Halloween (13 films)

Friday the 13th (12 films)

Saw (10 films)

A Nightmare on Elm Street (9 films)

Child's Play (8 films)

The Conjuring (8 films)

The Cognitive-Behavioral Perspective

Cognitive-behavioral theorists argue that biological factors are but one part of the cause of panic attacks. In their view, full panic reactions are experienced only by people who further *misinterpret* the physiological events that are taking place within their bodies. Cognitive-behavioral treatments are aimed at correcting such misinterpretations.

The Cognitive-Behavioral Explanation: Misinterpreting Bodily Sensations

Cognitive-behavioral theorists believe that panic-prone people may be very sensitive to certain bodily sensations; when they unexpectedly experience such sensations, they misinterpret them as signs of a medical catastrophe (Kyriakoulis & Kyrios, 2023; Bailey, 2022). Rather than understanding the probable cause of their sensations as "something I ate" or "an argument with the boss," those prone to panic grow increasingly upset about losing control, fear the worst, lose all perspective, and rapidly plunge into panic. For example, many people with panic disorder seem to "overbreathe," or *hyperventilate,* in stressful situations. The irregular breathing makes them think that they are in danger of suffocation, so they panic. They further develop the belief that these and other "dangerous" sensations may return at any time and so set themselves up for future panic attacks.

In **biological challenge tests,** researchers produce hyperventilation or other biological sensations by administering drugs or by instructing clinical research participants to breathe, exercise, or simply think in certain ways. As you might expect, participants with panic disorder experience greater upset during these tests than participants without the disorder, particularly when they believe that their bodily sensations are dangerous or out of control (Bailey, 2022).

Why might some people be prone to such misinterpretations? One possibility is that panic-prone individuals actually experience more frequent, confusing, or intense bodily sensations than other people do (Kyriakoulis & Kyrios, 2023). Indeed, the kinds of sensations that are most often misinterpreted in panic disorders seem to be carbon dioxide increases in the blood, shifts in blood pressure, and rises in heart rate, bodily events that are controlled in part by the brain's panic circuit—and, as you may recall, the panic circuit is overactive in people with panic disorder. Another possibility, supported by some research, is that panic-prone people have had more trauma-filled events over the course of their lives than other people, leading to higher expectations of catastrophe (Craske, 2022). Whatever the precise cause of such misinterpretations may be, once they take hold, they increasingly guide behaviors and choices in life. For example, panic-prone people may learn to display avoidance and safety behaviors that help control their bodily sensations. They may repeatedly hold onto people or objects to avoid feeling faint, or they may move slowly or sit still much of the time to avoid upsetting increases in heart rate. Given such misinterpretations, it is not surprising that people who are panic-prone generally have a high degree of what is called **anxiety sensitivity;** that is, they focus on their bodily sensations much of the time, are unable to assess them logically, and interpret them as potentially harmful (Bailey, 2022).

biological challenge test A procedure used to produce panic in participants or clients by having them exercise vigorously or perform some other potentially panic-inducing task in the presence of a researcher or therapist.

anxiety sensitivity A tendency to focus on one's bodily sensations, assess them illogically, and interpret them as harmful.

Cognitive-Behavioral Therapy

Cognitive-behavioral therapists use a combination of techniques to correct people's misinterpretations of their bodily sensations (Kyriakoulis & Kyrios, 2023; Craske, 2022). First, they educate clients about the general nature of panic attacks, the actual causes of bodily sensations, and the tendency of the clients to misinterpret their sensations. Next, they teach the clients to apply more accurate interpretations during stressful situations, thus short-circuiting the panic sequence at an early point. The therapists may also teach the clients ways to cope better with anxiety—for example, by using relaxation and breathing techniques—and to distract themselves from their sensations, perhaps by striking up a conversation with someone.

In addition, cognitive-behavioral therapists often use biological challenge procedures to induce panic sensations so that clients can apply their new interpretations and skills under watchful supervision (Bailey, 2022). Clients whose attacks typically are triggered by a rapid heart rate, for example, may be instructed to jump up and down for several minutes or to run up a flight of stairs. They can then practice interpreting the resulting sensations appropriately, without dwelling on them.

According to research, cognitive-behavioral treatment often helps people with panic disorder (Kyriakoulis & Kyrios, 2023; Craske, 2022). In studies across the world, at least two-thirds of participants who receive this treatment have become free of panic, compared with only 13 percent of control participants. Cognitive-behavioral therapy has proved to be at least as helpful as antidepressant drugs or benzodiazepines in the treatment of panic disorder, sometimes even more so (Roy-Byrne & Craske, 2022). In view of the effectiveness of both cognitive-behavioral and drug treatments, many clinicians have tried, with some success, to combine them. Similarly, research suggests that cognitive-behavioral therapy, drug therapy, or a combination of these approaches is helpful to those who display both panic disorder and agoraphobia (Roy-Byrne, 2022).

Richard Baker/In Pictures via Getty Images

LED tranquility London's popular Room to Breathe exhibition helps visitors develop new methods for managing anxiety. The exhibition's floor-through-ceiling LED screens, sized 20,000 square feet, make use of color, guided imagery, and music to teach deep breathing techniques to visitors, helping them gain control over anxiety-linked sensations throughout their bodies.

SUMMING UP

Panic Disorder

Panic attacks are periodic, discrete bouts of panic that occur suddenly. People with panic disorder experience panic attacks repeatedly and unexpectedly and without apparent reason. Panic disorder may be accompanied by agoraphobia in some cases, leading to two diagnoses.

Many biological theorists believe that panic disorder is caused by a hyperactive panic circuit in the brain. Biological therapists use certain antidepressant drugs or benzodiazepines to treat people with this disorder.

Cognitive-behavioral theorists suggest that panic-prone people become preoccupied with some of their bodily sensations, misinterpret them as signs of medical catastrophe, have panic attacks, learn to display avoidance and safety behaviors that help control their bodily sensations, and in some cases develop panic disorder. Cognitive-behavioral therapists teach clients to interpret their physical sensations more accurately and to cope better with anxiety.

Obsessive-Compulsive Disorder

OBSESSIONS ARE PERSISTENT thoughts, ideas, impulses, or images that seem to invade a person's consciousness. **Compulsions** are repetitive and rigid behaviors or mental acts that people feel they must perform in order to prevent or reduce anxiety. As **Figure 4-3** indicates, minor obsessions and compulsions are familiar to almost everyone. You may find yourself filled with thoughts about an upcoming performance or exam or keep wondering whether you forgot to turn off the stove or lock the door. You may feel better when you avoid stepping on cracks, turn away from black cats, or arrange your closet in a particular manner. Repetitive thoughts or behaviors of this kind, however, are hardly a reflection of psychopathology.

According to DSM-5-TR, a diagnosis of **obsessive-compulsive disorder** is called for when obsessions or compulsions feel excessive or unreasonable, cause great distress, take up much time, and interfere with daily functions (see **Table 4-8**). Although obsessive-compulsive disorder is not classified as an anxiety disorder in DSM-5-TR, anxiety does play a major role in this pattern. The obsessions cause intense anxiety, while the compulsions are aimed at preventing or reducing anxiety (APA, 2022). In addition, anxiety rises if the individuals try to resist their obsessions or compulsions. An individual with this disorder observed, "I can't get to sleep unless I am sure everything in the house is in its proper place so that when I get up in the morning, the house is organized. I work like mad to set everything straight before I go to bed, but, when I get up in the morning, I can think of a thousand things that I ought to do. . . . I can't stand to know something needs doing and I haven't done it" (McNeil, 1967, pp. 26–28).

Around 1.2 percent of the people in the United States and other countries throughout the world experience obsessive-compulsive disorder in any given year (NIMH, 2023; Simpson, 2023). Approximately 2.3 percent develop the disorder at some point during their lives. The rate of obsessive-compulsive disorder for transgender and nonbinary people is not yet known. Research conducted with mostly cisgender populations finds

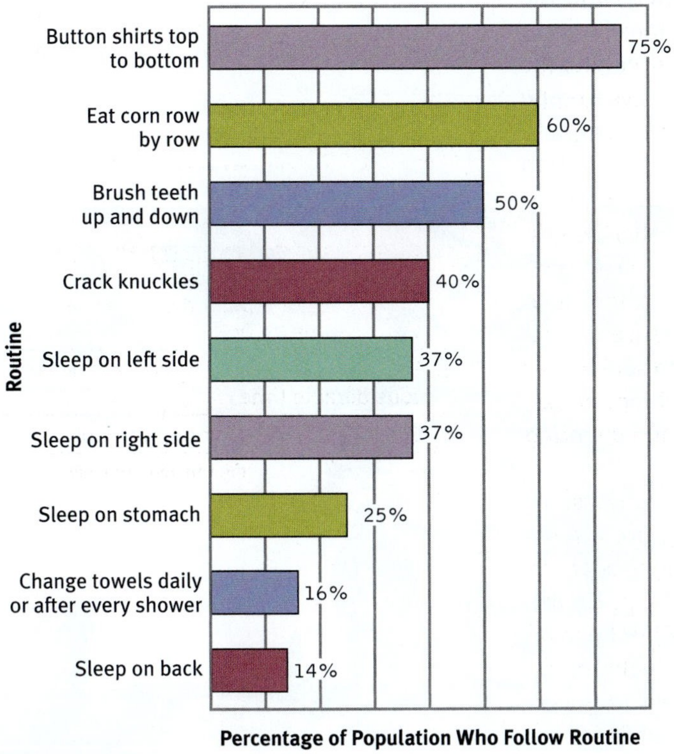

FIGURE 4-3

Common Routines

Most people find it comforting to follow set routines when they carry out everyday activities, and some become irritated if they must depart from their routines. (Information from: Purple.com, 2022; Crupain, 2017; Kanner, 2005, 1998, 1995.)

that the disorder is equally common for men and women. It is also equally prevalent across people of different races and ethnic groups and people of different sexual orientations. The disorder usually begins by childhood or young adulthood and typically persists for many years, although its symptoms and their severity may fluctuate over time (ADAA, 2022; Rosenberg, 2022). It is estimated that 40 percent of people with obsessive-compulsive disorder seek treatment, many for an extended period (NIMH, 2023, 2017; Swierkosz-Lenart et al., 2023).

obsession A persistent thought, idea, impulse, or image that is experienced repeatedly, feels intrusive, and causes anxiety.

compulsion A repetitive and rigid behavior or mental act that a person feels driven to perform in order to prevent or reduce anxiety.

obsessive-compulsive disorder A disorder in which a person has recurrent obsessions, compulsions, or both.

What Are the Features of Obsessions and Compulsions?

Obsessive thoughts feel both intrusive and foreign to the people who experience them. Attempts to ignore or resist these thoughts may arouse even more anxiety, and before long, they come back more strongly than ever. People with obsessions typically are quite aware that their thoughts are excessive.

Certain basic themes run through the thoughts of most people troubled by obsessive thinking (APA, 2022). The most common theme appears to be dirt or contamination (Forrester, 2022). Other common themes are violence and aggression, orderliness, religion, and sexuality. The prevalence of such themes may vary from culture to culture (Simpson, 2023). Religious obsessions, for example, seem to be more common in cultures or countries with strict moral codes and religious values.

Compulsions are similar to obsessions in many ways. For example, although compulsive behaviors are technically under voluntary control, the people who feel they must do them have little sense of choice in the matter. Most of these individuals recognize that their behavior is unreasonable, but they believe at the same time that something terrible will happen if they don't perform the compulsions. After performing a compulsive act, they usually feel less anxious for a short while. For some people, the compulsive acts develop into detailed *rituals*. They must go through the ritual in exactly the same way every time, according to certain rules.

Like obsessions, compulsions take various forms. *Cleaning compulsions* are very common. People with these compulsions feel compelled to keep cleaning themselves, their clothing, or their homes. The cleaning may follow ritualistic rules and be repeated dozens or hundreds of times a day. People with *checking compulsions* check the same items over and over—door locks, gas taps, important papers—to make sure that all is as it should be. Another common compulsion is the constant effort to seek *order* or *balance*. People with this compulsion keep placing certain items (clothing, books, foods) in perfect order in accordance with strict rules. *Touching, verbal,* and *counting* compulsions are also common.

Although some people with obsessive-compulsive disorder experience obsessions only or compulsions only, most experience both. In fact, compulsive acts are often a response to obsessive thoughts. In many cases, for example, compulsions seem to represent a *yielding* to obsessive doubts, ideas, or urges. A person who keeps doubting that their home is secure may yield to that obsessive doubt by repeatedly checking locks and gas jets, or a person who obsessively fears contamination may yield to that fear by performing cleaning rituals. In other cases, compulsions help *control* obsessions. The interplay of obsessions and compulsions is apparent in the case of Darcy:

TABLE 4-8

Dx Checklist

Obsessive-Compulsive Disorder
1. Occurrence of repeated obsessions, compulsions, or both.
2. The obsessions or compulsions take up considerable time.
3. Significant distress or impairment.

Information from: APA, 2022.

Now 37, Darcy reckoned that she had begun having obsessions around age 9. . . . She had fears of being hit by a speeding car if she stepped off the curb. She feared that [her] friends would be kidnapped by bad people. And she was terrified that, if she didn't do an elaborate prayer routine at night, all manner of terrible things would befall her family.

(continued on the next page)

> *The prayer routine . . . grew to gigantic proportions, containing many rules and restrictions. Darcy believed that she had to repeat each family member's full name 15 times, say a sentence that asked for each person to be kept safe, promise God that she would improve herself, clap her hands 20 times for each person, kneel down and get up 5 times, and then put her hands into a prayer position while bowing. She "had" to do this routine at least 10 times each night, and if she made a mistake anywhere along the way, she had to start totally over again from the beginning, or else something bad would happen to her parents or little brother. . . .*
>
> *When Darcy began [college] . . . she would worry incessantly about having written something offensive on an email or an assignment. Walking around campus, she would pick up rubbish: papers that she had never seen before; she would worry that she might have written something on one of them. She feared that she would accidentally hurt one of her fellow students by something that she might do or say. By this time Darcy was repeating certain phrases over and over again to ward off disaster.*
>
> (AIPC, 2013)

Obsessive-compulsive disorder was once among the least understood of the psychological disorders. In recent decades, however, researchers have begun to learn more about it. The most influential explanations and treatments come from the psychodynamic, cognitive-behavioral, and biological models.

The Psychodynamic Perspective

As you have read, psychodynamic theorists believe that an anxiety disorder develops when children come to fear their own id impulses and use ego defense mechanisms to lessen the resulting anxiety. What distinguishes obsessive-compulsive disorder, in their view, is that here the battle between anxiety-provoking id impulses and anxiety-reducing defense mechanisms is not buried in the unconscious but is played out in overt thoughts and actions. The id impulses usually take the form of obsessive thoughts, and the ego defenses appear as counterthoughts or compulsive actions. A person who keeps imagining their parent lying broken and bleeding, for example, may counter those thoughts with repeated safety checks throughout their home.

Sigmund Freud traced obsessive-compulsive disorder to the *anal stage* of development (occurring at about 2 years of age). He proposed that during this stage, some children experience intense rage and shame as a result of negative toilet-training experiences. Other psychodynamic theorists have argued instead that such early rage reactions are rooted in feelings of insecurity (Blum, 2023; Cludius et al., 2021). Either way, these children repeatedly feel the need to express their strong aggressive id impulses while at the same time knowing they should try to restrain and control the impulses. If this conflict between the id and the ego continues, it may eventually blossom into obsessive-compulsive disorder. Overall, research has not clearly supported the psychodynamic explanation (Meehan, O'Connor, & Keogh, 2022).

When treating patients with obsessive-compulsive disorder, psychodynamic therapists try to help the individuals uncover and overcome their underlying conflicts and defenses, using the customary techniques of free association and therapist interpretation. Research has offered little evidence, however, that a traditional psychodynamic approach is of much help (Blum, 2023; Meehan et al., 2022). Thus, some psychodynamic therapists now prefer to treat these patients with short-term psychodynamic therapies, which, as you read earlier, are more direct and action-oriented than the classical techniques.

of NOTE ...

After Using a Public Toilet:

18 percent of people do not wash their hands.

23 percent of hand-washers fail to use soap.

Only 5 percent of soap-users wash for longer than 15 seconds.

The CDC suggests washing with soap for at least 20 seconds.

(Information from: CDC, 2022; Borchgrevink, Cha, & Kim, 2013)

The Cognitive-Behavioral Perspective

Cognitive-behavioral theorists begin their explanation of obsessive-compulsive disorder by pointing out that everyone has repetitive, unwanted, and intrusive thoughts (Alcolado, 2022; Forrester, 2022). Anyone might have thoughts of harming others or being contaminated by germs, for example, but most people dismiss or ignore such thoughts with ease. Those who develop this disorder, however, typically blame themselves for such thoughts and expect that somehow terrible things will happen. To avoid such negative outcomes, they try to **neutralize** the thoughts—thinking or behaving in ways meant to put matters right or to make amends.

neutralizing A person's attempt to eliminate unwanted thoughts by thinking or behaving in ways that put matters right internally, making up for the unacceptable thoughts.

exposure and response prevention A cognitive-behavioral technique used to treat obsessive-compulsive disorder that exposes a client to anxiety-arousing thoughts or situations and then prevents the client from performing compulsive acts. Also called *exposure and ritual prevention.*

Neutralizing acts might include requesting special reassurance from others, deliberately thinking "good" thoughts, washing one's hands, or checking for possible sources of danger. When a neutralizing effort brings about a temporary reduction in discomfort, it is reinforced and will likely be repeated (Simpson, 2023; Sündermann & Veale, 2022). Eventually, the neutralizing thought or act is used so often that it becomes, by definition, an obsession or a compulsion. At the same time, the person becomes more and more convinced that their unpleasant intrusive thoughts are dangerous. As their fear of such thoughts increases, the thoughts begin to occur more frequently, and they, too, become obsessions.

In support of this explanation, studies have found that people with obsessive-compulsive disorder have intrusive thoughts more often than other people, resort to more elaborate neutralizing strategies, and experience reductions in anxiety after using neutralizing techniques (Alcolado, 2022; Forrester, 2022).

Cognitive-behavioral therapists use a combination of techniques to treat clients with obsessive-compulsive disorder. They begin by educating the clients, pointing out how misinterpretations of unwanted thoughts, an excessive sense of responsibility, and neutralizing acts have helped to produce and maintain their symptoms (Alcolado, 2022). The therapists then guide the clients to identify and challenge their distorted cognitions. Increasingly, the clients come to appreciate that their obsessive thoughts are inaccurate occurrences rather than valid and dangerous cognitions for which they are responsible. Correspondingly, they recognize their compulsive acts as unnecessary.

AP Photo/David Goldman

Outside the comfort zone A child gets a muddy hug from counselors at a camp for children with Tourette's disorder, a syndrome marked by sudden movements and vocalizations. Many people with Tourette's also display obsessive-compulsive disorders that feature cleaning compulsions and obsessions about dirt. Thus, the camp has a therapeutic mud obstacle course that exposes campers, in a supportive atmosphere, to conditions of mess and muck that might otherwise produce severe anxiety for them (*exposure and response prevention*).

With such gains in hand, the clients become willing to subject themselves to the rigors of a distinctly behavioral technique called **exposure and response prevention** (or **exposure and ritual prevention**) (Sündermann & Veale, 2022). In this technique, the clients are repeatedly exposed to objects or situations that produce anxiety, obsessive fears, and compulsive behaviors, but they are told to *resist* performing the behaviors they usually feel so bound to perform. Because people find it very difficult to resist such behaviors, the therapists may set an example first.

Therapists who conduct exposure and response prevention often use videoconferencing to go beyond the office and deliver specific instructions to clients directly in their home settings, where compulsions are most problematic (Luxton, Nelson, & Maheu, 2023; Patel, Comer, & Simpson, 2021). This telemental health approach gained even greater usage during the social-distancing period of the Covid-19 pandemic. At the very least, a number of therapists compose exposure-and-response-prevention exercises that clients must carry out in the form of homework (Forrester, 2022).

Techniques of this kind often help reduce the number and impact of obsessions and compulsions. Overall, between 50 and 70 percent of clients with obsessive-compulsive disorder have been found to improve considerably with cognitive-behavioral therapy, improvements that often continue indefinitely (Swierkosz-Lenart et al., 2023;

Rosenberg, 2022). The effectiveness of this approach brings to mind the old joke about a superstitious man who keeps snapping his fingers to keep elephants away. When someone points out, "But there aren't any elephants around here," the man replies, "See? It works!" Picking up on this analogy, one theorist asserts that people with obsessive-compulsive disorder are figuratively snapping their fingers, and "unless they stop (response prevention) and take a look around at the same time (exposure), they aren't going to learn much of value about elephants" (Berk & Efran, 1983, p. 546).

Have you ever tried an informal version of exposure and response prevention in order to stop behaving in certain ways?

The Biological Perspective

In recent years, researchers have uncovered direct evidence that biological factors play a key role in obsessive-compulsive disorder. For example, some genetic studies have identified gene anomalies that characterize individuals with this disorder (Leckman, 2022). In addition, using brain scan procedures, researchers have identified a brain circuit that helps regulate our primitive impulses, such as sexual desires, aggressive instincts, and needs to excrete (Simpson, 2023; Simpson et al., 2020). The circuit, which brings such impulses to our attention and leads us to act on or disregard them, includes brain structures such as the *orbitofrontal cortex* (just above each eye), *cingulate cortex*, *striatum* (including the *caudate nucleus* and *putamen*, two other structures at the back of the striatum), *thalamus*, and *amygdala* (see **Figure 4-4**). Among the most important neurotransmitters at work in this circuit are *serotonin*, *glutamate*, and *dopamine*.

Studies indicate that this brain circuit, called the *cortico-striato-thalamo-cortical circuit*, is hyperactive in people with obsessive-compulsive disorder, making it difficult for them to turn off or dismiss their various impulses, needs, and related thoughts (Bracco et al., 2023; Kammen et al., 2022). After most people use the bathroom, for example, they have concerns about contamination, and they act accordingly by washing their hands. When they perform this behavior, their brain circuit calms their contamination concerns and cleanliness needs. In contrast, because the cortico-striato-thalamo-cortical circuit of people with obsessive-compulsive disorder is hyperactive, these individuals may continue to experience contamination concerns and need to perform cleaning actions—again and again and again.

FIGURE 4-4

The Biology of Obsessive-Compulsive Disorder

The brain circuit whose dysfunction has been linked to obsessive-compulsive disorder includes structures such as the orbitofrontal cortex, cingulate cortex, striatum, thalamus, and amygdala (left). The illustration on the right highlights how the structures of this circuit work together and trigger each other into action to produce obsessive-compulsive reactions. The long axons of the neurons from each structure form fiberlike pathways across the brain that extend to the other structures in the circuit.

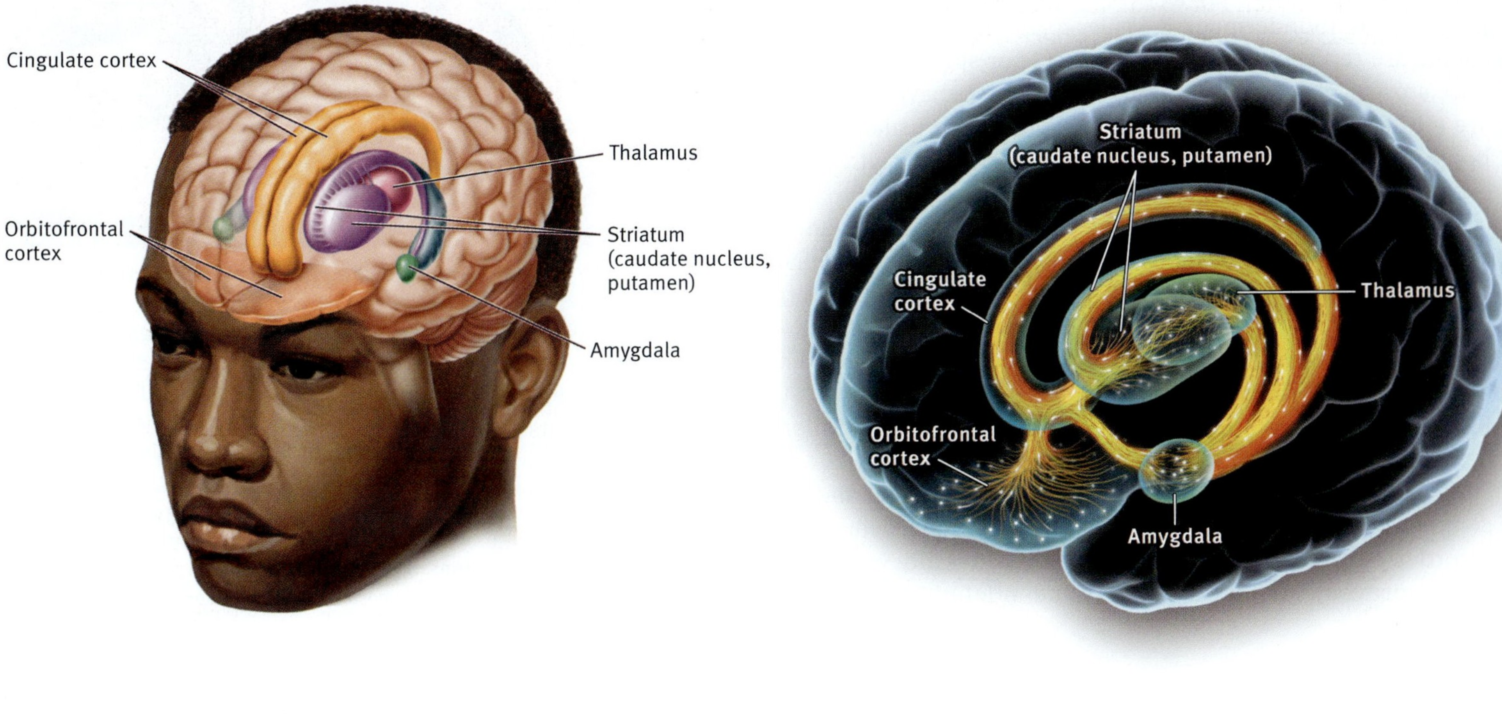

By far, the most widely used biological treatment for obsessive-compulsive disorder is *antidepressant drugs,* particularly ones that specifically increase activity of serotonin. Numerous studies have found that such drugs bring improvement to between 50 and 60 percent of those with obsessive-compulsive disorder (Swierkosz-Lenart et al., 2023; Rosenberg, 2022). Their obsessions and compulsions do not usually disappear totally, but on average, they are cut almost in half (Simpson, 2023).

Most researchers believe that these drugs bring improvement by increasing the activity of serotonin within the cortico-striato-thalamo-cortical circuit, thus helping to correct the brain circuit's hyperactivity. Consistent with this notion, studies have found that the structures in the circuit interconnect more appropriately after people with obsessive-compulsive disorder respond successfully to antidepressant treatment (Kammen et al., 2022).

While many clients with obsessive-compulsive disorder receive *either* cognitive-behavioral therapy or antidepressant drug therapy, a growing number are now being treated with a combination of those interventions. According to research, such combinations often yield higher levels of symptom reduction and bring relief to more clients than do each of the approaches alone—improvements that may continue for years (Rosenberg, 2022).

obsessive-compulsive-related disorders Disorders in which obsessive-like concerns drive people to repeatedly and excessively perform certain pathological behavior patterns.

hoarding disorder A disorder in which people feel compelled to save items and become very distressed if other people try to discard them, resulting in an excessive accumulation of items.

trichotillomania A disorder in which people repeatedly pull out hair from their scalp, eyebrows, eyelashes, or other parts of the body. Also called *hair-pulling disorder.*

excoriation (skin-picking) disorder A disorder in which people repeatedly pick at their skin, resulting in significant sores or wounds.

Obsessive-Compulsive-Related Disorders

Several additional patterns are similar to and closely related to obsessive-compulsive disorder. DSM-5-TR includes a grouping called **obsessive-compulsive-related disorders** and assigns four patterns to that group: *hoarding disorder, trichotillomania (hair-pulling disorder), excoriation (skin-picking) disorder,* and *body dysmorphic disorder.* Collectively, these disorders are displayed by at least 5 percent of all people (Phillips, 2023, 2022; Mansueto, 2022).

People who display **hoarding disorder** feel that they must save items, and they become very distressed if they try to discard them (APA, 2022). These feelings make it difficult for them to part with possessions, resulting in an extraordinary accumulation of items that clutter their lives and living areas. This pattern causes significant distress and may greatly impair personal, social, or occupational functioning (Stamatis, Roddy, & Timpano, 2022). It is common for people with hoarding disorder to wind up with numerous useless and valueless items, from junk mail to broken objects to unused clothes. Parts of their homes may become inaccessible because of the clutter. For example, sofas, kitchen appliances, or beds may be unusable. In addition, the pattern often results in fire hazards, unsanitary conditions, or other dangers.

Mark Ralston/AFP via Getty Images

Pandemic hoarding? In the early months of the Covid-19 pandemic, many people sought to stockpile essential items, like this man waiting in line to purchase 150 rolls of toilet paper. "Panic buying," however, should not be confused with hoarding disorder, an ongoing disturbance marked by significant personal distress and impairment in social, occupational, or other important areas of functioning.

People with **trichotillomania,** also known as *hair-pulling disorder,* repeatedly pull out hair from their scalp, eyebrows, eyelashes, or other parts of the body (APA, 2022). The disorder usually centers on just one or two of these body sites, most often the scalp. Typically, those with the disorder pull one hair at a time. It is common for anxiety or stress to trigger or accompany the hair-pulling behavior (Mansueto, 2022). Because of the distress, impairment, or embarrassment caused by this behavior, the individuals often try to reduce or stop the hair-pulling. The term *trichotillomania* is derived from the Greek word for "frenzied hair-pulling."

People with **excoriation (skin-picking) disorder,** keep picking at their skin, resulting in significant sores or wounds (APA, 2022). Like those with hair-pulling disorder, they often try to reduce or stop the behavior. Most individuals with excoriation disorder pick with their fingers and center their picking on one area, most often the face. Other common areas of focus include the arms, legs, lips, scalp, chest, and extremities, such as fingernails and cuticles. The behavior is typically triggered or accompanied by anxiety or stress (Park & Koo, 2023; Mansueto, 2022).

body dysmorphic disorder A disorder in which individuals become preoccupied with the belief that they have certain "defects" or flaws in their physical appearance. Such flaws are imagined or greatly exaggerated.

People with **body dysmorphic disorder** become preoccupied with the belief that they have a particular defect or flaw in their physical appearance. Actually, the perceived imperfection is imagined or greatly exaggerated in the person's mind (APA, 2022). Such beliefs drive the individuals to repeatedly check themselves in the mirror, groom themselves, pick at the perceived flaw, compare themselves with others, seek reassurance, or perform other, similar behaviors. Here too, those with the problem experience significant distress or impairment.

Body dysmorphic disorder is the obsessive-compulsive-related disorder that has received the most study to date. Researchers have found that, most often, individuals with this problem focus on wrinkles, spots on the skin, facial hair, swelling of the face, or the shape of the nose, mouth, jaw, or eyebrow (Phillips, 2023, 2022; Sündermann & Veale, 2022). Some worry about the appearance of their feet, hands, breasts, penis, or other body parts. Still others are concerned about bad odors coming from sweat, breath, genitals, or the rectum. Ben's all-consuming belief that his nose was misshapen began when he was 18 years old:

> *Whenever I saw my reflection I got this feeling in my stomach, a knot that was accompanied by a feeling that something was seriously wrong with the way I looked. . . . My preoccupation with my appearance was never far from my mind. I lived with a constant feeling of dread and started to compare myself to everyone around me. I began to mentally study other people's appearances and their noses in particular. Almost everyone looked better than me. . . . My iPhone became my worst enemy. I felt a compulsion to photograph and video myself from different angles and then spend hours studying them. I hated what I saw but I felt that I had to get an understanding of just how bad my nose was.*
>
> *(Schnackenberg & Petro, 2016, pp. 69–71)*

of NOTE ...

Looking Good

Seventy-two percent of facial plastic surgeons report that many of their patients seek cosmetic procedures in order to look better in selfies and on TikTok, Instagram, Snapchat, X, Facebook Live, and other social media (FPS, 2023, 2022, 2020).

Of course, it is common in our society to worry about appearance. Many teenagers and young adults worry about acne, for instance. The concerns of people with body dysmorphic disorder, however, are extreme. They may severely limit contact with other people, be unable to look others in the eye, or go to great lengths to conceal their "defects"—say, always wearing sunglasses to cover their supposedly misshapen eyes. As many as half of people with the disorder seek plastic surgery or dermatological treatment, and often they feel worse rather than better afterward (Phillips, 2023, 2022). A large number are homebound, 80 percent have suicidal thoughts, and as many as 25 percent may attempt suicide at some point in their lives.

As with the other obsessive-compulsive-related disorders, theorists typically account for body dysmorphic disorder by using the same kinds of explanations, both psychological and biological, that have been applied to obsessive-compulsive disorder. Similarly, clinicians typically apply the same kinds of treatment used with obsessive-compulsive disorder, particularly antidepressant drugs and cognitive-behavioral therapy (ADAA, 2023; Phillips, 2023). In recent years, clinical scientists have also had success developing apps for use with body dysmorphic disorder (Wilhelm et al., 2022).

SUMMING UP

Obsessive-Compulsive Disorder

People with obsessive-compulsive disorder are beset by obsessions, perform compulsions, or both. According to the psychodynamic view, obsessive-compulsive disorder arises out of a battle between id impulses and ego defense mechanisms. In contrast, cognitive-behavioral theorists believe that the disorder grows from a common human tendency to have unwanted and unpleasant thoughts. The efforts of some people to understand, eliminate, or avoid such thoughts actually lead to obsessions and compulsions. Cognitive-behavioral therapists educate clients and help them correct their misinterpretations of the unwanted thoughts. With such gains in hand, the therapists then conduct exposure and response prevention.

Biological researchers have tied obsessive-compulsive disorder to a hyperactive cortico-striato-thalamo-cortical circuit in the brain. Antidepressant drugs that raise serotonin activity are a widely used and useful form of treatment.

In addition to obsessive-compulsive disorder, DSM-5-TR lists a group of obsessive-compulsive-related disorders, disorders in which obsessive-like concerns drive individuals to repeatedly and excessively perform specific patterns of behavior that greatly disrupt their lives. This group consists of hoarding disorder, trichotillomania, excoriation (skin-picking) disorder, and body dysmorphic disorder.

Integrating the Models: The Developmental Psychopathology Perspective

WHILE READING THROUGH this chapter, you may have noticed that certain findings and principles from each of the models seem compatible, and you may have wondered whether the explanations offered by the models could sometimes be combined to provide a fuller understanding of the various anxiety, obsessive-compulsive, and obsessive-compulsive-related disorders. A number of clinical theorists have asked the same question and have looked for ways to integrate the variables cited by the models. As you read in the chapter on models of psychopathology, one of today's most influential integrative views is the *developmental psychopathology* perspective. This perspective focuses on the *intersection* and *context* of important factors at key points of *time* throughout an individual's life span.

What are the factors that developmental psychopathologists look at when seeking to understand the development of anxiety-related disorders (see **Figure 4-5**)? Drawing

FIGURE 4-5

Development of Anxiety Disorders

A range of variables may combine and intersect throughout a person's life to produce an anxiety disorder. However, the particular variables may differ from person to person. In line with the principle of *equifinality*, the two individuals in this illustration experience different negative variables, yet each winds up with an anxiety disorder.

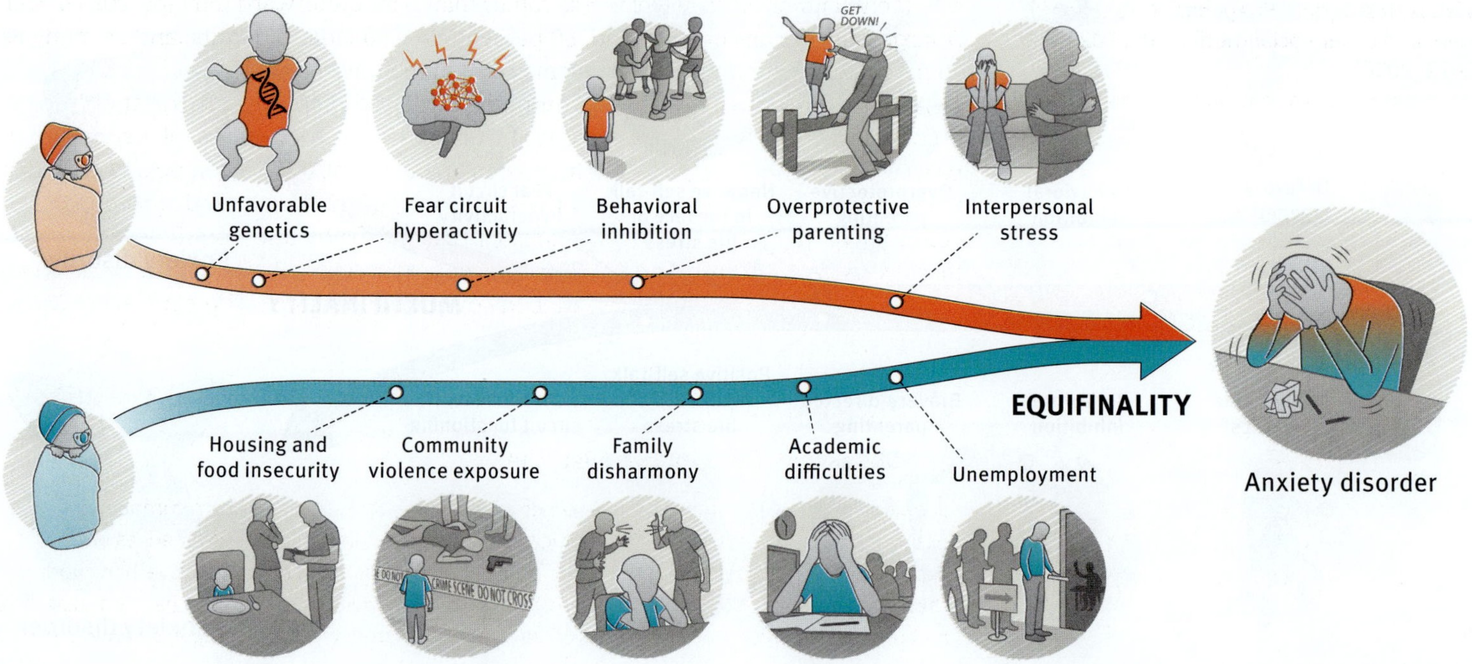

from the biological model, they have been interested in the growing number of studies that link particular genetic variations to hyperactive fear circuits and, in turn, to inhibited—that is, fearful—temperaments in certain infants and toddlers (Baldwin, 2023; Plomin & Viding, 2022). From the earliest days of life, such children show a withdrawn, isolated, and cautious pattern known as *behavioral inhibition*. They are wary of new objects, people, and environments, and they always seem on guard against potential threats. Research indicates that this inhibited temperament often endures throughout a person's life and places some individuals at heightened risk for the development of anxiety-related disorders (Fox et al., 2022).

Drawing from the cognitive-behavioral and psychodynamic models, developmental psychopathologists have also been interested in research findings that highlight the important role of *parenting styles* (Spadoni et al., 2022). Investigations indicate that as children grow, *overprotective parenting*—in which parents rush in too quickly to prevent or rescue their children from experiencing distress—denies them opportunities to learn how to manage distress by themselves and to build a strong sense of self-confidence (Mathijs et al., 2023). If children already have a biological vulnerability and an inhibited temperament, exposure to overprotective parenting can help promote repeated eruptions of anxiety, setting the stage for lifelong anxiety.

Finally, drawing from the sociocultural model, developmental psychopathologists have also been interested in research showing that life stress, poverty, discrimination, school difficulties, family disharmony, peer pressure, and community danger can heighten the likelihood of developing anxiety-related disorders (Baldwin, 2023; Nelemans et al., 2023, 2020). Indeed, a growing number of studies suggest that, in many cases, some such factors must be present for these disorders to emerge, in addition to any unfavorable biological factors, temperament, or parenting experiences the individual may have.

While the developmental psychopathology perspective helps us appreciate that the principles of the various models may often be combined to better account for anxiety-related disorders, it also highlights that the models have not typically addressed important questions about the *development* of these disorders. Precisely *how* and *when*, for example, do the variables from each of the models interact to produce the disorders? A growing body of research suggests that the various key

FIGURE 4-6

The Power of Protective Factors

Key positive factors throughout life can help "protect" some persons from developing anxiety disorders. Both individuals in this illustration are born with an unfavorable genetic makeup and an inhibited temperament. However, one person further experiences "bravery-directed" parenting and, in turn, an adaptive fear circuit in the brain, which together protect that person from developing an anxiety disorder.

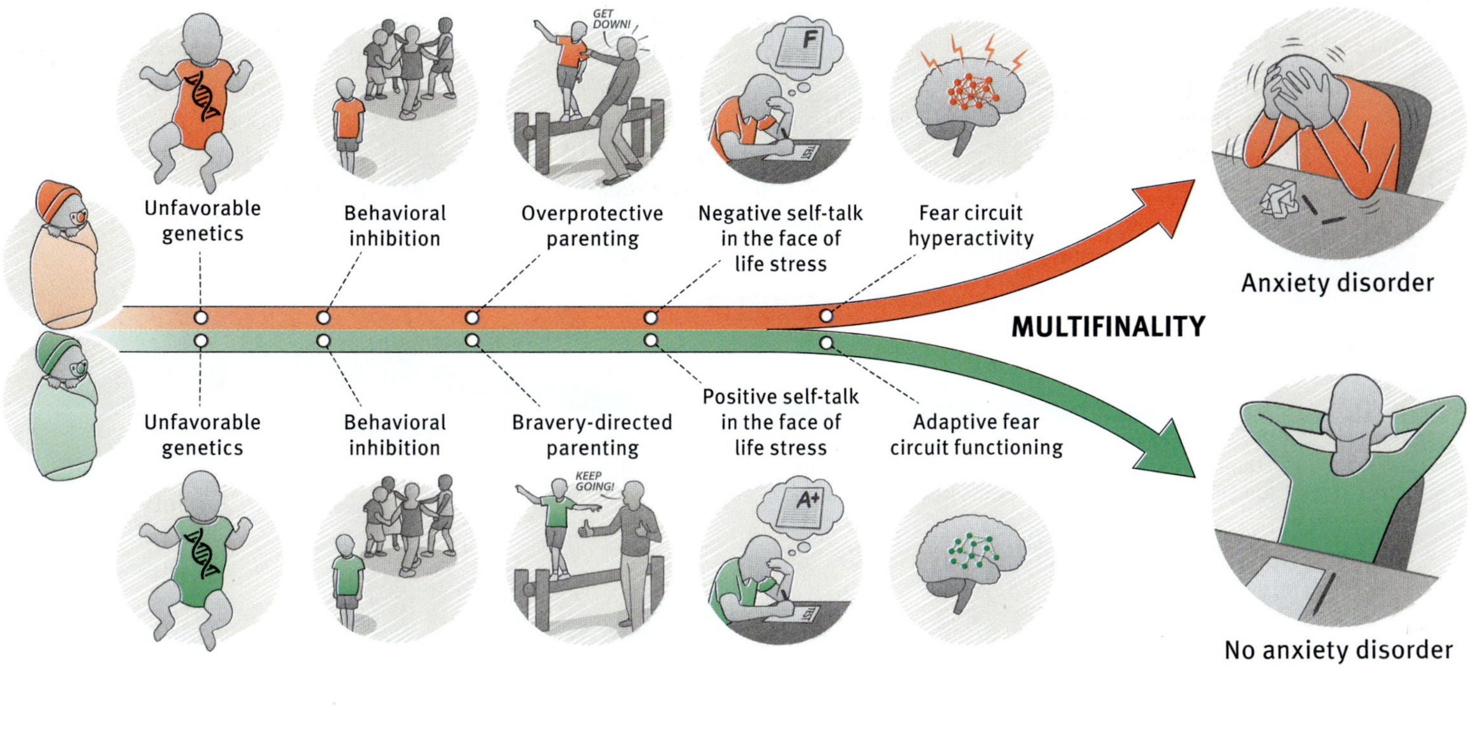

factors—from biology to temperament to parenting to life events—may have greater or lesser impact at different points of development (Cicchetti, 2023, 2018, 2016). The early establishment of a fearful temperament, for example, may impede the later impact of positive life events. Conversely, effective parenting may serve as a *protective* factor and reduce the impact of an unfavorable biological predisposition or of later negative life events (see **Figure 4-6**). Clearly, in order for anxiety-related disorders to be more fully understood and effectively treated, these important developmental issues need to be studied further.

of NOTE ...

Modern Comforts

Many children cling to blankets or cuddly toys to feel more secure. Similarly, researchers and clinicians find that many of today's adults cling to their cell phones as "digital security blankets" in uncomfortable situations.

SUMMING UP

Integrating the Models

To explain anxiety, obsessive-compulsive, and related disorders, proponents of the developmental psychopathology perspective examine how key factors emerge and intersect at points and contexts throughout an individual's life span. The factors of interest to them include genetic factors, a hyperactive fear circuit in the brain, an inhibited temperament, overprotective parenting, maladaptive thinking, avoidance behaviors, life stress, and negative social factors.

Quick Quiz

1. What are the key principles in the sociocultural, psychodynamic, humanistic, cognitive-behavioral, and biological explanations of generalized anxiety disorder? pp. 109–119
2. How effective have treatments been for generalized anxiety disorder? pp. 112–119
3. Define and compare specific phobias and agoraphobia. How do cognitive-behavioral theorists explain phobias? pp. 120–123
4. Describe the three exposure techniques used to treat specific phobias. pp. 124–125
5. What are the various components of social anxiety disorder, and how is this disorder treated? pp. 126–129
6. How do biological and cognitive-behavioral clinicians explain and treat panic disorder? pp. 131–134
7. Which factors do psychodynamic, cognitive-behavioral, and biological theorists believe are at work in obsessive-compulsive disorder? pp. 136–139
8. Describe and compare the effectiveness of exposure and response prevention and antidepressant medications as treatments for obsessive-compulsive disorder. pp. 137–139
9. Describe the four obsessive-compulsive-related disorders. pp. 139–140
10. How do developmental psychopathology theorists integrate the findings and principles from the various models to explain anxiety, obsessive-compulsive, and obsessive-compulsive-related disorders? pp. 141–143

CHAPTER 5

Disorders of Trauma and Stress

Army Corporal Xavier Jackson, now 28 years old, served two tours of duty in Afghanistan. Xavier grew up in an economically unstable household in Baltimore. His mother died when he was 5, and he and his two brothers lived with their father in a small, two-bedroom apartment. Nevertheless, Xavier was known as the most cheerful person in his circle of friends. He exuded optimism, and he always insisted everything would be fine. He chastised anyone who expressed doubts or pessimism. He joined the army because it made sense financially, but he was also drawn to the order of military life and the feeling that he was taking action to control his future.

During his time in Afghanistan, Xavier was beloved by everyone he served with, no matter what their ethnicity or race, but he also made a special effort to be a mentor to other Black soldiers in his unit. He received a commendation for evacuating two wounded members of his unit when they came under fire. Although in combat far from home, Xavier was a pretty happy guy.

Then, one day late in his second tour, near Kandahar, Xavier's unit came under heavy attack. As part of this larger attack, the soldiers confronted numerous explosive devices. Xavier's leg was severely damaged—almost shattered—by one such bomb, and two other soldiers in his unit lost their lives. Taken to a combat support hospital for repair and recovery, Xavier became increasingly testy with the staff during the hospitalization and angrily insisted to anyone who would listen that the United States was making strategic mistakes. He had frequent nightmares about the attack.

Due to his severe injury, Xavier received a medical discharge from the army and returned to the States to continue rehabilitation. His wife, Sarah, felt that he was a different person when he returned to her. He was anxious and argued with her often about raising their 2-year-old son, Xavier Jr., sometimes screaming at her out of the blue, which he had never done before. He recoiled every time he heard a loud noise outside, and he refused to ride in cars, except to go to physical therapy. It was often tough to get him into the car even for that.

Although Sarah hoped Xavier would return to being himself over time, his psychological challenges intensified over the following year. He cut himself off from friends and seemed constantly unhappy. Still avoiding cars, he left the house only to walk around his neighborhood, so he was unable to seek out-of-the-house employment. Sarah and Xavier Jr. came to dread the times when Xavier would start breathing heavily, tense up, sit down, and grab a table for support, saying his heart was racing and he was terrified something terrible would happen. Sarah also hated those nights when Xavier would awaken screaming. Although he would never tell her what he'd been dreaming about, she was sure it was his time in war. Sometimes, Xavier would return from a short walk and say vaguely that he suspected a neighbor was planning something against him.

Xavier rarely talked about his time "over there," but occasionally he told Sarah it wasn't right that he got to be with his family while many of his friends had died. He once said, "Maybe it would be better if I weren't around anymore," but he quickly assured her he would never leave her and their son. One night, five years after his return, Sarah was discussing a serious argument she'd had with her sister, and she realized he wasn't listening, just staring into space, pale, sweating, and trembling slightly. She asked, "What's wrong?," and he responded, quietly, "I don't know what just happened. It's like I was back there, the day that . . . you know, the day with my leg. It was all happening again." He admitted this had been happening a lot lately. Shaken, he finally agreed to Sarah's strong suggestion that he seek help, and they arranged for a therapist to talk to him over videoconference.

TOPIC OVERVIEW

autonomic nervous system (ANS) The network of nerve fibers that connect the central nervous system to all the other organs of the body.

endocrine system The system of glands located throughout the body that help control important activities, such as growth and sexual activity.

sympathetic nervous system The nerve fibers of the autonomic nervous system that quicken the heartbeat and produce other changes experienced as arousal.

During the horror of combat, soldiers often become highly anxious and depressed, confused and disoriented, and even physically ill. Moreover, for many, like Xavier, these and related reactions to extraordinary stress or trauma continue well beyond the combat event itself.

Of course, it is not just combat soldiers who are affected by stress. Nor does stress have to rise to the level of combat trauma to have a profound effect on psychological and physical functioning. Stress comes in all sizes and shapes, and we are all greatly affected by it.

We feel some degree of stress whenever we are faced with demands or opportunities that require us to change in some manner. The state of stress has two components: a *stressor,* the event that creates the demands, and a *stress response,* the person's reactions to the demands. The stressors of life may include annoying everyday hassles, such as rush-hour traffic; turning-point events, such as college graduation or marriage; long-term problems, such as poverty, discrimination, or poor health; or traumatic events, such as major accidents, assaults, or disasters. Our response to such stressors is influenced by the way we *judge* both the events and our capacity to react to them in an effective way (Chu et al., 2022; Lazarus & Folkman, 1984). People who sense that they have the ability and the resources to cope are more likely to take stressors in stride and to respond well.

When we view a stressor as threatening, a natural reaction is arousal and a sense of fear. Stress reactions—and the sense of fear they produce—are often at play in psychological disorders. People who experience a large number of stressful events are particularly vulnerable to the onset of the anxiety disorders that you read about in the previous chapter. Similarly, increases in stress have been linked to the onset of depression, schizophrenia, sexual dysfunctions, and other psychological difficulties.

Extraordinary stress and trauma play an even more central role in certain psychological disorders. In these disorders, the reactions to stress become severe and debilitating, linger for a long period of time, and may make it nearly impossible for the individual to live a comfortable life. Under the heading "Trauma- and Stressor-Related Disorders," DSM-5-TR lists several disorders in which trauma and extraordinary stress provoke a range of significant stress symptoms, including heightened arousal, anxiety and mood problems, memory and orientation difficulties, and behavioral disturbances. Two of these disorders, *acute stress disorder* and *posttraumatic stress disorder,* are discussed in this chapter. In addition, DSM-5-TR lists the "dissociative disorders," a group of disorders also triggered by traumatic events, in which the primary symptoms are severe memory and orientation problems. These disorders are also examined in this chapter.

Different strokes for different folks
Some people are exhilarated by the opportunity to chase bulls through the streets of Pamplona, Spain, during the annual "running of the bulls" (left). Others are terrified by such a prospect and prefer instead to engage tamer animals, such as ostriches, during the "running of the ostriches" fiesta in Irurzun, Spain (right).

Peio Hernandez/EPA/Newscom

Jon Dimis/AP Photo

To fully understand these various stress-related disorders, it is important to appreciate the precise nature of stress and how the brain and body typically react to stress. Thus, let's first discuss stress and arousal, then move on to discussions of acute and posttraumatic stress disorders and the dissociative disorders. ■

Stress and Arousal: The Fight-or-Flight Response

THE FEATURES OF AROUSAL are set in motion by the brain structure called the *hypothalamus*. When our brain interprets a situation as dangerous, neurotransmitters in the hypothalamus are released, triggering the firing of neurons throughout the brain and the release of chemicals throughout the body. Actually, the hypothalamus activates two important systems—the *autonomic nervous system* and the *endocrine system*. The **autonomic nervous system** (ANS) is the extensive network of nerve fibers that connect the *central nervous system* (the brain and spinal cord) to all the other organs of the body. These fibers help control the *involuntary* activities of the organs—breathing, heartbeat, blood pressure, perspiration, and the like (see **Figure 5-1**). The **endocrine system** is the network of *glands* located throughout the body. (As you read earlier in the textbook, glands release *hormones* into the bloodstream and on to the various body organs.) The ANS and the endocrine system often overlap in their responsibilities. There are two brain–body routes by which these systems produce arousal—the *sympathetic nervous system* and the *hypothalamic-pituitary-adrenal axis*.

When we face a dangerous situation, the hypothalamus first excites the **sympathetic nervous system**, a group of ANS fibers that work to quicken our heartbeat and produce the other changes that we experience as fear or anxiety (Alshak & Das, 2023). These nerves may stimulate the organs of the body directly—for example, they may directly stimulate the heart and increase the heart rate. The nerves may also influence the organs indirectly by stimulating the *adrenal glands* (glands located on top of the kidneys), particularly an area of these glands called the *adrenal medulla*. When the adrenal medulla is stimulated, the chemicals *epinephrine* (*adrenaline*) and *norepinephrine* (*noradrenaline*) are released. You have already learned earlier in the textbook that these chemicals are important neurotransmitters when they operate in the brain. When released from the adrenal medulla, however, they act as hormones and travel through the bloodstream to various organs and muscles, further producing arousal.

FIGURE 5-1

The Autonomic Nervous System (ANS)

When the sympathetic division of the ANS is activated, it stimulates some organs and inhibits others. The result is a state of general arousal. In contrast, activation of the parasympathetic division leads to an overall calming effect.

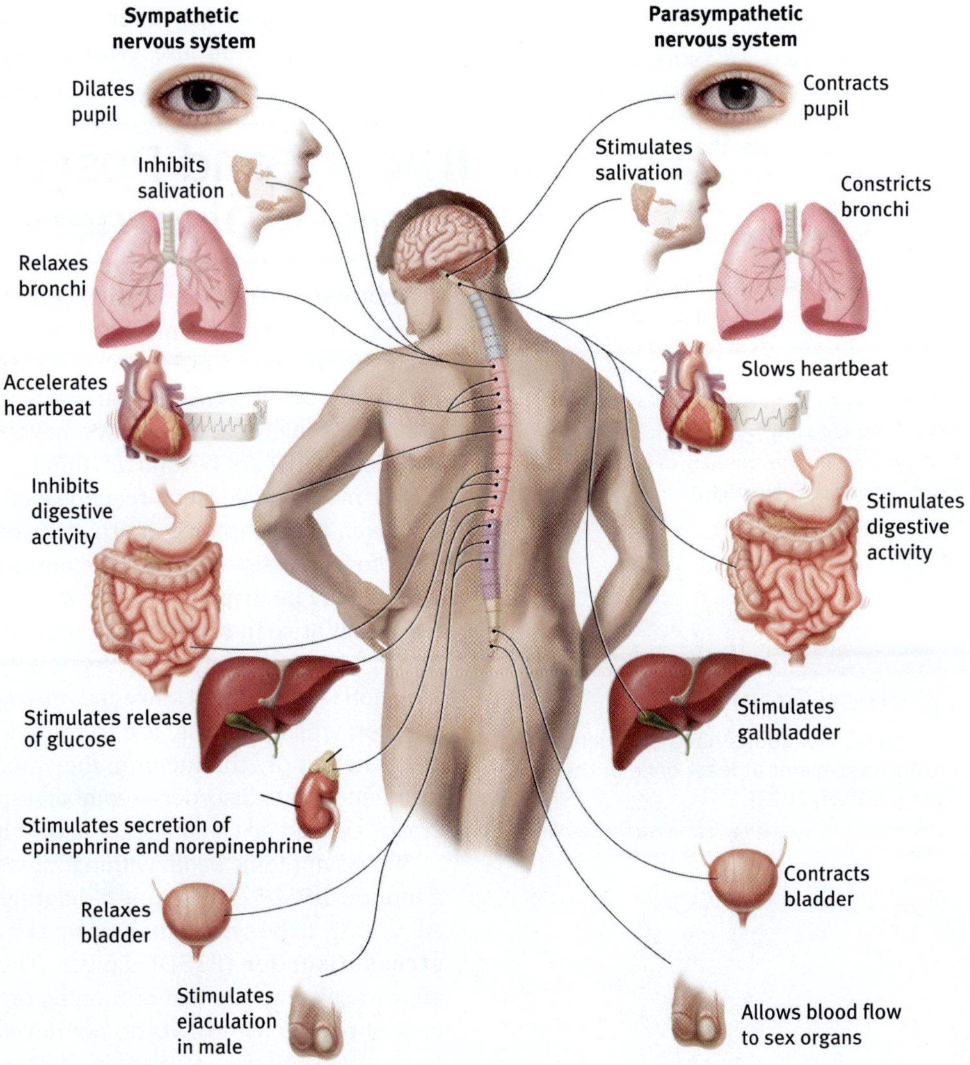

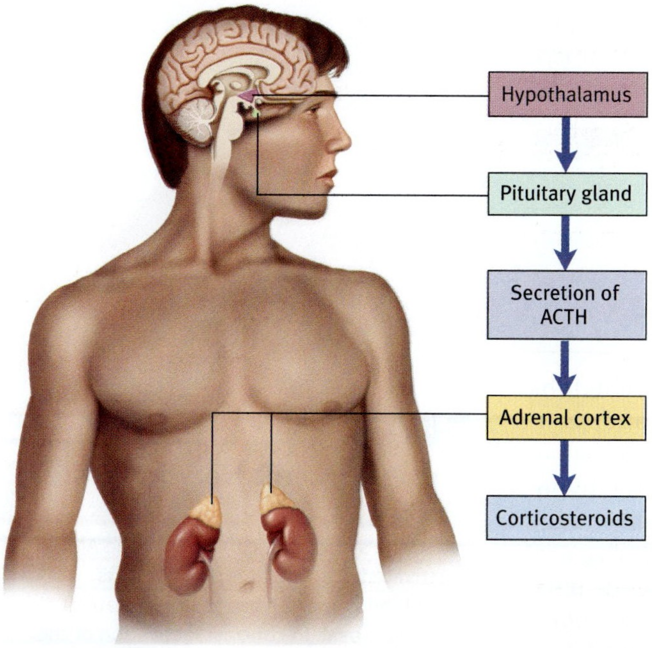

FIGURE 5-2

The HPA Axis

When a person perceives a stressor, the hypothalamus activates the pituitary gland to secrete the adrenocorticotropic hormone, or ACTH, which stimulates the adrenal cortex. The adrenal cortex releases stress hormones called corticosteroids that act on other body organs to trigger arousal and fear reactions.

When the perceived danger passes, a second group of ANS fibers, called the **parasympathetic nervous system,** helps return our heartbeat and other body processes to normal. Together the sympathetic and parasympathetic nervous systems help control our arousal reactions.

The second brain–body route by which arousal is produced is the **hypothalamic-pituitary-adrenal (HPA) axis** (see **Figure 5-2**). When we are faced by stressors, the hypothalamus also signals the *pituitary gland,* which lies nearby, to secrete the *adrenocorticotropic hormone (ACTH),* sometimes called the body's "major stress hormone." ACTH, in turn, stimulates the outer layer of the adrenal glands, an area called the *adrenal cortex,* triggering the release of a group of stress hormones called **corticosteroids,** including the hormone *cortisol.* These corticosteroids travel to various body organs, where they further produce arousal reactions.

The reactions on display throughout the sympathetic nervous system and the HPA axis are collectively referred to as the *fight-or-flight* response, precisely because they arouse our body and prepare us for a response to danger. Each person has a particular pattern of functioning in these two brain–body stress routes and so has a particular way of experiencing arousal when they confront stressors. Some people, for example, react with relatively little tension even in the face of significant threats, while others react with considerable tension even when they encounter minimal threats. People also differ in their sense of which situations are threatening. Flying in an airplane may arouse terror in some people and boredom in others.

Acute and Posttraumatic Stress Disorders

OF COURSE, WHEN we actually confront stressful situations, we do not think to ourselves, "Oh, there goes my autonomic nervous system" or "My fight-or-flight response seems to be kicking in." We just feel aroused psychologically and physically and experience a growing sense of fear. If the stressful situation is perceived as extraordinary and/or unusually dangerous, we may temporarily experience levels of arousal, fear, and depression that are beyond anything we have ever known.

For most people, such reactions subside soon after the danger passes. For others, however, the symptoms of arousal, anxiety, and depression, as well as other kinds of symptoms, persist well after the upsetting situation is over (Brewin et al., 2024). These people may be displaying *acute stress disorder* or *posttraumatic stress disorder,* patterns that arise in reaction to a psychologically traumatic event. A traumatic event is one in which a person is exposed to actual or threatened death, serious injury, or sexual violation (APA, 2022). Unlike the anxiety disorders that you read about in the previous chapter, which typically are triggered by situations that most people would not find overwhelmingly threatening, the situations that cause acute stress disorder or posttraumatic stress disorder—combat, rape, an earthquake, a mass shooting, an airplane crash—would be traumatic for almost anyone.

If the symptoms begin within four weeks of the traumatic event and last for less than a month, DSM-5-TR assigns a diagnosis of **acute stress disorder** (Morrison, 2023; APA, 2022). If the symptoms continue longer than a month, a diagnosis of **posttraumatic stress disorder** (PTSD) is given. The symptoms of PTSD may begin either shortly after the traumatic event or months or years afterward (see **Table 5-1**). In fact, 25 percent of people with PTSD do not develop a full clinical syndrome until six months or more after their trauma (Sareen, 2022).

of NOTE ...

Common Event

Around 60% of adults have experienced a traumatic event at least once in their lives (USDVA, 2023).

TABLE 5-1

Dx Checklist

Posttraumatic Stress Disorder
1. Person is exposed to a traumatic event—death or threatened death, severe injury, or sexual violation.
2. Person experiences at least one of the following intrusive symptoms: • Repeated, uncontrolled, and distressing memories • Repeated and upsetting trauma-linked dreams • Dissociative experiences such as flashbacks • Significant upset when exposed to trauma-linked cues • Pronounced physical reactions when reminded of the event(s)
3. Person continually avoids trauma-linked stimuli.
4. Person experiences negative changes in trauma-linked cognitions and moods, such as being unable to remember key features of the event(s) or experiencing repeated negative emotions.
5. Person displays conspicuous changes in arousal or reactivity, such as excessive alertness, extreme startle responses, or sleep disturbances.
6. Person experiences significant distress or impairment, with symptoms lasting more than a month.

Information from: APA, 2022.

Studies indicate that at least half of all cases of acute stress disorder develop into PTSD (Bryant, 2022; Sayer et al., 2022). Think back to Xavier, the soldier fighting in Afghanistan whose case opened this chapter. Within days of the attack on his unit, Xavier became overrun by arousal, anxiety, sleep problems, worry, anger, depression, irritability, intrusive thoughts, flashback memories, and social detachment—thus qualifying him for a diagnosis of acute stress disorder. As his symptoms worsened and continued beyond one month—even long after his return to the United States—this diagnosis became PTSD. Aside from the differences in onset and duration, the symptoms of acute stress disorder and PTSD are almost identical.

- **Increased Arousal, Negative Emotions, and Guilt** People may feel excessively alert (hyperalertness), be easily startled, have trouble concentrating, and develop sleep problems. They may display anxiety, anger, or depression, and these emotions may fluctuate markedly—a pattern called *emotion dysregulation* or *labile mood* (Zhou et al., 2023). Relatedly, many have difficulty experiencing positive emotions, such as joy, pride, and love. In addition, many individuals feel extreme guilt because they survived the traumatic event while others did not (Beck & Sloan, 2022). Some also feel guilty about what they may have had to do to survive.
- **Reexperiencing the Traumatic Event** People may be battered by recurring thoughts, memories, dreams, or nightmares connected to the event (Beck & Sloan, 2022). A few experience flashbacks, reliving the event so vividly in their minds that they think it is actually happening again (USDVA, 2022).
- **Reduced Responsiveness and Dissociation** People with these disorders may feel detached from other people, be unresponsive to external stimuli, and lose interest in activities that once brought enjoyment. Many endure symptoms of *dissociation*, or psychological separation; that is, they feel dazed, have trouble remembering things, experience *depersonalization* (feeling that their conscious state or body is unreal), or have a sense of *derealization* (feeling that the environment is unreal or strange) (Brand, 2023; DePrince et al., 2023).

parasympathetic nervous system The nerve fibers of the autonomic nervous system that help return bodily processes to normal.

hypothalamic-pituitary-adrenal (HPA) axis One route by which the brain and body produce arousal.

corticosteroids Hormones, including cortisol, released by the adrenal glands at times of stress.

acute stress disorder A disorder in which a person experiences fear and related symptoms soon after a trauma but for less than a month.

posttraumatic stress disorder (PTSD) A disorder in which a person experiences fear and related symptoms long after a traumatic event.

- **Avoidance** People usually avoid activities that remind them of the traumatic event and try to avoid related thoughts, feelings, or conversations (Beck & Sloan, 2022). Terry, an earthquake survivor, displayed many of these symptoms years after his traumatic ordeal:

> *He . . . worked hard to convince others that the earthquake had not affected him. He did this by avoiding people that knew he had gone through this experience and by quickly changing the topic when it came up. However, he found that whenever he had free time, he would have unwanted intrusive thoughts and images about the earthquake. In addition, he was having increasingly distressing nightmares that were causing him to lose several hours of sleep each night. His repeated violent awakenings throughout the night had also disturbed his wife's sleep, resulting in them no longer sharing a bedroom. Terry found that the harder he worked to avoid these thoughts, the more frequent they would become, and that they were getting stronger each day. He feared that if he thought about the memory he would lose control of his emotions and would not be able to cope. He was concerned that the fear and panic that occurred when he was reminded of the trauma would last forever.*
>
> *(Monson & Shnaider, 2014)*

Clinicians have come to appreciate that people who experience symptoms of dissociation and unresponsiveness as part of their stress syndrome tend to be more impaired and distressed than others without such additional symptoms (Lanius, Frewen, & Brand, 2022). Thus, DSM-5-TR requires diagnosticians to clarify the presence of such symptoms in a client with the label *PTSD with dissociative symptoms*. This pattern is particularly common among people with PTSD whose traumas involved military combat, sexual abuse, or other forms of physical abuse, especially repeated abuse or childhood abuse (TD, 2023).

An acute or posttraumatic stress disorder can occur at any age, even in childhood, and can affect one's personal, family, social, or occupational life (Copeland & McGinnis, 2023; McLaughlin, 2023). Surveys indicate that 3.5 to 6 percent of people in North America have one of the stress disorders in any given year; 7 to 12 percent experience one of them during their lifetimes (ADAA, 2022; Sareen, 2022). At least half of these individuals seek treatment, but relatively few do so initially. More than 20 percent attempt suicide (Roberge et al., 2022). People with these stress disorders often develop other psychological disorders as well, such as depressive, anxiety, or substance use disorders (Livingston et al., 2023). Individuals with PTSD also have an increased risk of developing physical ailments such as bronchitis, asthma, heart disease, and liver disease (Sareen, 2022).

of NOTE ...

Most Stressed Generation

Adults born since 1997 (*Gen Z*) are, on average, more stressed than other adults by several societal issues: mass shootings, financial uncertainty, the rise in suicide rates, climate change, separation and deportation of immigrants, and sexual harassment and assault (Kelly, 2023; Brownlee, 2022; APA, 2020).

People with low incomes are more likely than people with higher incomes to experience stress disorders (Sareen, 2022). Transgender people and nonbinary people are at least twice as likely as cisgender people to develop the disorders (Marchi et al., 2023; Livingston et al., 2022, 2020; Barr et al., 2021), and women are at least twice as likely as men to experience the disorders (ADAA, 2022). Similarly, the prevalence of stress disorders is at least twice as high in the lesbian, gay, and bisexual populations as in the overall population (Marchi et al., 2023; Valentine et al., 2022).

It is also the case that people of color are more likely than non-Hispanic White people to develop a stress disorder after confronting a severe trauma (Jones et al., 2022; Sareen, 2022). The reason for this racial-ethnic difference is not clear. Some theorists believe it is tied to the disadvantaged financial status experienced by many people of color, which may limit access to mental health care in the aftermath of traumas. Others point to the traumatic impact of ongoing discrimination and inequities endured by so many people of color (Harb et al., 2023; Nelson & Olson, 2023).

What Triggers Acute and Posttraumatic Stress Disorders?

Any traumatic event can trigger a stress disorder; however, some are particularly likely to do so (Korte et al., 2023; Biggs et al., 2022). Among the most common are combat, disasters, and victimization.

Combat For years, clinicians have recognized that many soldiers develop symptoms of severe anxiety and depression *during* combat. It was called "soldier's heart" during the Civil War, "shell shock" during World War I, and "combat fatigue" during World War II and the Korean War (Beck & Sloan, 2022; USDVA, 2022). Not until after the Vietnam War, however, did clinicians learn that a great many soldiers also experience serious psychological symptoms *after* combat.

By the late 1970s, it became apparent that many Vietnam combat veterans were still experiencing war-related psychological difficulties. We now know that as many as 29 percent of all Vietnam veterans had an acute or posttraumatic stress disorder, and indeed 15 percent of veterans continued to have PTSD when followed up 15 years after their military service (Sareen, 2022).

A similar pattern has unfolded among the nearly 2.7 million veterans of the wars in Afghanistan and Iraq. As many as 20 percent of the individuals deployed to those wars have so far reported symptoms of PTSD (USDVA, 2023). Among those directly exposed to prolonged periods of combat-related stress, the percentage with PTSD is higher still. Moreover, the emotional toll of combat-related PTSD ripples through the entire family (Monson et al., 2022). On average, families headed by combat veterans with PTSD display more parenting difficulties, child mental health problems, spousal marital dissatisfaction, and family dysfunction.

Craig F. Walker/Getty Images

Lingering impact More than four decades after the Vietnam War, over a quarter million veterans of that war are still experiencing PTSD. Until his death in 2016, one such veteran was King Charsa Bakari Kamau. He is seen here playing the piano at a mall in Denver, Colorado, an avocation that he considered to be his best therapy.

Disasters, Accidents, and Illnesses Acute and posttraumatic stress disorders may also follow natural and accidental disasters such as earthquakes, floods, tornadoes, fires, airplane crashes, and serious car accidents (see **Table 5-2**). Researchers have found, for example, unusually high rates of PTSD among the survivors of 2005's Hurricane Katrina; 2012's Superstorm Sandy; the devastating hurricanes that struck Puerto Rico, Florida, and Texas in 2017 and 2022; and the recurrent deadly wildfires in California, Hawaii, and Australia (Velez & Adam, 2023; Saeed & Gargano, 2022). In fact, because they occur more often, stress disorders linked to civilian traumas are much more common than those linked to combat traumas (Biggs et al., 2022). Studies have found, for example, that at least 25 percent of people involved in significant traffic accidents—adult or child—may develop PTSD within a year of the accident (McLaughlin, 2023; Daddah et al., 2022).

Research suggests that serious medical illnesses can also lead to PTSD (Bonnano et al., 2024). At least 20 percent of people with life-threatening illnesses or severe chronic conditions develop this disorder (Sareen, 2022). Studies also reveal that the rate of PTSD increases for those affected by epidemics (rapid spread of a disease within a community) and pandemics (rapid spread across multiple countries) (Taylor, 2022). According to worldwide surveys conducted just one month after the Covid-19 pandemic began, 54 percent of the population had developed ongoing feelings of severe stress, including 73 percent of all health care personnel, and 7 percent were already displaying PTSD (Liu et al., 2020; Wang et al., 2020). Moreover, the prevalence of PTSD was 14 percent among those who had actually contracted Covid-19 (Stavem et al., 2022). Such findings suggest that when long-term investigations into the psychological effects of Covid-19 are eventually completed, they will indicate a large total of people with PTSD.

TABLE 5-2

Worst Natural Disasters of the Past 100 Years

Disaster	Year	Location	Number Killed
Flood	1931	Huang River, China	3,700,000
Tsunami	2004	South Asia	280,000
Earthquake	1976	Tangshan, China	255,000
Heat wave	2003	Europe	35,000
Volcano	1985	Nevado del Ruiz, Colombia	23,000
Hurricane	1998	(Mitch) Central America	18,277
Landslide	1920	Haiyuan County, China	32,000
Blizzard	1972	Iran	4,000
Tornado	1989	Saturia, Bangladesh	1,300

Information from: Lake, 2022; Pappas & Means, 2022; Parogni, 2022; Gringer, 2020.

rape Forced sexual intercourse or another sexual act committed against a nonconsenting person or intercourse between an adult and an underage person.

Victimization

People who have been abused or victimized often have stress symptoms that linger. Research suggests that one-third of all survivors of physical or sexual assault or abuse develop PTSD (Sareen, 2022). As many as 28 percent of all people directly exposed to terrorism and mass shootings or torture may develop the disorder (NMVVRC, 2022).

SEXUAL ASSAULT AND ABUSE A common form of victimization in our society today is sexual assault (see ***InfoCentral***). **Rape** is forced sexual intercourse or another sexual act committed against a nonconsenting person or intercourse between an adult and an underage person. In the United States, approximately 144,000 cases of rape or attempted rape are reported to the police each year (Statista, 2023). Experts believe that these are only one-third of the actual number of rapes and rape attempts given the reluctance of many survivors to report their sexual assaults (RAINN, 2023). When there is an ongoing pattern of unwanted or coerced sexual activity and/or the victim is underage, the term *sexual abuse* is used. Approximately 75 percent of people who experience sexual assault or abuse are victimized by acquaintances, intimates, or relatives (RAINN, 2023).

According to research conducted with predominantly cisgender populations, women and girls are victims of sexual assault and abuse much more than men and boys. Around 1 in 6 women or girls report being raped at some time during their lives, compared to 1 in 33 men or boys (RAINN, 2023). Furthermore, around 1 in 5 women or girls report having experienced patterns of coerced sexual activity as a child, typically by a family member or close acquaintance, compared to 1 in 13 men or boys reporting such childhood sexual abuse. Research further suggests that transgender people are sexually assaulted or abused at an even higher rate than cisgender people; as many as 1 in 2 transgender people report being raped at some time during their lives (RAINN, 2023; Burley et al., 2022). Less is known about rates of sexual assault and abuse among nonbinary people.

The rates of rape and sexual abuse differ across racial-ethnic groups. For example, among people in the United States, at least 27 percent of Indigenous women have been raped at some point in their lives, compared with 22 percent of Black women, 19 percent of non-Hispanic White women, 18 percent of Asian American women, and

Gabrielle Lurie/AFP via Getty Images

Awareness and prevention on campus Over the past decade, amid growing concern that many universities underreport sexual assaults on campus, student activist groups have raised awareness about the scope of the problem and pushed officials to better address and prevent sexual dangers on campus. Here, students display important messages at Stanford University's graduation ceremonies in 2016. The "1 in 3" sign refers to the oft-quoted statistic that as many as one-third of female students across the country are sexually assaulted during college, a statistic that has decreased in recent years.

SEXUAL ASSAULT

People who are **sexually assaulted** have been forced to engage in a sexual act against their will. According to most definitions, people who are **raped** have been forced into sexual intercourse or other forms of sexual penetration. Rape survivors often experience **rape trauma syndrome (RTS)**, a pattern of problematic physical and psychological symptoms. RTS is actually a form of PTSD. Approximately **one-third** of rape survivors develop PTSD.

THE PSYCHOLOGICAL EFFECTS OF RAPE

suicidal thoughts
attempted **suicide**
vulnerability to develop **psychological disorders**
feelings of self-blame and **betrayal flashbacks**
panic attacks
sleep problems
memory problems

Rape survivors are more likely to:

3 X suffer from depression
4 X contemplate suicide
5 X suffer from PTSD
13 X abuse alcohol
20 X abuse drugs

(RAINN, 2023; CMSAC, 2023)

WHO IS RAPED?

Gender

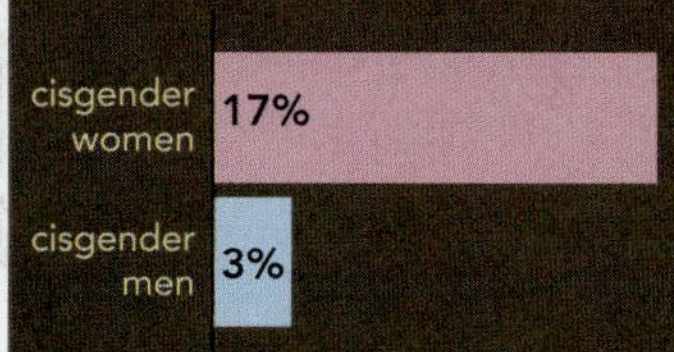

Age

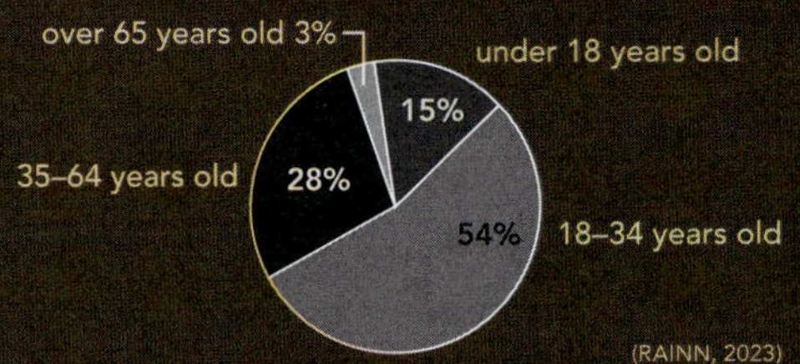

(RAINN, 2023)

Who commits rape?

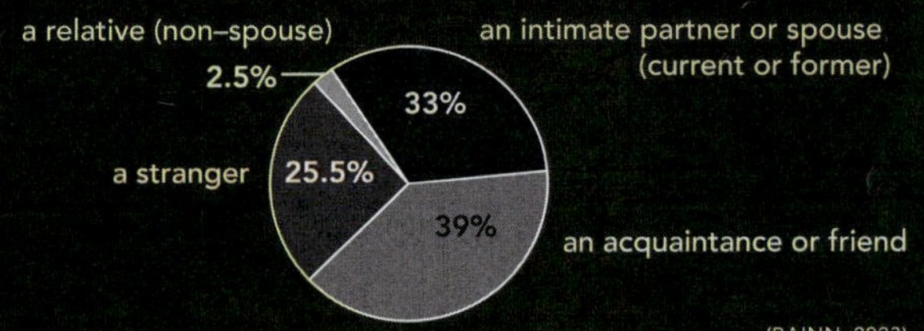

(RAINN, 2023)

SEXUAL ASSAULTS ON TRANSGENDER AND NONBINARY INDIVIDUALS

Transgender individuals

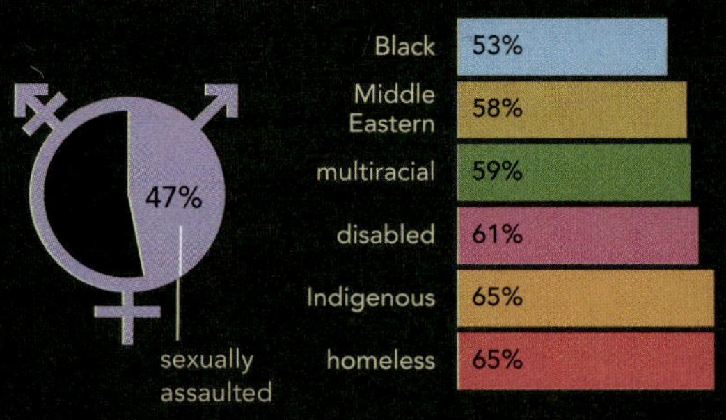

Non-binary and transgender schoolchildren

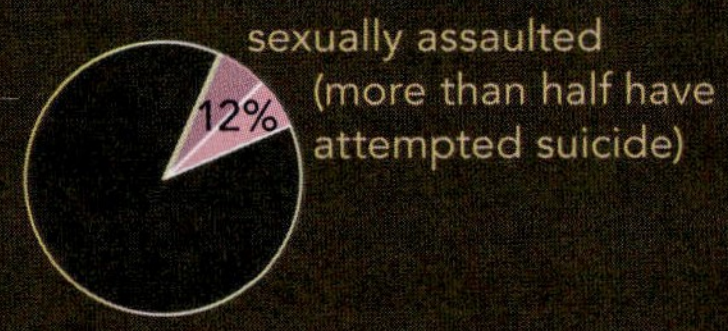

Reaching Out to Police

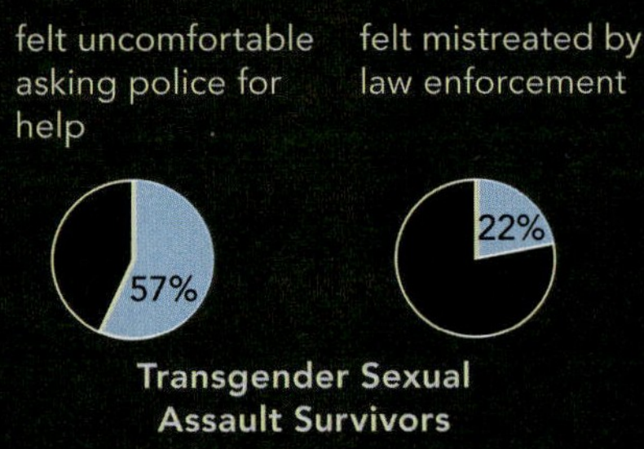

(MCASA, 2022, 2020; VAWnet, 2020; NSVRC, 2021, 2019)

CRISIS ON COLLEGE CAMPUSES

(RAINN, 2023; Weiner, 2014; Adams, 2013)

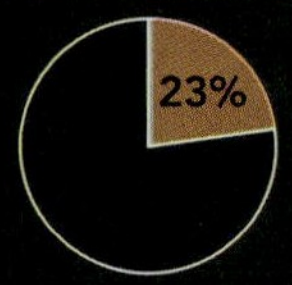

women sexually assaulted in college

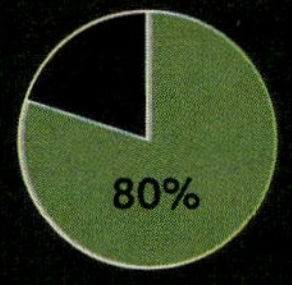

college rapes estimated to be unreported

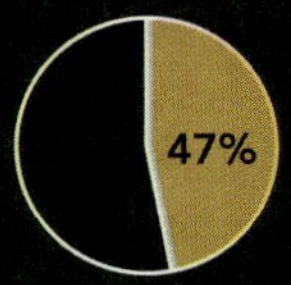

college rape victims sustain bodily injuries

144,000 rapes are reported to police per year, but the number of rapes per year is estimated to be *at least* **400,000**

(RAINN, 2023; Statista, 2023)

Factors Aiding Recovery

Positive self-esteem
Social support
Previous success in coping with stress
Economic security
Accurate information about rape and rape trauma syndrome
Constructive decision-making

(Smith & Segal, 2022; Kirkner & Ullman, 2019; NCVS, 2017, 2014)

Factors Delaying Recovery

Prior victimization
Chronic life stressors
Lack of social support
Low self-esteem
Degree of violence during attack

(Buchanan, 2023; Smith & Segal, 2022; NCVS, 2017, 2014)

15 percent of Hispanic women (BJS, 2023, 2020, 2017; DCCESV, 2022; WCSAP, 2022). The rates are even higher for transgender people of color (RAINN, 2023; Staples & Fuller, 2021).

The psychological impact of being raped is immediate and may last a long time (Buchanan, 2023). Although some rape survivors feel emotionally numb for a period of time after being raped, many experience enormous distress during the week after the assault—a level of stress that continues to rise for the next three weeks, peaks for another month or so, and then starts to improve. In a pioneering study, 94 percent of rape survivors fully qualified for a clinical diagnosis of acute stress disorder when they were observed around 12 days after the assault (Rothbaum et al., 1992). Although some individuals who are raped improve psychologically within 3 or 4 months, for many others the profound effects of their assault persist for up to 18 months or longer. Survivors typically continue to have higher-than-average levels of anxiety, suspiciousness, depression, self-esteem problems, self-blame, suicidal thoughts, flashbacks, sleep problems, and sexual dysfunction (Carroll & Banks, 2022). The following woman describes how her posttraumatic stress symptoms lingered for decades after she had been sexually assaulted.

The nationwide college campaign "It's On Us" obligates everyone on campus to help prevent and intervene in campus sexual assaults. What are the advantages of this broad focus of responsibility?

Somehow, I was back to that familiar place. Moments after waking up drenched in sweat, I lie still in bed—waiting for my heart to stop racing and for the feeling to return to my body. I was safe. It's been twenty years since I was raped, but PTSD makes it feel like it wasn't that long ago.

My nightmares are frequent, every dream is the same: my ex has found me and is going to finish me off. . . .

Days earlier, I accused my boyfriend of grabbing me by the ankles as I slept. That morning, I woke to find him standing at the foot of our bed and screamed. He was just saying goodbye before heading to work. I was experiencing flashbacks of the morning I was attacked.

The scars . . . have faded from my skin, but not my memory.

It's been nearly two decades since I was raped . . . . I began a new life, remarried, became a mother and now I advocate for other survivors of rape. But I am not immune to the effects of trauma in the aftermath of sexual assault. My night terrors come and go and I still cope with anxiety, paranoia and insomnia.

On the days when my symptoms are the worst, I stay at home and away from people. For the most part, I have learned to manage my phobias, accepting them as quirks I may never be rid of.

(Lee, 2017)

Survivors of rape and other crimes also are much more likely than other people to have serious long-term health problems. Research finds that over the course of their lives, rape and sexual abuse survivors develop a higher-than-usual rate of asthma, headaches, irritable bowel syndrome, chronic pain, sleep difficulties, and cardiovascular issues (Basile et al., 2020).

Ongoing victimization and abuse in the family—specifically child and spouse abuse—may also lead to psychological stress disorders (McLaughlin, 2023; La Greca et al., 2022). Because these forms of abuse may occur over the long term and violate family trust, many individuals who experience such mistreatment develop other symptoms and disorders as well.

of NOTE ...

Dangerous Consequence

According to reports by police and crisis hotlines, rates of domestic abuse rose significantly during the early phase of the Covid-19 pandemic, when families were required to stay at home for extended periods—increases attributed to social isolation, higher unemployment, greater financial pressure, higher stress levels, and increased alcohol consumption, among other factors (CCJ, 2023; Mineo, 2022).

TERRORISM AND MASS SHOOTINGS People who are victims of *terrorism* or who live under the threat of terrorism often experience posttraumatic stress symptoms (Watson, Canetti, & Hobfoll, 2023; NMVVRC, 2022). Unfortunately, this source of traumatic stress

Rhona Wise/Getty Images

Empowerment and resilience A week after 17 students and teachers were killed in a 2018 mass shooting at a high school in Parkland, Florida, thousands of students throughout the state staged this rally on the grounds of the stricken high school, demanding improvements in school safety and stricter gun-control laws. Clinical theorists believe that the qualities of empowerment and resilience demonstrated by the Parkland students have helped protect some of them from developing PTSD.

is on the rise. The terrorist events of September 11, 2001, for example, have left a lasting mark on the United States and the rest of the world. Hijacked airplanes crashed into and brought down the World Trade Center in New York City, partially destroyed the Pentagon in Washington, DC, and crashed into a field in Stonycreek Township, Pennsylvania, killing thousands of victims and rescue workers and forcing thousands more to desperately run, crawl, and even dig their way to safety. A number of studies have indicated that in the aftermath of that fateful day, many individuals developed immediate and long-term psychological effects, ranging from brief stress reactions, such as shock, fear, and anger, to enduring psychological disorders, such as PTSD (NYC, 2023).

Follow-up studies suggest that many such individuals continue to experience terrorism-related stress reactions (NYC, 2023; Hamwey et al., 2020). Indeed, even years after the attacks, 42 percent of all adults in the United States and 70 percent of all New York adults report high terrorism fears; 23 percent of all adults in the United States report feeling less safe in their homes; 15 percent of all U.S. adults report drinking more alcohol than they did prior to the attacks; and 9 percent of New York adults display PTSD, compared with the national annual prevalence of 3.5 percent. Studies of other high-profile acts of terrorism—such as the 1995 Oklahoma City federal building bombing; the 2013 Boston Marathon bombing; the 2016 Bastille Day truck attack in Nice, France; and the 2017 Ariana Grande concert bombing in Manchester, United Kingdom—tell a similar story.

Similarly, people who have survived *mass shootings* often experience posttraumatic stress symptoms (USDVA, 2023). Such shootings—sometimes perpetrated in the name of terrorism, sometimes not—have been increasing at an alarming rate at schools and other public places throughout the United States and other parts of the world, including the killings of 58 concertgoers in Las Vegas, Nevada, in 2017; 17 individuals at the Marjory Stoneman Douglas High School in Parkland, Florida, in 2018; 10 people in a supermarket in Buffalo, New York, in 2022; 19 children and 2 teachers at the Robb Elementary School in Uvalde, Texas, in 2022; and 260 attendees at a music festival in Israel in 2023.

TORTURE **Torture** refers to the use of "brutal, degrading, and disorienting strategies in order to reduce victims to a state of utter helplessness" (AI, 2023; Okawa & Hauss, 2007). Often, it is done on the orders of a government or another authority to force

torture The use of brutal, degrading, and disorienting strategies to reduce victims to a state of utter helplessness.

persons to yield information or make a confession. As you will read in the chapter on law and mental health, the question of the morality of torturing prisoners who are considered suspects in the "war on terror" has been the subject of much discussion, especially over the past two decades.

People from all walks of life are subjected to torture worldwide—from suspected terrorists to student activists and members of religious, ethnic, political, and marginalized groups. The techniques used on them may include *physical torture* (beatings, waterboarding, electrocution), *psychological torture* (threats of death, mock executions, verbal abuse, degradation), *sexual torture* (rape, violence to the genitals, sexual humiliation), or *torture through deprivation* (sleep, sensory, social, nutritional, medical, or hygiene deprivation). Torture victims often experience physical ailments as a result of their ordeal, from scarring and fractures to neurological problems and chronic pain. It also appears that more than 30 percent of torture victims develop PTSD (Sareen, 2022).

Why Do People Develop Acute and Posttraumatic Stress Disorders?

Anyone who experiences an extraordinary trauma will be affected by it, but only some people develop a stress disorder. To understand the development of these disorders more fully, researchers have looked at *biological factors, childhood experiences, cognitive factors and coping styles, social support systems,* and the *severity and nature of the traumas.* Our discussions in this section will center on PTSD because that is the stress disorder that is most researched.

Biological Factors

Investigators have linked PTSD to several biological factors. The ones that have received the most attention are the brain–body *stress routes,* the brain's *stress circuit,* and *inherited predispositions.*

THE BRAIN–BODY STRESS ROUTES As you'll recall, when we are stressed, the brain's hypothalamus activates two stress routes throughout the brain and body—the sympathetic nervous system and the hypothalamic-pituitary-adrenal (HPA) axis. These routes react to stress by producing a general state of arousal, the former through nerve cell firing and the latter through releasing hormones into the bloodstream.

Helpers at risk Rescue workers frantically carry a victim from the ruins of an earthquake in Nepal (left), and a health care worker sits outside a New York City hospital after working relentlessly to help save countless Covid-19 patients (right). Studies reveal that those called upon to help people during catastrophes may themselves be at high risk for stress disorders.

Omar Havana/Getty Images

Tayfun Coskun/Anadolu Agency via Getty Images

Roberto Schmidt/AFP via Getty Images

Adam Scotti/Prime Minister's Office/Handout via Reuters/Redux

Historical trauma *Historical trauma* refers to the cumulative psychological wounds carried across generations by the members of a cultural group that was subjected to extraordinary past oppression, such as slavery, genocide, forced migration, or violent colonialization. According to research, a variety of actions can help promote individual healing, reconciliation, and social change, including participation in community gatherings and peaceful demonstrations. Here, a Black woman in the United States (left) and an Indigenous woman in Canada (right) protest the generations of oppression experienced by their cultural groups.

While everyone reacts to traumatic events with increased arousal throughout these two routes, research suggests that people who develop PTSD react with especially heightened arousal in the routes (Engel et al., 2023). There is evidence that, even prior to confronting a severe trauma, such individuals' routes are overly reactive to modest stressors, thus setting up a predisposition to develop PTSD. There is also evidence that *after* confrontation with a severe trauma, those brain–body routes become even more overly reactive (Lissek & Berg, 2022). Small wonder that researchers have found irregular activity of the hormone *cortisol* and the neurotransmitter/hormone *norepinephrine*—major players in the two routes—in the urine, blood, and saliva of combat soldiers, rape survivors, concentration camp survivors, and survivors of other severe stresses (Rasmusson et al., 2023; Hakamata et al., 2022). In short, once PTSD sets in, an individual's brain–body stress routes are characterized by still greater overreactivity in the face of stress, and this persistent overreactivity may lock in brain and body dysfunction and the continuing symptoms of PTSD.

THE BRAIN'S STRESS CIRCUIT Researchers believe that the chronic overreactivity of the two stress routes may help bring about dysfunction in a distinct brain circuit, sometimes called the brain's *stress circuit*. As you have read in earlier chapters, emotional, behavioral, and cognitive reactions of various kinds are tied to brain circuits—networks of brain structures that communicate and trigger each other into action. Dysfunction in one such circuit, the stress circuit, apparently contributes to the symptoms of PTSD. The brain's stress circuit includes such structures as the *amygdala, prefrontal cortex, anterior cingulate cortex, insula,* and *hippocampus,* among others (Averill et al., 2023; Hakamata et al., 2022; Weems et al., 2021).

Researchers have found that dysfunctions within and between three structures in this circuit—the amygdala, prefrontal cortex, and hippocampus—play particularly key roles in PTSD (Harris et al., 2023; Kredlow et al., 2022). It appears, for example, that in people with PTSD, the interconnection between the amygdala and the prefrontal cortex is flawed: activity by the former is too high, and activity by the latter is too low. The net effect of this flawed interconnection is that the individuals persistently experience symptoms of arousal, such as intense startle reactions and increased heart rate, that interfere with adaptive functioning. Similarly, in people with PTSD, there appears to be a flawed interconnection between the amygdala, prefrontal cortex, and hippocampus, the structure that helps initiate memories and helps regulate the body's stress hormones. The net result of this problematic interconnection is that the individuals keep experiencing the emotional memories, dissociations, and (yet again) arousal symptoms that characterize PTSD (Raise-Abdullahi et al., 2023).

Denise Truscello/Getty Images

Childhood interrupted In 2022, singer, songwriter, and musician Marcus Mumford took a hiatus from his successful band Mumford & Sons to release a deeply personal solo album, *Self-Titled.* The album included several autobiographical songs about being sexually abused as a child and the emotional wounds Mumford has carried since. Studies find that an abusive childhood increases a person's risk for developing PTSD when the person confronts traumatic events later in life.

INHERITED PREDISPOSITION Researchers also believe that certain individuals *inherit* a tendency for overly reactive brain–body stress routes and for a dysfunctional brain stress circuit. In turn, such individuals may have a susceptibility to PTSD. Genetic studies have located several genes that might be involved in this inherited susceptibility (Bustamante et al., 2023; Marchese & Huckins, 2023). Similarly, family pedigree research supports the notion of an inherited susceptibility. Studies conducted on thousands of pairs of twins who have served in the military find that if one twin develops posttraumatic stress symptoms after combat, an identical twin is more likely than a fraternal twin to develop the same symptoms (MGH, 2023).

In related work, researchers have found that people with PTSD often transmit relevant biological irregularities to their children (Tappenden, Pratchett, & Yehuda, 2022; Yehuda, 2022). In one study, for example, investigators examined the cortisol levels of women who had been pregnant during the September 11, 2001, terrorist attack and had developed PTSD in its aftermath. Not only did these women have higher-than-average cortisol levels, but their babies born after the attacks also displayed higher cortisol levels, suggesting that the babies inherited a predisposition to develop PTSD.

Childhood Experiences

Some researchers believe that a predisposition to develop PTSD may also be *acquired during childhood* rather than inherited at birth (Brown, Becker-Weidman, & Saxe, 2023; McLaughlin, 2023). In support of this notion, a number of studies have found that young children who are chronically neglected or abused or otherwise traumatized develop overly reactive brain–body stress routes and a dysfunctional brain stress circuit that carry into later life (Leroux et al., 2023; Weems et al., 2021). Apparently, their unfortunate childhood experiences actually play a role in reprogramming their brain and body stress responses.

Consistent with these findings, researchers have also found that substantial negative occurrences in childhood (physical, psychological, and/or deprivational), collectively called **adverse childhood experiences** (ACEs), increase a person's risk for later PTSD, among other disorders (Brown et al., 2023; McLaughlin, 2023). People whose childhoods were marked by poverty, for example, appear more likely to develop PTSD in the face of later trauma. So do people whose childhoods included an assault, abuse, or a catastrophe; multiple traumas; parental conflict; or living with family members who have psychological disorders.

Cognitive Factors and Coping Styles

Cognitive factors appear to play a key role in the development and maintenance of stress disorders (Bryant, 2023; Ehlers et al., 2022; McLean, Cummings, & Litz, 2022). In particular, it has been found that individuals who develop PTSD often display significant memory difficulties prior to their exposure to trauma. For example, research indicates that persons who struggle when attempting to recall everyday information, such as items on a shopping list, have a heightened risk for developing PTSD when they confront traumas. Such preexisting memory impairments are consistent with the memory disturbances found in PTSD itself—for example, intrusive flashbacks and poor recollection of key aspects of the traumatic event.

Another cognitive factor that helps set the stage for stress disorders is having a high *intolerance of uncertainty,* that is, extreme discomfort with the fact that negative events can occur unpredictably in life. In the previous chapter, you read that such intolerance often contributes to generalized anxiety disorder. Research finds that it is also prominent among people who develop PTSD in the face of trauma (Clauss et al., 2023). Similarly, studies suggest that people who generally view life's negative events as beyond their control may develop more severe stress symptoms after sexual abuse or other kinds of traumatic events than people who feel they have more control over their lives (Smith et al., 2023; Tull, 2022).

In addition to cognitive factors, it appears that an *inflexible coping style* may increase the likelihood of developing PTSD (Comer et al., 2021). In past years, it was believed that certain coping styles (for example, positive thinking, problem-solving) were always good and that others were always bad (avoidance, distraction). However, it turns out that different stressors call for different forms of coping, and no one coping style is universally effective. People are best served by having access to a broad range of coping strategies—such as problem-solving, positive thinking, avoidance, distraction, and acceptance—each of which can be called upon or put aside in accord with the particular features of various life stressors. Not surprisingly, then, studies have found that people with a *flexible* coping style are less likely than other individuals to develop PTSD after encountering traumatic events (Baluku et al., 2023; Comer et al., 2021; Compas, Vreeland, & Henry, 2020).

In a similar vein, today's psychologists often focus on the importance of **resilience**—the process of adapting well in the face of adversity (Troy et al., 2023). Whenever people apply effective coping strategies in difficult situations, they are demonstrating resilience, and people who are repeatedly resilient in life are less likely than other individuals to develop PTSD upon encountering traumatic events (Bonanno et al., 2024; Averill et al., 2023). There is some evidence that genetic factors help determine one's level of resilience across various life situations, but studies also find that young children who are regularly exposed to *manageable* stress develop heightened resilience skills, a gain that may continue throughout childhood and adulthood (Park et al., 2022). Not surprisingly, studies also find that the brain–body stress routes and the brain stress circuit of persons who repeatedly demonstrate resilience tend to operate better than those of other people (Averill et al., 2023; Roberts & Karatsoreos, 2021).

AP Photo/Ahn Young-joon

Building resilience Noting that *resilient* responses to life pressures may protect people from developing stress disorders, many programs now claim to build resiliency skills. Here young South Korean schoolchildren fall on a mudflat at a five-day winter military camp designed to strengthen them mentally and physically.

Social Support Systems

People whose social and family support systems are limited are also more likely to develop PTSD after a traumatic event (Monson et al., 2022). Rape survivors who feel loved, cared for, valued, and accepted by their friends and relatives recover from their ordeal more successfully. So do those treated with dignity and respect by the criminal justice system (Murphy-Oikonen et al., 2022). In contrast, clinical reports have suggested that inadequate social support contributes to the development of PTSD in some combat veterans (NCPTSD, 2023).

The Severity and Nature of the Trauma

As you might expect, the severity and nature of the traumatic event a person encounters help determine whether the individual will develop a stress disorder (Kessler et al., 2022) (see ***Trending***). Moreover, some events may override a favorable biological foundation, nurturing childhood, positive attitudes, and/or social support. Generally, the more severe or prolonged the trauma and the more direct one's exposure to it, the greater the likelihood of developing a stress disorder (APA, 2022). Mutilation, severe physical injury, or sexual assault in particular seem to increase the risk of stress disorders,

adverse childhood experiences (ACEs) Negative events occurring during childhood (for example, mistreatment, abuse, neglect, household dysfunction) that can lead to immediate or later trauma.

resilience The process of adapting well in the face of adversity.

...TRENDING

A New Disorder: Prolonged Grief Disorder

Yui Mok/Press Association via AP Images

Never forget A flower is placed against the National Covid Memorial Wall in London. This public mural contains over 150,000 hand-painted hearts to commemorate the many lives lost in the United Kingdom during the pandemic. By 2023, almost 7 million people worldwide had died from Covid-19.

As you have read, in 2022, the American Psychiatric Association (APA) published DSM-5-TR. The APA used the publication of this text revision as an opportunity to add a brand new diagnostic category—*prolonged grief disorder*. DSM-5-TR lists this new disorder in its group of *trauma- and stressor-related disorders,* along with the other disorders you've been reading about in this chapter.

Persons qualify for a diagnosis of prolonged grief disorder if, a year or more after the death of a loved one, they continue to display severe, wide-ranging symptoms of grief almost every day. Their persistent grief may include such symptoms as intense yearning for the lost individual, preoccupation with thoughts or memories of the loved one, a sense that their own identity has died with the lost one, marked disbelief about the loss, avoidance of reminders about the loss, extreme emotional pain, detachment from people and activities, reduced emotions in current situations, a sense of meaninglessness, and profound loneliness. Moreover, these continuing grief symptoms produce significant distress or impairment. People with this continuing pattern have a heightened risk of suicidal thinking.

Prolonged grief disorder is different from a *common grief reaction*. The latter can also be very intense and overwhelming and includes many of the same symptoms, but in that reaction the symptoms are more likely to weaken, become less frequent, and subside over time; to interfere less with daily functioning; and to stay within the scope of reactions characteristic of the bereaved person's cultural, social, and religious networks (APA, 2022). Prolonged grief disorder is also different from a grief-triggered *depressive disorder*. As you'll read in the chapter on depressive disorders, the clinical symptoms of the latter are more restricted to the emotional realm than the wide range of trauma-linked symptoms found in prolonged grief disorder (APA, 2022).

Researchers do not yet know the precise prevalence of prolonged grief disorder, but some studies suggest that it is experienced by fewer than 10 percent of bereaved persons (APA, 2023). Research conducted with mostly cisgender populations finds that the disorder is equally common for men and women. It appears to be more common among people who have lost a child, lost a spouse, were very dependent on the loved one, or lost the loved one to a violent or unexpected death (Na et al., 2023). The disorder also seems to occur more often among bereaved older adults than younger ones and more often among Black Americans than non-Hispanic White Americans (APA, 2022). However, relatively little research has been done to support or explain these observed differences.

Although it was designated a DSM disorder only in 2022, the pattern of prolonged grief has actually been of interest to clinicians for years (Zachar, First, & Kendler, 2023). Indeed, back in 2013, the framers of DSM-5 cited it as a condition worthy of study for possible inclusion in a future DSM. (Back then, it was called *persistent complex bereavement disorder.*) In the years following the framers' suggestion, members of the DSM-5-TR task group conducted reviews of the research literature and eventually became convinced that the category's validity, reliability, and clinical usefulness warranted its inclusion as a diagnostic category in DSM-5-TR.

as does witnessing the gruesome injury or death of other people. In addition, people who experience intentionally inflicted traumas are more likely to develop a stress disorder than those who encounter unintentional traumas (Sareen, 2022).

There is also growing evidence that encounters with multiple or recurring traumas can lead to a particularly severe pattern called *complex PTSD* (Fung et al., 2023; Feeny, Klein, & Benhamou, 2022). Persons with complex PTSD experience virtually all of the symptoms mentioned throughout this chapter, including numerous dissociative experiences, as well as profound disturbances in their emotional control, self-concept, and relationships.

Stolen lives, complex trauma A model at the Cosmopolitan NYFW (New York Fashion Week) raises awareness about child sex trafficking, a widespread criminal practice in which individuals under the age of 18 are illegally transported from one area to another and induced or forced to perform sexual acts and/or pornography. Subjected to profound physical, sexual, and emotional abuse and denied basic human needs, 77 percent of survivors display PTSD symptoms, and 41 percent develop *complex PTSD*.

Putting the Factors Together: The Developmental Psychopathology Perspective

Most of today's stress theorists believe that the various factors we have been looking at work together to help produce PTSD. The *developmental psychopathology* perspective, which has received considerable research support in the realm of PTSD, provides one of the most influential explanations of how this might occur (Cicchetti, 2023, 2018, 2016; Weems et al., 2021).

As you'll recall from earlier chapters, theorists from this perspective focus on the *intersection* and *context* of important variables at key *points of time* throughout an individual's life span. In the case of PTSD, they suggest that certain people have a biological predisposition—either inherited or acquired—for overreactivity in their brain–body stress routes and for dysfunction in their brain's stress circuit. This predisposition sets the stage for but does not guarantee the later development of PTSD. If these individuals encounter extreme stressors throughout their childhood, however, their stress routes may become still more overreactive and their brain's stress circuit more dysfunctional, and their risk of later developing PTSD may continue to grow (Brown et al., 2023; Lissek & Berg, 2022). This risk may increase still further if, over the course of their lives, the individuals acquire ineffective coping mechanisms, develop certain cognitive tendencies, and/or have weak social supports (Park et al., 2022).

It is important to note that in the developmental psychopathology perspective, the relationship between the contributing factors is often a two-way street. For example, while overreactive brain–body stress routes can contribute to poor coping during childhood and beyond, it is also the case that a childhood filled with *protective factors* such as experiences of *manageable* stress can, as we observed earlier, improve the functioning of the stress routes and facilitate better coping skills, thus reducing the risk of an individual later developing PTSD (Averill et al., 2023; Grasso, 2022).

According to developmental psychopathologists, the developing brain is always interacting with stressful experiences, and so the *timing* of stressors and traumas over the course of development has a profound influence on whether an individual will develop PTSD (La Greca et al., 2022; Park et al., 2022). For example, extreme stressors in childhood disrupt and alter the person's newly developing brain–body stress routes and brain stress circuit, increasing the likelihood that the routes and circuit will operate poorly over the course of life (Hakamata et al., 2022). In contrast, stressors in adulthood are less likely to alter the stress routes and stress circuit because the routes and circuit are more deeply rooted by then (Weems et al., 2021). Thus, people who encounter profound traumas in life are particularly likely to develop PTSD if their *early* lives were marked by experiences of intense stress.

Do the vivid images children see frequently on the web, TV, social media and video games make them more vulnerable or less vulnerable to later developing stress disorders?

The consequence of all this, according to the developmental psychopathology perspective, is that one person with, say, overreactive brain–body stress routes in early childhood may eventually develop

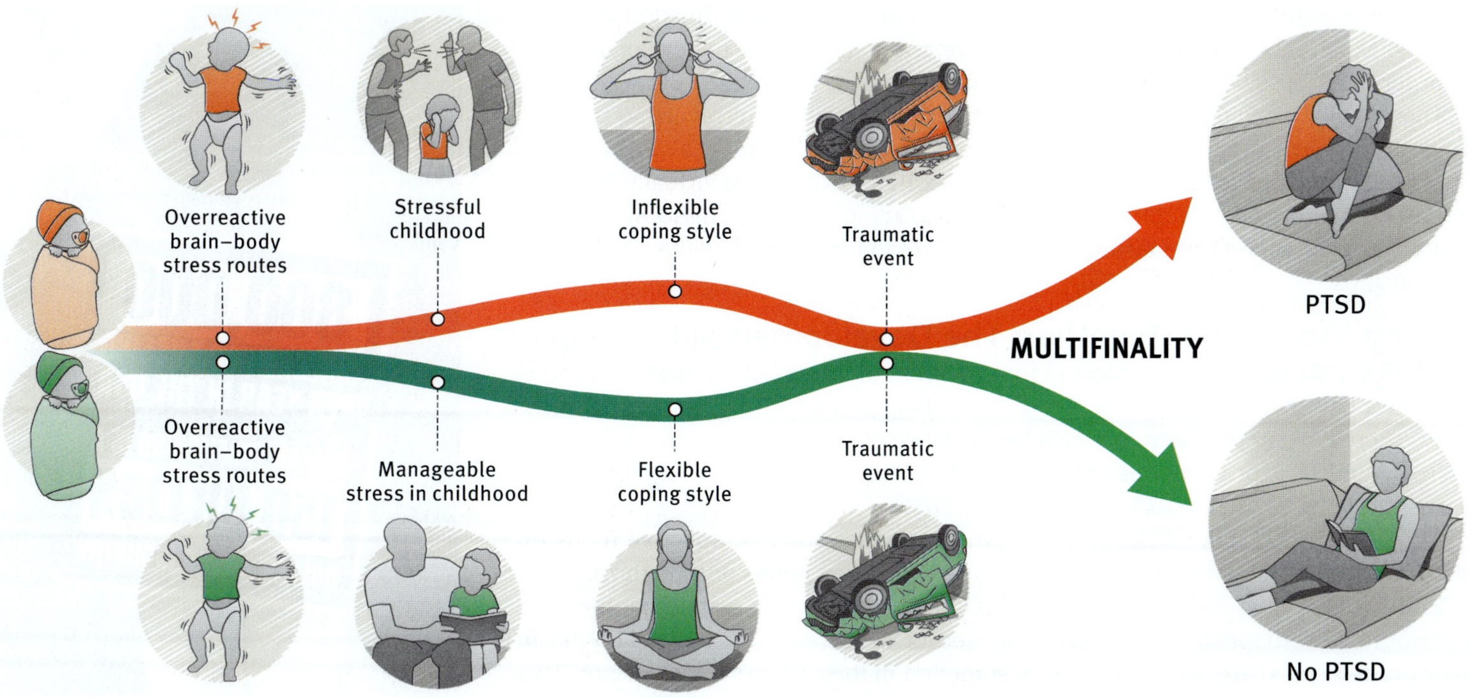

FIGURE 5-3

Multifinality and PTSD

According to the principle of *multifinality*, persons initially challenged by similar negative variables in childhood may wind up with different clinical outcomes. Both individuals in this illustration are born with overreactive brain–body stress routes. However, one individual further experiences intense childhood stress and acquires poor coping skills, setting the stage for PTSD in the face of a later traumatic event. In contrast, the other individual experiences manageable stress throughout childhood (a protective factor) and so remains clinically healthy when confronted by a later trauma.

PTSD when confronted by an extraordinary trauma, whereas another person with similar predisposing stress routes may not develop PTSD in the face of such trauma (see **Figure 5-3**). It all depends on the presence, timing, and intersections of the various factors we have been discussing. As you read in the chapter on models of psychopathology, this is the principle of *multifinality,* the notion that persons with similar beginnings may wind up at very different end points. Conversely, two persons — one with overreactive stress routes in early childhood and the other with appropriately reactive stress routes in early childhood — may both develop PTSD when eventually confronted by an extraordinary trauma (see **Figure 5-4**). In such cases, the person with the favorable early stress routes might nevertheless later come to develop overreactive routes as a result of aversive childhood experiences, inadequate social supports, and other such factors. This principle is known as *equifinality,* the notion that different developmental pathways may lead to the same end point.

How Do Clinicians Treat Acute and Posttraumatic Stress Disorders?

Treatment can be very important for people who have been overwhelmed by traumatic events. Overall, one-third of all cases of PTSD improve within 12 months. The remainder of cases may persist for longer, and, indeed, one-third of people with PTSD continue to be impaired by PTSD symptoms even after many years (Sareen, 2022).

Today's treatment procedures for troubled survivors often vary from trauma to trauma. Was it combat, an act of terrorism, sexual molestation, or a major accident? Yet all the treatment programs share basic goals: they try to help survivors put an end to their stress reactions, gain perspective on their painful experiences, and return to constructive living (Ruzek, Yalch, & Burkman, 2023). Programs for combat veterans with PTSD illustrate how these issues may be addressed.

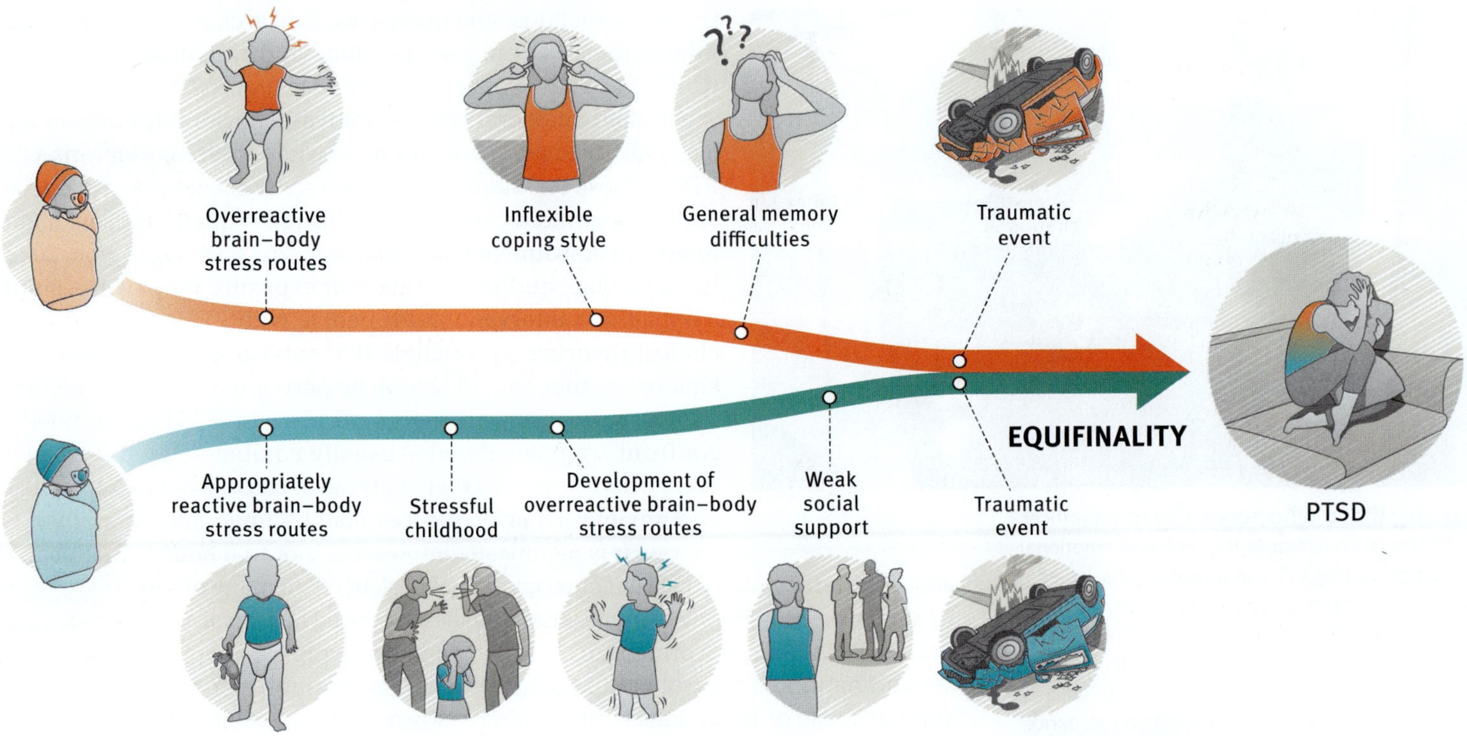

FIGURE 5-4

Equifinality and PTSD

The two individuals in this illustration experience different developmental variables. One, for example, is born with overreactive brain–body stress routes, and the other is born with brain–body stress routes that react appropriately. In each case, the initial variable combines with a particular cluster of subsequent negative variables to set the stage for the later development of PTSD, exemplifying the principle of *equifinality*.

Treatment for Combat Veterans

Therapists have used a variety of techniques to help reduce veterans' posttraumatic symptoms. Among the most common are *antidepressant drug therapy, cognitive-behavioral therapy, couple or family therapy,* and *group therapy*. Commonly, two or more of these approaches are combined, although such combinations do not always lead to better outcomes than just one of them (Keane, 2021). Regrettably, more than one-third of treated combat veterans prematurely discontinue their PTSD treatment (Duran et al., 2022).

ANTIDEPRESSANT DRUGS Antidepressant drugs are widely used for veterans with PTSD (Davis, Pilkinton, & Aikens, 2023; Stein, 2023). Typically, these medications are more helpful for the PTSD symptoms of increased arousal and negative emotions and less helpful for the recurrent negative memories, dissociations, and avoidance behaviors that also characterize the disorder. Around half of PTSD patients who take antidepressant drugs experience some symptom reductions. Other psychotropic drugs do not fare as well in PTSD research (West, Benedek, & Wynn, 2022).

COGNITIVE-BEHAVIORAL THERAPY Cognitive-behavioral therapy has proved to be of considerable help to many veterans with PTSD, bringing significant overall improvement to half or more of those who receive such treatment (Stein & Norman, 2023; McLean et al., 2022). On the cognitive side, the therapists guide the veterans to examine and change the dysfunctional attitudes and styles of interpretation they have developed as a result of their traumatic experiences. Over the course of such examinations and efforts, often called *cognitive processing therapy* (or *CPT*) when applied in cases of PTSD, the veterans learn to deal with difficult memories and feelings, come to accept what they have experienced and done, become less judgmental of themselves, and begin to trust other people once again (Galovski, Norman, & Hamblen, 2023; Chard & Wachen, 2022). Increasingly, a number of cognitive-behavioral therapists are adding mindfulness-based techniques to further help the clients become more accepting and less judgmental of their recurring

Carlos Osorio/Toronto Star via Getty Images

Serving those who serve Corrections officer Keith Hassel understands the profound emotional impact of working in trauma-related jobs, based on his years of service as a wartime navy veteran and a police officer and his personal struggles with PTSD. Thus, several years ago, he developed the Toronto PTSD Emergency Response Coalition, a network that provides peer support and guidance to first responders who experience significant psychological difficulties as a result of their work exposure to traumatic events.

thoughts, feelings, and memories. Research indicates that such mindfulness techniques produce additional improvements (USDVA, 2023; Wagner & Cáceres-Melillo, 2023).

On the behavioral side, cognitive-behavioral therapists typically apply *exposure* techniques when treating veterans with PTSD. These techniques have been quite successful at reducing specific symptoms and, in turn, bringing about improvements in overall adjustment (Galovski et al., 2023; Brown & Foa, 2022). In fact, some studies indicate that exposure may be the single most helpful intervention for people with PTSD, leading many clinical theorists to conclude that exposure techniques of one kind or another should always be part of the treatment picture.

During exposure therapy, veterans with PTSD are guided to confront trauma-related—usually combat-related—objects, events, and situations that continue to cause them extreme upset and anxiety. Their exposures may be imagined or in vivo. Of course, it is technically impossible, not to mention unethical, to expose veterans with PTSD to actual combat experiences, so many of today's exposure treatments rely on the vivid, multisensory images produced by *virtual reality* procedures (Ruzek, 2023; Stein & Norman, 2023). Here clients use wraparound goggles or a headset and handheld controllers to navigate their way through a computer-generated combat scene or bomb attack. Study after study suggests that virtual reality therapy is extremely helpful for combat veterans with PTSD as well as for people with other kinds of psychological challenges, such as social anxiety disorder and various phobias (Difede et al., 2022).

Perhaps the most widely applied exposure technique in cases of PTSD is **prolonged exposure** (Ruzek et al., 2023; Brown & Foa, 2022), in which therapists direct clients to confront not only trauma-related objects and situations but also their painful memories of traumatic experiences—memories they have been actively avoiding. The clients repeatedly recall and describe the memories—particularly "hot spots," pieces of the experiences that are especially dreadful—in great detail for extended periods of time, holding on to them until becoming less aroused, anxious, and upset by them. Here a therapist conducting prolonged exposure offers instructions to a client with PTSD:

> *Up to this point . . . you have been making great progress and have been experiencing the decrease in anxiety that we expect to see. Today we are going to do the exposure a little differently. . . . I will ask you to tell me . . . what the most distressing or upsetting parts of this memory are for you now. And then today, rather than going through the entire memory from beginning to end, I will ask you to focus the revisiting and recounting on each of these "hot spots," one at a time. We will pick one to begin with and you will repeat that one part of the memory over and over just by itself, focusing in closely and describing what happened in great detail, as if in slow motion, including what you felt, saw, heard, and thought. We will repeat it as many times as necessary to "wear it out" or bring about a big decrease in your [discomfort] level. When that part seems to have been sufficiently processed, we will move to the next one.*
>
> *(Foa, Hembree, & Rothbaum, 2007, pp. 100–101)*

Over the course of prolonged exposure, the client is expected to remember more and more details of each hot spot, experience less distress during such memories, become less fearful of the memories, and indeed display fewer symptoms of PTSD.

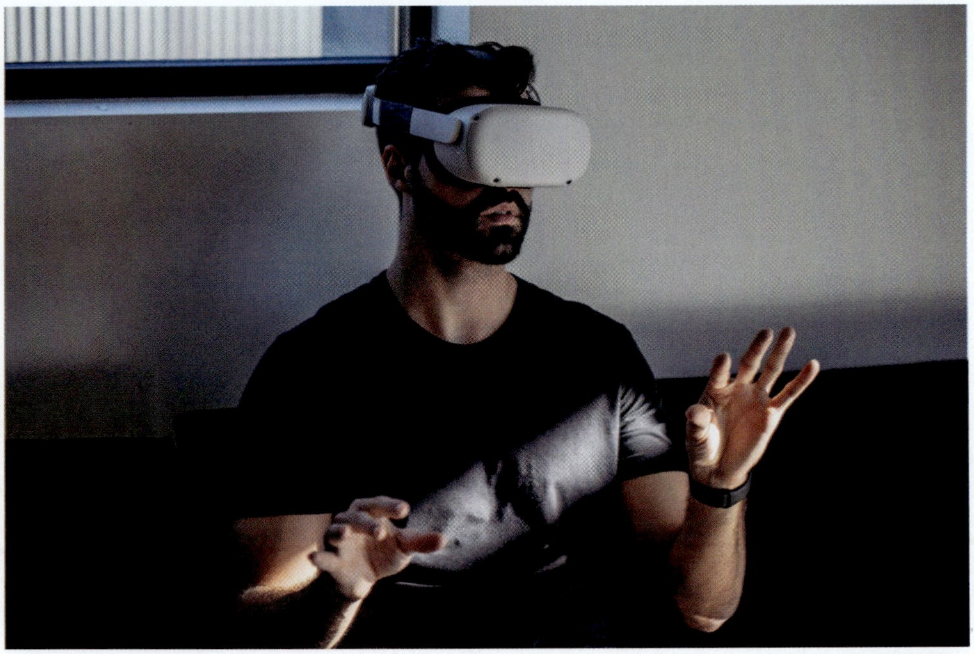

"Virtual" exposure A man demonstrates the operation of a Meta Quest 2 headset, a virtual reality device commonly used by cognitive-behavioral therapists as they conduct exposure therapy for PTSD and various anxiety disorders. The headset safely provides clients with realistic but controlled exposure to traumatic events and environments.

Research suggests that for clients who can stay with such intense memory exercises (many cannot), prolonged exposure is even more helpful than more gradual exposure interventions (Sloan et al., 2023; Brown & Foa, 2022).

Yet another form of exposure therapy, **written exposure therapy** (WET), has been used for veterans with PTSD. Many individuals tolerate this approach better than the intense and longer prolonged exposure approach, and it is often highly effective (Sloan et al., 2023, 2022; Stein & Norman, 2023). To help clients confront their troubling memories and express their difficult feelings, WET therapists have the individuals repeatedly write about them. This journaling approach is often preferred by clients who are looking to work through painful and traumatic memories but who do not wish to speak about them in detail with a therapist.

Finally, a popular form of exposure therapy is **eye movement desensitization and reprocessing** (EMDR), in which clients move their eyes in a rhythmic manner from side to side while flooding their minds with images of the objects and situations they ordinarily try to avoid. Although this approach has a number of skeptics, case studies and controlled studies suggest that the treatment can sometimes be helpful to people with PTSD (Stein & Norman, 2023; de Jongh et al., 2022). Many theorists argue that it is the exposure feature of EMDR, rather than the eye movement per se, that accounts for its success as a treatment.

COUPLE AND FAMILY THERAPY Veterans with PTSD may be helped further in couple therapy or family therapy formats (Monson et al., 2023, 2022; Stojek et al., 2022). The symptoms of PTSD are particularly apparent to spouses and other family members who may be directly affected by the client's anxieties, depressed mood, or angry outbursts. With the help and support of their family members, clients may come to examine their impact on others, learn to communicate better, improve their problem-solving skills, and reestablish feelings of closeness.

GROUP THERAPY In group therapy sessions, veterans meet with others like themselves to share experiences and feelings (particularly guilt and rage), develop insights, and give mutual support (AGPA, 2023; Ruzek et al., 2023). Today, hundreds of small *veterans outreach programs* across the country, as well as treatment programs in Veterans Administration hospitals and mental health clinics, provide group treatment (NCPTSD, 2023).

prolonged exposure A treatment approach in which clients confront not only trauma-related objects and situations but also their painful memories of traumatic experiences.

written exposure therapy (WET) A brief treatment approach for PTSD in which therapists guide clients to confront their troubling memories by having them repeatedly write about them.

eye movement desensitization and reprocessing (EMDR) An exposure treatment in which clients move their eyes in a rhythmic manner from side to side while flooding their minds with images of objects and situations they ordinarily avoid.

© Sarahbeth Maney/USA TODAY NETWORK

A shared trauma Survivors of the Oxford High School shooting in Pontiac, Michigan (left), and the Marjory Stoneman Douglas High School shooting in Parkland, Florida (right), come together and embrace in the city of Uvalde, Texas, in 2022. The two traveled over 1,500 miles from their respective hometowns to bring support and comfort to Uvalde students and family members following the Robb Elementary School shooting.

These agencies also offer individual therapy, counseling for spouses and children, family therapy, and aid in seeking jobs, education, and benefits. Clinical reports suggest that such programs offer a necessary, sometimes lifesaving, treatment opportunity.

Community Interventions

People who are traumatized by disasters, victimization, or accidents benefit from many of the same treatments that are used to help survivors of combat. In addition, because their traumas occur in their own community, where mental health resources are close at hand, they may, according to many clinicians, benefit further from immediate community interventions (Morganstein et al., 2023).

One such community approach is **psychological debriefing,** or **critical incident stress debriefing.** This intervention has survivors of trauma talk extensively about their feelings and reactions within days of the critical incident (Arancibia et al., 2022). The clinicians then clarify to the survivors that their reactions are common responses to a terrible event, offer stress management tips, and in some cases refer the individuals to professionals for long-term counseling. Such sessions may even be provided to trauma survivors who have not yet displayed any posttraumatic stress symptoms at all as well as to those who have. Over the past three decades, this intense approach has been applied in the aftermath of countless widescale traumatic events, from the 2001 World Trade Center attack to the 2017 mass killing of 58 individuals at a concert in Las Vegas, Nevada. In such cases, debriefing-trained counselors have come from far and wide to conduct debriefing sessions with the survivors.

In recent years, research has called into question the effectiveness and appropriateness of psychological debriefing and similar community programs (Bryant, 2023; Vignaud et al., 2022). In fact, some clinicians believe that intervention programs of this kind may encourage individuals to dwell too long on the traumatic events they have experienced or may unintentionally "suggest" problems to certain survivors, thus helping to *produce* stress disorders. In light of such concerns, several other early response interventions have gained popularity in recent years. One of the leading ones, **psychological first aid** (PFA), explicitly rejects the more controversial features of critical incident stress debriefing (APA, 2023; Everly & Lating, 2022). For example, although PFA encourages clinical helpers to promote adaptive functioning and address the immediate concerns and needs of survivors, it explicitly cautions helpers against providing on-site therapy, eliciting details of the traumatic event, assuming that everyone exposed to the event has

psychological debriefing A form of crisis intervention in which survivors are helped to talk about their feelings and reactions to traumatic incidents. Also called *critical incident stress debriefing.*

psychological first aid (PFA) A disaster response intervention that seeks to reduce the initial distress of survivors and foster their adaptive functioning, but without procedures that may be premature, intrusive, or inflexible.

been traumatized, or assuming that all survivors need to talk to a helper. PFA interventions have been used increasingly in recent years—offered, for example, to the communities and groups hardest hit by the Covid-19 pandemic and to the survivors, parents, and community members affected by the Uvalde, Texas, school shootings (DeAngelis, 2022; Zemel, 2022). Although PFA programs are promising and their use is clearly on the rise, their effectiveness has yet to be fully established by researchers.

dissociative disorders Disorders marked by major changes in memory that do not have clear physical causes.

SUMMING UP

Acute and Posttraumatic Stress Disorders

When we appraise a stressor as threatening, we often experience a stress response consisting of arousal and a sense of fear. The features of arousal are set in motion by the hypothalamus, a brain structure that activates two different stress routes—the sympathetic nervous system and the HPA axis.

People with acute stress disorder or PTSD react with arousal, anxiety, and other stress symptoms after a traumatic event, including reexperiencing the traumatic event, avoiding related events, being markedly less responsive than usual, and feeling guilt. Traumatic events may include combat experiences, disasters, or experiences of victimization.

In attempting to explain why some people develop a psychological stress disorder and others do not, researchers have focused on biological factors (particularly, overly reactive brain–body stress routes, a dysfunctional brain stress circuit, and an inherited predisposition), childhood experiences, cognitive factors and coping styles, social support systems, and the severity and nature of traumatic events as well as on how these factors may work together to produce such a disorder. Techniques used to treat the stress disorders include antidepressant drugs, cognitive-behavioral therapy (including exposure techniques), family therapy, and group therapy. Rapidly mobilized community interventions, such as psychological debriefing and psychological first aid, have also been applied.

Dissociative Disorders

AS YOU HAVE JUST READ, a number of people with acute and posttraumatic stress disorders have symptoms of dissociation along with their other symptoms. They may, for example, feel dazed, have trouble remembering things, or have a sense of depersonalization or derealization. Symptoms of this kind are also on display in **dissociative disorders,** another group of disorders triggered by traumatic events (Moskowitz et al., 2024). The memory difficulties and other dissociative symptoms found in these disorders are particularly intense, extensive, and disruptive. Moreover, in such disorders, dissociative reactions are the main or only symptoms. People with dissociative disorders do not typically have the significant arousal, negative emotions, sleep difficulties, and other symptoms that characterize acute and posttraumatic stress disorders. Nor are there clear physical factors at work in dissociative disorders.

Aftershocks In the aftermath of Turkey and Syria's massive earthquake in 2023, which killed more than 45,000 people, a dazed man separated from his loved ones sits and waits for information about their whereabouts. Survivors of natural disasters are particularly vulnerable to dissociative symptoms.

Burak Kara/Getty Images

TABLE 5-3

Dx Checklist

Dissociative Amnesia
1. Person cannot recall important life-related information, typically traumatic or stressful information. The memory problem is more than simple forgetting.
2. Significant distress or impairment.
3. The symptoms are not caused by a substance or a medical condition.

Information from: APA, 2022.

Most of us experience a sense of wholeness and continuity as we interact with the world. We perceive ourselves as being more than a collection of isolated sensory experiences, feelings, and behaviors. In other words, we have an *identity,* a sense of who we are and where we fit in our environment. *Memory* is a key to this sense of identity, the link between our past, present, and future. Without a memory, we would always be starting over; with it, our life and our identity move forward. In dissociative disorders, one part of a person's memory or identity becomes *dissociated,* or separated, from other parts of their memory or identity.

There are several kinds of dissociative disorders. People with *dissociative amnesia* are unable to recall important personal events and information. People with *dissociative identity disorder,* once known as *multiple personality disorder,* have two or more separate identities that may not always be aware of each other's memories, thoughts, feelings, and behavior. And people with *depersonalization-derealization disorder* feel as though they have become detached from their own mental processes or bodies or are observing themselves from the outside.

Dissociative Amnesia

People with **dissociative amnesia** are unable to recall important information, usually of a stressful nature, about their lives (APA, 2022). The loss of memory is much more extensive than typical forgetting and is not caused by physical factors, such as a blow to the head (see **Table 5-3**). Typically, an episode of amnesia is directly triggered by a traumatic or upsetting event (Spiegel, 2023; Ross, 2022).

Dissociative amnesia may be *localized, selective, generalized,* or *continuous.* In *localized amnesia,* the most common type of dissociative amnesia, a person loses all memory of events that took place within a limited period of time, almost always beginning with some very disturbing occurrence. A soldier, for example, may awaken a week after a horrific combat battle and be unable to recall the battle or any of the events surrounding it. The forgotten period is called the *amnestic episode.*

People with *selective amnesia,* the second most common form of dissociative amnesia, remember some but not all events that took place during a period of time. If the combat soldier mentioned in the previous paragraph had selective amnesia, they might remember certain interactions or conversations that occurred during the battle but not more disturbing events, such as the death of a friend or the screams of enemy soldiers.

In some cases, the loss of memory extends back to times long before the upsetting period. In addition to forgetting battle-linked events, the soldier may not remember events that occurred earlier in their life. In this case, they would have what is called *generalized amnesia.* In extreme cases, they might not even recognize relatives and friends.

In the forms of dissociative amnesia just discussed, the period affected by the amnesia has an end. In *continuous amnesia,* however, forgetting continues into the present. The soldier might forget new and ongoing experiences as well as what happened before and during the battle.

These various forms of dissociative amnesia are similar in that the amnesia interferes mostly with a person's memory of personal material. Memory for abstract or encyclopedic information usually remains, as does *procedural memory*—memory about how to perform procedures such as walking, talking, or riding a bike. People with dissociative amnesia are as likely as anyone else to know the name of the president of the United States and how to read or how to drive a car.

Studies suggest that around 2 percent of all adults experience dissociative amnesia in a given year (Almaazmi,

Paul Karasik/Conde Nast/The Cartoon Bank

"I'm concerned about his memory. He keeps asking, 'Who's a good boy? Who's a good boy?'"

Aldweik, & Mukhtar, 2023). Many cases seem to begin during serious threats to health and safety, as in wartime and natural disasters (Spiegel, 2023; Ross, 2022). Like the soldier in the earlier examples, combat veterans often report memory gaps of hours or days, and some forget personal information, such as their name and address.

Childhood abuse, particularly child sexual abuse, can also trigger dissociative amnesia (Linde-Krieger, Yates, & Carlson, 2022; Quiñones, 2022); indeed, in the 1990s, there were many reports in which adults claimed to recall long-forgotten experiences of childhood abuse (McNally, 2023) (see **PsychWatch**). In addition, dissociative amnesia

dissociative amnesia A dissociative disorder marked by an inability to recall important personal events and information.

PSYCHWATCH

Repressed Memories or False Memories?

Throughout the 1990s, clinicians reported numerous cases of *repressed childhood memory of abuse*. Adults with this type of dissociative amnesia seem to recover buried memories of sexual and physical abuse from their childhood. A woman might claim, for example, that her father sexually molested her repeatedly between the ages of 5 and 7. Or a young man might remember that a family friend made sexual advances on several occasions when he was very young. Often the repressed memories would surface during therapy for another problem.

Although the number of such claims has declined dramatically in recent years, clinicians remain divided on this issue (McNally, 2023; Otgaar et al., 2022). Some believe that recovered memories are just what they appear to be—horrible memories of abuse that have been buried for years in the person's mind. Other clinicians—the majority—believe that the memories are actually illusions, false images created during the process of therapy.

Bettmann/Getty Images

Early recall These siblings, all born on the same day in different years, have very different reactions to their cakes at a 1958 birthday party. But how do they each remember that party today? Research suggests that our memories of early childhood may be influenced by the reminiscences of family members, our dreams, television and movie plots, and our present self-image.

Opponents of the repressed memory concept point out that false memories of various kinds can actually be created in the laboratory by tapping into research participants' imaginations (Loftus & Klemfuss, 2023; McNally, 2023). Similarly, they argue, certain clients in treatment, especially those whose therapists use special *memory recovery techniques* such as hypnosis, may respond to those techniques by unknowingly forming false memories of abuse. In fact, in large surveys of individuals who have received therapy at some point over the past several decades, many report that their therapists initiated the possibility of repressed abuse and that they then came to uncover new memories of abuse over the course of treatment (Patihis, 2023; Patihis et al., 2022; Patihis & Pendergrast, 2018). The same surveys found that clients whose therapists raise the possibility of repressed memories of abuse are 20 to 29 times more likely than other clients to eventually experience abuse memories.

It is important to recognize that the theorists who question the recovery of repressed childhood memories do not in any way deny the problem of child sexual abuse. In fact, proponents and opponents alike are greatly concerned that the public may take this debate to mean that clinicians have doubts about the scope of the problem of child sexual abuse. Unfortunately, that problem is all too real and all too common.

dissociative fugue A form of dissociative amnesia in which a person travels to a new location and may assume a new identity, simultaneously forgetting their past.

may occur under more ordinary circumstances, such as the sudden loss of a loved one through rejection or death or extreme guilt over certain actions (Ross, 2022).

The personal impact of dissociative amnesia depends on how much is forgotten. Obviously, an amnestic episode of two years is more of a problem than one of two hours. Similarly, an amnestic episode during which a person's life changes in major ways causes more difficulties than one that is quiet.

An extreme version of dissociative amnesia is called **dissociative fugue.** Here people not only forget their personal identities and details of their past lives but also flee to an entirely different location. Some people travel a short distance and make few social contacts in the new setting (Spiegel, 2023; Daliri et al., 2022). Their fugue may be brief—a matter of hours or days—and end suddenly. In other cases, however, the person may travel far from home, take a new name, and establish a new identity, new relationships, and even a new line of work. Such people may also display new personality characteristics; often they are more outgoing.

Why do many people question the authenticity of people who seem to lose their memories at times of severe stress?

The majority of people who go through a dissociative fugue regain most or all of their memories and never have a recurrence. Since fugues are usually brief and totally reversible, those who have experienced them tend to have few aftereffects. People who have been away for months or years, however, often do have trouble adjusting to the changes that took place during their flight.

Dissociative Identity Disorder

Dissociative identity disorder is both dramatic and disabling, as we observe in the case of Clara:

Clara was first brought in for treatment after she was found walking in circles by the side of the road in a suburban neighborhood near Denver. Agitated, malnourished, and dirty, this 30-year-old woman told police that her name was Franny and that she was a 15-year-old who was running away from her home in Telluride. At first, the police officers suspected she was giving a false identity to avoid prosecution as a sex worker or for drug possession, but they found no evidence for either.

Once it became apparent that she fully believed what she was saying, the woman, who carried no identification of any kind, was transferred to a psychiatric hospital for observation. By the time she met with a therapist, she was no longer a young child speaking rapidly about a terrible family situation. She was now calling herself Clara, and she spoke in slow, measured, and sad tones—eloquent but often confused. At first, she did not want to answer questions, complaining that she had been brought there by police for no good reason, but once the therapist reassured her that he was there to help and she was not in any trouble, she began to open up.

Clara described how she had been physically and verbally abused for years by her stepfather. Her stepfather claimed this violence was her fault for misbehaving, but as the years went on, the abuse occurred any time her stepfather was in a bad mood or had been drinking. She said she had run away from home at the age of 15 and had not spoken since then to either her mother or her stepfather. She claimed that, although she had spent considerable time living on the streets over the years, she was currently living with her partner, Trish, in a small apartment. However, when pressed, she was unable to say what Trish did for a living, nor could she provide her address or last name. Thus, she remained in treatment.

Over the course of treatment, as her therapist continued to probe for details of her unhappy childhood and physical abuse, Clara became more and more agitated, until finally during one session she actually transformed back into 15-year-old Franny.

Her therapist wrote in his notes, "Her entire physical presence transformed itself suddenly and almost violently. Her face, previously relaxed and even flat, became tense and scrunched up, and her entire body hunched over. She moved her chair back almost two feet and repeatedly flinched from me if I even gestured in her direction. Her voice became high-pitched, clipped, and fast, spitting out words, and her vocabulary became limited to that which a child would display. She seemed to be a different person in every way possible."

Over the following several sessions, Clara's therapist wound up meeting still other personalities. One was Miss Johnson, a strict school principal who claimed to have taught Clara when she was younger. Another was Roger—unhoused, tough, and threatening—who made it clear he was in charge of Clara and the other personalities. Lilly, aged 24, was a math genius and accountant who seemed to appear whenever Clara needed to deal with money or complex mathematical issues.

dissociative identity disorder A dissociative disorder in which a person develops two or more distinct personalities. Previously known as *multiple personality disorder.*

subpersonalities The two or more distinct personalities found in individuals with dissociative identity disorder. Also known as *alternate personalities.*

A person with **dissociative identity disorder** develops two or more distinct personalities, often called **subpersonalities,** or **alternate personalities,** each with a unique set of memories, behaviors, thoughts, and emotions (see **Table 5-4**). At any given time, one of the subpersonalities takes center stage and dominates the person's functioning. Usually one subpersonality, called the *primary,* or *host,* personality, appears more often than the others.

The transition from one subpersonality to another, called *switching,* is usually sudden and may be dramatic. Clara, for example, twisted her face and hunched her shoulders and body forward violently. Switching is usually triggered by a stressful event, although clinicians can also bring about the change with hypnotic suggestion.

Cases of dissociative identity disorder were first reported almost three centuries ago. Around 1 percent of the population is reported to experience the disorder within a given year; however, some clinical theorists believe it may be more common than this (Mitra & Jain, 2023; Foote, 2022). Most cases are first diagnosed in late adolescence or early adulthood, but more often than not, the symptoms actually began in early childhood after episodes of trauma or abuse (often physical and/or sexual abuse) (Mitra & Jain, 2023; Quiñones, 2022). Initial research suggests that the prevalence of this disorder for transgender people and nonbinary people is about the same as the prevalence for cisgender people (Soldati et al., 2022). According to studies conducted with mostly cisgender populations, women receive this diagnosis at least three times as often as men (Foote, 2022).

Why might women be more likely than men to receive a diagnosis of dissociative identity disorder?

Media Drum World/ZUMA Press/Newscom

Media Drum World/ZUMA Press/Newscom

Subpersonalities at work Emma Laver-Scott is the picture of tranquility as she walks with her daughter along the English coastline (left). In fact, however, she has dissociative identity disorder, a condition that, for years, brought torment and terror to her life, as illustrated in a drawing by one of her 21 subpersonalities (right). Prior to her diagnosis at the age of 31, Emma had experienced 22 years of memory blackouts, strange injuries, depressive feelings, forgotten journeys, bizarre notes around the house, and mysterious voices and visions, all of which had eluded proper clinical assessment. For a while, Emma even attributed her symptoms to possession by spirits.

TABLE 5-4

Dx Checklist

Dissociative Identity Disorder
1. Person experiences a disruption to their identity, as reflected by at least two separate personality states or experiences of possession.
2. Person repeatedly experiences memory gaps regarding daily events, key personal information, or traumatic events, beyond ordinary forgetting.
3. Significant distress or impairment.
4. The symptoms are not caused by a substance or a medical condition.

Information from: APA, 2022.

How Do Subpersonalities Interact?

How subpersonalities relate to or recall one another varies from case to case. Generally, however, there are three kinds of relationships. In *mutually amnesic relationships,* the subpersonalities have no awareness of one another. Conversely, in *mutually cognizant patterns,* each subpersonality is well aware of the rest. They may hear one another's voices and even talk among themselves. Some are on good terms, while others do not get along at all.

In *one-way amnesic relationships,* the most common relationship pattern, some subpersonalities are aware of others, but the awareness is not mutual. Those who are aware, called *coconscious subpersonalities,* are "quiet observers" who watch the actions and thoughts of the other subpersonalities but do not interact with them. Sometimes while another subpersonality is present, the coconscious personality makes itself known through indirect means, such as auditory hallucinations (perhaps a voice giving commands) or "automatic writing" (the current personality may find itself writing down words over which it has no control).

Investigators used to believe that most cases of dissociative identity disorder involved two or three subpersonalities. Studies now suggest, however, that the average number of subpersonalities per patient is 5 to 10 (Foote, 2022). In fact, there have been cases in which 100 or more subpersonalities were observed. Often the subpersonalities emerge in groups of two or three at a time.

In the case of "Eve White," made famous in the book and movie *The Three Faces of Eve,* a woman had three subpersonalities—Eve White, Eve Black, and Jane (Thigpen & Cleckley, 1957). Eve White, the primary personality, was quiet and serious; Eve Black was carefree and mischievous; and Jane was mature and intelligent. According to the book, these three subpersonalities eventually merged into Evelyn, a stable personality who was really an integration of the other three.

The book was mistaken, however; this was not to be the end of Eve's dissociation. In an autobiography 20 years later, she revealed that altogether 22 subpersonalities had come forth during her life, including 9 subpersonalities after Evelyn. Usually they appeared in groups of three, and so the authors of *The Three Faces of Eve* apparently never knew about her previous or subsequent subpersonalities. She later overcame her disorder, achieving a single, stable identity, and was known as Chris Sizemore for four decades until her death in 2016 (Weber, 2016; Sizemore, 1991).

How Do Subpersonalities Differ?

As in Chris Sizemore's case, subpersonalities often exhibit dramatically different characteristics. They may also have their own names and different *identifying features, abilities and preferences,* and even *physiological responses.*

IDENTIFYING FEATURES The subpersonalities may differ in features as basic as age, gender, race, and family history, as in the case of Sybil Dorsett, whose disorder is described in the famous novel *Sybil* (Schreiber, 1973). According to the novel, Sybil displayed 17 subpersonalities, all with different identifying features. They included adults, a teenager, and even a baby. One subpersonality, Vicky, saw herself as attractive and blonde, while another, Peggy Lou, believed herself to be "a pixie with a pug nose." Yet another, Mary, was plump with dark hair, and Vanessa was a tall, thin redhead. (It is worth noting that the accuracy of the real-life case on which this novel was based has been challenged in recent years.)

ABILITIES AND PREFERENCES Although memories of abstract or encyclopedic information are not usually affected in dissociative amnesia, they are often disturbed in dissociative identity disorder. It is not uncommon for the different subpersonalities to have different abilities: one may be able to drive, speak a foreign language, or play a musical instrument, while the others cannot (APA, 2022; Foote, 2022). Their handwriting can also differ. In addition, the subpersonalities usually have different tastes

of NOTE ...

Treating Sybil

Over the past two decades, claims by several colleagues who worked closely with the author of *Sybil* and with Sybil's real-life therapist suggest that Shirley Mason (the person on whom Sybil was based) was highly hypnotizable, extremely suggestible, and anxious to please her therapist and that her disorder was in fact induced largely by hypnosis, sodium pentothal, and therapist suggestion (Carey, 2017; Nathan, 2011; Rieber, 2002, 1999).

in food, friends, music, and literature. Chris Sizemore ("Eve") later pointed out, "If I had learned to sew as one personality and then tried to sew as another, I couldn't do it. Driving a car was the same. Some of my personalities couldn't drive" (Sizemore & Pittillo, 1977, p. 4).

PHYSIOLOGICAL RESPONSES Researchers have discovered that subpersonalities may have physiological differences, such as differences in blood pressure levels and allergies (NAMI-M, 2022; Putnam, Zahn, & Post, 1990; Putnam, 1984). A pioneering study looked at the brain activities of different subpersonalities by measuring their *evoked potentials*—that is, brain-response patterns recorded on an electroencephalograph. The brain pattern a person produces in response to a specific stimulus (such as a flashing light) is usually unique and consistent. However, when an evoked potential test was administered to 4 subpersonalities of each of 10 people with dissociative identity disorder, the results were dramatic. The brain-activity pattern of each subpersonality was unique, showing the kinds of variations usually found in totally different people. A number of other studies conducted over the past two decades have yielded similar findings (Modesti et al., 2022).

of NOTE ...

Assessment Delay

People with dissociative identity disorder do not receive that diagnosis until they have been in therapy for an average of seven years (Mitra & Jain, 2023; Foote, 2022).

How Common Is Dissociative Identity Disorder?

As you have read, dissociative identity disorder has traditionally been thought of as relatively uncommon. Some researchers even argue that many or all cases are *iatrogenic*—that is, unintentionally produced by practitioners (Foote, 2022). They believe that therapists create this disorder by subtly suggesting the existence of other personalities during therapy or by explicitly asking a patient to produce different personalities while under hypnosis. In addition, they believe, a therapist who is looking for multiple personalities may reinforce these patterns by displaying greater interest when a patient displays symptoms of dissociation. In a related vein, some theorists note that dissociative identity disorder seems to be *culture-bound* (Spiegel, 2023; Krüger, 2020). While the prevalence of this disorder has grown in North America, it is rare or nonexistent in Great Britain, Sweden, Russia, India, and Southeast Asia.

These arguments seem to be supported by the fact that many cases of dissociative identity disorder first come to attention while the person is already in treatment for a less serious problem. But such is not true of all cases; many people seek treatment because they have noticed time lapses throughout their lives or because relatives and friends have observed their subpersonalities (Mitra & Jain, 2023).

What verdict is appropriate for accused criminals with dissociative identity disorder whose crimes are committed by one of their subpersonalities?

The number of people diagnosed with dissociative identity disorder increased dramatically in the 1980s and 1990s, only to decrease again in the twenty-first century. Notwithstanding this decline, thousands of cases have now been diagnosed in the United States and Canada alone. On the other side of the coin, many clinicians continue to question the legitimacy of this category.

How Do Theorists Explain Dissociative Amnesia and Dissociative Identity Disorder?

A variety of theories have been proposed to explain dissociative amnesia and dissociative identity disorder. Older explanations, such as that offered by psychodynamic theorists, have not received much investigation. However, newer viewpoints, which highlight such factors as *state-dependent learning* and *self-hypnosis*, have captured the interest of clinical scientists.

The Psychodynamic View

Psychodynamic theorists believe that these dissociative disorders are caused by *repression*, the most basic ego defense mechanism: people fight off anxiety by unconsciously preventing painful memories, thoughts, or impulses from reaching awareness. Everyone uses repression to a degree, but

Sam Marlow/CartoonStock Ltd.

people with dissociative amnesia and dissociative identity disorder are thought to repress their memories in an extreme way (Ross, 2022).

In the psychodynamic view, dissociative amnesia is a *single episode* of massive repression. A person unconsciously blocks the memory of an extremely upsetting event in order to avoid the pain of facing it (O'Neil, 2022). Repressing may be the individual's only protection from overwhelming anxiety.

In contrast, dissociative identity disorder is thought to result from a *lifetime* of extreme repression (Stern, 2022). Psychodynamic theorists believe that this continuous use of repression is motivated by traumatic childhood events, particularly abusive parenting (Mitra & Jain, 2023; O'Neil, 2022; Subramanyam et al., 2020). Children who experience such traumas may come to fear the dangerous world they live in and take flight from it by pretending to be another person who is looking on safely from afar. Abused children may also come to fear the impulses that they believe are the reasons for their excessive punishments. Whenever they experience "bad" thoughts or impulses, they unconsciously try to disown and deny them by assigning them to other personalities.

Support for the psychodynamic explanation of dissociative identity disorder comes from a variety of studies, largely case studies, that report such brutal childhood experiences as beatings, cuttings, burnings with cigarettes, imprisonment in closets, rape, and extensive verbal abuse (Linde-Krieger et al., 2022; Quiñones, 2022). Indeed, more than 70 percent of people with this disorder were abused physically and/or sexually as children (Foote, 2022). Yet some individuals with this disorder do not seem to have experiences of abuse in their background (Mitra & Jain, 2023; Dell, 2022; Ross, 2022, 2018).

State-Dependent Learning: A Cognitive-Behavioral View

If people learn something when they are in a particular situation or state of mind, they are likely to remember it best when they are again in that same condition. If they are given a learning task while under the influence of alcohol, for example, their later recall of the information may be strongest under the influence of alcohol. Similarly, if they smoke cigarettes while learning, they may later have better recall when they are again smoking.

This link between state and recall is called **state-dependent learning.** It was initially observed in animals that learned things during experiments while under the influence of certain drugs (Jafari-Sabet et al., 2022; Overton, 1966, 1964). Research with human participants later showed that state-dependent learning can be associated with mood states as well: material learned while the participant is in a happy mood is recalled best when the participant is again happy, and sad-state learning is recalled best during sad states (Faul & LaBar, 2022; Bower, 1981) (see **Figure 5-5**).

What causes state-dependent learning? One possibility is that *arousal* levels are an important part of learning and memory. That is, a particular level of arousal will have a set of remembered events, thoughts, and skills attached to it. When a situation produces that particular level of arousal, the person is more likely to recall the memories linked to it (Dev et al., 2022).

Although people remember certain events better in some arousal states than in others, most can recall events under a variety of states. However, some theorists suggest that people who are prone to develop dissociative disorders have state-to-memory links that are unusually rigid and narrow and are even tied to specific brain changes (Vissia et al., 2022; Barlow, 2011). Each of their thoughts, memories, and skills may be tied *exclusively* to a particular state of arousal, so that they recall a given event only when they experience an arousal state almost identical to the state in which the memory was first acquired. When such people are calm, for example, they may forget what

state-dependent learning Learning that becomes associated with the conditions under which it occurred so that it is best remembered under the same conditions.

self-hypnosis The process of hypnotizing oneself, sometimes for the purpose of forgetting unpleasant events.

happened during stressful times, thus laying the groundwork for dissociative amnesia. Similarly, in dissociative identity disorder, different arousal levels may produce entirely different groups of memories, thoughts, and abilities—that is, different subpersonalities. This could explain why personality transitions in dissociative identity disorder tend to be sudden and stress-related.

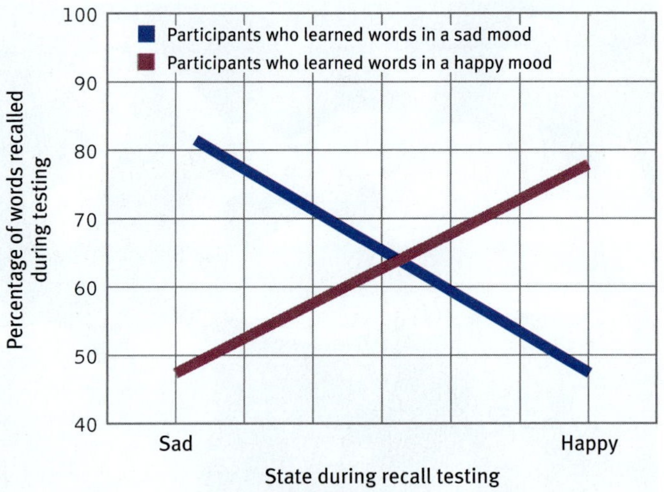

FIGURE 5-5

State-Dependent Learning

In one study, participants who learned a list of words while in a hypnotically induced happy state remembered the words better if they were in a happy mood when tested later than if they were in a sad mood. Conversely, participants who learned the words when in a sad mood recalled them better if they were sad during testing than if they were happy. (Information from: Bower, 1981.)

Self-Hypnosis As you first learned in the opening chapter of the textbook, people who are *hypnotized* enter a sleeplike state in which they become very suggestible. While in this state, they can behave, perceive, and think in ways that would ordinarily seem impossible. They may, for example, become temporarily blind, deaf, or insensitive to pain. Hypnosis can also help people remember events that occurred and were forgotten years ago, a capability used by many psychotherapists. Conversely, it can make people forget facts, events, and even their personal identities—an effect called *hypnotic amnesia*.

The parallels between hypnotic amnesia and the dissociative disorders we have been examining are striking. Both are conditions in which people forget certain material for a period of time yet later remember it. And in both, the people forget without any insight into why they are forgetting or any awareness that something is being forgotten. These parallels have led some theorists to conclude that dissociative disorders may be a form of **self-hypnosis** in which people hypnotize themselves to forget unpleasant events (Dell, 2022). Dissociative amnesia may develop, for example, in people who, consciously or unconsciously, hypnotize themselves into forgetting horrifying experiences that have recently taken place in their lives. If the self-induced amnesia covers all memories of a person's past and identity, that person may undergo a dissociative fugue.

The self-hypnosis theory might also be used to explain dissociative identity disorder (Dell, 2022). On the basis of several investigations, some theorists believe that this disorder often begins between the ages of 4 and 6, a time when children are generally very suggestible and excellent hypnotic subjects (Mitra & Jain, 2023; Dell, 2022). These theorists argue that some children who experience abuse or other horrifying events manage to escape their threatening world by self-hypnosis, mentally separating themselves from their bodies and fulfilling their wish to become some other person or persons (Foote, 2022; Quiñones, 2022). One patient with multiple personalities observed, "I was in a trance often [during my childhood]. There was a little place where I could sit, close my eyes and imagine, until I felt very relaxed just like hypnosis" (Bliss, 1980, p. 1392).

How Are Dissociative Amnesia and Dissociative Identity Disorder Treated?

As you have read, people with dissociative amnesia often recover on their own. Only sometimes do their memory problems linger and require treatment. In contrast, people with dissociative identity disorder usually require treatment to regain their lost memories and develop an integrated personality. Treatments for dissociative amnesia tend to be more successful than those for dissociative identity disorder, probably because the former pattern is less complex.

How Do Therapists Help People with Dissociative Amnesia?

The leading treatments for dissociative amnesia are *psychodynamic therapy, hypnotic therapy,* and *drug therapy,* although support for these interventions comes largely from case studies rather than controlled investigations (Spiegel, 2023). Psychodynamic therapists guide clients to search their unconscious in the hope of bringing forgotten experiences back to consciousness (Mitra & Jain, 2023; Loewenstein, 2022). The focus

of NOTE ...

Most Frequently Forgotten in Everyday Life

Online passwords
Where cell phone was left
Where keys were left
Where remote control was left
Names
Dream content
Birthdays/anniversaries

Erin Painter/Midland Daily News/AP Photo

Hypnotic recall Northwood University students react while under hypnosis to the suggestion of being on a beach in Hawaii and needing suntan lotion. Many clinicians use hypnotic procedures to help clients recall past events, but research reveals that such procedures often create false memories.

of psychodynamic therapy seems particularly well suited to the needs of people with dissociative amnesia. After all, the patients need to recover lost memories, and the general approach of psychodynamic therapists is to try to uncover memories—as well as other psychological processes—that have been repressed. Thus, many theorists, including some who do not ordinarily favor psychodynamic approaches, believe that psychodynamic therapy may be the most appropriate treatment for dissociative amnesia.

Another common treatment for dissociative amnesia is **hypnotic therapy,** or **hypnotherapy.** Therapists hypnotize patients and then guide them to recall their forgotten events (Mitra & Jain, 2023; Kluft, 2022). Given the possibility that dissociative amnesia may be a form of self-hypnosis, hypnotherapy may be a particularly useful intervention. It has been applied both alone and in combination with other approaches.

Sometimes, injections of barbiturates such as *sodium amobarbital* (Amytal) or *sodium pentobarbital* (Pentothal) have been used to help patients with dissociative amnesia regain their lost memories. These drugs are often called "truth serums," but actually their effect is to calm people and free their inhibitions, thus helping them to recall anxiety-producing events (Johnson & Sadiq, 2023; Spiegel, 2023). The drugs do not always work, however, and if used at all, they are likely to be combined with other treatment approaches.

How Do Therapists Help People with Dissociative Identity Disorder?

Treatment for dissociative identity disorder is complex and difficult, much like the disorder itself. Therapists usually try to help the clients (1) recognize fully the nature of their disorder, (2) recover the gaps in their memory, and (3) integrate their subpersonalities into one functional personality.

RECOGNIZING THE DISORDER Once a diagnosis of dissociative identity disorder is made, therapists typically try to bond with the primary personality and with each of the subpersonalities (Spiegel, 2023; Loewenstein, 2022). As bonds are formed, therapists try to educate patients and help them to recognize fully the nature of their disorder. Some therapists actually introduce the subpersonalities to one another by hypnosis, for example, or by having patients look at videos of their other personalities. A number of therapists have also found that group therapy helps to educate patients (Subramanyam et al., 2020). In addition, family therapy may be used to help educate spouses and children about the disorder and to gather helpful information about the patient (AAMFT, 2023).

of NOTE ...

Their Words

"Memory isn't like reading a book; it's more like writing a book from fragmentary notes."

John F. Kihlstrom, psychologist

RECOVERING MEMORIES To help patients recover the missing pieces of their past, therapists typically use the same approaches applied in dissociative amnesia, including psychodynamic therapy, hypnotherapy, and drug treatment (Mitra & Jain, 2023; Spiegel, 2023; Loewenstein, 2022). These techniques work slowly for patients with dissociative identity disorder, however, as some subpersonalities may keep denying experiences that the others recall. One of the subpersonalities may even assume a "protector" role to prevent the primary personality from enduring the pain of recollecting traumatic experiences.

INTEGRATING THE SUBPERSONALITIES The final goal of therapy is to merge the different subpersonalities into a single, integrated identity (Mitra & Jain, 2023; Ross, 2022). Integration is a continuous process that occurs throughout treatment until patients "own" all of their behaviors, emotions, sensations, and knowledge. **Fusion** is the final merging of two or more subpersonalities. Many patients distrust this final treatment goal, and their subpersonalities may consider integration to be a form of death (Spiegel, 2023; Howell, 2020, 2011). Therapists have used a range of approaches to help merge subpersonalities, including psychodynamic, supportive, cognitive-behavioral, and drug therapies.

Once the subpersonalities are integrated, further therapy is typically needed to maintain the complete personality and to teach social and coping skills that may help prevent later dissociations. In case reports, some therapists note high success rates, but others find that patients continue to resist full integration (Bachrach et al., 2023; Ross, 2022, 2018). In fact, a number of therapists question the need for full integration.

hypnotic therapy A treatment in which the patient undergoes hypnosis and is then guided to recall forgotten events or perform other therapeutic activities. Also known as *hypnotherapy*.

fusion The final merging of two or more subpersonalities in dissociative identity disorder.

depersonalization-derealization disorder A dissociative disorder marked by the presence of persistent and recurrent episodes of depersonalization, derealization, or both.

Depersonalization-Derealization Disorder

As you read earlier, DSM-5-TR categorizes **depersonalization-derealization disorder** as a dissociative disorder, even though it is not characterized by the memory difficulties found in the other dissociative disorders. Its central symptoms are persistent and recurrent episodes of *depersonalization* (the sense that one's own mental functioning or body is unreal or detached) and/or *derealization* (the sense that one's surroundings are unreal or detached) (Morrison, 2023).

Arun, a 28-year-old television production assistant, came to therapy complaining that he was spending more and more of his time questioning his reality. During waking hours, he often felt stuck in a chronic dream state, floating above himself, disconnected from his own thoughts, and watching his body go through the motions of his life. At work, when he would carry props to the set, he would sometimes look at his hands and perceive them as foreign and abnormally large. When getting actors to the right place on time, he often felt as if they might be robots.

By the third week of therapy, he also reported that his girlfriend's facial and body features often appeared in an altered manner when he was looking at her. When he walked by other people in his neighborhood in Cambodia Town in Long Beach, California, they often seemed to him too large to be human, and they sometimes appeared to change size as he walked by them, suddenly becoming quite small. Still later in therapy, he considered dropping out of treatment because he had doubts that his therapist was actually alive.

Like Arun, people experiencing depersonalization feel as though they have become separated from their body and are observing themselves from outside. Occasionally their mind seems to be floating a few feet above them—a sensation known as *doubling*. Their body parts feel foreign to them, their hands and feet smaller or bigger than usual. Many describe their emotional state as "mechanical," "dreamlike," or "dizzy." Throughout the whole experience, however, they are aware that their perceptions are distorted, and in that sense they remain in contact with reality. In some cases, this sense of unreality also extends to other sensory experiences and behavior. People may, for example, have distortions in their sense of touch or smell or their judgments of time or space, or they may feel that they have lost control over their speech or actions.

In contrast to depersonalization, derealization is characterized by the person feeling that the external world is unreal and strange. Objects may seem to change shape or size; other people may seem removed, mechanical, or even dead. Arun, for example, saw other people as excessively large or excessively small, perceived his girlfriend in a distorted manner, and later hesitated to return to therapy because he wondered whether his therapist was really alive.

of NOTE ...

Their Words

"I was trying to daydream, but my mind kept wandering."

Steven Wright, comedian

Depersonalization and derealization experiences by themselves do not indicate a depersonalization-derealization disorder. Transient depersonalization or derealization reactions are fairly common (Murphy, 2023; Simeon, 2022). One-half of all people say that on occasion, they have felt as though they were watching themselves in a movie (Spiegel, 2023). Similarly, one-third of individuals who confront a life-threatening danger encounter feelings of depersonalization or derealization. People sometimes have feelings of depersonalization after practicing meditation or after traveling to new places. Young children may also experience depersonalization from time to time as they are developing their capacity for self-awareness. In most such cases, the affected people are able to compensate for the distortion and continue to function with reasonable effectiveness until the temporary episode eventually ends.

If you have ever experienced feelings of depersonalization or derealization, how did you explain them at the time?

The symptoms of depersonalization-derealization disorder, in contrast, are persistent or recurrent, cause considerable distress, and may impair social relationships and job performance. The disorder is experienced by 1 to 2 percent of the population, most often adolescents and young adults; it is hardly ever experienced by people over 40 (Spiegel, 2023). It usually comes on suddenly and may be triggered by extreme fatigue, physical pain, intense stress, or recovery from substance use disorder. Survivors of traumatic events or people caught in life-threatening situations, such as hostages or kidnap victims, seem to be particularly vulnerable to this disorder. The disorder tends to be long-lasting; the symptoms may improve and even disappear for a time, only to return or intensify during times of severe stress (Michal, 2022). Like Arun in our case discussion, many people with the disorder fear that they are losing their minds and become preoccupied with worry about their symptoms. Few theories have been offered to explain depersonalization-derealization disorder (Michal, 2022). Several different forms of psychotherapy have been applied in cases of this disorder, but there has been relatively little research to test the efficacy of these approaches (Spiegel, 2023; Simeon, 2022).

SUMMING UP

III Dissociative Disorders

People with dissociative disorders experience major changes in memory and identity that are not caused by clear physical factors—changes that often emerge after a traumatic event. Typically, one part of the memory or identity is dissociated, or separated, from the other parts. People with dissociative amnesia are unable to recall important personal information or past events in their lives. Those with dissociative fugue, an extreme form of dissociative amnesia, not only fail to remember personal information but also flee to a different location and may establish a new identity. In another dissociative disorder, dissociative identity disorder, a person develops two or more distinct subpersonalities.

Dissociative amnesia and dissociative identity disorder are not well understood. Among the processes that have been cited to explain them are extreme repression, state-dependent learning, and self-hypnosis. Dissociative amnesia may end on its own or may require treatment. Dissociative identity disorder typically requires treatment.

People with yet another kind of dissociative disorder, depersonalization-derealization disorder, feel as though they are detached from their own mental processes or body and are observing themselves from the outside or feel as though the people or objects around them are unreal or detached.

Getting a Handle on Trauma and Stress

THE CONCEPTS OF TRAUMA and stress have been prominent in the field of psychopathology since its early days when, for example, Sigmund Freud proposed that most mental disorders begin with traumatic losses or events. But why and how do trauma and stress translate into psychopathology? The answer to that question has, in fact, eluded clinical theorists and researchers—until recent times. Researchers now better understand the relationship between trauma, stress, and psychological dysfunction—viewing it as a complex and unfolding interaction of many variables, including biological factors, childhood experiences, personal styles, and social supports. Similarly, clinicians are now developing more effective treatment programs for people with acute and posttraumatic stress disorders—programs that *combine* biological, cognitive-behavioral, family, and group interventions.

Insights and treatments for the dissociative disorders, the other group of trauma-triggered disorders discussed in this chapter, have not moved as quickly. However, the field's focus on these disorders has surged in recent decades—partly because of intense clinical interest in the memory disturbances on display in posttraumatic stress reactions and in physically rooted disorders such as Alzheimer's disease.

Amid the rapid developments in the realms of trauma and stress lies a cautionary tale. When problems are studied heavily, it is common for the public, as well as some researchers and clinicians, to draw conclusions that may be too bold. For example, many people—perhaps too many—are now receiving diagnoses of PTSD, partly because the symptoms of PTSD are many and because PTSD has received so much attention. Similarly, some of today's clinicians worry that the resurging interest in dissociative disorders may be creating a false impression of their prevalence. We will come across such potential problems again when we look at other forms of psychopathology that are currently receiving great focus, such as bipolar disorders among children and attention-deficit/hyperactivity disorder. The line between enlightenment and overenthusiasm is often thin.

of NOTE ...

Top Personal Sources of Stress Reported by Adults

- Work
- Money
- Relationships
- Health

(Information from: APA, 2022)

Quick Quiz

1. What factors determine how people react to stressors in life? pp. 146–148
2. What factors help influence whether persons will develop acute and posttraumatic stress disorders after experiencing a traumatic event? How does the developmental psychopathology perspective integrate these factors to explain the onset of posttraumatic stress disorder? pp. 148–162
3. What treatment approaches have been used with people who experience acute or posttraumatic stress disorder? pp. 162–167
4. List and describe the different dissociative disorders. pp. 167–178
5. What are the various patterns of dissociative amnesia? What is dissociative fugue? pp. 168–170
6. What are the different kinds of relationships that the subpersonalities may have in dissociative identity disorder? pp. 172–173
7. Describe the psychodynamic, state-dependent learning, and self-hypnosis explanations of dissociative amnesia and dissociative identity disorder. How well is each explanation supported by research? pp. 173–175
8. What approaches have been used to treat dissociative amnesia? pp. 175–176
9. What are the key features of treatment for dissociative identity disorder? Is treatment successful? pp. 176–177
10. Define and describe depersonalization-derealization disorder. How well is this pattern understood? pp. 177–178

CHAPTER 6

Depressive and Bipolar Disorders

The first conscious thought that all was not well with me came . . . when I was twenty-two. I had been living in Los Angeles for two years, working various temp jobs while trying to establish myself as a writer and performance artist. Out of nowhere and for no apparent reason—or so it seemed—I started feeling strong sensations of grief. I don't remember the step-by-step progression of the illness. What I can recall is that my life disintegrated; first, into a strange and terrifying space of sadness and then, into a cobweb of fatigue. I gradually lost my ability to function. It would take me hours to get up out of bed, get bathed, put clothes on. By the time I was fully dressed, it was well into the afternoon. . . .

After a while I stopped showing up at my temp job, stopped going out altogether, and locked myself in my home. It was over three weeks before I felt well enough to leave. During that time, I cut myself off from everything and everyone. Days would go by before I bathed. I did not have enough energy to clean up myself or my home. There was a trail of undergarments and other articles of clothing that ran from the living room to the bedroom to the bathroom of my tiny apartment. Dishes with decaying food covered every counter and tabletop in the place. Even watching TV or talking on the phone required too much concentration. . . . All I could do was take to my pallet of blankets and coats positioned on the living room floor and wait for whatever I was going through to pass. And it did. Slowly. . . .

. . . Deep down, I knew that something had gone wrong with me, in me. But what could I do? Stunned and defenseless, the only thing I felt I could do was move on. I assured myself that my mind and the behaviors it provoked were well within my control. In the future I would just have to be extremely aware. I would make sure that what happened did not happen again. But it did. Again and again, no matter how aware, responsible, or in control I tried to be. . . .

Each wave of the depression cost me something dear. I lost my job because the temp agencies where I was registered could no longer tolerate my lengthy absences. Unable to pay rent, I lost my apartment and ended up having to rent a small room in a boarding house. I lost my friends. Most of them found it too troublesome to deal with my sudden moodiness and passivity so they stopped calling and coming around.

(Danquah, 1998)

Most people's moods come and go. Their feelings of elation or sadness are understandable reactions to daily events and do not affect their lives greatly. However, the moods of certain people last a long time. As in the case of Meri Nana-Ama Danquah, a Ghanaian American writer and performance artist who described her disorder above, their moods color all of their interactions with the world and even interfere with normal functioning. Such people struggle in particular with depression, mania, or both. **Depression** is a low, sad state in which life seems dark and its challenges overwhelming. **Mania,** the opposite of depression, is a state of breathless euphoria, or at least frenzied energy, in which people may have an exaggerated belief that the world is theirs for the taking.

Mood problems of these kinds are at the center of two groups of disorders—depressive disorders and bipolar disorders. These groups are examined in this chapter. People with **depressive disorders** experience depression only, a pattern called

depression A low, sad state marked by significant levels of sadness, lack of energy, low self-worth, guilt, or related symptoms.

mania A state or episode of euphoria or frenzied activity in which people may have an exaggerated belief that the world is theirs for the taking.

depressive disorders The group of disorders marked by unipolar depression.

unipolar depression Depression without a history of mania.

bipolar disorder A disorder marked by alternating or intermixed periods of mania and depression.

unipolar depression (Robles, Fresán, &Ayuso-Mateos, 2024). They have no history of mania and return to a normal or nearly normal mood when their depression lifts. In contrast, those with **bipolar disorders** have periods of mania that alternate with periods of depression (Meyer et al., 2024).

Mood problems have always captured people's interest, in part because so many famous people have experienced them. The Bible speaks of the severe depressions of Nebuchadnezzar, Saul, and Moses. Queen Victoria of England and Abraham Lincoln seem to have experienced recurring depressions. Mood difficulties also have plagued writers Ernest Hemingway, James Baldwin, and Sylvia Plath; comedian Jim Carrey; and musical performers Bruce Springsteen, Beyoncé, and Kendrick Lamar. Their problems have been shared by millions.

Unipolar Depression and the Depressive Disorders

WHENEVER WE FEEL particularly unhappy, we may describe ourselves as "depressed." In all likelihood, we are merely responding to sad events, fatigue, or unhappy thoughts. This loose use of the term confuses an everyday mood swing with a clinical syndrome. All of us experience dejection from time to time, but only some experience a depressive disorder. Depressive disorders bring severe and long-lasting psychological pain that may intensify as time goes by. Those who experience such disorders may lose their will to carry out the simplest of life's activities; some even lose their will to live.

Beatriz Velasco/Getty Images

"Our superpower" Charismatic actor and former athlete Dwayne "The Rock" Johnson happily poses for a selfie with fans at a movie premier. Known for his high energy and quick wit, Johnson has opened up in recent years about his history of significant depression. In the same spirit, the larger-than-life strongman encourages others to reach out when they are experiencing dark moments, saying that "asking for help is our superpower."

How Common Is Unipolar Depression?

Around 8 percent of adults in the United States experience a severe unipolar pattern of depression in any given year, while as many as 5 percent display mild forms (NIMH, 2023; Krishnan, 2022). Around 20 percent of all adults experience an episode of severe unipolar depression at some point in their lives. These prevalence rates are relatively similar in Brazil, Canada, England, France, and many other countries. Moreover, the rate of depression—mild or severe—is higher among people of limited economic means than people of affluence (APA, 2022).

Research conducted with mostly cisgender populations finds that women are at least twice as likely as men to have episodes of severe unipolar depression (NIMH, 2023). As many as 26 percent of such women have an episode at some time in their lives, compared with 12 percent of such men. Research further indicates that the disorder is more common among transgender or nonbinary people than among cisgender people (Pinciotti et al., 2022; Pinna et al., 2022; Tordoff et al., 2022).

The rate of experiencing severe unipolar depression also varies by race and ethnicity (NIMH, 2023; Hasin et al., 2018). Surveys find that in the United States, around 28 percent of Indigenous people have an episode of severe depression at some time in their lives, compared with 23 percent of non-Hispanic White people, 16 percent of Hispanic people, 15 percent of Black people, and 12 percent of Asian American people. At the same time, however, there is evidence that, given the same depressive symptoms, people of color are less likely than non-Hispanic White persons to receive a formal diagnosis or professional treatment for the disorder (Adames & Bernal, 2024; MHA, 2023). Thus, communities of color may actually have higher rates of severe depression than those listed above.

An episode of severe depression can occur at any point throughout the life span. The average age of onset is 19 years, with the peak age being late adolescence or early adulthood (NIMH, 2023). In any given year, the rate of severe depression is higher among adults under 65 years of age than among those 65 years and older (Krishnan, 2022).

Many people with unipolar depression, including severe depression, recover within six months, some without treatment. More than half of those who recover from severe depression have at least one other episode later in their lives (Rush, 2023; Monroe & Harkness, 2022).

What Are the Symptoms of Depression?

The picture of depression may vary from person to person. Earlier you read how Meri's profound sadness, fatigue, and cognitive deterioration brought her job and social life to a standstill. Some depressed people have symptoms that are less severe. They manage to function, although their depression typically robs them of much effectiveness or pleasure.

As the case of Meri indicates, depression has many symptoms other than sadness. The symptoms, which often exacerbate one another, span five areas of functioning: emotional, motivational, behavioral, cognitive, and physical.

Mike Twohy/The New Yorker Collection/CartoonBank

Emotional Symptoms

Most people who are depressed feel sad and dejected. They describe themselves as feeling "miserable," "empty," and "humiliated." They tend to lose their sense of humor, report getting little pleasure from anything, and in some cases display *anhedonia*, an inability to experience any pleasure at all (Serretti, 2023). A number also experience anxiety, anger, or agitation (Van Ameringen, 2022). Terrie Williams, author of *Black Pain*, a book about depression in Black people, describes the agony she went through each morning as her depression was unfolding:

> *Nights I could handle. I fell asleep easily, and sleep allowed me to forget. But my mornings were unmanageable. To wake up each morning was to remember once again that the world by which I defined myself was no more. Soon after opening my eyes, the crying bouts would start and I'd sit alone for hours, weeping and mourning my losses.*
>
> (Williams, 2008, p. 9)

Motivational Symptoms

Depressed people typically lose the desire to pursue their usual activities. Almost all report a lack of drive, initiative, and spontaneity. They may have to force themselves to go to work, talk with friends, eat meals, or have sex. Terrie describes her social withdrawal during a depressive episode:

> *. . . I stayed in bed for three days with the shades drawn and the lights out. Three days. Three days not answering the phone. Three days not checking my e-mail. I was disconnected completely from the outside world, and I didn't care.*
>
> (Williams, 2008, p. xxiv)

major depressive disorder A severe pattern of depression that is disabling and not caused by such factors as drugs or a general medical condition.

persistent depressive disorder A chronic form of unipolar depression marked by ongoing and repeated symptoms of either major or mild depression.

premenstrual dysphoric disorder A disorder marked by repeated episodes of significant depression and related symptoms during the week before menstruation.

postpartum depression A disorder in which a major depressive episode typically begins within four weeks after delivering a child; many cases actually begin during pregnancy.

Suicide is perhaps the most extreme form that lack of motivation can take. As you will read in the chapter on suicide, many depressed people become uninterested in life or wish to die; others wish they could end their own lives, and some actually do. The risk of suicide by severely depressed people is 17 times that of people who are not depressed (APA, 2022). It has been estimated that between 6 and 15 percent of people who experience severe depression die by suicide (Ritchie, Roser, & Ortiz-Ospina, 2022).

Behavioral Symptoms

Depressed people are usually less active and less productive. They spend more time alone and may stay in bed for long periods. One man recalls, "My eyes would open at the crack of dawn, but getting out of bed was impossible. I just stayed there, and stayed there, and stayed there some more, virtually paralyzed, knowing that a day filled with misery awaited me." Depressed people may also move and even speak more slowly.

Cognitive Symptoms

Depressed people hold extremely negative views of themselves. They consider themselves inadequate, undesirable, inferior, perhaps even evil. They also blame themselves for nearly every unfortunate event, even things that have nothing to do with them, and they rarely credit themselves for positive achievements. Another cognitive symptom of depression is pessimism. The individuals are usually convinced that nothing will ever improve, and they feel helpless to change any aspect of their lives (Schreiber & Culpepper, 2023).

People with depression frequently complain that their intellectual ability is very poor. They feel confused, are unable to remember things, are easily distracted, and are unable to solve even the smallest problems. In laboratory studies, depressed people do perform somewhat (but not extremely) more poorly than nondepressed people on tasks of memory, attention, and reasoning (Lyness, 2023, 2022).

Physical Symptoms

People who are depressed frequently have such physical ailments as headaches, indigestion, constipation, dizzy spells, and general pain (McClintock & Choi, 2022). In fact, many cases of depression are misdiagnosed as medical problems at first. Disturbances in appetite and sleep are particularly common (Lyness, 2023, 2022). Most depressed people eat less, sleep less, and feel more fatigued than they did prior to the disorder. Some, however, eat and sleep excessively.

Diagnosing Unipolar Depression

According to DSM-5-TR, a *major depressive episode* is a period of two or more weeks marked by at least five symptoms of depression, including sad mood and/or loss of pleasure (see **Table 6-1**). In extreme cases, the episode may include psychotic symptoms, ones marked by a loss of contact with reality, such as *delusions*—bizarre ideas without foundation—or *hallucinations*—perceptions of things that are not actually present (Rothschild, 2023). A depressed person with psychotic symptoms may decide to stop eating "because my intestines are deteriorating and will soon stop working."

DSM-5-TR lists several types of depressive disorders. People who go through a major depressive episode without having any history of mania receive a diagnosis of **major depressive disorder** (APA, 2022) (see Table 6-1 again). The disorder may be further described as *seasonal* if it changes with the seasons (for example, if the depression recurs each winter), *catatonic* if it is marked by either immobility or excessive activity, or *melancholic* if the person is almost totally unaffected by pleasurable events.

People whose unipolar depression is chronic receive a diagnosis of **persistent depressive disorder** (see Table 6-1 again). Some people with this disorder have

of NOTE ...

Misdiagnosed

More than one-third of people with a bipolar disorder do not receive the correct diagnosis until 10 or more years after first seeking treatment (Suppes, 2022; Carvalho, Firth, & Vieta, 2020).

repeated major depressive episodes. Others have less disabling depressive symptoms, a pattern technically called *persistent depressive disorder with dysthymic syndrome*.

A third type of depressive disorder is **premenstrual dysphoric disorder,** a diagnosis given to people who repeatedly have clinically significant depressive and related symptoms during the week before they menstruate. The inclusion of this pattern in DSM-5-TR is controversial. Many clinicians believe that the category is sexist and "pathologizes" severe cases of *premenstrual syndrome* (*PMS*), premenstrual discomforts that are common and normal.

A fourth type of depressive disorder is **postpartum depression,** called *major depressive disorder with peripartum onset* in DSM-5-TR, a syndrome in which a major depressive episode typically begins within four weeks after delivering a child; many cases actually begin during pregnancy (APA, 2022). The depressive symptoms may adversely affect the parent–infant relationship, the self-image of the parent, and the psychological and physical health of the child (Sockol, 2022).

Yet another kind of depressive disorder, *disruptive mood dysregulation disorder,* is characterized by a combination of persistent depressive symptoms and recurrent outbursts of severe temper. This disorder emerges during mid-childhood or adolescence and so is discussed in the later chapter on disorders common among children and adolescents.

TABLE 6-1

Dx Checklist

Major Depressive Episode
1. For a 2-week period, person displays an increase in depressed mood for the majority of each day and/or a decrease in enjoyment or interest across most activities for the majority of each day.
2. For the same 2 weeks, person also experiences at least 3 or 4 of the following symptoms: • Considerable weight change or appetite change • Daily insomnia or hypersomnia • Daily agitation or decrease in motor activity • Daily fatigue or lethargy • Daily feelings of worthlessness or excessive guilt • Daily reduction in concentration or decisiveness • Repeated focus on death or suicide, a suicide plan, or a suicide attempt
3. Significant distress or impairment.
Major Depressive Disorder
1. Presence of a major depressive episode.
2. No pattern of mania or hypomania.
Persistent Depressive Disorder
1. Person experiences the symptoms of major or mild depression for at least 2 years.
2. During the 2-year period, symptoms are not absent for more than 2 months at a time.
3. No history of mania or hypomania.
4. Significant distress or impairment.

Information from: APA, 2022.

Stress and Unipolar Depression

Episodes of unipolar depression often seem to be triggered by stressful events in an individual's life (APA, 2022). In fact, researchers have found that 80 percent of all severe episodes occur within a month or two of a significant negative event (Anderson, Monden, & Bukodi, 2022; Hammen, 2018, 2016). Stressful life events also precede other psychological disorders, but depressed people report more of such events than anybody else.

Some clinicians consider it important to distinguish a *reactive* (*exogenous*) *depression,* which follows clear-cut stressful events, from an *endogenous depression,* which seems to be a response to internal factors. But one can never know for certain whether a depression is reactive. Thus, most of today's clinicians concentrate on recognizing both the situational aspects and the internal aspects of any given case of unipolar depression.

The Biological Model of Unipolar Depression

Medical researchers have been aware for years that certain diseases and drugs produce mood changes. Could unipolar depression itself have biological causes? Studies of genetic factors, biochemical factors, brain circuits, and the immune system suggest that often it does.

Genetic Factors

Three kinds of research—family pedigree studies, twin studies, and gene studies—suggest that some people inherit a predisposition to unipolar depression. *Family pedigree studies* select people with unipolar depression, examine their relatives, and see whether depression also afflicts other members of the family. If a predisposition to unipolar depression is inherited, the relatives of a person with depression should have a higher rate of depression than the population at large.

Tim Mosenfelder/Getty Images

"Idk what peace feels like" A few months after this 2016 concert in New Orleans, rap artist and actor Kid Cudi revealed on his Facebook page that he had entered an inpatient program to receive treatment for depression and suicidal urges. He wrote to his fans, "My anxiety and depression have ruled my life for as long as I can remember. . . . Idk what peace feels like." He returned to performing a month later.

In fact, researchers have found that as many as 30 percent of such a person's relatives are depressed (see **Table 6-2**), compared with less than 10 percent of the general population (Krishnan, 2022).

If a predisposition to unipolar depression is inherited, you might also expect to find a particularly large number of cases among the close relatives of depressed persons. *Twin studies* have supported this expectation. When an identical twin has unipolar depression, there is a 38 percent chance that the other twin has already had or will eventually have the same disorder. In contrast, when a fraternal twin has unipolar depression, the other twin has only a 20 percent chance of having the disorder (Krishnan, 2022).

Finally, today's scientists have at their disposal techniques from the field of molecular biology to help them directly identify genes and determine whether certain gene irregularities are related to depression (Berrettini, 2022). Using such techniques, researchers have found evidence that unipolar depression may be tied to genes on at least two-thirds of the body's 23 chromosomes.

Biochemical Factors

Low activity of two neurotransmitter chemicals, **norepinephrine** and **serotonin,** has been strongly linked to unipolar depression. One of the first clues to this relationship came in the 1950s, when the first truly effective antidepressant drugs were developed. Although these initial antidepressant drugs were discovered by accident, researchers soon learned that while the drugs were relieving depression, they also were bringing about increases in norepinephrine and/or serotonin activity.

For years, it was thought that low activity of *either* norepinephrine or serotonin directly produces depression, but theorists now believe that their relationship to depression is more complicated (Gillespie, 2022; Moncrieff et al., 2022). Research indicates that depression is probably linked to *interactions* between serotonin and norepinephrine activity or between them and additional key neurotransmitters, particularly **glutamate,** a neurotransmitter responsible for stimulating neurons and promoting connectivity and communication among neurons (Halaris & Cook, 2023). In addition, as you will read shortly, a number of studies suggest that the activity of these neurotransmitters may either reflect or help produce dysfunction of a *depression-related circuit* in the brain, dysfunction that may be the key to the development of depression.

Biological researchers have also learned that another group of chemicals—the body's *hormones*—are linked to depression. As you learned previously in the chapter

TABLE 6-2

Comparing Depressive and Bipolar Disorders

	One-Year Prevalence (%)	Typical Age at Onset (Years)	Prevalence Among First-Degree Relatives	Receiving Treatment Currently (%)
Major depressive disorder	8.0	18–29	Elevated	52
Persistent depressive disorder (with dysthymic syndrome)	1.5–5.0	10–25	Elevated	62
Bipolar I disorder	1.7	15–44	Elevated	49
Bipolar II disorder	1.1	15–44	Elevated	49
Cyclothymic disorder	0.4–2.5	15–25	Elevated	Unknown

Information from: NIMH, 2023, 2017; Stovall, 2023, 2022; APA, 2022; Krishnan, 2022; Kessing, 2020; Kessler et al., 2012, 2010; Wang et al., 2005.

about trauma and stress, whenever we confront stressors in life, our brain triggers into action two stress-related routes throughout the brain and body. One of those routes, the *hypothalamic-pituitary-adrenal* (*HPA*) *axis*, ultimately brings about the release of hormones at various locations throughout the body, and those hormones spur assorted body organs into action, causing us to temporarily experience a heightened state of arousal. You may recall that the HPA axis of people with posttraumatic stress disorder (PTSD) and certain anxiety disorders consistently *overreacts* when those individuals confront stressors. Research indicates that the HPA axis of people with depression is also overly reactive in the face of stress, causing excessive releases of *cortisol* and related hormones at times of stress (Krishnan, 2022; Sforzini et al., 2022). This relationship is not all that surprising given that stressful events so often seem to trigger depression. Once again, it is possible that the HPA axis overreactivity and heightened hormone activity found in depressed people either reflect or help produce dysfunction in a *depression-related circuit* in the brain, the biological focus that we turn to next.

Peter Macdiarmid/eyevine/Redux

Lighting up depression On one of the darkest days of the year, these Londoners try to beat the winter blues by soaking up the illumination from "The Light Station," a seasonal affective disorder lighting installation available in a tunnel under Southwark Bridge.

Brain Circuits

As you have read in previous chapters, biological researchers have determined that emotional reactions of various kinds are tied to brain *circuits*—networks of brain structures that work together, triggering each other into action and producing a particular kind of emotional or behavioral reaction. A brain circuit whose dysfunction contributes to unipolar depression has begun to emerge (Bertocci et al., 2022; McClintock & Choi, 2022). An array of brain-imaging studies point to several brain structures that are likely members of this depression-related brain circuit, including the *prefrontal cortex, hippocampus, amygdala,* and *subgenual cingulate* (also called *Brodmann Area 25*), among other structures (see **Figure 6-1**). You may notice that several of the structures in this circuit are also members of the brain circuits that contribute to certain anxiety disorders and PTSD. However, the subgenual cingulate is distinctly part of the depression-related circuit.

Unlike some of the other brain circuits we have discussed, dysfunctions of this depression-related brain circuit cannot be characterized in general terms, as, for example, a "hyperactive" or "underactive" circuit. But there are many indications that the circuit does malfunction in distinct ways for many persons with depression. Research suggests, for example, that among depressed people, activity and blood flow are unusually low in certain parts and unusually high in other parts of the prefrontal cortex; the hippocampus is undersized, and its production of new neurons is low; activity and blood flow are high in the amygdala; the subgenual cingulate is particularly small and active; and the communication, or *interconnectivity,* between these various structures is often problematic (Krishnan, 2022; McClintock & Choi, 2022).

Studies indicate that under usual circumstances the neurotransmitters serotonin and norepinephrine are both plentiful and active in this brain circuit. It appears, however, that among depressed people, the activity of serotonin and norepinephrine in this circuit is distinctly lower than among other people (Krishnan, 2022). This is not surprising, considering all the research we observed earlier linking depression to low activity by these neurotransmitters. The irregular activity of these neurotransmitters in this brain circuit might be the result of dysfunction within or between the circuit's various structures *or,* alternatively, the cause of such circuit dysfunction. At this point, researchers do not know which is the case.

norepinephrine A neurotransmitter whose irregular activity is linked to depression and panic disorder.

serotonin A neurotransmitter whose irregular activity is linked to depression, obsessive-compulsive disorder, and eating disorders.

glutamate A neurotransmitter responsible for stimulating neurons and promoting connectivity and communication among neurons.

The Immune System

As you will learn in the chapter on disorders that feature somatic symptoms, the *immune system* is the body's network of activities and body cells that fight off bacteria, viruses, and other foreign invaders. When people are under intense stress for a while, their immune systems may become dysregulated, leading to slower functioning of important white blood cells called *lymphocytes* and to increased

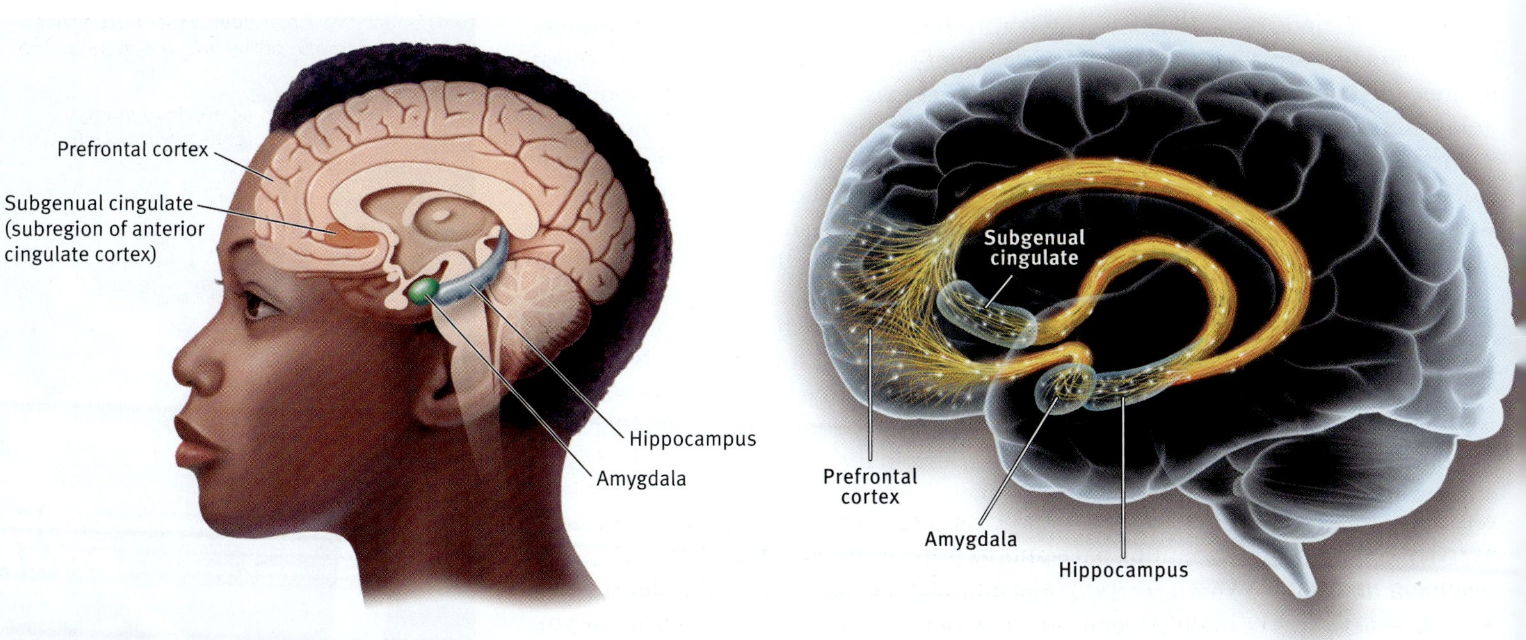

FIGURE 6-1

The Biology of Depression

Researchers believe that the brain circuit involved in unipolar depression includes structures such as the prefrontal cortex, hippocampus, amygdala, and subgenual cingulate (left). The illustration on the right highlights how the structures of this circuit work together and trigger each other into action, an interconnectivity that is flawed in people with depression. The long axons of the neurons from each structure form fiberlike pathways that extend to the other structures in the circuit.

production of *pro-inflammatory cytokines*, proteins that spread throughout the body and cause inflammation and various illnesses. There is a growing belief among some researchers that immune system dysregulation of this kind helps produce depression (Bertollo et al., 2024; Toups & Nemeroff, 2022).

What Are the Biological Treatments for Unipolar Depression?

Usually, biological treatment means *antidepressant drugs* or popular alternatives such as herbal supplements, but for people whose depression does not respond to these medications or to psychotherapy, biological treatment sometimes means *brain stimulation*.

ANTIDEPRESSANT DRUGS There are four kinds of drugs available to reduce the symptoms of depression: *monoamine oxidase (MAO) inhibitors, tricyclics,* the *second-generation antidepressants,* and *ketamine-based drugs.*

The effectiveness of **MAO inhibitors** as a treatment for unipolar depression was discovered accidentally back in 1952. Physicians noted that *iproniazid*, a drug being tested on patients with tuberculosis, had an interesting effect: it seemed to make the patients happier (Bloom, 2023). It was found to have the same effect on patients with depression (Kline, 1958). What this and several related drugs had in common biochemically was that they slowed the body's production of the enzyme *monoamine oxidase (MAO)*. Thus, they were called MAO inhibitors. By inhibiting (that is, blocking) the production of MAO, these drugs ultimately increased the activity level of the neurotransmitters serotonin and norepinephrine throughout the brain. Approximately half of depressed patients who take MAO inhibitors are helped by them (AAPP, 2022; Macaluso, 2022). However, the patients must stick to a rigid diet, avoiding foods containing the chemical *tyramine*—including such common foods as cheeses, bananas, and certain wines. Otherwise, their blood pressure rises dangerously.

The discovery of **tricyclics** in the 1950s was also accidental. Researchers who were looking for a new drug to combat schizophrenia ran some tests on a drug called *imipramine* (Kuhn, 1958). They discovered that imipramine was of little help in cases of schizophrenia, but it did relieve unipolar depression in many people (Healy, 2022). The new drug (trade name Tofranil) and related ones became known as tricyclic antidepressants because they all share a three-ring molecular structure.

MAO inhibitor An antidepressant drug that prevents the action of the enzyme monoamine oxidase.

tricyclic An antidepressant drug such as imipramine that has three rings in its molecular structure.

In hundreds of studies, depressed patients taking tricyclics have improved significantly more than similar patients taking placebos, although the drugs must be taken for at least 10 days before such improvements take hold (Macaluso, 2022). Around 50 to 60 percent of patients who take tricyclics are helped by them (Rush, 2023; AAPP, 2022). To avoid the risk of relapse, most clinicians keep patients on these drugs for at least five months after they are free of depressive symptoms, an extension called "continuation therapy" or "maintenance therapy" (Jarrett & Vittengl, 2022).

Many researchers have concluded that one of the ways in which tricyclics are able to reduce depression is by acting on the *neurotransmitter reuptake mechanisms* of key neurons (Ogbru, 2022). Remember from the chapter about models of psychopathology that brain messages are carried from a sending neuron across the synaptic space to a receiving neuron by a neurotransmitter, the chemical released from the end of the sending neuron. However, there is a complication in this process. While the sending neuron releases the neurotransmitter, a pumplike mechanism in the neuron's ending immediately starts to reabsorb it in a process called *reuptake*. The purpose of this reuptake process is to limit how long the neurotransmitter remains in the synaptic space and to prevent it from overstimulating the receiving neuron. However, the reuptake mechanisms for people with depression are apparently *too vigorous* in neurons that use either serotonin or norepinephrine, thus actually preventing messages from reaching the receiving neurons and so producing symptoms of depression. Tricyclics correct this problem by inhibiting the overly vigorous reuptake processes of depressed individuals, thus allowing serotonin and norepinephrine to remain in their synapses longer and to, in turn, properly stimulate receiving neurons (see **Figure 6-2**).

Some studies suggest that, for many depressed people, once these reuptake processes are corrected, serotonin and norepinephrine activity becomes smoother and more appropriate throughout their depression-related brain circuit (Yang et al., 2022).

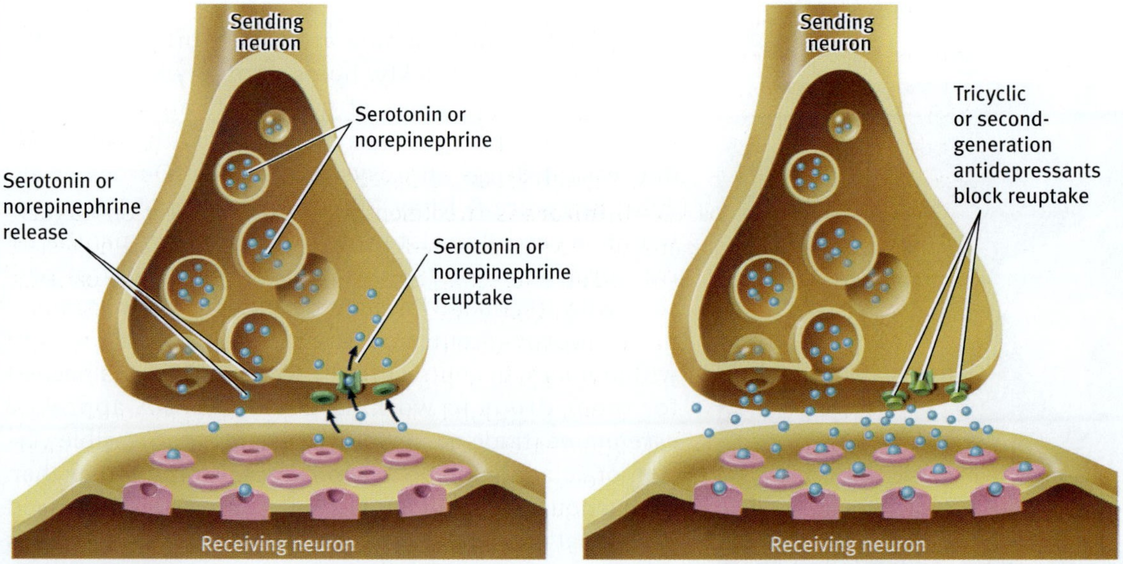

FIGURE 6-2

Reuptake and Antidepressants

(Left) Soon after a neuron releases neurotransmitters such as norepinephrine or serotonin into its synaptic space, it activates a pumplike reuptake mechanism to reabsorb excess neurotransmitters. In depression, however, this reuptake process is too active, removing too many neurotransmitters before they can bind to a receiving neuron. (Right) Tricyclic and most second-generation antidepressant drugs block the reuptake process, enabling norepinephrine or serotonin to remain in the synapse longer and bind to the receiving neuron.

selective serotonin reuptake inhibitors (SSRIs) A group of second-generation antidepressant drugs that increase serotonin activity specifically, without affecting other neurotransmitters.

ketamine An anesthetic drug that is also used as an antidepressant, bringing rapid relief to many people with depression.

Correspondingly, the interconnections between the structures in that circuit become more orderly and functional. With such biological corrections in place, depression subsides for many patients.

Second-generation antidepressants, the third group of effective drugs for depression, are structurally different from the MAO inhibitors and tricyclics. Developed over the past three decades, most of these drugs are called **selective serotonin reuptake inhibitors** (SSRIs) because they increase serotonin activity, largely without affecting norepinephrine or other neurotransmitters. The SSRIs include *fluoxetine* (trade name Prozac), *sertraline* (Zoloft), and *escitalopram* (Lexapro). Other second-generation antidepressants are *selective norepinephrine reuptake inhibitors* (such as *atomoxetine*, or Strattera), which increase norepinephrine activity only, and *serotonin–norepinephrine reuptake inhibitors* (such as *venlafaxine*, or Effexor), which increase both serotonin and norepinephrine activity (Nelson, 2023; AAPP, 2022). As their names imply, these various second-generation antidepressants act on the neurotransmitter reuptake mechanisms of key neurons in the brain, similar to the operation of the tricyclics (Shelton, 2022).

In effectiveness and speed of action, the second-generation antidepressant drugs are on a par with the tricyclics, yet their sales have skyrocketed (Hirsch & Birnbaum, 2023; Rush, 2023). They do not produce as many undesired effects as MAO inhibitors or tricyclics, although they can produce significant side effects of their own, including weight gain and reduced sex drive.

The fourth group of antidepressants is *ketamine-based drugs*. In recent years, researchers have learned that the drug **ketamine** brings significant relief to many people with depression (Derosa et al., 2024; Sanacora & Kitay, 2022). This drug has actually been available as a short-acting *anesthetic* since 1970, often used in surgery or to reduce pain in injured persons, and it has also gained notoriety as a party drug that can be abused (nicknamed "Special K" by many who abuse the drug). However, its antidepressant effect at lower dosages has now caught the attention of the clinical field, and the drug has been hailed by the U.S. Food and Drug Administration (FDA) as the "first truly new medication for depression" since the discovery of the second-generation antidepressants.

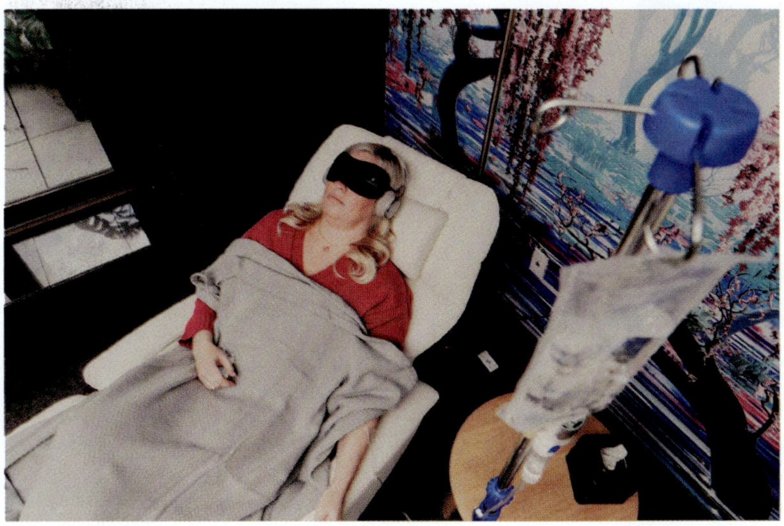

Victor Llorente/The New York Times/Redux

Ketamine for severe depression This patient is receiving an intravenous infusion of ketamine under medical supervision. In an alternative ketamine-based approach, some patients with severe depression take a recently approved drug called *esketamine*, which is available as a nasal spray.

The virtues of ketamine are that it often alleviates depression very quickly, helps people who are unresponsive to other kinds of treatments and those who are suicidal, and combines effectively with other antidepressant drugs and psychotherapies (Derosa et al., 2024; Sanacora & Kitay, 2022). Early tests of ketamine, which were administered *intravenously*, produced extraordinary results — as many as 70 percent of persons with treatment-resistant depression showed *immediate* improvement, and their symptoms decreased within hours, in contrast to the weeks or months needed for other drugs to work. In 2019, the FDA approved *esketamine* (trade name Spravato), a more accessible version of ketamine that is taken by *nasal spray* rather than intravenously. During a treatment session, the depressed individual receives several rounds of esketamine sprays into the nostrils (while under medical supervision) and is then monitored for a couple of hours. Like intravenous ketamine, the nasal spray drug brings very rapid relief for many people with depression (Halaris & Cook, 2023).

The nasal spray has become the ketamine treatment mode of choice. Typically, it is combined with other kinds of antidepressant drugs because esketamine alone has only a short-term effect and because such combinations seem to be more effective than any one of those treatments alone (Thase & Connolly, 2023).

The ketamine-based treatments appear to alleviate the symptoms of depression by increasing the activity of the neurotransmitter *glutamate* in the brain, in contrast to the increases in serotonin and norepinephrine produced by the other antidepressant drugs (Halaris & Cook, 2023). Thus, many clinical theorists now suspect that low glutamate activity may be equally or even more important than low serotonin or norepinephrine activity in depression or that low activity of all of these transmitters collectively helps produce the disorder. Some theorist suspect that by increasing glutamate activity throughout the depression-related brain circuit, ketamine improves connectivity between the structures in the circuit more directly or completely than the other antidepressant drugs do, accounting for its more immediate and powerful impact on depressed individuals (Derosa et al., 2024; Thase & Connolly, 2023).

If antidepressant drugs are effective, why do many people seek out herbal supplements, such as St. John's wort, for depression?

As popular as the different kinds of antidepressants are, it is important to recognize that they do not work for everyone. As you have read, even the most successful of them *fails* to help at least 30 percent of patients with depression (You et al., 2024; Thase & Connolly, 2023). In fact, a number of recent reviews have raised the strong possibility that the failure rate is higher still (see ***Trending***).

...TRENDING

How Effective Are Antidepressant Drugs, Really?

One of the most talked-about issues in the clinical field today is the possibility that many antidepressant drugs may not be as effective as previously thought. For years, clinical researchers believed that tricyclic and second-generation antidepressants help around 65 percent of people who are experiencing depression, an effectiveness rate that is much higher than the 35 percent of depressed people who seem to improve in response to placebo drugs. It turns out that this rate of 65 percent is correct with regard to *published* studies. But apparently the story is different when unpublished studies are considered.

This issue had its beginnings a decade ago when two separate teams of researchers decided to examine the possible impact of publication bias on the reported effectiveness rates of antidepressant drugs (Turner et al., 2022, 2020, 2008; Kirsch, 2019, 2014). *Publication bias* refers to the tendency of professional journals to accept for publication mainly those studies that have positive findings. For example, they may primarily publish antidepressant drug studies that find antidepressants to be significantly more effective than placebo drugs.

imageBROKER/Alamy Stock Photo

One of the research teams, headed by investigator Erick Turner, reviewed 74 antidepressant drug studies—some of them published and, very importantly, some that had not been published (Turner et al., 2022, 2020, 2008). The researchers found that only 38 of the 74 studies yielded positive findings (that is, the drug was clearly effective), and all but one of these studies were published. In contrast, the other 36 studies yielded findings that were negative or questionable (the drug was not particularly effective), and 22 of them were *not* published. When the reviewers combined the findings from all the studies—both published and unpublished—the percentage of people helped by antidepressant drugs turned out to be lower than the percentage yielded in published studies alone. That is, antidepressants helped improve the symptoms of approximately *50* percent of depressed people, not 65 percent. In short, antidepressant drugs may not be as superior to placebo drugs as previously believed. In recent years, other reviews have also examined the performance of antidepressant drugs, again combining findings from published and unpublished studies, and they have uncovered the same story.

This is a very serious matter, to be sure. When making decisions about treatment, clinicians must know how likely it is that depressed clients will be helped by the various available interventions. In light of these multiple reviews, it may be most prudent to conclude that today's antidepressant drugs are indeed helpful but, for many depressed people, perhaps not as helpful or as superior (to placebo treatments) as once believed.

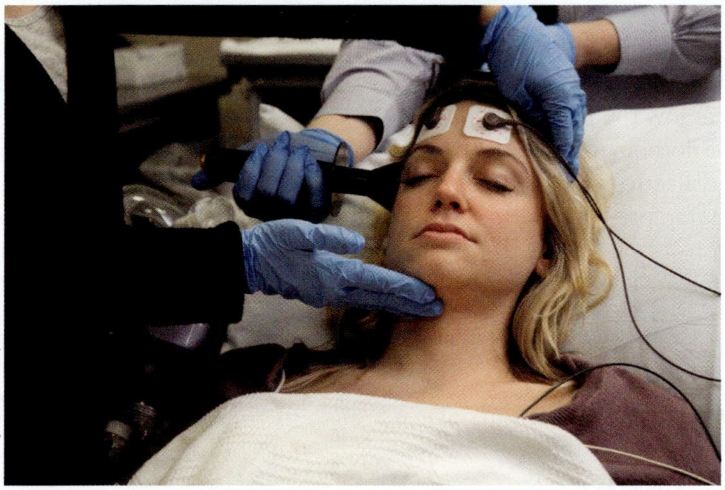

ECT Today Administering ECT has changed significantly since the treatment's early days. Today, patients are given drugs to help them sleep, muscle relaxants to prevent severe jerks of the body and broken bones, and oxygen to guard against brain damage.

BRAIN STIMULATION: ELECTROCONVULSIVE THERAPY As you read in the chapter about models of psychopathology, a different form of biological treatment, **brain stimulation,** refers to interventions that directly or indirectly stimulate certain areas of the brain. The oldest—and most controversial—such approach is **electroconvulsive therapy** (*ECT*). In recent years, some additional kinds of brain stimulation have been developed for the treatment of depressive disorders.

Clinicians and patients alike vary greatly in their opinions of ECT. Some consider it a safe biological approach with minimal risks; others believe it to be an extreme measure that can cause troublesome memory loss and even neurological damage. Despite this controversy, ECT is used frequently, largely because it can be a very effective and relatively fast-acting intervention for unipolar depression.

In an ECT procedure, two electrodes are attached to the patient's head, and 65 to 140 volts of electricity are passed through the brain for half a second or less. This results in a *brain seizure* that lasts from 15 to 70 seconds (Kellner, 2023, 2022). After 6 to 12 such treatments, spaced over two to four weeks, most patients feel less depressed (McDonald, 2022).

The discovery that electric shock can be therapeutic occurred by accident. In the 1930s, searching for a cure for the psychotic disorder schizophrenia, an Italian psychiatrist named Ugo Cerletti applied electric currents to a patient's head to produce seizures. ECT soon became popular and was tried out on a wide range of pathologies. Its effectiveness with severe depression, not schizophrenia, became apparent. In the early years of ECT, broken bones and dislocations of the jaw or shoulders sometimes resulted from patients' severe convulsions. Today's practitioners avoid these problems by giving patients strong *muscle relaxants* to minimize convulsions. They also use *anesthetics* (*barbiturates*) to put patients to sleep during the procedure, reducing their terror.

Patients who receive ECT typically have difficulty remembering some events, most often events that took place immediately before and after their treatments (Kellner, 2023, 2022). In most cases, this memory loss clears up within a few months, but some patients are left with gaps in more distant memory, and this form of amnesia can be permanent.

ECT is clearly effective in treating unipolar depression, although it has been difficult to determine why it works so well (McDonald, 2022; Li et al., 2020). Studies find that between 50 and 80 percent of ECT patients improve (Kellner, 2023, 2022). The approach is particularly effective when patients follow up the initial cluster of sessions with continuation, or maintenance, therapy—either ongoing antidepressant medications or periodic ECT sessions (Obbels et al., 2022).

OTHER FORMS OF BRAIN STIMULATION Over the past few decades, three additional kinds of brain stimulation have been developed for the treatment of depressive disorders—*vagus nerve stimulation, transcranial magnetic stimulation,* and *deep brain stimulation.*

The vagus nerve, the longest nerve in the human body, runs from the brain stem through the neck down the chest and on to the abdomen. A number of years ago, a group of depression researchers suspected that they might be able to stimulate the brain by electrically stimulating the vagus nerve. They were hoping to mimic the positive effects of ECT without producing the undesired effects or trauma associated with ECT. Their efforts gave birth to a new treatment for depression—**vagus nerve stimulation** (VNS).

brain stimulation Biological treatments that directly or indirectly stimulate certain areas of the brain.

electroconvulsive therapy (ECT) A treatment for depression in which electrodes attached to a patient's head send an electrical current through the brain, causing a convulsion.

vagus nerve stimulation (VNS) A treatment for depression in which an implanted pulse generator sends regular electrical signals to a person's vagus nerve; the nerve then stimulates the brain.

transcranial magnetic stimulation (TMS) A treatment in which an electromagnetic coil, which is placed on or above a patient's head, sends a current into the individual's brain.

deep brain stimulation (DBS) A treatment for depression in which a pacemaker powers electrodes that have been implanted in the patient's subgenual cingulate, thus stimulating that brain area.

As you read in the chapter on models of psychopathology, in this procedure a surgeon implants a small device called a *pulse generator* under the skin of the chest. The surgeon then guides a wire, which extends from the pulse generator, up to the neck and attaches it to the vagus nerve (see **Figure 6-3**). Electrical signals travel from the pulse generator through the wire to the vagus nerve. The stimulated vagus nerve then delivers electrical signals to the brain. The pulse generator is typically programmed to provide 30 seconds of stimulation to the vagus nerve (and, in turn, the brain) every five minutes. Research has found that VNS can bring significant relief to depressed patients, including those who do not respond to other forms of treatment (Holtzheimer, 2023; Meyer, Kilian, & Schlaepfer, 2022).

In another technique, **transcranial magnetic stimulation** (TMS), a clinician places an electromagnetic coil on or above the patient's head. The coil sends a current into the prefrontal cortex. As you'll remember, some parts of the prefrontal cortex of depressed people are underactive. TMS appears to increase neuron activity in that structure and, in turn, may improve functioning throughout the rest of the brain's depression-related circuit. A number of studies have found that the procedure reduces depression when it is administered daily for four to six weeks (Holtzheimer, 2023, 2022; Fakuda et al., 2022).

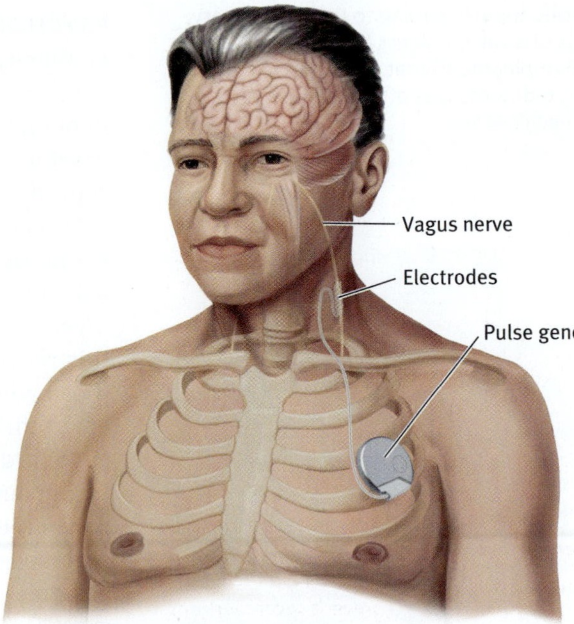

FIGURE 6-3

Vagus Nerve Stimulation

In this procedure, an implanted pulse generator sends electrical signals to the vagus nerve, which then delivers electrical signals to the brain.

Yet another brain stimulation procedure is called **deep brain stimulation** (DBS). As you have read, around 20 years ago researchers linked depression to high activity in the subgenual cingulate, a key member of the depression-related brain circuit. This finding led neurologist Helen Mayberg and her colleagues (2005) to administer a treatment, DBS, to six severely depressed patients who had previously been unresponsive to all other forms of treatment. The Mayberg team drilled two tiny holes into the patient's skull and implanted electrodes in the subgenual cingulate. The electrodes were connected to a battery, or "pacemaker," that was implanted in the patient's chest or stomach. The pacemaker powered the electrodes, sending a steady stream of low-voltage electricity to the brain structure. Mayberg's expectation was that this repeated stimulation would reduce activity in the structure to a normal level and help "recalibrate" the depression-related brain circuit. In the initial study of DBS, four of the six severely depressed patients became almost depression-free within a matter of months. Subsequent research with other severely depressed individuals has also yielded promising findings (Holtzheimer, 2023, 2022; Figee et al., 2022).

Stimulating the brain In this version of transcranial magnetic stimulation (TMS), a cushioned helmet is placed over the individual's head, sending brief electromagnetic currents to stimulate her brain.

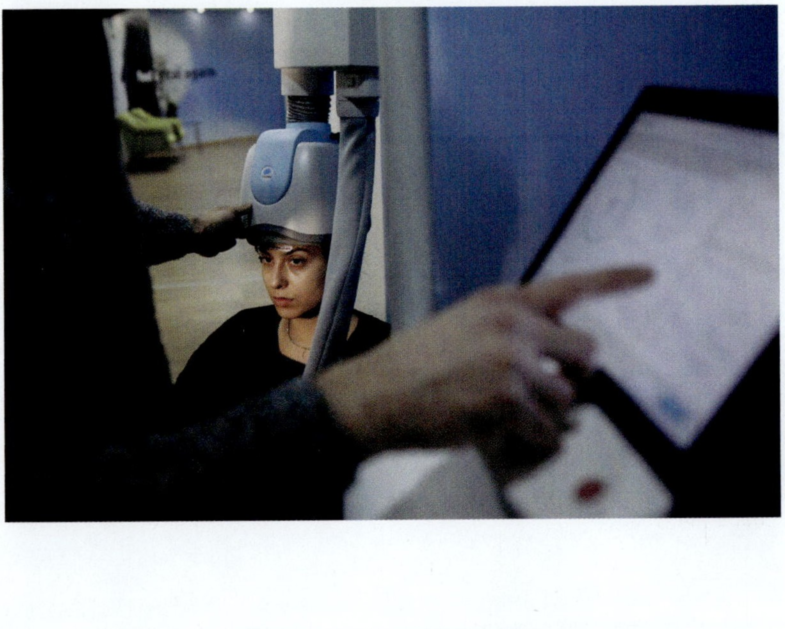

Corinna Kern/laif/Redux

The Psychological Models of Unipolar Depression

The psychological models that have been most widely applied to unipolar depression are the psychodynamic and cognitive-behavioral models. The psychodynamic model has not been strongly supported by research, but the cognitive-behavioral model has received considerable support and has gained a large following.

The Psychodynamic Model

Sigmund Freud (1917) and his student Karl Abraham (1916, 1911) developed the first psychodynamic explanation and treatment for depression. Their emphasis on *dependence* and *loss* continues to influence today's psychodynamic clinicians.

symbolic loss According to Freudian theory, the loss of a valued object (for example, a loss of employment) that is unconsciously interpreted as the loss of a loved one. Also called *imagined loss.*

PSYCHODYNAMIC EXPLANATIONS Freud and Abraham began by noting the similarity between clinical depression and grief in people who lose loved ones: constant weeping, loss of appetite, difficulty sleeping, loss of pleasure in life, and general withdrawal. According to the theorists, a series of unconscious processes is set in motion when a loved one dies. Unable to accept the loss, mourners at first regress to the *oral stage* of development, the period of total dependency when infants cannot distinguish themselves from their parents. By regressing to this stage, the mourners merge their own identity with that of the person they have lost and so symbolically regain the lost person. They direct all their feelings for the loved one, including sadness and anger, toward themselves. For most mourners, this reaction, called *introjection,* is temporary. For some, however—particularly those whose various dependency needs were improperly met during infancy and early childhood—grief worsens over time, and they develop clinical depression (Gabbard & DeJean, 2023; Gabbard, 2022).

Of course, many people become depressed without losing a loved one. To explain why, Freud proposed the concept of **symbolic loss,** or **imagined, loss**, in which a person equates other kinds of events with the loss of a loved one. Consider, for example, college students who believe that their parents love them only when they excel academically. Such individuals may experience a failure in a course as the loss of their parents.

Although many psychodynamic theorists have parted company with Freud and Abraham's theory of depression, it continues to influence current psychodynamic thinking (Gabbard & DeJean, 2023). For example, *object relations theorists* (the psychodynamic theorists who emphasize relationships) propose that depression results when people's relationships—especially their early relationships—leave them feeling unsafe, insecure, and dependent on others (Shahar, 2023).

Studies have offered general support for the psychodynamic idea that major losses, especially ones experienced early in life, may set the stage for later depression (Lee & Jung, 2024; Krishnan, 2022). For example, when a diagnostic survey was administered to thousands of adults in one study, the individuals whose fathers had died during their childhood scored higher on depression (Jacobs & Bovasso, 2009). Related research supports the psychodynamic idea that people whose childhood needs were poorly met are particularly likely to become depressed after experiencing loss (Krishnan, 2022; Tsehay, Necho, & Mekonnen, 2020). At the same time, research does not indicate that loss or problematic early relationships are always at the core of depression. Only a fraction of all people who have major losses in life actually become depressed (Anderson et al., 2022).

Cultural loss Natalia Pleshkova, who fled Ukraine in 2022, holds a precious reminder of her homeland—a 1937 photograph of her grandmother. Various theories link loss to depression. When refugees like Natalia experience the loss of their cultural norms, religious customs, social support, native language, and overall identity, they may develop a form of depression called *cultural bereavement.*

Theo Stroomer/The New York Times/Redux

WHAT ARE THE PSYCHODYNAMIC TREATMENTS FOR UNIPOLAR DEPRESSION? Because they believe that unipolar depression results from unconscious grief over real or imagined losses, compounded by excessive dependence on other people, psychodynamic therapists seek to help clients bring these underlying issues to consciousness and work them through (Summers, Barber, & Zilcha-Mano, 2024; Gabbard & DeJean, 2023). Using the arsenal of basic psychodynamic procedures, they encourage the depressed client to associate freely during therapy; suggest interpretations of the client's associations, dreams, and displays of resistance and transference; and help the person review past events and feelings. Free association, for example, helped one man recall the early experiences of loss that, according to his therapist, had set the stage for his depression:

> *Among his earliest memories, possibly the earliest of all, was the recollection of being wheeled in his baby cart under the elevated train structure and left there alone. Another memory that recurred vividly during the analysis was of an operation around the age of five. He was anesthetized and his mother left him with the doctor. He recalled how he had kicked and screamed, raging at her for leaving him.*
>
> (Lorand, 1968, pp. 325–326)

Despite case reports of such successes as this, researchers have found that long-term psychodynamic therapy is only occasionally helpful in cases of unipolar depression (Prochaska & Norcross, 2018). Two features of the approach may help limit its effectiveness. First, depressed clients may be too passive and feel too weary to join fully in the subtle therapy discussions. Second, they may become discouraged and end treatment too early when this long-term approach is unable to provide the quick relief that they desperately seek. Short-term psychodynamic therapies have performed better than the longer-term approaches (Summers et al., 2024; Caselli et al., 2023).

The Cognitive-Behavioral Model

As with other kinds of psychological disorders, cognitive-behavioral theorists contend that unipolar depression results from a combination of maladaptive behaviors and dysfunctional ways of thinking. These theories fall into three groups: explanations that focus mostly on the behavioral realm, those that give primary attention to negative thinking, and ones that feature a complex interplay between cognitive and behavioral factors.

THE BEHAVIORAL DIMENSION Clinical researcher Peter Lewinsohn was one of the first theorists to link depression to significant changes in the number of rewards and punishments people receive in their lives (Lewinsohn et al., 1990, 1984). He suggested that the positive rewards in life dwindle for some people, leading them to perform fewer and fewer constructive behaviors. The rewards of campus life, for example, may disappear when young people graduate from college and take a job, or the rewards of high salary and adulation may be lost for aging professional athletes when their skills deteriorate. Although many people manage to fill their lives with other forms of gratification, some become particularly disheartened. The positive features of their lives decrease even more, and the decline in rewards leads them to perform still fewer constructive behaviors. In this manner, they spiral toward depression.

In a number of studies, researchers have found that the number of rewards people receive in life is indeed related to the presence or absence of depression. Not only do depressed participants typically report fewer positive rewards than nondepressed participants, but when their rewards begin to increase, their mood improves as well (Colgan, Lejuez, & Magidson, 2022; Stein et al., 2020). Similarly, other investigations have found a strong relationship between positive life events and feelings of life satisfaction and happiness (Delhey et al., 2023).

Lewinsohn and other theorists have further proposed that *social* rewards are particularly important in the downward spiral of depression (Colgan et al., 2022). This claim has been supported by research showing that depressed people receive fewer social rewards than nondepressed people and that as their mood improves, their social

Mike Ehrmann/Getty Images

Eventually the applause stops After his final game in 2023, National Football League great Tom Brady walks off the field one last time to the cheers of adoring fans. The reduction in rewards brought about by retirement may place athletes and other high achievers at risk for depression unless they find new sources of gratification. Perhaps in anticipation of this, Brady quickly lined up a new career as a broadcaster.

...TRENDING

Gender Dysphoria: A Legitimate Diagnosis?

As you read in the chapter on assessment and diagnosis, DSM-5-TR no longer includes transgender functioning as a category of psychopathology. However, the manual does retain a depression-like category called *gender dysphoria*. According to the DSM-5-TR, a diagnosis of gender dysphoria should be assigned to people identifying as transgender or nonbinary who persistently experience significant distress and impairment, including feelings of depression, due to their gender identity and its contradiction to their assigned gender. The retention of gender dysphoria as a disorder is controversial. According to many clinical theorists, since transgender and nonbinary patterns reflect less common but healthy—not pathological—ways of experiencing and expressing one's gender identity, any unhappiness and upset that may accompany the patterns should likewise not be considered pathological.

Hesther Ng/SOPA Images/Sipa USA via AP Images

Living authentically Transgender people do not necessarily experience gender dysphoria. Here a person carries a transgender pride flag while participating in London's annual Trans+ Pride march.

Stress Among Transgender and Nonbinary People

To be sure, many people who identify as transgender or nonbinary do experience distress. Surveys reveal that 90 percent of such individuals experience at least a *moderate* degree of distress or dysfunction at home, school, or work or in social relationships, especially during adolescence (Collet et al., 2023; Nadal, 2023; Dolotina & Turban, 2022). However, research suggests that the primary cause for *intense* dysphoric reactions is the enormous prejudice, stigmatization, harassment, and inequities that the individuals typically face in their lives (Black, Humphrey, & Marquez, 2023; Nadal, 2023; Puckett et al., 2023). This is why so many clinicians favor the elimination of gender dysphoria from the DSM. That is, society's reactions to a person identifying as transgender or nonbinary may be much more responsible for the individual's psychological pain than the individual's dismay over gender issues themselves (Collet et al., 2023).

Treatments for Gender Dysphoria

That said, people in psychological pain still need help, and, indeed, many people who identify as transgender or nonbinary seek out psychotherapy (Puckett et al., 2023). No single form of psychotherapy has been more widely used than other forms to help the individuals to deal with feelings of stress, although *affirmative therapy,* a culturally responsive treatment that you read about earlier, is being used more and more (Comer et al., 2024; Dickey & Puckett, 2022; Pachankis et al., 2020).

Psychotherapy is often helpful, but therapy alone does not typically reduce all of the stress that these individuals experience. Two interventions that appear to be of further help to the psychological state of people with such dysphoria, particularly those identifying as transgender, are the biological procedures that many choose to undergo: hormone administration and/or gender-affirming surgery (Tangpricha & Safer, 2023; Restar et al., 2022).

Biological Procedures for Transgender People

It is important to recognize that transgender people undergo hormone administration and/or surgery not primarily as an intervention for gender dysphoria but to address the incongruence between their gender identity and their assigned gender. However, as noted above, these measures do often have the additional impact of preventing or reducing dysphoria. Let's examine those procedures.

Many transgender people change their sexual characteristics by means of *hormone administration*

(Ferrando, Zhao, & Nikolavsky, 2024). For transgender women, physicians prescribe the sex hormone *estrogen* as well as *antiandrogens* (drugs that suppress their bodies' production of the sex hormone testosterone). This leads to breast development, loss of body and facial hair, and changes in body fat distribution (Ferrando, 2023; Kim, 2020). In contrast, transgender men are administered the sex hormone *testosterone*, resulting in a deeper voice, increased muscle mass, and changes in facial and body hair.

Hormone administration enables many transgender persons to lead a fulfilling life in the gender that fits them. For others, however, this is not enough, and they may seek out *gender-affirming surgery*—also called *gender confirmation surgery*, *gender reassignment surgery*, and *gender change surgery* (Ferrando et al., 2024; Ferrando, 2023). Such surgery is usually preceded by one to two years of hormone administration. Gender-affirming surgery can involve facial reconstruction, breast reconstruction, and/or genital reconstruction.

Research into the outcomes of gender-affirming surgery has yielded generally positive findings. Across many studies, at least 70 percent of patients report satisfaction with the outcome of the surgery, improvement in the quality of their lives, a better psychological state, more positive body satisfaction, better interpersonal interactions, and improvements in sexual functioning (Bruce et al., 2023; Ferrando, 2023; Bränström & Pachankis, 2019).

Education and Support

Two positive developments in recent years for people who identify as transgender or nonbinary—particularly those with gender dysphoria—have been the growth of *education* programs and *support* programs (Boskey & Marchall, 2022; NCTE, 2022). Across the world, there has been a concerted effort to broaden knowledge about and awareness of transgender and nonbinary functioning. Many hundreds of educational programs, which are offered in locations ranging from schools to workplaces to the Internet, now target people grappling with gender identity issues, health care professionals, family members, and the general public. Similarly, numerous support, or mutual help, groups—both in person and online—are now available for people who identify as transgender and nonbinary, providing social support, advice, and relevant information. Research indicates that these various offerings help prevent or reduce gender dysphoria and other forms of psychological distress among the individuals (Selkie et al., 2020).

---

rewards increase. Although depressed people are sometimes the victims of social circumstances, it may also be that their down mood and flat behaviors help produce a decline in social rewards.

NEGATIVE THINKING Pioneering clinical theorist Aaron Beck believed that negative thinking lies at the heart of depression (Beck, 2016, 2002, 1967). According to Beck, *maladaptive attitudes*, a *cognitive triad*, *errors in thinking*, and *automatic thoughts* combine to produce unipolar depression.

Beck believed that some people develop *maladaptive attitudes* as children, such as "My general worth is tied to every task I perform" or "If I fail, others will feel repelled by me." The attitudes result from their own experiences, the judgments of the people around them, or their society (see **Trending**). In a full, active life, to experience a number of failures is inevitable, so such attitudes are inaccurate and set the stage for all kinds of negative thoughts and reactions. Beck suggested that later in these people's lives, upsetting situations may trigger an extended round of negative thinking. That thinking typically takes three forms, which he calls the **cognitive triad:** the individuals repeatedly interpret (1) their *experiences*, (2) *themselves*, and (3) their *futures* in negative ways that lead them to feel depressed. The cognitive triad is at work in the thinking of this depressed person:

> *I feel afraid and ashamed all the time. Everyone else in the world can manage their lives, take care of their responsibilities without any effort, but I can't cope with anything. On the surface, it may seem like I take care of things well enough, but I don't know what I'm doing and it's a miracle everything hasn't fallen apart for me so far. I know my boss thinks I'm incompetent, even though she doesn't say so; it's only a matter of time before I lose my job. My wife doesn't really love me; eventually she'll leave me and get custody of*

(continued on the next page)

cognitive triad The three forms of negative thinking that Aaron Beck theorized lead people to feel depressed. The triad consists of a negative view of one's experiences, oneself, and the future.

our daughter Alice. That's probably for the best, because it will only mess up Alice's life to have me as a mother. My wife's parents hate me because they don't like their daughter being married to another woman, and a Haitian woman to boot. All their words of love are attempts to lower my guard while they try to convince Janet to leave me and find someone they approve of to raise Alice with. I'm not good at anything, and I'm completely unlikable. I'm going to end up alone.

According to Beck, depressed people also make *errors in their thinking*. In one common error of logic, they draw arbitrary inferences—negative conclusions based on little evidence. While walking through the park, for example, Deion passes a woman who is looking at nearby flowers and concludes, "She's avoiding looking at me." Similarly, depressed people often minimize the significance of positive experiences or magnify that of negative ones. For example, Camila receives an A on a difficult college English exam but concludes that the grade reflects the professor's generosity rather than her own ability (minimization). Later in the week, Camila must miss an English class and becomes convinced that it will be impossible to keep up the rest of the semester (magnification).

Finally, depressed people have *automatic thoughts*, a steady train of unpleasant thoughts that keep suggesting to them that they are inadequate and their situation is hopeless. Beck labels these thoughts "automatic" because they seem to just happen, as if by reflex. In the course of only a few hours, depressed people may be visited by hundreds of such thoughts: "I'm worthless. . . . I'll never amount to anything. . . . I let everyone down. . . . Everyone hates me. . . . My responsibilities are overwhelming. . . . I've failed as a parent. . . . I'm stupid. . . . Everything is difficult for me. . . . Things will never change."

Might some nondepressed people experience *positive* automatic thoughts?

Many studies have produced evidence in support of Beck's explanation (Dozois & Dobson, 2023; Krishnan, 2022). Several of them confirm that depressed people hold maladaptive attitudes and that the more of these maladaptive attitudes they hold, the more depressed they tend to be. A number of studies have found the cognitive triad at work in depressed people. Still others have supported Beck's claims about errors of logic. And finally, research has supported Beck's notion that automatic thoughts are tied to depression. In a related line of research, it has been found that people who generally make *ruminative responses* during their depressed moods—that is, repeatedly dwell mentally on their mood without acting to change it—feel dejection longer and are more likely to develop clinical depression later in life than people who avoid such ruminations (Dozois & Dobson, 2023; Watkins, 2022).

LEARNED HELPLESSNESS: A COGNITIVE-BEHAVIORAL INTERPLAY According to psychologist Martin Seligman, feelings of helplessness are at the center of depression (Leonard, 2023; Scherer, 2022; Seligman, 2018, 1975). Since the mid-1960s, Seligman has been developing the **learned helplessness** theory of depression. It holds that people become depressed when they think that (1) they no longer have control over the reinforcements (the rewards and punishments) in their lives and (2) they themselves are responsible for this helpless state.

Seligman's theory first began to take shape when he was working with laboratory dogs. In one procedure, he strapped dogs into an apparatus called a hammock, in which they received shocks periodically no matter what they did. The next day, each dog was placed in a *shuttle box*, a box divided in half by a barrier over which the animal could jump to reach the other side (see **Figure 6-4**). Seligman applied shocks to the dogs in the box, expecting that they, like other dogs in this situation, would soon learn to escape by jumping over

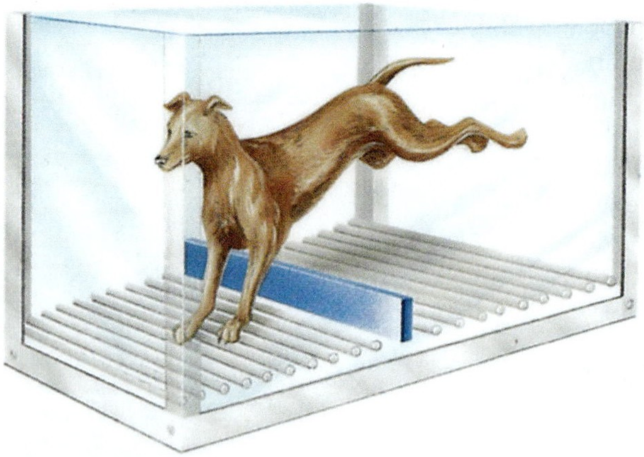

FIGURE 6-4

Jumping to Safety

Experimental animals learn to escape or avoid shocks that are administered on one side of a shuttle box by jumping to the other (safe) side.

the barrier. However, most of these dogs failed to learn anything in the shuttle box. After a flurry of activity, they simply "lay down and quietly whined" and accepted the shock.

Seligman decided that while receiving inescapable shocks in the hammock the day before, the dogs had learned that they had no control over unpleasant events (shocks) in their lives. That is, they had learned that they were helpless to do anything to change negative situations. Thus, when later they were placed in a new situation (the shuttle box) where they could in fact control their outcomes, they continued to believe that they were generally helpless. Seligman noted that the effects of learned helplessness greatly resemble the symptoms of human depression, and he proposed that people in fact become depressed after developing a general belief that they have no control over the outcomes in their lives.

© Michael Bunel/Le Pictorium Agency via ZUMA Press

Victimization and learned helplessness
At a 2019 demonstration in Paris, participants lie on the floor and hold placards with the names of French women who had been killed by their partners that year. Research suggests that some people who are abused by their spouses develop feelings of helplessness, thus helping to explain why they stay in such dangerous relationships.

In numerous human and animal studies, participants who undergo helplessness training have displayed reactions similar to depressive symptoms. For example, when human participants are exposed to uncontrollable negative events, they later score higher than other individuals on a depressive mood scale. Similarly, helplessness-trained animal subjects lose interest in sexual and social activities—a common symptom of human depression.

The learned helplessness explanation of depression has been revised somewhat over the past several decades. According to one modified version of the theory, the *attribution–helplessness theory*, when people view events as beyond their control, they ask themselves why this is so (Brouder & Haeffel, 2023; Scherer, 2022). If they attribute their present lack of control to some *internal* cause that is both *global* and *stable* ("I am inadequate at everything, and I always will be"), they may well feel helpless to prevent future negative outcomes, and they may experience depression. If they make other kinds of attributions, they are unlikely to have this reaction.

Consider Dylan, a college student whose romantic partner breaks up with him. If Dylan attributes this loss of control to an internal cause that is both global and stable—"It's my fault [internal], I ruin everything I touch [global], and I always will [stable]"—he then has reason to expect similar losses of control in the future and may generally experience a sense of helplessness. According to the learned helplessness view, the rejected student is a prime candidate for depression. If Dylan had instead attributed the breakup to causes that were more *specific* ("The way I've behaved the past couple of weeks blew this relationship"), *unstable* ("I don't know what got into me—I don't usually act like that"), or *external* ("My ex often makes poor judgments"), he might not expect to lose control again and would probably not experience helplessness and depression. Hundreds of studies have supported the relationship between styles of attribution, helplessness, and depression (Brouder & Haeffel, 2023; Scherer, 2022).

Although the learned helplessness theory of unipolar depression has been very influential, it too has imperfections. For example, much of the learned helplessness research relies on animal subjects. It is impossible to know whether the animals' symptoms do in fact reflect the clinical depression found in humans. In addition, the attributional feature of the theory raises difficult questions. What about the dogs and rats who learn helplessness? Can animals make attributions, even implicitly?

COGNITIVE-BEHAVIORAL THERAPY Cognitive-behavioral therapists combine behavioral and cognitive techniques to help clients with depression. On the behavioral side, they seek to get the clients moving again—to engage in and enjoy more activities. On the cognitive side, they guide the clients to think in more adaptive,

learned helplessness The perception, based on past experiences, that one has no control over the reinforcements in one's life.

China Photos/Getty Images

Reintroducing pleasure Following the principles of *behavioral activation*, depressed patients at the Zhongshan Mental Hospital in China are encouraged to weed a garden. Behavioral activation therapists guide clients to increase the number of pleasurable activities in their lives, particularly activities that brought them joy (in this case, gardening) prior to their disorders.

less negative ways. A variety of approaches have been developed to help bring about these changes (Dobson, 2024). Two of the leading ones are *behavioral activation* and *Beck's cognitive therapy*.

In **behavioral activation,** therapists work systematically to increase the number of constructive and rewarding activities and events in a client's life. The approach builds on the work of Peter Lewinsohn, the theorist who tied mood to the rewards one experiences in life. There are three key components to the approach. The therapists (1) reintroduce depressed clients to pleasurable events and activities, (2) consistently reward nondepressive behaviors and withhold rewards for depressive behaviors, and (3) help clients improve their social skills (Dobson, 2024; Colgan et al., 2022).

First, the therapist selects activities that the client considers pleasurable, such as going shopping or taking photos, and encourages the person to set up a weekly schedule for engaging in them. Studies have shown that adding positive activities to a person's life can indeed lead to a better mood. Second, while reintroducing pleasurable events into a client's life, the therapist makes sure that the person's various behaviors are reinforced correctly. Behavioral activation theorists argue that when people become depressed, their negative behaviors—crying, ruminating, complaining, or self-depreciation—keep others at a distance, reducing chances for rewarding experiences and interactions. To change this pattern, therapists guide clients to monitor their maladaptive behaviors and to try new, more positive ones. Dozens of smartphone apps are now available to help clients accurately record the negative and positive activities they perform in life and the mood changes that result, making behavioral activation a more precise approach than it once was (Colgan et al., 2022; Sakata et al., 2022). Finally, behavior activation therapists train clients in effective social skills. In group therapy programs, for example, members may work together to improve eye contact, facial expression, posture, and other behaviors that send social messages.

Can you think of other uses, advantages, and disadvantages that might result from the growing use of mood-tracking apps?

Behavioral activation techniques seem to be of only limited help when they are the sole feature of treatment, particularly if the severity of depression is more than modest. But when they are combined with cognitive techniques, they are, as you'll see next, often quite helpful (Dobson, 2024; Dimidjian, 2022).

To help depressed clients overcome their negative thinking, Aaron Beck developed a treatment approach he called **cognitive therapy.** He used this label because the approach focuses largely on guiding clients to recognize and change negative cognitive processes. However, as you will note, the approach also includes several behavioral techniques such as those we have just examined. The approach follows four phases and usually requires fewer than 20 sessions.

behavioral activation A therapy for depression in which the therapist works systematically to increase the number of constructive and pleasurable activities and events in a client's life.

cognitive therapy A therapy developed by Aaron Beck that helps people identify and change the maladaptive assumptions and ways of thinking that help cause their psychological disorders.

***PHASE 1: INCREASING ACTIVITIES AND ELEVATING MOOD** Using behavioral techniques to set the stage for the cognitive dimensions of treatment, therapists first encourage clients to become more active in their lives. As the clients become more active from week to week, their mood is expected to improve.

***PHASE 2: CHALLENGING AUTOMATIC THOUGHTS** Once people are more active and are feeling some emotional relief, therapists begin to educate them about their negative automatic thoughts. Here again, clients may use smartphone apps to accurately identify and document such thoughts as they arise in their daily lives (Denecke, Schmid, & Nüssli, 2022; Sakata et al., 2022). The therapist and client then test the reality behind the thoughts, often concluding that the thoughts are groundless.

***PHASE 3: IDENTIFYING NEGATIVE THINKING AND BIASES** As people begin to recognize the flaws in their automatic thoughts, the therapists show them how illogical thinking processes are contributing to these thoughts. The therapists also guide clients to recognize that almost all their interpretations of events have a negative bias and to change that style of interpretation, as in the following therapy discussion with a client who has concluded, after a recent breakup, that she must be unattractive:

Therapist: *You said your evidence of being unattractive is that you feel ugly and that Roger broke up with you.*

Client: *I just don't feel attractive. . . .*

Therapist: *Are there some men who think you're attractive?*

Client: *Well, there have been a number of men who find me attractive. But I'm not interested in them.*

Therapist: *As evidence that you are not attractive, you cite the fact that Roger broke up with you. What were the reasons for the breakup?*

Client: *We weren't getting along. He just can't commit to anyone. And he lies.*

Therapist: *So you personalized his shortcomings and concluded that you are not attractive?*

Client: *That's true.*

Therapist: *I wonder if we could look at the evidence that you use to support your negative beliefs and see if the evidence is relevant and convincing or if it is characterized by these kinds of distortions.*

(Leahy, 2017, pp. 66–67)

***PHASE 4: CHANGING PRIMARY ATTITUDES** Therapists help clients change the maladaptive attitudes that set the stage for their depression in the first place. As part of the process, therapists encourage clients to test their attitudes in discussion after discussion.

Numerous studies have shown that cognitive-behavioral approaches help with unipolar depression. Depressed adults who receive these therapies improve much more than those who receive placebos or no treatment at all (Dobson, 2024; Craighead, 2022; Garland, 2022). Around 50 to 60 percent show significant improvement in or elimination of their symptoms. To help prevent relapses, a number of therapists follow up successful cognitive-behavioral therapy with *preventive cognitive therapy*—a short

of NOTE ...

Serious Oversight

Family physicians, internists, and pediatricians fail to detect depression in at least 50 percent of their depressed patients (Lyness, 2023, 2022; Williams & Nieuwsma, 2022).

series of "booster" sessions conducted months later that focus on reducing negative automatic thoughts and developing a relapse prevention plan (Krishnan, 2022).

It is worth noting that many of today's cognitive-behavioral therapists do not agree with the proposition that individuals must *fully* discard their negative cognitions in order to overcome depression. These therapists, the *third wave* cognitive-behavioral therapists about whom you read in earlier chapters, including those therapists who practice *acceptance and commitment therapy* (*ACT*), use mindfulness training and other cognitive-behavioral techniques to help depressed clients *recognize* and *accept* their negative cognitions simply as unimportant streams of thinking that flow through their minds. As the clients increasingly accept their negative thoughts for what they are rather than use them as guides for behaviors and decisions, the individuals learn to work around them in life. Research suggests that thought acceptance of this kind helps prevent recurrences of depression after individuals have recovered (Segal, 2023; A-Tjak & Hayes, 2022).

of NOTE ...

Their Words

"No one can make you feel inferior without your consent."

Eleanor Roosevelt

The Sociocultural Model of Unipolar Depression

Sociocultural theorists propose that unipolar depression is strongly influenced by the social context that surrounds people. Their belief is supported by the finding, discussed earlier, that depression is often triggered by outside stressors. Once again, there are two kinds of sociocultural views—the *family-social perspective* and the *multicultural perspective*.

The Family-Social Perspective

Earlier, you read that some cognitive-behavioral theorists believe that a decline in social rewards is particularly important in the development of depression. This view is also consistent with the family-social perspective.

The connection between declining social rewards and depression is a two-way street. On the one hand, researchers have found that depressed people often display ineffective social skills and communicate poorly. They seek repeated reassurances from others, and they typically speak more slowly and quietly than nondepressed people, pause longer between words, and take longer to respond to others. Such social deficits

Luis Acosta/Getty Images

Is texting a relationship buster? Studies suggest that communicating excessively by text may affect intimate relationships negatively—producing needless misunderstandings and fewer face-to-face encounters.

make other persons uncomfortable and may cause them to avoid the depressed individuals. As a result, the social contacts and rewards of people with depression decrease, and, as they participate in fewer and fewer social interactions, their social skills deteriorate still further.

Consistent with these findings, depression has been tied repeatedly to the unavailability of social support such as that found in a happy intimate relationship (Dozois & Dobson, 2023; Krishnan, 2022). Research indicates that people in troubled intimate relationships are 25 times more likely to have a depressive disorder than people in untroubled relationships (Keitner, 2023). In some cases, the partner's depression may contribute to marital discord or divorce, but often the interpersonal conflicts and low social support found in troubled relationships seem to lead to depression (Williams & Nieuwsma, 2022; Whisman, Sbarra, & Beach, 2021). Studies have also found that people whose lives are generally characterized by limited social supports, isolation, and lack of intimacy are particularly likely to become depressed and to remain depressed longer than other people (Fisher et al., 2024; Krishnan, 2022).

Niall Carson/Press Association via AP Images

Everyone has social needs Researchers have found that macaque monkeys—like many other animals—are greatly affected by friends and relatives. Moreover, the facial expressions of macaques show emotions ranging from anger to fear to sadness—expressions that influence each other's social judgments, behaviors, and moods.

Research has likewise revealed that one of the most problematic features of disease epidemics is the social isolation and distancing imposed on people to help contain the spread of infection. Studies conducted across various epidemics, including the Covid-19 pandemic, find that the rate of clinical depression in stricken communities rises to as much as 37 percent among adults and 23 percent among children (Bertollo et al., 2024; NORC, 2023, 2022, 2020; CSP, 2022). Although economic, family, and health concerns certainly contribute to these increases, one of the most closely linked factors is the sense of loneliness that emerges during extended periods of isolation and distancing (Fisher et al., 2024; NORC, 2023, 2022, 2020; Ernst et al., 2022). Indeed, as many as 60 percent of people confined to their homes during epidemics report substantial feelings of loneliness—and the longer the social isolation, the greater the likelihood of developing both loneliness and depression (NORC, 2023, 2022, 2020). The link between isolation, loneliness, and depression seems to be implicitly recognized by people in these situations, as they often try to improve such matters on their own. Throughout the Covid-19 pandemic, for example, 87 percent of adults said they were communicating with friends and family by phone, text, social media, or Zoom every day, a significant increase over their rate of communication prior to the outbreak (NORC, 2023, 2022, 2020).

Why might problems in the social arena—for example, social loss, social ties, and social rewards—be particularly tied to depression?

Family-Social Treatments

Therapists who use family and social approaches to treat depression help clients change how they deal with the close relationships in their lives. The most effective family-social approaches are *interpersonal psychotherapy* and *couple therapy*.

INTERPERSONAL PSYCHOTHERAPY

As you read in the chapter about models of psychopathology, practitioners of **interpersonal psychotherapy (IPT)** address four interpersonal problem areas in their treatment of psychopathology (Markowitz, 2022; Mattos et al., 2022). As you'll recall, these therapists first encourage clients who have experienced recent *interpersonal losses* to develop new ways of remembering lost persons and to also look for new relationships. Second, IPT therapists help clients examine and resolve *interpersonal role disputes*—that is, differences they have with other people about the roles each should play in their relationships. Third, IPT therapists help

interpersonal psychotherapy (IPT) A treatment for unipolar depression that is based on the belief that clarifying and changing one's interpersonal problems helps lead to recovery.

of NOTE ...

Friendships in Decline

75% Percentage of Americans who reported having a "best" friend in 1990

59% Percentage of Americans who reported having a "best" friend in 2021

33% Percentage of Americans who reported having 10 or more close friends in 1990

13% Percentage of Americans who reported having 10 or more close friends in 2021

(Cox, 2021)

clients who are going through *interpersonal role transitions* (brought about by major life changes) to develop the social supports and skills their new roles require. And fourth, IPT therapists help clients who may display significant *interpersonal deficits*, such as extreme shyness or social awkwardness, to develop more effective social skills and assertiveness.

The IPT approach has been applied to unipolar depression more than most other psychological disorders. Studies suggest that it and related interpersonal treatments for depression have a success rate similar to that of cognitive-behavioral therapy (Dozois & Dobson, 2023; Swartz, 2023; Huibers et al., 2022). Not surprisingly, IPT is considered especially useful for depressed people who are struggling with social conflicts or undergoing changes in their careers or social roles.

COUPLE THERAPY As you have read, depression can result from discord in a marriage or other intimate relationship, and recovery from depression is often slower for people who do not receive support from their partner (Dozois & Dobson, 2023; Whisman et al., 2021). In fact, as many as half of all depressed clients may be in a dysfunctional relationship. Thus, it is not surprising that many cases of depression have been treated by **couple therapy,** the approach in which a therapist works with two people who share a long-term relationship.

Therapists who offer *integrative behavioral couple therapy* combine cognitive-behavioral and sociocultural techniques to teach couples specific communication and problem-solving skills, guide them to recognize that their problematic interactions often reflect basic differences between them, and steer them to become more accepting and supportive of each other. When the depressed person's intimate relationship is filled with conflict, this approach and similar ones may be as effective as—or even more effective than—individual cognitive-behavioral therapy, interpersonal psychotherapy, or medication in helping to reduce depression (Whisman, Beach, & Davilla, 2022; Christensen, Doss, & Jacobson, 2020).

The Multicultural Perspective

Two kinds of relationships have particularly captured the interest of multicultural theorists: (1) links between *gender and depression* and (2) ties between *cultural background and depression*. In the case of gender, a strong relationship has been found, but a clear explanation for that relationship has yet to emerge. The clinical field is still sorting out whether and what ties exist between cultural factors and depression.

GENDER AND DEPRESSION There are a number of strong links between gender and depression. For example, as you have read, depression is generally more common among people identifying as transgender or nonbinary than among cisgender people (Pellicane & Ciesla, 2022). Although research on this front is still in its early stages, initial findings suggest that this disparity is due, at least in part, to the increased experiences of discrimination, prejudice, stigmatization, and victimization that many transgender and nonbinary people experience in their lives (Pellicane & Ciesla, 2022; Zubair, 2021). Such experiences can foster profound senses of alienation and loneliness (Fisher et al., 2024). Furthermore, chronic exposure to these demoralizing experiences leads many transgender and nonbinary people to *internalize*—or adopt as their own—society's stigmatizing messages about their gender identity and expression (Pellicane & Ciesla, 2022). Many multicultural researchers believe that it is the internalization of these negative messages that particularly increases the risk of depression among transgender and nonbinary people (Tebbe & Budge, 2022).

In another important kind of gender effect, research conducted with predominantly cisgender populations finds that women are at least twice as likely as men to receive a diagnosis of unipolar depression. This relationship has been found in locations as far apart as France, Sweden, Lebanon, New Zealand, South Africa, China, and the United

couple therapy A therapy format in which the therapist works with two people who share a long-term relationship.

States. Why this huge gender difference? A variety of theories have been offered and studied (Morken et al., 2023; Hyde & Mezulis, 2020). The *artifact theory* holds that women and men are equally prone to depression but that clinicians often fail to detect depression in men. Perhaps many women with depression display more emotional symptoms, such as sadness and crying, which are easily diagnosed, while many men mask their depression behind traditionally "masculine" symptoms such as anger. Although this is a popular explanation, research indicates that most women are actually no more willing or able than most men to identify their depressive symptoms and to seek treatment.

The *hormone explanation* holds that hormone changes trigger depression in many women, particularly during puberty, pregnancy, and menopause. Research suggests, however, that the social and life events that accompany these developmental milestones are also profound and may account for experiences of depression as well as—or better than—the hormone shifts themselves. Hormone explanations have also been criticized as sexist since they imply that most women's normal biology can be flawed.

Steve Pfost/Newsday RM via Getty Images

Pursuing a legal remedy According to research, social media use by teenagers has been surging during the past decade, and, perhaps not so coincidentally, the rates of hopelessness, depression, and self-harm among teenage girls have risen during the same period. In 2022, 19-year-old Alexis Spence (shown here) and her parents filed a lawsuit against Meta, claiming that she developed depression, anxiety, an eating disorder, and suicidal behaviors as a result of her repeated exposure to unsuitable content on her Instagram feed, beginning at age 11.

The life stress theory suggests that most women in our society are subject to more stress than most men. On average, they face more poverty, more menial jobs, less adequate housing, more discrimination, and more victimization than most men—all factors that have been linked to depression. And in many families, women bear a disproportionate share of responsibility for child care and housework.

The *body dissatisfaction explanation* states that most girls in Western society are taught, almost from birth but particularly during adolescence, to seek a low body weight and a slender body shape—goals that are unreasonable, unhealthy, and often unattainable. As you'll read when we cover eating disorders, research finds that, as adolescence unfolds, many girls, for example, do become more and more dissatisfied with their weight and body and, on average, display an increased rate of depression. However, it is not clear that eating and weight concerns actually cause depression; they may instead be the result of depression.

The *lack-of-control theory,* which draws on the learned helplessness research, proposes that most women may be more prone to depression than most men because they feel less control over their lives. It has been found that victimization of any kind, from discrimination to burglary to rape, often produces a sense of helplessness and increases the symptoms of depression—and women in our society are, on average, more likely than men to be victimized across various domains (Mrejen et al., 2023).

A final explanation for the gender rate difference found in depression is the rumination theory. As you learned earlier, rumination is related to depression (Dozois & Dobson, 2023; Watkins, 2022). Research reveals that, on average, women are more likely than men to ruminate when they experience low moods, perhaps making them more vulnerable to the onset of clinical depression.

Each of these explanations for the observed gender differences in unipolar depression offers food for thought. Each has gathered just enough supporting evidence to make it interesting and just enough evidence to the contrary to raise questions about its usefulness. Thus, at present, this difference in depression rates remains one of the most talked-about but least understood phenomena in the clinical field.

CULTURAL BACKGROUND AND DEPRESSION Depression is a worldwide phenomenon, and certain symptoms of this disorder seem to be constant across all countries. The majority of depressed people across very different countries report symptoms of

Non-Western depression Depressed people in non-Western countries tend to have fewer cognitive symptoms, such as self-blame, and more physical symptoms, such as fatigue, weakness, and sleep disturbances.

sadness, joylessness, tension, lack of energy, loss of interest, loss of ability to concentrate, ideas of insufficiency, and thoughts of suicide (WHO, 2023). Beyond such core symptoms, however, research suggests that the precise picture of depression varies from country to country (APA, 2022; Vink et al., 2022). Depressed people in non-Western countries—China, Lebanon, and Nigeria, for example—are more likely to be troubled by physical symptoms such as fatigue, weakness, sleep disturbances, and weight loss. Depression in those countries is less often marked by cognitive symptoms such as self-blame, low self-esteem, and guilt.

Within the United States, as you read earlier, non-Hispanic White people appear to have higher rates of depression than Hispanic and Black people (MHA, 2023; NIMH, 2023; Hasin et al., 2018). On the other hand, according to research, Hispanic and Black Americans are 50 percent *more likely* than non-Hispanic White Americans to have *recurrent* episodes of depression (APA, 2022; Krishnan, 2022). Why this difference? Around 60 percent of depressed non-Hispanic White Americans receive treatment for their disorders (medication and/or psychotherapy), compared with 52 percent of depressed Black Americans and 40 percent of depressed Hispanic Americans (Adames & Bernal, 2024; BCBS, 2022; Alegria et al., 2015). It may be that people of color in the United States are more vulnerable to repeated experiences of depression partly because many of them have more limited treatment opportunities when they are depressed.

Research has also revealed that depression is distributed unevenly within some cultural groups (MHA, 2023). This is not totally surprising given that each cultural group itself consists of people of varied backgrounds and values. For example, depression is more common among Hispanic and Black people born in the United States than among Hispanic and Black immigrants. Moreover, within the Hispanic population, Puerto Ricans have a higher rate of depression than do Cuban American, Mexican American, and other Hispanic groups.

Multicultural Treatments

In an earlier chapter, you read that *culturally responsive therapies* are designed to draw on a person's cultural strengths and address the unique issues faced by people of color and other marginalized persons (Harkness & Pachankis, 2022; Williams & La Torre, 2022). For such approaches, therapists typically have cultural training, heightened awareness of their clients' cultural values and culture-related stressors, and appreciation of their own cultural identities and values. The therapists may also try to help clients identify and express their suppressed difficult emotions and pain and develop a comfortable (for them) bicultural balance.

Do you think culturally responsive therapies might be more useful for some kinds of disorders than for others? Why or why not?

In the treatment of unipolar depression, culturally responsive approaches increasingly are being combined with traditional forms of psychotherapy to help clients from marginalized groups overcome their disorders. A number of today's therapists, for example, offer cognitive-behavioral therapy for depressed clients from marginalized backgrounds while also focusing on the clients' cultural identity and unique cultural issues and pressures (Comer et al., 2024; Iwamasa, 2023; Jameel et al., 2022; Pachankis et al., 2022). Similarly, clinicians who practice *affirmative cognitive-behavioral therapy* to treat depression in LGBTQ+ clients draw on traditional cognitive and behavioral techniques—such as behavioral activation—while also working to validate and advocate for their clients' needs and help them achieve greater self-acceptance and pride regarding their sexual orientation, gender identity, and/or gender expression. A range of studies indicate that marginalized clients are indeed more likely to overcome their depressive disorders when a culturally responsive focus is added to other forms of psychotherapy (Pachankis et al., 2022, 2020; Sue et al., 2022).

Integrating the Models: The Developmental Psychopathology Perspective

As with their explanations of other psychological disorders, proponents of the *developmental psychopathology* perspective contend that unipolar depression is caused by a combination of the factors that we have been examining throughout this chapter. Moreover, they believe that the factors unfold and intersect in a developmental sequence, with early negative factors generally setting the stage for later negative factors and ultimately for depression, but with later positive factors, called *protective factors,* sometimes able to offset the lingering impact of early negative factors. Such explanations of unipolar depression have received considerable research support.

Consistent with biological findings, developmental psychopathologists believe that the road to unipolar depression often begins with a genetically inherited predisposition—a predisposition that is characterized by low activity of key neurotransmitters (serotonin, norepinephrine, or glutamate) in key brain structures, an overly reactive brain–body stress route (the HPA axis), and a dysfunctional depression-related brain circuit (Luyten & Fonagy, 2022; Lippard & Nemeroff, 2020). Researchers from this perspective have found that such biological predispositions will most likely result in later depression if the individual is *also* subjected to significant losses or other traumas early in life and/or inadequate parenting, such as parenting that is disrupted, depressive in style, inconsistent, or rejecting (Lee & Jung, 2024; Xiao et al., 2024; Maul et al., 2020). Still other studies indicate that this combination of biological and childhood factors often leads to a low self-concept, a temperament marked by guilt, a negative style of thinking, general feelings of helplessness, and interpersonal dependence—variables that are themselves each linked to depression (Xiao et al., 2024; Kalin, 2020). According to developmental psychopathologists, individuals who travel through this unfavorable developmental sequence are particularly likely to become depressed when they experience stress in adult life, especially interpersonal stress (Anderson et al., 2022).

Irvin Rivera/Getty Images

Broken beginnings and resilience
Successful television host and actor Terry Crews has entertained crowds across the world with his infectious personality and charming nature. Interestingly, he traces his accomplishments and positive outlook to an often dark and difficult past, including family violence during his childhood and later struggles with depression. From such experiences, he developed resilience and a commitment to be happy. Crews notes, "All of my fun things and great things come from sadness."

However, this precise sequence of intersecting factors is not the only avenue to later depression. Developmental psychopathology studies indicate, for example, that individuals who experience severe childhood traumas or inadequate parenting often develop depression when they later encounter life stress, even if they have no genetic predisposition for the disorder (Xiao et al., 2024; Luyten & Fonagy, 2022). Such findings are apparently related to the two-way relationship that exists between many of these factors. Research has found, for example, that exposure to severe traumas at key points early in life may negatively alter a child's HPA axis and depression-related brain circuit, even if that HPA axis and brain circuit had previously been functioning properly (Lee & Jung, 2024; Lippard & Nemeroff, 2020).

At the same time, the developmental psychopathology perspective is not all gloom and doom. The presence of negative developmental factors does not inevitably produce a march toward depression. Studies have found, for example, that individuals who experience *moderate* and *manageable* adversities throughout their childhood often develop *resilience*—an important protective factor—and become better able to withstand the depressive effects of life stress in adulthood (Oshri et al., 2022; Malhi, 2020). One study even found that participants who had repeatedly experienced moderate adversities throughout their lives were less likely to become depressed in the face of significant life stress than were participants who had faced little or no adversity in their lives (Seery, Holman, & Silver, 2010).

Jason Friend Photography Ltd/Alamy Stock Photo

Flower power *Hypericum perforatum,* known as *Saint John's wort,* is a low, wild-growing shrub, not an antidepressant drug. It is currently among the hottest-selling products in health stores, with studies indicating that it can be quite helpful in cases of mild or moderate depression.

SUMMING UP

People with unipolar depression experience depression without mania. According to the biological view, low activity of three neurotransmitters—norepinephrine, serotonin, and glutamate—is linked to depression. Hormonal factors, the result of an HPA axis that is overly reactive to stress, may also be at work. Research has also tied depression to irregularities in a circuit of brain structures, including the prefrontal cortex, hippocampus, amygdala, and subgenual cingulate. Most biological treatments for unipolar depression consist of antidepressant drugs, but several brain stimulation techniques are also used.

According to the psychodynamic view, certain people who experience real or imagined losses may regress to an earlier stage of development, fuse with the person they have lost, and eventually become depressed. Psychodynamic therapists try to help depressed persons uncover and work through their losses and their excessive dependence on others.

The cognitive-behavioral view features explanations of depression that are primarily behavioral, primarily cognitive, or a combination of behavioral and cognitive principles. On the behavioral side, the model says that when people experience a large reduction in their positive rewards in life, they become more and more likely to become depressed. On the cognitive side, Beck's theory of negative thinking holds that maladaptive attitudes, the cognitive triad, errors in thinking, and automatic thoughts help produce unipolar depression. Also, according to Seligman's learned helplessness theory, people become depressed when they believe that they have lost control over the reinforcements in their lives and when they attribute this loss to causes that are internal, global, and stable. Cognitive-behavioral therapists reintroduce clients to pleasurable events, reinforce nondepressive behaviors, teach interpersonal skills, and help the clients change or accept their dysfunctional cognitions.

Sociocultural theories propose that unipolar depression is influenced by social and cultural factors. Family-social theorists point, for example, to a low level of social support. Correspondingly, interpersonal psychotherapy and couple therapy are often helpful in cases of depression. Multicultural theorists note that the character and prevalence of depression may vary by gender and culture, an issue that culturally responsive therapies for depression seek to address.

Developmental psychopathology theorists contend that unipolar depression is caused by a combination of the factors cited by the various models and that these factors unfold and intersect in a developmental sequence.

Bipolar Disorders

PEOPLE WITH A BIPOLAR disorder experience both the lows of depression and the highs of mania. Many describe their lives as an emotional roller coaster as they shift back and forth between extreme moods. A number of persons with the disorder become suicidal. At least 5 percent of them eventually end their own lives, usually out of a sense of hopelessness (APA, 2022; Suppes, 2022). Their roller-coaster ride also has a dramatic impact on relatives and friends.

What Are the Symptoms of Mania?

Unlike people sunk in the gloom of depression, those in a state of mania typically experience dramatic and inappropriate rises in mood. The symptoms of mania span the same areas of functioning—*emotional, motivational, behavioral, cognitive,* and *physical*—as those of depression, but mania affects those areas in an opposite way.

A person in the throes of mania has active, powerful emotions in search of an outlet. The mood of euphoric joy and well-being is out of all proportion to the actual happenings in the person's life. Not every person with mania is a picture

of NOTE ...

World Count: Bipolar Disorder

More than 40 million people experience a bipolar disorder worldwide (WHO, 2022).

of happiness, however. Some instead become very irritable and angry, especially when others get in the way of their exaggerated ambitions.

In the motivational realm, people with mania seem to want constant excitement, involvement, and companionship. They enthusiastically seek out new friends and old, new interests and old, and have little awareness that their social style is overwhelming, domineering, and excessive.

The behavior of people with mania is usually very active. They move quickly, as though there were not enough time to do everything they want to do. They may talk rapidly and loudly, their conversations filled with jokes and efforts to be clever or, conversely, with complaints and verbal outbursts. Flamboyance is not uncommon: dressing in flashy clothes, giving large sums of money to strangers, or even getting involved in dangerous activities.

In the cognitive realm, people with mania usually show poor judgment and planning, as if they feel too good or move too fast to consider possible pitfalls. Filled with optimism, they rarely listen when others try to slow them down, interrupt their buying sprees, or prevent them from investing money unwisely. They may also hold an inflated opinion of themselves, and sometimes their self-esteem approaches grandiosity. During severe episodes of mania, some have trouble remaining coherent or in touch with reality.

Finally, in the physical realm, people with mania feel remarkably energetic. They typically get little sleep yet feel and act wide awake (Suppes, 2022). Even if they miss a night or two of sleep, their energy level may remain high.

"My mind and me" In interviews and the documentary *My Mind and Me*, talented singer and actress Selena Gomez has vividly described her years dealing with bipolar disorder. During her highs, she would feel the need to give away all of her wealth. But during her lows, she could barely get out of bed and sometimes contemplated suicide.

Diagnosing Bipolar Disorders

People are considered to be in a full *manic episode* when for at least one week they display an exceptionally high or irritable mood, increased activity or energy, and at least three other symptoms of mania (see **Table 6-3**). The episode may even include psychotic features such as delusions or hallucinations. When the symptoms of mania are less severe (causing little impairment), the person is said to be having a *hypomanic episode*.

TABLE 6-3

Dx Checklist

Manic Episode
1. For 1 week or more, person displays a continually irregular, inflated, unrestrained, or irritable mood as well as continually heightened energy or activity, for most of every day.
2. Person also experiences at least three of the following symptoms: • Grandiosity or overblown self-esteem • Reduced sleep need • Increased talkativeness, or drive to continue talking • Rapidly shifting ideas or the sense that one's thoughts are moving very fast • Attention pulled in many directions • Heightened activity or agitated movements • Excessive pursuit of risky and potentially problematic activities
3. Significant distress or impairment.
Bipolar I Disorder
1. Occurrence of a manic episode.
2. Hypomanic or major depressive episodes may precede or follow the manic episode.
Bipolar II Disorder
1. Presence or history of major depressive episode(s).
2. Presence or history of hypomanic episode(s).
3. No history of a manic episode.

Information from: APA, 2022.

DSM-5-TR distinguishes two kinds of bipolar disorders—bipolar I and bipolar II. People with **bipolar I disorder** have full manic and major depressive episodes (Morrison, 2023). Most of them experience an *alternation* of the episodes, for example, weeks of mania followed by a period of wellness followed in turn by an episode of depression. Some, however, have *mixed* features, in which they display both manic and depressive symptoms within the same episode—for example, having racing thoughts amidst feelings of extreme sadness. In **bipolar II disorder,** *hypomanic*—that is, mildly manic—episodes alternate with major depressive episodes over the course of time. Some people with this pattern accomplish huge amounts of work during their mild manic periods (see **PsychWatch**). In both bipolar I and bipolar II disorders, the individual's depressive episodes usually are more frequent and last longer than the manic episodes (Collier, 2023; NHS, 2023).

of NOTE ...

Frenzied Masterpiece

George Frideric Handel wrote his *Messiah* in less than a month during a manic episode (Roesch, 1991).

Without treatment, the mood episodes tend to recur for people with either type of bipolar disorder. If a person has four or more episodes within a one-year period, their disorder is considered to be *rapid cycling*. A woman describes her rapid cycling in the following excerpt, taken from a journal article she wrote anonymously a number of years ago:

> *My mood may swing from one part of the day to another. I may wake up low at 10 am, but be high and excitable by 3 pm. I may not sleep for more than 2 hours one night, being full of creative energy, but by midday be so fatigued it is an effort to breathe.*
>
> *If my elevated states last more than a few days, my spending can become uncontrollable. . . . I will sometimes drive faster than usual, need less sleep and can concentrate well, making quick and accurate decisions. At these times I can also be sociable, talkative and fun, focused at times, distracted at others. If this state of elevation continues I often find that feelings of violence and irritability towards those I love will start to creep in. . . .*
>
> *My thoughts speed up. . . . I frequently want to be able to achieve several tasks at the same moment. . . . Physically my energy levels can seem limitless. The body moves smoothly, there is little or no fatigue. I can go mountain biking all day when I feel like this and if my mood stays elevated not a muscle is sore or stiff the next day. But it doesn't last, my elevated phases are short. . . . The shift into severe depression or a mixed mood state occurs sometimes within minutes or hours, often within days and will last weeks often without a period of normality. . . .*
>
> *Initially my thoughts become disjointed and start slithering all over the place. . . . I start to believe that others are commenting adversely on my appearance or behaviour. . . . My sleep will be poor and interrupted by bad dreams. . . . The world appears bleak. . . . I become repelled by the proximity of people. . . . I will be overwhelmed by the slightest tasks, even imagined tasks. . . . Physically there is immense fatigue: my muscles scream with pain. . . . Food becomes totally uninteresting. . . .*
>
> *I start to feel trapped, that the only escape is death. . . . I become passionate about one subject only at these times of deep and intense fear, despair and rage: suicide. . . . I have made close attempts on my life . . . over the last few years. . . .*
>
> *Then inexplicably, my mood will shift again. The fatigue drops from my limbs like shedding a dead weight, my thinking returns to normal, the light takes on an intense clarity, flowers smell sweet and my mouth curves to smile at my children, my husband and I are laughing again. Sometimes it's for only a day but I am myself again, the person that I was a frightening memory. I have survived another bout of this dreaded disorder. . . .*
>
> (Anonymous, 2006)

Surveys indicate that between 1 and 2.8 percent of all adults experience a bipolar disorder at any given time (NIMH, 2023; Stovall, 2023). As many as 4.4 percent experience one of the bipolar disorders at some point in their life. According to research conducted with predominantly cisgender populations, bipolar disorders are equally common in women and men. Some preliminary research suggests that the disorders may be more common

bipolar I disorder A type of bipolar disorder marked by full manic and major depressive episodes.

bipolar II disorder A type of bipolar disorder marked by mildly manic (hypomanic) episodes and major depressive episodes.

PSYCHWATCH

Psychopathology and Creativity: A Delicate Balance

The ancient Greeks believed that various forms of "divine madness" inspired creative acts, from poetry to performance. Even today, many people expect "creative geniuses" to be psychologically disturbed. A popular image of the artist includes a glass of liquor, a cigarette, and a tormented expression. Classic examples include writer William Faulkner, who displayed alcohol use disorder and received electroconvulsive therapy for depression; poet Sylvia Plath, who was depressed for most of her life and eventually died by suicide at age 31; and ballet dancer Vaslav Nijinsky, who experienced schizophrenia and spent many years in institutions. In fact, a number of studies indicate that artists and writers are somewhat more likely than others to display certain mental disorders, particularly bipolar disorders (Nittle, 2023; Rothenberg, 2022).

Boaz Teitelbaum/Camera Press/Redux

Fuel for his art? Pioneering glass artist Dale Chihuly, seen here through one of his vibrant sculptures, is famous for his colorful and imaginative large-scale glass installations. Chihuly also experiences bipolar disorder, and his wife Leslie believes that the disorder—including his euphoric mania and flood of ideas—may help fuel and enhance his creativity.

Why might creative people be prone to such psychological disorders? Some may be genetically predisposed to such disorders (Greenwood, 2020). Another possibility is that their childhood or family environment may have contributed to the development of psychological problems, a vulnerability set in motion long before they begin their artistic careers. Consistent with this notion, creative people often have a family history of psychological problems (Nittle, 2023; Parnas et al., 2019), and a number have experienced intense psychological trauma during childhood (Zsedel, 2019). English writer Virginia Woolf, for example, endured sexual abuse as a child.

Yet another explanation for the link between creativity and psychological disorders is that the creative professions offer a welcome climate for those with psychological disturbances (Ivcevic, Grossman, & Ranjan, 2022; Collingwood, 2016). In the worlds of poetry, painting, and acting, for example, emotional expression, unusual thinking, and/or personal turmoil are valued as sources of inspiration and success.

Much remains to be learned about the relationship between emotional turmoil and creativity, but work in this area has already clarified two important points. First, psychological disturbance is hardly a requirement for creativity. Most "creative geniuses" are, in fact, psychologically stable and happy throughout their entire lives (Woo, 2023; Rothenberg, 2022, 2015). Second, mild psychological disturbances relate to creative achievement much more strongly than severe disturbances do (Woo, 2023; Donahue, 2020; Ehrenfeld, 2019). For example, nineteenth-century composer Robert Schumann produced 27 works during one hypomanic year but next to nothing during years when he was severely depressed and suicidal (Jamison, 1995).

Some artists worry that their creativity would disappear if their psychological disturbances were to stop. In fact, however, research suggests that successful treatment for severe psychological disorders more often than not improves the creative process (Rothenberg, 2022, 2015; Donahue, 2020). Romantic notions aside, severe mental dysfunction has little redeeming value, in the arts or anywhere else.

among people identifying as transgender or nonbinary than among cisgender people, but few studies have been conducted on this topic (Brickman & Fristad, 2022; Livingston et al., 2022). Research indicates that bipolar disorders are more common among people with low incomes than those with higher incomes (NIMH, 2023; Sletved et al., 2022). Onset usually occurs between the ages of 15 and 44 years (Stovall, 2023). In most untreated cases, the manic and depressive episodes eventually subside, only to recur at a later time.

Some people have numerous periods of hypomanic symptoms and *mild* depressive symptoms, a pattern that is called **cyclothymic disorder** in DSM-5-TR (Morrison, 2023). The symptoms of this milder form of bipolar disorder continue for two or more years, interrupted occasionally by normal moods that may last for only days or weeks. This disorder, like bipolar I and bipolar II disorders, usually begins in adolescence or early adulthood and is equally common across genders. Between 0.4 and 2.5 percent of the population develops cyclothymic disorder over the course of their lives (APA, 2022). In some cases, the milder symptoms eventually blossom into a bipolar I or bipolar II disorder.

What Causes Bipolar Disorders?

Biological research has produced some promising—though limited thus far—clues about the causes of bipolar disorders. The biological insights have come from studies of *neurotransmitter activity, ion activity, brain structure and circuitry,* and *genetic factors.*

Neurotransmitters Could irregular activity of neurotransmitters be related to bipolar disorders? This was the expectation of clinicians back in the 1960s after investigators first found a relationship between low norepinephrine activity and unipolar depression (Schildkraut, 1965). And indeed, over the years, a number of studies have found irregular activity of neurotransmitters—norepinephrine, serotonin, glutamate, and dopamine—in the brains of people with bipolar disorders (Guglielmo & Hasler, 2022; Mandal et al., 2022). But the kind of irregular neurotransmitter activity has varied from study to study (sometimes high and sometimes low, sometimes one neurotransmitter and sometimes another), leaving most of today's theorists unconvinced that neurotransmitters directly cause bipolar disorders.

Mark Lynch/CartoonStock Ltd.

Ion Activity While neurotransmitters play a significant role in the communication *between* neurons, *ions* seem to play a critical role in relaying messages *within* a neuron. That is, ions help transmit messages down the neuron's axon to the nerve endings. Positively charged *sodium ions* (Na^+) sit on both sides of a neuron's cell membrane. When the neuron is at *rest,* more sodium ions sit outside the membrane. When the neuron receives an incoming message at its receptor sites, pores in the cell membrane open, allowing the sodium ions to flow to the inside of the membrane, thus increasing the positive charge inside the neuron. This starts a wave of electrical activity that travels down the length of the neuron and results in its "firing."

If messages are to be relayed effectively down the axon, the sodium ions and nearby ions must be able to travel easily between the outside and the inside of the neural membrane. Some studies suggest that, among bipolar individuals, irregularities in the transport of these ions may cause neurons to fire too easily (resulting in mania) or to stubbornly resist firing (resulting in depression) (Karakurt & Pir, 2022; Qaswal, 2020).

Brain Structure and Circuitry Brain-imaging studies have identified a number of irregular brain structures in people with bipolar disorders (Stovall, 2023; Park et al., 2022). For example, these individuals tend to have a smaller hippocampus, basal ganglia, and cerebellum than other people do; further, they have smaller amounts of gray matter in the brain, and their raphe nuclei, striatum, amygdala, and prefrontal cortex have some structural irregularities. It is not clear what role such differences play in bipolar disorders. Some researchers believe that the irregularities collectively reflect dysfunction throughout a *bipolar-related brain circuit* (Bi, Che, & Bai, 2022; Phillips & Drevets, 2020). It may also be that such irregularities are related to the brain's depression-related circuit that you read about earlier in this chapter.

Genetic Factors Many theorists believe that people inherit a biological predisposition to develop bipolar disorders (Stovall, 2023). Family pedigree studies support this idea. Identical twins of those with a bipolar disorder have a 40 to 70 percent likelihood of developing the same disorder, and fraternal twins, siblings, and other close relatives of such persons have a 5 to 10 percent likelihood, compared with the 1 to 2.8 percent prevalence rate in the general population.

Researchers have also used techniques from *molecular biology* to more directly examine possible genetic factors in large families. Their work has linked bipolar disorders to a variety of genes located on at least 13 different chromosomes (Stovall, 2023). Such wide-ranging findings suggest that a number of genetic irregularities probably *combine* to help bring about bipolar disorders.

of NOTE ...

Higher Risk

The risk of developing bipolar disorder is six times higher for children of older men (over 45 years when their children were born) than children of young men (20 to 24 years). Why? One theory is that, as men age, they produce increased genetic mutations during the manufacture of sperm cells (Stovall, 2023; Chudal et al., 2014).

What Are the Treatments for Bipolar Disorders?

Until the latter part of the twentieth century, people with bipolar disorders were destined to spend their lives on an emotional roller coaster. Psychotherapists reported almost no success, and early antidepressant drugs were of limited help. In fact, those drugs sometimes triggered a manic episode (Serafini, Nasrallah, & Amore, 2022).

Mood-Stabilizing Drugs and Strategies

This gloomy picture changed dramatically in 1970 when the FDA approved the use of **lithium,** a silvery-white element found in various simple mineral salts throughout the natural world, as a treatment for bipolar disorder. It was lithium that first brought hope to those displaying bipolar disorder.

Determining the correct lithium dosage for a given patient is a delicate process requiring careful adjustments in dose, regular analyses of blood and urine samples, and other laboratory tests. Too low a dose will have little or no effect on the bipolar mood swings, but too high a dose can result in lithium toxicity (literally, poisoning), which can feature vomiting, diarrhea, tremors, seizures, kidney dysfunction, cardiac irregularities, and even death (Hedya, Avula, & Swoboda, 2023).

Despite such dangers, lithium is still used today for many persons with bipolar disorders. It is now one of several **mood-stabilizing drugs.** Effective alternative mood stabilizers include *lamotrigine* (Lamictal), *carbamazepine* (Tegretol), and *valproate* (Depakote)—antiseizure drugs that originally were used to treat brain seizure disorder (epilepsy). Such drugs do not require the frequent patient monitoring that lithium does. Additionally, certain *antipsychotic drugs,* originally developed to treat schizophrenia, are often included in the mix to help stabilize the moods of persons with bipolar disorders (Bobo & Shelton, 2022). The effects of these antipsychotics drugs tend to unfold sooner than those of the other mood-stabilizing drugs, although, as you will read in the chapter about schizophrenia, the antipsychotics pose serious health risks of their own.

All manner of research has attested to the mood-stabilizing effectiveness of lithium, antiseizure drugs, and antipsychotics—alone or in various combinations—in treating *manic* episodes (Nath & Gupta, 2023; Bobo & Shelton, 2022). More than 60 percent of patients with mania improve on these medications, and most such individuals have fewer new episodes of mania as long as they continue taking the medications, particularly those taking the antiseizure drug *lamotrigine* (Lamictal). These findings suggest that the mood stabilizers are also *prophylactic,* that they actually help prevent symptoms from developing (Healy, 2022). Thus, today's clinicians usually have patients continue taking some level of a mood-stabilizing drug even after their manic episodes subside.

Practitioners are less successful helping people with bipolar disorders overcome *depressive* episodes (Stovall, 2023; Serafini et al., 2022). The mood stabilizers do help reduce the suicidal thinking of bipolar individuals, but the other features of depression typically linger (Baldessarini et al., 2020). If a patient's depression does not respond to these drugs, a practitioner typically will add antidepressant drugs (Bobo & Shelton, 2023). Such combinations can be helpful, but, as noted earlier, most antidepressants have limited effectiveness in cases of bipolar depression. Some studies suggest that ketamine, the new kind of antidepressant drug that works so quickly in cases of unipolar depression, may be of help in cases of bipolar depression, but its potential for this kind of depression has yet to be fully clarified (Smith-Apeldoorn et al., 2022; Surjan et al., 2022).

cyclothymic disorder A disorder marked by numerous periods of hypomanic symptoms and mild depressive symptoms.

lithium A metallic element that occurs in nature as a mineral salt and is an effective treatment for bipolar disorders.

mood-stabilizing drugs Psychotropic drugs that help stabilize the moods of people with bipolar disorder. Also known as *antibipolar drugs.*

of NOTE ...

Special Danger

People with bipolar disorders have a higher rate of suicide than do people with any other mental disorder. Their rate may be as high as 10 to 30 times that of the general population (Gillette, 2022; Miller & Black, 2020).

Researchers do not fully understand why lithium and antiseizure drugs help in cases of bipolar disorder. One possibility is that the drugs change synaptic activity by operating *within* neurons (Mandal et al., 2022). The firing of a neuron consists of several phases that ensue at lightning speed. When a neurotransmitter binds to a receptor on the receiving neuron, a series of changes occur within the receiving neuron to set the stage for firing. The substances in the neuron that carry out those changes are often called *second messengers* because they relay the original message from the receptor site to the firing mechanism of the neuron. (The neurotransmitter itself is considered the *first messenger.*) Whereas antidepressant drugs affect a neuron's initial reception of neurotransmitters, mood stabilizers appear to affect a neuron's second messengers.

In a similar vein, it has been found that the mood-stabilizing drugs also increase the production of a protein called *brain-derived neurotrophic factor* (*BDNF*) and other proteins within certain neurons whose job it is to prevent cell death. The drugs may increase the health and functioning of those cells and thus reduce bipolar symptoms (Sharma et al., 2022; Lin & Huang, 2020).

Finally, it may be that effective mood stabilizers reduce bipolar symptoms by improving the functioning of or communications between key structures in the brain. In support of this possibility, it has been found that lithium actually increases the size of the hippocampus and the amount of gray matter in bipolar patients (Jahandideh et al., 2023; Anand et al., 2020). Recall that bipolar individuals have, among other brain irregularities, a smaller hippocampus and a smaller amount of gray matter than other people.

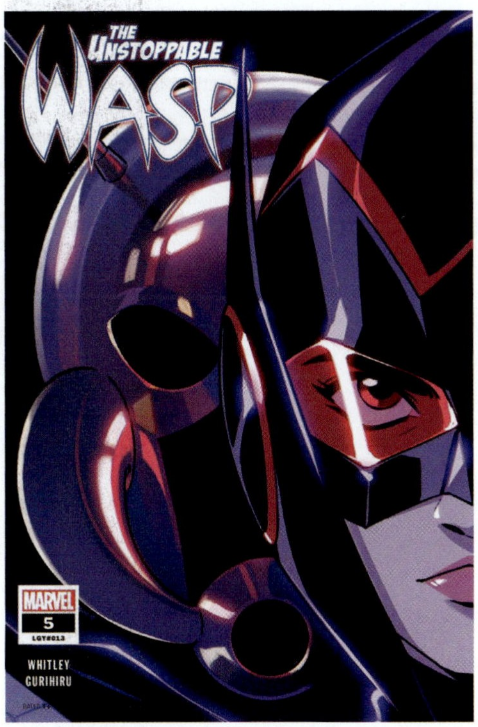

Marvel heroes trying to cope In Issue No. 5 of the *Unstoppable Wasp*, a Marvel Comics series, the title hero comes to the realization "I think I'm bipolar . . . and I don't think I can handle this alone." According to the storyline, her father, Ant-Man, also displayed a bipolar disorder.

Adjunctive Psychotherapy

Psychotherapy alone is rarely helpful for persons with bipolar disorders. At the same time, clinicians have learned that mood-stabilizing drugs alone are not always sufficient either. Of patients with these disorders, 30 percent or more may not respond to these drugs, may not receive the proper dose, or may relapse while taking them. In addition, individuals may stop taking mood stabilizers on their own because they are bothered by the drugs' unwanted effects, feel too well to recognize the need for the drugs, miss the euphoria felt during manic episodes, or worry about becoming less productive when they take the drugs (Vieta & Colom, 2023, 2022).

In view of these problems, many clinicians now provide individual, group, or family therapy as an *adjunct* to mood-stabilizing drugs (Post, 2023; Brickman & Fristad, 2022). Most often, therapists use these formats to emphasize the importance of continuing to take medications; to improve social skills and relationships that may be affected by bipolar episodes; to educate patients and families about bipolar disorders; to help patients solve the family, school, and occupational problems caused by their disorder; and to help prevent patients from attempting suicide. Studies have found that such adjunctive therapy at least doubles the likelihood that bipolar individuals will continue to take their medications properly, and it helps reduce hospitalizations, improve social functioning, and increase patients' ability to obtain and hold a job (Vieta & Colom, 2023, 2022). Psychotherapy commonly plays a more central role in the treatment of cyclothymic disorder. In fact, patients with cyclothymic disorder typically receive psychotherapy, alone or in combination with mood stabilizers.

SUMMING UP

Bipolar Disorders

In bipolar disorders, episodes of mania alternate or intermix with episodes of depression. These disorders are much less common than unipolar depression. They may take the form of bipolar I disorder, bipolar II disorder, or cyclothymic disorder.

Research has suggested various possible causes of bipolar disorders, including the irregular activity of neurotransmitters, irregularities in the transport of ions along their neural membranes, and certain brain structure irregularities that may reflect dysfunction in a bipolar-related brain circuit. A fourth possible cause of bipolar disorders points to genetic factors.

Lithium, antiseizure medications, and antipsychotic drugs have proved to be effective in the treatment of bipolar disorders, although they are typically more effective in the treatment and prevention of manic episodes than of depressive episodes. Patients tend to fare better when such drugs are combined with adjunctive psychotherapy.

Making Sense of All That Is Known

DURING THE PAST 50 years, researchers have made significant gains in the understanding and treatment of depressive and bipolar disorders. Numerous factors have been tied closely to unipolar depression. Indeed, more contributing factors have been associated with this disorder than with most other psychological problems. Developmental psychopathology theorists and researchers have done an admirable job of trying to put these various factors together; it is still not entirely clear, however, how all of these factors relate to unipolar depression.

As with unipolar depression, in recent decades clinicians and researchers have learned much about bipolar disorders. But bipolar disorders appear to be best explained by a focus on *one* kind of variable—biological factors. Whatever roles other factors may play, the primary one appears to lie in this realm.

In a similar vein, depressive and bipolar disorders are now among the most treatable of all psychological disorders. The choice of treatment for bipolar disorders is narrow and simple: drug therapy, often accompanied by psychotherapy, is the single most successful approach. The picture for unipolar depression is more varied and complex, although no less promising.

There is no question that investigations into depressive and bipolar disorders have been fruitful. And it is more than reasonable to expect that important research findings will continue to unfold in the years ahead. Now that clinical researchers have gathered so many important pieces of the puzzle, they must put the pieces together into a still more meaningful picture that will suggest even better ways to predict, prevent, and treat these disorders.

of NOTE ...

Exercise Really Helps

Research finds that physical exercise helps improve the moods of modestly or moderately depressed people, particularly when integrated with psychotherapy or antidepressant medication (Greer & Small, 2022; Dishman, McDowell, & Herring, 2021; Firth et al., 2020).

Quick Quiz

1. What is the difference between depressive disorders and bipolar disorders? pp. 181–182
2. What are the key symptoms of depression and mania? pp. 183–184, 208–209
3. Describe the roles of norepinephrine, serotonin, glutamate, hormones, and the depression-related brain circuit in unipolar depression. pp. 186–187
4. Describe Freud and Abraham's psychodynamic theory of depression and the evidence that supports it. pp. 193–194
5. How do cognitive-behavioral theorists describe the role of rewards, negative thinking, and learned helplessness in depression? pp. 195–199
6. What approaches do biological and cognitive-behavioral therapists use to treat people with unipolar depression? How effective are these various approaches? pp. 188–193, 199–202
7. How do sociocultural clinicians account for and treat unipolar depression? How might the character, causes, and treatments of depression vary by gender, race, ethnicity, and culture? pp. 202–206
8. How do developmental psychopathology theorists integrate the factors from the various models to help explain unipolar depression? p. 207
9. What roles do biological and genetic factors seem to play in bipolar disorders? pp. 212–213
10. Discuss the leading treatments for bipolar disorders, including their effectiveness. pp. 213–214

Suicide

CHAPTER 7

TOPIC OVERVIEW

Dorsey considered his life a great success. He was the first in his Irish American family to have graduated college, and by the age of 48, he had risen to the vice presidency of a small investment firm. He had a caring wife, Reena, and two sons in college who respected him. They lived in an upper-middle-class neighborhood, had a spacious house, and enjoyed a life of comfort. He was proud of his family and proud of himself. He also felt satisfaction that he had proven his parents wrong when they said that his relationship with Reena would never work out. He hardly acknowledged it to himself, but he felt vindicated when, in their sixties, his parents divorced over his father's relationship with a younger coworker. His relationship with Reena had outlasted his parents'.

In April of Dorsey's fiftieth year, everything changed. The early stages of the Covid-19 pandemic ravaged the economy. For months, Dorsey worked from home, and while he enjoyed spending more time with Reena, he felt like one day bled into the next, and he began to wish he could get out of the house. But with the pandemic raging, there was nowhere to go. More important, most of his clients were losing money—a situation that he felt would soon change but a very uncomfortable situation nevertheless.

Unfortunately, the Covid-related economic downturn stretched out longer than Dorsey had anticipated, and in August, he was fired from his job. Given the economic climate, the firm's president wanted to try new investment strategies and marketing approaches. He said Dorsey was "old school," that he didn't fully grasp today's financial scene—that he didn't know how to reach out to potential investors with Web-based advertising or how to engage with clients online. Dorsey's boss wanted to try a younger person.

The experience of failure, loss, and emptiness was overwhelming. Dorsey looked for another job, but he found only low-paying positions for which he was overqualified. Each day as he looked for work, Dorsey became more depressed, anxious, and desperate. He sometimes thought of starting his own investment company, but in the cold of night, he knew he was just fooling himself—not in this economy. It began to appear as if Reena and he might need to sell their home and move somewhere more affordable in order to get by. He kept sinking, withdrew from others, and felt increasingly hopeless.

Four months after losing his job, Dorsey began to think about ending his life. The pain was too great, the humiliation unending. He hated the present and dreaded the future. Throughout January, he went back and forth. On some days, he was sure he wanted to die. On other days, an enjoyable evening or uplifting conversation might change his mind temporarily.

In early February, Dorsey purchased a revolver from a local gun shop, supposedly to protect Reena and himself from a community crime wave that had arisen with the pandemic. Reena wasn't sure she liked the idea of a gun in the house, but Dorsey promised to keep it locked up and stressed how important her safety was to him. Although he kept telling himself that the gun was indeed for protection, he privately felt a sense of relief at the thought that the gun might give him an option if he decided he absolutely couldn't take his unrelenting pain and humiliation anymore.

On a Monday late in February, he heard about a job possibility, and it lifted his spirits. But the interview did not go well. His potential new boss, younger and less experienced than Dorsey, asked him to discuss online investment strategies. Although Dorsey had prepared furiously for the interview, knowing this subject would come up, he froze in the moment and stumbled through his answer. He was flooded with memories of his old boss

(continued on the next page)

Matt Manley

calling him out of touch, and he couldn't focus on what he was trying to say. He apologized at one point for stumbling and tried to laugh it off as if it was of no consequence, but his mind kept flashing onto the gun back at his house. At the end of the interview, his prospective employer thanked Dorsey and said he'd be hearing from them, but Dorsey knew there'd be no job offer.

He went home, took the gun from his locked desk drawer, and took his life.

MediaPunch Master/AP Images

A dance cut short Fans of dancer, choreographer, and DJ tWitch were shocked in 2022 when the entertainer died of a self-inflicted gunshot wound. According to reports, tWitch vaguely alluded to past challenges and struggles in a note left behind.

Salmon spawn and then die after an exhausting upstream swim to their breeding ground. Lemmings rush to the sea and drown. But only humans knowingly take their own lives. The actions of salmon and lemmings are instinctual responses that may even help their species survive in the long run. Only in the human act of suicide do beings act for the specific purpose of putting an end to their lives.

Suicide has been recorded throughout history. The Old Testament described King Saul's suicide: "There Saul took a sword and fell on it." The ancient Chinese, Greeks, and Romans also provided examples. In more recent times, suicides by such celebrated individuals as rock star Kurt Cobain, comedian Robin Williams, fashion designer Kate Spade, television correspondent and former Miss USA Cheslie Kryst, and celebrity chef Anthony Bourdain both shocked and fascinated the public.

Today, suicide is one of the leading causes of death in the world. By the time you finish reading this page and the next, someone in the United States will have died by suicide. In fact, approximately 131 Americans will have taken their own lives by this time tomorrow (CDC, 2023, 2022).

It has been estimated that worldwide, 1 million people die by suicide each year, more than 46,000 in the United States alone (CDC, 2023, 2022). At least 14 million other people throughout the world—1.2 million in the United States—make nonfatal attempts or gestures to end their lives, which are sometimes called **parasuicides** (CDC, 2023, 2022; WHO, 2022). Actually, it is difficult to obtain accurate figures on suicide, and many investigators believe that estimates are often low. For one thing, suicide can be difficult to distinguish from unintentional drug overdoses, automobile crashes, drownings, and other accidents. Many apparent "accidents" are probably intentional. For another, since suicide is frowned on in our society, relatives and friends often refuse to acknowledge that loved ones have taken their own lives.

Suicide is not officially classified as a mental disorder in DSM-5-TR, although the diagnostic manual proposes that a category called *suicidal behavior disorder* be studied for possible inclusion in future DSM revisions. In the meantime, the diagnostic manual designates suicidal behavior as a special condition that, whenever present, should be formally noted alongside a person's primary diagnosis—that is, alongside a primary diagnosis of PTSD, major depressive disorder, schizophrenia, or the like (APA, 2022). ■

What Is Suicide?

parasuicide A suicide attempt that does not result in death.

suicide A self-inflicted death in which the person acts intentionally, directly, and consciously.

NOT EVERY SELF-INFLICTED death is a suicide. A person who crashes their car into a tree after falling asleep at the steering wheel is not trying to end their life. Thus, Edwin Shneidman (2005, 1993, 1963), a pioneer in this field, defined **suicide** as an intentioned death—a self-inflicted death in which one makes an intentional, direct, and conscious effort to end one's life.

Intentioned deaths may take various forms. Consider the following examples. All three of these people intended to die, but their motives, concerns, and actions differed greatly:

Chaska, *until recently a police officer in the Oglala Sioux tribe, always found his name ironic. His name meant "eldest son" in the tribe, but his parents' plans had gone astray, and he was the only child they would ever have. His father died when he was 5, and his mother had raised him on her own, although many "aunties" helped shoulder the burden of his care. Growing up on the Pine Ridge Reservation had been hard. He remembered how little they had and that he was often hungry.*

As a tribal police officer, Chaska later witnessed the worst side of his community. He saw violent crimes and observed how some respected men abused their wives behind closed doors. He did not drink to excess, although he sometimes enjoyed smuggled beer with pals. He felt trapped by reservation life, distrusted by some who believed the tribal police were working with the federal government to oppress them. Although Chaska knew they were wrong, he understood the centuries of oppression and atrocities his people had suffered at the hands of the federal government that produced this distrust. Still, it hurt to feel outcast.

At the age of 35, Chaska tried to start over. Feeling isolated and sad, he left the police and the reservation and pursued life as a woodworker in the small Nebraska town of Rushville. But life in this new town proved to be just as isolated as life on the Pine Ridge Reservation. Here he felt strange around so many people who were not of the tribe. He felt distrusted as an outsider by the people of Rushville, just as he had felt distrusted by some of his own people. And, perhaps because of the new town's distrust, it was extremely hard to get carpentry work in Rushville. Although he'd been unhappy on the Pine Ridge Reservation, he now missed its sense of community.

When the Covid-19 pandemic hit, Chaska became even more isolated. Now there was no work at all, and he worried that he'd soon be out on the street. He went days without seeing another human being. One day, he heard that an old friend from the reservation had died by suicide, and despite his sadness, he envied his friend having found an escape. He didn't have anyone at all to talk to about his unhappiness. He was alone when he used his gun to end his life.

Demaine *never truly recovered from his mother's death. He was only 9 years old and unprepared for such a loss. His father sent him to live with his grandparents for a time, to a new school with new kids and a new way of life. In Demaine's mind, all these changes were for the worse. He missed the joy and laughter of the past. He missed his home, his father, and his friends. Most of all, he missed his mother. A few times, his grandparents took him to events at their mosque. Demaine had never before visited a mosque, as his family had always gone to his father's church. He found the mosque interesting, but being around others who shared his mother's religion only made him miss her more.*

He did not really understand her death. His father said that she was in heaven now, at peace, happy. Demaine's sadness and loneliness continued day after day, and he began to put things together in his own way. He believed he would be happy again if he could join his mother. He felt she was waiting for him, waiting for him to come to her. The thoughts seemed so right to him; they brought him comfort and hope. One evening, shortly after saying good night to his grandparents, Demaine climbed out of bed, went up the stairs to the roof of their apartment house, and jumped to his death. In his mind, he was joining his mother in heaven.

(continued on the next page)

of NOTE ...

Steady Rise

The rate of suicide in the United States has gone up fairly steadily throughout the twenty-first century. It was 10.4 suicides per 100,000 people in 2000; in 2022 it was 13.5 suicides per 100,000 people, an increase of 30 percent (CDC, 2023, 2022).

Tya and Cassidy had met on a speed date. Tya talked to dozens of prospects that night, but none of them appealed to her—except for Cassidy! She was quirky. She was witty. And she seemed as turned off by the whole speed date thing as Tya was. Tya hadn't wanted to come to this "Ladies' Night" speed dating event. Her close friend Dedra had insisted she go, saying Tya needed "to have a good time for a change." Now (although she didn't plan to admit it to Dedra), she was glad she had come.

Cassidy's was the only name that Tya put on her list. As it turned out, Cassidy also put Tya's name on her list, and a week later, each of them received an e-mail with contact information about the other. Before long, they were a couple. Tya marveled at her luck. She had beaten the odds. She had had a successful speed date experience.

It was Tya's first serious relationship; it became her whole life. Thus, she was truly shocked and devastated when, on the one-year anniversary of their speed date, Cassidy told her that she no longer loved her and was leaving her for someone else.

As the weeks went by, Tya was filled with both depression and anger. Several times, she texted or called Cassidy, begged her to reconsider, and pleaded for a chance to win her back. At the same time, she hated Cassidy for putting her through such misery.

Tya's friends became more and more worried about her. At first, they sympathized with her grief, but as time went on, her depression and anger worsened, and Tya began to act strangely. Always a bit of a drinker, she started to drink heavily and to mix her drinks with various drugs.

One night, Tya went into her bathroom, reached for a bottle of sleeping pills, and swallowed a handful of them. She wanted to make her pain go away, and she wanted Cassidy to know just how much pain she had caused. She continued swallowing pill after pill, crying and swearing as she gulped them down. When she began to feel drowsy, she decided to call her friend Dedra. She was not sure why she was calling, perhaps to say good-bye, to explain her actions, or to make sure that Cassidy was told or perhaps to be talked out of it. Dedra pleaded and reasoned with her and tried to motivate her to live. Tya was trying to listen, but she became less and less coherent. Dedra hung up the phone and quickly called Tya's neighbor and the police. When reached by the neighbor, Tya was already in a coma. Seven hours later, while her friends and family waited for news in the hospital lounge, Tya died.

of NOTE ...

Methods of Suicide

Firearms are used in 53 percent of the deaths by suicide in the United States. The second leading method, used in 27 percent of suicide deaths, is suffocation (for example, hanging). The third leading method, used in 12 percent of suicide deaths, is poisoning (for example, intentional drug overdose) (CDC, 2023, 2022).

While Tya seemed to have mixed feelings about her death, Chaska was clear in his wish to die. Whereas Demaine viewed death as a trip to heaven, Chaska saw it as an end to his existence. Such differences can be important in efforts to understand and treat people at risk for suicide. Accordingly, Shneidman distinguished four kinds of people who intentionally end their lives: the *death seeker, death initiator, death ignorer,* and *death darer.*

Death seekers clearly intend to end their lives at the time they attempt suicide. This singleness of purpose may last only a short time. It can change to confusion the very next hour or day and then return again in short order. Dorsey, the middle-aged investment counselor whose case opened this chapter, was a death seeker. He had many misgivings about suicide and was ambivalent about it for weeks, but on Tuesday night, he was a death seeker—clear in his desire to die and acting in a manner that virtually guaranteed a fatal outcome. Similarly, Chaska, the former tribal police officer who wanted to escape his unrelenting unhappiness and who feared the future, seemed to be a death seeker.

Death initiators also clearly intend to end their lives, but they act out of a belief that the process of death is already under way and that they are simply hastening the process. Some expect that they will die in a matter of days or weeks. A number of suicides among older adults or people who are very sick fall into this category. Robust novelist Ernest Hemingway was profoundly concerned about his failing body as he approached his 62nd birthday—a concern that some observers believe was at the center of his suicide in 1961. Similarly, a driving force in Robin Williams' suicide was the comedian's belief that his Parkinson's disease (later rediagnosed as Lewy body disease) spelled the end of his vibrant life and his career as a performer.

Death ignorers do not believe that their self-inflicted death will mean the end of their existence. They believe they are trading their present lives for a better or happier existence. Many child suicides, like Demaine's, fall into this category, as do those of adult believers in a hereafter who end their own lives to reach another form of life. In 1997, for example, the world was shocked to learn that 39 members of an unusual cult named Heaven's Gate had died by suicide at an expensive house outside San Diego. It turned out that these members had acted out of the belief that their deaths would free their spirits and enable them to ascend to a "higher kingdom."

Death darers experience mixed feelings, or ambivalence, about their intent to die, even at the moment of their attempt, and they show this ambivalence in the act itself. Although to some degree they wish to die, and they often do die, their risk-taking behavior does not guarantee death. The person who plays Russian roulette—that is, pulls the trigger of a revolver randomly loaded with one bullet—is a death darer. Tya might be considered a death darer. Although her unhappiness and anger were great, she was not sure that she wanted to die. Even while taking pills, she called her friend, reported her actions, and listened to her friend's pleas.

How should clinicians decide whether to hospitalize a person who is considering suicide or even one who has made an attempt?

When people play *indirect, covert, partial,* or *unconscious* roles in their own deaths, Shneidman (2001, 1993, 1981) classified them in a suicide-like category called **subintentional deaths.** Traditionally, clinicians have cited drug, alcohol, or tobacco use, recurrent physical fighting, and medication mismanagement as behaviors that may contribute to subintentional deaths. In recent decades, another behavioral pattern, **nonsuicidal self-injury** (NSSI), has been added to this list. The term "NSSI" refers to a direct and deliberate destruction of the body (for example, cutting or burning oneself) that is not accompanied by an actual intent to die. Like suicidal behavior, NSSI is not officially classified as a mental disorder in DSM-5-TR, but the diagnostic manual designates NSSI as a special condition that should, whenever present, be formally noted alongside a person's primary diagnosis.

Self-injurious behavior is more common than previously recognized, particularly among teenagers and young adults. Studies suggest that each year, more than 20 percent of all adolescents try to injure themselves, a rate that increased still further

subintentional death A death in which the individual plays an indirect, hidden, partial, or unconscious role.

nonsuicidal self-injury (NSSI) Direct and deliberate destruction of one's own body tissue that is not accompanied by an intent to die.

Majdi Fathi/NurPhoto via Getty Images

Death darers? A teenager jumps from one high rooftop to another, performing flips and other creative moves along the way, all part of the extremely dangerous "sport" called Parkour, or freerunning. Are practitioners of this increasingly popular activity searching for new challenges or highs, as many of them claim, or are some actually death darers?

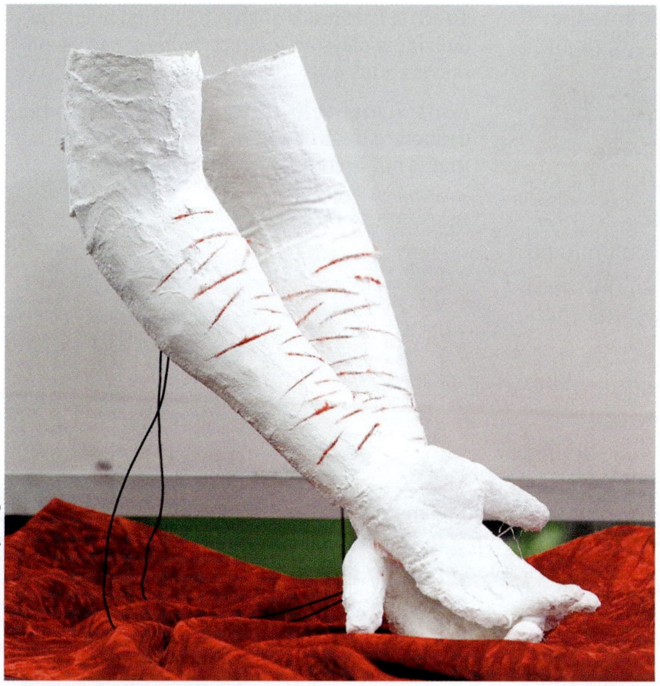

AAron Ontiveroz/Getty Images

Creative expression At least 20 percent of teenagers purposely injure themselves, particularly by skin cutting. Thus, Olivia Stewart, a high school student in Colorado, chose mental illness as the topic for her senior project and produced this remarkable sculpture on self-mutilation. Stewart, whose project also featured art representations of other psychological disorders, hopes that her work will help increase education and public awareness regarding mental disorders.

during the highly stressful social-distancing phase of the Covid-19 pandemic (Farkas et al., 2023; Mitchell et al., 2023; Xiao et al., 2022). It appears that the behavior can become reinforcing (and even somewhat addictive in nature). The pain brought on by self-injury seems to offer some relief from tension or other kinds of emotional distress, the behavior serves as a temporary distraction from problems, and the scars that result may document the person's anguish (Carpenter, Hepp, & Trull, 2023; Kuehn et al., 2022). More generally, self-injury may mitigate the person's chronic feelings of emptiness, boredom, negativity, isolation, and identity confusion. Although self-injury and the other risky behaviors mentioned earlier may indeed represent an indirect attempt at suicide, the true intent behind them is unclear, so, for the most part, these behaviors are not included in the discussions of this chapter.

How Is Suicide Studied?

Suicide researchers face a major obstacle: the people they study are no longer alive. How can investigators draw accurate conclusions about the intentions, feelings, and circumstances of those who can no longer explain their actions? Two research methods attempt to deal with this problem, each with only partial success.

One strategy is **retrospective analysis,** a kind of psychological autopsy in which clinicians and researchers piece together data from the suicide victim's past (Barman & Bairagi, 2023; Valero-Bover et al., 2022). Relatives, friends, therapists, or physicians may remember past statements, conversations, and behaviors that shed light on a suicide. Retrospective information may also be provided by the suicide notes some individuals leave behind. However, such sources of information are not always available or reliable. Many individuals do not leave notes. Moreover, a grieving relative or a distraught therapist may be incapable of objective recollections or simply reluctant to discuss an act that is so stigmatizing in our society. For more reliable information, retrospective analyses often turn to the suicide victim's medical records, which can help identify previous mental disorders or prior medications (Christl et al., 2022). However, such records uncover only the information that has been documented in a patient's medical history.

Because of these limitations, many researchers also use a second strategy—*studying people who survive their suicide attempts*. It is estimated that there are at least 20 nonfatal suicide attempts for every fatal suicide (WHO, 2022). However, it may be that people who survive suicide attempts differ in important ways from those who do not. Nevertheless, suicide researchers have found it useful to study survivors of suicide attempts, and this chapter shall draw upon clinical theories and studies of both those who attempt suicide and those who complete suicide.

Patterns and Statistics

Suicide happens within a larger social setting (see ***Trending***), and researchers have gathered many statistics regarding the social contexts in which such deaths take place. They have found, for example, that suicide rates vary from country to country (WPR, 2023, 2022). South Korea, Russia, South Africa, and Ukraine have very high rates—more than 20 suicides annually per 100,000 persons; conversely, Colombia, Egypt, Peru, Lebanon, Indonesia, and the Philippines have relatively low rates, fewer than 5 per 100,000. Falling in between are the United States (13.5), Germany (12.3), Canada (11.8), China (8.1), and England (7.9).

retrospective analysis A psychological autopsy in which clinicians piece together information about a person's suicide from the person's past.

...TRENDING

Internet and Social Media Horrors

Two current trends on the Internet and social media have produced enormous concern. One is the increasing availability and use of *pro-suicide websites*. These sites vary in their specific messages, but many of them celebrate acts of suicide and people who have died by suicide, others help set up appointments for joint or partner suicides, and several offer specific instructions about suicide methods, prospective suicide locations, and the writing of suicide notes (Moir et al., 2023; Wong, 2021).

The sites have spread across the Internet—on Web forums and chat groups; on social media platforms such as TikTok, Facebook, Instagram, and Reddit; and on video platforms such as YouTube and Vimeo. According to one study, although most suicide-related websites are dedicated to offering support, help, or constructive advice to people thinking about suicide, more than 20 percent of the sites provide information on how to hurt oneself or die by suicide (Eriksen, Konradsen, & Vildekilde, 2021).

A second trend of great concern is the *livestreaming of suicides* (Moir et al., 2023). On January 22, 2017, a 14-year-old girl named Nakia Venant hanged herself in her Florida bathroom while livestreaming the act on Facebook (see photo). Nakia had a long history of significant behavioral problems as well as a background of being physically abused and rejected. She had been in and out of numerous foster care homes for the previous eight years (Barnes, 2017).

Although precise numbers are not available, livestreaming of suicides seems to be on the rise (Moir et al., 2023; Shoib et al., 2022). Clinicians do not really know why certain people attempt suicide online. Some propose that, in addition to being in great psychological pain, the individuals may be trying to display their pain to others, memorialize their death, feel less alone in their final moments, or solicit interventions by others (Antara et al., 2022; Bever, 2017).

Nakia Venant facebook page

A tragic end On January 22, 2017, 14-year-old Nakia Venant broadcast her suicide on Facebook while sending and receiving texts.

Worried about the increase in broadcast suicides and the possible risk of copycat deaths, social media platforms have taken steps to help prevent livestreamed and other forms of suicides (Wong, 2021; Lopez-Castroman et al., 2020). Facebook, for example, has updated tools to make it easier for users to alert Facebook about suicide and self-harm postings that may come their way. Upon receiving such alerts, Facebook offers immediate guidance and resources to the concerned friends or acquaintances. In cases of livestreaming, it also tries to help the streamers directly by blocking their screens with messages that say, "Someone thinks you might need extra support right now and asked us to help." In turn, the streamer can contact a suicide helpline, view tips, and/or text a friend directly from that window.

A few social media platforms make it possible for troubled individuals to immediately chat with a trained counselor from the 988 Suicide & Crisis Lifeline, Crisis Text Line, or another crisis support service (Peters, 2020). In addition, they are developing pattern recognition software to help identify self-harm and suicide warning signals in user posts and comments—signals that the network's monitor team can then act upon proactively by reaching out to the posters (Aldhyani et al., 2022). Hopefully, these and other social media efforts will help prevent or reduce suicidal acts in general and the horrific phenomenon of livestream suicide in particular.

Religious affiliation and beliefs may help account for these national differences. For example, countries that are largely Catholic, Jewish, or Muslim tend to have low suicide rates. Perhaps in these countries, strict prohibitions against suicide or a strong religious tradition deter many people from attempting suicide. Yet there are exceptions to this tentative rule. For example, France, whose population is two-thirds Roman Catholic, has a relatively high suicide rate of 13.8 suicides per 100,000 persons.

AP Photo/Michael Albans

Continuing trend The rate of suicide in Indigenous populations is much higher than the national average. Here a memorial is held for a young suicide victim at a middle school on the Fort Peck Indian Reservation in Poplar, Montana.

Research suggests that religious doctrine may not help prevent suicide as much as the degree of an individual's *devoutness*. Regardless of their particular affiliation, very religious people seem less likely to die by suicide (Pulgar et al., 2022).

Suicide is also related to relationship status. Studies suggest that at least half of those who carry out suicide have a relatively low number of close personal friends and social contacts (Taylor et al., 2023; Olfson et al., 2022). In a related vein, never-married/never-partnered, divorced, and widowed people have a higher suicide rate than those who are married or partnered (Schreiber & Culpepper, 2023). Moreover, people in violent, high-conflict, or otherwise distressing relationships have a higher suicide rate than those in more harmonious relationships (CDC, 2023).

Suicide rates also differ for people with certain sexual orientations. Studies find that lesbian, gay, and bisexual people under the age of 40 attempt and/or die by suicide at substantially higher rates than heterosexual people of the same age (Ramchand et al., 2022; Lyons et al., 2019). As you will read later in the chapter, for example, the rate of suicide attempts by lesbian, gay, and bisexual teenagers is three times that of heterosexual teenagers, a difference attributed to factors such as personal angst, parent disapproval, and prejudice and victimization by peers (CDC, 2023, 2022). Moreover, the rate of suicide by lesbian, gay, and bisexual teenagers further doubles if they have undergone *sexual orientation change efforts* (*SOCEs*)—a range of psychological, medical, and/or religious techniques that attempt to change a person's sexual orientation (Comer et al., 2024; Fenaughty et al., 2023). Given the associations between SOCEs and various severe psychological difficulties and between SOCEs and suicide, today's leading professional medical organizations, such as the American Psychological Association and the American Medical Association, view SOCEs as unethical and have passed resolutions opposing their use in clinical practice (APA, 2023, 2021; Nakamura et al., 2022).

What factors might contribute to the even higher suicide risk among lesbian, gay, and bisexual people who have been subjected to SOCEs?

Suicide rates are also linked to gender. According to research conducted with largely cisgender populations, the rate of attempted suicides among women is 50 percent higher than among men, yet men die from their attempts at four times the rate of women (CDC, 2023, 2022; NIMH, 2022). Although various explanations have been proposed for this gender difference, a popular one points to the different methods used by men and women (De Vise, 2023; McKeon, 2021). Men tend to use more violent methods, such as shooting, stabbing, or hanging themselves, whereas women use less violent methods, such as drug overdose. Guns are used in 58 percent of the male suicides in the United States compared with 33 percent of the female suicides (NIMH, 2023, 2022).

In addition, transgender and nonbinary people have considerably higher rates of suicide attempts and fatalities than do cisgender people. Indeed, as many as 81 percent of transgender people have had thoughts about suicide, and 42 percent have attempted suicide due in part to their lifetime experiences of stigmatization, discrimination, and victimization (Kidd et al., 2023; Austin et al., 2022). In addition, research finds that the rate of suicide by young transgender and nonbinary people further doubles if they have undergone *gender identity change efforts* (*GICEs*)—a range of techniques that attempt to change the individual's gender identity to their birth-assigned sex (Comer et al., 2024; Fenaughty et al., 2023). Given such findings, today's leading professional organizations have also passed resolutions opposing the use of GICEs in clinical practice (APA, 2023, 2021).

Finally, in the United States at least, suicide rates vary according to race and ethnicity (see **Figure 7-1**). The overall suicide rate of non-Hispanic White people (16.9 suicides per 100,000 persons) is more than twice as high as that of many people of color, including Black, Hispanic, and Asian American people (CDC, 2023, 2022). A major exception to this pattern is the suicide rate of Indigenous people (23.9 per 100,000), which is higher than that of non-Hispanic White people. Although the marginalization of many Indigenous persons may partly explain their high suicide rate, studies show that factors such as alcohol use, modeling, and availability of firearms may also play a role (Stone et al., 2022).

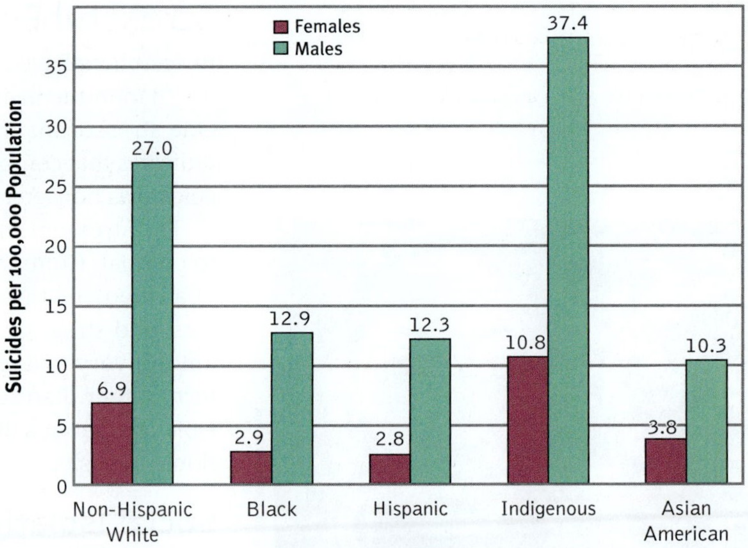

FIGURE 7-1

Suicide, Race/Ethnicity, and Gender

Research conducted with largely cisgender populations in the United States finds Indigenous people have the highest suicide rate, more than one-third higher than the next highest group, non-Hispanic White people. (Information from: NIMH, 2023, 2022.)

SUMMING UP

What Is Suicide?

Suicide is a self-inflicted death in which a person makes an intentional, direct, and conscious effort to end their life. Four kinds of people who intentionally end their lives have been distinguished: the death seeker, the death initiator, the death ignorer, and the death darer.

Two major strategies are used in the study of suicide: retrospective analysis (a psychological autopsy) and the study of people who survive suicide attempts. Suicide rates vary from country to country. One reason seems to be cultural differences in religious affiliation, beliefs, and degree of devoutness. Suicide rates also vary according to relationship status, sexual orientation, gender, and race and ethnicity.

What Triggers a Suicide?

SUICIDAL ACTS MAY be connected to recent events or current conditions in a person's life. Although such factors may not be the basic motivation for the suicide, they can precipitate it. Common triggering factors include *stressful events and situations, mood and thought changes, alcohol and other drug use, mental disorders,* and *modeling*.

Shannon Stapleton/Reuters/Redux

Deadly impact In 2015, Kalief Browder, a Bronx teenager, died by suicide after being imprisoned for three years, including two in solitary confinement, while *awaiting* trial for stealing a backpack. Browder's plight, memorialized in this New York City mural, has attracted widespread attention and outrage.

Stressful Events and Situations

Researchers have counted more stressful events in the recent lives of suicide attempters than in the lives of nonattempters (Choi, Marti, & Choi, 2022; Kuehn et al., 2022). One stressor that has been consistently linked to suicide is combat stress. Research indicates that combat veterans from various wars are more than twice as likely to die by suicide as nonveterans (Kime, 2022).

The stressors that help lead to suicide do not need to be as horrific as those tied to combat. Common forms of *immediate stress* seen in cases of suicide are the loss of a loved one through death, divorce, or rejection; loss of a job; significant financial loss; and stress caused by hurricanes, earthquakes, or other natural disasters, even among very young children. People may also attempt suicide in response to *long-term* rather than recent stress. Four such stressors are particularly common—social isolation, serious illness or injury, an abusive or repressive environment, and occupational stress.

Social Isolation

As you read in our earlier case descriptions, people from loving families or supportive social systems may carry out suicide. However, those without such social supports are particularly vulnerable to suicidal thinking and actions. Researchers have found a heightened risk for suicidal behavior among those who feel little sense of "belongingness," believe that they have limited or no social support, live alone, and have ongoing conflicts with other people (Schreiber & Culpepper, 2023).

Serious Illness or Injury

People whose illnesses cause them great pain or severe disability may attempt suicide, believing that death is unavoidable and imminent (Schreiber & Culpepper, 2023). They may also believe that the distress and problems caused by their illnesses are more than they can endure. Studies suggest that as many as one-third of those who die by suicide have been in poor physical health during the months prior to their suicidal acts. Illnesses that have been linked to higher suicide rates include cancer, heart disease, chronic lung disease, stroke, and diabetes mellitus.

Experiencing a traumatic brain injury more than doubles a person's likelihood of suicide, and this risk quadruples when the injury is particularly severe and in need of extensive medical care (Schreiber & Culpepper, 2023; Ineson et al., 2022). Those in the military have more such injuries than other people do, suggesting to many experts that traumatic brain injuries account for much of the increased suicide risk among combat veterans. These injuries can result in chronic headaches, loss of motor coordination, speech problems, seizures, sleep difficulties, hypersensitivity to light and sound, poor memory, confusion, impulsivity, depression, agitation and irritability, and mood swings. Collectively, such problems reduce the quality of an individual's life; moreover, as you will soon read, several of the mood and thought symptoms can trigger suicide in their own right.

of NOTE ...

The Impact of Internment

The suicide rate among 110,000 Japanese Americans who were interned (incarcerated) in "relocation centers" during World War II rose to double that of the national population (Des Marais, 2023; Jensen, 1998).

Abusive or Repressive Environment

Individuals in an abusive or repressive environment from which they have little or no hope of escape sometimes pursue suicide. For example, some prisoners of war, inmates of concentration camps, abused partners, abused children, and incarcerated people try to end their lives (LeMasters et al., 2023). Like those who have serious illnesses or injuries, these people may feel that they can endure no more distress and believe that there is no hope for improvement in their condition.

Occupational Stress

Some jobs create feelings of tension or dissatisfaction that may help trigger suicide attempts (CDC, 2023). Studies have revealed higher suicide rates among people working in nonspecialized, basic skills occupations. For people in advanced-skills occupations and professions, research has found relatively high suicide rates for psychiatrists and psychologists, physicians, nurses, dentists, lawyers, police officers, firefighters, emergency workers, and farmers (NIOSH, 2022). Of course, such correlations do not necessarily mean that occupational pressures directly cause suicidal actions. Perhaps workers in basic skills jobs are responding to financial insecurity rather than job stress when they attempt suicide. Similarly, rather than reacting to the emotional strain of their work, suicidal psychiatrists and psychologists may have long-standing emotional problems that stimulated their career interest in the first place.

Mood and Thought Changes

Many suicide attempts are preceded by a change in mood. The change may not be severe enough to warrant a diagnosis of a mental disorder, but it does represent a significant shift from the person's past mood. The most common change is an increase in sadness (Choi et al., 2022). Also common are increases in feelings of anxiety, tension, frustration, anger, or shame (Jones et al., 2024).

Suicide attempts may also be preceded by shifts in patterns of thinking. People may become preoccupied with their problems, lose perspective, and see suicide as the only solution to their difficulties (Schreiber & Culpepper, 2023). They often develop a sense of **hopelessness**—a pessimistic belief that their present circumstances, problems, or mood will never change (Pappas, 2023; Rukundo, Ogbolu, & Mugisha, 2023). Some clinicians believe that a feeling of hopelessness is the single most likely indicator of suicidal intent, and they take special care to look for signs of hopelessness when they assess the risk of suicide.

Many people who attempt suicide use **dichotomous thinking**, viewing problems and solutions in rigid either/or terms (Shneidman, 2005, 2001, 1993). Indeed, Shneidman said that the "four-letter word" in suicide is "only," as in "Suicide was the *only* thing I could do." In the following statement, a woman who survived her leap from a building describes her dichotomous thinking at the time. She saw death as the only alternative to her pain.

> *I was so desperate. I felt, my God, I couldn't face this thing. Everything was like a terrible whirlpool of confusion. And I thought to myself: There's only one thing to do. I just have to lose consciousness. That's the only way to get away from it. The only way to lose consciousness, I thought, was to jump off something good and high. . . .*
>
> *(Shneidman, 1987, p. 56)*

Daniele Venturelli/WireImage/Getty Images

"Out of the blue" In recent interviews, Deepika Padukone, one of Bollywood's most successful and glamorous film actresses, has disclosed her past struggles with depression and multiple suicide attempts. She says that her depression "just happened out of the blue." To help others with such issues, she has not only gone public but started the Live Love Laugh Foundation.

Alcohol and Other Drug Use

Autopsies reveal that about one-quarter of people who attempt suicide are intoxicated at the time of their act (Schreiber & Culpepper, 2023). It may be that the use of alcohol lowers a person's inhibitions, reduces fears of suicide, releases underlying aggressive feelings, or impairs judgment and problem-solving ability. Research shows that the use of other kinds of drugs may have a similar tie to suicide, particularly in teenagers and young adults. The likelihood of completing suicide is six times greater among those who engage in heavy alcohol and drug use (Mukamal, 2023).

Mental Disorders

Although people who attempt suicide may be troubled or anxious, they do not necessarily have a psychological disorder. Nevertheless, the vast majority of all suicide attempters do have such a disorder (Schreiber & Culpepper, 2023; King, 2021). Research suggests that as many as 70 percent of all suicide attempters had been

hopelessness A pessimistic belief that one's present circumstances, problems, or mood will not change.

dichotomous thinking Viewing problems and solutions in rigid either/or terms.

Ed Rode/Getty Images

"My descent into depression" Naomi Judd (*right*), performing here with her daughter Wynonna in Nashville, Tennessee, was the iconic matriarch of the country duo The Judds. In 2022, she took her own life at the age of 76, one day before she and Wynonna were to be inducted into the Country Music Hall of Fame. Back in 2016, Judd described her severe emotional challenges and her bipolar disorder in an autobiography, *River of Time: My Descent into Depression and How I Emerged with Hope*.

experiencing severe *depressive* or *bipolar disorders*, 20 percent *substance use disorder*, and 10 percent *schizophrenia*. Correspondingly, as many as 20 percent of people with each of these disorders try to end their lives. People who are both depressed and substance-dependent seem particularly prone to suicidal impulses (Ashrafioun et al., 2020). Certain anxiety disorders, posttraumatic stress disorder, and borderline personality disorder have also been linked to suicide.

Modeling: The Contagion of Suicide

It is not unusual for people, particularly teenagers, to attempt suicide after observing or reading about someone else who has done so (Martínez, Jiménez-Molina, & Gerber, 2023). Perhaps they have been struggling with major problems and the other person's suicide seems to reveal a possible solution, or perhaps they have been thinking about suicide and the other person's suicide seems to give them permission or finally persuades them to act. Either way, one suicidal act apparently serves as a *model* for another. Suicides by family members and friends, those by celebrities, and suicides by coworkers or colleagues are particularly common triggers.

Family Members and Friends

A recent suicide by a family member or a friend increases the likelihood that a person will attempt suicide (AFSP, 2023; King, 2021). Of course, the death of a family member or a friend, especially when self-inflicted, is a life-changing event, and suicidal thoughts or attempts may be tied largely to that trauma or sense of loss. Indeed, such losses typically have a lifelong impact on surviving relatives and friends, including a heightened risk of suicide that can continue for years (Schreiber & Culpepper, 2023). However, even when researchers factor out these issues, they find increases in the risk of suicide among the relatives and friends of people who recently died by their own hand. This additional risk factor is often called the *social contagion effect* (Martínez et al., 2023).

Celebrities

Research suggests that suicides by entertainers, political figures, and other well-known people are regularly followed by unusual increases in the number of suicides across the nation. Studies on this issue have found, for example, that the national suicide rate rose 5 to 16 percent during the weeks after the suicides of actress Marilyn Monroe, comedian Robin Williams, fashion designer Kate Spade, and celebrity chef Anthony Bourdain (Vinney, 2022; Sinyor et al., 2021).

of NOTE ...

Recent Suicides by Popular Musicians

Naomi Judd (2022)
David Berman (2019)
Goo Hara (2019)
Sulli (2019)
Avicii (2018)
Chester Bennington (2017)
Chris Cornell (2017)

Some clinicians argue that more responsible reporting could reduce this frightening impact of celebrity or other highly publicized suicides (Schreiber & Culpepper, 2023; Nordentoft, Madsen, & Erlangsen, 2020). A careful approach to reporting was seen in the media's coverage of the suicide of Kurt Cobain. MTV's repeated theme on the evening of the suicide was "Don't do it!" In fact, thousands of young people called MTV and other radio and television stations in the hours after Cobain's death, upset, frightened, and in some cases suicidal. Some of the stations responded by posting the phone numbers of suicide prevention centers, presenting interviews with suicide experts, and offering counseling services and advice directly to callers. Perhaps because of such efforts, the usual rate of suicide both in Seattle, where Cobain lived, and elsewhere held steady during the weeks that followed (Colburn, 1996).

Coworkers and Colleagues

The word-of-mouth publicity that attends suicides in a school, workplace, or small community may trigger suicide attempts. In an early example of this, the suicide of a recruit at a U.S. Navy training school was followed within two weeks by another and also by an attempted suicide at the school. To head off what threatened to become a suicide epidemic, the school began a program of staff education on suicide and group therapy sessions for recruits who had been close to the suicide victims (Grigg, 1988). Today, a number of schools, for individuals of all ages, put programs of this kind into action after a student dies by suicide. Such postsuicide programs are often referred to by clinicians as *postvention* (De Oliveira et al., 2023; McKeon, 2021).

of NOTE ...

Additional Risk

More police officers die by suicide each year than in the line of duty (Nissim et al., 2022).

Combination of Factors

Although any one of the factors we have been discussing can help precipitate suicide, research clarifies that a combination of them has an even stronger impact. Studies have found, for example, that people with bipolar disorder experiencing an episode of depression have an elevated suicide rate, as one might expect, but that bipolar people who are also unemployed, divorced, living alone, feeling hopeless, and/or abusing substances have particularly elevated rates of suicide (AIHW, 2023; Miller & Black, 2020). Moreover, on average, the more such factors, the greater an individual's inclination to pursue a suicidal act.

Because community-wide traumas often produce widespread feelings of depression and anxiety, severe economic losses, social isolation, and serious medical problems, clinicians often worry that such traumas will produce an increase in the number of suicides among residents (Panayi, 2020; Sher, 2020). In fact, however, suicide rates tend to hold steady or even fall during such events. For example, the first year of the Covid-19 pandemic, which some clinical theorists have called the "perfect storm" of multiple suicide risk factors, was accompanied by striking increases—between 45 and 300 percent—in the number of *calls* and *texts* to suicide prevention centers, but the rate of completed suicides in communities across the world did not increase (Loeb, 2022; Pirkis et al., 2022). A notable exception to this was the rate of completed suicides and suicide attempts among teenagers, which, as you will read later in this chapter, rose significantly during the pandemic (Charpignon et al., 2022).

Why might the Covid-19 pandemic have impacted suicide rates differently across various age groups?

SUMMING UP

What Triggers a Suicide?

Many suicidal acts are triggered by the current events or conditions in a person's life. The acts may be triggered by recent stressors, such as loss of a loved one and job loss, or long-term stressors, such as serious illness, an abusive environment, and job stress. They may also be preceded by changes in mood or thought, particularly increases in one's sense of hopelessness. In addition, the use of alcohol or other kinds of substances, mental disorders, or news of another's suicide may precede suicide attempts.

What Are the Underlying Causes of Suicide?

MOST PEOPLE FACED with difficult situations never try to end their lives. In an effort to understand why some people are more prone to suicide than others, theorists have proposed more fundamental explanations for self-destructive actions than the immediate triggers considered in the previous section. The leading theories come from the psychodynamic, sociocultural, and biological models. Some of these hypotheses, however, have received limited research support and fail to address the full range of suicidal acts. Thus, the clinical field currently lacks a satisfactory understanding of suicide.

A stranger's help Lauren Clements (*right*) sits peacefully next to Elliott Lopes (*left*) at the Natchez Trace Parkway Bridge in Franklin, Tennessee. Five years before this get-together, Clements was about to leap to her death from that very same bridge when Lopes, a cyclist pedaling by, quickly assessed the situation, grabbed hold of Clements, and saved her life.

The Psychodynamic View

Many psychodynamic theorists believe that suicide results from depression and from anger at others that is redirected toward oneself (Schechter et al., 2022; Ronningstam, Weinberg, & Maltsberger, 2021). To make this point, the influential psychiatrist Karl Menninger called suicide "murder in the 180th degree."

As you read in the previous chapter, Freud (1917) and Abraham (1916, 1911) proposed that when people experience the real or symbolic loss of a loved one, they come to "introject" the lost person; that is, they unconsciously incorporate the person into their own identity and feel toward themselves as they had felt toward the other. For a short while, anger toward the loved one may turn into intense anger against oneself and finally into depression. Suicide is thought to be an extreme expression of this self-hatred and self-punishment.

In partial support of Freud's view, researchers have often found a relationship between childhood losses—real or symbolic—and later suicidal behaviors (Jones et al., 2024; Islam et al., 2020). A classic study of 200 family histories, for example, found that early parental loss was much more common among suicide attempters (48 percent) than among nonsuicidal individuals (24 percent) (Adam, Bouckoms, & Streiner, 1982). Common forms of loss were death of the father and divorce or separation of the parents. Similarly, a study of 343 depressed individuals found that those who had felt rejected or neglected as children by their parents were more likely than other people to attempt suicide as adults (Ehnvall et al., 2008).

By the end of his career, Freud himself expressed dissatisfaction with his theory of suicide. Other psychodynamic theorists have also challenged his ideas over the years, yet themes of loss and self-directed aggression generally remain at the center of most psychodynamic explanations.

Durkheim's Sociocultural View

Toward the end of the nineteenth century, Emile Durkheim (1897), a sociologist, developed a broad theory of suicidal behavior. Today, this theory continues to be influential and is often supported by research (Na et al., 2022; Mueller et al., 2021). According to Durkheim, the probability of suicide is determined by how attached a person is to such social groups as the family, religious institutions, and community. The more thoroughly a person belongs, the lower the risk of suicide. Conversely, people who are disconnected from others and from society are at higher risk of dying by suicide. He defined several categories of suicide, including *egoistic, altruistic,* and *anomic* suicide.

Egoistic suicides are carried out by people over whom society has little or no control. These people are not concerned with the norms or rules of society, nor are they integrated into the social fabric. According to Durkheim, this kind of suicide is more likely in people who are isolated, alienated, and nonreligious. The larger the number of such people living in a society, the higher that society's suicide rate.

Altruistic suicides, in contrast, are undertaken by people who are so well integrated into the social structure that they intentionally sacrifice their lives for its well-being. Buddhist monks and nuns who protested the Vietnam War by setting themselves on fire and teachers who were killed while shielding students from mass shooters may have been undertaking altruistic suicide. According to Durkheim, societies that encourage people to sacrifice themselves for others and to preserve their own honor (as East Asian societies do) are likely to have higher suicide rates.

Anomic suicides, another category proposed by Durkheim, are those pursued by people whose social environment fails to provide stable structures, such as family and religion, to support and give meaning to life. Such a societal condition, called *anomie* (literally, "without law"), leaves people without a sense of belonging. Unlike egoistic suicide, which is the act of a person who rejects the structures of a society, anomic suicide is the act of a person who has been let down by a disorganized and often decaying society.

Durkheim argued that when societies go through periods of anomie, their suicide rates increase (Kar & Singh, 2023; Mueller et al., 2021). Historical trends support this claim. Periods of economic depression may bring about some degree of anomie in a country, and national suicide rates tend to rise during such times. Periods of population change and increased immigration, too, tend to bring about a state of anomie, and again suicide rates rise.

A major change in a person's immediate surroundings, rather than general societal problems, can also lead to anomic suicide. People who suddenly inherit a great deal of money, for example, may go through a period of anomie as their relationships with social, economic, and occupational structures are changed. Thus, Durkheim predicted

of NOTE ...

Suicide and Geography

In the United States, the highest rate of suicide is found in rural areas, where 20 per 100,000 people die by suicide. In contrast, in small or medium-sized cities, around 17 per 100,000 people end their lives, and in large cities, 13 per 100,000 people end their lives (Schreiber & Culpepper, 2023).

In the service of others According to Emile Durkheim, people who intentionally sacrifice their lives for others are completing altruistic suicide. In the 2016 movie *Rogue One*, renegade Jyn Erso leads a band of Rebel volunteers on a "suicide mission" to capture the schematic diagram of the Death Star, a powerful superweapon capable of destroying planets. Jyn and her group prevail, ultimately saving the galaxy, but all of them die in the process—as they knew they would.

interpersonal theory of suicide A theory that asserts that people with perceived burdensomeness, thwarted belongingness, and a psychological capability to carry out suicide are the most likely to attempt suicide.

that societies with more opportunities for changes in individual wealth or status would have higher suicide rates; this prediction has also been supported by research over the years (Er, Demir, & Sarei, 2023; Mobley & Taasoobshirazi, 2022).

Although today's sociocultural theorists do not always embrace Durkheim's particular ideas, most agree that interpersonal variables, social structure, and cultural stress often play major roles in suicide. The recent work of researcher Thomas Joiner, which is discussed in the following section, is a case in point.

The Interpersonal View

For more than a decade, clinical researcher Thomas Joiner and his colleagues have been developing the **interpersonal theory of suicide** (Robinson et al., 2024; Joiner et al., 2021, 2017; Joiner, 2009, 2005). According to this theory, people will be inclined to pursue suicide if they hold two key interpersonal beliefs—*perceived burdensomeness* and *thwarted belongingness*—and, at the same time, have a psychological *capability* to carry out suicide, a capability that they have acquired from life experiences. The theory does not dismiss the importance of the other factors you have been reading about in this chapter. However, says Joiner, without the further presence of perceived burdensomeness, thwarted belongingness, and acquired capability, those factors are not likely to result in self-inflicted death.

People with perceived burdensomeness believe that their existence places a heavy and permanent burden on their family, friends, and even society. This belief may produce the notion that "my death would be worth more than my life to my family and friends."

People with thwarted belongingness feel isolated and alienated from others—not an integral part of a family or social network. Their sense of social disconnect may be overstated or may be accurate, but, either way, it feels enduring, unchangeable, and confining.

Research indicates that people who experience *both* of these interpersonal perceptions are inclined to develop a desire for suicide. However, studies also indicate that such individuals are still unlikely to attempt suicide unless they further possess the third variable cited by the theory—the psychological capability to inflict lethal harm on themselves (Robinson et al., 2024; Magliocca et al., 2023; Allman, 2021). According to Joiner, people who are repeatedly exposed to painful or frightening life experiences, such as abuse, trauma, or severe illness, may develop a heightened tolerance for pain and a fearlessness about death, which in turn helps produce a psychological capability for suicidal acts (Kramer et al., 2020).

Wings of support At the gates of Joint Base San Antonio, a center for multiple military services, members of the U.S. Air Force greet military personnel and veterans with signs of encouragement on World Suicide Prevention Day. Their goal was to show support and solidarity to their military colleagues who might have thoughts of suicide.

Operation 2022/Alamy Stock Photo

Studies conducted across a range of populations—from adolescents to older adults—reveal that people with a combination of perceived burdensomeness, thwarted belongingness, and acquired suicide capability are significantly more likely to attempt suicide than people without these characteristics (Chung et al., 2022; Okan et al., 2022). Research further indicates that *hopelessness*—the pessimistic belief that you read about earlier—may help determine whether and when these three characteristics actually lead to suicide (Janackovski et al., 2022).

Although these factors have certainly been linked to civilian suicides, the theory's ability to help account for military suicides, which are twice as prevalent as civilian suicides, has stirred particular interest among clinical researchers. Studies have revealed that many soldiers and veterans, possibly due to the nature and impact of military training and combat, eventually develop feelings that they are a hardship on their families (perceived burdensomeness), have difficulty integrating into civilian life (thwarted belongingness), and grow accustomed to violence (acquired suicide capability). Correspondingly, studies have found that such individuals often develop suicidal thoughts and behaviors (Moceri-Brooks et al., 2023; Soberay et al., 2022).

The Biological View

For years, biological researchers have repeatedly found higher rates of suicide among the parents and close relatives of suicidal people than among those of nonsuicidal people (Schreiber & Culpepper, 2023). Moreover, studies have found higher rates of suicide among the identical twins of suicide victims than among the fraternal twins of victims. Such findings may suggest that genetic, and so biological, factors are at work.

Suicide sometimes runs in families. How might clinicians and researchers explain such family patterns?

Laboratory studies offer still more direct support for a biological view of suicide. One line of research focuses on *serotonin*. The activity level of this neurotransmitter has often been found to be low in people who die by suicide (Kennebeck & Bonin, 2023, 2021; Johnston et al., 2022). Moreover, brain scans reveal that the low serotonin activity of suicidal persons corresponds to dysfunction throughout their depression-related brain circuit, the circuit discussed in the previous chapter. At first glance, these findings may seem to tell us only that depressed people often attempt suicide. After all, depression is itself related to low serotonin activity and to dysfunction of the depression-related brain circuit. On the other hand, there is evidence of low serotonin activity and brain-circuit dysfunction even among suicidal people who have no history of depression (Bartlett et al., 2023; Melhem et al., 2022). That is, low serotonin activity and brain-circuit dysfunction also seem to play a role in suicide separate from depression.

How then might such serotonin and brain-circuit anomalies increase the likelihood of suicidal behavior? One possibility is that they contribute to aggressive and impulsive behaviors. It has been found, for example, that aggressive and impulsive people (including those who commit arson and murder) display lower serotonin activity and poorer brain-circuit functioning than do other people, suggesting that low serotonin activity and brain-circuit dysfunction may produce aggressive feelings and impulsive behavior (Desrochers, Spring, & Nautiyal, 2022; Mann & Currier, 2020). In people who are clinically depressed, these biological irregularities may lead to aggressive tendencies that cause these people to be particularly vulnerable to suicidal thoughts and acts. Even in the absence of a depressive disorder, however, people with low serotonin activity and a dysfunctional brain circuit may develop such aggressive feelings that they, too, are dangerous to themselves or to others.

of NOTE ...

Stunning Comparison

Nearly twice as many people die by suicide (45,979) as by homicide (24,576) in the United States each year (NIMH, 2023, 2022).

SUMMING UP

What Are the Underlying Causes of Suicide?

The leading explanations for suicide come from the psychodynamic, sociocultural, and biological models. Psychodynamic theorists believe that suicide usually results from depression and self-directed anger. Emile Durkheim's sociocultural theory defines three categories of suicide, based on the person's relationship with society: egoistic, altruistic, and anomic suicides. The interpersonal theory asserts that people with perceived burdensomeness, thwarted belongingness, and a psychological capability to carry out suicide are more likely to attempt suicide. And biological theorists suggest that low serotonin activity and irregularities in the depression-related brain circuit contribute to suicide.

Is Suicide Linked to Age?

of NOTE ...

Jarring Statistic

More people die by suicide (45,979) than by motor vehicle crashes (42,915) in the United States each year (NHTSA, 2022; NIMH, 2022).

ALTHOUGH PEOPLE OF ALL ages may attempt suicide, the likelihood of dying by suicide generally increases with age up through middle age, then decreases during the early stages of old age, and then increases again beginning at age 75 (see **Figure 7-2**). Currently, 3 of every 100,000 10- to 14-year-olds in the United States die by suicide each year, compared with a rate of 14 per 100,000 15- to 24-year-olds, 18 per 100,000 25- to 64-year-olds, 15 per 100,000 65- to 74-year-olds, and 21 per 100,000 people over age 85 (CDC, 2023, 2022).

Clinicians have paid particular attention to self-destructive behavior in three age groups: *children, adolescents,* and *older adults.* Although the features and theories of suicide discussed throughout this chapter apply to all age groups, each group faces unique challenges that may play key roles in the suicidal acts of its members.

Children

Suicide is infrequent among children, although it has been increasing over the past several decades (Kennebeck & Bonin, 2023, 2021; Schreiber & Culpepper, 2023). For children under age 10, one out of every million dies by suicide. That rate rises to 3 per 100,000 among 10- to 14-year-olds (CDC, 2023, 2022). In addition, it has been estimated that as many as 9 of every 100 children try to harm themselves, and many thousands of children are hospitalized each year for deliberately self-destructive acts, such as stabbing, cutting, burning, or shooting themselves; overdosing; or jumping from high places (Wharton, 2023; DeVille et al., 2020).

Researchers have found that suicide attempts by the very young are commonly preceded by such behavioral patterns as running away from home; accident-proneness; mood swings; aggressive acting out; temper tantrums; self-criticism; social withdrawal and loneliness; extreme sensitivity to criticism by others; low tolerance of frustration; sleep problems; dark fantasies, daydreams, or hallucinations; marked personality change; and overwhelming interest in death and suicide (Ehmke, 2022; Rodway et al., 2020). Studies further have linked child suicides to the recent or anticipated loss of a loved one, family stress, a parent's unemployment, abuse by parents, victimization by peers (for example, bullying), and a clinical level of depression (Kennebeck & Bonin, 2023, 2021). Around 80 percent of children who die by suicide do so by hanging or suffocation (CWLA, 2023; Ruch et al., 2021).

Most people find it hard to believe that children fully comprehend the meaning of a suicidal act. They argue that because a child's thinking is so limited, children who attempt suicide fall into Shneidman's category of "death ignorers," like Demaine, who sought to join his mother in heaven. Many child suicides, however, appear to be based on a clear understanding of death and on a clear wish to die (SMCH, 2023; Pfeffer, 2003). In addition, suicidal thinking among even typical children is apparently more common than most people once believed. Clinical interviews with schoolchildren have revealed that at least 33 percent have thought about suicide (DeVille et al., 2020).

FIGURE 7-2

Suicide and Age

In the United States, suicide rates generally increase through middle age, fall significantly during the early stages of old age, then rise again among people over the age of 74. (Information from: CDC, 2023, 2022.)

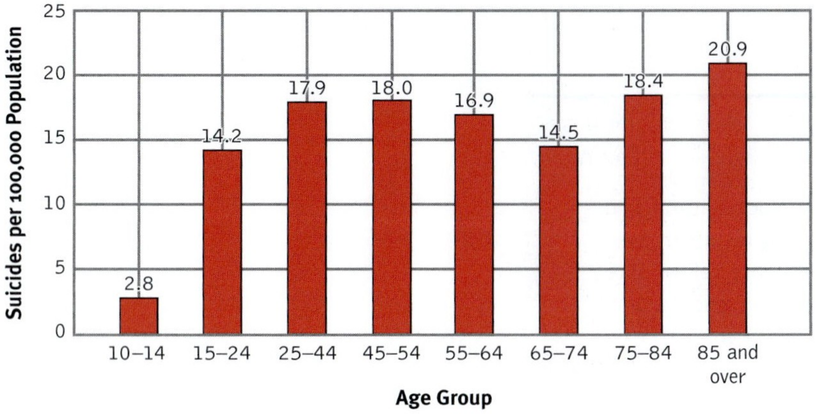

Adolescents

Dear Dad, Allie, Jonah, and Mittens,

I know you'll be upset about this, but please believe that this is the only way. I'll never be okay. People like Joey and Freddie will never stop calling me "loser" or "creep" or "nobody." There'll always be someone waiting to beat me up. I guess you might as well know, I didn't hurt my face falling off my bike. No one likes me. I wouldn't want to be around me either. But I hate them so much sometimes, I wish I was strong enough to fight back.

Well, I can't do this anymore. I hope you don't hate me for what I have to do. I want you to know, you're the best, and I love you. This isn't because of you. Don't ever think that it was. If I don't do it now, I'll do it someday, and this way I'm giving you more time to get over it. And I'll be much better off.

When I see Mom, I'll tell her how much you guys love and miss her.

Love,

Grady

As illustrated by Grady, age 17, suicidal actions by young people become much more common after age 13. According to official records, each year, 8 of every 100,000 15- to 19-year-olds in the United States end their lives (Kennebeck & Bonin, 2023, 2021). In addition, each year, as many as 20 percent of teenagers have serious suicidal thoughts, and 9 percent have made suicide attempts in the past year (CDC, 2023, 2022, 2020). Because fatal illnesses are uncommon among the young, suicide has become the third leading cause of death in this age group, after accidents and homicides (NIMH, 2023, 2022) (see **Table 7-1**). Around 18 percent of all adolescent deaths are the result of suicide. Moreover, suicidal thoughts and behaviors in adolescents are on the increase (Elia, 2023; Joseph et al., 2022). Over the past several years, adolescent visits to emergency departments for suicide-related reasons have increased by a factor of 6 (Brewer et al., 2022).

About half of teenage suicides have been tied to clinical depression, low self-esteem, and feelings of hopelessness, but many teenagers who attempt suicide also appear to have persistent anger and impulsiveness or to have serious alcohol or drug problems (Schreiber & Culpepper, 2023). Some also have deficiencies in their ability to sort out and solve problems.

Teenagers who consider or attempt suicide are often under great stress (Kennebeck & Bonin, 2023, 2021). They may be dealing with long-term pressures such as challenging (or missing) relationships with parents, family conflict, a history of abuse, inadequate peer relationships, social isolation, or repeated bullying (Jones et al., 2024; Rukundo et al., 2023). Indeed, suicide attempts are at least twice as common among teenage targets of bullying as among other teenagers. Alternatively, their actions may be triggered by more immediate stress, such as a parent's unemployment or illness or financial setbacks for the family. Recent interpersonal losses, such as breaking up with a romantic partner or falling out with friends, are particularly common among teenage suicide attempters (Rukundo et al., 2023). Stress at school is also a common problem for teenagers who attempt suicide (Elia, 2023). Some have trouble keeping up at school, while others may be high achievers who feel pressured to be perfect and to stay at the top of the class. Around 20 percent of teenagers who attempt suicide have alcohol or another drug in their body at the time of the attempt (Kennebeck & Bonin, 2023, 2021).

of NOTE ...

Youth Crisis Alert

In 2021, approximately two-thirds of all mental health–related hospitalizations and emergency department visits for children and adolescents were due to attempted suicide or self-injury. In contrast, one-third of all youth mental health hospitalizations and emergency department visits in 2009 were due to attempted suicide or self-injury (Arakelyan et al., 2023; Kim, Krause, & Lane, 2023).

TABLE 7-1

Most Common Causes of Death for Three Age Groups in the United States, 2020

Rank	Age 10–14 Years	Age 15–24 Years	Age 25–34 Years
1	Accident (881 deaths)	Accident (15,117 deaths)	Accident (31,315 deaths)
2	Suicide (581 deaths)	Homicide (6,466 deaths)	Suicide (8,454 deaths)
3	Cancer (410 deaths)	Suicide (6,062 deaths)	Homicide (7,125 deaths)
4	Homicide (285 deaths)	Cancer (1,306 deaths)	Heart disease (3,984 deaths)
5	Congenital illness (150 deaths)	Heart disease (870 deaths)	Cancer (3,573 deaths)

Information from: NIMH, 2023, 2022.

One group under particular stress is LGBTQ+ teenagers (Pappas, 2023). They often experience abuse, prejudice, stigmatization, and victimization by peers, including bullying. And many do not receive the same degree of parental acceptance as their non-LGBTQ+ peers. Studies indicate that almost one-quarter of lesbian, gay, or bisexual teenagers attempt suicide in a given year, nearly three times the rate found among heterosexual teenagers (CDC, 2023, 2022). Additionally, between 20 and 56 percent of transgender or nonbinary teenagers report attempting suicide within the past year, in contrast to 9 percent of cisgender teenagers (The Trevor Project, 2023, 2022; Austin et al., 2022).

Some theorists believe that the period of adolescence itself produces a stressful climate in which suicidal actions are more likely. Adolescence is a period of rapid growth that can be marked by conflicts, depressed feelings, tensions, and difficulties at home and at school. Adolescents tend to react to events more sensitively, angrily, dramatically, and impulsively than individuals in other age groups; thus, the likelihood of their engaging in suicidal acts during times of stress is high. In addition, the suggestibility of adolescents and their eagerness to imitate others, including others who attempt suicide, may set the stage for suicidal action (Kennebeck & Bonin, 2023, 2021; King, 2021). One study found that adolescents exposed to suicide by an acquaintance or a relative within the past year were more likely to attempt suicide than adolescents without a personal exposure of this kind (AAP, 2022; Swanson & Colman, 2013). It is believed that recent suicides by people on social media—including those who never met in person—may also raise the likelihood of attempted suicide by many young social media followers (Satariano, 2022; Hawton, Saunders, & Pitman, 2020).

Teen Suicides: Nonfatal Attempts Versus Completions

Far more teenagers attempt suicide than actually end their lives—research suggests that the ratio is as much as 100 to 1 (Kennebeck & Bonin, 2023; Pappas, 2023). In contrast, suicide attempts by older adults are much more likely to end in death (SPRC, 2023). The particularly large number of nonfatal teenage suicide attempts may mean that adolescents are less certain than middle-aged and older adults who make such attempts. While some do indeed wish to die, many may simply want to make others understand how desperate they are, or they may want to get help or teach others a lesson. Up to two-thirds of teenagers who make a suicide attempt try again in the future, and many die in their repeated attempt (Kennebeck & Bonin, 2023, 2021; Lesinskiene et al., 2022).

Teen Suicide Attempts: Why Is the Rate So High?

Why is the rate of suicide attempts so high among teenagers, and why does that rate continue to rise? Several explanations have been proposed. First, as the number and proportion of teenagers in the general population have risen, the competition for jobs, college positions, and academic and athletic honors has intensified for them, leading increasingly to shattered dreams and ambitions (Elia, 2023; Zide, 2022). Other explanations point to weakening ties in the family (which may produce feelings of alienation and rejection in many of today's young people) and to the easy availability of alcohol and other drugs and the pressure to use them (Kennebeck & Bonin, 2023, 2021; Rukundo et al., 2023).

Modeling of suicides by teenagers may also contribute to the rising rate of suicide attempts among the young (Schreiber & Culpepper, 2023; King, 2021). The detailed

Pandemic isolation A framed photo of Anaheim High School marching band saxophonist Rodney Moore Jr., who died by suicide in early 2021, sits on a music stand, flanked by the adolescent's former band teachers. According to Moore's parents, their son's mental well-being declined rapidly during the social isolation phase of the Covid-19 pandemic, contributing ultimately to this tragedy.

descriptions of teenage suicide that the media and the arts often offer may serve as models for young people who are contemplating suicide. In addition, an increasingly common event is that of teenagers who try to take their own lives just days after schoolmates or acquaintances die by suicide.

Some relatively recent societal occurrences have also been pointed to as explanations for the high and rising rate of teenage suicide attempts. One is the increasing influence that social media has on the lives and thinking of teenagers; add to that the heightened negativity, social pressures, status anxiety, and cyberbullying that reliance on social media can bring to some (Zide, 2022; Coyne et al., 2021). Another societal factor is the special negative impact that the Covid-19 pandemic has had on teenagers (Elia, 2023; Charpignon et al., 2022; HHS, 2021). While people of all ages were affected negatively by the pandemic and society's initial efforts to contain it by social distancing and isolation, teenagers had their very development interrupted by it. In-person social interactions and in-person schooling, for example, are key to the emotional, cognitive, and social growth of teenagers, and being deprived of such ongoing opportunities for an extended period of time posed special psychological dangers for young persons. Thus, it is not totally surprising that while the rates of suicide and suicide attempts did not rise (and even fell in some cases) for other age groups during the pandemic, they rose significantly for teenagers (Charpignon et al., 2022).

Teen Suicides: Multicultural Issues As you read earlier, the overall rate of suicide among teenagers in the United States is 8 per 100,000 (Kennebeck & Bonin, 2023, 2021). At the same time, teenage suicide rates vary by race and ethnicity. Each year, around 9 of every 100,000 non-Hispanic White teenagers die by suicide. In contrast, Black, Hispanic, and Asian American teenagers each display a rate of approximately 6 per 100,000 (AHR, 2023, 2022; Ramchand, Gordon, & Pearson, 2021;

Impassioned call to action Drawing on her own past experiences of anxiety, depression, and suicidal thinking, actress Taraji P. Henson is now an outspoken mental health advocate who seeks to promote psychological wellness and eradicate the stigma attached to psychological problems, especially in the Black community. Here, Henson delivers emotional testimony before the U.S. Congressional Black Caucus Emergency Taskforce on Black Youth Suicide and Mental Health, appealing for increased funding and more mental health resources, counselors, and programs in schools.

Lindsey et al., 2019). Although the rate of non-Hispanic White teens is obviously higher than the rates of the other groups of teenagers, the rates have in fact become closer in recent years as suicides by teenagers of color have steadily increased in number (Elia, 2023; Pappas, 2023).

The increase in suicides among Black male teenagers has been especially high over the past decade, a rate increase of 60 percent (AACAP, 2022; SHN, 2022; Ramchand et al., 2021). This sharp rise has been attributed to factors such as high family unemployment and economic instability, the many pressures associated with low income, and indignation or despair over racial inequities and discrimination in our society (Kennebeck & Bonin, 2023, 2021; AACAP, 2022).

The highest teenage suicide rate of all is displayed by Indigenous teenagers. Currently, each year, between 23 and 33 of every 100,000 Indigenous teenagers in the United States die by suicide, more than double the rate of non-Hispanic White teenagers and triple that of teenagers from other racial and ethnic groups (CDC, 2023, 2022; Ramchand et al., 2021). Clinical theorists attribute this extraordinarily high rate to factors such as extreme poverty, limited educational and employment opportunities, a particularly high rate of alcohol use disorder, and the geographical isolation of living on reservations (Stone et al., 2022; Davis & Matthies, 2021; SAMHSA, 2017). The very high numbers of suicides may also reflect the extensive *historical trauma* carried in many Indigenous communities, which (as you read in the chapter on disorders of trauma and stress) refers to the cumulative psychological wounds passed across generations by members of cultural groups subjected to legacies of oppression. In addition, it appears that certain Indigenous reservations have extreme suicide rates—called *cluster suicides*—and that teenagers who live in such communities are unusually likely to be exposed to suicide, have their lives disrupted, observe suicidal models, and be at risk for suicide contagion.

Older Adults

Approximately 15 of every 100,000 65- to 74-year-olds in the United States die by suicide, a rate that rises to more than 18 per 100,000 among 75- to 84-year-olds and around 21 per 100,000 among people over age 84, as you read earlier (CDC, 2023, 2022). Older adults, or people aged 65 and above, account for around 20 percent of all suicides in the United States, yet they make up only 17 percent of the total population (SAVE, 2023, 2022).

Many factors contribute to this high suicide rate. As people grow old, all too often they become ill, lose close friends and relatives, lose control over their lives, and lose status in our society (AAMFT, 2023; AHR, 2023, 2022). Such experiences may result in feelings of hopelessness, loneliness, depression, "burdensomeness," or inevitability among older people and so increase the likelihood that they will attempt suicide. One study found that two-thirds of people over age 80 who died by suicide had been hospitalized for medical reasons within two years preceding the suicide. Still other research has shown that the suicide rate of older adults who have recently lost a spouse is particularly high (Schreiber & Culpepper, 2023).

Older adults are typically more determined than younger people in their decision to die and give fewer warnings, so their suicide completion rate is much higher (De Leo, 2022). Given the determination of such individuals and their physical decline, some argue that older adults who want to die are clear in their thinking and should be allowed to carry out their wishes (see ***InfoCentral***). However, clinical depression appears to play an important role in as many as 60 percent of suicides by individuals in this age group, suggesting that more older adults who are suicidal should be receiving treatment for their depressive disorders (AAMFT, 2023; Nordentoft et al., 2020). In fact, research suggests that treating depression in older persons helps reduce their risk of suicide markedly.

of NOTE ...

Their Words

"What an amount of good nature and humor it takes to endure the gruesome business of growing old."

Sigmund Freud, letter to Lou Andreas-Salomé, 1935

Why do people often view the suicides of older adults or chronically sick people as less tragic than those of young or healthy people?

THE RIGHT TO DIE BY SUICIDE

In ancient Greece, citizens with a grave illness or mental anguish could obtain official permission from the Senate to take their own lives. In contrast, most Western countries have traditionally discouraged suicide, based on their belief in the "sanctity of life." Today, however, a person's "right to die by suicide" is receiving more and more support from the public, particularly in connection with ending great pain and terminal illness (Battin & Pope, 2022; Torrey, 2020).

WHO SUPPORTS THE RIGHT OF TERMINALLY ILL PATIENTS TO DIE BY SUICIDE?

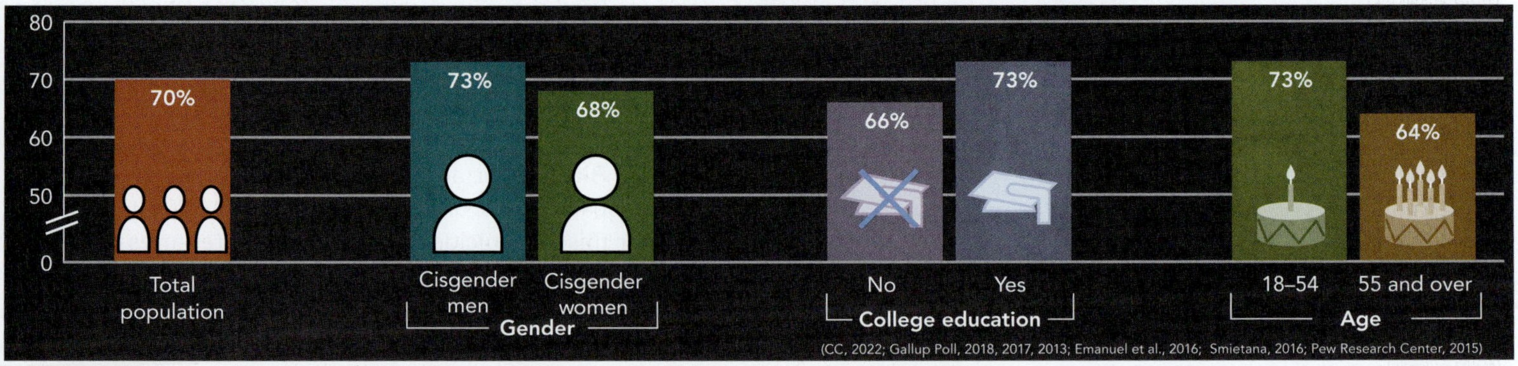

(CC, 2022; Gallup Poll, 2018, 2017, 2013; Emanuel et al., 2016; Smietana, 2016; Pew Research Center, 2015)

EUTHANASIA AND PHYSICIAN-ASSISTED SUICIDE

Euthanasia is the practice of ending the life of someone who is terminally sick or badly injured to stop the suffering. Euthanasia is not necessarily initiated by the patient. **Physician-assisted suicide** is a particular form of euthanasia, in which a physician helps a patient to end their life in response to the patient's request.

Should physicians provide indirect or direct assistance?

Physicians may *advise* patients about how to end their life (indirect assistance) or may *actually end* a patient's life (direct assistance). Many people who support physician-assisted suicide remain uncomfortable with the prospect of a doctor directly inducing a patient's death.

Around 55 percent of U.S. physicians believe that physician-assisted suicide should be available to terminally ill patients, while another 17 percent say "it depends" (CC, 2022). Around 49 percent of U.S. nurses personally support physician-assisted suicide, but 67 percent of nurses say that professionally they would help care for a patient during the final act of such suicides (CC, 2022).

Should doctors be allowed to *advise* or *directly end* the lives of patients?

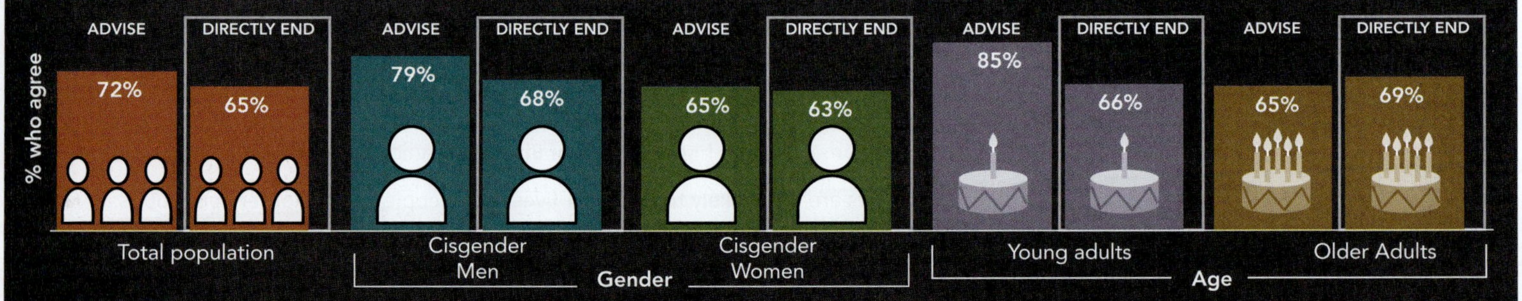

(CC, 2022; Hausdorff, 2019; Gallup Poll, 2018)

WHERE ARE EUTHANASIA AND PHYSICIAN-ASSISTED SUICIDE LEGAL?

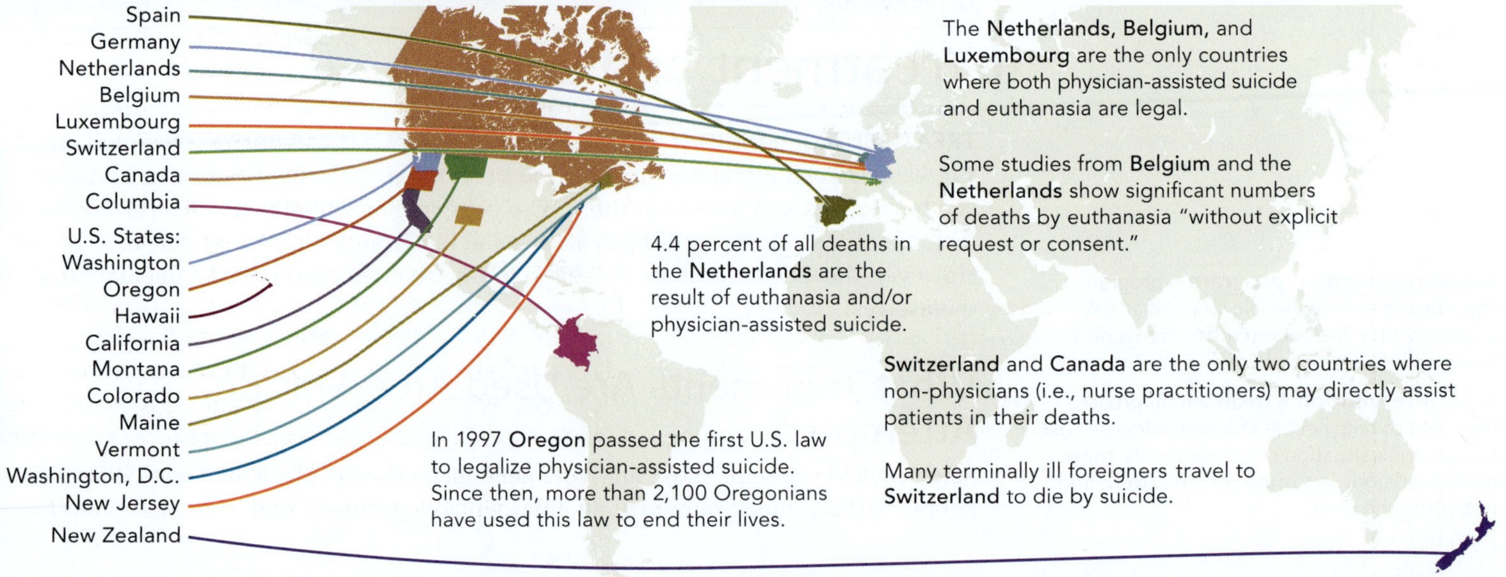

The **Netherlands, Belgium,** and **Luxembourg** are the only countries where both physician-assisted suicide and euthanasia are legal.

Some studies from **Belgium** and the **Netherlands** show significant numbers of deaths by euthanasia "without explicit request or consent."

4.4 percent of all deaths in the **Netherlands** are the result of euthanasia and/or physician-assisted suicide.

Switzerland and **Canada** are the only two countries where non-physicians (i.e., nurse practitioners) may directly assist patients in their deaths.

In 1997 **Oregon** passed the first U.S. law to legalize physician-assisted suicide. Since then, more than 2,100 Oregonians have used this law to end their lives.

Many terminally ill foreigners travel to **Switzerland** to die by suicide.

(Battin & Pope, 2022; Groenewoud et al., 2022; OHA, 2022; ProCon, 2022; MP, 2020; Pesut et al., 2019; Rodriguez, 2019)

ton koene/Alamy Stock Photo

The power of respect Older adults are held in high esteem in many Indigenous societies because of the store of knowledge they have accumulated. Perhaps not so coincidentally, the suicide rates among older adults in these cultures are relatively low. Here an older person teaches a younger one the ins and outs of building igloos—structures that are no longer used for housing but remain culturally significant.

The suicide rate among older adults in the United States is lower in certain marginalized racial and ethnic groups (OMH, 2023, 2021). Although Indigenous people have the highest overall suicide rate, for example, the rate among Indigenous older adults is relatively low. Elders are held in high esteem in Indigenous cultures and are looked to for the wisdom and experience they have acquired over the years, and this may help account for their relatively low suicide rate. Such high regard is in sharp contrast to the loss of status often experienced by non-Hispanic White older adults.

Similarly, the suicide rate is only one-quarter as high among Black older adults in the United States as among non-Hispanic White older adults (OMH, 2023, 2021). One reason for this low suicide rate may be the pressures faced by Black Americans. Those who reach an advanced age often have overcome significant adversity, and many feel proud of what they have accomplished. Because reaching old age is not in itself a form of success for non-Hispanic White Americans, their attitude toward aging may be more negative. Another possible explanation is that Black older adults have managed to overcome or reduce the feelings of indignation that prompt many suicides in younger Black people.

SUMMING UP

Is Suicide Linked to Age?

The likelihood of suicide varies with age. It is uncommon among children, although it has been rising in that age group during the past several decades. Adolescent suicide has been linked to clinical depression, anger, impulsiveness, major stress, and adolescent life itself. Suicide attempts by this age group are especially high. In the United States, the rate of suicide among Indigenous teens is more than twice as high as that among non-Hispanic White American teens and three times as high as those of Black, Hispanic, and Asian American teens.

Older adults are more likely to end their lives than people in most other age groups. The loss of health, friends, control, and status may produce feelings of hopelessness, loneliness, depression, or inevitability in older adults.

Treatment and Suicide

TREATMENT OF SUICIDAL people falls into two major categories: *treatment after suicide has been attempted* and *suicide prevention*. Treatment may also be beneficial to relatives and friends of those who complete or attempt suicide. Indeed, their feelings of loss, guilt, and anger after a suicide fatality or attempt can be intense. However, the discussion here is limited to the treatment afforded to suicidal people themselves.

suicide prevention program A program that tries to identify people who are at risk of ending their lives and to offer them crisis intervention.

crisis intervention A treatment approach that tries to help people in a psychological crisis to view their situation more accurately, make better decisions, act more constructively, and overcome the crisis.

What Treatments Are Used After Suicide Attempts?

After a suicide attempt, most survivors need medical care. More than one-half million people in the United States visit an emergency department and/or are admitted to a hospital each year for injuries resulting from efforts to harm themselves, and this number keeps rising (CDC, 2023, 2022). Some are left with severe injuries, brain damage, or other medical problems. Once the physical damage is treated, psychotherapy or drug therapy may begin on either an inpatient or an outpatient basis (Jobes, 2023). Unfortunately, even after attempting suicide, as many as 46 percent of suicidal people do not receive systematic follow-up care (Bommersbach, Rosenheck, & Rhee, 2022).

The goals of therapy for those who have attempted suicide are to keep the survivors alive, reduce their psychological pain, help them achieve a nonsuicidal state of mind, restrict their access to lethal suicide means, provide them with hope, and guide them to develop better ways of handling stress (Dattilio, Shapiro, & Greenaway, 2023; Jobes, 2023). Studies indicate that people who receive therapy after their suicide attempts have a lower risk of future suicide attempts and deaths than do attempters who do not receive such therapy (Kennebeck & Bonin, 2023, 2021; Schreiber & Culpepper, 2023). Various approaches have been employed, including drug, psychodynamic, cognitive-behavioral, group, and family therapies (Schechter et al., 2022; King, 2021).

Research suggests that cognitive-behavioral therapy may be particularly helpful (Dattilio et al., 2023; Wu et al., 2022). When clients are suicidal, the approach focuses largely on identifying and changing the painful thoughts, sense of hopelessness, dichotomous thinking, limited coping skills, impaired problem-solving abilities, and other cognitive and behavioral features that characterize suicidal people. Applying the principles of *mindfulness-based* cognitive-behavioral therapy, the therapists may also guide the clients to *accept* many of the painful thoughts and feelings that keep streaming through their minds rather than try to eliminate them (Ghosh et al., 2023; Tseng et al., 2023). Acceptance of this kind is expected to increase the clients' tolerance of psychological distress. All such treatment features are particularly prominent in a third wave cognitive-behavioral approach called *dialectical behavior therapy* (*DBT*), which is being used increasingly in cases of suicidal thinking and attempts (Goldstein et al., 2024; Alba et al., 2022). You will read much about DBT in the chapter on personality disorders.

Imaginechina via AP Images

Working with suicide A police officer catches and pulls to safety a distressed young woman who was trying to leap to her death off the edge of a six-story building. Police departments across the world typically provide special crisis intervention training so that officers can develop the skills to help suicidal people.

What Is Suicide Prevention?

During the past half-century, emphasis around the world has shifted from suicide treatment to suicide prevention. In some respects, this change is most appropriate: the last opportunity to keep many potential suicide victims alive comes before their first attempt.

The first **suicide prevention program** in the United States was founded in Los Angeles in 1955; the first in England, called the Samaritans, was started in 1953. There are now hundreds of suicide prevention centers in the United States and England. In addition, many of today's mental health centers, hospital emergency rooms, pastoral counseling centers, and poison control centers include suicide prevention programs among their services.

There are also hundreds of *suicide hotlines,* 24-hour-a-day telephone services, in the United States. Callers reach a counselor, typically a *paraprofessional*—a person trained in counseling but without a formal degree—who provides services under the supervision of a mental health professional.

Suicide prevention programs and hotlines respond to suicidal people as individuals *in crisis*—that is, under great stress, unable to cope, feeling threatened or hurt, and interpreting their situations as unchangeable. Thus, the programs offer **crisis intervention:** they try to help suicidal people see their situations more accurately, make better decisions, act more constructively, and overcome their crises

If you suspected that a friend or relative was suicidal, what actions might you take? What would you do if those actions were not successful initially?

Kevin Mazur/Getty Images for NARAS

Life-saving performance In a powerful moment at the 2018 Grammy Awards, rapper Logic (*center*) performs his song "1-800-273-8255," flanked by singer-songwriters Khalid and Alessia Cara and joined onstage by individuals personally affected by suicide. The song's title was the phone number of the National Suicide Prevention Lifeline. Help-seeking phone calls and website visits to the suicide prevention organization tripled during the hours following this performance. Although the phone number in the song title will still work, the hotline number has since been simplified to 988.

(Dattilio et al., 2023). Because crises can occur at any time, the centers advertise their hotlines and also welcome people who walk in without appointments. A growing number of centers also offer their services through modalities such as text messaging and Internet chat.

The broadest suicide prevention service in the United States is the **988 Suicide & Crisis Lifeline,** a nonprofit network consisting of more than 200 crisis centers across the country. When a person in crisis dials or texts the number 988, their call is routed to their nearest crisis center, where the person receives immediate counseling and mental health resources and referrals. Canadian crisis centers are also being made available through the 988 number.

While the 988 Suicide & Crisis Lifeline has the broadest outreach, other valuable and sizable crisis services are also available to persons in crisis. One is the *Crisis Text Line,* a service that offers text counseling, in partnership with a number of hotlines across the United States, to tens of thousands of persons in crisis. The Crisis Text Line has processed more than 100 million text messages since its launch a decade ago. Another important prevention service is the *TrevorLifeline,* a nationwide, around-the-clock hotline available specifically for LGBTQ+ teenagers who are thinking about suicide. This hotline is one of several services offered by the Trevor Project, a wide-reaching organization dedicated to providing support, guidance, and information to and promoting acceptance of LGBTQ+ teens (The Trevor Project, 2023).

Today, suicide prevention takes place not only at prevention centers and hotlines but also in more traditional therapist sessions (Jobes, 2023; Hawton et al., 2020). Suicide experts encourage all therapists to look for and address signs of suicidal thinking in their clients regardless of the broad reasons why the clients are seeking treatment. With this in mind, a number of guidelines have been developed to help therapists effectively uncover, assess, prevent, and treat suicidal thinking and behavior in their daily work (Jobes, 2023).

988 Suicide & Crisis Lifeline A national suicide prevention service, reachable at the 988 number, that routes calls or texts from persons in crisis to a nearby crisis center, where the individuals receive immediate counseling and mental health resources and referrals.

Specific techniques vary from therapist to therapist and from prevention center to prevention center, but the approach developed originally by the Los Angeles

Suicide Prevention Center continues to reflect the goals and techniques of many clinicians and organizations. During the initial contact at the center, the counselor has several tasks:

Establish a Positive Relationship As callers must trust counselors in order to confide in them and follow their suggestions, counselors try to set a positive and comfortable tone for the discussion. They convey that they are listening, understanding, interested, nonjudgmental, and available.

Understand and Clarify the Problem Counselors first try to understand the full scope of the caller's crisis and then help the person see the crisis in clear and constructive terms. In particular, they try to help callers see the central issues and the transient nature of their crisis and recognize the alternatives to suicide.

Assess Suicide Potential Crisis workers at the Los Angeles Suicide Prevention Center fill out a questionnaire, often called a *lethality scale,* to estimate the caller's potential for suicide. It helps them determine the degree of stress the caller is under, the caller's relevant personality characteristics, how detailed the suicide plan is, the severity of symptoms, and the coping resources available to the caller.

Assess and Mobilize the Caller's Resources Although they may view themselves as ineffectual, helpless, and alone, people who are suicidal usually have many strengths and resources, including relatives and friends. It is the counselor's job to recognize, point out, and activate those resources.

Formulate a Plan Together, the crisis worker and the caller develop a plan of action. In essence, they are agreeing on a way out of the crisis, an alternative to suicidal action. Most plans include a series of follow-up counseling sessions over the next few days or weeks either in person at the center or by phone. Each plan also requires the caller to take certain actions and make certain changes in their personal life. Counselors usually negotiate a *no-suicide contract* with the caller—a promise not to attempt suicide or at least a promise to reestablish contact if the caller again considers suicide. Although such contracts are popular, their effectiveness has been called into question in recent years (Schreiber & Culpepper, 2023). In addition, if callers are in the midst of a suicide attempt, counselors try to find out their whereabouts and get medical help to them immediately.

Although crisis intervention may be sufficient treatment for some suicidal people, long-term therapy is needed for most (Jobes, 2023). If a crisis intervention center does not offer this kind of therapy, its counselors will refer the clients elsewhere.

Yet another way to help prevent suicide may be to reduce the public's access to particularly lethal and common means of suicide through measures such as firearms control, safer medications, better bridge barriers, and car emission controls (CDC, 2023, 2022; Hawton et al., 2020). In the 1970s and 1990s, for example, Canada passed laws restricting the availability of and access to certain firearms. Since then, there has been a decrease in the number of suicides by firearms across the country, although this decrease was accompanied by an increase in suicides by other means (Langmann, 2021).

Preventing further harm In 2021, it was announced that New York City's extraordinary 16-story interactive art structure, *Vessel*, was being closed indefinitely, just two years after it had opened. The reason: the structure's safety measures failed to prevent several people from jumping to their deaths.

nycshooter/Getty Images

Do Suicide Prevention Programs Work?

It is difficult for researchers to measure the effectiveness of suicide prevention programs, but generally researchers have found that they can

Learning about suicide Students at Uplift Hampton Preparatory School in Dallas, Texas, participate in a role-playing exercise to help them understand mental health issues and suicide prevention. It's all part of the Youth Aware of Mental Health program offered to schools by the University of Texas Southwestern Medical Center.

AP Photo/Benny Snyder

be effective and should be widely implemented (Mishara et al., 2023; Doty et al., 2022). There are many kinds of programs, each with its own procedures and each serving populations that vary in number, age, and the like. Communities with high suicide risk factors, such as a high older-adult population or economic problems, may continue to have higher suicide rates than other communities regardless of the effectiveness of their local prevention centers.

Do suicide prevention centers reduce the number of suicides in a community? Clinical researchers do not know (Schlichthorst et al., 2023; Hawton et al., 2020). Studies comparing local suicide rates before and after the establishment of community prevention centers have yielded different findings. Some find a decline in a community's suicide rates, others find no change, and still others find an increase. Of course, even an increase may represent a positive impact if it is lower than the larger society's overall increase in suicidal behavior.

Do suicidal people contact prevention centers? Apparently, only a small percentage do; this is one of the reasons why in 2022, the 988 Suicide & Crisis Lifeline transitioned from a 10-digit number to an easier-to-remember 3-digit number and implemented a simpler linkage system (SAMHSA, 2022). At the same time, prevention programs do seem to reduce the number of suicides among those high-risk people who do call. An early but still influential study identified 8,000 high-risk individuals who contacted the Los Angeles Suicide Prevention Center (Farberow & Litman, 1970). Approximately 2 percent of these callers later died by suicide, compared with the 6 percent suicide rate usually found in similar high-risk groups. Clearly, centers need to be more visible and available to people who are thinking of suicide. The growing number of advertisements and announcements on social media, television, radio, and billboards indicates movement in this direction.

A key difficulty for suicide prevention programs is that they depend on accurate assessments of suicide risk, and accurate assessments are elusive (Campos et al., 2023; Jobes, 2023). People who are suicidal do not necessarily admit to or talk about their true feelings in discussions with professionals (McKeon, 2021). With this in mind, some researchers are working to develop tools of suicide assessment that rely less on verbal self-reports and more on nonverbal behaviors, psychophysiological measures, brain scans, and the like.

of NOTE ...

Prior to Suicide

Only 25 to 30 percent of people who die by suicide have had contact with a psychiatrist or psychotherapist within the year prior to their death (Schreiber & Culpepper, 2023).

One such assessment approach is the Self-Injury Implicit Association Test, developed by researcher Matthew Nock. Rather than asking people if they plan to attempt suicide, this cognitive test simply instructs them to pair various suicide-related words (for example, "dead," "lifeless," "suicide") with words that are personally relevant ("I," "myself," "mine") and with words that are not personally relevant ("they," "them," "other"). It turns out that people who are inclined to attempt suicide pair the suicide-related words with personally relevant words much more quickly than with non–personally relevant words. In a number of studies, this test has detected and predicted past and future suicide behavior more accurately than traditional self-report assessment scales (Moreno, Gutiérrez-Rojas, & Porras-Segovia, 2022; O'Shea et al., 2022). It is also worth noting that, according to research, an individual's quicker pairings of suicide-related words with personally relevant words are linked to increased activity in the person's insula and prefrontal cortex—key structures in the brain's depression-related, fear, and stress circuits (Ballard et al., 2019).

Yet another promising approach to suicide assessment makes use of mobile devices, including sensor-carrying wearable devices, to monitor suicidal individuals as they go about their daily lives. As you read earlier in this book, mobile devices can be used to periodically prompt individuals to report on their mood states and inner thoughts, and wearable devices can measure and report on heart rate and other relevant psychophysiological processes. The use of such technologies to assess suicide risk is still in the early stages, but recent studies suggest that mobile methods of this kind may indeed play an important role in the years to come (Cliffe et al., 2023; Barry, 2022). Because inclinations for self-harm can fluctuate greatly from day to day or even hour to hour, technology-based strategies that detect shifting risk indicators within suicidal individuals (for example, tone of voice, sleep changes, and physical activity levels) are able to provide important data for suicide assessment.

of NOTE ...

Deal Breaker

If clients state an intention to end their lives, therapists may break the doctor–patient confidentiality agreement that usually governs treatment discussions (Schreiber & Culpepper, 2023).

While the field awaits more accurate assessment tools and more effective interventions, many theorists believe that public education about suicide is the ultimate form of prevention—and a number of *suicide education programs* have emerged. Most of these programs take place in schools and concentrate on students and their teachers (AFSP, 2023; Pappas, 2023). Research finds that school-based suicide education programs significantly reduce suicidal thoughts and behaviors in adolescents. These programs typically have teachers or school counselors educate general populations of students about mental health, positive coping, and signs of suicide risk, and empower students to know how to seek help when they see suicide warning signs in themselves or their peers. These suicide education programs are most effective when they are accompanied by school-wide formal suicide risk screenings (Walsh, Herring, & McMahon, 2023). There are also a growing number of online sites that provide education about suicide—targeting troubled persons, their family members, and friends. These offerings agree with the statement made decades ago by the pioneering suicide researcher Edwin Shneidman:

Why might some schools be reluctant to offer suicide education programs, especially if they have never experienced a suicide attempt by one of their students?

> *The primary prevention of suicide lies in education. The route is through teaching one another and . . . the public that suicide can happen to anyone, that there are verbal and behavioral clues that can be looked for . . . and that help is available. . . .*
>
> *In the last analysis, the prevention of suicide is everybody's business.*
>
> (Shneidman, 1985, p. 238)

SUMMING UP

Treatment and Suicide

Treatment may follow a suicide attempt. When it does, therapists try to help the person achieve a nonsuicidal state of mind and develop better ways of handling stress and solving problems. People who receive therapy after their suicide attempt have a lower risk of future suicide attempts and suicide deaths. Various types of therapy have been employed after suicide attempts, including drug, psychodynamic, cognitive-behavioral, group, and family therapies.

Over the past half-century, emphasis has shifted to suicide prevention. Suicide prevention programs include 24-hour-a-day hotlines and walk-in centers staffed largely by paraprofessionals. The widest-ranging suicide prevention service in the United States is the 988 Suicide & Crisis Lifeline, which persons can reach by dialing or texting the number 988. During their initial contact with a suicidal person, counselors at suicide prevention programs try to establish a positive relationship, understand and clarify the problem, assess the potential for suicide, assess and mobilize the caller's resources, and formulate a plan for overcoming the crisis. To help improve suicide prevention, there are continuing efforts to develop more effective assessment techniques. Beyond crisis intervention, most suicidal people also need long-term therapy. In a still broader attempt at prevention, suicide education programs for the public are on the increase.

Psychological and Biological Insights Lag Behind

ONCE A MYSTERIOUS AND HIDDEN problem, hardly acknowledged by the public and barely investigated by professionals, suicide today is the focus of much attention. During the past 50 years in particular, investigators have learned a great deal about this life-or-death problem.

In contrast to most other problems covered in this textbook, suicide has received much more examination from the sociocultural model than from any other. Sociocultural theorists have, for example, highlighted the importance of societal change and stress, national and religious affiliation, marital status, gender, race, and the mass media. The insights and information gathered by psychological and biological researchers have been more limited.

Although sociocultural factors certainly shed light on the general background and triggers of suicide, they typically leave us unable to predict that a given person will attempt suicide. Clinicians do not yet fully understand why some people end their lives while others in similar circumstances manage to find ways to address their difficulties. Psychological and biological insights must catch up to the sociocultural insights if clinicians are truly to explain and understand suicide.

Treatments for suicide also pose some difficult problems. Although suicide prevention programs certainly show the clinical field's commitment to helping those who are suicidal, it is not yet clear how much such programs actually reduce the overall risk or rate of suicide.

At the same time, the growth in the amount of research on suicide offers great promise. And perhaps most promising of all, clinicians are now enlisting the public in the fight against this problem. They are calling for broader public education about suicide—for programs aimed at both young and old. It is reasonable to

of NOTE ...

Fatal Access

- The rate of gun-related suicides is 11 times higher in the United States than in all other industrialized countries.
- People who die by suicide are at least twice as likely to have a gun in their house as people who survive their suicide attempts.
- Suicide rates increase 4 to 10 times among teenagers who live in a house with a gun.

(Kennebeck & Bonin, 2023, 2021; Schreiber & Culpepper, 2023; Dempsey et al., 2019) expect that the current commitment will lead to a better understanding of suicide and to more successful interventions. Such goals are of importance to everyone. Although suicide itself is typically a lonely and desperate act, the impact of such acts is very broad indeed.

Quick Quiz

1. Define suicide and subintentional death. Describe four different kinds of people characterized by Shneidman who attempt suicide. What is nonsuicidal self-injury? pp. 218–222
2. What techniques do researchers use to study suicide? p. 222
3. How do statistics on suicide vary according to country, religion, relationship status, sexual orientation, gender, and race and ethnicity? pp. 222–225
4. What kinds of immediate and long-term stressors have been linked to suicide? pp. 226–227
5. What other conditions or events may help trigger suicidal acts? pp. 227–229
6. How do psychodynamic, sociocultural, interpersonal, and biological theorists explain suicide, and how well supported are their theories? pp. 230–233
7. Compare the risk, rate, and causes of suicide among children, adolescents, and older adults. pp. 234–240
8. How do theorists explain the high rate of suicide attempts by adolescents? pp. 236–238
9. Describe the nature and goals of treatment given to people after they have attempted suicide. Do such people often receive this treatment? pp. 240–241
10. Describe the principles of suicide prevention programs. What procedures are used by counselors in these programs? How effective are the programs? pp. 241–245

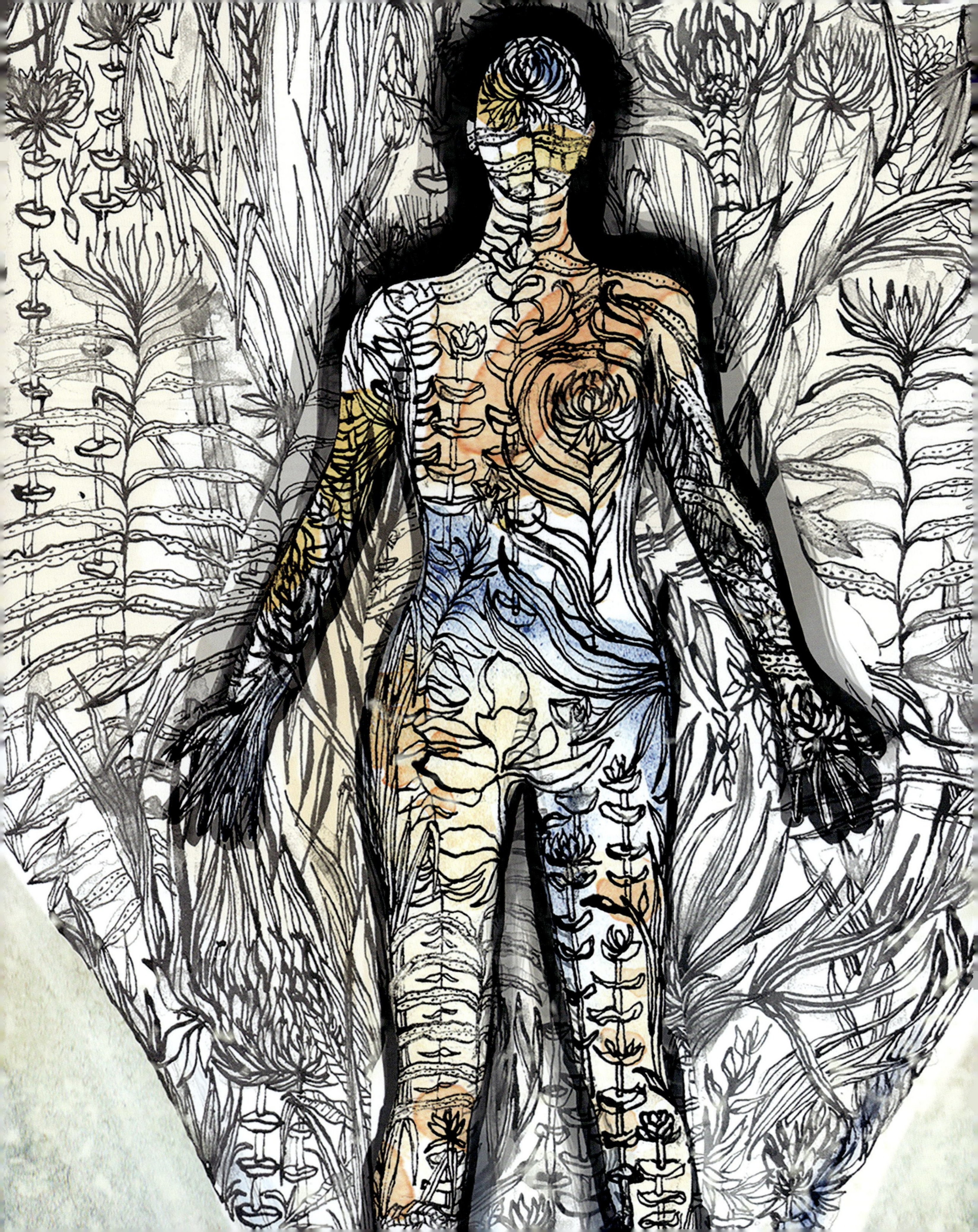

CHAPTER 8

Disorders Featuring Somatic Symptoms

TOPIC OVERVIEW

It was Wednesday. The big day. Midterms in history and physics back-to-back, beginning at 11:30, and an oral presentation in psych at 3:30. Jarell had been preparing for and dreading this day for weeks. He had been up until 3:30 A.M. the night before, studying, trying to nail everything down. It seemed like he had fallen asleep only minutes ago, yet here it was 9:30 A.M., and the nerve-racking day was under way.

Jarell had been confident about the history exam when he went to bed; it was the physics test and psych presentation that had scared him. Now, however, trying to wake up, he was so terrified that he couldn't keep straight which generals had commanded Union soldiers and which had commanded Confederate ones. And history was the field he was planning to major in! Physics, which had nothing to do with anything he intended to pursue professionally, he had already written off as a lost cause, his head swimming in causality, covariance, periodic wave frequencies, and quantum interactions. Psychology was interesting, but he was sure he would stammer through his presentation despite all his hard work. So now he was sure he would choke in all three subjects, and he cursed himself for going to sleep at all instead of doing some extra cramming.

As soon as he got out of bed, Jarell felt a tight pain grip his stomach. He also noticed buzzing in his ears, a light-headedness, and even aches throughout his body. He wasn't surprised given the day he was about to face. One test might bring a few butterflies of anxiety; two and a presentation were probably good for a platoon of dragonflies. He could not stop imagining having to explain his failure to his parents.

As he tried to get going, however, Jarell began to suspect that this was more than butterflies. His stomach pain soon turned to spasms, and his light-headedness became outright dizziness. He could barely make it to the bathroom without falling. Thoughts of breakfast made him nauseous. He knew he couldn't keep anything down.

Jarell tried to shake it off, but the symptoms stayed. Finally, his roommate convinced him that he had better go to a doctor. At 10:30, just an hour before the first exam, he entered the big brick building called "Student Health." He felt embarrassed, like a wimp, but what could he do? Persevering and taking tests under these conditions wouldn't prove anything—except maybe that he was foolish.

Psychological factors may contribute to somatic, or bodily, illnesses in a variety of ways. The physician who sees Jarell has some possibilities to sort out. Jarell could be *faking* his pain and dizziness to avoid taking some tough tests. Alternatively, he may be *imagining* his illness, that is, faking to himself. Or he could be *overreacting* to his pain and dizziness. Then again, his physical symptoms could be both real and significant yet triggered by *stress:* whenever he feels extreme pressure, such as a person can feel before an important test, Jarell's gastric juices may become more active and irritate his intestines, and his blood pressure may rise and cause him to become dizzy. Finally, he may be coming down with the flu. Even a "purely medical" problem like the flu, however, could be linked to psychological factors. Perhaps weeks of constant worry about the exams and presentation have weakened Jarell's body so that he was not able to fight off the flu virus. Whatever the diagnosis, Jarell's state of mind is affecting his body. The physician's view of the role played by psychological factors will in turn affect the treatment Jarell receives (Ouafik et al., 2023).

You have read throughout this book that psychological disorders frequently have physical causes. Dysfunctional brain circuits and irregular neurotransmitter activity, for example, contribute to generalized anxiety disorder, panic disorder, and posttraumatic stress disorder. Is it surprising, then, that bodily illnesses may have psychological causes? Today's clinicians recognize the wisdom of Socrates' assertion made many centuries ago: "You should not treat body without soul."

DSM-5-TR lists a number of psychological disorders in which bodily symptoms or concerns are the primary features of the disorders. These include *factitious disorder,* in which patients intentionally produce or feign physical symptoms; *conversion disorder,* which is characterized by medically unexplained physical symptoms that affect voluntary motor or sensory functioning; *somatic symptom disorder,* in which people become disproportionately concerned, distressed, and disrupted by bodily symptoms; *illness anxiety disorder,* in which people who are anxious about their health become preoccupied with the notion that they are seriously ill despite the absence of bodily symptoms; and *psychological factors affecting other medical conditions,* disorders in which psychological factors adversely affect a person's general medical condition. ■

Hagen/CartoonStock Ltd.

"Don't worry: It's perfectly normal for you to feel sluggish in the morning . . ."

Factitious Disorder Imposed on Self

LIKE JARELL, PEOPLE who become physically sick often go to a physician. Sometimes, however, the physician cannot find a medical cause for the problem and may suspect that other factors are involved. Perhaps the patient is *malingering*—intentionally feigning illness to achieve some external gain, such as financial compensation or time off from work (Mason, 2023). Jarell, for example, would be malingering if he knowingly made up his symptoms simply to avoid taking his midterm exams.

Alternatively, patients may intentionally produce or feign physical symptoms in themselves because they wish to be a patient; that is, the motivation for assuming the sick role may be the role itself. Physicians would then decide that the patients are manifesting **factitious disorder imposed on self** (see **Table 8-1**). Consider, for example, the symptoms of Adia, a patient with bacteremia—presence of bacteria in the blood, which can, if not corrected, lead to the life-threatening condition called sepsis. As you will note, the medical team's handling of Adia's right to privacy raises ethical issues, but the case itself illustrates the features of factitious disorder.

TABLE 8-1

Dx Checklist

Factitious Disorder Imposed on Self
1. False creation of physical psychological symptoms, or deceptive production of injury or disease, even without external rewards for such ailments.
2. Presentation of oneself as ill, damaged, or hurt.
Factitious Disorder Imposed on Another
1. False creation of physical or psychological symptoms, or deceptive production of injury or disease, in another person, even without external rewards for such ailments.
2. Presentation of another person (victim) as ill, damaged, or hurt.

Information from: APA, 2022.

[Adia] was referred to [the medical center] for evaluation of recurrent urinary tract infections and bacteremia. . . . She also had a skin disorder with blisters. An extensive workup showed . . . a completely normal genitourinary tract. . . .

Based on [Adia's unexplained] symptoms . . . one of the several doctors on this case suspected that the patient was inducing her own illness, and he decided to secretly search her personal possessions. . . .

While the patient was having an x-ray, her room was searched. Her purse contained a Petri dish with growing bacterial colonies, as well as needles, a syringe, and a tourniquet. The . . . Petri dish [was] replaced. Later that day, the patient was asked whether she might be harming herself by injection [of bacteria into her body]. She denied this, saying that she wanted to get better. Still later that day, the doctor told the patient that he knew she had some incriminating items in her purse. She then opened her purse so the doctor could see inside, and the items were apparently no longer present. To prove her point, the patient turned her purse upside down. At that point, one needle and a syringe fell out, which she had apparently overlooked when she returned from her x-ray and suspected that someone had searched her purse. The patient was upset about the room search but not visibly angry. She readily agreed to see a psychiatrist but continued to deny self-injection.

The next day, the patient tearfully confessed that she had had bacteriological materials in her purse, but she said she used them only to aspirate and culture some blisters on her skin. She still denied self-injection with bacteria and said she wanted the doctors to "keep looking for the cause of my problems."

(Savino & Fordtran, 2006, pp. 201–202)

Factitious disorder imposed on self is known popularly as *Munchausen syndrome,* a label derived from the exploits of Baron von Münchhausen, an eighteenth-century cavalry officer who journeyed from tavern to tavern in Europe telling fantastical tales about his supposed military adventures. People with factitious disorder often go to extremes to create the appearance of illness (APA, 2022). Many give themselves medications secretly. Some, like the person just described, inject drugs to cause bleeding, infections, or other problems (Vella, 2022). Still others use laxatives to produce chronic diarrhea (Wald, 2023). High fevers are especially easy to create. In studies of patients with a prolonged mysterious fever, 9 percent were eventually diagnosed with factitious disorder (Irwin & Bursch, 2023).

People with factitious disorder imposed on self often research their supposed ailments and are impressively knowledgeable about medicine. Many eagerly undergo painful testing or treatment, even surgery. When confronted with evidence that their symptoms are factitious, they typically deny the charges and leave the hospital; they may enter another hospital the same day (Stacey, 2021).

Clinical researchers have had a hard time determining the prevalence of factitious disorder imposed on self since patients with the disorder hide the true nature of their problem (Dickerman & Jiménez, 2023). Research conducted primarily with cisgender people finds around two-thirds of people with the disorder are women, although men may more often have severe cases (APA, 2022). Researchers have not studied differences in prevalence between cisgender and transgender or nonbinary people.

Factitious disorder imposed on self usually begins during early adulthood. It seems to be particularly common among people who (1) received extensive treatment for a medical problem as children, (2) carry a grudge against the medical profession, or (3) have worked as a nurse, laboratory technician, or medical aide (Carnahan & Jha, 2023; Jimenez et al., 2020). A number have poor social support, few enduring social relationships, and little family life (Irwin & Bursch, 2023).

The precise causes of factitious disorder imposed on self are not understood, although clinical reports have pointed to factors such as depression, unsupportive

of NOTE ...

Their Words

"I would rather have anything wrong with my body than something wrong with my head."

Sylvia Plath, *The Bell Jar*

factitious disorder imposed on self A disorder in which persons feign or induce physical symptoms on themselves, typically for the purpose of assuming the role of a sick person.

parental relationships during childhood, and extreme needs for attention and/or social support that are not otherwise available (Dickerman & Jiménez, 2023). Nor have clinicians been able to develop dependably effective treatments for this disorder.

Psychotherapists and medical practitioners often report feelings of annoyance or anger toward people with factitious disorder, feeling that these people are, at the very least, wasting their time. Yet people with the disorder feel they have no control over the problem, and they often experience great distress.

In a related pattern, *factitious disorder imposed on another,* known popularly as *Munchausen syndrome by proxy,* parents or other caretakers make up or produce physical illnesses in their children, leading in some cases to repeated painful diagnostic tests, medication, and surgery (Egge, 2023; Dimsdale, 2022) (see Table 8-1 again). If the children are removed from their parents and placed in the care of others, their symptoms disappear (see **PsychWatch**).

PSYCHWATCH

Munchausen Syndrome by Proxy

Tanya, a mere 8 years old, had been hospitalized 127 times over the past five years and has undergone 28 different medical procedures—from removal of her spleen to exploratory surgery of her intestines. Two months ago, her mother was arrested, charged with child endangerment. When Tanya's grandmother gently tried to talk to the girl about her mother's arrest (or, as she put it, "Mommy's going away"), Tanya was upset and confused.

"I miss Mommy so much. She's the best person in the world. She spent all her time with me in the hospital. They say Mommy was making me feel bad, putting bad stuff in my tube. But there's no way Mommy made me feel that bad."

Cases like Tanya's have horrified the public and called attention to *factitious disorder imposed on another,* popularly known as *Munchausen syndrome by proxy.* This form of factitious disorder is caused by a caregiver who uses various techniques to induce symptoms in a child—for example, giving the child drugs, tampering with medications, contaminating a feeding tube, or even smothering the child. The illness can take almost any form, but the most common symptoms are bleeding, seizures, asthma, comas, diarrhea, vomiting, "accidental" poisonings, infections, fevers, and sudden infant death syndrome.

The syndrome is very hard to diagnose (Egge, 2023). It is estimated that 1 in 200 children are victims of this Munchausen syndrome by proxy (Roesler & Jenny, 2022). Some victims die as a result of their symptoms, and a number of those who survive are permanently disfigured or physically impaired (Egge, 2023; Kugler, 2021). Psychological, educational, and physical development are also affected.

Convalescent, 1867, by Frank Holl

Frank Holl, Convalescent. Private Collection © Christopher Wood Gallery, London, UK/Bridgemanimages

The parent comes across as deeply devoted and caring, thus eliciting sympathy and admiration from others (Dimsdale, 2022). Yet the physical problems disappear when the child and parent are separated.

Should society treat or punish those parents who produce Munchausen syndrome by proxy in their children?

What kind of parent or caregiver carefully inflicts pain and illness on a child? The typical Munchausen parent or caregiver is emotionally needy and craves the attention and praise they receive for their devoted care of the sick child (Bursch, 2020). They may have little social support outside the medical system. Often, these caregivers have a medical background of some kind. A number have medically unexplained physical problems of their own (Roesler & Jenny, 2022). Typically, they deny their actions, even in the face of clear evidence, and initially may refuse to undergo therapy.

Law enforcement authorities approach Munchausen syndrome by proxy as a crime—a carefully planned form of child abuse (Kugler, 2021). They typically require that the child be separated from the parent at least for a period of time. At the same time, a parent who resorts to such actions is seriously disturbed and greatly in need of clinical help (Sanders & Bursch, 2020). In many cases, particularly those that are of moderate or modest severity, treatment makes it possible for the parent to be reintegrated into the family (Roesler & Jenny, 2022). Currently, clinical researchers and practitioners are working to develop still clearer insights and more effective treatments for such parents and their young victims.

SUMMING UP

Factitious Disorder

People with factitious disorder imposed on self feign or induce physical disorders, typically for the purpose of assuming the role of a sick person. In a related pattern, factitious disorder imposed on another, a parent fabricates or induces a physical illness in their child.

Conversion Disorder and Somatic Symptom Disorder

WHEN A BODILY AILMENT has an excessive and disproportionate impact on the person, has no apparent medical cause, or is inconsistent with known medical diseases, physicians may suspect a *conversion disorder* or a *somatic symptom disorder.* Consider the plight of Bassel:

of NOTE ...

Diagnostic Confusion

In the past, whiplash was regularly misdiagnosed as a psychologically caused condition.

Bassel was spending Saturday driving through the mountains with his wife, Zahra. They had been excited for this Montana vacation, as it gave them an opportunity to see more of the country and meet some people outside of their tight Egyptian American circle in their home near Los Angeles. They'd been having a great time so far. On this day, there was some light rain, but the views were still magnificent. They really didn't notice that the sky was getting darker until the rain came down harder and it was suddenly almost impossible to see. On this narrow winding mountain road, there was no place to pull over and wait for the storm to subside.

The rain intensified very quickly. Bassel had trouble with the sharp curves of the road. The last thing Zahra said to Bassel before the crash was, "Be careful! Watch it!" As Bassel tried to negotiate another curve, the car skidded off the road into the forest. As the car rolled and hit a tree, Bassel's instinctive thought was, "Thank goodness we were here when the storm came, so we didn't go off a cliff." After the impact, however, the intense pain in his left arm and leg told him immediately that they were broken. Then, after asking Zahra if she was all right and receiving no answer, Bassel turned and saw to his horror that she was bleeding from the head and was unconscious. In a panic, he called emergency services and gave the location as best he could. The wait for help to arrive seemed interminable, as he begged his still-breathing but unconscious wife to stay with him. Bassel noted ruefully that the rain let up almost immediately after the crash, but after they were loaded into the ambulance and he was administered painkillers, he wasn't aware of much else until he awoke from the surgery on his shattered leg.

He was met upon waking with the news that would destroy his world. Zahra hadn't made it. The next few months were a living nightmare. The funeral, his difficult rehabilitation, texts, e-mails, and conversations with family members and friends . . . self-blame . . . grief . . . and more. Compounding this despair and guilt, the accident had left Bassel with a severe physical impairment—he could not walk properly. He had made remarkable improvement rehabbing his broken left leg over the initial weeks, but once he was well enough to walk with a limp and was getting ready to return to work at the hardware store, he found himself unable to make his right leg work. After all his hard work to build up strength, now all he could do was crawl. Before long, he was back in the hospital for evaluation and treatment.

At first, Bassel and the hospital physician assumed that his right leg must have been hurt during the accident but that the injury had been overshadowed by the damage to his left leg or, alternatively, that he had injured the right leg by favoring it during his recovery. One by one, however, the hospital tests revealed nothing—no broken bones, no ligament or muscle damage, nothing. Nothing that could explain such severe impairment.

(continued on the next page)

Eventually, the weakness in his right leg turned into near paralysis and even spread to the recently rehabbed left leg. Because the physicians could not pin down the nature of his injuries, they decided Bassel should keep his activities to a minimum. To his deep regret, he had to extend his leave from work. During this leave, his boss ominously suggested that while Bassel just needed to focus on healing right now, once he was feeling better they would "have to have a discussion about your future here." After all he'd been through, Bassel began to doubt that he had much of a future to look forward to anyway.

The impact of the medical mystery deepened over the following weeks. As Bassel's paralysis continued and as all attempts at rehabilitation failed, he became more and more withdrawn, unable to see more than a few friends and family members and unable to take care of the many remaining tasks attached to Zahra's death. Texting, e-mailing, and phone conversations slowly came to a halt. Like the tragic accident itself, Bassel's paralysis left him self-absorbed and drained of emotion, unable to look back and unable to move forward.

Conversion Disorder (Functional Neurological Symptom Disorder)

Eventually, Bassel received a diagnosis of **conversion disorder**, or **functional neurological symptom disorder** (see **Table 8-2**). People with conversion disorder display physical symptoms that affect voluntary motor or sensory functioning, but the symptoms are inconsistent with known medical diseases (APA, 2022). In short, they have neurological-like symptoms—for example, paralysis, blindness, or loss of feeling—that have no neurological basis.

Conversion disorder often is hard, even for trained medical professionals, to distinguish from a genuine medical problem (Finkelstein & Popkirov, 2023; Stone & Sharpe, 2023). In fact, it is always possible that a diagnosis of conversion disorder is a mistake and that the patient's problem has an undetected neurological or other medical cause. Because conversion disorders are so similar to "genuine" medical ailments, physicians sometimes rely on significant irregularities in the patient's medical picture to help distinguish the two. The symptoms of a conversion disorder may, for example, be at odds with the way the nervous system is known to work (Mason, 2023; Perez & Finkelstein, 2023). In a conversion symptom called *glove anesthesia,* numbness begins sharply at the wrist and extends evenly right to the fingertips. As **Figure 8-1** shows, real neurological damage is rarely as abrupt or evenly spread out.

Unlike people with factitious disorder, those with conversion disorder do not consciously want or purposely produce their symptoms. Like Bassel, they almost always believe that their problems are genuinely medical. This pattern is called "conversion" disorder because clinical theorists used to believe that individuals with the disorder are converting psychological needs or conflicts into their neurological-like symptoms. Although some theorists still believe that conversion is at work in the disorder, others prefer alternative kinds of explanations, as you'll read later.

Conversion disorder often appears suddenly, at times of extreme stress (Stone & Sharpe, 2023). Many cases last just a matter of weeks, and most disappear within six months. When symptoms last longer than six months, a diagnosis of *persistent conversion disorder* is given. Some research suggests that people who develop the disorder tend to be generally suggestible (Wieder et al., 2020) (see ***MindTech***). Many are highly susceptible to hypnotic procedures, for example.

Conversion disorder is thought to be a rare problem, occurring in no more than 1 of every 10,000 persons (APA, 2022). It usually begins between late childhood and young adulthood. According to research conducted with largely cisgender populations, the disorder is at least twice as common in women as in men; its prevalence among transgender or nonbinary people is not known (Lerario et al., 2023; Perez & Finkelstein, 2023).

TABLE 8-2

Dx Checklist

Conversion Disorder (Functional Neurological Symptom Disorder)
1. Presence of at least one symptom or deficit that affects voluntary or sensory function.
2. Symptoms are found to be inconsistent with known neurological or medical disease.
3. Significant distress or impairment.

Information from: APA, 2022.

conversion disorder A disorder in which bodily symptoms affect voluntary motor and sensory functions but the symptoms are inconsistent with known medical diseases.

somatic symptom disorder A disorder in which people become excessively distressed and anxious about bodily symptoms they are experiencing and their lives are disproportionately disrupted by the symptoms.

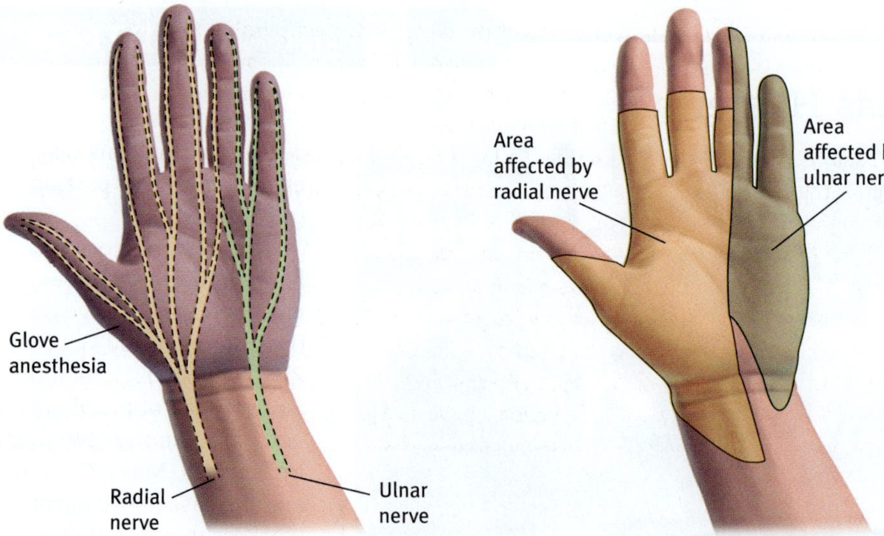

FIGURE 8-1

Glove Anesthesia

In this conversion symptom (left figure), the entire hand, extending from the fingertips to the wrist, becomes numb. Actual physical damage (right figure) to the ulnar nerve, in contrast, causes anesthesia in the ring finger and little finger and beyond the wrist partway up the arm; damage to the radial nerve causes loss of feeling only in parts of the ring, middle, and index fingers and the thumb and partway up the arm. (Information from: Gray, 1959.)

Somatic Symptom Disorder

People with **somatic symptom disorder** become excessively distressed, concerned, and anxious about bodily symptoms that they are experiencing, and their lives are greatly disrupted by those symptoms (APA, 2022) (see **Table 8-3**). The symptoms last longer but are less dramatic than those found in conversion disorder. In some cases, the somatic symptoms have no known cause; in others, the cause can be identified. Either way, the person's concerns are disproportionate to the seriousness of the bodily problems.

Two patterns of somatic symptom disorder have received particular attention. In one, sometimes called a *somatization pattern,* the individual experiences a large and varied number of bodily symptoms. In the other, called a *predominant pain pattern,* the person's primary bodily problem is the experience of pain.

Somatization Pattern

Keira baffled medical specialists with the wide range of her symptoms:

Keira first experienced severe abdominal and chest pains at age 25. A battery of tests and scans shed no light on the cause, and even after a surgical biopsy, doctors could not give her a diagnosis. Over the years, she had many episodes of this severe pain, along with nausea and dizziness. She and her wife Shari had planned to adopt a child, but after they had gotten deep into the process, they withdrew in fear that Keira's condition would prevent her from being an effective parent. This was devastating to both of them, as they had been so looking forward to being parents.

As Keira's pain and other symptoms persisted over the years, she saw doctor after doctor, nearly exhausting her and Shari's meager savings. She had her gallbladder removed by one surgeon who was convinced that gallstones were to blame, but her symptoms persisted. As she moved into her forties, she further began experiencing extreme light-headedness, often to the point of fainting, and she could not hold down solid food without vomiting. She developed significant blurry vision and intermittent hearing difficulties. She also felt extremely weak most of the time and was unable to work.

She and Shari eventually moved to a small apartment and tried to get by on Shari's nursing salary. Shari attempted to care for Keira, but they often quarreled over money, and Keira noticed that Shari was losing her spark and seemed depressed much of the time. As her symptoms continued and even expanded, a new wave of doctors came to suspect that Keira had a degenerative neurological disease. After also becoming distressingly thin and having trouble keeping her balance while walking, she was hospitalized, but, once again, various neurological and physical tests failed to produce a diagnosis.

MINDTECH

Can Social Media Spread "Mass Hysteria"?

In the opening chapter of this textbook, you read about outbreaks during the Middle Ages of *mass hysteria*, also called *mass madness* or *mass psychogenic illness*, in which large numbers of people would share psychological or physical maladies that had no medical causes. Instances of mass hysteria also occur in today's world. In a common occurrence, for example, large numbers of frenzied fans at music concerts collectively display extreme emotionality and lack of restraint during performances by their musical idols, accompanied in many cases by physical symptoms such as fainting, tremors, and even convulsions. Similarly, our world periodically witnesses outbreaks of mysterious illnesses that have no medical cause. In fact, the number of such cases may be on the increase (Müller-Vahl et al., 2022). Most of today's clinicians consider such outbreaks of mass hysteria a form of conversion disorder.

Marc Piasecki/FilmMagic/Getty Images

Modern mass hysteria? These frenzied fans display extreme emotionality and lack of restraint after seeing singer Justin Bieber at Hotel de Sers in Paris, France. Group patterns such as this often earn a label of mass hysteria.

Although incidents of mass hysteria date back over 400 years, social media seems to be a major factor in the current increase (Bartholomew, 2023, 2020, 2018, 2014). One notable outbreak in Le Roy, New York, demonstrates the suggestive role played by social media. Back in 2011, a student at a local high school began having facial spasms. After several weeks, others started having similar symptoms, and eventually 18 girls from the high school were affected. Apparently, a number of these teenagers began to show symptoms after they saw a YouTube video featuring a girl from a nearby town who had significant tics. Doctors eventually concluded that this was an example of mass psychogenic illness.

This case mirrors the many others that have emerged in recent years (Bartholomew, 2023, 2020; Zhao et al., 2021), including an outbreak of hiccups and vocal tics among teenagers in Danvers, Massachusetts, and the case of 400 garment workers in a Bangladesh factory who had severe gastrointestinal symptoms for which there was ultimately no physical explanation. In these and other cases, the symptoms seemed to be spread, at least in part, by social media exposure.

New Zealand sociologist Robert Bartholomew (2023, 2020, 2018, 2014) believes that due to the power of social media, future outbreaks of mass hysteria may be even more numerous, wide-ranging, and severe than any yet recorded. He observes that in the distant past "the local priests, who were . . . summoned to [treat mass psychogenic illnesses], faced a daunting task . . . but they were fortunate in one regard: they did not have to contend with mobile phones [and social media]."

Like Keira, people with a somatization pattern of somatic symptom disorder experience many long-lasting physical ailments—ailments that typically have little or no physical basis. This pattern, first described by Pierre Briquet in 1859, is also known as *Briquet's syndrome*. The person's ailments often include pain symptoms (such as headaches or chest pain), gastrointestinal symptoms (such as nausea or diarrhea), sexual symptoms (such as erectile or menstrual difficulties), and neurological-type symptoms (such as double vision or paralysis).

People with a somatization pattern usually go from doctor to doctor in search of relief. They often describe their many symptoms in dramatic and seemingly exaggerated terms. Most also feel anxious and depressed. The pattern typically lasts for many years, fluctuating over time but rarely disappearing completely without therapy.

In any given year, around 4 to 6 percent of all people in the United States experience a somatization pattern (APA, 2022; Levenson, 2022). According to research conducted with largely cisgender populations, the pattern is much more common among women than men; as with conversion disorder, its prevalence among transgender or nonbinary people is not known (Lerario et al., 2023; Perez & Finkelstein, 2023). The pattern often runs in families. It usually begins between adolescence and young adulthood.

Predominant Pain Pattern If the primary feature of somatic symptom disorder is pain, the person is said to have a predominant pain pattern. Patients with conversion disorder or a somatization pattern of somatic symptom disorder may also experience pain, but in this pattern, the pain is the key symptom. The source of the pain may be known or unknown. Either way, the concerns and disruption produced by the pain are disproportionate to its severity and seriousness.

Although the precise prevalence has not been determined, the predominant pain pattern appears to be fairly common (Levenson, 2022). It may begin at any age, and research conducted with predominantly cisgender populations finds that women are more likely than men to experience it. There are no data on the pattern's prevalence among transgender and nonbinary people.

Often this pattern develops after an accident or during an illness that has caused genuine pain, after which the pain takes on a life of its own. For example, Brianna reported pains and impairment that went far beyond her initial accident and her actual bodily condition:

At the age of 28, after lifting heavy boxes in her storage unit, Brianna developed mild pains in her back and across her chest. When the pains persisted for a few weeks, she saw a physician and was assigned to a round of physical therapy. Soon, however, her back and chest pain worsened. She took several days off from her paralegal job, and the pain, especially in her back, became so severe that she went to the emergency room. Every scan that was done during her emergency visit showed nothing unusual, and the doctors prescribed her muscle relaxants.

Two months later, the pain in her chest intensified and became intolerable, and she again went to see a doctor, who sent her to a cardiologist. Her ECG and echocardiogram were completely normal. She also underwent an endoscopy, but the procedure uncovered no sign of acid reflux, ulcers, or any other physical abnormality or condition.

As Brianna's pains continued over the next two years, several doctors and an array of physical therapists each came to the same conclusion—that, yes, Brianna might be having lingering effects from back and muscle strain, but the pains she was experiencing were, in all of their opinions, extremely disproportionate to her actual physical condition.

Throughout this ordeal, Brianna was mystified about the lingering pain, but she was most worried about taking too much time off work. She had always felt a bit isolated and scrutinized as the only Black woman on the administrative staff of the law firm. So she soldiered on through her intense pain, which rarely subsided. She eventually stopped getting out of bed except to go to work. She found that her boss didn't give her any trouble about missing time for medical tests, and she was pleased that coworkers frequently asked how she was doing. Nevertheless, after months and months of exams with a series of doctors, she was no closer to getting any answers.

TABLE 8-3

Dx Checklist

Somatic Symptom Disorder
1. Person experiences at least one upsetting or repeatedly disruptive physical (somatic) symptom.
2. Person experiences an unreasonable number of thoughts, feelings, and behavior regarding the nature or implications of the physical symptoms, including one of the following: (a) Repeated, excessive thoughts about their seriousness. (b) Continual high anxiety about their nature or health implications. (c) Disproportionate amounts of time and energy spent on the symptoms or their health implications.
3. Physical symptoms usually continue to some degree for more than 6 months.

Information from: APA, 2022.

of NOTE ...

Common Pain

- As many as 84 percent of the world's adults experience substantial low back pain *sometime* in their lifetime.
- As many as 33 percent of the world's adults are *currently* experiencing low back pain.
- As many as 23 percent of the world's adults experience *chronic* low back pain.

(Information from: Casiano et al., 2023, 2022)

Solving a painful mystery For years, singer-songwriter Billie Eilish was perplexed and discouraged by her ongoing struggles with chronic pain, and in fact, her songs often focused on the interplay between her physical and emotional pain. According to Eilish, a recent diagnosis suggests that the source of her previously puzzling problem is a connective tissue disorder called *joint hypermobility syndrome*. The condition, which is more complex and disabling than simple *hypermobility* (double-jointedness), produces severe pain and multiple injuries and has been linked to psychological challenges such as anxiety, depression, disordered eating, and neurodevelopmental problems—all challenges with which Eilish reports having struggled.

Rich Polk/Getty Images

What Causes Conversion and Somatic Symptom Disorders?

For many years, conversion and somatic symptom disorders were referred to as *hysterical* disorders (Stone & Sharpe, 2023). This label was meant to convey the prevailing belief that excessive and uncontrolled emotions underlie the bodily symptoms found in these disorders (see **Table 8-4**).

Work by Ambroise-Auguste Liébeault and Hippolyte-Marie Bernheim in the late nineteenth century helped foster the notion that such psychological factors were at the root of hysterical disorders. As you read in the opening chapter of this textbook, these researchers were able to produce hysterical symptoms in healthy people—deafness, paralysis, blindness, and numbness—by hypnotic suggestion, and they could remove the symptoms by the same means. If hypnotic suggestion could both produce and reverse physical dysfunctions, they concluded, hysterical disorders might themselves be caused by psychological processes.

Why do the terms "hysteria" and "hysterical" currently have such negative connotations in our society, as in "mass hysteria" and "hysterical personality"?

Today's leading explanations for conversion and somatic symptom disorders come from the psychodynamic, cognitive-behavioral, and multicultural models. None has received much research support, however, and the disorders are still poorly understood (Wu et al., 2023; Levenson, 2022).

The Psychodynamic View

As you read earlier, Freud's theory of psychoanalysis began with his efforts to explain hysterical symptoms. Indeed, he was one of the few clinicians of his day to treat patients with these symptoms seriously, as people with genuine problems. After studying hypnosis in Paris, Freud became interested in the work of an older physician, Josef Breuer (1842–1925). Breuer had successfully used hypnosis to treat a woman he called Anna O., who displayed hysterical deafness, disorganized speech, and paralysis (Ellenberger, 1972). On the basis of this and similar cases, Freud (1894/1962) came to believe that hysterical disorders represented a *conversion* of underlying emotional conflicts into physical symptoms and concerns (Peeling & Muzio, 2023).

Observing that most of his patients with hysterical disorders were women, Freud centered his explanation of such disorders on the needs of girls during their *phallic*

TABLE 8-4

Disorders That Have Somatic Symptoms

Disorder	Voluntary Control of Symptoms?	Symptoms Linked to Psychosocial Factor?	An Apparent Goal?
Malingering	Yes	Maybe	Yes
Factitious disorder	Yes	Yes	No*
Conversion disorder	No	Yes	Maybe
Somatic symptom disorder	No	Yes	Maybe
Illness anxiety disorder	No	Yes	No
Psychophysiological disorder	No	Yes	No
Physical illness	No	Maybe	No

*Except for medical attention.

stage (ages 3 through 5). At that time in life, he believed, all girls develop a pattern of desires called the *Electra complex:* each girl experiences sexual feelings for her father and at the same time recognizes that she must compete with her mother for his affection. However, aware of her mother's more powerful position and of cultural taboos, the child typically represses her sexual feelings and rejects these early desires for her father.

Freud believed that if a child's parents overreact to her sexual feelings—with strong punishments, for example—the Electra conflict will be unresolved and the child may reexperience sexual anxiety throughout her life. Whenever events trigger sexual feelings, she may feel an unconscious need to hide them from both herself and others. Freud concluded that some women hide their sexual feelings by unconsciously converting them into physical symptoms and concerns.

Today's psychodynamic theorists take issue with many of the specifics of Freud's explanation of conversion and somatic symptom disorders, but they continue to believe that persons with the disorders have unconscious conflicts carried forth from childhood that arouse anxiety and that they convert this anxiety into "more tolerable" physical symptoms (Peeling & Muzio, 2023).

Psychodynamic theorists propose that two mechanisms are at work in these disorders—primary gain and secondary gain (Mason, 2023). People derive **primary gain** when their bodily symptoms keep their internal conflicts out of awareness. During an argument, for example, a man who has underlying fears about expressing anger may develop a conversion paralysis of the arm, thus preventing his feelings of rage from reaching consciousness. People derive **secondary gain** when their bodily symptoms further enable them to avoid unpleasant activities or to receive sympathy from others. For example, when a conversion paralysis allows a soldier to avoid combat duty or conversion blindness prevents the breakup of a relationship, secondary gain may be at work. Similarly, the conversion paralysis of Bassel, the man who lost his wife in the automobile accident, seemed to help him avoid many painful duties after the accident, such as attending her funeral and returning to work.

primary gain In psychodynamic theory, the gain people derive when their somatic symptoms keep their internal conflicts out of awareness.

secondary gain In psychodynamic theory, the gain people derive when their somatic symptoms elicit kindness from others or provide an excuse to avoid unpleasant activities.

The Cognitive-Behavioral View

Cognitive-behavioral theorists point to somatic vigilance, rewards, and communication skills to help explain conversion and somatic symptom disorders.

In the realm of *somatic vigilance,* they suggest that some people are more attentive than others to their bodies, and this attentiveness causes them to focus more on their bodily discomforts, experience more unpleasant arousal in response to them, and

of NOTE ...

Diagnostic Controversy

Even people whose physical symptoms are caused by significant medical problems may qualify for a DSM-5-TR diagnosis of *somatic symptom disorder* if they are *overly* anxious or upset by their medical problems. Critics worry that many patients who are understandably upset by having cancer, heart disease, or other serious diseases may incorrectly receive a diagnosis of somatic symptom disorder.

worry about them more. This notion is similar to that of *anxiety sensitivity,* the personal inclination to focus on bodily sensations that is linked to panic disorder. Consistent with the somatic vigilance explanation of conversion and somatic symptom disorders, researchers have found that people with higher levels of such vigilance experience pain and pain-related anxiety more often than people with lower levels (French & Hameed, 2023; Perez & Finkelstein, 2023).

In the realm of *rewards,* cognitive-behavioral theorists propose that the physical symptoms of these disorders yield important benefits to patients. Perhaps the symptoms remove the individuals from an unpleasant relationship, or perhaps the symptoms bring attention from other people (Levenson, 2022; Godena et al., 2021). In response to such rewards, the individuals learn to display the bodily symptoms more and more prominently. The theorists also hold that people who are familiar with an illness will more readily adopt its physical symptoms (Peeling & Muzio, 2023). In fact, studies find that many patients develop their bodily symptoms after they or their close relatives or friends have had similar medical problems (Stone & Sharpe, 2023).

Clearly, this focus on the role of rewards is similar to the psychodynamic notion of secondary gain. The key difference is that psychodynamic theorists view the gains as indeed secondary—that is, as gains that come only after underlying conflicts produce the disorders. Cognitive-behavioral theorists view them as the primary cause of the development of the disorders.

Like the psychodynamic explanation, the reward explanation of conversion and somatic symptom disorders has received little research support. Even clinical case reports only occasionally support this position. In many cases, the pain and upset that surround the disorders seem to outweigh any rewards the symptoms might bring.

In the *communication* realm, some cognitive-behavioral theorists propose that conversion and somatic symptom disorders are forms of self-expression, providing a means for people to reveal emotions that would otherwise be difficult for them to convey (Peeling & Muzio, 2023; Reininger et al., 2023). Like their psychodynamic colleagues, these theorists hold that the emotions of people with the disorders are being converted into physical symptoms. They suggest, however, that the purpose of the conversion is not to defend against anxiety but to communicate extreme feelings—anger, fear, depression, guilt, jealousy—in a "physical language" that is familiar and comfortable for the person with the disorder.

According to this view, people who find it particularly hard to recognize or express their emotions are candidates for conversion and somatic symptom disorders (Krempel, Stricker, & Martin, 2023; Levenson, 2022). So are those who "know" the language of physical symptoms through firsthand experience with a genuine physical ailment. Because children are less able to express their emotions verbally, they are particularly likely to develop physical symptoms as a form of communication (Burton et al., 2020). Like the other explanations, this cognitive-behavioral view has not been widely tested or supported by research (Stone & Sharpe, 2023).

Why might Western and non-Western cultures differ sharply in their views of somatic discomforts?

The Multicultural View

Most Western clinicians believe that it is inappropriate to produce or focus excessively on somatic symptoms in response to personal distress. That is, in part, why conversion and somatic symptom disorders are included in DSM-5-TR. Some theorists believe, however, that this position reflects a Western bias—a bias that sees somatic reactions as an *inferior* way of dealing with stress and emotions (Salmon et al., 2022; Canna & Seligman, 2020) (see **Figure 8-2**).

In fact, the transformation of personal distress into somatic complaints is the norm in many non-Western cultures (Barbati et al., 2022; Levenson, 2022). In such cultures, the formation of such ailments is viewed as a socially and medically correct—and less stigmatizing—reaction to life's stressors. Studies have found very high rates of stress-caused bodily symptoms in non-Western medical settings throughout the world, including those in China, Japan, and Arab countries (MHN, 2023; Salmon et al., 2022). People throughout Latin America seem to display the most somatic reactions. Even within the United States, Hispanic people display more somatic reactions in the face of stress than do other populations.

The lesson to be learned from such multicultural findings is not that somatic reactions to stress are superior to psychological ones or vice versa but rather, once again, that both bodily and psychological reactions to life events are often influenced by one's culture. Overlooking this point can lead to knee-jerk mislabels or misdiagnoses.

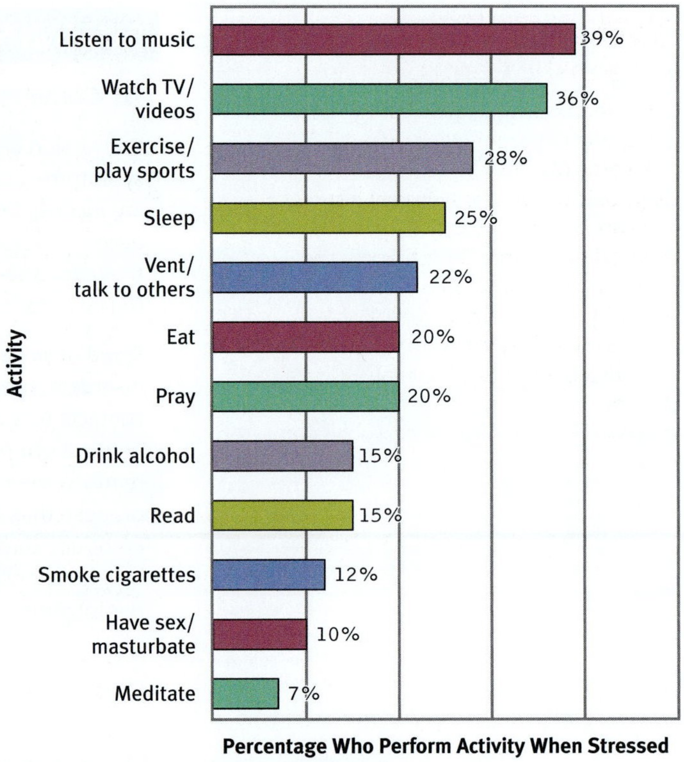

FIGURE 8-2

What Do People Do to Relieve Stress?

According to a survey of 6,700 adults in the United States, people are most likely to listen to music or watch television or videos when they are trying to reduce feelings of stress. (Information from: Everyday Health, 2022, 2018.)

How Are Conversion and Somatic Symptom Disorders Treated?

People with conversion and somatic symptom disorders usually seek psychotherapy only as a last resort (Levenson, 2022). They believe that their problems are completely medical, and at first, they reject all suggestions to the contrary. When a physician tells them that their symptoms or concerns have a psychological dimension, they often go to another physician. Eventually, however, many patients with these disorders do consent to psychotherapy, psychotropic drug therapy, or both (Finkelstein et al., 2023).

Many therapists focus on the *causes* of these disorders (the trauma or anxiety tied to the physical symptoms) and apply insight, exposure, and drug therapies (Patel & Chalder, 2024). Psychodynamic therapists, for example, try to help those with somatic symptoms become conscious of and resolve their underlying fears, thus eliminating the need to convert anxiety into physical symptoms (Russell, Abbass, & Allder, 2022). Alternatively, cognitive-behavioral therapists use exposure treatments. They expose clients to features of the horrific events that first triggered their physical symptoms, expecting that the clients will become less anxious over the course of repeated exposures and more able to face those upsetting events directly rather than through physical channels (Sardesai et al., 2023). And biological therapists most often use antidepressant drugs to help reduce anxiety and depression in patients with these disorders (Levenson, 2022).

Other therapists try to address the *physical symptoms* of these disorders rather than the causes, using techniques such as education, reinforcement, and cognitive restructuring (Patel & Chalder, 2024). Those who employ *education* explain the disorder to patients while also offering emotional support and hope that the physical symptoms may soon disappear. Therapists who take a *reinforcement* approach arrange for the removal of rewards for a client's "sickness" symptoms and an increase of rewards for healthy behaviors. And those who offer *cognitive restructuring* guide clients to think differently about the nature and causes of physical symptoms and illness. Researchers have not fully evaluated the effects of these approaches on conversion and somatic symptom disorders; several studies, however, have found them to be useful interventions (French & Hameed, 2023; Peeling & Muzio, 2023). It is also the case that antidepressant medications and other psychotropic drugs sometimes help alleviate the physical symptoms of people with these disorders in addition to reducing their feelings of anxiety and depression (Sardesai et al., 2023).

of NOTE ...

Seeking Relief

There are more than 430 million visits made each year to primary care physicians in the United States. Research suggests that 17 percent of patients under the care of primary care doctors display physical symptoms that have no apparent physical cause (CDC, 2023; Greenberg, 2016).

SUMMING UP

Conversion and Somatic Symptom Disorders

Conversion disorder, or functional neurological symptom disorder, involves bodily symptoms that affect voluntary motor and sensory functions, but the symptoms are inconsistent with known medical diseases. In somatic symptom disorder, people become excessively distressed, concerned, and anxious about bodily symptoms that they are experiencing, and their lives are greatly and disproportionately disrupted by the symptoms.

Freud developed the initial psychodynamic view of conversion and somatic symptom disorders, proposing that the disorders represent a conversion of underlying emotional conflicts into physical symptoms. According to cognitive-behavioral theorists, the physical symptoms of these disorders bring rewards to the individual, and such reinforcement helps maintain the symptoms. Some cognitive-behavioral theorists further propose that the disorders are forms of communication and that people express their emotions through their physical symptoms. Treatments for these disorders include insight, exposure, and drug therapies and may include techniques such as education, reinforcement, or cognitive restructuring.

Illness Anxiety Disorder

PEOPLE WITH **illness anxiety disorder,** previously known as *hypochondriasis,* are chronically anxious about their health and are convinced that they have or are developing a serious medical illness despite the absence of somatic symptoms. They repeatedly check their body for signs of illness and misinterpret various bodily events as signs of serious medical problems. Typically, the events are merely common bodily changes, such as occasional coughing, sores, or sweating. Those with illness anxiety disorder persist in such misinterpretations no matter what friends, relatives, and physicians say. Some such people recognize that their concerns are excessive, but many do not.

Although illness anxiety disorder can begin at any age, it starts most often in early adulthood, and it appears to be distributed equally across genders (APA, 2022). Fewer than 1 percent of all people experience the disorder (Levenson, 2022). Physicians report coming across many cases. As many as 3 percent of all patients seen by primary care physicians may display this pattern (APA, 2022). Their symptoms tend to rise and fall over the years.

Theorists typically explain illness anxiety disorder much as they explain anxiety disorders. Cognitive-behavioral theorists, for example, believe (1) that the illness fears are acquired through classical conditioning or modeling and (2) that people with the disorder are so sensitive to and threatened by bodily cues that they come to misinterpret them (French & Hameed, 2023; Arnáez et al., 2021).

People with illness anxiety disorder usually receive the kinds of treatments that are used to treat obsessive-compulsive disorder. Studies reveal, for example, that clients with the disorder often improve considerably when given the same *antidepressant drugs* that are helpful in cases of obsessive-compulsive disorder (French & Hameed, 2023). Many clients also improve when treated with the cognitive-behavioral approach of *exposure and response prevention* (Reuman & Abramowitz, 2022). The therapists repeatedly point out bodily variations to the clients while, at the same time, preventing them from seeking their usual medical attention. In addition, the cognitive-behavioral therapists guide the clients to identify, challenge, and change their beliefs about illness that are helping to maintain their disorder.

illness anxiety disorder A disorder in which people are chronically anxious about and preoccupied with the notion that they have or are developing a serious medical illness despite the absence of somatic symptoms.

psychophysiological disorders Disorders in which biological, psychological, and sociocultural factors interact to cause or worsen a physical illness. Also known as *psychological factors affecting other medical conditions.*

ulcer A lesion that forms in the wall of the stomach or of the duodenum.

insomnia Difficulty falling or staying asleep.

asthma A disease marked by narrowing of the trachea and bronchi, resulting in shortness of breath, wheezing, coughing, and a choking sensation.

SUMMING UP

Illness Anxiety Disorder

People with illness anxiety disorder are chronically anxious about and preoccupied with the notion that they have or are developing a serious medical illness despite the absence of substantial somatic symptoms. Theorists explain this disorder much as they do anxiety disorders. Treatment includes drug and cognitive-behavioral approaches originally developed for obsessive-compulsive disorder.

Psychophysiological Disorders: Psychological Factors Affecting Other Medical Conditions

ALMOST 100 YEARS AGO, clinicians identified a group of physical illnesses that seemed to be caused or worsened by an *interaction* of biological, psychological, and sociocultural factors (Bott, 1928). Early editions of the DSM labeled these illnesses **psychophysiological disorders** or **psychosomatic disorders**, but DSM-5-TR labels them as **psychological factors affecting other medical conditions** (see **Table 8-5**). The more familiar term "psychophysiological" will be used in this chapter.

It is important to recognize that significant medical symptoms and conditions are involved in psychophysiological disorders and that the disorders often result in serious physical damage. They are different from the factitious, conversion, and illness anxiety disorders, which are accounted for primarily by psychological factors.

TABLE 8-5

Dx Checklist

Psychological Factors Affecting Other Medical Conditions
1. The presence of a medical condition.
2. Psychological factors negatively affect the medical condition by: • Affecting the course of the medical condition. • Providing obstacles for the treatment of the medical condition. • Posing new health risks. • Triggering or worsening the medical condition.

Information from: APA, 2022.

Traditional Psychophysiological Disorders

Before the 1970s, clinicians believed that only a limited number of illnesses were psychophysiological. The best-known and most common of these disorders were ulcers, insomnia, asthma, chronic headaches, high blood pressure, and coronary heart disease. Recent research, however, has shown that many other physical illnesses—including bacterial and viral infections—may also be caused by an interaction of psychosocial and physical factors. Let's look first at the traditional psychophysiological disorders and then at the illnesses that are newer to this category.

Ulcers are lesions (holes) that form in the wall of the stomach or of the duodenum, resulting in burning sensations or pain in the stomach, occasional vomiting, and stomach bleeding. Around 1 percent of the population in the United States have ulcers in a given year (Vakil, 2022). Ulcers often are caused by an interaction of stress factors, such as environmental pressure or intense feelings of anger or anxiety, and physiological factors, such as the bacteria *Helicobacter pylori* (*H. pylori*) (Gillson, 2023).

Insomnia, difficulty falling asleep or maintaining sleep, plagues one-third of the population each year (Judd & Sateia, 2023). Although many of us have temporary bouts of insomnia that last a few nights or so, a large number of people—10 percent of the population—have insomnia that lasts months or years (Suni, 2022) (see ***InfoCentral***). Chronic insomnia may be caused by a combination of psychosocial factors, such as high levels of anxiety or depression, and physiological problems, such as an overactive arousal system or certain medical ailments (Bonnet & Arand, 2023).

Asthma causes the body's airways (the trachea and bronchi) to narrow periodically, making it hard for air to pass to and from the lungs. The resulting symptoms

Luca Sola/AFP via Getty Images

Breathing battles Asthma results from a combination of stress-related, environmental, and biological factors. Here, in the Mpumalanga province of South Africa, a child with asthma (center) interacts with her mother (left), who herself has severe breathing problems, and her grandmother. The high concentration of coal power plants in the region makes it one of the most dangerous air pollution hot spots in the world, resulting in thousands of breathing-related illnesses and deaths.

are shortness of breath, wheezing, coughing, and a terrifying choking sensation. Almost 8 percent of people in the United States currently have asthma (CDC, 2023), and most were children or young teenagers at the time of their first attack. The majority of asthma cases appear to be caused by an interaction of stress factors, such as environmental pressures or anxiety, and physiological factors, such as allergies to specific substances, a slow-acting sympathetic nervous system, or a weakened respiratory system (Lange-Vaidya, 2023; Wenzel, 2023).

Chronic headaches are frequent intense aches of the head or neck that are not caused by another physical disorder. There are two major types—*muscle contraction*, or *tension, headaches* and *migraine headaches*. **Muscle contraction headaches** are marked by pain at the back or front of the head or the back of the neck. These occur when the muscles surrounding the skull tighten, narrowing the blood vessels. Many millions of Americans experience them occasionally, while 5 percent of the population have such headaches chronically (Murphy & Hameed, 2023; NHF, 2023). **Migraine headaches** are extremely severe, often nearly paralyzing, headaches that are located on one side of the head and are sometimes accompanied by dizziness, nausea, or vomiting. Migraine headaches are thought by some medical theorists to develop in two phases: (1) blood vessels in the brain narrow so that the flow of blood to parts of the brain is reduced, and (2) the same blood vessels later expand so that blood flows through them rapidly, stimulating many neuron endings and causing pain. Around 10 percent of people in the United States experience migraines each year (NHF, 2023; Walter, 2022).

Research suggests that chronic headaches are caused by an interaction of stress factors, such as environmental pressures or general feelings of helplessness, anger, anxiety, or depression, and physiological factors, such as irregular activity of the neurotransmitter serotonin, vascular problems, or muscle weakness (Murphy & Hameed, 2023; NHF, 2023, 2022).

Hypertension is a state of chronic high blood pressure. That is, the blood pumped through the body's arteries by the heart produces too much pressure against the artery walls. Hypertension has few outward signs, but it interferes with the proper functioning of the entire cardiovascular system, greatly increasing the likelihood of stroke, heart disease, and kidney problems. It is estimated that 28 percent of the total population in the United States (almost 50 percent of adults) have hypertension, thousands die directly from it annually, and millions more perish because of illnesses caused by it (CDC, 2023; Egan, 2023). Some cases are caused by physiological irregularities alone, but most result from a combination of psychological and physiological factors and are called *primary*, or *essential, hypertension*. Some of the leading psychosocial causes of primary hypertension are constant stress, environmental danger, and general feelings of anger or depression. Physiological factors include obesity, smoking, poor kidney function, and an unusually high proportion of the gluey protein *collagen* in a person's blood vessels (Basile & Bloch, 2023).

Coronary heart disease is caused by a blocking of the *coronary arteries*, the blood vessels that surround the heart and are responsible for carrying oxygen to the heart muscle. The term actually refers to several problems, including blockage of the coronary arteries and *myocardial infarction* (a "heart attack"). In the United States, more than 28 million people currently have coronary heart disease—around 9 percent of the total population. It is the leading cause of death for adults, accounting for 697,000 deaths each year (CDC, 2023). If other heart-related diseases are added in, those numbers increase significantly. Approximately half of all middle-aged men and one-third of middle-aged women

muscle contraction headache A headache caused by a narrowing of muscles surrounding the skull. Also known as *tension headache*.

migraine headache A very severe headache that occurs on one side of the head, often preceded by a warning sensation and sometimes accompanied by dizziness, nausea, or vomiting.

hypertension Chronic high blood pressure.

coronary heart disease Illness of the heart caused by a blockage in the coronary arteries.

SLEEP AND SLEEP DISORDERS

Sleep is a naturally recurring state that features altered consciousness, suspension of voluntary bodily functions, muscle relaxation, and reduced perception of environmental stimuli. Researchers have acquired much data about the stages, cycles, brain waves, and mechanics of sleep, but they do not fully understand its precise purpose. We do know, however, that humans and other animals need sleep to survive and function properly.

HOW MUCH DAILY SLEEP DO PEOPLE NEED VS. GET?

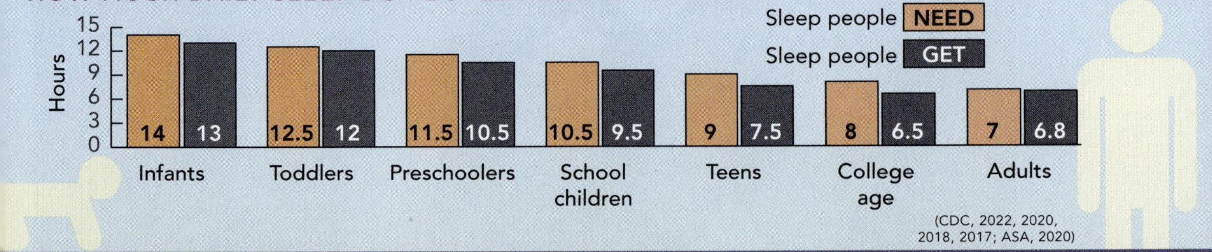

(CDC, 2022, 2020, 2018, 2017; ASA, 2020)

WHO GETS TOO LITTLE SLEEP?

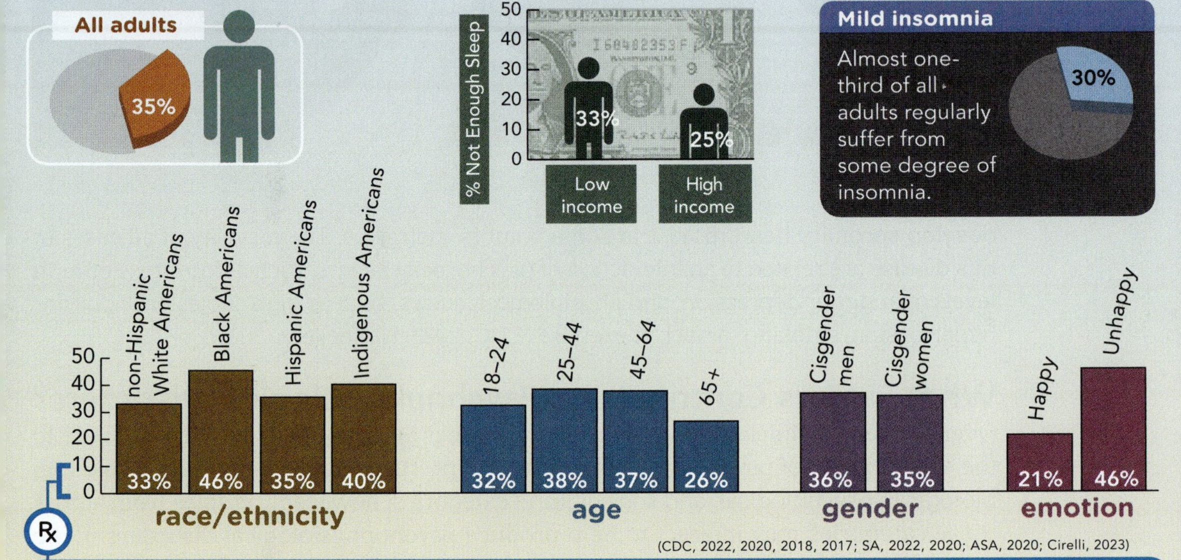

(CDC, 2022, 2020, 2018, 2017; SA, 2022, 2020; ASA, 2020; Cirelli, 2023)

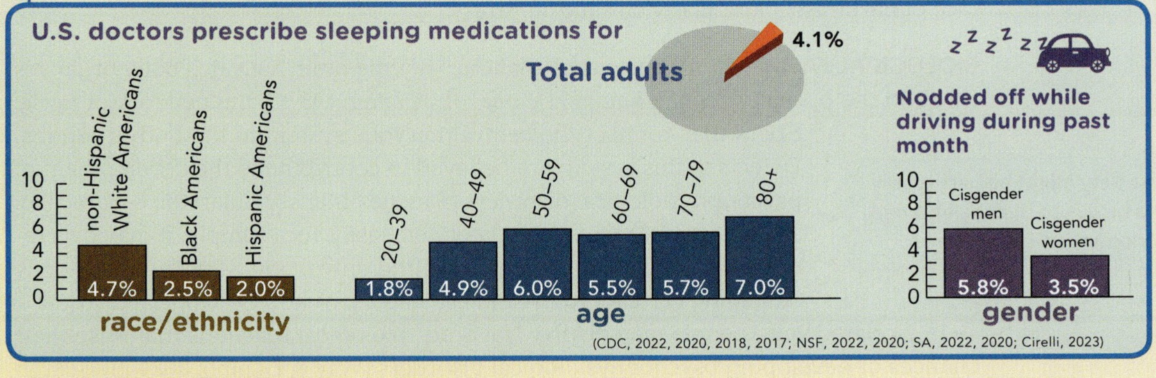

(CDC, 2022, 2020, 2018, 2017; NSF, 2022, 2020; SA, 2022, 2020; Cirelli, 2023)

Sleeplessness-produced problems

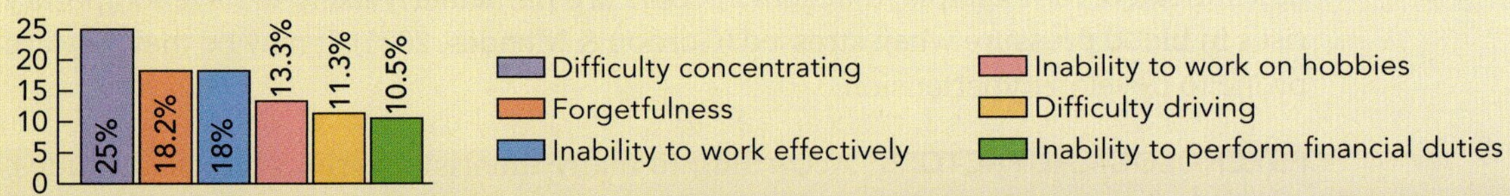

Tips for a good night's sleep

- Go to bed at the same time each night and awaken at the same time each morning.
- Avoid large meals before bedtime.
- Do not drink caffeine or alcohol before bedtime.
- Do not ingest nicotine before bedtime.
- Read or listen to soothing music before bedtime.
- Avoid viewing electronic media before bedtime.
- Create a cool, dark, and quiet bedroom atmosphere.
- If you cannot sleep, perform an interesting or productive activity until you feel sleepy.

(CDC, 2022, 2020, 2018, 2017; SF, 2022, 2020; ASA, 2020)

SLEEP-WAKE DISORDERS

Sleep-wake disorders are syndromes characterized by significant and repeated disruptions in the quantity, quality, timing, or nature of a person's sleep (APA, 2022).

% of people afflicted

Sleep apnea disorder: frequent awakenings each night due to periodic deprivation of oxygen to the brain during sleep — 21%

Insomnia disorder: severe difficulty falling asleep or maintaining sleep at least 3 nights per week — 10%

Parasomnias: disorders featuring frequent **sleepwalking** episodes, **sleep terrors**, or **nightmares** — 4%

Circadian rhythm disorder: mismatch between a person's sleep-wake pattern and the sleep-wake schedule of most other people — 3%

Hypersomnolence disorder: need for extra sleep, and excessive sleepiness — 2%

Narcolepsy: repeated sudden and irrepressible need to sleep during waking hours — .03%

(APA, 2022; Judd & Sateia, 2023; Foldvary-Schaefer, 2023)

Studying sleep This 5-year-old boy is being hooked up to monitors so that he can undergo a *polysomnographic* examination, a procedure that measures physiological activity during sleep, including measurements of brain, eye, lung, and heart activity.

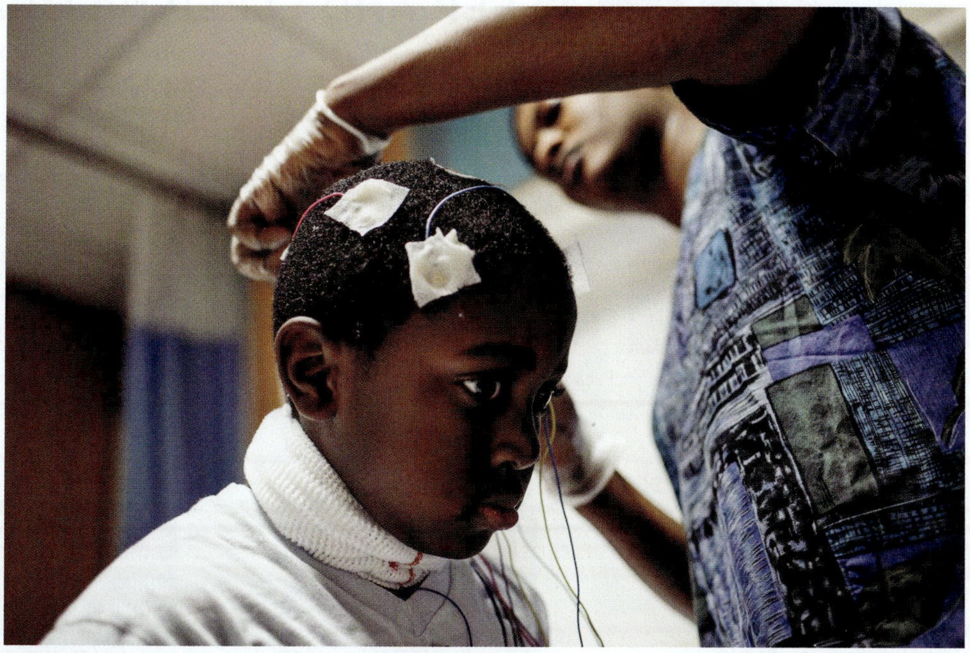

Melissa Golden/Redux

develop coronary heart disease at some point in their lives. The majority of all cases of this disease are related to an interaction of psychosocial factors, such as job stress or high levels of anger or depression, and physiological factors, such as high cholesterol, obesity, hypertension, smoking, or lack of exercise (CDC, 2022; Hennekens, 2022).

What Factors Contribute to Psychophysiological Disorders?

Over the years, clinicians have identified a number of variables that may contribute to the development of psychophysiological disorders. The variables can be separated into biological, psychological, and sociocultural categories; however, variables from across these categories may interact to help produce psychophysiological disorders in the face of life stress, particularly chronic life stress.

BIOLOGICAL FACTORS You have read that one way the brain activates body organs is through the operation of the *autonomic nervous system* (*ANS*), the network of nerve fibers that connect the central nervous system to the body's organs. Defects in this system are believed to contribute to the development of psychophysiological disorders (Sánchez-Manso, Gujarathi, & Varacallo, 2023). If one's ANS is stimulated too easily, for example, it may overreact to situations that most people find only mildly stressful, eventually damaging certain organs and causing a psychophysiological disorder.

Which jobs in our society might be particularly stressful? Might this be due to their heightened effects on the autonomic nervous system?

In a related vein, people may display "favored" biological reactions that raise their chances of developing psychophysiological disorders (Way & Uchino, 2024). Research has indicated, for example, that some people are particularly likely to have temporary rises in blood pressure when stressed (Gordon & Mendes, 2021). It may be that they are prone to develop hypertension.

PSYCHOLOGICAL FACTORS According to many theorists, various needs, attitudes, emotions, coping styles, or personality traits may cause people to overreact repeatedly to stressors, and so increase their chances of developing psychophysiological disorders (Vancheri et al., 2022). Some theorists have maintained, for example, that certain broad personality styles contribute to psychophysiological disorders. One is the **Type A personality style**, an idea introduced more than a half-century ago by two cardiologists, Meyer Friedman and Ray Rosenman (1959). People with this style are said to be consistently angry, cynical, driven, impatient, competitive, and ambitious. They interact with the world in a way that, according to Friedman and Rosenman, produces continual stress and often leads to coronary heart disease. People with a **Type B personality style,** by contrast, are thought to be more relaxed and less aggressive and thus are less likely to develop cardiovascular deterioration.

The link between the Type A personality style and coronary heart disease has been supported by some—but not all—studies. Thus, other researchers have tried to identify different personality styles that might be contributing more strongly to psychophysiological disorders. One of the most prominent is the **Type D personality style** (the D stands for "distress"), a style in which persons repeatedly experience strong negative emotions and reactions (worrying and ruminating, anxiety, sadness, pessimism) while, at the same time, feeling too inhibited and unsupported socially to express or test their feelings of distress. A body of research has indeed found that people with this broad personality style often are more inclined than other people to have coronary and other psychophysiological health problems; however, here again, the link does not hold up across all studies (Tunheim et al., 2022; Wang et al., 2022; Yi et al., 2022).

Many of today's theorists believe that Type A, Type D, and other personality styles fail to robustly predict coronary and other psychophysiological health problems because such personality groupings are too broad and consist of long lists of characteristics, some of which are less critical than others. Thus, many recent studies have looked instead at relationships between *specific characteristics* and psychophysiological illnesses, and these studies have revealed important trends. They have found, for example, that certain of the characteristics that make up the Type A style—anger, hostility—and certain of the characteristics in the Type D style—worrying, anxiety, depression, repression of negative emotions in social situations—each have a strong individual relationship to heart disease (Lee et al., 2022; Tunheim et al., 2022).

SOCIOCULTURAL FACTORS: THE MULTICULTURAL PERSPECTIVE Adverse social conditions may set the stage for psychophysiological disorders. Such conditions produce ongoing stressors that trigger and interact with the biological and personality factors just discussed. One of society's most negative social conditions, for example, is poverty. In study after study, it has been found that people of limited financial means have more psychophysiological disorders, poorer health in general, and poorer health outcomes

Type A personality style A personality pattern characterized by hostility, cynicism, drivenness, impatience, competitiveness, and ambition.

Type B personality style A personality pattern in which a person is more relaxed and less aggressive.

Type D personality style A personality style in which persons repeatedly experience strong negative emotions and reactions (worrying and ruminating, anxiety, sadness, pessimism) while, at the same time, feeling too inhibited and unsupported socially to express or test their feelings of distress.

Win McNamee/Getty Images

Religious protection? At a 2015 prayer vigil, church congregants hold up pictures of nine Bible study participants who were shot and killed at the Emanuel African Methodist Episcopal Church in Charleston, South Carolina. Some relatives of the victims told the mass murderer that they forgave him and were praying for him. Research indicates that people with strong institutional, religious, and social ties often recover more readily and healthfully from the effects of traumatic events.

than people with greater financial resources (HP, 2023; U.S. Census Bureau, 2023, 2022). One obvious reason for this relationship is that people with low incomes typically experience higher rates of crime, job dissatisfaction, unemployment, overcrowding, and other negative stressors than wealthier people. In addition, they typically receive inferior medical care.

The relationship of race and ethnicity to psychophysiological and other health problems is complicated. On the one hand, as one might expect from the economic trends just discussed, Black Americans (who, on average, have lower incomes and experience more poverty than non-Hispanic White Americans) encounter more health problems than do non-Hispanic White people. Black people have, for example, higher rates of hypertension, diabetes, and asthma (OMH, 2023). They are also more likely to die of heart disease, stroke, HIV/AIDS, and Covid-19. Certainly, economic factors may help account for this racial difference. Many Black people live in poverty, and those who do often must contend with the high rates of crime and unemployment and limited health care access that contribute to poor health (Ruiz et al., 2024; PUSA, 2022).

On the other hand, research further suggests that the high rate of psychophysiological and other medical disorders among Black Americans may also relate to factors beyond the economic sphere. Consider, for example, the finding that 57 percent of Black Americans have high blood pressure, compared with 44 percent of non-Hispanic White Americans (OMH, 2023). Although this difference may once again be linked to economic factors, it may also be the case that Black Americans have a physiological predisposition that increases their risk of developing high blood pressure. Or it may be that repeated experiences of racial discrimination constitute special stressors that raise blood pressure in Black people (Ruiz et al., 2024) (see **Figure 8-3**). Studies have found, for example, that the more discrimination people experience over a one-year period, the greater their daily rise in blood pressure, and the more discrimination Black Americans experience over the course of their lives, the more likely they are to have high blood pressure in middle age and old age (HP, 2023; Davis, 2020).

FIGURE 8-3

More Education, More Discrimination

In a large survey of Black American adults, the majority of respondents said that they have experienced race-related discrimination, at least occasionally. Moreover, the respondents who had attended college reported more experiences of discrimination than did the respondents who had not attended college. (Information from: Pew Research Center, 2022, 2019.)

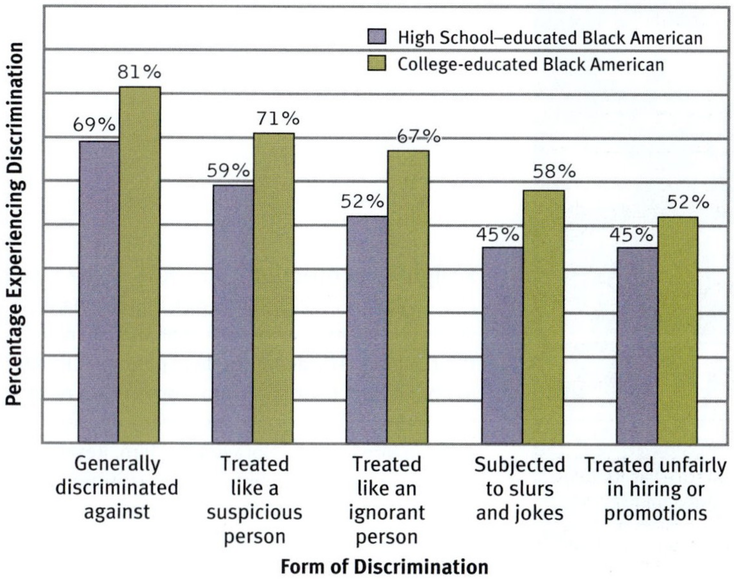

Looking at the health picture of Black Americans, one might expect to find a similar trend among Hispanic Americans. After all, a disproportionately high percentage of Hispanic Americans also have low incomes, are exposed to discrimination, are affected by high rates of crime and unemployment, and receive inferior medical care (Ruiz et al., 2024; PUSA, 2022). However, despite such disadvantages, the health of Hispanic Americans is, on average, at least as good as (and often better than) that of both non-Hispanic White Americans and Black Americans (OMH, 2023). For example, Hispanic Americans have lower rates of high blood pressure and live longer.

The relatively positive health picture for Hispanic people in the face of economic disadvantage has been referred to in the clinical field as the "Hispanic health paradox." Generally, many researchers are puzzled by this pattern, but some explanations have been offered (Fernandez, Garcia-Pérez, & Orozco-Aleman, 2023; Hernandez et al., 2022). It may be, for example, that the strong emphasis on social relationships, family support, and religiousness that characterizes many Hispanic cultures increases health resilience among their members (Uchino, Ong, & Sbarra, 2024). Or Hispanic people may have a physiological predisposition that improves their likelihood of having better health outcomes.

New Psychophysiological Disorders

Clearly, biological, psychological, and sociocultural factors combine to produce psychophysiological disorders. In fact, the interaction of such factors is now considered the *rule* of bodily functioning, not the exception (Way & Uchino, 2024). As the years have passed, more and more illnesses have been added to the list of traditional psychophysiological disorders, and researchers have found many links between psychosocial stress and a wide range of physical illnesses. Let's look at how these links were established and then look at *psychoneuroimmunology*, the area of study that ties stress and illness to the body's immune system.

Anadolu Agency/Getty Images

Too close for comfort Passengers press into a packed subway in Guangzhou, China. Overcrowding is a growing source of stress in today's world. As the global population soars above 8 billion people, researchers have found that those who live in overcrowded conditions experience more physical symptoms, such as stomachaches, headaches, hypertension, and respiratory problems.

Are Physical Illnesses Related to Stress? Back in 1967, two researchers, Thomas Holmes and Richard Rahe, developed the Social Readjustment Rating Scale, which assigns numerical values to the stresses that most people experience at some time in their lives (see **Table 8-6**). Answers given by a large sample of participants indicated that the most stressful event on the scale is the death of a long-term partner, which receives a score of 100 *life change units* (*LCUs*). Lower on the scale is retirement (45 LCUs), and still lower is a minor violation of the law (11 LCUs). This scale gave researchers a yardstick for measuring the total amount of stress a person faces over a period of time. If, for example, in the course of a year a woman started a new business (39 LCUs), sent her child off to college (29 LCUs), moved to a new house (20 LCUs), and had a close friend die (37 LCUs), her stress score for the year would be 125 LCUs, a considerable amount of stress for such a period of time.

With this scale in hand, Holmes and Rahe (1989, 1967) examined the relationship between life stress and the onset of illness. They found that the LCU scores of sick people during the year before they fell ill were much higher than those of healthy people.

TABLE 8-6

Most Stressful Life Events

Adults: Social Readjustment Rating Scale*	Students: Undergraduate Stress Questionnaire†
1. Death of spouse	1. Death (family member or friend)
2. Divorce	2. Had a lot of tests
3. Marital separation	3. It's finals week
4. Jail term	4. Applying to graduate school
5. Death of close family member	5. Victim of a crime
6. Personal injury or illness	6. Assignments in all classes due the same day
7. Marriage	7. Breaking up with romantic partner
8. Fired at work	8. Found out romantic partner cheated on you
9. Marital reconciliation	9. Lots of deadlines to meet
10. Retirement	10. Property stolen
11. Change in health of family member	11. You have a hard upcoming week
12. Pregnancy	12. Went into a test unprepared
*Full scale has 43 items. Information from Holmes, T. H., & Rahe, R. H. (1967). The Social Readjustment Rating Scale. *Journal of Psychosomatic Research*, 11, 213–218.	†Full scale has 83 items. Crandall, C. S., Preisler, J. J., & Aussprung, J. (1992). Measuring life event stress in the lives of college students: The Undergraduate Stress Questionnaire (USQ). *Journal of Behavioral Medicine*, 15(6), 627–662.

The ultimate mind–body connection?
Although rare, *sudden death* may occur among people who have just experienced the death of a loved one, extreme danger, or a severe loss of status (Engel, 1971, 1968). Here a photograph of Irma and Joe Garcia is displayed at a tribute in Uvalde, Texas, soon after the Robb Elementary School shooting in 2022. Just two days after Irma was killed while protecting her students, her husband Joe died of a sudden heart attack at her memorial.

If a person's life changes totaled more than 300 LCUs over the course of a year, that individual was particularly likely to develop serious health problems.

Using the Social Readjustment Rating Scale or similar scales, studies have since linked stresses of various kinds to a wide range of physical conditions, from trench mouth and upper respiratory infections to cancer (Way & Uchino, 2024; Bower & Kuhlman, 2023). Overall, the greater the amount of life stress, the greater the likelihood of illness. Researchers have even found a relationship between traumatic stress and death. People whose partner has died, for example, display an increased risk of death during their period of bereavement.

One shortcoming of Holmes and Rahe's Social Readjustment Rating Scale is that it does not take into consideration the particular life stress reactions of specific populations. For example, in their development of the scale, the researchers sampled non-Hispanic White Americans predominantly. Few of the respondents were Black Americans, Hispanic Americans, or other people of color. But since, on average, their ongoing life experiences often differ in key ways, might not people of color and non-Hispanic White people differ in their stress reactions to various kinds of life events? Research indicates that indeed they do (APA, 2022). One study found, for example, that Black and Hispanic teachers in the United States perceived and reacted to occupational stressors (e.g., heavy workload and administrator pressure) very differently than did non-Hispanic White teachers (Rauscher & Wilson, 2017). Similarly, Holmes and Rahe did not sample a number of other populations in the development of their scale, nor did they include life stressors particularly relevant to those populations, for example, LGBTQ+ people (social stigma and discrimination) and people with disabilities (accessibility barriers).

Finally, college students may face stressors that are different from those listed in the Social Readjustment Rating Scale. Instead of having marital difficulties, being fired, or applying for a job, a college student may have trouble with a roommate, fail a course, choose a major, or apply to graduate school. When researchers use special scales to measure life events in this population, they find the expected relationships between stressful events and illness (Alkhawaldeh et al., 2023; Wu et al., 2020) (see Table 8-6 again).

Psychoneuroimmunology

How do stressful events result in a viral or bacterial infection? Researchers in an area of study called **psychoneuroimmunology** seek to answer this question by uncovering the links between psychosocial stress, the immune system, and health (Bower & Kuhlman, 2023).

The **immune system** is the body's network of activities and cells that identify and destroy **antigens**—foreign invaders, such as bacteria, viruses, fungi, and parasites—and cancer cells. Among the most important cells in this system are billions of **lymphocytes,** white blood cells that circulate through the lymph system and the bloodstream. When stimulated by antigens, lymphocytes spring into action to help the body overcome the invaders. Our ability to fight off and overcome bacterial infections and viruses is dictated by how quickly and efficiently the lymphocytes and other white cells in our immune system operate.

One group of lymphocytes, called *helper T-cells,* identifies antigens and then multiplies and triggers the production of other kinds of immune cells. Another group, *natural killer cells,* seeks out and destroys body cells that have already been infected by viruses, thus helping to stop the spread of a viral infection. A third group of lymphocytes, *B-cells,* produces *antibodies,* protein molecules that recognize and bind to antigens, mark them for destruction, and prevent them from causing infection.

Various factors influence how effectively a person's immune system operates. Insufficient sleep and poor diet, for example, slow down the system. So too does old age (Grifoni et al., 2023). Researchers have also come to appreciate that stress can interfere significantly with the activity of lymphocytes and other parts of the immune system, slowing those cells down and thus increasing a person's susceptibility to viral and bacterial infections (Way & Uchino, 2024; Poller et al., 2022). In a landmark study, investigator Roger Bartrop and his colleagues (1977) in New South Wales, Australia, compared the immune systems of 26 people whose long-term partners had died eight weeks earlier with those of 26 matched control group participants whose partners had not died. Blood samples revealed that lymphocyte functioning was much lower in the bereaved people than in the controls. Still other studies have shown poor immune functioning in people who are exposed to long-term stress. For example, researchers have found poorer immune functioning among those who provide ongoing care for a relative with Alzheimer's disease (Alzheimer's Association, 2023).

If stress affects our capacity to fight off illness, it is no wonder that researchers have repeatedly found a relationship between life stress and illnesses of various kinds. But why and when does stress interfere with the immune system? A number of factors may influence whether stress will result in a slowdown of the system, including *biochemical activity, behavioral changes, personality factors,* and *degree of social support*. Once again, these factors sometimes operate in combination.

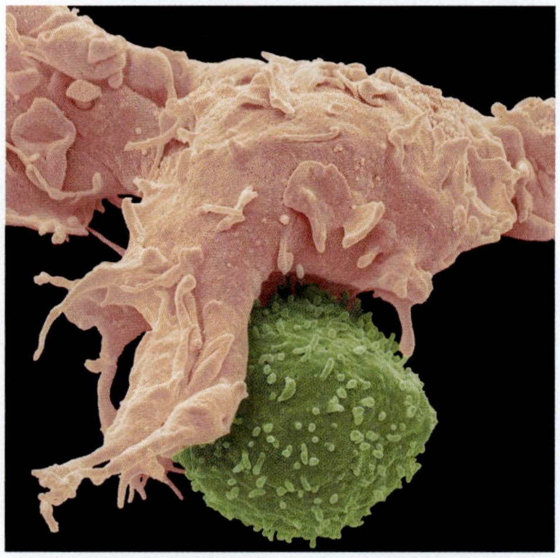
Steve Gschmeissner/Science Source

First line of defense When antigens first invade the body, lymphocytes are alerted by *macrophages*, big white blood cells in the immune system that engulf antigens and then deliver antigen fragments to the lymphocytes. Here a macrophage (pink) is handing off such fragments to a helper T-cell (green).

BIOCHEMICAL ACTIVITY As you'll recall from the chapter on stress disorders, there are two brain–body stress routes by which stressors produce arousal throughout the brain and body. One is the *sympathetic nervous system*, which, among its many actions, triggers the release of the neurotransmitter *norepinephrine*. It turns out that in addition to its role in producing arousal, an extended release of norepinephrine can influence the immune system adversely. Research indicates that if stress continues for too long a period, norepinephrine eventually travels to receptors on certain lymphocytes and gives them an *inhibitory message* to stop their activity, thus slowing down immune functioning (Way & Uchino, 2024; Johnson, 2022).

Recall also that the other brain–body stress route is the *hypothalamic-pituitary-adrenal (HPA)* axis, which, among its various actions, triggers the release of *cortisol* and other stress hormones. In addition to producing bodily arousal, an extended release of cortisol and other stress hormones can contribute to poorer immune system functioning. As in the case of norepinephrine, if stress continues for too long, the stress hormones travel to receptor sites located on certain lymphocytes and give an inhibitory message, again causing a slowdown of the activity of the lymphocytes (Way & Uchino, 2024; Johnson, 2022).

Research has further indicated that another action of norepinephrine and the various stress hormones is to trigger an increase in the production of *cytokines*, proteins that bind to receptors throughout the body. At moderate levels of stress, the cytokines, another key player in the immune system, help combat infection. But as stress continues and more norepinephrine and stress hormones are released, the growing production and spread of cytokines, particularly so-called pro-inflammatory cytokines, lead to *chronic inflammation* throughout the body, contributing at times to heart disease, stroke, and other illnesses (Bower & Kuhlman, 2023; Pahwa, Goyal, & Jialal, 2023).

BEHAVIORAL CHANGES Stress may set in motion a series of behavioral changes that indirectly affect the immune system. Some people under stress may, for example, become anxious or depressed, perhaps even develop an anxiety or depressive disorder. As a result, they may sleep badly, eat poorly, exercise less, or smoke or drink more—behaviors known to slow down the immune system (Wilson, Sweeney, & Zarrett, 2024; Bower & Kuhlman, 2023).

psychoneuroimmunology The study of the connections between stress, the body's immune system, and illness.

immune system The body's network of activities and cells that identify and destroy antigens and cancer cells.

antigen A foreign invader of the body, such as a bacterium or a virus.

lymphocytes White blood cells that circulate through the lymph system and bloodstream, helping the body identify and destroy antigens and cancer cells.

behavioral medicine A field that combines psychological and physical interventions to treat or prevent medical problems.

relaxation training A treatment procedure that teaches clients to relax at will so they can calm themselves in stressful situations.

biofeedback A technique in which a client is given information about physiological reactions as they occur and learns to control the reactions voluntarily.

PERSONALITY FACTORS According to research, people who generally respond to life stress with optimism, constructive coping, and resilience—that is, people who welcome challenges and are willing to take control in their daily encounters—experience stronger immune system functioning and are better prepared to fight off illness (Williams & Carlson, 2024; Pattakos, 2022). In a related vein, several studies suggest that people who are spiritual tend to be healthier than people without spiritual beliefs, and a few studies have linked spirituality to better immune system functioning (Park & Slattery, 2024; Ransome, 2020).

Researchers have further found a relationship between certain personality characteristics and a person's ability to cope effectively with cancer. They have found, for example, that patients with certain forms of cancer who display a helpless coping style and who cannot easily express their feelings, particularly anger, tend to have a poorer quality of life in the face of their disease than patients who do express their emotions (Hao et al., 2023). A few investigators have even suggested a relationship between personality and cancer *outcome,* but this claim has not been supported clearly by research (Antoni, Moreno, & Penedo, 2023; Bower & Kuhlman, 2023).

SOCIAL SUPPORT Finally, people who have few social supports and feel lonely tend to have poorer immune functioning in the face of stress than people who do not feel lonely (Uchino et al., 2024; Van Bogart et al., 2022). In a pioneering study, medical students were given the UCLA Loneliness Scale and then divided into "high" and "low" loneliness groups (Kiecolt-Glaser et al., 1984). The high-loneliness group showed lower lymphocyte responses during a final exam period.

Other studies have found that social support and affiliation may actually help protect people from stress, poor immune system functioning, and subsequent illness or help speed up recovery from illness or surgery (Uchino et al., 2024; Bower & Kuhlman, 2023). Similarly, some studies have suggested that patients with certain forms of cancer who receive social support in their personal lives or receive supportive therapy often have better immune system functioning and more successful recoveries than patients without such supports (Andersen et al., 2024; Antoni, Walsh, & Penedo, 2024; Antoni et al., 2023).

How might social distancing, isolation, and confinement—strategies used to contain epidemics and pandemics—actually hinder the ability of people to fight off other medical illnesses?

The power of support Cancer survivors clasp hands at the Susan G. Komen Race for the Cure, a 5K run held annually throughout the world. The run not only raises funds and increases awareness about cancer but also helps survivors encourage one another—applying research findings that social support can affect the immune system and improve recovery from various illnesses.

SUMMING UP

Psychophysiological Disorders

Psychological factors affecting other medical conditions, known commonly as psychophysiological disorders, are those in which biological, psychosocial, and sociocultural factors interact to cause or worsen a physical problem. Factors linked to these disorders are biological factors, such as defects in the autonomic nervous system or particular organs; psychological factors, such as particular needs, attitudes, or personality traits; and sociocultural factors, such as aversive social conditions and cultural pressures.

For years, clinical researchers singled out a limited number of physical illnesses as psychophysiological, such as ulcers, insomnia, asthma, chronic headaches, hypertension, and coronary heart disease. Recently many other psychophysiological disorders have been identified. Indeed, scientists have linked many physical illnesses to stress and have developed a new area of study called psychoneuroimmunology. Stress can slow lymphocyte activity, thereby interfering with the immune system's ability to protect against illness during times of stress. Factors that seem to affect immune functioning include norepinephrine and cortisol activity, behavioral changes, personality factors, and social support.

Psychological Treatments for Physical Disorders

AS CLINICIANS HAVE discovered that stress and related psychological and sociocultural factors may contribute to physical disorders, they have applied psychological treatments to more and more medical problems (Antoni et al., 2024; Meyers, 2023). The most common of these interventions are relaxation training, biofeedback, meditation, hypnosis, cognitive interventions, support groups, and therapies to increase awareness and expression of emotions. The field of treatment that combines psychological and physical approaches to treat or prevent medical problems is known as **behavioral medicine.**

Relaxation Training

As you read earlier in the textbook, therapists sometimes teach clients how to relax their muscles at will. The notion behind such **relaxation training** is that physical relaxation will lead to a state of psychological relaxation. Relaxation training, often in combination with medication, has been widely used in the treatment of high blood pressure. It has also been of some help in treating somatic symptom disorder, headaches, insomnia, asthma, diabetes, pain, certain vascular diseases, and the undesirable effects of certain cancer treatments (Andersen et al., 2024; Antoni et al., 2024, 2023).

Relaxing—and delicious! New stress relief programs, techniques, and products are constantly being introduced to the marketplace. These three individuals, for example, are able to unwind and relax in a chocolate spa at the Hakone Yunessun spa resort in Japan.

AP Photo/Itsuo Inouye

Biofeedback

In **biofeedback,** therapists use electrical signals from the body to train people to control physiological processes such as heart rate or muscle tension. Clients are connected to a monitor that gives them continuous information about

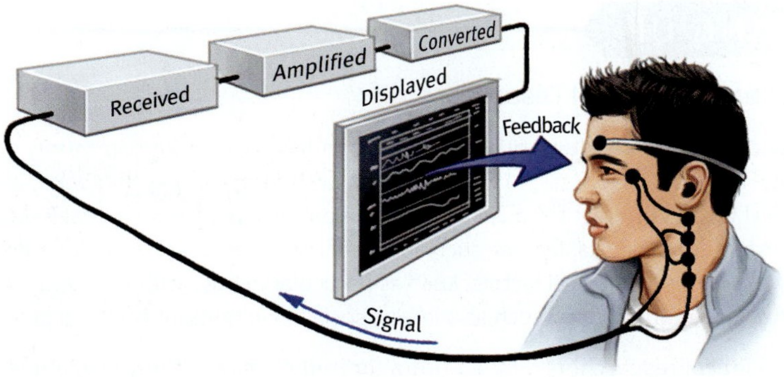

FIGURE 8-4

Biofeedback at Work

This biofeedback system records tension in the forehead muscles of a person with severe headaches. The system receives, amplifies, converts, and displays information about the tension, allowing the client to "observe" it and to try to reduce tension responses.

their bodily activities. By attending to the signals from the monitor, they may gradually learn to control even seemingly involuntary physiological processes.

The most widely applied method of biofeedback uses a device called an **electromyograph (EMG)**, which provides feedback about the level of muscular tension in the body. Electrodes are attached to the client's muscles—usually the forehead muscles—where they detect the minute electrical activity that accompanies muscle tension (see **Figure 8-4**). The device then converts the electric energy, or *potentials,* coming from the muscles into an image, such as lines on a screen, or into a tone whose pitch changes along with changes in muscle tension. Thus, clients "see" or "hear" when their muscles are becoming more tense or less tense. Through repeated trial and error, the individuals become skilled at voluntarily reducing muscle tension.

In a classic study, EMG feedback was used to treat 16 patients who had facial pain caused in part by tension in their jaw muscles (Dohrmann & Laskin, 1978). Changes in the pitch and volume of the tone indicate changes in muscle tension. After "listening" to EMG feedback repeatedly, the 16 patients in this study learned how to relax their jaw muscles at will and later reported that they had less facial pain.

EMG feedback has also been used successfully in the treatment of headaches and muscular disabilities caused by strokes or accidents. Still other forms of biofeedback training have been of some help in the treatment of heartbeat irregularities, asthma, high blood pressure, stuttering, and pain (Schmidt et al., 2023; Strada & Portenoy, 2022).

of NOTE ...

Additional Pain

32%	Percentage of low-income people with chronic knee pain or leg pain
19%	Percentage of high-income people with chronic knee pain or leg pain
37%	Percentage of low-income people with chronic neck pain or back pain
26%	Percentage of high-income people with chronic neck pain or back pain

(Information from: Anson, 2017)

Meditation

Although meditation has been practiced since ancient times, Western health care professionals have only recently become aware of its effectiveness in relieving physical distress. *Meditation* is a technique of turning one's concentration inward, achieving a slightly changed state of consciousness, and temporarily ignoring all stressors. Many people who meditate regularly report feeling more peaceful, engaged, and creative. Meditation has been used to help manage pain and to treat high blood pressure, heart problems, asthma, skin disorders, diabetes, insomnia, and even viral infections (Merschel, 2022; Strada & Portenoy, 2022).

One form of meditation that has been used in particular by patients experiencing severe pain is *mindfulness meditation* (Bower & Kuhlman, 2023; Edwards & Vowles, 2022). Here, as you read in other chapters, mindfulness meditators pay attention to the feelings, thoughts, and sensations that are flowing through their mind during

electromyograph (EMG) A device that provides feedback about the level of muscular tension in the body.

MediaNews Group/Orange County Register via Getty Images

"Downward goat" Yoga is a practice that combines physical and psychological techniques (including body posturing, controlled breathing, and relaxation and meditation exercises) to improve mental and physical well-being. An unusual version is *goat yoga*, which includes the techniques of traditional yoga but also has baby goats roaming around and interacting with the yogis (practitioners). Some goat yoga enthusiasts feel that their yoga experience is enhanced when the goats climb on their backs during planks (body postures). Others simply enjoy the unpredictability and added levity that the hoofed animals bring to the practice.

meditation, but they do so with detachment and objectivity and, most importantly, without judgment. By just being mindful but not judgmental of their feelings and thoughts, including feelings of pain, they are less inclined to label them, fixate on them, or react negatively to them.

Hypnosis

As you read earlier, people who undergo *hypnosis* are guided by a hypnotist into a sleep-like, suggestible state during which they can be directed to act in unusual ways, feel unusual sensations, remember seemingly forgotten events, or forget remembered events. With training, some people are even able to induce their own hypnotic state (*self-hypnosis*). Hypnosis is now used as an aid to psychotherapy and to help treat many physical conditions. It seems to be particularly helpful in the control of pain (Bai, 2023; Williams et al., 2022). It has also been used successfully to help treat such problems as skin diseases, asthma, insomnia, high blood pressure, warts, and other forms of infection (Anbar, 2022).

Cognitive-Behavioral Interventions

People with physical ailments have sometimes been taught new attitudes or cognitive responses toward their ailments as part of treatment (Abrahamsen et al., 2023; Antoni et al., 2024, 2023). For example, an approach called *self-instruction training*, or *stress inoculation training*, has helped patients cope with severe pain (Ashar et al., 2022; Meichenbaum, 2017, 1993, 1975). In this training, therapists teach people to identify and eventually rid themselves of unpleasant thoughts that keep emerging during pain episodes (so-called *negative self-statements*, such as "Oh no, I can't take this pain") and to replace them with *coping self-statements* instead (for example, "When pain comes, just pause; keep focusing on what you have to do").

Doctors now prescribe psychological interventions for a range of medical problems, but many patients resist such treatments. Why?

Support Groups and Emotion Expression

If anxiety, depression, anger, and the like contribute to a person's physical ills, interventions to reduce these negative emotions should help reduce the ills. Thus, it is not surprising that some medically ill people have profited from support groups, including

dpa picture alliance/Alamy Stock Photo

Arturo Holmes/Getty Images

Isolation stressbusters Although social isolation was instituted to contain the spread of Covid-19, it also generated immense personal stress that increased the risk of psychological difficulties and different medical problems. In order to help reduce such risks, a man in Germany strapped on his climbing gear to hang on a roof beam in his apartment living room (left), and a woman in New Jersey spent her housebound time practicing yoga and watching her favorite TV series (right).

online support groups, and from therapies that guide them to become more aware of and express their emotions and needs (Köstlin, Siem, & Rohmann, 2023; Pester et al., 2022). Research suggests that the discussion or even the writing down of past and present emotions or upsets may help improve a person's health, just as it may help one's psychological functioning (Gao, 2022; Maslej et al., 2020; Pennebaker & Smyth, 2016). In one study, asthma and arthritis patients who wrote down their thoughts and feelings about stressful events for a handful of days showed lasting improvements in their conditions. Similarly, stress-related writing was found to be beneficial for patients with either HIV or cancer.

Combination Approaches

Studies have found that the various psychological interventions for physical problems tend to be equally effective. Relaxation training and biofeedback training, for example, are equally helpful (and more helpful than placebos) in the treatment of high blood pressure, headaches, and asthma. Moreover, treatment is most helpful when multiple psychological interventions are used in combination with medical treatments (Antoni et al., 2024, 2023; Riley, 2022). For example, combinations of medication and psychological treatments such as support groups, mindfulness training, and relaxation training are often more effective than medication alone in the treatment of patients with coronary heart disease and related medical problems (Carlson, Baydoun, & Flynn, 2024; Tofler, 2023, 2022).

Clearly, the treatment picture for physical illnesses has been changing dramatically. While medical treatments continue to dominate, today's medical practitioners are traveling a course far removed from that of their counterparts in centuries past.

SUMMING UP

Psychological Treatments for Physical Disorders

Behavioral medicine combines psychological and physical interventions to treat or prevent medical problems. Psychological approaches such as relaxation training, biofeedback, meditation, hypnosis, cognitive-behavioral techniques, support groups, and therapies that heighten the awareness and expression of emotions and needs are increasingly being included in the treatment of various medical problems.

Expanding the Boundaries of Psychopathology

ONCE CONSIDERED OUTSIDE the field of psychopathology, bodily ailments and physical illnesses are now viewed as problems that fall squarely within its boundaries. Just as physical factors have long been recognized as playing a role in psychological difficulties, psychological conditions are now considered important contributors to problems in physical functioning. In fact, many of today's clinicians believe that psychological and sociocultural factors contribute to some degree to the onset and course of virtually all physical ailments.

The number of studies devoted to this relationship has risen steadily during the past 40 years. What researchers once viewed as a vague connection between stress and physical illness is now understood as a complex interaction of many variables. Such factors as life changes, a person's particular psychological state, social support, biochemical activity, and slowing of the immune system are all recognized as contributors to disorders that were once considered purely physical.

One of the most exciting aspects of these recent developments is the field's growing emphasis on the *interrelationship* of the social environment, the brain, and the rest of the body. Researchers have observed repeatedly that mental disorders are often best understood and treated when sociocultural, psychological, and biological factors are all taken into consideration. They now know that this interaction also helps explain medical problems. We are reminded that the brain is part of the body and that both are part of a social context. For better and for worse, the three are intertwined.

of NOTE ...

Strange Coincidence

On February 17, 1673, French actor-playwright Molière collapsed onstage and died while performing in *Le Malade Imaginaire* (*The Hypochondriac*).

Quick Quiz

1. What are the symptoms of factitious disorder, conversion disorder, and somatic symptom disorder? pp. 250–257
2. How do practitioners distinguish conversion disorder from a largely medical problem? What are two different patterns of somatic symptom disorder? pp. 254–257
3. What are the leading explanations and treatments for conversion and somatic symptom disorder? How well does research support them? pp. 258–261
4. What are the symptoms, causes, and treatments of illness anxiety disorder? p. 262
5. What are the specific causes of ulcers, asthma, insomnia, headaches, hypertension, and coronary heart disease? pp. 263–266
6. What kinds of biological, psychological, and sociocultural factors appear to contribute to psychophysiological disorders? pp. 266–268
7. What kind of relationship has been found between life stress and physical illnesses? What scale has helped researchers investigate this relationship? pp. 269–270
8. Describe the connection between stress, the immune system, and physical illness. Explain the specific roles played by various types of lymphocytes. pp. 270–271
9. Discuss how immune system functioning at times of stress may be affected by a person's biochemical activity, behavioral changes, personality style, and social support. pp. 271–272
10. What psychological treatments have been used to help treat physical illnesses? To which specific illnesses has each been applied? pp. 273–276

Eating Disorders

Shani, age 15: While I was learning to resist the temptation of hunger, I walked into the kitchen when no one was around, took a slice of bread out the packet, toasted it, spread butter on it, took a deep breath and bit. Guilty. I spat it in the trash and tossed the rest of it in and walked away. Seconds later I longed for the toast, walked back to the trash, popped open the lid and sifted around in the debris. I found it and contemplated, for minutes, whether to eat it. I brought it close to my nose and inhaled the smell of melted butter. Guilty. Guilty for trashing it. Guilty for craving it. Guilty for tasting it. I threw it back in the trash and walked away. No is no, I told myself. No is no.

. . . And no matter how hard I would try to always have The Perfect Day in terms of my food, I would feel the guilt every second of every day. . . . It was my desire to escape the guilt that perpetuated my compulsion to starve.

In time I formulated a more precise list of "can" and "can't" in my head that dictated what I was allowed or forbidden to consume. . . . It became my way of life. My manual. My blueprint. But more than that, it gave me false reassurance that my life was under control. I was managing everything because I had this list in front of me telling me what—and what not—to do. . . .

In the beginning, starving was hard work. It was not innate. Day by day I was slowly lured into another world, a world that was . . . as rewarding as it was challenging. . . .

That summer, despite the fact that I had lost a lot of weight, my mother agreed to let me go to summer camp with my fifteen-year-old peers, after I swore to her that I would eat. I broke that promise as soon as I got there. . . . At breakfast time when all the teens raced into the dining hall to grab cereal boxes and bread loaves and jelly tins and peanut butter jars, I sat alone cocooned in my fear. I fingered the plastic packet of a loaf of white sliced bread, took out a piece and tore off a corner, like I was marking a page in a book, onto which I dabbed a blob of peanut butter and jelly the size of a Q-tip. That was my breakfast. Every day. For three weeks.

I tried to get to the showers when everyone else was at the beach so nobody would see me. I heard girls behind me whispering, "That's the girl I told you about that looks so disgusting." Someone invariably walked in on me showering and covered her mouth with her hand like I was a dead body. I wished I could disappear into the drain like my hair that was falling out in chunks. . . .

On my return [to school], over the months everyone watched my body shrink as though it were being vacuum packed in slow motion. . . . At my lowest weight my hipbones protruded like knuckle bones under my dress and I had to minimize the increments of the belt holes until there was so much extra belt material dangling down that I did away with the belt completely. My shoes were too big for my feet; my ankles were so thin that I wore three pairs of socks at a time and still my shoes would slide off my heels. And my panties were so baggy I secured them with safety pins on the sides so they wouldn't fall down. . . .

On the home front things were worse than ever. . . . I locked my door and forbade anyone from entering. Even so, my mother and I had screaming matches every day, with her trying to convince me that "your body needs food as fuel" and me retaliating with "I'm not hungry." . . .

For nine months my mother stood by, forbidden to interfere, while I starved myself. She had no idea what was going on, nor did I. . . . She watched me transform from an innocent, soft, kind, loving girl into a reclusive, vicious, aggressive, defiant teenager. . . . And there was nothing she could say or do to stop me. . . .

(Raviv, 2010)

Matt Manley

CHAPTER 9

TOPIC OVERVIEW

anorexia nervosa A disorder marked by the pursuit of extreme thinness and by extreme weight loss.

It has not always done so, but Western society today equates thinness with health and beauty. In fact, in the United States, among other countries, thinness has become a national obsession. Most of us are as preoccupied with how much we eat as with the taste and nutritional value of our food. Thus, it is not surprising that during the past four decades, we have also witnessed an increase in two eating disorders that have at their core a morbid fear of gaining weight. Individuals with *anorexia nervosa,* like Shani, are convinced that they need to be extremely thin, and they lose so much weight that they may starve themselves to death. People with *bulimia nervosa* often go on eating binges, during which they uncontrollably consume large quantities of food and then force themselves to vomit or take other extreme steps to keep from gaining weight. A third eating disorder, *binge-eating disorder,* in which people frequently go on eating binges but do not force themselves to vomit or engage in other such behaviors, also is on the rise.

The news media have published many reports about eating disorders. One reason for the surge in public interest is the frightening medical consequences that can result from the disorders. The public first became aware of such consequences back in 1983 when Karen Carpenter died from medical problems related to anorexia. Carpenter, the 32-year-old lead singer of the soft-rock brother-and-sister duo called the Carpenters, had been enormously successful and was admired as a wholesome and healthy model to young persons everywhere. Another reason is the growing volume of celebrities who have acknowledged their battles with eating disorders and the negative impact the disorders have had on their lives. ■

Why do so many people in Western society struggle with at least some issues of eating and appearance?

Anorexia Nervosa

SHANI, 15 YEARS OLD and in the ninth grade, displays many symptoms of **anorexia nervosa** (APA, 2022). She purposely maintains a significantly low body weight, intensely fears becoming overweight, has a distorted view of her weight and shape, and is excessively influenced by her weight and shape in her self-evaluations (see **Table 9-1**).

Like Shani, at least half of the people with anorexia nervosa reduce their weight by restricting their intake of food, a pattern called *restricting-type anorexia nervosa.* First, they tend to cut out sweets and fattening snacks; then, increasingly, they eliminate other foods. Eventually, people with this kind of anorexia nervosa show almost no variability in diet. Others, however, lose weight by forcing themselves to vomit after meals or by abusing laxatives or diuretics, and they may even engage in eating binges, a pattern called *binge-eating/purging-type anorexia nervosa.*

Approximately 0.6 percent of people in Western countries develop anorexia nervosa in their lifetime, and many more display at least some of its symptoms (Guarda, 2023; NIMH, 2023). The prevalence of the disorder is higher among transgender and nonbinary people than among cisgender people (Arcelus & Witcomb, 2023; Simone et al., 2022). The prevalence may also be higher among gay, lesbian, and bisexual people than among heterosexual people (Arcelus & Witcomb, 2023; Shepherd, Brochu, & Rodriguez-Seijas, 2022). In addition, the prevalence is at least as high for people of color as it is for non-Hispanic White people (ANAD, 2023; Mitchison et al., 2023).

Around 75 percent of reported cases of anorexia nervosa occur in women and girls (NIMH, 2023). As you will also read later, a high female-to-male ratio holds across populations that are cisgender, transgender, heterosexual, and gay/lesbian/bisexual and across most racial and ethnic groups (Knight et al., 2022).

TABLE 9-1

Dx Checklist

Anorexia Nervosa
1. Individual purposely takes in too little nourishment, resulting in body weight that is very low and below that of other people of similar age and gender.
2. Individual is very fearful of gaining weight, or repeatedly seeks to prevent weight gain despite low body weight.
3. Individual has a distorted body perception, places inappropriate emphasis on weight or shape in self-judgments, or fails to appreciate the serious implications of their low weight.

Information from: APA, 2022.

Although anorexia nervosa can appear at any age, the peak age of onset is between 14 and 20 years (Guarda, 2023; NIMH, 2023). Typically, it begins after a person who is of average weight or slightly above average weight has been on a diet. The escalation toward anorexia nervosa may follow a stressful event, such as separation of parents, a move away from home, or an experience of personal failure (APA, 2022). Although most people with the disorder recover, as many as 6 percent of them become so seriously ill that they die, usually from medical problems brought about by starvation or from suicide (ANAD, 2023; Mehler, 2022). The suicide rate among people with anorexia nervosa is five times the rate found in the general population. At least 20 percent of individuals with this disorder continue to display severe eating disturbances for decades (NIMH, 2023).

Wallace Kirkland/Getty Images

Laboratory starvation Thirty-six volunteers who were put on a semistarvation diet for six months developed many of the symptoms found in anorexia nervosa and bulimia nervosa (Keys et al., 1950).

The Clinical Picture

Becoming thin is the key goal for people with anorexia nervosa, but *fear* provides their motivation. People with this disorder are afraid of becoming obese, of giving in to their growing desire to eat, and more generally of losing control over the size and shape of their bodies (Simonazzi et al., 2023). In addition, despite their focus on thinness and the severe restrictions they may place on their food intake, people with anorexia are *preoccupied with food*. They may spend considerable time thinking and even reading about food and planning their limited meals (Klein & Attia, 2023; Ekern, 2020). Many report that their dreams are filled with images of food and eating.

This preoccupation with food may in fact be a result of food deprivation rather than its cause. In a famous "starvation study" conducted in the late 1940s, 36 average-weight men volunteered to be on a semistarvation diet for six months (Keys et al., 1950). Like people with anorexia nervosa, the volunteers became preoccupied with food and eating. They spent hours each day planning their small meals, talked more about food than about any other topic, studied cookbooks and recipes, mixed food in odd combinations, and dawdled over their meals. Many also had vivid dreams about food.

Persons with anorexia nervosa also experience *distorted thoughts*. They usually have a low opinion of their body shape, for example, and consider themselves unattractive (Klein & Attia, 2023). In addition, they are likely to overestimate their actual proportions (Ambrosecchia et al., 2023). Here a 20-year-old with anorexia nervosa describes her feelings about her body:

I can't believe that other people, even my partner, see me as "thin." It seems so obvious to me that I'm too large. When I look at myself in a mirror or in the reflections of storefront windows on the street, I see a heavy person. Sometimes, if I stare long enough, I can force my mind to see a person who, while certainly not as thin as I should be, at least looks "barely adequate enough" that I can let it go and get on with my day. The scale says that I'm at a good weight, but I keep checking in the mirror, and what I see doesn't match what the scale is telling me.

This tendency to overestimate body size has been tested in the laboratory (Klein & Attia, 2023). In a popular assessment technique, research participants look at a photograph of themselves through an adjustable lens. They are asked to adjust the lens until the image that they see matches their actual body size. The image can be made to vary from 20 percent thinner to 20 percent larger than actual appearance. In one study, more than half of the individuals with anorexia nervosa overestimated their body size, stopping the lens when the image was larger than they actually were.

The distorted thinking found in people with anorexia nervosa also takes the form of certain maladaptive attitudes and misperceptions (Yager, 2022). People with the disorder tend to hold such beliefs as "I must be perfect in every way," "I will become a better person if I deprive myself," and "I can avoid guilt by not eating."

People with anorexia nervosa also have certain *psychological challenges,* such as depression, anxiety, low self-esteem, and insomnia or other sleep disturbances (NIMH, 2023; Zanella & Lee, 2022). A number grapple with substance abuse. And many display obsessive-compulsive patterns. They may set rigid rules for food preparation or even cut food into specific shapes. Broader obsessive-compulsive patterns are common as well. Many, for example, exercise compulsively, prioritizing exercise over most other activities in their lives (Plateau & Arcelus, 2023; Ioannidis et al., 2021). In some research, people with anorexia nervosa and others with obsessive-compulsive disorder score equally high for obsessiveness and compulsiveness (NEDA, 2022). Finally, persons with anorexia nervosa tend to be perfectionistic, a characteristic that typically precedes the onset of the disorder (Stackpole et al., 2023).

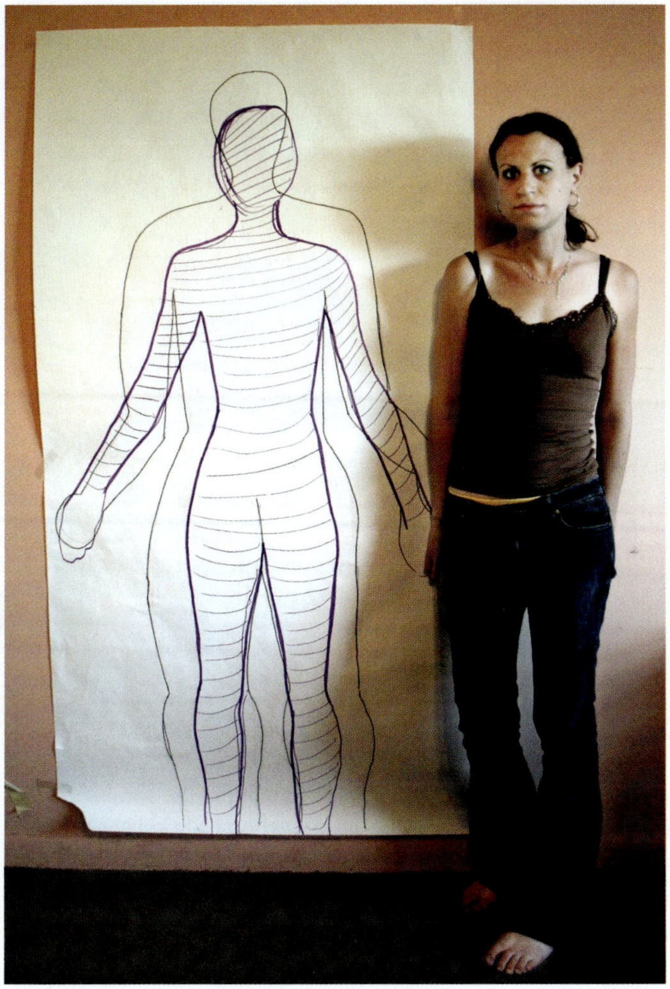

Emily Harris/Miami Herald/Tribune News Service via Getty Images

Distorted body perception In *body tracing,* an assessment and therapy technique, individuals draw an image they believe represents their own body size. Like many persons with eating disorders, this woman's self-drawing (black outline) is much larger than her actual body size (purple outline).

Medical Problems

The starvation habits of anorexia nervosa cause medical problems (Guarda, 2023; Mehler, 2022). Among menstruating (and soon-to-be menstruating) people, a major symptom is **amenorrhea,** the absence of (or failure to begin) menstrual cycles. Other problems include lowered body temperature, low blood pressure, body swelling, reduced bone mineral density, and slow heart rate. Metabolic and electrolyte imbalances also may occur and can lead to death by heart failure or circulatory collapse. The poor nutrition of people with anorexia nervosa may also cause skin to become rough, dry, and cracked; nails to become brittle; and hands and feet to be cold and blue. Some people lose hair from the scalp, and some grow *lanugo* (the fine, silky hair that covers some newborns) on their trunk, extremities, and face. Shani, the young woman whose self-description opened this chapter, recalls how her body deteriorated as her disorder was progressing: "Nobody knew that I was always cold no matter how many layers I wore, that my hair came out in thick wads whenever I wet it or washed it, that I stopped menstruating, [and] that my hipbones hurt to lie on my stomach and my coccyx hurt to sit on the floor" (Raviv, 2010).

SUMMING UP

Anorexia Nervosa

Rates of eating disorders have increased dramatically as thinness has become an obsession in Western countries. People with anorexia nervosa pursue extreme thinness and lose dangerous amounts of weight. They may follow a pattern of restricting-type anorexia nervosa or a pattern of binge-eating/purging-type anorexia nervosa. The central features of anorexia nervosa are a drive for thinness, intense fear of weight gain, and disturbed body perception and other cognitive disturbances. People with this disorder develop various medical problems, including amenorrhea. Approximately 0.6 percent of all people develop the disorder during their lives. Around 75 percent of cases occur among women and girls, a gender difference that holds relatively steady across cisgender, transgender, heterosexual, and gay/lesbian/bisexual populations and across most racial and ethnic groups.

Bulimia Nervosa

PEOPLE WITH bulimia nervosa—a disorder also known as *binge-purge syndrome*—engage in repeated episodes of uncontrollable overeating, or **binges.** A binge episode takes place over a limited period of time, often two hours, during which the person eats much more food than most people would eat during a similar time span (APA, 2022). In addition, people with this disorder repeatedly perform inappropriate *compensatory behaviors,* such as forcing themselves to vomit; misusing laxatives, diuretics, or enemas; fasting; or exercising excessively (see **Table 9-2**). Lindsey Hall, a noted writer on eating disorders who has since recovered from bulimia nervosa, describes a morning during her disorder:

Today I am going to be really good and that means eating certain predetermined portions of food and not taking one more bite than I think I am allowed. I am very careful to see that I don't take more than Doug does. I judge by his body. I can feel the tension building. I wish Doug would hurry up and leave so I can get going!

As soon as he shuts the door, I try to get involved with one of the myriad of responsibilities on the list. I hate them all! I just want to crawl into a hole. I don't want to do anything. I'd rather eat. I am alone, I am nervous, I am no good, I always do everything wrong anyway, I am not in control, I can't make it through the day, I just know it. It has been the same for so long.

I remember the starchy cereal I ate for breakfast. I am into the bathroom and onto the scale. It measures the same, but I don't want to stay the same! I want to be thinner! I look in the mirror, I think my thighs are ugly and deformed looking. I see a lumpy, clumsy, pear-shaped wimp. There is always something wrong with what I see. I feel frustrated trapped in this body and I don't know what to do about it.

I float to the refrigerator knowing exactly what is there. I begin with last night's brownies. I always begin with the sweets. At first I try to make it look like nothing is missing, but my appetite is huge and I resolve to make another batch of brownies. I know there is half of a bag of cookies in the bathroom, thrown out the night before, and I polish them off immediately. I take some milk so my vomiting will be smoother. I like the full feeling I get after downing a big glass. I get out six pieces of bread and toast one side in the broiler, turn them over and load them with patties of butter and put them under the broiler again till they are bubbling. I take all six pieces on a plate to the television and go back for a bowl of cereal and a banana to have along with them. Before the last toast is finished, I am already preparing the next batch of six more pieces. Maybe another brownie or five, and a couple of large bowlfuls of ice cream, yogurt or cottage cheese. My stomach is stretched into a huge ball below my ribcage. I know I'll have to go into the bathroom soon, but I want to postpone it. I am in never-never land. I am waiting, feeling the pressure, pacing the floor in and out of the rooms. Time is passing. Time is passing. It is getting to be time.

I wander aimlessly through each of the rooms again tidying, making the whole house neat and put back together. I finally make the turn into the bathroom. I brace my feet, pull my hair back and stick my finger down my throat, stroking twice, and get up a huge pile of food. Three times, four and another pile of food. I can see everything come back. I am glad to see those brownies because they are SO fattening. The rhythm of the emptying is broken and my head is beginning to hurt. I stand up feeling dizzy, empty and weak. The whole episode has taken about an hour.

(Hall & Cohn, 2010, p. 1)

TABLE 9-2

Dx Checklist

Bulimia Nervosa
1. Repeated binge-eating episodes.
2. Repeated performance of ill-advised compensatory behaviors (e.g., forced vomiting) to prevent weight gain.
3. Symptoms take place at least weekly for a period of 3 months.
4. Inappropriate influence of weight and shape on appraisal of oneself.

Information from: APA, 2022.

amenorrhea The absence of menstrual cycles.

bulimia nervosa A disorder marked by frequent eating binges followed by forced vomiting or other extreme compensatory behaviors to avoid gaining weight. Also known as *binge-purge syndrome.*

binge An episode of uncontrollable eating during which a person ingests a very large quantity of food.

TABLE 9-3

Comparing the Eating Disorders

	Lifetime Prevalence	Percentage Who Are Female	Typical Age at Onset	Percentage Who Receive Treatment	Successful Long-Term Recovery After Treatment
Anorexia nervosa	0.6%	75%	14–20 yrs	34%	34%
Bulimia nervosa	1.0%	83%	15–20 yrs	43%	75%
Binge-eating disorder	2.8%	67%	22–30 yrs	44%	60%

Information from: Crow, 2023; Engel et al., 2023; Klein & Attia, 2023; Mitchell, 2023; NIMH, 2023; Sysko & Devlin, 2023, 2022; Yager, 2022.

Around 1 percent of all people develop bulimia nervosa in their lifetime (Guarda, 2023; NIMH, 2023) (see **Table 9-3**). As with anorexia nervosa, the prevalence of this disorder is higher among transgender and nonbinary people than among cisgender people. The prevalence may also be higher among gay, lesbian, and bisexual people than among heterosexual people (Arcelus & Witcomb, 2023; Shepherd et al., 2022, Simone et al., 2022). And the prevalence is at least as high for people of color as it is for non-Hispanic White people (ANAD, 2023; Mitchison et al., 2023).

Also, like anorexia nervosa, bulimia nervosa occurs most frequently in women and girls—83 percent of reported cases—a high female-to-male ratio that holds across cisgender, transgender, heterosexual, and gay/lesbian/bisexual populations and across racial and ethnic groups (NIMH, 2023; Knight et al., 2022).

The disorder begins in adolescence or young adulthood (most often between 15 and 20 years of age) and often lasts for years, with periodic letup (Guarda, 2023; NIMH, 2023). The weight of people with bulimia nervosa usually stays within a healthy range, although it may fluctuate markedly within that range. Some people with this disorder, however, become seriously underweight and may eventually qualify for a diagnosis of anorexia nervosa instead.

Many teenagers and young adults go on occasional eating binges or experiment with vomiting or laxatives after they hear about these behaviors from their friends or the media. Indeed, according to global studies, 25 to 50 percent of all students report periodic binge eating or self-induced vomiting (Ekern, 2020). However, only some of these individuals (fewer than 5 percent of them) qualify for a diagnosis of bulimia nervosa (Engel, Steffen, & Mitchell, 2023).

of NOTE ...

Royal Bulimia

During her three years as queen of England, Anne Boleyn, King Henry VIII's second wife, displayed a habit, first observed during her coronation banquet, of vomiting during meals. In fact, she assigned a lady-in-waiting the task of holding up a sheet when the queen looked likely to vomit (Shaw, 2004).

Binges

Most people with bulimia nervosa have multiple binge episodes per week. Typically, they carry out the binges in secret. The person eats massive amounts of food very rapidly, with minimal chewing—usually sweet, high-calorie foods with a soft texture, such as ice cream, cookies, doughnuts, and sandwiches. The food is hardly tasted or thought about. Binge eaters consume an average of 2,000 to 3,400 calories during an episode (Engel et al., 2023; Fairburn & Murphy, 2020). Some individuals consume as many as 10,000 calories.

Binges are usually preceded by feelings of great tension (APA, 2022). The person feels irritable, "unreal," and powerless to control an overwhelming need to eat "forbidden" foods (Catania et al., 2023). During the binge, the person feels unable to stop eating. Although the binge itself may be experienced as pleasurable in the sense that it relieves the unbearable tension the individual has been experiencing, it is followed by feelings of extreme self-blame, shame, guilt, and depression, as well as fears of gaining weight and being discovered (Blythin et al., 2020).

Compensatory Behaviors

After a binge, people with bulimia nervosa try to compensate for and undo its effects. Many resort to vomiting, for example. But vomiting actually fails to prevent the absorption of half of the calories consumed during a binge. Furthermore, because repeated vomiting affects one's general ability to feel satiated, it leads to greater hunger and more frequent and intense binges. Similarly, the use of laxatives or diuretics largely fails to undo the caloric effects of bingeing (Mitchell, 2023).

What might be some other areas in life besides eating and food in which people sometimes binge and purge?

Vomiting and other compensatory behaviors may temporarily relieve the uncomfortable physical feelings of fullness or reduce the feelings of anxiety and self-disgust attached to binge eating. Over time, however, a cycle develops in which purging allows more bingeing, and bingeing necessitates more purging. The cycle eventually causes people with the disorder to feel powerless and disgusted with themselves (Engel et al., 2023). Most recognize fully that they have an eating disorder. Lindsey Hall, the writer we met earlier, recalls how the pattern of binge eating, purging, and self-disgust took hold while she was a teenager in boarding school.

> *The first time I stuck my fingers down my throat was during the last week of school. I saw a girl come out of the bathroom with her face all red and her eyes puffy. She had always talked about her weight and how she should be dieting even though her body was really shapely. I knew instantly what she had just done and I had to try it. . . .*
>
> *I began with breakfasts which were served buffet-style on the main floor of the dorm. I learned which foods I could eat that would come back up easily. When I woke in the morning, I had to make the decision whether to stuff myself for half an hour and throw up before class, or whether to try and make it through the whole day without overeating. . . . I always thought people noticed when I took huge portions at mealtimes, but I figured they assumed that because I was an athlete, I burned it off. . . . Once a binge was under way, I did not stop until my stomach looked pregnant and I felt like I could not swallow one more time.*
>
> *That year was the first of my nine years of obsessive eating and throwing up. . . . I didn't want to tell anyone what I was doing, and I didn't want to stop. . . . [Though] being in love or other distractions occasionally lessened the cravings, I always returned to the food.*
>
> *(Hall & Cohn, 2010, p. 55)*

As with anorexia nervosa, a bulimic pattern typically begins during or after a period of intense dieting, often one that has been successful and earned praise from family members and friends (Guarda, 2023; NEDA, 2022). Studies of both animals and humans have found that research participants without irregular eating patterns, when placed on very strict diets, also develop a tendency to binge. Some of the participants in the starvation study described earlier, for example, later binged when they returned to regular eating, and a number of them continued to be hungry even after large meals (Keys et al., 1950).

Bulimia Nervosa Versus Anorexia Nervosa

Bulimia nervosa is similar to anorexia nervosa in many ways. Both disorders typically begin after a period of dieting by people who are fearful of becoming obese; driven to become thin; preoccupied with food, weight, and appearance; and struggling with depression, anxiety, obsessiveness, and the need to be perfect (Guarda, 2023; NIMH, 2023). People with either of the disorders have a heightened risk of suicide attempts and fatalities. Substance abuse may accompany either disorder, perhaps beginning with

of NOTE ...

Diet Business

Worldwide, people spend $309 billion each year on weight-reduction foods, products, and services. The annual total in the United States is $58 billion (Business Wire, 2022; GlobeNewswire, 2022).

the excessive use of diet pills (Munn-Chernoff et al., 2021). People with either disorder believe that they weigh too much and look too heavy regardless of their actual weight or appearance. And both disorders are marked by disturbed attitudes toward eating.

Yet the two disorders also differ in important ways. Although people with either disorder worry about the opinions of others, those with bulimia nervosa tend to be more concerned about pleasing others, being attractive to others, and experiencing intimacy (Bellard et al., 2022). They also tend to be more sexually active than people with anorexia nervosa (Fairburn & Murphy, 2020). Particularly troublesome, they are more likely to have long histories of mood swings, become easily frustrated or bored, and have trouble coping effectively or controlling their impulses and strong emotions (Engel et al., 2023). More than one-third of those with bulimia nervosa display the characteristics of a personality disorder—particularly borderline or avoidant personality disorder, patterns you will be reading about in a later chapter (Lee & Vaillancourt, 2023; NEDA, 2022).

of NOTE ...

Early Publication

The apparent first diet book, *Letter on Corpulence*, was published in the mid-1800s (Wdowik, 2017; Herman, 2015).

Another difference is the nature of the medical complications that accompany the two disorders (Guarda, 2023; Mitchell & Zunker, 2022). For example, research conducted in largely cisgender populations finds that only half of women with bulimia nervosa are amenorrheic or have very irregular menstrual periods, compared with almost all of those with anorexia nervosa. In addition, repeated vomiting bathes teeth and gums in hydrochloric acid, leading some individuals with bulimia nervosa to have serious dental problems, such as breakdown of enamel and even loss of teeth. Moreover, cardiovascular disease and/or dangerous potassium deficiencies may occur among people with bulimia nervosa.

SUMMING UP

Bulimia Nervosa

People with bulimia nervosa go on frequent eating binges and then force themselves to vomit or perform other unhealthy compensatory behaviors. Around 1 percent of the population manifests bulimia nervosa in their lifetime. The binges are often in response to increasing tension and are followed by feelings of guilt and self-blame. Compensatory behavior is at first reinforced by the temporary relief from uncomfortable feelings of fullness or the reduction of feelings of anxiety, self-disgust, and loss of control attached to bingeing. Over time, however, individuals generally feel disgusted with themselves, depressed, and guilty. Around 83 percent of all cases of bulimia nervosa occur among women and girls, a gender difference that holds relatively steady across cisgender, transgender, heterosexual, and gay/lesbian/bisexual populations and across most racial and ethnic groups.

Binge-Eating Disorder

LIKE THOSE WITH bulimia nervosa, people with **binge-eating disorder** engage in repeated eating binges during which they feel no control over their eating (Catania et al., 2023). However, they do *not* perform inappropriate compensatory behavior (see **Table 9-4**). As a result of their frequent binges, around half of those with this disorder become overweight or even obese (Yager, 2022).

Although binge-eating disorder was not formally listed as a clinical category until the publication of DSM-5 in 2013, the syndrome was first recognized in the late 1950s as a pattern common among many people with obesity (Stunkard, 1959). At the same time, however, most people with obesity do not engage in repeated

binge-eating disorder A disorder marked by frequent binges without extreme compensatory acts.

binges; their excess weight results from frequent overeating, sedentary lifestyles, and/or a combination of biological, psychological, and sociocultural factors (ANAD, 2023).

Around 2.8 percent of people in the United States experience binge-eating disorder in their lifetime, making it the most prevalent eating disorder (NIMH, 2023; NEDA, 2022). As with the other eating disorders, women with this problem outnumber men—making up 67 percent of reported cases (Guarda, 2023). Researchers have not systematically investigated the disorder's prevalence rates and gender differences within specific populations—that is, within cisgender, transgender/nonbinary, heterosexual, gay/lesbian/bisexual, and racial/ethnic populations (Yager, 2022). One population that seems particularly at risk for binge-eating disorder is individuals who live with *food insecurity*—that is, a limited, uncertain, or unreliable availability of needed food due to limited financial means (Hazzard et al., 2023, 2020).

The binges that characterize binge-eating disorder are similar to those in bulimia nervosa, particularly the amount of food eaten and the sense of loss of control experienced by individuals during the binge (Catania et al., 2023). Moreover, like people with bulimia nervosa and anorexia nervosa, those with binge-eating disorder typically are preoccupied with food, weight, and appearance; tend to base evaluation of themselves largely on their weight and shape; often misperceive their body size and are extremely dissatisfied with their body; may struggle with feelings of depression, anxiety, self-disgust, and perfectionism; and sometimes abuse substances (Sysko & Devlin, 2023, 2022).

On the other hand, people with binge-eating disorder are not as driven to thinness as those with anorexia nervosa and bulimia nervosa, although they do aspire to limit their eating (see **Figure 9-1**). In addition, unlike those disorders, this problem does not necessarily begin with efforts at extreme dieting. People with this disorder typically first develop the pattern later than those with the other eating disorders; most often they are in their twenties (Guarda, 2023; NIMH, 2023).

People with binge-eating disorder have an increased risk of developing certain medical problems, and many people with the disorder describe their general health as poor. Because they do not lose excessive weight or perform unhealthy compensatory

TABLE 9-4

Dx Checklist

Binge-Eating Disorder
1. Recurrent binge-eating episodes.
2. Binge-eating episodes include at least three of these features: ■ Unusually fast eating ■ Absence of hunger ■ Uncomfortable fullness ■ Secret eating due to sense of shame ■ Subsequent feelings of self-disgust, depression, or severe guilt.
3. Significant distress.
4. Binge-eating episodes take place at least weekly over the course of 3 months.
5. Absence of excessive compensatory behaviors.

Information from: APA, 2022.

Cityfiles/Polaris

"The Biggest Loser" phenomenon These men participate in a group exercise program as part of the reality television show *Peso Pesado* (*Heavy Weight*), the Portuguese version of the American series *The Biggest Loser.* In these shows, contestants with excessive weight and obesity compete to lose the most weight for cash prizes. Most people with excess weight do not display binge-eating disorder, but many people with the disorder are obese.

FIGURE 9-1

Overlapping Patterns of Eating Disorders

Some people with anorexia nervosa binge and purge their way to weight loss, and some people with obesity binge eat. However, most people with bulimia nervosa are not obese, and most people with excess weight do not binge eat.

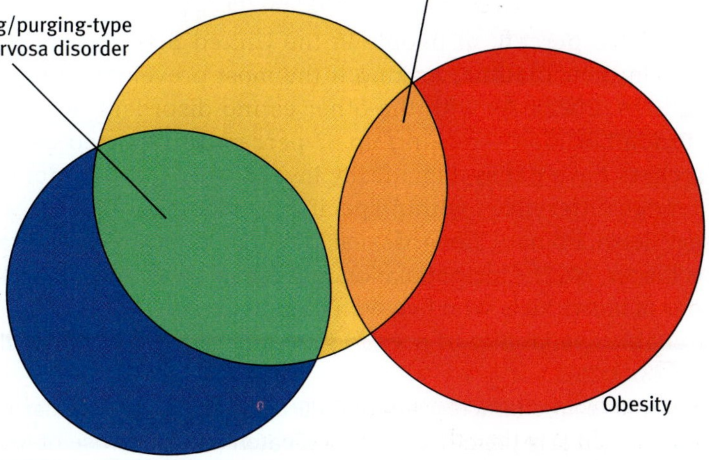

behaviors, their medical problems are different from the ones that characterize anorexia nervosa and bulimia nervosa (Mitchell & Zunker, 2022). Those whose disorder includes obesity are—like other people with excessive weight—more likely than the general population to develop diabetes, high blood pressure, heart disease, high cholesterol, and strokes, among other medical problems (Perreault & Laferrère, 2023).

SUMMING UP

Binge-Eating Disorder

People with binge-eating disorder have frequent binge-eating episodes but do not display unhealthy compensatory behaviors. Although most people with excess weight do not have binge-eating disorder, many individuals with binge-eating disorder become overweight. Around 2.8 percent of the population develop binge-eating disorder during their lives. Approximately 67 percent of people with this disorder are female.

What Causes Eating Disorders?

MOST OF TODAY'S theorists and researchers use a *multidimensional risk perspective* to explain eating disorders. That is, they identify several key factors that place a person at risk for these disorders (Guarda, 2023). Generally, the more of these factors that are present, the more likely it is that a person will develop an eating disorder. The multidimensional risk perspective for eating disorders is not as specific as the developmental psychopathology perspective, but it does share many principles with the latter perspective. That is, it too contends that the risk factors for eating disorders unfold over the course of development, that interactions between these factors are key, and that different risk factors and combinations of factors may lead to the same eating disorders.

As you will read, most of the risk factors that have been cited and investigated center on anorexia nervosa and bulimia nervosa. Binge-eating disorder, formally identified as a clinical syndrome more recently, is only now being broadly investigated. The factors that are further at work in this disorder will probably become clear in the coming years.

In addition, studies and explanations of the various risk factors have typically focused on cisgender and heterosexual individuals. Thus, it may be that some of the

of NOTE ...

Increased Vulnerability

According to research, survivors of sexual assault and sexual abuse are almost twice as likely as people without such experiences to develop bulimia nervosa (NEDA, 2022).

explanations you'll be reading about do not fully apply to eating disorders within LGBTQ+ populations. As more research on eating disorders is conducted on these populations, it is likely that a fuller understanding of the causes of the disorders will emerge.

Psychodynamic Factors: Ego Deficiencies

Hilde Bruch, a pioneer in the study and treatment of eating disorders, developed a largely psychodynamic theory of the disorders, a theory that is still influential. She argued that disturbed parent–child interactions lead to serious *ego deficiencies* in the child (including a poor sense of independence and control) and to severe *perceptual disturbances* that jointly help produce disordered eating (Wooldridge, 2022; Bruch, 2001, 1991, 1962).

According to Bruch, parents may respond to their children either effectively or ineffectively. *Effective parents* accurately attend to their children's biological and emotional needs, giving them food when they are crying from hunger and comfort when they are crying out of fear. *Ineffective parents,* by contrast, fail to attend to their children's needs, deciding that their children are hungry, cold, or tired without correctly interpreting the children's actual condition. They may feed their children when their children are anxious rather than hungry or comfort them when they are tired rather than anxious. Children who receive such parenting may grow up confused and unaware of their own internal needs, not knowing for themselves when they are hungry or full and unable to identify their own emotions.

Multiple eating disorders Mental health advocate Brittany Bergunder describes her decade-long struggle with eating disorders in her memoir *Safety in Numbers: From 56 to 221 Pounds*. Now recovered (middle photo), Brittany nearly died of anorexia nervosa at age 20 (left), then developed binge-eating disorder a few years later (right).

Splash News/Burgunder/Newscom

Because they cannot rely on internal signals, these children turn instead to external guides, such as their parents. They seem to be "model children," but they fail to develop genuine self-reliance and "experience themselves as not being in control of their behavior, needs, and impulses, as not owning their own bodies" (Bruch, 1973, p. 55). To overcome their sense of helplessness, they seek excessive control over their body size and shape and over their eating habits. Helen, an 18-year-old patient of Bruch's, described such needs and efforts:

> *You are afraid of not living up to what you think you are expected to do. You have one great fear, namely that of being ordinary, or average, or common—just not good enough. This peculiar dieting begins with such anxiety. You want to prove that you have control, that you can do it. The peculiar part of it is that it makes you feel good about yourself, makes you feel "I can accomplish something." It makes you feel "I can do something nobody else can do."*
>
> *(Bruch, 1978, p. 128)*

Clinical reports and research have provided some support for Bruch's theory. Clinicians have observed that many parents of teenagers with eating disorders do tend to define their children's needs rather than allow the children to define their own needs (MHN, 2023). When Bruch interviewed the mothers of 51 children with anorexia nervosa, many proudly recalled that they had always "anticipated" their young child's needs, never permitting the child to "feel hungry" (Bruch, 1973).

Research has also supported Bruch's belief that people with eating disorders perceive internal cues, including emotional cues, inaccurately (Friederich, Zipfel, & Wild, 2023; Ouellet-Courtois, Aardema, & O'Connor, 2021). When research participants with an eating disorder are anxious or upset, for example, many of them mistakenly think they are also hungry, and they respond as they might respond to hunger—by eating. And finally, studies support Bruch's argument that people with eating disorders rely excessively on the opinions, wishes, and views of others (Friederich et al., 2023; MHN, 2023) (see **MindTech**).

MINDTECH

Eating Disorders and Internet Toxicity

Mental health practitioners and researchers try to combat psychological disorders—in person, online, and in journals and books. Unfortunately, today there are also other—more negative—forces that run counter to the work of these professionals. Among the most common are Internet sites and social media communities whose goal is to promote behaviors that clinicians and most of society consider destructive. *Pro-anorexia sites and communities* are a prime example of this phenomenon.

It is estimated that there are hundreds of pro-anorexia (or *pro-Ana*) Internet sites, social media accounts, and online communities with names such as "Dying to Be Thin" and "Starving for Perfection" (Simons, Noteboom, & van Furth, 2023; Pruccoli et al., 2022). Many of these websites, groups, and influencers view anorexia nervosa as a lifestyle rather than a psychological disorder; others present themselves as nonjudgmental sites for people with anorexic symptoms. Either way, the sites and online communities are enormously popular. Comparable pro-bulimia sites are called *pro-Mia* sites.

Many visitors, members, and followers exchange tips on how they can starve themselves and disguise their weight loss from family, friends, and doctors (Simons et al., 2023; Mento et al., 2021; Gerrard, 2020). The platforms also offer support and feedback about starvation diets. Many offer mottoes, emotional messages, and photos and videos of extremely thin actresses and models as "thinspiration." Some encourage eating-related *challenges,* such as "waist challenges," in which users make videos vividly demonstrating their attempts to limit their eating and severely reduce their body size (Pruccoli et al., 2022).

Ting-Li Wang

Failure to filter High school student Naomi Sanders struggled with unhealthy eating habits for years, and so she tried to block pro–eating disorder posts from her TikTok feed. But her efforts were to no avail. Messages and videos promoting unsound dieting tips and extreme thinness continued to pop up multiple times each day.

As with the pro-suicide websites and online communities you read about in the chapter on suicide, the pro-Ana movement and its messages appear across the Internet and social media—on Web forums and chat groups and on video platforms, including TikTok, Instagram, Facebook, X, and YouTube. Many of the social media platforms try to seek out and delete pro-Ana material and groups by banning hashtags that glorify self-harm, and they have threatened to disable those accounts (Lai, 2022; Kersten, 2020). However, despite such efforts, the online communities—and their pro-Ana messages—continue to flourish as banned pro-Ana sites find alternative ways to reach users, for example, by creating new hashtags that reflect slight misspellings of the banned hashtags (SIRC, 2023; Pruccoli et al., 2022).

Research suggests that, on average, individuals who regularly contact these sites and communities experience a reduction in self-esteem and a rise in body dissatisfaction and depression, increase their dieting behavior, display more disordered eating, and attempt more self-harm as a result of their many visits (Simons et al., 2023; Pruccoli et al., 2022; Mento et al., 2021). This worries professionals and parents alike.

Many people are concerned that pro-Ana online material places vulnerable people at great risk, and they have called for greater efforts to ban such content (SIRC, 2023; Lai, 2022). Others argue, however, that despite their potential dangers, these online communities represent basic freedoms that should not be violated—freedom of speech, for example, and perhaps even the freedom to do oneself harm.

Cognitive-Behavioral Factors

If you examine Bruch's explanation of eating disorders closely, you'll note that it contains several *cognitive-behavioral* ideas. She held, for example, that people with eating disorders label their internal sensations and needs improperly, feel little control over their lives, and, in turn, want to have excessive levels of control over their body size, shape, and eating habits. According to cognitive-behavioral theorists, these deficiencies contribute to a broad cognitive distortion that lies at the center of disordered eating; namely, people with anorexia nervosa and bulimia nervosa judge themselves—often exclusively—based on their shape and weight and their ability to control them (Mitchell, 2023; Cooper & Mitchell, 2020). This "core pathology," say cognitive-behavioral theorists, contributes to all other aspects of the disorders, including the repeated efforts to lose weight and the preoccupation with shape, weight, and eating. As you read earlier in the chapter, research indicates that people with eating disorders do indeed display such cognitive deficiencies, although studies have not clarified that the deficiencies are necessarily the *cause* of eating disorders (Klein & Attia, 2023; Ouellet-Courtois et al., 2021).

Depression

Some theorists suggest that depressive disorders help set the stage for eating disorders (NIMH, 2023; Zanella & Lee, 2022). Their claim is supported by several kinds of evidence. First, many more people with an eating disorder qualify for a clinical diagnosis of major depressive disorder than do people in the general population. Second, people with depressive disorders have higher rates of eating disorders than do other people. Third, studies have revealed that when people with eating disorders experience depression-inducing circumstances, their disordered eating intensifies. For example, in the face of heightened social isolation during the initial wave of the Covid-19 pandemic, the symptoms of many people with eating disorders worsened considerably (Machado & Rodrigues, 2023; Gao, Bagheri, & Furuya-Kanamori, 2022). And fourth, as you will read, dysfunctions in the brain circuits of many people with eating disorders are similar to those of people with depressive disorders. Of course, although such findings suggest that depression may help cause eating disorders, other explanations are possible. For example, the pressure and pain of having an eating disorder may *cause* depression.

Body Dissatisfaction

People who evaluate their weight and shape negatively are experiencing *body dissatisfaction*. Around 83 percent of adolescent girls and adult women in the United States are dissatisfied with their bodies, compared with 74 percent of men and adolescent boys (Ipsos, 2022, 2018; Cass, Giltrap, & Talbot, 2020). Research suggests that people with high body dissatisfaction are more prone than others to develop eating disorders, depressive disorders, anxiety disorders, and body dysmorphic disorder (Guarda, 2023; Cass et al., 2020). Indeed, a number of clinical theorists believe that body dissatisfaction is the single most powerful contributor to dieting and the development of eating disorders (Canals & Arija Val, 2022; Zanella & Lee, 2022). Among the factors most closely tied to body dissatisfaction are perfectionism, unrealistic expectations, social media, societal bias, and family dynamics—factors that each help contribute to the onset of eating disorders, as you shall read shortly (Parra, Vandenbosch, & Mas-Manchón, 2023).

Biological Factors

Biological theorists suspect that certain genes may leave some people particularly susceptible to eating disorders (Arcelus & Witcomb, 2023; Watson, Davies, & Palmos, 2023). Consistent with this idea, relatives of people with eating disorders are up to six times more likely than other people to develop the disorders themselves. Moreover, if one identical twin has anorexia nervosa, the other twin also develops the disorder in

Dangerous professions Certain occupations place a premium on thinness, thus putting their professionals at particular risk for eating disorders. For example, former professional ballerina Anais Garcia (shown here) has described the unrealistic and relentless pressures she experienced in the professional ballet world, her dangerous obsession with thinness, and her near-fatal battle with anorexia nervosa. At her lowest, she weighed less than 80 pounds.

Andre Chung for The Washington Post via Getty Images

hypothalamus A brain structure that helps regulate various bodily functions, including eating and hunger.

lateral hypothalamus (LH) A brain region that produces hunger when activated.

ventromedial hypothalamus (VMH) A brain region that depresses hunger when activated.

weight set point The weight level that a person is predisposed to maintain, controlled in part by the hypothalamus.

as many as 70 percent of cases; in contrast, the rate for fraternal twins, who are genetically less similar, is 20 percent. Similarly, in the case of bulimia nervosa, identical twins display a concordance rate of 23 percent, compared with a rate of 9 percent among fraternal twins (Guarda, 2023; Yager, 2022; Kendler et al., 1995).

One factor that has captured the attention of biological investigators is the possible role of dysfunctional *brain circuits* in people with eating disorders (Prochazkova, Roubalova, & Papezova, 2023; Giacomini, Sadeghian, & Baldo, 2022). As you have read throughout this book, a *brain circuit* is a network of particular brain structures and their connecting pathways that work together, triggering each other into action to produce a distinct kind of behavioral, cognitive, or emotional reaction. Research suggests that each of the circuits linked to generalized anxiety, obsessive-compulsive, and depressive disorders also acts dysfunctionally to some degree in people with eating disorders (Frank et al., 2023; Prochazkova et al., 2023). For example, among individuals with eating disorders, the *insula* (a structure in the fear circuit) is unusually large and active, the *orbitofrontal cortex* (a structure in the obsessive-compulsive-related circuit) is uncommonly large, the *striatum* (another structure in the obsessive-compulsive-related circuit) is hyperactive, and the *prefrontal cortex* (a structure in the fear, obsessive-compulsive-related, *and* depression-related circuits) is unusually small. Similarly, the activity levels of serotonin, dopamine, and glutamate (key neurotransmitters in the fear, obsessive-compulsive-related, and depression-related circuits) are deviant in people with eating disorders (Guarda, 2023; Murray & Kaye, 2023). Given such findings, some researchers believe that dysfunctions across or within those various brain circuits collectively help cause eating disorders (Guarda, 2023; Prochazkova et al., 2023).

Finally, a number of biological theorists focus their explanation of eating disorders on one part of the brain in particular, the **hypothalamus,** a structure that regulates many bodily functions (Radin et al., 2024). The hypothalamus plays a central role in how the brain processes pleasurable and rewarding experiences, so it is not surprising that it helps control our appetite and govern our fluctuating desires for food intake. Researchers have located two separate areas in the hypothalamus that help control eating. One, the **lateral hypothalamus** (LH), produces hunger when it is activated. When the LH of a laboratory animal is stimulated electrically, the animal eats, even if it has been fed recently. In contrast, another area, the **ventromedial hypothalamus** (VMH), reduces hunger when it is activated. When the VMH is electrically stimulated, laboratory animals stop eating. These areas of the hypothalamus and related brain structures are apparently activated by chemicals from the brain and the body, depending on whether the person is eating or fasting.

Laboratory obesity Biological theorists believe that certain genes leave some individuals particularly susceptible to eating disorders. To help support this view, researchers have created mutant ("knockout") mice—mice without certain genes. The mouse on the left is missing a gene that helps produce obesity, and it is thin. In contrast, the mouse on the right, which retains that gene, is obese.

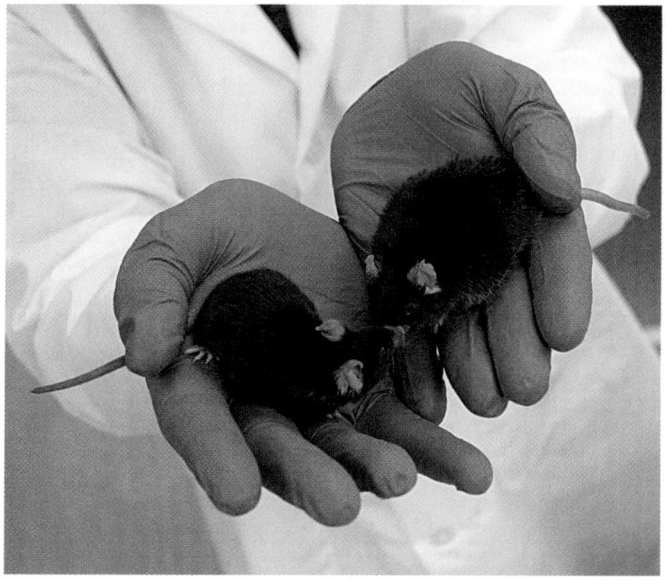

Some researchers believe that the hypothalamus, related brain structures, and certain hunger-related chemicals (such as a natural appetite suppressant called *GLP-1*) work together to provide a "weight thermostat" in the body, which is responsible for keeping an individual at a particular weight level called the **weight set point** (Ganipisetti & Bollimunta, 2023; Prochazkova et al., 2023). Genetic inheritance and early eating practices seem to determine each person's weight set point. According to the weight set point theory, when people diet and fall to a weight below their weight set point, their brain starts trying to restore the lost weight (Radin et al., 2024). Hypothalamic activity and related brain activity produce a preoccupation with food and a desire to binge. They also trigger bodily changes that make it harder to lose weight and easier to gain weight, however little is eaten. Once the brain and the body begin conspiring to raise weight in this way, dieters actually enter into a battle against themselves. Some people apparently manage to shut down the inner "thermostat" and control their eating almost completely. These people move toward restricting-type anorexia nervosa. For others, the battle spirals toward a binge-purge or binge-only pattern. Although the weight set point explanation has received considerable debate in the clinical field, it continues to be embraced by many theorists and practitioners.

Societal Pressures

Eating disorders are more common in Western countries than in other parts of the world. Thus, many theorists believe that Western standards of attractiveness—particularly female attractiveness—are partly responsible for the emergence of the disorders (Guarda, 2023; NEDA, 2022). Western standards of the ideal female shape, particularly for non-Hispanic White women, have slimmed steadily over the past 75 years, shifting from the "hourglass-ideal" of the 1950s (curvy figure) to the "thin-ideal" (very slender figure) and "fit-ideal" (slender figure but also toned) of the twenty-first century (McComb & Mills, 2022).

Because thinness is especially valued in the subcultures of performers, fashion models, and certain athletes, members of these groups are likely to be particularly concerned and/or criticized about their weight (Plateau & Arcelus, 2023). Correspondingly, studies have found that such individuals are indeed more prone than others to develop anorexia nervosa and bulimia nervosa (Kussman & Choo, 2024; ANAD, 2023). In fact, as noted at the beginning of this chapter, many famous young people from these fields have publicly acknowledged severely disordered eating patterns over the years. Surveys around the United States reveal that more than 9 percent of college students competing in women's athletics experience an eating disorder and that at least another 33 percent display eating behaviors that put them at risk for such disorders (NEDA, 2022; Levine, 2020).

Western society not only glorifies thinness but also creates a climate of prejudice against excess weight (Nelson & Olson, 2023; Abrams, 2022). Cruel jokes about people with excess weight and obesity are standard fare on the Web and television and in movies, books, and magazines (see ***Trending***). Research indicates that the prejudice against people with excess weight and obesity is deep-rooted. Prospective parents who were shown pictures of a chubby child and a medium-weight or thin child rated the former as less friendly, energetic, intelligent, and desirable than the latter. In another study, preschool children who were given a choice between a chubby rag doll and a thin rag doll chose the thin one, although they could not say why. Thus, it is small wonder that as many as 42 percent of 7-year-olds want to be thinner, 81 percent of 10-year-olds express concern about their weight and becoming overweight, and the number of children under 12 years who develop a full eating disorder is growing (ANAD, 2023; NEDA, 2022; Ekern, 2020).

Consistent with these trends, surveys of both adolescents and young adults have directly tied eating disorders and body dissatisfaction to social media use, Internet activity, and television viewing (Parra et al., 2023; McComb & Mills, 2022; NEDA, 2022). The surveys have found that the respondents who spent more time on social media were more likely to display eating disorders, have negative body image, eat in dysfunctional ways, and want to diet (see **Figure 9-2**). Those who spent more time on fashion and music

Nickolay Lamm of MyDeals.com/REX/Shutterstock

"Normal Barbie" For years, the ultra-slim measurements of the Barbie doll introduced young children to an unattainable ideal. Hoping to show instead that "average is beautiful," artist Nickolay Lamm has designed a Normal Barbie (right), using the measurements that health officials advocate for 19-year-old women. Normal Barbie turns out to be shorter, curvier, and bustier than the classic doll. In this spirit, the live-action film *Barbie* (2023) reenvisioned the classic doll as living in an inclusive "Barbieland" with dozens of fellow Barbies representing a broad and diverse range of body shapes and sizes.

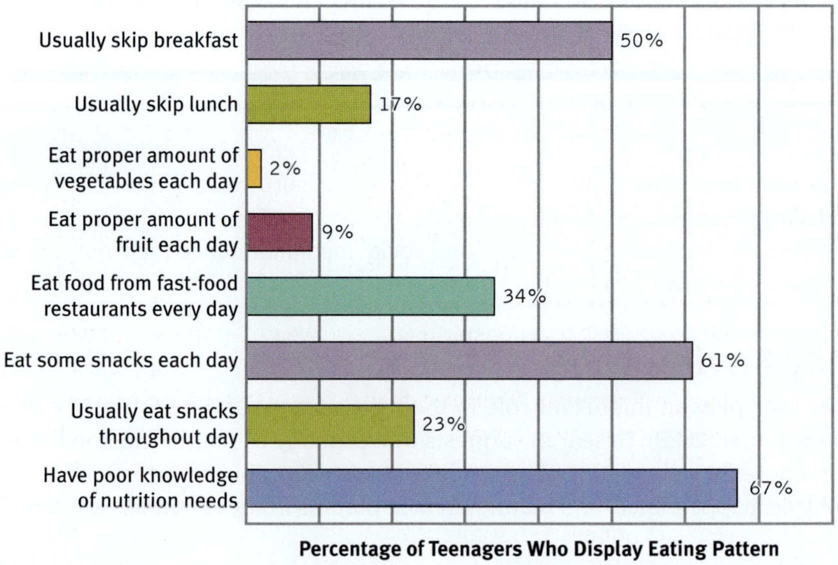

FIGURE 9-2

What Does Teenage Eating Look Like?

Teenage eating habits are not particularly healthful in general and are, in fact, poor for many teens, according to research. In fact, the majority of adolescents fail to meet dietary recommendations for nutrient intake. (Information from: CDC, 2023, 2020; Demory-Luce, 2023; Lehman, 2016; Johnson, 2011; Sebastian, Goldman, & Enns, 2010.)

...TRENDING

Shame on Body Shamers

"What happened to . . . ? Did she eat all her backup singers?" Thousands of cruel tweets like this one about the weight of a popular singer appear on social media every day. They are examples of *body shaming*, the practice of criticizing people publicly for being overweight or, less frequently, underweight.

Body shaming has actually been around since the mid-nineteenth century (Cox, 2022; Herman, 2015). What is new is the current volume and reach of this practice. Our world of tweets, social media, anonymous comment boards, provocative websites, opinionated talk shows, and the like has provided numerous platforms for cruel comments, including ones about people's appearance (ANAD, 2023; Cox, 2022).

Of course, the body shaming of celebrities receives the most attention, but comments of that kind have opened the door to an onslaught of body shaming in smaller circles and in everyday life. Surveys suggest that 60 percent or more of teenagers are body shamed in one way or another (Cox, 2022; Miller, 2016).

Body shaming can bring great personal pain to the targets of such comments (ANAD, 2023; Spratt, 2023). In addition, the practice appears to be contributing, along with other factors, to an increase in body dissatisfaction and disordered eating throughout our society (ANAD, 2023; MacPherson 2022).

The good news is that a countertrend is taking place across society. There is growing concern and anger by millions of people, including clinicians and educators, over the harmful impact of these communications, along with a determination to fight back. In a similar vein, hundreds of influential celebrities are now calling out the perpetrators.

Timothy A. Clary/AFP/Getty Images

Responding to shamers After Lady Gaga's halftime performance at the 2017 Super Bowl (above), many viewers took to social media to criticize her for daring to display the "flab" on her stomach. The superstar responded, "I'm proud of my body and you should be proud of yours too."

Over the past few years, for example, in response to negative tweets or posts about their bodies, celebrities have posted self-affirming messages such as the following:

"It's important for women and men to see and appreciate the beauty in their natural bodies."

—Singer Beyoncé Knowles

"I am not a woman whose self-worth comes from her chest size."

—Actress Kristen Bell

"Just because I am a male doesn't mean I'm impervious to your whispers. Body shaming hurts."

—Actor Chris Pratt

"I'm healthy and happy, and if you're hating on my weight, you obviously aren't."

— Singer Demi Lovato

"People . . . body shame me. . . . But at the end of the day I'm good enough for me."

—Model Ashley Graham

These are just a small fraction of the countershaming messages being posted by celebrities every day. Hopefully, the self-acceptance, independent thinking, and body satisfaction contained in such responses will come to influence readers more than the body-shaming messages do.

websites and those who viewed more gossip- and leisure-related television programs showed similar tendencies. And in one study, 69 percent of young girls said that the pictures of women they see in magazines and social media influence their notions of ideal body shape and make them want to lose weight.

Family Environment

Families may play an important role in the development and maintenance of eating disorders (Yager, 2022). Research suggests that as many as half of the families of people with anorexia nervosa or bulimia nervosa have a long history of emphasizing thinness, physical appearance, and dieting. In fact, parents in these families are more likely to diet themselves and to be generally perfectionistic and success-driven than are the parents in other families (MHN, 2023; NEDA, 2022). Camila, an 18-year-old, describes her view of the roots of her eating disorder:

I've always been aware of my mother being on one diet or another. At dinner, even though she cooked for us, she'd eat something different from the rest of us. Sometimes just a little bit of salad. Sometimes a tiny piece of chicken and brown rice. She always looked sad and made comments like, "I wish I could eat the lasagna you're eating. But this is what I need to eat." She signed up for workout classes and would go a few times—she looked cute in her leggings! Then I might not hear about it again until the next year, when she'd start again. I didn't even think of her as big—I always thought she was beautiful.

I was around 11 when she first said, laughing, "You little butterball, you're starting to look like me." I should have been flattered, but she didn't mean it positively. "You know, you could look just like Zoe Saldana if you ate less!" By the time I was 15, she had me going to exercise classes with her. One day, she just told me we were going. Then I started getting served the salad for dinner, and if I ever ate a cookie, she'd say to me, "I hope that's the only one of the day, young lady!"

Problematic interactions and forms of communication within a family may also set the stage for an eating disorder (Van Malderen et al., 2023; Zanella & Lee, 2022). Family systems theorists argue that the families of people who develop eating disorders are often dysfunctional to begin with and that the eating disorder of one member is a reflection of the larger problem. Influential family theorist Salvador Minuchin, for example, believed that an **enmeshed family pattern** often leads to eating disorders (MHN, 2023; Minuchin, 2020).

enmeshed family pattern A family system in which members are overinvolved with each other's affairs and overly concerned about each other's welfare.

In an enmeshed system, family members are overinvolved in each other's affairs and overconcerned with the details of each other's lives. On the positive side, enmeshed families can be affectionate and loyal. On the negative side, they can be clingy and foster dependency. Parents are too involved in the lives of their children, allowing little room for individuality and independence. Minuchin argued that adolescence poses a special problem for these families. The teenager's healthy push for independence threatens the family's apparent harmony and closeness. In response, the family may subtly force the child to take on a "sick" role—to develop an eating disorder or some other illness. The child's disorder enables the family to maintain its appearance of harmony. Sick children need their family, and family members can rally to protect them. Although some studies have supported such family systems explanations (MHN, 2023; Van Malderen et al., 2023; Zanella & Lee, 2022), they have failed to show that particular family patterns consistently set the stage for the development of eating disorders.

of NOTE ...

Family Teasing

Adolescents teased about their weight by family members are twice as likely as nonteased teens to become overweight within five years and are 1.5 times more likely to become binge eaters and use extreme weight control measures (Dahill et al., 2023, 2021; Pearlman et al., 2020; Neumark-Sztainer et al., 2007).

SUMMING UP

Explanations for Eating Disorders

Most theorists now use a multidimensional risk perspective to explain eating disorders and to identify several key contributing factors. Principal among these are ego deficiencies; cognitive factors; depression; body dissatisfaction; biological factors such as dysfunctional brain circuits, problematic activity of the hypothalamus, and disturbances of the body's weight set point; society's emphasis on thinness and bias against obesity; and family environment.

Chris Moore/Catwalking/Getty Images

Embracing diversity? The Western ideal of extreme thinness remains the leading standard for fashion models regardless of their nationality or cultural background. Psychologists worry that the success of supermodels such as Ethiopia's Liya Kebede (above) and Sudan's Alek Wek may contribute to thinner body ideals and more eating disorders in their African countries.

The Multicultural Picture

EARLIER IN THIS CHAPTER, you read that the prevalence of eating disorders may be particularly high among women and girls (both cisgender and transgender); nonbinary people; gay, lesbian, and bisexual people; and people of color. These multicultural trends will be examined in more detail in the following sections.

Racial and Ethnic Findings

Prior to the twenty-first century, studies indicated that the eating behaviors, body satisfaction, and weight goals of people of color in the United States, particularly young women, were considerably healthier than those of non-Hispanic White people (Lovejoy, 2001; Cash & Henry, 1995). However, research conducted over the past two decades suggests that people of color, again young women in particular, now express body dissatisfaction to the same degree as young non-Hispanic White American people, are even *more* likely to engage in disordered eating behaviors (particularly binge eating and purging), and may have a higher overall prevalence of eating disorders (Mitchison et al., 2023; NEDA, 2022). These relatively new trends are particularly prominent in certain racial and ethnic groups. Today's Black teenagers, for example, seem to be as much as 50 percent more likely than non-Hispanic White teenagers to binge eat, and in several studies, Asian American college students are found to have higher rates of restrictive eating and of anorexia nervosa than non-Hispanic White college students (ANAD, 2023; NEDA, 2022; Volpe, 2022).

Theorists have offered two explanations for the rise in disordered eating and eating disorders among people of color. One explanation suggests that levels of stress and disappointment have intensified significantly in the past two decades in communities of color, especially for many young people of color who are more activist and less accepting of racial and cultural inequities and discrimination than older people of color.

Sean Zanni/Getty Images

A precious shift Among today's most popular models is Precious Lee, seen here walking an outdoor runway at the 2022 Vogue World fashion show and fair in New York City. Lee is one of several young "curve models" expanding the shape of mainstream fashion who have soared to superstar status in recent years—perhaps indicating a shift away from the fashion industry's excessively slim standards. An activist for body shape diversity, Lee says that her goal is to "transform imagery as a whole [and] in fashion."

As you read earlier, stress and depression are key contributors to the onset and maintenance of disordered eating and eating disorders.

A second explanation for the shift points to possible *acculturation* in the realm of body ideals (Warren & Akoury, 2020; Ford, 2000). That is, given their repeated exposure to non-Hispanic White body ideals in social media, fashion magazines, and the like, it is possible that people of color (particularly women and girls) have been increasingly adopting the body size and shape standards of non-Hispanic White people. One study compared Black American women at a predominantly non-Hispanic White American university with those at a predominantly Black American university. Those at the former school had significantly higher depression and more eating challenges.

Why, in past years, were the eating behaviors and body satisfaction of people of color healthier than those of non-Hispanic White people in the United States, and why has that changed?

Clinical professionals have been slow to recognize these changing racial and ethnic trends. In one study, for example, clinicians were presented with identical case studies in which women of different races and ethnicities displayed disordered eating symptoms. When the person in the case study was Black or Hispanic as opposed to non-Hispanic White, the clinicians were less likely to assess the symptoms as problematic and less likely to recommend treatment (ANAD, 2023; NEDA, 2022). Given such research, it is small wonder that in the United States, people of color are less likely to receive treatment for their eating disorders than non-Hispanic White people.

Gender Findings

There are two kinds of gender trends that characterize eating disorders. One is a significant difference in the rate of these disorders for cisgender people versus the rate for transgender and nonbinary people. The other is the very high ratio of females to males with eating disorders, a ratio that holds across cisgender and transgender populations and across most racial and ethnic populations.

Regarding the first gender trend, people who are transgender or nonbinary have a higher prevalence of eating disorders and disordered eating habits than do cisgender people. Studies indicate that at least 9 percent of transgender or nonbinary people have displayed an eating disorder in the past year, compared to 2 percent of cisgender people (ANAD, 2023; Riddle & Safer, 2022). Similarly, transgender or nonbinary people, particularly teenagers, are significantly more likely to perform unhealthy behaviors to control their weight, including frequent fasting, diet pill use, steroid use, laxative use, and purging (Volpe, 2022; Parker & Harriger, 2020). Research has linked these higher rates to the heightened bullying and victimization experienced by these individuals, their particularly high degree of body dissatisfaction and drive for thinness, and their expectations that dietary restrictions may help suppress undesired secondary sex characteristics, such as large muscles for some or increased body fat and curves for others (ANAD, 2023; Riddle & Safer, 2022; Simone et al., 2022).

Frazer Harrison/Getty Images

Shedding weight stigma 2019 was a big year for singer and songwriter Sam Smith: the performer revealed that they are nonbinary and also opened up about years of struggle with extreme body dissatisfaction and disordered eating. Smith, shown here in 2023 winning a Grammy, has now become much more accepting of their body and is less preoccupied with body appearance and weight. The rate of eating disorders is higher for nonbinary people than cisgender people, a difference attributed to heightened stress, stigmatization, and other factors.

Regarding the second gender trend, research has consistently found much higher rates of eating disorders for women and girls than for men and boys, a difference that holds across cisgender and transgender populations and most racial and ethnic groups. Specifically, men and boys account for only 25 percent of all people with reported anorexia nervosa, 17 percent of those with bulimia nervosa, and 33 percent of individuals with binge-eating disorder (NIMH, 2023; NEDA, 2022). A key reason for this striking gender difference appears to be Western society's double standard for attractiveness. Our society's emphasis on a thin appearance is clearly aimed at women much more than men, and some theorists believe that this difference has made women much more inclined to diet and more prone to eating disorders.

Another reason for the male/female rate difference may be the different methods of weight loss favored by men and women. According to some studies, men are more likely to use exercise to lose weight, whereas women more often diet (NEDA, 2022; Thackray et al., 2016). And, as you have read, dieting often helps trigger the onset of eating disorders.

BEI/REX/Shutterstock

Everett Collection, Inc.

Not for women only A growing number of today's men are developing eating disorders. Some of them aspire to a very lean body shape and develop anorexia nervosa or bulimia nervosa. Singer Zayn Malik (left) has acknowledged falling into this pattern when he was a member of the boy band One Direction. Others want the muscular look displayed by body builders and may develop a disorder called muscle dysmorphia. Actor Michael B. Jordan (right) revealed that he temporarily developed "slight body dysmorphia" while training to build chiseled muscle mass for his role as boxer Adonis Creed in the film *Creed III*.

Why do some men develop anorexia nervosa or bulimia nervosa? For many men, body image appears to be the key factor, just as it is for so many women (Linardon et al., 2020). Many men with these disorders state that they were initially seeking to achieve a "lean, toned, thin" shape similar to the ideal female body rather than the muscular, broad-shouldered shape of society's ideal male body. In other cases of male eating disorders, studies suggest that initially, the persons were not addressing body image concerns but rather were trying to meet the requirements and pressures of a job or sport (NEDA, 2022; Cottrell & Williams, 2016).

Why do you think that the prevalence of eating disorders among men has been on the increase in recent years?

On a related matter, it is worth noting that a growing number of young men seem to be ensnared in a different pattern of dysfunctional eating in which they consider themselves too thin and perform *muscularity-oriented disordered eating behaviors*, behaviors marked by excessive eating and related efforts to gain weight and "bulk up" (Brown & Keel, 2023; Cooper et al., 2020). This pattern is particularly common among young Black American men. In some cases, the pattern escalates into a disorder called *muscle dysmorphia*, or *reverse anorexia nervosa*, in which persons who are actually quite muscular perceive themselves as scrawny and small and so continue to strive for a "perfect" body through excessive weight lifting, abuse of steroids, or other excessive measures.

Sexual Orientation Findings

The rates of eating disorders for people who are gay, lesbian, or bisexual appear to be higher than or at least as high as the rates for heterosexual people. Research findings are particularly clear and consistent for gay cisgender men, whose rate of eating disorders is at least seven times the rate for heterosexual cisgender men (Arcelus & Witcomb, 2023; Hallward et al., 2022). Indeed, as many as 42 percent of all cisgender men with eating disorders identify as gay (NEDA, 2022). Theorists and researchers have explained this exceptionally high prevalence for gay cisgender men by pointing to their high levels of body dissatisfaction, body image anxiety, and drives for thinness; their heightened concerns about attractiveness and appearance; and the stress and discrimination that pervade their lives (Knight et al., 2022; Shepherd et al., 2022).

Some studies similarly suggest that the rate of eating disorders for lesbian cisgender women is higher than the rate for heterosexual cisgender women; however, other studies suggest that the rate of eating disorders is about the same in both populations (NEDA, 2022; Parker & Harriger, 2020). Furthermore, although bisexuality and eating disorders is a relatively new area of study, early indications are that the prevalence of eating disorders for bisexual people is equal to or higher than the rate for their heterosexual peers (Knight et al., 2022).

Before we leave this discussion of multicultural factors and eating disorders, it is important to note the relationships between *intersectionality* and the disorders. As you read earlier in the textbook, multiple factors, such as race, ethnicity, gender, sexual orientation, and economic means, intersect in a given person to produce unique experiences and psychological effects. Correspondingly, researchers have repeatedly found intersectional effects in the development of eating disorders (Burke et al., 2022; Parker & Harriger, 2020). For example, while being Black *or* transgender *or* gay *or* financially disadvantaged may heighten one's risk of developing an eating disorder, researchers have found that being Black, transgender, gay, *and* financially disadvantaged increases the risk still more. The notion and impact of intersectionality offer a sobering reminder of the special vulnerability many people in our society have to eating disorders.

of NOTE ...

The Pandemic and Eating Disorders

During the first year of the Covid-19 pandemic, the number of eating disorders, especially among teenagers, increased at least 15 percent, and the number of eating disorder hospitalizations increased at least 48 percent (Rabayda & Hoover, 2023; Meier, van Hoeken, & Hoek, 2022; Volpe, 2022). LGBTQ+ individuals living in non-affirming households experienced particularly high increases in eating disorders (Schneider et al., 2023).

SUMMING UP

The Multicultural Picture

The rate of eating disorders for people of color is at least as high as and sometimes higher than the rate for non-Hispanic White people. Two explanations for the rise in eating disorders among people of color point to increases in their levels of stress and in their acculturation of White body ideals. The rate of eating disorders for transgender and nonbinary people is higher than that for cisgender people. One reason for this difference seems to be the heightened bullying and victimization experienced by transgender and nonbinary people. The rate of eating disorders for women is substantially higher than the rate for men across cisgender and transgender populations and most racial and ethnic populations. One reason for this difference is Western society's emphasis on thinness for women in particular. The rate of eating disorders for gay men is consistently higher than that for heterosexual men, a difference sometimes attributed to high levels of body dissatisfaction and drives for thinness among gay men.

How Are Eating Disorders Treated?

TODAY'S TREATMENTS FOR eating disorders have two goals. The first is to correct the dangerous eating pattern as quickly as possible. The second is to address the broader psychological and situational factors that have led to and maintain the eating problem (Van Huysse & Luzier, 2023). Family and friends can also play an important role in helping to overcome the disorder.

Treatments for Anorexia Nervosa

Around one-third of those with anorexia nervosa seek and receive treatment (NIMH, 2023). The immediate aims of treatment for anorexia nervosa are to help people regain their lost weight, recover from malnourishment, and eat healthily again (McElroy et al., 2020). Therapists must then help them to make psychological and perhaps family changes to lock in those gains.

Mauro Fermariello/Science Source

Nutrition plus education A woman receives food counseling and education while eating a meal at an eating disorders treatment clinic. Although it is not always a part of treatment, she is also being fed nutrients through a tube to help increase her weight.

How Are Proper Weight and Healthful Eating Restored?

A variety of treatment methods are used to help patients with anorexia nervosa gain weight quickly and return to health within weeks, a phase of treatment called *nutritional rehabilitation* (Steinglass, 2023; SAHM, 2022). In the past, treatment almost always took place in a hospital, but now it is often offered in day hospitals or outpatient settings.

In life-threatening cases, clinicians may need to force *tube and intravenous feedings* on a patient who refuses to eat (Marchili et al., 2023; Mitchell & Peterson, 2020). Unfortunately, this use of force may cause the client to distrust the treatment team. In contrast, clinicians using behavioral weight-restoration approaches offer social and other *rewards* whenever patients eat properly or gain weight and offer no rewards when they eat improperly or fail to gain weight.

Perhaps the most popular nutritional rehabilitation approach is a combination of supportive nursing care, nutritional counseling, and a relatively high-calorie diet. Here nurses and other staff members start the patient's diet at 1,500 calories per day, then gradually increase the caloric intake over the course of several weeks (Steinglass, 2023). The nurses educate patients about the program, track their progress, provide encouragement, and help them appreciate that their weight gain is under control and will not lead to obesity. In some programs, the nurses also use **motivational interviewing,** an intervention that uses a mixture of empathy and inquiring review to help motivate clients to recognize they have a serious eating problem and commit to making constructive choices and behavior changes (Miller & Rollnick, 2023; Yager, 2022). Studies find that patients in nutritional rehabilitation programs usually gain the necessary weight over 8 to 12 weeks.

How Are Lasting Changes Achieved?

Most people in treatment for anorexia nervosa gain weight successfully in the short term, but clinical researchers have found that those individuals must overcome their underlying psychological problems in order to create lasting improvement. Therapists typically use a combination of education, psychotherapy, and family therapy to reach this broader goal (Lock et al., 2024; Steinberg et al., 2023). Psychotropic drugs, particularly antipsychotic drugs, are sometimes used when patients do not respond to those other forms of treatments (Mutwalli et al., 2023). Studies suggest that such medications may help with weight gain but typically not with an individual's anorexia-related cognitive and emotional symptoms (McElroy et al., 2020).

COGNITIVE-BEHAVIORAL THERAPY

A combination of cognitive and behavioral interventions are included in most treatment programs for anorexia nervosa. These techniques are designed to help clients appreciate and change the behaviors and thought processes that keep their restrictive eating going (Dalle Grave & Pike, 2023; Fitzsimmons-Craft & Pike, 2022). On the behavioral side, clients are typically required to monitor (by written diaries or smartphone apps) their feelings, hunger levels, and food intake and the ties between these variables. On the cognitive side, they are taught to identify their "core pathology"—the deep-seated belief that they should in fact be judged by their shape and weight and by their ability to control these physical characteristics. The clients may also be taught alternative ways of coping with stress and of solving problems.

Cognitive-behavioral therapists are particularly careful to help patients with anorexia nervosa recognize their need for independence and teach them more appropriate ways

motivational interviewing A treatment that uses empathy and inquiring review to help motivate clients to recognize they have a serious psychological problem and commit to making constructive choices and behavior changes.

Carl De Souza/AFP via Getty Images

Jonathan Ferrey/Getty Images

"I changed my body for my sport" Two of U.S. track and field's most acclaimed stars several years ago, Lauren Fleshman (left) and Mary Cain (right), have recently revealed the patterns of disordered eating, unhealthy weight loss, and excessive training that accompanied their pursuit of athletic success. Fleshman also cited bodily damage, oppressive coaching demands, and body shaming as conditions female athletes are often subjected to in her article "I Changed My Body for My Sport. No Girl Should."

to exercise control (Dalle Grave & Pike, 2023; Fitzsimmons-Craft & Pike, 2022). The therapists may also teach them to better identify and trust their internal sensations and feelings. Finally, cognitive-behavioral therapists seek to help clients with anorexia nervosa change their attitudes about eating and weight (see **Table 9-5**). The therapists may guide the clients to identify, challenge, and change maladaptive assumptions, such as "I must always be perfect" or "My weight and shape determine my value." They may also educate the clients about the body distortions that are typical of anorexia nervosa and help them recognize that their assessments of their own size are incorrect (Dalle Grave & Pike, 2023; Artoni et al., 2021).

According to research, cognitive-behavioral techniques are often effective in cases of anorexia nervosa (Fitzsimmons-Craft & Pike, 2022). The treatment is most successful at preventing relapses when it continues for at least a year beyond a patient's recovery—a *maintenance,* or *preventive,* therapy strategy that you read about in the chapter on

TABLE 9-5

Sample Items from the Eating Disorder Inventory

For each item, decide if the item is true about you ALWAYS (A), USUALLY (U), OFTEN (O), SOMETIMES (S), RARELY (R), or NEVER (N). Circle the letter that corresponds to your rating.

A	U	O	S	R	N	I eat when I am upset.
A	U	O	S	R	N	I stuff myself with food.
A	U	O	S	R	N	I think about dieting.
A	U	O	S	R	N	I think that my thighs are too large.
A	U	O	S	R	N	I feel extremely guilty after overeating.
A	U	O	S	R	N	I am terrified of gaining weight.
A	U	O	S	R	N	I get confused as to whether or not I am hungry.
A	U	O	S	R	N	I have the thought of trying to vomit in order to lose weight.
A	U	O	S	R	N	I think my buttocks are too large.
A	U	O	S	R	N	I eat or drink in secrecy.

Information from: Cooper & Mitchell, 2020; Clausen et al., 2011; Garner, 2005; Garner, Olmsted, & Polivy, 2004, 1991, 1984.

Reuters/Stefano Rellandini

The beginning of a movement An early effort at responsible advertising regarding body shape occurred back in 2007 when the Nolita clothing brand launched an ad campaign against excessive thinness. One of the brand's billboards featured an emaciated naked woman appearing beneath the words "No Anorexia." The billboard model Isabelle Caro later died of complications from anorexia nervosa.

depressive disorders. At the same time, studies suggest that the cognitive-behavioral approach brings the best results when it is supplemented by other approaches. In particular, family therapy is often included in treatment.

CHANGING FAMILY INTERACTIONS Family therapy can be a valuable part of treatment for anorexia nervosa, particularly for children and adolescents with the disorder (Lock et al., 2024; Steinberg et al., 2023). As in other family therapy situations, the therapist meets with the family as a whole, points out troublesome family patterns, and helps the members make appropriate changes. In particular, family therapists may try to help the persons with anorexia nervosa separate their own feelings and needs from those of other family members. Although the role of family in the development of anorexia nervosa is not yet clear, research strongly suggests that family therapy (or at least parent counseling) can be helpful in the treatment of this disorder, (Gorrell, Simic, & Le Grange, 2023; Godart et al., 2022), as it ultimately was in the following case:

Leeanne *[mother]*:	*I blame myself for not seeing what was going on. It's so different these days from when I was younger. Back then, Black women were expected to be curvy. That's what the men wanted. I always told Janelle she was curvy as a compliment. It's my fault.*
Therapist:	*I haven't heard Janelle blame you once during our sessions. Janelle, do you think this is your mother's fault?*
Janelle *[patient]*	*It's not your fault, Mama, but you do mention my curves a lot. I can remember times when someone I liked went out with another girl, and you'd say, "Well, she is so skinny and pretty. It's not fair." And you'd hug me and act like what you said would make me feel better. A couple of times you talked about ways I might lose weight. But it's not you, it's a lot of things. Mainly me.*
Therapist:	*Leeanne, do you think it's true that only very thin women can be attractive?*
Leeanne (*after pause*):	*No. Heck, I really have no idea what men want, to tell the truth! (laughs) I see lots of good-looking men with really curvy women. What do I know?*
Therapist:	*Janelle and Grace, I'd like to ask you, what would you like to hear from your mother when you have a problem, like with relationships or something?*
Grace *[sister]*:	*Well, really, I'd love for you to just listen. Oh, and once in a while telling me it will be all right would be nice.*
Janelle:	*Me too, Mama. You really are a great listener and that's great, but you tend to jump in and start trying to talk me through solving my problems. Sometimes I just want to let you know I'm upset and have you tell me that I'm not crazy to be upset.*

What Is the Aftermath of Anorexia Nervosa?

The average lifetime duration of anorexia nervosa is six years (Yager, 2022). The use of combined treatment approaches, with cognitive-behavioral therapy typically at the center, has greatly improved the outlook for people with this disorder, although the road to recovery can be difficult. The course and outcome of this disorder vary from person to person, but researchers have noted certain trends.

On the positive side, as you read earlier, weight is often quickly restored once treatment for the disorder begins, and treatment gains may continue for years. As many as 75 percent of patients continue to show improvement—either full or partial—when interviewed several years or more after their initial recovery (Klein & Attia, 2023; Wentz, 2023).

Another positive note is that most of the medical complications from anorexia nervosa improve when individuals regain their weight (Mehler, 2022). Also encouraging is that the death rate from anorexia nervosa seems to be falling (Wentz, 2023). Earlier diagnosis and safer and faster weight-restoration techniques may account for this trend.

On the negative side, at least 20 percent of people with anorexia nervosa remain seriously troubled for years (Klein & Attia, 2023; Wentz, 2023). Furthermore, recovery, when it does occur, is not always permanent. At least one-third of recovered patients have recurrences of anorexic behavior, usually triggered by new stresses, such as marriage, pregnancy, or a major relocation (Steinglass, 2023). Even years later, many who have recovered continue to express concerns about their weight and appearance (Klein & Attia, 2023). Some still restrict their diets to a degree or hold distorted ideas about food, eating, and weight.

About half of those who have overcome anorexia nervosa continue to have certain psychological problems—particularly depression, obsessiveness, and social anxiety—years after treatment. Such problems are particularly common in those who had not reached a fully healthy weight by the end of treatment (Steinglass, 2023; Stewart et al., 2022).

The more weight persons have lost and the more time that passes before they enter treatment, the poorer the recovery rate (Klein & Attia, 2023; Zerwas et al., 2013). People who had psychological problems before the onset of the disorder tend to have a poorer recovery rate than those without such a history. People whose family or interpersonal relationships are troubled have less positive treatment outcomes. Younger individuals seem to have a better recovery rate than older ones.

Jeff Kravitz/Getty Images

A difficult trip back When actress and model Zoe Kravitz agreed to play an anorexic woman in the movie *The Road Within*, she believed her past history with eating disorders would be an asset. However, Kravitz found that dieting down to 90 pounds for the movie "triggered some old stuff," and she had difficulty calling an end to the new weight loss (Takeda, 2015).

Treatments for Bulimia Nervosa

Around 43 percent of those with bulimia nervosa seek and receive treatment (NIMH, 2023). Treatment programs for the disorder are often offered in eating disorder clinics. Such programs offer (1) nutritional rehabilitation, which, for bulimia nervosa, means helping clients eliminate their binge-purge patterns and establish healthful eating habits, and (2) a combination of therapies aimed at eliminating the underlying causes of bulimic patterns (Crow, 2023; Dodd, Wonderlich, & Peterson, 2023). The programs emphasize education as much as therapy.

Cognitive-Behavioral Therapy

When treating clients with bulimia nervosa, cognitive-behavioral therapists employ many of the same techniques that they use to help treat people with anorexia nervosa (Dalle Grave & Pike, 2023). However, they tailor the techniques to the unique features of bulimia (for example, bingeing and purging) and to the specific beliefs at work in bulimia nervosa.

The therapists often instruct clients with bulimia nervosa to keep diaries of their eating behavior, the changes in their sensations of hunger and fullness, and the ebb and flow of other feelings (Mitchell, 2023; Parker, Clark, & Juarascio, 2023). This helps the clients observe their eating patterns more objectively and recognize the emotions and situations that trigger their desire to binge. People have found smartphone apps particularly useful for keeping track of such changes throughout the day.

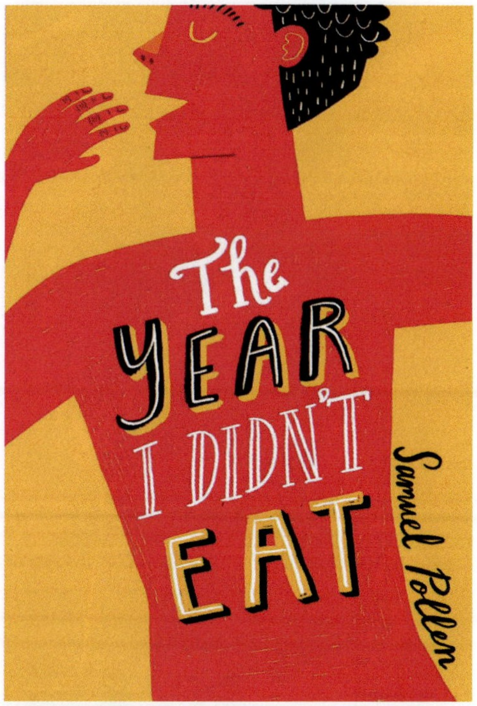

Artful presentations Eating disorders have been featured in many novels, films, videos, television dramas, and other forms of art. One recent offering is the novel *The Year I Didn't Eat*, about the emotional impact an eating disorder has on the life of a struggling 14-year-old boy.

Cognitive-behavioral therapists may also use the behavioral technique of *exposure and response prevention* to help break the binge-purge cycle. As you read earlier in the textbook, this approach consists of exposing people to situations that would ordinarily raise anxiety and then preventing them from performing their usual compulsive responses until they learn that the situations are actually harmless and their compulsive acts are unnecessary. For bulimia nervosa, the therapists require clients to eat particular kinds and amounts of food and then prevent them from vomiting to show that eating can be a harmless and even constructive activity that needs no undoing (Butler & Heimberg, 2023; Mitchell, 2023). Typically, the therapist sits with the client while the client eats the forbidden foods and stays until the urge to purge has passed. Studies find that this treatment often helps reduce eating-related anxieties, bingeing, and vomiting.

Beyond such behavioral techniques, a primary focus of cognitive-behavioral therapists is to help clients with bulimia nervosa recognize and change their maladaptive attitudes toward food, eating, weight, and shape. The therapists typically teach the clients to identify and challenge the negative thoughts that regularly precede their urge to binge—"I have no self-control," "I might as well give up," "I look fat." They may also guide clients to recognize, question, and eventually change their perfectionistic standards, sense of helplessness, and low self-concept. Cognitive-behavioral approaches help as many as 75 percent of patients stop or reduce bingeing and purging (Dalle Grave & Pike, 2023; Lebow et al., 2023; Parker et al., 2023).

Other Forms of Psychotherapy

Because of its effectiveness in cases of bulimia nervosa, cognitive-behavioral therapy is often tried first, before other therapies are considered. If clients do not respond to it, other approaches with promising but less impressive track records may then be tried (Crow, 2023; Castellini et al., 2022). A common alternative is *interpersonal psychotherapy*, the treatment that is used to help improve interpersonal functioning. *Psychodynamic therapy* has also been used in cases of bulimia nervosa, but relatively few research studies have tested and supported its effectiveness (Friederich et al., 2023). The various forms of psychotherapy—cognitive-behavioral, interpersonal, and psychodynamic—are often supplemented by *family therapy* (Lock et al., 2024; Gorrell et al., 2023).

Cognitive-behavioral, interpersonal, and psychodynamic therapy may each be offered in either an individual or a group therapy format. Group formats, including self-help groups, give clients with bulimia nervosa an opportunity to share their concerns and experiences with one another. Group members learn that their disorder is not unique or shameful, and they receive support from one another, along with honest feedback and insights. In the group, they can also work directly on underlying fears of displeasing others or being criticized. Research suggests that group formats are often as helpful as individual treatments for people with bulimia nervosa (Mitchell, 2023; AGPA, 2022).

Antidepressant Medications

During the past 20 years, antidepressant drugs have been used to help treat bulimia nervosa. In contrast to people with anorexia nervosa, those with bulimia nervosa are often helped considerably by these drugs, experiencing reductions in both their binges and their vomiting (Mutwalli et al., 2023; Monteleone et al., 2022). Studies suggest that antidepressants are less effective than psychotherapy, particularly cognitive-behavioral therapy, but that a combination of the two is more effective than either form of treatment alone (Crow, 2023).

of NOTE ...

Fashion Downsizing

Over the past 20 years, the dress size of the average fashion model has decreased almost 30 percent, from size 5.2 to 3.7, although the height of the average model has remained the same during that period (Maymone et al., 2020).

What Is the Aftermath of Bulimia Nervosa?

The average lifetime duration of bulimia nervosa is six years (Yager, 2022). Left untreated, the disorder is more likely to last longer, sometimes improving temporarily but then returning. Treatment, however, produces immediate, significant improvement in approximately 40 percent of clients: they stop or greatly reduce their bingeing and purging, eat properly, and maintain a healthy weight (Mitchell, 2023; Isomaa & Isomaa, 2014). Another 40 percent show a moderate response—at least some decrease in binge eating and purging. Follow-up studies, conducted years after treatment, suggest that around 75 percent of people with bulimia nervosa have recovered either fully or partially (Engel et al., 2023; Quadflieg, Voderholzer, & Fichter, 2023).

Relapse can be a problem even among people who respond successfully to treatment (Filipponi et al., 2022). Studies suggest that 31 percent of those who recover from bulimia nervosa may relapse within two years (Muhlheim, 2020). As with anorexia nervosa, relapses are usually triggered by a new life stress, such as an upcoming exam, a job change, marriage, or divorce. Relapse is more likely among people who had longer histories of bulimia nervosa before treatment, had vomited more frequently during their disorder, continued to vomit at the end of treatment, had histories of substance abuse, and continue to be lonely or to distrust others after treatment (Engel et al., 2023; Vall & Wade, 2015).

Why might some people who recover from anorexia nervosa and bulimia nervosa remain vulnerable to relapse even after recovery?

Treatments for Binge-Eating Disorder

The average lifetime duration of binge-eating disorder is 14 years (Yager, 2022). Approximately 44 percent of people with this problem receive treatment (NIMH, 2023). Given the key role of binges in this disorder (bingeing without purging), today's treatments for binge-eating disorder are often similar to those for bulimia nervosa. In particular, cognitive-behavioral therapy, certain other forms of psychotherapy, and, in some cases, antidepressant medications are provided to help reduce or eliminate the binge-eating patterns and to change disturbed thinking, such as being overly concerned with weight and shape (Dalle Grave & Pike, 2023; Scott, 2023). According to research, psychotherapy is generally more helpful than antidepressants. Group therapy is often as helpful as—and in some cases more helpful than—individual treatments for people with the disorder (AGPA, 2022).

Evidence indicates that these various interventions are indeed often effective, at least in the short run (Rösch & Hilbert, 2023). As many as 60 percent of clients no longer fit the criteria for binge-eating disorder by the end of treatment (Sysko & Devlin, 2023, 2022; McElroy et al., 2020). Many of their early gains may continue for years. However, only around one-third of the recovered individuals showed total improvement in those follow-up studies. As with the other eating disorders, many of those who initially recover from binge-eating disorder continue to have a relatively high risk of relapse (Rösch & Hilbert, 2023).

As you read earlier, many people with binge-eating disorder also are overweight, and that part of their challenges requires additional kinds of intervention. Their weight difficulties are often resistant to long-term improvement, even if their binge eating is reduced or eliminated (McElroy et al., 2020).

of NOTE ...

Why Some Do Not Seek Help for Eating Disorders

- Stigma regarding eating disorders
- Negative self-view
- Fear of treatment
- Mental health misinformation
- Doubts about clinical field
- Financial concerns

(Information from: Ali & Fassnacht, 2023; Liu, Hay, & Conti, 2022; Nicula et al., 2022)

SUMMING UP

Treatments for Eating Disorders

The first step in treating anorexia nervosa is to increase calorie intake and quickly restore the person's weight, a part of treatment called nutritional rehabilitation. The second step is to deal with the underlying psychological and family problems, often using a combination of education, cognitive-behavioral approaches, and family therapy. As many as 75 percent of people who are successfully treated for anorexia nervosa continue to show full or partial improvements years later. However, some of them relapse along the way.

Treatments for bulimia nervosa focus first on stopping the binge-purge pattern (nutritional rehabilitation) and then on addressing the underlying causes of the disorder. Often several treatment strategies are combined, including education, psychotherapy (particularly cognitive-behavioral therapy), and, in some cases, antidepressant medications. As many as 75 percent of those who receive treatment eventually improve either fully or partially. While relapse can be a problem and may be precipitated by a new stress, treatment leads to lasting improvements in psychological and social functioning for many people. Similar treatments are used to help people with binge-eating disorder. Some of these individuals, however, may also require interventions to address their unhealthy excess weight.

Prevention of Eating Disorders: Wave of the Future

CLEARLY, EATING DISORDERS are profoundly destructive. Moreover, the various treatments for these disorders, while they've improved greatly in recent years, do not bring about a full recovery for a number of people with these disorders. Thus, some clinical theorists believe that researchers must put more work into the development of programs that promote body positivity and *prevent* the onset of eating disorders (Le, Tan, & Wilksch, 2023; O'Mara et al., 2023). One of today's promising prevention programs, called the *Body Project,* has been developed and expanded by psychologists Eric Stice and Carolyn Black Becker and their colleagues (Stice et al., 2021, 2020; Becker et al., 2017). Keeping in mind the key factors that predispose people to the development of eating disorders, the Body Project offers a total of four weekly group sessions for high school and college-age students. In these sessions, group members are guided through a range of intense verbal, written, role-playing, and behavioral exercises that critique Western society's ultrathin ideal. The participants also engage in body acceptance exercises and eating-related activities that run counter to the ultrathin ideal; these are coupled with motivation enhancement techniques, skill-building training, and social support exercises.

Encouragingly, the Body Project prevention program has performed well in research (Stice et al., 2021, 2020, 2019). In comparison to other young people who received education-only prevention programs or no prevention programs at all, participants in the Body Project develop fewer eating disorders, hold more realistic and healthful appearance ideals, display fewer maladaptive eating attitudes and behaviors, have greater body satisfaction, and experience more positive emotions in follow-up studies conducted a year or more after the program.

Clearly, this program is promising and important. Whether in the form of the Body Project or other such undertakings, prevention programs address a critical need in the clinical field's commitment to helping people overcome eating disorders, and the number of such programs is likely to increase in the years to come (Le et al., 2023; O'Mara et al., 2023).

"You have potential, but you need to lose some weight."

Quick Quiz

1. What are the symptoms and main features of anorexia nervosa and bulimia nervosa? How are people with anorexia nervosa similar to those with bulimia nervosa? How are they different? pp. 280–286
2. What are the symptoms and main features of binge-eating disorder? How is this disorder different from bulimia nervosa? pp. 286–288
3. According to Hilde Bruch, how might parents' failure to attend appropriately to their baby's internal needs and emotions contribute to the later development of an eating disorder? pp. 289–290
4. How might a person's brain circuits, hypothalamus, and weight set point contribute to the development of an eating disorder? pp. 291–292
5. What evidence suggests that sociocultural pressures and factors may set the stage for eating disorders? pp. 293–295
6. How do the prevalence rates for eating disorders vary in accord with race and ethnicity, gender, and sexual orientation? pp. 296–299
7. What are the key goals and approaches used in the treatment of anorexia nervosa, and how successful are they? What factors affect a person's recovery? pp. 299–303
8. What are the key goals and approaches used in the treatment of bulimia nervosa, and how successful are they? What factors affect a person's recovery? pp. 303–305
9. How are treatments for binge-eating disorder similar to and different from treatments for bulimia nervosa? p. 305
10. What are some of the key features of eating disorder prevention programs such as the Body Project? p. 306

Substance Use and Addictive Disorders

CHAPTER 10

TOPIC OVERVIEW

"My name's Blake, and I'm an alcoholic." Blake took a breath to collect himself as the crowd in the room muttered, "Hi, Blake." He had been attending Alcoholics Anonymous (AA) meetings near his home in West Virginia for over two years now, but this was the first time he'd been asked to share his story fully at a meeting, and he was very nervous.

"I'll state right off the bat, it sure wasn't my idea to start coming around to these rooms. I wanted no part of AA. In fact, I wanted no part of not drinking. What happened was, I wrecked my truck, went off the road and into a field, and broke my leg. And wouldn't you know, I had a bottle in there with me, half drunk. Almost busted the breathalyzer when the cops came." There were a couple of knowing chuckles in the crowd.

"The lawyers and the judges hammered out a deal, seeing as I didn't hurt anybody but myself. I'd go to rehab, and when I get out, I have to show that I've been coming to these meetings so I don't have to go to jail. Oh, and they took my license away, too. So the deal seemed like something pretty easy to say yes to, and I did it. Couple of years ago, you would have seen me at a meeting, getting my paper signed at the end—of course they never sign it at the beginning of the meeting! But over time, my feelings about the meetings changed. In fact, six months ago they stopped making me bring them those signed papers. And here I am anyway, still coming around. I've come to find that this fellowship, and quitting drinking, saved my life.

"So, let's start at the beginning. I guess I'll go all the way back to when I was born. I think I knew what alcohol was before I knew what Legos were. I don't really have any memories of my dad when he didn't have a beer in his hand. Didn't seem like any big thing. I never suspected it had anything to do with all the screaming he and my mom did at each other. By the time I was eight or nine, I saw less and less of Dad. He didn't leave or anything, he was just always with his buddies at the bar. I think I wanted to get to be a grown-up so I could go to the bar too and see what this special place was all about. Mom did her drinking at home, sometimes having her friends over to help her with that.

"When I was twelve was the first time I snuck a beer out of the fridge when no one was looking. I was left alone a lot. My parents both worked themselves to the ground even though we barely had enough to eat most nights. I popped open that beer one night when I was home taking care of myself. Had it with my slice of turkey. As I drank it, it just felt warm all down my throat, into my stomach, so I drank some more. And as I felt that buzz hit me, just from one beer, I thought, 'Yeah, I get what all the fuss is about.'

"It was a couple more years before I got the chance to feel that buzz again. Some of my friends snuck beers from their parents. We would sit around drinking their beers and I couldn't believe how much cooler I felt. All my jokes were funnier, and I was sure my friends liked me more. Soon I was drinking at every high school party and sneaking drinks with my friends during classes, too. Everyone was doing it.

"After high school, I started working at a gas station. You people from around here can guess I wasn't exactly busy. There wasn't much to do most of the day but sneak in back and crack open a beer. I lost that job when they found out I took beer from the store. I guess me being drunk on the job didn't really help, either. That was the first of many jobs I lost.

"No matter how little I was working, I always found a way to get beer and get loaded. I had a few buddies and we had an understanding. Whichever of us was working that month would buy the beer. I got some construction work now and then. That's when I met some REAL drinkers. We'd sit around on the site after work and they'd pass a bottle of whiskey around. Some nights I didn't even make it home.

(continued on the next page)

"Years go on, and I had to start each day with a shot. If I didn't, I'd get real shaky and lay around in bed all day. My morning shot would get me up and out the door to work, if I was working. I hear a lot of stories where people say everyone got worried about their drinking. Friends tried to get them help and so on. There was nothing like that for me. Everyone I knew drank at least as much as me.

"Once in a blue moon I'd take a notion to cut back my drinking for a week or two, just to prove to myself I could. That usually lasted about half a day. Nerves and the shakes would get to me. However, I almost never had the thought, even in the back of my mind, that I might have a problem. I can't believe it now, but I drove drunk nearly every day. I knew the hours of every liquor store up and down the county, and I started planning where I'd buy my liquor a week ahead of time so I'd never run out. Food, I let myself run out of, never booze.

"Well, I already told you how it all ended up. After the nightmare of detoxing and then going through rehab, I started coming to these meetings. Yeah, I was trying to get a paper signed, but then you people kept telling me I was worth something, that you wanted to help me, and that I could actually help you too. Eventually, it sunk in. I actually feel pretty good most days now—but I know that I have to be on guard each day and commit myself again and again to not drinking."

of NOTE ...

Early Start, Bad Ending

An earlier onset of alcohol use has been linked to a faster development of alcohol use disorder and to worse outcomes (Bukstein, 2023).

Human beings enjoy a remarkable variety of foods and drinks. Every substance on Earth probably has been tried by someone, somewhere, at some time. We also have discovered substances that have interesting effects—both medical and pleasurable—on our brains and the rest of our bodies. We may swallow an aspirin to quiet a headache, an antibiotic to fight an infection, or a tranquilizer to calm us down. We may drink coffee to get going in the morning or wine to relax with friends. We may smoke cigarettes or vape to soothe our nerves. However, many of the substances we consume can harm us or disrupt our behavior or mood. The misuse of such substances has become one of society's biggest problems. Combining costs related to crime, lost work productivity, and health care, it is estimated that the overall cost of substance misuse is $740 billion each year in the United States alone (NIDA, 2023).

Not only are numerous substances available in our society, but new ones are introduced almost every day. Some are harvested from nature, others derived from natural substances, and still others produced in the laboratory. Some, such as antianxiety drugs, require a physician's prescription for legal use. Others, such as alcohol and nicotine, are legally available to adults throughout the United States. Still others, such as heroin, are illegal under just about all circumstances. In 1962, only 4 million people in the United States had ever used cocaine, heroin, or another illegal substance; today, the number has climbed to around 139 million (SAMHSA, 2023). In fact, 40 million people have used illegal substances within the past month. More than one-quarter of all teenagers have used an illegal substance.

A *drug* is defined as any substance other than food that affects our bodies or minds. It need not be a medicine or be illegal. The term "substance" is now frequently used in place of "drug," in part because many people fail to recognize that such substances as alcohol, tobacco, and caffeine are drugs, too. When a person ingests a substance—whether it be alcohol, cocaine, marijuana, or some form of medication—trillions of powerful molecules surge through the bloodstream and into the brain. Once there, the molecules set off a series of biochemical events that disturb the usual operation of the brain and body. Not surprisingly, then, substance misuse may lead to various kinds of atypical functioning.

substance intoxication A cluster of temporary undesirable behavioral or psychological changes that develop during or shortly after the ingestion of a substance.

substance use disorder A pattern of long-term maladaptive behaviors and reactions brought about by repeated use of a substance.

tolerance The brain's and body's need for ever-larger doses of a drug to produce desired effects.

withdrawal Unpleasant, sometimes dangerous reactions that may occur when people who use a drug regularly stop using it or reduce the dosage.

Substances may cause *temporary* changes in behavior, emotion, or thought; this cluster of changes is called **substance intoxication** in DSM-5-TR. As Blake found out, for example, an excessive amount of alcohol may lead to *alcohol intoxication,* a temporary state of poor judgment, mood changes, irritability, slurred speech, and poor coordination. Similarly, drugs such as LSD may produce *hallucinogen intoxication,* sometimes called *hallucinosis,* which consists largely of perceptual distortions and hallucinations.

Some substances can also lead to *long-term* problems. People who regularly ingest them may develop **substance use disorders,** patterns of maladaptive behaviors and reactions brought about by the repeated use of substances (Murray & Kiernan, 2024; APA, 2022). People with a substance use disorder may come to crave a particular substance and rely on it excessively, resulting in damage to their family and social relationships, poor functioning at work, and/or danger to themselves or others (see **Table 10-1**). In many cases, people with such a disorder also become physically dependent on the substance, developing a *tolerance* for it and experiencing *withdrawal* reactions. When people develop **tolerance,** they need increasing doses of the substance to produce the desired effect. **Withdrawal** reactions consist of unpleasant and sometimes dangerous symptoms—cramps, anxiety attacks, sweating, nausea—that occur when the person suddenly stops taking or cuts back on the substance. Blake, who described his problems to fellow members at an Alcoholics Anonymous meeting, was caught in a form of substance use disorder called *alcohol use disorder.* Over time, alcohol interfered with his daily functioning, helped lower his drive, and greatly damaged his work life. He also built up a tolerance for alcohol over time and had withdrawal symptoms such as anxiety and shaking when he tried to stop using it.

TABLE 10-1

Dx Checklist

Substance Use Disorder

1. Individual displays a maladaptive pattern of substance use leading to significant impairment or distress.
2. Presence of at least two of the following substance-produced symptoms within a 1-year period:
   - Substance is often taken in larger amounts.
   - Unsuccessful efforts to reduce or control substance use.
   - Much time spent trying to obtain, use, or recover from effects of substance.
   - Failure to fulfill major role obligations.
   - Continued use despite persistent interpersonal problems.
   - Reduction of important activities.
   - Continued use in dangerous situations.
   - Continued use despite worsening of physical or psychological problems.
   - Craving for substance.
   - Tolerance effects.
   - Withdrawal reactions.

Information from: APA, 2022.

In any given year, 16.5 percent of all people over age 11 in the United States, or more than 46 million people, have a substance use disorder (SAMHSA, 2023). The prevalence of substance use disorders tends to be higher among gay, lesbian, and bisexual people than heterosexual people (Wittgens et al., 2022; Ruppert, Sussman, & Kattari, 2020), and, according to emerging studies, it is higher among transgender and nonbinary people than cisgender people (Kidd et al., 2023; Ruppert, Kattari, & Sussman, 2021). You will read more about possible reasons for these various differences later in the chapter.

Indigenous people have the highest rate of substance use disorders in the United States (more than 27 percent), while Asian Americans have the lowest (8 percent). Hispanic Americans, non-Hispanic White Americans, and Black Americans have rates of between 15.7 and 17.2 percent (SAMHSA, 2023) (see **Figure 10-1**). The male-to-female ratio for substance use disorders is 4 to 3, a difference in prevalence that holds across cisgender and transgender populations and people of various races and ethnicities (SAMHSA, 2023).

The substances people misuse fall into several categories: *depressants, stimulants, hallucinogens,* and *cannabis.* In this chapter, you will read about some of the most problematic substances and the atypical patterns they may produce. In addition, at the end of the chapter, you'll read about *gambling disorder,* a problem that DSM-5-TR lists as an additional addictive disorder. By listing this behavioral pattern alongside the substance use disorders, DSM-5-TR is suggesting that this condition has symptoms and causes that share more than a passing similarity to those at work in substance use disorders. ■

FIGURE 10-1

How Do Racial and Ethnic Groups Differ in Substance Use Disorders?

In the United States, Indigenous people are more likely than members of other ethnic or racial groups to have substance use disorders. (Information from: SAMHSA, 2023.)

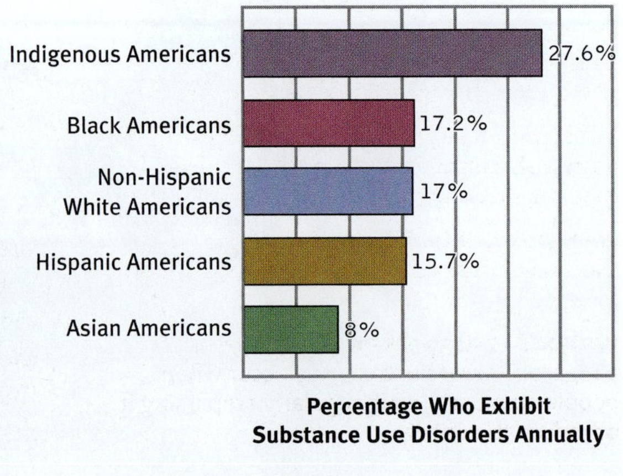

alcohol Any beverage containing ethyl alcohol, including beer, wine, and liquor.

binge drinking Consuming five or more alcoholic drinks in a single episode.

Depressants

DEPRESSANTS SLOW THE ACTIVITY of the central nervous system. They reduce tension and inhibitions and may interfere with a person's judgment, motor activity, and concentration. The three most widely used groups of depressants are *alcohol, sedative-hypnotic drugs,* and *opioids*.

Alcohol

More than 2 billion people worldwide consume **alcohol.** In the United States, around 67 percent of adults and 18 percent of teenagers drink beverages that contain alcohol, at least from time to time (SAMHSA, 2023). Purchases of beer, wine, and liquor amount to hundreds of billions of dollars each year in the United States (Statista, 2023).

When people consume five or more drinks on a single occasion, it is called a **binge drinking** episode. Almost 22 percent of people in the United States over age 11 binge-drink each month (SAMHSA, 2023). Around 5.8 percent of people over age 11 binge-drink at least five times each month. They are considered heavy drinkers. Among heavy drinkers, males outnumber females by almost 2 to 1.

All alcoholic beverages contain *ethyl alcohol,* a chemical that is quickly absorbed into the blood through the lining of the stomach and the intestine. The ethyl alcohol immediately begins to take effect as it is carried in the bloodstream to the central nervous system (the brain and spinal cord), where it acts to *depress,* or slow, functioning by binding to various neurons. One important group of neurons to which ethyl alcohol binds is those that typically receive the neurotransmitter GABA. As you read in the chapter on anxiety disorders, GABA carries an *inhibitory* message—a message to stop firing—when it is received at certain neurons. When alcohol binds to receptors on those neurons, it apparently helps GABA to shut down the neurons, thus helping to relax the drinker (Wang et al., 2022).

At first, ethyl alcohol depresses the areas of the brain that control judgment and inhibition; people become looser, more talkative, and often more friendly. As their inner control breaks down, they may feel relaxed, confident, and happy. When more alcohol is absorbed, it slows down additional areas in the central nervous system, leaving drinkers less able to make sound judgments, their speech less careful and less coherent, and their memory weaker. Many people become highly emotional and perhaps loud and aggressive.

Simulating alcohol's effects Air Force members operate pedal go-karts while wearing goggles that produce alcohol-like impairment. The exercise is part of an alcohol abuse prevention program designed to give airpersons experience with alcohol's effects on vision and balance.

Operation 2021/Alamy Stock Photo

Motor difficulties increase as a person continues drinking, and reaction times slow. People may be unsteady when they stand or walk and clumsy in performing even simple activities. They may drop things, bump into doors and furniture, and misjudge distances. Their vision becomes blurred, particularly their *peripheral,* or side, vision, and they have trouble hearing. As a result, people who have drunk too much alcohol may have great difficulty driving or solving simple problems (LoParco et al., 2024).

The extent of the effect of ethyl alcohol is determined by its *concentration,* or proportion, in the blood. Thus, a given amount of alcohol has less effect on a large person than on a small person. Gender also affects the concentration of alcohol in the blood. For example, cisgender women have less of the stomach enzyme *alcohol dehydrogenase,* which breaks down alcohol in the stomach before it enters the blood. So they become more intoxicated than cisgender men on equal doses of alcohol, and they may be at greater risk for physical and psychological damage from alcohol (Mukamal, 2023).

Levels of impairment are closely related to the concentration of ethyl alcohol in the blood. When the alcohol concentration reaches 0.06 percent of the blood volume, a person usually feels relaxed and comfortable. By the time it reaches 0.09 percent, however, the drinker crosses the line into intoxication. If the level goes as high as 0.55 percent, the drinker will likely die. Most people lose consciousness before they can drink enough to reach this level; nevertheless, each year, more than 1,000 people in the United States die from too high a blood alcohol level (Ackermann, 2023; Mukamal, 2023).

The effects of alcohol subside only when the alcohol concentration in the blood declines. Most of the alcohol is broken down, or *metabolized,* by the liver into carbon dioxide and water, which can be exhaled and excreted. The average rate of this metabolism is 25 percent of an ounce per hour, but different people's livers work at different speeds; thus, rates of "sobering up" vary. Despite popular belief, only time and metabolism can make a person sober. Drinking black coffee, splashing cold water on one's face, or "pulling oneself together" cannot hurry the process.

Matthew Horwood/Getty Images

Substance misuse and sports fans A problem that has received growing attention in recent years is excessive drinking by fans at sports events. These Welsh fans are surrounded by countless beer cans as they watch a soccer match between Wales and England, with an opportunity to participate in the 2022 World Cup at stake.

Alcohol Use Disorder

Though legal, alcohol is actually one of the most dangerous of recreational drugs, and its reach extends across the life span. In fact, 23 percent of middle school students admit to some alcohol use in a given year, while more than 28 percent of high school seniors drink alcohol each month (most to the point of intoxication), and almost 2 percent drink every day (Miech et al., 2023). Alcohol misuse is also a major problem on college campuses (Akua & Samek, 2023) (see **PsychWatch**).

Surveys indicate that over a one-year period, 10.6 percent of all people over age 11 in the United States display *alcohol use disorder,* known in popular terms as *alcoholism* (SAMHSA, 2023). For teenagers only, the rate is 3.4 percent. The prevalence for alcohol use disorder is higher for transgender and nonbinary people than for cisgender people; higher for lesbian, gay, and bisexual people than for heterosexual people; and higher for men than for women across most groups (a 4:3 ratio) (Kidd et al., 2023; Wittgens et al., 2022; Ruppert et al., 2021, 2020).

The one-year prevalence of alcohol use disorder in the United States is 11 percent for non-Hispanic White people, 10.3 percent for Hispanic people, and 10.1 percent for Black people (SAMHSA, 2023). Indigenous people display a much higher rate: around 15.6 percent of them experience the disorder, although specific prevalence rates differ widely across the various Indigenous communities (Downey & Chang, 2024). Asian Americans have a lower rate of alcohol use disorder (6 percent) than do people from other cultures. As many as half of them have a deficiency of *alcohol dehydrogenase,* the chemical responsible for breaking down alcohol, so they react quite negatively to even modest intakes of alcohol. Such reactions may, in turn, help prevent extended use (Cho et al., 2023).

Why do you think Indigenous people have a much higher rate of alcohol use disorder than members of other racial and ethnic groups?

CLINICAL PICTURE Generally speaking, people with alcohol use disorder drink large amounts of alcohol regularly and rely on it to enable them to do things that would otherwise make them anxious. Eventually, the drinking interferes with their social behavior and ability to think and work. They may have frequent arguments with family members or friends, miss work repeatedly, and even lose their jobs. MRI scans of chronic heavy drinkers have revealed damage in various structures of their brains and, correspondingly, impairments in their memory, speed of thinking, attention skills, and balance (Goodwin et al., 2024; Park, Jeon, & Baek, 2023).

PSYCHWATCH

College Binge Drinking: An Extracurricular Crisis

Drinking large amounts of alcohol in a short time, or *binge drinking,* is a serious problem on college campuses as well as in other settings. Studies show that more than 33 percent of college students binge-drink at least once each month, one-quarter of them six times or more per month (NIAAA, 2023; SAMHSA, 2023). In many circles, alcohol use is an accepted part of college life, but consider some of the following statistics:

- Alcohol-related arrests account for the majority of all campus arrests.
- More than half of all sexual assaults on college campuses involve the heavy consumption of alcohol.
- Alcohol is a factor in at least 25 percent of academic problems and instances of dropping out of college.
- Approximately 700,000 students each year are physically or emotionally traumatized or assaulted by a student drinker.
- Alcohol is tied to 1,500 fatal injuries, including car crashes, among college-age persons every year.
- Half of college students say "drinking to get drunk" is an important reason for drinking.
- Binge drinking often has a lingering effect on mood, memory, brain functioning, and heart functioning.
- The number of female binge drinkers among college students has increased by a third over the past decade.

(Akua & Samek, 2023; NIAAA, 2023; CDC, 2022)

© Andrew Lichtenstein/Sygma via Getty Images

Testing the limits College binge drinking, which involves behaviors similar to that shown here, has led to a number of deaths in recent years.

These findings have led some educators to describe binge drinking as "the number one public health hazard" for full-time college students, and many researchers and clinicians have turned their attention to it. Studies have collectively surveyed many thousands of students at college campuses around the United States (CDC, 2023, 2022; NIAAA, 2023). Among other useful information, the surveys have found that the students most likely to binge-drink are those who live in fraternity or sorority houses, pursue a party-centered lifestyle, and engage in high-risk behaviors such as substance misuse. The surveys have also suggested that students who are binge drinkers in high school are more likely to binge-drink in college.

Efforts to change such patterns have begun (NIAAA, 2023; DiGuiseppi et al., 2020). For example, many universities now provide substance-free dorms. Studies indicate that the rate of binge drinking by residents in these college housing facilities is half the rate displayed by students who live in a fraternity or sorority house. Such research efforts are promising. However, most people in the clinical field agree that more work is needed to help us fully understand, prevent, and treat what has become a major societal problem.

Individually, people's patterns of alcoholism vary. Some drink large amounts of alcohol every day and keep drinking until intoxicated. Others go on periodic binges of heavy drinking that can last weeks or months; they may remain intoxicated for days and later be unable to remember anything about the period. Still others may limit their excessive drinking to weekends, evenings, or both.

TOLERANCE AND WITHDRAWAL For many people, alcohol use disorder includes the symptoms of tolerance and withdrawal reactions. As their bodies build up a tolerance for alcohol, they need to drink ever-larger amounts to feel its desired effects. In addition, they have withdrawal symptoms when they stop drinking. Within hours, their hands, tongue, and eyelids begin to shake; they feel weak and nauseated; they sweat and vomit; their heart beats rapidly; and their blood pressure rises. They may also become anxious, depressed, unable to sleep, or irritable (APA, 2022).

A small percentage of people with alcohol use disorder go through a particularly dramatic withdrawal reaction called **delirium tremens** (DTs). It consists of terrifying visual hallucinations that begin within three days after they stop or reduce their drinking. Some people see small, frightening animals chasing or crawling on them or objects dancing about in front of their eyes. Shivering and profuse sweating are also common. Like most other alcohol withdrawal symptoms, DTs usually run their course in two to three days. However, people who have such severe withdrawal reactions may also have seizures, lose consciousness, experience a stroke, or even die. Today, certain medical procedures can help prevent or reduce such extreme reactions.

Poor estimates As part of the LessThanUThink alcohol education program, college students try to estimate the volume of a 12-ounce beer by pouring water from a pitcher. This student, like many others, said she was "amazed" to find out how much more than 12 ounces she had poured.

What Are the Personal and Social Impacts of Alcohol Use Disorder?

Alcohol use disorder destroys millions of families, social relationships, and careers (Mukamal, 2023). Alcohol-related medical treatments, lost productivity, and deaths cost society many billions of dollars annually. The disorder also plays a role in one-third or more of all suicides, homicides, assaults, rapes, and fatal automobile accidents in the United States (NIAAA, 2023; Kõlves, Crossin, & Witt, 2022). Intoxicated drivers are responsible for close to 12,000 deaths each year, and in the past year, more than 7 percent of all adults have driven while intoxicated (NHTSA, 2023, 2022; CDC, 2022). Although these are frightening numbers, they represent significant drops over the past decade.

Alcohol use disorder has serious effects on the 30 million children of people with this disorder (AAMFT, 2023; MHN, 2023). Home life for these children is likely to include much conflict and perhaps sexual or other forms of abuse. In turn, the children themselves have higher rates of psychological problems. Many have low self-esteem, poor communication skills, poor sociability, and marital problems.

Long-term excessive drinking can also seriously damage a person's physical health (Mukamal, 2023). It so overworks the liver that people may develop an irreversible condition called *cirrhosis,* in which the liver becomes scarred and dysfunctional. Alcohol-related cirrhosis accounts for almost 30,000 deaths each year (CDC, 2023). Alcohol use disorder may also damage the heart and lower the immune system's ability to fight off diseases and infections.

Long-term excessive drinking also causes major nutritional problems. Alcohol makes people feel full and lowers their desire for food, yet it has no nutritional value. As a result, chronic drinkers become malnourished, weak, and prone to disease. Their vitamin and mineral deficiencies may also cause problems. An alcohol-related deficiency of vitamin B1 (thiamine), for example, may lead to *Korsakoff's syndrome,* a disease marked by extreme confusion, memory loss, and other neurological symptoms (Mukamal, 2023).

Drinking while pregnant places the fetus at risk (Padilla-Valdez et al., 2024; CDC, 2023; Chang, 2023). Excessive alcohol use during pregnancy may cause a baby to be born with **fetal alcohol syndrome**, a pattern of conditions that can include intellectual disability, hyperactivity, malformations of the head and face, heart problems, and slow growth. It is estimated that in the overall population, around 1 of every 1,000 babies is born with this syndrome (0.001 percent). The rate increases to more than 50 of

delirium tremens (DTs) A dramatic alcohol withdrawal reaction that consists of confusion, clouded consciousness, and visual hallucinations.

fetal alcohol syndrome A cluster of problems in a child, including irregularities in the head and face and intellectual deficits, caused by an excessive alcohol intake during pregnancy.

sedative-hypnotic drug A drug used to reduce anxiety and to help people sleep. Also called an *anxiolytic drug*.

barbiturates Addictive sedative-hypnotic drugs that reduce anxiety and help people sleep.

benzodiazepines The most common group of antianxiety drugs; includes Xanax.

opioid Opium, drugs derived from opium, and similar synthetic drugs.

opium A highly addictive substance made from the sap of the opium poppy.

morphine A highly addictive substance derived from opium that is particularly effective in relieving pain.

heroin One of the most addictive substances derived from opium.

endorphins Neurotransmitters that help relieve pain and reduce emotional tension.

every 1,000 for babies born to drinkers (5 percent). If all alcohol-related congenital conditions (known as *fetal alcohol spectrum disorder*) are counted, the rate is greater than 80 per 1,000 for babies born to drinkers (8 percent). In addition, heavy drinking early in pregnancy can lead to miscarriage. According to surveys, 9.8 percent of pregnant people have drunk alcohol during the past month, and 4.3 percent of pregnant people have had binge drinking episodes (SAMHSA, 2023).

Sedative-Hypnotic Drugs

Sedative-hypnotic drugs, also called **anxiolytic** (meaning "anxiety-reducing") **drugs,** produce feelings of relaxation and drowsiness. At low dosages, the drugs have a calming or sedative effect. At higher dosages, they are sleep inducers, or hypnotics. For much of the twentieth century, a group of drugs called **barbiturates** were the most widely prescribed sedative-hypnotic drugs. Over the past 60 years, however, these drugs have been largely replaced by **benzodiazepines,** which are generally safer and less likely to lead to intoxication, tolerance effects, and withdrawal reactions.

As noted earlier in the textbook, benzodiazepines, developed in the 1950s, are the most popular sedative-hypnotic drugs available. Xanax, Ativan, and Valium are just three of the dozens of these compounds in clinical use. Around 9 percent of adolescents and adults, almost 26 million people, have taken benzodiazepines during the past year, a rate that has sharply increased over the past two decades (SAMHSA, 2023). Like alcohol and barbiturates, they calm people by binding to receptors on the neurons that receive GABA and by increasing GABA's activity at those neurons (Tietze & Fuchs, 2022). Benzodiazepines relieve anxiety without making people as drowsy as other kinds of sedative-hypnotics. They are also less likely to slow a person's breathing, so they are less likely to cause death in the event of an overdose.

When benzodiazepines were first discovered, they seemed so safe and effective that physicians prescribed them generously, and their use spread. Eventually, it became clear that in high enough doses the drugs can cause intoxication and lead to *sedative-hypnotic use disorder,* a pattern marked by craving for the drugs, tolerance effects, and withdrawal reactions (Kroenke & Hirschtritt, 2023). Over a one-year period, 0.8 percent of all adolescents and adults in the United States display this disorder (SAMHSA, 2023). Research suggests that the long-term use of benzodiazepines by older adults can cause severe cognitive impairments, including intellectual decline, confusion, and memory loss (Wu et al., 2023). Despite this repeated finding, as many as 17 percent of such individuals are prescribed benzodiazepine medications, including as many as 40 percent of older adults living in nursing homes.

Why do you think nursing homes continue to administer benzodiazepines to so many older adults despite the cognitive dangers the drugs pose for that age group?

Opioids

Opioids include *opium,* which is taken from the sap of the opium poppy; *heroin, morphine,* and *codeine,* which are derived from opium; and similar *synthetic* (laboratory-blended) drugs, such as *methadone* and *fentanyl.* **Opium** itself has been in use for thousands of years. In the past, it was used widely in the treatment of medical disorders because of its ability to reduce both physical and emotional pain. Eventually, however, physicians discovered that the drug was addictive.

In 1804, a new substance, **morphine,** was derived from opium. Named after Morpheus, the Greek god of sleep, this drug relieved pain even better than opium did and initially was considered safe. However, widespread use of the drug eventually revealed that it, too, could lead to addiction. During the U.S. Civil War, so many wounded soldiers received morphine injections that morphine addiction became known as "soldiers' disease."

In 1898, morphine was converted into yet another new pain reliever, **heroin.** For several years, heroin was viewed as a wonder drug and was used as a cough medicine and for other medical purposes. Eventually, however, physicians learned that heroin is even more addictive than its predecessors. By 1917, the U.S. Congress had concluded that all drugs derived from opium were addictive, and it passed a law making opioids illegal except when used for medical purposes.

Still other drugs have been derived from opium, and, as noted above, synthetic opioids, such as *methadone* and *fentanyl*, have also been developed. These various opioid drugs are also known collectively as *narcotics*. Each drug has a different strength, speed of action, and tolerance level. Morphine, fentanyl, *codeine*, and *oxycodone* (the key ingredient in OxyContin and Percocet) are medical opioids, usually prescribed to relieve pain. Between 26 million and 86 million people over age 11 have taken medical opioids in the past year (SAMHSA, 2023). Around 12 percent of them took the drugs illicitly—either without a physician's prescription or in doses that were larger, more frequent, or of longer duration than prescribed.

Most opioids are smoked, inhaled, snorted, injected, or, as in the case of many pain relievers, swallowed in pill or liquid form or absorbed into the body through a patch attached to the skin. In injections, the opioid may be deposited just beneath the skin ("skin-popping"), deep into a muscle ("muscle popping"), or directly into a vein ("mainlining"). An injection quickly brings on a *rush*—a spasm of warmth and ecstasy that is sometimes compared with orgasm. The brief spasm is followed by several hours of a pleasant feeling called a *high* or *nod*. During a high, the person using the drug feels relaxed, happy, and unconcerned about food, sex, or other bodily needs.

Opioids create these effects by depressing the central nervous system, particularly the centers that help control emotion. The drugs attach to brain receptor sites that ordinarily receive **endorphins**—neurotransmitters that help relieve pain and reduce emotional tension (Stolbach & Hoffman, 2023). When neurons at these receptor sites receive opioids, they produce pleasurable and calming feelings just as they would do if they were receiving endorphins. In addition to reducing pain and tension, opioids cause nausea, narrowing of the pupils ("pinpoint pupils"), and constipation—bodily reactions that can also be brought about by releases of endorphins in the brain.

Stringer /EPA/Newscom

Purer blend Heroin, derived from poppies such as this one in a poppy field in southern Afghanistan, is much purer and stronger today than it was decades ago.

Opioid Use Disorder

After taking powerful opioids repeatedly for a week or more, people may develop *opioid use disorder*. In such cases, the opioid use interferes significantly with their social and occupational functioning, and their lives center around the substance. They may also build a tolerance for the drug and experience a withdrawal reaction when they stop taking it (Sevarino, 2023; Strain, 2022). At first, the withdrawal symptoms are anxiety, restlessness, sweating, and rapid breathing; later, they include severe twitching, aches, fever, vomiting, diarrhea, loss of appetite, high blood pressure, and weight loss of up to 15 pounds (due to loss of bodily fluids). These symptoms usually peak by the third day, gradually subside, and disappear by the eighth day. A person in opioid withdrawal can either wait out the symptoms or end withdrawal by taking the drug again.

Mei, a 36-year-old property manager in Rockford, Illinois, was already dealing with lots of stress at work when her back, which had been giving her trouble for years, went out with a vengeance. She was unable to get out of bed for several days, and she had to use sick days. Mei tried to go back to work on the fifth day but had so much difficulty getting around the office that her boss insisted she go home for the day.

(continued on the next page)

of NOTE ...

Decreasing Prescriptions

Partly due to increased government monitoring, the number of prescriptions for opioid pain relievers has dropped more than 10 percent in the past few years and 19 percent since 2012 (CDC, 2023).

The next day, she saw a doctor, pleading with him to help her get back to work right away. When X-rays turned up nothing significant, the doctor prescribed physical therapy. He also prescribed Vicodin to help her manage until the therapy showed results. He cautioned her to take no more than four in a day. That night, she took the medicine, and within an hour, her pain lifted, and she felt a sense of elation, almost giddiness. When the drug wore off, however, she yelled in pain to her husband Lyle that she was ready for another pill. She resolved not to let her pain go that long again before taking another dose. It took over a month before she could make an appointment for physical therapy, and she began taking two and eventually three pills at a time. With the pills, she found herself able to work, and she even felt more on top of managing the construction projects. At night, she'd take an extra pill and drift blissfully to sleep.

When Mei explained the scheduling problems with the physical therapy, her doctor gave her another prescription. However, she ran out two weeks later, long before she could reasonably ask for another prescription. Her first day without the medicine, she felt nervous, and coworkers noticed her perspiring at work. She remembered that there were still some Percocets in the medicine cabinet from when Lyle broke his leg the year before. "Just this once," she thought, "because I have a big meeting today that I can't miss." But the next day, she took more from the leftover bottle, taking four this time. At the end of the week, when that bottle had run out, she was in agonizing pain, barely able to walk. She also felt nauseous. Alone in her bedroom, near tears trying to figure out how she could possibly get more of the medicine, she decided to call her mother in China, with whom she could discuss anything. "Mother," she said, quietly, "I think I have a problem."

Like Mei, people with opioid use disorder reach a point where they need the opioid drug not only to feel good but also to avoid going into withdrawal, and they must continually increase their doses in order to achieve that relief. The temporary high becomes less intense and less important. They may spend much time planning their next dose, in many cases turning to theft or other criminal activities to support the expensive addiction.

Surveys suggest that within a given year, 2 percent of adolescents and adults in the United States, a total of 5.5 million people, display opioid use disorder (SAMHSA, 2023). Emerging research suggests that the prevalence rates among LGBTQ+ people and people of color may be even higher than these overall population rates (Downey & Chang, 2024; Kidd et al., 2023; Waugh et al., 2023).

For 90 percent of people with opioid use disorder, the disorder features an addiction to prescription pain-reliever opioids such as oxycodone (SAMHSA, 2023) (see **Figure 10-2**). For 18 percent, the opioid use disorder includes an addiction to heroin.

FIGURE 10-2

Where Do People Obtain Painkillers for Nonmedical Use?

Around 34 percent get the drugs free from friends or relatives, and 43 percent obtain them from doctors. Only 8 percent buy them from drug dealers. (Information from: SAMHSA, 2023.)

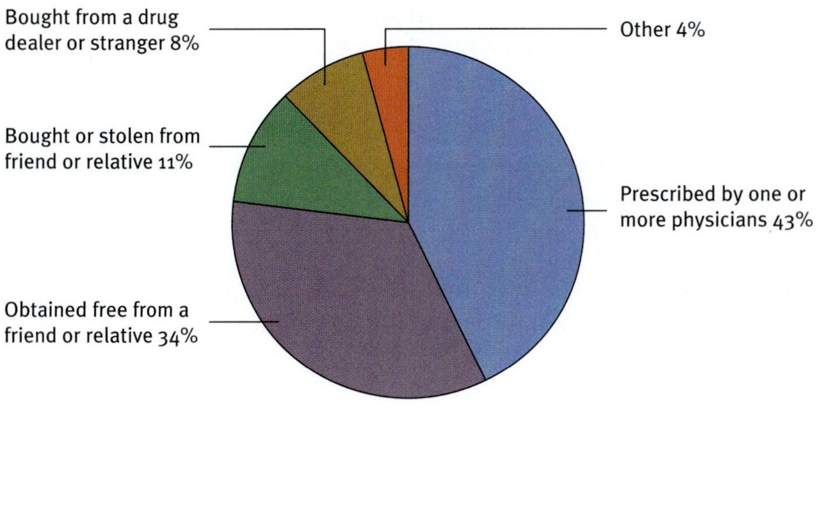

The rate of opioid dependence dropped considerably during the 1980s, rose in the early 1990s, fell in the late 1990s, and now is relatively high once again. Indeed, the striking increase of this rate over the past several years—including the increase among teenagers—and the growing number of deaths caused by opioid overdoses have many clinicians referring to it as an epidemic.

What Are the Dangers of Opioid Use? The most immediate danger of opioid use is an overdose, which closes down the respiratory center in the brain, almost paralyzing breathing and in many cases causing death (Coffin, 2023). Death is particularly likely during sleep, when a person is unable to fight this effect by consciously working to breathe. People who resume using heroin or a pain reliever after having avoided it for some time often make the fatal mistake of taking the same dose to which they had been accustomed before. Because their bodies have been without such opioids for some time, however, they can no longer tolerate the high dose (Kelty, Chrzanowska, & Preen, 2022).

Can you think of other substances or activities that, like opioids, can be helpful in controlled portions but dangerous when used excessively or uncontrollably?

In the past two decades, there has been a 400 percent increase in the number of deaths caused by opioid overdoses. Currently, each year, approximately 13,000 people in the United States die from heroin overdoses, and at least 56,000 die from overdoses of other opioids, primarily pain relievers (CDC, 2023, 2022; NIDA, 2023, 2022). These numbers represent the majority of all drug overdose deaths. The rate of opioid overdose deaths has been particularly high among Indigenous and Black people (Downey & Chang, 2024; Han et al., 2022).

Fentanyl is by far the opioid most commonly linked to overdose deaths. In fact, over the past decade, this synthetic drug has been responsible for around 60 percent of all opioid-related deaths (NIDA, 2023). It is at least 50 times more powerful than morphine and 20 times more powerful than heroin. Thus, it is approved for legal use only in surgery, the treatment of extreme pain, and/or end-of-life care.

At the same time, given the powerful feelings of euphoria and deep relaxation produced by fentanyl, the drug is often sold illegally. Over the past decade, fentanyl overdoses have increased dramatically in almost every city and town in the United States. Given the drug's extraordinary potency and relatively low cost, many street manufacturers and dealers mix it with other substances that they sell, such as heroin,

Mark Ralston/AFP/Getty Images

Deadly effects In 2016, music giant Prince died from an overdose of the opioid drug *fentanyl*, an extremely powerful prescription pain reliever. Immediately after his death, fans started leaving messages outside his residential compound in Minnesota, including this one with apt lyrics from Prince's song "Let's Go Crazy."

of NOTE ...

Diagnostic Controversy

DSM-5-TR combines two past disorders, *substance abuse* and *substance dependence,* into a single category—*substance use disorder.* Critics worry that clinicians may now fail to recognize and address the different prognoses and treatment needs of people who abuse substances and those who depend on substances.

cocaine, and marijuana. This allows them to extend the supplies of their more expensive drugs and increases the likelihood that their customers will return for more purchases, as fentanyl-laced substances are so addictive. One highly dangerous result is that many users of illicit drugs are unknowingly taking fentanyl in high quantities. For example, many heroin users may think they are taking their usual dose of heroin but are actually also taking the much more powerful fentanyl—a misperception that can quickly lead to their death (CDC, 2023).

Opioid users run other risks as well. Drug dealers often mix opioids with a cheaper drug or even a deadly substance, such as cyanide or battery acid, which can cause seizures and cardiac arrest. In addition, dirty needles and other unsterilized equipment used by opioid injectors spread infections such as HIV/AIDS, hepatitis C, and skin abscesses (Strain, 2022). This problem was exacerbated during the Covid-19-linked work shutdowns and social-distancing regulations, when many unhoused substance users had to go months without receiving their usual supplies of clean syringes from community aid workers (Saloner et al., 2022; Shapira & Neumark, 2022).

SUMMING UP

Substance Misuse and Depressants

Chronic and excessive use can lead to substance use disorders. Many people with such disorders also develop a tolerance for the substance in question and/or have unpleasant withdrawal symptoms when they abstain from it.

Depressants are substances that slow the activity of the central nervous system. Chronic and excessive use of these substances can lead to problems such as alcohol use disorder, sedative-hypnotic use disorder, or opioid use disorder. Alcohol intoxication occurs when the concentration of alcohol in the bloodstream reaches 0.09 percent. Among other actions, alcohol increases the activity of the neurotransmitter GABA at key sites in the brain. The sedative-hypnotic drugs, which produce feelings of relaxation and drowsiness, include barbiturates and benzodiazepines. These drugs also increase the activity of GABA. Opioids include opium and drugs derived from it, such as morphine and heroin, as well as laboratory-made opioids, such as methadone and opioid pain relievers. They operate by binding to neurons that ordinarily receive endorphins.

Stimulants

STIMULANTS ARE SUBSTANCES that increase the activity of the central nervous system, resulting in increased blood pressure and heart rate, more alertness, and sped-up behavior and thinking. One problematic stimulant is *nicotine,* which is typically ingested by smoking traditional cigarettes or by vaping e-cigarettes. In addition to the dangers posed by nicotine itself, these two forms of ingestion pose significant health risks (see ***InfoCentral***). Another stimulant is *caffeine,* which is found in coffee, tea, cola, energy drinks, chocolate, and certain medications. It is consumed daily by 90 percent of the world's population, but it too can cause certain problems when consumed excessively, including intoxication, withdrawal symptoms, and medical issues (Bordeaux & Lieberman, 2023; Giardina, 2023). Two of society's most problematic stimulants are *cocaine* and *amphetamines.*

What might the enormous popularity of caffeine products, such as coffee, cola, and energy drinks, say about the daily needs and desires of people in today's world?

SMOKING, TOBACCO, AND NICOTINE

Around **20%** percent of all Americans over the age of 11 regularly smoke tobacco—a total of **55 million** people (SAMHSA, 2023)

Similarly, **22%** of the world population over 11 smoke regularly—a total of **1.3 billion** people (WHO, 2023, 2022).

WHO SMOKES REGULARLY IN THE UNITED STATES?

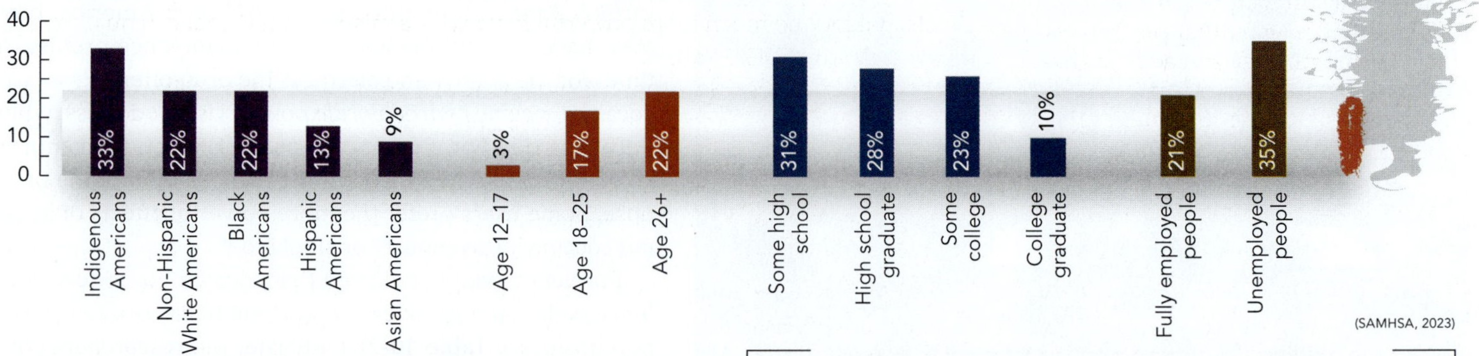

(SAMHSA, 2023)

SMOKING AND HEALTH

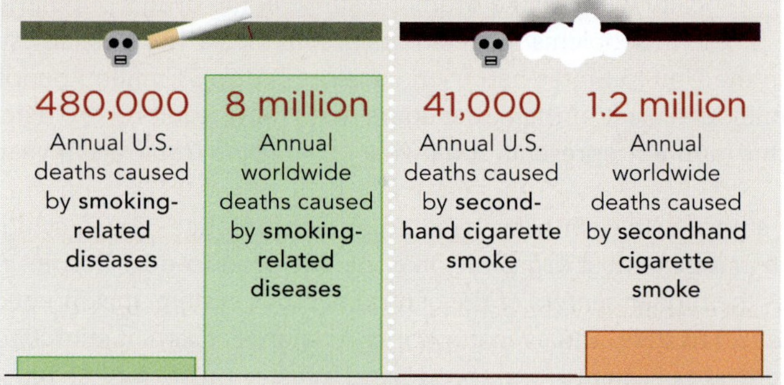

(WHO, 2023; CDC, 2022)

WHY DO PEOPLE CONTINUE TO SMOKE?

Fewer than 10% of smokers are able to successfully quit smoking each year because they are addicted to **nicotine**, the active substance in tobacco (CDC, 2022). Nicotine is a stimulant of the central nervous system that acts on the same neurotransmitters and reward centers in the brain as amphetamines and cocaine. It is as addictive as those drugs and heroin. Smokers addicted to nicotine are said to have **tobacco use disorder**.

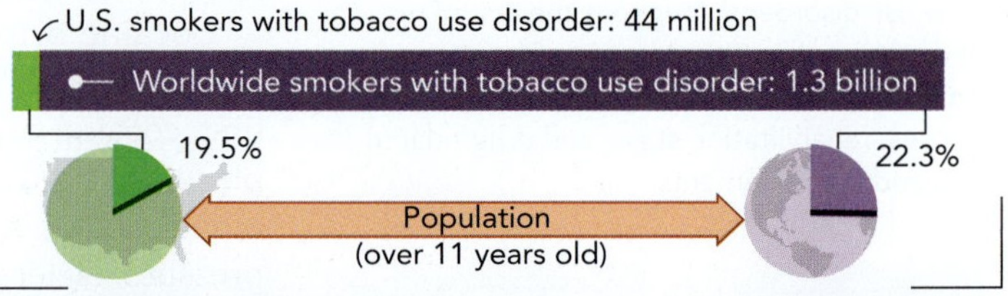

(SAMHSA, 2023; WHO, 2022)

QUITTING SMOKING

More and more smokers try to quit each year. One reason is that many studies have identified the severe health dangers smoking poses. Another is the outstanding job that health agencies have done spreading the word about these dangers. With the declining acceptability of smoking, a market for products and techniques to help people kick the habit has emerged.

Getting the Message

Teens who believe that frequent smoking is harmful

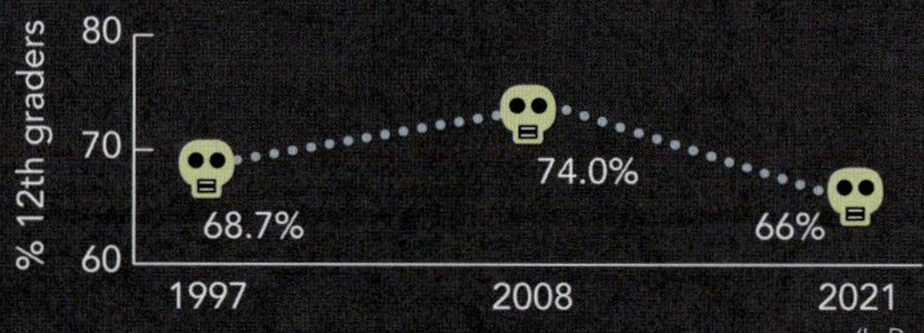

(L. D. Johnston et al., 2022)

Common Aids for Quitting

- **NICOTINE GUM**—Releases nicotine when chewed
- **NICOTINE PATCH**—Releases nicotine through the skin
- **NICOTINE LOZENGES**—Dissolve in the mouth and release nicotine
- **NASAL SPRAY AND INHALER**—Delivers aerosol nicotine into the nostrils
- **PSYCHOTROPIC DRUGS (VARENICLINE, BUPROPION)**—Reduce craving for nicotine
- **SELF-HELP GROUPS**—Offer psychological support
- **BEHAVIORAL COUNSELING**—Teaches alternative behaviors
- **HYPNOSIS**—Provides suggestion

(FDA, 2022; WMD, 2021)

Trying to Stop

(CDC, 2022)

Did You Know That...

- Nicotine is as or more addictive than heroin, alcohol, and cocaine.
- A tobacco cigarette contains 7,000 chemicals, hundreds of which are harmful.
- Smoking harms nearly every organ in the body.
- The life expectancy for smokers is at least 10 years shorter than for nonsmokers.
- Smoking causes 90% of all lung cancer deaths.
- 5 trillion cigarettes are smoked worldwide each year.
- Every day, 1,600 U.S. teens light up their first cigarette.

(OCF, 2023; WMD, 2023; ALA, 2022; CDC, 2022, 2021; Koh & Fiore, 2022)

Paras Griffin/Getty Images

Captive of crack cocaine In 2021, the popular rapper DMX died of a cocaine-induced heart attack at the age of 50. The entertainer, shown here in a mural in Atlanta, Georgia, first became addicted to crack when he was 14 years old, and he continued to struggle with cocaine use disorder throughout the rest of his life. Even throughout his decades of artistic and commercial success, DMX experienced multiple overdoses, rehabilitation stays, and drug-related arrests and imprisonments.

Cocaine

Cocaine—the central active ingredient of the coca plant, found in South America—is the most powerful natural stimulant now known. The drug was first separated from the plant in 1865. Many Indigenous people of South America, however, have chewed the leaves of the plant since prehistoric times for the energy and alertness the drug offers. Processed cocaine (*cocaine hydrochloride powder*) is an odorless, white, fluffy powder. For recreational use, it is most often snorted so that it is absorbed through the mucous membrane of the nose. Some users prefer the more powerful effects of injecting cocaine intravenously or smoking it.

For years, people believed that cocaine posed few problems aside from intoxication and, on occasion, temporary psychosis (see **Table 10-2**). Only later did researchers come to appreciate its many dangers. Their insights came after society witnessed a dramatic surge in the drug's popularity and in problems related to its use. In the early 1960s, an estimated 10,000 people in the United States had tried cocaine. Today, 51 million people have tried it, and 2.3 million—most of them teenagers and young adults—are using it currently, although this number represents somewhat of a decline from recent years (SAMHSA, 2023).

Cocaine brings on a euphoric rush of well-being and confidence. Given a high enough dose, this rush can be almost orgasmic, like the one produced by heroin. At first, cocaine stimulates the higher centers of the central nervous system, making people feel excited, energetic, talkative, and even euphoric. As more is taken, it stimulates other centers of the central nervous system, producing a faster pulse, higher blood pressure, faster and deeper breathing, and further arousal and wakefulness.

Cocaine apparently produces these effects largely by increasing supplies of the neurotransmitter *dopamine* at key neurons throughout the brain (Yuen et al., 2023). Excessive amounts of dopamine travel to receiving neurons throughout the central nervous system and overstimulate them. Cocaine appears to also increase the activity of the neurotransmitters *norepinephrine* and *serotonin* in some areas of the brain.

High doses of the drug produce *cocaine intoxication,* whose symptoms are poor muscle coordination, grandiosity, bad judgment, anger, aggression, compulsive

TABLE 10-2

Risks and Consequences of Drug Misuse

	Potential Intoxication	Addiction Potential	Risk of Organ Damage or Death	Risk of Severe Social or Economic Consequences	Risk of Severe or Long-Lasting Mental and Behavioral Changes
Opioids	High	High	High	High	High
Sedative-Hypnotics Barbiturates Benzodiazepines	 Moderate Moderate	 Moderate to High Moderate	 Moderate to High Low	 Moderate to High Low	 Low Low
Stimulants (cocaine, amphetamines)	High	High	Moderate	Low to Moderate	Moderate to High
Alcohol	High	Moderate	High	High	High
Cannabis	High	Low to Moderate	Low	Low to Moderate	Low
Mixed drugs	High	High	High	High	High

Information from: Boyer & Hernon, 2023; Gorelick, 2023, 2022; Mukamal, 2023; Strain, 2023, 2022; Park, 2022.

behavior, anxiety, and confusion (Nelson & Odujebe, 2023). Some people have hallucinations, delusions, or both, a condition called *cocaine-induced psychosis*.

> *A young man described how, after free-basing, he went to his closet to get his clothes, but his suit asked him, "What do you want?" Afraid, he walked toward the door, which told him, "Get back!" Retreating, he then heard the sofa say, "If you sit on me, I'll kick your ass." With a sense of impending doom, intense anxiety, and momentary panic, the young man ran to the hospital where he received help.*
>
> *(Allen, 1985, pp. 19–20)*

cocaine An addictive stimulant obtained from the coca plant. It is the most powerful natural stimulant known.

freebasing A technique for ingesting cocaine in which the pure cocaine basic alkaloid is chemically separated from processed cocaine, vaporized by heat from a flame, and inhaled with a pipe.

crack A powerful, ready-to-smoke freebase cocaine.

As the stimulant effects of cocaine subside, the user goes through a depression-like letdown, popularly called *crashing,* a pattern that may also include headaches, dizziness, and fainting. For occasional users, the aftereffects usually disappear within 24 hours, but they may last longer for people who have taken a particularly high dose. These people may sink into a stupor, deep sleep, or, in some cases, a coma.

Ingesting Cocaine

In the distant past, cocaine use and its impact were limited by the drug's high cost. Moreover, cocaine was usually snorted, a form of ingestion that has less powerful effects than either smoking or injection. Since 1984, however, the availability of newer, more powerful, and sometimes cheaper forms of cocaine has produced greater use of the drug. For example, many people now ingest cocaine by **freebasing,** a technique in which the pure cocaine basic alkaloid is chemically separated, or "freed," from processed cocaine, vaporized by heat from a flame, and inhaled through a pipe.

Many other people use **crack,** a powerful form of freebase cocaine that has been boiled down into crystalline balls. It is smoked with a special pipe and makes a crackling sound as it is inhaled (hence the name). Crack is sold in small quantities at a fairly low cost. Back in the 1980s, its affordability led to wide use among people who previously could not have afforded cocaine, primarily those in low-income, urban areas (Goulian et al., 2022). The prevalence of crack use has decreased during the past two decades; however, it is still the case that 0.4 percent of all people over age 11—almost 1 million individuals—use it over the course of a year (SAMHSA, 2023).

What Are the Dangers of Cocaine?

Aside from cocaine's harmful effects on behavior, cognition, and emotion, the drug poses serious physical dangers. Use of the more powerful forms of cocaine has caused the annual number of cocaine-related emergency room incidents in the United States to multiply more than 125 times over the past four decades (Armoon et al., 2023; Richards & Le, 2023).

The greatest immediate danger of cocaine use is an overdose (Nelson & Odujebe, 2023). Excessive doses have a strong effect on the respiratory center of the brain, at first stimulating it and then depressing it to the point where breathing may stop (Burnett, 2023; Mechem, 2021). Cocaine can also produce major, even fatal, heart irregularities or brain seizures that bring breathing or heart functioning to a sudden stop. Each year, at least 20,000 people in the United States die from an overdose involving cocaine, an enormous increase over the fatality rate of a decade ago, and other countries have shown a similar increase (Darke et al., 2023; NCDAS, 2023). In another kind of danger, pregnant people who use cocaine run the risk of miscarriage and of giving birth to children predisposed to drug use and to irregularities in their immune functioning, attention levels, learning, thyroid size, and dopamine and serotonin activity (Jansson, 2023).

Smoking crack Crack, a powerful form of freebase cocaine, is produced by boiling cocaine down into crystalline balls and is smoked with a crack pipe.

amphetamine A stimulant drug that is manufactured in the laboratory.

methamphetamine A powerful amphetamine drug that has surged in popularity in recent years, posing major health and law enforcement problems.

Amphetamines

Amphetamines are stimulant drugs manufactured in the laboratory. Some common examples are *amphetamine* (Benzedrine), *dextroamphetamine* (Dexedrine), a combination of the two (Adderall), and *methamphetamine* (Methedrine). First produced in the 1930s to help treat asthma, amphetamines soon became popular among people trying to lose weight; athletes seeking an extra burst of energy; soldiers, truck drivers, and pilots trying to stay awake; and students studying for exams through the night. Physicians now know that these drugs can carry serious risks, particularly when misused, and thus cannot be prescribed so casually. *Attention-deficit/hyperactivity disorder (ADHD)*, which is described in the chapter on disorders common among children and adolescents, is one of the few conditions for which amphetamines and related stimulant medications are still commonly prescribed today.

Amphetamine misuse is particularly common among college students. More than 1 of every 10 undergraduates reports acquiring amphetamines or related stimulants without a prescription in the past year and using them to enhance their academic performance, reduce their appetite, or get high (Bouchrika, 2023; Simão et al., 2022). Such students typically acquire the amphetamines from classmates with ADHD who share, sell, or trade their prescribed medications, a risky practice that clinicians refer to as *stimulant diversion* (Coleman et al., 2023).

Amphetamines are most often taken in pill or capsule form, although some people inject the drugs intravenously or smoke or snort them for a more rapid, powerful, and euphoric effect. Like cocaine, amphetamines increase energy and alertness and reduce appetite when taken in small doses; produce a rush, intoxication, and psychosis in high doses; and cause an emotional letdown as they leave the body. Also like cocaine, amphetamines stimulate the central nervous system by increasing the release of the neurotransmitters dopamine, norepinephrine, and serotonin throughout the brain, although the actions of amphetamines differ somewhat from those of cocaine (Martin & Le, 2023).

A particularly potent and addictive kind of amphetamine, **methamphetamine** (nicknamed *meth* or *crank*), has surged in popularity over the past decade and so warrants special focus. Around 6 percent of all people over the age of 11 in the United States (almost 17 million persons) have used methamphetamine at least once in their lives, with 0.9 percent (around 2.5 million persons) using it within the past year (SAMHSA, 2023). The drug is available in the form of crystals (also known by the street names *ice* and *crystal meth*), which users smoke. In the United States, the drug is popular among a wide range of people, from biker gangs to rural populations, and it has gained wide use as a "club drug," the term for drugs that regularly find their way to all-night dance parties, or "raves" (NIDA, 2023).

Methamphetamine: Spreading the word
Former drug user Joe Garcia (right) and his son hold signs at a Rapid City, South Dakota, street corner, warning pedestrians and motorists about methamphetamine use and addiction. Garcia and his family are on a mission, initiated after the methamphetamine-related death of Joe's twin, to educate others about the medical, psychological, and personal dangers of the drug and its devastating impact on families.

Adam Fondren/Rapid City Journal via AP

Much of the nonmedical methamphetamine in the United States is made in small mobile "stovetop laboratories" (converted RVs and campers), which typically operate for a few days in a remote area and then move on to a new—safer—location (Boyer & Hernon, 2023). Such laboratories have been around since the 1960s, but they have increased eightfold—in number, in production, and in being confiscated by authorities—this century. A major health concern is that the secret laboratories expel dangerous fumes and residue.

Since 1989, when the media first began reporting about the dangers of smoking methamphetamine crystals, the increase in usage has been dramatic. Methamphetamine-linked emergency room visits keep rising in hospitals, and use of this particular drug is now one of the leading reasons for admission to drug-related treatment programs, increasing from 15 percent to 24 percent of all admissions in recent years (Armoon et al., 2023; Jones et al., 2023, 2020).

Methamphetamine users are initially attracted to the increases in arousal, attention, and disinhibition produced by the drug, but, as they soon find out, this powerful stimulant may eventually have serious negative effects on their physical, mental, and social life (Paulus, 2023). For example, chronic methamphetamine users may develop open sores across their skin, and some may lose their teeth, a condition called "meth mouth." Some users experience serious damage to their nerve endings, a problem called *neurotoxicity*. And one-third of methamphetamine users develop paranoia, delusions, and hallucinations; some do not recover from this syndrome (Yasaei & Saadabadi, 2023; Hogarth, Manning, & van den Buuse, 2022).

Stimulant Use Disorder

Regular use of either cocaine or amphetamines may lead to *stimulant use disorder*. The stimulant comes to dominate the person's life, and the person may remain under the drug's effects much of each day and function poorly in social relationships and at work. People may develop tolerance and withdrawal reactions to the drug—they must take increasingly higher doses in order to gain the desired effects, and when they stop taking it, they may go through deep depression, fatigue, sleep problems, irritability, and anxiety (Mullen, Richards, & Crawford, 2023). These withdrawal symptoms usually peak and begin to subside around seven days after drug use has ended; however, the symptom of depression can last for weeks or even months. In a given year, 0.5 percent of all people over 11 years of age display a stimulant use disorder that is centered on cocaine (1.4 million people), 0.6 percent display one centered on methamphetamine (1.6 million people), and 0.5 percent display one centered on another kind of amphetamine (1.4 million people) (SAMHSA, 2023). Research has not systematically investigated whether the prevalence rates for LGBTQ+ people or people of color are any different from these overall population rates (Downey & Chang, 2024; Kidd et al., 2023; Lodge et al., 2022).

of NOTE ...

Recent Famous Drug Deaths in Music

- Taylor Hawkins, drummer (polydrug, 2022)
- DMX, rapper and actor (cocaine, 2021)
- Juice WRLD, rapper (opioid, 2019)
- Mac Miller, singer and rapper (polydrug, 2018)
- Tom Petty, singer and songwriter (polydrug, 2017)
- Lil Peep, rapper (polydrug, 2017)
- Prince, singer and songwriter (opioid, 2016)
- Whitney Houston, singer (cocaine and heart disease, 2012)
- Amy Winehouse, singer and songwriter (alcohol poisoning, 2011)
- Michael Jackson, singer, performer, and songwriter (polydrug, 2009)

SUMMING UP

Stimulants

Stimulants, including cocaine, amphetamines, caffeine, and nicotine, are substances that increase the activity of the central nervous system. Frequent use of cocaine or amphetamines can lead to stimulant use disorder. Stimulants produce their effects by increasing the activity of dopamine, norepinephrine, and serotonin in the brain.

Hallucinogens, Cannabis, and Combinations of Substances

OTHER KINDS OF SUBSTANCES may also cause problems for their users and for society. *Hallucinogens* produce delusions, hallucinations, and other sensory changes. *Cannabis* produces sensory changes, but it also has depressant and stimulant effects, and so it is considered apart from hallucinogens in DSM-5-TR. And many people take *combinations of substances*.

hallucinogen A substance that causes powerful changes primarily in sensory perception. Also called a *psychedelic drug*.

LSD (lysergic acid diethylamide) A hallucinogen derived from ergot alkaloids.

MDMA (3,4-methylenedioxymethamphetamine) A stimulant drug that also produces hallucinogenic effects and so is typically viewed as a hallucinogenic drug. Also called *Ecstasy*.

Hallucinogens

Hallucinogens are substances that cause powerful changes in sensory perception, from strengthening a person's typical perceptions to inducing illusions and hallucinations. They produce sensations so out of the ordinary that they are sometimes called "trips." The trips may be exciting or frightening, depending on how a person's mind interacts with the drugs. Also called *psychedelic drugs,* the hallucinogens include LSD, mescaline, psilocybin, and MDMA (Ecstasy). MDMA is technically a *stimulant,* similar to amphetamines, but it also produces hallucinogenic effects and so is grouped with the hallucinogens by the U.S. Department of Health and Human Services. Many hallucinogens come from plants or animals; others are produced in laboratories.

LSD (lysergic acid diethylamide)

LSD, one of the most famous and most powerful hallucinogens, was derived by Swiss chemist Albert Hoffman in 1938 from a group of naturally occurring drugs called *ergot alkaloids.* During the 1960s, a decade of social rebellion and experimentation, millions of people turned to the drug as a way of expanding their experience. Within two hours of being swallowed, LSD brings on a state of *hallucinogen intoxication,* sometimes called *hallucinosis,* marked by a general strengthening of perceptions, particularly visual perceptions, along with psychological changes and physical symptoms (Holze et al., 2023, 2022, 2020; Hwang & Saadabadi, 2023). People may focus on small details—the pores of the skin, for example, or individual blades of grass. Colors may seem enhanced or take on a shade of purple. People may have illusions in which objects seem distorted and appear to move, breathe, or change shape. A person under the influence of LSD may also hallucinate—seeing people, objects, or forms that are not actually present. In addition to such changes in visual perception, hallucinosis may cause one to hear sounds more clearly, feel tingling or numbness in the limbs, or confuse the sensations of hot and cold. The drug may also cause different senses to cross, an effect called *synesthesia.* Colors, for example, may be "heard" or "felt."

LSD can also induce strong emotions, from joy to anxiety or depression (Holze et al., 2023, 2022, 2020). The perception of time may slow dramatically. Long-forgotten thoughts and feelings may resurface. Physical symptoms can include sweating, palpitations, blurred vision, tremors, and poor coordination. All of these effects take place while the user is fully awake and alert, and they wear off in about six hours.

AP Photo/Martin Mejia

Mind-expanding tourism Under the supervision of an Indigenous guide, a tourist in Peru drinks *ayahuasca*, a plant-based psychedelic brew. The drug produces altered states of consciousness, including visual illusions and hallucinations, as well as intense vomiting. Although it has been around for centuries, the powerful drug has been popularized by several writers in recent years, with many tourists now traveling to South America for "healing" retreats in which their souls are supposedly purged, their minds expanded, and their psychological and physical ailments mended.

LSD produces these symptoms primarily by binding to some of the neurons that typically receive the neurotransmitter *serotonin,* changing the neurotransmitter's activity at those sites (Hwang & Saadabadi, 2023). These neurons ordinarily help the brain send visual information and control emotions (as you read in the chapter on depressive disorders); thus, LSD's activity there produces various visual and emotional symptoms.

Approximately 10.5 percent of all people above 11 years of age in the United States have used LSD at some point in their lives. Around 0.2 percent, or 524,000 people, use it currently (SAMHSA, 2023). A substance use disorder is relatively rare among LSD users; that is, people do not usually develop tolerance to the drug or have withdrawal symptoms when they stop taking it (Herian, 2022). However, LSD poses dangers for both one-time and long-term users. It is so powerful that any dose, no matter how small, is likely to produce enormous perceptual, emotional, and behavioral reactions. Sometimes the reactions are extremely unpleasant—a so-called bad trip. Consider Zack's experience.

of NOTE ...

Animal "Trips"

Many animals seek out particular natural substances in order to experience psychedelic reactions. For example, jaguars eat the caapi plant for its psychedelic properties, moose and reindeer eat amanita mushrooms, big horned sheep eat lichen, and lemurs eat certain toxic millipedes (Walters, 2022; Dy, 2021).

Zack arrived at the emergency room with his friend Artie. The 27-year-old coder for a Silicon Valley start-up had taken LSD for the first time earlier that evening. Artie had recommended Zack take "only" two doses for his first trip. Within 45 minutes, Zack had sensed that the walls and furniture in his house were rhythmically breathing, and while he at first found the sensation pleasant, he began to believe his recently deceased father knew what he was doing and was furious at him. Zack started crying uncontrollably and began to believe he had damaged his mind irreparably. Even though the lights in his house were low, the faintest light became intolerably bright. He found himself doubting whether he was truly who he thought he was or just a fraud pretending at everything. He became convinced he was dying, if not already dead, and he alternated between uncontrollable laughter, tears, and shouts for help. He also started shaking, and Artie decided to take him to the hospital. Zack was admitted for observation but within several hours had returned to himself, exhausted and embarrassed.

Another danger is the long-term effect that LSD may have. Some users eventually develop psychosis or a mood or anxiety disorder. And a number have *flashbacks*—a recurrence of the sensory and emotional changes after the LSD has left the body. Flashbacks may occur days or even months after the last LSD experience (Hwang & Saadabadi, 2023).

MDMA (3,4-methylenedioxymethamphetamine)

MDMA, best known to the public as *Ecstasy* or *Molly,* was developed in 1910, but it has gained life as a club drug in the past 30 years (Figurasin & Maguire, 2023). Altogether, 21 million people in the United States over the age of 11 have tried MDMA at least once in their lifetime, 2.2 million in the past year, and 600,000 in the past month (SAMHSA, 2023). Around 1.4 percent of all high school seniors have used it within the past year (Miech et al., 2023).

Why do various club drugs, often used at "raves," fall in and out of favor rather quickly?

Ecstasy's allure is that, as a stimulant and hallucinogen, it helps to raise the mood of many partygoers and provides them with an energy boost that enables them to keep dancing and partying. It may also produce strong feelings of attachment and connectedness in users.

As with LSD, users typically do not develop a substance use disorder centered on Ecstasy, but the drug can be dangerous, particularly when taken repeatedly (Figurasin & Maguire, 2023; Hoffman, 2023). In the psychological realm, it may cause immediate depression, anxiety, and memory impairment. In the physical realm, users may experience muscle tension, chills, increases in heart rate and blood pressure, reduced sweat production, heat stroke, and, in the long run, liver damage.

Scott Houston/Polaris

Feeling the effects Shortly after taking MDMA at a rave, this couple manifests a shift in mood, energy, and behavior.

MDMA works by causing the neurotransmitters serotonin and (to a lesser extent) dopamine to be released all at once throughout the brain, at first increasing and then depleting a person's overall supply of the neurotransmitters (Rizzo et al., 2022). The drug's impact on these neurotransmitters apparently accounts for its various psychological effects and associated problems (Figurasin & Maguire, 2023).

Cannabis

Cannabis sativa, the hemp plant, grows in warm climates throughout the world. The drugs produced from varieties of hemp are collectively called **cannabis**. The most powerful of them is *hashish;* the weaker ones include the best-known and most widely used form of cannabis, **marijuana,** a mixture derived from the buds, crushed leaves, and flowering tops of hemp plants. Around 128 million adolescents and adults have smoked marijuana during their lives (46 percent of people in those age groups), and more than 36 million smoke it at least monthly (13 percent of adolescents and adults) (SAMHSA, 2023). A growing number of cannabis users are opting to ingest cannabis through food products referred to as *cannabis edibles,* or simply "edibles" (Zamarripa et al., 2023), or by placing drops of a liquid containing cannabis under the tongue.

When smoked or ingested, cannabis produces a mixture of hallucinogenic, depressant, and stimulant effects. At low doses, the user typically has feelings of joy and relaxation and may become either quiet or talkative. Some users, however, become anxious, suspicious, or irritated, especially if they have been in a bad mood or are using in an upsetting environment. Many users report sharpened perceptions and fascination with the intensified sounds and sights around them. Time seems to slow down, and distances and sizes seem greater than they actually are. This overall "high" is technically called *cannabis intoxication*. Physical changes include reddening of the eyes, fast heartbeat, increases in blood pressure and appetite, dryness in the mouth, and dizziness. Some people become drowsy and may fall asleep.

The source of marijuana Marijuana is made from the leaves of the hemp plant, *Cannabis sativa*, such as the plants being cultivated in this grow room at a medical marijuana dispensary in Massachusetts. *Cannabis sativa* is grown in a wide range of altitudes, climates, and soils.

In high doses, cannabis produces odd visual experiences, changes in body image, and hallucinations. Users may become confused or impulsive. Some worry that other people are trying to hurt them. Most of the effects of cannabis last two to six hours when inhaled or 12 hours when eaten (Wang, 2023). The changes in mood, however, may continue longer.

Each cannabis drug comes in a variety of strengths. Potency is greatly affected by the climate in which the plant is grown, the way it was prepared, and the manner and duration of its storage. Of the several hundred active chemicals in cannabis, **tetrahydrocannabinol** (THC) appears to be the one most responsible for its psychoactive effects—the cannabis "high" and the perceptual, emotional, and cognitive reactions (Morland, Bretteville-Jensen, & Bramness, 2023). The higher the drug's THC content, the more powerful these effects. On average, hashish contains a large portion of THC, while marijuana contains a lower portion.

THC is absorbed in the body more quickly when it is inhaled than when it is ingested. Thus, marijuana smokers experience effects more quickly than those who ingest edibles. At the same time, because THC is absorbed more slowly when cannabis is eaten, the effects of edibles tend to last much longer than the effects of smoking marijuana (AAC, 2022; Johnson, 2020).

cannabis Drugs produced from the varieties of the hemp plant *Cannabis sativa*. They cause a mixture of hallucinogenic, depressant, and stimulant effects.

marijuana One of the cannabis drugs, derived from the buds, leaves, and flowering tops of the hemp plant *Cannabis sativa*.

tetrahydrocannabinol (THC) The main active ingredient of cannabis substances.

Cannabis Use Disorder

Until the early 1970s, the use of marijuana, the weak form of cannabis, rarely led to a pattern of *cannabis use disorder*. Today, however, many people regularly get quite high smoking marijuana or ingesting edibles, develop symptoms of tolerance and withdrawal, experience social or occupational (or academic) impairment, and come to display cannabis use disorder (Gorelick, 2023, 2022; Morissette et al., 2023) (see **Figure 10-3**). In the United States, 16.3 million people—5.8 percent of all persons above 11 years of age—have manifested this disorder within the past year (SAMHSA, 2023). It is particularly common among 18- to 25-year-olds; their annual rate is 14.4 percent. Several studies suggest that the prevalence rates for LGBTQ+ people and people of color may be even higher than these overall population rates (Downey & Chang, 2024; Struble et al., 2024; Kidd et al., 2023).

Why do so many of today's cannabis users fall into a pattern of cannabis use disorder, in contrast to users several decades ago? Mainly because marijuana itself has changed. The marijuana widely available in the United States today is at least seven times more powerful than that used in the early 1970s. The THC content of today's marijuana is typically 15 percent or more, compared with 2 percent in the 1970s (Morland et al., 2023; EPR, 2020). Marijuana is now grown in places with a hot, dry climate, which increases the THC content. The THC level when users vape cannabis is higher still (see ***Trending***).

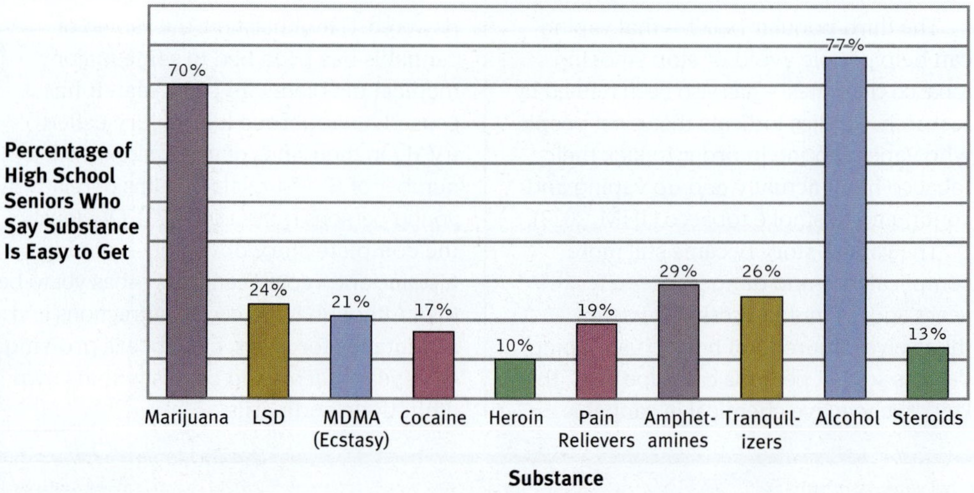

FIGURE 10-3

How Easy Is It for Teenagers to Acquire Problematic Substances?

Most surveyed high school seniors say it is easy to get alcohol and marijuana, and more than a quarter say it is easy to get amphetamines and tranquilizers. (Information from: Johnston et al., 2022.)

...TRENDING

Vaping: New Devices, New Problems

In 2007, a new way of inhaling nicotine was introduced in the United States—electronic cigarettes, or *e-cigarettes*. E-cigarettes are handheld battery-powered vaporizers that enable users to inhale aerosol (*vapor*) rather than cigarette smoke. In the case of nicotine, the device heats a solution that contains nicotine and converts it to vapor, which, in turn, is inhaled by the user.

Ever since vaping's introduction, its use for delivering nicotine has grown by leaps and bounds, especially among teenagers (Rigotti & Reddy, 2023). On average, the number of teenagers vaping nicotine was increasing by as much as 50 percent each year, until they entered social isolation and were closed out of school due to the Covid-19 pandemic. Currently, 21 percent of all high school seniors vape nicotine frequently, while only 4 percent of them smoke tobacco cigarettes frequently (Miech et al., 2023).

AleksandrYu/Getty Images

A new kind of bar Two teenagers smoke e-cigarettes at a vape bar. These bars, where users congregate to vape and try out new vapor mixtures, have popped up across the United States and throughout the world.

Teenagers give many reasons for vaping (FDA, 2023; JHM, 2023). Many like the flavorings (such as apple pie or watermelon). Others appreciate the lack of smoke (with no odor, the stigma of smoking is reduced). A number have also said they vape because it feels adventuresome, offers a good time with friends, and is relaxing. The explosion of vaping nicotine has been fueled by three popular beliefs—that vaping is safe, nonaddictive, and a way to avoid or reduce the smoking of tobacco cigarettes. These beliefs have not been supported by research.

The predominant belief by the public is that vaping nicotine is less dangerous to one's health than smoking tobacco, the latter of which is strongly linked to serious heart, lung, and liver diseases, cancer, and premature death. For example, more than 66 percent of today's high school seniors believe that regularly vaping nicotine is safe, compared to only 34 percent who think regular tobacco smoking is safe (Miech et al., 2023; Johnston et al., 2022). Consistent with these notions, studies suggest that vaping nicotine does not produce the number, range, or severity of health problems associated with smoking tobacco cigarettes (Rigotti & Reddy, 2023). However, the vapor that is inhaled during nicotine vaping does contain certain toxic chemicals that may, in certain cases, increase the risks of cancer, heart disease, and lung disease (JHM, 2023).

The second popular belief—that vaping nicotine is less addictive than smoking tobacco—has been clearly refuted by research. Nicotine is a very powerful and addictive substance that can lead to a pattern of substance use disorder, whether it is inhaled by vaping or by smoking tobacco (JHM, 2023; Rigotti & Reddy, 2023).

The third popular belief—that vaping can help people avoid or stop smoking tobacco cigarettes—has also been refuted by research. Studies indicate that most people who vape nicotine in order to kick their tobacco habit actually end up vaping *and* continuing to smoke tobacco (JHM, 2023).

The vaping story became still more complicated—and dangerous—a few years ago. Manufacturers and vapers themselves figured out how to use vaping devices so that persons can vape *THC*, the key psychoactive chemical in cannabis (JHM, 2023). Since then, the vaping of cannabis has been rising dramatically, among teenagers in particular. Today, nearly 15 percent of all high school seniors vape cannabis frequently, a rate that is steadily approaching the 21 percent rate of those who vape nicotine frequently (Miech et al., 2023). Moreover, the THC level in vaped cannabis is several times higher than the level in traditionally smoked marijuana, increasing the likelihood that regular users will fall into a pattern of cannabis use disorder (Keyes et al., 2022; SD, 2022).

Beyond the addiction potential of high-powered THC inhalation, the vaping of cannabis has been tied to some major medical problems. In particular, it has caused a dangerous lung injury called EVALI in thousands of users, along with a number of EVALI-related deaths of relatively young persons (Kathuria, 2023). Obviously, the complete story of vaping—vaping nicotine and vaping cannabis—has yet to be told. Although it has certain attractions and advantages for users, evidence is growing each year that vaping comes with its own limitations and perils.

Is Cannabis Dangerous? Researchers have discovered that using marijuana may pose certain dangers (Hashemi & Gray, 2023). It occasionally causes panic reactions, and some smokers fear they are losing their minds.

Because cannabis can interfere with cognitive functioning and the performance of complex sensorimotor tasks, it has caused many automobile accidents. Indeed, each year, 4.1 percent of adults drive (at least once) while under the influence of marijuana or another cannabis product (LoParco et al., 2024; SAMHSA, 2023). Furthermore, people under the effects of cannabis often fail to remember information, especially anything that has been recently learned, no matter how hard they try to concentrate; thus, heavy cannabis users are at a serious disadvantage at school or work (Morissette et al., 2023).

There are research indications that regular cannabis use may also lead to long-term health problems (Gorelick, 2023, 2022; Saviano, 2022). Marijuana smoking may, for example, contribute to lung disease, although there is considerable debate on this issue. Some studies suggest that marijuana smoking reduces the ability to expel air from the lungs, perhaps even more than tobacco smoking does. Another concern is the effect of regular marijuana smoking on human reproduction. Studies since the late 1970s have linked chronic marijuana smoking with lower sperm counts and atypical ovulation.

Ethan Miller/Getty Images

Tasty high An assortment of cannabis edibles are on display at this cannabis dispensary in Nevada, where purchases of both recreational or medical marijuana are legal. Edibles are absorbed in the body less rapidly than smoked cannabis, but their popularity is on the rise.

Efforts to educate the public about the dangers of repeated cannabis use appeared to have paid off throughout the 1980s. The percentage of high school seniors who smoked marijuana on a daily basis decreased from 11 percent in 1978 to 2 percent in 1992. Today, however, 6.3 percent of high school seniors smoke it daily (Miech et al., 2023), and 79 percent of high school seniors do not believe that regular use poses a great risk (Johnston et al., 2022).

Cannabis and Society: A Rocky Relationship For centuries, cannabis played a respected role in medicine. It was recommended as a surgical anesthetic by Chinese physicians 2,000 years ago and was used in other lands to treat cholera, malaria, coughs, insomnia, and rheumatism. When cannabis entered the United States in the early twentieth century, mainly in the form of marijuana, it was likewise used for various medical purposes. Soon, however, more effective medicines replaced it, and the favorable view of cannabis began to change. Marijuana began to be used as a recreational drug, and its illegal distribution became a law enforcement problem. Authorities assumed it was highly dangerous and outlawed the "killer weed."

In the 1980s, researchers developed precise techniques for measuring THC and for extracting pure THC from cannabis; they also developed laboratory forms of THC. These inventions opened the door to new medical applications for cannabis, such as its use in treating glaucoma, a severe eye disease (Duncan et al., 2024). Cannabis was also found to help patients with chronic pain or asthma, reduce the nausea and vomiting of cancer patients in chemotherapy, and improve the appetites of people with HIV/AIDS and so help them combat weight loss.

Given such findings, several interest groups campaigned during the late 1980s for the *medical legalization* of marijuana, which operates on the brain and body more quickly than the THC capsules developed in the laboratory. Government agencies resisted this movement, saying prescriptions for pure THC served all needed medical functions. However, medical marijuana advocates pressed on, and in 2009, the U.S. Attorney General directed federal prosecutors to not pursue cases against medical marijuana users or their caregivers who were complying with state laws. Today, at least 39 states (plus Washington, DC, Guam, and Puerto Rico) have laws allowing cannabis to be used for medical purposes, and several more have such laws pending (WPR, 2023). Medical marijuana is also legal in dozens of countries (Gorelick, 2023, 2022).

Heartened by mounting research support for the medical usefulness of marijuana, a movement to also legalize the recreational use of marijuana has gained enormous

of NOTE ...

Changing Course

- In 1913, California became one of the first states to declare marijuana a poison and to criminalize its sale or possession.
- In 1996, California was the first state to legalize medical marijuana.

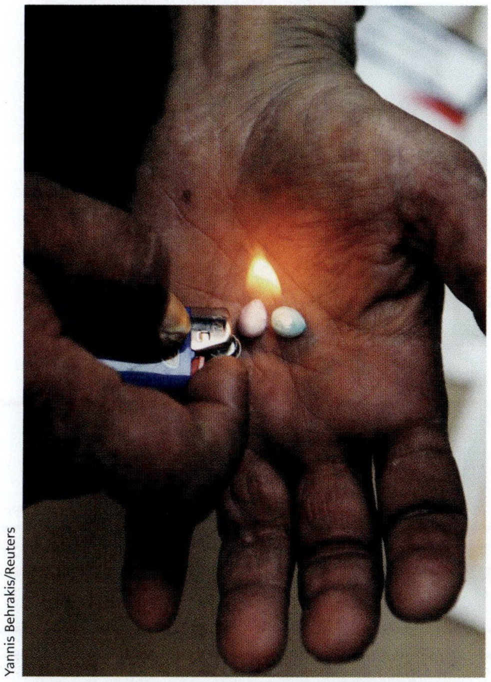

Easy to make, dangerous to take A drug user in Greece prepares a cocktail known as a speedball, a mixture of cocaine and heroin. The pink capsule in her hand contains heroin, and the blue one contains cocaine. Speedballs have been linked to numerous polysubstance deaths.

momentum in recent years. In fact, since 2012, the residents of at least 24 states have voted to legalize marijuana for use of any kind (WPR, 2023). Altogether, according to recent polls, 59 percent of the population now believes that marijuana should be made legal for all purposes, up from 12 percent in 1969 and 41 percent in 2010 (Van Green, 2022). Several countries around the world have moved even faster than the United States in this realm. Canada, for example, fully legalized the medical use of marijuana in 2017 and the recreational use in 2018.

Combinations of Substances

Many people take a combination of different substances rather than a single substance, a pattern called *polysubstance use*. Correspondingly, many substance abuse disorders are actually *polysubstance use disorders*. Jonah's pattern of substance abuse is a case in point.

If I was being honest—and of course I wasn't, not to anyone—I'd been getting high on one thing or another, usually a combination of things, for over 20 years. It was pot and drinking in high school and college. Back then, I'd smoke a joint before a concert and I'd get so lost in the music. I didn't even do it as often as some of my friends. Then one night at a party people were doing cocaine in the back bedroom and I got curious so I tried it. I felt a burst of energy but it didn't last long. I wound up returning to that back room over and over.

I felt I was fine. I later got a good job working as a middle school teacher—liked the work, loved the kids, and believed I was making an important difference in their lives. At the same time, however, I'd get wasted in bars with my buddies on the weekends, sleeping off hangovers all day Sunday. I got a number for a coke delivery service, and I bought from them sometimes. It never interfered with my job, I believed, just gave me something extra to look forward to. I started coming into work sometimes without having slept, but no one seemed to notice. One year I started buying Percocet on the internet through pill mills, so that drug entered the rotation. I still can't believe I was that reckless. I also tried heroin a couple of times and it was nice, but maybe I was lucky because I never really knew how to get it regularly.

When I was about 30, I moved in with Nikki, and I decided I wouldn't do anything but drink ever again. That lasted about two months, and then one of my old cocaine friends offered me a line of crystal meth. I loved it—so much stronger than coke, lasted all night. I tried to only do it when Nikki was out, but eventually I did it when she was home as well, telling her I needed to work all night on a contract so she'd stay out of my way. Sometimes I'd buy some molly too, which was a more relaxed, trippy experience.

Because people often take more than one drug at a time, researchers have studied the ways in which drugs interact with one another. When different drugs are in the body at the same time, they may *multiply*, or potentiate, each other's effects. The combined impact, called a *synergistic effect*, is often greater than the sum of the effects of each drug taken alone: a small dose of one drug mixed with a small dose of another can produce an enormous change in body chemistry.

One kind of synergistic effect occurs when two or more drugs have *similar actions*. For instance, alcohol, benzodiazepines, barbiturates, and opioids—all depressants—may severely depress the central nervous system when mixed. Combining them, even in small doses, can lead to extreme intoxication, coma, and even death. For example, a young man may have just a few alcoholic drinks at a party, and shortly afterward take a moderate dose of barbiturates to help him fall asleep. He believes he has acted with restraint and good judgment—yet he may never wake up.

A different kind of synergistic effect results when drugs have *opposite*, or *antagonistic, actions*. Stimulant drugs, for example, interfere with the liver's usual disposal of barbiturates and alcohol. Thus, people who combine barbiturates or alcohol with cocaine or amphetamines may build up toxic, even lethal, levels of the depressant drugs in their systems (Hammad et al., 2022). Students who take amphetamines to help them study late into the night and then take barbiturates to help them fall asleep are unknowingly placing themselves in serious danger.

Each year, tens of thousands of people are admitted to hospitals with a multiple-drug emergency, and several thousand of them die (Kelty et al., 2022). Sometimes the cause is carelessness or ignorance. Often, however, people use multiple drugs precisely because they enjoy the synergistic effects. In fact, many clinical observers believe that the majority of those who use one illicit drug are also using another to some extent.

of NOTE ...

Bad Age

By a strange coincidence, several of music's most famous stars and substance misusers have died at age 27. They include Jimi Hendrix, Jim Morrison, Janis Joplin, Kurt Cobain, Brian Jones, Russell (Ol' Dirty Bastard) Jones, and Amy Winehouse. The phenomenon has been called "The 27 Club" in some circles.

SUMMING UP

Hallucinogens, Cannabis, and Combinations of Substances

Hallucinogens, such as LSD, are substances that cause powerful changes primarily in sensory perception. People's perceptions are intensified, and they may have illusions and hallucinations. LSD apparently causes such effects by disturbing the release of the neurotransmitter serotonin. The stimulant drug MDMA also produces hallucinogenic effects and so is typically grouped with the hallucinogens.

The main ingredient of *Cannabis sativa*, a hemp plant, is tetrahydrocannabinol (THC). Marijuana, the most popular form of cannabis, is more powerful today than it was in years past. It can cause intoxication, and regular use can lead to cannabis use disorder.

Many people take more than one drug at a time, and the drugs interact. The use of two or more drugs at the same time—polysubstance use—has become increasingly common.

What Causes Substance Use Disorders?

CLINICAL THEORISTS HAVE developed sociocultural, psychological, and biological explanations for why people develop substance use disorders. No single explanation, however, has gained broad support. Like so many other disorders, excessive and chronic drug use is increasingly viewed as the result of a combination of these factors.

Sociocultural Views

Sociocultural theorists propose that people are most likely to develop substance use disorders when they live under stressful socioeconomic conditions (Sorensen et al., 2022). Studies have found that people who have lower socioeconomic status have higher rates of substance use disorders than those of higher socioeconomic status. Similarly, people who are unemployed have heightened rates of alcohol or opioid use disorder (AAC, 2023; Matthews et al., 2022). In a related vein, 26 percent of unemployed adults currently use an illegal drug, compared with around 15 percent of full-time employees and 18 percent of part-time employees (SAMHSA, 2023).

As you have read throughout this chapter, the prevalence of various substance use disorders is particularly high

Stress of stardom Taylor Hawkins of the rock band Foo Fighters struggled mightily with the special stressors that accompany touring, performing, and superstardom, according to several friends and colleagues. Hawkins died while the band was on tour in 2022, with 10 substances in his body, including heroin, benzodiazepines, and antidepressants.

Kevin Winter/Getty Images

Unhoused people and substance use
Two unhoused people inject themselves with a mixture of heroin and fentanyl on a street in Philadelphia. People who live under stressful economic conditions are relatively more likely to develop substance use disorders. Correspondingly, opioid abuse and opioid overdoses have shown a particularly sharp spike in unhoused environments in recent years.

among marginalized individuals such as LGBTQ+ people and people of color. Many theorists explain this heightened rate by pointing to the special stressors such people experience, including discrimination, stigmatization, fewer job opportunities, inadequate health care availability, and, often in the case of LGBTQ+ people, low social support (Kidd et al., 2023). Apparently, the more these individuals experience such stressors, the more likely they are to develop substance use disorders. For example, a range of studies conducted with Hispanic, Black, and LGBTQ+ people find higher rates of the disorders among those participants who live or work in environments of particularly intense discrimination (Downey & Chang, 2024; Gavurova, Ivankova, & Rigelsky, 2022).

Finally, still other sociocultural theorists propose that people are more likely to develop substance use disorders if they are part of a family or social environment in which substance use is valued or at least accepted. Researchers have learned that problem drinking is more common among teenagers whose parents and peers drink, as well as among teenagers whose family environments are stressful and unsupportive (AAC, 2023; Gallegos et al., 2021). In related work, relatively lower rates of alcohol use disorder are found among Jewish and Protestant people, groups in which drinking is typically acceptable only as long as it remains within clear limits (Shandrow, 2023).

What factors might explain the finding that different ethnic, religious, and national groups have different rates of alcohol use disorder?

Psychodynamic Views

Psychodynamic theorists believe that people with substance use disorders have powerful *dependency* needs that can be traced to their early years (Estévez et al., 2022). They suggest that when parents fail to satisfy a young child's need for nurturance, the child is likely to grow up depending excessively on others for help and comfort, trying to find the nurturance that was lacking during the early years. If this search for outside support includes experimentation with a drug, the person may well develop a dependent relationship with the substance.

Some psychodynamic theorists also believe that certain people respond to their early deprivations by developing a *substance abuse personality* that leaves them particularly prone to drug abuse. Personality inventories, patient interviews, and even animal studies have in fact indicated that individuals who abuse drugs tend to be more dependent, antisocial, impulsive, novelty seeking, risk taking, and depressive than other individuals (Xu et al., 2024; Gavurova et al., 2022). However, these findings are correlational (at least the findings from human studies are) and do not clarify whether such traits lead to chronic drug use or whether repeated drug use causes people to be dependent, impulsive, and the like.

In an effort to establish clearer causation, a pioneering longitudinal study measured the personality traits of a large group of young men who did not have alcohol use disorder and then kept track of each man's development (Jones, 1971, 1968). Years later, the traits of the men who developed alcohol problems in middle age were compared with the traits of those who did not. The men who developed alcohol problems had been more impulsive as teenagers and continued to be so in middle age, a finding suggesting that impulsive men are indeed more prone to develop alcohol use disorder (Halcomb, Yoder, & Cyders, 2022).

A major weakness of this line of argument is the wide range of personality traits that have been tied to substance use disorders. Different studies point to different "key" traits. Inasmuch as some people with these disorders appear to be dependent, others impulsive, and still others antisocial, researchers cannot presently conclude that any one personality trait or group of traits stands out in the development of the disorders (Schuckit et al., 2023; Lee, Ross, & Bothwell, 2022).

of NOTE ...

Family Risk

More than 10 percent of children currently live with a parent who misuses alcohol (NIAAA, 2023).

Cognitive-Behavioral Views

According to cognitive-behavioral theorists, *operant conditioning* may play a key role in substance use disorders. These theorists argue that the temporary reduction of tension or temporary elevation of spirits produced by a drug has a rewarding effect, thus increasing the likelihood that the user will seek this reaction again (Patrick et al., 2024). Similarly, the rewarding effects may eventually lead users to try higher dosages or more powerful methods of ingestion. Beyond these conditioning explanations, cognitive-behavioral theorists further argue that such rewards eventually produce an *expectancy* that substances will be rewarding, and this expectation helps motivate people to increase drug use at times of tension (Duncan, 2020).

Erik McGregor/LightRocket via Getty Images

Greed behind the opioid epidemic
These tombstones were planted outside a bankruptcy courthouse in New York by opioid abuse survivors and other demonstrators. The protestors were calling attention to a 2022 settlement in which the family that owned Purdue Pharma—the maker of the painkiller OxyContin—gained immunity from subsequent criminal and civil prosecution in exchange for the family's agreement to dissolve the pharmaceutical company, never produce opioids again, and pay $6 billion to fund treatment. Purdue had conducted false and misleading marketing that resulted in massive increases in opioid prescriptions.

In support of these views, studies have found that many people do drink more alcohol, seek heroin, or use cannabis when they feel tense (Patrick et al., 2024; Strain, 2022). In one study, as participants worked on a difficult anagram task, a confederate planted by the researchers unfairly criticized and belittled them. The participants were then asked to participate in an "alcohol taste task," supposedly to compare and rate alcoholic beverages. Those who had been harassed drank more alcohol during the taste task than did the control participants who had not been criticized.

In a manner of speaking, the cognitive-behavioral theorists are arguing that many people take drugs to "medicate" themselves when they feel tense. If that is the case, then one would expect higher rates of substance use disorders among people with anxiety, depression, and other such problems. And, in fact, at least 20 percent of all adults with psychological disorders also display substance use disorders (Xu et al., 2024; Gavurova et al., 2022).

A number of cognitive-behavioral theorists have proposed that *classical conditioning* may also play a role in these disorders (MHN, 2023; Kozanian et al., 2022). As you may remember from earlier chapters, classical conditioning occurs when two stimuli that appear close together in time become connected in a person's mind so that eventually the person responds similarly to each stimulus. Cues or objects present in the environment at the time a person takes a drug may act as classically conditioned stimuli and come to produce some of the same pleasure brought on by the drugs themselves. Just the sight of a hypodermic needle, "drug buddy," or regular supplier, for example, has been known to comfort people who are addicted to heroin or amphetamines and to relieve their withdrawal symptoms. In a similar manner, cues or objects that are present during withdrawal distress may *produce* withdrawal-like symptoms. For example, one man who had formerly been dependent on heroin became nauseated and had other withdrawal symptoms when he returned to the neighborhood where he had gone through withdrawal in the past—a reaction that led him to start taking heroin again.

Family legacy Drew Barrymore, shown here at the 2021 Rock & Roll Hall of Fame Induction Ceremony, has had a varied career extending from her 1982 breakout role in *E.T. the Extra-Terrestrial* to her current work as host of a popular daytime talk show. Barrymore's family is often pointed to as an example of family-linked and genetic-caused substance misuse. Drew's grandfather, famous actor John Barrymore, died of alcohol poisoning; her father struggled with substance use disorder; her sister died of a drug overdose; and she herself has recovered from substance abuse.

Kevin Mazur/Getty Images

Biological Views

Over the past few decades, researchers have learned that biological factors play a major role in drug misuse. Studies on *genetic predisposition, neurotransmitters,* and *brain circuits* have all pointed in this direction.

Genetic Predisposition

Research with human twins has suggested that people may inherit a predisposition to misuse substances (NIDA, 2023, 2020, 2019; Duncan, 2020). Numerous studies have found an alcoholism *concordance* rate of around 50 percent in identical twins; that is, if one identical twin displays alcoholism, the other twin also does in 50 percent of the cases. In contrast, in these same studies, fraternal twins have a concordance rate of only 30 percent. As you have read, however, such findings do not rule out other interpretations. For one thing, the parenting received by two identical twins may be more similar than that received by two fraternal twins.

A clearer indication that genetics may play a role in substance use disorders comes from studies of alcoholism rates in people adopted shortly after birth. These studies have compared adoptees whose biological parents misused alcohol with adoptees whose biological parents did not. By adulthood, the individuals whose biological parents misused alcohol typically show higher rates of alcohol use disorder than those whose biological parents did not misuse alcohol.

Genetic linkage strategies and *molecular biology* techniques provide more direct evidence in support of a genetic explanation. One line of investigation has found an atypical form of the *dopamine-2 (D2) receptor gene* in a majority of research participants with substance use disorders but in less than 20 percent of participants who do not have such disorders (Blum et al., 2023, 2022, 2018, 1990). Other studies have tied still other genes to substance use disorders (Dick et al., 2023; Hatoum et al., 2023).

reward circuit A dopamine-rich circuit in the brain that produces feelings of pleasure when activated.

Neurotransmitters

Over the past few decades, some researchers have pieced together a neurotransmitter-focused explanation of drug tolerance and withdrawal symptoms (Ciuca Anghel et al., 2023; Hayes et al., 2020). They contend that when a particular drug is ingested, it increases the activity of certain neurotransmitters whose usual purpose is to calm, reduce pain, lift mood, or increase alertness. When a person keeps on taking the drug, the brain apparently makes an adjustment and reduces its own production of the neurotransmitters. Because the drug is increasing neurotransmitter activity or efficiency, the brain's release of the neurotransmitter is less necessary. As drug intake increases, the body's production of the neurotransmitters continues to decrease, leaving the person in need of progressively more of the drug to achieve its effects. In this way, drug takers build tolerance for a drug, becoming more and more reliant on it rather than on their own biological processes to feel comfortable, happy, or alert. If they suddenly stop taking the drug, their natural supply of neurotransmitters will be low for a time, producing the symptoms of withdrawal. Withdrawal continues until the brain resumes its typical production of the neurotransmitters. To some extent, the misused substance dictates which neurotransmitters will be affected (Chester et al., 2022).

The Brain's Reward Circuit

The neurotransmitter-focused explanation of substance use disorder helps explain why people who regularly take substances have tolerance and withdrawal reactions. But why are drugs so rewarding, and why do certain people turn to them in the first place? Brain-imaging studies answer these questions by pointing to the operation of a particular brain circuit—the circuit within which the neurotransmitters under discussion do their work. As you read earlier, a brain circuit is a network of brain structures that work together, triggering each other into action to produce a distinct behavioral, cognitive, or emotional reaction. The circuit that has been tied to substance misuse is the **reward circuit,** also called the *reward center* and the *pleasure pathway* (Rasgado-Tolrdo et al., 2024; Volkow & Blanco, 2023; Weinstein, 2023).

Apparently, whenever a person ingests a substance (from foods to drugs), the substance eventually activates the brain's reward circuit. This circuit features the brain structure called the *ventral tegmental area* (in the midbrain), a structure known as the *nucleus accumbens* (also called the *ventral striatum*), and the *prefrontal cortex* (see **Figure 10-4**). In addition, the circuit includes the amygdala, the hippocampus, and several other structures. The key neurotransmitter in this reward circuit is *dopamine* (Manza et al., 2023). When dopamine is activated throughout the circuit, a person feels pleasure. Music may activate dopamine in the reward circuit. So may a hug or a word of praise. And so do drugs. Although other neurotransmitters also play roles in the reward circuit, dopamine is the primary one.

Certain drugs directly stimulate the structures in the brain's reward circuit. Remember that cocaine and amphetamines directly increase dopamine. Other drugs seem to stimulate the structures in roundabout ways. The biochemical reactions triggered by alcohol, opioids, and marijuana set in motion a series of chemical events that eventually lead to increased dopamine activity in the reward circuit and, in turn, excessive communications (that is, heightened interconnectivity) between the circuit's structures (Cadoni, 2022).

Crack cookies? Researchers at Connecticut College found that the lab-induced addiction of rats to Oreo cookies—particularly the creamy center—was as strong as their lab-induced addiction to cocaine and morphine. The study was conducted to test the growing theory that many high-fat, high-sugar foods stimulate the brain in the same ways and locations that addictive drugs do.

Photo by Bob MacDonnell, courtesy Connecticut College

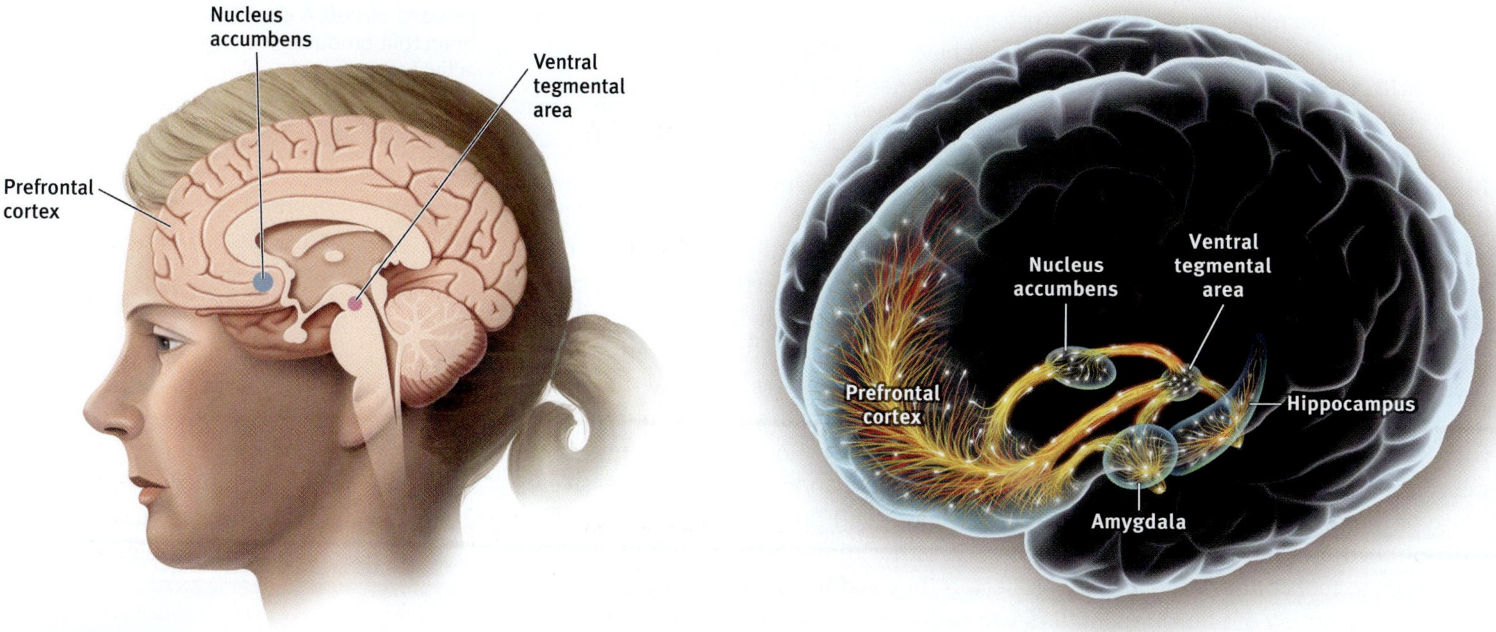

FIGURE 10-4

The Pleasure Pathway

Chronic dysfunction of the brain's reward circuit (left)—which includes the ventral tegmental area, nucleus accumbens, and prefrontal cortex—can lead to a substance use disorder. The illustration on the right highlights how the structures of the circuit work together and trigger each other into action to produce pleasure reactions. The long axons of the neurons from each structure form fiberlike pathways that extend to the other structures in the circuit.

Some theorists suspect that people who chronically use drugs may generally have a *reward deficiency syndrome:* their reward circuit is not readily activated by the usual events in their lives, so they turn to drugs to stimulate this pleasure pathway, particularly in times of stress (Blum et al., 2023, 2022; Kótyuk et al., 2022). Atypical genes, such as the form of the D2 receptor gene discussed earlier, have been cited as possible contributors to this syndrome.

The Developmental Psychopathology View

As with other psychological disorders, a number of substance use theorists have tried to integrate the variables identified by each of the models. Once again, developmental psychopathology theorists have been active in this effort.

According to this perspective, the road to substance use disorders often begins with genetically inherited predispositions—predispositions characterized by a less-than-optimal reward circuit in the brain and by a problematic temperament featuring some of the negative traits discussed earlier in this chapter. Developmental psychopathologists suggest that such predispositions will eventually result in a substance use disorder if the individual further experiences numerous stressors throughout childhood, inadequate parenting (such as substance misuse modeling), satisfying substance use experiences, relationships with peers who use drugs, and/or significant adult stressors (Bataineh et al., 2024; John-Henderson et al., 2024; Gallegos et al., 2021). At the same time, individuals who experience *manageable* adversities throughout childhood and adolescence can develop a level of resilience that may help counter such unfavorable predispositions, stressors, and negative family and peer influences.

Developmental psychopathology theorists propose that either of two very different temperaments may set the stage for later substance misuse. On the one hand, some individuals may begin with a *disinhibited* temperament, also called an *externalizing* temperament—featuring impulsivity, aggressiveness, overactivity, limited persistence, low frustration tolerance, and inattention (Elam et al., 2022; Halcomb et al., 2022). Such individuals have great difficulty controlling their behaviors, thus increasing their risk of having early family conflicts, behavioral problems, and school difficulties—variables that may, in turn, lead to social problems, relationships with undesirable peers, rewards

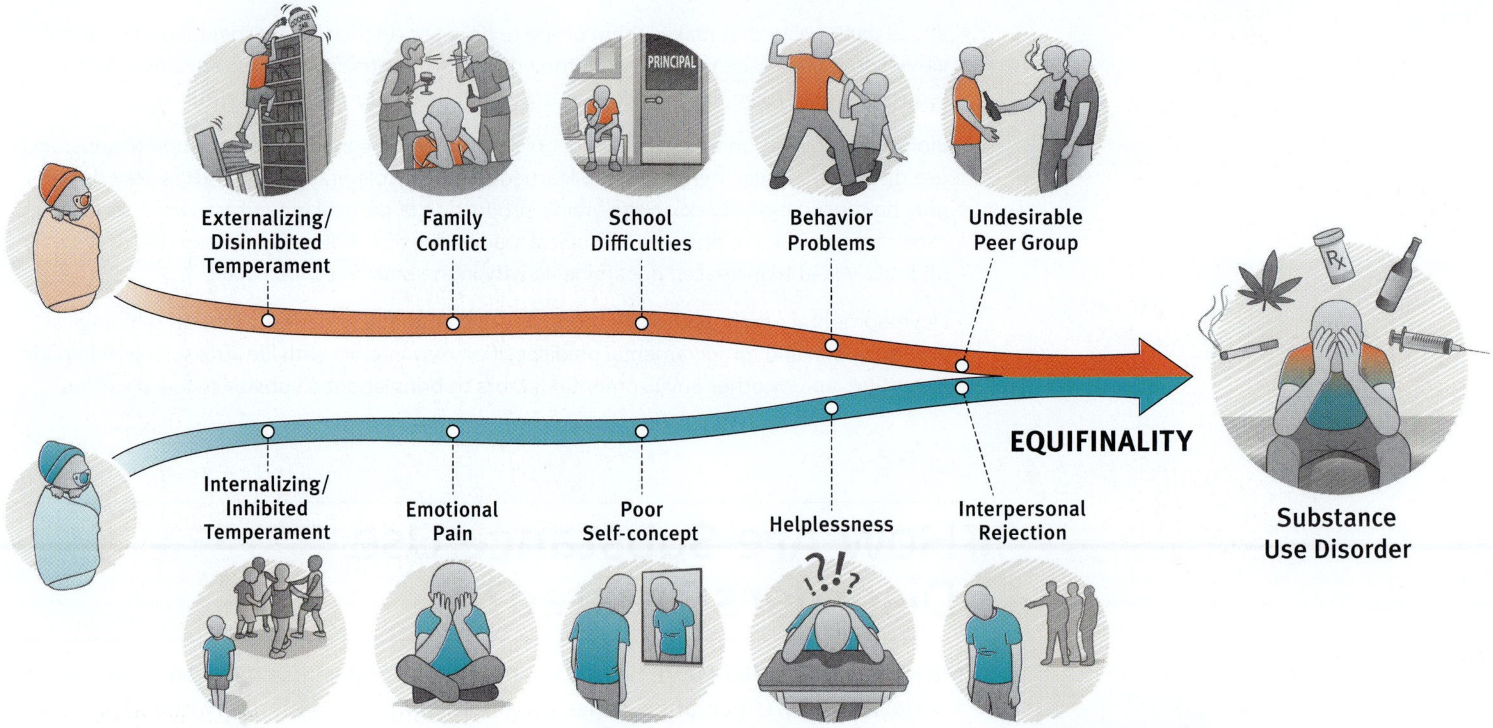

FIGURE 10-5

Development of Substance Use Disorders

In line with the principle of *equifinality*, these two individuals experience different negative variables, yet each winds up with a substance use disorder. For one, an externalizing (disinhibited) temperament interacts with family conflicts, school difficulties, behavioral problems, and an undesirable peer group to help produce the disorder. The substance use disorder of the other person results from interactions between an internalizing (inhibited) temperament, emotional pain, a poor self-concept, a sense of helplessness, and interpersonal rejections.

from those peers for repeated drug use, and, ultimately, the onset of substance use disorders. Studies have confirmed that this cluster and sequence of variables do indeed precede many cases of substance use disorder (Kovács et al., 2022).

On the other hand, according to the developmental psychopathology perspective, other individuals may begin with a temperament of *inhibition* and *negative affectivity,* sometimes called an *internalizing* temperament—characterized by multiple fears, depression, negative thinking, and dependence. This temperament may contribute to worrying and sadness throughout the individuals' development, low self-concept, a sense of helplessness, and interpersonal rejections. These individuals may eventually turn to alcohol and drugs largely because the substances reduce their emotional pain, quiet their troublesome thoughts, and help them through interpersonal difficulties (see **Figure 10-5**). Studies have indicated that this cluster and sequence of variables may also lead to substance use disorders (John-Henderson et al., 2024; Willis et al., 2022).

The notion that different temperaments may trigger and interact with different developmental factors to bring about substance use disorders is consistent with a key developmental psychopathology principle described earlier in the textbook, namely, *equifinality*—the principle that different developmental tracks can lead to the same psychological disorder.

SUMMING UP

What Causes Substance Use Disorders?

Several explanations for substance use disorders have been put forward. According to sociocultural theorists, the people most likely to develop these disorders are those who live in socioeconomic conditions that generate stress or whose families value or tolerate drug use. In the psychodynamic view, people who develop substance use disorders have excessive dependency needs that are traceable to the early stages of life. Some psychodynamic theorists also believe that certain people have a substance abuse personality that makes them prone to drug use. In the leading cognitive-behavioral views, drug use is seen as being reinforced initially because it reduces tensions, and such reductions lead to an expectancy that drugs will be comforting and helpful.

Biological explanations suggest that people may inherit a genetic predisposition to substance use disorders. Researchers have also learned that drug tolerance and withdrawal symptoms may be caused by cutbacks in the brain's production of particular neurotransmitters during excessive and chronic drug use. Biological studies suggest that many, perhaps all, drugs may ultimately lead to increased dopamine activity in the brain's reward circuit.

Developmental psychopathology theorists suggest that a genetically inherited biological predisposition and temperamental predisposition may interact with life stressors, problematic parenting, and/or other environmental factors to bring about a substance use disorder.

How Are Substance Use Disorders Treated?

MANY APPROACHES HAVE been used to treat substance use disorders (Swimmer & Sandelich, 2024). Such approaches are often combined with *motivational interviewing,* an intervention in which therapists help motivate the clients to make constructive choices and behavioral changes (Kiburi et al., 2023; Saxon, 2022). Although treatment sometimes meets with great success, more often it is only moderately helpful (Peavy, 2023; Strain, 2023, 2022). The various interventions are typically offered on either an outpatient or an inpatient basis, in person or by telemental health, or through a combination of these modalities. Only around 9 percent of people with substance use disorders receive treatment (SAMHSA, 2023).

Why might so many treatments for substance use disorders have only limited success?

Psychodynamic Therapies

Psychodynamic therapists first guide clients to uncover and work through the underlying needs and conflicts that they believe have led to the substance use disorder. The therapists then try to help the clients change their substance-related styles of living. Although this approach is often used, it has not been found to be highly effective (Zuccon et al., 2023; López et al., 2021). It may be that substance use disorders, regardless of their causes, eventually become stubborn independent problems that must be the direct target of treatment if people are to become drug-free. Psychodynamic therapy tends to be of more help when it is combined with other approaches in a multidimensional treatment program.

Cognitive-Behavioral Therapies

Cognitive-behavioral treatments for substance use disorders help clients identify and change the behaviors and cognitions that keep contributing to their patterns of substance misuse (Boness et al., 2023; Clevenger, Sturges, & Storie, 2023). The leading cognitive-behavioral interventions for these disorders are *aversion therapy, contingency management, relapse-prevention training,* and *acceptance and commitment therapy.*

Aversion Therapy

In **aversion therapy,** a widely used approach based on the behavioral principle of classical conditioning, clients are repeatedly presented with an unpleasant stimulus (for example, an electric shock) at the very moment that they are taking a drug. After repeated pairings, they are expected to react negatively to the substance itself and to lose their craving for it.

aversion therapy A treatment in which clients are repeatedly presented with unpleasant stimuli while they are performing undesirable behaviors, such as taking a drug.

relapse-prevention training An approach to treating alcohol use disorder in which clients are taught to plan ahead and to apply coping strategies in situations that typically trigger excessive drinking.

Aversion therapy has been used to treat alcohol use disorder more often than other substance use disorders. In one version of this therapy, drinking is paired with drug-induced nausea and vomiting. The pairing of nausea with alcohol is expected to produce negative responses to alcohol itself. Another version of aversion therapy requires people with alcohol use disorder to imagine extremely upsetting, repulsive, or frightening scenes while they are drinking. The pairing of the imagined scenes with alcohol is expected to produce negative responses to alcohol itself. Here is the kind of scene therapists may guide a client to imagine:

> *I'd like you to vividly imagine that you are tasting the (beer, whiskey, etc.). See yourself tasting it, capture the exact taste, color and consistency. Use all of your senses. After you've tasted the drink you notice that there is something small and white floating in the glass—it stands out. You bend closer to examine it more carefully, your nose is right over the glass now and the smell fills your nostrils as you remember exactly what the drink tastes like. Now you can see what's in the glass. There are several maggots floating on the surface. As you watch, revolted, one manages to get a grip on the glass and, undulating, creeps up the glass. There are even more of the repulsive creatures in the glass than you first thought. You realize that you have swallowed some of them and you're very aware of the taste in your mouth. You feel very sick and wish you'd never reached for the glass and had the drink at all.*
>
> *(Clarke & Saunders, 1988, pp. 143–144)*

Aversion therapy for substance use disorders has had only limited success when it is the sole form of treatment (Brooten-Brooks, 2022; Pontzen, Schomerus, & Steinberg, 2022). A major problem is that the approach can be effective only if people are motivated to subject themselves to multiple sessions of this unpleasant procedure, and many people are not.

Contingency Management

Based on the behavioral principle of operant conditioning, *contingency management* programs offer clients incentives (such as vouchers, prizes, cash, or privileges) that are contingent on the submission of drug-free urine specimens (McPherson et al., 2022). In essence, this procedure—usually lasting 8 to 16 weeks—is rewarding clients for abstaining from the use of the substances upon which they are dependent.

Studies indicate that clients in contingency management programs maintain a higher attendance record than those in other kinds of programs (HHS, 2023). However, unless the programs are part of a larger treatment approach, they are at best moderately effective at helping clients abstain from substances for an extended period (Kampman, 2023, 2021; Saxon, 2022). As with aversion therapy, a major limitation is that the approach can be effective only when people are motivated to continue despite its unpleasantness or demands.

Relapse-Prevention Training

One of the most prominent cognitive-behavioral approaches to substance misuse is **relapse-prevention training**. The overall goal of this approach is for clients to gain *control* over their substance-related behaviors. To help reach this goal, clients are taught to identify high-risk situations, appreciate the range of decisions that confront them in such situations, plan ahead of time, develop effective coping strategies, change their maladaptive lifestyles, and learn from mistakes and lapses.

Relapse-prevention training has been found to lower some people's frequency of alcohol intoxication and of binge drinking (Harada et al., 2022; McKay, 2022). People who are young and do not have the tolerance and withdrawal features of chronic

of NOTE ...

Endangered Athletes

College athletes are more likely to drink, drink heavily, and binge-drink than college students who are not athletes (McDuff et al., 2024; McNamara et al., 2022; SAMHSA, 2021; CR, 2020).

Relapse An all-too-common problem in substance use disorders is relapse. After six years of sobriety, popular singer Demi Lovato had a substance use relapse in 2018 and experienced a near-fatal overdose, leading to extended inpatient treatment. As shown here, Lovato returned to performing 18 months later when she movingly sang "Anyone" at the 2020 Grammy Awards, a song about feeling hopeless that she had written just days before her overdose.

Kevin Winter/Getty Images

detoxification Systematic and medically supervised withdrawal from a drug.

antagonist drugs Drugs that block or change the effects of an addictive drug.

naloxone A widely used opioid antagonist.

methadone maintenance program A treatment in which clients are given legally and medically supervised doses of methadone—a heroin substitute—to treat opioid use disorder.

alcohol use seem to do best with this approach. Relapse-prevention training has also been applied successfully in some cases of cannabis, opioid, and cocaine use disorders (Kiburi et al., 2023).

Acceptance and Commitment Therapy

Another form of cognitive-behavioral treatment used in cases of substance use disorder is *acceptance and commitment therapy* (*ACT*). As you read in earlier chapters, ACT therapists use a mindfulness-based approach to help clients become *aware* of their streams of thoughts as they are occurring and accept such thoughts as mere events of the mind. For people with substance use disorders, that means increasing their awareness and acceptance of their drug cravings, worries, and depressive thoughts. By accepting such thoughts rather than trying to eliminate them, the clients are expected to be less upset by them and less likely to act on them by seeking out drugs. Research indicates that ACT is more effective than placebo treatments and at least as effective as other cognitive-behavioral treatments for substance use disorders and sometimes more effective (Dela Cruz et al., 2023; McKay, 2022). In many cases, ACT has been combined with relapse-prevention training or other cognitive-behavioral interventions, a combination that typically yields more success than either approach alone (Stavrinaki, Kelly, & Karekla, 2022).

Biological Treatments

Biological treatments may be used to help people withdraw from substances, abstain from them, or simply maintain their level of use without increasing it further (Truong et al., 2024). As with the other forms of treatment, biological approaches alone rarely bring long-term improvement, but they can be helpful when combined with other approaches.

Detoxification

The systematic and medically supervised withdrawal from a drug is called **detoxification.** Some detoxification programs are offered on an outpatient basis. Others are located in hospitals and clinics and may also include individual and group therapy, a "full-service" institutional approach that has become popular. One detoxification approach is to have clients withdraw gradually from the substance, taking smaller and smaller doses until they are off the drug completely. A second—often medically preferred—detoxification strategy is to give clients other drugs that reduce the symptoms of withdrawal (Truong et al., 2024; Sevarino, 2023). Antianxiety drugs, for example, are sometimes used to help reduce severe alcohol withdrawal reactions such as delirium tremens and seizures. Detoxification programs seem to help motivated people withdraw from drugs. However, relapse rates tend to be high for those who do not receive a follow-up form of treatment—psychological, biological, or sociocultural—after successfully detoxifying (Strain, 2023, 2022).

In case of an emergency This vending machine at the Wayne State University library dispenses free packets of Narcan, a nasal spray version of the opioid antagonist drug *naloxone*, which quickly reverses the effects of opioid overdoses. Narcan was approved by the U.S. Food and Drug Administration in 2023 as the first naloxone product available without a prescription, opening the door for sales of the lifesaving drug to consumers in pharmacies, in convenience stores, online, and in various other locations.

Jim West/Report Digital-REA/Redux

Antagonist Drugs

After successfully stopping their use of a drug, people must avoid falling back into a pattern of chronic use. As an aid to resisting temptation, some people with substance use disorders are given **antagonist drugs,** which block or change the effects of the addictive drug. *Disulfiram* (Antabuse), for example, is often given to people who are trying to stay away from alcohol. A person who drinks alcohol while taking it will have intense nausea, vomiting, blushing, a faster heart rate, dizziness, and perhaps fainting. People taking disulfiram are less likely to drink alcohol because they know the terrible reaction that awaits them if they have even one drink. Disulfiram has proved helpful, but again only with people who are motivated to take it as prescribed (Holt, 2023).

For substance use disorders centered on opioids, several *opioid antagonist drugs,* such as **naloxone,** are used (Truong et al., 2024; Strain, 2023). These antagonists attach to *endorphin* receptor sites throughout the brain and make it impossible for the opioids to have their usual effect. Without the rush or high, continued drug use becomes pointless. In addition, by blocking endorphin receptors during an opioid overdose, opioid antagonists can actually reverse the deadly effect of respiratory depression, thus saving the user's life. Research indicates that opioid antagonists may also be useful in the treatment of alcohol use disorders or cocaine use disorders (Holt, 2023).

Drug Maintenance Therapy

A drug-related lifestyle may be a bigger problem than the drug's direct effects. Much of the damage caused by heroin addiction, for example, comes from overdoses, unsterilized needles, and an accompanying life of crime. Thus, clinicians were very enthusiastic when **methadone maintenance programs** were developed in the 1960s to treat heroin addiction (Dole & Nyswander, 1967, 1965). In these programs, people with an addiction are given the laboratory opioid *methadone* as a substitute, or *agonist,* for heroin. Although they then become dependent on methadone, their new addiction is maintained under safe medical supervision. Unlike heroin, methadone can be taken by mouth (thus eliminating the dangers of needles) and needs to be taken only once a day.

Why has the legal, medically supervised use of heroin (in Great Britain) or heroin substitutes (in the United States) sometimes failed to combat drug problems?

At first, methadone programs seemed very effective, and many of them were set up throughout the United States, Canada, and England. These programs became less popular during the 1980s, however, because of the addictive properties and dangers of methadone itself (Seligman, Cleary, & Berghella, 2023). However, maintenance treatment with methadone has sparked interest once again in recent years, partly because of new research support (Strain, 2023) and partly because of the rapid spread of the HIV and hepatitis C viruses among intravenous drug users and their sex partners and children (Frimpong et al., 2020). Today, thousands of clinics across the United States provide methadone treatment.

Another opioid substitute drug, *buprenorphine,* has also been gaining momentum as a form of maintenance therapy during the past decade (Truong et al., 2024). Like methadone, this drug is itself an opioid that is administered to patients as a safer alternative to heroin, painkillers, and the like (Gottlieb et al., 2023). At the same time, according to research, buprenorphine produces less tolerance and fewer withdrawal reactions than methadone (Seligman et al., 2023). Thus, buprenorphine is permitted by law to be prescribed by physicians in their offices rather than as part of a highly structured clinic program. It is worth noting that buprenorphine is sometimes combined with the opioid antagonist naloxone into a drug named *suboxone.* Research finds that suboxone is indeed a helpful intervention for opioid use disorder, but it is not clearly superior to the use of either of its components alone (Strain, 2023).

Drug maintenance therapies were particularly impacted during the Covid-19 pandemic (Saloner et al., 2022; Shapira & Neumark, 2022). Because stay-at-home orders were initially instituted to help slow the spread of Covid-19, the federal government had to relax its methadone and buprenorphine treatment regulations. For example, federal agencies allowed clinics to dispense extended quantities of methadone to patients so the patients would not have to visit clinics daily, and the agencies required less frequent physician office visits, urine samples, and counseling for patients in buprenorphine treatments. Many patients did not do well under these revised guidelines, leading to more relapses and overdoses than had previously occurred in such treatments.

Drug use . . . under medical supervision
Methadone is itself an opioid that can be as dangerous as other opioids when not taken under safe medical supervision. Here a nurse at a methadone treatment facility prepares the drug for administration to clients.

Chau Doan/LightRocket via Getty Images

Sociocultural Therapies

As you have read, sociocultural theorists believe that psychological problems emerge in a social setting and are best treated in a social context. Two sociocultural approaches that have been used to help people overcome substance use disorders are (1) *self-help and residential treatment programs* and (2) *community prevention programs*.

of NOTE ...

Street Tags

Alcohol	booze, brew
Cocaine	blow, Charlie, rock, snow
Heroin	black tar, horse, smack
Marijuana	grass, Mary Jane, reefer, weed
Amphetamines	bennies, speed, uppers
MDMA	Ecstasy, Molly, X, beans
Methamphetamine	meth, crank, crystal, ice
Pain relievers	Oxy, Percs, Vikes
Gambling	action, gaming, punting

Self-Help and Residential Treatment Programs

Many people with substance use disorders have organized among themselves to help one another recover without professional assistance (USAgov, 2023; Saxon, 2022). The drug self-help movement dates back to 1935, when two Ohio men with alcohol use disorder met and wound up discussing alternative treatment possibilities. The first discussion led to others and to the eventual formation of a self-help group whose members discussed alcohol-related problems, traded ideas, and provided support. The organization became known as **Alcoholics Anonymous** (AA).

Today, AA has over 2 million members in 123,000 groups across the world (AA, 2023). It offers peer support along with moral and spiritual guidelines to help people overcome alcoholism. Different members apparently find different aspects of AA helpful. For some, it is the peer support; for others, it is the spiritual dimension. Meetings take place regularly, and members are available to help each other 24 hours a day.

By offering guidelines for living, the organization helps members abstain "one day at a time," urging them to accept as "fact" the idea that they are powerless over alcohol and that they must stop drinking entirely and permanently if they are to live functional lives. AA views alcoholism as a disease and takes the position that "Once an alcoholic, always an alcoholic." Related self-help organizations, *Al-Anon* and *Alateen*, offer support for people who live with and care about people with alcoholism. Self-help programs such as Narcotics Anonymous and Cocaine Anonymous have been developed for other substance use disorders (Peavy, 2023).

It is worth noting that the abstinence goal of AA is in direct opposition to the controlled-drinking goal of relapse-prevention training and several other interventions for substance misuse. In fact, this issue—abstinence versus controlled drinking—has been debated for years.

Research indicates, however, that both controlled drinking and abstinence may be useful treatment goals, depending on the nature of the particular drinking problem (Bruce & Gross, 2023; Hammarberg et al., 2023).

Ilana Panich-Linsman/The New York Times/Redux

The group factor Clients at a treatment center for substance use disorders in Tennessee embrace during a group therapy session. Group approaches and relationships play a major role in virtually all substance abuse treatments—inpatient and outpatient, professional and self-help, psychosocial and biological.

Many self-help programs have expanded into **residential treatment centers**, or **therapeutic communities**—such as *Samaritan Daytop Village* and *Phoenix House*—where people formerly addicted to drugs live, work, and socialize in a drug-free environment while undergoing individual, group, and family therapies and transitioning back to community life (Saxon, 2022; Song, Kim, & Lee, 2022). Consider, once again, Jonah, the middle school teacher with polysubstance use disorder, whom you met earlier in the chapter:

Alcoholics Anonymous (AA) A self-help organization that provides support and guidance for people with alcohol use disorder.

residential treatment center A place where people who were formerly addicted to drugs live, work, and socialize in a drug-free environment. Also called a *therapeutic community*.

"Not on your life!" Those were my exact words when Nikki gave me the ultimatum. No way was I going away to rehab at 38 years old. What about my job? I'd probably get fired. And would it even be accessible for my wheelchair? I came up with every possible reason why I just couldn't go. "Listen, Jonah," she said, "you're going there or you're moving out. I won't have you here anymore until you get clean. You go from substance to substance, combo to combo—alcohol, marijuana, coke, meth, heroin, Ecstasy. It never stops, it keeps getting worse, and it will never end." I felt like I couldn't breathe. Everything was closing in on me and I thought my life was over.

It came crashing down when she found my stash, although she insisted she was about to leave me anyway because of my unpredictable and manipulative behavior. Terrified, I agreed to go to a place she picked out for me. I thought my life was ending and was scared to meet all the new people. I got there at night, and I nervously met a few people. They asked me what I was there for and I started telling them everything, which I had never done before. During the day we'd have groups, and I opened up about the drugs but also about a lot of other things. I read Narcotics Anonymous (NA) literature, and I recognized myself on nearly every page.

I initially went in just to get Nikki off my back, never thinking I'd stop for good, but after about a week I started to think, maybe this is something I would want to keep working on after I get out of here. The more I talked about my life, the less happy I realized I had been while I was using. And I was stunned by how close I got to the other patients, although there were strict rules about not becoming intimate with any of the patients. Some of the people in there with me were detoxing from heroin, alcohol, or benzos, and they were having a really tough time. One guy getting off Xanax was still hallucinating two weeks in. I surprised myself by really wanting to help them. Lou sort of took charge of always clearing the way for me to wheel through, and we became buddies.

After four weeks, it was time for me to leave, and I was excited not only to get back home but to start attending NA meetings. It was suggested I go to a meeting the day I get back, and the rehab people set me up for an outpatient program while I was still in rehab. I resolved to do, at least try to do, everything that was suggested, whether it made sense to me or not. So, by the time I went home, it felt like a beginning, not the end, of the substance work. Over time Nikki came to see how much better I was doing. I don't ever want to know what would happen if I use again, but I do know this is life and death for me.

The evidence that keeps self-help and residential treatment programs going comes largely in the form of individual testimonials like Jonah's. Many tens of thousands of people have revealed that they are members of these programs and credit them with turning their lives around. Studies of the programs have also had favorable findings, but the number of such studies has been limited (Mutschler et al., 2022; Song et al., 2022).

What impact might admissions by celebrities about past drug use have on people's willingness to seek treatment for a substance use disorder?

Community Prevention Programs

Perhaps the most effective approach to substance use disorders is to prevent them. Most schools have prevention programs. In addition, many substance misuse prevention programs are offered in the community—in-person or by video-conferencing (telemental health); in workplaces, activity centers, and other community settings; and even through the media (SAMHSA, 2023). More than 8 percent of adolescents report that they have

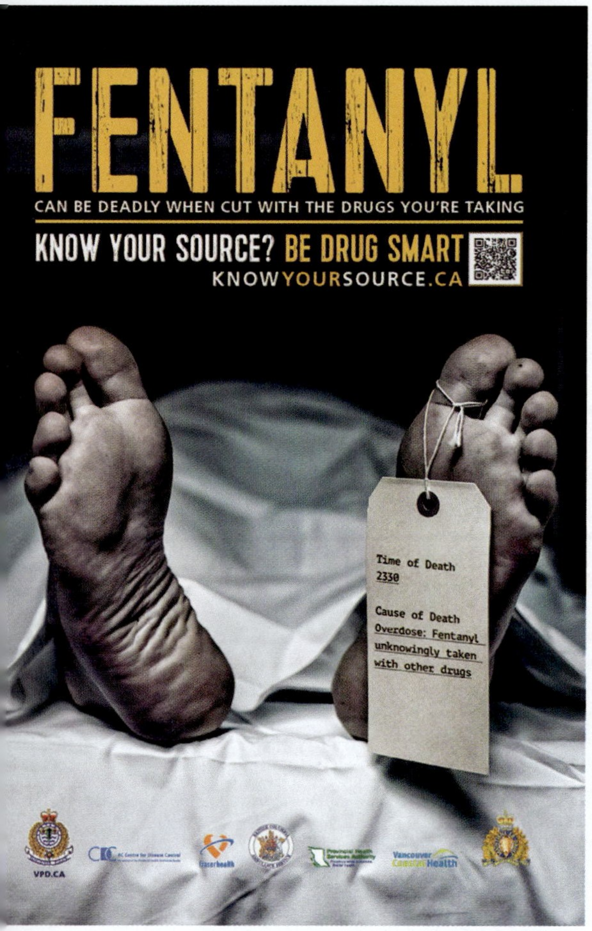

RMCP/Contraband Collection/Alamy

"Know Your Source" One far-reaching substance education program was Canada's *Know Your Source* campaign, launched in 2016 as fentanyl was becoming a growing problem and street drugs laced secretly with fentanyl were leading to more and more overdoses and deaths. In an effort to alert hard-to-reach substance users, posters such as this one were sent to bars, restaurants, and the like, educating potential and current users about the dangers of fentanyl, how to spot the symptoms of overdose, and how to be "drug smart" in one's use of substances.

participated in substance use prevention programs outside school within the past year. Around 65 percent have seen or heard substance use prevention messages. And around 53 percent have talked to their parents in the past year about the dangers of alcohol and other drugs.

Some prevention programs are based on a total abstinence model, while others teach responsible use. Some seek to interrupt drug use; others try to delay the age at which people first experiment with drugs. Programs may also differ in whether they offer drug education, teach alternatives to drug use, try to change the psychological state of the potential user, help people change their peer relationships, or combine these techniques. Prevention programs may focus on the *individual* (for example, by providing education about unpleasant drug effects), the *family* (by teaching parenting skills), the *peer group* (by teaching resistance to peer pressure), the *school* (by setting up firm enforcement of drug policies), or the *community* at large.

Two of today's leading community-based prevention programs are *Truth* and *Above the Influence*. Truth is an antismoking and antivaping campaign, aimed at young people in particular, that has "edgy" ads on social media, on television, and in magazines. Above the Influence is a similar advertising campaign that focuses on a range of substances misused by teenagers. Although such community-based prevention programs have many proponents, it has been difficult to design studies that might clarify their effectiveness in preventing ill-advised substance use.

Culturally Responsive Treatment

As noted earlier, the prevalence of various substance use disorders is particularly high among LGBTQ+ people and people of color, an elevated rate that is tied to the unique kinds of stress, discrimination, and mistreatment they experience and the inadequate health care services available to them. Thus, a growing number of clinicians now offer *culturally responsive* therapies and programs for such people, which combine affirmative (or related) approaches and existing substance-focused interventions (Downey & Chang, 2024; Harkness & Pachankis, 2022; Hereth & Durand, 2022). As you may recall from discussions earlier in the textbook, affirmative and other culturally responsive approaches address clients' unique cultural issues by including a focus on the individual's cultural issues and needs and featuring cultural humility and responsiveness by the therapist.

Similarly, therapists have become increasingly aware that women often require treatment methods that are different from those designed for men (Guttmacher Institute, 2023). For example, cisgender women and cisgender men often have different physical and psychological reactions to drugs. In addition, treatment of women with substance use disorders may be complicated by the impact of higher rates of sexual abuse, the unique stresses linked to traditional female roles in the family and society, the possibility in some that they may be or may become pregnant while taking drugs, the stresses of raising children, and the fear of criminal prosecution for abusing drugs during pregnancy (Thomas & Juckel, 2022). Thus, many women with such disorders feel more comfortable seeking help at gender-sensitive clinics or residential programs; some such programs also allow children to live with their recovering mothers.

Finally, many people with substance use disorders live in underserved and perhaps violent communities. Many of today's treatment programs try to be sensitive to the unique pressures and problems faced by substance users who are unhoused or have low socioeconomic status (APA, 2023). Therapists who are attuned to such challenges can do more to address the stressors that often lead to relapse. Of course, the nature of many clients' *intersectionality* may increase the likelihood that they will encounter interacting stressors: they may experience economic hardship, discrimination, *and* marginalization related to their race, ethnicity, gender, and/or sexual orientation. Such people are more likely to develop substance use disorders and may have still greater need for culturally responsive treatments.

of NOTE ...

Drug Arrest Consequences

Studies reveal that Black and Hispanic people are more likely than non-Hispanic White people to be imprisoned after drug arrests and are less likely to be ordered into treatment (Downey & Chang, 2024; Volkow, 2021).

SUMMING UP

How Are Substance Use Disorders Treated?

Usually, several approaches are combined to treat substance use disorders. Psychodynamic therapists try to help clients become aware of and correct the underlying needs and conflicts that may have led to their use of drugs. Cognitive-behavioral techniques include aversion therapy, contingency management, relapse-prevention training, and acceptance and commitment therapy. Biological treatments include detoxification, antagonist drugs, and drug maintenance therapy. Sociocultural treatments approach substance use disorders in a social context by means of self-help groups (for example, AA), residential treatment programs, and community prevention programs. A growing number of clinicians now offer culturally responsive substance use treatments for LGBTQ+ people and people of color.

Other Addictive Disorders

AS YOU READ at the beginning of this chapter, DSM-5-TR lists **gambling disorder** as an addictive disorder alongside the substance use disorders. This represents a significant broadening of the concept of addiction, which in previous editions of the DSM referred only to the misuse of substances. In essence, DSM-5-TR is suggesting that people may become addicted to behaviors and activities beyond substance use.

Gambling Disorder

It is estimated that 2 to 4 percent of adults and 3 to 10 percent of teenagers and college students experience *gambling disorder* (Domino, 2023; Black, 2020). Clinicians are careful to distinguish between this disorder and social gambling (APA, 2022). Gambling disorder is defined less by the amount of time or money spent gambling than by the addictive nature of the behavior. People with gambling disorder are preoccupied with gambling and typically cannot walk away from a bet. When they lose money repeatedly, they often gamble more in an effort to win the money back and continue gambling even in the face of financial, social, occupational, educational, and health problems (Macdonald-Gagnon & Potenza, 2022). They usually gamble more when they are feeling distressed, and they often lie to cover up the extent of their gambling. Many people with gambling disorder need to gamble with ever-larger amounts of money to reach the desired excitement, and they feel restless or irritable when they try to reduce or stop gambling—symptoms that are similar to the tolerance and withdrawal reactions displayed in substance use disorders (APA, 2022).

The explanations proposed for gambling disorder often parallel those for substance use disorders (Domino, 2023). Some studies suggest, for example, that people with gambling disorder may (1) inherit a genetic predisposition to develop the disorder; (2) experience heightened dopamine activity and dysfunction of the brain's reward circuit when they gamble; (3) have impulsive, novelty-seeking, and other personality styles that leave them prone to gambling disorder; and (4) make repeated cognitive mistakes, such as inaccurate expectations and misinterpretations of their emotions and bodily states. The research on these theories has been limited thus far, leaving such explanations tentative for now.

Several of the leading treatments for substance use disorders have been adapted for use with gambling disorder (Domino, 2023). These treatments include cognitive-behavioral approaches, such as relapse-prevention training, and biological approaches, such as opioid antagonists. In addition, the self-help group program Gamblers

of NOTE ...

Popular Titles

Addiction is a popular theme in music. Hit songs include Future's "Move That Dope," Amy Winehouse's "Rehab," the Rolling Stones' "Sister Morphine," Kenny Rogers's "The Gambler," Pink's "Sober," Eminem's "Drug Ballad," Missy Elliott's "Pass That Dutch," and The Weeknd's "Can't Feel My Face."

gambling disorder A disorder marked by persistent and recurrent gambling behavior, leading to a range of life problems.

rez-art/Getty Images

Increase in gambling venues This woman is playing a slot machine in a casino—harmless fun for her but not for everyone. Some theorists believe that recent increases in gambling disorder are related to the explosion of new gambling venues, including the spread of online gambling.

Anonymous, a network modeled after Alcoholics Anonymous, is available to the many thousands of people with gambling disorder. People who attend such groups seem to have a better recovery rate.

Internet Use Disorder and Internet Gaming Disorder

As people increasingly turn to the Internet for activities that used to take place in the "real world"—communicating, networking, shopping, playing games, and participating in a community—a new psychological problem has emerged: an uncontrollable need to be online (Derevensky et al., 2022). This pattern has been called *Internet use disorder* and *Internet addiction,* among other names.

People who have this pattern—at least 1 percent of all people—spend all or most of their waking hours texting, tweeting, networking, gaming, Internet browsing, e-mailing, blogging, visiting virtual worlds, shopping online, or viewing online pornography. Specific symptoms of this pattern parallel those found in substance use disorders and gambling disorder, extending from the loss of outside interests to possible withdrawal reactions when Internet use is not possible (APA, 2022).

Although clinicians, the media, and the public have shown enormous interest in this condition, it is not included as a disorder in DSM-5-TR. Rather, the DSM workgroup recommended that one version of the pattern, which it calls *Internet gaming disorder,* receive further study for possible inclusion in future editions (Müller, Dreier, & Wölfling, 2023).

of NOTE ...

Smart Phone Addiction?

- 47 percent of people in the United States say they are "addicted" to their smart phones.
- People check their smart phones an average of 352 times per day.

(Information from: Howarth, 2024)

SUMMING UP

Other Addictive Disorders

DSM-5-TR groups gambling disorder alongside the substance use disorders as an addictive disorder. Treatments for gambling disorder include cognitive-behavioral approaches, opioid antagonists, and self-help groups. Clinicians have also identified an addictive pattern called Internet use disorder.

New Wrinkles to a Familiar Story

IN SOME RESPECTS, the story of the misuse of drugs is the same today as in the past. Substance use is still rampant, often creating damaging psychological disorders. New drugs keep emerging, and the public goes through periods of believing, naïvely, that the new drugs are "safe." Only gradually do people learn that these, too, pose dangers. And treatments for substance use disorders continue to have only limited effect.

Yet there are positive new wrinkles in this familiar story. Researchers have begun to develop a clearer understanding of how substances act on the brain and body. In treatment, self-help groups and rehabilitation programs are flourishing. And preventive education to make people aware of the dangers of drug misuse is expanding and seems to be having an effect. One reason for these improvements is that investigators and clinicians have stopped working in isolation and are instead looking for intersections between their own work and work from other models.

Yet another new wrinkle to the addiction story is that the clinical field has now formally proclaimed that substances are not the only things to which people may develop an addiction. By grouping gambling disorder with the substance use disorders and targeting Internet gaming disorder for possible inclusion in the future, DSM-5-TR has opened the door for a broader view and perhaps broader treatments of addictive patterns—whether they are induced by substances or by other kinds of experiences.

of NOTE ...

The Pandemic and Alcohol

- During the first year of the Covid-19 pandemic, marked by social isolation, excessive drinking increased at least 20 percent (Hampton, 2022). Middle-aged people had the largest increase in alcohol consumption (Kerr et al., 2022; Hu et al., 2021).
- Alcohol-related deaths increased by more than 25 percent during that year (NIAAA, 2023, 2022). It is estimated that the one-year pandemic-related increase in alcohol consumption will result in 8,000 additional alcohol-related deaths by 2040 (Hampton, 2022).

Quick Quiz

1. What are substance use disorders? p. 311
2. How does alcohol act on the brain and body? What are the problems and dangers of alcohol misuse? pp. 312–316
3. Describe the features and problems of the misuse of barbiturates and benzodiazepines. p. 316
4. Compare the various opioids (opium, heroin, morphine). What problems may result from their use? pp. 316–320
5. List and compare two kinds of stimulant drugs. Describe their biological actions and the problems caused by each of them. pp. 320–325
6. What are the effects of hallucinogens, particularly LSD and MDMA? pp. 326–328
7. What are the effects of marijuana and other cannabis substances? Why is marijuana a greater danger today than it was decades ago? pp. 328–332
8. What special problems does polysubstance use pose? pp. 332–333
9. Describe the leading explanations and treatments for substance use disorders. How well supported are these explanations and treatments? pp. 333–346
10. Why is gambling disorder categorized as an addictive disorder in DSM-5-TR alongside substance use disorder? pp. 347–348

Sexual Disorders

CHAPTER 11

TOPIC OVERVIEW

Mike, a 34-year-old anesthesiologist in Mobile, Alabama, had not had an intimate relationship or sexual encounter for three years. More to the point, he had not had any interest in sex during this time. He decided to pursue therapy soon after Samantha, a woman he'd met through his friend Gianni, asked him out on a date. He cited his work schedule to avoid having to meet up with her, suggesting that "maybe" they could get a drink sometime next month. Mike liked Samantha very much, and he could see that she was beautiful. They had hit it off, and when out in groups, they had make in-jokes with each other in a flirtatious manner. However, the thought that Samantha was probably interested in a physical relationship made Mike feel uncomfortable. He himself was not interested in a relationship of that kind—with Samantha or any other person.

Mike had not always been disinterested in sex. In fact, growing up in Atmore, he had watched pornography repeatedly and masturbated frequently. As a teenager, he had also fantasized about many of the girls in his high school. And he had had sex several times while in medical school. While he enjoyed each sexual experience greatly, he afterward felt bad, either thinking he had disrespected these nice women or thinking that the women themselves had been too forward and so must be "deviants." Throughout medical school, he continued to pursue pornography regularly.

After he began his medical career at a hospital in Mobile, Mike increasingly focused on work. He wanted to excel. He had taken on the name Mike in place of his Muscogee name, Micca, thinking it might help him fit in with his coworkers. Although he performed his job well and advanced to a supervisory position, he was constantly terrified that he might make a mistake that could lead to the death of a patient. This fear had not come true, but his anxiety and concern about it were almost obsessive. Seeking to ensure that he would perform perfectly and succeed at work, he even resolved to stop watching pornography, fearing that his sexual thoughts might distract him at a critical time when performing his duties with a patient. He also feared that his viewing of pornography might somehow be discovered and cost him his job.

Mike assumed all along that he would meet the right person and begin a relationship and that his sexual thoughts would eventually be channeled in what he believed to be a positive, acceptable direction. As the years unfolded, he did indeed meet several appealing persons, but, more often than not, having a physical relationship with any of them was the last thing on his mind.

At one point, about three years ago, Mike went on a date with a charming and attractive person named Gina. They had a lovely dinner, and she invited him back to her house, where they had sex. He enjoyed both the social experience and the sexual experience, but afterward he found himself revolted that Gina had been willing to have sex with "a total stranger" on the first date. He ignored her subsequent phone calls, and since that encounter, he had not thought sexually at all about other people. He believed that he should have sexual desires and thoughts, and he was upset that he didn't—but he just didn't.

Mike became increasingly depressed. He devoted himself to his work, but, as much as he enjoyed anesthesiology, his lack of sexual desire and activity left him feeling incomplete. He wanted to feel such desire again; he wanted that part of his life back. When he avoided a date invitation from Samantha, he realized for certain that he was experiencing more than a passing phase and that he would need treatment to overcome this pattern.

sexual dysfunction A disorder marked by a persistent inability to function satisfactorily in some area of the sexual response cycle.

Sexual behavior is a major focus of both our private thoughts and our public discussions. Sexual feelings are a crucial part of our development and daily functioning, sexual activity is tied to the satisfaction of our basic needs, and sexual performance is linked to our self-esteem. Most people are fascinated by the different sexual behavior of others, and they worry about how typical their own sexuality is.

Experts recognize two general categories of sexual disorders: sexual dysfunctions and paraphilic disorders. People with *sexual dysfunctions* have problems with their sexual responses. Mike, for example, has a dysfunction referred to in DSM-5-TR as *male hypoactive sexual desire disorder,* a persistent, long-standing lack of interest in sex that causes significant distress for him. People with *paraphilic disorders* have repeated and intense sexual urges or fantasies in response to objects or situations that society deems it inappropriate to sexualize, and they may behave inappropriately as well. They may be aroused by the thought of sexual activity with a child, for example, or of exposing their genitals to strangers, and they may act on those urges. ■

Sexual Dysfunctions

SEXUAL DYSFUNCTIONS, DISORDERS IN WHICH people cannot respond satisfactorily in key areas of sexual functioning, make it difficult or impossible to enjoy sexual activity. Such dysfunctions are typically very distressing, and they often lead to sexual frustration, guilt, loss of self-esteem, and interpersonal problems (Lafortune et al., 2023). The sexual dysfunctions can be interrelated; many patients with one dysfunction have another as well. Studies suggest that as many as 35 percent of people around the world experience such a dysfunction during their lives (Shifren, 2023; Snyder & Rosen, 2020).

of NOTE ...

Their Words

"Sex is hardly ever just about sex."

Shirley McLaine, actress

Sexual Dysfunctions Across the Population

Before we examine the various sexual dysfunctions, it is important to clarify that most of the current information, theorizing, and research on them has been gathered from studies of cisgender, heterosexual, and non-Hispanic White people (Cheng, 2022; Whitney et al., 2022). Clinicians and researchers have typically assumed that other subpopulations display similar sexual dysfunctions and respond to similar treatments. In many cases, this assumption appears to be correct, but emerging clinical observations and investigations suggest that the character and explanations of some of the sexual dysfunctions might vary from subgroup to subgroup.

Gender and Sexual Dysfunctions

Although there are many similarities between the sexual dysfunctions of cisgender people and those of transgender and nonbinary people, experts believe that there are probably important differences between the dysfunctions of these groups as well (Fraiman et al., 2023; Campbell, 2022; Roncato Barcelos, Fransceschini, & Lara, 2022). After all, the groups often have key psychological and physical differences, some reflecting distinct life experiences and others produced by biological interventions such as hormone and/or surgical interventions for many transgender people—and such differences inevitably affect aspects of their sexual functioning. However, relatively few studies of distinct sexual dysfunctions among transgender and nonbinary people have been conducted to date (Blanken, 2022). A wave of such studies is emerging (Montejo, 2023; Whitney et al., 2022), but in the meantime, you should keep in mind that the features, prevalence rates, explanations, and treatments of sexual dysfunctions discussed in this chapter are based largely on investigations and observations of cisgender people.

Also of importance in the realm of gender are the male–female distinctions applied to sexual dysfunctions. As you will soon read, DSM-5-TR designates many of the

Bradley Secker/Panos Pictures/Redux

Expanding inclusivity Today's couples vary widely, as illustrated by this transgender woman (left) and her partner, enjoying a walk on a beautiful day. Correspondingly, sex theorists and therapists are now following a philosophy of *expanding inclusivity* and trying to adapt their professional thinking and techniques to best address the distinctive characteristics and needs of various populations and relationships.

sexual dysfunctions as either *male* or *female* (for example, male hypoactive sexual desire disorder or female sexual interest/arousal disorder). To avoid confusion, in this chapter, we will adhere to DSM-5-TR's male–female labels, distinctions, descriptions, and prevalence rates. However, once again, as you are reading, keep in mind that such discussions may not always apply in the same ways to sexual functioning among transgender men, transgender women, and nonbinary people.

Sexual Orientation and Sexual Dysfunctions To date, studies of sexual dysfunctions have focused largely on heterosexual people; research extending to sexual orientations outside this population is at a relatively early stage (Blanken, 2022). It appears that the information about sexual dysfunctions gathered from studies of heterosexual people does indeed often apply to people of other sexual orientations. However, experts also believe that the dysfunctions of heterosexual people are probably different in certain respects from those of gay and bisexual people given the groups' different partner choices and different stressors in life. And, in fact, a few early studies have found small differences in the character and prevalence of certain sexual dysfunctions in these groups (Mainwaring et al., 2023; Cheng, 2022). More such studies continue to emerge, but in the meantime, you should, once again, keep in mind that the field's knowledge of the ties between sexual dysfunctions and sexual orientation is relatively limited.

Rates for sexual behavior are typically based on population surveys. What factors might affect the accuracy of such surveys?

Similarly, given that a majority of the current research on sexual dysfunctions focuses on heterosexual people, the male-linked and female-linked prevalence rates and explanations reported throughout this chapter may not always apply to those of gay men, lesbian women, and bisexual people. Some preliminary research hints, for example, that lesbian and bisexual women may, on average, experience fewer sexual pain problems than heterosexual women and that gay men may display different rates of erectile dysfunction than heterosexual men (Cheng, 2022; McNabney et al., 2022).

Race and Ethnicity and Sexual Dysfunctions Relatively little is known about racial and ethnic differences in sexuality and sexual dysfunctions. Although different cultural groups have for years been labeled "insatiable," "hypersexual,"

desire phase The phase of the sexual response cycle consisting of sexual urges, fantasies, and attraction to others.

male hypoactive sexual desire disorder According to DSM-5-R, a male dysfunction marked by a persistent reduction or lack of interest in sex and a low level of sexual activity.

female sexual interest/arousal disorder According to DSM-5-TR, a female dysfunction marked by a persistent reduction or lack of interest in sex, low sexual activity, and, in some cases, limited excitement during sexual activity.

"hot blooded," "exotic," "passionate," "submissive," and the like, such incorrect stereotypes have grown strictly from ignorance or prejudice, not from objective observations or research.

In fact, sex clinicians and researchers have only recently begun to attend systematically to the importance of race and ethnicity (Azim et al., 2023; Chen, Li, & Eisenberg, 2022). Few past studies examined sexual dysfunctions among persons of color specifically, and surveys of the broader population typically had insufficient representation of participants of color in their samples (Battle et al., 2022). Moreover, it turns out that people of color have, on average, been particularly uncomfortable acknowledging their sexual dysfunctions in surveys and interviews, thus raising further questions about the accuracy of research findings and conclusions (Gaines et al., 2022). Studies that address these earlier research deficiencies are now being conducted and are expected to shed light on the role of race and ethnicity in sexual dysfunctions, but current information and insights in this realm are limited.

Disorders of Desire

The human sexual response can be described as a *cycle* with four phases: *desire, excitement, orgasm,* and *resolution* (Conn & Hodges, 2023) (see **Figure 11-1** and **Figure 11-2**). Sexual dysfunctions affect one or more of the first three phases. Resolution consists simply of the relaxation and reduction in arousal that typically follow orgasm. Some people struggle with a sexual dysfunction their whole lives; in other cases, effective sexual functioning preceded the dysfunction. In some cases, the dysfunction is present during all sexual situations; in others, it is tied to particular situations (APA, 2022).

The **desire phase** of the sexual response cycle consists of an interest in or urge to have sex, sexual attraction to others, and, for many people, sexual fantasies. Two dysfunctions affect the desire phase—what DSM-5-TR has termed *male hypoactive sexual desire disorder* and *female sexual interest/arousal disorder.* The latter disorder actually cuts across both the desire phase and the excitement phase of the sexual response cycle. It is considered a single disorder in DSM-5-TR because, according to research, desire and arousal overlap particularly highly for most women, and many women express difficulty distinguishing feelings of desire from feelings of arousal (APA, 2022).

A number of people generally lack feelings of sexual attraction to others but are comfortable with the absence of such feelings and consider themselves *asexual* rather than impaired or dysfunctional. These individuals are not diagnosed as having one of the sexual desire disorders. Still other people have sexual interest in others but choose, as a matter of lifestyle rather than sexual desire, to avoid engaging in sexual relations. Here again, these individuals are not diagnosed as having one of the sexual desire disorders.

FIGURE 11-1

The Sexual Response Cycle

Researchers studying predominantly cisgender populations have found a similar sequence of phases in both men and women. Sometimes, however, women do not experience orgasm; in that case, the resolution phase is less sudden. And sometimes women have two or more orgasms in succession before the resolution phase. (Information from: Conn & Hodges, 2023; Shifren, 2023, 2022; Kaplan, 1974; Masters & Johnson, 1970, 1966)

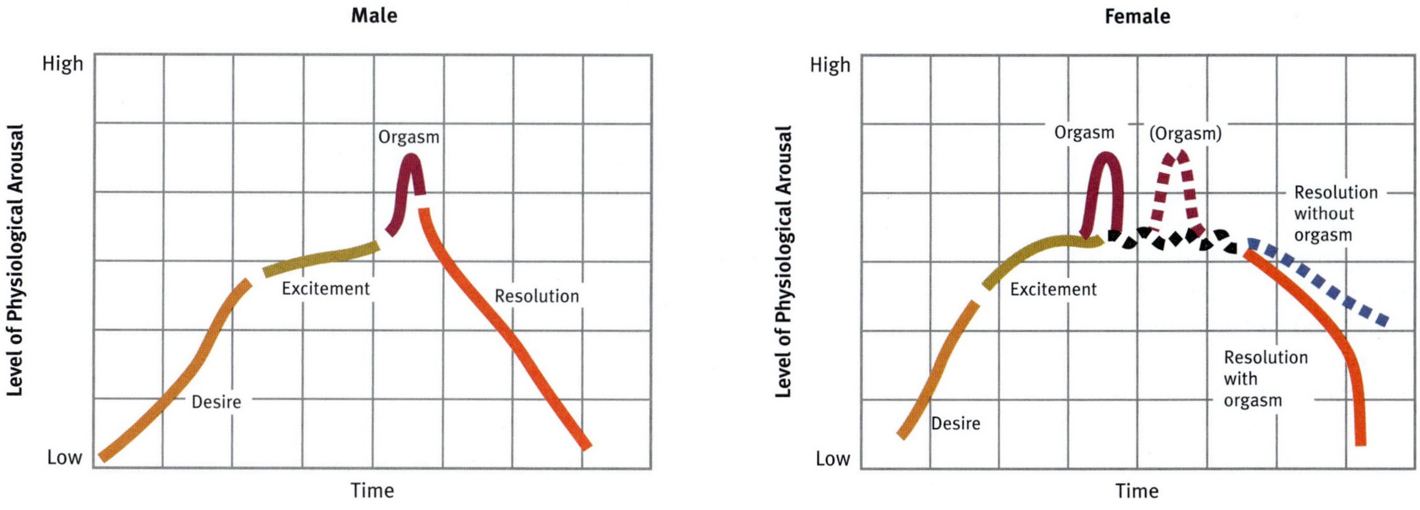

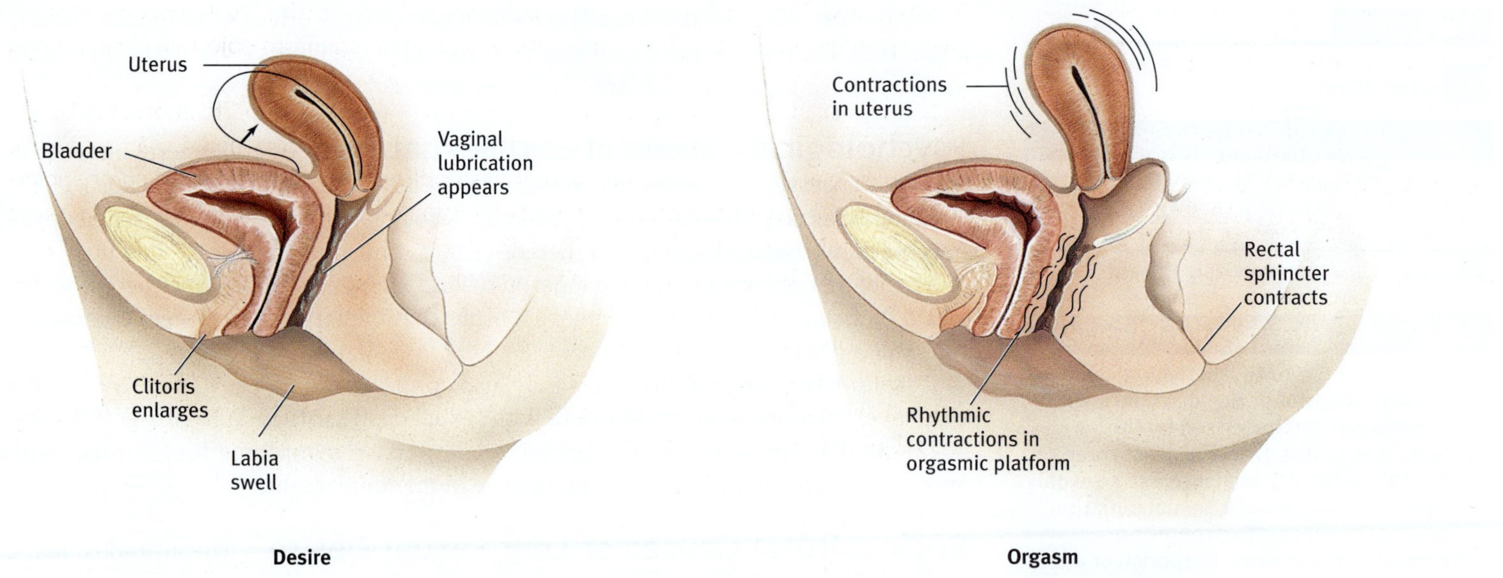

FIGURE 11-2

Female Sexual Anatomy

Changes in the female anatomy take place during the different phases of the sexual response cycle. (Information from: Conn & Hodges, 2023; Shifren, 2023, 2022; Hyde, 1990)

Individuals with what DSM-5-TR calls **male hypoactive sexual desire disorder** persistently lack or have reduced interest in sex, engage in little sexual activity, and, in turn, experience significant distress (see **Table 11-1**). Like Mike, the anesthesiologist whose case opened this chapter, their physical responses may be typical, and they may enjoy the experience when they do have sex. While most cultures portray men as wanting all the sex they can get, 5 to 15 percent of men worldwide have this disorder, and the number seeking therapy has increased during the past decade (Khera, 2023; Rosen & Khera, 2022).

Individuals with what DSM-5-TR calls **female sexual interest/arousal disorder** also lack typical interest in sex and rarely initiate sexual activity (see Table 11-1 again). In addition, many with the condition feel little excitement during sexual activity, are unaroused by erotic cues, and have few genital or nongenital sensations during sexual activity (Khoury et al., 2024; APA, 2022). Approximately 39 percent of women worldwide have reduced sexual interest and arousal (Shifren, 2023, 2022). About one-third of those individuals feel significant distress due to their lower level of arousal, and, as such, they qualify for a diagnosis of female sexual interest/arousal disorder. Note that many sex researchers and therapists believe it is inaccurate to combine desire and excitement symptoms into a single disorder. They would prefer that DSM-5-TR separate these problems into two separate dysfunctions.

A person's sex drive is determined by a combination of biological, psychological, and sociocultural factors, any of which may reduce sexual desire. Most cases of low sexual desire are caused primarily by sociocultural and psychological factors, but biological conditions can also lower sex drive significantly.

Biological Causes of Low Sexual Desire

A number of hormones interact to help produce sexual desire and behavior, and irregularities in their activity can lower a person's sex drive (Khera, 2023; Rosen & Khera, 2022). In all people, a high level of the hormone *prolactin*, a low level of the hormone *testosterone*, and either a high level or a low level of the hormone *estrogen* can lead to low sex drive. Low sex drive has been linked to the high levels of estrogen contained in some birth control pills, for example. Conversely, it has also been tied to the low level of estrogen found in many postpartum or postmenopausal women.

Clinical practice and research have further indicated that sex drive can be lowered by certain pain medications, psychotropic drugs, and illegal drugs, such as cocaine and heroin (Hirsch & Birnbaum, 2023, 2022). Low levels of alcohol may enhance the sex drive by lowering a person's inhibitions, but high levels may reduce it (Salari et al., 2023; Rosen & Khera, 2022).

TABLE 11-1

Dx Checklist

Male Hypoactive Sexual Desire Disorder
1. For at least 6 months, individual repeatedly experiences few or no sexual thoughts, fantasies, or desires.
2. Individual experiences significant distress about this.
Female Sexual Interest/Arousal Disorder
1. For at least 6 months, individual usually displays reduced or no sexual interest and arousal, characterized by the reduction or absence of at least three of the following: ■ Sexual interest ■ Sexual thought or fantasies ■ Sexual initiation or receptiveness ■ Excitement or pleasure during sex ■ Responsiveness to sexual cues ■ Genital or nongenital sensations during sex.
2. Individual experiences significant distress.

Information from: APA, 2022.

Long-term physical illness can also lower a person's sex drive (Hirsch, 2023; Shifren, 2023, 2022). The reduced drive may be a direct result of the illness or an indirect result of stress, pain, or depression brought on by the illness.

Psychological Causes of Low Sexual Desire

A general increase in anxiety, depression, or anger may reduce sexual desire in people (Shifren, 2023, 2022). Frequently, as cognitive-behavioral theorists have noted, people with low sexual desire have particular attitudes, fears, or memories that contribute to their dysfunction, such as a belief that sex is immoral or dangerous (Conn & Hodges, 2023). Other people are so afraid of losing control over their sexual urges that they try to resist them completely. And still others fear pregnancy.

Certain psychological disorders may also contribute to low sexual desire. Even a mild level of depression can interfere with sexual desire (Bruce, 2023; Rosen & Khera, 2022). And some people with obsessive-compulsive symptoms find contact with another person's body fluids and odors to be highly unpleasant.

Sociocultural Causes of Low Sexual Desire

The attitudes, fears, and psychological disorders that contribute to low sexual desire occur within a social context, and thus certain sociocultural factors have also been linked to disorders of sexual desire. Many people who have low sexual desire are feeling situational pressures—divorce, a death in the family, job stress, infertility difficulties, or having a baby (Conn & Hodges, 2023; Shifren, 2023, 2022). Other people may be having problems in their relationships. People who are in an unhappy relationship, have lost affection for their partner, or feel powerless and dominated by their partner can lose interest in sex (Khera, 2023; Rosen & Khera, 2022). Even in basically happy relationships, if one partner is a very unskilled, unenthusiastic lover, the other can begin to lose interest in sex (Graham & Bancroft, 2020). And sometimes partners differ in their needs for closeness. The one who needs more personal space may develop low sexual desire as a way of keeping distance.

The impact of situational stress and relationship problems on sexual desire was highlighted by surveys conducted during the highly stressful first year of the Covid-19 pandemic. In some surveys, at least 25 percent of people in intimate relationships reported pandemic-linked reductions in their sexual desire, a rate that reached 65 percent among particularly stressed hospital workers (De Rose et al., 2021; Li et al., 2020). In another study, 34 percent of surveyed individuals reported pandemic-related increases in conflict in their intimate relationships, increases that contributed to lower levels of sexual desire and lower frequencies of sexual behavior (Luetke et al., 2020).

Online desires Traffic on online pornography sites increased substantially during the early stages of the Covid-19 pandemic. In addition, during that period of widespread loneliness and alienation, online searches using the terms "romance," "passionate," and "swapping" (or "swinging") more than doubled.

Photo illustration by Adrien Fillon/NurPhoto via AP

Cultural factors can also set the stage for low sexual desire. Some heterosexual men, for example, adopt a cultural *double standard* and thus cannot feel sexual desire for a woman they love and respect (Hensums, Overbeek, & Jorgensen, 2022). More generally, because our society equates sexual attractiveness with youthfulness, many middle-aged and older people lose interest in sex as their self-image or their attraction to their partner diminishes with age.

The trauma of sexual molestation or assault is especially likely to produce the fears, attitudes, and memories found in disorders of sexual desire (Saadedine et al., 2023; Blais, 2021). Some survivors of sexual abuse may feel repelled by sex, sometimes for years, even decades. In some cases, survivors may have vivid flashbacks of the assault during adult consensual sexual activity.

Disorders of Excitement

The **excitement phase** of the sexual response cycle is marked by changes in the pelvic region, general physical arousal, and increases in heart rate, muscle tension, blood pressure, and rate of breathing. For penile arousal, blood pools in the pelvis and leads to an erection; for vaginal arousal, the clitoris and labia swell, and the vagina becomes lubricated. As you read earlier, female sexual interest/arousal disorder may include dysfunction during the excitement phase. In addition, a disorder of penile functioning—*erectile disorder*—involves dysfunction during the excitement phase only.

Erectile Disorder

Erectile disorder is characterized by a persistent failure to attain or maintain an erection during sexual activity (see **Table 11-2**). This problem occurs in at least 16 percent of the male population worldwide (Snyder & Rosen, 2020). Kasem has the disorder:

Kasem, a 44-year-old construction foreman originally from Thailand, entered therapy with his 40-year-old wife Gina to address problems in their marriage. For the past year, Kasem and Gina have not been sexually intimate, and their relationship has grown distant. Kasem has become withdrawn, and he retreats most evenings to watch cable news in a separate room. He and Gina chat briefly and politely as they go to bed. But at this point, he feels like he's in a sham marriage, and she is extremely unhappy as well.

The problem in their sex life began when Kasem started having difficulty maintaining an erection during sexual intercourse. On several occasions in a row, Kasem and Gina would begin making love, with Kasem very much enjoying the foreplay, but he would then start to feel tired during intercourse, and he would lose his erection. The first time, he thought to himself, "I guess I'm just not up to it tonight." The next few times, he further attributed the erectile difficulties to work-related stress. Kasem had many responsibilities managing his crew, and his arms and legs were often sore. Each of those initial times, he pretended to Gina that the loss of erection wasn't happening, and he continued trying to make love to her. In a panic, he faked orgasms to put an end to the ordeals, hoping she wouldn't notice.

As the weeks went by and his inability to perform sexually continued, he started to worry that there was something wrong with him. Work provided no escape from his concerns. The men in the crew were very macho, always bragging about their sexual exploits. Matt, in particular, seemed to have a story about a different date every few days. Around these Lotharios, Kasem privately felt ashamed. He couldn't hope to supervise these men if he was so inadequate and they were so accomplished in the bedroom. He thought back to his years growing up in Thailand. Even then, being a "ladies' man" had been very important to his various friends.

Eventually, Kasem's worries turned into fear—fear that he could no longer perform, fear that he was disappointing Gina, fear that he was no longer a man. He was afraid of being romantic with Gina. Although she had not complained, he could sense the concern in her. Eventually, he could not even get an erection during foreplay. The more he tried to concentrate on what he was supposed to do, the more elusive it all became. Sex had become a chore to him.

One night when they were trying to have sex, Gina asked with tears in her eyes, "Am I doing something wrong? What is it, Kay? Don't you love me? Is it because I gained this weight?" Kasem said, "No, don't be silly! You're the most beautiful woman in the world! I'm just really tired out from work."

(continued on the next page)

TABLE 11-2

Dx Checklist

Erectile Disorder
1. For at least 6 months, individual usually finds it very difficult to obtain an erection, maintain an erection, and/or achieve past levels of erectile rigidity during sex.
2. Individual experiences significant distress.

Information from: APA, 2022.

excitement phase The phase of the sexual response cycle marked by changes in the pelvic region, general physical arousal, and increases in heart rate, muscle tension, blood pressure, and rate of breathing.

erectile disorder A dysfunction in which a person repeatedly fails to attain or maintain an erection during sexual activity.

Privately, however, he did develop a suspicion that he might no longer be attracted to Gina. What did this mean? Was his love for her fading? Had he married the wrong woman? He was still sometimes able to achieve an erection when masturbating, but he was terrified when he was with his wife. What kind of man was he?

As the sexual domain grew increasingly unpleasant, giving rise to broader unhappiness and to endless questions and self-condemnations, Kasem stopped trying to have any sex at all. He did not explain his reasons to Gina. He just stopped approaching her. And before long, he stopped talking to her about other areas of their life as well. He thought that such distance would bring relief and protection from his sex-related fears and feelings of shame, but, in reality, it drove a still deeper wedge between Gina and him. So now, a year after Kasem's first episode of erectile disorder, to save their once-happy marriage, they decided to try therapy.

Unlike Kasem, most people with erectile disorder are over the age of 50, largely because so many cases are associated with ailments or diseases of older adults (Rosen & Khera, 2022). Around 8 percent of men in their twenties, for example, have the disorder, compared to 18 percent in their fifties and 37 percent in their seventies. Moreover, according to surveys, half of all adult men experience erectile difficulty during intercourse at least some of the time. Most cases of erectile disorder result from an interaction of biological, psychological, and sociocultural processes.

BIOLOGICAL CAUSES The same hormonal imbalances that can cause male hypoactive sexual desire disorder can also produce erectile disorder (Rosen & Khera, 2022). More commonly, however, vascular problems—problems with the body's blood vessels—are involved. An erection occurs when the chambers in the penis fill with blood, so any condition that reduces blood flow into the penis, such as heart disease or clogging of the arteries, may lead to erectile disorder (Sauer & Kimmel, 2022). It can also be caused by damage to the nervous system as a result of diabetes, spinal cord injuries, multiple sclerosis, kidney failure, or treatment by dialysis (Hirsch, 2023). In addition, as is the case with male hypoactive sexual desire disorder, the use of certain medications and various forms of substance abuse, from alcohol abuse to cigarette smoking, may interfere with erections (Hirsch & Birnbaum, 2023, 2022).

Medical procedures, including ultrasound recordings and blood tests, have been developed for diagnosing biological causes of erectile disorder. Measuring **nocturnal penile tumescence,** or erections during sleep, is particularly useful in assessing whether physical factors are responsible. Erections usually occur during *rapid eye movement (REM) sleep,* the phase of sleep in which dreaming takes place (Rosen & Khera, 2022). It is considered healthy to have two to five REM periods each night and several penile erections as well. Atypical or absent nightly erections usually (but not always) indicate some physical basis for erectile failure. A man, for example, may be instructed to fasten a simple "snap gauge" band around his penis before going to sleep and then check it the next morning. A broken band indicates that he has had an erection during the night. An unbroken band indicates that he did not have nighttime erections and suggests that his general erectile problem may have a physical basis. Newer versions of this device further attach the band to a computer, which provides precise measurements of erections throughout the night.

The STI factor For many people, sexually transmitted infections (STIs) affect sexual functioning. For example, many men with certain STIs, such as chlamydia (see photo), may develop infections of the prostate gland, which can lead to erectile disorder. More generally, persons' concerns about unsuspectedly contracting an STI from a sex partner can interfere with their comfort and behavior during sex.

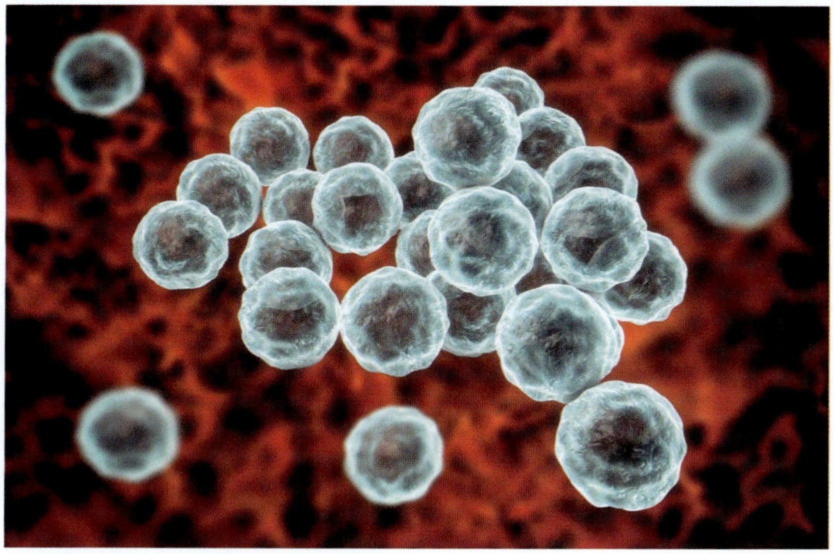

Science Photo Library

Such assessment devices are less likely to be used in clinical practice today than in past years. As you'll read later in the chapter, Viagra and other drugs for erectile disorder are typically given to patients, without much formal evaluation of their problem.

PSYCHOLOGICAL CAUSES Any of the psychological causes of male hypoactive sexual desire disorder can also interfere with arousal and lead to erectile disorder. Most men with severe depression, for example, can often experience some degree of erectile dysfunction (Khera, 2023).

One well-supported psychological explanation for erectile disorder is the cognitive-behavioral theory developed by William Masters and Virginia Johnson (1970). The explanation emphasizes **performance anxiety** and the **spectator role.** If a man, for example, begins to have erectile problems, he may become fearful about failing to have an erection and may worry during each sexual encounter (Hirsch, 2023, 2022). Instead of relaxing and enjoying the sensations of sexual pleasure, he remains distanced from the activity, watching himself and focusing on the goal of reaching erection. Instead of being an aroused participant, he becomes a judge and spectator. Whatever the initial reason for the erectile dysfunction, the resulting spectator role becomes the reason for the ongoing problem. In this vicious cycle, the original cause of the erectile failure becomes less important than fear of failure.

SOCIOCULTURAL CAUSES Each of the sociocultural factors that contribute to male hypoactive sexual desire disorder has also been tied to erectile disorder. For example, men who have lost their jobs and are under financial stress are more likely to develop erectile difficulties than other men. Relationship stress, too, has been tied to this dysfunction (Rosen & Khera, 2022).

Disorders of Orgasm

During the **orgasm phase** of the sexual response cycle, a person's sexual pleasure peaks and sexual tension is released as the muscles in the pelvic region contract, or draw together, rhythmically (see **Figure 11-3**). In a penile orgasm, semen is ejaculated; in a vaginal orgasm, the outer third of the vaginal wall contracts. DSM-5-TR lists two dysfunctions that are associated with a penile orgasm—*premature ejaculation* and *delayed ejaculation*. It lists one dysfunction associated with a vaginal orgasm—*female orgasmic disorder.*

nocturnal penile tumescence Erection during sleep.

performance anxiety The fear of performing inadequately and a related tension that are experienced during sex.

spectator role A state of mind that some people experience during sex, focusing on their sexual performance to such an extent that their performance and their enjoyment are reduced.

orgasm phase The phase of the sexual response cycle during which a person's sexual pleasure peaks and sexual tension is released as muscles in the pelvic region contract rhythmically.

FIGURE 11-3

Male Sexual Anatomy

Changes in the male anatomy occur during the different phases of the sexual response cycle. (Information from: Rosen & Khera, 2022; Hyde, 1990)

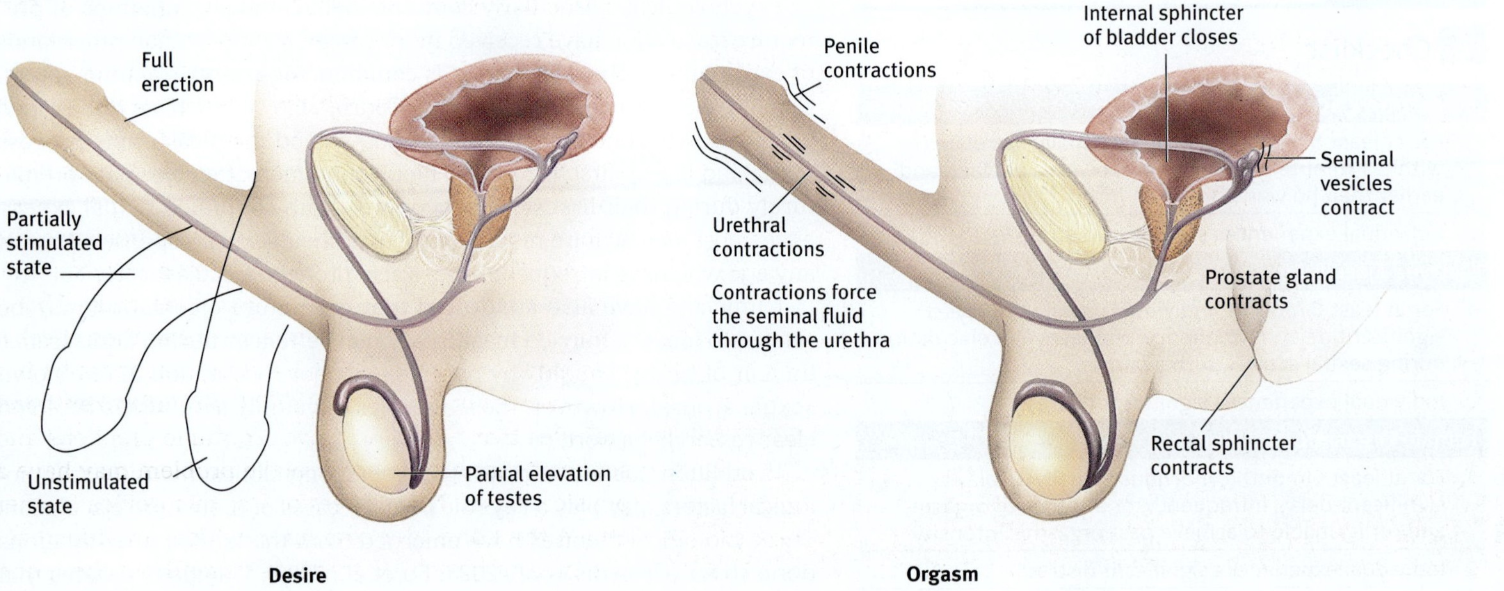

Premature Ejaculation

In several ways, Cedro is typical of others in his experience of premature ejaculation:

Cedro, a 20-year-old student, sought treatment after his girlfriend Adriana ended their relationship because his premature ejaculations had left her sexually frustrated. Even before Adriana left him, Cedro had begun to dread sex, embarrassed and ashamed by his performance. He found caressing her body and her touching his body so arousing that he typically ejaculated before completely entering her with his penis or after at most a minute of intercourse. This relationship had been his first sexual experience with any degree of privacy. Growing up, Cedro had shared a cramped one-bedroom apartment with his single mother. Throughout his adolescence, his experiences of masturbation had been hurried stolen moments in the bathroom just off the bedroom, with Cedro always knowing that his mother was just outside the door.

Prior to Adriana, Cedro had had only one sexual relationship, during his senior year in high school. Two of his older cousins would drive him to a neighboring town to locate a certain sex worker to help "turn him into a man." Not wanting to let down his cousins, Cedro would go along with this despite feeling uncomfortable about the situation for several reasons. After picking up the sex worker, they would drive to a deserted area, and Cedro would have sex with her while his cousins waited outside the car. Fearing that he and the sex worker would be discovered by the police, Cedro felt tremendous pressure to "hurry up." And besides, in the winter, it was very cold. Cedro felt particularly obliged to follow his cousins' demands because he always looked up to them and they seemed to always have his back. So, at the point when Cedro began his relationship with Adriana, his entire sexual history had consisted of rapid masturbation and then rapid intercourse, with virtually no foreplay.

Research suggests that 30 percent of men worldwide have ejaculated *early* at some point in time—that is, they have reached orgasm and ejaculated within one minute of beginning sexual activity with a partner and before they wished to (see **Table 11-3**). When a person experiences a persistent pattern of such early ejaculation, a diagnosis of **premature ejaculation** (also called *rapid* ejaculation) is given. Roughly 4 percent of men have this ongoing condition (Crowdis, Leslie, & Nazir, 2023; Rosen & Khera, 2022). The typical duration of intercourse in our society has increased over the past several decades, which has caused more distress among those who ejaculate prematurely. Research suggests that premature ejaculation can be experienced at any age.

Psychological, particularly cognitive-behavioral, explanations of premature ejaculation have received more research support than other kinds of explanations. The dysfunction is common, for example, among young, sexually inexperienced men such as Cedro, who simply have not learned to slow down, control their arousal, and extend the pleasurable process of making love (Hirsch, 2023). In fact, young men often ejaculate prematurely during their first sexual encounter. With continued sexual experience, most men acquire more control over their sexual responses. Men of any age who have infrequent sex are also prone to ejaculate early.

Clinicians have also suggested that premature ejaculation may be related to anxiety, hurried masturbation experiences during adolescence (in fear of being "caught" by parents), or poor recognition of one's own sexual arousal. However, these theories have only sometimes received clear research support.

In addition, there is a growing belief among clinical theorists that biological factors may play a key role in many cases of premature ejaculation. Three biological theories have emerged from the limited investigations done so far (Crowdis et al., 2023; Fu et al., 2020). One theory states that premature ejaculation stems from a genetic predisposition to develop this

TABLE 11-3

Dx Checklist

Premature Ejaculation
1. For at least 6 months, individual usually ejaculates within 1 minute of beginning sex with a partner, and earlier than he wants to.
2. Individual experiences significant distress.
Delayed Ejaculation
1. For at least 6 months, individual usually displays a significant delay, infrequency, or absence of ejaculation during sexual activity with a partner.
2. Individual experiences significant distress.
Female Orgasmic Disorder
1. For at least 6 months, individual usually displays a significant delay, infrequency, or absence of orgasm, and/ or is unable to achieve past orgasmic intensity.
2. Individual experiences significant distress.

Information from: APA, 2022.

dysfunction. Indeed, one study found that 91 percent of a small sample of men experiencing early ejaculation had first-degree relatives who also had the dysfunction. A second theory, based on animal studies, argues that the premature ejaculation is tied to overactive serotonin receptors in some parts of the brain and underactive serotonin receptors in other parts. A third explanation holds that the dysfunction results from greater sensitivity or nerve conduction in the area of the penis, a notion that has received inconsistent research support thus far.

AP Photo/Shuji Kajiyama

Grooming is key Humans are not the only animals that follow a sexual response cycle or, for that matter, display sexual dysfunctions. Here a male macaque monkey grooms a female monkey while they sit in a hot spring in the snow in central Japan. Such grooming triples the likelihood that the female will engage in sexual activity with the male.

Delayed Ejaculation

Between 1 and 10 percent of men worldwide experience **delayed ejaculation** (MacGill, 2023; Meston & Stanton, 2020), a condition in which the individual is unable to ejaculate or has very delayed ejaculations during sexual activity with a partner (see Table 11-3 again). Delayed ejaculation (previously called *male orgasmic disorder* or *inhibited male orgasm*) is typically a source of great frustration, as in the case of Leonard:

Leonard, the 42-year-old financial officer of a flourishing cybersecurity company, entered couples counseling with his wife Rachel, who had recently quit her teaching job to devote herself full-time to environmental and charitable causes. The problem that dismayed both of them was sexual—Leonard was having repeated difficulty ejaculating during intercourse, and many of their sexual encounters ended with him saying he didn't think he could continue. Rachel was frustrated that she was denied sexual satisfaction and was hurt that Leonard had seemingly lost his desire for her. She was also concerned that she might be doing something wrong. For his part, Leonard felt inadequate and angry with himself.

Leonard admitted to the counselor that the pressures of his high-stakes job made it difficult for him to relax at home—sometimes even when he and Rachel were having sex. While he was trying to be romantic, his mind might return to an important work deal or report he had to complete. Although they were wealthy enough to attend gala events and meet important people, he felt he had to keep pushing himself at work or they would fall into financial ruin. Once his mind traveled in those directions, his enjoyment of sex would "fritter away," and his performance would follow suit.

As Leonard described it, he would begin overthinking everything he was doing, second-guessing his technique, trying too hard to "get back into the spirit of things." To avoid such problems, he would sometimes try to plan their sexual encounters and his performance ahead of time, but then he would typically become unable to respond spontaneously. During sex, upon recognizing that he was nowhere near climax, he would begin to panic, and his excitement would wane to the point that he often lost his erection and had to beg off continuing. Not only had this become a regular pattern, but the sequence began unfolding earlier and earlier in their sexual encounters. Eventually he found himself bracing for a bad outcome even before he and Rachel would start a sexual activity.

A low testosterone level, certain neurological diseases, and head or spinal cord injuries can interfere with ejaculation (Hirsch, 2023, 2022; Rosen & Khera, 2022). Substances that slow down the sympathetic nervous system (such as alcohol, some medications for high blood pressure, and certain psychotropic medications) can also affect ejaculation. For example, serotonin-enhancing antidepressant drugs appear to interfere with ejaculation in at least 30 percent of men who take them (Hirsch & Birnbaum, 2023, 2022).

A leading psychological cause of delayed ejaculation appears to be performance anxiety and the spectator role, the cognitive-behavioral factors also involved in erectile disorder (Nimbi et al., 2020, 2018). Once an individual begins to focus on reaching orgasm during sex, that person may stop being an aroused participant and instead become a self-critical and fearful observer. Another psychological cause of delayed

premature ejaculation A dysfunction in which unintentional penile orgasm and ejaculation persistently occur within one minute of beginning sexual activity with a partner. Also called *early* or *rapid* ejaculation.

delayed ejaculation A penile dysfunction characterized by persistent inability to ejaculate or very delayed ejaculations during sexual activity with a partner.

of NOTE ...

Nightly Visits

People sometimes have an orgasm during sleep. Ancient Babylonians said that such orgasms were caused by "maids of the night" and "little night men" who visited people in their sleep (Kahn & Fawcett, 1993).

ejaculation may be past masturbation habits (MacGill, 2023). If, for example, a man has masturbated all his life by rubbing his penis against sheets, pillows, or other such objects, he may have difficulty reaching orgasm in the absence of the sensations tied to those objects. Finally, delayed ejaculation may develop out of male hypoactive sexual desire disorder. For example, a man who engages in sex without any real desire for it may not get aroused enough to ejaculate.

Female Orgasmic Disorder Fatima and her boyfriend Saad, in a relationship for three years, went for sex therapy because of her lack of orgasm:

Fatima had actually never had an orgasm. She had been faking orgasm during intercourse with Saad until recently. Finally, she told him the truth, and they sought therapy together.

Fatima was raised in a strict religious family. She could not recall seeing her parents kiss or show physical affection to each other. She was severely punished on one occasion when her mother found her looking at her own genitals, at about age 7. Fatima received no sex education from her parents, and when she began to menstruate, her mother told her only that this meant that she could become pregnant, so she mustn't kiss a boy or let a boy touch her. Correspondingly, her mother severely restricted her dating, with repeated warnings that "boys only want one thing." While Fatima's parents were demanding of her (for example, chastising her when she got a single B on her report card), they were loving parents, and their approval was very important to her.

During her childhood, Fatima took her mother's admonishments about sex and romance very seriously, and she paid careful attention to both parents' discomfort with the subject. It was, in her mind, an important part of a proper Muslim upbringing. She felt deeply that sexuality was tied up with sin and that sex should be only for purposes of having children within marriage. But when she went to college, she made friends with other young women of Pakistani Muslim descent, and, to her surprise, they were quite comfortable engaging in and discussing sex and romance. The friends described their own parents as encouraging of their romances and never making them feel wrong for having sexual desires.

Confused, Fatima decided to discuss this contradiction with her mother. One conversation led to another, and Fatima's mother eventually revealed that her father had had an affair with a coworker when Fatima was a toddler. As a result of his betrayal, Fatima's embittered mother had developed an aversion to the idea of sexuality—an aversion that she passed on to her daughter. Over the course of these revelations, Fatima's mother acknowledged how unfair this early indoctrination had been to her daughter, and she tearfully apologized.

Bolstered by these revelations, Fatima was eager to explore a relationship with Saad, a co-student whom she had found enormously appealing for some time. Given her new insights about her family and a broader perspective on sexuality, she was increasingly able to view Saad as a good and trustworthy person, a person who respected her, not someone who wanted "only one thing." Their mutual affection grew, and eventually they entered into a long-term relationship. In the sexual realm, Fatima was won over by Saad's gentleness and his interest in her needs, and she came to enjoy sex to a degree she had never anticipated.

But she did not enjoy sex in one way: she never developed the ability to have an orgasm. She envied her best friend, who described more than once what an orgasm felt like. And intellectually, she understood that female orgasms were acceptable, healthy, and in fact desirable. But despite such insights and despite her recognition that her upbringing had been a sexually unhealthy one, she could not have an orgasm. Fatima recognized that, at some level, she continued to feel she was doing something terrible when she and Saad made love, and she was unable to enjoy their sexual intimacy to its fullest. Eventually, she decided that her lack of orgasm was something she wanted to change if possible and something she wanted to reveal to Saad. She wanted orgasmic experiences for herself, and she also wanted to share such experiences while she and Saad were making love. So she opened up to him. After several caring and constructive discussions, they decided to seek help together in therapy.

female orgasmic disorder According to DSM-5-TR, a dysfunction in which a woman persistently fails to reach orgasm, has very-low-intensity orgasms, or has very delayed orgasms.

Like Fatima, 10 to 15 percent of women report having never had an orgasm, either alone or during intercourse, and at least another 9 percent rarely have orgasms (MLP, 2023). Those who experience extensive orgasm difficulties on an ongoing basis, accompanied by significant distress, meet the criteria for a diagnosis of what DSM-5-TR calls **female orgasmic disorder**—a persistent pattern of failing to reach orgasm, having very low-intensity orgasms, or having a very delayed orgasm despite sufficient stimulation (see Table 11-3 again). Roughly 5 to 10 percent of women meet the criteria for this condition (Shifren, 2023, 2022; Bradford, 2022, 2021). In one study, when participants with female orgasmic disorder were asked to pick a word that best describes their feelings about it, two-thirds of them chose "frustration" (Kingsberg et al., 2013).

Around 38 percent of all women regularly experience orgasm in intercourse, and another 43 percent experience it infrequently in intercourse (McIntosh, 2022). At the same time, most clinicians agree that orgasm during intercourse is not mandatory for healthy sexual functioning (Shifren, 2023, 2022). Many women instead reach orgasm by themselves or with their partners by direct stimulation of the clitoris. Although early psychodynamic theories considered a lack of orgasm during intercourse to be pathological, evidence shows that women who rely on stimulation of the clitoris for orgasm are entirely healthy—physically and psychologically (Bradford, 2022, 2021). It is important to note that a number of clinicians further believe that the achievement of orgasm, under any circumstance, should not be a defining feature of an acceptable and healthy sex life (Shifren, 2023, 2022).

Biological, psychological, and sociocultural factors may combine to produce female orgasmic disorder. Because arousal plays a key role in orgasms, arousal difficulties often are featured prominently in explanations of female orgasmic disorder.

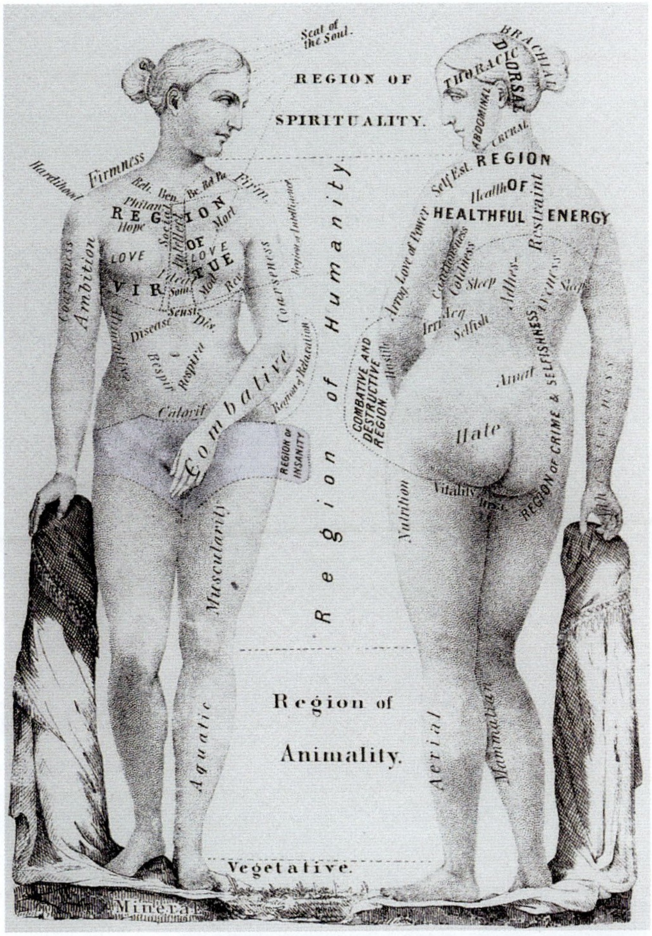

From Joseph R. Buchanan, Outlines of Lectures on the Neurological System of Anthropology, Cincinnati, 1854. Courtesy of Oskar Diethelm Library, DeWitt Wallace Institute of Psychiatry: History, Policy, & the Arts, Weill Cornell Medical College.

"The region of insanity" Medical authorities described "excessive passion" in Victorian women as dangerous and as a possible cause of insanity (Gamwell & Tomes, 1995). This illustration from a nineteenth-century medical textbook labels a woman's reproductive organs as her "region of insanity."

BIOLOGICAL CAUSES A variety of physiological conditions can affect a vaginal orgasm. Diabetes can damage the nervous system in ways that interfere with arousal, lubrication of the vagina, and orgasm. Lack of orgasm has sometimes been linked to multiple sclerosis and other neurological diseases, to the same drugs and medications that may interfere with a penile ejaculation, and to changes, often postmenopausal, in skin sensitivity and structure of the clitoris, vaginal walls, or the labia—the folds of skin on each side of the vagina (Conn & Hodges, 2023; Hirsch & Birnbaum, 2023, 2022; Salari et al., 2023).

PSYCHOLOGICAL CAUSES Research suggests that women with a high level of *sexual inhibition* are more likely to experience female orgasmic disorder (Bradford, 2022, 2021; Graham & Bancroft, 2020). These individuals may worry greatly about their sexual performance, have related negative thoughts about it, and be easily distracted during sexual activity.

More generally, the psychological causes of female sexual interest/arousal disorder, including depression, may also lead to female orgasmic disorder (MLP, 2023; Shifren, 2023, 2022). In addition, as both psychodynamic and cognitive theorists might predict, memories of childhood traumas and relationships have sometimes been associated with orgasm problems (MLP, 2023; Saadedine et al., 2023). In contrast, according to some studies, childhood memories of positive, dependable, and affectionate caregivers tend to predict positive orgasm outcomes (Heiman, 2007).

SOCIOCULTURAL CAUSES For years, many clinicians have believed that orgasmic problems in many women may result from society's recurrent message to women that they should repress and deny their sexuality, a message that supposedly causes many women to develop restrictive sexual attitudes and behaviors. And indeed, women with both arousal and orgasmic difficulties often report that they had an overly strict religious upbringing, were punished for childhood masturbation, received no preparation for the onset of menstruation, were restricted in their dating as teenagers, and were told that "nice girls don't" (Bradford, 2022, 2021).

It turns out, however, that a sexually restrictive history is just as common among women who function well during sexual activity. In addition, cultural messages about female sexuality have been more positive in recent years, while the rate of arousal and orgasmic problems remains the same for women. Why, then, do some women develop such difficulties and others do not? Researchers suggest that unusually stressful events or traumas may help produce the fears, memories, and attitudes that often characterize these sexual difficulties (Saadedine et al., 2023). For example, many women molested as children or raped as adults experience female orgasmic disorder (MLP, 2023; Blais, 2021).

Some theorists believe that the women's movement has helped to enlighten clinical views of sexual disorders. How might this be so?

Research has also related orgasmic behavior to certain qualities in a woman's intimate relationships (Shifren, 2023, 2022; Kingsberg et al., 2017). Studies have found, for example, that the likelihood of reaching orgasm may be tied to how much emotional involvement and pleasure a woman had during her first experience of intercourse, her current attraction to her partner's body, and her relationship happiness. Interestingly, the same studies have found that orgasmic women more often have erotic fantasies during sex with their current partner than do nonorgasmic women.

Disorders of Sexual Pain

Certain sexual dysfunctions are characterized by enormous physical discomfort during intercourse, a difficulty that does not fit neatly into a specific part of the sexual response cycle. Such dysfunctions, collectively called **genito-pelvic pain/penetration disorder,** particularly affect women (Khoury et al., 2024; Kingsberg & Spadt, 2023).

For some women with genito-pelvic pain/penetration disorder, the muscles around the vagina involuntarily contract, preventing entry (see **Table 11-4**). This problem, known in medical circles as *vaginismus,* can prevent a couple from ever having sexual penetration. The problem has received relatively little research, but estimates are that at least 1 percent of all women have vaginismus (Smith, 2022). A number of women with vaginismus enjoy sex greatly, have a strong sex drive, and reach orgasm with stimulation of the clitoris (Meana & Binik, 2022; Angin et al., 2020). They just fear the discomfort of penetration of the vagina.

TABLE 11-4

Dx Checklist

Genito-Pelvic Pain/Penetration Disorder
1. For at least 6 months, individual repeatedly experiences at least one of the following problems: ■ Difficulty having vaginal penetration during intercourse ■ Significant vaginal or pelvic pain when trying to have intercourse or penetration ■ Significant fear that vaginal penetration will cause vaginal or pelvic pain ■ Significant tensing of the pelvic muscles during vaginal penetration.
2. Individual experiences significant distress from this.

Information from: APA, 2022.

Most clinicians agree with the cognitive-behavioral position that this form of genito-pelvic pain/penetration disorder is usually a learned fear response, set off by an expectation that intercourse will be painful and damaging. A variety of factors apparently can set the stage for this fear, including anxiety and misinformation about intercourse, exaggerated stories about how painful and bloody the first occasion of sexual penetration is, trauma caused by an unskilled partner, and the trauma of childhood sexual abuse or adult rape (Anand, 2023; Kingsberg & Spadt, 2023).

Alternatively, this form of genito-pelvic pain/penetration disorder can be caused by an infection of the vagina or urinary tract, a gynecological disease such as herpes simplex, or the physical effects of menopause (Conn & Hodges, 2023; Kingsberg & Spadt, 2023). In such cases, the dysfunction can be overcome only if the individuals receive medical treatment for these conditions.

Some other women with genito-pelvic pain/penetration disorder do not have involuntary contractions of their vaginal muscles, but they do experience severe vaginal or pelvic pain during sexual penetration, a pattern known medically as *dyspareunia* (from Greek words meaning "painful mating"). Surveys suggest that 14 to 16 percent of all women (and 40 percent of all postmenopausal women) experience dyspareunia to some degree (Anand, 2023; Shifren, 2023, 2022). Those with this problem typically enjoy sex and get aroused but find their sex lives very limited by the pain that accompanies what used to be a positive event.

This form of genito-pelvic pain/penetration disorder usually has a physical cause (Tayyeb & Gupta, 2023; Meana & Binik, 2022). Among the most common is an injury (for example, to the vagina or the pelvic ligaments) during childbirth (Conn & Hodges, 2023). The scar left by an episiotomy (a cut often made to enlarge the vaginal entrance and ease delivery) also can cause pain (Berens, 2023; Bertozzi et al., 2010). More generally, such pain has also been tied to vaginal infections, wiry pubic hair rubbing against the labia during intercourse, a penis or digit colliding with remaining parts of the hymen, pelvic diseases, tumors, cysts, allergic reactions to the chemicals in vaginal douches and contraceptive creams, the rubber in condoms and diaphragms, and the protein in semen (Orr et al., 2020).

Although psychological factors (for instance, heightened anxiety or overattentiveness to one's body) or relationship problems may contribute to dyspareunia, psychosocial factors alone are rarely responsible for it (Kingsberg & Spadt, 2023; Meana & Binik, 2022). It is also the case that 1 to 5 percent of surveyed men have pain in the genitals during intercourse, and many of them also qualify for a diagnosis of genito-pelvic pain/penetration disorder (Hellstrom & DeLay, 2021).

of NOTE ...

Correlates of Positive Sexual Activity

- Stress reduction
- Mood boosts
- Improved immune system
- Memory improvements
- More efficient metabolism
- Better sleep
- Cardiovascular improvements

(Information from: Sauer & Walsh, 2022)

SUMMING UP

Sexual Dysfunctions

DSM-5-TR lists two disorders of the desire phase *of the* sexual response cycle: what the manual calls male hypoactive sexual desire disorder *and* female sexual interest/arousal disorder. Biological causes for these disorders include irregular hormone levels, certain drugs, and some medical illnesses. Psychological and sociocultural causes include specific fears, situational pressures, relationship problems, and the trauma of having been sexually molested or assaulted.

Disorders of the excitement phase include erectile disorder. Biological causes of erectile disorder include irregular hormone levels, vascular problems, medical conditions, and certain medications. Psychological and sociocultural causes include the combination of performance anxiety and the spectator role, situational pressures such as job loss, and relationship problems.

Disorders of orgasm include premature ejaculation. This dysfunction has been attributed most often to behavioral causes, such as inappropriate early learning and inexperience. In recent years, possible biological factors have been identified as well. Delayed ejaculation, a repeated absence of or long delay in reaching orgasm, can have biological causes, such as low testosterone levels, neurological diseases, and certain drugs, and psychological causes, such as performance anxiety and the spectator role. Female orgasmic disorder has been tied to biological causes such as medical diseases and changes that occur after menopause, psychological causes such as memories of childhood traumas, and sociocultural causes such as relationship problems.

Genito-pelvic pain/penetration disorder involves significant pain during intercourse. In one form of this disorder, vaginismus, involuntary contractions of the muscles around the vagina prevent entry of the penis. In another form, dyspareunia, the person has severe vaginal or pelvic pain during intercourse. This form of the disorder usually occurs in women and typically has a physical cause, such as injury resulting from childbirth.

Treatments for Sexual Dysfunctions

THE PAST HALF CENTURY has brought major changes in the treatment of sexual dysfunctions. A revolution in the treatment of sexual dysfunctions began with the publication of William Masters and Virginia Johnson's landmark book *Human Sexual*

genito-pelvic pain/penetration disorder A sexual dysfunction characterized by significant physical discomfort during intercourse.

Sexual pioneers William Masters and Virginia Johnson work with a couple in their office. The two researchers conducted their work from 1967 until the 1990s, writing two classic books, *Human Sexual Response* and *Human Sexual Inadequacy*.

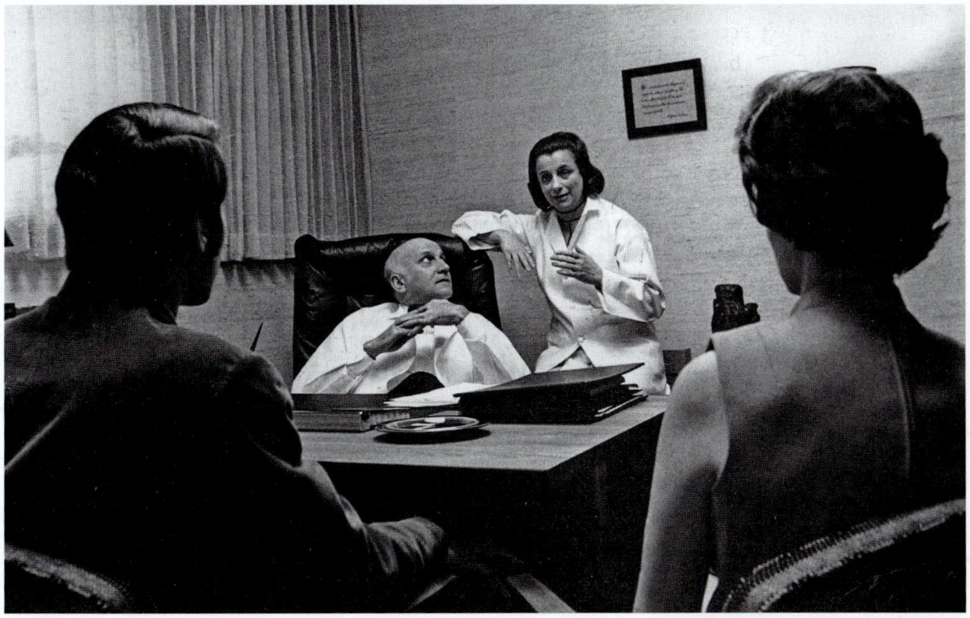

George Tames/The New York Times/Redux

Inadequacy in 1970. The *sex therapy* program they introduced has evolved into a complex approach that now includes interventions from the various models, particularly cognitive-behavioral, couple, and family systems therapies. The goal of sex therapy is to help clients function better sexually and achieve a higher level of sexual satisfaction and psychological well-being. In recent years, biological interventions, particularly drug therapies, have been added to the treatment arsenal.

As you have read, due to a lack of broader research, sexual dysfunctions are currently described, understood, and explained without much regard to differences in LGBTQ+ and racial and ethnic groups, although it is probable that some important differences exist and will be uncovered soon by emerging research. Correspondingly, many sex therapists currently use the same basic sex therapy techniques to treat clients of all gender identities, sexual orientations, and races and ethnicities, although some efforts are under way to also develop group-specific sex therapy techniques (Chen et al., 2022; Gaines et al., 2022). Beyond such techniques, a growing number of today's sex therapists also try to address broader pressures facing persons from various groups—issues that may impact clients' responsiveness to treatment (Campbell, 2022; Malone et al., 2021). And finally, as you will read, most current sex therapy techniques are geared to persons who identify as male or female, the majority of clients in sex therapy—a focus that is adjusted, when possible, if working with nonbinary clients (Fielding, 2021).

of NOTE ...

Not So Far Apart

In a survey of heterosexual couples, women say they want an average of 19 minutes of sexual foreplay and actually spend 11. Men say they want an average of 18 minutes of foreplay and actually spend 13 (Castleman, 2017).

What Are the General Features of Sex Therapy?

Modern sex therapy is short-term and instructive, typically lasting less than 20 sessions. It centers on specific sexual challenges rather than on broad personality issues. Kasem, the man with erectile disorder whom you met earlier, responded successfully to the multiple techniques of modern sex therapy:

During the initial therapy appointment, the therapist told Kasem and Gina that Kasem's problem was quite treatable, and he believed Kasem's sexual difficulties were probably the primary cause rather than the result of their relationship problems. After a detailed discussion of Kasem and Gina's personal, relationship, and sexual history, the therapist said Kasem's erectile disorder likely stemmed from a number of causes. Initially, it very well might have been due to work stress and/or physical exhaustion. Subsequently, however, Kasem's concerns, self-doubts, and endless evaluations about his sexual performance became the primary reason that his erectile disorder continued and intensified.

Kasem and Gina agreed to center their therapy on Kasem's erectile disorder, and they decided on a 15-session course of treatment. The following session, the therapist gave them "homework." They were to set aside some time at home to explore each other with touch. The therapist gave them instructions to not attempt any sexual stimulation or intercourse but merely to enjoy making each other feel good. When they followed through on this assignment at home, freed of the obligation to perform, Kasem found to his surprise that within a few minutes he developed an erection and experienced a desire to make love to Gina. When this occurred, the couple shared a look, and Gina asked, sheepishly, "What should we do? Should we . . . ?" After a moment of silence, Kasem laughed and said, "Come on, Gina, we're not children! Let's go for it." He was more excited than he'd been in some time, and that night they made love for the first time in almost a year.

At their next therapy session, the therapist congratulated them on their progress and said, with a grin, that many couples initially find themselves unable to abide by the no-sex rules of this exercise. However, he told them that Kasem's ability to perform that time did not necessarily mean that he'd be able to have an erection every time they did the exercise. The therapist gave them more homework, telling them that they should repeat the exercise during the coming week and add in some light foreplay, but he emphasized that they should not necessarily expect Kasem to again have an erection during the exercise. Moreover, either way, they should refrain from having intercourse.

Although he certainly heard the therapist's warning, Kasem was eager for them to do their homework during the coming week. He chuckled to himself that they would probably once again wind up breaking the rules of the exercise. After all, he reasoned, he was back to being a capable lover who could please his wife. Thus, he was aghast when he did not achieve an erection the second time around.

Their next therapy session focused on helping Kasem deal with the embarrassment and self-doubt produced by the results—in his mind, the "non-results"—of the latest homework exercise. The therapist reminded him that this was so common that he had predicted its possible occurrence last week. He reminded Kasem that a critical feature of the exercise was to have no expectation and no obligation to perform. The therapist instructed the couple to repeat the homework assignment during the coming week. Once again, Kasem did not achieve an erection during the exercise, but he and Gina did acknowledge how much they were enjoying caressing each other nonetheless.

Over the course of the next few sessions, the therapist emphasized that, in general, an erection is not the be-all and end-all of sexual pleasure. Kasem and Gina could please each other sexually in many ways. Gina picked up on this and enthusiastically assured Kasem that she enjoyed their homework sessions either way, and she was just happy they were being intimate. She said she was overjoyed that he was expressing his love and desire for her again, and they were closer than they had been in some time. It didn't matter whether they actually had intercourse. She added that she was even getting more pleasure from their recent attempts than she had from some of their past sexual activities—activities from before his erectile disorder. The reason? He was becoming a more sensitive lover. Gina's proclamations made Kasem feel more than a little happy and very relieved.

In the weeks that followed, the no-sex rules were lifted, and several of their homework exercises did indeed lead to intercourse. By the twelfth week, Kasem was regularly achieving and sustaining erections during lovemaking. At the same time, both he and Gina recognized that on those occasions when he didn't achieve erections, there were plenty of other ways they could please each other. This, in fact, was the abiding philosophy they adopted toward sex—for both now and in the future. They ended therapy after 14 weeks. At work, Kasem held his head high when the crew traded stories of their sexual exploits; he suspected that he now had a fuller and more satisfying romantic life and a stronger relationship than many of his bragging coworkers were experiencing.

of NOTE ...

Partnered Sex

- **67%** Percentage of U.S. men who have engaged in partnered sex in the past year
- **67%** Percentage of U.S. women who have engaged in partnered sex in the past year
- **41%** Percentage of U.S. men who desire more frequent partnered sex than they currently experience
- **21%** Percentage of U.S. women who desire more frequent partnered sex than they currently experience

(Information from: Herbenick et al., 2022)

As Kasem's treatment indicates, modern sex therapy includes a variety of principles and techniques. The following ones are used in almost all cases, regardless of the dysfunction:

Sex is one of the topics most commonly searched on the Internet. Why might it be such a popular search topic?

1. **Assessing and conceptualizing the difficulty.** Patients are initially given a medical examination and are interviewed concerning their sex history. The therapist's focus during the interview is on gathering information about past life events and, in particular, current factors that are contributing to the dysfunction (Khera, 2023). Sometimes proper assessment requires a team of specialists, perhaps including a psychologist, urologist, and neurologist.
2. **Mutual responsibility.** Therapists stress the principle of *mutual responsibility*. Both partners in the relationship are affected by the sexual problem, regardless of who has the actual dysfunction, so treatment is likely to be more successful when both are in therapy (Shifren, 2023).
3. **Education about sexuality.** Many patients who experience sexual dysfunctions know very little about the physiology and techniques of sexual activity (Conn & Hodges, 2023; Khera, 2023). Thus, sex therapists may discuss these topics and offer educational materials, including instructional books, videos, and websites.
4. **Emotion identification.** Sex therapists help patients identify and express upsetting emotions tied to past events that may keep interfering with sexual arousal and enjoyment (MLP, 2023).
5. **Attitude change.** Following one of the key principles of cognitive-behavioral therapy, sex therapists help patients examine and change any beliefs about sexuality that are preventing sexual arousal and pleasure (Meana & Hall, 2023). Some of these mistaken beliefs are widely shared in society and can result from past traumatic events, family attitudes, or cultural ideas (Saadedine et al., 2023).
6. **Mindfulness.** In another application of cognitive-behavioral therapy, sex therapists often provide *mindfulness training* to clients and help them employ this technique in the sexual realm so that the clients can develop a heightened awareness of the negative thoughts and feelings that travel through their

Jon Hall/©Netflix/Courtesy: Everett Collection

Sex therapy, high school style In the Netflix series *Sex Education*, high schooler Otis Milburn sets up a sex advice business in which he counsels classmates about their sexual problems. Here, Milburn, whose mother is a licensed sex therapist, provides guidance to a student with sexual performance anxiety, using the school bathroom as his office.

minds during sex, learn to accept and disregard such thoughts, and better tune into erotic sensations that can facilitate their sexual activity (Conn & Hodges, 2023).

7. **Elimination of performance anxiety and the spectator role.** Therapists often teach couples *sensate focus,* or *nondemand pleasuring,* a series of sensual tasks, sometimes called "petting" exercises, in which the partners focus on the sexual pleasure that can be achieved by exploring and caressing each other's body at home, without demands for penetration or to reach orgasm—demands that may be interfering with arousal. Couples are told at first to refrain from intercourse at home and to restrict their sexual activity to kissing, hugging, and sensual massage of various parts of the body but not of the breasts or genitals. Over time, they learn how to give and receive greater sexual pleasure, and they build back up to activities of sexual intercourse (Boskey, 2023; Meana & Hall, 2023).

Are there other problem areas in life that might also be explained by performance anxiety and the spectator role?

8. **Increasing sexual and general communication skills.** Couples are taught to use their sensate-focus skills and apply new sexual techniques and positions at home (Shifren, 2023; Bradford, 2022). They may, for example, try sexual positions in which the person being caressed can guide the other's hands and control the speed, pressure, and location of sexual contact. Couples are also taught to give instructions to each other in a nonthreatening, informative manner ("It feels better over here, with a little less pressure") rather than a threatening uninformative manner ("The way you're touching me doesn't turn me on"). Moreover, couples may be given broader training in how best to communicate with each other (Khera, 2023).
9. **Changing destructive lifestyles and couple interactions.** A therapist may encourage a couple to change their lifestyle or take other steps to improve a situation that is having a destructive effect on their relationship—to distance themselves from interfering family members, for example, or to change a job that is too demanding. Similarly, if the couple's general relationship is marked by conflict, the therapist will try to help them improve it.
10. **Addressing physical and medical factors.** Systematic increases in physical activity have proved helpful for persons with various kinds of sexual dysfunctions (Akers, 2022). In addition, when sexual dysfunctions are caused by a medical problem, such as disease, injury, medication, or substance abuse, therapists try to address that problem (Salari et al., 2023). If antidepressant medications are causing erectile disorder, for example, the clinician may suggest lowering the dosage of the medication or turning to a different antidepressant.

"It's not you, babe—I've been neutered."

What Techniques Are Used to Treat Particular Dysfunctions?

In addition to the general components of sex therapy, specific techniques can help in each of the sexual dysfunctions.

Disorders of Desire Male hypoactive sexual desire disorder and female sexual interest/arousal disorder are among the most difficult dysfunctions to treat because of the many issues that may feed into them. Thus therapists typically use a combination of techniques (Khera, 2023; Rice, 2020). In a technique called *affectual*

of NOTE ...

Sex Versus Cell Phones

- **10%** Percentage of survey respondents who admit to having checked their cell phones during sex
- **41%** Percentage of survey respondents who say they would rather give up sex for a year than give up their cell phones for a year

(Information from: Wheelwright, 2022; SC, 2018)

awareness, patients visualize sexual scenes in order to discover any feelings of anxiety, vulnerability, and other negative emotions they may have concerning sex. In another technique, patients receive cognitive *self-instruction training* to help them change their negative reactions to sex. That is, they learn to replace negative statements during sex with "coping statements," such as "I can allow myself to enjoy sex; it doesn't mean I'll lose control."

Therapists may also use behavioral approaches to help heighten the sex drive of individuals. They may instruct clients to keep a "desire diary" in which they record sexual thoughts and feelings, to read books and view videos with erotic content, and to fantasize about sex. They also may encourage pleasurable shared activities such as dancing and walking together. If the reduced sexual desire has resulted from sexual assault or childhood sexual abuse, additional techniques may be needed (Meana & Hall, 2023). A client may, for example, be encouraged to remember, talk about, and think about the assault until the memories no longer arouse fear or tension. These and related psychological approaches apparently help many people with low sexual desire eventually to have intercourse more than once a week (Khera, 2023).

Finally, biological interventions, such as *hormone* treatments, have been used, particularly to treat female sexual interest/arousal disorder arising from menopause or removal of the ovaries (Conn & Hodges, 2023). In addition, several pharmaceutical drugs have been developed to help heighten the sex drive of individuals. These interventions have received some research support (Charmley, 2023; Molkara et al., 2021).

Erectile Disorder

Treatments for erectile disorder focus on reducing performance anxiety, increasing stimulation of the penis, or both, using a range of behavioral, cognitive, and relationship interventions (Khera, 2023). In one technique, a couple is instructed to try the *tease technique* during sensate-focus exercises; for example, a man may be caressed by his partner, but if the man gets an erection, the partner stops caressing him until the erection subsides. This exercise reduces pressure to perform and at the same time teaches the couple that erections occur naturally in response to stimulation, as long as the partners do not keep focusing on performance.

AP Photo/Amr Nabil

Viagra around the world Technicians at a pharmaceutical factory in Cairo sort thousands of Viagra pills for distribution and marketing in Egypt's pharmacies.

Biological approaches gained great momentum with the development in 1998 of ***sildenafil*** (trade name Viagra). This drug increases blood flow to the penis within one hour of ingestion; the increased blood flow enables the user to attain an erection during sexual activity. In general, *sildenafil* appears to be safe; however, it may not be so for patients with certain coronary heart diseases and cardiovascular diseases, particularly those who are taking *nitroglycerin* and other heart medications (Khera, 2023). Three other erectile dysfunction drugs have also been approved since the introduction of Viagra—*tadalafil* (Cialis), *vardenafil* (Levitra), and *avanafil* (Stendra). All of these drugs are about equal in effectiveness. Collectively, the drugs are the most common form of treatment for erectile disorder. Research has found they effectively restore erections and enable sexual intercourse in 43 to 83 percent of people who use them, compared to a rate of 10 to 24 percent among people taking placebo drugs (Marshall, 2023; Graham & Bancroft, 2020). Some research, though, suggests that a combination of one of these erectile dysfunction drugs and a psychological intervention such as those mentioned above may be more helpful than either kind of treatment alone.

Prior to the development of Viagra, Cialis, Levitra, and Stendra, a range of other medical procedures were developed for erectile disorder. These procedures are now viewed as "second line"—often costly—treatments that are used primarily when the medications are unsuccessful or too risky for individuals (Hirsch, 2023, 2022). Such treatments include gel suppositories, injections of drugs into the penis, a surgical implantation of a penile prosthesis, and a *vacuum erection device* (*VED*), a hollow cylinder that is placed over the penis. For the VED, a hand pump is used to pump air out of the cylinder, drawing blood into the penis and producing an erection.

of NOTE ...

Their Words

"Some nights he said that he was tired, and some nights she said that she wanted to read, and other nights no one said anything."

Joan Didion, Writer, Play It as It Lays

Premature Ejaculation

Early ejaculation has been treated successfully for years by behavioral procedures (Crowdis et al., 2023; Khera, 2023). In one such approach, the *stop-start,* or *pause, procedure,* the penis is manually stimulated by the partner until the patient is highly aroused (Campbell, 2022). The couple then pauses until this arousal subsides, after which the stimulation is resumed. This sequence is repeated several times, so the man ultimately experiences much more total time of stimulation than he has ever experienced before. Eventually the couple progresses to intercourse, making sure the penis is withdrawn whenever the man becomes too highly aroused. According to clinical reports, after two or three months, many couples can enjoy prolonged intercourse without any need for pauses.

Many clinicians treat premature ejaculation with SSRIs, the serotonin-enhancing antidepressant drugs. Because these drugs often reduce sexual arousal or interfere with orgasm, the reasoning goes, they may be helpful to men who ejaculate prematurely. Many studies report positive results with this approach (Crowdis et al., 2023; Khera, 2023). The effect of the approach is consistent with the biological theory, mentioned earlier, that serotonin receptors in the brains of patients with early ejaculation may function irregularly.

Delayed Ejaculation

Therapies for delayed ejaculation include techniques to reduce performance anxiety and increase stimulation (Moore, 2023; Stratton, 2022). For example, a man may be instructed to masturbate to orgasm in the presence of his partner or to masturbate just short of orgasm before inserting his penis for intercourse. This increases the likelihood that he will ejaculate during intercourse. The man then is instructed to insert his penis at ever earlier stages of masturbation.

When delayed ejaculation is caused by physical factors such as neurological damage or injury, treatment may include a drug to increase arousal of the sympathetic nervous system (MacGill, 2023). However, few studies have systematically tested the effectiveness of such biological treatments.

Female Orgasmic Disorder

Specific treatments for female orgasmic disorder include cognitive-behavioral techniques, self-exploration, enhancement of body awareness, and directed masturbation training (Conn & Hodges, 2023; MLP, 2023). These procedures are especially useful for those with female orgasmic disorder who have never had an orgasm under any circumstances. Biological treatments, including hormone therapy, have also been tried, but research has not consistently found these to be helpful (Shifren, 2023, 2022).

In **directed masturbation training,** the individual with female orgasmic disorder is taught step-by-step how to masturbate effectively and eventually to reach orgasm during sexual interactions. The training includes the use of diagrams and reading material, private self-stimulation, erotic material and fantasies, "orgasm triggers" such as holding one's breath or thrusting one's pelvis, sensate focus with a romantic partner, and sexual positioning that produces stimulation of the clitoris during intercourse. This training program appears to be highly effective: over 90 percent of female clients, for example, learn to have an orgasm during masturbation, about 80 percent during caressing by their partners, and about 30 percent during intercourse (Bradford, 2022; Graham & Bancroft, 2020).

sildenafil One of the drugs used to treat erectile disorder that helps increase blood flow to the penis during sexual activity. Marketed as Viagra.

directed masturbation training A sex therapy approach that teaches clients with female arousal or orgasmic problems how to masturbate effectively and eventually to reach orgasm during sexual interactions.

of NOTE ...

Solo Sex

- **60%** Percentage of U.S. men who have engaged in solo masturbation in the past month
- **37%** Percentage of U.S. women who have engaged in solo masturbation in the past month
- **10%** Percentage of U.S. men who have never engaged in solo masturbation
- **24%** Percentage of U.S. women who have never engaged in solo masturbation

(Information from: Herbenick et al., 2022)

As you read earlier, a lack of vaginal orgasm during intercourse is not necessarily a sexual dysfunction, provided the individual enjoys sex. For this reason, some therapists believe that the wisest course is simply to educate clients whose only concern is lack of vaginal orgasm during intercourse, informing them that they are quite healthy, and to further teach them how to reach orgasm, if they wish, through caressing by oneself or by one's partner.

Genito-Pelvic Pain/Penetration Disorder

Specific treatment for involuntary contractions of the muscles around the vagina typically involves two approaches (Anand, 2023; Angin et al., 2020). A woman, for example, may practice tightening and relaxing her vaginal muscles until she gains more voluntary control over them. The woman may also receive gradual behavioral exposure treatment to help her overcome her fear of penetration, beginning, for example, by inserting increasingly large dilators in her vagina at home and at her own pace and eventually ending with sexual penetration. Most clients treated with such procedures eventually have pain-free intercourse. Some medical interventions have also been used. For example, several clinical investigators have injected the problematic vaginal muscles with Botox to help reduce spasms in those muscles. Studies of this approach have yielded promising results (Tayyeb & Gupta, 2023; Meana & Binik, 2022).

Different approaches are used to treat the other form of genito-pelvic pain/penetration disorder—severe vaginal or pelvic pain during intercourse. As you read earlier, the most common cause of this problem is physical, such as pain-causing scars, lesions, or infection aftereffects. When the cause is known, pain management procedures, such as those you learned about earlier in the textbook, and sex therapy techniques may be tried, including helping a couple to learn intercourse positions that avoid putting pressure on the injured area (Tayyeb & Gupta, 2023). Medical interventions—from topical creams to surgery—may also be tried, but typically they must be combined with other sex therapy techniques to overcome the years of sexual anxiety and lack of arousal (Conn & Hodges, 2023). Experts believe that, in most cases, both forms of genito-pelvic pain/penetration disorder are best assessed and treated by a *team* of professionals, including a gynecologist, physical therapist, and sex therapist or other mental health professional (Kingsberg & Spadt, 2023).

What Are the Current Trends in Sex Therapy?

Sex therapists have now moved well beyond the approach first developed by Masters and Johnson. In a movement called "expanding inclusivity," today's sex therapists regularly treat partners who are living together but not married. In addition, they work with LGBTQ+ clients, as you read earlier; older adults; people with severe medical illnesses; clients with disabilities; people with neurodevelopmental disorders; and individuals who have no long-term sex partner. Sex therapists are also paying more attention to *compulsive sexual behavior disorder,* sometimes called *persistent sexuality disorder, hypersexuality,* or *sexual addiction*—a pattern now listed in ICD-11 but not in DSM-5-TR (Draps et al., 2022).

Many sex therapists have expressed concern about the sharp increase in the use of drugs and other medical interventions for sexual dysfunctions, particularly for the disorders characterized by low sexual desire and erectile disorder. Their concern is that therapists will increasingly choose the biological interventions rather than integrating biological, psychological, and sociocultural interventions. In fact, a narrow approach of any kind probably cannot fully address the complex factors that cause most sexual problems. It took sex therapists years to recognize the considerable advantages of an integrated approach to sexual dysfunctions. The development of new medical interventions should not lead to its abandonment.

SUMMING UP

Treatments for Sexual Dysfunctions

In the 1970s, the work of William Masters and Virginia Johnson led to the development of sex therapy. Today, sex therapy combines a variety of cognitive, behavioral, couple, and family systems therapies. It generally includes features such as careful assessment, education, acceptance of mutual responsibility, attitude changes, sensate-focus exercises, improvements in communication, and couple therapy. In addition, specific techniques have been developed for each of the sexual dysfunctions. The use of biological treatments for sexual dysfunctions is also increasing.

Paraphilic Disorders

PARAPHILIAS ARE PATTERNS in which people repeatedly have intense sexual urges or fantasies or display sexual behaviors that involve objects or situations outside the usual sexual norms. The sexual focus may, for example, involve nonhuman objects or the experience of suffering or humiliation. Many people with a paraphilia can become aroused only when a paraphilic stimulus is present, fantasized about, or acted out. Others need the stimulus only during times of stress or under other special circumstances. Some people with one kind of paraphilia have others as well. The large consumer market in paraphilic pornography leads clinicians to suspect that paraphilias may be far more common than previously thought (Fox et al., 2022).

Is the abundance of sexual material on the Internet psychologically healthy or damaging?

According to DSM-5-TR, a diagnosis of **paraphilic disorder** should be applied when paraphilias currently cause a person significant distress or impairment *or* when the satisfaction of the paraphilias has placed the person or other people at risk of harm (APA, 2022) (see **Table 11-5**). People who initiate sexual contact with children, for example, warrant a diagnosis of *pedophilic disorder,* regardless of how troubled the individuals may or may not be over their behavior. People whose paraphilic disorder

"Leave it on"

Danny Shanahan/CartoonStock Ltd

paraphilias Patterns in which a person has recurrent and intense sexual urges, fantasies, or behaviors involving nonhuman objects, children, nonconsenting adults, or experiences of suffering or humiliation.

paraphilic disorder A disorder in which a person's paraphilia causes great distress, interferes with social or occupational activities, or has placed the person or others at risk of harm.

TABLE 11-5

Dx Checklist

Paraphilic Disorder
1. For at least 6 months, individual experiences recurrent and intense sexually arousing fantasies, urges, or behaviors involving objects or situations outside the usual sexual norms (nonhuman objects; nongenital body parts; the suffering or humiliation of oneself or one's partner; or children or other nonconsenting persons).
2. Individual experiences significant distress or impairment over the fantasies, urges, or behaviors. (In some paraphilic disorders—pedophilic disorder, exhibitionistic disorder, voyeuristic disorder, frotteuristic disorder, and sexual sadism disorder—the performance of the paraphilic behaviors indicates a disorder, even in the absence of distress or impairment.)

Information from: APA, 2022.

involves children or nonconsenting adults often come to the attention of clinicians as a result of legal issues generated by their inappropriate actions.

Research into paraphilic disorders is quite limited. Information about the patterns has generally been derived from clinical reports and studies of cisgender, heterosexual, and non-Hispanic White people. While much information may indeed carry over to other subpopulations, it is also likely that some important—as yet uncovered—differences exist in the paraphilias and paraphilic disorders displayed by people from LGBTQ+ groups and by people of color. Studies on sexual fantasies find notable differences in the content of the fantasies experienced by people from various subgroups (Lehmiller & Gormezano, 2023). Of course, fantasies are not necessarily paraphilias, nor are disorders, but fantasies are key elements of many such patterns, so this finding may have implications for group differences among paraphilic disorders.

Research conducted with mostly cisgender populations finds that men with paraphilic disorder outnumber women, although the precise prevalences of the various disorders are largely unknown (APA, 2022). Moreover, as you will read, although theorists have proposed various explanations for paraphilic disorders, there is little formal evidence to support such explanations (Martin & Levine, 2023; Fox et al., 2022). And finally, none of the many treatments applied to these disorders has received much research or proved clearly effective (Fisher & Marwaha, 2023). Psychological treatments have been available the longest, but today's professionals are also using biological interventions.

Some practitioners administer drugs, collectively called *antiandrogens*, that lower the production of testosterone, the male sex hormone, and reduce the sex drive (Fisher & Marwaha, 2023). Although antiandrogens may indeed reduce paraphilic patterns, several of them disrupt appropriate sexual feelings and behavior as well. Thus, the drugs tend to be used primarily when the paraphilic disorders are of particular danger either to the individuals themselves or to other people. Clinicians may also prescribe SSRIs, the serotonin-enhancing antidepressant medications, to treat people with paraphilic disorders, hoping that the SSRIs will reduce these compulsion-like sexual behaviors just as they help reduce other kinds of compulsions (Brown, 2023; Vayisoglu, 2023). In addition, of course, a common effect of SSRIs is to lower sexual arousal.

How might societal norms influence the diagnosis and treatment of certain nonsexual patterns, such as compulsions, stress reactions, manic behaviors, somatic reactions, gambling, and delusions?

A word of caution is in order before we examine the various paraphilic disorders. The definitions of these disorders, like those of sexual dysfunctions, are strongly influenced by the norms of the particular society in which they occur (Fox et al., 2022) (see ***MindTech***). Some clinicians argue that except when other people are hurt by them, at least some paraphilic behaviors should not be considered disorders at all. Especially in light of the stigma associated with sexual disorders and the self-revulsion that many people feel when they believe they have such a disorder, we need to be very careful about applying these labels to others or to ourselves. Keep in mind that for years, clinicians considered homosexuality a paraphilic disorder, and their judgment was used to justify laws and even police actions against gay people. Only in 1987, when the gay rights movement helped change society's understanding of and attitudes toward homosexuality, did clinicians officially stop considering it a disorder and remove it entirely from the DSM. Even then, as you read earlier in the textbook, many clinicians continued for years to recommend and offer *sexual orientation change efforts,* or *SOCEs*—that is, now widely discredited attempts to administer so-called *conversion,* or *reparative, therapy* to "fix" the sexual orientation of gay people. With such diagnostic views and treatment efforts, the clinical field had unintentionally contributed to the persecution, anxiety, and humiliation of millions of people because of personal sexual behavior that differed from the conventional norms (Comer et al., 2024).

fetishistic disorder A paraphilic disorder consisting of recurrent and intense sexual urges, fantasies, or behaviors that involve the use of a nonliving object or nongenital part, often to the exclusion of all other stimuli, accompanied by clinically significant distress or impairment.

Fetishistic Disorder

One relatively common paraphilic disorder is **fetishistic disorder.** Key features of this disorder are recurrent intense sexual urges, sexually arousing fantasies, or

MINDTECH

"Sexting": From Pathology to Respectability

"Sexting" is the sending of sexually explicit material—usually photos or text messages—between digital devices, such as cell phones. The term "sexting" did not make its debut until 2005. In its early days, this behavior was viewed by most clinical theorists as pathological. Around 15 percent of sexters sent sexual photos of themselves to nonconsenting strangers (Mori et al., 2022, 2020), and many of the sexters fit the criteria for *exhibitionistic disorder*, the paraphilic pattern in which people act on urges to expose their genitals to others. Like other forms of exhibitionism, sexting of this kind often caused significant distress for recipients.

Over the past decade, however, the nature and context of many sexting behaviors have changed, and sexting's stock has risen among many—although certainly not all—clinicians (Gassó et al., 2022, 2021, 2019). Sending sexual photos of oneself has evolved into a widely used form of sexual expression and mutually consensual communication in the relationships of many teenagers and adults—a development called the *normalization* of sexting.

Findings vary widely, but, collectively, they indicate that at least 27 percent of individuals send sexts and that at least 35 percent receive them (Mori et al., 2022, 2020). Researchers are scurrying to understand the characteristics, causes, and impact of these behaviors. Much remains to be learned, but the researchers recognize that, on average, people sext more and more each year as they move from early adolescence to their late twenties. Moreover, investigators now distinguish between sexting that occurs within a romantic relationship and sexting within a nonromantic one, sexting in a committed relationship and sexting in a casual relationship, sexting done in young adult relationships (ages 18 to 28 years) and sexting in teenage relationships (ages 12 to 17), and nonconsensual, or coerced, sexting and consensual sexting.

Studies find that, on average, individuals who sext with mutual consent within romantic and/or committed relationships report greater relationship and sexual satisfaction than those who sext within nonromantic and/or casual relationships (Gassó et al., 2022, 2021, 2019; Mori et al., 2022, 2020). The former also seem to have less anxiety and depression and display lower rates of substance abuse than the latter.

Lisa Werner/Alamy Stock Photo

Similarly, on average, individuals who sext within young adult relationships report greater relationship and sexual satisfaction and display more positive emotions than individuals who sext within teenage relationships (Gassó et al., 2022, 2020, 2019; Krishna, 2019). Research has also revealed that the former sext much more often than the latter: 38 percent of young adults send sexts compared to 19 percent of teens, and 42 percent of young adults receive sexts compared to almost 35 percent of teens (Mori et al., 2022, 2020; Gordon, 2020). In addition, young adults who sext tend to be more aware of its potential risks and wind up experiencing less online bullying and harassment than teenagers who perform this behavior.

While sexting has become a relatively positive element in many relationships, there remain certain negative consequences and risks attached to it (Gassó et al., 2022, 2021, 2019; Mori et al., 2022, 2020). It is, for example, still the case that 15 percent of persons receive nonconsensual sexts from strangers. Even within relationships, persons may receive nonconsensual sexts. Moreover, there are a number of sexting-related dangers that can lead to significant problems for sexters: (1) Teenagers who transmit sexually explicit images are breaking child pornography laws, even if they create the images themselves, and their sexting can cause legal problems for them. (2) At least 14 percent of people report knowing that their sexts have been forwarded to other people without their consent—for example, in the form of "revenge porn." (3) Nothing totally disappears from the Internet, meaning that sexts can come back to haunt individuals years later, affecting their job security, social standing, and the like. When these or other negative consequences of sexting have occurred, considerable psychological distress has often followed, including poorer mental health, feelings of humiliation and vulnerability, social withdrawal, low self-image, and even suicidal thoughts. Clearly, despite sexting's rise in status and its positive value in many relationships, sexters must proceed with awareness and caution.

behaviors that involve the use of a nonliving object or nongenital body part, often to the exclusion of all other stimuli (APA, 2022). The disorder, which causes the individual significant distress or impairment, usually begins in adolescence (Martin & Levine, 2023). Almost anything can be a fetish; underwear, shoes, and boots are particularly common. Some people with this disorder steal in order to collect as many of the desired objects as possible. The objects may be touched, smelled, worn, or used

Brandon Thibodeaux/The New York Times/Redux

An AI fetish? Originally developed as computer programs with which users could cultivate friendships and fulfill companionship needs, *chatbots* using AI (artificial intelligence) technology have added functions in recent years such as erotic role-play and sexually charged conversations. In fact, when the chatbot Replika (see photo) recently turned off the capacity for erotic functions, many of its users were outraged, leading the company to turn the sexual functions back on. Even more enticing to many people is the continuing development of *sex robots* (also called *sexbots* and *robot sex dolls*), in which AI technology is offered within a silicone-based human form that also moves in humanlike ways. Sexbots have generated much discussion—both pro and con—but fully functioning versions have not yet been manufactured.

in some other way while the person masturbates, or the person may ask a partner to wear the object when they have sex. Some of these features are on display in the case of Jaylen, a teenager whose mother, Kiara, discovered his fetishistic disorder over the course of six months:

> *[Kiara] reported that she first recognized [Jaylen's] sexual interest in women's shoes six months ago. He started to disappear repeatedly from their apartment and [one day, Kiara] found him on the stairs . . . handling the shoes of a female neighbor. Later on, [Kiara] came across [Jaylen] rubbing and smelling the shoes in such a fascinated manner that he did not even recognize his mother's presence. . . . [Kiara] also noticed that [Jaylen] was increasingly staying within their apartment building, taking the neighbor's shoes down to the ground floor rather than going outside. . . . After a week [Jaylen] visited the neighbor's home while helping her carry shopping goods. After an apparently normal visit, the neighbor recognized that her shoes were missing. [Kiara] tried to talk with [her son], but he became agitated and refused to talk. After several weeks, she recognized that her own shoes were missing. . . . The mother then started keeping track of [Jaylen] and recognized that he was awaking at night and was . . . rubbing and smelling her shoes. [Kiara] did not recognize the sexual nature of his behaviors and thought that he had a compulsive interest in shoes. [However, one day] she entered the bathroom and found [Jaylen] there masturbating while he was holding and rubbing her shoe in his hand. At that point, she recognized the sexual nature of his interest in shoes for the first time. Subsequently she came across some videos on his mobile phone. They were recordings of young women's feet with or without shoes, including videos of [Kiara's own] naked feet. There were dozens of these videos . . . dating back four months.*
>
> *(Coskun & Ozturk, 2013, p. 199)*

of NOTE ...

What's in a Name?

The term "fetish" originates from the Portuguese word *feticio*, meaning "charm with mysterious powers."

Researchers have not been able to pinpoint the causes of fetishistic disorder (Martin & Levine, 2023; Fox et al., 2022). Psychodynamic theorists consider fetishes to be defense mechanisms that help people avoid the anxiety produced by more typical sexual contact. Psychodynamic treatment for this problem, however, has met with little success.

Cognitive-behavioral theorists view fetishes as learned behaviors that are acquired by classical conditioning in particular (Brown, 2023; Longpre & Guay, 2022). In a pioneering behavioral study, men were shown a series of slides of nude women along with slides of boots (Rachman, 1966). After many trials, the participants became aroused by the boot photos alone. If early sexual experiences similarly occur in the presence of particular objects, perhaps the stage is set for the development of fetishes.

Cognitive-behavioral therapists have sometimes treated fetishistic disorder with *aversion therapy* (PT, 2022; Miner & Munns, 2021). In a famous study, an electric shock was administered to the arms or legs of men with this disorder while they imagined their objects of desire (Marks & Gelder, 1967). After two weeks of therapy, all participants in the study showed at least some improvement. In another aversion technique, *covert sensitization,* people with fetishistic disorder are guided to *imagine* the pleasurable object and repeatedly pair this image with an *imagined* aversive stimulus until the object of sexual pleasure is no longer desired.

Another cognitive-behavioral treatment for fetishistic disorder is *masturbatory satiation* (MHN, 2023; Miner & Munns, 2021). In this method, the client masturbates to orgasm while fantasizing about a sexually appropriate object, then switches to fantasizing about fetishistic objects while masturbating again, continuing the fetishistic fantasy for an hour. The procedure is meant to produce a feeling of boredom, which in turn becomes linked to the fetishistic object.

exhibitionistic disorder A paraphilic disorder in which persons have repeated sexually arousing urges or fantasies about exposing their genitals to others and either act on these urges with nonconsenting individuals or experience clinically significant distress or impairment.

Exhibitionistic Disorder

Persons with **exhibitionistic disorder** experience recurrent and intense sexual arousal from exposing their genitals to an unsuspecting individual—arousal reflected by fantasies, urges, or behaviors (APA, 2022). Most often, the person wants to provoke shock or surprise rather than initiate sexual activity with the target individual. Sometimes exhibitionists will expose themselves in a particular neighborhood at particular hours. In a survey of 2,800 men, 4.3 percent of them reported that they perform exhibitionistic behavior (Fedoroff, 2020; Långström & Seto, 2006). Yet between one-third and one-half of all women report having seen or had direct contact with an exhibitionist, or so-called flasher, and exhibitionistic acts are the sex crime most commonly reported to police, accounting for one-third to two-thirds of all reported offenses (Kaylor & Jeglic, 2021; Marshall et al., 2008). The urge to exhibit typically becomes stronger when the person has free time or is under significant stress.

Generally, exhibitionistic disorder begins before age 18 (APA, 2022). Some studies suggest that those with the disorder have difficulty in interactions with others and are immature in their intimate relationships (Seeman, 2020). Around 30 percent of them are in a partnered relationship, and another 30 percent are divorced or separated; their sexual relations with partners are not usually satisfactory (Brown, 2023; Doctor & Neff, 2001). Men with the disorder often have doubts or fears about their masculinity, and some seem to have a strong bond to a possessive parent (Longpre & Guay, 2022).

Psychodynamic theorists propose that exhibitionistic disorder reflects an individual's development of sexual anxiety during a repressive childhood and an ongoing defense against that anxiety by calling attention to one's sexual parts (Kaylor & Jeglic, 2021). Cognitive-behavioral theorists have proposed that the disorder may begin with an early accidental exposure of one's sexual parts in front of another person, which produces arousal. That initial experience is then fantasied about and masturbated to over time, making the event and exhibitionistic behavior increasingly exciting (Kaylor & Jeglic, 2021). Neither of these theories has received much research support.

of NOTE ...

Tattoos and Sexuality

- **31%** Percentage of people with tattoos who say that their tattoos make them feel more attractive and/or sexier
- **29%** Percentage of people without tattoos who say that tattoos make persons less attractive and/or less sexy

(Information from: Pew Research Center, 2023; Harris Poll, 2008)

Lady Godiva and "Peeping Tom" According to legend, Lady Godiva rode naked through the streets of Coventry, England, to persuade her husband, the earl of Mercia, to stop taxing the poor. All townspeople were ordered to stay in their homes with shutters drawn during her eleventh-century ride, but a tailor named Tom drilled a hole in his shutter to watch Lady Godiva pass by. Since then, the term "Peeping Tom" has referred to people with voyeuristic disorder.

As with other paraphilic disorders, treatments for people with exhibitionistic disorder generally include aversion therapy, masturbatory satiation, social skills training, and some form of insight therapy (Brown, 2023; Miner & Munns, 2021). Antidepressant drugs, which generally lower sexual desire in many people, have also been used to help reduce the sexual drive of people with this disorder (Vayisoglu, 2023).

Voyeuristic Disorder

A person with **voyeuristic disorder** experiences recurrent and intense sexual arousal from observing an unsuspecting individual who is naked, disrobing, or engaging in sexual activity. As with other paraphilic disorders, this arousal takes the form of fantasies, urges, or behaviors (APA, 2022). The disorder usually begins before the age of 18 and tends to persist.

A person with voyeuristic disorder may masturbate during the act of observing or when thinking about it afterward but does not generally seek to have sex with the person being spied on (Brown, 2023). The vulnerability of the people being observed and the probability they would feel humiliated if they knew they were under observation are often part of the watcher's enjoyment (Fedoroff, 2020). In addition, the risk of being discovered adds to the excitement, as you can observe in 25-year-old Sam's description of his disorder during an interview:

I've had girlfriends, but it's not the same. It's fun at first, but I get bored after a while in relationships. I never get that kick, that excitement, that I do when I look at others.

The biggest thrill is when I'm watching my neighbor having sex with one of her boyfriends or maybe watching Zoe down the block changing her clothes. Neither of them fully shuts their drapes, so there's always a little angle where I can see into their rooms if I get in just the right position on the lawn. Sometimes I'll take a walk and try to find someone I haven't watched before. One time, I looked out my apartment window across the courtyard and by chance saw the woman right across from me changing her clothes in front of a window without drapes. I don't think I'd ever been able to see into that apartment before—she always keeps the drapes closed. But that night, there she was. I turned out all the lights and just watched. She seemed to be trying to pick out an outfit. She kept taking clothes off and putting new clothes on. I admit, alone there in my dark apartment, I masturbated watching her.

Thinking about my adventures afterwards, I also get excited, especially if I came close to getting caught. I realize what a chance I was taking, and it gets my heart going and gets the rest of me going as well. Sometimes I'll make up extra details when remembering what happened, especially details about barely getting away or even being spotted, and that makes it even better. Of course, if I ever did get caught, it would be horrible.

Charley Gallay/Getty Images

Celebrity sex videos and voyeurism In 1995, a private video displaying sex between actress Pamela Anderson and her then-husband rock musician Tommy Lee was stolen from their home and made available on the Internet and on videotape. The video became a viral sensation and ushered in an industry of celebrity sex videos, a phenomenon that attests to society's fascination with the sex lives of celebrities. For her part, Anderson was traumatized by the world's voyeurism, as she reveals in her recent autobiography and in the Netflix documentary *Pamela: A Love Story*. In this photo, she speaks onstage at the documentary's premier.

The first time I ever spied was a total accident. I was in high school, in the school play, and we were all in costumes. When the play was over, I was already excited because there had been loud applause for my bows. When I went into the band room where I'd left my bag, I passed the closet and saw the door was slightly cracked. Peeking through, I saw Lynette Jackson changing her shirt. I ran away before she could see me and felt such a thrill! I had never seen a girl in her bra, so that was exciting. Also, she was so stuck up because her parents were rich. And where I came from, rich girls never dated guys like me, so there seemed to be something forbidden about seeing her like this.

Voyeurism, like exhibitionism, is often a source of sexual excitement in fantasy; it can also play a role in regular sexual interactions if a partner consents to voyeuristic-like behaviors. The clinical disorder of voyeuristic disorder is marked by the repeated invasion of other people's privacy. Some people with the disorder are unable to have typical sexual relations; others have a conventional sex life apart from their disorder.

Many psychodynamic clinicians propose that people with voyeuristic disorder are seeking by their actions to gain power over others, possibly because they feel inadequate or are sexually or socially shy (Fox et al., 2022; Kaylor & Jeglic, 2021). Cognitive-behavioral theorists explain the disorder as a learned behavior that can be traced to a chance and secret observation of a sexually arousing scene (Longpre & Guay, 2022). If the onlookers observe and dwell on such scenes on several occasions while masturbating, they may develop a voyeuristic pattern.

voyeuristic disorder A paraphilic disorder in which a person has repeated and intense sexual desires to observe unsuspecting people in secret as they undress or to spy on couples having intercourse and either acts on these urges with nonconsenting people or experiences clinically significant distress or impairment.

Frotteuristic Disorder

A person with **frotteuristic disorder** experiences repeated and intense sexual arousal from touching or rubbing against a nonconsenting person. Men make up the overwhelming majority of people with frotteuristic disorder. The arousal may, as with the other paraphilic disorders, take the form of fantasies, urges, or behaviors.

frotteuristic disorder A paraphilic disorder in which a person has repeated and intense sexual urges or fantasies that involve touching and rubbing against a nonconsenting person and either acts on these urges with the nonconsenting person or experiences clinically significant distress or impairment.

pedophilic disorder A paraphilic disorder in which a person has repeated and intense sexual urges or fantasies about watching, touching, or engaging in sexual acts with children and either acts on these urges or experiences clinically significant distress or impairment.

sexual masochism disorder A paraphilic disorder in which a person has repeated and intense sexual urges, fantasies, or behaviors that involve being humiliated, beaten, bound, or otherwise made to suffer, accompanied by clinically significant distress or impairment.

Frottage (from French *frotter,* "to rub") is usually committed in a crowded place, such as a subway or a busy sidewalk (Bhatia & Parekh, 2023). A man, for example, may rub his genitals against the thighs or buttocks of another person or fondle the person's genital area or breasts with his hands. Typically the individual will fantasize during the act that this contact is part of a caring relationship with the target individual. This pattern usually begins in the teenage years or earlier, often after the person observes others committing an act of frottage. After the age of about 25, people gradually decrease and often cease their acts of frottage (APA, 2022).

Pedophilic Disorder

A person with **pedophilic disorder** experiences sexual arousal from children. This arousal is expressed through fantasies, urges, or behaviors (APA, 2022). Those with the disorder may be attracted to prepubescent children, early pubescent children, or both. Some people with pedophilic disorder are satisfied by child pornography or seemingly innocent material such as children's underwear ads; others are driven to actually watch, touch, fondle, or engage in sexual intercourse with children (Geradt et al., 2018). Some people with the disorder are attracted only to children; others are attracted to adults as well (Brown, 2023). Research suggests that two-thirds of identified child victims are girls (NSOPW, 2023).

People with pedophilic disorder usually develop their pattern of sexual arousal during adolescence (APA, 2022). Some were themselves sexually abused as children, and many were neglected, excessively punished, or deprived of genuinely close relationships during their childhood (Leroux et al., 2020). (That said, it is important to note that most individuals who were abused or neglected as children do not develop pedophilic disorder.) It is not unusual for people with pedophilic disorder to be in a partnered relationship with an adult and to have sexual difficulties or other frustrations in life that lead them to seek an area in which they can be in control. Often these individuals are immature: their social and sexual skills may be underdeveloped, they may have limited self-control and poor planning skills, and thoughts of adult sexual relationships may fill them with anxiety (Fox et al., 2022).

Some people with pedophilic disorder also have distorted thinking, such as "It's all right to have sex with children as long as they agree" (Eberhaut et al., 2022; Molen, Ronis, & Benoit, 2022). It is not uncommon for pedophiles to blame the children for adult–child sexual contacts or to assert that the children benefited from the experience.

While many people with this disorder believe that their feelings are indeed wrong and disturbed, others consider adult sexual activity with children to be acceptable (Glina et al., 2022). Some even have joined pedophile organizations that advocate abolishing the age-of-consent laws. The Internet has opened the channels of communication among such individuals, and there is now a wide range of websites, newsgroups, chat rooms, forums, and message boards centered on pedophilia and adult–child sex (Steel et al., 2023; Quayle, 2021).

Studies have found that most people with pedophilic disorder also display at least one additional psychological disorder (Brown, 2023). Some theorists have proposed that

Controversial distinction A man in Tokyo, Japan, looks at a poster advertising child-focused, sexually charged anime videos and graphic novels. The possession of "real" child pornography is illegal in Japan, but "fictional" child pornography is legal.

Batchelder/Alamy Stock Photo

pedophilic disorder may be related to biochemical or brain structure irregularities, such as atypical patterns of activity in the amygdala or in the frontal areas of the brain, but such irregularities have yet to receive consistent research support (Baltodano-Calle, Onton-Diaz, & Gonzales, 2022; Kruger & Kneer, 2021).

Most pedophilic offenders are imprisoned or forced into treatment if they are caught. After all, they are committing child sexual abuse when they take any steps toward sexual contact with a child. There are now many residential registration and community notification laws across the United States that help law enforcement agencies and the public account for and control where convicted child sex offenders live and work (NSOPW, 2023, 2020).

Treatments for pedophilic disorder include those already mentioned for other paraphilic disorders, such as aversion therapy, masturbatory satiation, cognitive-behavioral therapy, and antiandrogen drugs (Fisher & Marwaha, 2023; Landgren et al., 2022). One widely applied cognitive-behavioral treatment for this disorder, *relapse-prevention training,* is modeled after the relapse-prevention training programs used in the treatment of substance use disorders. In this approach, clients identify the kinds of situations that typically trigger their pedophilic fantasies and actions (such as depressed mood or distorted thinking). They then learn strategies for avoiding those situations or coping with them more appropriately and effectively. Some but not all features of relapse-prevention training have been of help in this and certain other paraphilic disorders (Barros et al., 2022; Miner & Munns, 2021).

Scott Olson/Getty Images

Pedophilia, abuse, and justice In 2018, Larry Nassar, former USA Gymnastics national team doctor, was sentenced to a total of 360 years in prison for multiple crimes of sexual assault against girls and young women under his care, including the sexual assault of minors and child pornography.

of NOTE ...

A Problem That Keeps Growing

In 2021, tech companies reported 80 million online photos and videos of children being sexually abused, almost double what they found in 2019 and quadruple what they found in 2018 (Bischoff, 2023; RAINN, 2022; Keller & Dance, 2019).

Sexual Masochism Disorder

A person with **sexual masochism disorder** is repeatedly and intensely sexually aroused by the act of being humiliated, beaten, bound, or otherwise made to suffer. Again, this arousal may take such forms as fantasies, urges, or behaviors. Many people have fantasies of being forced into sexual acts against their will, but only those who are very distressed or impaired by the fantasies receive this diagnosis. Some people with the disorder act on the masochistic urges by themselves, perhaps tying, sticking pins into, or even cutting themselves. Others have their sexual partners restrain, tie up, blindfold, spank, paddle, whip, beat, electrically shock, "pin and pierce," or humiliate them (APA, 2022).

An industry of products and services has arisen to meet the desires of people with the paraphilia or the paraphilic disorder of sexual masochism. Here a 34-year-old woman describes her work as the operator of a facility that meets those desires:

> *I get people here who have been all over looking for the right kind of pain they feel they deserve. Don't ask me why they want pain, I'm not a psychologist; but when they have found us, they usually don't go elsewhere. . . . Among the things I do, that work really quickly and well, are: I put clothespins on their nipples, or pins in their [testicles]. Some of them need to see their own blood to be able to get off. . . .*

(continued on the next page)

> *All the time that a torture scene is going on, there is constant dialogue. . . . I scream at the guy, and tell him what a no-good rotten bastard he is, how this is even too good for him, that he knows he deserves worse, and I begin to list his sins. It works every time . . . I act very tough and hard, but I'm really a very sensitive woman. But you have to watch out for a guy's health . . . you must not kill him, or have him get a heart attack. . . . I know of other places that have had guys die there. I've never lost a customer to death, though they may have wished for it during my "treatment."*
>
> *(Janus & Janus, 1993, p. 115)*

of NOTE ...

Their Words

"How strange would appear to be this thing that [is called] pleasure! And how curiously it is related to what is thought to be its opposite, pain! . . . Wherever the one is found, the other follows up behind."

Plato, *Phaedo*, fourth century B.C.

In one form of sexual masochism disorder, *hypoxyphilia,* people strangle or smother themselves (or ask their partner to strangle them) in order to enhance their sexual pleasure (Brown, 2023). There have, in fact, been a number of clinical reports of *autoerotic asphyxia,* in which people, usually males and as young as 10 years old, may accidentally induce a fatal lack of oxygen by hanging, suffocating, or strangling themselves while masturbating (Mileva et al., 2022). There is some debate as to whether the practice should be characterized as sexual masochism disorder, but it is at least sometimes accompanied by other acts of bondage (Brown, 2023).

Most masochistic sexual fantasies begin in childhood. However, the person does not act out the urges until later, usually by early adulthood (APA, 2022). The pattern typically continues for many years. Some people practice more and more dangerous acts over time or during times of particular stress (Brown, 2023; Fox et al., 2022).

In many cases, sexual masochism disorder seems to have developed through the learning process of classical conditioning (Brown, 2023; Longpre & Guay, 2022). A classic case study tells of a teenage boy with a broken arm who was caressed and held close by an attractive nurse as the physician set his fracture, a procedure done in the past without anesthesia (Gebhard, 1965). The powerful combination of pain and sexual arousal the boy felt then may have been the cause of his later masochistic urges and acts.

© Em[illegible]nuele Contini/NurPhoto via ZUMA Press

A celebration of S/M Sexual sadism and sexual masochism have been viewed by the public with either bemusement or horror, depending on the circumstances that surround these paraphilias. On the light side, the annual Folsom Street Fairs in San Francisco and Europe celebrate S/M and invite people (like these participants) to display their trademark outfits.

Sexual Sadism Disorder

A person with **sexual sadism disorder,** usually male, is repeatedly and intensely sexually aroused by the physical or psychological suffering of another individual (APA, 2022). This arousal may be expressed through fantasies, urges, or behaviors, including acts such as dominating, restraining, blindfolding, cutting, strangling, mutilating, or even killing the target individual. The label is derived from the name of the famous Marquis de Sade (1740–1814), who tortured others in order to satisfy his sexual desires.

People who fantasize about sexual sadism typically imagine that they have total control over a sexual victim who is terrified by the sadistic act. Many carry out sadistic acts with a consenting partner, often a person with sexual masochism disorder (Brown, 2023). Some, however, act out their urges on nonconsenting targets. A number of rapists and sexual murderers, for example, exhibit sexual sadism disorder. In all cases, a real or fantasized individual's suffering is the key to arousal.

The Everett Collection

Cinematic introduction In one of filmdom's most famous scenes, Alex, the sexually sadistic character in *A Clockwork Orange*, is forced to observe violent images while he experiences painful stomach spasms.

Fantasies of sexual sadism, like those of sexual masochism, may first appear in childhood or adolescence (Fedoroff, 2020). People who engage in sadistic acts begin to do so by early adulthood (APA, 2022). The pattern is long-term. Some people with the disorder engage in the same level of cruelty in their sadistic acts over time, but often their sadism becomes more and more severe over the years (Mokros et al., 2019). Obviously, people with severe forms of the disorder may be highly dangerous to others (Reale et al., 2022).

Some cognitive-behavioral theorists believe that classical conditioning is at work in sexual sadism disorder (Longpre & Guay, 2022; Fedoroff, 2020). While inflicting pain, perhaps unintentionally, on an animal or a person, a young individual may feel intense emotions and sexual arousal. The association between inflicting pain and being aroused sexually sets the stage for a pattern of sexual sadism. Cognitive-behavioral theorists also propose that the disorder may result from modeling, when adolescents observe others achieving sexual satisfaction by inflicting pain. The many Internet sex sites and sexual videos, magazines, and books in our society make such models readily available.

Both psychodynamic and cognitive-behavioral theorists further suggest that people with sexual sadism disorder inflict pain in order to achieve a sense of power or control, necessitated perhaps by underlying feelings of sexual inadequacy. The sense of power in turn increases their sexual arousal (Reale et al., 2022; Fedoroff, 2020). Alternatively, some biological studies have found signs of possible brain and hormonal irregularities in people with sexual sadism (Wuyts & Morrens, 2022; Kruger & Kneer, 2021). None of these explanations, however, has been thoroughly investigated.

Cognitive-behavioral therapists have treated the disorder with aversion therapy (Miner & Munns, 2021; Ware, McIvor, & Fernandez, 2021). The public's view of and distaste for this procedure have been influenced by the novel and 1971 movie *A Clockwork Orange,* which depicts simultaneous presentations of violent images and drug-induced stomach spasms to a sadistic young man until he is conditioned to feel nausea at the sight of such images. It is not clear that aversion therapy is helpful in cases of sexual sadism disorder. However, relapse-prevention training, used in some criminal cases, may be of value (Fisher & Marwaha, 2023; Barros et al., 2022).

sexual sadism disorder A paraphilic disorder in which a person has repeated and intense sexual urges or fantasies that involve inflicting suffering on others and either acts on these urges with nonconsenting individuals or experiences clinically significant distress or impairment.

SUMMING UP

Paraphilic Disorders

Paraphilias are patterns characterized by recurrent and intense sexual urges, fantasies, or behaviors involving objects or situations outside the usual sexual norms—for example, nonhuman objects, children, nonconsenting adults, or experiences of suffering or humiliation. When an individual's paraphilia causes great distress, interferes with social or occupational functioning, or places the individual or others at risk of harm, a diagnosis of paraphilic disorder is applied.

Fetishistic disorder consists of recurrent and intense sexual fantasies, urges, or behaviors that involve the use of a nonliving object or nongenital part. Exhibitionistic disorder features repeated and intense sexual fantasies, urges, or behaviors that involve exposing one's genitals to others. In voyeuristic disorder, a person has repeated and intense sexual fantasies, urges, or behaviors that involve secretly observing unsuspecting people who are naked, undressing, or engaging in sexual activity. In frotteuristic disorder, a person has repeated and intense sexual fantasies, urges, or behaviors that involve touching or rubbing against a nonconsenting person. In pedophilic disorder, a person has repeated and intense sexual fantasies, urges, or behaviors that involve watching, touching, or engaging in sexual acts with children. Sexual masochism disorder is characterized by repeated and intense sexual fantasies, urges, or behaviors that involve being humiliated, beaten, bound, or otherwise made to suffer. Sexual sadism disorder is characterized by repeated and intense sexual fantasies, urges, or behaviors that involve inflicting suffering on others.

Although various explanations have been proposed for paraphilic disorders, research has revealed little about their causes. A range of treatments have been tried, including aversion therapy, masturbatory satiation, and relapse-prevention training.

Personal Topics Draw Public Attention

As you have just read, much work remains to be done with regard to paraphilic disorders. However, clinicians have successfully collected a considerable body of data for the other group of sexual disorders: sexual dysfunctions. As a result, people with sexual dysfunctions are no longer doomed to a lifetime of sexual frustration. Studies of these dysfunctions have uncovered various psychological, sociocultural, and biological causes, and significant progress has been made in the treatment of the dysfunctions. At the same time, more information about sexual dysfunctions is needed, and still better interventions for the dysfunctions are vital, especially for LGBTQ+ people and people of color.

It has also become clear that education about sexual dysfunctions can be as important as therapy. When taken seriously, sexual myths often lead to feelings of shame, self-hatred, isolation, and hopelessness—feelings that themselves contribute to sexual difficulty. Thus, public education about sexual functioning—through the Internet, social media, books, television and radio, school programs, group presentations, and the like—has become a major and invaluable clinical focus.

of NOTE ...

Lockdown Essentials

In the early weeks of the Covid-19 pandemic, many people stockpiled vibrators and condoms, resulting in a 30 percent increase in online sales (Basu, 2020).

Quick Quiz

1. How do gender, sexual orientation, and race and ethnicity relate to sexual dysfunctions? pp. 352–354
2. What sexual dysfunctions are associated with the desire phase of the sexual response cycle? How common are they, and what causes them? pp. 354–357
3. What are the symptoms and prevalence of erectile disorder? To which phase of the sexual response cycle is it related? pp. 357–358
4. What are the possible causes of erectile disorder? pp. 358–359
5. Which sexual dysfunctions seem to involve performance anxiety and the spectator role? pp. 359, 361, 363
6. What are the symptoms, rates, and leading causes of premature ejaculation, delayed ejaculation, and female orgasmic disorder? To which phase of the sexual response cycle are they related? pp. 360–364
7. Identify, describe, and explain disorders of sexual pain. pp. 364–365
8. What are the general features of modern sex therapy? What particular techniques are further used to treat specific sexual dysfunctions? pp. 366–372
9. List, describe, and explain the various paraphilic disorders. pp. 373–383
10. Describe the treatment techniques of aversion therapy, masturbatory satiation, and relapse-prevention training. Which paraphilic disorders have they been used to treat, and how successful are they? pp. 377–383

CHAPTER 12

Schizophrenia and Related Disorders

TOPIC OVERVIEW

CANDACE, 32 YEARS OLD: *Candace was seemingly happy and functional up until the age of 28. She grew up in Atlanta. Her family had struggled financially, and they lived in an apartment with just one bedroom for her and her two older sisters. Although she had often observed her parents worrying about money and their living space felt cramped, she maintained a positive and upbeat attitude.*

She worked very hard through school and graduated with good grades from a state college. She took an administrative job with a fashion designer and so impressed her employer that she became the office manager when she was 25. She appreciated that many of the people who modeled the company's clothing were Black. When she was growing up, she hadn't seen many models who looked like her in fashion ads. For the time being, much of her salary went to pay back her student loans, and she lived in an apartment that was even smaller than the one in which she grew up. But she felt optimistic about her future.

Over the next three years, the challenges of life began to dent that optimism. First, the heating system in her apartment broke, and the landlord would not fix it. Although she was in the right, the landlord was obstinate and unresponsive, and she had no money to hire attorneys to help her. She bought a small space heater and during the winter months could not be more than five feet from it. She shivered under the covers at night.

Then her father died of a sudden heart attack, and she was devastated. They had always been extremely close. She began to feel unmoored, and she started just going through the motions at work, distracted by unpleasant thoughts.

Next, a series of break-ins occurred on her block. This troubled her greatly, and, in fact, she soon became convinced that the burglars were targeting her, maybe even conducting practice runs for eventually breaking into her apartment. Such thoughts intensified over time. She came to believe that the burglars weren't really after money but were somehow planning to capture her and make her join a religious cult. The more she dwelled on this thought, the more alienating and potentially dangerous her friends and people at work seemed to her. She began to wonder if they were all part of the plot, having meticulously planned it years ago.

One night, in the cold of her apartment, she heard voices just outside her apartment door. At first, she could not make out what they were saying, as it sounded like whispering. The more attention she paid the voices, however, the more she felt she could understand what they were saying. She thought she was hearing a group of kidnappers discussing their plans to invade the apartment and capture her. They were waiting until everything was in place that very evening. As she waited, her heart pounding, she could also hear the voices discussing their own lives and casually chatting about their families. She summoned the courage to open the door to see what was going on, but no one was in the hall. Back inside, she decided they had likely scurried out of sight while she had been opening the door; then she heard them resume with their conversations.

In the coming days and months, no one broke in, but she was sure each night that this would be the night. Indeed, on some nights she heard one of the voices in the hall saying, "Candace. We need you. We have your father here." Over time, she further heard noises that she decided were recording devices, placed in the walls. She concluded that that was how the kidnappers were tracking her! The landlord must be in on it, she realized. And, finally, "That must be why they shut down my heat. The recorders must only work if it's very cold."

As all this continued and intensified over time, Candace was unable to face work. She told her boss that her mother was dying and she needed some time off. The employer was sympathetic but asked her to promise she'd be back, at least part time, within three

(continued on the next page)

weeks. Candace agreed, just wanting to get out of the job—but she knew she'd never go back. With no money coming in, she had nowhere to go to for help. She ignored calls from her sisters and mother and hid in her tiny apartment. On television, she saw someone wearing a dress like one of the ones designed by her company, and she became convinced that this was a sign her boss was onto her and would be alerting the police that she had lied about her mother's health.

of NOTE ...

Costly Disorder

Factoring in the costs of lost productivity and medical and psychological care, the lifetime cost to the U.S. economy for each 25-year-old person with schizophrenia is $3.8 million, or $92,000 per year (Kotzeva et al., 2023; Velligan & Rao, 2023).

KENJI, 22 YEARS OLD: *As a teenager, Kenji was sometimes called "Mr. Cool" by his friends because he seemed unflappable. Underneath, however, he was actually quite anxious and constantly worried about what others thought of him, and he consciously adopted an "above-it-all" air to reduce the chances of saying or doing something that might lead to embarrassment for him. After all, he knew what he was dealing with—frequent memory problems, confusion, and an inability to make plans or follow through. On more than a few occasions, he had great trouble expressing himself or getting to the point. He might start sentences and then totally lose his train of thought before the sentences reached their end.*

He struggled through college to achieve mediocre grades, but he did graduate. He knew that he would never be nearly as successful as his father, a best-selling author of mystery novels about the famous detective character Koji Mori. Throughout his teenage and college years, his father always pressed him about his grades, saying that he was worried about his son and that it had been so important to Kenji's late mother that Kenji be successful. But his father was busy with book tours and screenwriting jobs, and ultimately he allowed Kenji to go his own way with little interference.

Kenji came to live alone in a small house his father had bought for him when he graduated from college. He got a job working the front desk at a high-end beauty salon. After about six months on the job, he became very anxious that he was not good enough to work there and that he had been hired only because it looked good to have a Japanese face at the desk. He soon found it impossible even to speak to the customers. He would mutter, "Hello. Name?" when they walked in and then gesture them to a seat in the waiting area. When even that became too much for him, he quit the job. His father continued to pay his bills.

Going out with friends became a chore. He no longer laughed at anyone's jokes, and he stopped making jokes of his own. As the weeks went by, he talked to the friends less and less, until reaching a point where he'd be out with a crowd and spend the whole night staring at the table in front of him. When his best friend Finley told him at dinner one night that he'd been diagnosed with bone cancer, Kenji stared expressionlessly and simply said, "I see. Tell me how that goes." Finley was crestfallen and thought Kenji didn't care, but actually Kenji was shaken by the news. He was afraid of saying the wrong thing.

Kenji stopped going out with friends at all around that time and spent most of his days sitting in front of the television, watching marathons of old shows, but he could barely focus on the simple plots. He virtually stopped bathing, finding the whole process too much to undertake. He dreaded calling for food deliveries; when asked by the delivery service if he wanted anything else, he would agonize over why he was being asked that. "Did I not order enough?" he'd ask himself. "Should I get something else? Did I offend the delivery guy? Is something else going on here?" Before long, he was speaking only the names of the ordered foods into the phone, without using full sentences. And when the food arrived, he'd only stick his arm out the door to receive it.

He also stopped answering his father's calls. During their last conversation, his father had asked several times, "Are you angry with me, Kenji? Say something, anything, please. Give me a few words at least." Kenji had forced himself to give one- or two-word answers in order to finish that call. After that, he stopped answering his phone.

As another month passed, he stopped getting dressed, and on most days he either stayed in bed or on the couch, staring at the wall for the entire day. He seemed frozen, literally motionless. He could not think of anything that he wanted to do. In fact, he had trouble thinking at all. One day, he received a phone message from his father, demanding to know what was going on, saying he would come over there if Kenji didn't call back in two days. Kenji ignored the message and continued staring at the wall.

Eventually, Candace and Kenji each received a diagnosis of **schizophrenia.** People with schizophrenia, though they previously functioned adequately, deteriorate into an isolated wilderness of unusual perceptions, odd thoughts, disturbed emotions, and motor irregularities. Like Candace and Kenji, people with schizophrenia experience **psychosis,** a loss of contact with reality. Their ability to perceive and respond to the environment becomes so disturbed that they may not be able to function at home, with friends, in school, or at work. They may have hallucinations (false sensory perceptions) or delusions (false beliefs), or they may withdraw into a private world. DSM-5-TR calls for a diagnosis of schizophrenia only after the symptoms continue for six months or more (see **Table 12-1**).

schizophrenia A psychotic disorder in which personal, social, and occupational functioning deteriorate as a result of unusual perceptions, odd thoughts, disturbed emotions, and motor irregularities.

psychosis A state in which a person loses contact with reality in key ways.

As you read in the chapter on substance use disorders, taking LSD or abusing amphetamines or cocaine may also produce psychosis. So may injuries or diseases of the brain. And so may other severe psychological disorders, such as major depressive disorder or bipolar disorder (Kleiger & Khadivi, 2023). Most commonly, however, psychosis appears in the form of schizophrenia.

Approximately 1 of every 100 people in the world has schizophrenia during their lifetime (Fischer & Buchanan, 2023; Velligan & Rao, 2023). An estimated 20 million people worldwide are afflicted with it, including 3.2 million in the United States (MHN, 2023; WHO, 2022). Studies reveal that, within the total population, the prevalence of schizophrenia is at least three times higher among transgender and nonbinary people than cisgender people (Cheng, 2022; Barr, Roberts, & Thakkar, 2021). In addition, emerging research suggests that the prevalence may be higher among gay, lesbian, and bisexual people than heterosexual people (Barr, Bigdeli, & Meyers, 2022). Studies also indicate that Black Americans and Indigenous Americans receive a diagnosis of schizophrenia more often than Hispanic, non-Hispanic White, and Asian Americans (SAMHSA, 2023; Anglin, 2022; Barr et al., 2022). The reasons for these various differences in prevalence—including special stressors faced by marginalized people, discrimination, and possible overdiagnosis—will be discussed later in this chapter.

of NOTE ...

Surprisingly Common

An estimated 13 to 23 percent of people experience one or more psychotic symptoms sometime during their lives (Marder, 2022).

The rate of schizophrenia is about equal for men and women, a similarity that holds across cisgender, heterosexual, and LGBTQ+ populations and people of most races and ethnicities (NIMH, 2023; APA, 2022). The average age of onset for men is 23 years, compared with 28 years for women.

The financial cost of schizophrenia—from health care costs to losses of productivity—is enormous—almost $300 billion each year in the United States—and the emotional cost is even greater (Velligan & Rao, 2023). As you read earlier in the textbook, people with this disorder are much more likely to attempt suicide than the general population (Suekane et al., 2024). It is estimated that as many as 25 percent of people with

TABLE 12-1

Dx Checklist

Schizophrenia
1. For 1 month, individual displays two or more of the following symptoms much of the time: (a) Delusions (b) Hallucinations (c) Disorganized speech (d) Unusual motor activity, including catatonia (e) Negative symptoms
2. At least one of the individual's symptoms must be delusions, hallucinations, or disorganized speech.
3. The individual functions much more poorly in various life spheres than was the case prior to the symptoms.
4. Beyond this 1 month of intense symptomology, individual continues to display some degree of impaired functioning for at least 5 additional months.

Information from: APA, 2022.

Barcroft/BoClips

Students With Psychosis In her late teens, Cecilia McGough coauthored an important astrophysics journal paper and began studying astronomy in college. At the same time, she was developing schizophrenia, which featured daily frightening hallucinations. McGough—who still sees, hears, and feels things that are not present—went on to found Students With Psychosis, an organization that reaches out to students worldwide, providing validation, support, resources, and perspective to those trying to cope and succeed in life in spite of their symptoms.

schizophrenia attempt suicide and 5 percent die from suicide (Bareis et al., 2023; Fischer & Buchanan, 2023). Given this high risk, it is strongly recommended that patients with schizophrenia receive thorough suicide risk assessments during treatment and when they are discharged from treatment programs (Lawrence & Bernstein, 2024; Siris & Braga, 2023). In addition, people with the disorder have an increased risk of physical—often fatal—illness (Dragioti et al., 2023). On average, they live 10 to 20 fewer years than other people (Velligan & Rao, 2023). In a related vein, a study of more than 7,000 patients with Covid-19 during the height of the pandemic found that the patients with schizophrenia were 2.7 times more likely to die from the virus than those without schizophrenia (Nemani et al., 2021).

Although schizophrenia appears in all socioeconomic levels, it is found more frequently in the lower levels (APA, 2022) (see **Figure 12-1**). This has led some theorists to believe that the stress of poverty is itself a cause of the disorder. However, it could be that schizophrenia causes individuals to fall from a higher to a lower socioeconomic level or to remain economically deprived because they are unable to meet the demands of many workplaces. This is sometimes called the *downward drift* theory.

People have long shown great interest in schizophrenia, flocking to plays and movies that explore or exploit our fascination with the disorder. Yet, as you will read, all too many people with schizophrenia are neglected in the United States. Although effective interventions have been developed, many persons with the disorder live without adequate treatment and never fully achieve their potential as human beings. ■

FIGURE 12-1

Socioeconomic Class and Schizophrenia

Consistent with findings from other countries, a study conducted in Denmark found that people with lower family incomes were more likely than people with higher family incomes to experience schizophrenia. (Information from: Hakulinen et al., 2020.)

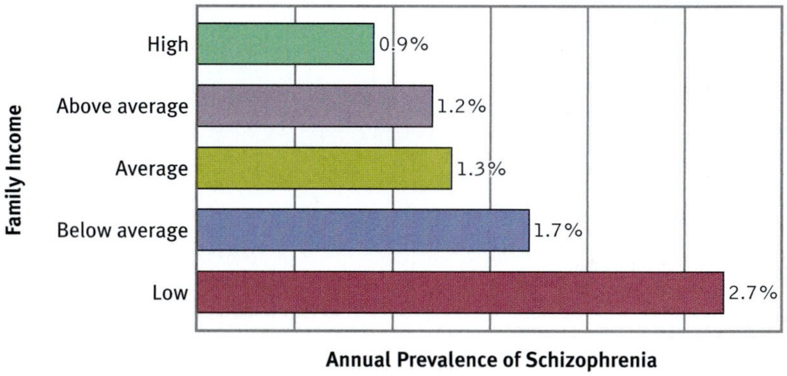

The Clinical Picture of Schizophrenia

The symptoms of schizophrenia vary greatly, and so do its warning signs, course, and responsiveness to treatment. In fact, most of today's clinicians believe that schizophrenia is actually a group of distinct disorders that happen to have some features in common (Fischer & Buchanan, 2023).

What Are the Symptoms of Schizophrenia?

Think back to Candace and Kenji, the two people described at the beginning of the chapter. Both of them deteriorated from a relatively adequate level of functioning to become ineffective in dealing with the world. Each had some of the symptoms found in schizophrenia. The symptoms can be grouped into three categories: *positive symptoms* (excesses of thought, emotion, and behavior), *negative symptoms* (deficits of thought, emotion, and behavior), and *psychomotor symptoms* (unusual movements or gestures). Some people with schizophrenia are more dominated by positive symptoms and others by negative symptoms, although most tend to have both kinds of symptoms to some degree. In addition, around half of those with schizophrenia have significant difficulties with memory, attention, and other kinds of cognitive functioning (Fischer & Buchanan, 2023; Javitt, 2023).

positive symptoms Symptoms of schizophrenia that seem to be pathological excesses of or out-of-the-ordinary and peculiar additions to typical thoughts, emotions, or behaviors.

delusion A strange false belief firmly held despite evidence to the contrary.

formal thought disorder A disturbance in the production and organization of thought.

loose associations A common thinking disturbance in schizophrenia, characterized by rapid shifts from one topic of conversation to another. Also known as *derailment*.

Positive Symptoms

Positive symptoms are "pathological excesses," or out-of-the-ordinary and peculiar additions, to a person's cognition and behavior (Velligan & Rao, 2023). *Delusions, disorganized thinking and speech, heightened perceptions and hallucinations,* and *incongruent affect* are the ones most often found in schizophrenia.

DELUSIONS Many people with schizophrenia develop **delusions,** ideas that they believe wholeheartedly but that have no basis in fact (Hardy & Turkington, 2024). The deluded person may consider the ideas enlightening or may feel confused by them. Some people hold a single delusion that dominates their lives and behavior; others have many delusions. *Delusions of persecution* are the most common in schizophrenia (APA, 2022). People with such delusions believe that they are being plotted or discriminated against, spied on, slandered, threatened, attacked, or deliberately victimized. Candace, for example, believed that neighborhood burglars were planning to kidnap her and force her into a cult and that her friends, workmates, and landlord were also in on the plot.

Philosopher Friedrich Nietzsche said, "Insanity in individuals is something rare—but in groups, parties, nations and epochs, it is the rule." What did he mean?

People with schizophrenia may also have *delusions of reference:* they attach special and personal meaning to the actions of others or to various objects or events. Candace interpreted a familiar-looking dress on television as a sign that her boss was onto her and would be calling the police. People with *delusions of grandeur* believe themselves to be great inventors, religious saviors, or other specially empowered persons. And those with *delusions of control* believe their feelings, thoughts, and actions are being controlled by other people.

DISORGANIZED THINKING AND SPEECH People with schizophrenia may not be able to think logically and may speak in peculiar ways. These difficulties, collectively called **formal thought disorders,** can cause the individual great confusion and make communication extremely difficult. Often, such thought disorders take the form of positive symptoms (pathological excesses), as in *loose associations, neologisms, perseveration,* and *clang.*

People who have **loose associations,** or **derailment,** the most common formal thought disorder, rapidly shift from one topic to another, believing that their incoherent statements make sense to others. A single, perhaps unimportant word in one sentence becomes the focus of the next. One man with schizophrenia, asked about his itchy arms, responded with this:

> *The problem is insects. My brother used to collect insects. He's now a man 5 foot 10 inches. You know, 10 is my favorite number. I also like to dance, draw, and watch television.*

hallucination The experiencing of sights, sounds, or other perceptions in the absence of external stimuli.

Some people with schizophrenia use *neologisms,* made-up words that typically have meaning only to the person using them. One person said, for example, "I am here from a foreign university . . . and you have to have a *'plausity'* of all acts of amendment to go through for the children's code . . . it is an *'amorition'* law . . . the children have to have this *'accentuative'* law so they don't go into the *'mortite'* law of the church" (Vetter, 1969, p. 189). Others may have the formal thought disorder of *perseveration,* in which they repeat their words and statements again and again. Finally, some use *clang,* or rhyme, to think or to express themselves. When asked how he was feeling, one man replied, "Well, hell, it's well to tell." Another described the weather as "So hot, you know it runs on a cot." Research suggests that some people may have disorganized speech or thinking long before their full pattern of schizophrenia unfolds (Adamowicz et al., 2024; Fischer & Buchanan, 2023).

HEIGHTENED PERCEPTIONS AND HALLUCINATIONS The perceptions and attention of some people with schizophrenia seem to intensify (Zeljic et al., 2021). The persons may feel that their senses are being flooded by all the sights and sounds that surround them. This makes it almost impossible for them to attend to important matters and details. Such problems may develop years before the onset of the actual disorder (Adamowicz et al., 2024; Fischer & Buchanan, 2023). It is also possible that these challenges further contribute to the memory impairments that are common to many people with schizophrenia (Javitt, 2023).

Another kind of perceptual problem in schizophrenia consists of **hallucinations,** perceptions that a person has in the absence of external stimuli (see ***InfoCentral***). People who have *auditory* hallucinations, by far the most common kind in schizophrenia, hear sounds and voices that seem to come from outside their heads. The voices may talk directly to the hallucinator, perhaps giving commands or warning of dangers, or they may be experienced as overheard.

Research suggests that people with auditory hallucinations actually produce the nerve signals of sound in their brains, "hear" them, and then believe that external sources are responsible (Yang et al., 2020). Some studies, for example, have measured blood flow in *Broca's area,* the region of the brain that helps people produce speech (Dabiri et al., 2022). The investigators have found more blood flow in Broca's area while patients are having auditory hallucinations. A related study instructed six men with schizophrenia to press a button whenever they had an auditory hallucination (Silbersweig et al., 1995). Brain scans revealed increased activity in their auditory cortex, the brain region that enables people to hear sounds, when they pressed the button.

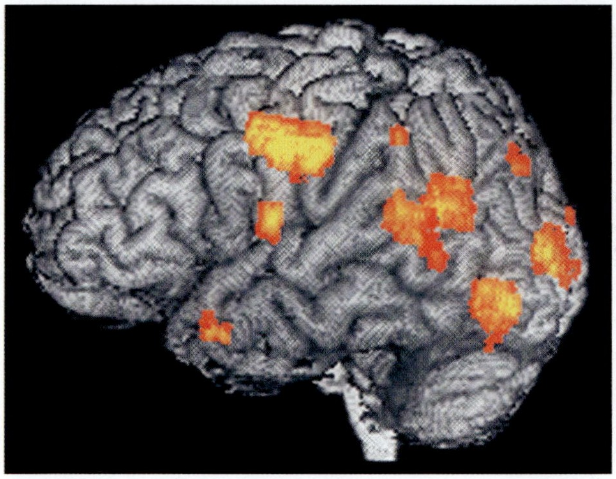

From "A functional neuroanatomy of hallucinations in schizophrenia," reprinted by permission from Macmillan Publishers Ltd. D. A. Silbersweig, E. Stern, C. Frith, C. Cahill, A. Holmes, Sylke Grootoonk, J. Seaward, P. McKenna, S. E. Chua, L. Schnorr, T. Jones, R. S. J. Frackowiak, 378, 6553, Nov 9,1995, *Nature* © 1995. Courtesy D. A. Silbersweig.

The human brain during hallucinations
This PET scan, taken when a patient was having auditory hallucinations, shows heightened activity (yellow-orange) in brain areas that help *produce* speech and *hear* sounds but not in the area that determines the *source* of sounds. Thus, people who are hallucinating seem to hear sounds produced by their own brains, but their brains cannot recognize that the sounds are actually coming from within (Yang et al., 2020; Silbersweig et al., 1995).

Hallucinations can also involve any of the other senses. *Tactile* hallucinations may take the form of tingling, burning, or electric-shock sensations. *Somatic* hallucinations feel as if something is happening inside the body, such as a snake crawling inside one's stomach. *Visual* hallucinations may produce vague perceptions of colors or clouds or distinct visions of people or objects. People with *gustatory* hallucinations regularly find that their food or drink tastes strange, and people with *olfactory* hallucinations smell odors that no one else does, such as the smell of poison or smoke.

Hallucinations and delusional ideas often occur together (Hardy & Turkington, 2024). A woman who hears voices issuing commands, for example, may have the delusion that the commands are being placed in her head by someone else. A man with delusions of persecution may hallucinate the smell of poison in his bedroom or the taste of poison in his coffee. Might one symptom cause the other? Whatever the cause and whichever comes first, the hallucination and delusion eventually feed into each other.

HALLUCINATIONS

Hallucinations are the experiencing of sights, sounds, smells, and other perceptions that occur in the absence of external stimuli.

TYPES OF HALLUCINATIONS

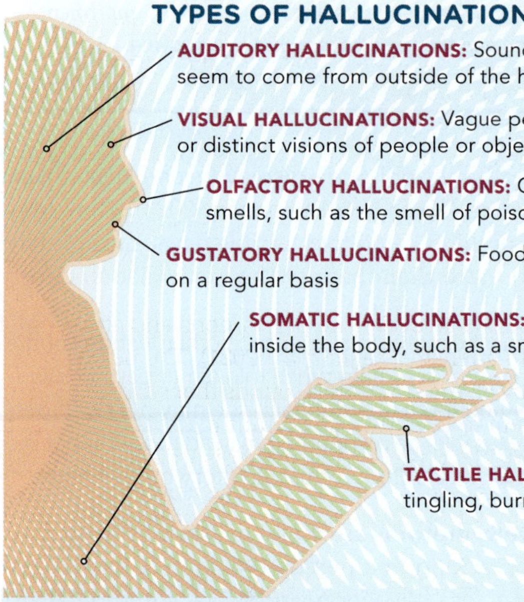

AUDITORY HALLUCINATIONS: Sounds and voices that seem to come from outside of the head

VISUAL HALLUCINATIONS: Vague perceptions of colors, clouds, or distinct visions of people or objects

OLFACTORY HALLUCINATIONS: Odors that no one else smells, such as the smell of poison or smoke

GUSTATORY HALLUCINATIONS: Food or drink tastes strange on a regular basis

SOMATIC HALLUCINATIONS: Feelings that something is happening inside the body, such as a snake crawling inside one's stomach

TACTILE HALLUCINATIONS: Perceptions of tingling, burning, or electric-shock sensations

Hallucinations are also experienced by people with:

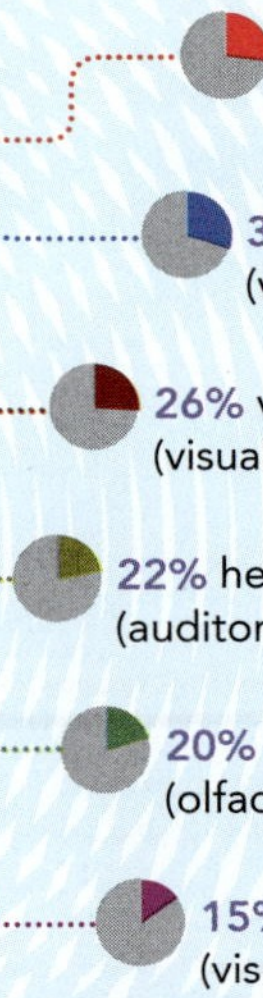

- 27% delirium (visual type)
- 30% neurocognitive disorder (visual and auditory types)
- 26% vision impairment (visual type)
- 22% hearing impairment (auditory type)
- 20% loss of smell (olfactory type)
- 15% migraines (visual and olfactory types)

(Press, 2022; Zhang et al., 2022; O'Brien et al., 2020; Lynn, 2019; Villines, 2019; Monson et al., 2018; Sacks, 2017, 2012; Mandal, 2014)

Hallucinations are different from:

Illusions: Distorted or misinterpreted real perceptions

Imagery: Under voluntary control and does not mimic real perception

Dreaming: Occurs when person is asleep

Pseudohallucinations: Internally triggered, vivid perceptions that are recognized by individual as unreal, and partly under voluntary control

SCHIZOPHRENIC HALLUCINATIONS

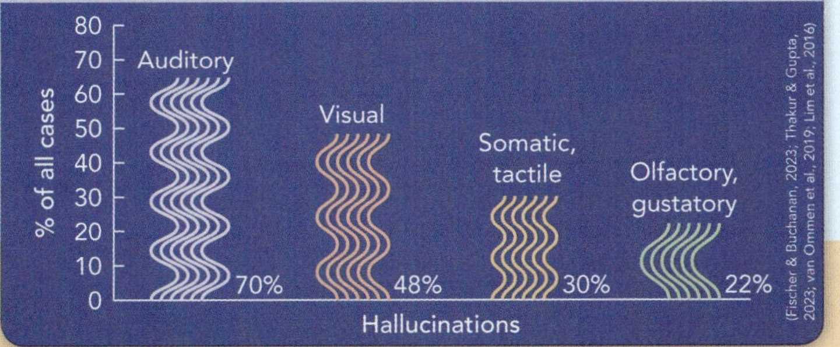

(Fischer & Buchanan, 2023; Thakur & Gupta, 2023; van Ommen et al., 2019; Lim et al., 2016)

HALLUCINATIONS CAN BE "NORMAL"

Many people experience hallucinations that are unrelated to disorders or substance ingestion. These hallucinations...

- affect as many as 10–28% of the population
- occur every 3 days, on average
- last for 2–3 minutes
- can be controlled around 60% of the time
- cause little distress or disruption, unless misinterpreted

(Thakur & Gupta, 2023; Aynsworth et al., 2022; Lin et al., 2019; Pelak, 2021; Villines, 2019; Sheikh, 2017; Daalman et al., 2011)

37% Hypnagogic hallucinations
Geometric patterns, faces, or landscapes experienced by some people falling asleep

12.5% Hypnopompic hallucinations
Geometric patterns, faces, or landscapes experienced by some people as they are awakening

(Summer, 2023, 2022)

BRAIN EXPLANATIONS FOR AUDITORY HALLUCINATIONS

ATYPICAL ACTIVATION of the primary **auditory cortex**.

FAILURE to recognize **internally generated speech** as one's own. Cross-activation with the **auditory areas**, so what most people experience as thoughts become "voiced."

EXCESSIVE ATTENTION to the **subvocal stream** that accompanies verbal thinking.

MUSICAL HALLUCINATIONS result from activation of the brain network involving **auditory areas, the motor cortex, visual areas, basal ganglia, cerebellum, hippocampus,** and **amygdala.**

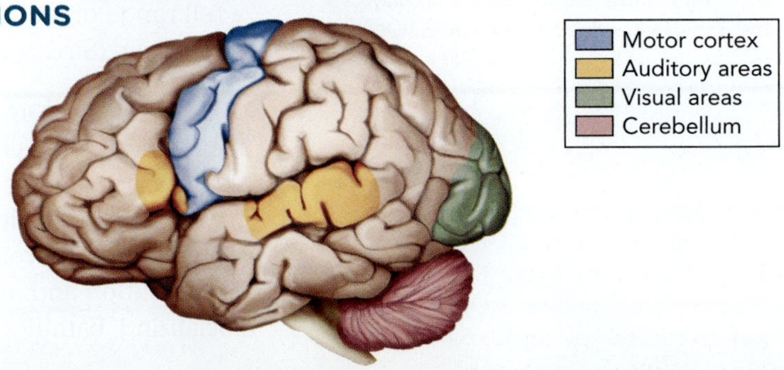

HALLUCINATIONS OVER THE AGES

Ancient times: Attributed to gifts from the gods or the Muses

Prior to 18th century: Caused by supernatural forces, such as gods or demons, angels or djinns

Middle of 18th century: Caused by the overactivity of certain centers in the brain

1990s: Resulting from a circuit of cortical and subcortical structures

(Thakur & Gupta, 2023; Hare, 2021; Carota & Bogousslavsky, 2019; Lin et al., 2019; Pelak, 2021, 2019; Groopman, 2017; Sacks, 2017, 2012; Shergill et al., 2000)

I thought the voices I heard were being transmitted through the walls of my apartment and through the washer and dryer and that these machines were talking and telling me things. I felt that the government agencies had planted transmitters and receivers in my apartment so that I could hear what they were saying and they could hear what I was saying.

(Anonymous, 1996, p. 183)

INCONGRUENT AFFECT Many people with schizophrenia display *incongruent affect,* emotions that are unsuited to the situation (Fischer & Buchanan, 2023). They may smile when making a somber statement or upon being told terrible news, or they may become upset in situations that should make them happy. They may also undergo abrupt and unforeseen shifts in mood.

In at least some cases, these emotions may be merely a response to other features of the disorder. Consider a woman with schizophrenia who smiles when told of her partner's serious illness. She may not actually be happy about the news; in fact, she may not be understanding or even hearing it. She could, for example, be responding instead to another of the many stimuli flooding her senses, perhaps a joke coming from an auditory hallucination.

Negative Symptoms

Negative symptoms are those that seem to be "pathological deficits," characteristics that are lacking in a person (Velligan & Rao, 2023). *Poverty of speech, blunted and flat affect, loss of volition,* and *social withdrawal* are commonly found in schizophrenia. Such deficits greatly affect one's life and activities.

POVERTY OF SPEECH People with schizophrenia often have **alogia,** or **poverty of speech,** a reduction in speech or speech content. Some people with this negative kind of formal thought disorder think and say very little. Others say quite a bit but still manage to convey little meaning.

RESTRICTED AFFECT Many people with schizophrenia have a *blunted affect*—they display less anger, sadness, joy, and other feelings than most people (Shang et al., 2024). Indeed, a number show almost no emotions at all, a condition known as *flat affect*. Their faces are still, their eye contact is poor, and their voices are monotonous.

Restricted affect of this kind may actually reflect an inability to *express* emotions as others do. An early study on this matter had participants view very emotional film clips. The participants with schizophrenia showed less facial expression than the others; however, they reported feeling just as much positive and negative emotion and in fact displayed more skin arousal (Kring & Neale, 1996). There is, in fact, a growing recognition in the clinical field that many people with schizophrenia not only experience a full range of emotions internally but also grapple with high levels of anxiety and/or depression (Siris & Braga, 2023; Lee et al., 2022).

of NOTE ...

Their Words

"Those of us who have not had [schizophrenia] should ask ourselves . . . how we would feel if our brain began playing tricks on us, if unseen voices shouted at us, if we lost the capacity to feel emotions and if we lost the ability to reason logically."

E. Fuller Torrey
Psychiatrist, research scientist and advocate

LOSS OF VOLITION Many people with schizophrenia experience *avolition,* or apathy, feeling drained of energy and of interest in common goals and unable to start or follow through on a course of action. This problem is particularly common in people who have had schizophrenia for many years, as if they have been worn down by it. Similarly, people with schizophrenia may feel *ambivalence,* or conflicting feelings, about most things. The avolition and ambivalence of Kenji, the young man you read about earlier, made socializing, bathing, dressing, and undressing almost impossible ordeals for him.

SOCIAL WITHDRAWAL People with schizophrenia may withdraw from their social environment and attend only to their own ideas and fantasies (Kent & Pinkham, 2024). Because their ideas are often quite illogical and confused, the withdrawal has the effect of distancing them still further from reality. The social withdrawal seems also to lead to a breakdown of social skills, including the ability to recognize other people's needs and emotions accurately (Wang et al., 2023).

Courtesy of Oskar Diethelm Library, DeWitt Wallace Institute of Psychiatry: History, Policy, & the Arts, Weill Cornell Medical College

A catatonic pose These patients, photographed in the early 1900s, show features of catatonia, including catatonic posturing, in which they assume bizarre positions for long periods of time.

Psychomotor Symptoms

People with schizophrenia sometimes experience *psychomotor symptoms.* Many move relatively slowly, and a number make awkward movements or repeated grimaces and odd gestures that seem to have a private purpose—perhaps ritualistic or magical.

The psychomotor symptoms of schizophrenia may take certain extreme forms, collectively called **catatonia.** People in a *catatonic stupor* stop responding to their environment, remaining motionless and silent for long stretches of time. Recall how Kenji would lie motionless and nearly mute in his house for days. People with *catatonic rigidity* maintain a rigid, upright posture for hours and resist efforts to be moved. Still others exhibit *catatonic posturing,* assuming awkward, peculiar positions for long periods of time. They may, for example, spend hours holding their arms out at a 90-degree angle or balancing in a squatting position. Finally, people with *catatonic excitement,* a different form of catatonia, move excitedly, sometimes wildly waving their arms and legs.

Around 10 percent of people with schizophrenia experience some degree of catatonia (Coffey, 2022). Individuals with other severe psychological disorders, such as major depressive disorder or bipolar disorder, may also experience these symptoms.

What Is the Course of Schizophrenia?

Schizophrenia usually first appears between the person's late teens and mid-thirties. Although its course varies widely from case to case, many individuals seem to go through three phases—prodromal, active, and residual. During the *prodromal phase,* symptoms are not yet obvious, but deterioration is already beginning. The person may withdraw socially, speak in vague or seemingly odd ways, develop strange ideas, or express little emotion. During the *active phase,* symptoms become apparent. Sometimes this phase is sparked by stress or trauma in the person's life (Rahme et al., 2023). For Candace, the 32-year-old fashion company office manager described earlier, the immediate activators were an unresolved apartment heating problem, the loss of her father, and a series of break-ins on her block.

Many people with schizophrenia eventually enter a *residual phase* in which they return to a prodromal-like level of functioning. They may retain some negative symptoms, such as blunted emotion, but have a lessening of the striking symptoms of the active phase. Although a quarter or more of patients recover completely from schizophrenia, usually through quality treatment or other supports, the majority continue to have at least some residual symptoms for the rest of their lives (Asbø et al., 2022).

In order to help predict the course of schizophrenia, it can be useful to note the particular pattern of an individual's symptoms. In 80 to 85 percent of cases, the disorder is dominated by positive symptoms, such as delusions, hallucinations, and certain formal thought disorders—a clinical picture sometimes called *Type I* schizophrenia, or *excess* schizophrenia (Fischer & Buchanan, 2023; Orsolini, Pompili, & Volpe, 2022). In 15 to 20 percent of cases, the individual displays mostly negative symptoms, such as restricted affect, poverty of speech, and loss of volition—a picture called *Type II* schizophrenia, or *deficit* schizophrenia (Mosolov & Yaltonskaya, 2022).

There are, in fact, a number of schizophrenia-like disorders listed in DSM-5-TR, each distinguished by particular durations and sets of symptoms (see **Table 12-2**). Because these psychotic disorders all bear a similarity to schizophrenia, they—along with schizophrenia itself—are collectively called *schizophrenia spectrum disorders* (APA, 2022). Schizophrenia is the most prevalent of these disorders. Clinical theorists believe that most of the explanations and treatments offered for schizophrenia are applicable to the other disorders as well.

negative symptoms Symptoms of schizophrenia that seem to be deficits in typical thought, emotions, or behaviors.

alogia A decrease in speech or speech content; a symptom of schizophrenia. Also known as *poverty of speech.*

catatonia A pattern of extreme psychomotor symptoms, found in some forms of schizophrenia, which may include catatonic stupor, rigidity, or posturing.

SUMMING UP

The Clinical Picture of Schizophrenia

Schizophrenia is a disorder in which personal, social, and occupational functioning deteriorate as a result of unusual perceptions, odd thought processes, disturbed emotions, and motor irregularities. Approximately 1 percent of the world's population experiences this disorder. The symptoms of schizophrenia fall into three groupings. Positive symptoms include delusions, certain formal thought disorders, hallucinations and other disturbances in perception and attention, and incongruent affect. Negative symptoms include poverty of speech, restricted affect, loss of volition, and social withdrawal. Schizophrenia may also include psychomotor symptoms, collectively called catatonia in their extreme form. Schizophrenia usually emerges during late adolescence or early adulthood and tends to progress through three phases: prodromal, active, and residual. Type I schizophrenia is often distinguished from Type II schizophrenia.

How Do Theorists Explain Schizophrenia?

AS WITH MANY other kinds of disorders, biological, psychological, and sociocultural theorists have each proposed explanations for schizophrenia. So far, the biological explanations have received by far the most research support. This is not to say that psychological and sociocultural factors play no role in the disorder. Rather, a *diathesis–stress relationship* may be at work: people with a biological predisposition will develop schizophrenia only if certain kinds of events or stressors are also present (Rahme et al., 2023; Demke, 2022). Similarly, a diathesis–stress relationship often seems to be operating in the development of other kinds of psychotic disorders (see **PsychWatch**).

TABLE 12-2

Schizophrenia Spectrum Disorders: An Array of Psychosis

Disorder	Key Features	Duration	Lifetime Prevalence
Schizophrenia	Various psychotic symptoms, such as delusions, hallucinations, disorganized speech, restricted or inappropriate affect, and catatonia	6 months or more	1.0%
Brief psychotic disorder	Various psychotic symptoms, such as delusions, hallucinations, disorganized speech, restricted or inappropriate affect, and catatonia	Less than 1 month	Unknown
Schizophreniform disorder	Various psychotic symptoms, such as delusions, hallucinations, disorganized speech, restricted or inappropriate affect, and catatonia	1 to 6 months	0.2%
Schizoaffective disorder	Marked symptoms of both schizophrenia and a major depressive episode or a manic episode	6 months or more	0.3%
Delusional disorder	Persistent delusions that are not bizarre and not due to schizophrenia; persecutory, jealous, grandiose, and somatic delusions are common	1 month or more	0.2%
Psychotic disorder due to another medical condition	Hallucinations, delusions, or disorganized speech caused by a medical illness or brain damage	No minimum length	0.2%–0.5%
Substance/medication-induced psychotic disorder	Hallucinations, delusions, or disorganized speech caused directly by a substance, such as an abused drug	No minimum length	Unknown

Information from: APA, 2022.

PSYCHWATCH

Postpartum Psychosis: A Dangerous Syndrome

On the morning of June 20, 2001, the nation's television viewers watched in horror as officials escorted 36-year-old Andrea Yates to a police car. Just minutes before, she had called police and explained that she had drowned her five children in the bathtub because "they weren't developing correctly" and because she "realized [she had not been] a good mother to them."

As many as 80 percent of people experience "baby blues" soon after giving birth, and at least 10 percent display clinical levels of depression, called *postpartum depression*. In addition, there is another postpartum disorder—*postpartum psychosis*—that has become all too familiar to the public by way of cases such as that of Andrea Yates.

Postpartum psychosis affects about 1 to 2 of every 1,000 individuals who have recently given birth (Friedman, Reed, & Ross, 2023). Within days or weeks, the person develops signs of losing touch with reality, such as delusions (for example, becoming convinced that the baby is the devil); hallucinations (perhaps hearing voices); extreme anxiety, confusion, and disorientation; disturbed sleep; and illogical, chaotic, or dangerous thoughts (for example, thoughts about harming or killing oneself or the child).

Although researchers do not fully understand the causes of the disorder, it has been linked to the enormous shift in hormone levels that takes place after delivery, birth-related dysregulation of the immune system, changes in dopamine activity, genetic factors, sleep deprivation, and early life stress for the parent (Friedman et al., 2023; Payne, 2022, 2021).

People with a history of bipolar disorder or schizophrenia are particularly vulnerable to postpartum psychosis (Friedman et al., 2023; Ortega et al., 2023). In addition, those who have previously experienced postpartum depression or postpartum psychosis have an increased likelihood of developing postpartum psychosis after subsequent births.

John Tlumacki/The Boston Globe via Getty Images

Family tragedy On January 24, 2023, in a case hauntingly similar to that of Andrea Yates, a Massachusetts woman named Lindsay Clancy strangled to death her three children (ages 7 months, 3 years, and 5 years) and then attempted to end her own life. At her arraignment, Clancy's attorney argued that the 32-year-old parent had been overmedicated and may have been experiencing postpartum psychosis. In the days and weeks following the killings, neighbors built this memorial for the children on the grounds outside their home.

Treatment typically consists of mood stabilizers such as lithium, antipsychotic drugs, and psychotherapy (Payne, 2022; Forde, Peters, & Wittkowski, 2020). Around 80 percent of patients fully recover from a given episode and return to their previous lifestyle, although, as noted above, they now have a heightened risk of developing the disorder again after future pregnancies (Ortega et al., 2023). Andrea Yates had symptoms of postpartum depression (and perhaps postpartum psychosis) and had attempted suicide after the birth of her fourth child (Denno, 2017). Then, after the birth of her fifth child a few years later, the symptoms of depression did in fact recur, along with features of psychosis. Yates again attempted suicide. Although she was hospitalized twice and treated with various medications, her condition failed to improve. Six months after giving birth to Mary, her fifth child, she drowned her children.

Between 4 and 11 percent of untreated individuals with postpartum psychosis die of suicide, and 1 to 4 percent kill their children (Friedman et al., 2023; Payne, 2022, 2021). These statistics and cases such as that of Yates remind us that the disorder can lead to terrible consequences and that early detection and treatment are critical.

On July 26, 2006, after an initial conviction for murder was overturned by an appeals court, Yates was found *not guilty by reason of insanity* and sent to a state mental hospital, where she continues to receive treatment today.

of NOTE ...

Their Words

"No great genius was ever without some tincture of madness."

Aristotle

Biological Views

What is arguably the most enlightening research on schizophrenia during the past several decades has come from genetic and biological investigations (Lawrence & Bernstein, 2024). These studies have revealed the key roles of inheritance and brain activity in the development of schizophrenia and have opened the door to important treatment changes.

Genetic Factors

Following the principles of the diathesis–stress perspective, genetic researchers believe that some people inherit a biological predisposition to schizophrenia and develop the disorder later when they face extreme stress, usually during late adolescence or early adulthood (Lieberman, 2024). The genetic view has been supported by studies of (1) relatives of people with schizophrenia, (2) twins with schizophrenia, and (3) people with schizophrenia who are adopted and by (4) direct genetic research.

ARE RELATIVES VULNERABLE? Family pedigree studies have found repeatedly that schizophrenia and schizophrenia-like brain irregularities are more common among relatives of people with the disorder (Hany et al., 2023). And the more closely related the relatives are to the person with schizophrenia, the more likely they are to develop the disorder (see **Figure 12-2**).

Of course, this trend by itself does not establish a genetic basis for the disorder. As the famous neuroscientist Solomon Snyder (1980) once pointed out, "Attendance at Harvard University also runs in families but would hardly be considered a genetic trait." Close family members are exposed to many of the same environmental influences as the person with schizophrenia, and it may be these influences that lead to the disorder.

IS AN IDENTICAL TWIN MORE VULNERABLE THAN A FRATERNAL TWIN? Twins, who are among the closest of relatives, have in particular been studied by schizophrenia researchers. If both members of a pair of twins have a particular trait, they are said to be *concordant* for that trait. If genetic factors are at work in schizophrenia, identical twins (who share all their genes) should have a higher concordance rate for schizophrenia than

Chris Ashford/Camera Press/Redux

Kevin Mazur/Getty Images

Elevated risk Comedian/actress Tiffany Haddish (left) and musical superstar Bruce Springsteen (right) have each revealed that one of their parents was diagnosed with schizophrenia. Like these performers, most children of people with schizophrenia do not develop this disorder or another severe mental disorder. However, the prevalence rate of severe mental disorders is higher among such offspring than among the general population, an elevated risk that may be due to genetic factors and/or a uniquely difficult upbringing.

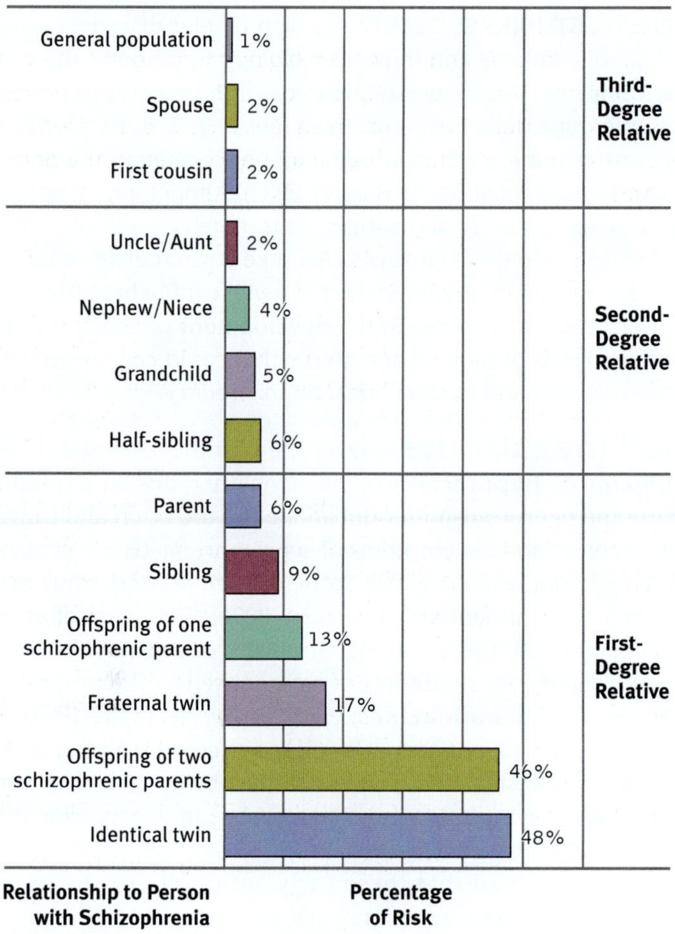

FIGURE 12-2

Family Links

People who are biologically related to someone with schizophrenia have a heightened risk of developing the disorder during their lifetimes. The closer the biological relationship (that is, the more similar the genetic makeup), the greater the risk of developing the disorder. (Information from: Fischer & Buchanan, 2023; Hany et al., 2023; Henriksen, Nordgaard, & Jansson, 2017; Gottesman, 1991, p. 96.)

fraternal twins (who share only some genes). This expectation has been supported consistently by research (Fischer & Buchanan, 2023; Crawford & Go, 2022; Gottesman, 1991). Studies have found that if one identical twin develops schizophrenia, there is a 48 percent chance that the other twin will do so as well. If the twins are fraternal, on the other hand, the second twin has approximately a 17 percent chance of developing the disorder.

What factors, besides genetic ones, might account for the elevated rate of schizophrenia among relatives of people with this disorder?

Once again, however, factors other than genetics may explain these concordance rates. For example, if one twin is exposed to a particular danger during the prenatal period, such as an injury or a virus, the other twin is likely to be exposed to it as well. This is especially true for identical twins, whose prenatal environment is especially similar. Thus, a predisposition to schizophrenia could be the result of a prenatal problem, and twins, particularly identical twins, would still be expected to have a higher concordance rate.

ARE THE BIOLOGICAL RELATIVES OF AN ADOPTEE VULNERABLE? Adoption studies look at adults with schizophrenia who were adopted as infants and compare them with both their biological relatives and their adoptive relatives. Because they were reared apart from their biological relatives, similar symptoms in those relatives would indicate genetic influences. Conversely, similarities to their adoptive relatives would suggest environmental influences. Researchers have repeatedly found that the biological relatives of adoptees with schizophrenia are more likely than their adoptive relatives to develop schizophrenia or another schizophrenia spectrum disorder (Fischer & Buchanan, 2023; Kendall, Walters, & Donovan, 2020).

WHAT DO GENETIC STUDIES SUGGEST? As with bipolar disorders, researchers have run studies of *genetic linkage* and *molecular biology* to pinpoint the possible genetic factors in schizophrenia. Using such genetic research procedures, investigators have identified possible gene defects on chromosomes 1, 2, 6, 8, 10, 13, 15, 18, 20, and 22 and on the X chromosome, each of which may help predispose a person to develop this disorder (Andreassen et al., 2023; Bassett, 2023). Altogether, more than 100 specific gene sites have been linked to schizophrenia to date (Wen et al., 2023)! These varied findings may indicate that schizophrenia, like a number of other disorders, is a *polygenic disorder,* caused by a combination of genetic influences (Rogers, 2023).

How might genetic factors lead to the development of schizophrenia? Research has pointed to two kinds of biological patterns that could conceivably be inherited—*biochemical irregularities* and *dysfunctional brain circuitry.*

of NOTE ...

Paternal Impact

People whose fathers were over 50 years of age when they were born are more likely to develop schizophrenia than people born to younger fathers. As in cases of bipolar disorder, this phenomenon may be explained by the tendency of aging men to produce increased genetic mutations during the manufacture of sperm cells (Fischer & Buchanan, 2023; Gourinat et al., 2023; Kendall et al., 2020).

Biochemical Irregularities

Over the past four decades, researchers have developed a **dopamine hypothesis** to explain their findings on schizophrenia: certain neurons that use the neurotransmitter dopamine fire too often and transmit too many messages, thus producing the symptoms of schizophrenia (Hany et al., 2023; Velligan & Rao, 2023). This hypothesis has undergone challenges and adjustments in recent years, but it is still very influential (Lieberman, 2024). The chain of events leading to this hypothesis began with the accidental discovery of **antipsychotic drugs,** medications that help remove the symptoms of schizophrenia. The first group of antipsychotic medications, the **phenothiazines,** were discovered in the 1950s by researchers who were looking for better *antihistamine* drugs to combat allergies. Although phenothiazines failed as antihistamines, it soon became obvious that they were effective in reducing schizophrenic symptoms, and clinicians began to prescribe them widely for this purpose (Jibson, 2023).

Researchers later learned that these early antipsychotic drugs often produce troublesome muscular tremors, symptoms that are identical to the central symptom of *Parkinson's disease,* a disabling neurological illness (Deik, 2022). This undesired reaction to antipsychotic drugs offered the first important clue to the biology of schizophrenia. Scientists already knew that people with Parkinson's disease have unusually low levels of the neurotransmitter dopamine in some areas of the brain and that lack of dopamine is the reason for their uncontrollable shaking. If antipsychotic drugs produce Parkinsonian symptoms in people with schizophrenia while removing their psychotic symptoms, perhaps the drugs reduce dopamine activity. And, scientists reasoned further, if lowering dopamine activity helps remove the symptoms of schizophrenia, perhaps schizophrenia is related to excessive dopamine activity in the first place.

Since the 1960s, research has supported and helped clarify the dopamine hypothesis. It has been found, for example, that some people with Parkinson's disease develop schizophrenia-like symptoms if they take too much *L-dopa,* a medication that raises Parkinson's patients' dopamine levels. The L-dopa apparently raises the dopamine activity so much that it produces psychosis. Support has also come from research on *amphetamines,* drugs that, as you read in the chapter on substance use disorders, stimulate the central nervous system by increasing dopamine activity in the brain. Clinical investigators have observed that people who take high doses of amphetamines may develop *amphetamine psychosis*—a syndrome very similar to schizophrenia (Mullen, Richards, & Crawford, 2023).

Researchers have located areas of the brain that are rich in dopamine receptors and have found that phenothiazines and related antipsychotic drugs bind to many of these receptors (Jibson, 2023). Apparently, the drugs are dopamine *antagonists*—drugs that bind to dopamine receptors, *prevent* dopamine from binding there, and so prevent the neurons from firing. Researchers have identified five kinds of dopamine receptors in the brain—called the D-1, D-2, D-3, D-4, and D-5 receptors—and have found that phenothiazines bind most strongly to the *D-2 receptors* (Longstreth & Hesketh, 2023).

dopamine hypothesis The theory that schizophrenia results from excessive activity of the neurotransmitter dopamine.

antipsychotic drugs Drugs that help correct grossly confused or distorted thinking.

phenothiazines A group of antihistamine drugs that became the first group of effective antipsychotic medications.

These and related findings suggest that in schizophrenia, messages traveling from dopamine-sending neurons to dopamine receptors on other neurons, particularly to the D-2 receptors, may be transmitted too easily or too often.

Although enlightening, the dopamine hypothesis has certain problems. The biggest challenge has come with the discovery of an additional group of antipsychotic drugs, initially referred to as *atypical antipsychotic drugs* and now called *second-generation antipsychotic drugs,* which are often more effective than the phenothiazines and related early drugs, now collectively called *first-generation antipsychotic drugs.* The newer drugs bind not only to D-2 dopamine receptors, like the first-generation antipsychotic drugs did, but also to many D-1 receptors and to receptors for other neurotransmitters, such as *serotonin, glutamate,* and *GABA* (Fischer & Buchanan, 2023; Zahid et al., 2023). Thus, it may be that schizophrenia is related to irregular activity or interactions of both dopamine and other neurotransmitters rather than to irregular dopamine activity alone (Lieberman, 2024; Velligan & Rao, 2023).

Dysfunctional Brain Structures and Circuitry

As you have read, reactions of various kinds are tied to brain circuits—networks of brain structures that work together, triggering each other into action and producing particular behaviors, cognitions, or emotions. Although research is far from complete, the brain circuit whose dysfunction contributes to schizophrenia has begun to emerge (Kang et al., 2023; Sabaroedin, Tiego, & Fornito, 2023; He et al., 2021). The structures that make up this schizophrenia-related circuit include the prefrontal cortex, hippocampus, amygdala, thalamus, striatum, and substantia nigra, among other brain regions (see **Figure 12-3**). These structures typically work together to bring about effective functioning in such realms as thought, perception, attention, memory, and planning—realms that are disturbed for people with schizophrenia. You may notice that several of the structures in this circuit are also members of brain circuits that contribute to other disorders, but in cases of schizophrenia, the structures function and interconnect in problematic ways that are, collectively, unique to this disorder.

The dysfunction of this schizophrenia-related circuit cannot be characterized in broad terms as, for example, a generally "hyperactive" or generally "underactive"

FIGURE 12-3

Biology of Schizophrenia

The brain circuit that has been linked to schizophrenia includes structures such as the prefrontal cortex, hippocampus, amygdala, thalamus, striatum, and substantia nigra (left). The illustration on the right highlights how the structures of this circuit typically trigger each other into action, an interconnectivity that is flawed in people with schizophrenia.

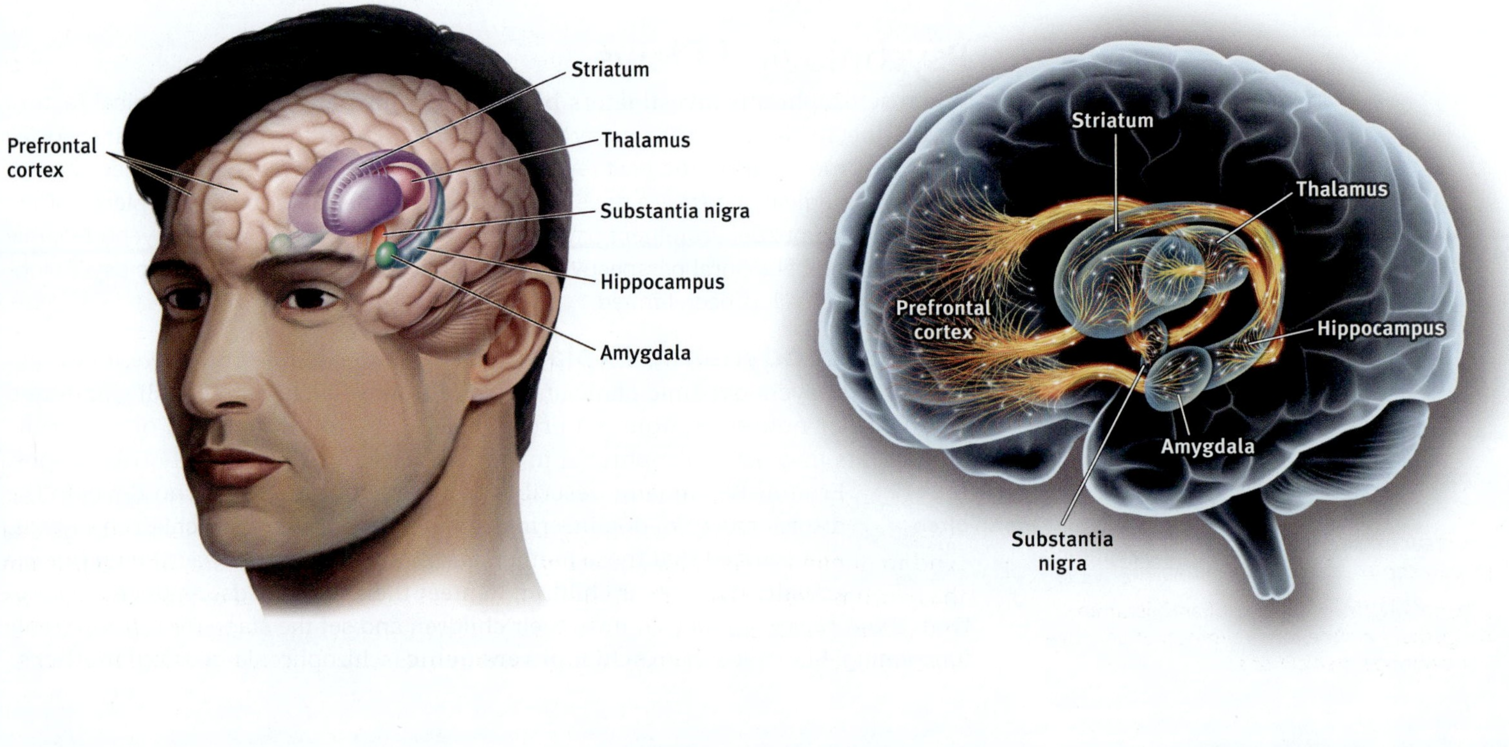

circuit. But numerous studies suggest that the circuit does indeed operate uncharacteristically in persons with schizophrenia (Dabiri et al., 2022; Modinos et al., 2020). For example, the *interconnectivity* (flow of communication) is unusually low between their substantia nigra and prefrontal cortex and between their striatum and thalamus, while it is unusually high between their substantia nigra and striatum, their thalamus and prefrontal cortex, and their hippocampus and prefrontal cortex (Du et al., 2023; Kang et al., 2023; Wang et al., 2017).

of NOTE ...

Their Words

"I shouldn't precisely have chosen madness if there had been any choice, but once such a thing has taken hold of you, you can't very well get out of it."

Vincent van Gogh, 1889

Keep in mind that this focus on brain circuitry is compatible with the dopamine hypothesis of schizophrenia, which monopolized biological explanations for so many years. After all, dopamine activity is very prominent throughout the schizophrenia-related brain circuit, particularly in the substantia nigra and striatum structures (Sabaroedin et al., 2023; He et al., 2021). The key difference between the dopamine hypothesis and the newer brain circuit view is that unusual activity by this neurotransmitter is now viewed as *part of* a broader circuit dysfunction that can propel people toward schizophrenia.

Viral Problems

What might cause the biochemical and structural irregularities found in many cases of schizophrenia? Various studies have pointed to genetic factors, poor nutrition, fetal development, birth complications, immune reactions, and toxins (Fischer & Buchanan, 2023; Hany et al., 2023). In addition, some investigators suggest that the brain irregularities may result from exposure to *viruses* before birth (Velligan & Rao, 2023; DeLisi, 2021). That is, in certain cases, a viral infection may activate an immune system response in the mother that is passed on to the developing fetus, enters the developing brain, and interrupts typical brain development.

Some of the evidence for the viral theory comes from animal model investigations, and other evidence is circumstantial, such as the finding that an uncommonly large number of people with schizophrenia are born during the late winter. The late winter birth rate among people with schizophrenia is 5 to 10 percent higher than among other people (Hany et al., 2023). This could be because of an increase in fetal or infant exposure to viruses at that time of year. More direct evidence for the viral theory of schizophrenia comes from many studies showing that mothers of people with schizophrenia were more likely to have been exposed to the influenza virus during pregnancy than were mothers of people without schizophrenia (Fischer & Buchanan, 2023).

Psychological Views

When schizophrenia investigators began to identify genetic and biological factors during the 1950s and 1960s, many clinicians abandoned the psychological theories of the disorder. During the past few decades, however, the tables have been turned, and psychological factors are once again being considered as important pieces of the schizophrenia puzzle. Prominent psychological theories come from the psychodynamic and cognitive-behavioral perspectives, although research support for these psychological perspectives has been limited.

The Psychodynamic Explanation

In the middle of the twentieth century, noted psychodynamic clinician Frieda Fromm-Reichmann (1948) elaborated on an earlier notion by Sigmund Freud (1924, 1915, 1914) that cold or unnurturing parents may set schizophrenia in motion. Based on her clinical observations, Fromm-Reichmann described the mothers of people who develop the disorder as cold, domineering, and uninterested in their children's needs. She claimed that these mothers may appear to be self-sacrificing but are actually using their children to meet their own needs. At once overprotective and rejecting, they confuse their children and set the stage for schizophrenic functioning. She called them **schizophrenogenic** (schizophrenia-causing) **mothers.**

Why have parents and family life so often been blamed for schizophrenia?

Although famous, Fromm-Reichmann's theory has received little research support (Garson, 2022; Hahn, 2020). The majority of people with schizophrenia do not appear to have parents who fit the schizophrenogenic description.

schizophrenogenic mother A type of mother—supposedly cold, domineering, and uninterested in the needs of her children—who was once thought by many clinicians to cause schizophrenia in her child.

Cognitive-Behavioral Explanations

Cognitive-behavioral theorists have offered two explanations of how and why people develop schizophrenia. One focuses largely on the behaviors of people with schizophrenia and applies the principles of *operant conditioning*. The other focuses on the peculiar thoughts of such individuals and stresses the possible role of *misinterpretations*.

OPERANT CONDITIONING As you have read, operant conditioning is the process by which people learn to perform behaviors for which they have been rewarded frequently. The operant explanation of schizophrenia holds that some people are, for one reason or another, not reinforced for their attention to social cues—that is, attention to other people's smiles, frowns, and comments. As a result, they stop attending to such cues and focus instead on irrelevant cues—the brightness of light in a room, a bird flying above, or the sound of a word rather than its meaning. As they attend to irrelevant cues more and more, their responses become increasingly bizarre (Kent & Pinkham, 2024; Catalano et al., 2020). Much of the support for this explanation has been circumstantial, and so the operant view is usually considered to be at best a partial explanation for schizophrenia. Although it may help explain why a given person displays more psychotic behavior in some situations than in others, it is too limited, in the opinion of many, to account for schizophrenia's origins and its many symptoms.

MISINTERPRETING PECULIAR SENSATIONS The misinterpretation explanation of schizophrenia begins by accepting the biological position that the brains of people with schizophrenia are actually producing strange and unreal sensations—sensations triggered by biological factors—when these people have hallucinations and related perceptual experiences. According to this cognitive-behavioral explanation, however, when the individuals attempt to understand their peculiar experiences, more features of their disorder emerge (Johnson et al., 2022; Knappik, Bless, & Larøi, 2022). When first confronted by voices or other troubling sensations, these people turn to friends and relatives. Naturally, the friends and relatives deny the reality of the sensations,

"I still see polka dots everywhere" For more than a half-century, famous artist Yayoi Kusama has created works of art that prominently feature polka dots and infinite nets, as shown in this installation, Dots Obsession, which immerses visitors in a mirrored corridor of red spotty balloons. Kusama, who chooses to live in a mental hospital, says her work is inspired by lifelong hallucinations. She noted recently, "I still see polka dots everywhere."

of NOTE ...

Private Notions

According to a survey of 2,000 adults in the United States,

- 56 percent believe some people can see and predict the future.
- 51 percent believe some people can read minds.
- 39 percent believe Earth has been visited by beings from outer space.
- 35 percent believe they have felt an unexplained presence in their homes.
- 27 percent believe in Bigfoot.

(Melore, 2021)

and eventually the persons conclude that the others are trying to hide the truth. They come to reject all feedback, and some develop beliefs (delusions) that they are being persecuted. In short, according to this theory, people with schizophrenia take a "rational path to madness" (Zimbardo, 1976). This process of drawing incorrect and bizarre conclusions (delusions) may be helped along by a cognitive bias that many people with schizophrenia have—a tendency to jump to conclusions (Javitt, 2023). Although researchers have established that people with schizophrenia do indeed experience sensory and perceptual problems, they have yet to provide clear, direct support for the cognitive-behavioral notion that misinterpretations of such sensory problems actually produce a syndrome of schizophrenia.

Sociocultural Views

Sociocultural theorists, recognizing that people with mental disorders are subject to a wide range of social and cultural forces, believe that *multicultural factors, social labeling,* and *family dysfunction* all contribute to schizophrenia. Research has yet to clarify what the precise causal relationships might be.

Multicultural Factors As you read earlier in the chapter, the prevalence of schizophrenia is higher for transgender and nonbinary people than cisgender people; higher for gay, lesbian, and bisexual people than heterosexual people; and higher for Black Americans and Indigenous Americans than non-Hispanic White Americans (Barr et al., 2022; Cheng, 2022). The higher rates of schizophrenia in these populations are often attributed to the special pressures that marginalized people experience in our society (for example, discrimination, stigmatization, violence, and inadequate health care), pressures that often contribute to feelings of severe stress (Herbst, 2022; Barr et al., 2021). As you read earlier, even in the face of biological causes, life stress plays a key role in the onset of schizophrenia, so the special stressors faced by marginalized people may increase their vulnerability to this disorder.

A second explanation for the heightened rates of schizophrenia among these various groups may lie in the economic sphere (Barr et al., 2022). On average, people in such groups have lower incomes than the rest of the population, and, as you read earlier, economically disadvantaged people have relatively high rates of schizophrenia.

A third explanation for the higher rates of schizophrenia among marginalized groups holds that clinicians are often unintentionally biased in their diagnoses of people who are different from themselves or that clinicians misread cultural differences as symptoms of schizophrenia. Studies have revealed, for example, that Black Americans with severe depression are more likely than non-Hispanic White Americans to receive a misdiagnosis of schizophrenia (Jegarl et al., 2023; Herbst, 2022). Similarly, in diagnoses of transgender and nonbinary people, it is possible that some clinicians confuse gender diversity with psychosis (Anglin, 2022).

How might bias by diagnosticians contribute to race-linked differences in the diagnosis of schizophrenia?

Yet another important multicultural finding is that of a relationship between schizophrenia and immigration (Fischer & Buchanan, 2023; Velligan & Rao, 2023). Studies from various countries have determined that the prevalence of this disorder can be up to four times higher in immigrant groups than in native-born groups, and this difference extends to the children of immigrants as well. The causes of the relationship between immigrant populations and schizophrenia are not fully understood. It may be that schizophrenia is overdiagnosed in immigrant groups, just as it is in other marginalized groups. Alternatively, the special stressors tied to immigration—for example, the stress of the relocation, becoming part of an outsider group, and/or being discriminated against—may leave immigrants particularly vulnerable to developing schizophrenia. Consistent with this explanation, research in various countries has revealed that immigrant groups that experience more discrimination have higher rates of schizophrenia than those that face less discrimination.

Social Labeling Many sociocultural theorists believe that the features of schizophrenia are influenced by the diagnosis itself. In their opinion, society assigns the label "schizophrenic" to people who fail to conform to certain norms of behavior. Once the label is assigned, whether justified or not, it becomes a self-fulfilling prophecy that promotes the development of many psychotic symptoms (Mesholam-Gately, Johnston, & Kechavan, 2023). It may be, for example, that the label-based expectations of other people subtly encourage the individuals to display psychotic behaviors, and they come to accept their assigned role and learn to play it convincingly.

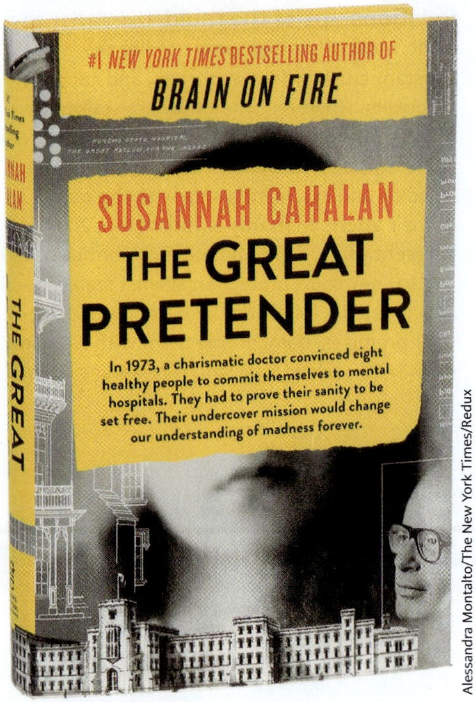

Alessandra Montalto/The New York Times/Redux

The fall of an influential study After conducting an extensive investigation, journalist and author Susannah Cahalan wrote a book in 2019 challenging the merits and authenticity of one of clinical psychology's most influential studies, Rosenhan's "On Being Sane in Insane Places."

For years, one of psychology's most famous studies—"On Being Sane in Insane Places" by clinical investigator David Rosenhan (1973)—seemed to support the social labeling theory. In this study, eight mentally healthy people, actually colleagues of Rosenhan, presented themselves at various mental hospitals, falsely complaining that they had been hearing voices say the words "empty," "hollow," and "thud." According to the author, on the basis of this complaint alone, each was diagnosed as having schizophrenia and admitted. Once hospitalized, the pseudopatients had a hard time convincing others that they were well, even though they behaved appropriately and stopped reporting symptoms as soon as they were admitted. The label "schizophrenia" kept influencing the way the staff viewed and dealt with them; for example, one pseudopatient who paced the corridor out of boredom was, in clinical notes, described as "nervous." And overall, the pseudopatients came to feel powerless, invisible, and bored.

In the decades following the publication of this study, its deceptive design and possible implications generated much debate and aroused both positive and negative emotions among clinicians and researchers. This reaction reached a still higher pitch in 2019, when author Susannah Cahalan wrote a book about the study after gaining access to Rosenhan's own notes, conducting key interviews, and uncovering new information. In her book, Cahalan (2019) built the case that the details and claims of the study were largely inaccurate and, at times, fraudulent. Among her key points: (1) the pseudopatients actually presented symptoms to their hospital clinicians in more disturbing and graphic detail than the study claimed, (2) the pseudopatients actually had little training about how to act in the hospital and were largely on their own, (3) the hospital experiences of the pseudopatients were sometimes much more positive than those presented in the study, (4) the study cut out at least one pseudopatient whose hospital experiences had been particularly positive, (5) at least some of the pseudopatients reported in the study were made up, and (6) the study's data and sources were never disclosed.

Even as originally presented, Rosenhan's study was very controversial. What kinds of ethical, legal, and therapeutic concerns might its purported design raise?

When a theory is built upon a major piece of work and the merits of that work turn out to be questionable, it is difficult to properly assess the merits of the theory itself. This is the position that proponents of the social labeling theory of schizophrenia find themselves in at the present time. It is important to recognize, however, that numerous other studies on social labeling have been undertaken in the half-century since the Rosenhan study, and, collectively, their findings do indeed suggest that the label of schizophrenia (and of other mental disorders) often has a profound, negative, and stigmatizing impact that may influence the further development and treatment of the disorder (Fischer & Buchanan, 2023).

Family Dysfunction Many studies suggest that schizophrenia, like a number of other mental disorders, is often linked to *family stress* (Adrien et al., 2023; Hahlweg & Baucom, 2022). Parents of people with schizophrenia often (1) display more conflict, (2) have more difficulty communicating with one another, and (3) are more critical of and overinvolved with their children than other parents are.

Family theorists have long recognized that some families are high in **expressed emotion**—that is, members frequently express criticism, disapproval, and hostility toward each other and intrude on one another's privacy. People who are trying to recover from schizophrenia are as much as four times more likely to relapse if they live

expressed emotion The general level of criticism, disapproval, and hostility expressed in a family. People recovering from schizophrenia are considered more likely to relapse if their families rate high in expressed emotion.

Relationships of the mind Like Taylor Swift, most celebrities grow used to the constant crush of fans, reporters, and curious onlookers. However, when they are stalked, the matter grows more serious. Some stalkers have *erotomanic delusions*, false beliefs that they are loved by and in a relationship with the object of their attention (Hardy & Turkington, 2024). In recent years, Swift and other celebrities have had to seek court protection against stalkers who are constantly following them, trying to enter their premises, bombarding them with calls and messages, seeking love, and threatening them.

with such a family than if they live with one that is low in expressed emotion (Shetty et al., 2023; Hahlweg & Baucom, 2022). Do such findings mean that family dysfunction helps cause and maintain schizophrenia? Not necessarily. It is also the case that the symptoms of people with schizophrenia greatly disrupt family life. In so doing, these symptoms themselves may help produce the family problems that clinicians and researchers continue to observe.

Developmental Psychopathology View

As they do with other psychological disorders, developmental psychopathology theorists offer an integrative and developmental framework to explain why and how the factors discussed in this chapter may lead to schizophrenia. The theorists contend that the road to schizophrenia begins with a genetically inherited predisposition to the disorder—a predisposition that is expressed by the dysfunctional brain circuit you read about earlier (Addington et al., 2022; Walker et al., 2016). The theorists further argue that this genetic predisposition may eventually lead to schizophrenia if, over the course of development, the individual experiences significant life stressors, difficult family interactions, and/or other negative environmental factors (Lee & Jung, 2024; Myllyaho et al., 2022).

Of course, as you read earlier, theorists of all kinds have, for years, proposed that a diathesis–stress relationship is at work in schizophrenia—that is, people with a biological predisposition to this disorder will develop it if they further experience significant life stress or other negative events. Thus, the developmental psychopathology perspective does not represent a totally new way of understanding schizophrenia. What theorists and researchers from this perspective have done, however, is provide much more detail about the diathesis–stress processes at work in schizophrenia. In particular, they have clarified two key points:

1. Schizophrenia typically begins to unfold long before the actual onset of the disorder in young adulthood. Previously, you read that people with this disorder often display cognitive, perception, and attention problems earlier in their lives (Adamowicz et al., 2024; Li et al., 2024). Developmental psychopathology researchers have found that such people also tend to be more socially withdrawn, disagreeable, and disobedient and to have more motor difficulties

of NOTE ...

Their Words

"In the past 40 years, I've had auditory hallucinations in my head, all day, every day, and I can't get them out."

Brian Wilson, cofounder of the Beach Boys

throughout their early development (Kelleher, 2023; Velligan & Rao, 2023). Some of those early problems seem to result largely from the individual's inherited predisposition, but, according to research, the problems may also be due to repeated experiences of childhood stress, family dysfunction, and/or difficult social interactions (Lee & Jung, 2024; Myllyaho et al., 2022).

2. One of the key ways that a dysfunctional brain circuit may adversely affect the functioning of people who later become schizophrenic is through the circuit's impact on the operation of the *hypothalamic-pituitary-adrenal (HPA) axis.* As you'll recall from the chapter on disorders of trauma and stress, whenever we are stressed, the brain's hypothalamus activates this brain–body stress route, leading, in turn, to the secretion of cortisol and other stress hormones and to a broad experience of arousal. Developmental psychopathology researchers have found that dysfunction by the schizophrenia-related brain circuit leads to repeated overreactions by the HPA axis in the face of stress (Leroux et al., 2023; Zhu et al., 2022; Ji et al., 2021). Such chronic overreactions leave individuals highly sensitive to and unsettled by stressors throughout their development. The individuals become all the more inclined to later develop schizophrenia in the face of stress.

Developmental psychopathology researchers and other investigators have further discovered that an overly reactive HPA axis and chronic stress reactions lead to the development of a dysfunctional *immune system,* characterized by heightened inflammation throughout the brain (see **Figure 12-4**). Thus, it is not surprising that numerous studies conducted in recent years have found significant immune system problems in people with schizophrenia, including a heightened production and spread of *pro-inflammatory cytokines,* proteins that cause chronic inflammation throughout the brains of people with this disorder (Adamowicz et al., 2024; Zhang et al., 2024).

In addition to adding depth to the diathesis–stress view of schizophrenia, the developmental psychopathology perspective provides an important service by emphasizing the advantages of *prevention* in dealing with this disorder (Kelleher, 2023). According to this perspective, the factors discussed in this chapter (from brain circuit

FIGURE 12-4

Developing Schizophrenia

According to developmental psychopathology theorists, these individuals illustrate the principle of *multifinality* and wind up with different clinical outcomes even though they are challenged by similar developmental risk factors (brain circuit dysfunction, HPA axis overreactivity, and brain inflammation). The first individual further experiences social withdrawal and substantial life stress, setting the stage for schizophrenia, while the second individual experiences a life of social engagement and only modest life stress (protective factors) and so remains psychologically healthy.

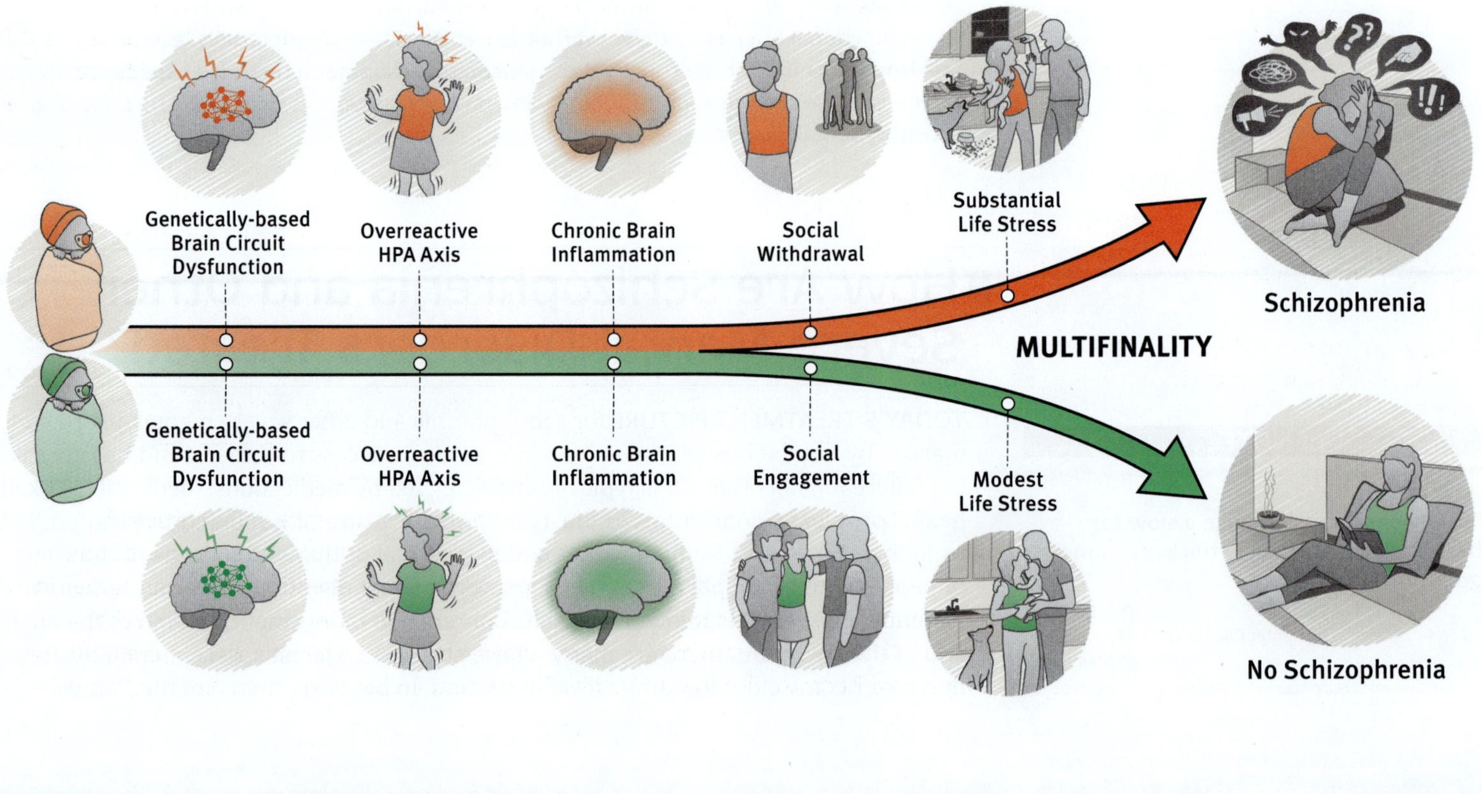

dysfunction to family dynamics to stress reactions) can all affect each other. Just as an overreactive HPA axis can make children particularly vulnerable to stress, so too can their acquisition of resilience and coping skills improve the operation of their HPA axis. This two-way relationship argues for better identification of children at risk for schizophrenia and for stronger preventive interventions that might reverse the factors predisposing them to schizophrenia (Lieberman, 2024; Kelleher, 2023). Unfortunately, as you will learn in the next section, most of today's approaches to schizophrenia involve treatment after the onset of the disorder rather than prevention.

How might children at risk for schizophrenia be identified at home, in school, and/or in social settings?

SUMMING UP

How Do Theorists Explain Schizophrenia?

Many theorists believe that biological and environmental factors combine in a diathesis–stress relationship to help produce schizophrenia.

The biological explanations of schizophrenia point to genetic, biochemical, brain structure and circuitry, and viral causes. The genetic view is supported by studies of relatives, twins, adoptees, and genes. The leading biochemical explanation holds that dopamine may be overactive in the brains of people with schizophrenia. Studies have also identified a brain circuit whose dysfunction may lead to schizophrenia. Finally, some researchers believe that schizophrenia is related to a virus that affects the developing fetus.

Prominent psychological explanations for schizophrenia come from the psychodynamic and cognitive-behavioral models. The psychological explanations have not typically received compelling research support.

One sociocultural theory holds that multicultural differences may be linked to the prevalence of schizophrenia. Another sociocultural explanation says that society expects people who are labeled as having schizophrenia to behave in certain ways and that such expectations actually lead to further symptoms. Other sociocultural theorists point to family dysfunction as playing a role in the development of schizophrenia.

Applying an integrative and developmental framework, developmental psychopathology theorists contend that an individual's genetic predisposition—implemented by a dysfunctional brain circuit and overreactive HPA axis—may eventually lead to schizophrenia if, over the course of the person's development, they also experience significant life stressors, difficult family interactions, and/or other negative environmental factors.

How Are Schizophrenia and Other Severe Mental Disorders Treated?

TODAY'S TREATMENT PICTURE for schizophrenia and other severe mental disorders is marked by miraculous triumphs for some, modest success for others, and heartbreaking failure for still others. It is typically characterized by medications, medication-linked health problems, compromised lifestyles, and a mixture of hope and frustration. Let us look at the case of Cathy, whose journey is typical of that of hundreds of thousands of people with schizophrenia and other severe mental disorders. To be sure, there are patients whose efforts to overcome schizophrenia go more smoothly. And at the other end of the spectrum, there are many whose struggles against severe mental dysfunction never come close to Cathy's level of success. In between, there are the Cathys.

of NOTE ...

Their Words

"Schizophrenia rolls in like a slow fog, becoming imperceptibly thicker as time goes on."

Elyn R. Saks
The Center Cannot Hold: My Journey Through Madness

During [Cathy's] second year in college . . . her emotional troubles worsened. . . . and [she was] put on Haldol and lithium.

For the next sixteen years, Cathy cycled in and out of hospitals. She "hated the meds"—Haldol stiffened her muscles and caused her to drool, while the lithium made her depressed—and often she would abruptly stop taking them. . . . The problem was that off the drugs, she would "start to decompensate and become disorganized."

In early 1994, she was hospitalized for the fifteenth time. She was seen as chronically mentally ill, occasionally heard voices now . . . and was on a cocktail of drugs: Haldol, Ativan, Tegretol, Halcion, and Cogentin, the last drug an antidote to Haldol's nasty side effects. But after she was released that spring, a psychiatrist told her to try Risperdal, a new antipsychotic that had just been approved by the FDA. "Three weeks later, my mind was much clearer," she says. "The voices were going away. I got off the other meds and took only this one drug. I got better. I could start to plan. I wasn't talking to the devil anymore. Jesus and God weren't battling it out in my head." Her father put it this way: "Cathy is back." . . .

She went back to school and earned a degree in radio, film, and television. . . . In 1998, she began dating the man she lives with today. . . . In 2005, she took a part-time job. . . . Still, she remains on SSDI (Social Security Disability Insurance)—"I am a kept woman," she jokes—and although there are many reasons for that, she believes that Risperdal, the very drug that has helped her so much, nevertheless has proven to be a barrier to full-time work. Although she is usually energetic by the early afternoon, Risperdal makes her so sleepy that she has trouble getting up in the morning. . . .

Risperdal has also taken a physical toll. . . . "I can go toe-to-toe with an old lady with a recital of my physical problems," she says. "My feet, my bladder, my heart, my sinuses, the weight gain—I have it all." . . . But she can't do well without Risperdal. . . .

Such has been her life's course on medication. Sixteen terrible years, followed by fourteen pretty good years. . . . Still, if you look at the long-term course of her illness . . . you have to ask: Is hers a story of a life made better by our drug-based . . . care for mental disorders, or a story of a life made worse? . . . Cathy believes that this is a question that psychiatrists never contemplate.

(Whitaker, 2010)

As Cathy's journey illustrates, schizophrenia is extremely difficult to treat, but clinicians are much more successful at doing so today than they were in the past. Much of the credit goes to *antipsychotic drugs*—imperfect, troubling, and even dangerous though they may be. These medications help many people with schizophrenia and other psychotic disorders to think clearly and profit from psychotherapies that previously would have had little effect for them (Lawrence & Bernstein, 2024).

To best convey the plight of people with schizophrenia, this chapter will depart from the usual format and discuss the treatments from a historical perspective. A look at how treatment has changed over the years will help us understand the nature, problems, and promise of today's approaches. As we consider past treatments for schizophrenia, it is important to keep in mind that throughout much of the twentieth century, the label "schizophrenia" was assigned to most people with psychosis. Clinical theorists now realize that many people with psychotic symptoms are instead experiencing a severe form of bipolar disorder or major depressive disorder and that such people were in past times inaccurately diagnosed with schizophrenia (Ravan et al., 2024). Thus, our discussions of past treatments for schizophrenia, particularly the failures of institutional care, are as applicable to those other severe mental disorders as they are to schizophrenia. Similarly, our discussions about current approaches to schizophrenia, such as the community mental health movement, often apply to other severe mental disorders as well.

of NOTE ...

Their Words

"I believe that if you grabbed the nearest normal person off the street and put them in a psychiatric hospital, they'd be diagnosable as mad within weeks."

Clare Allan, novelist, *Poppy Shakespeare*

state hospitals Public mental hospitals in the United States, run by the individual states.

milieu therapy A humanistic approach to institutional treatment based on the premise that institutions can help patients recover by creating a climate that promotes self-respect, responsible behavior, and meaningful activity.

Institutional Care in the Past

For more than half of the twentieth century, most people diagnosed with schizophrenia were *institutionalized* in a public mental hospital. Because patients with schizophrenia did not respond to traditional therapies, the primary goals of these hospitals were to restrain them and give them food, shelter, and clothing. Patients rarely saw therapists and generally were neglected. Many were abused. Oddly enough, this state of affairs unfolded in an atmosphere of good intentions.

As you read in the textbook's opening chapter, the move toward institutionalization in hospitals began in 1793, when French physician Philippe Pinel "unchained the insane" at La Bicêtre asylum and began the practice of "moral treatment." For the first time in centuries, patients with severe disturbances were viewed as human beings who should be cared for with sympathy and kindness. As Pinel's ideas spread throughout Europe and the United States, they led to the creation of large *mental hospitals* rather than asylums to care for those with severe mental disorders (Berdzenishvili, 2022).

These new mental hospitals, typically located in isolated areas where land and labor were cheap, were meant to protect patients from the stresses of daily life and offer them a healthful psychological environment in which they could work closely with therapists. States throughout the United States were even required by law to establish public mental institutions, **state hospitals,** for patients who could not afford private ones.

Eventually, however, the state hospital system encountered serious problems. Between 1845 and 1955, nearly 300 state hospitals opened in the United States, and the number of hospitalized patients on any given day rose from 2,000 in 1845 to nearly 600,000 in 1955. During this expansion, wards became overcrowded, admissions kept rising, and state funding was unable to keep up.

The priorities of the public mental hospitals and the quality of care they provided changed over those 110 years (D'Antonio, 2023). In the face of overcrowding and understaffing, the emphasis shifted from giving humanitarian care to keeping order. In a throwback to the asylum period, more challenging patients were restrained, isolated, and punished; individual attention disappeared. Patients were transferred to *back wards,* or chronic wards, if they failed to improve quickly. Most of the patients on these wards experienced schizophrenia. The back wards were human warehouses

Institutional life In a scene reminiscent of public mental hospitals in the United States during the first half of the twentieth century, these patients spend their days crowded together on a hospital ward in Shanghai. Because of a shortage of therapists, only a small fraction of Chinese people with psychological disorders receive proper professional care today.

John Stanmeyer/VII/Redux

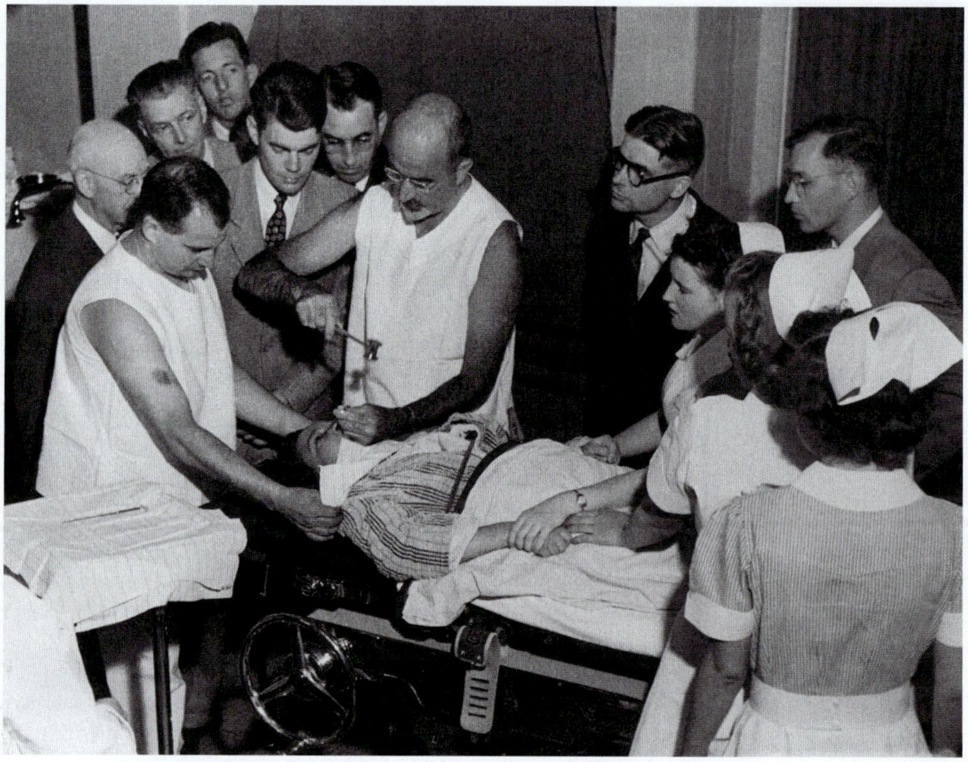

Bettmann/Getty Images

Lessons in psychosurgery Neuropsychiatrist Walter Freeman performs a lobotomy in 1949 before a group of interested onlookers by inserting a needle through a patient's eye socket into the brain.

filled with hopelessness. Staff members relied on straitjackets and handcuffs to deal with patients they could not manage. More "advanced" forms of treatment included medical approaches such as *lobotomy,* a now-notorious procedure in which surgeons would insert an instrument resembling an icepick through the side of the skull or the eye socket into the brain to cut or destroy nerve fibers (De Jesus et al., 2023).

Why have people with schizophrenia so often been subjected to horrific treatments such as overcrowded wards, lobotomy, and, later, deinstitutionalization?

Institutional Care Takes a Turn for the Better

In the 1950s, Clinicians developed two institutional approaches that finally brought some hope to patients who had lived in institutions for years: *milieu therapy,* based on humanistic principles, and the *token economy program,* based on behavioral principles. These approaches particularly helped improve patients' personal care and self-image, problem areas that had been worsened by institutionalization.

Milieu Therapy

In the opinion of humanistic theorists, institutionalized patients deteriorate because they are deprived of opportunities to exercise independence, responsibility, and positive self-regard and to engage in meaningful activities. Thus, the premise of **milieu therapy** is that institutions cannot be of help to patients unless they can somehow create a social climate, or milieu, that promotes productive activity, self-respect, and individual responsibility.

The pioneer of this approach was Maxwell Jones, a London psychiatrist who in 1953 converted a ward of patients with various psychological disorders into a therapeutic community. The patients were referred to as "residents" and were regarded as capable of running their own lives and making their own decisions. They participated in community government, working with staff members to establish rules and determine sanctions. Residents and staff members alike were valued as important therapeutic agents. The atmosphere was one of mutual respect, support, and openness. Patients could also take on special projects, jobs, and recreational activities. In short, their daily schedule was designed to resemble life outside the hospital.

Ian Hanning/REA/Redux

The healing arts Based on findings that artistic activities and expression can be therapeutic for people with severe mental disorders, many institutions include art therapy and music therapy. At a program in France, a patient seen here participates in a drawing workshop.

Milieu-style programs have since been set up in institutions throughout the Western world. The programs vary from setting to setting, but at a minimum, staff members try to encourage interactions (especially group interactions) between patients and staff, to keep patients active, and to raise their expectations about what they can accomplish. Research over the years has shown that people with schizophrenia and other severe mental disorders in milieu hospital programs often improve and that they leave the hospital at higher rates than patients in programs offering primarily custodial care (Clemmensen et al., 2023; Belsiyal, Rentala, & Das, 2022). Many remain impaired, however, and must live in sheltered settings after their discharge.

Despite its limitations, milieu therapy continues to be practiced in many institutions, often combined with other hospital approaches. Moreover, you will read later in this chapter that many of today's supervised group houses (previously known as halfway houses) and other community programs for people with severe mental disorders are run in accordance with the same principles of resident self-government and work schedules that have proved effective in hospital milieu programs.

The Token Economy

In the 1950s, clinicians interested primarily in behaviors and in principles of conditioning discovered that the systematic use of *operant conditioning* techniques on hospital wards could help change the behaviors of patients with schizophrenia (SCP, 2023; Ayllon & Michael, 1959). Programs that apply these techniques are called **token economy programs.**

In token economies, patients are rewarded when they behave acceptably and are not rewarded when they behave unacceptably. The immediate rewards for acceptable behavior are often tokens that can later be exchanged for food, cigarettes, hospital privileges, and other desirable items, all of which compose a "token economy." Acceptable behaviors likely to be included are caring for oneself and for one's possessions (making the bed, getting dressed), going to a work program, speaking appropriately, following ward rules, and showing self-control. Researchers have found that token economies do help reduce psychotic and related behaviors (SCP, 2023).

Some clinicians have voiced reservations about the claims made regarding token economy programs. Are operant conditioning procedures changing a patient's psychotic thoughts and perceptions, or are such procedures simply improving the patient's ability to imitate acceptable behavior? This issue is illustrated by the case of a middle-aged man named John, who had the delusion that he was the U.S. government and always spoke as such: "We are happy to see you. . . . We need people like you in our service. . . . We are carrying out our activities in John's body." When John's hospital ward converted to using a token economy, the staff members targeted his delusional statements and required him to identify himself properly to earn tokens. If he called himself John, he received tokens; if he described himself as the government, he received nothing. After a few months on the token economy program, John stopped referring to himself as the government. When asked his name, he would say, "John." Although staff members were understandably pleased with his improvement, John himself had a different view of the situation. In a private discussion he said this:

We're tired of it. Every damn time we want a cigarette, we have to go through their bullshit. "What's your name? . . . Who wants the cigarette? . . . Where is the government?" Today, we were desperate for a smoke and went to Simpson, the damn nurse, and she made us do her bidding. "Tell me your name if you want a cigarette. What's your name?" Of course,

of NOTE ...

Inside View

Experiencing delusions, businessman Clifford Beers spent 2 years in mental institutions during the early 1900s. His later description of conditions there in an autobiography, *A Mind That Found Itself*, spurred a reform movement in the United States called the "mental hygiene movement," which led to some key improvements in hospital conditions.

Apic/Getty Images

Few treatment options The seventeenth-century physicist and mathematician Isaac Newton was one of history's most influential scientists, whose accomplishments included developing the laws of planetary motion, building the first reflecting telescope, and formulating a prism-based theory of color. He also experienced schizophrenia, marked by delusions and hallucinations. However, as historians point out, the treatment options for Newton and others with this disorder were few and far between back in the late 1600s, consisting largely of "bloodletting, purging, potions of mixed sedatives, prayer, a walk in the woods, or a good book" (PT, 2016).

we said, "John." We needed the cigarettes. If we told her the truth, no cigarettes. But we don't have time for this nonsense. We've got business to do, international business, laws to change, people to recruit. And these people keep playing their games.

(Comer, 1973)

Token economy programs are no longer as popular as they once were, but they are still used in many mental hospitals, usually along with medication and psychotherapy, and in many community residences as well (Hangen et al., 2023; SCP, 2023). The approach has also been applied to other clinical conditions, including intellectual developmental disorders, delinquency, and hyperactivity, as well as in other fields, such as education and business.

Antipsychotic Drugs

Milieu therapy and token economy programs helped improve the gloomy outlook for patients diagnosed with schizophrenia, but it was the discovery of *antipsychotic drugs* in the 1950s that truly revolutionized treatment for schizophrenia. As noted earlier, these drugs eliminate many of schizophrenia's symptoms, and today they are almost always a part of treatment (Bustillo, 2023; Jibson, 2023).

The discovery of antipsychotic medications dates back to the 1940s, when researchers developed the first *antihistamine drugs* to combat allergies. The French surgeon Henri Laborit soon discovered that one group of antihistamines, *phenothiazines,* could also be used to help calm patients about to undergo surgery (Ban, 2023; Goff, 2020). One of the phenothiazines, *chlorpromazine,* was eventually tested on six patients with psychotic symptoms and was found to reduce their symptoms sharply. In 1954, chlorpromazine was approved for sale in the United States as an antipsychotic drug under the trade name Thorazine.

Since the discovery of the phenothiazines, other kinds of antipsychotic drugs have been developed. As you read earlier, the ones developed throughout the 1960s, 1970s, and 1980s are now referred to as **first-generation antipsychotic drugs** in order to distinguish them from the **second-generation antipsychotic drugs** that have been developed subsequently. The first-generation drugs are also known in some clinical circles as *neuroleptic drugs* because they often produce undesired movement effects

token economy program A behavior-focused program in which a person's desirable behaviors are reinforced systematically by the awarding of tokens that can be exchanged for goods or privileges.

first-generation antipsychotic drugs The initial group of antipsychotic drugs, developed throughout the 1960s, 1970s, and 1980s. Also known as *neuroleptic drugs.*

second-generation antipsychotic drugs A relatively newer group of antipsychotic drugs whose biological action is different from that of the first-generation antipsychotic drugs. Also known as *atypical antipsychotic drugs.*

similar to the symptoms of neurological diseases. Among the best-known first-generation drugs are *thioridazine* (Mellaril), *fluphenazine* (Prolixin), *trifluoperazine* (Stelazine), and *haloperidol* (Haldol). As you read earlier, the various antipsychotic drugs reduce psychotic symptoms at least in part by blocking excessive activity of the neurotransmitter *dopamine* (Jibson, 2023).

How Effective Are Antipsychotic Drugs?

Research has shown that antipsychotic drugs reduce symptoms in around 70 percent of patients diagnosed with schizophrenia (Stroup & Marder, 2023; Weston-Green, 2022; Goff, 2021). Moreover, in direct comparisons, the drugs appear to be a more effective treatment for schizophrenia than any of the other approaches used alone, such as psychotherapy, milieu therapy, or electroconvulsive therapy.

For patients who are helped by the drugs, the medications bring about clear improvement within a period of weeks and maximum improvement within six months (Jibson, 2023). However, symptoms may return if the patients stop taking the drugs too soon (Kidron & Nguyen, 2023). The antipsychotic drugs reduce the positive symptoms of schizophrenia (such as hallucinations and delusions) more completely (or at least more quickly) than the negative symptoms (such as restricted affect, poverty of speech, and loss of volition) (Weston-Green, 2022; Goff, 2021, 2020).

Unwanted effects The hand in this photo is that of neurologist Julie Kurek, who is conducting a telehealth treatment session and modeling hand movements for a patient with Parkinson's disease, a disorder caused by low dopamine activity. As a result of his disease, the patient has significant muscle tremors and movement difficulties. Antipsychotic drugs, particularly the first-generation drugs, often produce Parkinsonian-like symptoms.

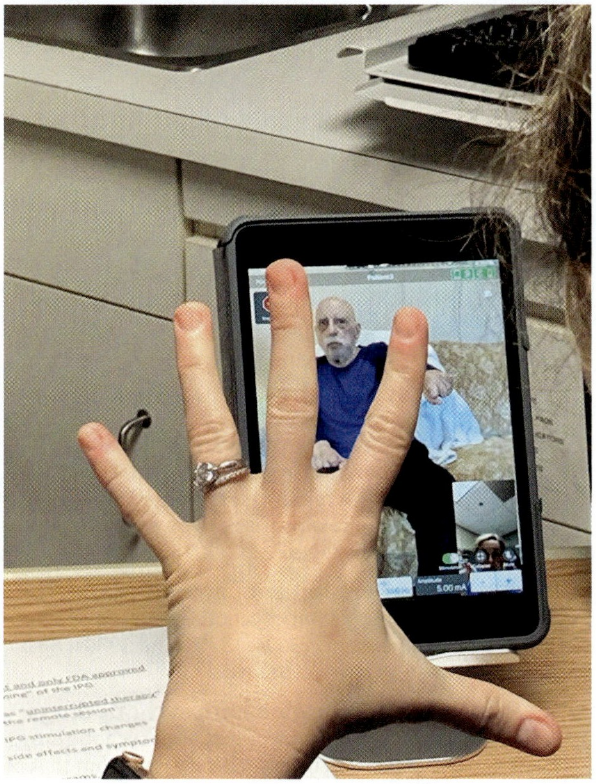

The Unwanted Effects of First-Generation Antipsychotic Drugs

In addition to reducing psychotic symptoms, the first-generation antipsychotic drugs sometimes produce disturbing movement problems (D'Souza & Hooten, 2023). These effects are usually called **extrapyramidal effects** because they appear to be caused by the drugs' impact on the extrapyramidal areas of the brain, areas that help control motor activity. DSM-5-TR has recently indicated a preference for the term *antipsychotic medication-induced movement disorder* to describe the effects.

The most common extrapyramidal effect is *parkinsonism*, a cluster of reactions that closely resemble the features of the neurological disorder Parkinson's disease (APA, 2022). At least half of patients on first-generation antipsychotic drugs have muscle tremors and muscle rigidity at some point in their treatment; they may shake, move slowly, shuffle their feet, and show little facial expression. Some also have muscle contractions of the face, neck, tongue, and back (symptoms called *dystonia*), and a number of them experience significant restlessness and discomfort in their limbs, which causes them to move their arms and legs continually in search of relief (symptoms called *akathisia*). These various symptoms seem to be the result of medication-induced reductions of dopamine activity in the *striatum*, the brain structure that coordinates movement and posture, among other functions (Liang, 2023; Deik, 2022). In most cases, the symptoms can be reversed if the person takes an *antiparkinson drug* along with the antipsychotic drug (Wyant & Chou, 2023).

Whereas most undesired drug effects appear within days or weeks, a reaction called **tardive dyskinesia** (meaning "late-appearing movement disorder") does not usually unfold until after a person has taken first-generation antipsychotic drugs for more than six months (Liang, 2023; Deik, 2022). Sometimes it does not even appear until after the medications are stopped. This syndrome may include involuntary writhing or ticlike movements of the tongue, mouth, face, or whole body; involuntary chewing, sucking, and lip smacking; and jerky movements of the arms, legs, or entire body.

Most cases of tardive dyskinesia are mild and involve a single symptom, such as tongue flicking; however, some are severe and include such features as continual rocking back and forth, irregular breathing, and extreme twisting of the face and body (APA, 2022). It is believed that more than 20 percent of the people who take first-generation antipsychotic drugs for an extended time, especially the most powerful such drugs, develop tardive dyskinesia to some degree, and the longer the drugs are taken, the higher the risk becomes. Patients over age 50 are at greater risk—perhaps three to five times the risk of younger patients (APA, 2022). Tardive dyskinesia can be difficult, sometimes impossible, to eliminate (Liang, 2023; Deik, 2022). Several medications have been developed that help reduce this pattern. In addition, certain vitamins have proved helpful.

Clinicians today are more knowledgeable and more cautious about prescribing first-generation antipsychotic drugs than they were in the past (Moncrieff et al., 2023; Guinart & Correll, 2020; Takeuchi & Remington, 2020). Previously, when patients did not improve with such a drug, their clinician would keep increasing the dose; today, a clinician will typically supplement the antipsychotic drug with a different drug, try an alternative antipsychotic drug, or stop all medications. Today's clinicians also try to prescribe the lowest effective doses for each patient and to gradually reduce medications weeks or months after the patient begins functioning appropriately (Goff, 2021). Research indicates that, for many such patients, reductions of this kind do not lead to a return of symptoms. For others, however, only small reductions in dosage are possible, and treatment for these patients typically involves the long-term use of carefully monitored high dosages of antipsychotic drugs (Moncrieff et al., 2023; Glick et al., 2020).

Why did psychiatrists in the past keep administering high dosages of antipsychotic drugs to patients who had adverse effects from the medications?

Second-Generation Antipsychotic Drugs

As you read earlier in the chapter, *second-generation* antipsychotic drugs have been developed in recent decades. The most widely used of these newer drugs are *clozapine* (trade name Clozaril), *risperidone* (Risperdal), *olanzapine* (Zyprexa), *quetiapine* (Seroquel), *ziprasidone* (Geodon), and *aripiprazole* (Abilify). As noted earlier, these drugs are received at somewhat fewer dopamine D-2 receptors, more D-1 receptors, and more serotonin receptors than the first-generation drugs (Deik, 2022; Weston-Green, 2022).

Second-generation antipsychotic drugs appear to be at least as effective as and often more effective than the first-generation drugs (Jibson, 2023; Stroup & Marder, 2023). Clozapine is often the most effective such drug, but the other second-generation drugs also bring significant change for many people. Recall, for example, Cathy, the woman whom we met earlier, and how well she responded to risperidone after years of faring poorly on first-generation antipsychotic drugs. Unlike the first-generation drugs, the newer drugs reduce not only the positive symptoms of schizophrenia but—to a small degree—the negative ones as well (Weston-Green, 2022). Another major benefit of the second-generation antipsychotic drugs is that they cause fewer extrapyramidal symptoms and seem less likely to produce tardive dyskinesia (D'Souza & Hooten, 2023; Deik, 2022). Approximately 7 percent of patients who take second-generation antipsychotic drugs for an extended time develop tardive dyskinesia (in contrast to at least 20 percent of those on the first-generation drugs). Clozapine is, by far, the least likely of the second-generation drugs to cause tardive dyskinesia (Jibson, 2023).

Given such advantages, more than half of all patients with schizophrenia who are medicated now take the second-generation drugs, which are considered the first line of treatment for the disorder (Jibson, 2023). As you read in the chapter on depressive and bipolar disorders, many patients with bipolar or other severe mental disorders also seem to be helped by several of these antipsychotic drugs (Johnson-Davis & Ly, 2024). Clinicians use the same general prescription strategies for the second-generation antipsychotic drugs as they do for the first-generation drugs (Stroup & Marder, 2023).

Yet the second-generation antipsychotic drugs have serious problems as well. For example, people who use one of these drugs, clozapine, have around a 1 to 1.5 percent risk of developing **agranulocytosis,** a life-threatening drop in white blood cells (other second-generation drugs do not produce this undesired effect) (Coates, 2022; Weston-Green, 2022). Patients who take clozapine must therefore have frequent blood tests so that agranulocytosis can be spotted early and the drug

extrapyramidal effects Unwanted movements, such as severe shaking, unusual grimaces, twisting of the body, and extreme restlessness, sometimes produced by antipsychotic drugs. Also known as *antipsychotic medication-induced movement disorder.*

tardive dyskinesia Extrapyramidal effects involving involuntary movements that some patients have after they have taken antipsychotic drugs for an extended time.

agranulocytosis A life-threatening drop in white blood cells. This condition is sometimes produced by the second-generation antipsychotic drug *clozapine.*

MINDTECH

Putting a Face on Auditory Hallucinations

Many of today's therapists use avatars to help clients overcome their psychological problems. In this form of virtual reality therapy, clinicians have the clients interact with computer-generated on-screen virtual human figures. One of the boldest applications of avatar therapy is its use with people experiencing schizophrenia. Clinical researcher Julian Leff and several colleagues have developed an approach that seems to offer particular promise (Rus-Calafell et al., 2022; Garety et al., 2021; Leff et al., 2014, 2013).

Can you think of any negative effects—short-term or long-term—that might result from putting a face on auditory hallucinations?

For a pilot study, the researchers selected 16 participants who were being tormented by imaginary voices (auditory hallucinations). In each case, the therapist presented the individual with a mean-sounding and mean-looking avatar that appeared on-screen. The avatar's voice pitch and appearance were designed based on the patient's description of the auditory hallucination and what the patient believed would be a corresponding face (Edwards et al., 2023; Rus-Calafell et al., 2022).

The patient was placed alone in a room with the computer simulation while the therapist generated the on-screen avatar from another room. Initially, the avatar spewed all sorts of frightening and upsetting statements at the patient. Then the therapist encouraged the patient to fight back—to tell the avatar things such as "I will not put up with this," "What you are saying is nonsense," "I don't believe these things," "You must go away and leave me alone," and "I do not need this kind of torment."

After seven 30-minute sessions, most of the participants in the pilot study had less frequent and less intense auditory hallucinations and reported being less upset by the voices that they did continue to hear. The participants also reported improvements in their feelings of depression and suicidal thinking. Of the 16 participants, 3 reported a total cessation of their auditory hallucinations after the sessions. These promising results have now been followed up by larger studies with more participants—each producing similar findings (Beaudoin et al., 2023; Kapadia, 2022; Ward et al., 2020). The collective results of these studies suggest that confronting one's hallucinations in a virtual world can indeed help at least some people with schizophrenia.

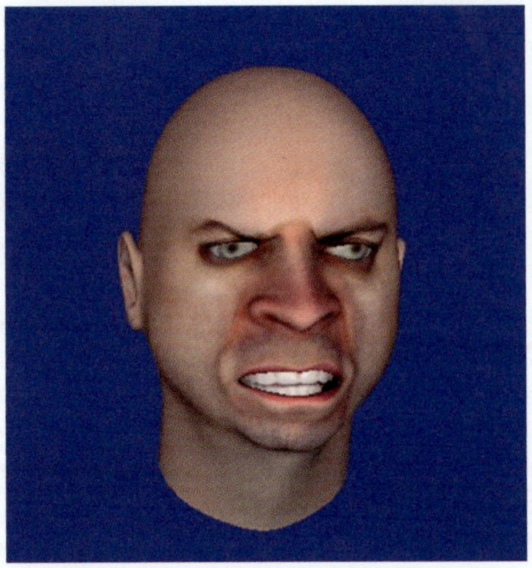

Virtual voices This is one of the sinister-looking avatars developed by clinical researcher Julian Leff and his colleagues in their treatment for people with schizophrenia.

stopped (Freudenreich & McEvoy, 2023). Also, research indicates that although these medications do reduce the symptoms of psychosis in many cases, they, like the first-generation antipsychotic drugs, may produce only mild changes in the quality of life for many of the patients who have chronic schizophrenia (Martinez & Peplow, 2024; Beaudoin et al., 2022).

Psychotherapy

By helping to relieve thought disturbances and perceptual disturbances, antipsychotic drugs allow people with schizophrenia to learn about their disorder, participate actively in therapy (see ***MindTech***), think more clearly about themselves and their relationships, make changes in their behavior, and cope with stressors in their lives. The most helpful forms of psychotherapy include cognitive-behavioral therapy and two sociocultural interventions—family therapy and coordinated specialty care. Often the various approaches are combined.

Cognitive-Behavioral Therapies

Two kinds of cognitive-behavioral therapy are now used for people with schizophrenia: (1) *cognitive remediation* and (2) *hallucination reinterpretation and acceptance*. Research indicates that both approaches are helpful, each in a different way.

COGNITIVE REMEDIATION Earlier, you read about a number of cognitive impairments displayed by people with schizophrenia, including difficulties in attention, planning, memory, speech, thinking, and social cue perception (Kent & Pinkham, 2024). Over the past decade, more and more theorists have come to believe that such deficits are actually a core feature of schizophrenia from which other symptoms of the disorder emerge (Li et al., 2024; McCutcheon, Keefe, & McGuire, 2023). Correspondingly, a treatment intervention called **cognitive remediation** has been developed (Singh et al., 2023).

In cognitive remediation, clients are required to complete increasingly difficult information-processing tasks on a computer. They may start with a simple task such as responding as quickly as possible to various stimuli that are flashed on the screen—a task designed to improve their attention skills. Once they can perform this task with considerable speed, they move on to more complex computer tasks, such as tasks that challenge their short-term memory. As they succeed at each computer task, they keep moving up the ladder until eventually reaching computer tasks that require planning and social awareness.

Studies indicate that, for many people with schizophrenia, cognitive remediation produces moderate improvements in attention, planning, memory, and problem-solving—improvements that surpass those produced by other treatment interventions (Bustillo, 2023; Singh et al., 2023). Moreover, these improvements extend to the client's everyday life and social relationships (Zhu et al., 2020).

cognitive remediation A treatment that focuses on the cognitive impairments that often characterize people with schizophrenia—particularly their difficulties in attention, planning, and memory.

HALLUCINATION REINTERPRETATION AND ACCEPTANCE As you also read earlier, one of the cognitive-behavioral explanations for schizophrenia starts with the premise that people with the disorder do indeed actually hear voices (or experience other kinds of hallucinations) as a result of biologically triggered sensations. According to this theory, the journey into schizophrenia takes shape when people try to make sense of these strange sensations and conclude incorrectly that the voices are coming from external sources, that they are being persecuted, or another such notion. These misinterpretations are essentially delusions.

With this explanation in mind, many clinicians now employ a cognitive-behavioral treatment for schizophrenia to help change how people view and react to their hallucinations (Hardy & Turkington, 2024; Johns et al., 2021). The therapists believe that if people can be guided to interpret such experiences in a more accurate way, they will not feel the fear and confusion produced by their delusional misinterpretations. The clinicians may, for example, provide clients with education and evidence about the biological causes of hallucinations, challenge their inaccurate ideas about the power of their hallucinations, and teach them to reattribute and more accurately interpret their hallucinations. Clients may, for example, adopt and apply alternative conclusions such as "It's not a real voice, it's my illness." These cognitive-behavioral techniques often help people with schizophrenia feel like they have more control over their hallucinations and reduce their delusional ideas (Hardy & Turkington, 2024; Bustillo, 2023).

The approach of *third-wave cognitive-behavioral therapists,* including practitioners of *acceptance and commitment therapy,* has gained particular prominence as a way to lessen the personal impact of hallucinations. As you read earlier in the textbook, third-wave cognitive-behavioral therapists believe that the most useful goal of treatment is often to help clients *accept* their streams of problematic thoughts rather than to judge them, act on them, or try fruitlessly to change them. The therapists, for example, help highly anxious individuals to become simply *mindful* of the worries that engulf their thinking and to *accept* such negative thoughts as harmless events of the mind. Similarly, in cases of schizophrenia, third-wave cognitive-behavioral therapists try to help clients become detached and comfortable observers of their hallucinations—merely mindful of the unusual sensations and accepting of them—while otherwise moving forward with the tasks and events of their lives.

Paul Brown/REX/Shutterstock

Shared delusions When two or more persons share a delusion or hallucination, it is called *folie à deux* or *shared psychosis.* An Internet version of this seems to be the online preoccupation by many users with *Slender Man,* a mythical "boogie man" whom some people report seeing in their everyday lives. (He is portrayed here at a science fiction convention.) In an infamous case, two 12-year-old girls stabbed a classmate multiple times to appease and impress Slender Man. Clinicians later testified that each assailant had a schizophrenia spectrum disorder.

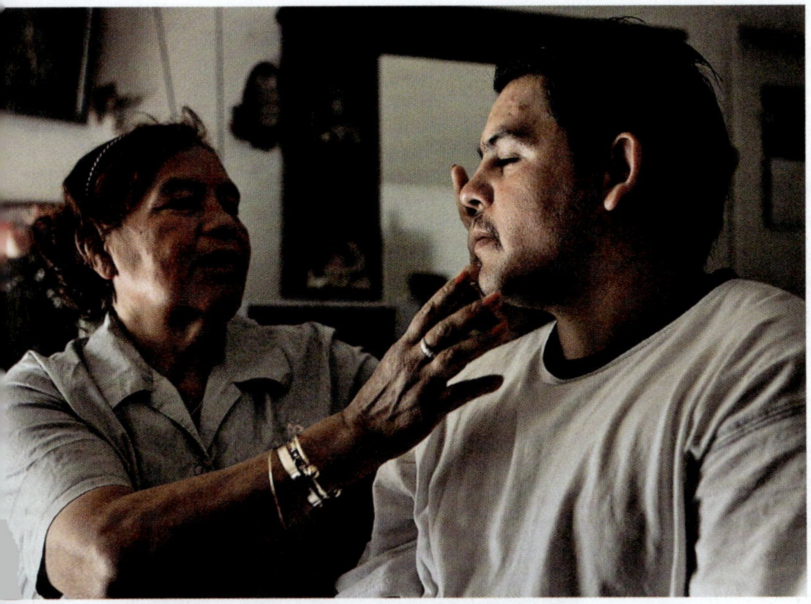

Robert Gauthier/Los Angeles Times via Getty Images

Engaging the family Research indicates that people with schizophrenia make more progress in treatment when they feel positive toward their family. Thus, family involvement, including family therapy, is now often a significant part of treatment. Here a loving mother, Maria Orduna, caresses her son Alfredo during his visit to her apartment. Alfredo has suffered through housing insecurity, poverty, and jail, largely because of his schizophrenic disorder.

Studies indicate that these various cognitive-behavioral treatments are often very helpful to clients with schizophrenia (Gaudiano & Ellenberg, 2022; Johns et al., 2021; Liu, Li, & Hsiao, 2021). Many clients who receive such treatments report that they feel less distressed by their hallucinations and that they have fewer delusions. Indeed, they are often able to shed the diagnosis of schizophrenia. Rehospitalizations decrease considerably among clients treated with cognitive-behavioral therapy.

Family Therapy

Many persons who are recovering from schizophrenia and other severe mental disorders live with their families: parents, siblings, spouses, or children. Such situations create special pressures; even if family stress was not a factor in the onset of the disorder, a patient's recovery may be strongly influenced by the behavior and reactions of relatives at home.

Generally speaking, people with schizophrenia who feel positive toward their relatives do better in treatment (Bustillo, 2023). As you read earlier, recovered patients living with relatives who display high levels of *expressed emotion*—that is, relatives who are very critical, emotionally overinvolved, and hostile—often have a much higher relapse rate than those living with more positive and supportive relatives (Shetty et al., 2023; Hahlweg & Baucom, 2022). Moreover, for their part, family members may be very upset by the social withdrawal and unusual behaviors of a relative with schizophrenia (Jones, 2020).

To address such issues, clinicians now commonly include family therapy in their treatment of schizophrenia, providing family members with guidance, training, practical advice, education about the disorder, and emotional support and empathy (Bustillo, 2023; Tessier et al., 2023). In family therapy, relatives develop more realistic expectations and become more tolerant, less guilt-ridden, and more willing to try new patterns of communication. Family therapy also helps the person with schizophrenia cope with the pressures of family life, make better use of family members, and avoid troublesome interactions. Research has found that family therapy—particularly when it is combined with drug therapy—helps reduce tensions within the family and so helps relapse rates and hospital readmissions go down (Tessier et al., 2023; Rodolico et al., 2022).

The families of people with schizophrenia and other severe mental disorders may also turn to *family support groups* and *family psychoeducational programs* for encouragement and advice (NIMH, 2023; Tessier et al., 2023; Issac et al., 2022). In such programs, family members meet with others in the same situation to share their thoughts and emotions, provide mutual support, and learn about schizophrenia.

Coordinated Specialty Care

Many clinicians believe that, in addition to therapy, treatment for people with schizophrenia must address the social and personal difficulties in their lives. These clinicians offer practical advice; work with clients on problem-solving, memory enhancement, decision-making, and social skills; make sure that the clients are taking their medications properly; and may even help them find work, financial assistance, appropriate health care, and proper housing (NIMH, 2023).

This practical, active, and broad approach is called **coordinated specialty care** (CSC) because it is typically offered by a team of health specialists rather than a single therapist. It is provided particularly to people with newly developing schizophrenia and is applied as early as possible. Research finds that CSC does indeed help keep such individuals out of the hospital (Bustillo, 2023; NIMH, 2022).

coordinated specialty care (CSC) A treatment approach for people with severe mental disorders in which clinicians provide interventions ranging from therapy and practical advice to medication monitoring, housing guidance, and vocational counseling.

deinstitutionalization The discharge of large numbers of patients from long-term institutional care so that they might be treated in community programs.

AP Photo/John Minchillo

The pandemic and community mental health During the shutdown phase of the Covid-19 pandemic, mental health professionals journeyed into the community to treat clients rather than have the clients travel to their offices. Here Dr. Jeanie Tse (right), chief medical officer at the Institute for Community Living in New York City, treats a patient with schizophrenia on the street outside his home during a 2020 treatment session.

The Community Approach

The broadest approach for the treatment of schizophrenia and other severe mental disorders is the *community approach*. In 1963, partly in response to the terrible conditions in public mental institutions and partly because of the emergence of antipsychotic drugs, the U.S. government ordered that patients be discharged and treated in the community. Congress passed the *Community Mental Health Act*, which stipulated that patients with psychological disorders were to receive a range of mental health services—outpatient therapy, inpatient treatment, emergency care, preventive care, and aftercare—in their communities rather than being transported to institutions far from home. The act was aimed at a variety of psychological disorders, but patients diagnosed with schizophrenia and other severe disorders, especially those who had been institutionalized for years, were affected most. Other countries around the world put similar sociocultural treatment programs into action shortly thereafter.

Thus began several decades of **deinstitutionalization,** an exodus of hundreds of thousands of patients with schizophrenia and other long-term mental disorders from state institutions into the community. On a given day in 1955, close to 600,000 patients were living in state institutions; today, the daily patient population in the same kinds of hospitals is between 38,000 and 75,000 (AHA, 2023, 2019; BH, 2023, 2022, 2020; Hudson, 2021). Clinicians have learned that patients recovering from schizophrenia and other severe disorders can benefit greatly from community programs (Bustillo, 2023). As you will read, however, the actual quality of community care for these people has often been inadequate throughout the United States. The result is a "revolving door" pattern for many patients. They are discharged to the community, readmitted to an institution within months, discharged a second time, admitted yet again, and so on, over and over (Bravo et al., 2022).

How might the "revolving door" pattern itself worsen the symptoms and outlook of people with schizophrenia?

What Are the Features of Effective Community Care?

Consistent with the philosophy of coordinated specialty care, an important principle of the community mental health approach is that people with schizophrenia and other

"Court to Community" Denver, Colorado, has established a program called "Court to Community," which diverts people with severe mental disorders—especially those who keep committing misdemeanor offenses—into court-monitored mental health programs rather than jails and prisons. People who are repeatedly charged with crimes, like this man with schizophrenia who has been in jail more than 30 times, plead their cases to the program's judges, who determine whether the individuals are taking their medications, avoiding illicit drug use, and attending therapy sessions.

Craig F. Walker/Getty Images

severe mental disorders do best when they are treated by a multidisciplinary team of health professionals and have access to multiple services. In a leading community approach—called **assertive community treatment**—the team provides medication, psychotherapy, numerous patient–staff contacts, help in handling daily pressures and responsibilities, guidance in making decisions, social skills training, residential supervision, and vocational counseling (Mueser, 2022). When this kind of approach is available in a community, residents with schizophrenia and other severe mental disorders make more progress, have fewer hospitalizations, and avoid houselessness more successfully than do people living in communities without the approach (NIMH, 2023).

Some other key features of effective community care programs are (1) coordination of patient services, (2) short-term hospitalization, (3) partial hospitalization, (4) supervised residencies, and (5) occupational training.

of NOTE ...

Their Words

"It must . . . have been profoundly demoralizing for him to have conversations always focused on fixing up his illness."

Anne Deveson
Tell Me I'm Here: One Family's Experience of Schizophrenia

COORDINATED SERVICES When the Community Mental Health Act was first passed, it was expected that community care would be provided by **community mental health centers,** treatment facilities that would supply medication, psychotherapy, and inpatient emergency care to people with severe disturbances as well as help coordinate the services offered by other community agencies. When community mental health centers are available and provide these services, clients with schizophrenia and other severe disorders often make significant progress (Bustillo, 2023; Mueser, 2022). Coordination of services is particularly important for clients who display both a severe mental disorder and a substance use disorder, a pattern called *dual diagnosis,* or *co-occurring disorder* (Campbell, Caroff, & Mann, 2022).

SHORT-TERM HOSPITALIZATION When people develop severe psychotic symptoms, today's clinicians first try to treat them on an outpatient basis, usually with a combination of antipsychotic medication and psychotherapy. If this approach fails, they may try *short-term hospitalization*—in a mental hospital or a general hospital's psychiatric unit—that lasts days or a few weeks (rather than months or years) (NAMI, 2023; Burns & Kendrick, 2020). Soon after the patients improve, they are discharged and move on to **aftercare,** a general term for follow-up care and treatment in the community. Because short-term hospitalization often leads to more improvement and a lower rehospitalization rate than extended institutionalization, countries throughout the world now favor it over long-term institutionalization.

PARTIAL HOSPITALIZATION People's needs may fall between full hospitalization and outpatient therapy, and so some communities offer **day centers,** or **day hospitals,** all-day programs in which patients return to their homes for the night. Day centers provide patients with daily supervised activities, therapy, and programs to improve social skills. People recovering from severe disorders in day centers often do better and have fewer relapses than those who spend extended periods in a hospital or in traditional outpatient therapy (Bustillo, 2023; NAMI, 2023). Another kind of institution that has become a popular setting for the treatment of people with schizophrenia and other severe disorders is the *residential crisis center* (NAMI, 2023). These are structures in the community that provide 24-hour nursing care for people with severe mental disorders. Many individuals who would otherwise be cared for in state hospitals are now being transferred to these centers.

SUPERVISED GROUP HOUSES Many people do not require hospitalization but are unable to live alone or with their families. **Supervised group houses,** also known as *halfway houses, crisis houses,* or *group homes,* often serve individuals well (NAMI, 2023). Such residences may shelter between one dozen and two dozen people. The live-in staff usually are *paraprofessionals*—laypeople who receive training and ongoing supervision from outside mental health professionals. The houses are typically run with a *milieu therapy* philosophy that emphasizes mutual support, resident responsibility, and self-government. Some supervised group houses, called *partially supervised group houses,* provide less than 24/7 staff support. Research indicates that supervised group houses help many people recovering from schizophrenia and other severe disorders adjust to community life and avoid rehospitalization (NAMI, 2023; Mueser, 2022). Here is how one man described living in such a house after multiple hospitalizations:

Overall, my group home was a good experience. I probably couldn't have lived on my own at the time. The word was that our home was one of the better ones—I was lucky my parents paid. People who'd been in other group homes said the staff was disorganized and turned over constantly, and the meals weren't good.

At our home, we got three solid meals a day. After the hospital, it seemed like total freedom. I could do what I wanted, no one forced me to bathe on their schedule, staff didn't boss me around. I just had to go to therapy sessions, take my medicine, and stick to our "code of conduct." Of course, it was tough living with so many people, supervised all the time. Plus, the curfew was a drag.

There were 18 of us when I first got there, and I think it got as high as 21. There were six staff members, a couple of them former residents. Decisions got voted on by everyone, which I liked, except one time when the group voted to discipline a buddy of mine for breaking curfew repeatedly.

The best part was making friends. We were going through the same thing, and we looked out for each other. If one of us improved, it felt like we were all improving. I'd always been nervous around people who weren't like me, but I learned I could be friends with different kinds of people, including a Black guy and Chilean guy that I got especially close to. There were a few people who kept to themselves, but the rest of us supported each other. In group sessions, I heard from people who had lived in the community on their own—they'd talk about what to do if the hallucinations started again or how to readjust to living on the outside. Altogether, I stayed at the group home for a year. I'm not sure I would have made it if I hadn't lived there.

OCCUPATIONAL TRAINING AND SUPPORT Paid employment provides income, independence, self-respect, and the stimulation of working with others. It also brings companionship and order to one's daily life. For these reasons, occupational training and placement are important services for people with schizophrenia and other severe mental disorders (Bustillo, 2023; Gjerdalen et al., 2023).

assertive community treatment A community approach for people with severe mental disorders in which a multidisciplinary team provides interventions ranging from medications and therapy to residential and vocational guidance.

community mental health center A treatment facility that provides medication, psychotherapy, and emergency care for psychological problems and coordinates treatment in the community.

aftercare A program of posthospitalization care and treatment in the community.

day center A program that offers hospital-like treatment during the day only. Also known as a *day hospital.*

supervised group house A residence for people with schizophrenia or other severe problems, often staffed by paraprofessionals. Also known as *halfway house, crisis house,* or *group home.*

Community outreach Unhoused people are more likely to develop schizophrenia, and having schizophrenia increases one's chances of becoming unhoused. Thus, Briana Daniel founded and directs the Street Team Movement, a volunteer program that helps people experiencing housing insecurity in Orlando, Florida, to address their clothing, laundry, hygiene, and mental health needs.

Kevin Spear/Orlando Sentinel/TNS via Getty Images

Many people recovering from such disorders receive occupational training in a **sheltered workshop**—a supervised workplace for employees who are not ready for competitive or complicated jobs. The workshop replicates a typical work environment: products such as toys or simple appliances are manufactured and sold, workers are paid according to performance, and they are expected to be at work regularly and on time. In the United States, however, occupational training of this kind is not consistently available to people with severe mental disorders.

An alternative work opportunity for people with severe psychological disorders is **supported employment,** an increasingly popular approach in which vocational agencies and counselors help clients find competitive jobs in the community and provide psychological support while the clients are employed (NIMH, 2023; Zürcher et al., 2023). According to research, the supported employment approach is more effective than sheltered workshops in helping people with severe disorders to enter or return to competitive employment (Park et al., 2022). Nevertheless, like sheltered workshops, supported employment opportunities are often in short supply, and fewer than 25 percent of individuals with severe psychological disorders have jobs in the competitive job market (Gjerdalen et al., 2023; Holm et al., 2021).

How Has Community Treatment Failed?

There is no doubt that effective community programs can help people with schizophrenia and other severe mental disorders recover. However, fewer than half of all the people who need appropriate community mental health services receive them (Vece, 2020). In fact, as you read earlier in the chapter, in any given year, 40 percent of people with severe mental disorders do not receive treatment from any kind of mental health specialist or program (TAC, 2022). Two factors are primarily responsible: *poor coordination* of services and a *shortage* of services.

sheltered workshop A supervised workplace for people who are not yet ready for competitive jobs.

supported employment An approach to employment in which vocational agencies and counselors help clients find competitive jobs in the community and provide psychological support while the clients are employed.

case manager A community therapist who offers and coordinates a full range of services for people with severe mental disorders, including therapy, advice, medication supervision, guidance through the community system, and protection of patients' rights.

POOR COORDINATION OF SERVICES The various mental health agencies in a community often fail to communicate with one another (McBain et al., 2021; Burns & Kendrick, 2020). There may be an opening at a nearby supervised group house, for example, and the therapist at the community mental health center may not know about it. In addition, even within a community agency, a patient may not have continuing contacts with the same staff members and may fail to receive consistent services. Still another problem is

Jorge Sanz/SOPA Images/LightRocket via Getty Images

Perilous impact During the Covid-19 pandemic, firefighters on a balcony in Spain search for a missing man who experiences psychosis—later found safe in a nearby forest. Research has shown that during epidemics and pandemics, people with schizophrenia tend to experience poorer functioning, heightened confusion, and a greater suicide risk—effects linked to their symptoms, elevated vulnerability to stressful situations, special needs for social support, and relatively low use of cell phones, texting, Zoom, and social media (Brown et al., 2020).

poor communication between mental hospitals and community mental health centers, particularly at times of patients' discharge.

To help deal with such problems in communication and coordination, community therapists may act as **case managers** for people with schizophrenia and other severe mental disorders (Bustillo, 2023). In addition to providing therapy, advice, and medication guidance, they try to coordinate available community services, guide clients through the community system, and help protect clients' legal rights. Many professionals now believe that effective case management is the key to success for a community program, and emerging research supports their view (Lim et al., 2022).

SHORTAGE OF SERVICES The number of community programs—community mental health centers, supervised group houses, and sheltered workshops—available to people with severe mental disorders falls woefully short (NYTEB, 2022; McBain et al., 2021). In addition, a number of the community mental health centers that do exist generally fail to provide adequate services for people with severe disorders. They tend to devote their efforts and money to people with less disabling problems, such as anxiety disorders or problems in social adjustment (SAMHSA, 2023; Torrey, 2019).

There are various reasons for this shortage of services. One of the primary factors is economic. On the one hand, more public funds are available for people with psychological disorders now than in the past. (*Public funds* refers to money provided by federal, state, and local governments as opposed to patient out-of-pocket payments and private insurance payments.) In 1963, a total of $1 billion in public funding was spent on mental health needs, whereas in 2020, approximately $179 billion in public funding was devoted to this realm (Statista, 2023; SAMHSA, 2020, 2014; AHA, 2019). This represents a significant increase even when inflation and so-called real dollars are factored in. At the same time, however, rather little of the additional money is going to community treatment programs for people with severe disorders (NYTEB, 2022; McBain et al., 2021). Much of it goes instead to prescription drugs, monthly income payments such as Social Security Disability Insurance, services for people with mental disorders in nursing homes and general hospitals, and community services for people who are experiencing less dysfunction. Moreover, today, much of the cost of community treatment for people with severe mental disorders falls on state and local governments rather than the federal government, and these more local sources of funding cannot always meet the challenge.

of NOTE ...

Addressing the Shortage

Clinical administrators estimate that an additional 123,000 beds are needed in mental hospitals in the United States to meet the inpatient needs of people with severe mental disorders (BH, 2023, 2020; Cahalan, 2020).

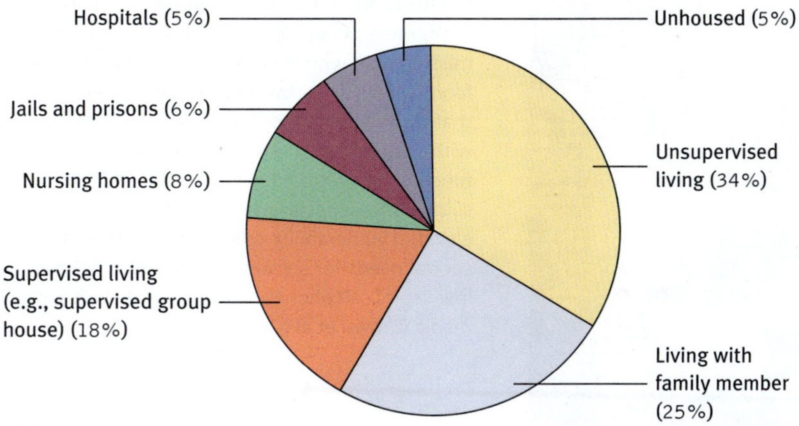

FIGURE 12-5

Where Do People with Schizophrenia Live?

According to some calculations, more than one-third live in unsupervised residences, 6 percent are incarcerated, and 5 percent are unhoused. (Information from Torrey, 2019, 2001.)

The shortages and unavailability of community services seem to particularly affect people of color. Research indicates, for example, that Black Americans and other people of color with schizophrenia are less likely than non-Hispanic White Americans with the disorder to receive proper community care, preventive interventions, cognitive-behavioral therapy, family therapy, or the more effective second-generation antipsychotic drugs, and they are more likely to be attended to in hospital emergency departments or to receive no care at all (AHRQ, 2023, 2022; Heun-Johnson et al., 2021; Petti et al., 2021). Various explanations have been proposed for such inferior care, including poverty-linked factors, transportation issues, inadequate health insurance, bias and discrimination in some mental health settings, and negative beliefs by people of color about mental health services. Many clinicians believe that LGBTQ+ people with schizophrenia similarly receive less adequate community care and fewer positive interventions than cisgender and heterosexual people with the disorder; however, systematic research into this impression has not yet been conducted (DeLuca et al., 2022; Keuroghlian, 2022).

What Are the Consequences of Inadequate Community Treatment?

What happens to people with schizophrenia and other severe disorders whose communities do not provide the services they need and whose families cannot afford private treatment (see **Figure 12-5**)? As you have read, 40 percent receive no treatment at all; many others spend a short time in a state hospital or residential crisis center and are then discharged prematurely, often without adequate follow-up treatment (NAMI, 2023).

These individuals live in various settings (MHA, 2023; Torrey, 2019, 2001). Many return to their families and receive medication and perhaps emotional and financial support but little else in the way of treatment. According to some estimates, around 8 percent enter an alternative institution such as a nursing home or rest home, where they receive only custodial care and medication. As many as 18 percent are placed in privately run residences where supervision often is provided by untrained staff—foster

© Renée C. B[illegible]/ZUMA Press Wire

Mental health needs versus civil rights

Known as "the most famous 'homeless' man in California" during his 16 years of living on the streets, Mark Rippee (right) became the face of ongoing policy battles between civil libertarians who oppose involuntary treatment and families who want to intervene on behalf of loved ones with severe psychological and medical conditions. Rippee's sisters repeatedly petitioned to have their unhoused brother cared for, saying that he himself was unable to appreciate the depths of his problems and needs, including schizophrenia and full vision loss, but the state's protective civil rights laws prevented any interventions against Rippee's will. Rippee died of pneumonia and sepsis in 2022.

George Etheredge/The New York Times/Redux

The slide Friends gather at a heated grate in New York City to hold a 2016 memorial service for Nakesha Williams, who died at age 46 of a pulmonary embolism and related health problems after living on the streets for eight years. A standout 1993 graduate of Williams College, Williams eventually developed deeply entrenched psychotic symptoms that severely limited her ability to cope. She resisted all efforts by outreach workers, friends, and acquaintances to help her get shelter, psychological help, and medication.

homes (small or large), boardinghouses, care homes, and similar facilities. These residences vary greatly in quality. Some of them are legitimate "bed and care" facilities, providing three meals a day, medication reminders, and at least a small degree of staff supervision. However, many do not offer even these minimal services.

Another 34 percent of people with schizophrenia and other severe disorders live in totally unsupervised settings. Some are equal to the challenge of living alone, supporting themselves effectively and maintaining nicely furnished apartments. But others cannot really function independently and wind up in run-down single-room occupancy hotels (SROs) or rooming houses. They may live in conditions that are substandard and unsafe, which may exacerbate their disorder. Many survive on government disability payments, and a number spend their days wandering through neighborhood streets.

Finally, a great number of people with schizophrenia and other severe disorders have become unhoused. There are 565,000 unhoused people in the United States, and approximately 140,000 of them have a severe mental disorder, commonly schizophrenia (MIPO, 2022). Many have been discharged from hospitals. Others are young adults who were never hospitalized in the first place. Moreover, in the United States, as many as 450,000 people with severe mental disorders are in prisons and jails (that is, one-third of all incarcerated people), often because their disorders have led them to break the law (WPB, 2023; MIPO, 2022; Ornstein & Leifman, 2022). Certainly, deinstitutionalization and the community mental health movement have failed them.

of NOTE ...

Unmet Treatment Needs

- People with severe mental disorders are 10 times more likely to be in a prison than in a mental hospital.
- The Los Angeles jail system, with thousands of inmates requiring mental health services, is now in effect the largest mental institution in the United States.
- 63 percent of people with a history of mental disorders do not receive mental health treatment while incarcerated in state and federal prisons.

(Binswanger & Elmore, 2023; NAMI, 2023; McCann, 2022; Ornstein & Leifman, 2022)

The Promise of Community Treatment

Despite these serious problems, proper community care has shown great potential for assisting people in recovering from schizophrenia and other severe disorders, and clinicians and many government officials continue to press to make it more available (NYTEB, 2022).

In addition, a number of *national interest groups* have formed in countries around the world that push for better community treatment. In the United States, for example, the *National Alliance on Mental Illness* (*NAMI*) began in 1979 with 300 members and has expanded into an organization composed of 650 local affiliates and state organizations and many tens of thousands of members (NAMI, 2023). Made up largely of families and people affected by severe mental disorders (particularly schizophrenia, bipolar disorders, and major depressive disorder), NAMI has become not only a source of information, support, and guidance for its members but also a powerful lobbying force in state and national legislatures, and it has pressured community mental health centers to treat more people with schizophrenia and other severe disorders.

Today, community care is a major feature of treatment for people recovering from severe mental disorders in countries around the world. Both in the United States and abroad, well-coordinated community treatment is seen as an important part of the solution to the problem of severe mental dysfunction (Bustillo, 2023).

SUMMING UP

How Are Schizophrenia and Other Severe Mental Disorders Treated?

For more than half of the twentieth century, the main treatment for schizophrenia and other severe mental disorders was institutionalization and custodial care. In the 1950s, two in-hospital approaches were developed that often brought improvement: milieu therapy and token economy programs.

The discovery of antipsychotic drugs in the 1950s revolutionized the treatment of schizophrenia and other disorders marked by psychosis. Theorists believe that the first-generation antipsychotic drugs operate by reducing excessive dopamine activity in the brain. They can, however, also produce movement disorders called extrapyramidal effects, which include parkinsonism and tardive dyskinesia. An important development in the field has been the discovery and use of second-generation antipsychotic drugs such as clozapine and risperidone; these cause fewer extrapyramidal effects than the first-generation drugs.

Psychotherapy is often employed successfully in combination with antipsychotic drugs. Helpful forms include cognitive-behavioral therapy, family therapy, and coordinated specialty care. Family support groups and family psychoeducational programs are also growing in number.

A community approach to the treatment of schizophrenia and other severe mental disorders began in the 1960s, when a policy of deinstitutionalization in the United States brought about a mass exodus of hundreds of thousands of patients from state institutions into the community. An important feature of community care is assertive community treatment. Unfortunately, the quality and funding of community care for people with schizophrenia and other severe disorders have been inadequate throughout the United States, often resulting in a "revolving door" pattern. One consequence is that many people with such disorders are now unhoused or in prison.

An Important Lesson

AFTER YEARS OF frustration and failure, clinicians now have an arsenal of services and supports with which to treat schizophrenia and other disorders marked by psychosis—medication, institutional programs, psychotherapy, and community programs. It has become clear that antipsychotic medications open the door for recovery from these disorders, but in most cases other kinds of treatment are also needed to help the recovery process along. The various approaches must be combined in a way that meets each individual's specific needs.

Working with schizophrenia and other severe disorders has taught therapists an important lesson: no matter how compelling the evidence for biological causation may be, a strictly biological approach to the treatment of psychological disorders is

of NOTE ...

Their Words

"I doubt if ever the history of the world . . . could show a larger amount of insanity than that of the present day."

John Hawkes, physician and author
On the Increase of Insanity, 1857

a mistake more often than not. Largely on the basis of biological discoveries and pharmacological advances, hundreds of thousands of patients with schizophrenia and other severe mental disorders were released to their communities in the 1960s. Little attention was paid to their psychological and sociocultural needs, and many have been trapped in their pathology ever since. Clinicians must remember this lesson, especially in today's climate, when managed care and government priorities often promote medication as the sole treatment for psychological problems.

Why do so many people continue to perceive most people with schizophrenia as dangerous and violent despite evidence to the contrary?

The treatment and recovery picture for people with schizophrenia has progressed considerably over the past 125 years, especially during the past half-century, but it still has far to go. Studies suggest that the recovery rates—both partial and full—could be considerably higher than they are. It is unacceptable that so many people with this and other severe mental disorders receive few or none of the effective community interventions that have been developed, and it is worse still that hundreds of thousands of these people have become unhoused or imprisoned. It is now up to clinicians, along with public officials, to address the needs of all people with schizophrenia and other severe disorders.

Quick Quiz

1. What is schizophrenia, and how prevalent is it? What is its relation to socioeconomic class? pp. 389–390
2. What are the positive, negative, and psychomotor symptoms of schizophrenia? pp. 391–395
3. Describe the genetic, biochemical, brain circuitry, and viral explanations of schizophrenia and discuss how they have been supported in research. pp. 398–402
4. What are the key features of the psychodynamic, cognitive-behavioral, multicultural, social labeling, family, and developmental psychopathology explanations of schizophrenia? pp. 402–408
5. Describe institutional care for people with schizophrenia and other severe mental disorders over the course of the twentieth century. How effective are the milieu and token economy treatment programs? pp. 411–413
6. How do antipsychotic drugs operate on the brain? How do first-generation antipsychotic and second-generation antipsychotic drugs differ? pp. 413–416
7. How effective are antipsychotic drugs in the treatment of schizophrenia? What are the unwanted effects of first-generation antipsychotic drugs? pp. 413–416
8. What kinds of psychotherapy seem to help people with schizophrenia and other disorders marked by psychosis? pp. 416–418
9. What is deinstitutionalization? What features of community care seem critical for helping people with schizophrenia and other severe mental disorders? pp. 419–422
10. How and why has the community mental health approach been inadequate for many people with severe mental disorders? pp. 422–425

CHAPTER 13

Personality Disorders

TOPIC OVERVIEW

While interviewing for the job of editor of a start-up news website, Frederick said, "This may sound self-serving, but I am extraordinarily gifted. I am certain that I will do great things in this position. I and the Osterman Post will soon set the standard for journalism and blogging in the country. Within a year, we'll be looking at the HuffPost in the rearview mirror." The committee was impressed. Frederick's self-confidence and boldness had wowed them.

A year later, many of the same individuals were describing Frederick differently—arrogant, self-serving, cold, egomaniacal, draining. He had performed well as editor (though not as spectacularly as he seemed to think), but that performance could not outweigh his impossible personality. Colleagues below and above him had grown weary of his manipulations, emotional outbursts, refusal ever to take the blame, nonstop boasting, and grandiose plans. Once again, Frederick had outworn his welcome.

To be sure, Frederick had great charm, and he knew how to make others feel important—when it served his purpose. Thus, he always had his share of friends and admirers. But in reality, they were just passing through—until Frederick would tire of them or feel betrayed by their lack of enthusiasm for one of his self-serving interpretations or grand plans or until they simply could take Frederick no longer.

Bright and successful though he was, Frederick always felt entitled to more than he was receiving—to higher grades at school, greater compensation at work, more attention from friends. If criticized even slightly, he reacted with fury and was certain that the critic was jealous of him. At first glance, Frederick seemed to have a lot going for him socially. Typically, he could be found in the midst of a romantic relationship—in which he might be tender and seemingly devoted. But Frederick would always tire of his partner within a few weeks or months and would turn cold or even mean. He often had affairs with other people while still involved with the current partner. The breakups rarely brought sadness or remorse to him, and he would almost never think about his former partners again. He always had himself.

Each of us has a *personality*—a set of uniquely expressed characteristics that influence our behaviors, emotions, thoughts, and interactions. Our particular characteristics, often called *personality traits,* lead us to react in fairly predictable ways as we move through life. Yet our personalities are also flexible. We learn from experience. As we interact with our surroundings, we try out various responses to determine which feel better and which are more effective. This is a flexibility that people with a personality disorder usually do not have.

People with a **personality disorder** display an enduring, rigid pattern of inner experience and outward behavior that impairs their sense of self, emotional experiences, goals, capacity for empathy, and/or capacity for intimacy (APA, 2022; see **Table 13-1**). Put another way, they have personality traits that are much more extreme and dysfunctional than those of most other people in their culture, leading to significant problems and psychological pain for themselves or others.

Frederick appears to display a personality disorder. For most of his life, his extreme narcissism, grandiosity, and insensitivity have led to poor functioning in both the personal and the social realms. They have caused him to repeatedly feel angry and unappreciated, deprived him of close personal relationships, and brought considerable pain to others. Note also the upset and turmoil felt by Frederick's coworkers and romantic partners.

Matt Manley

TABLE 13-1

Dx Checklist

Personality Disorder
1. Individual displays a long-term, rigid, and wide-ranging pattern of inner experience and behavior that leads to dysfunction in at least two of the following realms: ■ Cognition ■ Emotion ■ Social interactions ■ Impulsivity
2. The individual's pattern is significantly different from ones usually found in their culture.
3. Individual experiences significant distress or impairment.

Information from: APA, 2022.

The symptoms of personality disorders last for years and typically become recognizable in adolescence or early adulthood, although some symptoms may begin during childhood. These disorders are among the most difficult psychological disorders to treat. Many people with the disorders are not even aware of their personality problems and fail to trace their difficulties to their maladaptive style of thinking and behaving. Surveys indicate that as many as 11 percent of all adults in the United States display a personality disorder at any given time (Zimmerman, 2023; APA, 2022).

It is common for a person with a personality disorder to also experience another disorder, a relationship called *comorbidity* (McGrath & Reynolds, 2024). As you will read later in this chapter, for example, many people with avoidant personality disorder, who fearfully shy away from all relationships, also display social anxiety disorder. The presence of a personality disorder complicates a person's chances for a successful recovery from other psychological problems.

DSM-5-TR identifies 10 personality disorders (APA, 2022). Often these disorders are separated into three groups, or *clusters*. One cluster, marked by odd or eccentric behavior, consists of the *paranoid, schizoid,* and *schizotypal* personality disorders. A second cluster features dramatic behavior and consists of the *antisocial, borderline, histrionic,* and *narcissistic* personality disorders. The final cluster features a high degree of anxiety and includes the *avoidant, dependent,* and *obsessive-compulsive* personality disorders.

These 10 personality disorders are each characterized by a group of problematic personality symptoms. For example, as you will soon learn, *paranoid personality disorder* is diagnosed when a person has unjustified suspicions about being harmed by others, has persistent unfounded doubts about the loyalty of friends, reads threatening meanings into benign events, persistently bears grudges, and has recurrent unjustified suspicions about the faithfulness of life partners.

The DSM's listing of 10 distinct personality disorders is called a *categorical* approach. Like a light switch that is either on or off, this kind of approach assumes that (1) problematic personality traits are either present or absent in people, (2) a personality disorder is either displayed or not displayed by a person, and (3) a person with a personality disorder is not markedly troubled by personality traits outside of that disorder.

It turns out, however, that these assumptions are frequently contradicted in clinical practice. In fact, the symptoms of the personality disorders listed in DSM-5-TR overlap so much that clinicians often find it difficult to distinguish one disorder from another, resulting in frequent disagreements about which diagnosis is correct for a person with a personality disorder (McGrath & Reynolds, 2024). Diagnosticians sometimes even determine that particular people have more than one personality disorder (Widiger, Hines, & Crego, 2024). This lack of agreement has raised serious questions about the *validity* (accuracy) and *reliability* (consistency) of the 10 DSM-5-TR personality disorder categories.

Is hatred a disorder? With the term "Skinhead" tattooed on the back of his head, this man awaits trial in Germany for committing neo-Nazi crimes against foreigners and liberals. Clinicians sometimes confront extreme racism and intolerance, particularly among clients with paranoid, antisocial, and certain other personality disorders. Some in the clinical field would like to classify extreme hatred and prejudice as a psychological disorder.

Reuters/Matthias Hiekel

Given this state of affairs, many theorists have challenged the use of a categorical approach to personality disorders. They believe that personality disorders differ more in *degree* than in type of dysfunction and should instead be classified by the severity of personality traits rather than by the presence or absence of specific traits—a procedure called a *dimensional* approach. In a dimensional approach, each trait is viewed as varying along a continuum extending from nonproblematic to extremely problematic. People with a personality disorder are those who display extreme degrees of problematic traits—degrees not commonly found in the general population.

As noted above, despite the growing enthusiasm for a dimensional approach, DSM-5-TR retains a categorical approach for the classification of personality disorders. At the same time, however, it describes an *alternative* dimensional approach that should be considered for adoption in future editions of the DSM. Most of the discussions in this chapter are organized around the 10-disorder categorical approach used in DSM-5-TR. Later in the chapter, we will examine possible alternative—dimensional—approaches of the future, including the one presented in DSM-5-TR.

As you read about the various personality disorders, you should be clear that diagnoses of such disorders can be assigned too often. We may catch glimpses of ourselves or of people we know in the descriptions of these disorders and be tempted to conclude that we or they have a personality disorder. In the vast majority of instances, such interpretations are incorrect. We all display personality traits. Only occasionally are they so maladaptive, distressing, and inflexible that they can be considered disorders. ■

personality disorder An enduring, rigid pattern of inner experience and outward behavior that repeatedly impairs one's sense of self, emotional experiences, goals, capacity for empathy, and/or capacity for intimacy.

paranoid personality disorder A personality disorder marked by a pattern of distrust and suspiciousness of others.

SUMMING UP

Personality Disorders and DSM-5-TR

People with a personality disorder display an enduring, rigid pattern of inner experience and outward behavior. Their personality traits are much more extreme and dysfunctional than those of most other people in their culture, resulting in significant problems for them or those around them. It has been estimated that as many as 11 percent of adults display such a disorder at any given time. DSM-5-TR uses a categorical approach that lists 10 distinct personality disorders. In addition, the framers of DSM-5-TR have proposed a dimensional approach to the classification of personality disorders.

"Odd" Personality Disorders

THE CLUSTER OF "odd" personality disorders, as DSM-5-TR characterizes them, consists of the *paranoid, schizoid,* and *schizotypal* personality disorders. People with these disorders typically have odd or eccentric behaviors that are similar to but not as extensive as those on display in schizophrenia, including extreme suspiciousness, social withdrawal, and peculiar ways of thinking and perceiving things. Such behaviors often leave the person isolated. Some clinicians believe that these personality disorders are related to schizophrenia. Directly related or not, people with an odd-cluster personality disorder often qualify for an additional diagnosis of schizophrenia or have close relatives with schizophrenia.

Why do you think personality disorders attract so many efforts at amateur psychology?

Clinicians have learned much about the symptoms of the odd-cluster personality disorders but have not been so successful in determining their causes or how to treat them. In fact, as you will soon read, people with these disorders rarely seek treatment.

Paranoid Personality Disorder

People with **paranoid personality disorder** deeply distrust other people and are suspicious of others' motives (APA, 2022). Because they believe that everyone intends them harm, they shun close relationships. Their trust in their own ideas and abilities can be excessive, though, as you can observe in the case of Eduardo:

For Eduardo, a researcher at a genetic engineering company, this was the last straw. He had been severely chastised by his supervisor for deviating from the research procedure on a major study. He knew where this was coming from. He had been "ratted out" by his jealous, conniving lab colleagues. Eduardo demanded a meeting with his supervisor and the three other researchers in the lab.

At the outset of the meeting, Eduardo insisted that he would not leave the room until he was told the name of the person who had ratted him out. He acknowledged that he had, in fact, changed the study's design in key ways, but then he quickly shifted the focus onto his lab colleagues. He stated that the other scientists were intimidated by his visionary ideas,

(continued on the next page)

and he accused them of trying to get him out of the way. He said that their desire to get rid of him was always apparent to him, revealed by their coldness toward him each and every day and their nastiness whenever he tried to correct them or offer constructive criticism. Nor did it escape his attention that they were always laughing at him, talking about him behind his back, and, on more than one occasion, trying to copy or destroy his notes.

The other researchers were aghast as Eduardo laid out his suspicions. They pointed out that it was Eduardo, not they, who was always behaving in an unfriendly manner. He had stopped speaking to all of them two months ago, and he regularly tried to antagonize them—giving them dirty looks and slamming doors.

Next, Eduardo's supervisor, Lisa, spoke up. She said that in her objective opinion, none of Eduardo's accusations were true. First, none of his colleagues had informed on him. She herself had reviewed videos from the lab cameras as a matter of routine and had noticed him feeding rats that were supposed to be left hungry. Second, she said that it was his coworkers' accounts, not Eduardo's, that rang true. In fact, she had received many complaints from people outside the lab about Eduardo's cold and aloof manner.

Later, in the privacy of her office, Lisa told Eduardo that she had no choice but to let him go. Eduardo was furious but not completely surprised. His past two jobs had ended badly as well.

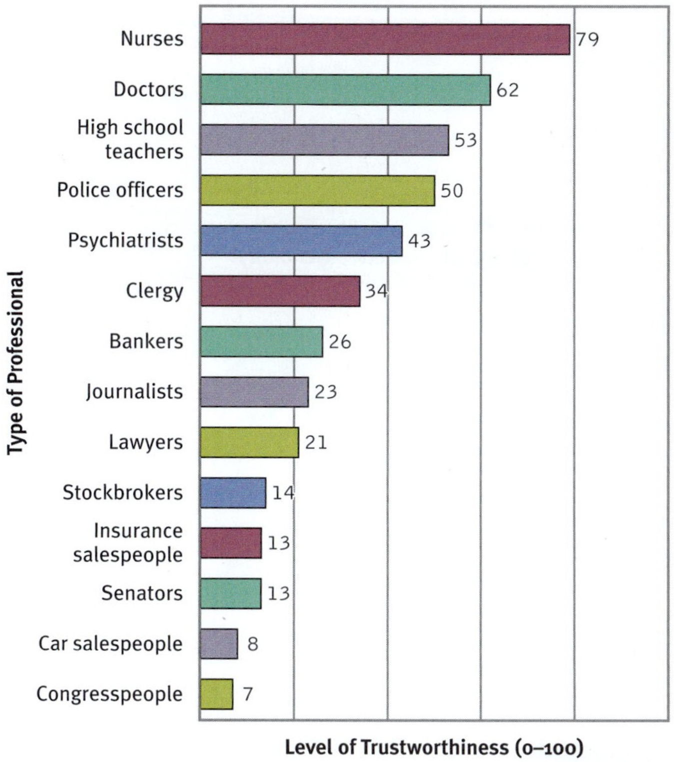

FIGURE 13-1

Whom Do You Trust?

Although distrust and suspiciousness are the hallmarks of paranoid personality disorder, even people without this disorder are often untrusting. In one survey, respondents said they believe certain professionals are particularly untrustworthy, including congresspeople and car salespeople. (Information from: Gallup News, 2023, 2020)

Ever on guard and cautious and noticing threats everywhere, people like Eduardo continually expect to be the targets of some trickery (see **Figure 13-1**). They find "hidden" meanings, which are usually belittling or threatening, in everything (Zimmerman, 2023). In an early study that required people to role-play, participants with paranoia were more likely than control participants to read hostile intentions into the actions of others (Turkat, Keane, & Thompson-Pope, 1990). In addition, they more often chose anger as the appropriate role-play response.

Quick to challenge the loyalty or trustworthiness of acquaintances, people with paranoid personality disorder remain cold and distant. A person might avoid confiding in anyone, for example, for fear of being hurt, or an individual might, without any justification, persist in questioning their partner's faithfulness. Although inaccurate and inappropriate, their suspicions are not usually *delusional;* the ideas are not so strange or so firmly held as to clearly remove the individuals from reality (Zimmerman, 2023).

People with this disorder are critical of weakness and find fault in others, particularly at work. They are unable to recognize their own mistakes, though, and are extremely sensitive to criticism. They often blame others for the things that go wrong in their lives, and they repeatedly bear grudges. As many as 4.4 percent of adults in the United States experience this disorder (APA, 2022).

How Do Theorists Explain Paranoid Personality Disorder? The theories that have been proposed to explain paranoid personality disorder, like those about most other personality disorders, have received little systematic research. Psychodynamic theories, the oldest of these explanations, trace the pattern to early interactions with demanding parents, particularly distant, rigid fathers and overcontrolling, rejecting mothers (Paris, 2022, 2020, 2018). (You will find that psychodynamic explanations for almost all the personality disorders begin the same way—with repeated mistreatment during childhood and lack of love.) According to one psychodynamic view, some people come to view

Jason Adam Katzenstein The New Yorker Collection/The Cartoon Bank

their environment as hostile as a result of their parents' persistently unreasonable demands. They must always be on the alert because they cannot trust others, and they are likely to develop feelings of extreme anger. They also project these feelings onto others and, as a result, feel increasingly persecuted. Similarly, some cognitive-behavioral theorists suggest that people with paranoid personality disorder generally hold broad maladaptive assumptions, such as "People are evil" and "People will attack you if given the chance" (Greenburgh & Raihani, 2022; Beck, Davis, & Freeman, 2015).

Biological theorists propose that paranoid personality disorder has genetic causes (Fariba, Gupta, & Kass, 2023; Tesli et al., 2023). A widely reported study that looked at self-reports of suspiciousness in 3,810 Australian twin pairs found that if one twin was excessively suspicious, the other had an increased likelihood of also being suspicious (Kendler, Heath, & Martin, 1987). Once again, however, it is important to note that such similarities between twins might also be the result of common environmental experiences.

Treatments for Paranoid Personality Disorder

People with paranoid personality disorder do not typically view themselves as needing help, and few come to treatment willingly (Skodol & Bender, 2022). Furthermore, many who are in treatment view the role of patient as inferior, and they distrust and rebel against their therapists. Thus, it is not surprising that therapy for this disorder has limited effect and moves slowly.

Object relations therapists—the psychodynamic therapists who give center stage to relationships—try to look past the client's anger and work on what they view as the individual's deep wish for a satisfying relationship (Normandin, Weiner, & Ensink, 2023; Kernberg, 2022, 2020, 2018). Cognitive-behavioral therapy has also been used to treat people with paranoid personality disorder. On the behavioral side, therapists help clients to utilize anxiety-reduction techniques and to improve their skills at solving interpersonal problems. On the cognitive side, therapists guide the clients to develop more realistic interpretations of other people's words and actions and to become more aware of other people's points of view (Kramer, Levy, & McMain, 2024). Low dosages of antipsychotic drug therapy seem to be of limited help (Zimmerman, 2023; Nelson, 2021).

of NOTE ...

Trusting Oneself, Distrusting Others

According to a national survey, during the Covid-19 pandemic, 86 percent of people across the United States trusted that they were doing the right things and making good decisions, but only 46 percent trusted that their community neighbors were doing the same (Pew Research Center, 2020). Only 28 percent trusted that people across the country were doing the right things.

schizoid personality disorder A personality disorder featuring persistent avoidance of relationships and little expression of emotion.

schizotypal personality disorder A personality disorder characterized by extreme discomfort in close relationships, very odd patterns of thinking and perceiving, and behavioral eccentricities.

Schizoid Personality Disorder

People with **schizoid personality disorder** persistently avoid and are removed from social relationships and demonstrate little in the way of emotion (APA, 2022). Like people with paranoid personality disorder, they do not have close ties with other people. The reason they avoid social contact, however, has nothing to do with paranoid feelings of distrust or suspicion; it is because they genuinely prefer to be alone. Take Deion:

Deion's days followed a routine from which he rarely deviated. He woke up, ate his breakfast of cereal and an orange, and sat down to his data entry job. He worked until noon, ate a salad, then resumed work until 5:00. He ate dinner, watched game shows on television, then settled into bed. Once a week, he endured a phone call with his mother, and once a month, he spoke to his brother on the phone to hear the latest about his niece, Thulani. He made an effort to feign interest in Thulani's excellent grades, privately frustrated that he had to take the time out of his day to hear about the 11-year-old's education.

Prior to the Covid-19 pandemic, Deion had to go into the office of the IT firm for which he worked. He had found it a chore but kept his head down, performed his job, and stayed clear of the insipid chatter of his coworkers. Not long after he started at the firm, the coworkers stopped inviting him out for drinks after work—he had always said no to their overtures. He found it odd that some of his coworkers were also friends outside of the office. Chance had thrown these people together, and he saw no need to spend time with them voluntarily. Over time, he found himself attracted to Josh, a man who worked in the office, but he saw no reason to strike up any sort of relationship with Josh just because he liked the way he looked. When Josh tried to get to know Deion, Deion would give short, matter-of-fact answers, and Josh eventually stopped trying to talk to him. Deion had been more than a little relieved when the pandemic closed the office; he found working from home much simpler. He no longer had to talk to his coworkers at all. When the firm later gave employees the option of returning to the workplace or continuing to work at home, Deion was delighted, and he immediately chose home.

Deion's mother, Tanya, certainly noticed and was concerned about Deion's isolation, especially as he grew more and more secluded and detached from others. He was the only person she knew who actually had liked the social isolation that characterized the first year of the pandemic. Increasingly, their relationship felt empty to her, and their conversations were flat. Eventually, he stopped pretending to care about her social activism and human rights advocacy, endeavors to which she'd devoted so much of her life. For example, when she discussed a voting rights march that she had organized, Deion asked why he should care about the needs of other people just because they looked like him. On another occasion, when she asked him why he was no longer talking to his father (Tanya's ex-husband), Deion explained that they hadn't had a fight or anything like that, but "I just don't know what I'd even talk to him about." Given her concerns, Tanya asked Deion if he would consider going into therapy, but Deion insisted that he was fine and that people were simply a hassle.

People like Deion, often described as "loners," make no effort to start or keep friendships, take little interest in having sexual relationships, and even seem indifferent to their families. They seek out jobs that require little or no contact with others. When necessary, they can form work relations to a degree, but they prefer to keep to themselves. Many live by themselves as well. Not surprisingly, their social skills tend to be weak. If they do marry or enter into an exclusive relationship, their lack of interest in intimacy may create significant problems.

People with schizoid personality disorder focus mainly on themselves and are generally unaffected by praise or criticism. They rarely show any feelings, expressing neither joy nor anger. They seem to have no need for attention or acceptance; are typically viewed as cold, humorless, or dull; and generally succeed in being

of NOTE ...

Their Words

"There was a point when I was 15 or 16 that I realized that my father wanted me to be a loner. I decided, It's okay to be an introvert, but I don't want to be a loner. I want a few other people in my life."

Mark Vonnegut, physician and author, son of famous writer Kurt Vonnegut ignored. Based on surveys in the United States, it is estimated that as many as 4.9 percent of the adult population display this disorder (APA, 2022).

How Do Theorists Explain Schizoid Personality Disorder?

Many psychodynamic theorists, particularly object relations theorists, propose that schizoid personality disorder has its roots in an unsatisfied need for human contact (Normandin et al., 2023; Kernberg, 2022, 2020, 2018). The parents of people with this disorder, like those of people with paranoid personality disorder, are believed to have been unaccepting or even abusive of their children (Zimmerman, 2023). Whereas people with paranoid symptoms react to such parenting chiefly with distrust, those with schizoid personality disorder are left with limited abilities to give or receive love. They cope by avoiding all relationships.

Cognitive-behavioral theorists propose, not surprisingly, that people with schizoid personality disorder display irregularities in their thinking. Their thoughts are often vague, empty, and without much meaning, and they have trouble scanning the environment to arrive at accurate perceptions (Zimmerman, 2023; Cherry, 2022). Unable to pick up emotional and/or social cues from others, they simply cannot respond appropriately.

Warner Bros/DCComics/Kobal/REX/Shutterstock

A darker knight In recent years, Batman movies have presented the crime fighter as a singularly driven loner incapable of forming or sustaining relationships, a portrayal true to the original comic book presentation. In the film *Batman v Superman: Dawn of Justice*, for example, his asocial personality, including his hatred and distrust of Superman, is evident. Some clinical observers have argued that in these recent presentations, Batman displays some of the symptoms of schizoid personality disorder.

Treatments for Schizoid Personality Disorder

Their social withdrawal prevents most people with schizoid personality disorder from entering therapy unless some other disorder, such as alcohol use disorder, makes treatment necessary. These clients are likely to remain emotionally distant from the therapist, seem not to care about their treatment, and make limited progress at best (Skodol & Bender, 2022).

Cognitive-behavioral therapists have sometimes been able to help people with this disorder experience more positive emotions and more satisfying social interactions (Kramer et al., 2024; Beck et al., 2015). On the cognitive end, their techniques include presenting clients with lists of emotions to think about or having them write down and remember pleasurable experiences. On the behavioral end, therapists have sometimes had success teaching social skills to such clients, using role-playing, exposure techniques, and homework assignments as tools (Zimmerman, 2023). Group therapy is apparently useful when it offers a safe setting for social contact, although people with schizoid personality disorder may resist pressure to take part (Cherry, 2022). As with paranoid personality disorder, drug therapy seems to offer limited help (Fariba, Madhanagopal, & Gupta, 2022; Nelson, 2021).

Schizotypal Personality Disorder

People with **schizotypal personality disorder** display a range of interpersonal problems marked by extreme discomfort in close relationships, very odd patterns of thinking and perceiving, and behavioral eccentricities (APA, 2022). Anxious around others, they seek isolation and have few close friends. Some feel intensely lonely. The disorder is more severe than the paranoid and schizoid personality disorders, as illustrated in the case of 46-year-old Linh:

Linh began therapy at the insistence of her brother Tuan. She began the intake interview by insisting that there was nothing wrong with her, she did not need to be there, and this was merely to get her brother off her back. She made little eye contact and had to be asked questions repeatedly before she responded. A picture of aloofness, along with

(continued on the next page)

minimal and often strange answers, characterized this therapy session and subsequent ones. Moreover, her aloof behavior in therapy paralleled her demeanor throughout the other parts of her life—inexpressive, bland, and indifferent.

Linh used a wheelchair, having lost the use of her legs in a car accident as a teenager; her then-boyfriend Mark had been driving while intoxicated and wound up serving time in prison following the accident. When the therapist asked Linh how she had dealt with the accident and its aftermath, Linh answered brusquely that for years she avoided thinking about it but had recently come to realize that it was actually a message that she should avoid dating anyone who wasn't of Vietnamese descent. Linh hadn't spoken to Mark since his trial and had no interest in how his life had been impacted. "The accident really didn't have anything to do with him. Mark was just the vessel for the message to me." She also explained that she didn't care about the state of her body because "that's not the real me."

Linh opined that her brother Tuan couldn't handle the fact that she didn't need to constantly have their parents in her life as Tuan did. In fact, she had not spoken to her parents in about a year, and she never returned their calls. She shrugged, indicating that she wasn't interested in speaking to them, but when pressed, she acknowledged that she felt anxious when talking with them, although they usually tried to be quite loving. She also said that, in a way, she had been checking in on her parents the past year: she had repeated visions that they were doing well. Thus, she was surprised when Tuan recently told her that her father was being treated for bone cancer.

Linh had no friends, but she reported not being lonely. She liked being by herself. She acknowledged that most people thought she was strange. Linh explained away having no friends by saying, "People are afraid of me because I have telepathic skills that enable me to change the way they think, if I choose to. Also, people are always trying to make jokes, and I don't understand that at all. It's easier to stay by myself. I help people write grant proposals on a freelance basis and talk to my clients as little as I can. That's why I never say yes to schools that offer me grant-related positions with salaries and benefits."

Recently, Linh gave Tuan's son Louis an unusual gift for his eighth birthday—a scrapbook of graphic car crash photographs. When asked about the gift choice, she explained that she was passing on the message that had been given to her and that Louis needed to see those photos. She refused to explain further why this was necessary.

of NOTE ...

Common Beliefs

People who think they have extrasensory experiences are not necessarily experiencing schizotypal personality disorder. In fact, according to surveys, at least 57 percent of adults believe in paranormal entities—demons, ghosts, vampires, or other supernatural beings (Melore, 2021).

As with Linh, the thoughts and behaviors of people with schizotypal personality disorder can be noticeably disturbed. These symptoms may include *ideas of reference*—beliefs that unrelated events pertain to them in some important way—and *bodily illusions,* such as sensing an external "force" or presence. A number of people with this disorder consider themselves to have special extrasensory abilities, and some believe they have magical control over others. Examples of schizotypal eccentricities include repeatedly arranging cans to align their labels, organizing closets extensively, or wearing an odd assortment of clothing. The emotions of these individuals may be inappropriate, flat, or humorless.

People with schizotypal personality disorder often have great difficulty keeping their attention focused. Correspondingly, their conversation is typically digressive and vague, even sprinkled with loose associations. They tend to drift aimlessly and, like Linh, to lead an idle, relatively unproductive life. They are likely to choose undemanding jobs in which they can work below their capacity and are not required to interact with other people. Based on surveys in the United States, it is estimated that as many as 3.9 percent of adults display schizotypal personality disorder (APA, 2022).

How Do Theorists Explain Schizotypal Personality Disorder?

Because the symptoms of schizotypal personality disorder so often resemble those of schizophrenia, researchers have hypothesized that similar factors may be at work in both disorders. A range of studies have supported such expectations. Investigators have found that schizotypal symptoms, like schizophrenic patterns, are often linked to family conflicts and to psychological disorders in parents. They have also learned that cognitive impairments, such as difficulties in attention and short-term memory, may contribute to schizotypal personality disorder, just as they apparently do to schizophrenia (Zahid & Best, 2023; Zouraraki et al., 2023). Finally, researchers have linked schizotypal personality disorder to some of the same biological factors found in schizophrenia, such as high activity of the neurotransmitter dopamine, enlarged brain ventricles, smaller temporal lobes, and loss of gray matter (Fariba et al., 2023; Attademo, Bernardini, & Verdolini, 2021). As you read in the chapter on schizophrenia, there are indications that these biological factors may have a genetic basis (Tesli et al., 2023).

Although these findings do suggest a close relationship between schizotypal personality disorder and schizophrenia, the personality disorder also has been linked to disorders of mood. More than half of people with schizotypal personality disorder also experience major depressive disorder or bipolar disorder at some point in their lives (Rosell, 2023; Zimmerman, 2023). Moreover, relatives of people with depression have a higher-than-usual-rate of schizotypal personality disorder and vice versa. Thus, at the very least, this personality disorder is not tied exclusively to schizophrenia.

Sipa Press

When personality disorders explode

In this 2007 video, Seung-Hui Cho, a student at Virginia Tech, described the slights he experienced throughout his life. After mailing the video to *NBC News*, he proceeded to kill 32 people, including himself, and wound 25 others in a massive campus shooting. Most clinical observers agree that he displayed a combination of features from the antisocial, borderline, paranoid, schizoid, schizotypal, and narcissistic personality disorders, including boundless fury and hatred, extreme social withdrawal, persistent distrust, strange thinking, intimidating behavior and arrogance, and disregard for others.

Treatments for Schizotypal Personality Disorder

Therapy is as difficult in cases of schizotypal personality disorder as it is in cases of paranoid and schizoid personality disorders. Most therapists agree on the need to help these clients "reconnect" with the world and recognize the limits of their thinking and their powers. The therapists may thus try to set clear limits—for example, by requiring punctuality—and work on helping the clients recognize where their views end and those of the therapist begin (Rosell, 2023). Other therapy goals are to increase positive social contacts, reduce overstimulation, and help the individuals become more aware of their personal feelings (Nielsen et al., 2023; Skodol & Bender, 2022).

Cognitive-behavioral therapists further try to teach clients to evaluate their unusual thoughts or perceptions objectively and to ignore the inappropriate ones (Rosell, 2023; Zimmerman, 2023). The therapists may keep track of clients' odd or magical predictions, for example, and later point out their inaccuracy. When clients are speaking and begin to digress, the therapists might ask them to sum up what it is they are trying to say. In addition, specific behavioral methods, such as speech lessons, social skills training, and tips on appropriate dress and manners, have sometimes helped clients learn to blend in better with and be more comfortable around other people (Kramer et al., 2024).

Antipsychotic drugs have been given to people with schizotypal personality disorder, again because of the disorder's similarity to schizophrenia. In low doses, the drugs appear to have helped some people, usually by reducing their thought problems (Rosell, 2023).

SUMMING UP

"Odd" Personality Disorders

Three of the personality disorders in DSM-5-TR are marked by the kinds of odd or eccentric behavior often on display in schizophrenia. People with paranoid personality disorder display a broad pattern of distrust and suspiciousness. Those with schizoid personality disorder persistently avoid social relationships, have little or no social interest, and show little emotional expression. People with schizotypal personality disorder display a range of interpersonal problems marked by extreme discomfort in close relationships, very odd forms of thinking and behavior, and behavioral eccentricities. People with these three kinds of disorders usually are resistant to treatment, and treatment gains tend to be modest at best.

antisocial personality disorder A personality disorder marked by a general pattern of disregard for and violation of other people's rights.

"Dramatic" Personality Disorders

THE CLUSTER OF "dramatic" personality disorders includes the *antisocial, borderline, histrionic,* and *narcissistic* personality disorders. The behaviors of people with these problems are so dramatic, emotional, or erratic that it is often almost impossible for them to have relationships that are truly giving and satisfying.

These personality disorders are more commonly diagnosed than the others. However, only the antisocial and borderline personality disorders have received much study, partly because they create so many problems for other people. The causes of these disorders, like those of the odd-cluster personality disorders, are not well understood. Treatments range from ineffective to moderately effective.

Antisocial Personality Disorder

Sometimes described as "psychopaths" or "sociopaths," people with **antisocial personality disorder** persistently disregard and violate others' rights (APA, 2022). Aside from substance use disorders, this is the disorder most closely linked to adult criminal behavior. DSM-5-TR stipulates that a person must be at least 18 years of age to receive this diagnosis; however, most people with antisocial personality disorder displayed some patterns of misbehavior before they were 15, including truancy, running away, cruelty to animals or people, and destroying property. Robert Hare, an influential Canadian psychologist in the field of criminal psychology, brings this disorder to life in this classic case description of Ray, an inmate Hare met at the beginning of his career:

of NOTE ...

Previous Identity

During the nineteenth century, antisocial personality disorder was referred to as "moral insanity" (Jones, 2017).

In the early 1960s, I found myself employed as the sole psychologist at the British Columbia Penitentiary. . . . I wasn't in my office for more than an hour when my first "client" arrived. He was a tall, slim, dark-haired man in his thirties. The air around him seemed to buzz, and the eye contact he made with me was so direct and intense that I wondered if I had ever really looked anybody in the eye before. That stare was unrelenting. . . .

Without waiting for an introduction, the inmate—I'll call him Ray—opened the conversation: "Hey, Doc, how's it going? Look, I've got a problem. I need your help. I'd really like to talk to you about this." . . . He pulled out a knife and waved it in front of my nose, all the while smiling and maintaining that intense eye contact. . . . He explained that he intended to use the knife not on me but on another inmate. . . .

From that first meeting on, Ray managed to make my eight-month stint at the prison miserable. His constant demands on my time and his attempts to manipulate me into doing things for him were unending. On one occasion, he convinced me that he would make a good cook . . . and I supported his request for a transfer from the machine shop (where he had apparently made the knife). . . . Several months after I had recommended the transfer, . . . it was discovered that Ray was the brains behind the bootleg operation [in the prison kitchen, and] he spent some time in solitary confinement.

Once out of "the hole," Ray appeared in my office as if nothing had happened and asked for a transfer from the kitchen to the auto shop—he really felt he had a knack, he saw the need to prepare himself for the outside world . . . eventually he wore me down.

Soon afterward I decided to leave the prison to pursue a Ph.D. in psychology, and about a month before I left, Ray almost persuaded me to ask my father, a roofing contractor, to offer him a job as part of an application for parole. . . . Ray had an incredible ability to con not just me but everybody. He could talk, and lie, with a smoothness and a directness that sometimes momentarily disarmed even the most experienced and cynical of the prison staff. When I met him he had a long criminal record behind him (and, as it turned out, ahead of him); about half his adult life had been spent in prison, and many of his crimes had been violent. . . . He lied endlessly, lazily, about everything, and it disturbed him not a whit whenever I pointed out something in his file that contradicted one of his lies. . . . Finally convinced that he might not make the perfect job candidate in my father's firm, I turned down Ray's request—and was shaken by his nastiness at my refusal.

Before I left the prison for the university, I took advantage of the prison policy of letting staff have their cars repaired in the institution's auto shop—where Ray still worked, thanks (he would have said no thanks) to me. . . . With all our possessions on top of the car and our baby . . . in the backseat, my wife and I headed for Ontario. . . . Later, when we encountered some moderate inclines, the radiator boiled over. A garage mechanic discovered ball bearings in the carburetor's float chamber; he also pointed out where one of the hoses to the radiator had clearly been tampered with. These problems were repaired easily enough, but the next one, which arose while we were going down a long hill, was more serious. The brake pedal became very spongy and then simply dropped to the floor—no brakes, and it was a long hill. Fortunately, we made it to a service station, where we found that the brake line had been cut so that a slow leak would occur. Perhaps it was a coincidence that Ray was working in the auto shop when the car [had been] tuned up, but [then again, perhaps not].

(Hare, 1993)

Like Ray, people with antisocial personality disorder lie repeatedly (APA, 2022). Many cannot work consistently at a job; they are absent frequently and are likely to quit their jobs altogether (Black, 2023). Usually they are also careless with money and frequently fail to pay their debts. They are often impulsive, taking action without thinking of the consequences. Correspondingly, they may be irritable, aggressive, and quick to start fights.

Recklessness is another common trait: people with antisocial personality disorder have little regard for their own safety or for that of others, even their children. They are self-centered as well and are likely to have trouble maintaining close relationships. Usually they develop a knack for gaining personal profit at the expense of others. Because the pain or damage they cause seldom concerns them, clinicians often say that they lack a moral conscience. They think of their victims as weak and deserving of being conned, robbed, or even physically harmed (see **Trending**).

Popular sociopaths Television and movie audiences love characters with the symptoms of antisocial personality disorder. One popular villain is the cruel, self-centered, and amoral Logan Roy (left), who has consistently manipulated and disregarded the needs of other people, including family members, while overseeing a financial empire in the HBO series *Succession*. Similarly, the notorious Joker (right) has displayed antisocial qualities since his initial comic book appearance in 1940, although his additional psychotic symptoms in the 2019 film *Joker* suggested a comorbid diagnosis of schizophrenia.

Macall B. Polay/©HBO/Courtesy Everett Collection, Inc

Niko Tavernise/© Warner Bros./Courtesy Everett Collection

...TRENDING

Mass Murders: Where Does Such Violence Come From?

At approximately noon on May 24, 2022, an 18-year-old man entered the Robb Elementary School in Uvalde, Texas, with a semiautomatic rifle and proceeded to kill 19 children and 2 teachers and injure another 17 individuals. The Uvalde horror was preceded by numerous other mass killings, including those of students and teachers at Virginia Tech in Blacksburg, Virginia (2007); children and teachers at the Sandy Hook Elementary School in Newtown, Connecticut (2012); Bible study members at a church in Charleston, South Carolina (2015); patrons at the Pulse nightclub in Orlando, Florida (2016); attendees at a country music concert in Las Vegas, Nevada (2017); students and teachers at the Marjory Stoneman Douglas High School in Parkland, Florida (2018); congregants at the Tree of Life synagogue in Pittsburgh, Pennsylvania (2018); customers at a Walmart store in El Paso, Texas (2019); shoppers at a Tops grocery store in Buffalo, New York (2022); and patrons at a bowling alley and nearby bar in Lewiston, Maine (2023). Moreover, in the 12 months following the Uvalde shooting, an additional 600 mass shootings occurred.

These numbers are numbing. Clinicians have offered various theories about why individuals commit such murders, but enlightening research and effective interventions have been elusive.

What do we know about mass killings? We know they involve, by definition, the murder of four or more people in the same location and at around the same time. Records indicate that, on average, mass killings now occur in the United States as often as 10 times each week, 75 percent of them feature a lone killer, 70 percent involve the use of firearms, 67 percent are committed by non-Hispanic White persons, and 96 percent are carried out by men or teenage boys (Girgis et al., 2023; NTAC, 2023; FBI, 2022, 2020).

We also know that despite public perceptions, mass killings are not a new phenomenon. They have occurred—with regularity—for centuries (Bonn, 2022, 2020, 2019). What is new, however, is the large increase in mass *public* shootings (for example, schools, concerts, stores, and workplaces). And the number of such shootings keeps rising each year (FBI, 2022).

Theorists have suggested a number of factors to help explain mass killings, including the availability of guns, bullying behavior, substance abuse, the proliferation of violent media and video games, dysfunctional homes, and contagion effects (NTAC, 2023; Metzl, Piemonte, & McKay, 2021). Moreover, regardless of one's position on gun control, media violence, or the like, almost everyone, including most clinicians, believe that mass killers typically experience a mental disorder (Glick et al., 2021; Cowan & Cole, 2020). Which mental disorder? On this, there is little agreement. Each of the following has been suggested (NTAC, 2023; Brucato et al., 2021):

- Antisocial, narcissistic, borderline, paranoid, or schizotypal personality disorder
- Psychotic disorder
- Intermittent explosive disorder—an impulse-control disorder featuring repeated, unprovoked verbal and/or behavioral outbursts
- Severe depression, stress, or anxiety
- Substance use disorder

Although these and yet other disorders have been proposed, none has received clear support in the research on mass killings. On the other hand, several psychological variables have emerged as common denominators across the various studies: severe feelings of anger and resentment, feelings of being persecuted or grossly mistreated, desires for revenge, social isolation or estrangement, and an interest in violence (Bonn, 2022; Cerfolio et al., 2022; FBI, 2022; Silva et al., 2021). That is, regardless of which mental disorder a mass killer may display, the individual usually is driven by feelings and circumstances of this kind. For many clinical investigators, this finding suggests that research should focus less on diagnosis and more on identifying and understanding these particular variables.

Clearly, clinical research must expand its focus on this area of enormous social concern. It is a difficult problem to investigate, partly because so few mass killers survive their crimes (more than half die by suicide or are killed at the scene of the shooting), but the clinical field has managed to gather useful insights about other elusive areas (Girgis et al., 2023; NTAC, 2023). And, indeed, in the aftermath of the horrific murders mentioned at the beginning of this box, a wave of heightened determination seems to have seized the clinical community.

Wang Ying/Xinhua News Agency/eyevine/Redux

Unthinkable Employees and friends of victims take part in a prayer and vigil in El Paso, Texas, after a 2019 mass shooting at a Walmart store left 23 dead and another 23 wounded, believed to be the deadliest attack on Hispanic Americans in modern American history.

Based on surveys in the United States, it is estimated that as many as 3.6 percent of adults meet the criteria for antisocial personality disorder (APA, 2022). Because people with this disorder are often arrested, researchers frequently look for people with antisocial patterns in prison populations (Trestman, Rahmani, & Bhatia, 2022; Azevedo et al., 2020). It is estimated that at least 30 percent of people in prison meet the diagnostic criteria for this disorder (Swaim, 2022). Among men in urban jails, the antisocial personality pattern has been linked strongly to past arrests for crimes of violence. The criminal behavior of many people with this disorder declines after the age of 35; some, however, continue their criminal activities throughout their lives (Fisher & Hany, 2023).

How do various institutions in our society—government, business, science, religion—view lying? How might such views affect lying by individuals?

Studies and clinical observations also indicate that people with antisocial personality disorder have higher rates of alcohol use disorder and other substance use disorders than do the rest of the population (Anona et al., 2024). Indeed, some research indicates that more than 80 percent of people with this personality disorder display a substance use disorder at some point in their lives (Black, 2023). Thus, some theorists speculate that antisocial personality disorder and substance use disorders both have the same cause, such as a deep-seated need to take risks. Consistent with this notion, a number of people with antisocial personality disorder also display gambling disorder. In fact, the personality disorder is manifested by 23 percent of all people with gambling disorder (Black, 2023).

How Do Theorists Explain Antisocial Personality Disorder?

Most explanations of antisocial personality disorder come from the psychodynamic, cognitive-behavioral, and biological models. Although researchers have linked a number of factors to this disorder, complete explanations have been elusive.

PSYCHODYNAMIC FACTORS As with many other personality disorders, *psychodynamic* theorists propose that this one begins with an absence of parental love during infancy, leading to a lack of basic trust (De Wit-De Visser et al., 2023; Ling et al., 2022). In this view, some children—the ones who develop antisocial personality disorder—respond to the early inadequacies by becoming emotionally distant, and they bond with others through the use of power and destructiveness. In support of the psychodynamic explanation, researchers have found that people with this disorder are more likely than others to have had significant stress in their childhoods, particularly in such forms as family poverty, family violence, child abuse, and parental conflict or divorce (Fisher & Hany, 2023; Logan-Greene et al., 2023).

COGNITIVE-BEHAVIORAL FACTORS *Cognitive-behavioral* theorists have argued that a combination of behavioral and cognitive factors contributes to antisocial personality disorder. On the behavioral side, they suggest that antisocial symptoms may be learned through principles of conditioning, particularly *modeling*, or imitation. As evidence, they point to the higher rate of antisocial personality disorder found among the parents and close relatives of people with this disorder (APA, 2022). The modeling explanation is also supported by studies of friends and associates of people with antisocial personality disorder. For example, one investigation found that middle school students who were attracted to antisocial peers went on to engage in antisocial behavior themselves in order to gain acceptance (Black, 2023; Juvonen & Ho, 2008).

Bruce Eric Kaplan The New Yorker Collection/The Cartoon Bank

"You'll have to excuse me—I'm myself today."

Cognitive-behavioral theorists also point to *operant conditioning* to help explain this disorder. They suggest that some parents unintentionally teach antisocial behavior by regularly rewarding a child's aggressive behavior (Black, 2023; Yang et al., 2022). When the child misbehaves or becomes violent in reaction to the parents' requests or orders, for example, the parents may give in to restore peace. Without meaning to, they may be teaching the child to be stubborn and perhaps even violent.

On the cognitive side, cognitive-behavioral theorists say that people with antisocial personality disorder often hold attitudes that trivialize the importance of other people's needs (Zahn-Waxler, 2023; Kaseweter, Browne, & Prkachin, 2022). They believe that such a philosophy of life may be far more common in our society than people recognize. In a related explanation, a number of cognitive-behavioral theorists propose that people with this disorder have genuine difficulty recognizing points of view or feelings other than their own.

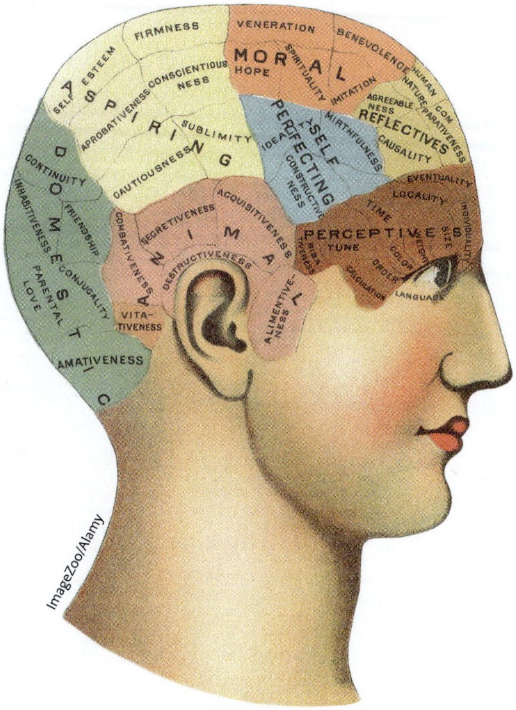

Early notions of personality In the once popular but thoroughly debunked nineteenth-century theory of phrenology, Franz Joseph Gall (1758–1828) suggested that the brain consists of distinct portions, each responsible for some aspect of personality. Phrenologists tried to assess personality by feeling bumps and indentations on a person's head. People with antisocial personalities, for example, were expected to have head bumps near the "Animal" area of the brain, where traits such as combativeness, destructiveness, and secretiveness were believed to be located.

BIOLOGICAL FACTORS A wide range of studies suggest that *biological* factors play an important role in antisocial personality disorder. First, there are indications that people may inherit a biological predisposition to the disorder (Black, 2023; Fisher & Hany, 2023; Tesli et al., 2023). For example, twin research has found that 67 percent of the identical twins of people with antisocial personality disorder also display the disorder themselves, in contrast to 31 percent of fraternal twins of people with the disorder. Similarly, some genetic research suggests that the disorder may be linked to particular genes (Li et al., 2023; Adanty et al., 2022).

In addition, biological researchers have found that antisocial people, particularly those who are highly impulsive and aggressive, have lower activity of the neurotransmitter serotonin than other people (Rosell et al., 2023). As you may recall from the chapter on suicide, other kinds of studies have linked both impulsivity and aggression to low serotonin activity, so the presence of this biological factor in people with antisocial personality disorder is not surprising.

In related work, studies indicate that individuals with this disorder display deficient functioning in their *prefrontal cortex, anterior cingulate cortex, amygdala, hippocampus,* and *temporal cortex*—brain structures that, collectively, help people follow rules; plan and execute realistic strategies; and display sympathy, judgment, and empathy (Rosell et al., 2023; Miglin et al., 2022; Kolla et al., 2021). These are, of course, all abilities found wanting in people with antisocial personality disorder.

A different line of biological research has found that research participants with this disorder often respond to warnings or expectations of stress with low brain and bodily arousal, such as slow autonomic arousal and slow EEG waves (Fariba et al., 2023; Black & Kolla, 2022). It is believed that such underarousal may enable people with the disorder to readily tune out threatening or emotional situations and so be unaffected by them. This could help explain a phenomenon often observed by clinicians—that people with antisocial personality disorder seem to feel less anxiety than other people and so lack a key ingredient for learning from negative life experiences or tuning in to the emotional cues of others (Mirandola et al., 2023). Such physical underarousal may also help explain why people with antisocial personality disorder take more risks and seek more thrills than other people do. That is, they may be drawn to antisocial activity precisely because it meets an underlying biological need for more excitement and arousal. In support of this idea, as you read earlier, antisocial personality disorder often goes hand in hand with sensation-seeking behavior.

These numerous biological factors may be connected more closely than first meets the eye. Consistent with the field's increasing emphasis on dysfunctional brain circuits, many theorists now suspect that antisocial personality disorder is ultimately related to poor functioning by a brain circuit consisting of the structures mentioned above. Poor communication (that is, poor *interconnectivity*) between those structures in the circuit may produce chronic low reactions to stress by the two brain–body stress routes—the *sympathetic nervous system* and the *hypothalamic-pituitary-adrenal axis*—leading, in turn, to a state of low arousal, weak stress reactions, insufficient empathy for the pain of others, and other features of antisocial personality disorder (Bell et al., 2022; Black & Kolla, 2022). Although enthusiasm for this explanation is growing, research regarding its specifics and merits has been limited to date.

Treatments for Antisocial Personality Disorder

Treatments for people with antisocial personality disorder are typically ineffective (Black, 2023, 2022; De Wit-De Visser et al., 2023). Major obstacles to treatment include the individual's lack of a clear conscience, desire to change, or respect for therapy. Most of those in therapy have been forced to participate by an employer, their school, or the law, or they come to the attention of therapists when they also develop another psychological disorder.

Cognitive-behavioral therapists may try to guide clients with antisocial personality disorder to think about moral issues and about the needs of other people. However, research has not found this approach to be particularly helpful (Black, 2022; McGuire, 2022). In a similar vein, a number of hospitals and prisons have tried to create a therapeutic community for people with this disorder, a structured environment that teaches responsibility toward others (NHSE, 2023). Some such individuals seem to profit from approaches of this kind, but it appears that most do not. In recent years, clinicians have also used psychotropic medications, particularly antipsychotic drugs, to treat people with antisocial personality disorder. However, research has not found medication to be consistently useful in addressing the overall antisocial pattern (Moscovici & Jones, 2022; Nelson, 2021).

borderline personality disorder A personality disorder characterized by repeated instability in interpersonal relationships, self-image, and mood and by impulsive behavior.

Borderline Personality Disorder

People with **borderline personality disorder** display great instability, including major shifts in mood, an unstable self-image, and impulsivity (APA, 2022). These characteristics combine to make their relationships very unstable as well. In her first treatment session, Dal displays or reveals all of these difficulties, as described by her therapist:

Dal . . . seems to be unable to maintain a stable sense of self-worth and self-esteem. Her confidence in her ability to "hold on to men" is at a low ebb, having just parted ways with "the love of her life." In the last year alone she confesses to having had six "serious relationships."

. . . The commencement of each affair was "a dream come true" and the men were all and one "Prince Charming." But then she invariably found herself in the stormy throes of violent fights over seeming trifles. She tried to "hang in there," but the more she invested in the relationships, the more distant and "vicious" her partners became. Finally, they abandoned her. . . .

*She shrugs and . . . her posture [becomes] almost violent: "No one f***s with me. I stand my ground, you get my meaning?" She admits that she physically assaulted three of her last six paramours, hurled things at them, and, amidst uncontrollable rage attacks and temper tantrums, even threatened to kill them. What made her so angry? She can't remember now. . . .*

As she recounts these sad exploits, she alternates between boastful swagger and self-chastising, biting criticism of her own traits and conduct. Her affect swings wildly, in the confines of a single therapy session, between exuberant and fantastic optimism and unbridled gloom.

One minute she can conquer the world, careless and "free at last" ("It's their loss. . . .")—the next instant, she hyperventilates with unsuppressed anxiety, bordering on a panic attack. . . .

Dal likes to "live dangerously, on the edge." She does drugs occasionally—"not a habit, just for recreation," she assures me. She is a shopaholic and often finds herself mired in debts. She went through three personal bankruptcies. . . . She also binges on food, especially when she is stressed or depressed which seems to occur quite often.

She sought therapy because she is having intrusive thoughts about killing herself. [She often performs] self-injury and self-mutilation (she shows me a pair of pale, patched wrists, more scratched than slashed).

(Vaknin, 2016, 2015)

of NOTE ...

Their Words

"Anger is a brief lunacy."

Horace, Roman poet

of NOTE ...

Experiencing Anger

12%	Percentage of adults who report they have trouble controlling their anger
28%	Percentage who say they worry about how angry they feel sometimes
45%	Percentage who say they regularly lose their temper at work
50%	Percentage who say they have reacted to computer problems by screaming, shouting, or hitting their computer

(BAAM, 2023, 2020, 2017)

Like Dal, people with borderline personality disorder swing in and out of very depressive, anxious, and irritable states that last anywhere from a few hours to a few days or more (see **Table 13-2**). Their emotions seem to be always in conflict with the world around them (Waite et al., 2024). They are prone to bouts of anger, which sometimes result in physical aggression and violence. Just as often, however, they direct their impulsive anger inward and inflict bodily harm on themselves. Many seem troubled by deep feelings of emptiness (Lopez-Villatoro et al., 2023).

Borderline personality disorder is a complex disorder, and it is fast becoming one of the more common conditions seen in clinical practice. As many as 85 percent of individuals with this syndrome also experience another psychological disorder, such as major depressive disorder, posttraumatic stress disorder, or an eating disorder, at some point in their lives (Anona et al., 2024; Kawada, 2023). Their impulsive, self-destructive activities may range from substance misuse to delinquency, unsafe sex, and reckless driving (Waite et al., 2024). Many engage in behaviors that involve self-injury or self-mutilation, such as cutting or burning themselves or banging their heads (Scheunemann et al., 2023). As you read in the chapter on suicide, such behaviors typically cause immense physical discomfort, but those with borderline personality disorder often feel as if the physical discomfort offers relief from their emotional distress. It may serve as a distraction from their emotional or interpersonal upsets, "snapping" them out of an "emotional overload." Many try to hurt themselves as a way of dealing with their chronic feelings of emptiness, boredom, and identity confusion (Lopez-Villatoro et al., 2023).

Suicidal threats and actions are also common (Anona et al., 2024). Studies suggest that around 70 percent of people with borderline personality disorder attempt suicide at least once in their lives; around 6 percent actually die of suicide (NYP, 2023; APA, 2022). It is common for people with this disorder to enter clinical treatment by way of the emergency room after a suicide attempt (Besch et al., 2023).

People with borderline personality disorder frequently form intense, conflict-ridden relationships in which their feelings are not necessarily shared by the other person (Skodol, 2022). They may come to idealize another person's qualities and abilities after just a brief first encounter. They also may violate the boundaries of relationships. Thinking in dichotomous (black-and-white) terms, they quickly feel rejected and become furious when their expectations are not met, yet they remain very attached to the relationships. In fact, they have recurrent fears of impending abandonment and frequently engage in frantic efforts to avoid real or imagined separations from important people

TABLE 13-2

Comparison of Personality Disorders

	Cluster	Similar Disorders	Responsiveness to Treatment
Paranoid	Odd	Schizophrenia; delusional disorder	Modest
Schizoid	Odd	Schizophrenia; delusional disorder	Modest
Schizotypal	Odd	Schizophrenia; delusional disorder	Modest
Antisocial	Dramatic	Conduct disorder	Poor
Borderline	Dramatic	Depressive disorder; bipolar disorder	Moderate
Histrionic	Dramatic	Somatic symptom disorder; depressive disorder	Modest
Narcissistic	Dramatic	Cyclothymic disorder (mild bipolar disorder)	Poor
Avoidant	Anxious	Social anxiety disorder	Moderate
Dependent	Anxious	Separation anxiety disorder; depressive disorder	Moderate
Obsessive-Compulsive	Anxious	Obsessive-compulsive disorder	Moderate

Krista Schlueter/The New York Times/Redux

Of public interest When comedian Pete Davidson joined the cast of *Saturday Night Live* in 2014, he had no idea that, as his career blossomed, he would receive a diagnosis of borderline personality disorder and that this would be of great interest to his fans (and social media trolls). Davidson has spoken openly about his mental health problems and his pursuit of treatment.

in their lives. Sometimes they cut themselves or carry out other self-destructive acts to prevent partners from leaving (LeWine, 2023; Titus & DeShong, 2020).

People with borderline personality disorder typically have dramatic identity shifts. Because of this unstable sense of self, their goals, aspirations, friends, and even sexual orientation may shift rapidly. They may also occasionally have a sense of dissociation, or detachment, from their own thoughts or bodies (Zimmerman, 2023). At times they may have no sense of themselves at all, leading to the feelings of emptiness described earlier (Lopez-Villatoro et al., 2023).

According to surveys in the United States, as many as 5.9 percent of the adult population experience borderline personality disorder (APA, 2022). The course of the disorder varies from person to person. In the most common pattern, the person's instability and risk of suicide peak during young adulthood and then gradually wane with advancing age.

How Do Theorists Explain Borderline Personality Disorder?

Theorists have pointed to a range of possible psychological, biological, and sociocultural factors in their explanations of borderline personality disorder. In addition, over the past several years, there have been productive efforts to determine how such factors may interact to produce the disorder.

PSYCHOLOGICAL, BIOLOGICAL, AND SOCIOCULTURAL FACTORS Because so many people with borderline personality disorder fear abandonment, *psychodynamic* theorists have looked once again to early parental relationships to explain the disorder. Object relations theorists, for example, propose that an early lack of acceptance by parents may lead to a loss of self-esteem, increased dependence, and an inability to cope with separation (Normandin et al., 2023; Kernberg, 2022, 2020, 2018). In support of this theory, research has found that the parents of many people with borderline personality disorder did indeed neglect or reject them during their childhood, verbally abuse them, or otherwise behave inappropriately (Armour et al., 2022). The childhoods were often marked by multiple parent substitutes, divorce, death, or traumas such as physical or sexual abuse (Chapman, Jamil, & Fleisher, 2023; Yuan et al., 2023). At the same time, it is important to recognize that the vast majority of people with histories of physical, sexual, or psychological abuse do not go on to develop borderline personality disorder.

of NOTE ...

Venting Myth

Contrary to the notion that "letting off steam" reduces anger, angry participants in one study acted much more aggressively after hitting a punching bag than did angry participants who sat quietly for a while (Fosslien & Duffy, 2022; Salters-Pedneault, 2019; Bushman, Baumeister, & Stack, 1999).

"Stained Glass" Popular singer Madison Beer, performing here at a music festival in 2022, has openly discussed her diagnosis of borderline personality disorder, her self-harm behaviors, and her experiences with sexual abuse as a child. In her single "Stained Glass," the singer focuses on her mental health struggles and urges people to be gentle and nonjudgmental toward others because one never knows what painful experiences others have endured.

Borderline personality disorder also has been linked to *biological* factors. There are indications that people may inherit a biological predisposition to this disorder (Tesli et al., 2023). In twin research, for example, it has been found that 35 percent of the identical twins of people with borderline personality disorder also display the disorder themselves, in contrast to 19 percent of fraternal twins of people with the disorder (Chapman et al., 2023; Skodol, 2022). In a similar vein, studies suggest that the disorder may be linked to particular genes (Fariba et al., 2023).

Beyond genetic studies, researchers have found that people with borderline personality disorder, particularly those who are most impulsive—individuals who attempt suicide or are very aggressive toward others—have lower brain serotonin activity (Chapman et al., 2023; O'Higgins et al., 2022). Recall once again, from the chapters on depression and suicide, that low serotonin activity has been linked repeatedly to depression, suicide, aggression, and impulsivity.

Borderline personality disorder also has been tied to irregular activity in certain brain structures, including the amygdala (hyperactive), hippocampus (underactive), prefrontal cortex (underactive), and other structures in the frontal lobes—structures that collectively help people plan well, form accurate judgments, makegood decisions, exercise self-control, and express emotions properly (Fernando et al., 2023; Geurts et al., 2022). A number of theorists further believe that these structures are members of a particular brain circuit and that the problems displayed by each structure actually reflect dysfunction (that is, poor interconnectivity) throughout that entire brain circuit, dysfunction that results in frequent emotional outbursts, impulsive acts, wrong judgments, and bad decisions (Xiao et al., 2023; Sverak et al., 2022).

Finally, some *sociocultural* theorists suggest that cases of borderline personality disorder are particularly likely to emerge in cultures that change rapidly (Fariba et al., 2023; Choudhary & Gupta, 2020). As a culture loses its stability, they argue, it inevitably leaves many of its members with problems of identity, a sense of emptiness, high anxiety, and fears of abandonment. Family units may come apart, leaving people with little sense of belonging. Changes of this kind in society today may explain growing reports of the disorder (Paris, 2022, 2020, 2018).

Integrative Explanations

In recent years, two explanations—the *biosocial* and the *developmental psychopathology* explanations—have examined how these various factors might intersect to more fully account for borderline personality disorder. As you will read, the two explanations are quite compatible and often overlap.

According to the *biosocial* explanation, the disorder results from a combination of internal forces (for example, difficulty identifying and controlling one's emotions, social skill deficits, and irregular neurotransmitter activity) and external forces (for example, an environment in which a child's emotions are punished, ignored, trivialized, or disregarded; Bertele et al., 2022; McQuade et al., 2022). Parents may, for instance, misinterpret their child's intense emotions as exaggerations or attempts at manipulation rather than as serious expressions of unsettled internal states. According to the biosocial explanation, if children have intrinsic difficulty identifying and controlling their emotions and if their parents teach them to ignore their intense feelings, they may never learn how to properly recognize and control their emotional arousal, how to tolerate emotional distress, or when to trust their emotional responses. Such children will be at risk for the development of borderline personality disorder. Most of the internal and external factors cited by biosocial theorists are the very factors focused on in the preceding section. This theory has received some (but not consistent) research support (Bertele et al., 2022; McQuade et al., 2022).

Proponents of the other integrative explanation of borderline personality disorder, the *developmental psychopathology* explanation, build on and add details to the biosocial view. Like the biosocial theorists, developmental psychopathologists believe that

©Netflix/Courtesy Everett Collection

"Inside" In 2021, the multimedia special *Inside* was released to wide acclaim by comedian and performance artist Bo Burnham, who is shown here in a scene from the special. Burnham filmed the show entirely inside his guesthouse during the pandemic, without a crew or audience, using songs, sketches, and monologues to depict his mental health struggles, both lifelong and pandemic-induced, including his intense feelings of depression, anxiety, and anger; experiences of dissociation and derealization; suicidal thoughts; and overwhelming isolation and emptiness. According to posts, many viewers with psychological challenges identified with the various emotions depicted in the special, including people with borderline personality disorder, who typically struggle with a wide range of such emotions.

internal and external factors may intersect over the course of a person's life to help produce this disorder (Herzog, Kube, & Fassbinder, 2022; Wilson & Olino, 2021). While these theorists are interested in all such factors—from genetic to environmental—they believe that early parent–child relationships are particularly influential in the development of borderline personality disorder.

Consistent with the position held by the psychodynamic model's *object relations* theorists, developmental psychopathologists contend that children who experience early trauma and abuse and whose parents are markedly inattentive, uncaring, confusing, threatening, and dismissive are likely to enter adulthood with a *disorganized attachment style*—a severely flawed capacity for healthy relationships (Fonagy, Campbell, & Luyten, 2023; Pollard, Bucci, & Berry, 2023). That is, their attachments to other people throughout life will parallel their problematic attachments to their parents and will be filled with anxiety, emotional instability, and inconsistency.

According to developmental psychopathology theorists, people whose early childhoods are marked by traumas and dysfunctional attachments with their parents may avoid developing a disorganized attachment style of their own if they are fortunate enough to also experience positive developmental factors (positive genetic predispositions, positive life events, sensitive role models, opportunities to build resilience, and the like) that help counter their early negative experiences (Fonagy et al., 2023). However, those who do not experience such positive factors are high-risk candidates for borderline personality disorder. Studies repeatedly confirm that, on average, people with borderline personality disorder display a disorganized attachment style and have indeed experienced unfavorable parenting and early childhood traumas (Martin-Gagnon et al., 2023; Armour et al., 2022).

In recent years, developmental psychopathology theorists have also come to believe that a central psychological deficit in borderline personality disorder is the person's inability to *mentalize* (Chapman et al., 2023). **Mentalization** refers to people's capacity to understand their own mental states and those of other people—that is, to recognize needs, desires, feelings, beliefs, and goals. When people mentalize effectively, they can predict the behaviors of other people, and they can react to others in appropriate and trusting ways. The theorists suspect that persons who emerge from childhood with a disorganized attachment style have a weakened ability to mentalize and, correspondingly, a poor ability to control their own emotions, attention, thinking, and behavior and their relationships. Poor mentalization skills are on display in several psychological disorders, but studies find that mentalization is particularly flawed in people with borderline personality disorder (Gagliardini et al., 2023; Martin-Gagnon et al., 2023).

mentalization The capacity to understand one's own mental states and those of other people.

dialectical behavior therapy (DBT) A comprehensive treatment approach, applied in cases of borderline personality disorder, suicidal intent, and/or other psychological problems; includes both individual sessions and group sessions.

The developmental psychopathology explanation of borderline personality disorder has excited many in the clinical field as multiple studies keep finding clear relationships between poor parent–child attachments and the development of disorganized attachment styles and between disorganized attachment styles and borderline personality disorder.

Treatments for Borderline Personality Disorder

It is extraordinarily difficult for a therapist to strike a balance between challenging the thinking of a client with borderline personality disorder and empathizing with the person's dependency and anger (McKenzie, Gregory, & Hogg, 2022). The fluctuating interpersonal attitudes of clients with the disorder can also make it difficult for therapists to establish collaborative working relationships with them (Kramer et al., 2024). Moreover, clients with borderline personality disorder may violate the boundaries of the client–therapist relationship (for example, repeatedly calling the therapist's emergency contact number to discuss matters of a less urgent nature). When, however, such difficulties are overcome, it appears that psychotherapy can eventually lead to at least moderate improvement for people with borderline personality disorder.

PSYCHODYNAMIC THERAPIES Traditional psychoanalytic therapy has not been effective for people with borderline personality disorder (Keefe et al., 2021). However, contemporary psychodynamic approaches, particularly *relational psychoanalytic therapy* and a related treatment called *transference-focused psychotherapy*—approaches in which therapists take a more supportive posture and focus largely on issues that occur within the therapist–client relationship—have had some success (Chapman et al., 2023; Normandin et al., 2023). In these treatments, therapists work to provide an empathic setting within which clients with borderline personality disorder can explore their unconscious conflicts and pay attention to their central relationship disturbance, poor sense of self, and pervasive loneliness and emptiness.

DIALECTICAL BEHAVIOR THERAPY Over the past 25 years, a third wave cognitive-behavioral therapy for borderline personality disorder, called **dialectical behavior therapy** (DBT), has received considerable research support and is now considered the treatment of choice for people with borderline personality disorder (Rizvi et al., 2024; Bender et al., 2023; Marco, Mayoral, & Hervas, 2023). DBT, developed by psychologist Marsha Linehan, consists of individual therapy and group skill-building sessions held weekly for approximately one year. While targeting all of the features of borderline personality disorder, DBT places special emphasis on clients' efforts at self-harm and/or suicide.

Advice from the Hulk As all Marvel Comics readers know, the Incredible Hulk struggles with the regulation of his emotions and with severe swings in his moods and behaviors. In an episode of the Marvel TV show *She-Hulk: Attorney at Law*, Bruce Banner (the Hulk) reveals to his cousin Jennifer Walters (She-Hulk) that his efforts to control his anger have been helped by dialectical behavior therapy (DBT) and that she too should pursue that form of treatment to be an effective superhero. The Hulk explains that DBT "allows us to hold two opposing truths at the same time," and he clarifies that the approach is "about accepting the situation you're in."

The individual therapy sessions of DBT include many of the same behavioral and cognitive techniques that are applied to other disorders: mindfulness skill training, homework assignments, psychoeducation, the teaching of coping and related skills, modeling by the therapist, clear goal setting, reinforcements for appropriate behaviors, ongoing assessment of the client's behaviors and treatment progress, and collaborative examinations by the client and therapist of the client's ways of thinking.

Although primarily cognitive-behavioral, the individual DBT sessions also borrow heavily from the contemporary psychodynamic and humanistic approaches, placing the client–therapist relationship itself at the center of treatment interactions, making sure that appropriate treatment boundaries are adhered to, and providing an environment of acceptance and validation of the client. Indeed, DBT therapists regularly empathize with their borderline clients and with the emotional turmoil they are experiencing, locate kernels of truth in the clients' complaints or demands, and examine alternative ways for them to address valid needs.

DBT clients also participate in groups where they build their needed skills. In these groups, clients practice new ways of relating to other people in a safe environment and receive validation and support from other group members (Shaw et al., 2024).

DBT has received more research support than any other treatment for borderline personality disorder (Rizvi et al., 2024; Chapman et al., 2023; Gillespie, Murphy, & Joyce, 2022). Many clients who undergo DBT become more able to tolerate stress, develop more social skills, respond more effectively to life situations, and develop a more stable identity, gains that typically continue for years. They also display significantly fewer self-harm and suicidal behaviors and require fewer hospitalizations than those who receive other forms of treatment. In addition, they are more likely to remain in treatment and to report less anger, more social gratification, improved work performance, and reductions in substance abuse.

of NOTE ...

Their Words

"I honestly didn't realize at the time that I was dealing with myself. . . . But I suppose it's true that I developed a therapy [DBT] that provides the things I needed for so many years and never got."

Marsha Linehan, psychologist, 2011

MENTALIZATION-BASED THERAPY As you read earlier in this section, a number of theorists believe that a core deficit for people with borderline personality disorder is their inability to *mentalize*—to accurately recognize their own mental states and those of other people, particularly such mental states as needs, desires, feelings, beliefs, and goals. Thus, an increasingly popular treatment for this disorder is *mentalization-based therapy*, an approach in which therapists use cognitive-behavioral techniques to help clients improve their mentalization skills. Focusing on the here-and-now therapy interaction, therapists raise and lower clients' emotional arousal, guide the clients to repeatedly observe their state of mind, help them appreciate the inaccuracy of their mentalizing efforts, guide them to try out more flexible perspectives, and help them achieve greater accuracy in the identification of their own mental states and those of the therapist. Over time, therapy progress is expected to produce improvements in the everyday mentalization skills of clients and, in turn, a more stable sense of self, better regulation of emotions and behaviors, and calmer and more gratifying stable relationships.

Studies find that mentalization-based therapy does indeed help improve the functioning of people with borderline personality disorder and reduce many of their symptoms (Bateman et al., 2023; Fonagy et al., 2023). However, it is not yet clear whether such improvements are as wide-ranging as those brought about by the more comprehensive DBT approach.

PSYCHOTROPIC DRUGS Antidepressant, mood-stabilizing, antianxiety, and antipsychotic drugs have helped calm the emotional and aggressive storms of some people with borderline personality disorder (Chapman et al., 2023; Lunghi et al., 2023). However, given the numerous suicide attempts by people with this disorder, some clinicians believe that the use of drugs on an outpatient basis, in the absence of structured psychological support, is unwise. Most professionals

Why do most clinicians believe that medications alone are not sufficient for the treatment of borderline personality disorder?

histrionic personality disorder A personality disorder characterized by a pattern of excessive emotionality and attention seeking. Once called *hysterical personality disorder.*

believe that psychotropic drug treatment for this disorder should be used largely as an adjunct to psychotherapy approaches, and indeed many clients seem to benefit from a combination of psychotherapy and psychotropic drug therapy.

Histrionic Personality Disorder

People with **histrionic personality disorder,** once called *hysterical personality disorder,* are extremely emotional—they are typically described as "emotionally charged"—and continually seek to be the center of attention (APA, 2022). Their exaggerated moods and neediness can complicate life considerably, as we observe in the case of Lucinda:

Unhappy over her impending divorce, Lucinda decided to seek counseling. She arrived at her first session wearing a very provocative outfit, including a revealing blouse and extremely short skirt.

When asked to discuss her separation, Lucinda first insisted that the therapist call her Cindy, saying, "All my close friends call me that, and I like to think that you and I will become very good friends here." She said that her husband, Morgan, had suddenly abandoned her—"probably brainwashed by some young trollop." She proceeded to describe their breakup in a theatrical manner. Over a span of five minutes, her voice ranged from whispers to cries of agony and back again to whispers; she waved her arms dramatically while making some points and sat totally still while making others.

Lucinda said that when Morgan first told her that he wanted a divorce, she did not know whether she could go on. After all, they had been so "incredibly and irrevocably" close, and he had been so very devoted to her. She said that initially she even had thoughts of doing away with herself. But, of course, so many people needed her to be strong. So many people relied on her, particularly her "dear friends" and her sister. She had deep and special relationships with them all.

She told the therapist that without Morgan, she would now need a man to take care of her—emotionally and every other way. She asked the therapist if she looked like a 30-year-old woman. When he declined to answer, she said, "I know you're not supposed to say."

When the therapist attempted to steer the conversation back to Morgan, Lucinda became petulant and asked, "Do we really need to talk about that abusive lout?" Morgan had, after all, always called her inadequate and worthless throughout their marriage and told her that everything good in her life had been due to him. When her therapist pointed out that this seemed to contradict the rosy picture she had just painted of Morgan and their married life, she quickly changed the subject.

As the session came to a close, Lucinda's therapist suggested that it might be useful for him to meet with Morgan. She loved the idea, saying, "Then he'll know the competition he has!"

When he met with Morgan a few days later, the therapist heard a very different story. Morgan said, "I really loved Cindy—still do—but she was always flying off the handle, telling me I'm no good or that I didn't care about her. She would often complain that I spent too much time at work—keep in mind that I never work more than 30 hours a week—and too little time attending to her and her needs. I just can't take life with her anymore. It's too draining."

Morgan also indicated that Lucinda had virtually no close friends. She and her sister might talk on the phone once a month. He acknowledged that she drew a lot of attention from people. But, he noted, "Look at the way she dresses and her constant flirting. That'll certainly get people's attention, keep them around for a while."

of NOTE ...

"Egoist" Versus "Egotist"

An *egoist* is a person concerned primarily with their own interests. An *egotist* has an inflated sense of self-worth. A boastful egotist is not necessarily a self-absorbed egoist.

Based on surveys in the United States, it is estimated that as many as 1.8 percent of adults experience histrionic personality disorder (APA, 2022). People with this disorder are always "onstage," using theatrical gestures and mannerisms and grandiose language to describe ordinary everyday events. Like chameleons, they keep changing themselves to attract and impress an audience, and in their pursuit they change not only their surface characteristics—according to the latest fads—but also their opinions and beliefs. In fact, their speech is actually scanty in detail and substance, and they seem to lack a sense of who they really are.

Approval and praise are their lifeblood; they must have others present to witness their exaggerated emotional states. Vain, self-centered, demanding, and unable to delay gratification for long, they overreact to minor events that get in the way of their quest for attention. Some make suicide attempts, often to manipulate others (APA, 2022).

People with histrionic personality disorder may draw attention to themselves by exaggerating their physical illnesses or fatigue. They may also behave very provocatively and try to achieve their goals through sexual seduction. Most obsess over how they look and how others will perceive them, often wearing bright, eye-catching clothes. They exaggerate the depth of their relationships, considering themselves to be the intimate friends of people who view them as no more than casual acquaintances (Zimmerman, 2023; French & Shrestha, 2022).

of NOTE ...

Their Words

"The hysterical find too much significance in things. The depressed find too little."

Mason Cooley, American aphorist

How Do Theorists Explain Histrionic Personality Disorder? As you read in the chapter on disorders featuring somatic disorders, the psychodynamic perspective was originally developed to help explain cases of hysteria. Thus, it is no surprise that psychodynamic theorists continue to have a strong interest in histrionic personality disorder. Most psychodynamic theorists believe that as children, people with this disorder had cold and controlling parents who left them feeling unloved and afraid of abandonment (Fariba et al., 2023; Yalch, Ceroni, & Dehart, 2023). To defend against deep-seated fears of loss, the children learned to behave dramatically, inventing crises that would require other people to act protectively.

Anthony Smith/CartoonStock, Ltd

Cognitive-behavioral explanations look instead at the lack of substance and the extreme suggestibility that people with histrionic personality disorder have. Cognitive-behavioral theorists view these individuals as becoming less and less interested in knowing about the world at large because they are so self-focused and emotional. With no detailed memories of what they never learned, they must rely on hunches or on other people to provide them with direction in life. Some such theorists also believe that people with this disorder hold a general assumption that they are helpless to care for themselves, and so they constantly seek out others who will meet their needs (MH, 2023; Weishaar & Beck, 2006).

Sociocultural, particularly multicultural, theorists believe that the very category of histrionic personality disorder, like other personality disorders, is produced in part by cultural norms and expectations (Tyrer & Mulder, 2022). Until recent decades, for example, society encouraged women to hold on to childlike dependency throughout their development. Correspondingly, some theorists assert that the vain, dramatic, and selfish behavior characteristic of the histrionic personality may actually be an exaggeration and stereotype of femininity as society once defined it, just as antisocial personality disorder may reflect an extreme version of traits once associated with stereotypic masculinity (Wang, 2023; Widiger & Gore, 2016). Some sociocultural theorists and critics, thus, question whether a diagnosis of histrionic personality disorder is ever appropriate and valid.

narcissistic personality disorder A personality disorder marked by a broad pattern of grandiosity, need for admiration, and lack of empathy.

Treatments for Histrionic Personality Disorder

Working with clients with histrionic personality disorder can be very difficult because of the demands, tantrums, and seductiveness they may deploy (Skodol & Bender, 2022). Another problem is that they may pretend to have important insights or pretend to change during treatment merely to please the therapist (Magid & Fox, 2022). To head off such problems, therapists must remain objective and maintain strict professional boundaries.

Cognitive-behavioral therapists have tried to help people with this disorder change their belief that they are helpless and develop better, more deliberate ways of thinking and solving problems (Babl et al., 2023; Beck et al., 2015). Psychodynamic therapy and various group therapy formats have also been used (Koppers et al., 2023; Zimmerman, 2023). In all of these approaches, therapists ultimately aim to help the clients recognize their excessive dependency, find inner satisfaction, cope better, and become more self-reliant (French & Shrestha, 2022). Clinical case reports suggest that each of the approaches can be useful. Drug therapy tends to be of limited help except as a means of relieving the depressive symptoms some clients have (Lunghi et al., 2023).

Narcissistic Personality Disorder

Think back to Frederick, the newly hired news editor described at the beginning of this chapter. As you may recall, within weeks of his being hired, Frederick's nonstop boasting, arrogance, insensitivity, and oversized plans had repelled and worn down everyone working at the website, an impact that characterized every area of his life. Eventually, Frederick received a diagnosis of **narcissistic personality disorder,** a disorder marked by a pervasive pattern of grandiosity, need for admiration, and lack of empathy for others (APA, 2022). Convinced of their own great success, power, or beauty, people with this disorder expect constant attention and applause from those around them.

In the Greek myth, Narcissus died enraptured by the beauty of his own reflection in a pool, pining away with longing to possess his own image. His name has come to be synonymous with extreme self-involvement, and indeed people with narcissistic personality disorder have a monumental sense of self-importance. They exaggerate their achievements and talents, expecting others to recognize them as superior. They are very choosy about their friends and associates, believing that their problems are unique and can be appreciated only by other "special," high-status people. Because of their charm, they often make favorable first impressions, as Frederick did when he first interviewed for his job, yet they can rarely maintain long-term relationships (Melli et al., 2024; Caligor & Petrini, 2022).

People with narcissistic personality disorder are seldom interested in the feelings of others. They may not even be able to empathize with such feelings (di Giacomo et al., 2023). Many take advantage of other people to achieve their own ends. Their actions are often driven at some level out of envy of others; at the same time they believe others envy them. Although they have a grandiose self-image, some react to criticism or frustration with rage or embitterment (Mitra & Fluyau, 2023). Others may react with cold indifference. And still others experience a sense of inadequacy, humiliation, pessimism, or depression (Kwon, 2023; Caligor & Petrini, 2022). They may have periods of effervescence that alternate with periods of disappointment.

Based on surveys in the United States, it is estimated that as many as 6.2 percent of adults may display narcissistic personality disorder (APA, 2022). Narcissistic-type behaviors and thoughts are common among teenagers but do not usually lead to adult narcissism (see **MindTech**).

William Haefeli/CartoonStock

"Sometimes you act like you're the only narcissist in this marriage"

MINDTECH

Selfies: Narcissistic or Not?

Peter Bernik/Shutterstock

In the art world, people have been drawing self-portraits for centuries. More recently, digital technology has ushered in the *selfie,* a cousin to the self-portrait. Safe to say, just about every cell phone user has taken selfies. Around 72 percent of all people and 82 percent of young adults have posted photos of themselves, 92 million selfies are posted every day, and selfies are the most reposted of all messages (Statista, 2023; Broz, 2022; Mason, 2020). These self-photos have created such a stir that the word *selfie* was elected "Word of the Year" by the *Oxford English Dictionary* at one point.

As the selfie phenomenon has grown, opinions about selfies have intensified. It seems like people either love them or hate them. This is true in the field of psychology as well. Some psychologists view taking selfies as a form of narcissistic behavior, while others view them more positively.

First, the negative perspective. As noted elsewhere in this chapter, many sociocultural theorists detect a link between narcissistic personality disorder and "eras of narcissism" in society. They suggest that social values in society break down periodically, producing generations of self-centered, materialistic youth. Some of these theorists consider today's selfie generation a perfect example of a current era of narcissism. This theory has gained a large following, but it is not consistently supported by research. Several teams of investigators have found no relationship between how many selfies people post and how high they score on narcissism personality scales (Wu, 2022; Boursier, Gioia, & Griffiths, 2020). Other researchers have found that many people who score high on narcissism scales do not necessarily enjoy taking selfies (Jin & Ryu, 2022; Monacis et al., 2020). Moreover, the vast majority of people who post selfies do not score especially high on narcissism scales.

What other trends in behavior—digital or otherwise—might suggest that our society is currently in an era of narcissism?

This lack of support for the narcissism viewpoint does not mean that selfies, especially repeated selfie behaviors, are completely harmless. Sherry Turkle, an influential technology psychologist, believes that the near-reflexive instinct to photograph oneself may limit deeper engagements with the environment or prevent a full experience of events (Turkle, 2021, 2017, 2015, 2013). Turkle also suggests that people who post an endless stream of selfies are often seeking external validation of their self-worth, even if that pursuit does not rise to a level of clinical narcissism. Several studies support Turkle's notions (Jin & Ryu, 2022; Liu, Zhu, & He, 2022). Small wonder that 68 percent of selfie-takers admit to editing their photos before posting them (Almanza, 2020; Reynolds, 2020).

On the positive side, a number of psychologists believe that the criticisms and concerns about the selfie movement have been overstated. They agree with media psychologist Pamela Rutledge that, for the most part, selfies are an inevitable by-product of "technology-enabled self-expression" (Rutledge, 2023, 2017, 2013). Rutledge contends that selfie behaviors are simply confusing to individuals of a predigital generation. Moreover, she concludes that the selfie trend can enhance explorations of identity, help identify one's interests, develop artistic expression, help people craft a meaningful narrative of their life experiences, and even reflect more realistic body images (for example, posting selfies without makeup). Indeed, several studies have supported these points and have also uncovered additional positive motives and effects of selfie-taking (Ivusic, 2022; Wu, 2022).

In short, like other technological trends you've read about, the selfie phenomenon has received mixed grades from psychology researchers and practitioners so far.

How Do Theorists Explain Narcissistic Personality Disorder?

Psychodynamic theorists more than others have theorized about narcissistic personality disorder, and they again propose that the problem begins with cold, rejecting parents (Mitra & Fluyau, 2023; Lenzenweger, 2022). They argue that some people with this background spend their lives defending against feeling unsatisfied, rejected, unworthy, ashamed, and wary of the world. They do so by repeatedly telling themselves that they are actually perfect and desirable and also by seeking admiration from others. Object relations theorists — the psychodynamic theorists who emphasize relationships — interpret the grandiose self-image as a way for these people to convince themselves that they are totally self-sufficient and without need of warm relationships with their parents or anyone else (Normandin et al., 2023; Caligor & Stern, 2020). In support of the psychodynamic theories, research has found that children who are neglected and/or abused or who lose parents through adoption, divorce, or death are at particular risk for the later development of narcissistic personality disorder (Caligor & Petrini, 2022; Lenzenweger, 2022).

A number of cognitive-behavioral theorists propose that narcissistic personality disorder may develop when people are treated *too positively* rather than too negatively in early life. They hold that certain children acquire a superior and grandiose attitude when their "admiring or doting parents" teach them to "overvalue their self-worth," repeatedly rewarding them for minor accomplishments or for no accomplishment at all (Mitra & Fluyau, 2023; Caligor & Petrini, 2022).

Why do people often admire arrogant deceivers — art forgers, jewel thieves, or certain kinds of "con" artists, for example?

Many sociocultural theorists detect a link between narcissistic personality disorder and "eras of narcissism" in society (Colby, 2022; Gorun, Scherban, & Auchincloss, 2022). They suggest that family values and social ideals in certain societies periodically break down, producing generations of young people who are self-centered and materialistic and have short attention spans. Western cultures in particular, which encourage self-expression, individualism, and competitiveness, are considered likely to produce such generations of narcissism. In fact, one worldwide study found that respondents from the United States had the highest narcissism scores, followed, in descending order, by those from Europe, Canada, Asia, and the Middle East (Foster, Campbell, & Twenge, 2003). Still another study found that the narcissism survey scores of college students in the United States increased by 30 percent between 1979 and 2006, a trend that appears to be continuing today with the ever-growing use of social media (Mortell, 2022; Twenge & Foster, 2008).

Treatments for Narcissistic Personality Disorder

Narcissistic personality disorder is one of the most difficult personality patterns to treat because the clients are unable to acknowledge weaknesses, to appreciate the effect of their behavior on others, or to incorporate feedback from others (Kwon, 2023). The clients who consult therapists usually do so because of a related disorder such as depression (Mitra & Fluyau, 2023). Once in treatment, the clients may try to manipulate the therapist into supporting their sense of superiority (Skodol & Bender, 2022). Some also seem to project their grandiose attitudes onto their therapists and develop a love–hate stance toward them (Gorun et al., 2022).

Psychodynamic therapists seek to help people with this disorder recognize and work through their underlying insecurities and defenses (Zimmerman, 2023; Crisp & Gabbard, 2020). Cognitive-behavioral therapists, focusing on the self-centered thinking of such individuals, try to redirect the clients' focus onto the opinions of others, teach them to interpret criticism more rationally, increase their ability to empathize, and change their all-or-nothing notions (Kramer et al., 2024; Nook et al., 2022). None of these approaches have received systematic study, nor have they had clear success (Kwon, 2023; Mitra & Fluyau, 2023). Psychotropic drugs may be used to treat co-occurring psychological disorders but not the personality disorder itself (Lunghi et al., 2023).

of NOTE ...

Vain Portrait

King Frederick V, ruler of Denmark from 1746 to 1766, had his portrait painted at least 70 times by the same artist, Carl Pilo (Shaw, 2004).

SUMMING UP

"Dramatic" Personality Disorders

Four of the personality disorders in DSM-5-TR are marked by highly dramatic, emotional, or erratic symptoms. People with antisocial personality disorder display a pattern of disregard for and violation of the rights of others. No known treatment is notably effective. People with borderline personality disorder display a pattern of instability in interpersonal relationships, self-image, and mood, along with extreme impulsivity. Treatment, particularly dialectical behavior therapy, apparently can be helpful and lead to some improvement. People with histrionic personality disorder display a pattern of extreme emotionality and attention seeking. Clinical case reports suggest that treatment is helpful on occasion. Finally, people with narcissistic personality disorder display a pattern of grandiosity, need for admiration, and lack of empathy. It is one of the most difficult disorders to treat.

"Anxious" Personality Disorders

THE CLUSTER OF "anxious" personality disorders includes the *avoidant, dependent,* and *obsessive-compulsive personality disorders*. People with these patterns typically display anxious and fearful behavior. As with most of the other personality disorders, research support for the various explanations of these disorders is limited. At the same time, treatments for the disorders appear to be modestly to moderately helpful—considerably better than for other personality disorders.

of NOTE ...

Their Words

"We continue to shape our personality all our life."

Albert Camus

Avoidant Personality Disorder

People with **avoidant personality disorder** are very uncomfortable and inhibited in social situations, overwhelmed by feelings of inadequacy, and extremely sensitive to negative evaluation (APA, 2022). They are so fearful of being rejected that they give no one an opportunity to reject them—or to accept them either:

Santi starts his first therapy session by imploring the new counselor to offer tips for becoming more popular. He says he is always certain that people must find him ridiculous. He had a few friends in the past, including his college friend Javier and Javier's high school friend Adolfo. But after Santi's college graduation, Javi and Adi seemed to tease him mercilessly about his torn clothes and small apartment. He knew that they also made fun of each other, but he feared it was more than good-natured banter when they were focusing on him. Santi tells the counselor, "I believe they thought of me as pathetic, and because I have no money, that stuff about my clothes and home really hurt." Santi eventually stopped calling them back when they tried to contact him to make plans, and he hasn't spoken to either in about two years. Better to be alone—even lonely—than to live in constant fear of criticism or embarrassment.

Since then, Santi has struggled to make new friends. A number of people work at his place of employment, a shipping factory sorting center, but he keeps to himself, avoiding contact with the others, steering clear of their judgments, and blending into the woodwork as much as possible. His coworkers seem nice enough, but he is terrified to

(continued on the next page)

avoidant personality disorder A personality disorder characterized by consistent discomfort and restraint in social situations, overwhelming feelings of inadequacy, and extreme sensitivity to negative evaluation.

speak to them about anything other than work, even if they approach him. He's sure that they would laugh at him if they knew he was looking to make friends, and he does not want to face that kind of embarrassment. Worse, even if he were to become friends with them, they'd eventually realize that he is unintelligent and inept. He already knows he is unlikable and untalented; he doesn't need more confirmation. He is always vigilant not to say too much in conversation; he doesn't want to give anyone ammunition to criticize and humiliate him. He just cannot not bear the thought of looking foolish.

His mother often asks him, "Santiago, why don't you do something with your business degree? All those scholarships. Your father and I thought you'd be the first in our family to own a house." Santi always tells her that he is happy with the job he has. He does not mention his certainty that he would fail at any high-level job he might attempt, a failure that would lead to intolerable embarrassment and humiliation. Nor could he face the rejection of not getting the jobs he might apply for.

No, in his mind, his life is where it has to be. Although he is profoundly unhappy and actually craves acceptance and close relationships, he is better off where he is. At the least, his lifestyle and job minimize the dangers of social interaction and keep unbearable feelings of embarrassment and disgrace at a safe distance.

of NOTE ...

Shyness Alert

Between 40 and 60 percent of people in the world consider themselves to be shy (PT, 2023; Rettew, 2019).

People like Santi actively avoid occasions for social contact. At the center of this withdrawal lies not so much poor social skills as a dread of criticism, disapproval, or rejection. They are timid and hesitant in social situations, afraid to say something foolish or to embarrass themselves by blushing or acting nervous. Even in intimate relationships, they express themselves very carefully, afraid of being shamed or ridiculed.

People with this disorder believe themselves to be unappealing or inferior to others. They exaggerate the potential difficulties of new situations, so they seldom take risks or try out new activities. They usually have few or no close friends, though they actually yearn for intimate relationships, and frequently feel depressed and lonely.

Avoidant personality disorder is similar to *social anxiety disorder,* the condition you read about in the chapter on anxiety disorders, and many people with one of these two disorders also experience the other (APA, 2022). The similarities include a fear of humiliation and low confidence. Some theorists believe that there is a key difference between the two disorders—namely, that people with social anxiety disorder primarily fear

Walter Pietsch/Alamy Stock Photo

Just a stage A shy child watches from afar while schoolmates and adults play together during a visit to Paris's 60-acre Jardin du Luxembourg (Luxembourg Gardens). Early temperament is often linked to adult personality, but research has not shown that extreme shyness, a common part of childhood, necessarily predicts an avoidant personality disorder in adulthood.

social *circumstances,* while people with avoidant personality disorder tend to fear close social *relationships*. Other theorists, however, believe that the two disorders reflect the same core psychopathology and should be combined (Fariba & Sapra, 2023).

Based on surveys in the United States, it is estimated that at least 2.4 percent of adults have avoidant personality disorder (APA, 2022). Many children and teenagers are also painfully shy and avoid other people, but this is usually just a typical part of their development.

How Do Theorists Explain Avoidant Personality Disorder?

Theorists often assume that avoidant personality disorder has the same causes as anxiety disorders—such as early traumas, conditioned fears, upsetting beliefs, or biochemical irregularities (Crisan et al., 2023). However, with the exception of social anxiety disorder, research has not tied the personality disorder directly to the anxiety disorders. Psychodynamic and cognitive-behavioral explanations of avoidant personality disorder are the most popular among clinicians.

Psychodynamic theorists focus mainly on the general feelings of shame and insecurity that people with avoidant personality disorder have (Fariba & Sapra, 2023). Some trace the shame to childhood experiences such as early bowel and bladder accidents. If parents repeatedly punish or ridicule a child for having those accidents, the child may develop a negative self-image. This may lead to the child feeling unlovable throughout life and distrusting the love of others. Other psychodynamic theorists believe that a variety of childhood traumas are capable of producing shame and insecurity in a child—and later feelings of distrust and unworthiness—especially if they are dealt with by excessive punishments, rejection, or ridicule.

Similarly, cognitive-behavioral theorists believe that harsh criticism and rejection in early childhood may lead certain people to assume that others in their environment will always judge them negatively. These people come to expect rejection, misinterpret the reactions of others to fit that expectation, discount positive feedback, and generally fear social involvements—setting the stage for avoidant personality disorder (Weme, Sorensen, & Binder, 2023; McQuillan, 2022). In several studies, when participants with this disorder were asked to recall their childhood, their descriptions supported both the psychodynamic and cognitive-behavioral predictions. They remembered, for example, feeling criticized, rejected, and isolated; receiving little encouragement from their parents; and experiencing few displays of parental love or pride (Crisan et al., 2023; Cuncic, 2020).

Cognitive-behavioral theorists also suggest that most people with avoidant personality disorder fail to develop effective social skills and that failure helps maintain the disorder. In support of this position, several studies have found social skills deficits among some people with avoidant personality disorder (Weme et al., 2023; Pedersen, 2022). Most of the theorists agree, however, that these deficits first develop as a result of the individuals avoiding so many social situations.

Treatments for Avoidant Personality Disorder

People with avoidant personality disorder come to therapy in the hope of finding acceptance and affection. Keeping them in treatment can be a challenge, however, for many of them soon begin to avoid the sessions (Skodol & Bender, 2022). They may distrust the therapist's sincerity and start to fear the clinician's rejection. Thus, as with several of the other personality disorders, a key task of the therapist is to gain the person's trust.

Beyond building trust, therapists tend to treat people with avoidant personality disorder much as they treat people with social anxiety disorder and other anxiety disorders. Such approaches have had at least modest success (Fariba et al., 2023). Psychodynamic therapists try to help clients recognize and resolve the unconscious conflicts that may be operating (Timberlake & Fesel, 2023; Cuncic, 2020). Cognitive-behavioral therapists help the individuals change their distressing beliefs and thoughts, carry on in the face of painful emotions, and improve their self-image (Fariba & Sapra, 2023; McQuillan,

of NOTE ...

Shyness Rocks

Rock music has been strongly influenced by stars with extremely shy, reticent demeanors.

- Influential singer-songwriter and famous introvert David Bowie was so uncomfortable performing that he created alternate stage personas, such as the alien rock star Ziggy Stardust, so that he could sing his songs "in disguise."
- Known for his shyness, the guitarist Buckethead performs with a bucket on his head and his face covered.
- The alternative rock band My Bloody Valentine often played with their backs to the audience and spearheaded a pop movement called "shoegaze" based on their tendency to look away or at the floor during shows.
- For some of her initial concerts, folk singer Cat Power (Chan Marshall) would not look at the audience and would weep or run offstage during shows.

of NOTE ...

Big Overlap

Suspiciousness, self-absorption, anxiety, and depression are prominent features in almost all 10 personality disorders in DSM-5-TR.

2022). They also provide social skills training and exposure treatments that require people to gradually increase their social contacts (Weme et al., 2023; Zimmerman, 2023). Group therapy formats, especially groups that follow cognitive and behavioral principles, have the added advantage of providing clients with practice in social interactions (Koppers et al., 2023; Weme et al., 2023). Antianxiety and antidepressant drugs are sometimes useful in reducing the social anxiety of people with the disorder (Sperry & Casteleiro, 2022).

Dependent Personality Disorder

People with **dependent personality disorder** have a pervasive, excessive need to be taken care of (APA, 2022). As a result, they are clinging and obedient, fearing separation from their parent, partner, or other person with whom they are in a close relationship. They rely on others so much that they cannot make the smallest decision for themselves. Lucas is a case in point:

Lucas, an assistant graphics programmer, is a 42-year-old single man who lives with his father. He is currently grappling with intense feelings of depression and anxiety. These feelings began when he ended his relationship of two years with Orena, whom he had viewed as the woman of his dreams and his future wife. But Lucas's father just didn't like Orena, and he certainly didn't like the idea of Lucas marrying her. In fact, he forbade it—forbade his middle-aged son from marrying the woman of his dreams.

Inside, Lucas was furious at his father, although he knew he could never express his anger. He simply could not—now or ever—risk his father getting angry at him, being disappointed in him, not talking to him, or being unsupportive. Then he might have to fend for himself, and that was unthinkable. At some level, he also thought that maybe his father might be right. He always went along with his father's advice and decisions. He thought of himself as a person of poor judgment—too poor to make a decision, big or small, on his own.

So eventually, Lucas did what he always knew he would have to do—he broke up with Orena. He was more than ashamed and critical of himself, for hurting Orena, for being such a weakling, for giving up his dream so readily. But he felt helpless and incapable of taking any other course of action.

Lucas is not particularly accomplished in the various areas of his life. His job of 15 years is at least two levels below what he is capable of. Over the years, he rejected promotion offers and did not respond to overtures from other graphic design companies. The reason was always the same: he didn't want—no, he was afraid to take on—additional responsibilities, especially responsibilities for making decisions and leading other workers. He is considered dependable and hardworking—a never-changing fixture in the work setting.

His social life is similarly modest and uneventful. Outside of Orena, his social life is limited to a single lifelong friend. They get together for dinner and an activity three nights a week. If his friend ever cancels, Lucas feels lost.

Growing up, Lucas's older sisters, mother, and father always pampered and protected him, catering to his every need. Still he remembers being fearful and tentative throughout his childhood, afraid to do anything on his own. When his sisters grew older and moved away and after his mother died, it became just him and his father. Going away to college in another city was unthinkable. His father is now the most important person in his life. Although more than a little domineering, he loves Lucas and continues the family tradition of protecting and guiding him.

dependent personality disorder A personality disorder characterized by a pattern of clinging and obedience, fear of separation, and an ongoing need to be taken care of.

It is usual and healthy to depend on others, but those with dependent personality disorder constantly need assistance with even the simplest matters and have extreme feelings of inadequacy and helplessness. Afraid that they cannot care for themselves, they cling desperately to friends or relatives. Surveys in the United States suggest that 0.6 percent or less of adults experience this disorder (APA, 2022).

As you observed previously, people with avoidant personality disorder have difficulty *initiating* relationships. In contrast, people with dependent personality disorder have difficulty with *separation*. They feel completely helpless and devastated when a close relationship ends, and they quickly seek out another relationship to fill the void. Many cling persistently to relationships with partners who physically or psychologically abuse them (APA, 2022).

Lacking confidence in their own ability and judgment, people with this disorder seldom disagree with others and allow even important decisions to be made for them. They may depend on a parent or partner to decide where to live, what job to have, and which neighbors to befriend. Because they so fear rejection, they are overly sensitive to disapproval and keep trying to meet other people's wishes and expectations, even if it means volunteering for unpleasant or demeaning tasks.

Many people with dependent personality disorder feel distressed, lonely, and sad; often they dislike themselves. Thus, they are at risk for depressive and anxiety disorders (APA, 2022). Their fear of separation and their feelings of helplessness may leave them particularly prone to suicidal thoughts, especially when they believe that a relationship is about to end (Bornstein, 2024, 2020; Bornstein & Natoli, 2022).

of NOTE ...

Their Words

"The deepest principle of human nature is the craving to be appreciated."

William James, psychologist, 1896

How Do Theorists Explain Dependent Personality Disorder?

Psychodynamic explanations for dependent personality disorder are similar to those for depression. Freudian theorists argue, for example, that unresolved conflicts during the oral stage of development can give rise to a lifelong need for nurturance, thus heightening the likelihood of a dependent personality disorder (Fariba et al., 2023; Bornstein & Natoli, 2022). Similarly, object relations theorists say that early parental loss or rejection may prevent typical experiences of *attachment* and *separation*, leaving some children with fears of abandonment that persist throughout their lives (Normandin et al., 2023; Kernberg, 2022, 2020, 2018). Still other psychodynamic theorists suggest that, to the contrary, many parents of people with this disorder were overcontrolling and overprotective, thus increasing their children's dependency, insecurity, and separation anxiety.

Cognitive-behavioral theorists point to both behavioral and cognitive factors in their explanation of dependent personality disorder. In the behavioral realm, they propose that parents of people with dependent personality disorder unintentionally rewarded their children's clinging and "loyal" behavior while at the same time punishing acts of independence, perhaps through the withdrawal of love. Alternatively, some parents' own dependent behaviors may have served as models for their children (Bornstein, 2024, 2020; Bornstein & Natoli, 2022). In the cognitive realm, the theorists identify maladaptive attitudes as further helping to produce and maintain this disorder, such as "I am inadequate and helpless to deal with the world" and "I must find a person to provide protection so I can cope." Dichotomous (black-and-white) thinking may also play a key role: "If I am to be dependent, I must be completely helpless," or "If I am to be independent, I must be alone." Such thinking prevents the individuals from making efforts to be autonomous (APA, 2022; Beck et al., 2015).

Bruce Eric Kaplan The New Yorker Collection/The Cartoon Bank

"My self-esteem was so low I just followed her around everywhere she would go."

Treatments for Dependent Personality Disorder

In therapy, people with dependent personality disorder usually place all responsibility for their treatment and well-being on the clinician. Thus, a key task of therapy is to help patients accept responsibility for themselves (Skodol & Bender, 2022). Because the domineering behaviors of a partner or parent may help foster a

obsessive-compulsive personality disorder A personality disorder marked by such an intense focus on orderliness, perfectionism, and control that the person loses flexibility, openness, and efficiency.

client's symptoms, some clinicians suggest couple or family therapy as well or even separate therapy for the partner or parent.

Treatment for dependent personality disorder can be at least modestly helpful. Psychodynamic therapy for this pattern focuses on many of the same issues as therapy for depressed people, including the *transference* of dependency needs onto the therapist (Bornstein, 2024, 2020; Bornstein & Natoli, 2022). Cognitive-behavioral therapists combine behavioral and cognitive interventions to help the clients take control of their lives (Fariba et al., 2023; Beck et al., 2015). On the behavioral end, the therapists often provide assertiveness training to help the individuals better express their own wishes in relationships. On the cognitive end, the therapists also try to help the clients challenge and change their assumptions of incompetence and helplessness. As with avoidant personality disorder, a group therapy format can be useful because it provides opportunities for clients to receive support from a number of peers rather than from a single dominant person (Koppers et al., 2023). In addition, group members may serve as models for one another as they practice better ways to express feelings and solve problems. Antidepressant drug therapy has been helpful for people whose personality disorder is accompanied by depression (Zimmerman, 2023).

Obsessive-Compulsive Personality Disorder

People with **obsessive-compulsive personality disorder** are so preoccupied with order, perfection, and control that they lose all flexibility, openness, and efficiency (Rizvi & Torrico, 2023; APA, 2022). Their concern for doing everything "right" impairs their productivity, as in the case of Talay:

of NOTE ...

Their Words

"If everything seems under control, you're just not going fast enough."

Mario Andretti, racing driver

Talay, a 32-year-old chemical researcher from Thailand living in Boston, had been urged by his partner Kurt to seek couples counseling in an attempt, as Kurt put it, "to save our marriage." Talay remarked several times during the initial interview that therapy was taking him away from an important work project—even though the therapist had arranged to see the couple in the evening to accommodate Talay's work schedule.

Kurt explained to the therapist that Talay frequently belittled him and shut him out, behaviors that had been escalating in recent months. Almost every night, Talay would spend endless hours alone poring over data and results—from studies that had, for the most part, been completed and analyzed months ago. Whenever Kurt would complain, Talay would get furious, insisting that he needed to check and recheck every detail to make sure that no mistakes had been made. After all, anything he put his name on had to be completely accurate.

At the lab, Talay was a "good soldier," always wanting to do a good job, usually deferential to his bosses, and rarely giving them a hard time—unless they asked to move faster on his projects! He had been reprimanded twice for being behind schedule. Each time, he tried to explain to his superiors that everything needed to be perfect and that that takes time and attention to detail. When the supervisors suggested that he have assistants handle the administrative tasks, Talay hid his irritation but said pointedly that he could not trust any of the "kids" they'd hired, that he really had to do everything himself, because precision and organization were needed at each point in the data analysis.

It wasn't just Talay's work-related behavior that made things stressful and unpleasant for Kurt. It was Talay's home-related behavior as well. For example, Talay refused to allow Kurt any involvement in financial matters or any control over the construction of their new house—even though Kurt was a roofer and had a lot more experience than Talay in the construction business. Trusting only himself—his own organizational skills and work ethic—Talay would tell Kurt, "You don't know what you're doing. You'll only mess things up." Kurt was both exasperated and hurt by such an absurd statement. Moreover, he knew the new house would never reach completion under Talay's supervision.

Kurt felt that slowly but surely, Talay's perfectionistic, detailed, and controlling style had taken over their personal life and was now ruining their relationship. With Talay, there was a right and a wrong for every behavior, every decision, every plan. Talay's black-and-white standards had also worked their way into the couple's social life. When, for example, Theo, a close friend, left his wife several months ago, Talay responded by cutting him off totally, saying that such behavior was disgraceful. A few months later, when Kurt brought up his own unhappiness in their marriage, Talay accused him of being "just like Theo, no respect for marriage at all," adding as a kicker, "I'd have been better off staying in Thailand, where people have better values, are more competent, and know how to be a loving partner." He apologized immediately, but the statement had done great damage and had clarified for Kurt that things had to change or their marriage had to end.

In Talay's concern with rules, standards, and order and doing things right, he has trouble recognizing the larger picture. When faced with a task, he and others who have obsessive-compulsive personality disorder may become so focused on organization and details that they fail to grasp the point of the activity. As a result, their work is often behind schedule (some seem unable to finish any job), and they may neglect leisure activities, friendships, and relationships.

People with this personality disorder set unreasonably high standards for themselves and others. Their behaviors extend well beyond the realm of conscientiousness. They can never be satisfied with their performance, but they typically refuse to seek help or to work with a team, convinced that others are too careless or incompetent to do the job right. Because they are so afraid of making mistakes, they may be reluctant to make decisions.

They also tend to be rigid and stubborn, particularly in their morals, ethics, and values. They live by a strict personal code and use it as a yardstick for measuring others. They may have trouble expressing much affection, and their relationships are sometimes stiff and superficial. In addition, they are often stingy with their time or money. Some cannot even throw away objects that are worn out or useless (Grant & Chamberlain, 2020). Based on surveys in the United States, it is estimated that as many as 7.9 percent of adults experience obsessive-compulsive personality disorder (Rizvi & Torrico, 2023; APA, 2022).

Many clinicians believe that obsessive-compulsive personality disorder and *obsessive-compulsive disorder* are closely related. Certainly, the two disorders share a number of features, and many people who experience one of the disorders meet the diagnostic criteria for the other disorder (Rizvi & Torrico, 2023). However, it is worth noting that people with the personality disorder are more likely to experience either a depressive, bipolar, or anxiety disorder than to experience obsessive-compulsive disorder (Pozza et al., 2021).

How Do Theorists Explain Obsessive-Compulsive Personality Disorder?

Most explanations of obsessive-compulsive personality disorder borrow heavily from those of obsessive-compulsive disorder despite the doubts concerning a link between the two disorders. Research evidence for these explanations is limited.

Freudian theorists suggest that people with obsessive-compulsive personality disorder are *anal retentive* (Fariba et al., 2023; Rizvi & Torrico, 2023). That is, because of overly harsh toilet training during the anal stage, they become filled with anger, and they remain *fixated* at this stage. To keep their anger under control, they persistently resist both their anger and their instincts to have bowel movements. In turn, they become extremely orderly

Toilet trouble According to Freud, toilet training often produces rage in a child. If parents are too harsh in their approach, the child may become fixated at the anal stage and prone to obsessive-compulsive functioning later in life.

Design Pics/Misty Bedwell/Getty Images

and restrained; many become passionate collectors. Other psychodynamic theorists suggest that any early struggles with parents over control and independence may ignite the aggressive impulses at the root of this personality disorder.

Cognitive-behavioral theorists have little to say about the origins of obsessive-compulsive personality disorder, but they do propose that illogical thinking processes help keep it going (Rizvi & Torrico, 2023; Reddy, 2020). They point, for example, to dichotomous thinking, which may produce rigidity and perfectionism. Similarly, they note that people with this disorder tend to misread or exaggerate the potential outcomes of mistakes or errors.

of NOTE ...

Critical Difference

People with obsessive-compulsive disorder typically do not want or like their symptoms; those with obsessive-compulsive personality disorder often embrace their symptoms and rarely seek to resist them.

Treatments for Obsessive-Compulsive Personality Disorder

People with obsessive-compulsive personality disorder do not usually believe there is anything wrong with them. They therefore are not likely to seek treatment unless they are also experiencing another disorder, most frequently an anxiety disorder or depression, or unless someone close to them insists that they get treatment (Pinto, 2020). Because of this, therapists often feel as though they must "win over" and engage the clients in the therapy process (Kramer et al., 2024; Skodol & Bender, 2022).

People with this personality disorder sometimes respond well to psychodynamic or cognitive-behavioral therapy (Daniels et al., 2023; Fariba et al., 2023; Rizvi & Torrico, 2023). Psychodynamic therapists typically try to help these clients recognize, experience, and accept their underlying feelings and insecurities and perhaps take risks and accept their personal limitations. Cognitive-behavioral therapists focus on helping the clients to change their dichotomous—"all or nothing"—thinking, perfectionism, intolerance of uncertainty, indecisiveness, procrastination, and chronic worrying. A number of clinicians report that people with obsessive-compulsive personality disorder, like those with obsessive-compulsive disorder, respond well to SSRIs, the serotonin-enhancing antidepressant drugs; however, researchers have yet to study this issue fully (Gecaite-Stonciene et al., 2022).

SUMMING UP

"Anxious" Personality Disorders

Three of the personality disorders in DSM-5-TR are marked by anxious and fearful behavior. People with avoidant personality disorder are consistently uncomfortable and inhibited in social situations, overwhelmed by feelings of inadequacy, and extremely sensitive to negative evaluation. People with dependent personality disorder have a persistent need to be taken care of, are submissive and clinging, and fear separation. People with obsessive-compulsive personality disorder are so preoccupied with order, perfection, and control that they lose their flexibility, openness, and efficiency. A variety of treatment strategies have been used for people with these disorders and apparently have been modestly to moderately helpful.

Multicultural Factors: Emerging Research

ACCORDING TO THE criteria of DSM-5-TR, a pattern diagnosed as a personality disorder must "deviate markedly from the expectations of the individual's culture" (APA, 2022). Given the importance of culture in this diagnosis and given the enormous clinical interest in personality disorders, it is striking how little multicultural research was conducted on these conditions until recent years. Clinical theorists had suspicions but little compelling evidence that there are cultural differences in this realm.

Studies conducted over the past decade indicate that the rates of personality disorder diagnoses vary considerably from country to country (APA, 2022; Sansone & Sansone, 2011; Huang et al., 2009). The United States has among the highest reported rates, while Nigeria, China, and countries in Western Europe have lower reported rates. Studies have not yet determined the reasons for such variations; however, many theorists speculate that cultural differences among countries are responsible (APA, 2022; Munson et al., 2022). For example, in countries that strongly encourage collectivist behavior (as opposed to individualistic behavior and personal autonomy), the likelihood of developing narcissistic personality disorder may be relatively low.

In a related vein, studies in the United States are increasingly finding that the diagnostic rates of personality disorders often vary across race and ethnicity, sexual orientation, and gender identity. Focusing primarily on borderline personality disorder, emerging research suggests that the diagnostic rate of this disorder may be higher among Black and Hispanic people than non-Hispanic White people (Wu et al., 2022). It may be that their heightened stressors of marginalization, economic hardship, and discrimination predispose many people of color to develop borderline personality disorder or, alternatively, that clinicians unintentionally display diagnostic bias and too readily assign a personality disorder diagnosis to clients of color when the clients experience context-related occurrences of anger, mood fluctuation, and relationship stress (Burke et al., 2024; APA, 2022).

Why have researchers given relatively little attention to the study of cultural, racial, sexual orientation, and gender differences in personality disorders?

Research on personality disorders in LGBTQ+ populations is limited, but a few studies, focusing once again on borderline personality disorder, suggest that the diagnostic rate of this disorder is higher for transgender and nonbinary people than cisgender people and higher for lesbian, gay, and bisexual people than heterosexual people (Denning et al., 2022; Wu et al., 2022; Rodriguez-Seijas, Morgan, & Zimmerman, 2021). Once again, the reason for these differences may be the heightened stressors experienced by these groups or the impact of diagnostic bias.

Finally, the rates of personality disorders often differ for men and women. Men have higher rates than women for the paranoid, schizoid, schizotypal, antisocial, and narcissistic personality disorders, and women have higher rates for the histrionic, avoidant, and dependent personality disorders. (Only for borderline personality disorder and obsessive-compulsive personality disorder do men and women have the same rates.) Such differences are not well understood, but DSM-5-TR suggests that they may be tied to society's different expectations for the behaviors and emotions displayed by men and women (APA, 2022).

Although multicultural research into personality disorders is a relatively recent phenomenon and useful data are still modest, it is welcome news that studies of this kind are now unfolding. It is expected that such investigations will soon shed considerable light on the impact that cultural factors and diagnostic bias have on the development, assessment, and diagnosis of these disorders as well as open the door for wider-ranging and culturally responsive treatments (Haft et al., 2022).

SUMMING UP

Multicultural Factors

Until recent years, relatively little research was done on the ties between personality disorders and multicultural factors. However, current investigations are beginning to suggest that the disorders vary among people of different countries, races and ethnicity, gender, and sexual orientation. The reasons for such differences may include (1) variations in experiences of stress and (2) diagnostic bias.

Are There Better Ways to Classify Personality Psychopathology?

AS YOU READ EARLIER, a leading criticism of DSM-5-TR's approach to personality disorders is that the classification system defines such disorders by using *categories*—rather than *dimensions*—of personality. Many of today's theorists believe that personality disorders differ more in *degree* than in type of dysfunction. Therefore, they propose that the disorders should be classified by the severity of key personality traits (or dimensions) rather than by the absolute presence or absence of specific traits (Monaghan & Bizumic, 2023). In such an approach, each key trait (for example, disagreeableness, dishonesty, or self-absorption) would be viewed as varying along a continuum in which there is no clear boundary between typical and atypical. People with a personality disorder would be those who display extreme degrees of several of these key traits—degrees not commonly found in the general population (see ***InfoCentral***).

Why do some observers suggest that personality disorders are little more than descriptions of undesirable personal styles?

Which key personality dimensions should clinicians use to help identify people with personality problems? Some theorists believe that they should rely on the dimensions identified in the "Big Five" theory of personality, dimensions that have received enormous attention by personality psychologists over the years. Others favor the dimensions featured in the "HiTOP" model of classification.

The "Big Five" Theory of Personality and Personality Disorders

A large body of research conducted with diverse populations consistently suggests that the basic structure of personality may consist of five "supertraits," or factors—*neuroticism, extroversion, openness to experiences, agreeableness,* and *conscientiousness* (Bornstein, 2024; Cai et al., 2023). Each of these factors, which are frequently referred to as the "Big Five," consists of a number of subfactors. Anxiety and hostility, for example, are subfactors of the neuroticism factor, while optimism and friendliness are subfactors of the extroversion factor. Theoretically, everyone's personality can be summarized by a combination of

Photo courtesy of Everett Collection

Dysfunctional toons Today's animated film characters often have significant personality flaws, illustrated, for example, by the cluster of problematic traits found among the *South Park* kids. Observers note that the kids (especially Cartman, second from left) display enduring grumpiness, disrespect for authority, irreverence, self-absorption, disregard for the feelings of others, general lack of conscience, and a tendency to get into trouble.

THE DARK TRIAD

Over the past 20 years, researchers have studied the **Dark Triad**, a trio of "malicious" traits that work together to produce socially offensive behaviors (Kowalski et al., 2021; Paulhus & Williams, 2002). People with these traits — *narcissism*, *psychopathy*, and *Machiavellianism* — tend to undermine others, perhaps secretly, to achieve their own ends.

Individuals with just one of these traits often offend, manipulate, or disregard the needs of others. But those with **all three** traits are particularly self-absorbed and create serious problems for others. People who score high on Dark Triad rating scales may display a personality disorder, but more often, they experience little distress or impairment and function adequately, sometimes quite effectively, in the personal, social, and occupational realms.

WHAT IS THE DARK TRIAD?

Narcissism
Self-admiring
Self-absorbed
Admiration-seeking
Special treatment–seeking
Overly entitled
Gratification-seeking

Psychopathy
Callous
Insensitive
Antisocial
Unempathetic
Remorseless
Disinhibited

Machiavellianism
Manipulative
Self-interested
Duplicitous
Cynical
Amoral
Focused on personal gain

(Bader et al., 2022; Kowalski et al., 2021; Pilch, 2020; Somma et al., 2020)

PEOPLE WITH THE DARK TRIAD SEEK . . .

- Power
- Status
- Social dominance
- Immediate rewards
- Boundless personal gains
- Thrills
- Substance-related highs

(Bader et al., 2022; Jonason et al., 2020, 2017; Dåderman & Ragnestål-Impola, 2019; Jauk & Dieterich, 2019; Vedel & Thomsen, 2017)

THE DARK TRIAD AFFECTS ALL SPHERES OF LIFE

The PERSONAL realm

People are more likely to be...
Immodest
Disagreeable
Greedy
Suspicious
Dishonest
Substance abusers
Aggressive drivers

(Bader et al., 2022; Gardiner & Lawson, 2022; Karras et al., 2022: Kowalski et al., 2021; Somma et al., 2020; Jauk & Dieterich, 2019)

The SOCIAL sphere

People are more likely to be...
Dominant
Prejudiced
Unethical
Bullies
Extroverted
Aggressive
Insensitive

(Bader et al., 2022; Somma et al., 2020; Dåderman & Ragnestål-Impola, 2019)

THE DARK TRIAD

The SEXUAL realm

People are more likely to...
Pursue quick gratification
Seek casual sex
Display aggressive strategies
Exhibit sexual opportunism
Seek more sexual partners
Commit sexual infidelities
Poach mates from others

(Kowalski et al., 2021; Jonason et al., 2020, 2017, 2011, 2010, 2009; Lyons et al., 2020)

At WORK

People are more likely to...
Have troubled work relationships
Exhibit toxic leadership
Ruthlessly seek self-advancement
Cheat
Commit sexual harassment
Hinder career success of subordinates
Adversely affect personal well-being of subordinates

(Hogrefe, 2023; Schwarzinger, 2023; Schyns et al., 2022; Schattke & Marion-Jetten, 2021; Somma et al., 2020; Dåderman & Ragnestål-Impola, 2019)

WHO IS MORE LIKELY TO DISPLAY THE DARK TRIAD?

THE DARK TRIAD

Men > Women
Non-Hispanic White people > People of color
CEOs/upper managers > Nonmanagement workers
Internet trolls > Nonmalevolent users

(Cesinger et al., 2022; Jonason et al., 2022; Wu et al., 2022; Dahling et al., 2008; Twenge & Foster, 2008)

THE DARK TRIAD AND SUCCESS

People tend to...
- Attain leadership positions
- Earn higher salaries
- Experience career satisfaction
- Negotiate effectively

THE DARK TRIAD

(Cesinger et al., 2022; Diller et al., 2021; Adam, 2019)

> **of NOTE ...**
>
> **As Suspected**
>
> Research finds that people who like dogs may be psychologically different from those who like cats (Cherry, 2020; Gosling, Sandy, & Potter, 2015). Almost 5,000 participants filled out a Big Five personality inventory. On average, the "dog people" scored higher than the "cat people" on extroversion, agreeableness, and conscientiousness. In contrast, the cat people scored higher on introversion and curiosity (that is, openness to experiences).

these supertraits. One person may display high levels of neuroticism and agreeableness, medium extroversion, and low conscientiousness and openness to experiences. In contrast, another person may display high levels of agreeableness and conscientiousness, medium neuroticism and extroversion, and low openness to experiences. And so on.

Many proponents of the Big Five model have argued further that it would be best to describe all people with personality disorders as being high, low, or in between on the five supertraits and to drop the use of personality disorder categories altogether (Smith, McCabe, & Widiger, 2022; Conway & Krueger, 2020). Thus, a particular person who currently qualifies for a diagnosis of avoidant personality disorder might instead be described as displaying a high degree of neuroticism, medium degrees of agreeableness and conscientiousness, and very low degrees of extroversion and openness to new experiences. Similarly, a person currently diagnosed with narcissistic personality disorder might be described in the Big Five approach as displaying very high degrees of neuroticism and extroversion, medium degrees of conscientiousness and openness to new experiences, and a very low degree of agreeableness.

HiTOP and Personality Disorders

A number of clinical theorists have looked elsewhere for a dimensional classification system of personality pathology. As you read in the chapter on assessment and diagnosis, some influential researchers have developed the Hierarchical Taxonomy of Psychopathology (HiTOP), a dimensional system that focuses primarily on *maladaptive* symptoms and traits likely to result in clinical impairment (Ringwald, Forbes, & Wright, 2023; Conway, Forbes, & the HiTOP Consortium, 2022). Whereas the Big Five model looks at personality dimensions such as extraversion, agreeableness, and conscientiousness, the HiTOP model looks at more clinically relevant and impairing dimensions, such as detachment, antagonism, and disinhibition.

The HiTOP model offers a hierarchical organization that enables assessors to list and rate *narrow* dimensions of pathology (specific symptoms and traits) and the *broader* dimensions in which those narrow dimensions cluster together and produce more severe dysfunction. For example, whereas DSM-5-TR's categorical system might use the single category of *avoidant personality disorder* to describe a particular client, HiTOP would indicate the client's symptoms (avoidance, social anxiety), traits (sensitivity, timidity), and broad maladjustments (fear, distress).

Although the HiTOP model is a relatively recent addition to the clinical field, it is already being actively embraced by many professionals. Clinicians like its detailed and informative dimensional scheme and also find the model useful for guiding treatment planning (Balling et al., 2023). Moreover, researchers appreciate the large number of studies that support the validity, reliability, and clinical utility of the model (Watson et al., 2022; Kotov et al., 2020).

"Personality Disorder—Trait Specified": DSM-5-TR's Proposed Dimensional Approach

In addition to the Big Five approach and the HiTOP approach, the framers of the DSM (the classification system used in the United States) and the ICD (the classification system used in most countries outside the United States) have each developed their own dimensional approach for classifying personality disorders. DSM-5-TR's approach is currently offered in the form of a *proposed* dimensional scheme that may eventually become official. ICD-11 has already adopted its dimensional approach.

A look at DSM-5-TR's proposed dimensional approach to personality disorders, which was actually introduced in DSM-5, reveals just how different a dimensional approach is from a categorical approach. It begins with the notion that people whose traits significantly impair their functioning should receive a diagnosis called **personality disorder—trait specified (PDTS)** (APA, 2022). When assigning this diagnosis, clinicians would also

personality disorder—trait specified (PDTS) A personality disorder undergoing study for possible inclusion in the DSM. People would receive this diagnosis if they had significant impairment in functioning as a result of one or more very problematic traits.

PDTS in action The Netflix series *Beef* focuses on two characters, Danny Cho (in photo) and Amy Lau. The two characters have a near car accident, each experiences road rage, and they develop an ongoing antagonistic relationship, marked by repeated displays of utter rage and zero empathy. Some clinicians have suggested that both Danny and Amy might qualify for a diagnosis of *personality disorder—trait specified (PDTS)*, with emphasis on their traits of intense hostility (from the *antagonism* and *negative affectivity* groupings) and suspiciousness and emotional lability (from the *negative affectivity* grouping).

identify and list the problematic traits and rate the severity of impairment caused by them. According to the proposal, five groups of problematic traits would be eligible for a diagnosis of PDTS: *negative affectivity, detachment, antagonism, disinhibition,* and *psychoticism.*

- **Negative affectivity.** People who display negative affectivity experience negative emotions frequently and intensely. In particular, they exhibit one or more of the following traits: *emotional lability* (unstable emotions), *anxiousness, separation insecurity, perseveration* (repetition of certain behaviors despite repeated failures), *submissiveness, hostility, depressivity, suspiciousness,* and *strong emotional reactions* (overreactions to emotionally arousing situations).
- **Detachment.** People who manifest detachment tend to withdraw from other people and social interactions. They may exhibit any of the following traits: *restricted emotional reactivity* (little reaction to emotionally arousing situations), *depressivity, suspiciousness, withdrawal, anhedonia* (inability to feel pleasure or take interest in things), and *intimacy avoidance.* You'll note that two of the traits in this group—depressivity and suspiciousness—are also found in the negative affectivity group.
- **Antagonism.** People who display antagonism behave in ways that put them at odds with other people. They may exhibit any of the following traits: *manipulativeness, deceitfulness, grandiosity, attention seeking, callousness,* and *hostility.* Hostility is also found in the negative affectivity group.
- **Disinhibition.** People who manifest disinhibition behave impulsively, without reflecting on potential future consequences. They may exhibit any of the following traits: *irresponsibility, impulsivity, distractibility, risk taking,* and *imperfection/disorganization.*
- **Psychoticism.** People who display psychoticism have unusual and bizarre experiences. They may exhibit any of the following traits: *unusual beliefs and experiences, eccentricity,* and *cognitive and perceptual dysregulation* (odd thought processes and sensory experiences).

If a person is impaired significantly by any of the five trait groups or even by just one of the 25 traits that make up those groups, they would qualify for a diagnosis of *personality disorder—trait specified.* In such cases, the diagnostician would indicate which traits are impaired.

of NOTE ...

Character Ingestion

As late as the Victorian era, many English parents believed that babies absorbed personality and moral uprightness as they took in milk. Thus, if a parent could not nurse, it was important to find a wet nurse of good character (Asimov, 1997).

Consider, for example, Lucas, the unhappy 42-year-old assistant graphics programmer described in the section on dependent personality disorder. As you may recall, Lucas met the criteria for a diagnosis of that disorder under DSM-5-TR's current categorical approach, based largely on his lifetime of extreme dependence on his father, mother, sisters, friends, and coworkers. Using the alternative dimensional approach presented in DSM-5-TR, a diagnostician would instead observe that Lucas is significantly impaired by several of the traits that characterize the negative affectivity trait group. He is, for example, greatly impaired by "separation insecurity." This trait has prevented him from ever living on his own, marrying Orena, disagreeing with his father, advancing at work, and broadening his social life. In addition, Lucas seems to be impaired significantly by the traits of "submissiveness," "anxiousness," and "depressivity." Given this picture, his therapist might assign him a diagnosis of *personality disorder—trait specified, with problematic traits of separation insecurity, submissiveness, anxiousness, and depressivity.*

According to this dimensional approach, when clinicians assign a diagnosis of personality disorder—trait specified, they also must rate the degree of dysfunction caused by each of the person's traits, using a five-point scale ranging from "little or no impairment" (rating = 0) to "extreme impairment" (rating = 4).

Consider Lucas once again. He would probably warrant a rating of "0" on most of the 25 traits listed in the DSM-5-TR proposal, a rating of "3" on the traits of anxiousness and depressivity, and a rating of "4" on the traits of separation insecurity and submissiveness. Altogether, he would receive the following cumbersome but informative diagnosis:

Diagnosis: *Personality Disorder—Trait Specified*

Separation insecurity: Rating 4

Submissiveness: Rating 4

Anxiousness: Rating 3

Depressivity: Rating 3

Other traits: Rating 0

It is important to note that this alternative approach to personality disorders has opponents in the clinical community. Some clinicians worry that the proposed changes would give too much latitude to diagnosticians—allowing them to apply diagnoses of personality disorder to an enormous range of personality patterns (Herpertz & Bertsch, 2022). Still others worry that the requirements of the newly proposed system are too cumbersome or complicated. Nevertheless, according to studies and reports spanning more than a decade, many clinicians have found the alternative approach to be usable and helpful in the diagnosis and treatment of people with personality disorders, and enthusiasm for the new approach has been growing (Bach & Tracy, 2022; Widiger & Hines, 2022). Thus, it would appear that the next edition of the DSM, like the current edition of the ICD, will feature a largely dimensional approach to the classification and diagnosis of personality disorders.

of NOTE ...

Animal Traits

Researchers have found that animals of every kind—from spiders and birds to lions and elephants—display distinct differences in their personalities, behaviors, and preferences. Among sheep, for example, some are leaders and others are followers. Similarly, sheep differ in their individual levels of fearfulness, vocalization, friendliness, and distraction. These differences often hold steady throughout their lives (Cherry, 2020; Angier, 2010).

SUMMING UP

Are There Better Ways to Classify Personality Psychopathology?

Given the significant problems posed by DSM-5-TR's current categorical approach, a number of today's theorists believe that personality disorders should instead be described and classified by a dimensional approach. Some well-supported dimensional approaches include the Big Five model and the Hierarchical Taxonomy of Psychopathology model. And, indeed, DSM-5-TR itself proposes an alternative approach for consideration—a dimensional approach called the personality disorder—trait specified model. This approach is under study for possible inclusion in a future revision of the DSM.

Rediscovered, Then Reconsidered

DURING THE FIRST HALF of the twentieth century, clinicians believed deeply in the unique, enduring patterns we call personality, and they tried to define important personality traits. They then discovered how readily people can be shaped by the situations in which they find themselves, and a backlash developed. The concept of personality seemed to lose legitimacy, and for a while it became almost an obscene word in some circles. The clinical category of personality disorders went through a similar rejection. When psychodynamic and humanistic theorists dominated the clinical field, *neurotic character disorders*—a set of diagnoses similar to today's personality disorders—were considered useful clinical categories, but their popularity declined as other models grew in influence.

In the twenty-first century, however, serious interest in personality and personality disorders has rebounded. In case after case, clinicians have concluded that rigid personality traits do seem to pose special problems, and they have developed new objective tests and interview guides to assess these disorders, setting in motion a wave of systematic research. So far, the antisocial and borderline personality disorders have received the most study. However, with dimensional classification approaches gaining momentum, additional research is being conducted. Such investigations will enable clinicians to better answer some pressing questions: How common are the various personality disorders? How useful are personality disorder categories? How effective is a dimensional approach to diagnosing these disorders? And which treatments are most effective?

of NOTE ...

Their Words

"Personality disorders . . . are the only things left in psychiatry where people think you are bad."

Gary M. Flaxenberg, psychiatrist, 1998

Quick Quiz

1. What is a personality disorder? p. 429
2. Describe the social relationship problems caused by each of the personality disorders. pp. 431–461
3. What are the three "odd" personality disorders, and what are the symptoms of each? pp. 431–436
4. What explanations and treatments have been applied to the paranoid, schizoid, and schizotypal personality disorders? pp. 432–437
5. What are the "dramatic" personality disorders, and what are the symptoms of each disorder? pp. 438–452
6. How have theorists explained antisocial personality disorder and borderline personality disorder? What are the leading treatments for these disorders, and how effective are they? pp. 441–450
7. What are the leading explanations and treatments for the histrionic and narcissistic personality disorders? How strongly does research support these explanations and treatments? pp. 451–455
8. What is the name of the cluster that includes the avoidant, dependent, and obsessive-compulsive personality disorders? What are the leading explanations and treatments for these disorders, and to what extent are they supported by research? pp. 455–462
9. How comprehensively have researchers studied variations in the rates of personality disorders across nationality, race and ethnicity, sexual orientation, and gender identity? pp. 462–463
10. Describe three of the dimensional approaches that have been proposed to identify and describe personality disorders. pp. 464–468

CHAPTER 14

Disorders Common Among Children and Adolescents

Cecilia was, by far, the funniest and most entertaining kid in her family. Living with her five siblings, her mother and father, and her beloved Abuela, Cecilia always enjoyed taking "center stage" in her living room, belting out hysterical impressions of everyone's favorite pop stars. "Va a crecer para ser comediante," her Abuela would always say ("She's going to be a comedian"). When it was time to go to bed, after the lights were turned out, Cecilia would often get in some trouble for blurting out funny noises and jokes and making her siblings laugh uncontrollably.

Going into the first parent–teacher conference of the year, her parents imagined they might have to apologize for Cecilia's silly antics and attention-grabbing behavior. And so they were quite pleased at first when her teacher, Ms. Gossman, actually described the 6-year-old as the portrait of behavioral control in the classroom. But their reactions quickly shifted to shock when Ms. Gossman further shared that Cecilia actually hadn't uttered a single word out loud in front of the class all year. The teacher described Cecilia as extraordinarily shy and reserved at school, never wanting to be in the spotlight. In the classroom, Cecilia had become adept at communicating without using any words, mostly responding to questions with head nods, facial expressions, and hand gestures. If Cecilia needed to communicate something fairly complex, she would whisper her words to the child sitting next to her, Maisie from around the corner, who would then share them out loud on Cecilia's behalf.

Finally, Ms. Gossman shared her concerns about Cecilia's social development, suggesting that the parents should consider having her social functioning evaluated by a specialist. At school she rarely joined other kids at play, even when they directly invited her to play with them. She always looked pained and uncomfortable when kids asked her questions; she might just stare blankly at them and stay silent as a stone.

It was almost impossible for Cecilia's parents to believe that their bubbly chatterbox, who never passed up an opportunity to perform or ham it up in front of others at home, was the same child now being described by her teacher.

During her initial call to the clinic, Mrs. Smith said her [7-year-old son Ricky] was "out of control." She said Ricky "was all over the place" and "constantly getting into trouble." . . .

Ricky . . . said his teacher, Mrs. Candler, was always yelling at him and sending notes home to his mother. Ricky initially said he did not know why the teacher yelled at him but then said it was mostly about not paying attention or following class rules. . . .

Ricky . . . said he had a few friends but often had to keep to himself. This was because Mrs. Candler made him spend much of the school day in a corner of the classroom to complete his work. Unfortunately, little of the work was successfully finished. Ricky said he felt bored, sad, tired, and angry in the classroom. . . .

Ricky said his mother yelled at him a lot. . . . He said he felt happiest when riding his bike because nobody yelled at him and he could "go wherever I want." . . .

(continued on the next page)

TOPIC OVERVIEW

> *Mrs. Smith said Ricky was almost intolerable in the classroom, . . . crying when asked to do something, stomping his feet, and being disrespectful to the teacher. . . . [She also said] her son was generally "out of control" at home. He would not listen to her commands and often ran around the house until he got what he wanted. She and her son often argued about his homework, chores, [and] misbehavior. . . . [In addition,] Ricky often fidgeted and lost many of his school materials. He was disorganized and paid little attention to long-term consequences. The child was also difficult to control in public places, such as a supermarket or church. . . . [At school, he was] getting out of his seat more and more, requiring a constant response. . . .*
>
> (Kearney, 2016, pp. 62–64)

Cecelia and Ricky are both displaying psychological disorders. The disorders are disrupting their school performance and social relationships, but each disorder does so in a particular way and for particular reasons. Cecelia, who may qualify for a diagnosis called *selective mutism,* displays markedly different social behavior across the home setting and the school setting. Her extreme social reticence outside of the home prevents her from developing many friendships and from fully demonstrating her academic abilities and school readiness. On the other hand, Ricky's behaviors and problems are on display across most settings. He cannot concentrate and is overly active and impulsive at home, at school, and in social interactions—difficulties that characterize a disorder called *attention-deficit/hyperactivity disorder* (*ADHD*).

Psychological difficulties can occur at any time in life. Some patterns of psychopathology, however, are more likely to emerge during particular periods—during childhood, for example, or, at the other end of the spectrum, during older adulthood. In this chapter, you will read about disorders that commonly have their onset during childhood or early adolescence. In the next chapter, you'll learn about problems that are more prevalent among older adults. ■

of NOTE ...

Counseling Deficit

Currently there is 1 school counselor for every 415 students in the United States. The recommended ratio is 1 per 250 students (ASCA, 2023).

Stress During Childhood and Adolescence

PEOPLE OFTEN THINK of childhood as a carefree and happy time—yet it can also be frightening and upsetting. In fact, children of all countries typically have at least some emotional and behavioral challenges as they encounter new people and situations. Surveys reveal that *worry* is a common experience: Close to half of all children in the United States have multiple fears, particularly concerning school, health, and personal safety (CDC, 2023). Bed-wetting, nightmares, temper tantrums, and restlessness are other problems that many children contend with. Adolescence can also be a difficult period. Physical and sexual changes, social and academic pressures, school violence, personal doubts, and temptations cause many teenagers to feel nervous, confused, and depressed (Abrams, 2023).

A particular concern among children and adolescents is that of being bullied (see ***InfoCentral***). Surveys throughout the world have revealed repeatedly that **bullying** ranks as a major problem in the minds of most young respondents. Over 20 percent of students report being bullied frequently, and more than 50 percent report having been bullied at least once (DTL, 2023, 2019; NBPC, 2023, 2020). The rates are even higher among students of color and those in the LGBTQ+ community (Wittlin, Kuper, & Olson, 2023). Typically, kids who have been bullied react with feelings of humiliation, anxiety, dislike

bullying The repeated infliction of force, threats, or coercion in order to intimidate, hurt, or dominate another, less powerful person; particularly common among children and adolescents.

Frederick Florin/AFP via Getty Images

Death by bullying? At this memorial site, a person lays down white roses next to a banner that reads, "Dinah Rest in Peace." In 2021, people throughout France protested and created memorials for Dinah, a 14-year-old who died by suicide. The adolescent's family and friends attributed her suicide to "two years of racist and homophobic" harassment and bullying by several schoolmates. The school and local authorities denied these claims and closed the case, which in turn triggered more public protests.

for school, or life dissatisfaction (Abrams, 2023; Armitage et al., 2021). In extreme cases, they may attempt suicide (Vojinovic, 2023). Moreover, the psychological effects of being bullied can reach far into adulthood. Also troubling, the technological advances of today's world have broadened the ways in which children and adolescents can be bullied, and *cyberbullying*—bullying and humiliating by social media, text messaging, and e-mail—is now on the rise (Abrams, 2023). Given these findings, the past two decades have witnessed a rise in antibullying legislation across the United States. The number of states enacting antibullying laws has grown from one state in 1999 (Georgia) to all 50 states today (CRC, 2023).

The pressures and stresses of childhood and adolescence increased all the more with the emergence of the Covid-19 pandemic in 2020 and society's efforts to contain the virus. During the initial years of the pandemic, most young people were confronted by circumstances such as in-home confinement with their families, social distancing or isolation from friends and peers, online rather than in-person

Phil Mislinski/Getty Images

Cavan Images/Getty Images

Today's worries A kindergarten student (left) hides under her desk during a school-shooting lockdown drill, while a teenager (right) experiences the stress of pandemic-induced isolation—events and measures that have raised anxiety among today's children. Children have always had multiple fears and concerns, but the specific worries change from generation to generation.

CHILD AND ADOLESCENT BULLYING

Bullying is the repeated infliction of force, threats, or coercion in order to intimidate, hurt, or dominate another, less powerful person. It is particularly common among children and adolescents. LGBTQ+ people are much more likely to be bullied. Over the past decade, clinicians and educators have learned that bullying is much more common and more harmful than previously thought (NBPC, 2023, 2020; Armitage et al., 2021).

TYPES OF BULLYING

Physical — hitting, pushing, tripping

Verbal — name-calling, mean taunting, sexual comments, threatening

Relational/Social — spreading rumors, posting embarrassing images, rejecting from group

BULLYING IS ON THE RISE...

39%	50%
over age 50	under age 50

people bullied as teenagers

(DTL, 2023, 2019; NBPC, 2023, 2020; Harris Interactive, 2014; NFER, 2010)

BULLIES TEND TO:

- Display antisocial behaviors
- Have low empathy
- Perform poorly in school
- Drop out of school
- Bring weapons to school
- Drink alcohol
- Use drugs

(Hong et al., 2021; Morin, 2020; BSA, 2017)

EFFECTS OF BULLYING

- Depression
- Suicidal thinking and attempts
- Anxiety
- Low self-esteem
- Sleep problems
- Somatic symptoms
- Substance use and abuse
- School problems and/or phobias
- Antisocial behavior

(NBPC, 2023, 2020; Choi & Park, 2021; Hong et al., 2021; Malhi & Bharti, 2021; O'Reilly et al., 2021; Petrov, 2020)

SCHOOL BULLYING

Much bullying takes place at school. Around **two-thirds** of all school bullying occurs in hallways, schoolyards, bathrooms, cafeterias, or buses. Almost **one-third** occurs in classrooms, while teachers are present. It is estimated that over **30%** of school bullying goes unreported (DTL, 2023, 2019; NBPC, 2023, 2020; CDC, 2021, 2019; SB, 2021, 2019).

The Nature of School Bullying

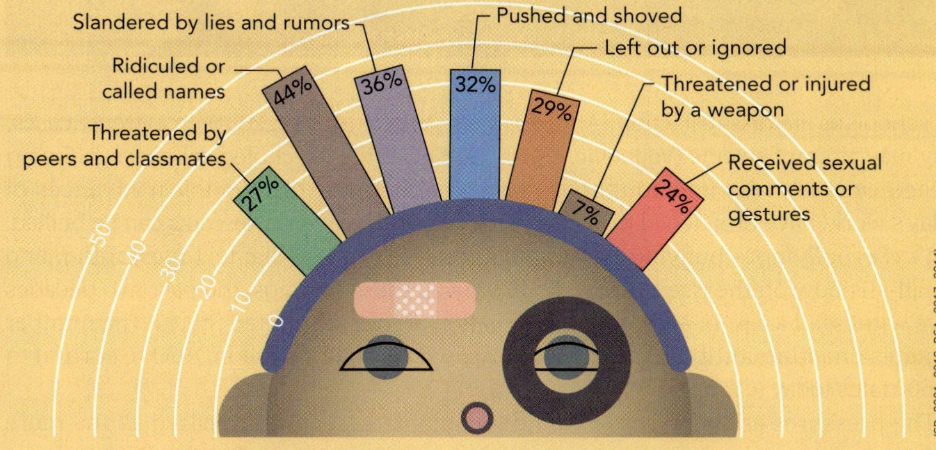

(SB, 2021, 2019; BSA, 2017, 2014)

Features of School Antibullying Programs

- Increased supervision of students
- Delivery of consequences for bullying
- Schoolwide implementation of antibullying policies
- Cooperation among school staff, parents, and professionals across disciplines
- Identification of risk factors for bullying

(CDC, 2021, 2019, 2018)

Bullying prevention programs in schools reduce bullying by around 25%. (NBPC, 2023, 2020)

CYBERBULLYING

Cyberbullying takes place through social media, texting, websites, e-mail, instant messaging, chat rooms, or posted videos or photos. Around **37%** of all children and teens have been bullied online at least once. About **21%** are bullied online frequently (DTL, 2023, 2019; CDC, 2021, 2019; NBPC, 2020; Petrov, 2020; Skrba, 2020).

Like

Why Do Teens Cyberbully?

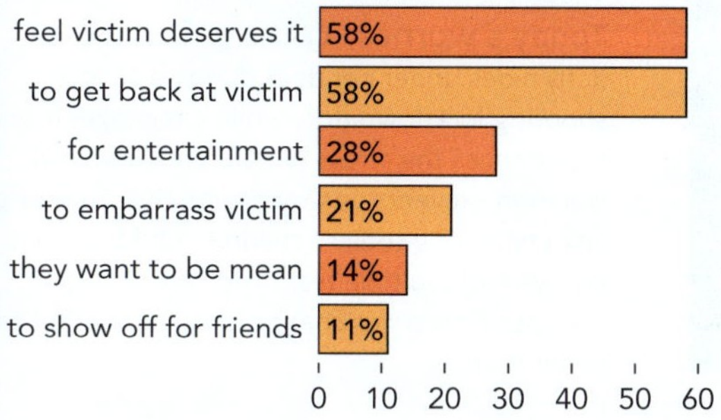

(Gordon, 2020; NBPC, 2020; NB, 2017; BSA, 2014; Knowthenet, 2013)

Social Media and Cyberbullying

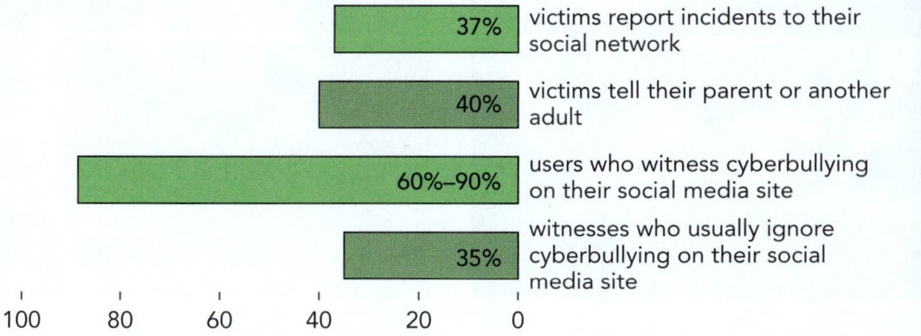

(NBPC, 2020; Petrov, 2020; EIE, 2017; NB, 2017; Pew Research Center, 2017; BSA, 2014; Knowthenet, 2013)

schooling, reductions in school-related and after-school activities, irregular sleep patterns, lack of structure in their lives, and economic hardships (Abrams, 2023). And some children and adolescents were further subjected to increases in parent drinking, psychopathology, and abusive behavior (Calvano et al., 2023). These extraordinary circumstances greatly affected the emotions and behaviors of young people (Malloy et al., 2024; Sáez-Clarke, et al., 2022; Trucco et al., 2022). Surveys conducted during the pandemic found increases in the number of children who generally felt edgy (54 percent), annoyed (47 percent), worried (47 percent), sad (44 percent), and apathetic (54 percent), as well as increases in the intensity of such negative feelings (Gindt et al., 2021; Zhou et al., 2020).

Psychological Disorders of Childhood and Adolescence

BEYOND THE VARIOUS CONCERNS and stresses of childhood, at least one-fifth of all children and adolescents also experience a diagnosable psychological disorder (CDC, 2023). Boys with disorders outnumber girls, even though most of the adult psychological disorders are more common among women. Moreover, research suggests that children and adolescents in the LGBTQ+ community experience even higher rates of psychological disorders than their peers, due in part to the particularly high degree of victimization, trauma, and discrimination to which they are subjected (Wittlin et al., 2023; Jonas et al., 2022).

of NOTE ...

Their Words

"The true character of society is revealed in how it treats its children."

Nelson Mandela, anti-apartheid activist and president of South Africa

Some disorders displayed by children—childhood anxiety disorders, childhood depression, and disruptive disorders—have adult counterparts, although they are also distinct in certain ways. Other childhood disorders—elimination disorders, for example—usually disappear or radically change form by adulthood. There are also disorders, called *neurodevelopmental disorders,* that begin at birth or in very early childhood and persist in stable forms into adult life. These include attention-deficit/hyperactivity disorder, autism spectrum disorder, and intellectual disability.

While reading about the disorders of childhood and adolescence throughout this chapter, you should keep in mind, once again, that the Covid-19 pandemic has had a special impact on the nature and prevalence of such disorders. The already high rates of several disorders—particularly childhood anxiety disorders and childhood depression—increased significantly during the early years of the pandemic (Gotlib et al., 2022; Glynn et al., 2021). In addition, the symptoms of preexisting psychological disorders often worsened throughout the pandemic (Breaux et al., 2021). Such trends are consistent with findings from past epidemics and pandemics (Loades et al., 2020).

Covid-19-related reductions in in-person schooling also made it difficult for young people with psychological disorders to receive full treatment and support for their problems. Prior to the pandemic, almost 60 percent of adolescents with psychological needs received some or all of their mental health services at school—services that became less available without in-person schooling (Abrams, 2023; Golberstein, Wen, & Miller, 2020).

What other in-person school services might also be important to the mental health of children and adolescents?

The mental health of children and adolescents from marginalized groups was particularly impacted during the Covid-19 pandemic. For example, a study of over 30,000 LGBTQ+ teenagers found that at the height of the pandemic, more than 70 percent of the teenagers were experiencing poor mental health and more than 40 percent were seriously considering suicide (The Trevor Project, 2023, 2022, 2021). According to many theorists, this exceptionally high number of mental health problems and disorders among LGBTQ+ children and adolescents was caused by their pandemic-linked confinement to their homes—homes that over two-thirds of them felt were unsafe or unsupportive of their gender identity or sexual orientation (The Trevor Project, 2023, 2022, 2021). Children of color and children in households experiencing economic hardships also experienced particularly poor mental health during the pandemic (Xiao et al., 2022).

Childhood Anxiety Disorders

of NOTE ...

Rising Tide

The rate of anxiety among children and teenagers in the United States increased by 29 percent between 2016 and 2020. The rate of depression rose 27 percent for children and teenagers during those same years (Lebrun-Harris et al., 2022).

ANXIETY IS, to a degree, a common part of childhood. Since children have had fewer experiences than adults, their world is often new and scary. They may be frightened by common events, such as the beginning of school, or by special upsets, such as moving to a new house or becoming seriously ill. In addition, each generation of children is confronted by new sources of anxiety. Today's children, for example, have been repeatedly warned, both at home and at school, about the need for social distancing, the dangers of Internet browsing and online predators, drugs, school shootings, and terrorism. Moreover, they are bombarded by violent images online, on television, and in films—both animated and live action. And for many of today's children, climate change, social unrest, experiences of discrimination, and declining economic opportunities also produce feelings of anxiety (Abrams, 2023).

Children may also be strongly affected by parental problems or family disruptions (Bogat, Levendosky, & Cochran, 2023; Calvano et al., 2023). If, for example, parents typically react to events with high levels of anxiety or uncertainty, or if they overprotect their children, the children may be more likely to respond to the world with anxiety (Cabrera et al., 2023). And if parents become seriously ill or must be separated from their children for a long period, childhood anxiety may result. Beyond such environmental problems, genetic studies suggest that some children are prone to an anxious temperament (Tan et al., 2024).

For some children, these anxieties become long-lasting and debilitating, interfering with their daily lives and their ability to function appropriately. Such children may be experiencing an *anxiety disorder.* Surveys indicate that at least 25 percent of all children and adolescents experience an anxiety disorder at some point in time (Bennett & Walkup, 2022).

Some of the childhood anxiety disorders are similar to their adult counterparts. Specific phobias in childhood, for example, usually look and operate much like the phobias of adulthood, and a number of untreated childhood phobias grow into adult ones (Johnsen, Wichstrøm, & Dahllöf, 2024). More often, however, the anxiety disorders of childhood take on a different character from that of adult anxiety disorders. Inasmuch as certain cognitive functions are beyond the capacity of children, especially young children, their anxiety disorders are typically dominated by behavioral and somatic symptoms rather than cognitive ones—symptoms such as clinging, sleep difficulties, avoidance, irritability, and stomach pains (Roy & Comer, 2020). They tend to center on specific, sometimes imaginary, objects and events, such as monsters, ghosts, or thunderstorms, rather than broad concerns about the future or one's place in the world (Strawn et al., 2020).

Separation Anxiety Disorder and Selective Mutism

Two patterns of childhood anxiety, *separation anxiety disorder* and *selective mutism,* have received considerable attention in recent years, partly because they cause children emotional pain and partly because they leave the parents feeling helpless as they try to help their children.

separation anxiety disorder A disorder marked by excessive anxiety, even panic, whenever the person is separated from home, a parent, or another attachment figure.

selective mutism A disorder marked by failure to speak in certain social situations when speech is expected despite an ability to speak in other situations.

Separation anxiety disorder, which you learned about in the chapter on anxiety disorders, is one of the most common anxiety disorders among children. The disorder often begins as early as the preschool years, and at least 4 percent of all children experience it (Bennett & Walkup, 2022). As you'll recall, children experiencing this disorder have enormous difficulty being away from their parents or other major attachment figures, and often they are reluctant—or they outright refuse—to go anywhere

where they might be separated from their parents—friends' houses, birthday parties, or even their own bedrooms. Children with the disorder often worry that when they are separated, their parents might get seriously hurt or die or that they themselves might get kidnapped or lost, preventing them from ever seeing their parents again. Separation anxiety disorder in childhood may further take the form of *school refusal,* in which children fear going to school and often stay home for a long period (Biswas & Sahoo, 2023). However, many cases of school refusal, particularly those in later childhood, have causes other than separation fears, such as social or academic concerns, depression, fears of specific objects or persons at school, or a desire to resist authority.

William Haefeli/CartoonStock Ltd

"When you go off to camp, your parents are going to want to see some separation anxiety."

In **selective mutism,** children consistently fail to speak in certain social situations but show no difficulty at all speaking in others (ASHA, 2024; Furr et al., 2020). Like Cecelia, whom you read about at the beginning of this chapter, a child with this disorder may have no problem talking, laughing, or singing at home with family members but will offer absolutely no words in other key situations, such as the classroom. Some go an entire school year without speaking a word to their teacher or classmates. People who see a selectively mute child only at school often find it hard to believe that the child is an absolute chatterbox at home. In addition, some children with selective mutism exhibit significant irritability when interacting with their close family members despite showing overall patterns of extreme shyness around others (Freitag et al., 2024). Around 1 percent of all children display this disorder (APA, 2022).

Many researchers believe that selective mutism is an early version of *social anxiety disorder,* appearing in children before they have fully developed the cognitive capacities to worry about future embarrassment or anticipate potential judgment from others. And, in fact, many (but not all) older children with selective mutism do develop social anxiety disorder (Koskela et al., 2023; APA, 2022). At the same time, there are many features unique to selective mutism. For example, some children with this disorder have delays in their development of communication and language skills.

Like Cecelia's teacher, educators and clinicians often underestimate the capabilities of children when they refuse to speak in a classroom or during an evaluation. Thus, some children with selective mutism are misclassified as having an *intellectual disability* or *autism spectrum disorder* (two conditions that you will read about later in this chapter). This can, in turn, lead to incorrect interventions that focus on intellectual functioning and language development rather than on anxiety difficulties.

Reluctant to speak Children with selective mutism fail to speak in their classrooms and/or other social situations. Often the children use whispering, either directly to a teacher or through a go-between, to communicate important messages. Here, a child with the disorder whispers to her counselor at Florida International University's Center for Children and Families.

© Melissa Lyttle

Treatments for Childhood Anxiety Disorders

Despite the high prevalence of childhood and adolescent anxiety disorders, as many as two-thirds of anxious children go untreated (CDC, 2023; Radez et al., 2021). Among the children who do receive treatment, psychodynamic, cognitive-behavioral, family, and group therapies, separately or in combination, have been used most often. Each approach has had some degree of success; however, studies have found that cognitive-behavioral therapy fares best (Hong et al., 2023; Kendall et al., 2023). These various therapies parallel the adult anxiety approaches you read about in the chapter on anxiety disorders, but they are tailored to the child's cognitive abilities,

Al Diaz/Miami Herald/TNS via Getty Images

Never too young? Seeking to optimize psychological wellness, young campers at the Camp Honey Shine in Miami, Florida, learn mindfulness meditation and other techniques for dealing with stress.

unique life situation, and limited control over life events. In addition, clinicians may offer psychoeducation, provide parenting intervention, and arrange school interventions to treat anxious children (Conroy et al., 2022; Comer et al., 2021). For the treatment of selective mutism, group formats of cognitive-behavioral therapy have received the most support (Georgiadis, Furr, & Comer, 2024; Hong et al., 2023).

Clinicians have also used psychotropic drug therapy in a number of cases of childhood anxiety disorders, often in combination with psychotherapy (Schatzberg & Nemeroff, 2024). They prescribe not only antianxiety drugs but antidepressant and antipsychotic drugs as well (Strawn et al., 2022). In a landmark study called the Child/Adolescent Anxiety Multimodal Study, clinicians treated almost 500 children and adolescents with anxiety disorders across the United States and compared the effectiveness of cognitive-behavioral therapy alone, antidepressant therapy alone, cognitive-behavioral and antidepressant therapy combined, and placebo therapy (Bai et al., 2023; Crane et al., 2021). They found that combining cognitive-behavioral and antidepressant therapy led to the most favorable outcomes.

Because children typically have difficulty recognizing and understanding their feelings and motives, many therapists, particularly psychodynamic therapists, use **play therapy** as part of treatment. In this approach, the children play with toys, draw, and make up stories; in doing so, they are thought to reveal and work through the conflicts in their lives and their related feelings.

play therapy An approach to treating childhood disorders that helps children express their conflicts and feelings indirectly by drawing, playing with toys, and making up stories.

SUMMING UP

Childhood Stress and Disorders of Anxiety

Emotional and behavioral problems are common in childhood and adolescence, but, in addition, at least 20 percent of all children and adolescents in the United States have a diagnosable psychological disorder. A particular concern among children is that of being bullied. The stresses and psychological disorders of children and adolescents intensified and increased throughout the early stages of the Covid-19 pandemic.

Anxiety disorders are particularly common among children and adolescents. This group of problems includes adultlike disorders, such as social anxiety disorder and generalized anxiety disorder, the childhood form of separation anxiety disorder, and selective mutism.

Depressive and Bipolar Disorders During Childhood

When Cameron was 8 years old, his mother started to worry about him. Not so coincidentally, his teacher was becoming concerned at the same time. What they both saw was a sad and seemingly lost little boy. At home, Cameron just wanted to lie around and watch TV. He would do his chores and answer his parents' questions—in as few words as possible—but he initiated almost nothing. He ate only when told to eat. He showed little interest in his beloved iPad and stopped playing video games. Nor did Cameron seek out playmates anymore. His mother had to virtually drag him to their houses. Nothing gave him pleasure. Cameron also seemed to have more than a few physical problems—from headaches to stomach pains, it was always something, yet the doctor said he checked out fine.

The story was similar at school. Cameron was obedient and compliant, always did what his teacher asked, but seemed sad and joyless. He rarely joined in class discussions. He stayed in a group with the other kids as they traveled from the classroom to the cafeteria or the schoolyard, but he interacted very little with anyone in particular. When the school psychologist interviewed him, she noticed that he made no eye contact, offered little, and rarely smiled.

When the counselor asked Cameron's mother and teacher if anything special had triggered his unhappiness, they both pointed to the departure of his two best friends—twins who had moved to another state two months ago. But, at the same time, the more they thought about it, that was not really the beginning of Cameron's slide. It certainly worsened things, but his sad mood, inactivity, and isolation had been increasing for quite a while before that.

LIKE CAMERON, around 2 percent of children and as many as 8 percent of adolescents currently experience a major depressive disorder (CDC, 2023; ADAA, 2021). As many as 20 percent of adolescents experience at least one depressive episode during their teen years. In addition, children can experience a bipolar disorder.

of NOTE ...

Their Words

"It is an illusion that youth is happy, an illusion of those who have lost it."

W. Somerset Maugham, playwright and novelist

Major Depressive Disorder

Very young children lack some of the cognitive skills that help produce clinical depression, thus accounting for the relatively low rate of depression among the very young. For example, in order to experience the sense of hopelessness typically found in depressed adults, children must be able to hold expectations about the future, a skill rarely in full bloom before the age of 7.

Nevertheless, if life situations or biological predispositions are significant enough, even very young children sometimes have severe downward turns of mood (Bogat et al., 2023; Bonin, 2022). Depression in the young may be triggered by negative life events (particularly losses), major changes, rejection, or ongoing abuse (Hoffmann et al., 2024; Wang et al., 2024) (see **PsychWatch**). Childhood depression commonly features symptoms such as irritability, headaches, stomach pain, and a disinterest in toys and games.

Clinical depression is much more common among teenagers than among young children. Adolescence is, under the best of circumstances, a difficult and confusing time, marked by angst, hormonal and bodily changes, mood changes, complex

PSYCHWATCH

Child Abuse

A problem that affects all too many children and has an enormous impact on their psychological development is *child abuse,* the nonaccidental use of excessive physical or psychological force by an adult on a child, often with the intention of hurting or destroying the child. Between 5 and 16 percent of children in the United States are physically abused each year (Boos, 2023; CDC, 2022). Surveys suggest that 1 of every 10 children is the victim of severe violence, such as being kicked, bitten, hit, beaten, or threatened with a knife or a gun. Although child abuse is perpetrated in all socioeconomic groups, it is apparently more common among those who are economically disadvantaged (Boos, 2023; Holbrook & Hudziak, 2020).

Abusers are usually the child's parents (Christian, 2022). Clinical investigators have learned that abusive parents often have poor impulse control, low self-esteem, higher levels of depression, and weak parenting skills (Boos, 2023). Many were abused themselves as children and have had poor role models (MacIntosh & Ménard, 2021). In some cases, they are dealing with stressors such as marital discord or unemployment (Christian, 2022).

Studies suggest that the survivors of child abuse may experience both immediate and long-term psychological effects (Schlensog-Schuster et al., 2024). Research has shown, for example, that they may experience psychological symptoms such as anxiety, depression, or bed-wetting and may display performance and behavior problems in school (Hoffmann et al., 2024; WHO, 2023, 2022). Long-term negative effects include lack of social acceptance, a higher number of medical and psychological disorders during adulthood, more abuse of alcohol and other substances, more impulsive and risk-taking behaviors, more arrests during adolescence and adulthood, a greater risk of becoming criminally violent, a higher unemployment rate, and a higher suicide rate (Schlensog-Schuster et al., 2024; Brown, Yilanli, & Rabbitt, 2023). Finally, as many as one-third of those who are abused grow up to be abusive, neglectful, or inadequate parents themselves (WHO, 2023, 2022).

Early detection This is one of many current posters reaching out to children to report abuse.

Two forms of child abuse have received special attention: emotional abuse and sexual abuse. *Emotional abuse* may include severe rejection, excessive discipline, scapegoating and ridicule, isolation, and refusal to provide help for a child with psychological problems (Gonzalez, Mirabal, & McCall, 2023). It probably accompanies all forms of physical abuse and neglect and often occurs by itself. *Child sexual abuse,* the use of a child for gratification of sexual desires, may occur outside or within the home (Melmer & Gutovitz, 2023). Surveys suggest that 20 percent of women were forced into sexual contact with an adult during childhood, many of them with a parent or stepparent (Brown et al., 2023; RAINN, 2023). Around eight percent of men were forced into such contact during childhood. Child sexual abuse appears to be equally common across all socioeconomic classes, races, and ethnic groups.

A variety of therapies have been used in cases of child abuse, including therapeutic and educational groups such as *Parents Anonymous,* which help parents develop insight into their behavior, provide training on alternatives to abuse, and teach coping and parenting skills (Backhaus et al., 2023; WHO, 2023, 2022). In addition, prevention programs, often in the form of home visitations and parenting interventions, have proved promising (PCAA, 2024).

Research suggests that the psychological needs of children who have been abused should be addressed as early as possible (Misurell, Zocca, & Anderson, 2023; WHO, 2023, 2022). Clinicians and educators have launched valuable *early detection programs* that (1) educate all children about child abuse, (2) teach them skills for avoiding or escaping from abusive situations, (3) encourage children to tell another adult if they are abused, and (4) assure them that abuse is never their fault.

relationships, and new explorations. For some teens, these typical upsets of adolescence cross the line into clinical depression. As you learned in the chapter on suicide, suicidal thoughts and attempts are particularly common among adolescents, and depression is the leading cause of such thoughts and attempts. Recall that as many as 20 percent of teenagers in the United States have had serious suicidal thoughts in the past year and 9 percent have made suicide attempts (CDC, 2023, 2020).

The Washington Post/Getty Images

Separation and depression A young boy hugs his father as the soldier departs for deployment to Afghanistan. Given evidence that extended family separations often produce depression in children, clinical theorists have been concerned about the thousands of children from military families who were left behind during the wars in Afghanistan and Iraq.

Interestingly, while there are no gender differences in the rates of depression before the age of 13, girls are twice as likely as boys to be depressed by the age of 16 (NIMH, 2023). Why this gender shift? Several factors have been suggested, including hormonal changes in adolescence, the fact that teenage girls increasingly experience more stressors than teenage boys, and the tendency of teenage girls, on average, to become more emotionally invested than boys in social relationships and social media judgments as they mature. One explanation also focuses on the growing dissatisfaction that so many teenage girls feel about their bodies. Whereas puberty for most boys is accompanied by socially desired increases in muscle mass and other body changes, puberty for the majority of girls is often accompanied by unwelcome increases in body fat and weight gain. Raised in a society that values and demands extreme thinness as the aesthetic female ideal, many adolescent girls feel imprisoned by their own bodies, have low self-esteem, and become depressed (Klein & Attia, 2023). Many also develop eating psychopathology, as you learned in the chapter on eating disorders.

Most studies of teenage gender differences in depression have been conducted on the broad population; however, emerging research suggests that LGBTQ+ teens experience still higher rates of depression and suicidal behavior than their cisgender and heterosexual peers (Randall et al., 2023; The Trevor Project, 2023, 2022; Wittlin et al., 2023). For example, as you read in the chapter on suicide, some studies indicate that almost one-quarter of lesbian, gay, or bisexual teenagers attempt suicide in a given year, nearly three times the rate found among heterosexual teenagers (CDC, 2023). Similarly, between 20 and 56 percent of transgender or nonbinary teenagers report attempting suicide within the past year, in contrast to 9 percent of cisgender teenagers (The Trevor Project, 2023, 2022; Austin et al., 2022). The rate of suicide attempts appears to be reduced by as much as 30 percent among transgender and nonbinary teenagers living in homes that support and affirm their gender identity (The Trevor Project, 2022).

For years, it has generally been believed that childhood and teenage depression will respond well to the same treatments that have helped depressed adults—particularly, cognitive-behavioral therapy, interpersonal psychotherapy, and antidepressant drugs—and, in fact, many studies have indicated the effectiveness of such approaches, especially when one of the psychotherapies is combined with antidepressant drugs (Kovacs, 2023). Moreover, clinicians have sometimes found success treating children and adolescents with family-focused approaches that aim to improve parent–child relationships, increase shared family activities, and build child coping skills (van Aswegen et al., 2023; Waraan et al., 2023). At the same time, one development over the past two decades has raised a significant concern about the treatment of depressed teenagers. This is the discovery that antidepressant drugs may be dangerous for some depressed children and teenagers.

In the 1990s, most psychiatrists believed that second-generation antidepressants were safe and effective for children and adolescents, and they prescribed them readily.

David M. Benett/Getty Images

Teenage heartache Since the release of her successful first album *Sour* in 2021, the songs of singer-songwriter Olivia Rodrigo have become the "voice" of teenage heartbreak, angst, and depression. The songs in *Sour* are about painful feelings—from despair to anger—surrounding relationship breakups.

However, based on a number of clinical reports, the U.S. Food and Drug Administration (FDA) concluded in 2004 that the drugs may produce a real, though small, increase in the risk of suicidal behavior for certain children and adolescents, especially during the first few months of treatment. In turn, the agency ordered that antidepressant containers carry a "black box" warning to that effect. Arguments about the wisdom of this FDA order have since ensued. Although most of today's practitioners agree that the drugs may indeed increase the risk of suicidal thoughts and attempts in as many as 2 percent of young patients, they have since concluded that the overall risk of suicide is actually reduced for the vast majority of children and adolescents who take the drugs and that, on balance, the drugs are a useful and relatively safe treatment (Schatzberg & Nemeroff, 2024; Moreland & Bonin, 2022). Nevertheless, the "black box" controversy has highlighted the importance of research, particularly in the treatment realm. We are reminded that treatments that work for individuals of a certain age, gender, race, or ethnic background may be less effective or even dangerous for other groups of people.

Bipolar Disorder and Disruptive Mood Dysregulation Disorder

For decades, bipolar disorder was thought to be almost exclusively an *adult* disorder whose earliest age of onset was the late teens (APA, 2022). However, beginning in the mid-1990s, clinical theorists did an about-face, and a large number of them came to believe that many children display bipolar disorder (Bram & Edwards, 2023; Birmaher, 2022). Indeed, reviews of national diagnostic trends found that the number of children and adolescents diagnosed and treated for bipolar disorder in the United States increased at least 40-fold from 1994 to 2013 (Hendrickson, Girma, & Miller, 2020).

During that 20-year period, some theorists came to suspect that such increases reflected not a rise in the prevalence of bipolar disorders among children but rather a new—often inaccurate—diagnostic trend. They believed that the diagnosis of bipolar disorder was being overapplied to children and adolescents and being assigned to the majority of extremely explosive, aggressive children (Malhi, Jadidi, & Bell, 2023). In support of these claims, studies revealed that symptoms of irritability, rage, or aggression, along with depression, were in fact dominating the clinical picture of most children who were receiving a bipolar diagnosis (Janiri et al., 2024; Hendrickson et al., 2020). Many such children were not even displaying the symptoms of mania or the mood swings that characterize adult bipolar disorder.

In 2013, the framers of DSM-5, the DSM edition that preceded the current DSM-5-TR, came to the same conclusion—that the childhood bipolar label had been overapplied. In an attempt to rectify this, they included a new category in the classification manual, **disruptive mood dysregulation disorder (DMDD),** for children with patterns of severe rage (see **Table 14-1**). It was expected that, henceforth, most children with severe anger and temper outbursts would receive this diagnosis and that the number of childhood bipolar disorder diagnoses and associated medication prescribing practices would decrease correspondingly. And, indeed, the rate of childhood bipolar disorder diagnoses has declined since the publication of DSM-5, as DMDD diagnoses have risen (Bram & Edwards, 2023; APA, 2022). That said, it is important to note that the new category has its own share of critics and that its validity and clinical usefulness are currently receiving considerable research (Burke et al., 2024; Evans et al., 2021). Moreover, contrary to original expectations, research shows that children with a diagnosis of DMDD have actually been prescribed antipsychotic medications and complex drug combinations at a higher rate than children with a diagnosis of bipolar disorder (Findling et al., 2022).

TABLE 14-1

Dx Checklist

Disruptive Mood Dysregulation Disorder
1. For at least a year, individual repeatedly displays severe and disproportionate outbursts of temper.
2. The outbursts occur at least three times per week and are present in at least two settings (home, school, with peers).
3. Individual repeatedly displays irritable or angry mood between the outbursts.
4. Individual receives initial diagnosis between 6 and 18 years of age.

Information from: APA, 2022.

SUMMING UP

Depressive and Bipolar Disorders During Childhood

Depression in childhood is often characterized by such symptoms as irritability, headaches, stomach pain, and a disinterest in toys and games. Clinical depression is much more common among teenagers than among young children. Studies indicate that second-generation antidepressant drugs may produce an increase in the risk of suicidal behavior for a small number of children and adolescents; however, most practitioners believe that the overall risk of suicide is actually reduced for the vast majority of young patients who take the drugs.

During the decades leading up to the 2013 publication of DSM-5, there was an enormous increase in the number of children and adolescents who received diagnoses of bipolar disorder and who were thus prescribed mood stabilizing drugs and antipsychotic drugs. Diagnoses of bipolar disorder have decreased now that DSM-5 and DSM-5-TR have added a new childhood category, disruptive mood dysregulation disorder, although this has not decreased the prescribing of antipsychotic drugs and complex drug combinations in children and adolescents.

Oppositional Problems

MOST CHILDREN BREAK rules or misbehave on occasion. If they consistently display extreme hostility and defiance, however, they may qualify for a diagnosis of *oppositional defiant disorder* or *conduct disorder*.

What are some ways that one might distinguish between developmentally common misbehaviors and misbehaviors requiring clinical attention?

Oppositional Defiant Disorder: A Legitimate Category?

Children with what the DSM-5-TR calls **oppositional defiant disorder** are described as argumentative and defiant, angry, irritable, and in some cases vindictive (APA, 2022). They may argue repeatedly with adults, ignore adult rules and requests, deliberately annoy other people, and feel much anger and resentment. Between 3 percent and 11 percent of children qualify for a diagnosis of oppositional defiant disorder (Hawes et al., 2023; Aggarwal & Marwaha, 2022). Before puberty, the disorder is most common in boys, but rates are equal across genders after puberty.

The diagnostic category of oppositional defiant disorder is controversial (Burke et al., 2024; Gerlach, 2023; Beltrán, Sit, & Ginsburg, 2021). Clinical theorists have raised three areas of concern: (1) The label "defiant" is stigmatizing, essentially labeling children with behavioral challenges as "difficult" or "bad." (2) Many of the symptoms included in the definition of *oppositional defiant disorder*—for example, tantrums, irritability, and poor self-control—are common reactions to childhood experiences of trauma and chronic stress; hence, in many cases, these symptoms do not reflect fixed underlying patterns of defiant behavior. And indeed, research has found higher rates of trauma in the lives of children meeting criteria for oppositional defiant disorder than in the lives of their peers. (3) The diagnostic category may be culturally insensitive or biased given that judgments about what constitutes disrespectful, challenging, or otherwise problematic behavior are highly subjective and culture-bound.

disruptive mood dysregulation disorder (DMDD) A childhood disorder marked by severe recurrent temper outbursts along with a persistent irritable or angry mood.

oppositional defiant disorder A controversial DSM-5-TR disorder in which children are repeatedly argumentative, defiant, angry, irritable, and perhaps vindictive.

Lee Lorenz The New Yorker Collection/The Cartoon Bank

"Is this the story you want to tell on your college application?"

Conduct Disorder

In contrast to the subjective judgments at the center of a diagnosis of oppositional defiant disorder, **conduct disorder** is characterized by a more observable and severe pattern of aggressive behavior in which the basic rights of others are repeatedly violated (APA, 2022). For example, children with conduct disorder may be physically cruel to people or animals, deliberately destroy other people's property, steal or lie, skip school, or run away from home (see **Table 14-2**). Many threaten or harm their victims, committing such crimes as arson, shoplifting, forgery, breaking into buildings or cars, mugging, and armed robbery. As they get older, their acts of physical violence may include rape or, in rare cases, homicide. The symptoms of conduct disorder are apparent in this summary of a clinical interview with a 15-year-old boy named Derek:

> *Questioning revealed that Derek was getting into . . . serious trouble of late and was arrested for shoplifting 4 weeks before. Derek was caught with one other youth when he and a dozen friends swarmed a convenience store and took everything they could before leaving in cars. This event followed similar others at two retail clothing stores. Derek blamed his friends for his arrest because they apparently left him behind as he straggled out of the store. He was charged only with shoplifting, however, after police found him holding just three candy bars and a bag of potato chips. Derek expressed no remorse for the theft or any care for the store clerk who was injured when one of the teens pushed her into a glass case. When informed of the clerk's injury, for example, Derek replied, "I didn't do it, so what do I care?"*
>
> *The psychologist questioned Derek further about other legal violations and discovered a rather extended history of trouble. Derek was arrested for vandalism 10 months earlier for breaking windows and damaging cars on school property. He received probation for 6 months because this was his first offense. Derek also boasted of other exploits for which he was not caught, including several shoplifting episodes, . . . joyriding, and missing school. Derek missed 23 days (50 percent) of school since the beginning of the academic year. In addition, he described break-in attempts at his neighbors' apartments. . . . Only rarely during the interview did Derek stray from his bravado.*
>
> *(Kearney, 2016, pp. 87–88)*

Conduct disorder usually begins between 7 and 15 years of age (APA, 2022). Between 2 and 10 percent of children, three-quarters of them boys, qualify for this diagnosis (Mohan, Yilanli, & Ray, 2023). Children with a relatively mild conduct disorder often improve over time, but a severe case may continue into adulthood and develop into antisocial personality disorder, another psychological problem, and/or a criminal lifestyle (Mohan et al., 2023; Perlstein et al., 2023). Usually, the earlier the onset of the conduct disorder, the poorer the eventual outcome. Research indicates that more than 80 percent of those who develop conduct disorder have first displayed the symptoms described in the DSM-5-TR category of oppositional defiant disorder (Aggarwal & Marwaha, 2022; APA, 2022). More than one-third of children with conduct disorder also display attention-deficit/hyperactivity disorder (ADHD), a disorder that you will read about shortly, and a number experience depression and anxiety (Bansal et al., 2024; Evans et al., 2024).

conduct disorder A disorder in which children repeatedly violate the basic rights of others and display significant aggression.

DSM-5-TR instructs diagnosticians to distinguish those individuals whose conduct disorder is marked by particularly callous and unemotional behaviors, as they may be qualitatively different from others with the disorder (APA, 2022). A number of researchers distinguish yet another pattern of aggression found in certain cases of conduct disorder: *relational aggression,* in which the individual is socially isolated and primarily performs social misdeeds such as slandering others, spreading rumors, and manipulating friendships (Li et al., 2023; Brandes et al., 2021).

Many children with conduct disorder are suspended from school, placed in foster homes, or incarcerated (OJJDP, 2024; Perera & Diliberti, 2023). When children between the ages of 8 and 18 break the law, the legal system often labels them *juvenile delinquents* or *young offenders.* More than half of the juveniles who are arrested each year are *recidivists,* meaning they have a history of having been arrested. Data indicate that Black American youths are more likely to be arrested, labeled juvenile delinquents, and imprisoned than non-Hispanic White American youths who commit similar offenses (DOJ, 2023; Manaba, 2020). This suggests that, on average, the former are more likely to receive punishment, while the latter are more likely to receive treatment for their conduct disorders or other antisocial behaviors.

Boys have the highest rates of involvement with the juvenile justice system. Most commonly, their arrests are for drug possession and crimes against property. Girls' arrests are most often for drug possession, sexual offenses, and running away. Emerging research suggests that transgender and nonbinary teens involved with the justice system are arrested most often for school truancy, running away from home, and sexual offenses (Wittlin et al., 2023; Mallon & Perez, 2020). It is encouraging that the overall number of arrests of teenagers for serious crimes has fallen by more than one-half over the past two decades (DOJ, 2023).

TABLE 14-2

Dx Checklist

Conduct Disorder
1. Individual repeatedly behaves in ways that violate the rights of other people or ignores the norms or rules of society, beyond the violations displayed by most other people of the same age.
2. At least three of the following features are present over the past year (and at least one in the past 6 months): ■ Frequent bullying or threatening of others ■ Frequent provoking of physical fights ■ Using dangerous weapons ■ Physical cruelty to people ■ Physical cruelty to animals ■ Stealing during confrontations with a victim ■ Forcing someone into sexual activity ■ Fire-setting ■ Deliberately destroying others' property ■ Breaking into a house, building, or car ■ Frequent lying ■ Stealing items of value under nonconfrontational circumstances ■ Frequent staying out beyond curfews, starting before the age of 13 ■ Running away from home overnight at least twice ■ Frequent truancy from school, starting before the age of 13.
3. Significant impairment.

Information from: APA, 2022.

What Are the Causes of Conduct Disorder?

Many cases of conduct disorder, particularly those marked by destructive behaviors, have been linked to genetic and biological factors, including several of the factors tied to antisocial personality disorder, the adult disorder you read about in the previous chapter (Chan et al., 2023; Dash et al., 2023). A number of cases have also been tied to drug abuse, poverty, traumatic events, and exposure to violent peers, community violence, or marginalization (Mohan et al., 2023). In addition, conduct disorder is often related to troubled parent–child relationships, harsh and excessively critical parenting, family conflict, marital conflict, and family hostility (Bogat et al., 2023). Children whose parents reject, leave, coerce, or abuse them or fail to provide appropriate and consistent supervision are apparently more likely to develop conduct problems. Children also seem more prone to this disorder when their parents themselves have poor empathy skills, are antisocial, display excessive anger, or have substance use, mood, or schizophrenic disorders (Elia, 2023; Pelham et al., 2021).

As you learned in the chapter on models of psychopathology, *developmental psychopathologists* explain conduct disorder by pointing to *interactions* between these various developmental factors (Shaw, 2023; Fonagy, 2021). Research shows, for example, that some (but certainly not all) children who are maltreated go on to develop conduct disorder. Why only some? According to several studies, maltreated individuals are especially likely to develop conduct problems if they were also born with a particular variation of a gene called the *MAOA gene* (nicknamed the "human warrior gene"), one of several genes implicated in conduct disorder (Sleek, 2023; Mentis et al., 2021). On the other hand, children who are similarly maltreated but who do *not* carry this particular genetic vulnerability are not as likely to develop conduct disorder. Moreover, *unless* they are maltreated, people with this genetic variability do not have a particularly high risk for developing conduct disorder. In short, children with a problematic variation of the MAOA gene *and* a childhood filled with maltreatment are at high risk for conduct disorder, but children with only one of these factors are significantly less likely to develop the disorder.

OF NOTE …

Help Needed

Around 70 percent of children and teens in the juvenile justice system have at least one mental health condition (NAMI, 2023).

How Do Clinicians Treat Conduct Disorder?

Because aggressive behaviors become more locked in with age, treatments for conduct disorder are generally most effective with children younger than age 13 (Frick, 2023; McMahon & Frick, 2021). Several different treatments have had moderate success, but no one of them alone appears to be the answer for this difficult problem.

of NOTE ...

Their Words

"It is so much easier to try to help a six-month-old child or a six-year-old child than it is a 16-year-old troubled kid."

Nicholas Kristof, journalist and author

PARENTING INTERVENTIONS Given the importance of family factors in conduct disorder, many therapists use a combination of family and cognitive-behavioral interventions, collectively known as **parenting interventions,** to help improve family functioning and teach parents how to stop rewarding unwanted behaviors and consistently reward proper behaviors (Engelbrektsson et al., 2023; Lindhiem & Birmaher, 2022). Parenting interventions can take various forms, depending on the age of the child with conduct problems.

One form of parenting intervention, used with children as young as 2 years, is called *parent–child interaction therapy* (*PCIT*) (Sanchez, Javadi, & Comer, 2023). Here therapists teach parents to work with their child positively, set appropriate limits, act consistently, be fair and structured in their discipline, and establish appropriate expectations regarding the child. Ideally, these efforts strengthen the parent–child relationship, improve the parents' attitudes, increase appropriate parental control, promote a consistent home environment, and produce improvements in the child's behavior. A related family intervention for young children, *video modeling,* uses video tools to help achieve the same goals.

In recent years, researchers have successfully used *video-conferencing* technology to offer parent–child interaction therapy in the homes of children with severe conduct problems. In this approach, referred to as *iPCIT* (*Internet-delivered parent–child interaction therapy*), parents use webcams and stream home family interactions, as they are occurring, to a therapist located elsewhere, while the therapist, in turn, coaches the parents through a Bluetooth earpiece. Research suggests that this video-conferencing technique can sometimes lead to even more positive child improvements than those seen in parent–child interaction therapy delivered in a clinic (Bagner et al., 2023; Sanchez et al., 2023; Comer et al., 2021).

Why might some children show more improvement when therapists use technology to treat them in their homes than when they are treated in a clinic?

If children with conduct problems are of school age, therapists may engage the parents and child more directly through *family therapy,* in which the entire family identifies problematic behaviors and participates in collaborative problem-solving (Carr, 2023; Sheidow, McCart, & Drazdowski, 2022). Like parenting interventions for younger children with conduct disorder, this enhanced approach for school-age children has often achieved a measure of success.

Many therapists further supplement parenting interventions with interventions in the children's schools, social lives, and the broader community—a combination of interventions called *multisystemic therapy.* Multisystemic therapists not only treat family dynamics but also work to increase the amount of time that children spend with positive children and role models instead of with antisocial peers. Although this integrative approach is typically applied to particularly severe and complex cases of conduct disorder, research finds that it often results in positive effects for these cases (Littell et al., 2021).

CHILD-FOCUSED TREATMENTS Treatments that focus primarily on the child with conduct disorder rather than on the whole family have sometimes been helpful (Awhangansi et al., 2023; Lochman, Powell, & Jones, 2022). In an effective cognitive-behavioral approach called *problem-solving skills training,* therapists combine modeling, practice, role-playing, and systematic rewards to teach children constructive thinking and positive social behaviors. The therapists may play games and solve tasks with the children and later help them apply the lessons and skills derived

parenting intervention A treatment approach for conduct disorder, ADHD, autism spectrum disorder, and intellectual disability in which therapists combine family and cognitive-behavioral interventions to help improve family functioning and help parents deal with their children more effectively.

Norma Jean Gargasz/Alamy Stock Photo

Antisocial behavior and the law Many young persons with conduct disorder are incarcerated in *juvenile detention centers* when their behaviors place them in conflict with the law. Despite improved conditions at some centers, the inmates, like this individual at a program in Arizona, often spend much time sitting around and disengaged—hardly a prescription for better behavior or mental health.

from the games and tasks to real-life situations. In another helpful cognitive-behavioral intervention called the Coping Power Program, children with conduct problems participate in group sessions that teach them to manage their anger more effectively, view situations in perspective, solve problems, become aware of their emotions, build social skills, set goals, and handle peer pressure. Yet another child-focused approach is psychotropic drug therapy, particularly stimulant drugs that may help reduce the aggressive and/or impulsive behaviors of children with conduct problems at home and at school.

Residential Treatment Residential treatment in the community has also helped some children. In one such approach, *treatment foster care,* children with conduct disorder engaging in serious delinquent behaviors are assigned by the juvenile justice system to a foster home in the community. While there, the children, foster parents, and birth parents all receive support and treatment interventions, including family therapy with both sets of parents, individual treatment for the child, and meetings with the school and with parole and probation officers. In addition, the children and their parents continue to receive treatment and support after the children leave foster care. Research shows that treatment foster care helps reduce teen participation in violent crimes, such as assaults, robberies, and rapes (Vimefall, Sahrblom, & Nordlöf, 2022).

In contrast to this form of residential treatment, institutionalization in so-called *juvenile detention centers* has not met with much success (Mendel, 2023). In fact, such institutions frequently serve to strengthen delinquent behavior rather than resocialize young persons who display such behavior. Moreover, as noted earlier, young Black children who display antisocial behaviors are more likely to wind up in juvenile detention centers than are young non-Hispanic White Americans who display similar antisocial patterns.

How might juvenile detention centers themselves contribute to the high recidivism rate among teenagers involved with the justice system?

Prevention It may be that the best hope for dealing with the problem of conduct disorder lies in *prevention* programs that begin in the earliest stages of childhood (CDC, 2023). These programs try to change unfavorable social conditions before a conduct disorder is able to develop. Typically, the programs offer training opportunities for young people, recreational facilities, and health care. They may also seek to ease the stresses of poverty, promote more positive school environments, and provide home support for improved child-rearing practices (Milburn, Rice, & Petry, 2024). All such approaches work best when they educate and involve the family.

Elimination Disorders

CHILDREN WITH ELIMINATION disorders repeatedly urinate or pass feces in their clothes, in bed, or on the floor. They already have reached an age at which they are expected to control these bodily functions, and their symptoms are not caused by physical illness.

of NOTE ...

Their Words

"The boy will come to nothing."

Jacob Freud, 1864 (referring to his 8-year-old son Sigmund after he had urinated in his parents' bedroom)

Enuresis

Enuresis is repeated involuntary (or in some cases intentional) bed-wetting or wetting of one's clothes. It typically occurs at night during sleep but may also occur during the day. Children must be at least 5 years of age to receive this diagnosis (APA, 2022; Tu, Baskin, & Arnhym, 2022). The condition may be triggered by stressful events, such as a hospitalization, entrance into school, or family problems.

The prevalence of enuresis decreases with age. As many as 33 percent of 5-year-old children have some bed-wetting, and 16 percent meet the criteria for enuresis; in contrast, 5 percent of 10-year-olds and less than 2 percent of 15-year-olds have enuresis (APA, 2022; Tu et al., 2022). Boys with the disorder outnumber girls by 2 to 1. Those with enuresis typically have a close relative (parent, sibling) who has had or will have the same disorder.

Research has not favored one explanation for enuresis over the others (Gomez Rincon, Leslie, & Lotfollahzadeh, 2023). Psychodynamic theorists explain it as a symptom of broader anxiety and underlying conflicts. Family theorists point to disturbed family interactions. Cognitive-behavioral theorists view the problem as the result of improper, unrealistic, or coercive toilet training. And biological theorists suspect that children with this disorder often have a small bladder capacity, weak bladder muscles, and/or disturbed sleep patterns.

Most cases of the disorder correct themselves even without treatment. However, treatments, particularly cognitive-behavioral therapy, can speed up the process (Tu & Baskin, 2022). In a widely used classical conditioning approach, the *bed-wetting alarm treatment* (or *bell-and-pad technique*), a bell and a battery are wired to a pad consisting of two metallic foil sheets, and the entire apparatus is placed under the child at bedtime (Mello et al., 2023; Mowrer & Mowrer, 1938). A single drop of urine sets off the bell, awakening the child as soon as any wetting takes place. Thus, the bell (unconditioned stimulus) paired with the sensation of a full bladder (conditioned stimulus) produces the response of waking. Eventually, a full bladder alone awakens the child.

Another cognitive-behavioral treatment method is *dry-bed training*. In this approach, children receive training in retention control, are awakened periodically during the night, practice getting out of bed and going to the bathroom, and are appropriately rewarded. Like the bell-and-pad technique, this behavioral approach is often effective.

Encopresis

Children with **encopresis,** also called soiling, repeatedly defecate into their clothing. The disorder is less common than enuresis, and it is also less well researched (Sood, 2023, 2022). This problem seldom occurs at night during sleep. It is usually involuntary, starts at the age of 4 or older, and affects about 1.5 to 4 percent of all children (see **Table 14-3**). At least two-thirds of children with this disorder are boys.

Encopresis causes intense social problems, shame, and embarrassment. Children who experience it usually try to hide their condition and try to avoid situations, such as camp or school, in which they might embarrass themselves. It may stem from

enuresis A childhood disorder marked by repeated bed-wetting or wetting of one's clothes.

encopresis A childhood disorder characterized by repeated defecating in inappropriate places, such as one's clothing.

TABLE 14-3

Comparison of Disorders Beginning in Childhood or Adolescence

Disorder	Usual Age of Identification	Prevalence Among All Children	Gender with Greatest Prevalence	Elevated Family History	Recovery by Adulthood
Separation anxiety disorder	Before 12 years	4%	Females	Yes	Usually
Selective mutism	2–4 years	1%	Females	Yes	Often
Unipolar depression	7 years–adolescence	5%–8%	Females (after age 13)	Yes	Often, but may have episodic recurrences
Conduct disorder	7–15 years	2%–10%	Males	Yes	Often
Enuresis	5–8 years	7%	Males	Yes	Usually
Encopresis	4 years or older	1.5%–4%	Males	Unclear	Usually
ADHD	Before 12 years	7%–10%	Males	Yes	Often
Autism spectrum disorder	0–3 years	2%	Males	Yes	Sometimes
Specific learning disorders	6–9 years	5%–10%	Males	Yes	Often
Intellectual disability	Before 10 years	1%	Males	Unclear	Sometimes

Information from: Augustyn, 2023, 2022; Baldor, 2023; Hamilton, 2023, 2022; Krull & Chan, 2023; Mohan et al., 2023; NAA, 2023; von Hahn, 2023; APA, 2022; Bennett & Walkup, 2022; Tu et al., 2022.

constipation or other biological factors, stress, improper toilet training, or a combination of these factors (Sood, 2023, 2022; APA, 2022). Constipation, by far the most common cause, is a factor in 80 percent of cases. Because physical problems are so often linked to this disorder, a medical examination is typically conducted first.

The most common and successful treatments for encopresis are cognitive-behavioral and medical approaches or a combination of the two (Sood, 2023; Lomas Mevers et al., 2020). Treatment may include interventions to eliminate the children's constipation, biofeedback to help the children better detect when their bowels are full, and the stimulation of regular bowel functioning with high-fiber diets, mineral oil, laxatives, and lubricants. Family therapy has also proved helpful.

SUMMING UP

Oppositional Problems and Elimination Disorders

Those meeting the DSM-5-TR diagnostic criteria for oppositional defiant disorder, a controversial category, argue repeatedly with adults, ignore adult rules and requests, and feel intense anger and resentment. Those with conduct disorder, a more severe pattern, repeatedly violate the basic rights of others. Children with this latter disorder often exhibit violent and cruel behavior and may deliberately destroy property, steal, and run away.

Clinicians have treated children with conduct disorders by using approaches such as parenting interventions, including parent–child interaction therapy, multisystemic therapy, problem-solving skills training, the Coping Power Program, and treatment foster care. Some individuals with this disorder have instead been institutionalized in juvenile training centers. A number of prevention programs have also been developed.

Children with one of the elimination disorders, enuresis, repeatedly urinate in their beds or their clothes, usually involuntarily. Cognitive-behavioral approaches, such as the bed-wetting alarm treatment, are effective treatments for enuresis. Children with another elimination disorder, encopresis, repeatedly defecate into their clothing.

Neurodevelopmental Disorders

NEURODEVELOPMENTAL DISORDERS ARE a group of disabilities linked with brain functioning that emerge at birth or during very early childhood and affect the individual's behavior, memory, concentration, and/or ability to learn. DSM-5-TR categorizes *attention-deficit/hyperactivity disorder, autism spectrum disorder,* and *intellectual disability* as neurodevelopmental disorders (APA, 2022). As you read at the beginning of this chapter, neurodevelopmental disorders often have a significant impact throughout the person's life (Conant & Miller, 2024).

Attention-Deficit/Hyperactivity Disorder

Children with **attention-deficit/hyperactivity disorder (ADHD)** have great difficulty attending to tasks, behave overactively and impulsively, or both (APA, 2022) (see **Table 14-4**). Because all children are inattentive and impulsive to a certain extent, the symptoms must be beyond what is developmentally typical in order to qualify for a diagnosis of ADHD. ADHD often appears before the child starts school, as with Ricky, one of the children we met at the beginning of this chapter.

As in Ricky's case, the symptoms of ADHD often feed into one another. Children who have trouble focusing attention may keep turning from task to task until they end up trying to run in several directions at once. Similarly, children who move constantly may find it hard to attend to tasks or show good judgment. In many cases, one of these symptoms stands out much more than the other. About half of the children with ADHD also have learning or communication problems, many perform poorly in school, a number have difficulty interacting with other children, and about 80 percent misbehave, often quite seriously (Bansal et al., 2024; Evans et al., 2024). The children may also have great difficulty controlling their emotions, and some have anxiety or mood problems (Todzia-Kornas, Szczegielniak, & Gondek, 2024).

of NOTE ...

ADHD's Associated Challenges

According to research, people with ADHD tend to have . . .

- More difficulty succeeding in school.
- More problems at work.
- Reduced earning power.
- More relationship problems.
- More driving citations and accidents.
- More problems with the law.

(Information from: ADHDAM, 2024.)

TABLE 14-4

Dx Checklist

Attention-Deficit/Hyperactivity Disorder
1. Individual presents one or both of the following patterns:
(a) For 6 months or more, individual frequently displays at least six of the following symptoms of inattention, to a degree that is maladaptive and beyond that shown by most similarly aged persons: ■ Unable to properly attend to details, or frequently makes careless errors ■ Finds it hard to maintain attention ■ Fails to listen when spoken to by others ■ Fails to carry out instructions and finish work ■ Disorganized ■ Dislikes or avoids mentally effortful work ■ Loses items that are needed for successful work ■ Easily distracted by irrelevant stimuli ■ Forgets to do many everyday activities. (b) For 6 months or more, individual frequently displays at least six of the following symptoms of hyperactivity and impulsivity, to a degree that is maladaptive and beyond that shown by most similarly aged persons: ■ Fidgets, taps hands or feet, or squirms ■ Inappropriately wanders from seat ■ Inappropriately runs or climbs ■ Unable to play quietly ■ In constant motion ■ Talks excessively ■ Interrupts questioners during discussions ■ Unable to wait for turn ■ Barges in on others' activities or conversations
2. Individual displayed some of the symptoms before 12 years of age.
3. Individual shows symptoms in more than one setting.
4. Individual experiences impaired functioning.

Information from: APA, 2022.

Laurence Griffiths/Getty Images

Competition of another kind Simone Biles, the most decorated American gymnast in history, performs in the balance beam competition at the 2016 Olympic Games at age 19. Biles has proudly announced that she experiences ADHD, and indeed she received an exemption from the World Anti-Doping Association to take methylphenidate for her condition. She has tweeted, "Having ADHD and taking medicine for it is nothing to be ashamed of."

Between 7 and 10 percent of all children display ADHD at any given time, most of them boys (Krull & Chan, 2023; APA, 2022). Those whose parents have had ADHD are more likely than others to develop it. The disorder usually persists throughout childhood. Many children show a lessening of symptoms as they move into mid-adolescence, but as many as 60 percent of them, particularly those with more severe symptoms, continue to have ADHD as adults (Bukstein, 2023; Solanto, 2023). The symptoms of restlessness and overactivity are not usually as pronounced in adult cases. Adults with ADHD have higher-than-average rates of substance misuse, insomnia, risky sexual behavior, driving accidents, and job changes, and they tend to earn a lower income (Fairbank, 2023; Pelham et al., 2022; Sultan et al., 2021).

ADHD is difficult to assess properly (Chugh, Aggarwal, & Balyan, 2024). Ideally, the child's behavior should be observed in several environments (at school, at home, with friends) because the symptoms of hyperactivity and inattentiveness must be present across multiple settings in order for ADHD to be diagnosed (Krull & Chan, 2023). Because children with ADHD often give poor descriptions of their symptoms, it is important to obtain reports of the symptoms from parents and teachers (Eng et al., 2024). A range of diagnostic interviews, rating scales, and psychological tests should be used, but many children receive their diagnosis from pediatricians or family physicians rather than from a systematic mental health assessment. Extensive studies indicate that ADHD is, in fact, overdiagnosed in the United States and other parts of the world (Kazda et al., 2023, 2021). At the same time, ADHD remains underdiagnosed in certain subpopulations, such as in girls and in children of color (Morgan & Hu, 2023), a concern we will return to in our later discussion of multicultural factors and ADHD.

What Are the Causes of ADHD?

Most of today's clinicians consider ADHD to result from several interacting causes. In many cases, for example, biological factors have been identified, with genetic studies suggesting that certain children have a predisposition to display inattention, impulsivity, and overactivity (Doherty et al., 2024; Rosenberg et al., 2024).

To appreciate the brain factors that may contribute to ADHD, it is necessary to first understand regular human attention. There are two complementary processes that make up our moment-to-moment attention (Nigg et al., 2023, 2020; Nigg, 2017, 2016). *Type 1 attention processes* are beyond our voluntary control and focus our attention

neurodevelopmental disorders A group of disabilities—including ADHD, autism spectrum disorder, and intellectual disability—in the functioning of the brain that emerge at birth or during very early childhood and affect one's behavior, memory, concentration, or ability to learn.

attention-deficit/hyperactivity disorder (ADHD) A neurodevelopmental disorder marked by the inability to focus attention, overactive and impulsive behavior, or both.

The brain, attention, and ADHD This is a 3D graphical representation, created with MRI technology, of the brain connections at work during the act of paying attention. The graphical representation is a side view of the brain, in which a person's eyes would be at the left side and the back of the head on the right side. The yellow tint shows brain fiber pathways that are key to effective attention—fibers that interconnect in a less-than-ideal manner for people with ADHD.

on unexpected things that occur in our surroundings, such as sudden sounds or startling information. In contrast, *Type 2 attention processes* are mental activities that we control, and they involve our effortful focus of attention. In order to attend to our environment properly, we must have an appropriate interplay between our Type 1 and Type 2 attention processes. In many situations, for example, it is important that our Type 2 attention processes suppress our Type 1 attention alerts so that we can achieve our goals. If you were reading a book and suddenly there was lightning and thunder outside, your Type 1 attention processes might automatically reorient your focus momentarily to the unanticipated sight and sound. In order to resume reading, however, you would need to engage your Type 2 attention processes to consciously divert your attention from the distracting weather outside and back to your book.

The symptoms of poor attention found in ADHD are commonly understood as a breakdown in the balance between Type 1 and Type 2 attention processes. Children with ADHD have particular difficulty engaging Type 2 attention processes to override Type 1 "emergency alarms," and as a result, they have trouble deliberately refocusing their attention to successfully function at home, at school, and in social situations. If there is a loud lawn mower running outside of a classroom, most students can keep their focus on the teacher despite the distraction. In contrast, students with ADHD may have significant difficulty recruiting Type 2 attention processes to turn their focus back to the teacher.

Brain scan studies have identified an *attention circuit*—a number of structures that work together throughout the brain to bring about attention and to maintain a proper balance between Type I and Type 2 attention processes. You have read about some of the brain structures in this circuit (the *prefrontal cortex, anterior cingulate,* and *striatum,* for example) in our earlier discussions of other brain circuits (Agoalikum et al., 2023; da Silva et al., 2023). Other structures in the attention brain circuit, such as the *corona radiata,* are new to your reading and are tied to a narrower range of behaviors and cognitive processes, including attention (Jones et al., 2023). Research on the possible ties between the brain's attention circuit and ADHD is still unfolding, but indications are that individuals with ADHD have a dysfunctional attention circuit, marked by poor communication (faulty *interconnectivity*) between the structures in this circuit as well as by atypical activity of the neurotransmitter *dopamine* throughout the brain circuit (da Silva et al., 2023). Given the dysfunctional attention circuit of these individuals, their Type 2 attention processes are, more often than not, simply unable to override their Type 1 attention processes.

In addition to biological factors, ADHD has been linked to high levels of stress and to family dysfunction (Krull & Chan, 2023). In fact, some studies suggest that these negative factors interfere with the development of effective Type 2 attention processes (Nigg et al., 2023, 2020; Nigg, 2017, 2016). In addition, sociocultural theorists have noted that ADHD symptoms and a diagnosis of ADHD may themselves create interpersonal problems and produce further symptoms in the child. That is, children who are hyperactive tend to be viewed negatively by their peers, parents, and teachers; have impaired peer relationships; and, in turn, come to view themselves negatively (APA, 2022).

Interventions and Treatments for ADHD

Almost 80 percent of all children and adolescents with ADHD receive interventions and treatments (CDC, 2023). The most commonly used approaches are drug therapy, cognitive-behavioral therapy, or a combination of the two (Krull & Chan, 2023).

methylphenidate A stimulant drug, better known by the trade names Ritalin or Concerta, commonly used to treat ADHD.

DRUG THERAPY Millions of children and adults with ADHD are currently treated with **methylphenidate,** a stimulant drug that actually has been available for decades, or with certain other stimulants. Although a variety of manufacturers now produce methylphenidate, the drug is often known to the public by its famous trade names, Ritalin or Concerta. As researchers have confirmed methylphenidate's quieting effects on children with ADHD and its ability to help them focus, behave better at school, interact better with their families, and control aggression, use of the drug has increased enormously—according to some estimates, at least a threefold increase since 1990 alone (Vertessen, Luman, & Oosterlaan, 2024; Krull & Chan, 2023; Campez et al., 2022). This increase in use also extends to preschoolers.

Why has there been a sizable increase in the diagnosis and treatment of ADHD over the past few decades?

Methylphenidate is the most common medication for children with ADHD, although amphetamines (such as Adderall) are also often prescribed for children and in fact are now the medication of choice for adults with ADHD (Schatzberg & Nemeroff, 2024; Brent, Bukstein, & Solanto, 2023). Altogether, more than 4 million children in the United States regularly take either methylphenidate or an amphetamine drug for ADHD (CDC, 2023). It is worth noting that although both methylphenidate and amphetamines are stimulant drugs, they are somewhat different in structure and in certain actions.

Although widely used, methylphenidate and amphetamines have raised certain concerns (Vertessen et al., 2024; Krull & Chan, 2023). First, many clinicians worry about the possible long-term effects of these various drugs, and others question whether the favorable findings of the drug studies (most of which have been done with non-Hispanic White American children) are applicable to children from other racial and ethnic backgrounds. Second, because ADHD is overdiagnosed in the United States, many children who are receiving these stimulants may in fact have been inaccurately diagnosed. Third, although research suggests that stimulant medications are safe for the majority of people with ADHD, the drugs may, in some cases, lead to mild tremors or tics, growth interference, psychotic symptoms, or heart problems. And, finally, the stimulants can be addictive if misused, as you read in the chapter on substance use and addictive disorders. Indeed, the drugs used to treat ADHD have become popular recreational drugs among teenagers and young adults; some snort them to get high, and others use them to stay alert or improve their performance at school or work. A number of young adults have become dependent on the stimulants. In fact, recent spikes in the use of stimulant medications by people who do *not* have ADHD have led, in part, to a national shortage of stimulant medications in the United States—a shortage that has seriously disrupted care for many children with ADHD. Indeed, since the stimulant shortage began in 2022, around 40 percent of individuals with ADHD and their caregivers have reported difficulties finding and filling their needed prescription medications (ADDitude, 2023).

of NOTE ...

Their Words

"I want to thank my mom and my dad up in heaven for disobeying the doctor's orders and not medicating their hyperactive girl and finding out what she was into instead."

Audra McDonald, Tony Award–winning actress and singer

COGNITIVE-BEHAVIORAL THERAPY AND TREATMENT COMBINATIONS Cognitive-behavioral therapy, particularly interventions that seek to change and/or manage specific behaviors, is often used for individuals with ADHD (Krull & Chan, 2023; Barkley, 2022, 2020). In many cases, parents and teachers are taught how to apply the principles of operant conditioning—systematically rewarding the children for attentiveness or self-control. They may, for example, set up a *token economy program* in which the children receive tokens whenever they attend and respond appropriately—tokens that can later be exchanged for rewards of various kinds. Many children with ADHD also participate in eight-week therapeutic summer camps that provide systematic cognitive-behavioral interventions in classroom-like formats.

Parents of children with ADHD may also receive a *parenting intervention,* in which cognitive-behavioral techniques are combined with family interventions to help the parents manage their children's behaviors more effectively, similar to the parenting interventions used in cases of conduct disorder (CDC, 2023; Doffer et al., 2023).

More than fun These campers at Florida International University's Summer Treatment Program learn to work together, plan, and delay gratification while participating in group activities—all part of a model program for children with ADHD and related challenges. The program applies cognitive-behavioral principles, exercise, and fitness training to help campers develop better attention, behavioral control, coping, teamwork, and social skills.

Courtesy Summer Treatment Program, Center for Children and

Moreover, parenting interventions and operant techniques may be combined with *school interventions* (Pfiffner et al., 2023). In one such combination program, the Daily Report Card (DRC), a child's target behaviors—staying in the classroom seat, raising a hand to speak, and using an "inside voice"—are carefully evaluated, recorded on a DRC, and reinforced by teachers throughout the school day. At the end of the day, the teacher further provides the report card for the parents to see, and, if a sufficient number of target behaviors had been performed satisfactorily that day, the child is also given rewards at home.

Research suggests that children with ADHD may improve most when they receive a combination of stimulant drug therapy and the cognitive-behavioral treatments we have been discussing (Krull & Chan, 2023). Combining drug therapies and cognitive-behavioral therapy is also desirable because, according to research, children who receive both treatments require lower levels of medication, meaning, of course, that they are less subject to any undesired effects from the medications.

Multicultural Factors and ADHD

Throughout this book, you have learned that race and ethnicity often affect how people are diagnosed and treated for various psychological disorders. Thus, you should not be surprised that race and ethnicity seem similarly important with regard to the quality of care for ADHD.

A number of studies indicate that in the United States Black and Hispanic children with significant attention and activity problems are less likely than non-Hispanic White children with similar symptoms to be assessed for ADHD or to receive a diagnosis of ADHD (Morgan & Hu, 2023; APA, 2022). Moreover, among those who do receive an ADHD diagnosis, children of color are less likely than non-Hispanic White children to be treated with stimulant drugs or a combination of stimulants and cognitive-behavioral therapy—the interventions that seem to be of most help to individuals with ADHD (Morgan & Hu, 2023; Davis et al., 2021). They are also less likely to receive adequate follow-up care to monitor their medication responses.

In part, these racial and ethnic differences are tied to economic factors. Studies consistently show that children from economically disadvantaged households are less likely than those from economically secure households to be identified as having ADHD and are less likely to receive effective treatment, and that families of color are, on average, more economically disadvantaged and inadequately insured. Some clinical theorists further believe that social bias and stereotyping may contribute to the racial and ethnic differences in diagnosis and treatment. They argue that our society often views the symptoms of ADHD as clinical problems when exhibited by non-Hispanic White children but as indicators of poor parenting, lower IQ, substance use, or violence when displayed by Black and Hispanic children (APA, 2022; Evans, Owens, & Power, 2021). This notion has been supported by the finding that, all symptoms being equal, teachers and parents in the United States are more likely to conclude that overactive non-Hispanic White children have ADHD but that overactive Black or Hispanic children have other kinds of difficulties (Morgan & Hu, 2023; Zablotsky & Alford, 2020).

Whatever the precise reasons may be, it appears that children of color are less likely to receive a proper ADHD diagnosis and treatment. While many of today's clinical theorists correctly alert us to the possibility that ADHD may be generally overdiagnosed and overtreated, it is important to also recognize that children from marginalized backgrounds may, in fact, be underdiagnosed and undertreated.

autism spectrum disorder A neurodevelopmental disorder that, according to DSM-5-TR, is marked by substantial unresponsiveness to others, significant communication deficits, and highly rigid and repetitive behaviors, interests, and activities.

Autism Spectrum Disorder

Autism spectrum disorder, a pattern first identified by psychiatrist Leo Kanner in 1943, is, according to DSM-5-TR, marked by substantial unresponsiveness to other people, significant communication deficits, and highly rigid and repetitive behaviors, interests, and activities (APA, 2022) (see **Table 14-5**). These symptoms appear early in life, typically before 3 years of age. Just two decades ago, this pattern of functioning seemed to characterize around 1 out of every 2,000 children. In recent years, however, there has been a steady increase in the number of children who are considered to be part of the autism spectrum, and it now appears that at least 1 in 36 children display autism spectrum disorder (Augustyn, 2023; NAA, 2023). Jennie and Carter are two such individuals:

TABLE 14-5

Dx Checklist

Autism Spectrum Disorder
1. Individual displays continual deficiencies in various areas of communication and social interaction, including the following: ▪ Social-emotional reciprocity ▪ Nonverbal communication ▪ Development and maintenance of relationships.
2. Individual displays significant restriction and repetition in behaviors, interests, or activities, including two or more of the following: ▪ Exaggerated and repeated speech patterns, movements, or object use ▪ Inflexible demand for same routines, statements, and behaviors ▪ Highly restricted, fixated, and overly intense interests ▪ Over- or underreactions to sensory input from the environment.
3. Individual develops symptoms by early childhood.
4. Individual experiences impaired functioning.

Information from: APA, 2022.

*Ms. D'Angelo [a special education teacher] first observed **Jennie** in a small classroom over a five-day period. Jennie was often nonresponsive to others, especially her classmates, and rarely made eye contact with anyone. When left alone, Jennie would usually stand, put her hands over her throat, stick out her tongue, and make strange but soft noises. This would last for hours if she were left alone. When seated, Jennie rocked back and forth in her chair but never fell. Her motor skills seemed excellent and she could use crayons and manipulate paper when asked to do so. Her dexterity was also evident in her aggression, however. Jennie often grabbed people's jewelry and eyeglasses and flung them across the room. She moved quickly enough to accomplish this in less than 6 seconds. . . . Ms. D'Angelo noticed that Jennie was most aggressive when introduced to something or someone new. . . .*

Ms. D'Angelo noticed that Jennie did not speak and vocalized only when making her soft sounds. . . . [She] made no effort to communicate with others and was often oblivious to others. . . . Despite her lack of expressiveness, Jennie did understand and adhere to simple requests from others. She complied readily when told to get her lunch, use the bathroom, or retrieve an item in the classroom. . . .

Jennie had a "picture book" with photographs of items she might want or need. . . . When shown the book and asked to point, Jennie either pushed the book onto the desk if she did not want anything or pointed to one of five photographs (i.e., a lunch box, cookie, glass of water, favorite toy, or toilet) if she did want something. . . .

[Her parents] said Jennie "had always been like this" and gave examples of her early impairment. Both said Jennie was "different" as a baby when she resisted being held and when she failed to talk by age 3 years. . . . [They] enrolled their daughter in her current school when she was 4 years old.

(Kearney, 2016, pp. 125–126)

(continued on the next page)

***Carter's** parents, Vanessa and Reginald, were concerned about him as early as the age of 2. He was not affectionate with them the way his older brothers Kevin and Darius had been, and he at times seemed to recoil from their attempts to talk to or hold him. He did not begin to speak until he was 3, when he finally did begin speaking, albeit infrequently. While Kevin and Darius were rambunctious, teasing each other constantly and enjoying pranks, Carter was aloof from the merriment and preferred his own company.*

Reggie and Vanessa went in for a conference with Carter's teacher, who expressed her concerns. She said Carter was quite bright, and his arithmetic work was excellent, but his language work was less accomplished, and he did not seem to socialize with his classmates. Carter was one of only three Black children in the class, but the teacher had seen him brush off friendly overtures from Black and White classmates alike. When spoken to, Carter would typically answer flatly, using the fewest possible words, and he almost physically shrank back from any interpersonal approach.

At the teacher's suggestion, Carter's parents took him to a child psychologist, and after several sessions, the psychologist diagnosed the child as autistic. Vanessa, in particular, found this hard to believe, saying, "Look, I admit he's a bit shy and awkward around people, but he gets by just fine. He dresses himself, does okay in school, and he's not a problem at home. Okay, maybe there's an issue, but I really don't see it being something as big as autism." The psychologist explained that autism doesn't always present as dramatically as Vanessa and Reggie may have seen it portrayed in movies and on TV, and their son was in fact an autistic person who would benefit from additional support.

Carter was placed in a special educational program at age 6, and he also began a cognitive-behavioral intervention. Vanessa stepped back from her role as editor in chief of a popular magazine to spend more time at home trying to supplement Carter's educational and treatment interventions.

Carter is now 10 years of age, and over the past several years, he has made improvements. In fact, he is highly accomplished in his school program. At home, he does his chores, like cleaning his room and taking out the trash. Vanessa and Reggie have attended a number of workshops that have helped them view Carter and his autistic ways as "different" from their other children, not as "abnormal" or "deficient"—an attitude the workshop leader calls neurodiversity. Correspondingly, they try to arrange the family environment and household so that it is in sync with his needs and abilities as much as possible. For example, they tailor his chores toward more solitary duties, whereas Kevin and Darius often work together.

He joins the family every mealtime, but usually he eats without joining in the conversation or commenting on the food they're eating. He watches the news on TV every night, becoming anxious if he ever misses it, but he does not choose to engage when his father tries to discuss the news with him.

Carter likes to draw, and he is quite good at it for his age. All his drawings are of analog clocks. Reggie and Vanessa find this narrow focus unusual, but they take care to encourage the development of his artistic skill. A few times, they suggested that he might enjoy drawing something else, but each time he strongly indicated "No," and the discussions ended there.

of NOTE ...

Their Words

"No two people with autism are the same. Its precise form of expression is different in every case."

Oliver Sacks, neurologist and writer

Autistic people vary widely in strengths, abilities, needs, and difficulties. Some, like Jennie, have very severe challenges that pervade every aspect of their lives. Many others, like Carter, exhibit social and communication patterns that make it hard to succeed in some settings, but they may also enjoy great success and effectiveness in other settings. That is, Jennie and Carter have common threads running through their autistic patterns, but the challenges posed by their respective patterns certainly differ.

For decades, the term *autistic disorder* was applied only to cases with severe symptoms such as those experienced by Jenny. Individuals like Carter, who displayed different, often less severe autistic-like features, were assigned to different diagnostic

Through a different lens An 8-year-old autistic child peers through a hole in the netting of a baseball batting cage, seemingly unaware of other children and activities at the playground.

categories such as "Asperger's disorder" or "pervasive developmental disorder not otherwise specified." In 2013, however, the framers of DSM-5 determined that autistic disorder and the other autistic-like syndromes should no longer be considered separate disorders, and they combined them under the category of *autism spectrum disorder*. To help distinguish the diverse challenges faced by people assigned to this single category, DSM-5 (and now DSM-5-TR) requires diagnosticians to further specify how much support the person needs, whether the person also has intellectual impairment, and whether the individual also displays language impairment (APA, 2022).

Altogether, around 80 percent of diagnosed autistic children are boys (Augustyn, 2023; NAA, 2023). Research conducted with predominantly cisgender populations finds that it takes autistic girls much longer than it takes autistic boys to receive a formal autism diagnosis after displaying initial signs of the condition (McDonnell et al., 2021). As many as 90 percent of autistic children continue to experience significant impediments into adulthood. Many have enormous difficulty maintaining employment, performing household tasks, and leading independent lives. Even autistic adults with relatively few language or other cognitive challenges may experience difficulties with closeness and empathy and have restricted interests and activities.

Competing Viewpoints and Terminology in Autism

Before proceeding further in our discussion of autism spectrum disorder, we should take note of a few points. The first is to recognize a perspective called **neurodiversity**, a viewpoint that has been embraced by a growing number of persons in both the clinical field and the public arena (CC, 2023; Dwyer, 2022). You will be reading more about neurodiversity shortly in the section on explanations for autism, but, simply put, it refers to the notion that all brains differ from each other and that some people's brains (those of *neurodivergent* people) simply develop or work differently from the brains of most other people (those of *neurotypical* people). The former people should not be thought of as "abnormal," "pathological," or "mentally disordered," nor should the latter people be thought of as "normal" or "mentally healthy."

Some believe that autism should be viewed through the lens of neurodiversity, not as a mental or medical disorder (Hamilton & Petty, 2023). In turn, they consider it ill-advised to think of autism as a diagnostic category that consists of problematic symptoms and is in need of significant repair. Thus, as you are reading the upcoming

neurodiversity A perspective, sometimes applied to autism, ADHD, and certain other neurodevelopmental disorders, that holds that all brains differ from each other and that some people's brains (those of *neurodivergent* people) develop or work differently from the brains of most other people (those of *neurotypical* people) without implying that the neurodivergent people are pathological or deficient.

Christoph Soeder/picture-alliance/dpa/AP Images

"Embracing neurodiversity" Today, many autistic people embrace the perspective of neurodiversity. Like the person in this photo, they do not view their autism as a disorder but rather a reflection of neurodivergent brain development and operation—alternative brain functioning that can, in fact, produce certain strengths and advantages if accommodated by the person's surrounding environment.

sections on autism, you should keep in mind that not everyone agrees with the notions that will be described. (It should also be pointed out that, according to some theorists, a number of other disorders, including ADHD and specific learning disorders, can also be viewed through the lens of neurodiversity.)

A second point to take note of centers on descriptive language. For almost every clinical disorder, clinicians and researchers use a "person-first" descriptor, such as "person with schizophrenia" or "person with borderline personality disorder." Such language is meant to convey that the person is more than their disorder. However, research indicates that the majority of adults with an autistic pattern (at least, those who do not have accompanying intellectual challenges) prefer an "autism-first" descriptor—"autistic person"—a preference consistent with the neurodiverse view that autistic functioning does not reflect psychopathology (Buijsman, Begeer, & Scheeren, 2023). Given that preference, we shall use the autism-first descriptor in our discussions of autism.

The Features of Autism

As we mentioned at the beginning of this section on autism spectrum disorder, the key features of autism are substantial unresponsiveness to other people, significant communication deficits, and highly rigid and repetitive behaviors, interests, and activities (APA, 2022).

The individual's *limited display of social-emotional reciprocity*—extreme aloofness, seeming lack of interest in other people, low empathy, and inability to share attention with others—has long been considered a central feature of autism (You et al., 2024). Like Jennie and Carter, autistic children typically do not reach for their parents during infancy. Instead, they may arch their backs when they are held and appear not to recognize or care about those around them. In a similar vein, unlike other children of the same age, autistic children typically do not include others in their play and do not represent social experiences when they are playing; that is, they may not see themselves as others see them, and they have little desire to imitate or be like others (Augustyn & von Hahn, 2023).

Communication challenges take various forms in autism spectrum disorder. Many autistic people have great difficulty understanding speech or using language for conversational purposes. In fact, like Jennie, at least one-third do not say more than a few words (NAA, 2023). Those who do talk may have rigid and repetitious speech patterns. One of the most common speech patterns is *echolalia,* the exact echoing of phrases

of NOTE ...

Their Words

"Being on the spectrum and having other learning differences, I am used to working harder and have a great drive to succeed. I interpret things differently, which helps with analyzing scripts, engulfing myself into roles, to achieve realism. [It] also drives me to make strong choices."

Kayla Cromer, actress

spoken by others. The individuals repeat the words with the same accent or inflection but with no sign of understanding or intent of communicating. Some even repeat a sentence days after they have heard it.

The nonverbal behaviors of these individuals are often at odds with their efforts at verbal communication. For example, they may not use a conventional tone when talking. They may display few or no facial expressions or body gestures. And they may not maintain much eye contact during interactions. Recall, for example, that Jennie "rarely made eye contact with anyone."

Autistic people also display a wide range of *highly rigid and repetitive behaviors, interests, and activities* that extend beyond speech patterns (Augustyn & von Hahn, 2023). Typically they become very upset at minor changes in objects, persons, or routines and resist any efforts to change their own repetitive behaviors. Jennie's special education teacher noticed that she was most aggressive when introduced to something or someone new. And Carter became uncomfortable and abrupt when his parents suggested that he make drawings of objects other than analog clocks.

Similarly, some autistic children react with tantrums if a parent wears an unfamiliar pair of glasses, a chair is moved to a different part of the room, or a word in a song is changed. These reactions are sometimes called a *perseveration of sameness* (Kanner, 1943). Many also become strongly attached to particular objects such as plastic lids, rubber bands, buttons, or water. They may collect these objects, carry them, or play with them constantly. Some are fascinated by movement and may watch spinning objects, such as fans, for hours.

Autistic people may display *motor movements* that are rigid, repetitive, and atypical (Miller et al., 2024). They may jump, flap their arms, twist their hands and fingers, rock, walk on their toes, spin, and make faces. These acts are called *self-stimulatory behaviors*, or "stimming." Some severely challenged autistic individuals also perform *self-injurious behaviors,* such as repeatedly lunging into a wall or banging their head against a wall, pulling their hair, or biting themselves (Augustyn & von Hahn, 2023).

The features of autism spectrum disorder suggest a very challenging and contradictory pattern of reactions to stimuli (Patil & Kaple, 2023). Sometimes the individuals seem overstimulated by sights and sounds and appear to be trying to block them out (called *hyperreactivity*), while at other times they seem understimulated and appear to be performing self-stimulatory actions (called *hyporeactivity*). For example, they may be unresponsive to loud noises yet turn around when they hear a drink being poured.

Autistic and artistic An autistic child enjoys a wall-painting activity at the 2019 World Autism Awareness Day celebration in Malaysia, attended by more than 200 autistic children. Art therapy is offered in many educational and treatment programs for autistic persons to help improve the children's visual and tactile functioning, fine motor skills, communication capacity, and self-image.

Mohd Samsul Mohd Said/Getty Images

What Are the Explanations for Autism Spectrum Disorder?

A variety of explanations have been offered for autism spectrum disorder. Over the years, researchers and theorists have pointed to sociocultural, psychological, and biological factors.

SOCIOCULTURAL EXPLANATIONS Early on, theorists thought that family dysfunction was the primary cause of autism spectrum disorder. When psychiatrist Leo Kanner first identified this disorder in 1943, he argued that particular personality characteristics of the parents created an unfavorable climate for development and contributed to the disorder (Kanner, 1954, 1943). He and other clinicians saw these parents as very intelligent yet cold—"refrigerator parents." These claims had enormous influence on the public and on the self-image of the parents themselves, but research has totally failed to support a picture of rigid, cold, rejecting, or disturbed parents (Augustyn, 2023).

PSYCHOLOGICAL EXPLANATIONS According to some theorists, autistic people have a central cognitive pattern that makes typical communication and interactions challenging and sometimes impossible.

theory of mind An awareness that other people base their behaviors on their own beliefs, intentions, and other mental states, not on information that they have no way of knowing.

joint attention Sharing focus with other people on items or events in one's immediate surroundings, whether through shared eye gazing, pointing, referencing, or other verbal or nonverbal indications that one is paying attention to the same object.

One influential explanation holds that autistic people do not develop a **theory of mind**—an awareness that other people base their behaviors on their own beliefs, intentions, and other mental states, not on information that they have no way of knowing (Nijhof, 2023; Askham, 2022). (You may notice that theory of mind is similar to *mentalization,* which was discussed in the previous chapter on personality disorders.)

By 3 to 5 years of age, typically developing children can usually take the perspective of another person into account and use it to anticipate what that other person will do. In a way, they learn to read other peoples' minds. Let us say, for example, that we watch Simón place a marble in a container and then we observe Ayita move the marble to a nearby room while Simón is taking a nap. We know that later Simón will search first in the container because he is not aware that Ayita moved the marble. We know this because we take Simón's perspective into account. A typically developing child would also anticipate Simón's search correctly after observing the scene. An autistic child might not. The autistic child might expect Simón to look in the nearby room because that is where the marble actually is. Simón's own mental processes would be unimportant to the child.

Studies show that many autistic people do indeed experience this kind of cognitive difficulty (sometimes called "mind-blindness"), although they are not the only group of individuals with this cognitive challenge. As a result, they have difficulty taking part in make-believe play, using language in ways that include the perspectives of others, developing relationships, or participating in various kinds of human interaction.

Autistic people also experience difficulties in **joint attention,** a cognitive challenge that is probably related to their theory of mind difficulty. They struggle to share focus with other people on items and events in their immediate surroundings through mutual eye gazing, making reference to observed objects, pointing, or other such acts (de Belen et al., 2023). Indeed, when autistic individuals with severe cognitive restrictions are around other people, they simply are not having a "shared" experience. Joint attention challenges can greatly impair not only social interactions but also language development since a core function of language is to direct someone else's attention.

Why do autistic people have these cognitive differences? Most theorists point to biological factors that affect cognitive development and functioning.

Images by Tang Ming Tung/Getty Images

Joint attention By pointing out flowers to her mother, this child is displaying effective *joint attention*. Joint attention refers to the cognitive ability to share focus with other people on items in one's immediate surroundings through pointing, mutual eye gazing, and/or making reference to observed objects. Autistic people often display limited joint attention skills.

BIOLOGICAL EXPLANATIONS For years, researchers have tried to determine what biological factors might underlie the features of autism spectrum disorder. They have not yet developed a complete biological explanation, but they have uncovered promising leads. First, examinations of the relatives of autistic people keep suggesting a *genetic factor*. The prevalence of autism among their siblings, for example, is 10 to 20 percent, a rate much higher than the general population's (Augustyn, 2023). Moreover, the prevalence of autism among the identical twins of autistic people is greater than 60 percent (APA, 2022). Genetic studies are increasingly identifying specific genes that, in combination, increase the likelihood of autistic spectrum disorder (Doherty et al., 2024; APA, 2022).

Some studies have also linked autism spectrum disorder to *prenatal difficulties* or *birth complications* (Augustyn, 2023). The chances of persons developing autism are higher if they were exposed prenatally to a significant infection such as rubella, to toxic chemicals such as aluminum and mercury, or to alcohol or drugs. Additionally, complications during labor or delivery—such as a knotted umbilical cord or inadequate oxygen supply—significantly increase the chances of developing autism.

In addition, researchers have identified specific *biological factors* that may contribute to autism spectrum disorder. Initially, investigators believed that the atypical activity or atypical anatomy of a single brain structure, the *cerebellum*, might be responsible for autism, partly because this structure helps control a person's ability to rapidly shift attention (Cundari et al., 2023). Cerebellum irregularities are still considered a possible factor, but research over the past two decades has also tied autism spectrum disorder to other brain structures, including the *corpus callosum, prefrontal cortex, amygdala, orbitofrontal cortex, cingulate cortex, striatum,* and *thalamus* (Evans et al., 2024; Lee, 2024; Ayub et al., 2021).

Dysfunction by any of these brain structures may contribute to the disorder. However, in line with scientists' heightened appreciation of the importance of brain circuits, a growing number of theorists believe that atypical communication among these and perhaps other brain structures may be the key. In support of this belief, many studies of autistic people and of animals that display autistic-like behavior indicate atypical interconnectivity—sometimes hyperconnectivity and sometimes hypoconnectivity—between these various structures (Leyhausen et al., 2024; Leisman, Melillo, & Melillo, 2023). It is tempting to conclude from such findings that there is an *autism-related brain circuit* whose dysfunction is the key to the development of autism, but research has yet to establish the existence or nature of such a circuit.

Finally, because it has received so much attention over the past 25 years, the *MMR vaccine* theory, a biological explanation for autism spectrum disorder that has *not* been borne out, should be mentioned. In 1998, a team of investigators published a study suggesting that a *postnatal event*—the vaccine for measles, mumps, and rubella (*MMR vaccine*)—might produce autistic symptoms in some children (Wakefield et al., 1998). Specifically, the researchers thought that for certain children, this vaccine, which is usually given to children between the ages of 12 and 15 months, produces an increase in the measles virus throughout the body, which in turn causes the onset of a powerful stomach disease and, ultimately, autism spectrum disorder.

However, virtually all research conducted since 1998 has argued against this theory (Augustyn, 2023). For example, epidemiological studies repeatedly have found that children throughout the world who receive the MMR vaccine have the same prevalence of autism as those who do not receive the vaccine. Moreover, careful reexaminations of the original study have indicated that it was methodologically flawed and that, in fact, it falsified certain facts about the participants' medical histories; its main investigator had a financial conflict of interest in the study; and it actually failed to demonstrate any relationship between the MMR vaccine and the development of autism spectrum

Why do many people still believe that the MMR vaccine causes autism spectrum disorder despite so much evidence to the contrary?

of NOTE ...

Autism's Associated Challenges

- Around 31 percent of autistic children experience intellectual disability.
- Between 30 and 61 percent of autistic children display ADHD.
- More than 50 percent of autistic children have chronic sleep problems.
- Between 11 and 40 percent of autistic children experience an anxiety disorder.
- Around 7 percent of autistic children and 26 percent of autistic adults experience depression.
- As many as 33 percent of autistic persons have a seizure disorder.
- Between 4 and 35 percent of autistic adults experience schizophrenia.

disorder (*Lancet,* 2010). Indeed, *Lancet,* the journal that had published the study, eventually retracted it and its findings. Unfortunately, despite this clear refutation and decades of evidence challenging the 1998 study, many concerned parents now choose to withhold the MMR vaccine from their young children, leaving them highly vulnerable to diseases that can be very dangerous.

THE NEURODIVERSITY EXPLANATION As you read earlier, proponents of the neurodiversity perspective believe that autistic people are, in fact, *neurodivergent* people whose brains develop and work differently, not less well or less healthfully, than the brains of neurotypical people. That is, the features that characterize autistic individuals are "disabling" only to the extent that their surrounding environments fail to accommodate the individuals' specific needs (CC, 2023; Hamilton & Petty, 2023).

In turn, proponents of the neurodiversity perspective believe that the psychological and biological explanations for autism described above—cognitive and perceptual deficits, genetic anomalies, and brain circuit dysfunctions—are misguided and misleading. They acknowledge that the brains of autistic people do indeed pose significant challenges as the individuals navigate through their world, but the primary cause of such challenges is the ongoing mismatch between their particular brain operations and a social and physical environment that is tailored to the needs of neurotypical people (CC, 2023; Hamilton & Petty, 2023). In fact, the brains of autistic people often have many strengths (recall, for example, Carter's superior math skills and artistic ability), but these tend to be undervalued when clinicians and other people view their overall functioning as pathological and deficient (Axbey et al., 2023).

The neurodiversity view of autism is one of the most strongly debated issues in the clinical field today. Why might this be so?

Not surprisingly, supporters of the neurodiversity perspective also believe that some of the interventions and treatments for autistic persons that you will be reading about next are misguided and, at times, harmful. The supporters are in favor of those interventions that change the environment to accommodate the brain functioning of autistic people (for example, noise-canceling headphones that address the individual's sensitivity to loud sounds, job environments that build on the skills of autistic employees, and social environments that are less demanding of conventional interactions) (Blankenship, 2023; Jellett & Flower, 2023). However, they strongly disapprove of interventions that teach autistic persons to mimic neurotypical behavior or that try to convert the autistic individual into a neurotypical person (CC, 2023).

Interventions and Treatments for Autism

Certain interventions and treatments seek to help autistic people adapt better to their environment, although no treatment yet known totally reverses the autistic pattern. The most widely applied approaches are *cognitive-behavioral therapy, communication training, parenting interventions,* and *community integration.* In addition, psychotropic drugs and certain vitamins have sometimes helped when combined with other approaches (Weissman, 2023, 2021).

COGNITIVE-BEHAVIORAL THERAPY For more than 50 years, cognitive-behavioral approaches have been used in cases of autism, particularly behavior-focused interventions that teach the individuals new, adaptive behaviors—including speech, social skills, classroom skills, and self-help skills—while seeking to reduce dysfunctional behaviors (You et al., 2024). Using the principles of *modeling,* therapists often demonstrate desired behaviors and guide the autistic persons to imitate them. Using the principles of *operant conditioning,* the clinicians reinforce adaptive behaviors, first by "shaping" them—breaking them down so they can be learned step-by-step—and then rewarding each step clearly and consistently. With careful planning and execution, these procedures often produce new, more adaptive behaviors.

of NOTE ...

Their Words

"The one common denominator for all of the young [autistic] children is that early intervention does work, and it seems to improve the prognosis."

Temple Grandin, professor and autistic individual

Multiple long-term studies have compared the progress of autistic children who receive behavioral interventions to those who do not receive such interventions

Li Ran/Xinhua via Getty Images

Facilitating community integration To achieve a fuller life, autistic people need to be involved in the community. With this in mind, Wu Guixiang (left) has set up an autism training center in Tianjin, northern China, where she works with her adult autistic son Zhang Hao (right) and other autistic persons, providing them with courses on life and the building of social and vocational skills. With such training, the individuals have developed skills at cooking, traveling, shopping, and other community activities.

(You et al., 2024; Rodgers et al., 2021). Findings show that the autistic children who receive behavior-focused interventions by the age of 3 typically perform better in school and score higher on intelligence tests by the age of 7. Moreover, these gains often continue into the teenage years and beyond. Given such favorable findings, most clinicians now consider early intensive behavior-focused programs to be a helpful intervention for many of the challenges faced by autistic children (Weissman, 2023).

Interventions for autistic individuals seem to provide the most benefit when they are started early in life (Yu, Ozonoff, & Miller, 2024). Very young autistic children often begin with services at home, but ideally, by the end of toddlerhood, they attend special programs outside the home. Typically, services are provided by education, health, or social service agencies until the children reach the preschool years, and then the department of education for each state determines which specific services the children will receive. In the United States, each autistic child in public education receives an *Individualized Education Program* (*IEP*), a legal document that details the support services, therapies, and special accommodations to be afforded the child so that appropriate educational goals can be met.

Given the recent increases in the prevalence of autism, many school districts are now trying to provide education and training for autistic children in special classes that operate at the district's own facilities (Rudy, 2023). However, most school districts remain ill-equipped to meet the needs of autistic students, particularly those students who are severely challenged by their autistic symptoms. The most fortunate of these students are sent by their school districts to attend *special schools,* where education and therapy are combined. Some of the children who attend these special schools eventually spend at least part of their school day returning to standard classrooms in their own school district (Weissman, 2023).

COMMUNICATION TRAINING As you learned earlier, even when given intensive treatment, at least one-third of autistic people remain speechless. To help address this, they are often taught other forms of communication, including *sign language* and *simultaneous communication,* a method combining sign language and speech. They may also learn to use **augmentative communication systems,** such as "communication boards" or computers that use pictures, symbols, or written words to represent

augmentative communication system A method for enhancing the communication skills of autistic people, people with intellectual disability, or those with cerebral palsy by teaching them to point to pictures, symbols, letters, or words on a communication board or computer.

AP Photo/Albuquerque Journal, Pat Vasquez-Cunningham

Learning to communicate Cognitive-behavioral clinicians and educators have had success teaching many autistic children to communicate. Here a speech language specialist combines cognitive-behavioral techniques with the use of a communication board to teach a 3-year-old child how to express herself better and understand others.

objects or needs (Schlosser & Koul, 2023). A child may point, for instance, to a picture of a fork to give the message "I am hungry" or to a picture of a radio for "I want music." Recall, for example, the use of a "picture book" by Jennie, the child whose case introduced this section.

Some programs now use *child-initiated interactions* to help improve the communication skills of autistic children. In such programs, teachers try to identify *intrinsic* reinforcers rather than trivial ones like food or candy. First, the children are encouraged to choose items that they are interested in, and then they learn to initiate questions ("What's that?" "Where is it?" "Whose is it?") in order to obtain the items. Studies find that child-directed interventions of this kind often increase self-initiated communications, language development, and social participation (Higgins-Walsh, 2023; Schlosser & Koul, 2023).

Some autism programs further try to improve language and communication skills by working on the individual's *joint attention* ability. The clinician teaches the individual to gaze into the eyes of others, make reference to observed objects, point at objects, and perform other "sharing" behaviors when involved in joint activities with other people. Studies have found that bolstering joint attention skills, particularly during the preschool years, can have a positive impact on communication, language, and social development (Özkan et al., 2023).

PARENTING INTERVENTIONS Today's intervention programs for autism spectrum disorder involve parents in a variety of ways. Cognitive-behavioral programs, for example, help parents apply conditioning and skill-building techniques at home (Ros-DeMarize, Klein, & Carpenter, 2023; Dai et al., 2021). Printed, online, and/or in-person instructions for parents and home visits by teachers and other professionals are typically included in such programs. Research consistently has demonstrated that the behavioral gains produced by parents who receive such instructions are often equal to or greater than those generated by teachers.

In addition to parenting interventions of this kind, individual therapy and support groups are becoming more available to help the parents of autistic children deal with their own emotions and needs (Lee, Cascella, & Marwaha, 2023). A number of parent associations and lobbies also offer emotional support and practical help to parents.

COMMUNITY INTEGRATION Many of today's programs teach self-help, self-management, and living, social, recreational, and work skills to autistic persons as early as possible to help the individuals function better in their communities (Brighenti et al., 2023; Rudy, 2023). In addition, greater numbers of carefully run *group homes* and *sheltered workshops* are now available for autistic teenagers and adults who cannot live independently. These and related programs help the individuals become a part of their community; they also reduce the concerns of aging parents whose children will always need supervision.

Intellectual Disability (Intellectual Developmental Disorder)

Our intellectual functioning and assorted practical skills together affect our ability to meet the demands of everyday living. People receive a diagnosis of **intellectual disability (ID)** when they display general *intellectual functioning* that is well below

intellectual disability (ID) A neurodevelopmental disorder marked by intellectual functioning and adaptive behavior that are significantly below average. Also called *intellectual developmental disorder.*

intelligence quotient (IQ) A score derived from intelligence tests that theoretically represents a person's overall intellectual capacity.

average, in combination with poor *adaptive behavior* (APA, 2022). That is, in addition to having a low IQ (a score of 70 or below), a person with intellectual disability has great difficulty in areas such as communication, home living, self-direction, work, or safety. The individual's intellectual and adaptive limitations also must appear before the age of 18 (see **Table 14-6**).

In recent years, DSM-5-TR introduced the term "intellectual developmental disorder" as an alternative to "intellectual disability" while, at the same time, pointing out that the two terms are equivalent and that intellectual disability remains the term most commonly used by educational and other professions, advocacy groups, and the public (APA, 2022). Consistent with the broad use of "intellectual disability," we are using that term throughout this chapter.

People with intellectual disability are varied, including children in institutional wards who continuously rock back and forth, young people who work in special job programs, and adults who raise and support their families by working at jobs that meet their abilities. At least 1 of every 100 people meets the criteria for this diagnosis (Baldor, 2023; APA, 2022). Around three-fifths of them are male, and the vast majority experience relatively *mild* functional impairments and require only minimal levels of support and assistance.

Ben McCanna/Portland Press Herald via Getty Images

Common needs People with intellectual disability have typical interpersonal and sexual needs—needs for which they may receive training and supervision in various programs. Here a couple with Down syndrome twirl each other on the dance floor during the Night to Shine—a dance party in Portland, Maine, for people with special needs.

Assessing Intelligence

As you learned in the chapter on clinical assessment and diagnosis, educators and clinicians administer *intelligence tests* to measure intellectual functioning. These tests consist of a variety of questions and tasks that rely on different aspects of intelligence, such as knowledge, reasoning, and judgment. Having difficulty in just one or two of these subtests or areas of functioning does not necessarily reflect low intelligence (see **PsychWatch**). It is an individual's overall test score, or **intelligence quotient (IQ),** that is thought to indicate general intellectual ability.

Many theorists have questioned whether IQ tests are indeed valid. Do they actually measure what they are supposed to measure? The correlation between IQ and school performance is around 0.50, indicating that IQ scores are somewhat predictive—but far from perfectly predictive—of school achievements (Pishghadam et al., 2022). Correlations between IQ and performances in most other areas of life are even less strong. Moreover, the accuracy of IQ tests at measuring extremely low intelligence has not been evaluated adequately, so it is difficult to properly assess people with severe intellectual disability.

Intelligence tests also appear to be socioculturally biased, as you read in the chapter on clinical assessment and diagnosis. Children reared in households at the middle and upper socioeconomic levels tend to have an advantage on the tests because they are regularly exposed to the kinds of language and thinking that the tests evaluate. The tests rarely measure the common sense, practical knowledge, and resourcefulness needed for success and survival by people who live in economically distressed, crime-ridden areas—a kind of know-how that certainly requires intellectual skills. People of color and people for whom English is a second language also often appear to be at a disadvantage in taking these tests.

TABLE 14-6

Dx Checklist

Intellectual Disability (Intellectual Developmental Disorder)
1. Individual displays deficient intellectual functioning in areas such as reasoning, problem-solving, planning, abstract thinking, judgment, academic learning, and learning from experience. The deficits are reflected by clinical assessment and intelligence tests.
2. Individual displays deficient adaptive functioning in at least one area of daily life, such as communication, social involvement, or personal independence, across home, school, work, or community settings. The limitations extend beyond those displayed by most other persons of the same age and necessitate ongoing support at school or work, or with independent living.
3. The deficits begin before the age of 18.

Information from: APA, 2022.

PSYCHWATCH

Reading and 'Riting and 'Rithmetic

Around 10 to 15 percent of all children develop particularly slowly and function poorly in a single area such as learning, communication, or motor coordination (Hamilton, 2023, 2022). The children do not display intellectual disability, and in fact they are often very bright, yet their problems may interfere with school performance, daily living, or social interactions (Fletcher & Miciak, 2024). According to DSM-5-TR, many of these children are experiencing a specific learning disorder, communication disorder, or developmental coordination disorder—each a kind of neurodevelopmental disorder (APA, 2022).

Children with a *specific learning disorder* have significant difficulties acquiring reading, writing, arithmetic, or mathematical reasoning skills (von Hahn, 2023). Some display *dyslexia*, a pattern marked by very slow or inaccurate reading, difficulty understanding the meaning of what one is reading, and/or spelling difficulties (Dominguez & Carugno, 2023).

The *communication disorders* feature language, speech sound, or speech fluency difficulties. These disorders include *stuttering*, or *childhood-onset fluency disorder*, in which individuals may frequently repeat, prolong, or interject sounds when they speak; pause before finishing a word; or experience excessive tension in the muscles they use for speech.

Finally, children with *developmental coordination disorder* perform coordinated motor activities very poorly (APA, 2022; Hamilton, 2022). Younger children with this disorder are clumsy and slow to master skills such as tying shoelaces, buttoning shirts, and zipping pants. Older children with the disorder may have great difficulty assembling puzzles, building models, playing ball, and printing or writing.

Studies have linked these various disorders to genetic factors, brain irregularities, birth injuries, lead poisoning, inappropriate diet, sensory or perceptual dysfunction, and poor teaching (Dominguez & Carugno, 2023; Hamilton, 2023, 2022). Some of the disorders respond to special treatments (Thapliyal & Ahuja, 2023). Reading therapy, for example, is very helpful in mild cases of dyslexia. Furthermore, a number of the disorders disappear before adulthood, even without any treatment.

If IQ tests do not always measure intelligence accurately and objectively, then the diagnosis of intellectual disability also may be biased. That is, some people may receive the diagnosis partly because of test inadequacies, cultural differences, discomfort with the testing situation, or the bias of a tester.

Assessing Adaptive Functioning

Diagnosticians cannot rely solely on a cutoff IQ score of 70 to determine whether a person experiences intellectual disability. Some people who receive a low IQ score are quite capable of managing their lives and functioning independently, while others are not. The cases of Alec and Jeffrey show the range of adaptive abilities and needs for support.

***Alec** comes from a family of limited economic means. He functions fairly effectively at home and in his community. He dresses and feeds himself, and he also takes great care of his pet turtle. Each day after school, he takes care of himself for two hours until his mother returns home from work. He enjoys riding his bike and following major league baseball, and he plays well with his friends. At school, however, Alec refuses to participate or do his homework. He seems ineffective, at times lost, in the classroom. Referred to a school psychologist by his teacher, he received an IQ score of 60.*

***Jeffrey** comes from an affluent home. He was always slow to develop, and he sat up, stood, and talked late. During his infancy and toddler years, he was put in a special stimulation program and given special help and attention at home. Jeffrey still has trouble dressing himself today, and he cannot be left alone in the backyard lest he hurt himself or wander off into the street. Schoolwork is very difficult for him. The teacher must work slowly and provide individual instruction for him. Tested at age 6, Jeffrey received an IQ score of 60.*

Alec seems well adapted to his environment outside school. Jeffrey's difficulties, however, are pervasive. In addition to his low IQ score, Jeffrey has difficulty meeting challenges at home and elsewhere. Thus, a diagnosis of intellectual disability may be more appropriate for Jeffrey than for Alec.

Several scales have been developed to assess adaptive behavior (McKenzie et al., 2024; Bertelli et al., 2021). Here again, however, some people function better in their lives than the scales predict, while others fall short. Thus, to properly diagnose intellectual disability, clinicians should probably observe the adaptive functioning of individuals in their everyday environments, taking both the person's background and the community's standards into account.

Jim West/Alamy Stock Photo

Getting a head start Studies suggest that IQ scores and school performances of children from economically deprived neighborhoods can be improved by enriching their daily environments at a young age. This is, in part, the basis for Head Start programs, which serve more than 1 million children each year across the United States, including this group of preschoolers.

What Are the Features of Intellectual Disability?

The most consistent feature of intellectual disability is that the person learns very slowly. Other areas of difficulty are attention, short-term memory, planning, and language (Bertelli et al., 2021; Zagaria et al., 2021). Those with intellectual disability who are living in institutions are particularly likely to have these limitations.

Traditionally, four levels of intellectual disability have been distinguished: *mild, moderate, severe,* and *profound*. In past times, these four levels were defined strictly by the individual's IQ score—mild ID reflected an IQ score of 50 to 70, moderate ID a score of 35 to 49, severe ID a score of 20 to 34, and profound ID a score below 20. Today, however, rather than determining the ID levels by IQ scores, the clinical field finds it more useful and informative to focus on the extent of the person's adaptive skills and functional impairment and the degree of support and assistance the person needs (APA, 2022).

MILD ID Some 80 to 85 percent of all people with intellectual disability fall into the category of *mild ID*. Individuals classified with mild ID typically have the adaptive skills needed to benefit from schooling, require only intermittent supports as children, and can support themselves as adults with minimal, if any, assistance. Mild ID is not usually recognized until children enter school and are assessed there (McKenzie et al., 2024). These children demonstrate rather typical language, social, and play skills, but they need assistance in challenging and difficult circumstances—a limitation that becomes increasingly apparent as academic and social demands increase (Pivalizza & Lalani, 2023). As adults, their jobs tend to be nontechnical support positions, entry-level placements, and/or labor-intensive work.

Research has often linked mild ID to sociocultural and psychological causes—in particular, to restricted and unstimulating environments during a child's early years, problematic parent–child interactions, and insufficient learning experiences (Pivalizza & Lalani, 2023). These relationships have been observed in studies comparing deprived and enriched environments. In fact, some community programs have sent workers into the homes of young children who score low on IQ tests to help enrich the home environment, and such interventions have often improved the children's functioning (Tooley, Bassett, & Mackey, 2021; Ramey & Ramey, 2007, 2004).

Some biological factors may also be at work in mild ID. Studies suggest, for example, that fetal exposure to alcohol, drugs, or malnutrition may lower a child's intellectual potential (Baldor, 2023).

MODERATE, SEVERE, AND PROFOUND ID Approximately 10 percent of those with intellectual disability are classified with *moderate ID*. These individuals can function relatively well in familiar places with moderate levels of assistance. They typically receive their diagnosis earlier in life than do individuals with mild ID, as they demonstrate clear deficits in language development and play during their preschool years. By middle school, they further show significant delays in their acquisition of reading and number skills and adaptive skills. By adulthood, however, many people with moderate ID manage to develop a fair degree of communication skill, benefit from vocational training, and can work in nontechnical or labor-intensive jobs, usually under supervision.

Approximately 3 to 4 percent of people with intellectual disability receive a classification of *severe ID*. They typically demonstrate basic motor and communication deficits during infancy. Many also show signs of neurological dysfunction and have an increased risk for brain seizure disorder. In school, they may be able to use two or three words when speaking. They usually require careful supervision, profit somewhat from vocational training, and can perform only basic work tasks in structured and sheltered settings. Most can function well in the community if they live in group homes, in nursing homes, or with their families (AAIDD, 2024).

Around 1 to 2 percent of all people with intellectual disability are classified with *profound ID*. This level is very noticeable at birth or early infancy. With training, people with profound ID may learn or improve basic skills such as walking, some talking, and feeding themselves. They need a very structured environment, with continuous close supervision and considerable help, in order to develop to the fullest (AAIDD, 2024). Profound and severe ID often appear as part of larger syndromes that include severe physical disabilities.

of NOTE ...

Their Words

"The IQ test was invented to predict academic performance, nothing else. If we wanted something that would predict life success, we'd have to invent another test completely."

Robert Zajonc, psychologist, 1984

What Are the Biological Causes of Intellectual Disability?

As you read earlier, the primary predictors of mild ID are environmental. In contrast, the main causes of moderate, severe, and profound ID are biological, although people who function at these levels also are strongly affected by their family and social environment (Baldor, 2023; Lee et al., 2023). The biological causes include chromosomal irregularities, metabolic disorders, prenatal problems, birth complications, and childhood diseases and injuries.

CHROMOSOMAL CAUSES The most common of the chromosomal disorders that lead to intellectual disability is **Down syndrome,** named after Langdon Down, the British physician who first identified it. Down syndrome occurs in fewer than 1 of every 700 live births, but the possibility of a Down syndrome birth increases significantly as the biological parents enter middle age (Powell-Hamilton, 2023). For example, if a woman of age 30 conceives a child, the baby has a 1 in 900 chance being born with Down syndrome, whereas the odds increase to 1 in 350 at age 35 and to 1 in 85 at age 40.

People with Down syndrome may have a relatively small head, flat face, almond-shaped eyes, high cheekbones, and, in some cases, protruding tongue (Gelbar, 2023; Ostermaier, 2022). This last feature may affect their ability to pronounce words clearly. They are often particularly affectionate with family members but in general display the same range of personality characteristics as the rest of the population.

Several types of chromosomal irregularities may cause Down syndrome. The most common type (94 percent of cases) is *trisomy 21,* in which the person has three free-floating twenty-first chromosomes instead of two. Most people with Down syndrome range in IQ from 35 to 55. The individuals appear to age early, and many even show signs of neurocognitive decline as they approach age 40 (Jacobs et al., 2023). It appears that Down syndrome and early neurocognitive decline often occur together because the genes that produce them are located close to each other on chromosome 21.

Fragile X syndrome is the second most common chromosomal cause of intellectual disability (Schwartz et al., 2023). One of every 6,000 persons is born with this pattern (Powell-Hamilton, 2023). Children born with a fragile X chromosome (that is, an X chromosome with a genetic irregularity that leaves it prone to breakage and loss) generally display mild to moderate degrees of intellectual dysfunction, language impairments, and, in some cases, behavioral problems (Baldor, 2023). Typically, they are shy and anxious.

Reaching higher Today, people with Down syndrome are viewed as individuals who can learn and accomplish many things in their lives. Eddie Gordon, a teenager with Down syndrome, is lifted into the air in celebration by his Timberline High School baseball teammates. He has just rounded the bases during his turn as an honorary leadoff batter.

AP Photo/The Idaho Statesman, Kyle Green

METABOLIC CAUSES In metabolic disorders, the body's breakdown or production of chemicals is disturbed. The metabolic disorders that affect intelligence and development are typically caused by the pairing of two defective *recessive* genes, one from each biological parent. Although one such gene would have no influence if it were paired with a nondefective gene, its pairing with another defective gene leads to major difficulties for the child.

The most common metabolic disorder to cause intellectual disability is *phenylketonuria (PKU)*, which strikes 1 of every 14,000 children. The functioning of babies with PKU seems ordinary at birth, but they cannot break down the amino acid *phenylalanine*. The chemical builds up and is converted into substances that poison the system, causing severe intellectual dysfunction and several other symptoms. Today, infants can be screened for PKU, and if started on a special diet before 3 months of age, they may develop typical intellectual abilities (Baldor, 2023; Lee et al., 2023).

PRENATAL AND BIRTH-RELATED CAUSES As a fetus develops, major physical problems in the pregnancy can threaten the child's later prospects for ordinary development (AAIDD, 2024; Lee et al., 2023). When a pregnant woman, for example, has too little iodine in her diet, the child may be born with *severe congenital hypothyroidism*, marked by an irregular thyroid gland, slow development, intellectual disability, delayed bone maturation, and smaller stature into adulthood. This condition is rare today because the salt in most diets now contains extra iodine. Also, any infant born with this problem may quickly be given thyroid extract to bring about typical development.

Other prenatal problems may also cause intellectual disability. As you learned in the chapter on substance use and addiction disorders, too much alcohol use during pregnancy can result in children born with **fetal alcohol syndrome,** a group of very serious problems that includes mild to severe ID (CDC, 2023; Weitzman & Rojmahamongkol, 2022). It is estimated that each year, more than 50 of every 1,000 pregnancies marked by heavy alcohol use lead to fetal alcohol syndrome—a total of 120,000 infants worldwide. In fact, a generally safe level of alcohol consumption during pregnancy has not been established by research. In addition, prenatal exposure to certain infections—*rubella* (German measles) and *syphilis*, for example—may cause childhood problems that include intellectual disability (Lee et al., 2023).

Birth complications also can lead to problems in intellectual functioning. A prolonged period without oxygen (*anoxia*) during or after delivery can cause brain damage and intellectual disability in a baby. In addition, although premature birth does not necessarily lead to long-term problems for children, researchers have found that some babies with a premature birth weight of less than three pounds display low intelligence (Molad et al., 2023; Pierrat et al., 2021).

CHILDHOOD PROBLEMS After birth, particularly up to age 6, certain injuries and accidents can affect intellectual functioning and in some cases lead to intellectual disability (Baldor, 2023). Poisoning by certain toxins, serious head injuries caused by accident or abuse, excessive exposure to X-rays, and excessive use of certain drugs pose special dangers. For example, a serious case of *lead poisoning*, from eating lead-based paints or inhaling high levels of automobile fumes, can cause intellectual disability in children. Mercury, radiation, nitrite, and pesticide poisoning may do the same. In addition, certain infections, such as *meningitis* and *encephalitis*, can lead to intellectual disability if they are not diagnosed and treated in time (Lee et al., 2023).

Interventions and Treatments for People with Intellectual Disability The quality of life attained by people with intellectual disability depends largely on sociocultural factors: where they live and with whom, how they are educated, and the growth opportunities available at home and in their community (Esteban et al., 2023). Thus, intervention programs for people with intellectual disability try to provide comfortable and stimulating residences, a proper education, and social and economic opportunities.

Down syndrome A form of intellectual disability caused by irregularities in the twenty-first chromosome.

fetal alcohol syndrome A group of problems in a child, including lower intellectual functioning, low birth weight, and irregularities in the hands and face, that result from a fetus's exposure to excessive alcohol during the pregnancy.

of NOTE ...

Their Words

"I have one chromosome more than you . . . So what?"

Karen Gaffney, famous distance swimmer, intellectual disability advocate, and individual with Down syndrome

The power of mainstreaming The goal of mainstreaming, or inclusion, programs—in which children with intellectual disability are placed in general education classes—is apparent in this photo. Nandor Szecsi (front), who has Down syndrome and is mainstreamed, is hugged lovingly by his classmate in Budapest, Hungary.

WHAT IS THE PROPER RESIDENCE? Until recent decades, parents of children with intellectual disability would typically send them to live in public institutions—**state schools**—as early as possible (USDOE, 2023). These overcrowded institutions provided basic care, but residents were neglected, often abused, and isolated from society.

During the 1960s and 1970s, the public became more aware of these sorry conditions and, as part of the broader *deinstitutionalization* movement (see the chapter on schizophrenia), demanded that many people with intellectual disability be released from the state schools. In many cases, the releases were done without adequate preparation or supervision. Like people with schizophrenia who were suddenly deinstitutionalized, those with intellectual disability were virtually dumped into the community. Often they were unable to adjust and had to be institutionalized once again.

Since that time, reforms have led to the creation of *small institutions* and other *community residences* that teach self-sufficiency, devote more staff time to patient care, and offer educational and medical services. The community residences range from fully supervised group homes to semi-independent residences to local branches of larger institutions. Many of these settings follow the principles of **normalization** first started in Denmark and Sweden—they attempt to provide living conditions similar to those enjoyed by the rest of society, flexible routines, and common developmental experiences, including opportunities for self-determination, sexual fulfillment, and economic freedom (van der Weele et al., 2021).

Today, the vast majority of children with intellectual disability live at home rather than in an institution. During adulthood and as their parents age, however, some people with intellectual disability require levels of assistance and opportunities that their families are unable to provide. A community residence becomes an appropriate alternative for them. Most people with intellectual disability, including almost all with mild ID, now spend their adult lives either in the family home or in a community residence (NCD, 2023; Zabidi, Hastings, & Totsika, 2023).

WHICH EDUCATIONAL PROGRAMS WORK BEST? Because early intervention seems to offer such great promise, educational programs for people with intellectual disability may begin during the earliest years. The appropriate education depends on the person's level of adaptive functioning and needed assistance. Educators hotly debate whether special education or mainstreaming is most effective once the children enter school (Lee et al., 2023; MHN, 2023). In traditional **special education** formats, children with intellectual disability may be grouped together in a separate, specially designed educational program. In contrast, in **mainstreaming,** or **inclusion,** they are placed in general education classes with students from the typically developing school population. Neither approach seems consistently superior. It may be that mainstreaming is better for some areas of learning and for some children and that special education classes are better for others. Today, a hybrid approach is common for some children with mild ID—the children are placed in general education classrooms, but they receive supplemental instruction, accommodations, and resources in order to provide tailored support and assistance. As is the case for autistic students, in the United States, each public school student with intellectual disability receives an *Individualized Education Program* (IEP)—the legally binding document discussed previously that details the support services, therapies, and special accommodations to be afforded the child so that proper educational goals can be achieved.

What might be the benefits of mainstreaming compared with special education classes, and vice versa?

Teachers who work with students with intellectual disability often use operant conditioning principles to improve their students' self-help, communication, social, and academic skills (Pivalizza, 2022; Wakeman et al., 2021). They break learning tasks down into small steps, giving positive reinforcement for each increment of progress. Additionally, many institutions, schools, and private homes have set up *token economy programs*—the operant conditioning programs that have also been used to treat children with ADHD and institutionalized patients who have schizophrenia.

state school A state-supported institution for people with intellectual disability.

normalization The principle that institutions and community residences for people with intellectual disability should provide living conditions and opportunities similar to those enjoyed by the rest of society.

special education An approach to educating children with intellectual disability in which their differences and needs are supported and accommodated in the least restrictive ways possible, sometimes but not always in separate, specially designed programs.

mainstreaming The placement of children with intellectual disability in general school classes. Also known as *inclusion*.

WHEN IS THERAPY NEEDED? Like anyone else, people with intellectual disability sometimes have significant emotional and behavioral challenges. Around 30 percent or more have a psychological disorder in addition to the intellectual disability (Landgren et al., 2024; Eaton et al., 2021). Furthermore, some experience low self-esteem, interpersonal problems, and difficulties adjusting to community life (Komenda et al., 2023). These problems are helped to some degree by either individual or group therapy (Lee et al., 2023). Large numbers of people with intellectual disability also take psychotropic medications (Adams et al., 2023). Many clinicians argue, however, that too often the medications are used simply for the purpose of making the individuals easier to manage.

PROMOTING PERSONAL, SOCIAL, AND OCCUPATIONAL GROWTH People need to feel effective and competent in order to move forward in life. Those with intellectual disability are most likely to have such feelings if their communities allow them to grow and to make many of their own choices (Garcia-Lee, Strnadova, & Dowse, 2024). Denmark and Sweden, where the normalization movement began, have again been leaders in this area, developing youth clubs that encourage those with intellectual disability to take risks and function independently. The Special Olympics program has also encouraged those with intellectual disability to be active in setting goals, to participate in their environment, and to interact socially with others (Lee et al., 2023; SO, 2023). More generally, a number of "befriending" programs enlist volunteers from the community to provide companionship and support to people with intellectual disability, efforts that often increase community participation and help lift moods (Brand, Scior, & Loewenberger, 2024).

Socializing, sex, and marriage can be difficult issues for people with intellectual disability and their families, but with proper training and practice, they usually can learn to use contraceptives and carry out responsible family planning (Perez-Curiel et al., 2023). National advocacy organizations and a number of clinicians currently offer guidance in these matters, and some have developed *dating skills programs* (AAIDD, 2024).

Some states restrict marriage for people with intellectual disability. These laws are rarely enforced, though, and in fact many people with mild ID marry. Contrary to popular myths, the marriages can be very successful. And although some people with intellectual disability may be incapable of raising children, many are quite able to do so, either on their own or with special help and community services (Perez-Curiel et al., 2023).

Finally, adults with intellectual disability—whatever the level of their adaptive functioning—need the personal and financial rewards that come with holding a job (AAIDD, 2024; Randall, Bernard, & Durah, 2023). Many work in *sheltered workshops*, protected and supervised workplaces that train them at a pace and level tailored to their abilities. After training in the workshops, a number of people with mild or moderate ID move on to hold regular jobs. Although training programs for people with intellectual disability have improved greatly in quality over the past 40 years, there are too few of them. Thus, additional programs are needed so that more people with intellectual disability may achieve their full potential as workers and as human beings.

Working for money, independence, and self-respect Marvin Haquin (left), who works as a kitchen employee at a restaurant in Paris, France, is supervised by kitchen manager Regine Kha (right) to prepare meals for the customers. The restaurant promotes the employment of individuals with intellectual disability and/or autism spectrum disorder, like Marvin—providing them with job opportunities and dignity through training and placement.

Anne-Christine Poujoulat/AFP via Getty Images

SUMMING UP

Neurodevelopmental Disorders

Neurodevelopmental disorders are a group of disabilities in the functioning of the brain that emerge at birth or during very early childhood and affect the person's behavior, memory, concentration, and/or ability to learn. They often have a significant impact throughout the person's life.

Children with attention-deficit/hyperactivity disorder (ADHD) attend poorly to tasks, behave overactively and impulsively, or both. Many of the attention difficulties seen in ADHD may be associated with a dysfunctional attention brain circuit whose structures display problematic interconnectivity. Drug therapy—methylphenidate or amphetamines—and cognitive-behavioral programs can be effective treatments.

Autistic people display substantial unresponsiveness to other people, significant communication deficits, and highly rigid and repetitive behaviors, interests, and activities. The leading explanations of autism spectrum disorder point to cognitive deficits, such as failure to develop a theory of mind and joint attention skills, and biological factors, such as a dysfunctional brain circuit. Although no intervention or treatment totally reverses the autistic pattern, significant help is available in the form of cognitive-behavioral treatments, communication training, parenting interventions, and community integration. At the same time, an alternative perspective, neurodiversity, has gained increased attention in the clinical field, challenging the merits of viewing autism as a clinical disorder and taking issue with many of today's explanations and treatments for autism.

People with intellectual disability display intellectual functioning that is significantly below average and experience challenges in adaptive functioning and independence. Mild ID has often been linked to environmental factors such as unstimulating environments during a child's early years, problematic parent–child interactions, and insufficient learning experiences. Moderate, severe, and profound ID are caused primarily by biological factors. The leading biological causes of intellectual disability are chromosomal irregularities, metabolic disorders, prenatal problems, birth complications, and childhood diseases and injuries.

Today's intervention programs for people with intellectual disability typically emphasize the importance of a comfortable and stimulating residence—the family home, a small institution or group home, or a semi-independent residence; proper education; therapy for psychological problems; and programs offering training in socializing, sex, marriage, parenting, and occupational skills. A current debate in the field of education centers on whether people with intellectual disability profit more from special education or from mainstreaming.

Clinicians Discover Childhood and Adolescence

EARLY IN THE twentieth century, mental health professionals virtually ignored children. At best, they viewed them as small adults and treated their psychological disorders as they would adult problems. Today, the problems and needs of young people have caught the attention of researchers and clinicians.

This increased attention has zeroed in on the importance of the family. Because children and adolescents have limited control over their lives, they are particularly

of NOTE ...

Their Words

"The hurt that troubled children create is never greater than the hurt they feel."

L. Tobin, author

affected by the attitudes and reactions of family members. Clinicians must therefore deal with those attitudes and reactions as they try to address the problems of the young. Treatments for conduct disorder, ADHD, intellectual disability, and other problems of childhood and adolescence typically fall short unless clinicians educate and work with the family as well. At the same time, clinicians who work with children and adolescents have learned that concentrating on the family alone can lead to problems. For years, autism spectrum disorder was explained exclusively by family factors, misleading theorists and therapists alike and adding to the pain of parents already dealing with the significant challenge of meeting their autistic children's needs.

Why do you think mental health professionals largely overlooked child mental health problems in past times?

Given society's ever-increasing focus on the challenges, needs, rights, and, at times, mistreatment of young people, the study and treatment of psychological disorders among children and adolescents are likely to continue at a rapid pace. Now that clinicians and public officials have "discovered" this population, they are not likely to underestimate their needs and importance again.

Quick Quiz

1. What are the prevalence rates for the various disorders found among children and adolescents? pp. 475–508
2. What are the different kinds of childhood anxiety disorders? What are today's leading explanations and treatments for these disorders? pp. 476–478
3. What childhood disorders feature depression, and what are today's leading explanations and treatments for these disorders? Why might DSM-5-TR's inclusion of the new category disruptive mood dysregulation disorder affect diagnoses of childhood bipolar disorder? pp. 479–482
4. Describe oppositional defiant disorder and conduct disorder. What factors help cause conduct disorder, and how is this disorder treated? pp. 483–487
5. What are enuresis and encopresis? How are these disorders explained and treated? pp. 488–489
6. What are the symptoms of ADHD? What are today's leading explanations for it? What are the current treatments for ADHD, and how effective are they? pp. 490–495
7. What is autism spectrum disorder, and what are its possible causes? What are the overall goals of treatment for this pattern, and which interventions have been most useful? What is the neurodiversity perspective? pp. 495–507
8. Describe the different levels of intellectual disability. pp. 507–508
9. What are the leading environmental and biological causes of intellectual disability? pp. 507–509
10. What kinds of residences, educational programs, treatments, and community programs are helpful to persons with intellectual disability? pp. 509–511

CHAPTER

15

Disorders of Aging and Cognition

Nelson was a 61-year-old utilities worker in a small town not far from Memphis, Tennessee. He was a strong, healthy individual, very happy with his wife, Josephine. Their son, Nelson Jr., had recently graduated with a master's degree in architecture. Although Nelson's work was demanding, he and Josephine considered themselves blessed.

Then, seemingly out of the blue, Nelson began displaying episodes of explosive anger at Josephine, something that had never happened before. The first time this occurred, Josephine had forgotten to buy Nelson's favorite brand of soda pop in the weekly grocery shopping. As soon as Nelson realized he would have to drink water or juice instead of pop with dinner, he yelled, "I swear, Jo, you are as dumb as any person I've ever met! How could you do this to me? I have to go out there all day into the homes of ungrateful people to work on their pipes, and I come home to this. I'm sick of it!" Nelson soon snapped out of it, however, and apologized, and they both tacitly agreed to write it off as stress from his job.

However, similar episodes followed, and they became more frequent. Josephine began to brace herself whenever it was time for Nelson to arrive home from work, not knowing what "unforgivable crime" she would be accused of.

These episodes began to affect Nelson at work as well. He was reprimanded for unleashing a torrent of abuse at an apartment resident who refused to allow him access to read the meter, although such refusals were common in cases where the building superintendent was not present. He had screamed and screamed that the resident just didn't want a Hispanic man in the building despite explanations by the flustered resident.

Nelson also started behaving in uncharacteristic ways. He came home late some nights, in a bad mood, saying he had lost a lot of money in a poker game with his coworkers, the same individuals he had previously called "degenerate gamblers"—in fact, the same guys whose poker night invitations he had always rejected. On other nights, Nelson often came home with armfuls of purchases—a radio, lottery tickets, and a stack of LPs—even though he had no record player.

Around six months into these changes in Nelson's behavior, he also began saying odd things, often using the wrong words. In tender moments, he called his wife "my little caterpillar," which she thought was odd but decided to receive as an endearment. However, when he would say things like "I have to go into the garage" when he actually meant it was time for him to go to work, she became alarmed. Nelson also repeatedly bemoaned that he and Josephine had foolishly spent too much money for their son "to go design ships." Not only was it out of character for Nelson to complain about helping their son, but Nelson Jr. designed buildings, not ships.

The following year, Nelson was fired from his job for excessive absenteeism, which shocked Josephine, who believed he had been going off to work every day. Nelson explained to her that sometimes he simply preferred to go sit in the park instead of working, reasoning that it really didn't make any difference what he did. Josephine insisted that Nelson must see a doctor because something was terribly wrong with him. He reluctantly agreed.

After a series of interviews, a thorough medical history, and multiple physical, psychological, and neurological exams and scans, Nelson's medical team determined that he had a major neurocognitive disorder called Pick's disease. Pick's disease is a close relative of Alzheimer's disease, a disease similarly characterized by progressive and irreversible dementia—a pattern of severe difficulties in thinking, behavior, judgment, language, and memory. Josephine was told that Nelson would not only deteriorate further but also die from this disease in a matter of years.

(continued on the next page)

Matt Manley

TOPIC OVERVIEW

Josephine cared for Nelson over the next three years as best she could, hiring a caretaker so she could continue with her job to pay for everything. During this time, the Nelson she knew slipped away, slowly at first but then rapidly. His speech problems intensified until he rarely spoke. Josephine could not get him to eat enough, and he began losing weight and becoming weak. And his memory all but disappeared. Josephine was devastated the first time he asked her who she was, but eventually she came to accept his blank stares and his lack of recognition when they interacted.

Nelson was eventually moved to a facility where he could receive full-time care. Josephine visited him regularly. However, he was now in rapid decline, and his medical condition deteriorated precipitously. Nelson soon succumbed to a major infection and took his final breaths—less than five years after his first signs of Pick's disease.

Nelson experienced a *major neurocognitive disorder*. There are various kinds of such disorders. *Alzheimer's disease* is one kind—indeed the most common kind—but in fact many people loosely use the term "Alzheimer's" to refer to several of the major neurocognitive disorders (Alzheimer's Association, 2023).

The term "Alzheimer's disease" is familiar to almost everyone in our society. It is a diagnosis no one wants to hear because it feels like a death sentence. At present, this disorder, along with some of the other major neurocognitive disorders, remains incurable and almost untreatable, although, as you will learn later, researchers are currently making enormous progress toward understanding it and reversing—or at least slowing—its march.

What makes Alzheimer's disease and several of the other major neurocognitive disorders particularly frightening is that they mean not only eventual physical death but also, as in Nelson's case, a kind of psychological death—a progressive deterioration of one's memory and related cognitive faculties. Disorders marked primarily by substantial cognitive decline (including memory impairment) used to be called *dementia*. Dementia is still a technically acceptable term, but, over time, the term came to be used pejoratively in everyday language (for example, "That person is demented"). Therefore, a disorder marked primarily by substantial cognitive deterioration is now categorized as a *major neurocognitive disorder* in DSM-5-TR. In addition, a disorder marked primarily by less severe cognitive deterioration is called a *mild neurocognitive disorder.*

Although major neurocognitive disorders are the most publicized and feared psychological problems among older adults, they are hardly the only ones. A variety of psychological disorders are tied closely to later life. As with childhood disorders, some of the disorders of old age are caused primarily by pressures that are particularly likely to appear at that time of life, others by unique traumatic experiences, and still others—like neurocognitive disorders—by biological irregularities. ■

of NOTE ...

Average Life Expectancy

83.5 years	Asian Americans
77.7 years	Hispanic Americans
76.4 years	Non-Hispanic White Americans
70.8 years	Black Americans
65.2 years	Indigenous Americans

(KFF, 2023; Arias et al., 2022)

Older Adults and Stress

OLD AGE, ALSO CALLED OLDER ADULTHOOD OR LATER ADULTHOOD, IS usually defined in our society as the years past age 65. By this account, over 52 million people in the United States are older adults, representing 18 percent of the total population; this is a 15-fold increase since 1900 (Alzheimer's Association, 2023; U.S. Census Bureau, 2023, 2020). It has also been estimated that there will be 95 million older adults in the United States by 2060—23 percent of the population (PRB, 2023). Not only is the overall population of older adults on the rise, but also the number of people over age 85 will double in the next 10 years. Indeed, people over age 85 represent the fastest-growing segment of the population in the United States and in most countries around the globe (PRB, 2023).

Like childhood, old age brings special pressures, unique upsets, and major biological changes (Heflin, 2023). People become more prone to illness and injury as they age (Mindlis & Federman, 2024). About half of adults over age 65 have two or three chronic illnesses, and 15 percent have four or more. And at least half of older adults have some measure of insomnia or other sleep problems (APA, 2023; Winkelman, 2023). In addition, these individuals are likely to be contending with the stress of loss—of spouses, friends, and adult children; of former activities and roles; of hearing and vision (Lu et al., 2024; Kaplan, 2023). Many lose their sense of purpose after they retire. Some also have to adjust to the loss of beloved pets and possessions.

Charles Barsotti/CartoonStock Ltd.

"My advice is to learn all the tricks you can while you're young."

The stresses of aging need not necessarily cause psychological problems (see **PsychWatch**). In fact, some older people, particularly those who seek social contacts and those who maintain a sense of control over their lives, use the changes that come with aging as opportunities for learning and growth (Ballmer & Gantschnig, 2024; Choi, Hill, & Parmelee, 2024). For example, 75 percent of older adults now use the Internet to connect with people of similar ages and interests (more than a 16-fold increase since 2000), and more than half of these users are on social media (Faverio, 2022).

For other older people, however, the stresses of old age do lead to psychological difficulties. Studies indicate that 25 percent of older adults meet the criteria for a mental disorder, and as many as half of all older adults would benefit from some degree of mental health services, yet fewer than 20 percent actually receive them (APA, 2023; Johnson, 2022). **Geropsychology**, the field of psychology dedicated to the mental health of people above the age of 65, has developed almost entirely within the past four decades, and at present, only 4 percent of clinicians work primarily with such individuals (IPA, 2023; Comer et al., 2022).

What kinds of attitudes and activities might help people enter old age with peace of mind and positive anticipation?

The psychological problems of older adults can be divided into two groups. One group consists of disorders that may be common among people in all age groups but are often connected to the process of aging when they occur in an older adult. These include *depressive, anxiety,* and *substance use disorders.* The other group consists of disorders of cognition, such as *delirium, mild neurocognitive disorders,* and *major neurocognitive disorders,* that result from brain irregularities. As in Nelson's case, these irregularities are most often tied to aging, but they can sometimes occur when people are younger.

It is important to note that the various pressures of old age and their impact on older adults often intensify during times of community-wide stress. This was, for example, on vivid display during the Covid-19 pandemic. While everyone was heavily affected by this enduring event, its impact on older adults was particularly profound. They had (and still have) a higher risk than other persons of developing severe cases of Covid-19, and, indeed, 80 percent of Covid-19 deaths have been among people over age 65 (CDC, 2023, 2020; NCOA, 2023). Similarly, the social distancing and stay-at-home procedures employed during the pandemic tended to have their greatest impact on older adults, who generally depend more on others—physically, emotionally, and socially (Choi et al., 2024). Thus, it is not surprising that, while the pandemic substantially impacted the mental health of people from all age groups, it

geropsychology The field of psychology concerned with the mental health of older adults.

PSYCHWATCH

The Centenarians

Clinicians suggest that aging need not inevitably lead to psychological problems. Nor, apparently, does it always lead to physical problems.

There are currently more than 100,000 *centenarians* in the United States (600,000 worldwide)—people who are 100 years old or older (Statista, 2023; Dakic et al., 2022). When researchers have studied these people—often called the "oldest old"—they have been surprised to learn that centenarians are on average more healthy, positive, clearheaded, and agile than those in their eighties and early nineties (Perls, 2023; Leung et al., 2022). Although many experience cognitive decline, at least half remain quite alert. Many of them are, in fact, still employed, sexually active, and able to enjoy the outdoors and the arts. What is their greatest fear? The fear of significant cognitive decline. According to some studies, a number of people in their nineties and older fear the prospect of mental deterioration more than they fear death (Arosio et al., 2017; Boeve et al., 2003).

Some scientists believe that people who live this long carry "longevity" genes and have favorable "aging proteins" that make them resistant to disabling or terminal infections (Coenen et al., 2023; Simon et al., 2023). Correspondingly, some studies comparing the brain MRIs of centenarian participants to those of younger older adult participants found smoother brain functioning and brain circuit connectivity among the centenarians (Merenstein & Bennett, 2022; Jiang et al., 2020). Still other research points to active and engaged lifestyles, effective coping and problem-solving skills, "robust" personalities, attitudes of acceptance, and favorable environmental and economic conditions that help centenarians meet life's challenges with optimism and a sense of challenge (Perls, 2023; Uittenhove et al., 2023). The centenarians themselves often credit a good frame of mind or regular behaviors that they have maintained for many years—for example, eating healthful food and proper portions, getting regular exercise, and not smoking (Dakic et al., 2022; da Silva et al., 2018). Said one such individual, a retired math and science teacher, "You can't sit. . . . You have to keep moving" (Duenwald, 2003).

Christian Hartmann/Reuters/Redux

Key to his longevity Robert Marchand, age 106 at the time of this photo, cycles at an indoor track near Paris, France, an activity he continued to pursue until his death in 2021. Marchand attributed his longevity to eating lots of fruits and vegetables and to working out for an hour each day on a cycling home trainer.

had, on average, its greatest psychological effects on people above age 65. According to research, people in this age group had particularly high increases in their rates of anxiety, depression, loneliness, chronic stress, PTSD, insomnia, feelings of burdensomeness, confusion, and cognitive dysfunction (Statista, 2023; Webb & Chen, 2022). This special psychological impact on older adults was similarly on display during past epidemics and pandemics.

Depression in Later Life

DEPRESSION IS ONE of the most common mental health challenges of people over age 65 (Bhalla, Terpstra, & Butters, 2024; Comer et al., 2022). The features of depression are the same for older people as for younger people, including feelings of profound sadness and emptiness; low self-esteem, guilt, and pessimism; and loss of appetite and sleep disturbances. Depression is particularly common among those who have recently undergone a trauma, such as the loss of a spouse or close friend or the development of a serious physical illness (Ameen, Williams, & Guthrie, 2024; Mindlis & Federman, 2024).

Harrison, a 76-year-old retired attorney, started therapy for what his therapist would later diagnose as major depressive disorder. He maintained that he was coming to therapy at the insistence of his wife, Docia, who was concerned because Harrison had virtually stopped leaving the house, was spending much of his time in bed, was eating less and losing weight, and was usually in a bleak mood.

Harrison conceded that he had actually been feeling "down" over the past several years. He had been caught by surprise by the loss of purpose he experienced when he retired four years earlier. He was surprised that he rarely heard from any of his former law colleagues. He had expected panicked calls from them whenever they would be faced with a difficult case, perhaps even pleas for him to come in and consult on occasion, but he had received only a few check-in calls from the head of the firm—calls that felt patronizing.

Harrison told the therapist that when he retired, he had envisioned spending time traveling the world with Docia, doing the things he had missed out on while he was focusing on his career. However, several months into the retirement, Docia broke her hip, which led to months of rehab and recovery. Harrison helped her, of course, but he was surprised by how draining the effort was. He felt in over his head and exhausted caring for Docia—he, Harrison, who had always been in full command of any situation.

Then, just as Docia's recovery was almost complete, a major blow came—Harrison's closest friend Darren died suddenly of a stroke. This devastated both Harrison and Docia. The world stopped for them. After a few months, Docia began proposing that the two of them pick themselves up and go on vacation. But Harrison demurred, always suggesting they wait a couple of months more. He couldn't face the effort required to plan and go on a big trip.

It was now two years since Darren's death, and Harrison had just about ceased leaving the house. He insisted that this state of affairs was only natural since most of his social activities had involved him and Docia going out with Darren and Leslie. When the therapist asked if they had reached out to Leslie, Harrison sheepishly explained that Docia saw her sometimes but that he hadn't been able to bring himself to see her since the funeral. Asked if he and Docia ever did things alone, just the two of them, Harrison replied, "For a while a couple of years ago, we'd go on some 'dates,' but really, what's the point? I'm tired all the time, and I don't have much interest in getting out of bed."

Overall, as many as 20 percent of people become depressed at some point during old age (Sekhon, Patel, & Sapra, 2023). This rate among older adults is about the same as that among younger adults—even lower, according to some studies. However, it climbs much higher (as much as 50 percent) among older adults who live in nursing homes (Espinoza & Unützer, 2023).

To date, there have been few studies that examine the rates of depression among LGBTQ+ older adults and older adults of color. However, emerging research suggests that in the United States, the prevalence of depression is higher among transgender and nonbinary older adults than cisgender older adults (Feinstein et al., 2023; Hughto et al., 2023); among lesbian, gay, and bisexual older adults than heterosexual older adults (Feinstein et al., 2023; Miller, 2023); and among adults of color, particularly those who are Black or Hispanic, than non-Hispanic White older adults (Masa et al., 2023; Jimenez et al., 2022). These trends are similar to those in younger adults, which you read about in the chapter on depressive disorders. Moreover, as with younger adults, the higher rates of depression among older adults in marginalized groups are apparently linked to the health care barriers and experiences of discrimination, prejudice, stigmatization, and victimization that many such older adults have experienced in their lives (Hash & Hicks Patrick, 2024; Hughto et al., 2023; Masa et al., 2023).

of NOTE ...

Social Downturn

27%	Percentage of older adults who felt isolated from others before the Covid-19 pandemic
56%	Percentage of older adults who felt isolated from others during the Covid-19 pandemic

(Statista, 2023)

Making a difference To help prevent feelings of unimportance and low self-esteem, some older adults now offer their expertise to young people who are trying to master new skills, undertake business projects, and the like. This volunteer at an elementary school is teaching numbers to two kindergarteners.

Carol Kaliff/Hearst Connecticut Newspapers via AP

Several studies suggest that depression raises an older adult's chances of developing significant medical problems (Chen et al., 2024; Cai et al., 2023). For example, depressed older adults with high blood pressure are almost three times as likely to have a stroke as nondepressed older adults with the same condition. Similarly, older adults who are depressed recover more slowly and less completely from heart attacks, hip fractures, pneumonia, and other infections and illnesses. Small wonder that among older people, increases in clinical depression are tied to increases in the mortality rate (Heflin, 2023).

Is it more likely that positive thinking leads to good health or that good health produces positive thinking?

As you read in the chapter on suicide, older adults are also more likely to die from suicide than young people, and often their suicides are related to depression (Kaplan, 2023; Comer et al., 2022). The overall rate of suicide in the United States is 13.5 per 100,000 people. In contrast, the rate is 15 per 100,000 for those 65 to 74 years of age, 18 per 100,000 for those 75 to 84 years of age, and 21 per 100,000 for those 85 years of age and above (WPR, 2024, 2022; CDC, 2022).

Like younger people, older adults who are depressed may be helped by cognitive-behavioral therapy, interpersonal psychotherapy, antidepressant medications, or a combination of these approaches (Sekhon et al., 2023). Both individual and group therapy formats have been used. More than half of older adults with depression improve with these various treatments. It is sometimes difficult, however, for older people to use antidepressant drugs effectively and safely because the body breaks the drugs down differently in later life (Schatzberg & Nemeroff, 2024; Rochon, 2023). Moreover, among older people, antidepressant drugs have a higher risk of causing some cognitive impairment. Electroconvulsive therapy, applied with certain modifications, has been used for older adults who are severely depressed and have not been helped by other approaches (Kellner, 2022, 2021).

Some older adults experience depression as part of a bipolar disorder rather than a unipolar type of depressive disorder (Sajatovic & Chen, 2023; Shobassy, 2021). Around 1 percent of all persons over 65 years of age display a bipolar disorder in any given year. For more than 70 percent of them, the disorder began well before they reached old age. In most cases, the individuals receive the kinds of treatment that younger individuals with bipolar disorder receive—mood-stabilizing medications and adjunctive psychotherapy.

© Matthew A. Turner 2013

kali9/Getty Images

In pursuit of stimulation Gerontologists propose that older adults need to pursue pleasurable and personally meaningful activities. To help address this need, the people on the left race in the National Senior Games, and those on the right engage in a challenging game of chess.

Anxiety Disorders in Later Life

ANXIETY IS ALSO common among older adults (APA, 2023). At any given time, at least 10 percent of older adults experience one or more anxiety disorders (Graham, 2023; Liu et al., 2023). Surveys indicate that generalized anxiety disorder is particularly common (Baldwin, 2023). The prevalence of anxiety also increases throughout the course of old age (Karim et al., 2021). For example, people over 85 years of age report higher rates of anxiety than those between 65 and 84 years.

As with depression, emerging research suggests that in the United States, the prevalence of anxiety disorders is higher among transgender and nonbinary older adults than cisgender older adults (Feinstein et al., 2023; Hughto et al., 2023); among lesbian, gay, and bisexual older adults than heterosexual older adults (Feinstein et al., 2023; Miller, 2023); and among adults of color than non-Hispanic White older adults (Masa et al., 2023; Jimenez et al., 2022). Once again, these trends are similar to those in younger adults, which you read about in the chapter on anxiety disorders.

There are many things about aging that may heighten the anxiety levels of older adults. Declining health, for example, has often been pointed to, and, in fact, older adults who have significant medical illnesses or injuries report more anxiety than those who are healthy or injury-free (Mindlis & Federman, 2024) (see ***InfoCentral***). In addition, for older adults from marginalized groups, factors such as limited health care access and experiences of discrimination, prejudice, stigmatization, and victimization may help raise their levels of anxiety (Masa et al., 2023; Miller et al., 2023).

Older people with anxiety disorders have been treated with psychotherapy of various kinds, particularly cognitive-behavioral therapy (Ando et al., 2023). Many also receive benzodiazepines or other antianxiety medications, just as younger people with such disorders do. And a number are treated with serotonin-enhancing antidepressant drugs. Again, however, all such drugs must be used cautiously with older adults (Graham, 2023; Rochon, 2023).

THE AGING POPULATION

The number and proportion of older adults in the United States and around the world are ever-growing. This acceleration has important consequences, requiring each society to pay particular attention to aging-related issues in health care, housing, the economy, and other such realms. In particular, as the number and proportion of older adults increases, so too do the number and proportion of the population who experience aging-related psychological difficulties.

Worldwide percentage of older adults is increasing

In 2018 older adults, for the first time, outnumbered children under 5 years of age. In 2035, they will outnumber children under 18 years of age.

(WHO, 2022; U.S. Census Bureau, 2020, 2019)

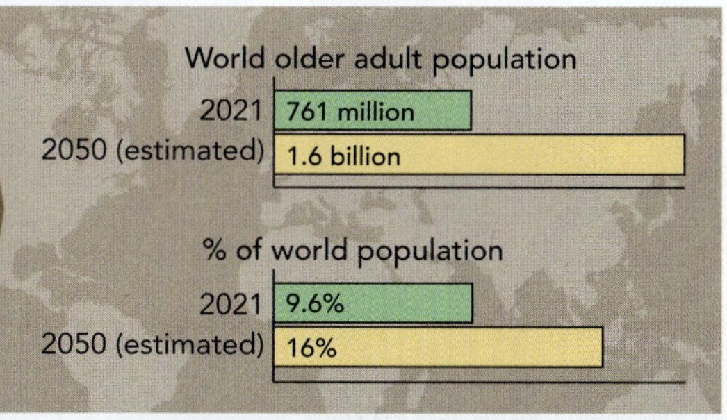

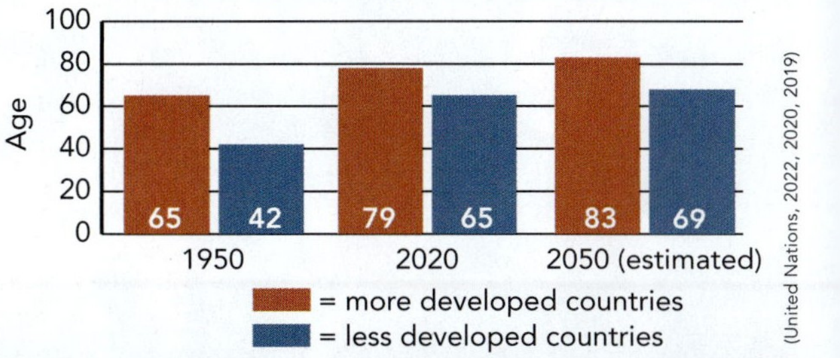

PSYCHOLOGICAL DISORDERS AMONG OLDER ADULTS

Common triggers for psychological disorders among older adults

- Physical disability
- Long-term illness
- Change of residence or environment
- Illness of a loved one
- Loss of a loved one
- Medication misuse
- Poor diet or malnutrition

(Lu et al., 2023; Paul, 2023; Meichsner et al., 2020; East, 2018)

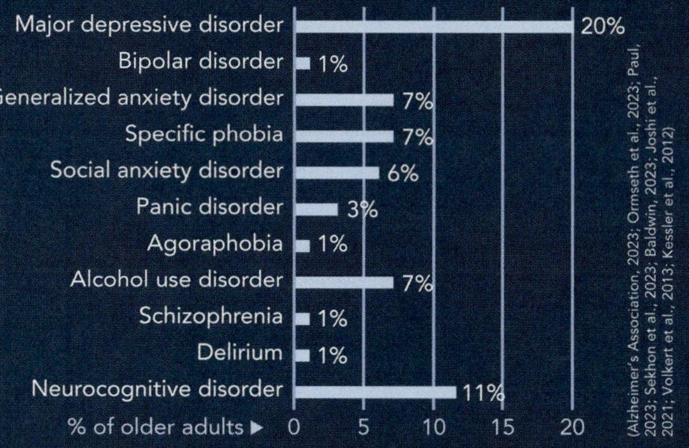

Psychological problems contribute to medical problems

Both aging itself and aging-related psychological disorders contribute to the development of medical disorders

(Paul, 2023; Woolston 2020)

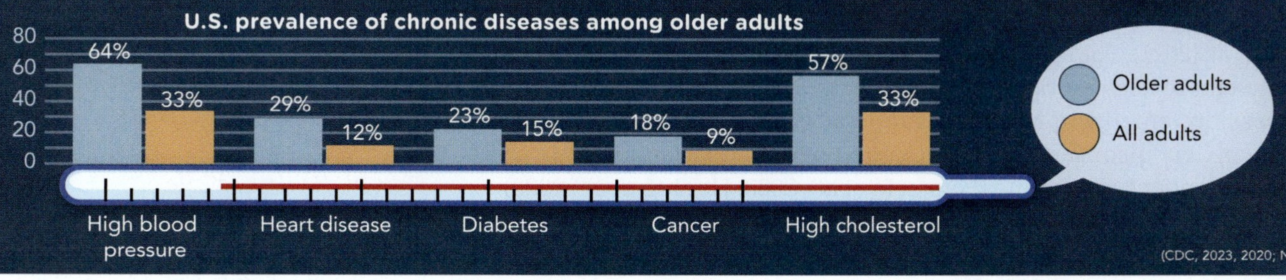

(CDC, 2023, 2020; NCOA, 2023; NCHS, 2020)

THE OLDER ADULT POPULATION IS ITSELF AGING

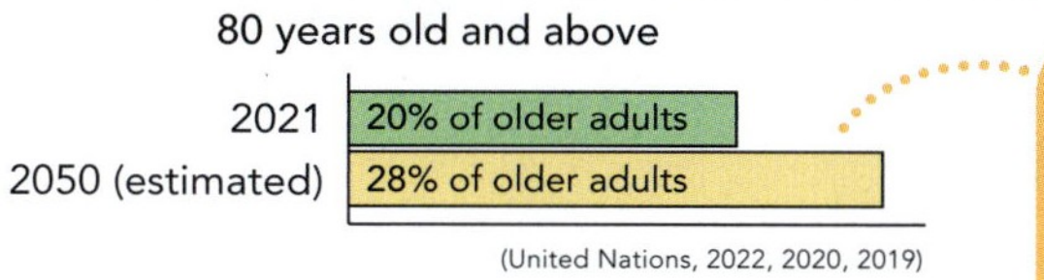

If you make it to age 80, you can expect to live an additional 9 years on average.

(SSA, 2023)

Staying Active

Around 20 percent of older adults are still in the work force. Around half of older adults do some form of volunteer work.

(EO, 2023; PRB, 2019)

WHERE DO OLDER ADULTS LIVE?

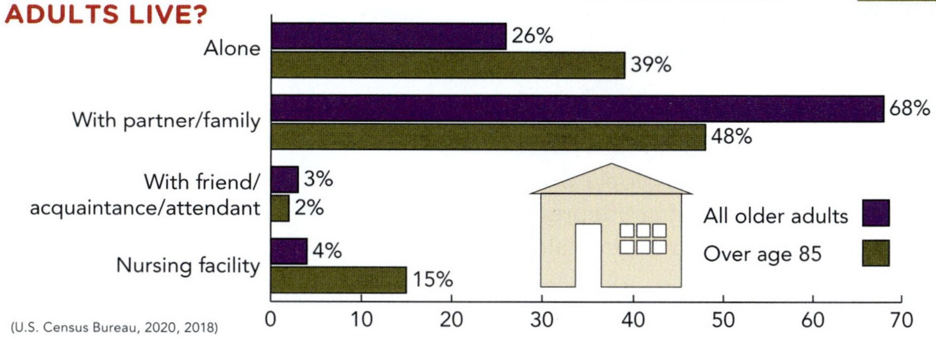

Embracing Social Media

Older adults are currently the fastest-growing age group on social media.

(EO, 2023)

Khadejeh Nikouyeh/News & Record via AP

Simulating old age Health care workers in North Carolina wear glasses that mimic a loss of color vision and gloves that produce arthritic-like functioning, part of a program to help such workers better understand the obstacles faced by their older adult clients.

Substance Misuse in Later Life

ALTHOUGH ALCOHOL USE disorder and other substance use disorders are significant problems for many older adults, the prevalence of such patterns actually appears to decline after age 65, perhaps because of declining health or reduced income (Leahy, 2023). The majority of older adults do not misuse alcohol or other substances despite the fact that aging can sometimes be a time of considerable stress, which, in our society, often causes people to turn to alcohol and drugs.

Surveys find that 11 to 15 percent of older adults are binge drinkers and that 3 to 7 percent of older adults have alcohol use disorder in a given year (NIAAA, 2024; Joshi et al., 2021; NPOHA, 2021). Men under 30 are four times as likely as men over 60 to display a behavioral problem associated with excessive alcohol use, such as repeated falling, spells of dizziness or blacking out, secretive drinking, or social withdrawal. Older patients who are institutionalized, however, do display high rates of problem drinking. For example, the estimated number of alcohol problems among older adults admitted to general and mental hospitals is at least 15 percent, and estimates of alcohol-related problems among patients in nursing homes are as high as 50 percent (Leahy, 2023; NCAC, 2020).

Researchers often distinguish between older problem drinkers who have had alcohol use disorder for many years and those who do not start abusing alcohol until their fifties or sixties. The latter group typically begins abusive drinking as a reaction to the negative events and pressures of growing older, such as the death of a spouse or close friend, living alone, or unwanted retirement (NIA, 2022). Alcohol use disorder in older adults is treated much as it is in younger adults: through interventions such as detoxification, Alcoholics Anonymous (AA), and cognitive-behavioral therapy (Lin et al., 2023; Joshi et al., 2021).

A leading substance problem in older adults is the *misuse of prescription drugs* (Anlay et al., 2024). Most often, the misuse is unintentional. In the United States, people over the age of 65 buy more than one-third of all prescription drugs. At any given time, older adults are taking, on average, five prescription drugs and two over-the-counter drugs (Heflin, 2023; Rochon, 2023). Thus, their risk of confusing medications or skipping doses is high. To help address this problem, physicians and pharmacists often try to simplify medications, educate older patients about their prescriptions, clarify directions, and teach them to watch for undesired effects (Anlay et al., 2024).

of NOTE ...

Hazardous Event

One of every four older adults falls each year. Such falls are the leading cause of fatal and nonfatal injuries in this age group, including hip fractures, head trauma, and death (Sioutis et al., 2024; NCOA, 2023).

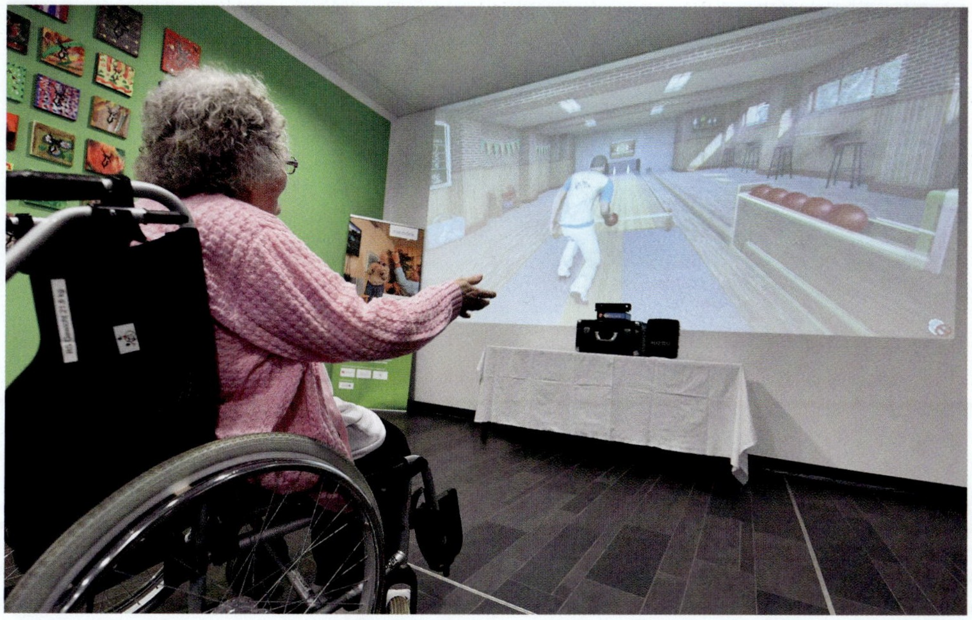

Virtual vitality Digital technology can help improve the cognitive and physical functioning of older adults. Using virtual reality technology, this retirement home resident is able to participate in her favorite sport of bowling, take a bike ride through various environments, and revisit old haunts.

Martin Schutt/picture alliance via Getty Images

On the other hand, physicians themselves are sometimes to blame in cases of prescription drug misuse, perhaps overprescribing medications for older adult patients or unwisely mixing certain medicines. If the multiple drugs taken by a person interact poorly, it can lead to significant medical problems, called *adverse drug events*. Between 3 and 10 percent of all hospitalizations for older adults are caused by adverse drug events (Rochon, 2023).

Yet another drug-related problem, apparently on the increase, is the misuse of powerful medications at nursing homes. Research indicates that antipsychotic drugs are currently being given to at least 22 percent of the total nursing home population in the United States despite the fact that many of the residents do not display psychotic functioning (Ausmed, 2023; Rochon, 2023). Apparently, these powerful and (for some older patients) dangerous drugs are often given to sedate and manage the patients. Indeed, research suggests that 17 percent of new nursing home patients who have never before taken an antipsychotic drug are administered such drugs within 100 days of admission (Rochon, 2023).

What changes in medical practice, patient education, or family interactions might address the problem of prescription drug misuse by older adults?

Psychotic Disorders in Later Life

OLDER ADULTS HAVE a higher rate of psychotic symptoms than younger people. Their psychotic symptoms are usually caused by underlying medical conditions such as neurocognitive disorders, the disorders of cognition that you will read about in the next section of this chapter (Creese et al., 2023). Some older adults, though, experience *schizophrenia* or *delusional disorder*, one of the other schizophrenia spectrum disorders.

Actually, schizophrenia is less common in older people than in younger ones. In fact, many people with schizophrenia find that their symptoms lessen in later life (Walker & Harrison, 2023; Cohen & Reinhardt, 2020). Improvement can occur in people who have had schizophrenia for 30 or more years, particularly in such areas as social skills and work capacity, as we are reminded by the remarkable late-life improvement of the Nobel Prize recipient John Nash, the subject of the book and movie *A Beautiful Mind*.

It is uncommon for *new* cases of schizophrenia to emerge in late life (Meesters, 2023; APA, 2022). Thus, some of the older adults with schizophrenia began receiving antipsychotic drugs and psychotherapeutic interventions many years earlier and are continuing to do so in old age. Once again, though, antipsychotic drugs may pose more dangers (cognitive impairment, stroke, seizures) for older people than younger people, given the metabolism changes in older people (Lunghi et al., 2023; Hoertel et al., 2021). It is also the case that a number of older adults with schizophrenia go untreated and wind up in nursing homes, in run-down apartments, unhoused, or incarcerated.

Another kind of psychotic disorder found among older adults is *delusional disorder*, in which people develop beliefs that are false but not bizarre (Gonzalez-Rodriguez et al., 2022). This disorder, which you read about in the chapter on schizophrenia, is rare in most age groups—around 2 of every 1,000 persons—but its prevalence appears to increase in older adults (APA, 2022). Those with a delusional disorder may develop deeply held suspicions of persecution; they believe that other people—often family members, doctors, or friends—are conspiring against, cheating, spying on, or maligning them. They may become irritable, angry, or depressed or pursue legal action because of such ideas. It is not clear why this disorder increases among older people, but some clinicians suggest that the rise is related to the deficiencies in hearing, the social isolation, the greater stress, or the heightened poverty with which many such persons contend (Chen et al., 2024; Marder, 2023).

delirium A rapidly developing, acute disturbance in attention and orientation that makes it very difficult to concentrate and think in a clear and organized manner.

SUMMING UP

Disorders of Later Life

The problems of older adults are often linked to the losses and other stresses and changes that accompany advancing age. As many as 50 percent of older adults would benefit from mental health services, yet fewer than 20 percent receive them. Depression is a common mental health problem among those in this age group. Older people may also experience anxiety disorders. Between 3 and 7 percent exhibit alcohol use disorder in any given year, and many others misuse prescription drugs. In addition, some older adults display psychotic disorders such as schizophrenia or delusional disorder.

Disorders of Cognition

MOST OF US worry from time to time that we are losing our memory and other mental abilities. You rush out the door without your keys, you meet a familiar person and cannot remember their name, or you forget that you have seen a particular film. Actually, such mishaps are a common and quite typical feature of stress or of aging. As people move through middle age, these memory difficulties and lapses of attention increase, and by the age of 60 or 70, they may occur regularly (see ***MindTech***). Sometimes, however, people have memory difficulties and other cognitive changes that are far more extensive and problematic.

In an earlier chapter, you read that problems in memory and related cognitive processes can occur without biological causes in the form of *dissociative disorders*. More often, though, cognitive problems do have organic roots, particularly when they appear late in life. The leading such disorders among older adults are *delirium*, *major neurocognitive disorder*, and *mild neurocognitive disorder*.

Delirium

Delirium is a major disturbance in attention and orientation to the environment (see **Table 15-1**). As the person's focus becomes less clear, they have great difficulty concentrating and thinking in an organized way, leading to misinterpretations, illusions, and

TABLE 15-1

Dx Checklist

Delirium
1. Over the course of hours or a few days, individual experiences fast-moving and fluctuating disturbances in attention and orientation to the environment.
2. Individual also displays a significant cognitive disturbance.

Information from: APA, 2022.

MINDTECH

Remember to Tweet; Tweet to Remember

Social media and the Internet in general are often thought of as the province of the young. However, older adults are also going online and joining social media at increasing rates. Three of every four people over age 65 now use the Internet, and more than half of those users are on social media (Statista, 2024; Faverio, 2022).

Mike Kemp/In Pictures via Getty Images

Online gaming for all ages An older adult sits at a kitchen table with her iPad to tackle her daily Wordle puzzle. Like other Wordle aficionados, she has six attempts to guess a five-letter word in this stimulating Web-based word game that has become a must-do activity for people of all ages.

Online activity by older adults is much more than just an interesting statistic; it may be downright therapeutic. Several studies have found that such activity actually helps older adults maintain and possibly improve their cognitive skills, coping skills, social pleasures, emotions, self-competence, and physical well-being (Choi et al., 2024; Rennoch, Schlomann, & Zank, 2024). In one early study on this matter, for example, researchers recruited 42 older adult non-Internet users and trained 14 of them on Facebook. The study found a 25 percent improvement in the cognitive performances of the 14 participants, including improvements in their mental "updating" skills—the ability to quickly add or delete material from their working memory (Blue, 2013).

Clinical theorists have offered several explanations for the positive effects of social media on older adults. It may be, for example, that the cognitive stimulation derived from social media participation activates memory and other cognitive faculties or that the engagement with the world and family provided by the Internet directly satisfies social and emotional needs (Choi et al., 2024; Benge et al., 2023). Whatever the reason, more and more studies indicate that older adults who are online often function and feel better than those who do not pursue online activities.

Of course, social media can sometimes be problematic for older adults, just as it can have a negative impact on younger persons. One older user—a clinical psychologist!—put it this way: "Even at my age, it's easy to feel competitive, jealous, left out on social media. . . . It stirs up those feelings and juvenile thoughts of 'I'm not cool.' . . . You think you've outgrown those decades ago, but, no" (Pennoyer, 2017). Despite such concerns, the growing body of research suggests that reluctant older adults should probably forge ahead and embrace social media and the Internet—for better functioning and for better mental health.

sometimes hallucinations. People with delirium may believe that it is morning in the middle of the night or that they are home when actually they are in a hospital room.

This state of massive confusion typically develops over a short period of time, usually hours or days (APA, 2022). Delirium may occur in any age group, including children, but it is most common in older adults (Ormseth et al., 2023). Fewer than 0.5 percent of people under 55 years of age experience delirium, compared with 2 percent of people over that age and 14 percent of those over 85 years of age. When older adults enter a hospital—which represents a major change in their environment and routine—to be treated for a general medical condition, more than 18 percent of them show symptoms of delirium (ANA, 2024; Ali & Cascella, 2022). Altogether, 29 to 64 percent experience delirium during their stay in the hospital (Francis & Young, 2023, 2022; Ormseth et al., 2023). As many as 20 percent of older adults receiving surgery develop some degree of delirium, and as many as 50 percent experience delirium after high-risk surgery (Dilmen et al., 2024; Ramirez Echeverria, Schoo, & Paul, 2023). Between 20 and 50 percent of older adult nursing home residents have some delirium (ANA, 2024; APA, 2022).

Fever, certain diseases and infections, poor nutrition, head injuries, strokes, and stress (including the trauma of surgery) may all cause delirium (Dilmen et al., 2024; Ramirez Echeverria et al., 2023). So may intoxication by certain substances, such as prescription drugs (Huang, 2023). Partly because older people face so many of these problems, they are more likely than younger people to experience delirium (Fischer & Corsetti, 2024). If a clinician accurately identifies delirium, it can sometimes be corrected relatively quickly—by treating the underlying infection, for example, or reducing or changing the patient's drug prescription (Mattison, 2023; Ormseth et al., 2023). However, the syndrome typically fails to be recognized for what it is. Incorrect diagnoses are relatively common and can, in many cases, lead to significant medical and psychological difficulties, including a heightened death rate for older adults with delirium (Fischer & Corsetti, 2024).

neurocognitive disorder A disorder marked by a significant decline in at least one area of cognitive functioning.

major neurocognitive disorder A neurocognitive disorder in which the decline in cognitive functioning is substantial and interferes with a person's ability to be independent.

mild neurocognitive disorder A neurocognitive disorder in which the decline in cognitive functioning is modest and does not interfere with a person's ability to be independent.

Alzheimer's disease The most common type of neurocognitive disorder, usually occurring after the age of 65, marked most prominently by memory impairment.

Alzheimer's Disease and Other Neurocognitive Disorders

People with a **neurocognitive disorder** experience a significant decline in at least one (often more than one) area of cognitive functioning, such as memory, attention, visual perception, planning and decision-making, language ability, or social awareness (APA, 2022). Like Nelson, the individual whose case opened this chapter, people with certain types of neurocognitive disorders may also undergo personality changes—they may behave inappropriately, for example—and their symptoms may worsen steadily.

If the person's cognitive decline is substantial and interferes significantly with the ability to be independent, a diagnosis of **major neurocognitive disorder** is in order. If the decline is modest and does not interfere with independent functioning, the appropriate diagnosis is **mild neurocognitive disorder** (see **Table 15-2**).

There are currently 55 million people with neurocognitive disorders around the world, with 10 million new cases emerging each year (WHO, 2023). The number of cases is expected to reach 150 million by 2050 unless a cure is found. The occurrence of neurocognitive disorders is closely related to age. Among people 65 years of age, the prevalence is around 1 to 2 percent, increasing to as much as 50 percent for those over the age of 85 (Heflin, 2023).

As you read earlier, **Alzheimer's disease** is the most common type of neurocognitive disorder, accounting for at least two-thirds of all cases (WHO, 2023). Around 6.7 million people in the United States currently have this disease, a number that is expected to reach 13 million by 2050 (Alzheimer's Association, 2023; CDC, 2023). Alzheimer's disease sometimes appears in middle age (early onset), but in the vast majority of cases, it occurs after the age of 65 (late onset), and its prevalence increases markedly among people in their late seventies. Around 5 percent of people age 65 to 74, 13 percent of people age 75 to 84, and 33 percent of those age 85 and older have this disease (Alzheimer's Association, 2023) (see **Figure 15-1**). Research conducted with mostly cisgender populations finds that women are twice as likely as men to develop this disease, a difference that has been attributed primarily to biological differences (for example, hormonal differences) and the longer average life span of women (Alzheimer's Association, 2023; Huang, 2023).

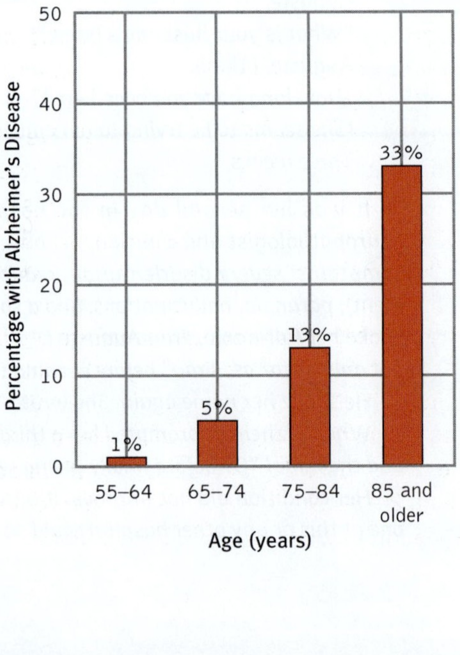

FIGURE 15-1

Substantial Cognitive Decline and Age

The occurrence of Alzheimer's disease is closely related to age. Around 6 percent of all people under the age of 75 have the disease, compared with 33 percent of those who are age 85 or older. (Information from: Alzheimer's Association, 2023)

TABLE 15-2

Dx Checklist

Major Neurocognitive Disorder
1. Individual displays substantial decline in at least one of the following areas of cognitive function: ■ Memory and learning ■ Attention ■ Perceptual-motor skills ■ Planning and decision-making ■ Language ability ■ Social awareness.
2. Cognitive deficits interfere with the individual's everyday independence.
Mild Neurocognitive Disorder
1. Individual displays modest decline in at least one of the following areas of cognitive function: ■ Memory and learning ■ Attention ■ Perceptual-motor skills ■ Planning and decision-making ■ Language ability ■ Social awareness.
2. Cognitive deficits do not interfere with the individual's everyday independence.

Information from: APA, 2022.

Research has been limited, but a few studies suggest that LGBTQ+ people are somewhat more likely to experience Alzheimer's disease than cisgender people and heterosexual people (Alzheimer's Association, 2023). One explanation for this difference is that the heightened stress, victimization, and health care challenges faced by many LGBTQ+ people over the course of their lives adversely affect their cardiovascular system, sleep patterns, diet, and economic status—factors that are known to increase the risk of developing Alzheimer's disease (Cheng et al., 2024; Hash & Hicks Patrick, 2024). In addition, except for Asian Americans, people of color in the United States are considerably more likely to experience Alzheimer's disease than non-Hispanic White people (Fazeli et al., 2024). The reasons for this significant racial and ethnic difference are not known. The difference may be related to the heightened risk factors just mentioned or to the Alzheimer-linked genetic factors that you will be reading about shortly (Hash & Hicks Patrick, 2024; Alzheimer's Association, 2023).

Alzheimer's disease is a gradually progressive disease in which memory impairment is, by far, the most prominent cognitive dysfunction (Zhang et al., 2024). Technically, people with the disease receive a DSM-5-TR diagnosis of *mild neurocognitive disorder due to Alzheimer's disease* during the early and mild stages of the syndrome and *major neurocognitive disorder due to Alzheimer's disease* during the later, more severe stages.

Alzheimer's disease is named after Alois Alzheimer, the German physician who formally identified it in 1907. Alzheimer first became aware of the syndrome in 1901 when a new patient, Auguste D., was placed under his care:

On November 25, 1901, a . . . woman with no personal or family history of mental illness was admitted to a psychiatric hospital in Frankfurt, Germany, by her husband, who could no longer ignore or hide quirks and lapses that had overtaken her in recent months. First, there were unexplainable bursts of anger, and then a strange series of memory problems. She became increasingly unable to locate things in her own home and began to make surprising mistakes in the kitchen. By the time she arrived at Städtische Irrenanstalt, the Frankfurt Hospital for the Mentally Ill and Epileptics, her condition was as severe as it was curious. The attending doctor, senior physician Alois Alzheimer, began the new file with these notes. . . .

She sits on the bed with a helpless expression.
"What is your name?"
Auguste.
"Last name?"
Auguste.
"What is your husband's name?"
Auguste, I think.
"How long have you been here?"
(She seems to be trying to remember.)
Three weeks.

It was her second day in the hospital. Dr. Alzheimer, a thirty-seven-year-old neuropathologist and clinician, . . . observed in his new patient a remarkable cluster of symptoms: severe disorientation, reduced comprehension, aphasia (language impairment), paranoia, hallucinations, and a short-term memory so incapacitated that when he spoke her full-name, Frau Auguste D ______, and asked her to write it down, the patient got only as far as "Frau" before needing the doctor to repeat the rest.

He spoke her name again. She wrote "Augu" and again stopped.

When Alzheimer prompted her a third time, she was able to write her entire first name and the initial "D" before finally giving up, telling the doctor, "I have lost myself."

Her condition did not improve. It became apparent that there was nothing that anyone at this or any other hospital could do for Frau D. except to insure her safety and try to keep her as clean and comfortable as possible for the rest of her days. Over the next four and a half years, she became increasingly disoriented, delusional, and incoherent. She was often hostile.

"Her gestures showed a complete helplessness," Alzheimer later noted in a published report. "She was disoriented as to time and place. From time to time she would state that she did not understand anything, that she felt confused and totally lost. . . . Often she would scream for hours and hours in a horrible voice."

By November 1904, three and a half years into her illness, Auguste D. was bedridden, incontinent, and largely immobile. . . . Notes from October 1905 indicate that she had become permanently curled up in a fetal position with her knees drawn up to her chest, muttering but unable to speak, and requiring assistance to be fed.

(Shenk, 2001, pp. 12–14)

Although some people with Alzheimer's disease may survive for as many as 20 years, the time between onset and death is typically four to eight years (Alzheimer's Association, 2023; Kumar et al., 2022). It usually begins with mild memory problems, lapses of attention, and difficulties in language and communication. As symptoms worsen, the person has trouble completing complicated tasks or remembering important appointments. Eventually, the individual also has difficulty with simple tasks, forgets distant memories, and has changes in personality that often become very noticeable. For example, a gentle man may become uncharacteristically aggressive.

People with Alzheimer's disease may at first deny that they have a problem, but they soon become anxious or depressed about their state of mind; many also become agitated (Grossberg et al., 2024; Singh et al., 2024). As many as 40 percent of them develop a depressive disorder (Alzheimer's Association, 2024). Here, a person describes their experiences with memory loss as the disease progressed:

Jim Davis/The Boston Globe via Getty Images

Slipping away Because of their short-term memory problems, people with advanced cases of Alzheimer's disease are often unable to easily draw, paint, or do simple tasks. In addition, their long-term memory deficits may prevent them from recognizing even close relatives or friends.

More than once I found myself walking down the street in my neighborhood with great purpose, headed confidently in a particular direction, when suddenly I realized I had no idea where I was trying to go. I'd look around, try to orient myself, and stare in the direction I was headed to figure out what store I might have been aiming for. But nothing came to me. So I would head home, dejected, and my partner Dante would say, with an exasperated sigh, "Honey, you were picking up dinner at the Vietnamese restaurant."

Eventually, during one of these episodes, when I was trying to head home, I couldn't even remember the way back to our apartment, and I panicked. Then I saw the laundromat and I remembered with great relief how to get home. Crying, I told Dante what had happened, and we decided from now on he would run all errands and I would not go out without him. Each day, I feel more frustrated and embarrassed. And I feel like I'm not pulling my weight.

As the neurocognitive symptoms intensify, people with Alzheimer's disease show less and less awareness of their limitations. They may withdraw from others during the late stages of the disorder, become more confused about time and place, wander, speak little, and show very poor judgment (Alzheimer's Association, 2024; Kumar et al., 2022). Eventually, they become fully dependent on other people. They may lose almost all knowledge of the past and fail to recognize the faces of even close relatives. They also become increasingly uncomfortable at night and take frequent naps during the day. During the late phases of the disorder, they require constant care.

People with Alzheimer's usually remain in fairly good health until the later stages of the disease. As their mental functioning declines, however, they become less active and

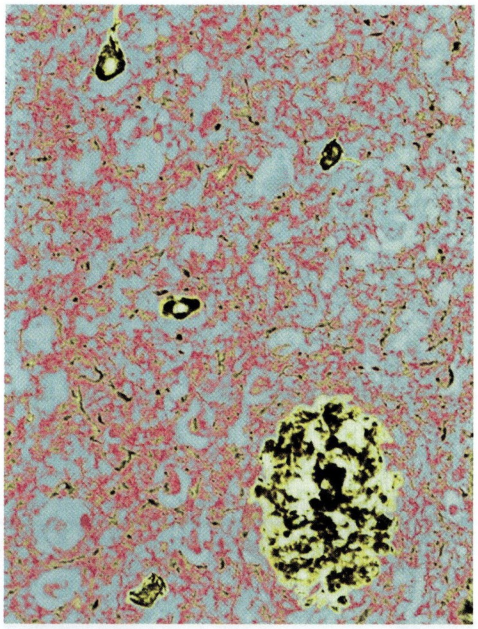

Simon Fraser/Science Source

Biological culprits Tissue from the brain of a person with Alzheimer's disease shows excessive amounts of plaque (large yellow-black sphere at lower right of photo) and neurofibrillary tangles (several smaller yellow blobs throughout photo).

spend much of their time just sitting or lying in bed. This makes them prone to develop serious infections such as pneumonia, which can result in death. Alzheimer's disease is currently responsible for 122,000 deaths each year in the United States, a number more than 50 percent higher than it was a decade ago (Alzheimer's Association, 2024, 2023; CDC, 2023). It is the seventh leading cause of death in the country.

In most cases, Alzheimer's disease can be diagnosed with certainty only after death, when structural changes in the person's brain, such as excessive *senile plaques* and *neurofibrillary tangles,* can be fully examined (Vromen et al., 2023). **Senile plaques** are sphere-shaped deposits of a small molecule known as the *beta-amyloid protein* that form in the spaces *between* neurons in the hippocampus, cerebral cortex, and certain other brain structures, as well as in some nearby blood vessels. The formation of plaques is a typical part of aging, but it is exceptionally high in people with Alzheimer's disease (Gharat et al., 2024; Alzheimer's Association, 2023).

Neurofibrillary tangles, twisted protein fibers found *within* the neurons of the hippocampus and certain other brain structures, also occur in all people as they age, but again people with Alzheimer's disease form an extraordinary number of them.

Scientists do not fully understand what role excessive numbers of plaques and tangles play in Alzheimer's disease, but most agree that both do their ultimate damage by contributing to the death of neurons (Balusu et al., 2023). The plaques (which occur between neurons) accomplish this by interfering with neuron-to-neuron communications, while the tangles (which occur inside neurons) accomplish it by blocking the transportation of essential molecules within neurons (Tampellini, 2024; Alzheimer's Association, 2023, 2020). Today's leading explanations for Alzheimer's disease center on plaques and tangles and on the various factors that may contribute to their formation and excessive buildup.

What Are the Genetic Causes of Alzheimer's Disease?

To understand the genetic theories of Alzheimer's disease, we must first appreciate the nature and role of *proteins*. Proteins are fundamental components of all living cells, including, of course, brain cells. They are large molecules made up of chains of carbon, hydrogen, oxygen, nitrogen, and sulfur. There are many different kinds of proteins, each with a different function. Collectively, they are essential for the proper functioning of an organism.

The plaques and tangles that are so plentiful in the brains of Alzheimer's patients seem to occur when two important proteins start acting in a frenzied manner. Atypical activity by the beta-amyloid protein is, as you just read, key to the repeated formation of plaques. Atypical activity by another protein, *tau,* is key to the excessive formation of tangles (Ye et al., 2024; Alzheimer's Association, 2023). One of the leading theories holds that the many plaques formed by beta-amyloid proteins also cause tau proteins within neurons to start breaking down, resulting in tangles and the death of many neurons (Keene, Montine, & Kuller, 2022).

What causes this chain of events? Genetic factors are a major culprit (Zhang et al., 2024). However, the genetic factors that are responsible differ for the early-onset and late-onset types of Alzheimer's disease.

EARLY-ONSET ALZHEIMER'S DISEASE

Alzheimer's disease occurs before the age of 65 in fewer than 10 percent of cases (Brosch & Farlow, 2023; WHO, 2023). This relatively rare form of the disorder typically runs in families. Researchers have learned that it is caused by irregularities in genes responsible for the production of two proteins—the *beta-amyloid precursor protein* (*beta-APP*) and the *presenilin protein*. Apparently, some families transmit mutations, or atypical forms, of one or both of these genes—mutations that lead ultimately to irregular beta-amyloid protein buildups and, in turn, to plaque formations (Murphy, Buzinova, & Johnson, 2024; Alzheimer's Association, 2023; Huang, 2023).

senile plaques Sphere-shaped deposits of beta-amyloid protein that form in the spaces between certain neurons and in certain blood vessels of the brain as people age. People with Alzheimer's disease have an excessive number of such plaques.

neurofibrillary tangles Twisted protein fibers that form within certain neurons as people age. People with Alzheimer's disease have an excessive number of such tangles.

Lucas Oleniuk/Toronto Star via Getty Images

An early good-bye Lyndon Blackbird (left) takes a leave of absence from work to spend what he suspects will be the last summer with his 54-year-old wife, Evelyn Davis. Davis was diagnosed with early-onset Alzheimer's disease.

LATE-ONSET ALZHEIMER'S DISEASE The vast majority of Alzheimer cases develop after the age of 65. Although most people with Alzheimer's disease do not have a family history of it, people whose parents or siblings have the disease are more likely than others to develop it (Alzheimer's Association, 2023). This late-onset form of the disease appears to result from a combination of genetic, environmental, and lifestyle factors. However, the genetic factors at play in late-onset Alzheimer's disease are different from those involved in early-onset Alzheimer's disease. The genetic factor that has received the most attention from clinical theorists and researchers is a gene called the apolipoprotein E (ApoE) gene (Ji et al., 2024).

The ApoE gene, located on chromosome 19, is generally responsible for the production of a protein that helps transport cholesterol in the bloodstream. This gene comes in three forms: E-2, E-3, and E-4. About 30 percent of the population inherit the E-4 form, called the ApoE-4 form, and those people may be particularly vulnerable to the development of Alzheimer's disease (Ji et al., 2024; Sherva & Kowall, 2022). Apparently, this ApoE-4 gene form promotes the excessive formation of beta-amyloid proteins, helping to spur the formation of plaques and, in turn, the breakdown of the tau protein, the formation of numerous tangles, the death of many neurons, and, ultimately, the onset of Alzheimer's disease (Alzheimer's Association, 2023).

Although the ApoE-4 gene form appears to be a major contributor to the development of Alzheimer's disease, it is important to recognize that not everyone with this form of the gene develops the disease. Other factors—perhaps environmental, lifestyle, or stress-related—may also have a significant impact in the development of late-onset Alzheimer's disease (Zhang et al., 2024; Alzheimer's Association, 2023, 2020).

AN ALTERNATIVE GENETIC THEORY OF ALZHEIMER'S DISEASE As you have just read, a number of genetic theories of Alzheimer's disease point to gene forms—

10/66 Psychiatric investigator Mariella Guerra works with research participant Consuelo Klingenber Perez (left) as part of a study done by the 10/66 Dementia Research Group. Only 10 percent of Alzheimer's disease studies focus on individuals from developing countries despite the fact that 66 percent of all people with the disease live in those countries. Thus, the 10/66 research group makes a point of conducting better-represented studies across the world.

Steve Russell/Toronto Star via Getty Images

of NOTE ...

Typical Aging?

DSM-5 and DSM-5-TR have added the category *mild neurocognitive disorder*, characterized by modest declines in memory or other cognitive functions, in order to help clinicians detect people in the early stages of *major neurocognitive disorder*. Critics worry, however, that many people who display common age-related forgetfulness and other relatively ordinary features of growing older could incorrectly receive a diagnosis of mild neurocognitive disorder.

most often ApoE-4—that produce atypical beta-amyloid protein buildups and plaque formations. These gene forms, in turn, lead to irregular activity of tau proteins and the formation of numerous tangles. In recent years, however, some researchers have come to believe that irregular tau protein activity is not always the result of these atypical beta-amyloid protein buildups (Chu et al., 2024; Ye et al., 2024; Zhang et al., 2023). These researchers have identified other gene forms in Alzheimer's patients that seem to be directly associated with tau protein irregularities and tangle formations within neurons. Thus, it may be that there are multiple genetic causes for the formation of numerous tangle formations and the onset of Alzheimer's disease: (1) gene forms that start the ball rolling by first promoting beta-amyloid protein formations and plaques and (2) gene forms that more directly promote tau protein irregularities and tangle formations.

How Do Brain Structure and Brain Circuitry Relate to Alzheimer's Disease? Granting that genetic factors may predispose people to Alzheimer's disease, we still need to know what aberrations in brain structure and brain circuitry eventually result from such factors and help promote Alzheimer's disease. Researchers have identified a number of possibilities.

Certain brain structures seem to be especially important in memory. Among the most important structures in short-term memory is the *prefrontal cortex*. Among the most important structures in transforming short-term memory into long-term memory are the *hippocampus, amygdala, thalamus,* and *hypothalamus*. Studies indicate that Alzheimer's disease involves improper functioning of one or more of these brain structures (Grieco, Holmes, & Xu, 2023; Kumar et al., 2022) (see **Figure 15-2**). In addition, consistent with the field's increasing emphasis on dysfunctional brain circuits, research suggests that Alzheimer's disease may ultimately be related to poor

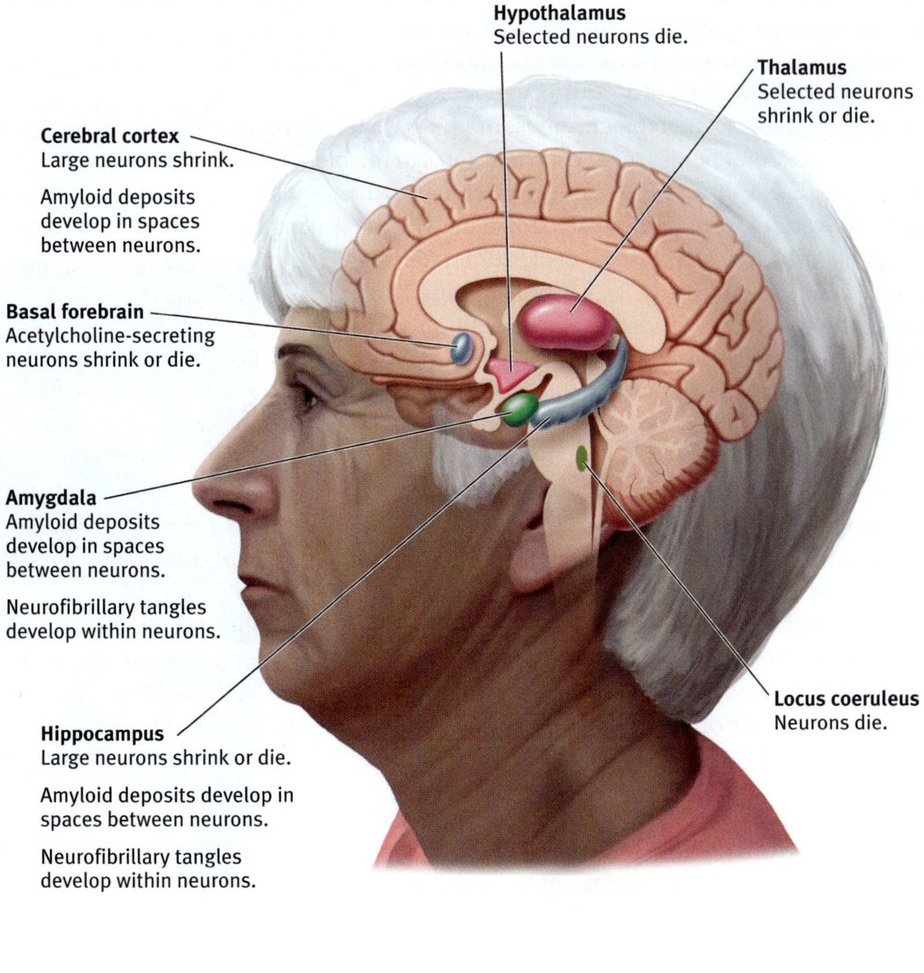

FIGURE 15-2

The Aging Brain

In old age, the brain undergoes changes that affect cognitive functions such as memory, learning, and reasoning to some degree. The same changes occur to an excessive degree in people with Alzheimer's disease. (Information from: Alzheimer's Association, 2023; Kumar et al., 2022; Sun, Ueno, & Narumoto, 2022; Selkoe, 2011, 1992) communication (poor *interconnectivity*) among these structures. In short, the brain circuit consisting of these and related structures may function improperly (Grieco et al., 2023).

What Biochemical Changes in the Brain Relate to Alzheimer's Disease? In order for new information to be acquired and remembered, certain proteins must be produced in key brain cells. Several brain chemicals—for example, *acetylcholine, glutamate, RNA* (*ribonucleic acid*), and *calcium*—are responsible for the production of the memory-linked proteins. If the activity of any of these chemicals is disturbed, the proper production of proteins may be prevented and the formation of memories interrupted. Thus, it is not surprising that research has linked atypical activity by these various chemicals to Alzheimer's disease. Studies have found, for example, deficient activity levels of acetylcholine and glutamate in the brains of people with Alzheimer's disease as well as irregularities in the breakdown of calcium (Song, Tang, & Law, 2024; Wu et al., 2023).

What kinds of psychological and physical functioning might be negatively affected by a person's inability to form memories properly?

Other Explanations of Alzheimer's Disease Several lines of investigation suggest that certain substances found in nature may act as toxins, damage the brain, and contribute to the development of Alzheimer's disease (Zhang et al., 2024). For example, some studies have detected high levels of *zinc* in the brains of some Alzheimer's patients (Li et al., 2022). Still other studies have suggested that the environmental toxin *lead* may contribute to the development of Alzheimer's disease (Islam et al., 2022). It is worth noting, in this regard, that many of today's older adults were exposed to high levels of lead in the 1960s and 1970s, regularly inhaling air pollution from vehicle exhausts—an exposure that might have damaged or destroyed many of their neurons (George, 2022).

Two other explanations for Alzheimer's disease have also been offered. One is the *autoimmune theory*. On the basis of certain irregularities found in the immune systems of people with Alzheimer's disease, several researchers have speculated that changes in aging brain cells may trigger an *autoimmune response* (that is, a mistaken attack by the immune system against itself) that helps lead to the disease (Fang et al., 2024; Weaver, 2023). The other explanation is the *prion* theory. Because Alzheimer's disease resembles *Creutzfeldt-Jakob disease*, another type of neurocognitive disorder that is known to be caused by misshapen proteins called *prions*, some researchers propose that prions may also help cause Alzheimer's disease (Huang, 2023). Although prion activity has indeed been detected in the brains of people with Alzheimer's disease, it is not clear that these misshapen proteins play a causal role in the disease (Joshi & Ahuja, 2023).

Assessing and Predicting Alzheimer's Disease As you read earlier, cases of Alzheimer's disease can be diagnosed with absolute certainty only after death, when an autopsy is performed. However, by using a battery of assessment tools—including neuropsychological tests (tests that measure a person's cognitive, perceptual, and motor performances on certain tasks), brain scans, blood tests and other laboratory work, and careful history-taking—diagnosticians are usually able to build a strong circumstantial case and arrive at an accurate diagnosis (Vromen et al., 2023; Kumar et al., 2022).

When diagnosticians administer brain scans, laboratory tests, and other biological tests, they are looking for **biomarkers**—biochemical, molecular, genetic, or structural characteristics that usually accompany Alzheimer's disease (Huang, 2023). There are many such biomarkers, but one that is always important, not surprisingly, is the indication of a large number of beta-amyloid proteins and tau proteins, the building blocks for plaques and tangles (Gao et al., 2024).

It turns out that many of these biomarkers appear in the brain years before the obvious onset of Alzheimer's disease. Thus, many researchers have tried to determine whether certain combinations of biomarkers might be able to *predict* cases of

biomarkers Biochemical, molecular, genetic, or structural characteristics that usually accompany a disease.

Alzheimer's disease and other neurocognitive disorders—perhaps even years before the onset of symptoms (Gao et al., 2024; Mosconi et al., 2018, 2014, 2010, 2008). One pioneering study, for example, used brain scans and other biological tests to measure a combination of biomarkers in dozens of older adult research participants—all of them seemingly healthy—and then followed the cognitive functioning of the individuals for up to 24 years. Eventually, 43 percent of the study's participants developed Alzheimer's disease. The researchers found that those who developed the disease had displayed more biomarker irregularities on their initial brain tests than the participants who remained healthy. Overall, the biomarker tests, administered years before the onset of symptoms, predicted *mild* neurocognitive impairment with an accuracy rate of 71 percent and *major* neurocognitive impairment with an accuracy rate of 83 percent.

Would people be better off knowing that they will eventually develop a disease that has no known cure?

As you will learn shortly, the most effective interventions for Alzheimer's disease and other neurocognitive disorders are those that help *prevent* these problems, or at least ones that are applied early. Clearly, then, it is essential to have tools that identify the disorders as early as possible, preferably years before the onset of symptoms.

Other Types of Neurocognitive Disorders

There are a number of neurocognitive disorders in addition to Alzheimer's disease (Morrow, 2024; Huang, 2023; Uwagbai & Kalish, 2023) (see **Trending**). *Vascular neurocognitive disorder,* for example, follows a cerebrovascular accident, or *stroke,* during which blood flow to specific areas of the brain was cut off, thus damaging the areas. *Frontotemporal neurocognitive disorder,* also known as *Pick's disease,* is a rare disorder that affects the frontal and temporal lobes. *Neurocognitive disorder due to prion disease,* also called *Creutzfeldt-Jakob disease,* has symptoms that include spasms of the body. As you read earlier, this disorder is caused by misshapen proteins called prions. *Neurocognitive disorder due to Huntington's disease* is an inherited disease in which memory problems—along with personality changes, mood difficulties, and severe twitching and spasms—worsen over time. *Parkinson's disease,* the slowly progressive neurological disorder marked by tremors, rigidity, and unsteadiness, can result in *neurocognitive disorder due to Parkinson's disease,* particularly in older people or those whose cases are advanced. In recent years, it has become clear that many people who used to receive this diagnosis were, in fact, experiencing a different disorder, *neurocognitive*

"My toughest fight" Boxing great Muhammad Ali described his decades-long struggle with Parkinson's disease as "my toughest fight." In that spirit, 75-year-old Nancy Van Der Stracten trains regularly at a boxing gym in Turkey, seeking to slow down her Parkinson's disease. Although far from a cure, specialists believe that various exercises—especially ones that facilitate balance, coordination, and strengthening—may help slow the progression of the disease.

...TRENDING

Damaging the Brain: Football and CTE

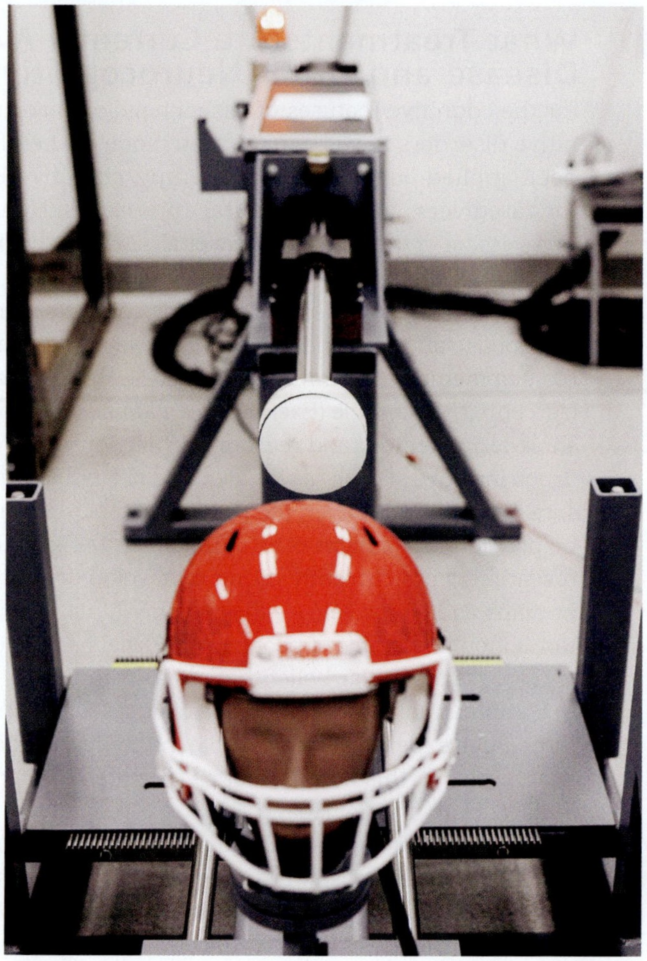

Anastasiia Sapon/The New York Times/Redux

An engineering approach Engineering scientists are trying to prevent CTE and other brain injuries by developing safer and more protective football helmets. Here a dummy head wearing a helmet shock absorber is prepped for trauma simulation at a Stanford University lab.

Tens of millions of people in the United States build their Sunday schedules around professional football. They watch their favorite National Football League (NFL) teams go "head-to-head" in what has arguably become America's favorite viewer pastime. For years, it was generally believed that the obvious dangers of this sport were outweighed by the enjoyment it brought to so many and the riches it offered the players. But that thinking has changed dramatically over the past few decades. The reason? The discovery that many NFL players experience *chronic traumatic encephalopathy (CTE),* a degenerative brain disease, largely as a result of the repeated head blows they receive over the course of their years in the game (Munakomi & Puckett, 2023).

Research has clarified that, like various other neurocognitive disorders, CTE features excessive formations of *tangles*—produced by the *tau protein*—in neurons throughout the brain (Huang, 2023; Ruchika et al., 2023). These tangles, along with related irregularities in brain structures such as the hippocampus, thalamus, substantia nigra, and amygdala, produce a range of neurocognitive symptoms that unfold over a period of years—disorientation, memory loss, erratic behavior, personality changes, progressive cognitive decline, Parkinsonian symptoms, suicidal thinking, and death (Huang, 2023; Ruchika et al., 2023).

CTE and its lethal impact were not identified until 2005, when neuropathologist Bennet Omalu was conducting an autopsy on former NFL player Mike Webster and discovered indications of this "new" disease in Webster's brain. Webster had displayed severe cognitive, behavioral, and emotional deterioration prior to his death, but his symptoms had been a medical mystery. Since Omalu's breakthrough discovery, CTE has been identified in the autopsied brains of many former football, hockey, soccer, and rugby players, as well as boxers, wrestlers, martial artists, and military personnel (Hageman, Hageman, & Nihorn, 2024; Ayubcha et al., 2021).

The recognition of CTE and its impact unfolded slowly for several reasons (Hageman et al., 2024; Ruchika et al., 2023). First, it can result not only from one obvious episode of major brain trauma but also from a series of relatively mild concussions and mild blows to the head. Second, brain scans of living persons cannot easily detect the disease in progress because mild concussions do not result in bleeding or obvious brain structure damage. Like Alzheimer's disease, a definitive diagnosis of CTE can be made only when the brain is examined after death (Ayubcha et al., 2021; Grashow et al., 2020). However, what *is* clear, while individuals with CTE are still alive, is that something profoundly wrong is happening to them.

Now that CTE is "on the map," research into this problem is on the rise, and, just as important, a growing number of precautions and actions are being taken—by individuals and officials alike (Abdalazem, 2022; McCambridge & Stinson, 2020). For example, the NFL has changed its "return-to-play" procedures, making sure that players fully recover from all symptoms of even mild concussions before they resume playing. The league has also reduced the number of "contact" practice sessions a team may conduct. Moreover, the NFL has created a multi-million-dollar CTE compensation fund from which former players and their families can collect as their symptoms unfold and/or after their deaths.

In the meantime, CTE reminds us all too well that neurocognitive disorders are not only the result of genetic and/or lifestyle factors. They can also be brought about by head injuries—even seemingly mild ones—or, for that matter, by drugs, brain surgery, or factors yet to be determined.

disorder with Lewy bodies, which is characterized by the buildup of clumps of protein deposits, called Lewy bodies, within many neurons. Finally, yet other neurocognitive disorders may be caused by *HIV infections, traumatic brain injury, substance abuse,* or various *medical conditions* such as meningitis or advanced syphilis.

of NOTE ...

Costly Disease

In the United States, the total annual cost for Alzheimer's disease and other neurocognitive disorders is $345 billion (Alzheimer's Association, 2023).

What Treatments Are Currently Available for Alzheimer's Disease and Other Neurocognitive Disorders?

Treatments for the cognitive features of Alzheimer's disease and most other types of neurocognitive disorders have been, at best, modestly helpful. A number of approaches have been applied, including drug therapy, cognitive-behavioral interventions, support for caregivers, and sociocultural approaches. None of these interventions stops the progression of the disorder (Chu et al., 2024; Alzheimer's Association, 2023).

DRUG TREATMENT Most of the drugs currently prescribed for Alzheimer's patients are designed to affect acetylcholine and glutamate, the neurotransmitters that play important roles in memory (Karimi Tari et al., 2024; Wu et al., 2023). The drugs include *donepezil* (Aricept), *rivastigmine* (Exelon), *galantamine* (Reminyl), and *memantine* (Namenda). The short-term memory and reasoning ability of some Alzheimer's patients who take these drugs improve slightly, as do their use of language and their ability to cope under pressure. Generally, however, the benefits of the drugs are limited, and their side effects can be problematic (Gharat et al., 2024; Huang, 2023). Given the limitations of such drugs, researchers are currently trying to develop drugs that work directly on beta-amyloid proteins and tau proteins—the proteins at play in the formation of plaques and tangles throughout the brains of people with Alzheimer's disease (Zhang et al., 2023)

There is a popular belief that another approach—taking vitamin E, either alone or in combination with one of these drugs—will help slow down some of the cognitive difficulties experienced by people in the mild stage of Alzheimer's disease; however, as it turns out, this notion is, at best, modestly supported by various studies (Charbit, Vidal, & Hanon, 2024; Huang, 2023).

The drugs just discussed are prescribed *after* a person has developed Alzheimer's disease. In contrast, some studies have suggested that several substances now available on the marketplace for other kinds of problems might help prevent or delay the onset of Alzheimer's disease. For example, certain studies have found that cisgender women who took the hormone *estrogen* for years after menopause seemed to reduce

Lloyd Fox/Baltimore Sun/Tribune News Service via Getty Images

Singing out Norma Griner, a woman with advanced Alzheimer's disease, sings out in perfect pitch in one of many videos posted by her son and enjoyed by people around the world. Given her musical background, Griner's son encouraged her to sing in locations extending from her kitchen table to Lake Roland Park, Maryland, an activity rooted in the principle that music memory tends to continue for people with neurocognitive disorders even as their other memories may fade. Griner died at age 91 in 2022.

their risk of developing Alzheimer's disease; on balance, however, research has not provided consistent evidence that estrogen therapy helps to prevent or treat the disease (Press & Buss, 2021). Similarly, certain studies have suggested that the long-term use of *nonsteroidal anti-inflammatory drugs* such as *ibuprofen* and *naprosyn* (drugs found in Advil, Motrin, Nuprin, and other pain relievers) might help reduce the risk of Alzheimer's disease (Chu et al., 2024); once again, however, research overall has not found consistent evidence that these drugs effectively prevent or treat the disease (Nayak et al., 2024).

Jonathan Goldberg/Alamy

Fitness of all kinds Clinicians stress the value of *cognitive fitness* to help prevent or slow down cognitive decline in old age. At the same time, *physical exercise* may be even more effective at slowing down cognitive decline—thus the emergence of numerous physical fitness programs for older adults.

COGNITIVE-BEHAVIORAL TECHNIQUES Cognitive-behavioral treatments have been used in cases of Alzheimer's disease with some degree of success (Luo et al., 2023; Comer et al., 2022). In Japan, for example, a number of people with the disease meet regularly in classes, performing simple calculations and reading essays and novels aloud (Okazaki, 2020). Similarly, research suggests that cognitive activities, including computer-based cognitive stimulation programs, sometimes help prevent or delay the onset of Alzheimer's disease (Bai et al., 2024; Alzheimer's Association, 2023). Indeed, some studies suggest that the regular pursuit of leisure activities that are cognitively simulating—writing letters, following the news, reading, playing musical instruments, and attending concerts or plays—seems to decrease the risk of developing the disease (Czaja, 2024; Kumar et al., 2022).

Interestingly, strategies that focus primarily on behaviors rather than on cognitions seem to be even more useful in preventing and managing this disease. It has become clear across many studies that physical exercise helps improve cognitive functioning—for people of all ages and states of health (Echeverria & Stein, 2024; Morey, 2022). There is also evidence that regular physical exercise may specifically help reduce the risk of developing Alzheimer's disease and other neurocognitive disorders (Zhang et al., 2024; Alzheimer's Association, 2023, 2020). Thus, physical exercise is often a part of treatment programs for people with the disorders.

Behavior-focused interventions of a different kind have been used to help improve specific symptoms displayed by Alzheimer's patients. The approaches typically focus on changing everyday patient behaviors that are stressful for the family, such as wandering at night, loss of bladder control, demands for attention, and inadequate personal care (Alzheimer's Association, 2023; Press & Buss, 2021). The therapists use a combination of role-playing exercises, modeling, and practice to teach family members how and when to use reinforcement in order to shape more positive behaviors.

of NOTE ...

Busy Body, Busy Mind, Healthier Brain

Researchers have found fewer plaques and tangles in the brains of lab mice that live in intellectually and physically stimulating environments—with chew toys, running wheels, and tunnels—than in those of mice that live in less stimulating settings (Azevedo et al., 2023; Rashid et al., 2020; Lazarov et al., 2005).

SUPPORT FOR CAREGIVERS Caregiving can take a heavy toll on the close relatives of people with Alzheimer's disease and other neurocognitive disorders (Levenson et al., 2024; Kaplan, 2023). To say the least, it is hard to take care of someone who is becoming increasingly lost, helpless, and medically ill (Bai et al., 2024). And it is very painful to witness mental and physical decline in someone you love. More than 80 percent of all people with Alzheimer's disease are cared for by their relatives, usually their adult children or spouses (Alzheimer's Association, 2023, 2020). One of the most frequent reasons for the institutionalization of people with Alzheimer's disease is that overwhelmed caregivers can no longer cope with the difficulties of keeping them at home.

Many Alzheimer's caregivers experience anger and depression, and their own physical and mental health often declines (Levenson et al., 2024; Wiegelmann et al., 2021). Clinicians now recognize that one of the most important aspects of treating Alzheimer's disease and other types of neurocognitive disorders is to focus on the emotional needs of the caregivers, including their needs for regular time out, education about the disease, and psychotherapy (Thodis et al., 2023). Some clinicians also provide caregiver support groups (Huang, 2023).

Karsten Moran for The Washington Post via Getty Images

Toll on caregivers A woman comforts her mother, who has advanced Alzheimer's disease, while they sit together on a couch. The psychological and physical burdens of caring for close relatives with neurocognitive disorders typically take a heavy toll on caregivers.

SOCIOCULTURAL APPROACHES Sociocultural approaches play an important role in treatment (Alzheimer's Association, 2023, 2020). A number of *day-care facilities* for patients with neurocognitive disorders have been developed, providing treatment programs and activities for outpatients during the day and returning them to their homes and families at night. There are also many *assisted-living facilities* in which those with neurocognitive impairments live in cheerful apartments, receive needed supervision, and take part in stimulating activities. These apartments are typically designed to meet the special needs of the residents—providing more light, for example, or enclosing gardens with circular paths so the residents can go for strolls alone without getting lost. Studies suggest that such facilities bring some degree of improvement to the cognitive deficits of residents and enhance their enjoyment of life. In addition, a growing number of practical devices, such as tracking beacons worn on the wrists of Alzheimer's patients and shoes that contain a GPS tracker, have been developed to help locate patients who may wander off (Levenson et al., 2024; Huang, 2023).

Given the progress now unfolding in the understanding and treatment of Alzheimer's disease and other neurocognitive disorders, researchers are looking forward to life-changing advances in the coming years. The brain changes responsible for these disorders are complex, but most investigators believe that exciting breakthroughs are just over the horizon (Delrieu, Andrieu, & Vellas, 2024).

of NOTE ...

Long-Term Care

Around 49 percent of the long-term residents in nursing homes have a neurocognitive disorder (Alzheimer's Association, 2023). Approximately 34 percent of people living in residential care facilities (housing that provides assistance for everyday living activities) have a neurocognitive disorder.

SUMMING UP

Disorders of Cognition

Older adults are more likely than people of other age groups to experience delirium, a fast-developing disturbance marked by great difficulty focusing attention, staying oriented, concentrating, and following an orderly sequence of thought.

Neurocognitive disorders, characterized by a significant decline in cognitive function, become increasingly common in older age groups. There are many types of neurocognitive disorders, the most common being Alzheimer's disease. Alzheimer's disease has been linked to an unusually high number of senile plaques and neurofibrillary tangles in the brain. According to a leading explanation of late-onset Alzheimer's disease, people who inherit ApoE-4, a particular form of the apolipoprotein E (ApoE) gene, are especially vulnerable to the development of Alzheimer's disease. Other causes have also been proposed for this disease.

Researchers are making some significant strides at better assessing Alzheimer's disease and other types of neurocognitive disorders and even at identifying those who will eventually develop these disorders. Drug therapy and cognitive-behavioral therapies have been used to treat Alzheimer's disease, with limited success. Addressing the needs of caregivers is now a key part of treatment. In addition, sociocultural approaches such as day-care facilities are on the rise.

Issues Affecting the Mental Health of Older Adults

AS THE STUDY and treatment of older adults have progressed, three issues have raised concern among clinicians: the special problems faced by older people of color and by older LGBTQ+ people, the inadequacies of long-term care, and the need for a health-maintenance approach to medical care in an aging world.

First, as you have read throughout this textbook, *discrimination based on race and ethnicity, gender, and sexual orientation* has long been a problem in the United States, and many people are affected negatively as a result, particularly older adults. To be both old and a member of a marginalized group is considered a kind of "double jeopardy" by many observers (Miller, 2023). For older women in marginalized groups, the difficulties are sometimes termed "triple jeopardy," as more older women than older men live alone, are widowed, and are economically disadvantaged. Clinicians must take into account their older patients' race, ethnicity, gender, sexual orientation, and economic situation as they try to diagnose and treat their mental health problems (Hash & Hicks Patrick, 2024) (see **Figure 15-3**).

On average, proper medical and mental health care tends to be less adequate and less accessible for older adults in marginalized groups, just as it is for younger individuals in those groups, a state of affairs tied to economic factors and discrimination, among other variables (CMA, 2023; KFF, 2023; Miller, 2023) In addition, some older adults in marginalized groups face language barriers that interfere with their medical

FIGURE 15-3

Race, Ethnicity, and Older Adults

The population of older adults in the United States is becoming racially and ethnically more diverse. Currently, around 76 percent of all older adults are non-Hispanic White people. By 2060, non-Hispanic White people will comprise 55 percent of all older adults. (Information from: KFF, 2023; PRB, 2023; Mather, Scommegna, & Kilduff, 2019; Frey, 2018; Mather, 2016)

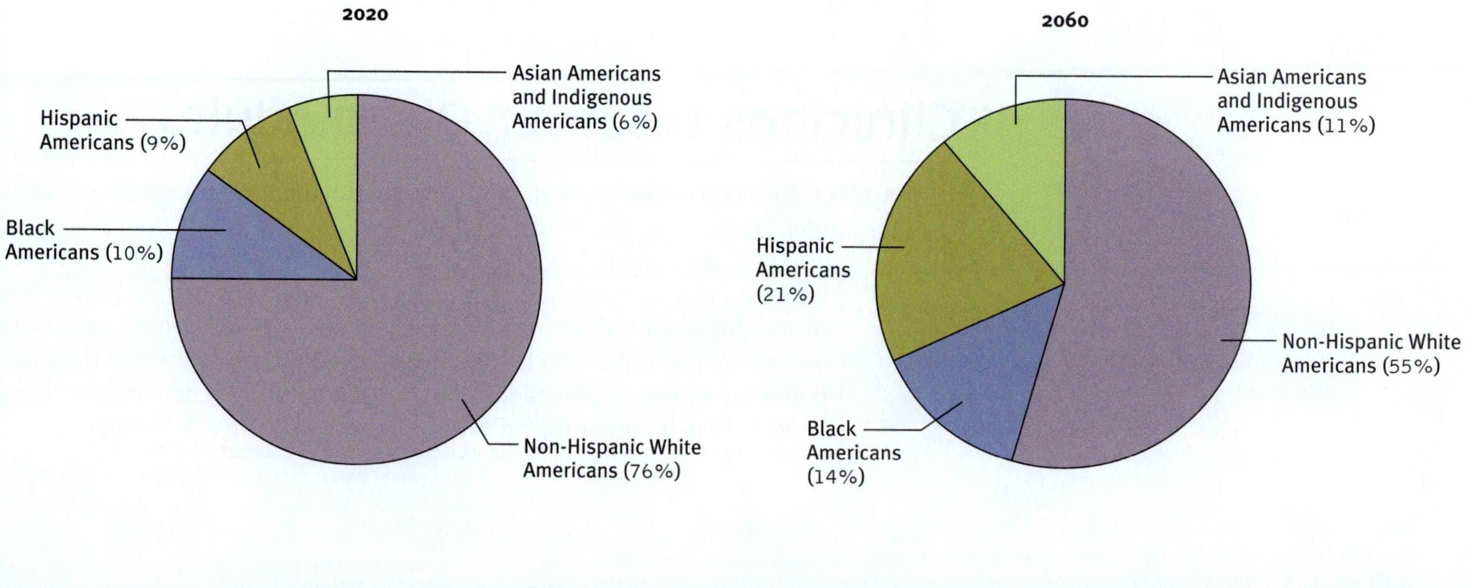

of NOTE ...

Unaffordable

Around 21 percent of older adults say they do not take medications as prescribed because of the cost (Bunis, 2022; Kirzinger et al., 2019). The rate of Black Americans and Hispanic Americans unable to afford prescription medications is 1.5 to 2 times higher than that of non-Hispanic White Americans (ASPE, 2022).

and mental health care, others may hold cultural beliefs that prevent them from seeking services, and some do not know about medical and mental health services that are sensitive to their particular needs (Hash & Hicks Patrick, 2024; Thodis et al., 2023). As a result, it is common for many older people in marginalized communities to rely largely on family members or friends for remedies and health care.

Second, many older people require *long-term care,* a general term that may refer variously to the services offered outside the family in a partially supervised apartment, a senior housing complex for older adults with mild impairment, or a nursing home where skilled medical and nursing care is available around the clock. The quality of care in such residences varies widely (Mitchell et al., 2024).

At any given time in the United States, only about 4 percent of all older adults actually live in nursing homes (1.5 million people), but at least 15 percent of people 85 years and older do eventually wind up living in such facilities (McCain, 2023; HA, 2023, 2020). Thus, many older adults live in fear of being "put away." They fear having to move, losing independence, and living in a medical environment. Many also worry about the cost of long-term care facilities. Around-the-clock nursing care is expensive, and nursing home costs continue to rise. The average cost for a nursing home room in the United States is $100,000 per year (Alzheimer's Association, 2023). Most health insurance plans available today do not adequately cover the costs of long-term or permanent placement.

Finally, clinical scientists suggest that the current generation of young adults should take a *health-maintenance,* or *wellness promotion, approach* to their own aging process (Echeverria & Stein, 2024; Heflin, 2023). In other words, they should do things that promote physical and mental health—avoid smoking, eat well-balanced and healthful meals, exercise regularly, engage in positive social relationships, and take advantage of psychoeducational, stress management, and other mental health programs (Charbit et al., 2024; Zhang et al., 2024). There is a growing belief that older adults will adapt more readily to changes and negative events if their physical and psychological health is good (Czaja, 2024; Xu et al., 2024).

SUMMING UP

Issues Affecting Older Adults

In studying and treating the problems of old age, clinicians have become concerned about three issues: the problems of older adults in marginalized groups, inadequacies of long-term care, and the need for health maintenance by young adults.

Clinicians Discover Older Adults

JUST A HALF-CENTURY ago, mental health professionals focused relatively little on older adults. But like the problems of children, those of aging people have now caught the attention of researchers and clinicians. Current work is changing how we understand and treat the psychological problems of people in this age group. No longer do clinicians simply accept depression or anxiety in old age as inevitable. No longer do they overlook the dangers of prescription drug misuse by older adults. And no longer do they underestimate the dangers of delirium or the prevalence of neurocognitive disorders.

Why do you think relatively little mental health research was conducted on older adults until recent years?

Kyodo via AP Images

Timeless beats Clinicians recommend that people young and old pursue activities that promote their mental health. For 88-year-old Sumiko Iwamuro, one such activity is to work as a DJ each night at clubs in the heart of Tokyo's Red Light district. A restaurant owner by day, Iwamuro first developed her passion for spinning the turntables at a music school for DJs that she enrolled in after her husband died 15 years ago.

As older people live longer and their number grows ever larger, their needs are becoming more visible. Particularly urgent is neurocognitive impairment and its devastating impact. The complexity of the brain makes neurocognitive disorders difficult to understand, diagnose, and treat. However, researchers are now making important discoveries on a regular basis. To date, this research has focused largely on the biological aspects of the disorders, but the disorders have such a powerful impact on patients and their families that psychological and sociocultural investigations are also now growing by leaps and bounds.

Quick Quiz

1. What is geropsychology? What kinds of special pressures and upsets are faced by older adults? pp. 516–518
2. How common is depression among older adults? What are the possible causes of this disorder in this age group, and how is it treated? pp. 518–520
3. How prevalent are anxiety disorders among older adults? How do theorists explain the onset of these disorders in this age group, and how do clinicians treat them? pp. 521–522
4. Describe and explain the kinds of substance misuse patterns that sometimes emerge among older adults. pp. 522–524
5. What kinds of psychotic disorders may be experienced by older adults? pp. 524–525
6. What is delirium? pp. 525–527
7. How common are neurocognitive disorders among older adults? Describe the clinical features and course of Alzheimer's disease. pp. 527–530
8. What are the possible causes of Alzheimer's disease? pp. 530–533
9. Can Alzheimer's disease be predicted? What kinds of interventions are applied in cases of this and other neurocognitive disorders? pp. 533–534, 536–538
10. What issues regarding aging have raised particular concern among clinicians? pp. 539–540

Law, Society, and the Mental Health Profession

CHAPTER 16

TOPIC OVERVIEW

Dear Jodie:

There is a definite possibility that I will be killed in my attempt to get Reagan. It is for this very reason that I am writing you this letter now. As you well know by now, I love you very much. The past seven months I have left you dozens of poems, letters and messages in the faint hope you would develop an interest in me. . . . Jodie, I would abandon this idea of getting Reagan in a second if I could only win your heart and live out the rest of my life with you, whether it be in total obscurity or whatever. I will admit to you that the reason I'm going ahead with this attempt now is because I just cannot wait any longer to impress you. I've got to do something now to make you understand in no uncertain terms that I am doing all of this for your sake. By sacrificing my freedom and possibly my life I hope to change your mind about me. This letter is being written an hour before I leave for the Hilton Hotel. Jodie, I'm asking you please to look into your heart and at least give me the chance with this historical deed to gain your respect and love. I love you forever.

John Hinckley

John W. Hinckley Jr. wrote this letter to actress Jodie Foster in March 1981. Soon after writing it, he stood waiting, pistol ready, outside the Washington Hilton Hotel. Moments later, President Ronald Reagan came out of the hotel, and the popping of pistol fire was heard. As his Secret Service detail pushed Reagan into the limousine, a police officer, the president's press secretary, and a Secret Service agent fell to the pavement. The president had been shot, and by nightfall, most of America had seen the face and heard the name of the disturbed young man from Colorado.

As you have read throughout this book, the psychological dysfunction of an individual does not occur in isolation. It is influenced—sometimes caused—by societal and social factors, and it affects the lives of relatives, friends, and acquaintances. The case of John Hinckley demonstrates in powerful terms that individual psychopathology may, in some cases, also affect the well-being and rights of people the person does not know.

By the same token, clinical scientists and practitioners do not conduct their work in isolation. As they study and treat people with psychological difficulties, they affect and are affected by other institutions of society. We have observed, for example, how the government regulates the use of psychotropic medications, how clinicians helped carry out the government's policy of deinstitutionalization, and how clinicians have called the psychological ordeals of Vietnam, Iraq, and Afghanistan combat veterans to the attention of society.

In short, like their clients, clinical professionals operate within a complex social system—for clinicians, it is the system that defines and often regulates their professional responsibilities. Just as we must understand the social context in which psychopathology occurs in order to understand the behavior, so must we understand the context in which this behavior is studied and treated. This chapter focuses on the relationship between the mental health field and three major forces in society—the *legislative/judicial system*, the *business/economic* arena, and the world of *technology*. ■

Law and Mental Health

TWO SOCIAL INSTITUTIONS have a particularly strong impact on the mental health profession: the legislative and judicial systems. These institutions—collectively, the *legal field*—have long been responsible for protecting both the public good and the rights of individuals. Sometimes the relationship between the legal field and the mental health field has been friendly, and those in the two fields have worked together to protect the rights and meet the needs of troubled people and of society at large. At other times they have clashed, and one field has imposed its will on the other.

This relationship has two distinct aspects. On the one hand, mental health professionals often play a role in the criminal justice system, as when they are called upon to help the courts assess the mental stability of people accused of crimes. They responded to this call in the Hinckley case, as you will read, and in thousands of other cases. This aspect of the relationship is sometimes termed *psychology in law;* that is, clinical practitioners and researchers operate within the legal system. On the other hand, there is another aspect to the relationship, called *law in psychology.* The legislative and judicial systems act upon the clinical field, regulating certain aspects of mental health care. The courts may, for example, force some people to enter treatment, even against their will. In addition, the law protects the rights of patients.

of NOTE ...

Their Words

"I think John Hinckley will be a threat the rest of his life. He is a time bomb."

U.S. Attorney, 1982

"Without doubt, [John Hinckley] is the least dangerous person on the planet."

Attorney for John Hinckley, 2003

The intersections between the mental health field and the legal and judicial systems are collectively referred to as **forensic psychology** (FP, 2024; Bouchrika, 2023). Forensic psychologists or psychiatrists (or related mental health professionals) may perform such varied activities as testifying in trials, researching the reliability of eyewitness testimony, or helping police profile the personality of a serial killer on the loose.

How Do Clinicians Influence the Criminal Justice System?

To arrive at just and appropriate punishments, the courts need to know whether defendants are *responsible* for the crimes of which they are accused and *capable* of defending themselves in court. If not, it would be inappropriate to find defendants guilty or punish them in the usual manner. The courts have decided that in some instances, people who experience severe mental disturbances may not be responsible for their actions or may not be able to defend themselves in court and so should not be punished in the usual way. Although the courts make the final judgment as to mental instability, their decisions are guided to a large degree by the opinions of mental health professionals (Peay, 2023).

When people accused of crimes are judged to be impaired by a severe mental disturbance, they usually are sent to a mental institution for treatment, a process called **criminal commitment.** Actually, there are several forms of criminal commitment. In one, people are judged mentally unstable *at the time of their crimes* and so innocent of wrongdoing. They may plead **not guilty by reason of insanity** and bring mental health professionals into court to support their claim. When people are found not guilty on this basis, they are committed for treatment until they improve enough to be released.

forensic psychology The branch of psychology concerned with intersections between psychological practice and research and the judicial system.

criminal commitment A legal process by which people accused of a crime are instead judged mentally unstable and sent to a treatment facility.

not guilty by reason of insanity A verdict stating that defendants are not guilty of a crime because they were insane at the time of the crime.

In a second form of criminal commitment, people are judged mentally unstable *at the time of their trial* and so are considered unable to understand the trial procedures and to defend themselves in court. They are committed for treatment until they are competent to stand trial. Once again, the testimony of mental health professionals helps determine the defendant's psychological functioning.

These judgments of mental instability have stirred many arguments. Some people consider the judgments to be loopholes in the legal system that allow criminals to escape proper punishment for wrongdoing. Others argue that a legal system simply cannot be just unless it allows for extenuating circumstances, such as impairment by a severe mental disturbance. The practice of criminal commitment differs from country to country. In this chapter, you will read primarily about how it operates in the United States. Although the specific principles and procedures of each country may differ, most countries grapple with the same issues, concerns, and decisions that you will read about here.

AP Photo

Would-be assassin Few courtroom decisions have spurred as much debate or legislative action as the jury's verdict that John Hinckley, captured in the act of shooting President Ronald Reagan, was not guilty by reason of insanity.

Criminal Commitment and Insanity During Commission of a Crime

Consider once again the case of John Hinckley. Was he insane at the time he shot the president? If insane, should he be held responsible for his actions? On June 21, 1982, 15 months after he shot four men in the nation's capital, a jury pronounced Hinckley not guilty by reason of insanity. Hinckley thus joined Richard Lawrence, a house painter who shot at Andrew Jackson in 1835, and John Schrank, a saloonkeeper who shot former president Teddy Roosevelt in 1912, as a would-be assassin who was found not guilty by reason of insanity.

It is important to recognize that "insanity" is a *legal* term (Parmigiani et al., 2023). That is, the definition of "insanity" used in criminal cases was written by legislators, not by clinicians. Defendants may have mental disorders but not necessarily qualify for a legal definition of "insanity." Modern Western definitions of "insanity" can be traced to the murder case of Daniel M'Naghten in England in 1843 (Collins, Hinkebein, & Schorgl, 2023; Kaplan, 2023). M'Naghten shot and killed Edward Drummond, the secretary to British Prime Minister Robert Peel, while trying to shoot Peel. Because of M'Naghten's apparent delusions of persecution, the jury found him to be not guilty by reason of insanity. The public was outraged by this decision, and their angry outcry forced the British lords to define the insanity defense more clearly. This legal definition, known as the **M'Naghten test,** or **M'Naghten rule,** stated that having a mental disorder at the time of a crime does not by itself mean that the person was insane; the defendant also had to be *unaware of the nature of their act* or *unable to know right from wrong*. The state and federal courts in the United States adopted this test as well.

In the late nineteenth century, some state and federal courts in the United States, dissatisfied with the M'Naghten rule, adopted a different test—the **irresistible impulse test.** This test, which had first been used in Ohio in 1834, emphasized the inability to control one's actions. A person who committed a crime during an uncontrollable "fit of passion" was considered insane and not guilty under this test.

For years, state and federal courts chose between the M'Naghten test and the irresistible impulse test to determine the sanity of criminal defendants. For a while, a third test, called the **Durham test,** also became popular, but it was soon replaced in most courts. This test, based on a decision handed down by the U.S. Supreme Court in 1954 in the case of *Durham v. United States,* stated simply that people are not criminally responsible if their "unlawful act was the product of mental disease or mental defect." This test was meant to offer more flexibility in court decisions, but it proved too flexible. Insanity defenses could point to such problems as alcohol abuse or other forms of substance abuse and conceivably even headaches or ulcers, which were listed as psychophysiological disorders in DSM-I (Callaghan, 2023; Appelbaum, 2022).

In 1955, the American Law Institute formulated a test that combined aspects of the M'Naghten, irresistible impulse, and Durham tests. The **American Law Institute (ALI) test** held that people are not criminally responsible if, at the time of a crime, they had a mental disorder or defect that prevented them from knowing right from wrong *or* from being able to control themselves and to follow the law. For a time, the new test became the most widely accepted legal test of insanity. After the Hinckley verdict, however, there was a public uproar over the wide-ranging ALI guidelines, and people called for tougher standards.

M'Naghten test A legal test that holds people to be insane at the time of a crime if, because of a mental disorder, they did not know the nature of their act or did not know right from wrong. Also called the *M'Naghten rule*.

irresistible impulse test A legal test that holds people to be insane at the time of a crime if they were driven by an uncontrollable "fit of passion."

Durham test A legal test that holds people to be insane at the time of a crime if their act was the result of a mental disorder.

American Law Institute (ALI) test A legal test for insanity that holds people to be insane at the time of a crime if, because of a mental disorder, they did not know right from wrong or could not resist an uncontrollable impulse to act.

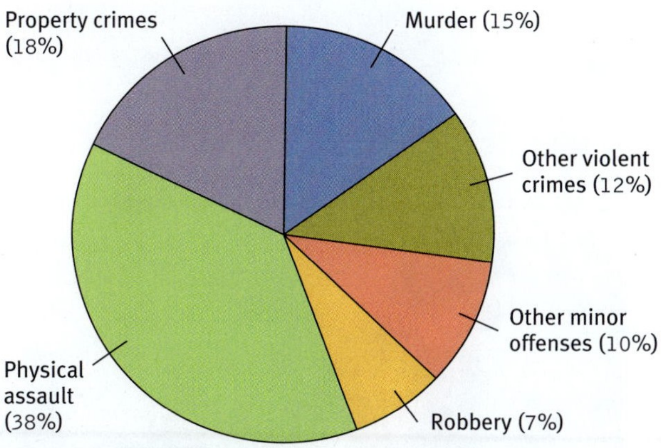

FIGURE 16-1

Crimes for Which People Are Found Not Guilty by Reason of Insanity

Reviews of not guilty by reason of insanity verdicts show that most people who are acquitted on this basis had been charged with a violent crime. (Information from: LLALLI, 2023; Perlin, 2021; Melton et al., 2020, 2017; Steadman et al., 1993; Callahan et al., 1991.)

Partly in response to this uproar, the American Psychiatric Association recommended in 1983 that people should be found not guilty by reason of insanity *only* if they did not know right from wrong at the time of the crime; an inability to control themselves and to follow the law should no longer be sufficient grounds for a judgment of insanity. In short, the association was calling for a return to the M'Naghten test. This test is now used in all cases tried in federal courts and in about half of the state courts. The broader ALI standard is still used in the remaining state courts, except in Idaho, Kansas, Montana, and Utah, which have more or less done away with the insanity plea altogether (Collins et al., 2023; Justia, 2023).

People experiencing severe mental disorders in which confusion is a major feature may not be able to tell right from wrong or to control their behavior. It is therefore not surprising that the majority of defendants who are acquitted of a crime by reason of insanity qualify for a diagnosis of schizophrenia or another form of psychosis (Antar, 2023; LLALLI, 2023). Moreover, most of these acquitted defendants have a history of past hospitalization, arrest, or both. The crimes for which defendants are found not guilty by reason of insanity vary greatly, although most are violent crimes of some sort. Around 15 to 30 percent of those acquitted are accused specifically of murder (LLALLI, 2023) (see **Figure 16-1**).

WHAT CONCERNS ARE RAISED BY THE INSANITY DEFENSE? Despite the changes in the insanity criteria, criticism of the insanity defense continues. One concern is the fundamental difference between the law and the science of human behavior. The law assumes that individuals have free will and are generally responsible for their actions. Several models of human behavior, in contrast, assume that physical or psychological forces act to determine the individual's behavior. Inevitably, then, legal definitions of *insanity* and *responsibility* will differ from those suggested by clinical research.

A second criticism points to the uncertainty of scientific knowledge about pathological behavior. During a typical insanity defense trial, the testimony of defense clinicians conflicts with that of clinicians hired by the prosecution, and so the jury must weigh the claims of "experts" who disagree in their assessments. Some people view this lack of professional agreement as evidence that clinical knowledge in some areas may be too incomplete to be allowed to influence important legal decisions. Others counter that the field has made great strides—for example, developing several psychological scales to help clinicians discriminate more consistently between *sane* and *insane* as defined by the M'Naghten standard (FP, 2024; Parmigiani et al., 2023).

Even with helpful scales in hand, however, clinicians making judgments of legal insanity face a problem that is difficult to overcome: they must evaluate a defendant's state of mind during an event that took place weeks, months, or years earlier. Because mental states can and do change over time and across situations, clinicians can never be entirely certain that their assessments of mental instability at the time of the crime are accurate.

Perhaps the most common criticism of the insanity defense is that it allows people who commit crimes to escape punishment. Granted, some people who successfully plead insanity are released from treatment facilities just months after their acquittal. Yet the number of such cases is quite small (Justia, 2023; Perlin, 2021; Steadman et al., 1993). According to surveys, the public dramatically overestimates the percentage of defendants who plead insanity, guessing it to be 30 to 40 percent, when in fact it is less than 1 percent. Moreover, only a small proportion of these defendants fake or exaggerate their psychological symptoms, and only 25 percent of those who plead insanity are actually found not guilty on this basis. In all, fewer than 1 of every 400 defendants in the United States is found not guilty by reason of insanity (see ***PsychWatch***). It is also worth noting that in as many as 75 percent of those cases in which defendants are acquitted by reason of insanity, the prosecution has agreed to the appropriateness of the plea (MHA, 2024; LLALLI, 2023).

PSYCHWATCH

Famous Insanity Defense Cases

Although the plea of not guilty by reason of insanity is used infrequently, some of the most famous cases in history have featured this defense strategy. You have already learned about the cases of John Hinckley (in this chapter) and Andrea Yates (in the chapter on schizophrenia and related disorders). Here are some other famous insanity defense cases:

emka74/Alamy

Changing pleas The Lennon Wall in Prague, Czech Republic, built shortly after the murder of John Lennon by Mark David Chapman, is filled with Lennon-inspired graffiti and Beatles song lyrics. Chapman eventually changed his initial plea of not guilty by reason of insanity to guilty.

1977 In Michigan, Francine Hughes poured gasoline around the bed where her husband lay in a drunken stupor. Then she lit a match and set him on fire. At her trial, she explained that he had beaten her repeatedly for 14 years and had threatened to kill her if she tried to leave him. The jury found her not guilty by reason of insanity, making her into a symbol for many abused women across the nation.

1978 David "Son of Sam" Berkowitz, a serial killer in New York City, explained that a barking dog had sent him demonic messages to kill. Although two psychiatrists assessed him as psychotic, he was found guilty of his crimes. Long after his trial, he said that he had actually made up the delusions.

1979 Kenneth Bianchi, one of the pair known as the Hillside Strangler, entered a plea of not guilty by reason of insanity but was found guilty, along with his cousin, of sexually assaulting and murdering women in the Los Angeles area in late 1977 and early 1978. He claimed that he had multiple personalities.

1980 In December, Mark David Chapman murdered John Lennon. Chapman later explained that he had killed the rock music legend because he believed Lennon to be a "sellout." He initially pleaded not guilty by reason of insanity, describing hearing the voice of God and comparing himself with Moses. However, he eventually changed his plea to guilty and was given a life sentence for murder.

1992 Jeffrey Dahmer, a 31-year-old mass murderer in Milwaukee, was tried for the killings of 15 young men. Dahmer drugged some of his victims, performed crude lobotomies on them, and dismembered their bodies and stored their parts to be eaten. Despite a plea of not guilty by reason of insanity, the jury found him guilty as charged. He was beaten to death by another inmate in 1995.

1994 On June 23, 1993, 24-year-old Lorena Bobbitt cut off her husband's penis with a 12-inch kitchen knife while he slept. During her trial, defense attorneys argued that after years of abuse by John Bobbitt, his wife experienced a brief psychotic episode and was seized by an "irresistible impulse" to cut off his penis after he raped her. In 1994, the jury found her not guilty by reason of insanity. She was committed to a state mental hospital and released a few months later.

2011 In 2002, Brian David Mitchell abducted a 14-year-old teenager named Elizabeth Smart from her home and held her until she was rescued nine months later. After years of trial delays, Mitchell pleaded not guilty by reason of insanity in 2010, saying that he was acting out delusions ("revelations from God") when he committed this crime. The jury found him guilty of kidnapping in 2011 and sentenced him to life in prison without parole.

2015 In 2012, James Holmes, a 25-year-old neuroscience doctoral student, entered a cinema in Aurora, Colorado, and opened fire on the moviegoers, killing 12 and wounding 20. In the months after his arrest, Holmes, who had no prior criminal record, tried three times to kill himself. Holmes pleaded not guilty by reason of insanity, but a jury found him guilty of murder in 2015 and sentenced him to life in prison without parole.

2017 In 2014, two 12-year-old girls stabbed a classmate multiple times, saying they were trying to appease and impress Slender Man, a mythical "boogie man" whom a number of Internet users report seeing and fearing in their everyday lives. In separate 2017 trials, each of the assailants pleaded guilty to attempted intentional homicide, but in each case they were further deemed to have been mentally ill at the time of the attack and were assigned to extended treatment in a mental hospital rather than imprisonment.

AP Photo/Douglas D. Pizac

"Effectively misleading psychopath" In 2002, Brian David Mitchell abducted 14-year-old Elizabeth Smart at knifepoint from her home and held her until she was rescued nine months later. After being declared incompetent to stand trial for seven years, Mitchell was called an "effectively misleading psychopath" by a judge, found guilty of kidnapping, and sentenced to life in prison, despite his not guilty by reason of insanity plea.

During most of U.S. history, a successful insanity plea amounted to the equivalent of a long-term prison sentence (Collins et al., 2023; Roth, 2020). In fact, on average, treatment in a mental hospital resulted in confinement that was twice as long as imprisonment for the same crime would have been. Because hospitalization resulted in little if any improvement, clinicians were reluctant to predict that persons who had been found not guilty by reason of insanity would not repeat their criminal behavior.

Today, however, people acquitted of crimes by reason of insanity are being released from mental hospitals earlier and earlier (Reynolds, 2023). This trend is the result of the increasing effectiveness of drug therapy and other treatments in institutions, the growing reaction against extended institutionalization, and more emphasis on patients' rights (Collins et al., 2023). In 1992, in the case of *Foucha v. Louisiana,* the U.S. Supreme Court clarified that the *only* acceptable basis for determining the release of patients who have been hospitalized through the criminal justice system is whether they are still "insane"; they cannot be kept indefinitely in mental hospitals solely because they are dangerous. Some states are able to maintain control over such people even after their release from hospitals (Reynolds, 2023). Adopting a procedure called "outpatient commitment," the states may insist on community treatment, monitor the patients closely, and rehospitalize them if necessary (MHA, 2024; Wipond, 2023).

WHAT OTHER VERDICTS ARE AVAILABLE? Over the past four decades, at least 20 states have added another verdict option—**guilty but mentally ill.** Defendants who receive this verdict are found to have had a mental illness at the time of their crime, but the illness was not fully related to or responsible for the crime. The option of guilty but mentally ill enables jurors to convict a person they view as dangerous while also suggesting that the individual receive needed treatment. Defendants found to be guilty but mentally ill are given a prison term with the added recommendation that they also undergo treatment if necessary (Callaghan, 2023; Collins et al., 2023).

After initial enthusiasm for this verdict option, legal and clinical theorists have increasingly found it unsatisfactory. According to research, it has not reduced the number of not guilty by reason of insanity verdicts, and it often confuses jurors (MHA, 2024). In addition, as critics point out, appropriate mental health care is supposed to be available to all people in prisons anyway, regardless of the verdict. That is, the verdict of guilty but mentally ill may differ from a guilty verdict in name only.

Some states allow still another kind of defense, *guilty with diminished capacity,* in which a defendant's mental dysfunction is viewed as an extenuating circumstance that the court should take into consideration in determining the precise crime of which the person is guilty (Frierson & Joshi, 2023). The defense lawyer argues that because of mental dysfunction, the defendant could not have *intended* to commit a particular crime. The person can then be found guilty of a lesser crime—of manslaughter (unlawful killing without intent), say, instead of murder in the first degree (planned murder). The famous case of Dan White, who shot and killed Mayor George Moscone and City Supervisor and gay rights icon Harvey Milk of San Francisco in 1978, illustrates the use of this verdict.

Defense attorney Douglas Schmidt argued that a patriotic, civic-minded man like Dan White—high school athlete, decorated war veteran, former fireman, policeman, and city supervisor—could not possibly have committed such an act unless something had snapped inside him. The brutal nature of the two final shots to each man's head only proved that White had lost his wits. White was not fully responsible for his actions because he suffered from "diminished capacity." Although White killed Mayor George Moscone and Supervisor Harvey Milk, he had not planned his actions. On the day of the shootings, White was mentally incapable of planning to kill, or even of wanting to do such a thing.

Well known in forensic psychiatry circles, Martin Blinder, professor of law and psychiatry at the University of California's Hastings Law School in San Francisco, brought a good measure of academic prestige to White's defense. White had been, Blinder explained to the jury, "gorging himself on junk food: Twinkies, Coca-Cola. . . . The more he consumed, the worse he'd feel and he'd respond to his ever-growing depression by consuming ever more junk food." Schmidt later asked Blinder if he could elaborate on this. "Perhaps if it were not for the ingestion of this junk food," Blinder responded, "I would suspect that these homicides would not have taken place." From that moment on, Blinder became known as the author of the Twinkie defense. . . .

Dan White was convicted only of voluntary manslaughter, and was sentenced to seven years, eight months. (He was released on parole January 6, 1984.) Psychiatric testimony convinced the jury that White did not wish to kill George Moscone or Harvey Milk.

The angry crowd that responded to the verdict by marching, shouting, trashing City Hall, and burning police cars was in good part homosexual. Gay supervisor Harvey Milk had worked well for their cause, and his loss was a serious setback for human rights in San Francisco. Yet it was not only members of the gay community who were appalled at the outcome. Most San Franciscans shared their feelings of outrage.

(Coleman, 1984, pp. 65–70)

San Francisco Chronicle

115th Year No. 108 ★★★★• TUESDAY, MAY 22, 1979 777-1111 20 CENTS

It's Voluntary Manslaughter — Maximum Penalty 8 Years

Several Jurors Weep in Court

City Officials Shocked by The Verdict

A Bloody Protest at City Hall

Verdict Angers Gays

Index

Justice served? After his lawyers employed the so-called Twinkie defense, San Francisco politician Dan White was convicted of voluntary manslaughter rather than premeditated murder in the 1978 killings of Mayor George Moscone and Supervisor Harvey Milk. That unpopular verdict led to a significant decrease in the use of "diminished capacity" defenses.

Because of possible miscarriages of justice, many legal experts have argued against the "diminished capacity" defense. A number of states have even eliminated it, including California shortly after the Dan White verdict (MHA, 2024).

WHAT ARE THE STATUTES FOR SEX OFFENSES? Since 1937, when Michigan passed the first "sexual psychopath" law, a number of states have placed people convicted of sex crimes in a special legal category (Mascolo, 2023; Slobogin, Hafemeister, & Mossman, 2020). These states believe that some of those who are repeatedly found guilty of sex crimes have a mental disorder, so the states categorize them as *mentally disordered sex offenders*.

People classified in this way are convicted of a criminal offense and are thus judged to be responsible for their actions. Nevertheless, the individuals are sent to a mental health facility instead of a prison. In part, such laws reflect a belief held by many legislators that people committing such sex crimes are psychologically disturbed. On a practical level, the laws help protect people who commit sex crimes from the physical abuse that they often receive in prison.

Over the past two decades, however, most states have been changing or abolishing their "mentally disordered sex offender" laws, and at this point, only a handful still have them. One reason for this trend is that, according to state laws, a person must be a good candidate for treatment in order to be classified as a "mentally disordered sex offender," a judgment that is difficult for clinicians to make, especially for this population (Moretti et al., 2024).

But perhaps the primary reason that "mentally disordered sex offender" laws have lost favor is that state legislatures and courts are now less concerned than they used to be about the rights and needs of people who commit sex crimes, given the large number of sex crimes taking place across the country, particularly ones in which children are targets (MHA, 2024; Amos, 2023). In fact, in response to public outrage over the high number of sex crimes, more than 20 states and the federal government have instead passed *sexually violent predator* laws (or *sexually dangerous persons* laws). These relatively new laws call for people convicted of certain sex crimes and who have served their sentence in prison to be removed from prison before their release and committed involuntarily to a mental hospital for treatment if a court judges them likely to engage in further "predatory acts of sexual violence" as a result of "mental abnormality" or "personality disorder" (MHA, 2024; Ambroziak et al., 2023). That is, in contrast to

guilty but mentally ill A verdict stating that defendants are guilty of a crime but are also experiencing a mental illness that should be treated during their imprisonment.

mentally incompetent A state of mental instability that leaves defendants unable to understand the legal charges and proceedings they are facing and unable to prepare an adequate defense with their attorney.

the "mentally disordered sex offender" laws, which call for people convicted of sex crimes to receive treatment *instead* of imprisonment, the "sexually violent predator" laws require people convicted of certain sex crimes to receive imprisonment and then, *in addition,* be committed for a period of involuntary treatment. The constitutionality of the "sexually violent predator" laws was upheld by the Supreme Court in the 1997 case of *Kansas v. Hendricks* by a 5-to-4 margin.

Criminal Commitment and Incompetence to Stand Trial

Regardless of their state of mind at the time of a crime, defendants may be judged to be **mentally incompetent** to stand trial. The competence requirement is meant to ensure that defendants understand the charges they are facing and can work with their lawyers to prepare and conduct an adequate defense. This minimum standard of competence was specified by the Supreme Court in the case of *Dusky v. United States* (1960).

The issue of competence is most often raised by the defendant's attorney, although prosecutors, arresting police officers, and even the judge may raise it as well (FP, 2024). When the issue of competence is raised, the judge orders a psychological evaluation, usually on an inpatient basis (see **Table 16-1**). If the court decides that the defendant is incompetent, the individual is typically assigned to a mental health facility until competent to stand trial (Heilbrun et al., 2023).

The exact number of competency evaluations conducted in the United States each year is not known; recent estimates range from 26,000 to 94,000 (FP, 2024; Morris, McNiel, & Binder, 2021). Observers agree that the number keeps increasing. Approximately 20 to 25 percent of defendants who receive a competency evaluation are found to be incompetent to stand trial. Competency decisions appear to be subject to racial bias. According to research, given the same psychological difficulties, people of color are more likely than non-Hispanic White people to be ruled incompetent to stand trial (Knight et al., 2023, 2022; Barer & Hinkle, 2022).

A famous case of incompetence to stand trial is that of Jared Lee Loughner. On January 8, 2011, Loughner went to a political gathering at a shopping center in Tucson, Arizona, and opened fire on 20 persons. Loughner killed 6 people and injured 14, including U.S. Representative Gabrielle Giffords. Giffords, the apparent target of the attack, survived, although she was shot in the head. After Loughner underwent five weeks of psychiatric assessment, a judge ruled that he was incompetent to stand trial. It was not until 18 months later, after extended treatment with antipsychotic drugs, that Loughner was ruled competent to stand trial. In November 2012, he pleaded guilty to murder and was sentenced to life in prison.

of NOTE ...

Their Words

"Our [legal] confusion is eliminated, we believe, if we resort to that quintessential twentieth-century solution to hard problems: We refer the problem to an expert."

Winslade & Ross
The Insanity Plea (1983)

TABLE 16-1

Race and Forensic Psychology

People of Color	Non-Hispanic White People
Psychologically disturbed lawbreakers *more* likely to be sent to prison.	Psychologically disturbed lawbreakers *more* likely to be sent to mental health facilities.
Defendants *more* likely to be judged incompetent to stand trial.	Defendants *less* likely to be judged incompetent to stand trial.
Individuals *more* likely to be ordered into involuntary mental hospital commitment.	Individuals *less* likely to be ordered into involuntary mental hospital commitment.
Individuals *more* likely to be ordered into involuntary outpatient commitment.	Individuals *less* likely to be ordered into involuntary outpatient commitment.

Information from: Schölin et al., 2024; Haroon et al., 2023; Knight et al., 2023, 2022; Barer & Hinkle, 2022; Shea et al., 2022; Winick, 2020; Swartz & Swanson, 2019; Judd & Parker, 2018; Kisely & Xiao, 2017; NCBH, 2015; Zaejian, 2014; Swanson et al., 2009; Pinals et al., 2004.

Dennis Fujimoto/The Garden Island via AP

Competency restoration In a case that attracted worldwide attention, Idaho resident Lori Vallow was accused of killing her two children, ages 7 and 16, in 2020. During her initial court hearings, she was declared incompetent to stand trial, based in part on her doomsday beliefs and her notions that some people have dark souls, are overtaken by zombies, and must be killed. A year later, a judge ruled that Vallow's legal competency had been reestablished during an 11-month period of competency restoration; thus, she went on trial, and in 2023 she was found guilty of murdering her children.

Many more cases of criminal commitment result from decisions of mental incompetence than from verdicts of not guilty by reason of insanity (BHC, 2022; Melton et al., 2020). However, in the United States, the majority of people currently institutionalized for psychological treatment through the criminal justice system are not from either of these two groups. Rather, they are convicted people in prison whose psychological problems have led prison officials to decide they need treatment, either in mental health units within the prison or in mental hospitals (MHA, 2024).

It is possible that an innocent defendant, ruled incompetent to stand trial, could spend years in a mental health facility with no opportunity to disprove the criminal accusations against them (Heilbrun et al., 2023; Winick, 2020). Some defendants have, in fact, served longer "sentences" in mental health facilities awaiting a ruling of competence than they would have served in prison had they been convicted. Such a possibility was reduced when the Supreme Court ruled, in the case of *Jackson v. Indiana* (1972), that an incompetent defendant cannot be indefinitely committed. After a reasonable amount of time, the person should either be found competent and tried, set free, or transferred to a mental health facility under *civil* commitment procedures, procedures you will learn about in the next section.

Until the early 1970s, most states required that mentally incompetent defendants be committed to maximum security institutions for the "criminally insane." Under current law, however, the courts have more flexibility. In fact, when the charges are relatively minor, such defendants are often treated on an outpatient basis, an arrangement frequently called *jail diversion* because the person with mental disturbances is "diverted" from jail to the community for mental health care (NCSC, 2023).

SUMMING UP

III How Do Clinicians Influence the Criminal Justice System?

Mental health professionals may help assess the mental stability of people accused of crimes. If defendants are judged to have been mentally unstable at the time they committed a crime, they may be found not guilty by reason of insanity and placed in a treatment facility rather than a prison. In federal courts and about half the state courts, insanity is judged in accordance with the M'Naghten test, which holds that defendants were insane at the time of a criminal act if they did not know the nature of the act or did not know right from wrong at the time they committed it. Other states use the broader American Law Institute test, which additionally includes defendants who were unable to control their actions at the time of the crime.

Some states have added an alternative verdict option, guilty but mentally ill. Still another verdict option is guilty with diminished capacity. Depending on state laws, it is also the case that people convicted of certain sex crimes may receive treatment under a mentally disordered sex offender law or, more commonly, under the state's sexually violent predator law.

Regardless of their state of mind at the time of the crime, defendants may be found mentally incompetent to stand trial, that is, incapable of fully understanding the charges or legal proceedings that confront them. These defendants are commonly sent to a mental health facility until they are competent to stand trial.

How Do the Legislative and Judicial Systems Influence Mental Health Care?

Just as clinical science and practice have influenced the legal system, so the legal system has had a major impact on clinical practice. First, courts and legislatures have developed the process of **civil commitment,** which allows certain people to be forced into mental health treatment. Although many people who show signs of severe mental disturbance seek treatment voluntarily, a large number are not aware of their problems or are simply not interested in undergoing therapy. For such people, civil commitment procedures may be put into action.

Second, the legal system, on behalf of the state, has taken on the responsibility of protecting patients' rights during treatment. This protection extends not only to patients who have been involuntarily committed but also to those who seek treatment voluntarily, even on an outpatient basis (MHA, 2024).

Dangerous to oneself There are various ways that people may be dangerous to themselves, in need of treatment, and subject to civil commitment. This sequence of photos shows a man being attacked by a lion at the zoo after he crossed a barbed-wire fence to "preach" to two of the animals.

AFP/Getty Images

Civil Commitment

Every year in the United States, large numbers of people with mental disorders are involuntarily committed to treatment (WPR, 2024). Typically, they are committed to *mental institutions*, but at least 47 states also have some form of *outpatient* civil commitment laws that allow patients to be forced into community treatment programs (NCSC, 2023). Canada and Great Britain have similar laws (Dawson, 2023). Civil commitments have long caused controversy and debate (NCSC, 2023). In some ways, the law provides more protection for people suspected of being criminals than for people suspected of being psychotic.

civil commitment A legal process by which a person can be forced to undergo mental health treatment.

WHY COMMIT? Generally our legal system permits involuntary commitment of individuals when they are considered to be *in need of treatment* and *dangerous to themselves or others* (Hare et al., 2024). People may be dangerous to themselves if they are suicidal or if they act recklessly (for example, drinking a drain cleaner to prove that they are immune to its chemicals). They may be dangerous to others if they seek to harm them or if they unintentionally place others at risk. The state's authority to commit people with psychological disturbances rests on its duties to protect the interests of the individual and of society (Zhong, Moreno, & Wasser, 2023).

WHAT ARE THE PROCEDURES FOR CIVIL COMMITMENT? Civil commitment laws vary from state to state (Hare et al., 2024; Zhong et al., 2023). Some basic procedures, however, are common to most of these laws. Often, family members begin commitment proceedings. For example, in response to a person's psychotic behavior and repeated assaults on other people, family members may try to persuade the individual to seek admission to a mental institution. If the person refuses, the members may go to court and seek an involuntary commitment order. The Supreme Court has ruled that if the person is a minor, a hearing is not necessary for involuntary commitment, as long as a qualified mental health professional considers commitment necessary. If the person is an adult, however, the process is more involved. The court usually will order a mental examination and allow the individual to contest the commitment in court, often represented by a lawyer.

The Supreme Court has ruled that before a person can be committed, there must be "clear and convincing" proof the individual is mentally ill and has met the state's criteria for involuntary commitment. That is, whatever the state's criteria, clinicians must offer clear and convincing proof that the person meets those criteria (MHA, 2024; Zhong et al., 2023). When is proof clear and convincing, according to the court? When it provides 75 percent certainty that the criteria of commitment have been met. This is far less than the near-total certainty ("beyond a reasonable doubt") required to convict people of committing a crime.

Fatal intervention A mother grieves shortly after her son, Lavall Hall, a 25-year-old man with schizophrenia, was shot and killed during a 2015 struggle with police, whom she herself had called to facilitate an emergency civil commitment in response to Hall's agitated psychotic state. Because of repeated tragedies like this, a growing number of police departments have begun teaching officers how to employ *verbal de-escalation* and empathy when interacting with persons in the throes of a mental health crisis.

Joe Raedle/Getty Images

EMERGENCY COMMITMENT Many situations require immediate action; no one can wait for commitment proceedings when a life is at stake. Consider, for example, an emergency patient who is suicidal or hearing voices demanding hostile actions against others. The person may need immediate treatment and around-the-clock supervision. If treatment could not be given in such situations without the patient's full consent, the consequences could be tragic.

Therefore, many states give clinicians the right to certify that certain patients need temporary commitment and medication (Rozel, Toohey, & Amin, 2023). In past years, these states required certification by two *physicians* (not necessarily psychiatrists in some of the

of NOTE ...

Waiting for Care

In a survey, nearly 90 percent of hospital emergency physicians reported psychiatric patients being held in their emergency departments for extended periods while waiting for inpatient psychiatric beds (Goldstein, 2022; Snook, 2018).

states). Today, states may allow certification by other mental health professionals as well. The clinicians must declare that the state of mind of the patients makes them dangerous to themselves or others. By tradition, the certifications are often referred to as *two-physician certificates*, or *2 PCs*. The length of such emergency commitments varies from state to state, but three days is often the limit (OMH, 2024; McCall, 2023). Should clinicians come to believe that a longer stay is necessary, formal commitment proceedings may be initiated during the period of emergency commitment.

WHO IS DANGEROUS? In the past, people with mental disorders were actually less likely than others to commit violent or dangerous acts. This low rate of violence was apparently related to the fact that so many such people lived in institutions. As a result of deinstitutionalization, however, hundreds of thousands of people with severe mental disorders now live in the community, and many of them receive little, if any, treatment. Some are indeed dangerous to themselves or others (SAMHSA, 2023; Trägårdh et al., 2023; Weinberger & Markowitz, 2022).

It is important to be clear that, according to research, the vast majority of people with mental disorders are in no way violent or dangerous, and only a small percentage of all violent acts are committed by people with mental disorders (Ghiasi, Azhar, & Singh, 2023; Hong et al., 2023). That said, studies do suggest that untreated people with severe mental disorders are, on average, somewhat more likely than the general population to perform violent behaviors. The disorders with the strongest relationships to violence are severe substance use disorder, impulse control disorder, antisocial personality disorder, and psychotic disorders (Buchanan, 2020; Large & Nielssen, 2020). Of these, substance use disorder appears to be the single most influential factor (Ghiasi et al., 2023). For example, schizophrenia compounded by substance use disorder has a stronger relationship to violence than schizophrenia alone does (CMHA, 2023).

A determination of *dangerousness* is often required for involuntary civil commitment. But can mental health professionals accurately predict who will commit violent acts? Research suggests that psychiatrists and psychologists are wrong more often than right when they make *long-term* predictions of violence (Large, Callaghan, & Ryan, 2023; Watts et al., 2022). Most often, they overestimate the likelihood that a patient will eventually be violent. Their *short-term* predictions—that is, predictions of imminent violence—tend to be more accurate. Researchers are now working, with some success, to develop new assessment techniques that use statistical approaches and are more objective in their predictions of dangerousness than are the subjective judgments of clinicians (FP, 2024; Connors & Large, 2023).

Failure to predict A school surveillance camera shows Dylan Klebold and Eric Harris in the midst of their killing rampage at Columbine High School in Littleton, Colorado, in 1999. Although the teenagers had built a violent website, threatened other students, had problems with the law, and displayed psychological problems, professionals were not able to predict or prevent their violent behavior.

WHAT ARE THE PROBLEMS WITH CIVIL COMMITMENT? Civil commitment has been criticized on several grounds (Hare et al., 2024; Fariba & Gupta, 2023; Wipond, 2023). First is the difficulty of assessing a person's dangerousness. If judgments of dangerousness are often inaccurate, how can one justify using them to deprive people of liberty? Second, the legal definitions of "mental illness" and "dangerousness" are vague. The terms may be defined so broadly that they could be applied to almost anyone an evaluator views as undesirable. Indeed, many civil libertarians worry about involuntary commitment being used to control people, as is often done in countries ruled by authoritarian governments, where mental hospitals house people with unpopular political views. A third problem is the sometimes questionable therapeutic value of civil commitment. Research suggests that many people committed involuntarily do not respond well to therapy. A fourth problem is that decisions about civil commitment are apparently subject to racial bias. Studies show that people of color are much more likely than non-Hispanic White people to be involuntarily committed (Schölin et al., 2024; Knight et al., 2023; Shea et al., 2022).

Don Bartletti/Los Angeles Times via Getty Images

Prisoners also have a right to treatment These prisoners at the San Diego County jail are receiving daylong classes on subjects like anger management and PTSD. The Supreme Court has upheld the right of prisoners to receive mental health treatment during their incarceration. However, prison systems are often ill-equipped to provide proper care.

TRENDS IN CIVIL COMMITMENT The flexibility of the involuntary commitment laws probably reached a peak in 1962. That year, in the case of *Robinson v. California,* the Supreme Court ruled that imprisoning people who experienced substance use disorders might violate the Constitution's ban on cruel and unusual punishment, and it recommended involuntary civil commitment to a mental hospital as a more reasonable action. This ruling encouraged the civil commitment of many kinds of "social deviants," and many such individuals found it difficult to obtain release from the hospitals to which they were committed.

During the late 1960s and early 1970s, reporters, novelists, civil libertarians, and others spoke out against the ease with which so many people were being unjustifiably committed to mental hospitals. As the public became more aware of these issues, state legislatures started to pass stricter standards about involuntary hospital commitment, and, as mentioned earlier, many launched *outpatient commitment* programs in which courts may order people with severe mental disorders into community treatment (NCSC, 2023; Dlugacz, Wimmer, & Nettesheim, 2022). In turn, rates of involuntary hospital commitment declined, and release rates rose. Fewer people are institutionalized through civil commitment procedures today than in the past (Segal, Rimes, & Badran, 2023; Schmidt & Gilboy, 2020).

Protecting Patients' Rights

Over the past several decades, court decisions and state and federal laws have significantly expanded the rights of patients with mental disorders, in particular the *right to treatment* and the *right to refuse treatment.*

HOW IS THE RIGHT TO TREATMENT PROTECTED? When people are committed to mental institutions and do not receive treatment, the institutions become, in effect, prisons for the unconvicted. To many patients in the late 1960s and the 1970s, large state mental institutions were just that, and some patients and their attorneys began to demand that the state honor the patients' **right to treatment** (Ferleger, 2023; Weinberger & Markowitz, 2022). In the landmark case of *Wyatt v. Stickney,* a suit on behalf of institutionalized patients in Alabama in 1972, a federal court ruled that the state was constitutionally obligated to provide "adequate treatment" to all people who had been committed involuntarily. Because conditions in the state's hospitals were so terrible, the judge laid out goals that state officials had to meet, including more therapists, better living conditions, more privacy, more social interactions and physical exercise, and a more proper use of physical restraint and medication. Other states—and indeed many other countries—have since adopted similar standards (CLRP, 2024; Pedersen et al., 2023).

Another important decision was handed down in 1975 by the Supreme Court in the case of *O'Connor v. Donaldson.* After being held in a Florida mental institution for more than 14 years, Kenneth Donaldson sued for release. Donaldson repeatedly had sought release and had been overruled by the institution's psychiatrists. He argued that he and his fellow patients were receiving poor treatment, were being largely ignored by the staff, and were allowed little personal freedom. The Supreme Court ruled in his favor,

right to treatment The legal right of patients, particularly those who are involuntarily committed, to receive adequate treatment.

Hospital neglect While some countries increasingly have attended to the rights of patients, including their rights to treatment and to humane treatment conditions, other countries, especially economically challenged ones, have lagged behind. For example, although the government of Indonesia banned *pasung*—the chaining or close-quarter confinement of mentally ill persons—back in 1977, the practice apparently continues today, as shown at this center for mental patients in Jakarta.

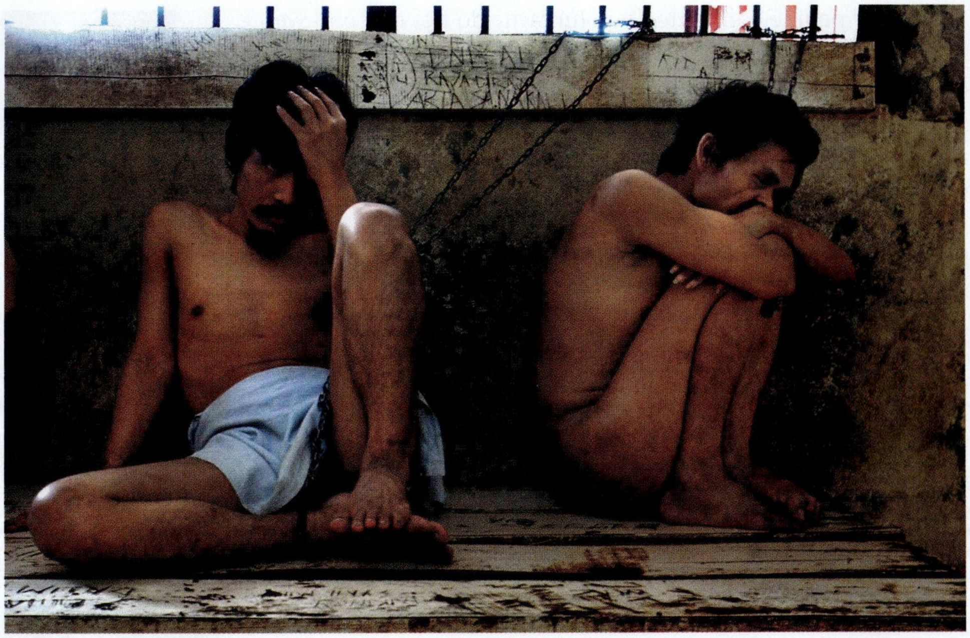

John Stanmeyer/VII/Redux

fined the hospital's superintendent, and said that such institutions must review patients' cases periodically. The justices also ruled that the state cannot continue to institutionalize people against their will if they are not dangerous and are capable of surviving on their own or with the willing help of responsible family members or friends (McCall, 2023).

To help protect the rights of patients, Congress passed the Protection and Advocacy for Mentally Ill Individuals Act in 1986. This law set up *protection and advocacy systems* in all states and U.S. territories and gave public advocates who worked for patients the power to investigate possible abuse and neglect and to correct those problems legally.

In more recent years, public advocates have argued that the right to treatment also should be extended to the tens of thousands of people with severe mental disorders who are repeatedly released from hospitals into communities ill-equipped to care for them (Perlin, 2021). Many such people have no place to go and are unable to care for themselves, often winding up unhoused or in prisons (CLRP, 2024; Roth, 2020). A number of advocates are now suing federal and state agencies throughout the country, demanding that they fulfill the promises of the community mental health movement.

of NOTE ...

Arresting Unhoused People with Mental Disorders

Many unhoused people with severe mental disorders wind up in jail rather than in treatment. Most are charged with such infractions as disorderly conduct, public intoxication, trespassing, not paying for a meal, menacing panhandling, loitering, or "lewd and lascivious behavior" (for example, public urination) (Harrell & Nam-Sonenstein, 2023; NLIHC, 2022; Head, 2021).

HOW IS THE RIGHT TO REFUSE TREATMENT PROTECTED? The courts have also decided that patients, particularly those in institutions, have the **right to refuse treatment** (CLRP, 2024; Ferleger, 2023). Most of the right-to-refuse-treatment rulings center on *biological treatments*. These treatments are easier to impose on patients without their cooperation than psychotherapy, and they often are more hazardous. For example, state rulings have consistently granted patients the right to refuse *psychosurgery,* the most irreversible form of physical treatment—and often the most dangerous (CLRP, 2024; Slobogin et al., 2020).

Some states have also acknowledged a patient's right to refuse *electroconvulsive therapy (ECT)*, the treatment you read about in the chapter on depressive disorders. However, the right-to-refuse issue is more complex with regard to ECT than to psychosurgery. ECT is very effective for many people with severe depression, but it can cause great upset and can also be misused. Today, many states grant patients—particularly voluntary patients—the right to refuse ECT (OMH, 2024; Iltis et al., 2023). Usually, a patient must be informed fully about the nature of the treatment and must give written consent to it. A number of states continue to permit ECT to be forced on committed patients, whereas others require the consent of a close relative or other third party in such cases.

right to refuse treatment The legal right of patients to refuse certain forms of treatment.

In the past, patients did not have the right to refuse *psychotropic medications*. As you have read, however, many psychotropic drugs are very powerful, and some produce effects that are unwanted and dangerous. As these harmful effects have become more apparent, some states have granted patients the right to refuse medication (OMH, 2024; Dlugacz et al., 2022). Typically, these states require physicians to explain the purpose of the medication to patients and obtain their written consent. If a patient's refusal is considered incompetent, dangerous, or irrational, the state may allow it to be overturned by an independent psychiatrist, medical committee, or local court. However, the refusing patient is supported in this process by a lawyer or other patient advocate.

WHAT OTHER RIGHTS DO PATIENTS HAVE? Court decisions have protected still other patient rights over the past several decades. Patients who perform work in mental institutions, particularly private institutions, are now guaranteed at least a *minimum wage*. In addition, according to a court decision, patients released from state mental hospitals have a right to *aftercare* and to an *appropriate community residence*, such as a group home (CLRP, 2024). And, more generally, people with psychological disorders should receive treatment in the *least restrictive facility* available (McCall, 2023; Weinberger & Markowitz, 2022). If an inpatient program at a community mental health center is available and appropriate, for example, then that is the facility to which they should be assigned, not a mental hospital.

THE "RIGHTS" DEBATE Certainly, people with psychological disorders have civil rights that must be protected at all times. However, many clinicians express concern that the patients' rights rulings and laws may unintentionally deprive these patients of opportunities for recovery. Consider the right to refuse medication. If medications can help a patient with a severe mental disorder to recover, doesn't the patient have the right to that recovery? If confusion causes the patient to refuse medication, can clinicians in good conscience delay medication while legal channels are being cleared?

Despite such legitimate concerns, keep in mind that the clinical field has not always done an effective job of protecting patients' rights. Over the years, many patients have been overmedicated and received improper treatments. Furthermore, one must ask

Robin Rayne/ZUMA Wire/Newscom

The person behind the ruling The principle that people with mental disorders must receive treatment in the least restrictive facility available is based on the 1999 Supreme Court decision in the case of *Olmstead v. L. C.* The "L. C." in the case title was the plaintiff Lois Curtis, a person diagnosed with schizophrenia who spent years being moved from one institution to another. After her release to the community, Curtis, shown in this photo, became a successful disability advocate, public speaker, and artist. She died at age 55 in 2022.

of NOTE ...

No Vote

Around 80 percent of states deny or place restrictions on the voting privileges of certain people with mental disorders. The wording in some of the state laws refers to the ineligible individuals as "incompetent," "insane," "incapacitated," "idiot," "lunatic," and of "unsound mind" (Bazelon Center, 2024).

whether the field's present state of knowledge justifies clinicians' overriding of patients' rights. Can clinicians confidently say that a given treatment will help a patient? Can they predict when a treatment will have harmful effects? Since clinicians themselves often disagree, it seems appropriate for patients, their advocates, and outside evaluators to also play key roles in decision making.

SUMMING UP

How Does the Legal system Influence Mental Health Care?

Courts may be called upon to commit people who have not committed crimes to mental hospitals for treatment, a process called civil commitment. Society allows involuntary commitment of people considered to be in need of treatment and dangerous to themselves or others. Laws governing civil commitment procedures vary from state to state, but the Supreme Court has ruled that in order for individuals to be committed, there must be clear and convincing proof that they are mentally ill and meet their state's criteria for involuntary commitment. In addition to mental hospital commitment, many states have established outpatient civil commitment programs.

The courts and legislatures significantly affect the mental health profession by specifying legal rights to which patients are entitled. The rights that have received the most attention are the right to treatment and the right to refuse treatment.

In What Other Ways Do the Clinical and Legal Fields Interact?

Mental health and legal professionals may influence each other's work in other ways as well. During the past 30 years, their paths have crossed in four key areas: *malpractice suits, professional boundaries, jury consultation,* and *psychological research of legal topics.*

Malpractice Suits

The number of **malpractice suits** against therapists has risen sharply in recent years. Claims have been made against clinicians in response to a patient's attempted suicide, sexual activity with a patient, failure to obtain informed consent for a treatment, negligent drug therapy, omission of drug therapy that would speed improvement, improper termination of treatment, and wrongful commitment (Barsky, 2024; Ash, Frierson, & Hatters Friedman, 2022). Studies suggest that malpractice suits—or the fear of them—can have significant effects on clinical decisions and practice, for better or for worse.

Professional Boundaries

Over the past 30 years, the legislative and judicial systems have helped change the *boundaries* that distinguish one clinical profession from another. In particular, they have given more authority to psychologists and blurred the lines that once separated psychiatry from psychology. A growing number of states, for example, are ruling that psychologists can admit patients to hospitals, a power previously held only by psychiatrists.

Most psychiatrists oppose the idea of prescription rights for psychologists. Why do some psychologists also oppose the idea?

In 1991, with the blessing of Congress, the Department of Defense started to reconsider the biggest difference of all between the practices of psychiatrists and psychologists—the authority to prescribe drugs, a role previously denied to psychologists. The Department of Defense set up a trial training program for army psychologists. Given the apparent success of this trial program, the American Psychological Association later recommended that all psychologists be allowed to pursue extensive educational and training programs in prescription services and receive certification to prescribe medications if they pass (Curtis, Hoffmann, & O'Leary Sloan, 2023; Kennedy, 2023). Several states and territories in the United States—including New Mexico, Louisiana, Illinois, Iowa, Idaho, Colorado, and the U.S. territory of Guam—now do grant prescription privileges to psychologists who receive special pharmacology training.

malpractice suit A lawsuit charging a therapist with improper conduct in the course of treatment.

Jury Consultation

During the past 30 years, more and more lawyers have turned to clinicians for psychological advice in conducting trials (FP, 2024). A new breed of clinical specialists, known as "jury specialists," has evolved. They advise lawyers about which potential jurors are likely to favor their side and which strategies are likely to win jurors' support during trials. The jury specialists make their suggestions on the basis of surveys, interviews, analyses of jurors' backgrounds and attitudes, and laboratory simulations of upcoming trials. However, it is not clear that a clinician's advice is more valid than a lawyer's instincts or that the judgments of either are particularly accurate.

Psychological Research of Legal Topics

Psychologists have sometimes conducted studies and developed expertise on topics of great importance to the criminal justice system. In turn, these studies influence how the system carries out its work. Psychological investigations of two topics, *eyewitness testimony* and *patterns of criminality,* have gained particular attention.

EYEWITNESS TESTIMONY

In criminal cases, testimony by eyewitnesses is extremely influential. It often determines whether a defendant will be found guilty or not guilty. But how accurate is eyewitness testimony? This question has become urgent, as a troubling number of people in prisons (many on death row) have had their convictions overturned after DNA evidence revealed that they could not have committed the crimes of which they had been convicted. It turns out that almost 70 percent of such wrongful convictions were based in large part on mistaken eyewitness testimony (Innocence Project, 2024).

Most eyewitnesses undoubtedly try to tell the truth about what or whom they saw. Yet research indicates that eyewitness testimony can be highly unreliable, partly because eyewitnesses sometimes hold subtle biases and partly because most crimes are unexpected, stressful, and fleeting and therefore not the sort of events remembered well (Ikier et al., 2024; Bergman, 2023). During the crime, for example, lighting may be poor, or other distractions may be present. Witnesses may have had other things on their minds, such as concern for their own safety or that of bystanders. Such concerns may greatly impair later memory.

In laboratory studies, researchers have found it easy to fool participants who are trying to recall the details of an observed event simply by introducing misinformation (Connor Desai & Reimers, 2023; Johnson et al., 2023). After a suggestive description by the researcher, stop signs can be transformed into yield signs, white cars into blue ones, and Mickey Mouse into Minnie Mouse. In addition, laboratory studies indicate that persons who are highly suggestible have the poorest recall of observed events (Brown et al., 2022).

Eyewitness error Research indicates that eyewitness testimony is often invalid. Here a woman talks to the man whom she had identified as her rapist back in 1984. DNA testing eventually proved that a different person had raped her, and the incorrectly identified man was released. In the meantime, however, he had served 11 years of a life sentence in prison.

Chuck Burton/AP Photo

As for identifying actual perpetrators, research has found that accuracy is heavily influenced by the method used in identification (Quigley-McBride & Wells, 2023). For example, police lineups, particularly ones conducted poorly, are not always reliable, and the errors that witnesses make when looking at lineups tend to stick (O'Donnell et al., 2023; Shen et al., 2023). Researchers have also learned that the confidence of witnesses is not always related to accuracy (Bergman, 2023). Yet the degree of a witness's confidence often influences whether jurors believe the person's testimony (Garrett et al., 2023).

Psychological investigations into the memories of eyewitnesses have not yet undone the judicial system's reliance on or respect for those witnesses' testimony. Nor should it. The distance between laboratory studies and real-life events is often great, and the findings from such studies must be applied with care. Still, eyewitness research has begun to make an impact. Instructions to jurors about the accuracy of eyewitness confidence may now be included in eyewitness cases (Garrett et al., 2023). In addition, studies of hypnosis and of its ability to create false memories have led most states to prohibit eyewitnesses from testifying about events or details if their recall of the events was initially helped by hypnosis.

PATTERNS OF CRIMINALITY A growing number of television shows, movies, and books suggest that clinicians often play a major role in criminal investigations by providing police with *psychological profiles* of perpetrators—"He's probably White, in his thirties, has a history of animal torture, has few friends, and is subject to emotional outbursts." The study of criminal behavior patterns and of profiling has increased in recent decades; however, it is not nearly as revealing or influential as the media and the arts would have us believe (Rossmo, 2023; Innes & Doncaster, 2022).

On the positive side, researchers have gathered information about the psychological features of various groups of people who commit criminal behaviors, and they have indeed found that perpetrators of particular kinds of crimes—serial murder or serial sexual assault, for example—frequently share a number of traits and background features (see **PsychWatch**). But while such traits are *often* present, they are not *always* present, and so applying profile information to a particular crime can be wrong and misleading. Increasingly, police are consulting psychological profilers, and this practice appears to be helpful as long as the limitations of profiling are recognized.

A reminder of the limitations of profiling comes from the case of the snipers who terrorized the Washington, DC, area for three weeks in October 2002, shooting 10 people dead and seriously wounding 3 others. Most of the profiling done by FBI psychologists had suggested that the sniper was acting alone; it turned out that the attacks were conducted by a pair: a middle-aged man, John Allen Muhammad, and a teenage boy, Lee Boyd Malvo. Although profiles had suggested a young thrill seeker, Muhammad was 41. Profilers had believed the attacker to be a non-Hispanic White person, but neither Muhammad nor Malvo was White. The prediction of a *male* attacker was correct, but then again female serial killers are relatively rare.

of NOTE ...

Recent TV Profilers

- *The Irrational*
- *Found*
- *Criminal Minds*
- *Mindhunter*
- *Killing Eve*
- *The Blacklist*
- *Luther*

Misleading profiles From 2001 to 2008, the FBI searched for the serial killer who was sending anthrax-tainted letters to people throughout the United States, resulting in 5 deaths and 13 cases of severe illness. Here a hazardous-material worker sprays his colleagues after they searched the Senate Office Building for traces of the deadly bacterium. As it turned out, psychological profiling—both solicited and unsolicited—was of limited help in this famous case and, in some instances, misled the FBI.

PSYCHWATCH

Serial Murderers: "Madness" or Badness?

On April 24, 2018, police arrested former police officer Joseph James DeAngelo outside his home near Sacramento, California. Based on DNA evidence, they accused DeAngelo of being the so-called Golden State Killer, a murderer of at least 12 people in separate incidents during a crime spree that terrorized Californians from 1974 to 1986. DeAngelo later pleaded guilty and so officially joined a growing list of serial killers who have fascinated and horrified the public over the years: Bruce Ivins ("anthrax killer"), Theodore Kaczynski ("Unabomber"), Ted Bundy, David Berkowitz ("Son of Sam"), Albert DeSalvo ("Boston Strangler"), John Wayne Gacy ("Killer Clown"), Jeffrey Dahmer ("Milwaukee Cannibal"), Dennis Rader ("BTK killer"), and more.

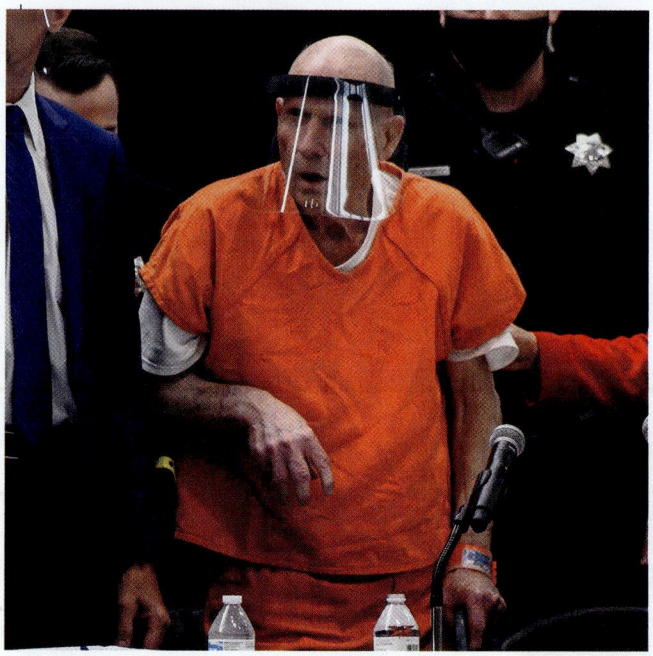

Daniel Kim/Sacramento Bee/Tribune News Service via Getty Images

"The Golden State Killer" On June 29, 2020, two years after his capture, Joseph James DeAngelo, wearing a face shield because of the Covid-19 pandemic, pleaded guilty to killing at least 12 people over a 12-year period.

By definition, serial killers commit a series of murders (three or more) in separate incidents over an extended period of time. They are different from mass killers, whom you read about in the chapter on personality disorders—individuals who murder four or more people at a single time, usually in a single location.

The FBI estimates that there are between 25 and 50 serial killers at large in the United States at any given time (FBI, 2023; WA, 2023; Moss & Wylde, 2020). Worldwide, 4,500 such killers have been identified since the year 1900 (Aamodt, Leary, & Southard, 2020, 2018; Aamodt, 2016). The number of serial killers seems to have decreased significantly in recent decades (WPR, 2024; Cottier, 2022). The reasons for this decrease are not clear; however, criminologists suspect it may be related to the increasing use of DNA technology in capturing such killers and to better tools of protection, such as cell phones and cell cameras, for potential victims (Weiss, 2020).

Serial killers each follow a unique pattern, but many of them appear to have certain characteristics in common (WPR, 2024; FBI, 2023; Fox, Levin, & Fridel, 2023, 2018). The majority—but certainly not all—are non-Hispanic White males between 30 and 45 years old, of average to high intelligence, seemingly clean-cut, smooth-talking, attractive, and skillful manipulators.

As many as half of serial killers may have severe personality disorders (FBI, 2023; Fox et al., 2023, 2018; Moss & Wylde, 2020). Lack of conscience and an utter disregard for people and the rules of society—key features of antisocial personality disorder—are typical. Narcissistic thinking is quite common as well. Feelings of being special may even give the killers an unrealistic belief that they will not get caught. Often it is this sense of invincibility that leads to their capture.

Sexual dysfunctions, paraphilic disorders, and fantasies may also play a part (FBI, 2023; Fox et al., 2023, 2018). Studies have found that vivid fantasies, often sexual and sadistic, may help drive the killer's behavior. A number of the killers were abused as children—physically, sexually, and/or emotionally (FBI, 2023; Keatley et al., 2018).

Law enforcement agencies and behavioral researchers have gathered an impressive body of statistical information about serial killings and killers in recent years. These data are often of help to criminal investigators as they seek to capture these repeat perpetrators of particularly heinous acts. At the same time, it would be inaccurate to say that clinical theorists understand why serial killers behave as they do.

SUMMING UP

Other Clinical–Legal Interactions

Mental health and legal professionals also cross paths in four other areas. First, malpractice suits against therapists have increased in recent years. Second, the legislative and judicial systems help define professional boundaries. Third, lawyers may solicit the advice of mental health professionals regarding the selection of jurors and case strategies. Fourth, psychologists may investigate legal phenomena such as eyewitness testimony and patterns of criminality.

What Ethical Principles Guide Mental Health Professionals?

DISCUSSIONS OF THE legal and mental health systems may sometimes give the impression that clinicians as a group are uncaring and are considerate of patients' rights and needs only when they are forced to be. This, of course, is not true. Most clinicians care greatly about their clients and strive to help them while at the same time respecting their rights and dignity (MHA, 2024; Campbell, 2023). In fact, clinicians do not rely exclusively on the legislative and court systems to ensure proper and effective clinical practice. They also regulate themselves by continually developing and revising ethical guidelines for their work and behavior. Many legal decisions do nothing more than place the power of the law behind these already existing professional guidelines.

Each profession within the mental health field has its own **code of ethics.** The code of the American Psychological Association (APA, 2023, 2017) is typical. This code, highly respected by other mental health professionals and by public officials, includes specific guidelines:

Barry Brecheisen/Getty Images

The ethics of giving professional advice
Psychologists are bound by the field's ethics code to base their advice on psychological theories and findings. In 2006, the enormously popular Phil McGraw ("Dr. Phil") surrendered his Texas psychologist license so that he could be free to use his own best judgment when giving advice on television and in books.

1. **Psychologists are permitted to offer advice** online, on social media, in self-help books, on DVDs, on television and radio programs, in newspapers and magazines, through mailed material, and in other places provided that they do so responsibly and professionally and base their advice on appropriate psychological literature and practices. Of these, Internet-based professional advice has proved particularly difficult to regulate because the number of online clinical offerings keeps growing, especially since the onset of the Covid-19 pandemic, and numerous online advice givers do not appear to have any professional training or credentials (Starvaggi, Dierckman, & Lorenzo-Luaces, 2023; Stoll, Müller, & Trachsel, 2020).
2. **Psychologists may not conduct fraudulent research, plagiarize the work of others, or publish false data.** During the past 30 years, cases of scientific fraud or misconduct have been discovered in all of the sciences, including psychology. These acts have led to misunderstandings of important issues, taken scientific research in the wrong direction, and damaged public trust. Unfortunately, the impressions created by false findings may continue to influence the thinking of both the public and other scientists for years.
3. **Psychologists must acknowledge their limitations** with regard to patients who are disabled or whose gender identity, ethnicity, language, socioeconomic status, or sexual orientation differs from that of the therapist. This guideline often requires psychotherapists to obtain additional training or supervision, consult with more knowledgeable colleagues, or refer clients to more appropriate professionals.
4. **Psychologists who make evaluations and testify in legal cases must base their assessments on sufficient information and substantiate their findings appropriately.** If an adequate examination of the individual in question is not possible, psychologists must make clear the limited nature of their testimony (Callaghan, 2023).
5. **Psychologists may not participate or assist in torture—acts in which severe pain, suffering, or degradation is intentionally inflicted on people.** This guideline was added to the code of ethics in 2017, a year after an APA-sponsored evaluation revealed that, over a period of several years, the APA had aided and advised the Department of Defense and the Central

Intelligence Agency in the development of "enhanced interrogation" techniques (that is, torture-based questioning) and had adjusted professional guidelines to allow psychologist involvement in such interrogations (see **PsychWatch**).

6. **Psychologists may not take advantage of clients or students, sexually or otherwise.** This guideline relates to the widespread social problem of sexual harassment as well as the problem of therapists who take sexual advantage of clients in therapy. The code specifically forbids a sexual relationship with a present or former therapy client for at least two years after the end of treatment—and even then, such a relationship is permitted only in "the most unusual circumstances." Furthermore, psychologists may not accept as clients people with whom they have previously had a sexual relationship.

   Research has clarified that clients may experience great emotional damage from sexual involvement with their therapists (Vesentini et al., 2023, 2022; Pope et al., 2021; MacIntyre & Appel, 2020). How many therapists actually have a sexual relationship with a client? On the basis of various surveys, reviewers have estimated that 3 to 5 percent of today's therapists engage in some form of sexual misconduct with patients, down from 10 percent more than a decade ago.

   Although the vast majority of therapists do not engage in sexual behavior of any kind with clients, their ability to control private feelings is apparently another matter. In surveys, more than 80 percent of therapists reported having been sexually attracted to a client, at least on occasion (Pope et al., 2023, 2021; Vesentini et al., 2023, 2022). Although few of these therapists acted on their feelings, most of them felt guilty, anxious, or concerned about the attraction. Given such issues, it is not surprising that sexual ethics training is given high priority in many of today's clinical training programs.

7. **Psychologists must follow the principle of confidentiality.** All of the state and federal courts have upheld laws protecting therapy **confidentiality.** For peace of mind and to ensure effective therapy, clients must be able to trust that their private exchanges with a therapist will not be repeated to others. There are times, however, when the principle of confidentiality must be compromised (Barnett & Coffman, 2023; Pope et al., 2021). A therapist in training, for example, must discuss cases on a regular basis with a supervisor, and clients must be informed that such discussions are taking place.

   Another exception to the principle of confidentiality arises in cases of outpatients who are clearly dangerous. The 1976 case of *Tarasoff v. Regents of the University of California,* one of the most important cases to affect client–therapist relationships, concerned an outpatient at a University of California hospital. He had confided to his therapist that he wanted to harm his former girlfriend, Tanya Tarasoff. Several days after ending therapy, the former patient stabbed Tanya Tarasoff to death.

   Should confidentiality have been broken in this case? The therapist, in fact, felt that it should. Campus police were notified, but the patient was released after some questioning. In their suit against the hospital and therapist, the victim's parents argued that the therapist should have also warned them and their daughter that the patient intended to harm Ms. Tarasoff. The California Supreme Court agreed: "The protective privilege ends where the public peril begins."

   The current code of ethics for psychologists thus declares that therapists have a **duty to protect**—a responsibility to break confidentiality, even without the client's consent, when it is necessary "to protect the client or others from harm." Since the Tarasoff ruling, most states have passed "duty to protect" bills that clarify the rules of confidentiality for therapists and protect them from certain civil suits (Barnett & Coffman, 2023; Slobogin et al., 2020).

Can you think of other instances in which the principle of therapy confidentiality should be broken?

code of ethics A body of principles and rules for ethical behavior, designed to guide decisions and actions by members of a profession.

confidentiality The principle that certain professionals will not divulge the information they obtain from a client.

duty to protect The principle that therapists must break confidentiality in order to protect a person who may be the intended target of a client.

of NOTE ...

Legal Knowledge

75%	Percentage of psychologists who are misinformed about their legal responsibilities regarding potentially dangerous clients
90%	Percentage of the same psychologists who feel confident that their legal knowledge in this realm is accurate

(Information from: Barnett & Coffman, 2023; Slobogin et al., 2020; Thomas, 2014.)

PSYCHWATCH

Doctor, Do No Harm

The Hippocratic Oath requires that doctors, first and foremost, "do no harm"—a principle also embraced by the code of ethics for each mental health profession. However, events uncovered a decade ago suggest that in the realm of torture, some psychologists did indeed bring harm to individuals.

In 2014 and 2015, several investigations and reports concluded that certain psychologists and, indeed, the American Psychological Association (APA) had participated for years in the Central Intelligence Agency (CIA) program of *enhanced interrogation*, or *torture-based questioning*, to obtain information from suspected terrorists. The investigations and reports revealed the following events (Opotow, 2022; APA, 2020, 2017; McDermott, 2020; Wise, 2018; Fink & Risen, 2017; Melechi, 2016; Patel & Elkin, 2015).

In 2002, shortly after the September 11, 2001, terrorist attacks in New York City and Washington, DC, the White House gave approval for a CIA program of "enhanced interrogation" of national security prisoners, or "detainees." In a series of so-called torture memos, it stated that enhanced interrogations could proceed if consulting mental health experts indicated that the procedures were not causing or were not likely to cause significant physical injury or severe mental distress.

Later in 2002, two psychologists, commissioned by the CIA, developed a package of enhanced interrogation procedures (including sleep deprivation, repeated waterboarding, physical assault, binding in stressful positions, deafening noise, and imprisonment in a box), and the CIA tested those procedures on a prisoner with possible ties to the terrorist organization Al Qaeda. Officials declared the test a success, and from that point forward, enhanced interrogations became an accepted national security policy. The two psychologists continued to serve as major advisers for the CIA program.

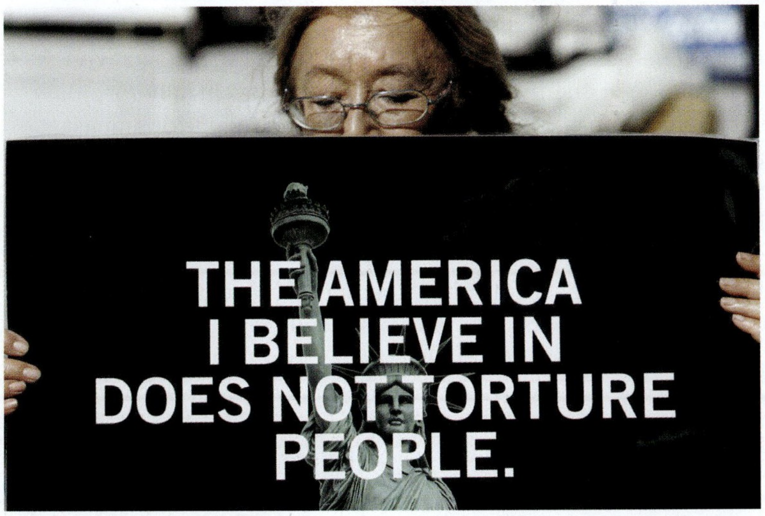

AP Photo/Jeff Chiu

No place for psychologists Along with many other protestors at an APA conference, this individual rallies against psychologist involvement in CIA-enhanced interrogation programs.

In order for the enhanced interrogation program to proceed, the CIA needed psychologists to observe the interrogations and declare them acceptable; it also needed ongoing advice and input from various psychologists to further develop the program. As a result, the CIA and key administrators at the APA developed a cooperative relationship that continued for several years. Although the APA did not participate in the actual administration of torture procedures, some of its administrators did have a series of communications, discussions, and brainstorming sessions with the CIA about the enhanced interrogation program and the possible role of psychologists.

Moreover, certain APA administrators manipulated the language of the organization's code of ethics, apparently to allow individual psychologists to participate in the enhanced interrogation program without fear of being accused of professional wrongdoing. After all, psychologists could not work with the program if that meant they were violating their profession's ethical standards. This concern disappeared in 2005 when the APA's Presidential Task Force on Psychological Ethics and National Security (PENS) ruled, in subtle language, that psychologists are not violating their "do no harm" obligation if they do not break any laws in their work, including possible work in the realm of enhanced interrogations. That is, even if their enhanced interrogation involvement contributed to the development of PTSD, anxiety disorders, depression, or the like, psychologists would not be violating their profession's ethical principles. In turn, the relationship between certain APA officials and the CIA was able to continue.

All this came to a head in 2014 and 2015, when the investigations and reports mentioned earlier unfolded. A year after those revelations, the APA, with its members now fully informed about what had taken place, sought to end this ugly episode and to ensure that it would not occur again. The entire APA membership voted to bar psychologists from direct and indirect involvement in any national security interrogations—both enhanced and noncoercive. In doing so, it was reaffirming that, even in a complex and dangerous world, a primary obligation of psychologists is to "do no harm" of any kind to individuals.

Mental Health, Business, and Economics

THE LEGISLATIVE AND judicial systems are not the only social institutions with which mental health professionals interact. *Business* and *economic* fields are two other sectors that influence and are influenced by clinical practice and study.

Work-Related Stress and Mental Health Services

According to numerous surveys, work is by far the leading source of stress for people (AIS, 2023; APA, 2023). Over 40 percent of workers find their jobs very stressful and believe them to be bad for their mental health and general health. Stressed-out workers report that the primary causes of their upsets are excessive workload (41 percent of workers), people and personnel issues (32 percent), difficulties balancing work with personal life (18 percent), and lack of job security (9 percent).

All of this work-related stress not only affects the personal functioning of employees. It also impairs their work performance. According to surveys, almost everyone occasionally takes days off from their job due to work stress; at least 15 percent of people miss six days or more each year (AIS, 2023). Furthermore, studies find that work stress contributes to poorer productivity and more accidents, employee mistakes, employee departures, insurance costs, and worker compensation expenses.

For both humane and financial reasons, many employers try to address the work-related stress and other mental health needs of their employees. Two common approaches, provided by at least half of employers, are *employee assistance programs* and *stress-reduction programs* (AIS, 2023; APA, 2023; Handrick, 2020). **Employee assistance programs** are mental health services made available by a place of business. They are run either by mental health professionals who work directly for a company or by outside mental health agencies. **Stress-reduction and problem-solving programs** are workshops or group sessions in which mental health professionals teach employees techniques for coping, solving problems, and handling and reducing stress. For example, as you read in the chapter on anxiety disorders, employers often make *mindfulness training* available to employees. Businesses believe that employee assistance and

employee assistance program A mental health program offered by a business to its employees.

stress-reduction and problem-solving program A workshop or series of group sessions offered by a business in which mental health professionals teach employees how to cope with and solve problems and reduce stress.

Julio Cortez/AP Photo

Uncommon work stress While all jobs feature some degree of stress, no occupation is more stressful than that of firefighters, and a number of programs and techniques have been developed to help these individuals deal with their stress. Here several Baltimore firefighters sit on a stoop across the street from a house in which three of their colleagues had just been killed battling a two-alarm blaze. The festive balloons given to them by a neighbor actually bring their loss and shock into even closer focus.

managed care program An insurance program in which the insurance company decides the cost, method, provider, and length of treatment.

peer review system A system by which clinicians paid by an insurance company may periodically review a patient's progress and recommend the continuation or termination of insurance benefits.

stress-reduction programs save them money in the long run by preventing psychological difficulties from interfering with work performance and by reducing employee insurance claims, a notion that has been supported in various studies. And, for their part, nearly half of workers agree that they need help learning how to manage stress.

The Economics of Mental Health

Personal finances and job security play major roles in a person's mental health. For example, as you learned in earlier chapters, sudden financial losses and unemployment brought about by the Covid-19 pandemic were often accompanied by increases in anxiety, depression, and/or substance misuse.

It is also the case that broad economic decisions by the government may influence the clinical field's treatment of people with severe mental disorders. For example, the desire of the state and federal governments to reduce costs was an important consideration in the country's *deinstitutionalization* movement, which contributed to the premature release of hospital patients into the community, beginning in the 1960s.

Economic decisions by government agencies may affect other kinds of clients and treatment programs as well. As we discussed earlier in the book, government funding for services to people with psychological disorders has risen sharply over the past six decades, from $1 billion in 1963 to around $179 billion today (Statista, 2024; SAMHSA, 2023, 2014; AHA, 2019). Some of that money is spent on prescription drugs and therapy, but much of the rest is targeted for income support, housing subsidies, and other such expenses rather than direct mental health services. The result is that government funding for mental health services is, in fact, insufficient, and people with severe mental disorders are hit hardest by the funding shortage.

Government funding currently covers around 64 percent of all mental health services, leaving a mental health expense of tens of billions of dollars for individual patients and their private insurance companies (SAMHSA, 2023, 2020, 2014). This large economic role of private insurance companies has had a significant effect on the way clinicians go about their work. As you read in the opening chapter, to reduce their expenses, most insurance companies have developed **managed care programs,** in which the company determines which therapists clients may choose from, the cost of sessions, and the number of sessions for which a client may be reimbursed (Hughes, 2023; McCarthy, 2022). These and other insurance plans may also control expenses through the use of **peer review systems,** in which clinicians who work for the insurance company periodically review a client's treatment program and recommend that insurance benefits be either continued or stopped. Typically, insurers require reports or session notes from the therapist, often including intimate personal information about the patient.

What are the costs to clients and practitioners when insurance companies make decisions about the methods, frequency, and duration of treatment?

As you also learned in the opening chapter, many therapists and clients dislike managed care programs and peer reviews (Goldman, 2022; Smith et al., 2022). They believe that the reports required of therapists breach confidentiality, even when efforts are made to protect anonymity. They also argue that the priorities of managed care programs inevitably shorten therapy, even if longer-term treatment would be advisable in particular cases. The priorities may also favor treatments that offer short-term results (for example, psychotropic medications) over more costly approaches that might yield more promising long-term improvement.

Yet another major problem with insurance coverage in the United States—whether managed care or other kinds of insurance programs—is that reimbursements for mental disorders are, on average, lower than those for physical disorders, placing people with psychological difficulties at a significant disadvantage. As we discussed earlier in the book, the federal government has tried to address this problem for more than a decade, and Congress has passed several federal *parity* laws that mandate equal insurance coverage for mental and physical problems (APA, 2023). However, it appears that many insurance companies still manage to shortchange the mental health claims of their members (MHA, 2024; Meyersohn, 2023; SAMHSA, 2022).

Caught in an economic spiral Group home residents and mental health advocates rally at the legislative office building in Raleigh, North Carolina, to protest a Medicaid payment law change. This change could result in residents with severe mental disorders losing their group homes and having nowhere to live.

Technology and Mental Health

AS YOU HAVE READ throughout this book, today's ever-changing technology has had significant effects—both positive and negative—on the mental health field, and it will undoubtedly affect the field even more in the coming years. The effects include the development of new sources of psychological dysfunction, the production of new psychological disorders, increased access to mental health information, and the expansion of clinical treatment approaches.

Our digital world provides *new sources* for psychological dysfunction. For example, the maladaptive functioning of many persons with gambling disorder has been exacerbated by the ready availability of Internet gambling. Similarly, social media, the Internet, and texting are now used frequently by those who wish to stalk or bully others, express sexual exhibitionism, pursue pedophilic desires, or satisfy other paraphilic disorders. And, in the opinion of many clinical theorists, constant texting, social media posting, and Internet browsing may help establish a foundation for attention problems.

As we have noted throughout this book, even everyday social networking can contribute to psychological dysfunction. In addition to its many virtues, social media may, according to research, provide a new venue for peer pressure and social anxiety in some adolescents. It may, for example, cause some people to develop fears that others in their network will exclude them socially. Similarly, clinicians worry that social networking may lead shy or socially anxious people to withdraw from valuable face-to-face relationships.

Can you think of innovative ways society could better curb the negative impact of social media on people's mental health?

Beyond providing new sources for psychological dysfunction, research indicates that today's technology also is helping to produce *new psychological disorders*. As you read in the chapter on substance use and addictive disorders, one such pattern is *Internet use disorder*, a problem marked by excessive and dysfunctional levels of texting, social media scrolling and posting, networking, Internet browsing, e-mailing, online shopping, or online pornographic use.

Similarly, the Internet has brought a new exhibitionistic feature to certain kinds of psychopathology. For example, as you learned in the chapter on suicide, a number of people now use social media to post videos of themselves engaging in self-cutting or suicidal acts, acts that traditionally had been conducted in private.

Still another major impact of today's technology is the enormous body of *mental health information* that the Internet and social media provide to the public and to clinicians as well. On the positive side, such information enables people to better inform themselves, their friends, and their family members about psychological problems and treatment options. However, along with this wealth of useful online information comes considerable misinformation about psychological problems and their treatments. And such misinformation is further accompanied by the problem of quality control. There are, for example, now numerous antitreatment sites online, such as pro-suicide and pro-Ana networks, that try to guide people away from seeking help for their psychological problems.

of NOTE ...

Multitasking

In one survey, more than half of the respondents reported that they sometimes multitask during their telehealth and/or telemental health visits, including surfing the Web, checking e-mails, and texting (25%); scrolling through social media (21%); and playing a video game (19%) (DF, 2020).

Finally, the face of clinical *treatment* has expanded in our fast-moving digital world. For example, computerized intervention programs, Internet-based support groups, smartphone mental health apps, and wearable monitoring devices like "smart" watches are now widely available (Kalman et al., 2023; Timmons et al., 2023). And *telemental health,* the use of remote technologies such as long-distance videoconferencing to provide real-time therapy sessions without the therapist being physically present, is now common, especially since being propelled into the clinical mainstream during the Covid-19 pandemic (Bagner et al., 2023; Meyersohn, 2023; Comer et al., 2021). Moreover, although *artificial intelligence* (*AI*) technology is just starting to play a role in mental health services and research, there is little doubt that it will eventually have a major impact on the clinical field (Grabb & Angelotta, 2023; Timmons et al., 2023; WHO, 2023).

Clearly, the growing impact of technological change on the mental health field presents formidable challenges for clinicians and researchers alike. Relatively few of the technological applications discussed throughout this book are well understood, and few have been subjected to comprehensive research. Yet, as mentioned earlier, the relationship between technology and mental health is growing precipitously. It behooves everyone in the field to understand this growth and its implications.

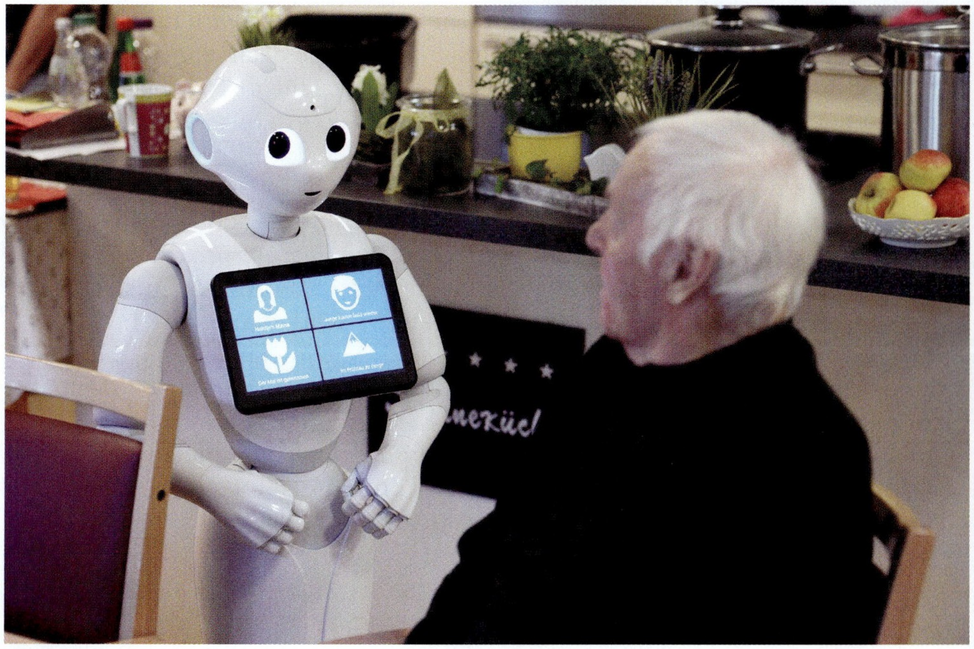

New technological help on the way At this Alzheimer's facility in Germany, a resident interacts with "Emma." Robots like this—which speak, play music, take photos, and follow simple commands—can be of significant help in the care of people with neurocognitive disorders.

The Person Within the Profession

THE ACTIONS OF clinical researchers and practitioners not only influence and are influenced by other forces in society but also are closely tied to their personal needs and goals (see ***InfoCentral***). You have observed that the human strengths, imperfections, wisdom, and clumsiness of clinical professionals may affect their theoretical orientations, their interactions with clients, and the kinds of clients with whom they choose to work. You have also learned how personal leanings may sometimes override professional standards and scruples and, in extreme cases, lead clinical scientists to commit research fraud and clinical practitioners to engage in sexual misconduct with clients.

Surveys of the mental health of therapists have found that as many as 84 percent report having been in therapy at least once (Pope et al., 2021; Pope & Wedding, 2019; Pope & Vasquez, 2016). Their reasons are largely the same as those of other clients, with relationship problems, depression, and anxiety topping the list. And, like other people, therapists often are reluctant to acknowledge their psychological difficulties.

It is not clear why so many therapists have psychological difficulties. Perhaps it is because their jobs are highly stressful; research suggests that therapists often experience some degree of job burnout (Lin, Assefa, & Stamm, 2023; Barnett, 2020; Horton, 2020). Indeed, more than half of surveyed therapists report that such feelings have, on occasion, affected the quality and effectiveness of their work. Or perhaps therapists are simply more aware of their own negative feelings or are more likely to pursue treatment for their challenges. Alternatively, people with personal concerns may be more inclined to choose clinical work as a profession. Whatever the reason, clinicians bring to their work a set of psychological issues that may, along with other important factors, affect how they listen and respond to clients (Öri et al., 2023).

The science and profession of psychopathology seek to understand, predict, and change psychological dysfunctions. But we must not lose sight of the fact that mental health researchers and clinicians are human beings, living within a society of human beings, working to serve human beings. The mixture of discovery, misdirection, promise, and frustration that you have encountered throughout this book is thus to be expected. When you think about it, could the study and treatment of human behavior really proceed in any other way?

of NOTE ...

Silent Struggle

In one survey, only 42 percent of psychiatrists who had experienced mental disorders said they would disclose their difficulties to family members or friends (Yasgur, 2019).

SUMMING UP

Ethical, Economic, Technological, and Personal Factors

Each clinical profession has a code of ethics. The psychologist's code includes prohibitions against engaging in fraudulent research, taking advantage of clients and students (sexually or otherwise), and participating or assisting in torture. It also establishes guidelines for respecting patient confidentiality. The case of *Tarasoff* v. *Regents of the University of California* helped determine the circumstances in which therapists have a duty to protect the client or others from harm and must break confidentiality.

Clinical practice and study also intersect with the business and economic worlds. Clinicians often help to address psychological problems relating to work. In addition, private insurance companies often set up managed care programs whose structure and reimbursement procedures influence and often reduce the duration and focus of therapy.

The remarkable technological advances of recent times have affected the mental health field by contributing to new sources of psychological dysfunction, new psychological disorders, increased access to mental health information, and the expansion of clinical treatment approaches.

Mental health activities are affected by the personal needs, values, and goals of the human beings who provide the clinical services. These factors inevitably affect the choice, direction, and even quality of their work.

PERSONAL AND PROFESSIONAL ISSUES

Like everyone else, clinicians have personal needs, perspectives, goals, and problems, each of which may affect their work. Therapists typically try to minimize the impact of such variables on their interactions with clients—called **countertransference** by Freud. However, research suggests that, to at least some degree, personal therapist issues influence how clinicians deal with clients.

THE EARLY YEARS

Common events in the early lives of therapists

- Experiencing personal distress
- Witnessing the distress of others
- Observing the behaviors and emotions of others; becoming psychologically minded
- Reading
- Being in therapy
- Being a confidant to others
- Modeling the behavior of others
- Learning from a mentor

(Pope et al., 2023, 2021; BPF, 2020; Miller, 2017; Pope & Vasquez, 2016; Farber et al., 2005)

Top 5 reasons people become therapists

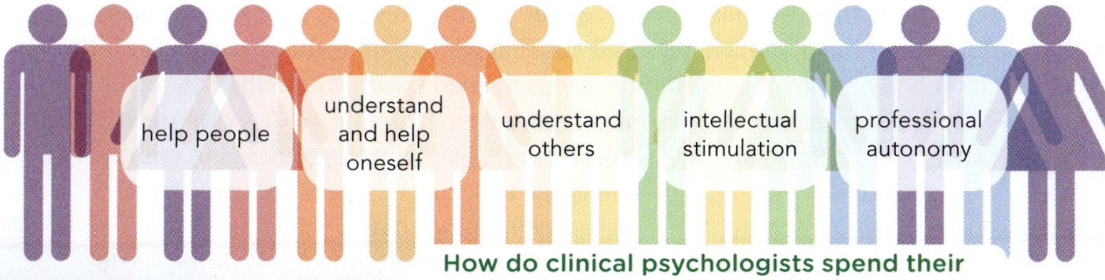

(Tirel, 2023, OCP, 2020; Conroy et al., 2019; Lin et al., 2019; Miller, 2017; Waters, 2015; Farber

CLINICAL CAREERS

How satisfied are clinical psychologists with their careers?

(Tirel, 2023; Conroy et al., 2019; Lin et al., 2019; Goetz et al., 2018; Rupert et al., 2012; Norcross et al., 2005)

How do clinical psychologists spend their professional time?

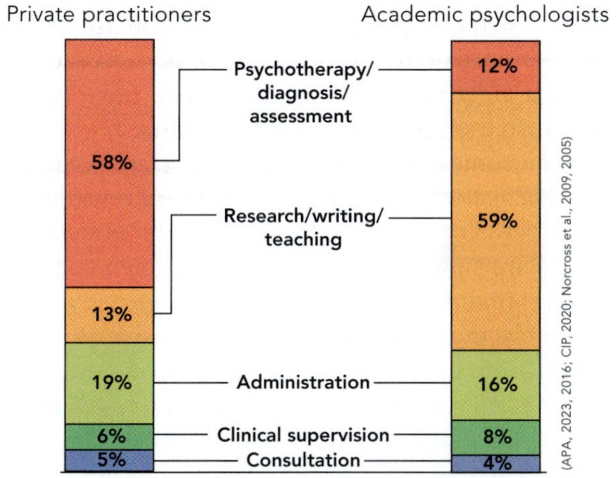

(APA, 2023, 2016; CIP, 2020; Norcross et al., 2009, 2005)

ETHICS IN CLINICAL PRACTICE

Although the field's code of ethics explicitly forbids it, some therapists engage in sexual relationships with their clients. This is the profession's most egregious violation of trust and boundaries and typically causes significant psychological harm to clients.

Who has had a sexual relationship with a client?

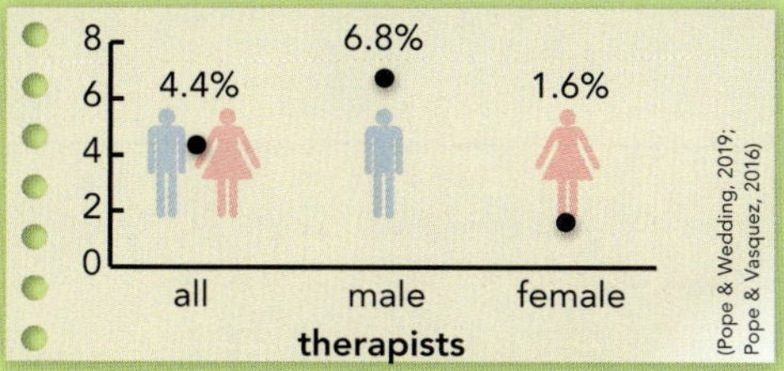

(Pope & Wedding, 2019; Pope & Vasquez, 2016)

Effects on clients

- Ambivalence
- Guilt
- Emptiness and isolation
- Sexual confusion
- Inability to trust
- Confusion of roles and boundaries
- Emotional damage
- Suppressed rage
- Heightened risk of suicide
- Cognitive dysfunction

(Pope et al., 2023, 2021; Pope & Wedding, 2019; Pope & Vasquez, 2016; Pope, 1994, 1988)

CLINICIANS IN THERAPY

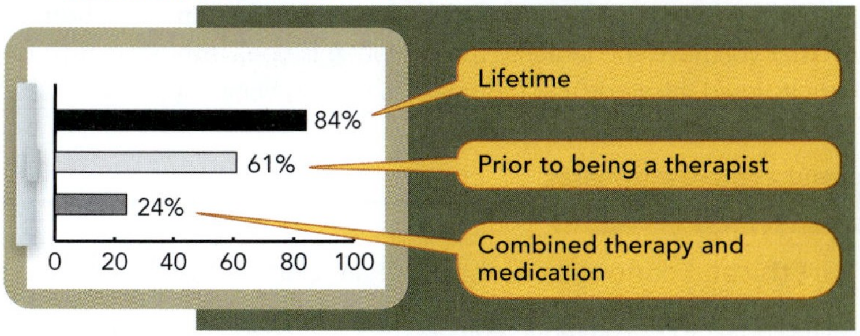

(Pope et al., 2023, 2021; AIPC, 2019; Pope & Vasquez, 2016; Bearse et al., 2014)

Top qualities clinicians look for in choosing a therapist

- Competence
- Warmth and caring
- Clinical experience and professional reputation
- Openness
- Active therapeutic style
- Flexibility

(Fagan, 2022, Hill et al., 2017; Norcross et al., 2009, 2005)

THE EMOTIONAL SIDE

Therapists' fears regarding clients

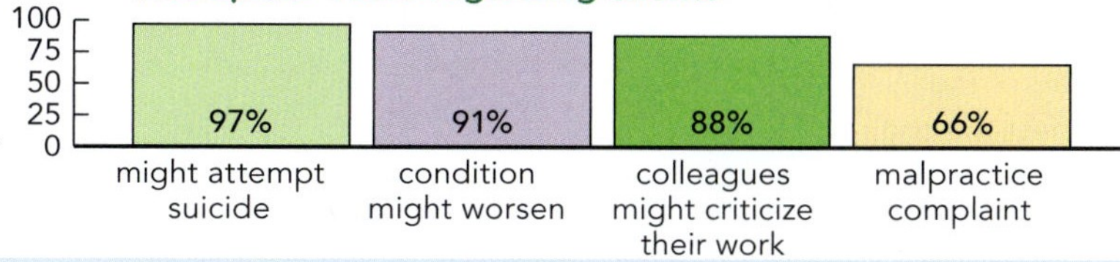

Therapists' anger toward clients

(Pope et al., 2023, 2021; Pope & Wedding, 2019; Clay, 2017; Pope & Vasquez, 2016; Pope & Tabachnick, 1993; Pope et al., 1987)

Within a Larger System

AT ONE TIME, clinical researchers and professionals conducted their work largely in isolation. Today, their activities have numerous ties to the legislative, judicial, and economic systems and to technological forces as well. One reason for this growing interconnectedness is that the clinical field has reached a high level of respect and acceptance in our society. Clinicians now serve millions of people in many ways. They have much to say about almost every aspect of society, from education to ecology, and are widely looked to as sources of expertise. When a field becomes so prominent, it inevitably affects how other institutions are run. It also attracts public scrutiny, and various institutions begin to keep an eye on its activities.

When people with psychological challenges seek help from a therapist, they are entering a complex system consisting of many interconnected parts. Just as their personal challenges have grown within a social structure, so will their treatment be affected by the various parts of a larger system—the therapist's values and needs, legal and economic factors, societal attitudes, technological changes, and yet other forces. These many forces influence clinical research as well.

The effects of this larger system on an individual's psychological needs can be positive or negative, like a family's impact on each of its members. When the system protects a client's rights and confidentiality, for example, it is serving the client well. When economic, legal, or other societal forces limit treatment options, cut off treatment prematurely, or stigmatize a person, the system is adding to the person's difficulties.

Because of the enormous growth and impact of the mental health profession in our society, it is important that we understand the profession's strengths and weaknesses. As you have read throughout this book, the field has gathered much knowledge, especially during the past several decades. What mental health professionals do not know and cannot do, however, still outweighs what they do know and can do. Everyone who turns to the clinical field—directly or indirectly—must recognize that it is young and imperfect. Society is vastly curious about behavior and often in need of information and help. What we as a society must remember, however, is that the field is still unfolding.

of NOTE ...

Their Words

"I spent . . . two hours chatting with Einstein. . . . He is cheerful, assured and likable, and understands as much about psychology as I do about physics, so we got on together very well."

Sigmund Freud, 1927

Quick Quiz

1. Briefly explain the M'Naghten, irresistible impulse, Durham, and ALI tests of insanity. Which tests are used today to determine whether defendants are not guilty by reason of insanity? pp. 545–546
2. Explain the guilty but mentally ill, diminished capacity, mentally disordered sex offender, and sexually violent predator verdicts and laws. pp. 548–550
3. What are the reasons behind and the procedures for determining whether defendants are mentally incompetent to stand trial? pp. 550–551
4. What are the reasons for civil commitment, and how is it carried out? What criticisms have been made of civil commitment? pp. 552–555
5. What rights have court rulings and legislation guaranteed to patients with psychological disorders? pp. 555–558
6. How do the legislative and judicial systems affect the issue of professional boundaries of clinical practice? pp. 558–559
7. What have clinical researchers learned about eyewitness memories and about patterns of criminality? How accurate and influential is the practice of psychological profiling in criminal cases? pp. 559–560
8. What key issues are covered by the psychologist's code of ethics? Under what conditions must therapists break the principle of confidentiality? pp. 562–563
9. What kinds of programs for the prevention and treatment of psychological problems have been established in work settings? What trends have emerged in recent years in the funding and insurance of mental health care? pp. 565–567
10. Describe how the mental health field has been affected by and dealt with the technological advances of recent years. pp. 567–568

Glossary

ABAB design A single-subject experimental design in which behavior is measured during a baseline period, after a treatment has been applied, after baseline conditions have been reintroduced, and after the treatment has been reintroduced. Also called a *reversal design*.

Abnormal psychology A term, no longer in common use, to describe the scientific study of atypical behavior undertaken to describe, predict, explain, and change pathological patterns of functioning.

Acceptance and commitment therapy (ACT) A cognitive-behavioral therapy that teaches clients to accept and be mindful of (that is, just notice) their dysfunctional thoughts or worries.

Acetylcholine A neurotransmitter that has been linked to depression and dementia.

Acute stress disorder A disorder in which a person experiences fear and related symptoms soon after a trauma but for less than a month.

Addiction Persistent, compulsive dependence on a substance or behavior.

Adjustment disorders Disorders characterized by clinical symptoms such as depressed mood or anxiety in response to significant stressors.

Adverse childhood experiences (ACEs) Negative events occurring during childhood (for example, mistreatment, abuse, neglect, household dysfunction) that can lead to immediate or later trauma.

Affect An experience of emotion or mood.

Affirmative therapy One kind of culturally responsive treatment, which validates and advocates for the needs of LGBTQ+ clients and helps them achieve greater self-acceptance and pride regarding their sexual orientation, gender identity, and/or gender expression.

Aftercare A program of posthospitalization care and treatment in the community.

Agoraphobia An anxiety disorder in which a person is afraid to be in public situations from which escape might be difficult or help unavailable if panic-like or embarrassing symptoms were to occur.

Agranulocytosis A life-threatening drop in white blood cells. This condition is sometimes produced by the second-generation antipsychotic drug *clozapine*.

Alcohol Any beverage containing ethyl alcohol, including beer, wine, and liquor.

Alcohol dehydrogenase An enzyme that breaks down alcohol in the stomach before it enters the blood.

Alcohol use disorder A pattern of behavior in which a person repeatedly abuses or depends on alcohol. Also known as *alcoholism*.

Alcoholics Anonymous (AA) A self-help organization that provides support and guidance for people with alcohol use disorder.

Alcoholism A pattern of behavior in which a person repeatedly abuses or depends on alcohol. Also known as *alcohol use disorder*.

Alogia A decrease in speech or speech content; a symptom of schizophrenia. Also known as *poverty of speech*.

Alprazolam A benzodiazepine drug shown to be effective in the treatment of anxiety disorders. Marketed as Xanax.

Altruistic suicide Suicide by people who intentionally sacrifice their lives for the well-being of society.

Alzheimer's disease The most common type of neurocognitive disorder, usually occurring after the age of 65, marked most prominently by memory impairment.

Amenorrhea The absence of menstrual cycles.

American Law Institute test A legal test for insanity that holds people to be "insane" at the time they committed a crime if, because of a mental disorder, they did not know right from wrong or could not resist an uncontrollable impulse to act.

Amnesia Loss of memory.

Amphetamine A stimulant drug that is manufactured in the laboratory.

Amphetamine psychosis A syndrome characterized by psychotic symptoms brought on by high doses of amphetamines. Similar to *cocaine psychosis*.

Amygdala A structure in the brain that plays a key role in emotion and memory.

Anal stage In psychoanalytic theory, the second 18 months of life, during which the child's focus of pleasure shifts to the anus.

Analogue experiment A research method in which the experimenter produces pathological-like behavior in laboratory participants and then conducts experiments on the participants.

Analogue observation A method for observing behavior in which people are observed in artificial settings such as clinicians' offices or laboratories.

Anesthesia A lessening or loss of sensation of touch or of pain.

Anomic suicide Suicide by individuals whose social environment fails to provide stability, thus leaving them without a sense of belonging.

Anorexia nervosa A disorder marked by the pursuit of extreme thinness and by extreme weight loss.

Anoxia A complication of birth in which the baby is deprived of oxygen.

Antabuse (disulfiram) A drug that causes intense nausea, vomiting, increased heart rate, and dizziness when taken with alcohol. It is often taken by people who are trying to refrain from drinking alcohol.

Antagonist drugs Drugs that block or change the effects of an addictive drug.

Antianxiety drugs Psychotropic drugs that help reduce tension and anxiety. Also called *minor tranquilizers* or *anxiolytics*.

Antibipolar drugs Psychotropic drugs that help stabilize the moods of people experiencing a bipolar disorder. Also known as *mood stabilizers*.

Antibodies Bodily chemicals that seek out and destroy foreign invaders such as bacteria or viruses.

Antidepressant drugs Psychotropic drugs that improve the mood of people with depression.

Antigen A foreign invader of the body, such as a bacterium or a virus.

Antipsychotic drugs Drugs that help correct grossly confused or distorted thinking.

Antipsychotic medication-induced movement disorder Unwanted movements, such as severe shaking, bizarre-looking grimaces, twisting of the body, and extreme restlessness, sometimes produced by antipsychotic drugs. Also called *extrapyramidal effects*.

Antisocial personality disorder A personality disorder marked by a general pattern of disregard for and violation of other people's rights.

Anxiety The central nervous system's physiological and emotional response to a vague sense of threat or danger.

Anxiety disorder A disorder in which anxiety is a central symptom.

Anxiety sensitivity A tendency to focus on one's bodily sensations, assess them illogically, and interpret them as harmful.

Anxiolytics Drugs that reduce anxiety.

ApoE-4 gene One form of the ApoE gene that is inherited by about 30 percent of the population. Those people may be particularly vulnerable to the development of Alzheimer's disease.

Arbitrary inference An error in logic in which a person draws negative conclusions on the basis of little or even contrary evidence.

Aripiprazole A second-generation antipsychotic drug whose brand name is Abilify.

Asperger's disorder A pattern previously distinguished from autism, in which people display profound social impairment yet maintain a relatively high level of cognitive functioning and language skills. The pattern is now one of the patterns included in autism spectrum disorder.

Assertive community treatment A community approach for people with severe mental disorders in which clinicians provide interventions ranging from medications and psychotherapy to residential and vocational guidance.

Assertiveness training A cognitive-behavioral approach to increasing assertive behavior that is socially desirable.

Assessment The process of collecting and interpreting relevant information about a client or research participant.

Asthma A disease marked by narrowing of the trachea and bronchi, resulting in shortness of breath, wheezing, coughing, and a choking sensation.

Asylum A type of institution that first became popular in the sixteenth century to provide care for persons with mental disorders. Most asylums became virtual prisons.

Attention circuit A number of brain structures that work together to bring about attention and to maintain a proper balance between Type 1 and Type 2 attention processes.

Attention-deficit/hyperactivity disorder (ADHD) A disorder marked by the inability to focus attention, or by overactive and impulsive behavior, or both.

Attribution An explanation of things we see going on around us that points to particular causes.

Auditory hallucination A hallucination in which a person hears sounds or voices that are not actually present.

Augmentative communication system A method for enhancing the communication skills of autistic people, people with intellectual disability, or those with cerebral palsy by teaching them to point to pictures, symbols, letters, or words on a communication board or computer.

Aura A warning sensation that may precede a migraine headache.

Autism spectrum disorder A neurodevelopmental disorder which, according to DSM-5-TR, is marked by substantial unresponsiveness to others, significant communication deficits, and highly repetitive and rigid behaviors, interests, and activities.

Autoerotic asphyxia A fatal lack of oxygen that people may unintentionally produce while hanging, suffocating, or strangling themselves during masturbation.

Automatic thoughts Numerous unpleasant thoughts that help to cause or maintain depression, anxiety, or other forms of psychological dysfunction.

Autonomic nervous system (ANS) The network of nerve fibers that connect the central nervous system to all the other organs of the body.

Aversion therapy A treatment in which clients are repeatedly presented with unpleasant stimuli while they are performing undesirable behaviors, such as taking a drug.

Avoidant personality disorder A personality disorder characterized by consistent discomfort and restraint in social situations, overwhelming feelings of inadequacy, and extreme sensitivity to negative evaluation.

Avolition A symptom of schizophrenia marked by apathy and an inability to start or complete a course of action.

Axon A long fiber extending from the body of a neuron.

Barbiturates Addictive sedative-hypnotic drugs that reduce anxiety and help people sleep.

Baseline data A person's initial response level on a test or scale.

Basic irrational assumptions The inaccurate and inappropriate beliefs held by people with various psychological disorders, according to Albert Ellis.

Battery A series of tests, each of which measures a specific skill area.

B-cell A lymphocyte that produces antibodies.

Behavior-focused therapy A therapeutic approach that seeks to identify problem-causing behaviors and change them. Also known as *behavior modification.*

Behavioral activation A therapy for depression in which the therapist works systematically to increase the number of constructive and pleasurable activities and events in a client's life.

Behavioral medicine A field that combines psychological and physical interventions to treat or prevent medical problems.

Behaviors The responses an organism makes to its environment.

Bender Visual-Motor Gestalt Test A neuropsychological test in which a subject is asked to copy a set of nine simple designs and later reproduce the designs from memory.

Benzodiazepines The most common group of antianxiety drugs, which includes Valium and Xanax.

Bereavement The process of working through the grief that one feels when a loved one dies.

Beta-amyloid protein A small molecule that forms sphere-shaped deposits called senile plaques, linked to aging and to Alzheimer's disease.

"Big Five" theory of personality A leading theory that holds that personality can be effectively organized and described by five broad dimensions of personality—openness, conscientiousness, extroversion, agreeableness, and neuroticism.

Binge An episode of uncontrollable eating during which a person ingests a very large quantity of food.

Binge drinking A pattern of alcohol consumption in which a person consumes five or more drinks on a single occasion.

Binge-eating disorder A disorder marked by frequent binges without extreme compensatory acts.

Binge-eating/purging-type anorexia nervosa A type of anorexia nervosa in which people have eating binges but still lose excessive weight by forcing themselves to vomit after meals or by abusing laxatives or diuretics.

Biofeedback A technique in which a client is given information about physiological reactions as they occur and learns to control the reactions voluntarily.

Biological challenge test A procedure used to produce panic in participants or clients by having them exercise vigorously or perform some other potentially panic-inducing task in the presence of a researcher or therapist.

Biological model The theoretical perspective that points to biological processes as the key to human behavior.

Biological therapy The use of physical and chemical procedures to help people overcome psychological problems.

Biomarkers Biochemical, molecular, genetic, or structural characteristics that usually accompany a disease.

Biopsychosocial theories Explanations that attribute the cause of psychopathology to an interaction of genetic, biological, developmental, emotional, behavioral, cognitive, social, and societal influences.

Biosocial theory A theory that points to a combination of internal and external factors to explain borderline personality disorder and certain other disorders.

Bipolar disorder A disorder marked by alternating or intermixed periods of mania and depression.

Bipolar I disorder A type of bipolar disorder marked by full manic and major depressive episodes.

Bipolar II disorder A type of bipolar disorder marked by mildly manic (hypomanic) episodes and major depressive episodes.

Birth complications Problematic biological conditions during birth that can affect the physical and psychological well-being of the child.

Blunted affect A symptom of schizophrenia in which a person shows less emotion than most people.

Body dysmorphic disorder A disorder in which individuals become preoccupied with the belief that they have certain defects or flaws in their physical appearance. Such defects or flaws are imagined or greatly exaggerated.

Body shaming The practice of criticizing people publicly for being overweight or (less frequently) underweight.

Borderline personality disorder A personality disorder characterized by repeated instability in interpersonal relationships, self-image, and mood and by impulsive behavior.
Brain circuit A network of particular brain structures that work together, triggering each other into action to produce a distinct kind of behavioral, cognitive, or emotional reaction.
Brain stimulation Interventions that directly or indirectly stimulate the brain in order to bring about psychological improvement.
Brain structure A distinct area or region of the brain formed by a large group of neurons.
Brain wave The fluctuations of electrical potential that are produced by neurons in the brain.
Breathing-related sleep disorder A sleep disorder in which sleep is frequently disrupted by a breathing problem, causing excessive sleepiness or insomnia.
Brief psychotic disorder Psychotic symptoms that appear suddenly after a very stressful event or a period of emotional turmoil and last anywhere from a few hours to a month.
Brodmann Area 25 A brain structure whose irregular activity has been linked to depression. Also called the *subgenual cingulate*.
Bulimia nervosa A disorder marked by frequent eating binges followed by forced vomiting or other extreme compensatory behaviors to avoid gaining weight. Also known as *binge-purge syndrome*.
Bullying The repeated infliction of force, threats, or coercion in order to intimidate, hurt, or dominate another, less powerful person; particularly common among children and adolescents.
Buprenorphine An opioid substitute drug that is administered as a form of maintenance therapy for substance use disorder.

Caffeine The world's most widely used stimulant, most often consumed in coffee.
Cannabidiol (CBD) A chemical in cannabis that can also be useful for treating some medical conditions, such as seizure disorders. Unlike THC, the main active chemical in cannabis, CBD does not produce a high.
Cannabis Drugs produced from the varieties of the hemp plant *Cannabis sativa*. They cause a mixture of hallucinogenic, depressant, and stimulant effects.
Cannabis edibles Food products that contain cannabis.
Case manager A community therapist who offers and coordinates a full range of services for people with severe mental disorders, including psychotherapy, advice, medication supervision, guidance through the community system, and protection of patients' rights.
Case study A detailed account of a person's life and psychological problems.
Catatonia A pattern of extreme psychomotor symptoms, found in some forms of schizophrenia, which may include catatonic stupor, rigidity, or posturing.
Catatonic excitement A form of catatonia in which a person moves excitedly, sometimes with wild waving of the arms and legs.
Catatonic stupor A symptom associated with schizophrenia in which a person becomes almost totally unresponsive to the environment, remaining motionless and silent for long stretches of time.
Catharsis The reliving of past repressed feelings in order to settle internal conflicts and overcome problems.
Caudate nuclei Structures in the brain, within the region known as the basal ganglia, that help convert sensory information into thoughts and actions.
Centenarians People who are 100 years old or older.
Central nervous system The brain and spinal cord.
Cerebellum An area of the brain that coordinates movement in the body and perhaps helps control a person's ability to shift attention rapidly.
Checking compulsion A compulsion in which people feel compelled to check the same things over and over.
Child abuse The nonaccidental use of excessive physical or psychological force by an adult on a child, often aimed at hurting or destroying the child.
Childhood-onset fluency disorder A communication disorder in which individuals repeat, prolong, or interject sounds when they speak; pause before finishing a word; or experience excessive tension in the muscles they use for speech. Also called *stuttering*.
Chlorpromazine A phenothiazine drug commonly used for treating schizophrenia. Marketed as Thorazine.
Chromosomes The structures, located within a cell, that contain genes.
Chronic headaches A medical problem marked by frequent intense aches in the head or neck that are not caused by another medical disorder.
Chronic traumatic encephalopathy (CTE) A degenerative brain disease that is experienced by many NFL players, among others, that is caused by repeated head blows over the course of time.
Circadian rhythm disorder A sleep–wake disorder characterized by a mismatch between a person's sleep–wake pattern and the sleep–wake schedule of most other people.
Circadian rhythms Internal "clocks" consisting of repeated biological fluctuations.
Cirrhosis An irreversible condition, often caused by excessive drinking, in which the liver becomes scarred and begins to change in anatomy and functioning.
Cisgender Individuals whose gender identity is consistent with their assigned gender.
Civil commitment A legal process by which a person can be forced to undergo mental health treatment.
Clang A rhyme used by some people with schizophrenia as a guide to forming thoughts and statements.
Classical conditioning A process of learning by temporal association in which two events that repeatedly occur close together in time become fused in a person's mind and produce the same response.
Classification system A list of disorders, along with descriptions of symptoms and guidelines for making appropriate diagnoses.
Cleaning compulsion A common compulsion in which people feel compelled to keep cleaning themselves, their clothing, and their homes.
Client-centered therapy The humanistic therapy developed by Carl Rogers in which clinicians try to help clients by conveying acceptance, accurate empathy, and genuineness.
Clinical interview A face-to-face encounter in which clinicians ask questions of clients, weigh their responses and reactions, and learn about them and their psychological problems.
Clinical psychologist A mental health professional who has earned a doctorate in clinical psychology.
Clinical psychology The study, assessment, treatment, and prevention of psychopathology.
Clinical social worker A mental health specialist who is qualified to conduct psychotherapy upon earning a master's degree or doctorate in social work.
Clinical test A device for gathering information about a few aspects of a person's psychological functioning from which broader information about the person can be inferred.
Clitoris The female sex organ located in front of the urinary and vaginal openings. It becomes enlarged during sexual arousal.
Clozapine A commonly prescribed second-generation antipsychotic drug.
Cocaine An addictive stimulant obtained from the coca plant. It is the most powerful natural stimulant known.
Code of ethics A body of principles and rules for ethical behavior, designed to guide decisions and actions by members of a profession.
Cognition The capacity to think, remember, and anticipate.
Cognitive-behavioral model A theoretical perspective that emphasizes both behavior and the process and content of thinking as causes of psychological problems.
Cognitive-behavioral therapies Therapy approaches that seek to help clients change both counterproductive behaviors and dysfunctional ways of thinking.

Cognitive processing therapy A cognitive-focused intervention for people with PTSD in which therapists guide individuals to examine and change the dysfunctional attitudes and styles of interpretation they have developed as a result of their traumatic experiences, thus enabling them to deal with difficult memories and feelings.

Cognitive remediation A treatment that focuses on the cognitive impairments that often characterize people with schizophrenia—particularly their difficulties in attention, planning, and memory.

Cognitive therapy A therapy developed by Aaron Beck that helps people identify and change the maladaptive assumptions and ways of thinking that help cause their psychological disorders.

Cognitive triad The three forms of negative thinking that Aaron Beck theorizes lead people to feel depressed. The triad consists of a negative view of one's experiences, oneself, and the future.

Communication disorders Neurodevelopmental disorders characterized by marked impairment in language, speech, sound, or speech fluency.

Community-based participatory research (CBPR) A research tradition that has members of an affected community work collaboratively with academically trained researchers at all stages of the research process.

Community mental health center A treatment facility that provides medication, psychotherapy, and emergency care for psychological problems and coordinates treatment in the community.

Community mental health treatment A treatment approach that emphasizes community care.

Comorbidity The occurrence of two or more disorders in the same person.

Complex PTSD A particularly severe pattern in which individuals experience virtually all of the symptoms of PTSD, including numerous dissociative experiences, as well as profound disturbances in their emotional control, self-concept, and relationships.

Compulsion A repetitive and rigid behavior or mental act that a person feels driven to perform in order to prevent or reduce anxiety.

Compulsive ritual A detailed, often elaborate, set of actions that a person often feels compelled to perform, always in an identical manner.

Computerized axial tomography (CT scan) A composite image of the brain created by compiling X-ray images taken from many angles.

Concerta A trade name of methylphenidate, a stimulant drug that is helpful in many cases of attention-deficit/hyperactivity disorder (ADHD).

Concordance A statistical measure of the frequency with which family members (often both members of a pair of twins) have the same particular characteristic.

Concurrent validity The degree to which the measures gathered from one assessment tool agree with the measures gathered from other assessment techniques.

Conditioned response (CR) A response previously associated with an unconditioned stimulus that comes to be produced by a conditioned stimulus.

Conditioned stimulus (CS) A previously neutral stimulus that comes to be associated with a nonneutral stimulus and can then produce responses similar to those produced by the nonneutral stimulus.

Conditioning A simple form of learning.

Conditions of worth According to client-centered theorists, the internal standards by which a person judges their own lovability and acceptability, determined by the standards to which the person was held as a child.

Conduct disorder A disorder in which children repeatedly violate the basic rights of others and display significant aggression.

Confederate An experimenter's accomplice, who helps create a particular impression in a study while pretending to be just another research participant.

Confidentiality The principle that certain professionals will not divulge the information they obtain from a client.

Confound In an experiment, a variable other than the independent variable that is also acting on the dependent variable.

Contingency management An operant conditioning treatment program that offers clients incentives (such as vouchers, prizes, cash, or privileges) that are contingent on the submission of drug-free urine specimens.

Continuation therapy A treatment strategy in which patients continue to receive therapy well after they are free of symptoms. Also known as *maintenance therapy.*

Continuous amnesia An inability to recall newly occurring events as well as certain past events.

Control group In an experiment, a group of participants who are not exposed to the independent variable.

Conversion disorder A disorder in which bodily symptoms affect voluntary motor and sensory functions, but the symptoms are inconsistent with known medical diseases. Also known as *functional neurological symptom disorder.*

Conversion therapy An intervention, widely discredited, that attempts to change the sexual orientation of a person from lesbian, gay, or bisexual to heterosexual, or to change the gender identity of a person from transgender or nonbinary to their assigned gender. Also called *reparative therapy.*

Convulsion A brain seizure.

Coordinated specialty care (CSC) A treatment approach for people with severe mental disorders in which clinicians provide interventions ranging from psychotherapy and practical advice to medication monitoring, housing guidance, and vocational counseling.

Coronary arteries Blood vessels that surround the heart and are responsible for carrying oxygen to the heart muscle.

Correlation The degree to which events or characteristics vary along with each other.

Correlation coefficient (*r*) A statistical term that indicates the direction and the magnitude of a correlation, ranging from –1.00 to +1.00.

Correlational method A research procedure used to determine how much events or characteristics vary along with each other.

Coronary heart disease Illness of the heart caused by a blockage in the coronary arteries.

Cortico-striato-thalamo-cortical brain circuit A brain circuit that includes such brain structures as the orbitofrontal cortex (just above each eye), cingulate cortex, striatum (including the caudate nucleus and putamen, two other structures at the back of the striatum), and thalamus. The circuit is hyperactive in people with obsessive-compulsive disorder.

Corticosteroids Hormones, including cortisol, released by the adrenal glands at times of stress.

Cortisol A hormone released by the adrenal glands when a person is under stress.

Counseling psychology A mental health specialty similar to clinical psychology that offers its own graduate training program.

Countertransference A phenomenon of psychotherapy in which therapists' own feelings, history, and values subtly influence the way they interpret a client's problems.

Couple therapy A therapy format in which the therapist works with two people who share a long-term relationship.

Covert desensitization Desensitization that focuses on imagining confrontations with frightening objects or situations while in a state of relaxation.

Covert sensitization A treatment for eliminating unwanted behavior by pairing the behavior with unpleasant mental images.

Covid-19 pandemic A global outbreak of Covid-19, a virus caused by severe acute respiratory syndrome coronavirus 2 (SARS-CoV-2). Also known as *coronavirus pandemic.*

C-reactive protein (CRP) A protein that spreads throughout the body and causes inflammation and various illnesses and disorders.

Crack A powerful, ready-to-smoke freebase cocaine.

Creutzfeldt–Jakob disease A neurocognitive disorder caused by misshapen proteins called prions.

Criminal commitment A legal process by which people accused of a crime are instead judged mentally unstable and sent to a treatment facility.

Crisis intervention A treatment approach that tries to help people in a psychological crisis to view their situation more accurately, make better decisions, act more constructively, and overcome the crisis.
Cross-tolerance Tolerance that a person develops for a substance as a result of regularly using another substance similar to it.
Cultural humility A process in which clinical scientists or practitioners continuously examine their own beliefs and cultural identities, explore individuals' cultures and historical realities that differ from their own, seek to understand the cultural context of each person's mental health challenges, and respond accordingly.
Culturally responsive therapies Treatment approaches that are designed to help address the unique issues faced by members of different cultural groups.
Culture A people's common history, values, institutions, habits, skills, technology, and arts.
Cyberbullying The use of social media, e-mail, texting, chat rooms, cell phones, or other digital devices to harass, threaten, or intimidate people.
Cyclothymic disorder A disorder marked by numerous periods of hypomanic symptoms and mild depressive symptoms.
Cytokines Proteins that bind to receptors throughout the body; includes proinflammatory cytokines that spread throughout the body and cause inflammation when persons are under chronic stress.

Daily Report Card (DRC) A treatment for ADHD in which a child's target classroom behaviors—for example, staying in the classroom seat or raising a hand to speak—are carefully evaluated, recorded on a DRC, and reinforced by teachers throughout the school day. At the end of the day, the teacher further provides the report card for the parents to see, and, if target behaviors had been performed satisfactorily, the child is also given rewards at home.
Dark triad A trio of negative traits—narcissism, psychopathy, and Machiavellianism—displayed by some people, resulting in socially offensive behaviors.
Day center A program that offers hospital-like treatment during the day only. Also known as a *day hospital.*
Death darer A person who is ambivalent about the wish to die even as they attempt suicide.
Death ignorer A person who attempts suicide without recognizing the finality of death.
Death initiator A person who attempts suicide believing that the process of death is already underway and that they are simply quickening the process.
Death seeker A person who clearly intends to end their life at the time of a suicide attempt.
Deep brain stimulation (DBS) A treatment for depression in which a pacemaker powers electrodes that have been implanted in the patient's subgenual cingulate, thus stimulating that brain area.
Deinstitutionalization The practice of releasing patients from public mental hospitals; begun in the 1960s with the release of hundreds of thousands of patients.
Delayed ejaculation A penile dysfunction characterized by persistent inability to ejaculate or very delayed ejaculations during sexual activity with a partner.
Delirium A rapidly developing, acute disturbance in attention and orientation that makes it very difficult to concentrate and think in a clear and organized manner.
Delirium tremens (DTs) A dramatic alcohol withdrawal reaction that consists of confusion, clouded consciousness, and visual hallucinations.
Delusion A strange false belief firmly held despite evidence to the contrary.
Delusion of control The belief that one's impulses, feelings, thoughts, or actions are being controlled by other people.
Delusion of grandeur The belief that one is a great inventor, historical figure, or other specially empowered person.
Delusion of persecution The belief that one is being plotted or discriminated against, spied on, slandered, threatened, attacked, or deliberately victimized.
Delusion of reference A belief that attaches special and personal meaning to the actions of others or to various objects or events.
Delusional disorder A disorder consisting of persistent, nonbizarre delusions that are not part of a schizophrenic disorder.
Demonology The belief that psychopathology results from supernatural causes such as evil spirits.
Dendrite An extension located at one end of a neuron that receives impulses from other neurons.
Denial An ego defense mechanism in which a person fails to acknowledge unacceptable thoughts, feelings, or actions.
Dependent personality disorder A personality disorder characterized by a pattern of clinging and obedience, fear of separation, and an ongoing need to be taken care of.
Dependent variable The variable in an experiment that is expected to change as the independent variable is manipulated.
Depersonalization-derealization disorder A dissociative disorder marked by the presence of persistent and recurrent episodes of depersonalization, derealization, or both.
Depressant A substance that slows the activity of the central nervous system and in sufficient dosages causes a reduction of tension and inhibitions.
Depression A low, sad state marked by significant levels of sadness, lack of energy, low self-worth, guilt, or related symptoms.
Depression-related brain circuit A brain circuit whose dysfunction contributes to unipolar depression. It includes the prefrontal cortex, hippocampus, amygdala, and subgenual cingulate (also called Brodmann Area 25), among other structures.
Depressive disorders The group of disorders marked by unipolar depression.
Derailment A common thinking disturbance in schizophrenia, involving rapid shifts from one topic of conversation to another. Also called *loose associations.*
Desensitization *See* Systematic desensitization.
Desire phase The phase of the sexual response cycle consisting of an urge to have sex, sexual fantasies, and sexual attraction to others.
Detoxification Systematic and medically supervised withdrawal from a drug.
Developmental coordination disorder A neurodevelopmental disorder marked by poor performance of coordinated motor activities.
Developmental psychopathology A perspective that uses a developmental framework to understand how variables and principles from the various models may collectively account for human functioning.
Deviance Variance from common patterns of behavior.
Diagnosis A determination that a person's difficulties reflect a particular disorder.
***Diagnostic and Statistical Manual of Mental Disorders* (DSM)** The classification system for mental disorders developed by the American Psychiatric Association. *See* DSM-5 *and* DSM-5-TR.
Dialectical behavior therapy (DBT) A comprehensive treatment approach, applied in cases of borderline personality disorder, suicidal intent, and/or other psychological problems; includes both individual therapy sessions and group sessions.
Diathesis–stress view The view that a person must first have a predisposition to a disorder and then be subjected to immediate psychosocial stress in order to develop the disorder.
Diazepam A benzodiazepine drug, marketed as Valium.
Dichotomous thinking Viewing problems and solutions in rigid either/or terms.
Diencephalon A brain area (consisting of the mammillary bodies, thalamus, and hypothalamus) that plays a key role in transforming short-term memory to long-term memory, among other functions.
Directed masturbation training A sex therapy approach that teaches women with female arousal or orgasmic problems how to masturbate effectively and eventually to reach orgasm during sexual interactions.
Disorganized attachment style A severely flawed capacity for human relationships, marked by an inconsistent pattern of responses in close relationships.

Displacement An ego defense mechanism that channels unacceptable id impulses toward a safer substitute.

Disruptive mood dysregulation disorder A childhood disorder marked by severe recurrent temper outbursts along with a persistent irritable or angry mood.

Dissociative amnesia A disorder marked by an inability to recall important personal events and information.

Dissociative disorders Disorders marked by major changes in memory that do not have clear physical causes.

Dissociative fugue A form of dissociative amnesia in which persons travel to a new location and may assume a new identity, simultaneously forgetting their past.

Dissociative identity disorder A dissociative disorder in which a person develops two or more distinct personalities. Previously known as *multiple personality disorder.*

Disulfiram (Antabuse) An antagonist drug used in treating alcohol abuse or dependence.

Dominant population The societal group that holds, on average, the greatest power, privilege, and social status.

Dopamine The neurotransmitter whose high activity has been shown to be related to schizophrenia.

Dopamine hypothesis The theory that schizophrenia results from excessive activity of the neurotransmitter dopamine.

Double-bind hypothesis A theory that some parents repeatedly communicate pairs of messages that are mutually contradictory, helping to produce schizophrenia in their children.

Double-masked design Experimental procedure in which neither the participant nor the experimenter knows whether the participant has received the experimental treatment or a placebo.

Down syndrome A form of intellectual disability caused by an irregularity in the twenty-first chromosome.

Drug Any substance other than food that affects the body or the mind.

Drug maintenance therapy An approach to treating substance dependence in which clients are given legally and medically supervised doses of the drug on which they are dependent, or a substitute drug.

Drug therapy The use of psychotropic drugs to reduce the symptoms of psychological disorders.

Dream A series of ideas and images that form during sleep.

DSM-5 (*Diagnostic and Statistical Manual of Mental Disorders,* Fifth Edition) The fifth edition of the DSM, published in 2013.

DSM-5-TR (*Diagnostic and Statistical Manual of Mental Disorders,* Fifth Edition, Text Revision) The current edition of the DSM, published in 2022. It is primarily a revision of the background text information found in DSM-5.

Dual diagnosis A pattern in which individuals experience both schizophrenia (or another severe psychological disorder) and a substance use disorder.

Durham test A legal test that holds people to be "insane" at the time they committed a crime if their act was the result of a mental disorder.

Duty to protect The principle that therapists must break confidentiality in order to protect a person who may be the intended target of a client.

Dyslexia A type of specific learning disorder in which people show a marked impairment in the speed and accuracy of reading, reading comprehension, and/or spelling.

Dyspareunia A type of genito-pelvic pain/penetration disorder in which a person experiences severe vaginal or pelvic pain during sexual intercourse.

Dyssomnias Sleep–wake disorders, such as insomnia disorder and hypersomnolence disorder, in which the amount, quality, or timing of sleep is disturbed.

Dysthymia A pattern of persistent depressive disorder that is chronic but less severe and less disabling than repeated episodes of major depression.

Early-onset Alzheimer's disease A relatively rare form of Alzheimer's disease that occurs before the age of 65. It typically runs in families.

Eccentric A person who deviates from conventional norms in odd, irregular, or even bizarre ways, but who is not displaying a psychological disorder.

Echolalia A symptom of autism or schizophrenia in which a person responds to statements by repeating the other person's words.

Ecstasy (MDMA) A drug chemically related to amphetamines and hallucinogens, used illicitly for its euphoric and hallucinogenic effects.

Ego According to Freud, the psychological force that employs reason and operates in accordance with the reality principle.

Ego defense mechanisms According to psychoanalytic theory, strategies developed by the ego to control unacceptable id impulses and to avoid or reduce the anxiety they arouse.

Egoistic suicide Suicide by people over whom society has little or no control, people who are not concerned with the norms or rules of society.

Ejaculation Contractions of the muscles at the base of the penis that cause sperm to be ejected.

Electra complex According to Freud, the pattern of desires all girls experience during the phallic stage, in which they develop a sexual attraction to their father.

Electroconvulsive therapy (ECT) A biological treatment in which a brain seizure is triggered when an electric current passes through electrodes attached to the patient's forehead.

Electroencephalograph (EEG) A device that records electrical impulses in the brain.

Electromyograph (EMG) A device that provides feedback about the level of muscular tension in the body.

Emergency commitment The temporary commitment to a mental hospital of a patient who is behaving in a bizarre or violent way.

Empirically supported treatment A movement in the clinical field that seeks to identify which therapies have received clear research support for each disorder, to develop corresponding treatment guidelines, and to spread such information to clinicians. Also known as *evidence-based treatment.*

Employee assistance program A mental health program offered by a business to its employees.

Encopresis A childhood disorder characterized by repeated defecating in inappropriate places, such as one's clothing.

Endocrine system The system of glands located throughout the body that help control important activities, such as growth and sexual activity.

Endogenous depression A depression that appears to develop without external reasons and is assumed to be caused by internal factors.

Endorphins Neurotransmitters that help relieve pain and reduce emotional tension. They are sometimes referred to as the body's own opioids.

Enhanced interrogation program A torture-based form of questioning that has been used to try to obtain information from suspected terrorists.

Enmeshed family pattern A family system in which members are overinvolved with each other's affairs and overly concerned about each other's welfare.

Enuresis A childhood disorder marked by repeated bed-wetting or wetting of one's clothes.

Epidemiological study A study that measures the incidence and prevalence of a problem, such as a disorder, in a given population.

Equifinality The principle that a number of different developmental pathways can lead to the same psychological disorder.

Erectile disorder A dysfunction in which a person repeatedly fails to attain or maintain an erection during sexual activity.

Ergot alkaloid A naturally occurring compound from which LSD is derived.

Essential hypertension High blood pressure caused by a combination of psychosocial and physiological factors.

Estrogen The primary female sex hormone.

Ethyl alcohol The chemical compound in all alcoholic beverages that is rapidly absorbed into the blood and immediately begins to affect the person's functioning.

Evidence-based treatment Treatment that has received clear research support for a particular disorder and has corresponding treatment guidelines.

Evoked potentials The brain response patterns recorded on an electroencephalograph while a person performs a task such as observing a flashing light.

Excitement phase The phase of the sexual response cycle marked by changes in the pelvic region, general physical arousal, and increases in heart rate, muscle tension, blood pressure, and rate of breathing.

Excoriation disorder A disorder in which people repeatedly pick at their skin, resulting in significant sores or wounds. Also called *skin-picking disorder*.

Exhibitionistic disorder A paraphilic disorder in which persons have repeated sexually arousing urges or fantasies about exposing their genitals to others, and either act on these urges with nonconsenting individuals or experience clinically significant distress or impairment.

Existential anxiety According to existential theorists, a universal fear of the limits and responsibilities of one's existence.

Existential model The theoretical perspective that human beings are born with the total freedom either to face up to one's existence and give meaning to one's life or to shrink from that responsibility.

Existential therapy A therapy that encourages clients to accept responsibility for their lives and to live with greater meaning and value.

Exorcism The practice, common in early societies, of treating psychopathology by coaxing evil spirits to leave the person's body.

Experiment A research procedure in which a variable is manipulated and the effect of that manipulation on another variable is observed.

Experimental group In an experiment, the participants who are exposed to the independent variable under investigation.

Exposure and response prevention A cognitive-behavioral technique used to treat obsessive-compulsive disorder that exposes clients to anxiety-arousing thoughts or situations and then prevents them from performing their compulsive acts. Also called *exposure and ritual prevention*.

Exposure therapy A behavior-focused intervention in which fearful people are repeatedly exposed to the objects or situations they dread.

Expressed emotion The general level of criticism, disapproval, and hostility expressed in a family. People recovering from schizophrenia are considered more likely to relapse if their families rate high in expressed emotion.

External validity The degree to which the results of a study may be generalized beyond that study.

Extrapyramidal effects Unwanted movements, such as severe shaking, bizarre-looking grimaces, twisting of the body, and extreme restlessness, sometimes produced by antipsychotic drugs. Also called *antipsychotic medication-induced movement disorder*.

Eye movement desensitization and reprocessing (EMDR) An exposure treatment in which clients move their eyes in a rhythmic manner from side to side while flooding their minds with images of objects and situations they ordinarily avoid.

Factitious disorder imposed on another A form of factitious disorder in which a caregiver uses various techniques to induce symptoms in a child or other person—for example, giving the individual drugs, tampering with medications, contaminating a feeding tube, or even smothering the individual. Also known as *Munchausen syndrome by proxy*.

Factitious disorder imposed on self A form of factitious disorder in which persons feign or induce physical symptoms on themselves, typically for the purpose of assuming the role of a sick person.

Family pedigree study A research design in which investigators determine how many and which relatives of a person with a disorder have the same disorder.

Family systems theory A theory that views the family as a system of interacting parts whose interactions exhibit consistent patterns and unstated rules.

Family therapy A therapy format in which the therapist meets with all members of a family and helps them to change in therapeutic ways.

Fantasy An ego defense mechanism in which a person uses imaginary events to satisfy unacceptable impulses.

Fear The central nervous system's physiological and emotional response to a serious threat to one's well-being.

Fear brain circuit The brain circuit that produces and manages fear reactions. Generalized anxiety disorder is related to dysfunction in this circuit, which includes such brain structures as the prefrontal cortex, anterior cingulate cortex, insula, and amygdala.

Fear hierarchy A list of objects or situations that frighten a person, starting with those that are slightly feared and ending with those that are feared greatly; used in systematic desensitization.

Female orgasmic disorder According to DSM-5-TR, a dysfunction in which a woman persistently fails to reach orgasm, has very-low-intensity orgasms, or has very delayed orgasms.

Female sexual interest/arousal disorder According to DSM-5-TR, a female dysfunction marked by a persistent reduction or lack of interest in sex and low sexual activity, as well as, in some cases, limited excitement and few sexual sensations during sexual activity.

Fentanyl A powerful opioid pain relief drug that is much more powerful than morphine and heroin. It is by far the pain reliever most commonly linked to overdose deaths.

Fetal alcohol syndrome A cluster of problems in a child, including lower intellectual functioning, low birth weight, and irregularities in the head and face, that results from a fetus's exposure to excessive alcohol during the pregnancy.

Fetishistic disorder A paraphilic disorder consisting of recurrent and intense sexual urges, fantasies, or behaviors that involve the use of a nonliving object or nongenital part, often to the exclusion of all other stimuli, accompanied by clinically significant distress or impairment.

First-generation antipsychotic drugs The group of antipsychotic drugs developed throughout the 1960s, 1970s, and 1980s, that comprised the first wave of antipsychotic drugs and are still in use today. Also called *neuroleptic drugs*.

Fixation According to Freud, a condition in which the id, ego, or superego do not mature properly and are frozen at an early stage of development.

Flashback The recurrence of LSD-induced sensory and emotional changes long after the drug has left the body, or, in posttraumatic stress disorder, the reexperiencing of past traumatic events.

Flat affect A marked lack of apparent emotions; a symptom of schizophrenia.

Flooding An exposure treatment for phobias in which clients are exposed repeatedly and intensively to a feared object and made to recognize that it is actually harmless.

Food insecurity Limited, uncertain, or unreliable availability of needed food due to limited financial means.

Forensic psychology The branch of psychology concerned with intersections between psychological practice and research and the judicial system. Also related to the field of *forensic psychiatry*.

Formal thought disorder A disturbance in the production and organization of thought.

Fragile X syndrome A pattern displayed by people whose X chromosome features a genetic irregularity that leaves it prone to breakage and loss. The individuals may generally display mild to moderate degrees of intellectual dysfunction, language impairments, and, in some cases, behavioral problems.

Free association A psychodynamic technique in which the patient describes any thought, feeling, or image that comes to mind, even if it seems unimportant.

Free-floating anxiety Chronic and persistent feelings of anxiety that are not clearly attached to a specific, identifiable threat.

Freebasing A technique for ingesting cocaine in which the pure cocaine basic alkaloid is chemically separated from processed cocaine, vaporized by heat from a flame, and inhaled with a pipe.

Frotteuristic disorder A paraphilic disorder in which a person has repeated and intense sexual urges or fantasies that involve touching and rubbing against a nonconsenting person, and either acts on these urges with the nonconsenting person or experiences clinically significant distress or impairment.

Functional magnetic resonance imaging (fMRI) A neuroimaging technique used to visualize internal functioning of the brain or body.

Fusion The final merging of two or more subpersonalities in dissociative identity disorder.

GABA *See* Gamma-aminobutyric acid.

Gambling disorder A disorder marked by persistent and recurrent gambling behavior, leading to a range of life problems.

Gamma-aminobutyric acid (GABA) A neurotransmitter whose low activity in the brain's fear circuit has been linked to anxiety.

Gender dysphoria A diagnostic category that, according to DSM-5-TR, may be assigned to transgender or nonbinary people if they persistently experience significant distress and impairment due to their gender identity and its contradiction to their assigned gender.

Gender-affirming surgery A surgical procedure that changes a person's sex organs and gender features. Also known as *gender reassignment surgery.*

Gender-sensitive therapies Approaches geared to the pressures of being a particular gender in society.

Gender fluid Individuals whose gender identity is not fixed and who instead display different mixtures of gender characteristics over time.

Gender identity change efforts (GICE) Interventions, widely discredited, that attempt to change the gender identity of a person from transgender or nonbinary to their assigned gender.

Gender reassignment surgery A surgical procedure that changes a person's sex organs and gender features. Also known as *gender-affirming surgery.*

General paresis An irreversible medical disorder whose symptoms include psychological disturbances, such as delusions of grandeur; caused by syphilis.

Generalized amnesia A loss of memory for events that occurred over a limited period of time as well as for certain events that occurred prior to that period.

Generalized anxiety disorder A disorder marked by persistent and excessive feelings of anxiety and worry about numerous events and activities.

Generic drug A marketed drug that is comparable to a trade-named drug in dosage form, strength, and performance.

Genes Chromosome segments that control the characteristics and traits we inherit.

Genetic linkage study A research approach in which extended families with high rates of a disorder over several generations are observed in order to determine whether the disorder closely follows the distribution pattern of other family traits.

Genital stage In Freud's theory, the stage beginning at approximately 12 years old, when the child begins to find sexual pleasure in sexual relationships.

Genito-pelvic pain/penetration disorder A sexual dysfunction characterized by significant physical discomfort during intercourse.

Geropsychology The field of psychology concerned with the mental health of older adults.

Gestalt therapy The humanistic therapy developed by Fritz Perls in which clinicians actively move clients toward self-recognition and self-acceptance by using techniques such as role-playing and self-discovery exercises.

Glia Brain cells that support the neurons.

Glutamate A neurotransmitter responsible for stimulating neurons in the brain and promoting connectivity and communication among neurons.

Group therapy A therapy format in which a group of people with similar problems meet together with a therapist to work on those problems.

Guided participation A modeling technique in which a client systematically observes and imitates the therapist while the therapist confronts feared items.

Guilty but mentally ill A verdict stating that defendants are guilty of committing a crime but are also experiencing a mental illness that should be treated during their imprisonment.

Guilty with diminished capacity A legal defense argument that states that because of limitations posed by mental dysfunction, a defendant could not have intended to commit a particular crime and thus should be convicted of a lesser crime.

Halfway house A residence for people with schizophrenia or other severe problems, often staffed by paraprofessionals. Also known as a *supervised group house, group home,* or *crisis house.*

Hallucination The experiencing of sights, sounds, or other perceptions in the absence of external stimuli.

Hallucinogen A substance that causes powerful changes primarily in sensory perception, including strengthening perceptions and producing illusions and hallucinations. Also called a *psychedelic drug.*

Hallucinosis A form of intoxication caused by hallucinogens, consisting of perceptual distortions and hallucinations.

Health maintenance The principle that young adults should act to promote their physical and mental health to best prepare for the aging process. Also called *wellness.*

Helper T-cell A lymphocyte that identifies foreign invaders and then both multiplies and triggers the production of other kinds of immune cells.

Heroin One of the most addictive substances derived from opium.

Hierarchical Taxonomy of Psychopathology (HiTOP) A dimensional system for classifying psychopathology that focuses on different levels of maladaptive symptoms and traits that collectively may result in clinical impairment.

High The pleasant feeling of relaxation and euphoria that follows the rush from certain recreational drugs.

Hippocampus A brain structure located below the cerebral cortex that is involved in memory.

Histrionic personality disorder A personality disorder characterized by a pattern of excessive emotionality and attention seeking. Once called *hysterical personality disorder.*

Hoarding disorder A disorder in which individuals feel compelled to save items and become very distressed if they try to discard them, resulting in an excessive accumulation of items.

Hopelessness A pessimistic belief that one's present circumstances, problems, or mood will not change.

Hormones The chemicals released by endocrine glands into the bloodstream.

Humanistic model The theoretical perspective that human beings are born with a natural inclination to be friendly, cooperative, and constructive, and are driven to self-actualize.

Humanistic therapy A system of therapy in which clinicians try to help clients look at themselves accurately and acceptingly so that they can fulfill their positive inborn potential.

Humors According to the early Greeks and Romans, bodily chemicals that influence mental and physical functioning.

Huntington's disease An inherited disease, characterized by progressive problems in cognition, emotion, and movement, that results in a neurocognitive disorder.

Hypersomnolence disorder A sleep–wake disorder characterized by an extreme need for extra sleep and feelings of excessive sleepiness.

Hypertension Chronic high blood pressure.

Hypnosis A sleeplike suggestible state during which a person can be directed to act in unusual ways, to experience unusual sensations, to remember seemingly forgotten events, or to forget remembered events.

Hypnotic amnesia Loss of memory produced by hypnotic suggestion.

Hypnotic therapy A treatment in which the patient undergoes hypnosis and is then guided to recall forgotten events or perform other therapeutic activities. Also known as *hypnotherapy.*

Hypnotism A procedure that places people in a trancelike mental state during which they become extremely suggestible.

Hypochondriasis A disorder in which people mistakenly fear that minor changes in their physical functioning indicate a serious disease. Now known as *illness anxiety disorder.*

Hypomanic episode An episode of mania in which the symptoms cause relatively little impairment.

Hypomanic pattern A pattern in which a person displays symptoms of mania, but the symptoms are less severe and cause less impairment than those of a manic episode.

Hypothalamic-pituitary-adrenal (HPA) axis One route by which the brain and body produce arousal.

Hypothalamus A brain structure that helps regulate various bodily functions, including eating and hunger.

Hypothesis A hunch or prediction that certain variables are related in certain ways.

Hypoxyphilia A pattern in which people strangle or smother themselves, or ask their partners to strangle or smother them, to increase their sexual pleasure.

Hysteria A term once used to describe what are now known as conversion disorder, somatic symptom disorder, and illness anxiety disorder.

Hysterical disorder A disorder in which physical functioning is changed or lost, without an apparent physical cause.

Iatrogenic Produced or caused inadvertently by a clinician.

ICD-11 (International Classification of Diseases, Eleventh Edition) The newest edition of the ICD, published in 2018 and put into operation in 2022.

Id According to Freud, the psychological force that produces instinctual needs, drives, and impulses.

Ideas of reference Beliefs that unrelated events pertain to oneself in some important way.

Identification Unconsciously incorporating the values and feelings of one's parents and fusing them with one's identity. Also, an ego defense mechanism in which a person takes on the values and feelings of a person who is causing them anxiety.

Idiographic information An individualistic understanding of a single person's psychopathology.

Illness anxiety disorder A disorder in which people are chronically anxious about and preoccupied with the notion that they have or are developing a serious medical illness, despite the absence of significant somatic symptoms.

Illogical thinking According to cognitive theories, illogical ways of thinking that may lead to self-defeating conclusions and psychological problems.

Immune system The body's network of activities and cells that identify and destroy antigens and cancer cells.

Inappropriate affect Displays of emotions that are unsuited to the situation.

Incidence The number of new cases of a disorder occurring in a population over a specific period of time.

Inclusion The placement of children with intellectual disability in general school classes. Also known as *mainstreaming.*

Independent variable The variable in an experiment that is manipulated to determine whether it has an effect on another variable.

Individual therapy A therapeutic approach in which a therapist sees a client alone for sessions that may last from 15 minutes to 2 hours.

Informed consent The requirement that researchers provide sufficient information to participants about the purpose, procedure, risks, and benefits of a study.

Insanity defense A legal defense in which a person charged with a criminal offense claims to be not guilty by reason of insanity at the time of the crime.

Insomnia Difficulty falling or staying asleep.

Insomnia disorder A sleep–wake disorder characterized by severe difficulty falling asleep or maintaining sleep at least three nights per week.

Institutional Review Board (IRB) An ethics committee in a research facility that is empowered to protect the rights and safety of human research participants.

Integrity test A test that is designed to measure whether the test-taker is generally honest or dishonest.

Intellectual developmental disorder A neurodevelopmental disorder marked by intellectual functioning and adaptive behavior that are significantly below average. Also called *intellectual disability.*

Intellectual disability (ID) A neurodevelopmental disorder marked by intellectual functioning and adaptive behavior that are significantly below average. Also called *intellectual developmental disorder.*

Intelligence quotient (IQ) An overall score derived from intelligence tests that theoretically represents a person's overall intellectual capacity.

Intelligence test A test designed to measure a person's intellectual ability.

Intermittent explosive disorder An impulse-control disorder in which people periodically fail to resist aggressive impulses and commit serious assaults on others or destroy property.

Internal validity The accuracy with which a study can pinpoint one factor as the cause of a phenomenon.

International Classification of Diseases (ICD) The classification system for medical and mental disorders that is used by the World Health Organization.

Internet gaming disorder A disorder marked by persistent, recurrent, and excessive Internet gaming activity. Recommended for further study by DSM-5-TR.

Internet use disorder An addictive pattern in which individuals have an uncontrollable need to be online, characterized by spending all or most of their waking hours texting, tweeting, networking, gaming, Internet browsing, e-mailing, blogging, visiting virtual worlds, shopping online, or viewing online pornography.

Interpersonal psychotherapy (IPT) A therapy that addresses four interpersonal problem areas that may be leading to psychopathology: interpersonal losses, interpersonal role disputes, interpersonal role transitions, and interpersonal deficits.

Interpersonal theory of suicide A theory that asserts that people with perceived burdensomeness, thwarted belongingness, and a psychological capability to carry out suicide are the most likely to attempt suicide. Also called *interpersonal-psychological theory.*

Interrater reliability A measure of the reliability of a test or of research results in which the consistency of evaluations across different judges is assessed. Also called *interjudge reliability.*

Intersectionality A multicultural framework that examines how each individual's memberships in multiple cultural groups and social identities—including race, ethnicity, socioeconomic class, gender, and sexual orientation—combine to shape their particular experiences, opportunities, outlook, and functioning.

Intersex A condition in which individuals are born with a combination of sex organs, reproductive organs, sex characteristics, chromosomes, and hormones that are ambiguous or inconsistent with each other.

Intolerance of uncertainty theory An explanation for generalized anxiety disorder that states that certain individuals cannot tolerate the knowledge that negative events may occur, even if the possibility of occurrence is very small.

Intoxication A cluster of undesirable behavioral or psychological changes, such as slurred speech or mood changes, that may develop during or shortly after the ingestion of a substance.

In vivo desensitization Desensitization that makes use of actual objects or situations, as opposed to imagined ones.

Ion An atom or group of atoms that has a positive or negative electrical charge.

Irresistible impulse test A legal test that holds people to be "insane" at the time they committed a crime if they were driven to do so by an uncontrollable "fit of passion."

Isolation An ego defense mechanism in which people unconsciously isolate and disown undesirable and unwanted thoughts, experiencing them as foreign intrusions.

Jail diversion An arrangement in which mentally disturbed criminal defendants are treated for their disorders on an outpatient basis. That is, they are diverted from jail to the community for mental health care.

Joint attention Sharing focus with other people on items or events in one's immediate surroundings, whether through shared eye-gazing, pointing, referencing, or other verbal or nonverbal indications that one is paying attention to the same object.

Juvenile delinquent A label sometimes applied by the legal system to children or teenagers who break the law.

Juvenile detention centers Facilities in which children or teenagers who break the law are sometimes incarcerated.

Ketamine An anesthetic drug that is also used as an antidepressant, bringing rapid relief to many people with depression.

Korsakoff's syndrome An alcohol-related disorder marked by extreme confusion, memory impairment, and other neurological symptoms.

Lamotrigine An antiseizure medication commonly used as a mood-stabilizing drug in the treatment of bipolar disorder. Also known by the brand name Lamictal.

Late-onset Alzheimer's disease By far the most common form of Alzheimer's disease, developing after the age of 65.

Latent content The symbolic meaning behind a dream's content.

Lateral hypothalamus (LH) A brain region that produces hunger when activated.

L-dopa A drug used in the treatment of Parkinson's disease, a disease in which dopamine is low.

Learned helplessness The perception, based on past experiences, that one has no control over the reinforcements in one's life.

Lewy body disease A type of neurocognitive disorder that involves a buildup of clumps of protein deposits, called Lewy bodies, within many neurons. In addition to progressive cognitive problems, this disease features significant movement difficulties.

Libido The sexual energy that fuels the id.

Life change units (LCUs) A system for measuring the stress associated with various life events.

Light therapy A treatment for seasonal affective disorder in which patients are exposed to extra light for several hours. Also called *phototherapy.*

Lithium A metallic element that occurs in nature as a mineral salt and is an effective treatment for bipolar disorders.

Lobotomy Psychosurgery in which a surgeon cuts the connections between the brain's frontal lobes and the lower centers of the brain.

Localized amnesia An inability to recall any of the events that occurred over a limited period of time.

Locus coeruleus A small area of the brain that seems to be active in the regulation of emotions. Many of its neurons use norepinephrine.

Long-term care Extended personal and medical support provided to older adults and other persons who may be impaired. It may range from partial support in a supervised apartment to intensive care at a nursing home.

Long-term memory The memory system that contains all the information that a person has stored over the years.

Longitudinal study A study that observes the same participants on many occasions over a long period of time.

Loose associations A common thinking disturbance in schizophrenia, characterized by rapid shifts from one topic of conversation to another. Also known as *derailment.*

LSD (lysergic acid diethylamide) A hallucinogen derived from ergot alkaloids.

Lycanthropy A condition in which persons believe themselves to be possessed by wolves or other animals.

Lymphocytes White blood cells that circulate through the lymph system and bloodstream, helping the body identify and destroy antigens and cancer cells.

Mainstreaming The placement of children with intellectual disability in general school classes. Also known as *inclusion.*

Major depressive disorder A severe pattern of depression that is disabling and not caused by such factors as drugs or a general medical condition.

Major neurocognitive disorder A neurocognitive disorder in which the decline in cognitive functioning is substantial and interferes with a person's ability to be independent.

Male hypoactive sexual desire disorder According to DSM-5-TR, a male dysfunction marked by a persistent reduction or lack of interest in sex and hence a low level of sexual activity.

Malingering Intentionally faking illness to achieve some external gains, such as financial compensation or military deferment.

Malpractice suit A lawsuit charging a therapist with improper conduct in the course of treatment.

Managed care program Health care coverage in which the insurance company largely controls the nature, scope, and cost of medical or psychological services.

Mania A state or episode of euphoria or frenzied activity in which people may have an exaggerated belief that the world is theirs for the taking.

Manifest content The consciously remembered content of a dream.

Mantra A sound, uttered or thought, used to focus one's attention and to turn away from ordinary thoughts and concerns during meditation.

MAO inhibitor An antidepressant drug that prevents the action of the enzyme monoamine oxidase.

Marginalized people People whose communities experience discrimination, as well as social, political, and economic exclusion, due to unequal power relationships across a society.

Marijuana One of the cannabis drugs, derived from the buds, leaves, and flowering tops of the hemp plant *Cannabis sativa.*

Marital therapy A therapy approach in which the therapist works with two people who share a long-term relationship. Also known as *couple therapy.*

Masked design A feature of an experiment in which participants do not know whether they are in the experimental condition or the control condition.

Mass murder The murder of four or more people in the same location and at around the same time.

Masturbation Self-stimulation of the genitals to achieve sexual arousal.

Masturbatory satiation A behavioral treatment in which a client masturbates for a very long period of time while fantasizing in detail about a paraphilic object. The procedure is expected to produce a feeling of boredom that becomes linked to the object.

Matched design A research design that matches the experimental participants with control participants who are similar on key characteristics.

MDMA A popular stimulant drug that also produces hallucinogenic effects and so is typically viewed as a hallucinogenic drug. Also called *Ecstasy.*

Mean The average of a group of scores.

Meditation A technique of turning one's concentration inward and achieving a slightly changed state of consciousness.

Melancholia A condition described by early Greek and Roman philosophers and physicians as consisting of unshakable sadness. Today it is known as *depression.*

Melatonin A hormone released by the pineal gland when a person's physical surroundings are dark.

Memory The faculty for recalling past events and past learning.

Mental incompetence A state of mental instability that leaves defendants unable to understand the legal charges and proceedings they are facing and unable to prepare an adequate defense with their attorney.

Mentalization The capacity to understand one's own mental states and those of other people.

Mentally disordered sex offender A legal category that some states apply to certain people who are repeatedly found guilty of sex crimes.

Mesmerism The method employed by Austrian physician F. A. Mesmer to treat hysterical disorders; a precursor of *hypnotism*.

Meta-analysis A statistical method that combines results from multiple independent studies.

Metabolism An organism's chemical and physical breakdown of food and the process of converting it into energy. Also, an organism's biochemical transformation of various substances, as when the liver breaks down alcohol into acetaldehyde.

Metacognitive theory A theory suggesting that people with generalized anxiety disorder implicitly hold both positive and negative beliefs about worrying.

Meta-worry Worrying about the fact that one is worrying so much.

Methadone A laboratory-made opioid-like drug.

Methadone maintenance program A treatment in which clients are given legally and medically supervised doses of methadone—a heroin substitute—to treat various opioid use disorders.

Methamphetamine A powerful amphetamine drug that has surged in popularity in recent years, posing major health and law enforcement problems.

Methylphenidate A stimulant drug, better known by the trade names Ritalin or Concerta, commonly used to treat ADHD.

Migraine headache A very severe headache that occurs on one side of the head, often preceded by a warning sensation and sometimes accompanied by dizziness, nausea, or vomiting.

Mild intellectual disability (mild ID) Level of intellectual disability where individuals typically have the adaptive skills needed to benefit from schooling, require only intermittent supports as children, and can support themselves as adults with minimal, if any, assistance.

Mild neurocognitive disorder A neurocognitive disorder in which the decline in cognitive functioning is modest and does not interfere with a person's ability to be independent.

Milieu therapy A humanistic approach to institutional treatment based on the premise that institutions can help patients recover by creating a climate that promotes self-respect, responsible behavior, and meaningful activity.

Mind–body dualism The position advocated by the seventeenth-century French philosopher René Descartes that the mind is separate from the body.

Mindfulness meditation A type of meditation in which people are mindful of (just notice) the various thoughts, emotions, sensations, and other private experiences that pass through their minds and bodies.

Mindfulness-based cognitive-behavioral therapy A type of therapy that teaches clients to be mindful of (just notice) and accept their dysfunctional thoughts or worries.

Minnesota Multiphasic Personality Inventory (MMPI) A widely used personality inventory consisting of a large number of statements that subjects mark as being true or false for them.

Mixed-methods research A research tradition that combines, or mixes, both quantitative and qualitative approaches within the same research project.

M'Naghten test A legal test that holds people to be "insane" at the time they committed a crime if, because of a mental disorder, they did not know the nature of the act or did not know right from wrong.

Model A set of assumptions and concepts that help scientists explain and interpret observations. Also called a *paradigm*.

Modeling A process of learning in which an individual acquires responses by observing and imitating others.

Moderate intellectual disability (moderate ID) Level of intellectual disability where individuals can function relatively well in familiar places with moderate levels of assistance.

Monoamine oxidase (MAO) A body chemical that destroys the neurotransmitter norepinephrine.

Monoamine oxidase (MAO) inhibitors Antidepressant drugs that lower MAO activity and thus increase the level of norepinephrine activity in the brain.

Mood disorder A disorder affecting one's emotional state, including major depressive disorder and bipolar disorders.

Mood-stabilizing drugs Psychotropic drugs that help stabilize the moods of people with bipolar disorder. Also known as *antibipolar drugs*.

Moral treatment A nineteenth-century approach to treating people with mental dysfunction that emphasized moral guidance and humane and respectful treatment.

Morphine A highly addictive substance derived from opium that is particularly effective in relieving pain.

Motivational interviewing A treatment that uses empathy and inquiring review to help motivate clients to recognize they have a serious psychological problem and commit to making constructive choices and behavior changes.

Multicultural perspective The view that each culture in a society has particular values, beliefs, and pressures that influence the behavior and functioning of its members.

Multicultural psychology The field that seeks to understand how the varied histories, opportunities, and barriers experienced by people of different races, ethnicities, genders, sexual orientations, abilities, languages, and other such factors affect behavior, emotion, and thought.

Multidimensional risk perspective A theory that identifies several kinds of risk factors that are thought to combine to help cause a disorder. The more factors present, the greater the risk of developing the disorder.

Multifinality The principle that persons with similar developmental histories may nevertheless have different clinical outcomes or react to comparable current situations in very different ways.

Munchausen syndrome An extreme and long-term form of factitious disorder in which a person produces symptoms, gains admission to a hospital, and receives treatment.

Munchausen syndrome by proxy A form of factitious disorder in which a caregiver uses various techniques to induce symptoms in a child or other person—for example, giving the individual drugs, tampering with medications, contaminating a feeding tube, or even smothering the individual. Also known as *factitious disorder imposed on another*.

Muscle contraction headache A headache caused by a narrowing of muscles surrounding the skull. Also known as *tension headache*.

Muscle dysmorphia Disorder in which men who are actually quite muscular perceive themselves as scrawny and small and so continue to strive for a "perfect" body through excessive weight lifting, abuse of steroids, or other excessive measures.

Muscularity-oriented disordered eating behaviors A dysfunctional pattern of eating in which men who consider themselves too thin eat excessively in order to gain weight and "bulk up."

Naloxone A widely used opioid antagonist drug. Marketed as Narcan.

Narcissistic personality disorder A personality disorder marked by a broad pattern of grandiosity, need for admiration, and lack of empathy.

Narcolepsy A sleep–wake disorder characterized by a repeated sudden and irrepressible need to sleep during waking hours.

Narcotic Any natural or synthetic opioid-like drug.

National Alliance on Mental Illness (NAMI) A nationwide grassroots organization that provides support, education, advocacy, and research for people with severe mental disorders and their families.

National interest groups Groups and organizations such as NAMI that have formed in countries around the world to push for better community treatment.

Natural experiment An experiment in which nature, rather than an experimenter, manipulates an independent variable.

Natural killer cell A lymphocyte that seeks out and destroys body cells that have already been infected by viruses, thus helping to stop the spread of a viral infection.

Naturalistic observation A method of observing behavior in which clinicians or researchers observe people in their everyday environments.

Negative correlation A statistical relationship in which the value of one variable increases while the value of the other variable decreases.

Negative symptoms Symptoms of schizophrenia that seem to be deficits in typical thought, emotions, or behaviors.

Neologism A made-up word that has meaning only to the person using it.

Nerve ending The region at the end of a neuron from which an impulse is sent to a neighboring neuron.

Neurocognitive disorder A disorder marked by a significant decline in at least one area of cognitive functioning.

Neurodevelopmental disorders A group of disabilities—including ADHD, autism spectrum disorder, and intellectual disability—in the functioning of the brain that emerge at birth or during very early childhood and affect one's behavior, memory, concentration, or ability to learn.

Neurodiversity A perspective, sometimes applied to autism, ADHD, and certain other neurodevelopmental disorders, that holds that all brains differ from each other and that some people's brains (those of *neurodivergent* people) develop or work differently from the brains of most other people (those of *neurotypical* people), without implying that the neurodivergent people are pathological or deficient.

Neurofibrillary tangles Twisted protein fibers that form within certain neurons as people age. People with Alzheimer's disease have an excessive number of such tangles.

Neuroimaging techniques Neurological tests that provide images of brain structure or activity, such as CT scans, PET scans, and MRIs. Also called *brain scanning*.

Neuroleptic drugs An alternative term for first-generation antipsychotic drugs, so called because they often produce undesired effects similar to the symptoms of neurological disorders.

Neuroleptic malignant syndrome A severe, potentially fatal reaction to antipsychotic drugs, marked by muscle rigidity, fever, altered consciousness, and autonomic dysfunction.

Neurological Relating to the structure or activity of the brain.

Neurological test A test that directly measures brain structure or activity.

Neuromodulator A neurotransmitter that helps modify or regulate the effect of other neurotransmitters.

Neuron A nerve cell.

Neuropsychological test A test that detects brain impairment by measuring a person's cognitive, perceptual, and motor performances.

Neurosis Freud's term for disorders characterized by intense anxiety, attributed to failure of a person's ego defense mechanisms to cope with unconscious conflicts.

Neurotransmitter A chemical that, released by one neuron, crosses the synaptic space to be received at receptors on the dendrites of neighboring neurons.

Neutralizing A person's attempt to eliminate unwanted thoughts by thinking or behaving in ways that put matters right internally, making up for the unacceptable thoughts.

Nicotine An alkaloid (nitrogen-containing chemical) derived from tobacco or produced in the laboratory.

Nicotine patch A patch attached to the skin like a Band-Aid, with nicotine content that is absorbed through the skin; it may ease the withdrawal reaction of an individual who has quit cigarette smoking.

Nightmare disorder A parasomnia characterized by chronic distressful, frightening dreams.

988 Suicide & Crisis Lifeline A national suicide prevention service, reachable at the 988 number, that routes calls or texts from persons in crisis to a nearby crisis center, where the individuals receive immediate counseling and mental health resources and referrals.

Nocturnal penile tumescence (NPT) Erection during sleep.

Nomothetic understanding A general understanding of the nature, causes, and treatments of psychopathology, in the form of laws or principles that apply across people.

Nonbinary Individuals who identify as neither male nor female, but rather as a blend of both or as neither.

Nonsuicidal self-injury (NSSI) Direct and deliberate destruction of one's own body tissue that is not accompanied by an intent to die.

Norepinephrine A neurotransmitter whose irregular activity is linked to depression and panic disorder.

Normalization The principle that institutions and community residences for people with intellectual disability should provide living conditions and opportunities similar to those enjoyed by the rest of society.

Norms A society's stated and unstated rules for proper conduct.

Not guilty by reason of insanity (NGRI) A verdict stating that defendants are not guilty of a crime because they were "insane" at the time of the crime.

Nutritional rehabilitation An initial phase of treatment in a number of cases of anorexia nervosa that includes supportive nursing care, day-to-day increased caloric intake, nutrition counseling, support, and, in some programs, motivational interviewing.

Object relations theory The psychodynamic theory that views the desire for relationships as the key motivating force in human behavior.

Observer drift The tendency of an observer who is rating subjects in an experiment to change criteria gradually and involuntarily, thus making the data unreliable.

Obsession A persistent thought, idea, impulse, or image that is experienced repeatedly, feels intrusive, and causes anxiety.

Obsessive-compulsive disorder A disorder in which a person has recurrent obsessions, compulsions, or both.

Obsessive-compulsive personality disorder A personality disorder marked by such an intense focus on orderliness, perfectionism, and control that the person loses flexibility, openness, and efficiency.

Obsessive-compulsive-related disorders Disorders in which obsessive-like concerns drive people to repeatedly and excessively perform certain pathological patterns of behavior.

Oedipus complex In Freudian theory, the pattern of desires emerging during the phallic stage in which boys become attracted to their mother as a sexual object and see their father as a rival they would like to push aside.

Olanzapine A second-generation antipsychotic drug whose brand name is Zyprexa.

Operant conditioning A process of learning in which individuals come to behave in certain ways as a result of experiencing consequences of one kind or another whenever they perform the behavior.

Opioid Opium, drugs derived from opium, and similar synthetic drugs.

Opioid antagonist A substance that attaches to opioid receptors in the brain and, in turn, blocks the effects of opioids.

Opium A highly addictive substance made from the sap of the opium poppy.

Oppositional defiant disorder A controversial DSM-5-TR disorder in which children are repeatedly argumentative, defiant, angry, irritable, and perhaps vindictive.

Oral stage The earliest developmental stage in Freud's conceptualization of psychosexual development, during which the infant's main gratification comes from feeding and from the body parts involved in feeding.

Orbitofrontal cortex A brain structure in which impulses involving excretion, sexuality, violence, and other primitive activities arise.

Orgasm A peaking of sexual pleasure, consisting of rhythmic muscular contractions in the pelvic region, during which a man's semen is ejaculated and the outer third of a woman's vaginal wall contracts.

Orgasm phase The phase of the sexual response cycle during which a person's sexual pleasure peaks and sexual tension is released as muscles in the pelvic region contract rhythmically.

Outpatient A person who receives a diagnosis or treatment in a clinic, hospital, or therapist's office but is not hospitalized overnight.

Outpatient civil commitment program A legal process in which courts order people with severe mental disorders into community treatment.

Oxycodone The key ingredient in OxyContin and Percocet, medical opioids prescribed to relieve pain.

Panic attacks Periodic, short bouts of panic that occur suddenly, reach a peak within minutes, and gradually pass.

Panic brain circuit The brain circuit that helps produce panic reactions, consisting of structures such as the amygdala, hippocampus, ventromedial nucleus of the hypothalamus, central gray matter, and locus coeruleus.

Panic disorder An anxiety disorder marked by recurrent and unpredictable panic attacks.

Paranoid personality disorder A personality disorder marked by a pattern of distrust and feelings of suspicion toward others.

Paraphilias Patterns in which a person has recurrent and intense sexual urges, fantasies, or behaviors involving nonhuman objects, children, or nonconsenting adults, or experiences of suffering or humiliation.

Paraphilic disorder A disorder in which a person's paraphilia causes great distress, interferes with social or occupational activities, or has placed the person or others at risk of harm.

Paraprofessional A person without previous professional training who provides services under the supervision of a mental health professional.

Parasomnias Sleep–wake disorders, such as sleepwalking, sleep terrors, and nightmare disorder, characterized by the occurrence of atypical events during sleep.

Parasuicide A suicide attempt that does not result in death.

Parasympathetic nervous system The nerve fibers of the autonomic nervous system that help return bodily processes to their usual state.

Parenting intervention A treatment approach for conduct disorder, ADHD, autism, and intellectual disability in which therapists combine family and cognitive-behavioral interventions to help improve family functioning and help parents deal with their children more effectively.

Parity laws Laws that direct insurance companies to provide equal coverage for mental problems and physical problems.

Parkinsonian symptoms Symptoms similar to those found in Parkinson's disease. Patients with schizophrenia who take antipsychotic medications may display one or more of these symptoms.

Parkinson's disease A slowly progressive neurological disease, marked by tremors and rigidity, that may also cause a neurocognitive disorder.

Participant An individual chosen to participate in a study. Also called a *subject*.

Participant modeling A behavioral treatment in which people with fears observe a therapist (model) interacting with a feared object and then interact with the object themselves.

Pedophilic disorder A paraphilic disorder in which a person has repeated and intense sexual urges or fantasies about watching, touching, or engaging in sexual acts with children, and either acts on these urges or experiences clinically significant distress or impairment.

Peer review system A system by which clinicians paid by an insurance company may periodically review a patient's progress and recommend the continuation or termination of insurance benefits.

Penile prosthesis A surgical implant consisting of a semirigid rod that produces an artificial erection.

People of color A general term for people who are Black, Hispanic, Indigenous, and/or Asian American.

Performance anxiety The fear of performing inadequately during sex, and the related tension that is experienced as a result.

Perseveration The persistent repetition of words and statements.

Persistent depressive disorder A chronic form of unipolar depression marked by ongoing and repeated symptoms of either major or mild depression.

Personality A unique and long-term pattern of inner experience and outward behavior that leads to consistent reactions across various situations.

Personality disorder An enduring, rigid pattern of inner experience and outward behavior that repeatedly impairs a person's sense of self, emotional experiences, goals, capacity for empathy, and/or capacity for intimacy.

Personality disorder—trait specified (PDTS) A personality disorder undergoing study for possible inclusion in the DSM. People would receive this diagnosis if they had significant impairment in functioning as a result of one or more very problematic traits.

Personality inventory A test, designed to measure broad personality characteristics, consisting of statements about behaviors, beliefs, and feelings that people evaluate as either characteristic or uncharacteristic of them.

Phallic stage In psychoanalytic theory, the period between the third and fourth years when the focus of sexual pleasure shifts to the genitals.

Phalloplasty A surgical procedure designed to create a functional penis.

Phenothiazines A group of antihistamine drugs that became the first group of effective antipsychotic medications.

Phenylketonuria (PKU) A metabolic disorder caused by the body's inability to break down the amino acid phenylalanine, resulting in intellectual disability and other symptoms.

Phobia A persistent and unreasonable fear of a particular object, activity, or situation.

Pick's disease A neurological disease that affects the frontal and temporal lobes, causing a neurocognitive disorder.

Placebo therapy A pretend treatment that the participant in an experiment believes to be genuine.

Play therapy An approach to treating childhood disorders that helps children express their conflicts and feelings indirectly by drawing, playing with toys, and making up stories.

Pleasure principle The pursuit of gratification that characterizes id functioning.

Plethysmograph A device used to measure sexual arousal.

Polygraph test A test that seeks to determine whether the test-taker is telling the truth by measuring physiological responses such as respiration level, perspiration level, and heart rate. Also known as a *lie detector test*.

Polysubstance use The use of two or more substances at the same time.

Positive correlation A statistical relationship in which the values of two variables increase together or decrease together.

Positive psychology The study and enhancement of positive feelings, traits, and abilities.

Positive symptoms Symptoms of schizophrenia that seem to be excesses of or bizarre additions to typical thoughts, emotions, or behaviors.

Positron emission tomography (PET scan) A computer-produced motion picture showing rates of metabolism throughout the brain.

Postpartum depression A disorder in which a major depressive episode typically begins within four weeks after delivering a child; many cases actually begin during pregnancy. Called *major depressive disorder with peripartum onset* in DSM-5-TR.

Postpartum psychosis An episode of psychosis experienced by a small percentage of new mothers that begins within days or weeks after giving birth.

Posttraumatic stress disorder (PTSD) A disorder in which a person experiences fear and related symptoms long after a traumatic event.

Poverty of speech A decrease in speech or speech content found in some people with schizophrenia. Also known as *alogia*.

Predictive validity The ability of a test or other assessment tools to predict future characteristics or behaviors.

Predisposition An inborn or acquired vulnerability for developing certain symptoms or disorders.

Prefrontal lobes Structures of the brain that play a key role in short-term memory, among other functions.

Premature ejaculation A dysfunction in which unintentional penile orgasm and ejaculation persistently occur within one minute of beginning sexual activity with a partner. Also called *early* or *rapid* ejaculation.

Premenstrual dysphoric disorder A disorder marked by repeated episodes of significant depression and related symptoms during the week before menstruation.

Premenstrual syndrome (PMS) A common and typical cluster of psychological and physical discomforts that precede menses.

Premorbid The period prior to the onset of a disorder.

Preparedness A predisposition to develop certain fears.

Prevalence The total number of cases of a disorder occurring in a population over a specific period of time.

Prevention Interventions aimed at deterring mental disorders before they can develop.

Preventive cognitive therapy A follow-up feature of cognitive-behavioral therapy characterized by a short series of "booster" sessions conducted months later that focus on further reducing dysfunctional thinking and developing a relapse prevention plan.

Primary gain In psychodynamic theory, the gain people derive when their somatic symptoms keep their internal conflicts out of awareness.

Primary personality The subpersonality that appears more often than the others in individuals with dissociative identity disorder.

Primary prevention Prevention interventions that are designed to prevent disorders altogether.

Private psychotherapy An arrangement in which a person directly pays a therapist for counseling services.

Pro-anorexia (or *pro-Ana*) online sites and communities Websites and groups that often view anorexia nervosa as a positive lifestyle rather than a psychological disorder and provide advice for maintaining anorexic behaviors and thinking.

Proband The person who is the focus of a genetic study.

Procedural memory Memory of learned skills that a person performs without needing to think about them.

Prodromal phase The period during which the symptoms of schizophrenia are not yet prominent, but the person has begun to deteriorate from previous levels of functioning.

Profound intellectual disability (profound ID) Level of intellectual disability, very noticeable at birth or in early infancy, where persons must learn or improve such basic skills as walking, some talking, and feeding themselves. These individuals need a very structured environment, with continuous close supervision and considerable help throughout their lives.

Projection An ego defense mechanism whereby individuals attribute to other people characteristics or impulses they do not wish to acknowledge in themselves.

Projective test A test consisting of ambiguous material that people interpret or respond to.

Prolonged exposure A treatment approach in which clients confront not only trauma-related objects and situations but also their painful memories of traumatic experiences.

Prolonged grief disorder A disorder in which, a year or more after the death of a loved one, people continue to display severe, wide-ranging symptoms of grief almost every day—symptoms that cause them distress or impairment.

Protection and advocacy system The system by which lawyers and advocates who work for patients may investigate the patients' treatments and protect their rights.

Protective factor A positive developmental variable such as effective parenting that helps to offset the impact of negative variables such as unfavorable genes or a difficult temperament.

Prozac The trade name for fluoxetine, a second-generation antidepressant.

Psychedelic drugs Substances such as LSD that cause profound perceptual changes. Also called *hallucinogenic drugs*.

Psychiatrist A physician who in addition to medical school has completed three to four years of residency training in the treatment of psychopathology.

Psychoanalysis Either the theory or the treatment of psychopathology that emphasizes unconscious psychological forces as the cause of psychological dysfunction.

Psychodynamic model The theoretical perspective that sees all human functioning as being shaped by dynamic (interacting) psychological forces and explains people's behavior by reference to unconscious internal conflicts.

Psychodynamic therapy A system of therapy whose goals are to help clients uncover past traumatic events and the inner conflicts that have resulted from them, settle those conflicts, and resume personal development.

Psychogenic perspective The view that the chief causes of psychopathology are psychological.

Psychological autopsy A procedure used to analyze information about a deceased person, for example, in order to determine whether the person's death was a suicide.

Psychological debriefing A form of crisis intervention in which survivors are helped to talk about their feelings and reactions to traumatic incidents. Also called *critical incident stress debriefing*.

Psychological First Aid (PFA) A disaster response intervention that seeks to reduce the initial distress of survivors and foster their adaptive functioning, but without procedures that may be premature, intrusive, or inflexible.

Psychological profile A method of suspect identification that seeks to predict an unknown criminal's psychological, emotional, and personality characteristics based on the individual's pattern of criminal behavior and on research into the psychological characteristics of people who have committed similar crimes.

Psychology The study of mental processes and behaviors.

Psychomotor symptoms Disturbances in movement sometimes found in certain disorders such as schizophrenia.

Psychoneuroimmunology The study of the connections between stress, the body's immune system, and illness.

Psychopathology The scientific study of mental difficulties or disorders, including their explanations, causes, progression, symptoms, assessment, diagnosis, and treatment. The word also is used as a synonym for the disorders (or symptoms) themselves.

Psychopathy *See* antisocial personality disorder.

Psychopharmacologist A psychiatrist who primarily prescribes medications.

Psychophysiological disorders Disorders in which biological, psychological, and sociocultural factors interact to cause or worsen a physical illness. Also known as *psychological factors affecting other medical conditions*.

Psychophysiological test A test that measures physical responses (such as heart rate and muscle tension) as possible indicators of psychological problems.

Psychosexual stages The developmental stages defined by Freud in which the id, the ego, and the superego interact.

Psychosis A state in which a person loses contact with reality in key ways.

Psychosurgery Brain surgery for mental disorders.

Psychotherapy A treatment system in which words and acts are used by a client (patient) and a therapist in order to help the client overcome psychological difficulties.

Psychotropic medications Drugs that mainly affect the brain and reduce many symptoms of mental dysfunction.

Qualitative methods Natural and unfiltered research methods intended to seek out each participant's direct perspective—gathering information that is offered in the participant's own words.

Qualitative study An exploratory research strategy that examines variables in their unfiltered and natural states, often through open-ended questioning, to gather rich descriptive accounts in great depth.

Quasi-experimental design A research design that fails to include key elements of a "pure" experiment and/or intermixes elements of both experimental and correlational studies.

Random assignment A selection procedure in an experiment that ensures that participants are randomly placed either in the control group or in the experimental group.

Rape Forced sexual intercourse or another sexual act committed against a nonconsenting person, or intercourse between an adult and an underage person.

Rapid eye movement (REM) sleep The period of the sleep cycle during which the eyes move quickly back and forth, indicating that the person is dreaming.

Rapprochement movement A movement to identify a set of common factors, or common strategies, that run through all successful therapies.

Rational-emotive therapy A cognitive therapy, developed by Albert Ellis, that helps clients identify and change the irrational assumptions and thinking that contribute to their psychological disorder.

Rationalization An ego defense mechanism in which a person creates acceptable reasons for unwanted or undesirable behavior.

Reaction formation An ego defense mechanism whereby a person counters an unacceptable desire by taking on a lifestyle that directly opposes the unwanted impulse.

Reactive depression A depression that appears to be triggered by clear events. Also known as *exogenous depression*.

Reactivity The extent to which the very presence of an observer affects a person's behavior.

Reality principle The recognition, characterizing ego functioning, that we cannot always express or satisfy our id impulses.

Receptor A site on a neuron that receives a neurotransmitter.

Regression An ego defense mechanism in which a person returns to a more primitive mode of interacting with the world.

Reinforcement The desirable or undesirable stimuli that result from an organism's behavior.

Relapse-prevention training An approach to treating alcohol use disorder in which clients are taught to plan ahead and to apply coping strategies in situations that typically trigger excessive drinking.

Relational psychoanalytic therapy A form of psychodynamic therapy that considers therapists to be active participants in the formation of patients' feelings and reactions and therefore calls for therapists to disclose their own experiences and feelings in discussions with patients.

Relaxation training A treatment procedure that teaches clients to relax at will so they can calm themselves in stressful situations.

Reliability A measure of the consistency of test or research results.

Repressed memory of childhood abuse A form of dissociative amnesia in which memories of sexual and physical abuse from childhood are repressed and recovered during adulthood.

Repression A defense mechanism whereby the ego prevents unacceptable impulses from reaching consciousness.

Residential treatment center A place where people who were formerly addicted to drugs live, work, and socialize in a drug-free environment. Also called a *therapeutic community*.

Resilience The process of adapting well in the face of adversity.

Resistance An unconscious refusal to participate fully in therapy.

Resolution phase The fourth phase in the sexual response cycle, characterized by relaxation and a decline in arousal following orgasm.

Response inventories Tests designed to measure a person's responses in one specific area of functioning, such as affect, social skills, or cognitive processes.

Restricting-type anorexia nervosa A type of anorexia nervosa in which people reduce their weight by severely restricting their food intake.

Reticular formation The brain's arousal center, which helps people to be awake, alert, and attentive.

Retrograde amnesia A lack of memory about events that occurred before the event that triggered amnesia.

Retrospective analysis A psychological autopsy in which clinicians piece together information about a person's suicide from the person's past.

Reversal design A single-subject experimental design in which behavior is measured to provide a baseline (A), then again after the treatment has been applied (B), then again after the conditions during baseline have been reintroduced (A), and then once again after the treatment is reintroduced (B). Also known as *ABAB design*.

Reward A pleasurable stimulus given to an organism that encourages a specific behavior.

Reward circuit A dopamine-rich circuit in the brain that produces feelings of pleasure when activated.

Reward-deficiency syndrome A condition, suspected to be present in some people, in which the brain's reward circuit is not readily activated by the usual events in their lives.

Right to refuse treatment The legal right of patients to refuse certain forms of treatment.

Right to treatment The legal right of patients, particularly those who are involuntarily committed to an institution, to receive adequate treatment.

Risk factor A life event, condition, or attribute that increases a person's susceptibility to developing a particular disorder.

Risperidone A commonly prescribed second-generation antipsychotic drug.

Ritalin A trade name of methylphenidate, a stimulant drug that is helpful in many cases of attention-deficit/hyperactivity disorder (ADHD).

Role-playing A therapy technique in which clients are instructed to act out roles assigned to them by the therapist.

Rorschach test A projective test in which a person reacts to inkblots designed to help reveal psychological features of the person.

Rosenthal effect The general finding that the results of any experiment often conform to the expectations of the experimenter.

Rush A spasm of warmth and ecstasy that occurs when certain drugs, such as heroin, are taken into the body.

Savant A person with a mental disorder or with significant intellectual deficits who has some extraordinary ability despite the disorder or deficits.

Schizoaffective disorder A disorder in which symptoms of both schizophrenia and a mood disorder are prominent.

Schizoid personality disorder A personality disorder featuring persistent avoidance of social relationships and little expression of emotion.

Schizophrenia A disorder of psychosis, in which personal, social, and occupational functioning deteriorate as a result of unusual perceptions, odd thoughts, disturbed emotions, and motor irregularities.

Schizophrenia-related brain circuit A brain circuit whose dysfunction contributes to schizophrenia. It includes the prefrontal cortex, hippocampus, amygdala, thalamus, striatum, and substantia nigra, among other brain structures.

Schizophreniform disorder A disorder in which all of the key features of schizophrenia are present but last only from one to six months.

Schizophrenogenic mother A type of mother—supposedly cold, domineering, and uninterested in the needs of her children—who was once thought to cause schizophrenia in her child.

Schizotypal personality disorder A personality disorder characterized by extreme discomfort in close relationships, very odd patterns of thinking and perceiving, and behavioral eccentricities.

School refusal A pattern in which children fear going to school and often stay home for a long period of time. Also called *school phobia*.

Scientific method The process of systematically gathering and evaluating information, through careful observations, to understand a phenomenon.

Seasonal affective disorder (SAD) A mood disorder in which mood episodes are related to changes in season.

Second messengers Chemical changes within a neuron just after the neuron receives a neurotransmitter message and just before it responds.

Second-generation antipsychotic drugs Antipsychotic drugs developed in recent decades, whose biological actions are different from that of the first-generation antipsychotic drugs. Also called *atypical antipsychotic drugs*.

Secondary gain In psychodynamic theory, the gain that people derive when their somatic symptoms elicit kindness from others or provide an excuse to avoid unpleasant activities.

Secondary prevention Prevention interventions that are designed to address disorders quickly, before they become more serious problems.

Sedative-hypnotic drugs Drugs that calm people at lower doses and help them fall asleep at higher doses.

Selective amnesia An inability to recall some of the events that occurred over a limited period of time.

Selective mutism A disorder marked by failure to speak in certain social situations when speech is expected, despite ability to speak in other situations.

Selective serotonin reuptake inhibitors (SSRIs) A group of second-generation antidepressant drugs that increase serotonin activity specifically, without affecting other neurotransmitters.

Self theory The psychodynamic theory that emphasizes the role of the self—our unified personality.

Self-actualization The humanistic process by which people fulfill their potential for goodness and growth.

Self-efficacy The belief that one can master and perform needed behaviors whenever necessary.

Self-help group A group made up of people with similar problems who help and support one another without the direct leadership of a clinician. Also called a *support group, peer group,* or *mutual help group*.

Self-hypnosis The process of hypnotizing oneself, sometimes for the purpose of forgetting unpleasant events.

Selfie A photograph that one has taken of oneself, typically with a smartphone or a webcam, and that is usually shared on social media.

Self-Injury Implicit Association Test A cognitive test used to help assess suicidal risk. Rather than asking people if they plan to attempt suicide, this test instructs them to pair various suicide-related words (for example, "dead," "lifeless," "suicide") with words that are personally relevant ("I," "myself," "mine") and with words that are not personally relevant ("they," "them," "other").

Self-instruction training A treatment developed by Donald Meichenbaum that teaches people to use coping self-statements at times of stress, discomfort, or significant pain. Also called *stress inoculation training*.

Self-monitoring Clients' observation of their own behavior.

Self-statements According to some theorists, statements about oneself, sometimes counterproductive, that come to mind during stressful situations.

Senile plaques Sphere-shaped deposits of beta-amyloid protein that form in the spaces between certain neurons and in certain blood vessels of the brain as people age. People with Alzheimer's disease have an excessive number of such plaques.

Sensate focus A treatment for sexual disorders that instructs couples to take the focus away from orgasm or intercourse and instead spend time concentrating on the pleasure achieved by such acts as kissing, hugging, and mutual massage. Also known as *nondemand pleasuring*.

Separation anxiety disorder A disorder marked by excessive anxiety, even panic, whenever the person is separated from home, a parent, or another attachment figure.

Serial murders A series of three or more killings carried out separately by the same individual(s) over a period of time—usually a month or more.

Serotonin A neurotransmitter whose irregular activity is linked to depression, obsessive-compulsive disorder, and eating disorders.

Severe congenital hypothyroidism A disorder in a baby marked by intellectual deficiencies and physical irregularities; caused by low levels of iodine in diet during pregnancy.

Severe intellectual disability (severe ID) Level of intellectual disability where persons demonstrate basic motor and communication deficits during infancy. Many also show signs of neurological dysfunction and have an increased risk for brain seizure disorder.

Sex offender statute The presumption by some state legislatures that people who are repeatedly found guilty of certain sex crimes have a mental disorder and should be categorized as "mentally disordered sex offenders." Such laws have been changed or abolished by many states over the past two decades.

Sexting The sending of sexually explicit material—particularly photos or text messages—between cell phones or other digital devices.

Sexual abuse A pattern in which a person is subjected to unwanted or coerced sexual activity and/or the victim is underage.

Sexual assault An act in which a person is forced to engage in a sexual act against their will.

Sexual dysfunction A disorder marked by a persistent inability to function satisfactorily in some area of the sexual response cycle.

Sexual masochism disorder A paraphilic disorder in which a person has repeated and intense sexual urges, fantasies, or behaviors that involve being humiliated, beaten, bound, or otherwise made to suffer, accompanied by clinically significant distress or impairment.

Sexual orientation change efforts (SOCE) Interventions, widely discredited, that attempt to change the sexual orientation of a person from lesbian, gay, or bisexual to heterosexual.

Sexual response cycle The general sequence of behavior and feelings that occurs during sexual activity, consisting of desire, excitement, orgasm, and resolution.

Sexual sadism disorder A paraphilic disorder in which a person has repeated and intense sexual urges or fantasies that involve inflicting suffering on others, and either acts on these urges with nonconsenting individuals or experiences clinically significant distress or impairment.

Sexually violent predator laws Laws passed by the federal government and many states that call for certain sex offenders who have been convicted of sex crimes and have served their sentence in prison to be removed from prison before their release and committed involuntarily to a mental hospital for treatment if a court judges them likely to engage in further acts of sexual violence due to a mental dysfunction. Also called *sexually dangerous persons laws*.

Shaping A learning procedure in which successive approximations of the desired behavior are rewarded until finally the exact and complete behavior is learned.

Sheltered workshop A supervised workplace for people who are not yet ready for competitive jobs.

Short-term memory The memory system that collects new information. Also known as *working memory*.

Shuttle box A box separated in the middle by a barrier that an animal can jump over in order to escape or avoid a shock.

Sildenafil One of the drugs used to treat erectile disorder that helps increase blood flow to the penis during sexual activity. Marketed as Viagra.

Single-case experimental design A research method in which a single participant is observed and measured both before and after the manipulation of an independent variable. Also called *single-subject experimental design*.

Sleep apnea disorder A sleep–wake disorder characterized by frequent awakenings each night due to periodic deprivation of oxygen to the brain during sleep.

Sleep terror disorder A parasomnia in which a person awakens suddenly during the first third of sleep, screaming out in extreme fear and agitation.

Sleep–wake disorders Syndromes characterized by significant and repeated disruptions

in the quantity, quality, timing, or nature of a person's sleep.
Sleepwalking disorder A parasomnia in which people repeatedly leave their beds and walk around without being conscious of the episode or remembering it later.
Social anxiety disorder A psychological disorder in which people fear social situations.
Social communication disorder A disorder marked by persistent problems in communication and social relationships, but without significant language difficulties or cognitive impairment. The communication and social problems are different in nature and less severe than those displayed by some autistic people.
Social skills training A therapy approach that helps people learn or improve social skills and assertiveness through role-playing and rehearsing of desirable behaviors.
Sociocultural model The theoretical perspective that emphasizes the effects of society, culture, and social and family groups on individual behavior.
Sociopathy *See* antisocial personality disorder.
Sodium amobarbital (Amytal) A drug used to put people into a near-sleep state during which some can better recall forgotten events.
Sodium pentobarbital (Pentothal) A drug used to put people into a near-sleep state during which some can better recall forgotten events.
Somatic symptom disorder A disorder in which people become excessively distressed, concerned, and anxious about bodily symptoms they are experiencing, and their lives are disproportionately disrupted by the symptoms.
Somatogenic perspective The view that psychopathology has physical causes.
Special education An approach to educating children with intellectual disability in which their individual difference and needs are supported and accommodated by grouping the children together in a separate, specially designed educational program.
Specific learning disorder A neurodevelopmental disorder marked by impairments in cognitive skills such as reading, writing, arithmetic, or mathematical skills.
Specific phobia A severe and persistent fear of a specific object or situation.
Spectator role A state of mind that some people experience during sex, focusing on their sexual performance to such an extent that their performance and their enjoyment are reduced.
Standardization The process in which a test is administered to a large group of people whose performance then serves as a standard or norm against which any individual's score can be measured.
State hospitals State-run public mental institutions in the United States.
State school A state-supported institution for people with intellectual disability.
State-dependent learning Learning that becomes associated with the conditions under which it occurred, so that it is best remembered under the same conditions.
Statistical analysis The application of principles of probability to the findings of a study in order to learn how likely it is that the findings have occurred by chance.
Statistical significance A measure of the probability that a study's findings occurred by chance rather than because of the experimental manipulation.
Stimulant drug A substance that increases the activity of the central nervous system.
Stimulus generalization A phenomenon in which responses to one stimulus are also produced by similar stimuli.
Stress brain circuit The brain circuit whose dysfunction contributes to PTSD. It includes such brain structures as the amygdala, prefrontal cortex, anterior cingulate cortex, insula, and hippocampus, among others.
Stress response A person's particular reactions to stress.
Stress-management program An approach to treating generalized and other anxiety disorders that teaches clients techniques for reducing and controlling stress.
Stress-reduction and problem-solving program A workshop or a series of group sessions offered by a business, in which mental health professionals teach employees how to cope with and solve problems and reduce stress.
Stressor An event that creates a sense of threat by confronting a person with a demand or opportunity for change of some kind.
Structured interview An interview format in which the clinician asks prepared questions.
Stuttering A communication disorder in which individuals repeat, prolong, or interject sounds when they speak; pause before finishing a word; or experience excessive tension in the muscles they use for speech. Also called *childhood-onset fluency disorder*.
Subgenual cingulate A brain structure whose irregular activity has been linked to depression. Also called *Brodmann Area 25*.
Subintentional death A death in which the individual has played an indirect, hidden, partial, or unconscious role.
Subject An individual chosen to participate in a study. Also called a *participant*.
Sublimation In psychoanalytic theory, the rechanneling of id impulses into endeavors that are both socially acceptable and personally gratifying. Sublimation can also be used as an ego defense mechanism.
Subpersonalities The two or more distinct personalities found in individuals with dissociative identity disorder. Also known as *alternate personalities*.
Substance intoxication A cluster of temporary undesirable behavioral or psychological changes that develop during or shortly after the ingestion of a substance.
Substance use disorder A pattern of maladaptive behaviors and reactions brought about by repeated use of a substance, sometimes also including tolerance for the substance and withdrawal reactions.
Suicidal behavior disorder A classification being studied for possible inclusion in a future revision of DSM-5, in which individuals have tried to die by suicide within the last two years.
Suicide A self-inflicted death in which the person acts intentionally, directly, and consciously.
Suicide education programs Suicide prevention programs that usually take place in schools and concentrate on students and their teachers. There are also a growing number of online sites that provide education about suicide—targeting troubled persons, their family members, and friends.
Suicide prevention program A program that tries to identify people who are at risk of ending their lives and to offer them crisis intervention.
Superego According to Freud, the psychological force that represents a person's values and ideals.
Supervised group house A residence for people with schizophrenia or other severe problems, often staffed by paraprofessionals. Also called *halfway house, crisis house,* or *group home*.
Support group A group made up of people with similar problems who help and support one another without the direct leadership of a clinician. Also called a *self-help group, peer group,* or *mutual-help group*.
Supported employment An approach to employment for people with psychological or physical conditions in which vocational agencies and counselors help clients find competitive jobs in the community and provide psychological support while the clients are employed.
Symbolic loss According to Freudian theory, the loss of a valued object (for example, a loss of employment) that is unconsciously interpreted as the loss of a loved one. Also called *imagined loss*.
Sympathetic nervous system The nerve fibers of the autonomic nervous system that quicken the heartbeat and produce other changes experienced as arousal.
Symptom A physical or psychological sign of a disorder.
Synapse The tiny space between the nerve ending of one neuron and the dendrite of another.
Syndrome A cluster of symptoms that usually occur together.
Synergistic effect In pharmacology, an increase of effects that occurs when more than one substance is acting on the body at the same time.
Synesthesia A crossing over of sensory perceptions. For example, a loud sound may be seen or a color may be felt.

Systematic desensitization An exposure treatment that uses relaxation training and a fear hierarchy to help clients with phobias react calmly to the objects or situations they dread.

Tarantism A disorder occurring throughout Europe between 900 and 1800 C.E. in which people would suddenly start to jump around, dance, and go into convulsions. Also known as *St. Vitus's dance*.

Tardive dyskinesia A group of late-developing involuntary movements that some patients experience after they have taken antipsychotic drugs for an extended time.

Telemental health The use of remote technologies, such as long-distance videoconferencing, to deliver mental health services without the therapist being physically present.

Temporal lobes Regions of the brain that play a key role in transforming short-term memory to long-term memory, among other functions.

Tension headache *See* Muscle contraction headache.

Tertiary prevention Prevention interventions that are designed to provide effective treatment for moderate or severe disorders as soon as it is needed so that the disorders do not become long-term problems.

Test A device for gathering information about a few aspects of a person's psychological functioning from which broader information about the person can be inferred.

Testosterone The principal male sex hormone.

Tetrahydrocannabinol (THC) The main active ingredient of cannabis substances.

Thanatos According to the Freudian view, the basic death instinct that functions in opposition to the life instinct.

Thematic Apperception Test (TAT) A projective test consisting of pictures that show people in ambiguous situations that the client is asked to interpret.

Theory of mind An awareness that other people base their behaviors on their own beliefs, intentions, and other mental states, not on information that they have no way of knowing.

Therapist A professional clinician who applies a system of therapy to help a person overcome psychological difficulties.

Therapy A systematic process for helping people overcome their psychological problems. Therapy consists of a client (patient), a trained therapist, and a series of contacts between them.

Third wave cognitive-behavioral therapies A group of relatively recent cognitive-behavioral approaches, including acceptance and commitment therapy (ACT), that help clients to accept many of their problematic thoughts rather than judge them, act on them, or try fruitlessly to change them.

Token economy program A behavior-focused program in which a person's desirable behaviors are reinforced systematically by the awarding of tokens that can be exchanged for goods or privileges.

Tolerance The brain and body's need for ever-larger doses of a drug to produce earlier effects.

Torture The use of brutal, degrading, and disorienting strategies to reduce victims to a state of utter helplessness.

Tranquilizer A drug that reduces anxiety.

Transcranial magnetic stimulation (TMS) A treatment in which an electromagnetic coil, which is placed on or above a patient's head, sends a current into the individual's brain.

Transference According to psychodynamic theorists, the redirection toward the psychotherapist of feelings associated with important figures in a patient's life, now or in the past.

Transference-focused psychotherapy A contemporary psychodynamic therapy, used primarily for people with a personality disorder, in which therapists focus largely on issues that occur within the therapist–patient relationship.

Transgender Individuals whose gender identity is different from their assigned gender.

Treatment A systematic procedure designed to change dysfunctional behavior into more functional behavior. Also called *therapy*.

Trephination An ancient operation in which a stone instrument was used to cut away a circular section of the skull to treat severe psychopathology.

Trichotillomania A disorder in which people repeatedly pull out hair from their scalp, eyebrows, eyelashes, or other parts of the body. Also called *hair-pulling disorder*.

Tricyclic An antidepressant drug such as imipramine that has three rings in its molecular structure.

Trisomy A chromosomal irregularity in which a person has three chromosomes of one kind rather than the usual two.

Tube and intravenous feeding Forced nourishment sometimes provided to people with anorexia nervosa when their condition becomes life-threatening.

Type A personality style A personality pattern characterized by hostility, cynicism, drivenness, impatience, competitiveness, and ambition.

Type B personality style A personality pattern in which a person is more relaxed, less aggressive, and less concerned about time.

Type D personality style A personality style in which persons repeatedly experience strong negative emotions and reactions (worrying and ruminating, anxiety, sadness, pessimism) while, at the same time, feeling too inhibited and unsupported socially to express or test their feelings of distress.

Type I schizophrenia According to some theorists, a type of schizophrenia dominated by positive symptoms, such as delusions, hallucinations, and certain formal thought disorders.

Type II schizophrenia According to some theorists, a type of schizophrenia dominated by negative symptoms, such as flat affect, poverty of speech, and loss of volition.

Ulcer A lesion that forms in the wall of the stomach or the duodenum.

Unconditional positive regard Full, warm acceptance of a person regardless of what they say, think, or feel; a critical component of client-centered therapy.

Unconditioned response (UCR) The natural, automatic response produced by an unconditioned stimulus.

Unconditioned stimulus (UCS) A stimulus that produces an automatic, natural response.

Unconscious The deeply hidden mass of memories, experiences, and impulses that is viewed in Freudian theory as the source of much behavior.

Undoing An ego defense mechanism in which a person unconsciously cancels out an unacceptable desire or act by performing another act.

Unipolar depression Depression without a history of mania.

Unstructured interview An interview format in which the clinician asks spontaneous questions that are based on issues that arise during the interview.

Vaginismus A type of genito-pelvic pain/penetration disorder in which the muscles around the vagina involuntarily contract, preventing sexual entry.

Vagus nerve stimulation (VNS) A treatment for depression in which an implanted pulse generator sends regular electrical signals to a person's vagus nerve; the nerve then stimulates the brain.

Validity A measure of the accuracy of a test's or study's results.

Valium The trade name of diazepam, an antianxiety drug.

Vaping The use of e-cigarettes or other devices that enable persons to inhale nicotine or other drugs as vapor rather than smoke.

Variable Any characteristic or event that can vary across time, locations, or persons.

Ventromedial hypothalamus (VMH) A brain region that depresses hunger when activated.

Virtual reality treatment Cognitive-behavioral intervention that uses virtual reality—3D computer graphics that simulate real-world objects and situations—as an exposure tool.

Visual hallucinations Hallucinations in which a person may either experience vague visual perceptions, perhaps of colors or clouds, or have distinct visions of people, objects, or scenes that are not there.

Voyeuristic disorder A paraphilic disorder in which a person has repeated and intense sexual desires to observe unsuspecting people in secret as they undress or to spy on couples having intercourse, and either acts on these urges with nonconsenting people or experiences clinically significant distress or impairment.

Wearable therapy Psychosocial interventions featuring the use of small and low-profile computer devices that can be worn, such as "smart" watches/wristbands and "smart" glasses, to help monitor and manage the emotional and behavioral problems of clients.

Weight set point The weight level that a person is predisposed to maintain, controlled in part by the hypothalamus.

Withdrawal Unpleasant, sometimes dangerous reactions that may occur when people who use a drug regularly stop taking it or reduce the dosage.

Working through The psychoanalytic process of facing conflicts, reinterpreting feelings, and overcoming one's problems.

Written exposure therapy (WET) A brief treatment approach for PTSD in which therapists guide clients to confront their troubling memories by having them repeatedly write about them.

References

AA (Alcoholics Anonymous). (2023). *A.A. around the world.* Retrieved from https://www.aa.org/aa-around-the-world.

AAC (American Addiction Centers). (2022). *Marijuana edibles: Risks, side effects and dangers.* Retrieved from https://americanaddictioncenters.org/marijuana-rehab/risks-of-edibles.

AAC (American Addiction Centers). (2023, July 7). *Alcohol and drug abuse statistics (facts about addiction).* Brentwood, TN: Author.

AACAP (American Academy of Child & Adolescent Psychiatry). (2022). *AACAP policy statement on increased suicide among Black youth in the U.S.* Washington, DC: Author.

AAIDD (American Association on Intellectual and Developmental Disabilities). (2024). *Intellectual disability.* Silver Spring, MD: Author.

AAMFT (American Association for Marriage and Family Therapy). (2023). *Children of alcoholics.* Retrieved from https://aamft.org/Consumer_Updates.

AAMFT (American Association for Marriage and Family Therapy). (2023). *Dissociative identity disorder.* Alexandria, VA: Author.

AAMFT (American Association for Marriage and Family Therapy). (2023). *Suicide in the elderly.* Arlington, VA: Author.

Aamodt, M. G. (2016, September 4). *Serial killer statistics.* Retrieved from http://maamodt.asp.radford.edu.

Aamodt, M. G., Leary, T. G., & Southard, L. (2018, October 2). Are you smarter than a serial killer? Norms, methods and interpretations cautions. Paper presented at the Annual Meeting of the Society for Police and Criminal Psychology, Sarasota, FL.

Aamodt, M. G., Leary, T., & Southard, L. (2020, June). Radford/FGCU annual report on serial killer statistics: 2020. *ResearchGate.*

AAP (American Academy of Pediatrics). (2022, November 17). *Teen suicide risk: What parents should know.* HealthyChildren.org. Retrieved from https://www.healthychildren.org/English/health-issues/conditions/emotional-problems/Pages/Which-Kids-are-at-Highest-Risk-for-Suicide.aspx.

AAPP (American Association of Psychiatric Pharmacists). (2022). *Monoamine oxidase inhibitors (MAOI): Role of MAOIs in pharmacotherapy.* Lincoln, NE: Author.

Abdalazem, R. (2022, July 5). What is CTE? Is the NFL doing anything about it? *AS USA.*

Abdoli, N., Sadeghi-Bahmani, D., Salari, N., Khodamoradi, M., Farnia, V., Jahangiri, S., . . . Brand, S. (2023). Nomophobia (No Mobile Phone Phobia) and psychological health issues among young adult students. *European Journal of Investigation in Health, Psychology and Education, 13*(9), 1762–1775.

Abi-Jaoude, E., Naylor, K. T., & Pignatiello, A. (2020). Smartphones, social media use and youth mental health. *Canadian Medical Association Journal, 192*(6), E136–E141.

ABMP (Associated Bodywork and Massage Professionals). (2016, December 20). *Mindfulness programs on the rise in U.S. medical schools.* Golden, CO: Author.

Abraham, K. (1911). Notes on the psychoanalytic investigation and treatment of manic-depressive insanity and allied conditions. In *Selected papers on psychoanalysis* (pp. 137–156). New York: Basic Books. (Work reprinted in 1960.)

Abraham, K. (1916). The first pregenital stage of the libido. In *Selected papers on psychoanalysis* (pp. 248–279). New York: Basic Books. (Work reprinted in 1960.)

Abrahamsen, C., Reme, S. E., Wangen, K. R., Lindbaek, M., & Werner, E. L. (2023). The effects of a structured communication tool in patients with medically unexplained physical symptoms: A cluster randomized trial. *eClinicalMedicine, 65,* 102262.

Abrams, Z. (2022, March 1). The burden of weight stigma. *Monitor on Psychology, 53*(2), 52.

Abrams, Z. (2023, January 1). Kids' mental health is in crisis. Here's what psychologists are doing to help. *Monitor on Psychology, 54*(1), 63.

Abrams, A. (2023, July 7). What happens when someone has a nervous breakdown? *Verywellmind.* Retrieved from https://www.verywellmind.com/what-is-a-nervous-breakdown-4172381.

Ackermann, K. (2023, March 27). Blood alcohol concentration levels and how they affect the body. *American Addiction Centers.* Retrieved from https://alcohol.org/health-effects.

ACS (American Cancer Society). (2020, February 1). *Depression.* Atlanta: Author. Retrieved from https://www.cancer.org/treatment.

ACS (American Cancer Society). (2023). *Emotional, mental health, and mood changes.* Atlanta: Author.

ADAA (Anxiety and Depression Association of America). (2021). *Anxiety and depression in children.* Silver Spring, MD: Author.

ADAA (Anxiety and Depression Association of America). (2021). *Childhood depression.* Silver Spring, MD: Author.

ADAA (Anxiety and Depression Association of America). (2022, June 16). *LGBTQ+ communities.* Silver Spring, MD: ADAA. Retrieved from https://adaa.org/find-help/by-demographics/lgbtq.

ADAA (Anxiety and Depression Association of America). (2022, June 27). *Anxiety disorders: Facts.* Silver Spring, MD: Author.

ADAA (Anxiety and Depression Association of America). (2022, September 27). *Black and African American communities.* Silver Spring, MD: ADAA. Retrieved from https://adaa.org/find-help/by-demographics/black-african-american communities.

ADAA (Anxiety & Depression Association of America). (2022, October 25). *Post-traumatic Stress Disorder (PTSD).* Silver Spring, MD: Author.

ADAA (Anxiety and Depression Association of America). (2023, June 22). *Body dysmorphic disorder.* Silver Spring, MD: Author.

Adam, D. (2019, March 12). Does a "dark triad" of personality traits make you more successful? *ScienceMag.*

Adam, K. S., Bouckoms, A., & Streiner, D. (1982). Parental loss and family stability in attempted suicide. *Archives of General Psychiatry, 39*(9), 1081–1085.

Adames, C., & Bernal, G. (2024). Psychotherapy for depression in adult Latinos: A systematic review of the science. In F. T. L. Leong, G. Bernal, & N.-C. T. Buchanan (Eds.). *Clinical psychology in communities of color: Integrating research and practice* (Chap. 8). Washington, DC: American Psychological Association.

Adamowicz, D. H., Wu, T.-C., Daly, R., Irwin, M. R., Jeste, D. V., Tu, X. M., . . . Lee, E. E. (2024). Executive functioning trajectories and their prospective association with inflammatory biomarkers in schizophrenia and non-psychiatric comparison participants. *Progressive Neuropsychopharmacological Biological Psychiatry, 128,* 110866.

Adams, D., Hastings, R. P., Maidment, I., Shah, C., & Langdon, P. E. (2023). Deprescribing psychotropic medicines for behaviours that challenge in people with intellectual disabilities: A systematic review. *BMC Psychiatry, 23*(1), 202.

Adams, J. G. (2013). Sexual assault. In J. G. Adams (Ed.). *Emergency medicine: Clinical essentials* (2nd ed., Chap. 128). Elsevier Health Services. [Kindle edition]

Adams, T. (2020, June 30). 10 tips to implement mindfulness in the workplace. *WellSteps.* Retrieved from https://www.wellsteps.com/blog.

Adanty, C., Ma, Z., Roy, A., Srivastava, A., Dai, N., & De Luca, V. (2022). Molecular genetics of antisocial personality disorder. In D. W. Black & N. J. Kolla (Eds.). *Textbook of antisocial personality disorder* (Chap. 8). Washington, DC: American Psychiatric Association Publishing.

Addington, J., Liu, L., Brummitt, K., Bearden, C. E., Cadenhead, K. S., Cornblatt, B. A., . . . Cannon, T. D. (2022). North American Prodrome Longitudinal Study (NAPLS 3): Methods and baseline description. *Schizophrenia Research, 243,* 263–267.

ADDitude (2023, September). "A daily nightmare": One year into the ADHD stimulant shortage. *ADDitude.* Retrieved from https://www.additudemag.com/adhd-medication-shortage-adderall-vyvanse.

ADHDAM (ADHD Awareness Month). (2024). ADHD: 7 Facts. https://www.adhdawarenessmonth.org/adhd-7-facts/

Adrien, V., Liewig, J., Diot, T., Ferreri, F., Mouchabac, S., Dubertret, C., & Bourgin, J. (2023). Association between family functioning and psychotic transition in ultra-high risk adolescents and young adults. *Frontiers in Psychiatry, 14,* 1177311.

AFSP (American Foundation for Suicide Prevention). (2023). *K–12 school suicide prevention.* New York: Author.

AFSP (American Foundation for Suicide Prevention). (2023). *Risk factors, protective factors, and warning signs.* Retrieved from https://afsp.org.

Agarwal, S., Jalan, M., Wilcox, H. C., Sharma, R., Hill, R., Pantalone, E., . . . Robinson, K. A. (2022, May). *Evaluation of mental health mobile applications.* Report No. 2022-EHC106. Rockville, MD: Agency for Healthcare Research and Quality,

Aggarwal, A., & Marwaha, R. (2022, September 19). Oppositional defiant disorder. *StatPearls.*

Agoalikum, E., Klugah-Brown, B., Wu, H. Hu, P., Jing, J., & Biswal, B. (2023). Structural differences among children, adolescents, and adults with attention-deficit/hyperactivity disorder and abnormal Granger causality of the right pallidum and whole-brain. *Frontiers in Human Neuroscience, 17,* 1076873.

AGPA (American Group Psychotherapy Association). (2022). *Group treatment of eating disorders.* New York: Author.

AGPA (American Group Psychotherapy Association). (2023). *Group interventions for treatment of psychological trauma.* New York: Author.

AHA (American Hospital Association). (2019). *Fast facts on U.S. hospitals.* Retrieved from https://www.aha.org/statistics.

AHA (American Hospital Association). (2019). *Trendwatch: Increasing access to behavioral health-care advances value for patients, providers and communities.* Retrieved from https://www.aha.org.

AHA (American Hospital Association). (2022). *Fast facts on U.S. hospitals, 2022.* Chicago: Author.

AHA (American Hospital Association). (2023). *Fast facts on U.S. hospitals, 2023.* Washington, DC: Author.

AHR (America's Health Rankings). (2022). *Health of women and children.* Minneapolis: United Health Group. Retrieved from https://www.americashealthrankings.org.

AHR (America's Health Rankings). (2022). *Senior report.* Minneapolis: United Health Group. Retrieved from https://www.americashealthrankings.org.

AHR (America's Health Rankings). (2023). *2022 health of women and children report.* Minneapolis: United Health Group. Retrieved from https://www.americashealthrankings.org/learn/reports.

AHR (America's Health Rankings). (2023). *2023 senior report.* Minneapolis: United Health Group. Retrieved from https://www.americashealthrankings.org/learn/reports.

AHRQ (Agency for Healthcare Research and Quality). (2022). *2022 National healthcare quality and disparities report.* Rockville, MD: Author.

AHRQ (Agency for Healthcare Research and Quality). (2023). *National healthcare quality and disparities reports.* Rockville, MD: Author.

AI (Amnesty International). (2023). *Torture.* Retrieved from https://www.amnesty.org/en/what-we-do/torture.

AIHW (Australian Institute of Health and Welfare). (2023). *Suicide & self-harm monitoring.* Canberra: Author.

Aiken, L. R. (1985). *Psychological testing and assessment* (5th ed.). Boston: Allyn & Bacon.

AIPC (Australian Institute of Professional Counselors). (2013, June 7). *Case study: Obsessive-compulsive disorder.* Retrieved from https://www.aipc.net.au/articles/case-study-obsessive-compulsive-disorder.

AIPC (Australian Institute of Professional Counselors). (2019). *Why counselors need mental health therapy.* Counselling Connection. Retrieved from https://www.counselling connection.com.

AIS (American Institute of Stress). (2023). *Workplace stress: Are you experiencing workplace stress?* Weatherford, TX: Author.

Akerele, O., McCall, M., & Aragam, G. (2021). Healing ethno-racial trauma in Black communities: Cultural humility as a driver of innovation. *JAMA Psychiatry, 78*(7), 703–704.

Akers, A. S. (2022, April 28). What to know about sex therapy. *Medical News Today.*

Aknin, L. B., Whillans, A. V., Norton, M. I., & Dunn, E. W. (2019). Happiness and prosocial behavior: An evaluation of the evidence. In J. Helliwell, R. Layard, & J. Sachs (Eds.), *World happiness report 2019* (Chap. 4). New York: Sustainable Development Solutions Network.

Akua, B. A., & Samek, D. R. (2023). The developmental unfolding of substance use disorder symptoms and academic achievement in the transition into and out of college. *Addictive Behaviors, 137,* 107530.

ALA (American Lung Association). (2022, November 17). *Harmful effects of smoking.* Chicago: Author.

ALA (American Lung Association). (2022, November 17). *What's in a cigarette?* Chicago: Author.

Alba, M. C., Bailey, K. T., Coniglio, K. A., Finkelstein, J., & Rizvi, S. L. (2022). Risk management in dialectical behavior therapy: Treating life-threatening behaviors as problems to be solved. *Psychotherapy, 59*(2), 163–167.

Albano, A. M. & Silverman, W. K. (2023). *Anxiety and related disorders interview schedule for DSM-5, Child and parent version.* New York: Oxford University Press.

Alcolado, G. M. (2022). Obsessive-compulsive disorder: Treating obsessions and associated behavioral responses. In G. Todd (Ed.). *Evidence-based treatment for anxiety disorders and depression: A cognitive behavioral therapy compendium* (Chap. 13). Cambridge: Cambridge University Press.

Aldhyani, T. H. H., Alsubari, S. N., Alshebami, A. S., Alkahtani, H., & Ahmed, Z. A. T. (2022). Detecting and analyzing suicidal ideation on social media using deep learning and machine learning models. *International Journal of Environmental Research and Public Health, 19,* 12635.

Alegria, M., Chatterji, P., Wells, K., Cao, Z., Chen, H., Takeuchi, D., . . . & Meng, X.-L. (2015). Disparity in depression treatment among racial and ethnic minority populations in the United States. *Psychiatric Services, 59*(11), 1264–1272.

Alfaro, A. J., Sakai, E., Carlson, C., Mehta, P. S., Anderson, J., Wynn, M., & Gould, C. E. (2022, August 23). Gero-mobile health: Feasibility of a VA mental health mobile apps coaching program for older veterans. *Clinical Gerontologist.* doi:10.1080/07317115.2022.2115433. [Online ahead of print]

Ali, A. M., Hendawy, A. O., Abd Elhay, E. S., Ali, E. M., Alkhamees, A. A., Kunigu, H., & Hassan, N. (2022). The Bergen Facebook Addiction Scale: Its psychometric properties and invariance among women with eating disorders. *BMC Women's Health, 22*(1), 99.

Ali, K., & Fassnacht, D. B. (2023). Barriers to treatment in eating disorders. In P. Robinson, T. Wade, B. Herpertz-Dahlann, F. Fernandez-Aranda, J. Treasure, & S. Wonderlich (Eds.). *Eating disorders.* Edinburgh: Springer.

Ali, M., & Cascella, M. (2022, August 8). ICU delirium. *StatPearls.*

Alkhawaldeh, A., Al Omari, O., Al Aldawi, S., Al Hashmi, I., Ann Ballad, C., Ibrahim, A., . . . Al Bashtawy, M. (2023). Stress factors, stress levels, and coping mechanisms among university students. *Scientific World Journal, 2023,* 2026971.

Allderidge, P. (1979). Hospitals, madhouses and asylums: Cycles in the care of the insane. *British Journal of Psychiatry, 134,* 321–334.

Allen, D. F. (Ed.). (1985). *The cocaine crisis.* New York: Plenum Press.

Allman, R. (2021, January 5). Profile: Thomas Joiner and the study of suicide. *Psychology Tools.* Retrieved from https://www.psychologytools.com/articles/profile-thomas-joiner-and-the-study-of-suicide.

Almaazmi, B. M., Aldweik, A. N., & Mukhtar, M. A. (2023). Dissociative amnesia: A mist over psychosis. *Cureus, 15*(9), e44619.

Almanza, A. (2020). 14 mind-blowing facts about selfies. *Reader's Digest.* Retrieved from https://www.rd.com/list/selfie-facts.

Alshak, M. N., & Das, J. M. (2023, May 8). Neuroanatomy, sympathetic nervous system. *StatPearls.*

Alzheimer's Association. (2020). *2020 Alzheimer's disease facts and figures: On the front lines: Primary care physicians and Alzheimer's care in America.* Chicago: Author.

Alzheimer's Association. (2023). Alzheimer's disease facts and figures. *Alzheimer's & Dementia Journal, 19*(4). Retrieved from https://doi.org/10.1002/alz.13016.

Alzheimer's Association. (2023). *2023 Alzheimer's disease facts and figures.* Chicago: Author.

Alzheimer's Association. (2024). *Depression.* Chicago: Author.

Alzheimer's Association. (2024). *Stages of Alzheimer's.* Chicago: Author.

Amadeo, K. (2017, July 11). *Deinstitutionalization: How does it affect you today?* Retrieved from https://www.thebalance.com/deinstitutionalization-3306067.

Ambrosecchia, M., Ardizzi, M., Russo, E. C., Ditaranto, F., Speciale, M., Vinai, P., . . . Gallese, V. (2023). Bodily self-recognition and body size overestimation in restrictive anorexia nervosa: Implicit and explicit mechanisms. *Frontiers in Psychology, 14,* 1197319.

Ambroziak, G., Vincent, S. R., Kahn, R. E., Mundt, J. C., & Thornton, D. (2023). Recidivism and violations among sexually violent persons on supervised release. *Psychology, Public Policy, and Law, 29*(1), 93–105.

Ameen, A., Williams, N., & Guthrie, D. M. (2024). Language and pain predict persistent depression among seriously ill home care clients. *Palliative & Support Care, 22*(1), 137–145.

Amos, M. (2023, March 5). Have sex offender laws gone too far? *The Public Purpose.* American University School of Public Affairs.

ANA (American Nurses Association). (2024). *Delirium: Prevent, identify, treat.* Silver Spring, MD: Author. Retrieved from https://www.nursingworld.org.

ANAD (Anorexia Nervosa and Associated Disorders). (2023). *Body shaming.* Chicago: Author.

ANAD (Anorexia Nervosa and Associated Disorders). (2023). *Eating disorder statistics.* Chicago: Author.

Anand, A., Nakamura, K., Spielberg, J. M., Cha, J., Karne, H., & Hu, B. (2020). Integrative analysis of lithium treatment associated effects on brain structure and peripheral gene expression reveals novel molecular insights into mechanism of action. *Translational Psychiatry, 10*(1), 103.

Anand, M. (2023, February 15). Female sexual pain: Differential diagnosis. *UpToDate.* Retrieved from http://www.uptodate.com.

Anbar, R. D. (2022, April 9). Treating skin conditions with hypnosis. *Psychology Today.* Retrieved from https://www.psychologytoday.com/us/blog/understanding-hypnosis/202204/treating-skin-conditions-hypnosis.

Andersen, B. L., Arrato, N. A., Conley, C. C., & Blevins, T. R. (2024). Psychological/behavioral interventions for patients with cancer. In N. Schneiderman (Ed.). *APA handbook of health psychology: Vol. 1. Foundations and context of health psychology; Vol. 2. Clinical interventions and disease management in health psychology; Vol. 3. Health psychology and public health* (Chap. 16). Washington, DC: American Psychological Association.

Anderson, E., Dvorin, K., Etingen, B., Barker, A. M., Rai, Z., Herbst, A. N., . . . Bokhour, B. G. (2022, August 11). "It makes you sit back and think where you wanna go": Veteran experiences in virtual whole health peer-led groups. *Health Expectations, 25*(5), 2548–2556. https://doi.org/10.1111/hex.13581.

Anderson, L. R., Monden, C. W. S., & Bukodi, E. (2022). Stressful life events, differential vulnerability, and depressive symptoms: Critique and new evidence. *Journal of Health and Social Behavior, 63*(2), 283–300.

Ando, M., Kao, Y.-C., Lee, Y.-C., Tai, S.-A., Mendez, S. R., Sasaki, K., Tang, W., & Papatheodorou, S. (2023, February 16). Remote cognitive behavioral therapy for older adults with anxiety symptoms: A systematic review and meta-analysis. *Journal of Telemedicine and Telecare.* https://doi.org/10.1177/1357633X231151788.

Andreassen, O. A., Hindley, G. F. L., Frei, O., & Smeland, O. B. (2023). New insights from the last decade of research in psychiatric genetics: Discoveries, challenges and clinical implications. *World Psychiatry, 22*(1), 4–24.

Andrews, J. A., Craven, M. P., Lang, A. R., Guo, B., Morriss, R., Hollis, C., & RADAR-CNS Consortium. (2022). Making remote measurement technology work in multiple sclerosis, epilepsy and depression: Survey of healthcare professionals. *BMC Medical Informatics and Decision Making, 22*(1), 125.

Angier, N. (2010, April 5). Even among animals: Leaders, followers and schmoozers. *New York Times.* Retrieved from https://www.nytimes.com/2010/04/06/science/06angi.html.

Angin, A. D., Gün, I., Sakin, Ö., Çikman, M. S., Eserdag, S., & Angın, P. (2020). Effects of predisposing factors on the success and treatment period in vaginismus. *JBRA Assisted Reproduction, 24*(2), 180–188.

Anglin, D. M. (2022, July 11). *The social patterning of psychosis.* Workshop on Early interventions for psychosis. National Academies of Sciences, Engineering and Medicine. New York: City University of New York.

Anlay, D. Z., Paque, K., Van Leeuwen, E., Cohen, J., & Dilles, T. (2024). Tools and guidelines to assess the appropriateness of medication and aid deprescribing: An umbrella review. *British Journal of Clinical Pharmacology, 90*(1), 12–106.

Anona, K., Olaomi, O., Udegbe, E., Uwumiro, F., Tuaka, E.-B., Okafor, N., . . . Opeyemi, M. (2024). Co-occurrence of bipolar disorder and personality disorders in the United States: Prevalence, suicidality, and the impact of substance abuse. *Journal of Affective Disorders, 345,* 1–7.

Anonymous. (1996). First person account: Social, economic, and medical effects of schizophrenia. *Schizophrenia Bulletin, 22*(1), 183.

Anonymous. (2006). On madness: A personal account of rapid cycling bipolar disorder. *British Journal of General Practice, 56*(530), 726–728.

Anson, P. (2017, February 9). Sex, poverty and education linked to chronic pain. *Pain News Network.* Retrieved from https://www.painnewsnetwork.org.

Antar, A. Y. (2023). Guilty or not guilty by reason of insanity? A comparative study of murderers referred for psychiatric examination by court order. *Health Justice, 11*(1), 35.

Antara, N. F. (2022, March 21). Is suicide becoming an epidemic on social media? *Dhaka Tribune.* Retrieved from https://www.dhakatribune.com/bangladesh.

Anto, A., Asif, R. O., Basu, A., Kanapathipillai, D., Salam, H., Selim, R., . . . Eisingerich, A. B. (2023). Exploring the impact of social media in anxiety among university students in the United Kingdom: Qualitative study. *JMIR Formative Research, 7,* e43037.

Antoni, M. H., Moreno, P. I., & Penedo, F. J. (2023). Stress management interventions to facilitate psychological and physiological adaptation and optimal health outcomes in cancer patients and survivors. *Annual Review of Psychology, 74,* 423–455.

Antoni, M. H., Walsh, E. A., & Penedo, F. J. (2024). The use of stress management interventions to facilitate adaptation to medical conditions. In N. Schneiderman (Ed.). *APA handbook of health psychology: Vol. 1, Foundations and context of health psychology; Vol. 2. Clinical interventions and disease management in health psychology; Vol. 3. Health psychology and public health* (Chap. 7). Washington, DC: American Psychological Association.

APA (American Psychiatric Association). (2022). *Diagnostic and statistical manual of mental disorders, text revision DSM-5-TR* (5th ed.). Washington, DC: Author.

APA (American Psychiatric Association). (2022). *Mental health disparities: Diverse populations.* Washington, DC: Author.

APA (American Psychiatric Association). (2022). *What is mental illness?* Washington, DC: Author.

APA (American Psychiatric Association). (2023). *Mental health disparities: Diverse populations.* Washington, DC: Author.

APA (American Psychiatric Association). (2023, September 21). *Mental health parity: New proposed rule.* Washington, DC: Author.

APA (American Psychiatric Association). (2023). *Prolonged grief disorder: Symptoms and diagnosis.* Retrieved from https://www.psychiatry.org/patients-families.

APA (American Psychiatric Association). (2023). *What are anxiety disorders?* Retrieved from https://www.psychiatry.org/patients-families.

APA (American Psychiatric Association). (2023). *What is psychotherapy?* Washington, DC: Author.

APA (American Psychological Association). (2016, September). 2015 APA survey of psychology health service providers. Retrieved from https://www.apa.org/workforce/publications/15-health-service-providers.

APA (American Psychological Association). (2017). *APA reaction to settlement of torture case against psychologists Mitchell, Jessen.* Washington, DC: Author.

APA (American Psychological Association). (2017). *Ethical principles of psychologists and code of conduct.* Washington, DC: Author.

APA (American Psychological Association). (2020). *Gen Z more likely to report mental health concerns.* Washington, DC: Author.

APA (American Psychological Association). (2020). *Timeline of APA policies & actions related to detainee welfare and professional ethics in the context of interrogation and national security.* Washington, DC: Author.

APA (American Psychological Association). (2021). *APA resolution on gender identity change efforts.* Washington, DC: Author.

APA (American Psychological Association). (2021). *APA resolution on sexual orientation change efforts.* Washington, DC: Author.

APA (American Psychological Association). (2022). *APA dictionary of psychology.* Washington, DC: Author.

APA (American Psychological Association). (2022). *Frequently asked questions about institutional review boards.* Washington, DC: Author.

APA (American Psychological Association). (2022). *Stress in America.* Washington, DC: Author.

APA (American Psychological Association). (2022). *Stress in America 2022.* Washington, DC: Author.

APA (American Psychological Association). (2022). The APA guidelines for psychological practice with sexual minority persons: An executive summary of the 2021 revision. *American Psychologist, 77*(8), 953–962.

APA (American Psychological Association). (2023). *APA dictionary of psychology.* Washington, DC: Author.

APA (American Psychological Association). (2023). *APA ethics office.* Washington, DC: Author.

APA (American Psychological Association). (2023). *APA's 2022 work and well-being survey results.* Washington, DC: Author.

APA (American Psychological Association). (2023). *Banning sexual orientation and gender identity change efforts.* Washington, DC: Author.

APA (American Psychological Association). (2023). *Careers in psychology.* Washington, DC: Author.

APA (American Psychological Association). (2023). *Disaster mental health information for psychologists.* Washington, DC: Author.

APA (American Psychological Association). (2023). *Ethnicity and health in America Series: Addiction in the African-American community.* Washington, DC: Author.

APA (American Psychological Association). (2023). *Older adults: Health and age-related changes.* Washington, DC: Author.

APA (American Psychological Association). (2023). *Stress in America 2022: Concerned for the future, beset by inflation.* Washington, DC: Author.

Appel, E. (2022). *Charitable giving statistics in 2022.* Madison, WI: Kindness Financial Planning.

Appelbaum, P. S. (2022). Settled insanity: Substance use meets the insanity defense. *Psychiatric Services, 73*(1), 105–107. https://doi.org/10.1176/appi.ps.202100518.

APsA (American Psychoanalytic Association). (2023). *Psychoanalytic psychotherapy.* New York: Author.

Arakelyan, M., Freyleue, S., Avula, D., McLaren, J. L., O'Malley, A. J., & Leyenaar, J. K. (2023). Pediatric mental health hospitalizations at acute care hospitals in the US, 2009–2019. *JAMA, 329*(12), 1000–1011. https://doi.org/10.1001/jama.2023.1992.

Arancibia, M., Leyton, F., Morán-Kneer, J., Muga, A., Rios, U., Sepúlveda, E., & Vallejo, V. (2022). Psychological debriefing in acute traumatic events: Evidence synthesis. *Medwave, 22,* 002538.

Arcelus, J., & Witcomb, G. L. (2023). Eating disorders in the LGBTQ+ population. In P. Robinson, T. Wade, B. Herpertz-Dahlann, F. Fernandez-Aranda, J. Treasure, & S. Wonderlich (Eds.). *Eating disorders.* Edinburgh: Springer.

Arias, E., Tejada-Vera, B., Kochanek, K. D., & Ahmad, F. B. (2022). Provisional life expectancy estimates for 2021. *Vital statistics rapid release report 23.* National Vital Statistics System. Atlanta: Centers for Disease Control and Prevention.

Ariel, B., Bland, M. P., & Sutherland, A. (2022). *Experimental designs (The SAGE Quantitative Research Kit).* Thousand Oaks, CA: Sage Publications.

Armitage, J. M., Wang, R. A. H., Davis, O. S. P., Bowes, L., & Haworth, C. M. A. (2021). Peer victimisation during adolescence and its impact on wellbeing in adulthood: A prospective cohort study. *BMC Public Health, 21*(1), 148.

Armoon, B., Fleury, M.-J., Griffiths, M. D., Bayani, A., Mohammadi, R., & Ahounbar, E. (2023). Emergency department use, hospitalization, and their sociodemographic determinants among patients with substance-related disorders: A worldwide systematic review and meta-analysis. *Substance Use and Misuse, 58*(3), 331–345.

Armour, J.-A., Joussemet, M., Mageau, G. A., & Varin, R. (2022, January 11). Perceived parenting and borderline personality features during adolescence. *Child Psychiatry and Human Development.* doi:10.1007/s10578-021-01295-3. [Online ahead of print]

Arnáez, S., García-Soriano, G., López-Santiago, J., & Belloch, A. (2021). Illness-related intrusive thoughts and illness anxiety disorder. *Psychology and Psychotherapy: Theory, Research and Practice, 94*(1), 63–80.

Arosio, B., Ostan, R., Mari, D., Damanti, S., Ronchetti, F., Arcudi, S., . . . Monti, D. (2017). Cognitive status in the oldest old and centenarians: A condition crucial for quality of life methodologically difficult to assess. *Mechanisms of Ageing and Development, 165* (Part B), 185–194.

Arsenovic, M. (2021, March 17). 16 fascinating mindfulness statistics to know in 2022. *Modern Gentlemen.*

Artoni, P., Chierici, M. L., Arnone, F., Cigarini, C., De Bernardis, E., Galeazzi, G. M., . . . Pingani, L. (2021). Body perception treatment, a possible way to treat body image disturbance in eating disorders: A case-control efficacy study. *Eating and Weight Disorders: Studies on Anorexia, Bulimia and Obesity, 26*(2), 499–514.

ASA (American Sleep Association). (2020). *Sleep disorder statistics.* Boston: Author.

Asbø, G., Ueland, T., Haatveit, B., Bjella, T., Flaaten, C. B., Wold, K. F., . . . Simonsen, C. (2022). The time is ripe for a consensus definition of clinical recovery in first-episode psychosis: Suggestions based on a 10-year follow-up study. *Schizophrenia Bulletin, 48*(4), 839–849.

ASCA (American School Counselor Association). (2023). *Student-to-school counselor ratio 2020–2021.* Alexandria, VA: Author.

Asch, D. A., Islam, M. N., Sheils, N. E., et al. (2021). Patient and hospital factors associated with differences in mortality rates among black and white US Medicare beneficiaries hospitalized with COVID-19 infection. *JAMA Network Open, 4*(6), e2112842.

Ash, P., Frierson, R. L., & Hatters Friedman, S. (2022). *Malpractice and liability in psychiatry.* New York: Springer.

ASHA (American Speech-Language-Hearing Association). (2024). *Selective mutism.* Rockville, MD: Author.

Ashar, Y. K., Gordon, A., Schubiner, H., Uipi, C., Knight, K., Anderson, Z., . . . Wager, D. (2022). Effect of pain reprocessing therapy vs placebo and usual care for patients with chronic back pain: A randomized clinical trial. *JAMA Psychiatry, 79*(1), 13–23.

Ashrafioun, L., Zerbo, K. R. A., Bishop, T. M., & Britton, P. C. (2020). Opioid use disorders, psychiatric comorbidities, and risk for suicide attempts among veterans seeking pain care. *Psychological Medicine, 50*(12), 2017–2112.

Asimov, I. (1997). *Isaac Asimov's book of facts.* New York: Random House (Wing Books).

Askham, A. V. (2022, April 8). "Theory of mind" in autism: A research field reborn. *Spectrum.*

ASPE (Assistant Secretary for Planning and Evaluation). (2022). *Prescription drug affordability among Medicare beneficiaries.* Washington, DC: Author.

Assari, S. (2019). Race, education attainment, and happiness in the United States. *International Journal of Epidemiologic Research, 6*(2), 76–82.

A-Tjak, J., & Hayes, L. (2022). Depression. In M. P. Twohig, M. E. Levin, & J. M. Petersen (Eds.). *The Oxford handbook of acceptance and commitment therapy* (Chap. 14). New York: Oxford University Press.

Attademo, L., Bernardini, F., & Verdolini, N. (2021). Neural correlates of schizotypal personality disorder: A systematic review of neuroimaging and EEG studies. *Current Medical Imaging, 17*(11), 1283–1298.

Augustyn, M. (2022, June 27). Overview of fears and phobias in children and adolescents. *UpToDate.* Retrieved from https://www.uptodate.com.

Augustyn, M. (2023, April 19). Autism spectrum disorder in children and adolescents: Terminology, epidemiology, and pathogenesis. *UpToDate.* Retrieved from https://www.uptodate.com.

Augustyn, M., & von Hahn, L. E. (2023, May 17). Autism spectrum disorder: Clinical features. *UpToDate.* Retrieved from https://www.uptodate.com.

Ausmed. (2023). *Restrictive practices: Chemical restraint in Australia.* Retrieved from https://www.ausmed.com/cpd/articles/what-is-chemical-restraint.

Austin, A., Craig, S. L., D'Soluza, S., & McInroy, L. B. (2022, July 29). Suicidality among transgender youth: Elucidating the role of interpersonal risk factors. *Journal of Interpersonal Violence, 37*(5–6), NPO2696–NP2718.

Averill, L. A., Averill, C. L., Akiki, T. J., & Abdallah, C. G. (2023). Examining neurocircuitry and neuroplasticity in PTSD. In M. J. Friedman, P. P. Schnurr, & T. M. Keane (Eds.). *Handbook of PTSD: Science and practice* (3rd ed., Chap. 9). New York: Guilford Press.

Averill, L. A., Averill, C. L., Pietrzak, R. H., Charney, D. S., & Southwick, S. M. (2023). Psychoneurobiology of resilience. In M. J. Friedman, P. P. Schnurr, & T. M. Keane (Eds.). *Handbook of PTSD: Science and practice* (3rd ed., Chap. 30). New York: Guilford Press.

Avery, R. J., Niederdeppe, J., Eisenberg, M. D., Sood, N., Welch, B., & Kim, J. J. (2022). Messages in prescription drug advertising for four chronic diseases, 2003–2016: A content analysis. *Preventive Medicine, 158,* 107015.

Awhangansi, S., Lewis, M., Karim, K., Abdulmalik, J., Archard, P. J., Okewole, A., & O'Reilly, M. (2023). *Impact of problem-solving skills and attributional retraining on conduct disorder among students at public secondary schools in Nigeria.* Lancashire, UK: University of Central Lancashire.

Axbey, H., Beckmann, N., Fletcher-Watson, S., Tullo, A., & Crompton, C. J. (2023, March 7). Innovation through neurodiversity: Diversity is beneficial. *Autism, 27*(7), 2193–2198.

Ayano, G., Demelash, S., Yohannes, Z., Haile, K., Tulu, M., Assefa, D., . . . Tsegay, L. (2021). Misdiagnosis, detection rate, and associated factors of severe psychiatric disorders in specialized psychiatry centers in Ethiopia. *Annals of General Psychiatry, 20*(1), 10.

Ayllon, T., & Michael, J. (1959). The psychiatric nurse as a behavioural engineer. *Journal of Experimental Analytical Behavior, 2,* 323–334.

Aynsworth, C., Rolinson, J., Pervez, M., Collerton, D., & Dudley, R. (2022, December 11). What is the frequency and nature of visual hallucinations in non-clinical participants? *Psychology and Psychotherapy.* doi:10.1111/papt.12440. [Online ahead of print]

Ayub, R., Sun, K. L., Flores, R. E., Lam, V. T., Jo, B., Saggar, M., & Fung, L. K. (2021). Thalamocortical connectivity is associated with autism symptoms in high-functioning adults with autism and typically developing adults. *Translational Psychiatry, 11*(1), 93.

Ayubcha, C., Revheim, M.-E., Newberg, A., Moghbel, M., Rojulpote, C., Werner, T. J., & Alavi, A. (2021). A critical review of radiotracers in the positron emission tomography imaging of traumatic brain injury: FDG, tau, and amyloid imaging in mild traumatic brain injury and chronic traumatic encephalopathy. *European Journal of Nuclear Medicine and Molecular Imaging, 48*(2), 623–641.

Azevedo, C. V., Hashiguchi, D., Campos, H. C., Figueiredo, E. V., Otaviano, S. F. S. D., Penitente, A. R., . . . Longo, B. M. (2023). The effects of resistance exercise on cognitive function, amyloidogenesis, and neuroinflammation in Alzheimer's disease. *Frontiers in Neuroscience, 17,* 1131214.

Azevedo, J., Vieira-Coelho, M., Castelo-Branco, M., Coelho, R., & Figueiredo-Braga, M. (2020). Impulsive and premeditated aggression in male offenders with antisocial personality disorder. *PLoS One, 15*(3), e0229876.

Azhari, A., Toms, Z., Pavlopoulou, G., Esposito, G., & Dimitriou, D. (2022). Social media use in female adolescents: Associations with anxiety, loneliness, and sleep disturbances. *Acta Psychologica, 229,* 103706.

Azim, K. A., Happel-Parkins, A., Moses, A., & Haardoerfer, R. (2023). Racialized differences across experiences and measurements of pain in genitopelvic pain/penetration disorder. *Journal of Sexual Medicine, 20*(2), 224–228.

BAAM (British Association of Anger Management). (2017). *Mental health organization: Boiling point report 2008.* BAAM. Retrieved from https://www.angermanage.co.uk.

BAAM (British Association of Anger Management). (2020). *Anger statistics.* West Sussex, UK: Author.

BAAM (British Association of Anger Management). (2023). *Drowning in anger—Don't be another statistic.* West Sussex, UK: BAAM.

Babl, A., Penedo, J. M. G., Berger, T., Schneider, N., Sachse, R., & Kramer, U. (2023). Change processes in psychotherapy for patients presenting with histrionic personality disorder. *Clinical Psychology and Psychotherapy, 30*(1), 64–72.

Bach, B., & Tracy, M. (2022). Clinical utility of the alternative model of personality disorders: A 10th year anniversary review. *Personality Disorders: Theory, Research, and Treatment, 13*(4), 369–379.

Bachrach, N., Rijkeboer, M. M., Arntz , A., & Huntjens, R. J. C. (2023). Schema therapy for dissociative identity disorder: A case report. *Frontiers in Psychiatry, 14,* 1151872.

Backhaus, S., Leijten, P., Jochim, J., Melendez-Torres, G. J., & Gardner, F. (2023, June). Effects over time of parenting interventions to reduce physical and emotional violence against children: A systematic review and meta-analysis. *eClinicalMedicine, 60,* 102003.

Bader, M., Hilbig, B. E., Zettler, I., & Moshagen, M. (2022, October 18). Rethinking aversive personality: Decomposing the dark triad traits into their common core and unique flavors. *Journal of Personality.* doi:10.1111/jopy.12785. [Online ahead of print]

Bagby, E. (1922). The etiology of phobias. *Journal of Abnormal Psychology, 17,* 16–18.

Bagner, D. M., Berkovits, M. D., Coxe, S., Frech, N., Garcia, D., Golik, A., . . . Comer, J. S. (2022). Telehealth treatment of behavior problems in young children with developmental delay: A randomized controlled trial. *JAMA Pediatrics.* doi:10.1001/jamapediatrics.2022.5204.

Bagner, D. M., Berkovits, M. D., Coxe, S., Frech, N., Garcia, D., Golik, A., . . . Comer, J. S. (2023). Telehealth treatment of behavior problems in young children with developmental delay: A randomized controlled trial. *JAMA Pediatrics, 177*(3), 231–239.

Bai, L., Liang, W., Wang, Y., Fan, N., Zhang, Q., Bian, Y., & Yang, F. (2023). Effects of adjunctive betahistine therapy on lipid metabolism in patients with chronic schizophrenia: A randomized double-blind placebo-controlled study. *Neuropsychiatric Disease and Treatment, 19,* 453–460.

Bai, N. (2023, April 14). Hypnotherapy: How hypnosis can alter the brain's perception of pain. *Stanford Medicine.* Retrieved from https://scopeblog.stanford.edu/2023/004/14.

Bai, S., Rolon-Arroyo, B., Walkup, J. T., Kendall, P. C., Ginsburg, G. S., Keeton, C. P., . . . Peris, T. S. (2023). Anxiety symptom trajectories from treatment to 5- to 12-year follow-up across childhood and adolescence. *Journal of Child Psychology and Psychiatry, 64*(9), 1336–1345.

Bai, Y.-L., Shyu, Y.-I. L., Huang, H.-L., Chiu, Y.-C., & Hsu, W.-C. (2024). The enrichment process for family caregivers of persons living with dementia: A grounded theory approach. *Journal of Advanced Nursing, 80*(1), 252–263.

Bailey, R. D. (2022). CBT for panic disorder. In G. Todd (Ed.). *Evidence-based treatment for anxiety disorders and depression: A cognitive behavioral therapy compendium* (Chap. 4). Cambridge: Cambridge University Press.

Bailey, R. J., & Ogles, B. M. (2023). *Common factors therapy: A principle-based treatment framework.* Washington, DC: American Psychological Association.

Bakeman, R., & Quera, V. (2023). Behavioral observation. In H. Cooper, M. N. Coutanche, L. M. McMullen, A. T. Panter, D. Rindskopf, & K. J. Sher (Eds.). *APA handbook of research methods in psychology: Foundations, planning, measures, and psychometrics* (pp. 251–274). Washington, DC: American Psychological Association.

Balakrishnan, A., & Akshaya, I. (2023). Self-labeling as having mental health illness among psychology students. *International Journal of Indian Psychology, 11*(3), July–September.

Baldessarini, R. J., Vázquez, G. H., & Tondo, L. (2020). Bipolar depression: A major unsolved challenge. *International Journal of Bipolar Disorders, 8*(1), 1.

Baldor, R. (2023, February 21). Primary care of the adult with intellectual and developmental disabilities. *UpToDate.* Retrieved from https://www.uptodate.com.

Baldwin, D. (2023, July 10). Generalized anxiety disorder in adults: Epidemiology, pathogenesis, clinical manifestations, course, assessment, and diagnosis. *UpToDate.* Retrieved from https://www.uptodate.com.

Ballard, E. D., Reed, J. L., Szczepanik, J., Evans, J. W., Yarrington, J. S., Dickstein, D. P., . . . Zarate, C. A. (2019). Functional imaging of the implicit association of the self with life and death. *Suicide and Life-Threatening Behavior, 49*(6), 1600–1608.

Balling, C. E., South, S. C., Lynam, D. R., & Samuel, D. B. (2023). Clinician perception of the clinical utility of the Hierarchical Taxonomy of Psychopathology (HiTOP) system. *Clinical Psychological Science, 11*(6), 1108–1121.

Ballmer, T., & Gantschnig, B. (2024). Maintaining autonomy: How older persons with chronic conditions and their significant others interpret, navigate, and overcome everyday difficulties. *Scandinavian Journal of Occupational Therapy, 31*(1), 2249959.

Baltodano-Calle, M. J., Onton-Diaz, M., & Gonzales, G. F. (2022). Androgens, brain and androgen deprivation therapy in paraphilic disorders: A narrative review. *Andrologia, 54*(10), e14561.

Baluku, M. M., Nansubuga, F., Kibanja, G. M., Ourna, S., Balikoowa, R., Nansambe, J., . . . Musanje, K. (2023). Associations of psychological inflexibility with posttraumatic stress disorder and adherence to COVID-19 control measures among refugees in Uganda: The moderating role of coping strategies. *Journal of Contextual Behavioral Science, 28,* 278–288.

Balusu, S., Horré, K., Thirupp, N., Craessaerts, K., Snellinx, A., Serneels, L., . . . De Strooper, B. (2023). MEG3 activates necroptosis in human neuron xenografts modeling Alzheimer's disease. *Science, 381*(6663), 1176–1182.

Ban, T. A. (2023). *Chlorpromazine after 50 years.* Cordoba: International Network for the History of Neuropsychopharmacology. Retrieved from http:www.inhn.org/archives.

Banducci, A. N., Cooper, B. N., Betts, J. M., & Serier, K. N. (2023). Exposure-based and behavioral theory in psychotherapy. In F. T. L. Leong, J. L. Callahan, J. Zimmerman, M. J. Constantino, & C. F. Eubanks (Eds.). *APA handbook of psychotherapy* (Vol. 1, Chap. 10). Washington, DC: APA.

Bandura, A., & Rosenthal, T. (1966). Vicarious classical conditioning as a function of arousal level. *Journal of Personality and Social Psychology, 3,* 54–62.

Bansal, P. S., Goh, P. K., Southward, M. W., Sizemore, Y. J., & Martel, M. M. (2024). Impulsivity as key bridge symptoms in cross-sectional and longitudinal networks of ADHD and ODD. *Journal of Child Psychology and Psychiatry, 65*(1), 52–63.

Barbati, A., Geraci, A., Niro, F., Pezzi, L., & Sarchiapone, M. (2022). Do migration and acculturation impact somatization? A scoping review. *International Journal of Environmental Research and Public Health, 19,* 16011.

Barber, J. P., Muran, J. C., McCarthy, K. S., Keefe, J. R., & Zilcha-Mano, S. (2021). Research on dynamic therapies. In M. Barkham, W. Lutz, & L. Castonguay (Eds.). *Bergin and Garfield's handbook of psychotherapy and behavior change* (Chap. 12, pp. 387–420). New York: Wiley.

Bareis, N., Olfson, M., Gerhard, T., Rolin, S., & Stroup, T. S. (2023, January). Means of suicide among adults with schizophrenia across the life span. *Schizophrenia Research, 251,* 82–90.

Barer, D., & Hinkle, J. (2022, March 15). State hospital staffing "emergency" looms as record 2,100 wait in jail for treatment. *KXAN Austin.*

Barkham, M., & Lambert, M. J. (2021). The efficacy and effectiveness of psychological therapies. In M. Barkham, W. Lutz, & L. G. Castonguay (Eds.). *Bergin and Garfield's handbook of psychotherapy and behavior change* (7th ed., Chap. 5). New York: Wiley.

Barkham, M., Lutz, W., & Castonguay, L. G. (2021, October). *Bergin and Garfield's handbook of psychotherapy and behavior change* (7th ed.). New York: Wiley.

Barkley, R. A. (2020). *12 Principles for raising a child with ADHD.* New York: Guilford Press.

Barkley, R. A. (2022). *Treating ADHD in children and adolescents: What every clinician needs to know.* New York: Guilford Press.

Barlow, M. R. (2011). Memory for complex emotional material in dissociative identity disorder. *Journal of Trauma & Dissociation, 12*(1), 53–66.

Barman, S., & Bairagi, K. (2023). Analysis of socio-demographic profiles of suicidal hanging cases to formulate a preventive strategy: An autopsy-based study conducted at a tertiary care hospital in the north-east region of India. *Cureus, 15*(7), e42483.

Barnes, M. (2017, March 14). Mom thought daughter's Facebook suicide was fake, posts cruel comment. *Rolling Out.* Retrieved from https://rollingout.com/2017/03/14.

Barnett, J. E. (2020). *Distress, therapist burnout, self-care, and the promotion of wellness for psychotherapists and trainees.* Mesa, AZ: Society for the Advancement of Psychotherapy. Retrieved from https://societyforpsychotherapy.org.

Barnett, J. E., & Coffman, C. (2023). *Confidentiality and its exceptions: The case of duty to warn.* Mesa, AZ: Society for the Advancement of Psychotherapy. Retrieved from https://societyforpsychotherapy.org.

Barnhill, J. W. (2023, August). Agoraphobia. In *Merck manual professional version.* Retrieved from https://www.merckmanuals.com/professional/psychiatric-disorders/anxiety-and-stressor-related-disorders/agoraphobia.

Barr, P. B., Bigdeli, T. B., & Meyers, J. L. (2022). Prevalence, comorbidity, and sociodemographic correlates of psychiatric diagnoses reported in the All of Us research program. *JAMA Psychiatry, 79*(6), 622–628.

Barr, S. M., Roberts, D., & Thakkar, K. N. (2021). Psychosis in transgender and gender non-conforming individuals: A review of the literature and a call for more research. *Psychiatry Review, 306,* 114272.

Barr, S. M., Snyder, K. E., Adelson, J. L., & Budget, S. L. (2021). Posttraumatic stress in the trans community: The roles of anti-transgender bias, non-affirmation, and internalized transphobia. *Psychology of Sexual Orientation and Gender Diversity, 9*(4), 410–421.

Barros, S., Oliveira, C., Araújo, E., Moreira, D., Almeida, F., & Santos, A. (2022). Community intervention programs for sex offenders: A systematic review. *Frontiers in Psychiatry, 13,* 949899.

Barry, E. (2022, September 30). Can smartphones help predict suicide? *New York Times.* Retrieved from https://www.nytimes.com/2022/09/30/health/suicide-predict-smartphone.html.

Barsky, A. E. (2024). *Clinicians in court: A guide to subpoenas, depositions, testifying, and everything else you need to know* (3rd ed., Chap. 9). New York: Guilford Press.

Barsova, T., Cheong, Z. G., Mak, A. R., & Liu, J. C. (2022). Predicting psychological symptoms when Facebook's digital well-being features are used: Cross-sectional survey study. *MJIR Formative Research, 6*(8), e39387.

Bartholomew, R. (2014). *Mass hysteria in schools: Worldwide since 1566.* Jefferson, NC: McFarland.

Bartholomew, R. (2018, January 16). Sonic attack claims are unjustified: Just follow the facts. *Skeptical Inquirer.* Retrieved from https://skepticalinquirer.org/exclusive.

Bartholomew, R. (2020). The coronavirus and the search for scapegoats. *Psychology Today.* Retrieved from https://www.psychologytoday.com/us/blog/its-catching/202002.

Bartholomew, R. (2023). Why mass hysteria is thriving in the 21st century. *Skeptical Inquirer Presents series.* Retrieved from https://skepticalinquirer.org/video.

Bartlett, E. A., Zanderigo, F., Stanley, B., Choo, T.-H., Galfalvy, H. C., Pantazatos, S. P., . . . Mann, J. J. (2023). In vivo serotonin transporter and 1A receptor binding potential and ecological momentary assessment (EMA) of stress in major depression and suicidal behavior. *European Neuropsychopharmacology, 70,* 1–13.

Bartrop, R. W., Lockhurst, E., Lazarus, L., Kiloh, L. G., & Penny, R. (1977). Depressed lymphocyte function after bereavement. *Lancet, 1,* 834–836.

Basile, J., & Bloch, M. J. (2023, January 5). Overview of hypertension in adults. *UpToDate.* Retrieved from http://www.uptodate.com.

Basile, K. C., Smith, S. G., Chen, J., & Zwald, M. (2020). Chronic diseases, health conditions, and other impacts associated with rape victimization of U.S. women. *Journal of Interpersonal Violence, 36*(23–24), NP12504–NP12520.

Bassett, A. S. (2023). Clinical genetics of schizophrenia and related neuropsychiatric disorders. *Psychiatry Research, 319,* 114992.

Basu, T. (2020, March 26). How coronavirus is transforming online dating and sex. *MIT Technology Review.* Retrieved from https://www.technologyreview.com/2020/03/26/950282.

Bataineh, B. S., Wilkinson, A. V., Sumbe, A., Clendennen, S. L., Chen, B., Messiah, S. E., & Harrell, M. B. (2024). Anxiety as a predictor of the age of initiation of tobacco and cannabis use in adolescents and young adults. *Addictive Behaviors, 148,* 107876.

Bateman, A., Fonagy, P., Cambell, C., Luyten, P., & Debbané, M. (2023, May 18). A history of mentalizing and mentalization-based treatment. In *Cambridge guide to mentalization-based treatment (MBT)* (Chap. 1). Cambridge: Cambridge University Press.

Battaglia, A. M., Mamak, M., & Goldberg, J. O. (2022). The impact of social media coverage on attitudes toward mental illness and violent offending. *Journal of Community Psychology, 50*(7), 2938–2949.

Battin, M. P., & Pope, T. M. (2022, March 25). Physician-assisted dying. *UpToDate.* Retrieved from https://www.uptodate.com.

Battle, C. R., Rubin, R. S., Kingsberg, S. A., & Alzweri, L. (2022). Ethnic minority representation in female sexual dysfunction questionnaire validation: A scoping review. *Journal of Sexual Medicine, 19*(12), 1824–1838.

Bazelon Center. (2024). *Voting rights.* Washington, DC: Author.

Bazzano, A. N., Sun, Y., Chavez-Gray, V., Akintimehin, T., Gustat, J., Barrera, D., & Roi, C. (2022). Effect of yoga and mindfulness intervention on symptoms of anxiety and depression in young adolescents attending middle school: A pragmatic community-based cluster randomized controlled trial in a racially diverse urban setting. *International Journal of Environmental Research and Public Health, 19*(19), 12076.

BCBS (Blue Cross/Blue Shield). (2022, May 31). *Racial disparities in diagnosis and treatment of major depression*. Washington, DC: Author.

Bearse, J. L., McMinn, M. R., Seegobin, W., & Free, K. (2014). Healing thyself: What barriers do psychologists face when considering personal psychotherapy and how can they be overcome? *APA Monitor on Psychology, 45*(4), 62.

Beaudoin, M., Hudon, A., Giguere, C.-E., Potvin, S., & Dumais, A. (2022). Prediction of quality of life in schizophrenia using machine learning models on data from Clinical Antipsychotic Trials of Intervention Effectiveness (CATIE) schizophrenia trial. *Schizophrenia, 8,* 29.

Beaudoin, M., Potvin, S., Phraxayavong, K., & Dumais, A. (2023). Changes in quality of life in treatment-resistant schizophrenia patients undergoing avatar therapy: A content analysis. *Journal of Personalized Medicine, 13,* 522.

Beck, A. T. (1967). *Depression: Clinical, experimental and theoretical aspects*. New York: Harper & Row.

Beck, A. T. (2002). Cognitive models of depression. In R. L. Leahy & E. T. Dowd (Eds.). *Clinical advances in cognitive psychotherapy: Theory and application* (pp. 29–61). New York: Springer.

Beck, A. T. (2016). Cognitive therapy: Nature and relation to behavior therapy [Republished article]. *Behavior Therapy, 47*(6), 776–784.

Beck, A. T., Davis, D. D., & Freeman, A. (Eds.). (2015). *Cognitive therapy of personality disorders* (3rd ed.). New York: Guilford Press.

Beck, A. T., Ward, C. H., Mendelson, M., Mock, J. E., & Erbaugh, J. (1962). Reliability of psychiatric diagnosis: 2. A study of consistency of clinical judgments and ratings. *American Journal of Psychiatry, 119,* 351–357.

Beck, J. G., & Sloan, D. M. (2022). *The Oxford handbook of traumatic stress disorders* (2nd ed.). New York: Oxford University Press.

Beck, J. G., & Sloan, D. M. (2022). *Traumatic stress disorders: Historical context and current focus*. In J. G. Beck & D. M. Sloan (Eds.). *The Oxford handbook of traumatic stress disorders* (Chap. 1). New York: Oxford University Press.

Beck, J. S. (2020, October 9). *Cognitive behavior therapy: Basics and beyond* (3rd ed.). New York: Guilford Press.

Becker, C. B., Perez, M., Kilpela, L. S., Diedrichs, P. C., Trujillo, E., & Stice, E. (2017). Engaging stakeholder communities as body image intervention partners: The Body Project as a case example. *Eating Behaviors, 25,* 62–67.

Beckers, T., Hermans, D., Lange, I., Luyten, L., Scheveneels, S., & Vervliet, B. (2023). Understanding clinical fear and anxiety through the lens of human fear conditioning. *Nature Reviews Psychology, 2,* 233–245.

Behan, D. (2022). Do clients train therapists to become eclectic and use the common factors? A qualitative study listening to experienced psychotherapists. *BMC Psychology, 10*(1), 183.

Bell, C., Tesli, N., Gurholt, T. P., Rokicki, J., Hjell, G., Fischer-Vieler, T., . . . Haukvik, U. K. (2022). Associations between amygdala nuclei volumes, psychosis, psychopathy, and violent offending. *Psychiatry Research: Neuroimaging, 319,* 111416.

Bell, M. (2023, August 29). 2023 update: Can lie detectors be used in court? *GA Accountability Courts*. Retrieved from https://gaaccountabilitycourts.org.

Bellard, A., Trotter, P., McGlone, F., & Cazzato, V. (2022). Vicarious ratings of self vs. other-directed social touch in women with and recovering from anorexia nervosa. *Scientific Reports, 12*(1), 13429.

Belsiyal, C. X., Rentala, S., & Das, A. (2022). Use of therapeutic milieu interventions in a psychiatric setting: A systematic review. *Journal of Education and Health Promotion, 11,* 234.

Beltrán, S., Sit, L., & Ginsburg, K. R. (2021). A call to revise the diagnosis of oppositional defiant disorder: Diagnosis are for helping not harming. *JAMA Psychiatry, 78*(11), 1181–1182.

Bender, A. M., Wilson, R. L. H., Borntrager, L., Orlowski, E. W., Gryglewicz, K., & Karver, M. S. (2023). Evaluating dialectical behavior therapy training with mental health clinicians. *Journal of Personality Disorders, 37*(1), 95–111.

Benge, J. F., Kiselica, A. M., Aguirre, A., Hilsabeck, R. C., Douglas, M., Paydarfar, D., & Scullin, M. K. (2023). Technology use and subjective cognitive concerns in older adults. *Archives of Gerontology and Geriatrics, 106,* 104877.

Bennett, S., & Walkup, J. T. (2022, August 19). Anxiety disorders in children and adolescents: Assessment and diagnosis. *UpToDate*. Retrieved from https://www.uptodate.com.

Bennett, S., & Walkup, J. T. (2022, May 12). Anxiety disorders in children and adolescents: Epidemiology, pathogenesis, clinical manifestations, and course. *UpToDate*. Retrieved from https://www.uptodate.com.

Berdzenishvili, I. (2022, February 20). *History of mental health 101: The first asylums*. Retrieved from https://www.byarcadia.org/post.

Berens, P. (2023, September 5). Overview of the postpartum period: Disorders and complications. *UpToDate*. Retrieved from http://www.uptodate.com.

Berens, P. (2023, May 31). Overview of the postpartum period: Normal physiology and routine maternal care. *UpToDate*. Retrieved from http://www.uptodate.com.

Bergman, P. (2023). *The psychology of eyewitness identification*. Retrieved from https://www.nolo.com.

Berk, R. (2022). *What are the chances of becoming a homicide victim? University of Pennsylvania*. Retrieved from https://crim.sas.upenn.edu/fact-check/what-are-chances-becoming-homicide-victim.

Berk, S. N., & Efran, J. S. (1983). Some recent developments in the treatment of neurosis. In C. E. Walker (Ed.). *The handbook of clinical psychology: Theory, research, and practice* (Vol. 2). Homewood, IL: Dow Jones-Irwin.

Berman, R. (2021, January 20). Many psychiatry patients prefer online therapy. *Medical News Today*.

Berrettini, W. (2022). Genetics of mood disorders. In C. B. Nemeroff, A. F. Schatzberg, N. Rasgon, & S. M. Strakowski (Eds.). *The American Psychiatric Association Publishing textbook of mood disorders* (2nd ed., Chap. 12). Washington, DC: American Psychiatric Association Publishing.

Berry, K. R., Gliske, K., Schmidt, C., Ballard, J., Killian, M., & Fenkel, C. (2023). The impact of family therapy participation on youths and young adult engagement and retention in a telehealth intensive outpatient program: Quality improvement analysis. *JMIR Formative Research, 7,* e45305.

Bertele, N., Talmon, A., Gross, J. J., Schmahl, C., Schmitz, M., & Niedtfeld, I. (2022). Childhood maltreatment and borderline personality disorder: The mediating role of difficulties with emotion regulation. *Journal of Personality Disorders, 36*(3), 264–276.

Bertelli, M. O., Deb, S., Munir, K., Hassiotis, A., & Salvador-Carulla, L. (2021). *Textbook of psychiatry for intellectual disability and autism spectrum disorder*. New York: Springer.

Bertocci, M. A., de Almeida, J. R. C., Strakowski, S. M., & Phillips, M. L. (2022). Brain imaging. In C. B. Nemeroff, A. F. Schatzberg, N. Rasgon, & S. M. Strakowski (Eds.). *The American Psychiatric Association Publishing textbook of mood disorders* (2nd ed., Chap. 11). Washington, DC: American Psychiatric Association Publishing.

Bertollo, A. G., Galvan, A. C. L., Mingoti, M. E. D., Gallagnol, C., & Ignácio, Z. M. (2024). Impact of COVID-19 on anxiety and depression: Biopsychosocial factors. *CNS & Neurological Disorders–Drug Targets, 23*(1), 122–133.

Bertozzi, S., Londero, A. P., Fruscalzo, A., Driul, L., & Marchesoni, D. (2010). Prevalence and risk factors for dyspareunia and unsatisfying sexual relationships in a cohort of primiparous and secondiparous women after 12 months postpartum. *International Journal of Sexual Health, 22*(1), 47–53.

Besch, V., Magnin, C., Greiner, C., Prada, P., Debbané, M., & Poulet, E. (2023, February 9). Examining readmission factors in psychiatric emergency care for individuals with personality disorders: A 6-year retrospective study. *Personality Disorders: Theory, Research, and Treatment, 14*(3), 321–333.

Bever, L. (2017, June 6). The disturbing trend of live-streamed suicides. *Chicago Tribune*. Retrieved from https://www.chicagotribune.com/lifestyles/health.

BH (Becker's Healthcare). (2020). *Becker's hospital review*. Chicago: Author.

BH (Becker's Healthcare). (2022). *Becker's hospital review*. Chicago: Author.

BH (Becker's Healthcare). (2023). *Becker's hospital review*. Chicago: Author.

Bhalla, R. K., Terpstra, A. R., & Butters, M. A. (2024). Late life depression. In M. W. Parsons & M. M. Braun (Eds.). *Clinical neuropsychology: A pocket handbook for assessment* (4th ed., Chap. 24). Washington, DC: American Psychological Association.

Bhatia, K., & Parekh, U. (2023, August 8). Frotteurism. *StatPearls*.

BHC (Behavioral Health Commission). (2022). *Commission meeting, December 2022*. Rialto, CA: Author.

Bi, B., Che, D., & Bai, Y. (2022). Neural network of bipolar disorder: Toward integration of neuroimaging and neurocircuit-based treatment strategies. *Translational Psychiatry, 12*(1), 143.

Bieling, P. J., McCabe, R. E., & Antony, M. M. (2022). *Cognitive-behavioral therapy in groups* (2nd ed.). New York: Guilford Press.

Biggs, Q. M., Vance, M. C., Fullerton, C. S., & Ursano, R. J. (2022). The epidemiology of acute stress disorder and other early responses to trauma in adults. In J. G. Beck & D. M. Sloan (Eds.). *The Oxford handbook of traumatic stress disorders* (Chap. 5). New York: Oxford University Press.

Bilodeau-Houle, A., Morand-Beaulieu, S., Bouchard, V., & Marin, F.-F. (2023). Parent-child physiological concordance predicts stronger observational fear learning in children with a less secure relationship with their parent. *Journal of Experimental Child Psychology, 226*, e10553.

Binet, A., & Simon, T. (1916). *The development of intelligence in children (The Binet-Simon Scale).* Philadelphia: Williams & Wilkins.

Binswanger, I., & Elmore, J. G. (2023, May 18). Clinical care of incarcerated adults. *UpToDate.* Retrieved from https://www.uptodate.com.

Birmaher, B. (2022, January 10). Pediatric bipolar disorder: Epidemiology and pathogenesis. *UpToDate.* Retrieved from https://www.uptodate.com.

Bischoff, P. (2023, January 25). *The rising tide of child abuse content on social media.* Retrieved from https://www.comparitech.com.

Biswas, H., & Sahoo, M. K. (2023). A study on psychiatric conditions in children with school refusal: A clinic based study. *Journal of Family Medicine and Primary Care, 12*(1), 160–164.

BJS (Bureau of Justice Statistics). (2017). *Victims and offenders.* Washington, DC: Author.

BJS (Bureau of Justice Statistics). (2020). *Data collection: National Crime Victimization Survey (NCVS).* Washington, DC: Author.

BJS (Bureau of Justice Statistics). (2023). *National Crime Victimization Survey (NCVS).* Washington, DC: Author.

Black, D. W. (2020). Impulse control and its disorders: Including pathological gambling. In J. R. Geddes, N. C. Andreason, & G. M. Goodwin (Eds.). *New Oxford textbook of psychiatry* (3rd ed., Chap. 123). New York: Oxford University Press.

Black, D. W. (2022). Treatment issues with antisocial personality disorder. In D. W. Black & N. J. Kolla (Eds.). *Textbook of antisocial personality disorder* (Chap. 19). Washington, DC: American Psychiatric Association Publishing.

Black, D. W. (2022, November 2). Treatment of antisocial personality disorder. *UpToDate.* Retrieved from http://www.uptodate.com.

Black, D. W. (2023, July 24). Antisocial personality disorder: Epidemiology, clinical manifestations, course and diagnosis. *UpToDate.* Retrieved from https://www.uptodate.com.

Black, D. W., & Kolla, N. J. (2022). *Textbook of antisocial personality disorder.* Washington, DC: American Psychiatric Association Publishing.

Black, L., Humphrey, N., & Marquez, J. (2023). The influence of minority stress-related experiences on mental wellbeing for trans/gender-diverse and cisgender youth: A comparative longitudinal analysis. *Royal Society Open Science, 10*(7), 221230.

Black, R. (2022). Psychodynamic therapy for depression and anxiety: How it works. *Psycom.* Retrieved from https://www.psycom.net/psychodynamic-therapy-for-depression.

Blais, R. K. (2021, January 5). The association of exposure to military sexual trauma and romantic relationship satisfaction among partnered men service members/veterans: The influence of compulsive sexual behavior. *Family Process, 60*(4), 1295–1306.

Blakemore, E. (2022, July 27). Women are still underrepresented in clinical trials. *Washington Post.*

Blanken, A. E. (2022, October). Sexual functioning of peri- and postmenopausal women Veterans may differ by sexual orientation. Paper presented at the North American Menopause Society Annual Meeting, October 12–15, Atlanta, GA.

Blankenship, L. (2023, March 31). *Removing barriers to success for neurodivergent workers.* Retrieved from https://business.vanderbilt.edu/news/2023/03/31.

Blashfield, R. K., Keele, J. W., Flanagan, E. H., & Miles, S. R. (2014). The cycle of classification: DSM-I through DSM-5. *Annual Review of Clinical Psychology, 10*, 25–51.

Bliss, E. L. (1980). *Multiple personality, allied disorders and hypnosis.* New York: Oxford University Press.

Bloom, F. E. (2020, January 31). Antidepressant. *Britannica.* Retrieved from https://www.britannica.com.

Bloom, F. E. (2023, September 25). Antidepressant. *Britannica.* Retrieved from https://www.britannica.com.

Bloom, S. L. (2020). *The Sanctuary Model: Moral treatment.* Retrieved from https://sanctuaryweb.com/TheSanctuaryModel/Origins of the Sanctuary Model.aspx.

BLS (Bureau of Labor Statistics). (2022, March 31). *Occupational employment and wages, May 2021.* Retrieved from https://www.bls.gov/oes/current/oes291223.htm.

BLS (Bureau of Labor Statistics). (2022, April 18). *Occupational Outlook Handbook: Psychologists.* Retrieved from https://www.bls.gov/ooh/life-physical-and-social-science/psychologists.htm.

BLS (Bureau of Labor Statistics). (2022, April 18). *Occupational Outlook Handbook: Social workers.* Retrieved from https://www.bls.gov/ooh/community-and-social-service/social-workers.htm.

BLS (Bureau of Labor Statistics). (2022, April 18). *Occupational Outlook Handbook: Substance abuse, behavioral disorder, and mental health counselors.* Retrieved from https://www.bls.gov/ooh/community-and-social-service/substance-abuse-behavioral-disorder-and-mental-health-counselors.htm.

Blue, A. (2013, February 18). *Should Grandma join Facebook? It may give her a cognitive boost, study finds.* University of Arizona News. Retrieved from https://news.arizona.edu/story.

Blum, K., Bowirrat, A., Elman, I., Baron, D., Thanos, P. K., Gold, M. S., . . . Badjaiyan, R. D. (2023). Evidence for the *DRD2* gene as a determinant of reward deficiency syndrome (RDS). *Clinical and Experimental Psychology, 9*(4), 8–11.

Blum, K., Chen, A. L. C., Thanos, P. K., Febo, M., Demetrovics, Z., Dushaj, K., . . . Badgaiyan, R. D. (2018). Genetic addiction risk score (GARS), a predictor of vulnerability to opioid dependence. *Frontiers in Bioscience (Elite Edition), 10*, 175–196.

Blum, K., Dennen, C. A., Elman, I., Bowirrat, A., Thanos, P. K., Badgalyan, R. D., . . . Gold, M. S. (2022). Should reward deficiency syndrome (RDS) be considered an umbrella disorder for mental illness and associated genetic and epigenetic induced dysregulation of brain reward circuitry? *Journal of Personalized Medicine, 12*(10), 1719.

Blum, K., Noble, E. P., Sheridan, P. J., Montgomery, A., Ritchie, T., Jagadeeswaran, P., . . . Cohn, J. B. (1990). Allelic association of human dopamine D2 receptor gene in alcoholism. *Journal of the American Medical Association, 263*(15), 2055–2060.

Blum, L. D. (2023). Minding our minds: Obsessive-compulsiveness, psychiatry, and psychology. *Culture, Medicine and Psychiatry, 47*(2), 543–554.

Blume, A. W. (2022, July 4). Back to the basics and fast forward to multiculturalism. *Psychology of Addictive Behaviors, 36*(6), 736–740.

Blythin, S. P. M., Nicholson, H. L., Macintyre, V. G., Dickson, J. M., Fox, J. R. E., & Taylor, P. J. (2020). Experiences of shame and guilt in anorexia and bulimia nervosa: A systematic review. *Psychology and Psychotherapy, 93*, 134–159.

Bobo, W. V., & Shelton, R. C. (2022, August 1). Bipolar major depression in adults: Efficacy and adverse effects of second-generation antipsychotics. *UpToDate.* Retrieved from https://www.uptodate.com.

Bobo, W. V., & Shelton, R. C. (2023, August 21). Bipolar major depression in adults: Efficacy and adverse effects of antidepressants. *UpToDate.* Retrieved from https://www.uptodate.com.

Bobo, W. V., & Shelton, R. C. (2023, March 19). Bipolar major depression in adults: General principles of treatment. *UpToDate.* Retrieved from https://www.uptodate.com.

Boeve, B., McCormick, J., Smith, G., Ferman, T., Rummans, T., Carpenter, T., . . . Petersen, R. (2003). Mild cognitive impairment in the oldest old. *Neurology, 60*(3), 477–480.

Bogat, G. A., Levendosky, A. A., & Cochran, K. (2023, February 15). Developmental consequences of intimate partner violence on children. *Annual Review of Clinical Psychology, 19*, 303–329.

Bohart, A. C., & Watson, J. C. (2020). Person-centered and emotion-focused psychotherapies. In S. B. Messer & N. J. Kaslow (Eds.), *Essential psychotherapies: Theory and practice* (4th ed., Chap. 7, pp. 221–256). New York: Guilford Press.

Bommersbach, T. J., Rosenheck, R. A., & Rhee, T. G. (2022). National trends of mental health care among US adults who attempted suicide in the past 12 months. *JAMA Psychiatry, 79*(3), 219–231.

Bonanno, G. A., Chen, S., Bagrodia, R., & Galatzer-Levy, I. R. (2024). Resilience and disaster: Flexible adaptation in the face of uncertain threat. *Annual Review of Psychology*. https://doi.org/10.1146/annurev-psych-011123-024224. [Online ahead of print]

Boness, C. L., Votaw, V. R., Schwebel, F. J., Moniz-Lewis, D. I. K., McHugh, R. K., & Witkiewitz, K. (2023). An evaluation of cognitive behavioral therapy for substance use disorders: A systematic review and application of the society of clinical psychology criteria for empirically supported treatments. *Clinical Psychology: Science and Practice, 30*(2), 129–142.

Bonin, L. (2022, September 13). Pediatric unipolar depression: Epidemiology, clinical features, assessment, and diagnosis. *UpToDate*. Retrieved from https://www.uptodate.com.

Bonn, S. A. (2019, January 7). Serial murder versus mass murder. *Psychology Today*. Retrieved from https://www.psychologytoday.com/us/blog.

Bonn, S. A. (2020). Wicked deeds. *Psychology Today*. Retrieved from https://www.psychologytoday.com/us/blog/wicked-deeds.

Bonn, S. A. (2022, June 20). The real reason mass shootings are on the rise. *Psychology Today*. Retrieved from https://www.psychologytoday.com/us/blog/wicked-deeds/202206.

Bonnet, M. H., & Arand, D. L. (2023, August 23). Risk factors, comorbidities, and consequences of insomnia in adults. *UpToDate*. Retrieved from http://www.uptodate.com.

Boos, S. C. (2023, June 14). Physical child abuse: Diagnostic evaluation and management. *UpToDate*. Retrieved from https://www.uptodate.com.

Boos, S. C. (2023, May 10). Physical child abuse: Recognition. *UpToDate*. Retrieved from https://www.uptodate.com.

Borchgrevink, C. P., Cha, J.-M., & Kim, S.-H. (2013). Hand washing practices in a college town environment. *Journal of Environmental Health, 75*(8), 18–24.

Bordeaux, B., & Lieberman, H. R. (2023, July 20). Benefits and risks of caffeine and caffeinated beverages. *UpToDate*. Retrieved from http://www.uptodate.com.

Bornstein, R. F. (2020). Dependent personality disorder. In B. J. Carducci & C. Nave (Eds.). *The Wiley encyclopedia of personality and individual differences* (Vol. 4, pp. 193–198). Hoboken, NJ: Wiley.

Bornstein, R. F. (2024, January). *Elements of personality: Discovering connections*. Washington, DC: American Psychological Association.

Bornstein, R. F., & Natoli, A. P. (2022). Dependent personalities. In R. Feinstein (Ed.). *Personality disorders* (Chap. 23). New York: Oxford University Press.

Boskey, E. (2023, November 27). Sex therapy with sensate focus. *Verywellmind*. Retrieved from https://www.verywellmind.com.

Boskey, E., & Marschall, A. (2022, February 28). Online transgender support groups. *Verywellmind*. Retrieved from https://www.verywellmind.com/best-online-transgender-support-groups-4800840.

Botanov, Y., Williams, A., & Sakaluk, J. (2022, May 19). Bad therapy. *Aeon Essays*.

Bott, E. (1928). Teaching of psychology in the medical course. *Bulletin of the Association of American Medical Colleges, 3*, 289–304.

Bouchrika, I. (2023, March 24). *How to become a forensic psychologist*. Retrieved from https://research.com/careers.

Bouchrika, I. (2023, July 27). 75 college drug abuse statistics: 2021/2023 data, facts & predictions. Retrieved from https://research.com/education/college-drug-abuse-statistics.

Boursier, V., Gioia, F., & Griffiths, M. D. (2020). Selfie-engagement on social media: Pathological narcissism, positive expectation, and body objectification—Which is more influential? *Addictive Behaviors Reports, 11*, 100263.

Bower, G. H. (1981). Mood and memory. *American Psychologist, 36*(2), 129–148.

Bower, J. E., & Kuhlman, K. R. (2023). Psychoneuroimmunology: An introduction to immune-to-brain communication and its implications for clinical psychology. *Annual Review of Clinical Psychology, 19*, 331–359.

Boyce, B., Salzberg, S., Selassie, S., & Morey, J. (2022, June 28). Summer meditation retreat: 6 mindfulness practices for self-care. *Mindful*.

Boyer, E. W., & Hernon, C. (2023, October 13). Methamphetamine: Acute intoxication. *UpToDate*. Retrieved from http://www.uptodate.com.

BPF (British Psychotherapy Foundation). (2020). *Why become a psychotherapist? (Part I)*. London: Author. Retrieved from https://www.britishpsychotherapyfoundation.org.uk.

Bracco, L., Dusi, N., Moltrasio, C., Brambilla, P., & Delvecchio, G. (2023, October 9). Structural and functional brain imaging after treatment with selective-serotonin reuptake-inhibitors in obsessive-compulsive disorder: A mini review. *Journal of Affective Disorders*. doi:10.1016/j.jad.2023.10.034. [Online ahead of print]

Bradford, A. (2021, May 13). Female orgasmic disorder: Epidemiology, pathogenesis, clinical manifestations, course, assessment, and diagnosis. *UpToDate*. Retrieved from http://www.uptodate.com.

Bradford, A. (2022, July 14). Treatment of female orgasmic disorder. *UpToDate*. Retrieved from http://www.uptodate.com.

Bram, A. D., & Edwards, K. G. (2023, June). Assessment of bipolar spectrum disorders, disruptive mood dysregulation disorder, and ADHD in children and adolescents. In J. H. Kleiger & I. B. Weiner (Eds.). *Psychological assessment of bipolar spectrum disorders* (Chap. 12). Washington, DC: American Psychological Association.

Brand, B. L. (2023). *The concise guide to the assessment and treatment of trauma-related dissociation*. Washington, DC: American Psychological Association.

Brand, F., Scior, K., & Loewenberger, A. (2024). Psychological and social outcomes of befriending interventions for adults with intellectual disabilities: A systematic review. *Journal of Applied Research in Intellectual Disabilities, 37*(1), e13168.

Brandes, C. M., Reardon, K. W., Shields, A. N., & Tackett, J. L. (2021). Towards construct validity of relational aggression. *Multivariate Behavioral Research, 56*(1), 161–162.

Bränström, R., & Pachankis, J. E. (2019, October 4). Reduction in mental health treatment utilization among transgender individuals after gender-affirming surgeries: A total population study. *American Journal of Psychiatry, 177*(8), 727–734.

Bratskeir, K. (2013, September 16). The habits of supremely happy people. *Huffington Post*.

Bravo, J., Buta, F. L., Talina, M., & Silva-Dos-Santos, A. (2022). Avoiding revolving door and homelessness: The need to improve care transition interventions in psychiatry and mental health. *Frontiers in Psychiatry, 13*, 1021926.

Breaux, R., Dvorsky, M. R., Marsh, N. P., Green, C. D., Cash, A. R., Shroff, D. M., . . . Becker, S. P. (2021, February 4). Prospective impact of COVID-19 on mental health functioning in adolescents with and without ADHD: Protective role of emotion regulation abilities. *Journal of Child Psychology and Psychiatry, and Allied Disciplines, 62*(9), 1132–1139.

Brennen, T., & Magnussen, S. (2023). Lie detection: What works? *Sage Journals, 32*(5), https://doi.org/10.1177/09637214231173095.

Brent, D., Bukstein, O., & Solanto, M. V. (2023, February 1). Management of attention deficit hyperactivity disorder in adults. *UpToDate*. Retrieved from https://www.uptodate.com.

Brewer, A. G., Doss, W., Sheehan, K. M., Davis, M. M., & Feinglass, J. M. (2022). Trends in suicidal ideation-related emergency department visits for youth in Illinois: 2016–2021. *Pediatrics, 150*(6), e2022056793.

Brewer, A., Leon, Y., Kuhn, S. C., Kuhn, D., & Schlund, M. W. (2024). Fear conditioning, anxiety and phobias: Considerations for operant-respondent interactions. In H. S. Roane, A. R. Craig, V. Saini, & J. E. Ringdahl (Eds.). *Behavior analysis: Translational perspectives and clinical practice* (Chap. 8). New York: Guilford Press.

Brewin, C. R., Cloitre, M., Chow, A. Y. M., & Maercker, A. (2024). Disorders specifically associated with stress. In G. M. Reed, P. L.-J. Ritchie, & A. Maercker (Eds.). *A psychological approach to diagnosis: Using the ICD-11 as a framework* (Chap. 10). Washington, DC: American Psychological Association.

Brickman, H. M., & Fristad, M. A. (2022). Psychosocial treatments for bipolar disorder in children and adolescents. *Annual Review of Clinical Psychology, 18*, 291–327.

Brighenti, S., Mustacchia, L., Cicinelli, G., Chieregato, S., Comella, C., Torrero, L., . . . Keller, R. (2023). Social skills and cognitive training to support work-related skills and job placement in a group of autistic adults: Effectiveness of a neuropsychological and social skills intervention: A case series study on a pilot program. *Community Mental Health Journal, 59*(8), 1610–1618.

Brooks, A. C. (2013, December 14). A formula for happiness. *New York Times*.

Brooks, A. C. (2021, May 20). What introverts and extroverts can learn from each other. *The Atlantic*.

Brooten-Brooks, M. C. (2022, March 3). What is aversion therapy and is it effective? *Verywellhealth*. Retrieved from https://www.verywellhealth.com.

Brosch, J. R., & Farlow, M. R. (2023, February 16). Early-onset dementia in adults. *UpToDate*. Retrieved from http://www.uptodate.com.

Brouder, L. M., & Haeffel, G. J. (2023, October). Stable-Global attributions, but not emotional valence, predict future depressive symptoms and event-specific inferences. *Journal of Social and Clinical Psychology, 42*(5), 471–486.

Broudy, M. S. (2022, July). Therapy treatments for anxiety disorders. *eCounseling*.

Brown, A. D., Becker-Weidman, E., & Saxe, G. N. (2023). A developmental perspective on childhood traumatic stress. In M. J. Friedman, P. P. Schnurr, & T. M. Keane (Eds.). *Handbook of PTSD: Science and practice* (3rd ed., Chap. 14). New York: Guilford Press.

Brown, C. L., Yilanli, M., & Rabbitt, A. L. (2023, May 29). Child physical abuse and neglect. *StatPearls*.

Brown, E., Gray, R., Lo Monaco, S., O'Donoghue, B., Nelson, B., Thompson, A., . . . McGorry, P. (2020). The potential impact of COVID-19 on psychosis: A rapid review of contemporary epidemic and pandemic research. *Schizophrenia Research, 222*, 79–87.

Brown, G. R. (2023). Exhibitionistic disorder. *Merck Manual Professional Version*. Retrieved from https://www.merckmanuals.com.

Brown, G. R. (2023). Fetishistic disorder. *Merck Manual Professional Version*. Retrieved from https://www.merckmanuals.com.

Brown, G. R. (2023). Overview of paraphilias and paraphilic disorders. *Merck Manual Professional Version*. Retrieved from https://www.merckmanuals.com.

Brown, G. R. (2023). Pedophilic disorder. *Merck Manual Professional Version*. Retrieved from https://www.merckmanuals.com.

Brown, G. R. (2023). Sexual masochism disorder. *Merck Manual Professional Version*. Retrieved from https://www.merckmanuals.com.

Brown, G. R. (2023). Sexual sadism disorder. *Merck Manual Professional Version*. Retrieved from https://www.merckmanuals.com.

Brown, G. R. (2023). Transvestic disorder. *Merck Manual Professional Version*. Retrieved from https://www.merckmanuals.com.

Brown, G. R. (2023). Voyeuristic disorder. *Merck Manual Professional Version*. Retrieved from https://www.merckmanuals.com.

Brown, J., Dodson, K. D., Spiller, V., & Carter, M. N. (2022, April 6). Suggestibility in police interviews and interrogations: A beginner's guide for law enforcement professionals. *Police Chief Online*.

Brown, L. A., & Foa, E. B. (2022). Empirically supported psychological treatments: Prolonged exposure. In J. G. Beck & D. M. Sloan (Eds.). *The Oxford handbook of traumatic stress disorders* (Chap. 30). New York: Oxford University Press.

Brown, T. A., & Barlow, D. H. (2021, January 2). *Anxiety and related disorders interview schedule for DSM-5 (ADIS-5) — Adult version: Client interview schedule 5-copy set (Treatments that work)*. New York: Oxford University Press.

Brown, T. A., & Keel, P. K. (2023). Eating disorders in boys and men. *Annual Review of Clinical Psychology, 19*, 177–205.

Brownlee, D. (2022, May 9). 82% of employed Gen Zers want mental health days, study finds. *Forbes*.

Broz, M. (2022, July 19). *28 selfie statistics, demographics, & fun facts (2023)*. Photutorial. Retrieved from https://photutorial.com/selfie-statistics.

Brucato, G., Appelbaum, P. S., Hesson, H., Shea, E. A., Dishy, G., Lee, K., . . . Girgis, R. R. (2021, February 17). Psychotic symptoms in mass shootings v. mass murders not involving firearms: Findings from the Columbia mass murder database. *Psychological Medicine, 52*(15), 3422–3430.

Bruce, D. F. (2023, February 14). Sexual problems and depression. *WebMD*.

Bruce, J., & Gross, Y. (2023). In adults with alcohol use disorder, what is the comparative effectiveness of Alcoholics Anonymous or Twelve Step Facilitation versus behavioral therapy in alcohol abstinence outcomes? *Evidence-Based Practice, 26*(8), 23–24.

Bruce, L., Khouri, A. N., Bolze, A., Ibarra, M., Richards, B., Khalatbari, S., . . . Lane, M. (2023). Long-term regret and satisfaction with decision following gender-affirming mastectomy. *JAMA Surgery, 158*(10), 10709–1077.

Bruch, H. (1962). Perceptual and conceptual disturbances in anorexia nervosa. *Psychosomatic Medicine, 24*, 187–194.

Bruch, H. (1973). *Eating disorders: Obesity, anorexia nervosa and the person within*. New York: Basic Books.

Bruch, H. (1978). *The golden cage: The enigma of anorexia nervosa*. Cambridge, MA: Harvard University Press.

Bruch, H. (1991). The sleeping beauty: Escape from change. In S. I. Greenspan & G. H. Pollock (Eds.). *The course of life: Vol. 4. Adolescence*. Madison, CT: International Universities Press.

Bruch, H. (2001). *The golden cage: The enigma of anorexia nervosa* (2nd ed.). Cambridge, MA: Harvard University Press.

Bryant, R. (2022, May 10). Treatment of acute stress disorder in adults. *UpToDate*. Retrieved from https://www.uptodate.com.

Bryant, R. (2023, June 22). *"Psychological debriefing" right after an accident or trauma can do more harm than good: Here's why*. Sydney: University of New South Wales.

Bryant, R. A. (2023). Psychological models of PTSD. In M. J. Friedman, P. P. Schnurr, & T. M. Keane (Eds.). *Handbook of PTSD: Science and practice* (3rd ed., Chap. 6). New York: Guilford Press.

BSA (Bullying Statistics of America). (2014). *A 2014 presentation of statistics and graphs on bullying*.

BSA (Bullying Statistics of America). (2017). *A 2017 presentation of statistics and graphs on bullying*.

Buchanan, A. (2020). Assessing and managing the risk of violence to others. In J. R. Geddes, N. C. Andreason, & G. M. Goodwin (Eds.). *New Oxford textbook of psychiatry* (3rd ed., Chap. 144). New York: Oxford University Press.

Buchanan, J. A. (2023, July 11). Evaluation and management of adult and adolescent sexual assault victims in the emergency department. *UpToDate*. Retrieved from http://www.uptodate.com.

Budiman, A., & Ruiz, N. G. (2021, April 9). *Asian Americans are the fastest-growing racial or ethnic group in the U.S.* Pew Research Center.

Buijsman, R., Begeer, S., & Scheeren, A. M. (2023). "Autistic person" or "person with autism"? Person-first language preference in Dutch adults with autism and parents. *Autism, 27*(3), 788–795.

Bukstein, O. (2023, November 27). Attention deficit hyperactivity disorder in adults: Epidemiology, pathogenesis, clinical features, course, assessment, and diagnosis. *UpToDate*. Retrieved from https://www.uptodate.com.

Bukstein, O. (2023, November 2). Substance use disorder in adolescents: Epidemiology, clinical features, assessment, land diagnosis. *UpToDate*. Retrieved from https://www.uptodate.com.

Bunis, D. (2022, January 19). Millions of older Americans can't afford their prescriptions. *AARP*. Retrieved from https://www.aarp.org/health/medicare-insurance/info-2022/drug-costs-survey.html.

Burke, J. D., Butler, E. J., Shaughnessy, S., Karlovich, A. R., & Evans, S. C. (2024). Evidence-based assessment of DSM-5 disruptive, impulse control, and conduct disorders. *Assessment, 31*(1), 75–93.

Burke, N. L., Hazzard, V. M., Schaefer, L. M., Simone, M., O'Flynn, J. L., & Rodgers, R. F. (2022, May 16). Socioeconomic status and eating disorder prevalence: At the intersections of gender identity, sexual orientation, and race/ethnicity. *Psychological Medicine*, 1–11. https://doi.org/10.1017/S0033291722001015.

Burley, J. F., Mont, J. D., Reid, A., & Macdonald, S. (2022). Promoting awareness to counter damaging attitudes, beliefs, and reactions related to sexual assault against trans people: A social media campaign for health and social service providers. *Health Promotion Practice*.

Burnett, L. B. (2023, March 11). Cocaine toxicity. *Medscape*. Retrieved from https://emedicine.medscape.com/article/813959.

Burns, T., & Kendrick, T. (2020). Planning and providing mental health services for a community. In J. R. Geddes, N. C. Andreason, & G. M. Goodwin (Eds.). *New Oxford textbook of psychiatry* (3rd ed., Chap. 135). New York: Oxford University Press.

Bursch, B. (2020). Munchausen by proxy: Five core principles. *Annals of Pediatrics & Child Health, 8*(2), 1171.

Burton, M., Maples-Keller, J., Hoskins, M., Tang, Y., Wyka, K., Difede, J., & Rothbaum, B. O. (2020). Combined psychotherapy and medication treatment. In D. Forbes, J. I. Bisson, C. M. Monson, & L. Berliner (Eds.). *Effective treatments for PTSD* (3rd ed., Chap. 17). New York: Guilford Press.

Bushman, B. J., Baumeister, R. F., & Stack, A. D. (1999). Catharsis, aggression, and persuasive influence: Self-fulfilling or self-defeating prophecies? *Journal of Personality and Social Psychology, 76*(3), 367–376.

Business Wire. (2022). *Weight management global market report 2022: Focus on health clubs, consultation services, online weight loss services, functional beverages, functional food, & dietary supplements: Forecasts for 2031*. Retrieved from https://www.businesswire.com.

Bustamante, D., Bountress, K., Sheerin, C., Koenen, K. C., Guffanti, G., Yan, L., . . . Amstadter, A. B. (2023). Genetics of PTSD. In M. J. Friedman, P. P. Schnurr, & T. M. Keane (Eds.). *Handbook of PTSD: Science and practice* (3rd ed., Chap. 11). New York: Guilford Press.

Bustillo, J. (2023, September 1). Schizophrenia in adults: Psychosocial management. *UpToDate*. Retrieved from https://www.uptodate.com.

Butler, R. M., & Heimberg, R. G. (2023). Imaginal exposure for disordered eating related fears: An initial randomized controlled trial. *Behavior Modification, 47*(1), 46–70.

Cabrera, V. M., Buitron, V., Patriarca, G. C., Rey, Y., Lebowitz, E. R., Silverman, W. K., & Pettit, J. W. (2023). Parent accommodation contemporaneously mediates the association between youth irritability and youth anxiety treatment outcome. *Behavior Therapy, 54*(5), 852–862.

Cadoni, C. (2022). Opioid reinforcement: What it is and how it can be modulated by cannabinoids. In V. B. Patel & V. R. Preedy (Eds.). *Handbook of substance misuse and addictions: From biology to public health* (pp. 1893–1920). New York: Springer.

Cahalan, S. (2019). *The great pretender: The undercover mission that changed our understanding of madness*. New York: Grand Central Publishing.

Cahalan, S. (2020, May 5). Mental illness treatment in meltdown. *Saturday Evening Post*. Retrieved from https://www.saturdayeveningpost.com/2020/05.

Cai, L., He, J., Wu, Y., & Jia, X. (2023). The relationship between big five personality and quality of life of people with disabilities: The mediating effect of social support. *Frontiers in Psychology, 13*, 1061455.

Cai, W., Ma, W., Mueller, C., Stewart, R., Ji, J., & Shen, W.-D. (2024). Association between late-life depression or depressive symptoms and stroke morbidity in elders: A systematic review and meta-analysis of cohort studies. *Acta Psychiatrica Scandinavica, 148*(5), 405–415.

Caire, M. J., Reddy, V., & Varacallo, M. (2023, March 27). Physiology, synapse. *StatPearls*.

Caletti, E., Massimo, C., Magliocca, S., Moltrasio, C., Brambilla, P., & Delvecchio, G. (2022). The role of the acceptance and commitment therapy in the treatment of social anxiety: An updated scoping review. *Journal of Affective Disorders, 310*, 174–182.

Caligor, E., & Petrini, M. J. (2022, October 21). Narcissistic personality disorder: Epidemiology, pathogenesis, clinical manifestations, course, assessment, and diagnosis. *UpToDate*. Retrieved from http://www.uptodate.com.

Caligor, E., & Stern, B. L. (2020). Diagnosis, classification, and assessment of narcissistic personality disorder within the framework of object relations theory. *Journal of Personality Disorders, 34*(Suppl.), 104–121.

Callaghan, C. B. (2023). *Psychological & scientific evidence in criminal trials* (2023–2024 ed.). Toronto: Thomson Reuters.

Callahan, L. A., Steadman, H. J., McGreevy, M. A., & Robbins, P. C. (1991). The volume and characteristics of insanity defense pleas: An eight-state study. *Bulletin of the American Academy of Psychiatry Law, 19*(4), 331–338.

Calvano, C., Engelke, L., Holl-Etten, A. K., Renneberg, B., & Winter, S. M. (2023, February 4). Almost 2 years into the COVID-19 pandemic: An update on parental stress, parent mental health, and the occurrence of child maltreatment. *European Child and Adolescent Psychiatry, 32*(12), 2593–2609.

Campbell, C. (2022). *Sex therapy: The basics*. New York: Routledge.

Campbell, E. C., Caroff, S. N., & Mann, S. C. (2022, March 17). Psychosocial interventions for co-occurring schizophrenia and substance use disorder. *UpToDate*. Retrieved from https://www.uptodate.com.

Campbell, L. (2023). The relationship between ethics and law in mental healthcare. In B. D. Kelly & M. Donnelly (Eds.). *Routledge handbook of mental health law* (Chap. 3). New York: Routledge.

Campez, M., Raiker, J. S., Little, K., Altszuler, A. R., Merrill, B. M., Macphee, F. L., . . . Pelham, W. E. (2022). An evaluation of the effect of methylphenidate on working memory, time perception, and choice impulsivity in children with ADHD. *Experimental and Clinical Psychopharmacology, 30*(2), 209–219.

Campos, A., Van Velzen, L. S., Veitman, D. J., Pozzi, E., Ambrogi, S., Ballard, E. D., . . . Rentería, M. E. (2023). Concurrent validity and reliability of suicide risk assessment instruments: A meta-analysis of 20 instruments across 27 international cohorts. *Neuropsychology, 37*(3), 315–329.

Canals, J., & Arija Val, V. (2022). Risk factors and prevention strategies in eating disorders. *Nutrición Hospitalaria, 39*(Spec. No. 2), 16–26.

Canna, M., & Seligman, R. (2020). Dealing with the unknown: Functional neurological disorder (FND) and the conversion of cultural meaning. *Social Science & Medicine, 246*, 112725.

CareerBuilder. (2023). 60% of employers are peeking into candidates' social media profiles. *CareerBuilder*. Retrieved from https://www.careerbuilder.com/advice/blog.

Carey, B. (2017, August 30). *The true story behind Sybil*. Retrieved from http://www.cbc.ca/books.

Carl, J. R., Jones, D. J., Lindhiem, O. J., Doss, B. D., Weingardt, K. R., Timmons, A. C., & Comer, J. S. (2022). Regulating digital therapeutics for mental health: Opportunities, challenges, and the essential role of psychologists. *British Journal of Clinical Psychology, 61*(Suppl. 1), 130–135.

Carlson, L. E., Baydoun, M., & Flynn, M. (2024). Emerging integrative medicine approaches to disease management. In N. Schneiderman (Ed.). *APA handbook of health psychology: Vol. 1. Foundations and context of health psychology; Vol. 2. Clinical interventions and disease management in health psychology; Vol. 3. Health psychology and public health* (Chap. 8). Washington, DC: American Psychological Association.

Carlton, C. N., Sullivan-Toole, H., Strege, M. V., Ollendick, T. H., & Richey, J. A. (2020). Mindfulness-based interventions for adolescent social anxiety: A unique convergence of factors. *Frontiers in Psychology, 11*, 1783.

Carnahan, K. T., & Jha, A. (2023, January 2). Factitious disorder. *StatPearls*.

Carota, A., & Bogousslavsky, J. (2019). Neurology versus psychiatry? Hallucinations, delusions, and confabulations. *Frontiers in Neurology and Neuroscience, 44*, 127–140.

Carpenter, R. W., Hepp, J., & Trull, T. J. (2023, August 21). Pain before, during, and after nonsuicidal self-injury: Findings from a large web study. *Journal of Psychopathology and Clinical Science*. doi:10.1037/abn0000853. [Online ahead of print]

Carr, A. (2023). Family therapy. In J. L. Matson (Ed.). *Handbook of clinical child psychology*. Springer, Cham: Springer.

Carroll, N. M., & Banks, A. (2022, November 4). Health care for female trauma survivors (with posttraumatic stress disorder or similarly severe symptoms). *UpToDate*. Retrieved from http://www.uptodate.com.

Carvalho, A. F., Firth, J., & Vieta, E. (2020). Bipolar disorder. *New England Journal of Medicine, 383*(1), 58–66.

Carvalho, D., Sequeira, C., Querido, A., Tomás, A., Morgado, T., Valentim, O., . . . Laranjeira, C. (2022). Positive mental health literacy: A concept analysis. *Frontiers in Psychology, 13*, 877611.

Caselli, I., Ielmini, M., Bellini, A., Zizoldi, D., & Callegari, C. (2023). Efficacy of short-term psychodynamic psychotherapy (STPP) in depressive disorders: A systematic review and meta-analysis. *Journal of Affective Disorders, 325*, 169–176.

Cash, T. F., & Henry, P. E. (1995). Women's body images: The results of a national survey in the U.S.A. *Sex Roles, 33*(1/2), 19–28.

Casiano, V. E., Sarwan, G., Dydyk, A. M., & Varacallo, M. (2022, September 4). Back pain. *StatPearls*.

Casiano, V. E., Sarwan, G., Dydyk, A. M., & Varacallo, M. (2023, February 20). Back pain. *StatPearls*.

Cass, J., Giltrap, G., & Talbot, D. (2020). Female body dissatisfaction and attentional bias to body images evaluated using visual search. *Frontiers in Psychology, 10*, 2821.

Castellini, G., Cassioli, E., Rossi, E., Mancini, M., Ricca, V., & Stanghellini, G. (2022). Bridging cognitive, phenomenological and psychodynamic approaches to eating disorders. *Eating and Weight Disorders, Studies on Anorexia, Bulimia and Obesity, 27*, 2273–2289.

Castleman, M. (2017, August 1). Surprise: Men enjoy—and want—foreplay. *Psychology Today*. Retrieved from https://www.psychologytoday.com/us/blog/all-about-sex/201708.

Catalano, L. T., Green, M. F., Wynn, J. K., & Lee, J. (2020). People with schizophrenia do not show the normal benefits of social versus nonsocial attentional cues. *Neuropsychology, 34*(6), 620–628.

Catania, J., Spirou, D., Gascoigne, M., & Raman, J. (2023). Loss of control as a transdiagnostic feature in obesity-related eating behaviours: A systematic review. *European Eating Disorders Review, 31*(1), 24–45.

Cavanaugh, C., & Nelson, T. (2022). A national study of the influence of adverse childhood experiences on depression among Black adults in the United States. *Journal of Affective Disorders, 311,* 523–529.

CC (Cleveland Clinic). (2023). *Neurodivergent.* Cleveland, OH: Author.

CC (Compassion & Choices). (2022). *Polling on medical aid in dying.* Retrieved from https://compassionandchoices.org.

CC (Compassion & Choices). (2022). *Polling on voter support for medical aid in dying.* Retrieved from https://compassionandchoices.org.

CCJ (Council on Criminal Justice). (2023). *New analysis shows 8% increase in U.S. domestic violence incidents following pandemic stay-at-home orders.* Retrieved from https://counciloncj.org/new-analysis-shows-8-increase-in-u-s-domestic-violence-incidents-following-pandemic-stay-at-home-orders.

CDC (Centers for Disease Control and Prevention). (2017). *Sleep and sleep disorders: Data and statistics.* Atlanta: Author.

CDC (Centers for Disease Control and Prevention). (2018). *Adolescent and school health: Anti-bullying policies and enumeration: An Infobrief for local education agencies.* Atlanta: Author.

CDC (Centers for Disease Control and Prevention). (2018). *Sleep and sleep disorders.* Atlanta: Author.

CDC (Centers for Disease Control and Prevention). (2019). *Violence prevention: Preventing bullying.* Atlanta: Author.

CDC (Centers for Disease Control and Prevention). (2020). *Coronavirus disease 2019: Older adults.* Atlanta: Author.

CDC (Centers for Disease Control and Prevention). (2020). *Data & statistics.* Atlanta: Author.

CDC (Centers for Disease Control and Prevention). (2020). *Fast food intake among children and adolescents in the United States, 2015–2018.* Atlanta: Author.

CDC (Centers for Disease Control and Prevention). (2020). *Increase in suicide mortality in the United States, 1999–2018* (NCHS Data Brief 362). Atlanta: Author.

CDC (Centers for Disease Control and Prevention). (2020, April 15). *Sleep and sleep disorders.* Atlanta: Author.

CDC (Centers for Disease Control and Prevention). (2020). *Youth Risk Behavior Survey: Data summary and trends report 2009–2019.* Atlanta: Author.

CDC (Centers for Disease Control and Prevention). (2021). *Fast fact: Prevent bullying.* Atlanta: Author.

CDC (Centers for Disease Control and Prevention). (2021). *Health effects of cigarette smoking.* Atlanta: Author.

CDC (Centers for Disease Control and Prevention). (2022). *Binge drinking.* Atlanta: Author.

CDC (Centers for Disease Control and Prevention). (2022, November 2). *Children (4 months to 14 years) sleep data.* Atlanta: Author.

CDC (Centers for Disease Control and Prevention). (2022). *Disparities in suicide.* Atlanta: Author.

CDC (Centers for Disease Control and Prevention). (2022, December 21). *Drug overdose deaths in the United States, 2001–2021* (NCHS Data Brief No. 457). Atlanta: Author.

CDC (Centers for Disease Control and Prevention). (2022). *Fast facts and fact sheets: Smoking and cigarettes.* Atlanta: Author.

CDC (Centers for Disease Control and Prevention). (2022). *Heart disease and stroke.* Atlanta: Author.

CDC (Centers for Disease Control and Prevention). (2022). *Impaired driving: Get the facts.* Atlanta: Author.

CDC (Centers for Disease Control and Prevention). (2022). *Smoking and tobacco use: Diseases and death.* Atlanta: Author.

CDC (Centers for Disease Control and Prevention). (2022). *Smoking cessation: Fast facts.* Atlanta: Author.

CDC (Centers for Disease Control and Prevention). (2022). *Suicide data and statistics.* Atlanta: Author.

CDC (Centers for Disease Control and Prevention). (2022). *Suicide prevention: Prevention strategies.* Atlanta: Author.

CDC (Centers for Disease Control and Prevention). (2022). *Underage drinking.* Atlanta: Author.

CDC (Centers for Disease Control and Prevention). (2022). *Underlying cause of death, 1999–2020 results: Deaths occurring through 2020.* Atlanta: Author.

CDC (Centers for Disease Control and Prevention). (2022, March 14). *When and how to wash your hands.* Atlanta: Author.

CDC (Centers for Disease Control and Prevention). (2022). *Youth Risk Behavior Surveillance System (YRBSS).* Atlanta: Author.

CDC (Centers for Disease Control and Prevention). (2023). *About Alzheimer's disease.* Atlanta: Author.

CDC (Centers for Disease Control and Prevention). (2023, January 18). *Alcohol use.* Atlanta: Author. Retrieved from https://www.cdc.gov/nchs/fastats/alcohol.htm.

CDC (Centers for Disease Control and Prevention). (2023, June 3). *Ambulatory care use and physician office visits.* Atlanta: Author.

CDC (Centers for Disease Control and Prevention). (2023). *Anxiety and depression in children: Get the facts.* Atlanta: Author.

CDC (Centers for Disease Control and Prevention). (2023). *Behavior or conduct problems in children.* Atlanta: Author.

CDC (Centers for Disease Control and Prevention). (2023). *Comprehensive suicide prevention: Program profiles.* Atlanta: Author.

CDC (Centers for Disease Control and Prevention). (2023). *COVID-19 risks and information for older adults.* Atlanta: Author.

CDC (Centers for Disease Control and Prevention). (2023). *Data and statistics about ADHD.* Atlanta: Author.

CDC (Centers for Disease Control and Prevention). (2023). *Data and statistics on children's mental health.* Atlanta: Author.

CDC (Centers for Disease Control and Prevention). (2023). *Data and statistics on FASDs.* Atlanta: Author.

CDC (Centers for Disease Control and Prevention). (2023). *Diet/nutrition.* Atlanta: CDC.

CDC (Centers for Disease Control and Prevention). (2023). *Disparities in suicide.* Atlanta: Author.

CDC (Centers for Disease Control and Prevention). (2023, July 6). *Facts about hypertension.* Atlanta: Author.

CDC (Centers for Disease Control and Prevention). (2023). *Fast facts: Preventing child abuse and neglect.* Atlanta: Author.

CDC (Centers for Disease Control and Prevention). (2023). *Fetal alcohol spectrum disorders (FASDs).* Atlanta: Author. Retrieved from https://www.cdc.gov/ncbddd/fasd.

CDC (Centers for Disease Control and Prevention). (2023, May 15). *Heart disease facts.* Atlanta: Author.

CDC (Centers for Disease Control and Prevention). (2023). *Leading causes of death.* Atlanta: Author.

CDC (Centers for Disease Control and Prevention). (2023, April 24). *Marriage and divorce.* Atlanta: Author.

CDC (Centers for Disease Control and Prevention). (2023, May 10). *Most recent national asthma data.* Atlanta: Author.

CDC (Centers for Disease Control and Prevention). (2023). *Older persons' health.* Atlanta: Author.

CDC (Centers for Disease Control and Prevention). (2023). *Parent training in behavior management for ADHD.* Atlanta: Author.

CDC (Centers for Disease Control and Prevention). (2023). *Suicide data and statistics.* Atlanta: Author.

CDC (Centers for Disease Control and Prevention). (2023, August 8). *Understanding the opioid overdose epidemic.* Atlanta: Author. Retrieved from https://www.cdc.gov/opioids/basics/epidemic.html.

CDC (Centers for Disease Control and Prevention). (2023). *Youth Risk Behavior Surveillance System (YRBSS): 2021 YRBS results now available.* Atlanta: Author.

Cénat, J. M., Blais-Rochette, C., Kokou-Kpolou, C. K., Noorishad, P.-G., Mukunzi, J. N., McIntee, S.-E., . . . Labelle, P. R. (2021). Prevalence of symptoms of depression, anxiety, insomnia, posttraumatic stress disorder, and psychological distress among populations affected by the COVID-19 pandemic: A systematic review and meta-analysis. *Psychiatry Research, 295,* 113599.

Cerfolio, N. E., Glick, I., Kamis, D., & Laurence, M. (2022). A retrospective observational study of psychosocial determinants and psychiatric diagnoses of mass shooters in the United States. *Psychodynamic Psychiatry, 50*(3), 513–528.

Cesinger, B., Gundolf, K., Hughes, M., Khedhaouria, A., & Montani, F. (2022, August 29). The bright and dark sides of the dark triad traits among senior managers: Effects on organizational commitment. *Review of Managerial Science*. https://doi.org/10.1007/s11846-022-00571-3. [Open access]

Chambless, D. L., & Hollon, S. D. (2023). Treatment validity for intervention studies. In H. Cooper, M. N. Coutanche, L. M. McMullen, A. T. Panter, D. Rindskopf, & K. J. Sher (Eds.). *APA handbook of research methods in psychology: Vol. 2. Research designs: Quantitative, qualitative, neuropsychological, and biological* (2nd ed., Chap. 3). Washington, DC: American Psychological Association.

Chan, L., Simmons, C., Tillem, S., Conkley, M., Brazil, I. A., & Baskin-Sommers, A. (2023). Classifying conduct disorder using a biopsychosocial model and machine learning method. *Biological Psychiatry: Cognitive Neuroscience and Neuroimaging, 8*(6), 599–608.

Chand, S. P., Kuckel, D. P., & Huecker, M. R. (2023, May 23). Cognitive behavior therapy. *StatPearls*.

Chang, G. (2023, September 13). Alcohol intake and pregnancy. *UpToDate*. Retrieved from http://www.uptodate.com.

Chao, Y.-S., Wu, C.-J., Lai, C., Cheng, Y.-P., Huang, Y., & Chen, W.-C. (2022, April 29). Why mental illness diagnoses are wrong: A pilot study on the perspectives of the public. *Frontiers in Psychiatry, 13*. https://doi.org/10.3389/fpsyt.2022.860487.

Chapman, J., Jamil, R. T., & Fleisher, C. (2023, June 2). Borderline personality disorder. *StatPearls*.

Charbit, J., Vidal, J. S., & Hanon, O. (2024). The role of nutrition in the prevention of cognitive decline. *Current Opinion in Clinical Nutrition and Metabolic Care, 27*(1), 9–16.

Chard, K. M., & Wachen, J. S. (2022). Empirically supported psychological treatments: Cognitive processing therapy. In J. G. Beck & D. M. Sloan (Eds.). *The Oxford handbook of traumatic stress disorders* (Chap. 31). New York: Oxford University Press.

Charmley, S. (2023, October 20). Female viagra: Drugs that increase sex drive, and can women take viagra? *Medical News Today*.

Charpignon, M.-L., Ontiveros, J., Sundaresan, S., Puri, A., Chandra, J., Mandl, K. D., & Majumder, M. S. (2022). Evaluation of suicides among US adolescents during the COVID-19 pandemic. *JAMA Pediatrics, 176*(7), 724–726.

CheckVideo. (2022). Crime statistics: Crime victim rates in the U.S. *CheckVideo*. Retrieved from https://www.checkvideo.com/blog-post/crime-victim-statistics.

Chen, M., & Xiao, X. (2022). The effect of social media on the development of students' affective variables. *Frontiers in Psychology, 13*, 1010766.

Chen, R., Fitzgerald, P. B., & Blumberger, D. M. (2022). *A practical guide to transcranial magnetic stimulation and neurophysiology and treatment studies*. New York: Oxford University Press.

Chen, T., Li, S., & Eisenberg, M. L. (2022). Associations between race and erectile dysfunction treatment patterns. *AUA Journals, 9*(5), 423–430.

Chen, T.-C., Zhang, X.-M., Liu, X.-Y., Bai, Y.-F., Feng, Y.-Y., & Wu, X.-J. (2024). Comment on "Association between late-life depression or depressive symptoms and stroke morbidity in elders: A systematic review and meta-analysis of cohort studies." *Acta Psychiatrica Scandinavica, 149*(1), 80–82.

Cheng, C. P. (2022, November 17). Higher psychosis rates in transgender population likely due to minority stress and clinical bias. *Mad in America*. Retrieved from https://www.madinamerica.com.

Cheng, M., Sommet, N., Jopp, D. S., & Spini, D. (2024). Income-related inequalities in physical and cognitive health domains over the later life course: Longitudinal evidence from the U.S. (1992–2016). *Research on Aging, 46*(1), 59–71.

Cheng, P. J. (2022). Sexual dysfunction in men who have sex with men. *ScienceDirect, 10*(1), 130–141.

Cherry, K. (2020, February 5). Paranoid personality disorder. *Verywellmind*. Retrieved from https://www.verywellmind.com.

Cherry, K. (2020, March 29). 10 fascinating facts about personality. *Verywellmind*. Retrieved from https://www.verywellmind.com.

Cherry, K. (2022). Sigmund Freud's life, theories, and influence. *Verywellmind*. Retrieved from https://verywellmind.com.

Cherry, K. (2022, July 22). What is a case study? *Verywellmind*. Retrieved from https://www.verywellmind.com.

Cherry, K. (2022, April 15). What is a correlation? *Verywellmind*. Retrieved from https://www.verywellmind.com.

Cherry, K. (2022, July 13). What is happiness? *Verywellmind*. Retrieved from https://www.verywellmind.com.

Cherry, K. (2022, May 30). What is naturalistic observation? *Verywellmind*. Retrieved from https://www.verywellmind.com/what-is-naturalistic-observation-2795391.

Cherry, K. (2022, October 18). What is schizoid personality disorder? *Verywellmind*. Retrieved from https://www.verywellmind.com.

Cherry, K. (2022, July 25). What is self-monitoring? *Verywellmind*. Retrieved from https://www.verywellmind.com/what-is-self-monitoring-5179838.

Cherry, K. (2023, May 5). How psychoanalysis influenced the field of psychology. *Verywellmind*. Retrieved from https://verywellmind.com.

Chester, L. A., Englund, A., Chesney, E., Oliver, D., Wilson, J., Sovi, S., . . . McGuire, P. (2022, December 9). Effects of cannabidiol and delta-9 tetrahydrocannabinol on plasma endocannabinoid levels in healthy volunteers: A randomized double-blind four-arm crossover study. *Cannabis and Cannabinoid Research*. doi:10.1089/can.2022.0174. [Online ahead of print]

Cho, Y., Lin, K., Lee, S.-H., Yu, C., Valle, D. S., Avery, D., . . . Walters, R. G. (2023). Genetic influences on alcohol flushing in East Asian populations. *BMC Genomics, 24*, 638.

Choi, B., & Park, S. (2021, January 11). Bullying perpetration, victimization, and low self-esteem: Examining their relationship over time. *Journal of Youth and Adolescence, 50*(4), 739–752.

Choi, N. G., Marti, C. N., & Choi, B. Y. (2022). Job loss, financial strain, and housing problems as suicide precipitants: Associations with other life stressors. *Population Health, 19*, 101243.

Choi, S. L., Hill, K. C., & Parmelee, P. A. (2024). Communication modalities, personality traits, and change in perceived control over social life following onset of the COVID-19 pandemic among older Americans. *Research on Aging, 46*(1), 29–42.

Choudhary, S., & Gupta, R. (2020). Culture and borderline personality disorder in India. *Frontiers in Psychology, 11*, 714.

Christensen, A., Dimidjian, S., Martell, C. R., & Doss, B. D. (2022). Integrative behavioral couple therapy. In J. L. Lebow (Ed.). *Clinical handbook of couple therapy* (Chap. 4). New York: Guilford Press.

Christensen, A., Doss, B., & Jacobson, N. S. (2020). *Integrative behavioral couple therapy: A therapist's guide to creating acceptance and change* (2nd ed.). New York: W. W. Norton.

Christensen, L., Turner, L. A., & Johnson, R. B. (2023). Randomized designs in psychological research. In H. Cooper, M. N. Coutanche, L. M. McMullen, A. T. Panter, D. Rindskopf, & K. J. Sher (Eds.). *APA handbook of research methods in psychology: Vol. 2. Research designs: Quantitative, qualitative, neuropsychological, and biological* (2nd ed., Chap. 27). Washington, DC: American Psychological Association.

Christian, C. (2022, June 30). Child abuse: Epidemiology, mechanisms, and types of abusive head trauma in infants and children. *UpToDate*. Retrieved from https://www.uptodate.com.

Christl, J., Schröder, N., Mennicken, R., Jänner, M., & Supprian, T. (2022). Inpatient suicides in late life: A retrospective analysis of a hospital group with nine psychiatric clinics. *Archives of Suicide Research, 26*(3), 1436–1446.

Chrysopoulos, P. (2022, April 18). Hippocrates: The Greek father of modern medicine. Retrieved from https://greekreporter.com.

Chu, D., Yang, X., Wang, J., Zhou, Y., Gu, J.-H., Miao, J., . . . Liu, F. (2024). Tau truncation in the pathogenesis of Alzheimer's disease: A narrative review. *Neural Regeneration Research, 19*(6), 1221–1232.

Chu, G. M., Goger, P., Malaktaris, A., & Lang, A. J. (2022). The role of threat appraisal and coping style in psychological response to the COVID-19 pandemic among university students. *Journal of Affective Disorders Reports, 8*(4), 100325.

Chu, J., Zhang, W., Liu, Y., Gong, B., Ji, W., Yin, T., . . . Yin, Y. (2024). Biomaterials-based anti-inflammatory treatment strategies for Alzheimer's disease. *Neural Regeneration Research, 19*(1), 100–115.

Chudal, R., Gissler, M., Sucksdorff, D., Lehti, V., Suominen, A., Kinkka-Yli-Salomaki, S., . . . Sourander, A. (2014). Parental age and the risk of bipolar disorders. *Bipolar Disorders, 16*, 624–632.

Chugh, N., Aggarwal, S., & Balyan, A. (2024). The hybrid deep learning model for identification of attention-deficit/hyperactivity disorder using EEG. *Clinical EEG and Neuroscience, 55*(1), 22–33.

Chung, S., Hovmand, P., McBride, A. M., & Joiner, T. (2022). Suicide attempts during adolescence: Testing the system dynamics of the interpersonal theory of suicide. *Journal of Adolescence, 94*(4), 628–641.

Cicchetti, D. (Ed.). (2016). *Developmental psychopathology* (3rd ed., 4 vols.). New York: Wiley.

Cicchetti, D. (2018). A multilevel developmental approach to the prevention of psychopathology in children and adolescents. In J. Butcher (Ed. in Chief), *APA handbook of psychopathology: Vol. 2. Psychopathology in children and adolescents* (Chap. 3). Washington, DC: American Psychological Association.

Cicchetti, D. (2023). A multiple levels of analysis developmental psychopathology perspective on adolescence and young adulthood. In L. J. Crockett, G. Carlo, & J. E. Schulenberg (Eds.). *APA handbook of adolescent and young adult development* (pp. 487–503). Washington, DC: American Psychological Association.

CIP (Careers in Psychology). (2020). *Careers as a psychologist.* Retrieved from https://careersinpsychology.org.

Cirelli, C. (2023, October 17). Insufficient sleep: Definition, epidemiology, and adverse outcomes. *UpToDate.* Retrieved from https://www.uptodate.com.

CISCRP (Center for Information and Study on Clinical Research Participation). (2023). *Perceptions and insights study.* Boston: Author.

Ciuca Anghel, D.-M. C., Nitescu, G. V., Tiron, A.-D., Gutu, C. M., & Baconi, D. L. (2023). Understanding the mechanisms of action and effects of drugs of abuse. *Molecules, 28,* 4969.

Clark, D. A. & Beck, A. T. (2023). *The anxiety and worry workbook: The cognitive behavioral solution* (2nd ed.). New York: Guilford Press.

Clarke, J. C., & Saunders, J. B. (1988). *Alcoholism and problem drinking: Theories and treatment.* Sydney: Pergamon Press.

Clarke, L. S., Riley, H. E., Corwin, E. J., Dunlop, A. L., & Hogue, C. J. R. (2022, January–December). The unique contribution of gendered racial stress to depressive symptoms among pregnant Black women. *Frontiers in Public Health, 18,* 17455057221104657. https://doi.org/10.1177/17455057221104657. [Free PMC article]

Clausen, L., Rosenvinge, J. H., Friborg, O., & Rokkedal, K. (2011). Validating the Eating Disorder Inventory-3 (EDI-3): A comparison between 561 female eating disorders patients and 878 females from the general population. *Journal of Psychopathology and Behavioral Assessment, 33*(1), 101–110.

Clauss, K., Houtsma, C., Shapiro, M. O., McDermott, M. J., Macia, K. S., Laurel, F. C., & Raines, A. M. (2023). Anxiety sensitivity and intolerance of uncertainty among veterans with subthreshold versus threshold PTSD. *Traumatology.* https://doi.org/10.1037/trm0000437. [Online ahead of print]

Clay, R. A. (2017). Coping with challenging clients. *Monitor on Psychology, 48*(7), 55.

Clay, R. A. (2022). Telehealth proves its worth. *APA Monitor, 53*(1), 85.

Clayton, S., & Swim, J. K. (2024, September). Climate change impacts on mental health and well-being. In N. Schneiderman (Ed.). *APA handbook of health psychology* (Vol. 1, Chap. 22). Washington, DC: American Psychological Association.

Clemmensen, L., Jorgensen, G., Gundersen, K. B., Smith, L. C., Midtgaard, J., Bouchard, S., . . . Glenthoj, L. B. (2023). Study protocol for virtual leisure investigating the effect of virtual reality-delivered stress reduction, entertainment and distraction on the use of coercion and need-based medication and patient satisfaction at a closed psychiatric intensive care unit: A mixed-methods pilot clinical trial. *BMJ Open, 13*(9), e070566.

Clevenger, S. M. F., Sturges, J. W., & Storie, M. (2023). Crises in substance misuse and dependence. In J. M. Dattilio, D. J. Shapiro, & D. S. Greenaway (Eds.). *Cognitive-behavioral strategies in crisis intervention* (4th ed., Chap. 8). New York: Guilford Press.

Cliffe, B., Gore-Rodney, J., Linton, M.-J., & Biddle, L. (2023). Developing suicide prevention tools in the context of digital peer support: Qualitative analysis of a workshop with multidisciplinary stakeholders. *MJIR Formative Research, 7,* e47178.

CLRP (Connecticut Legal Rights Project, Inc.). (2024). *Patients' bill of rights.* Middletown, CT: Author.

Cludius, B., Mannsfeld, A. K., Schmidt, A. F., & Jelinek, L. (2021). Anger and aggressiveness in obsessive-compulsive disorder (OCD) and the mediating role of responsibility, non-acceptance of emotions, and social desirability. *European Archives of Psychiatry and Clinical Neuroscience, 271*(6), 1179–1191.

CMA (Center for Medicare Advocacy). (2023). *Racial and ethnic health care disparities.* Willimantic, CT: Author.

CMHA (Canadian Mental Health Association). (2023). *Violence and mental health: Unpacking a complex issue.* Toronto: Author.

CMSAC (Central MN Sexual Assault Center). (2023). *Facts about sexual assault.* St. Cloud, MN: Author.

Coates, T. D. (2022, September 21). Drug-induced neutropenia and agranulocytosis. *UpToDate.* Retrieved from http://www.uptodate.com.

Coelho, C. M., Polák, J., Suttiwan, P., & Zsido, A. N. (2021). Fear inoculation among snake experts. *BMC Psychiatry, 21*(1), 539.

Coenen, L., Lehallier, B., de Vries, H. E., & Middeldorp, J. (2023). Markers of aging: Unsupervised integrated analyses of the human plasma proteome. *Frontiers in Aging, 4,* 1112109.

Coffey, M. J. (2022, August 15). Catatonia in adults: Epidemiology, clinical features, assessment, and diagnosis. *UpToDate.* Retrieved from http://www.uptodate.com.

Coffin, P. (2023, September 28). Prevention of lethal opioid overdone in the community. *UpToDate.* Retrieved from http://www.uptodate.com.

Cohen, C. I., & Reinhardt, M. M. (2020, April 2). Recovery and recovering in older adults with schizophrenia: A 5-tier model. *American Journal of Geriatric Psychiatry, 28*(8), 872–875.

Cohen, R. J., Schneider, W. J., & Tobin. R. (2022). *Psychological testing and assessment* (10th ed.). New York: McGraw-Hill.

Colburn, D. (1996, November 19). Singer's suicide doesn't lead to "copycat" deaths. *Washington Post Health.* Retrieved from https://www.washingtonpost.com/archive/lifestyle/wellness/1996/11/19.

Colby, A. (2022, September 29). The end of the culture of narcissism. *UnHerd.* Retrieved from https://unherd.com/2022/09/the-end-of-the-culture-of-narcissism.

Coleman, J., Kido, J., Xing, J., Aquino, C., Goday, B., Eckman, C., . . . Bavarian, N. (2023). Perspectives on deterrents from students who have discontinued prescription stimulant misuse and diversion behaviors. *Journal of Prevention, 44*(2), 193–206.

Coleman, L. (1984). *The reign of error: Psychiatry, authority, and law.* Boston: Beacon Press.

Colgan, C., Lejuez, C. W., & Magidson, J. F. (2022). Behavioral activation. In G. Todd & R. Branch (Eds.). *Evidence-based treatment for anxiety disorders and depression: A cognitive behavioral therapy compendium* (pp. 367–382). Cambridge: Cambridge University Press.

Collet, S., Kiyar, M., Martens, K., Vangeneugden, J., Simpson, V. G., Guillamon, A., . . . T'Sjoen, G. (2023). Gender minority stress in transgender people: A major role for social network. *Journal of Sexual Medicine, 20*(6), 905–917.

Collier, S. (2023, March 8). Bipolar disorder (manic depressive illness or manic depression). *Harvard Health Publishing.* Retrieved from https://www.health.harvard.edu/a_to_z.

Collingwood, J. (2016). The link between bipolar disorder and creativity. *Psych Central.* Retrieved from https://psychcentral.com/bipolar.

Collins, K., Hinkebein, G., & Schorgl, S. (2023). The John Hinckley trial and its effect on the insanity defense. *Famous Trials.* Retrieved from http://law2.umkc.edu/faculty/projects/ftrials/hinckley/hinckleytrial.html.

Colom, R. (2020). Intellectual abilities. *Handbook of Clinical Neurology, 173,* 109–120.

Comer, J. S. (2021). Rebooting mental health care delivery for the COVID-19 pandemic (and beyond): Guiding cautions as telehealth enters the clinical mainstream. *Cognitive and Behavioral Practice, 28,* 743–748.

Comer, J. S., Conroy, K., Cornacchio, D., Furr, J. M., Norman, S., & Stein, M. (2022). Psychometric evaluation of a caregiver-report adaptation of the Overall Anxiety Severity and Impairment Scale (OASIS) for use with youth populations. *Journal of Affective Disorders, 300,* 341–348.

Comer, J. S., Darling, L. N., Musser, E., del Busto, C., & Pincus, D. B. (2020). Stress and stress management in children and adolescents. In P. Lehrer & R. Woolfolk (Eds.). *Principles and practice of stress management* (4th ed.). New York: Guilford Press.

Comer, J. S., Furr, J. M., del Busto, C., Silva, K., Hong, N., Poznanski, B., . . . & Puliafico, A. C. (2021). Therapist-led, internet-delivered treatment for early child social anxiety: A waitlist-controlled evaluation of the iCALM Telehealth Program. *Behavior Therapy, 52*(2), 1171–1187.

Comer, J. S., Georgiadis, C., Schmarder, K., Chen, D., Coyne, C. A., Gudiño, O., . . . Pachankis, J. (2024). Reckoning with our past: An editorial review and affirmation of modern ethical practices from the Behavior Therapy Task Force on Sexual Orientation and Gender Identity/Expression Change Efforts (SOGI-ECEs). *Behavior Therapy.*

Comer, J. S., Nelson, C. L., Freitag, G., Silva, K., & Molinari, V. (2022). Clinical psychology and developmental considerations across the lifespan. In G. J. G. Asmundson (Ed.). *Comprehensive clinical psychology* (2nd ed., Vol. 1, pp. 168–184). Amsterdam: Elsevier.

Comer, R. (1973). *Therapy interviews with a schizophrenic patient.* Unpublished manuscript.

Compas, B. E., Vreeland, A., & Henry, L. (2020). Coping models of stress and resilience. In K. L. Harkness & E. P. Hayden (Eds.). *The Oxford handbook of stress and mental health* (Chap. 26, pp. 585–600). New York: Oxford University Press.

Conant, L., & Miller, L. (2024). Intellectual disability, and autism spectrum disorder, attention deficit/hyperactivity disorder, and specific learning disorders across the lifespan. In M. W. Parsons & M. M. Braun (Eds.). *Clinical neuropsychology: A pocket handbook for assessment* (4th ed., Chap. 22). Washington, DC: American Psychological Association.

Conn, A., & Hodges, K. R. (2023, July). Female orgasmic disorder. *Merckmanuals.* Retrieved from https://www.merckmanuals.com/professional/gynecology-and-obstetrics.

Conn, A., & Hodges, K. R. (2023, July). Genito-pelvic pain/penetration disorder. *Merckmanuals.* Retrieved from https://www.merckmanuals.com/professional/gynecology-and-obstetrics.

Conn, A., & Hodges, K. R. (2023, July). Overview of female sexual function and dysfunction. *Merckmanuals.* Retrieved from https://www.merckmanuals.com/professional/gynecology-and-obstetrics-and-dysfunction.

Conn, A., & Hodges, K. R. (2023, July). Pregnancy-related and postpartum sexual dysfunction. *Merckmanuals.* Retrieved from https://www.merckmanuals.com/professional/gynecology-and-obstetrics...and-dysfunction.

Conn, A., & Hodges, K. R. (2023, July). Sexual interest/arousal disorder. *Merckmanuals.* Retrieved from https://www.merckmanuals.com/professional/gynecology-and-obstetrics.

Connor Desai, S., & Reimers, S. (2023). Does explaining the origins of misinformation improve the effectiveness of a given correction? *Memory & Cognition, 51,* 422–436.

Connors, M. H., & Large, M. M. (2023). Calibrating violence risk assessments for uncertainty. *General Psychiatry, 36*(2), e100921.

Conroy, J., Lin, L., & Christidis, P. (2019). How satisfied are psychology-degree holders with their jobs? *Datapoint, 50*(6), 19. https://www.apa.org/monitor/2019/06/datapoint.

Conroy, K., Green, J. G., Phillips, K., Poznanski, B., Coxe, S., Kendall, P. C., & Comer, J. S. (2022). School-based accommodations and supports for anxious youth: Benchmarking reported practices against expert perspectives. *Journal of Clinical Child and Adolescent Psychology, 51*(4), 419–427.

Constant, A., Badcock, P., Friston, K., & Kirmayer, L. J. (2022). Integrating evolutionary, cultural, and computational psychiatry: A multilevel systemic approach. *Frontiers in Psychiatry, 13,* 763380.

Conway, C. C., Forbes, M. K., & the HiTOP Consortium. (2022). A hierarchical taxonomy of psychopathology (HiTOP) primer for mental health researchers. *Clinical Psychological Science, 10*(2), 236–258.

Conway, C. C., & Krueger, R. F. (2020). Personality disorders. In M. M. Antony & D. H. Barlow (Eds.). *Handbook of assessment and treatment planning for psychological disorders* (3rd ed., Chap. 16). New York: Guilford Press.

Cooper, M. (2008). *Essential research findings in counselling and psychotherapy: The facts are friendly.* Los Angeles: Sage.

Cooper, M., & Di Malta, G. (2023, December). Person-centered theory in psychotherapy. In F. T. L. Leong, J. L. Callahan, J. Zimmerman, M. J. Constantino, & C. F. Eubanks (Eds.). *APA handbook of psychotherapy* (Vol. 1, Chap. 5). Washington, DC: American Psychological Association.

Cooper, M., Eddy, K. T., Thomas, J. J., Franko, D. L., Carron-Arthur, B., Keshishian, A. C., & Griffiths, K. M. (2020). Muscle dysmorphia: A systematic and meta-analytic review of the literature to assess diagnostic validity. *International Journal of Eating Disorders, 53*(10), 1583–1604.

Cooper, Z., & Mitchell, K. S. (2020). Eating disorders. In M. M. Antony & D. H. Barlow (Eds.). *Handbook of assessment and treatment planning for psychological disorders* (3rd ed., Chap. 12). New York: Guilford Press.

Cooperman, J. (2022). Does labeling mental illness do more harm than good? *Common Reader.* Retrieved from https://commonreader.wustl.edu.

Copeland, W. E., & McGinnis, E. W. (2023). Epidemiology of trauma and PTSD in childhood and adolescence. In M. J. Friedman, P. P. Schnurr, & T. M. Keane (Eds.). *Handbook of PTSD: Science and practice* (3rd ed., Chap. 5). New York: Guilford Press.

Coppersmith, D. D. L., Dempsey, W., Kleiman, E. M., Bentley, K. H., Murphy, S. A., & Nock, M. K. (2022, July 18). Just-in-Time adaptive interventions for suicide prevention: Promise, challenges, and future directions. *Psychiatry, 85*(4), 317–333. https//doi.org/10.1080/00332747.2022.2092828.

Corrigan, P. W. (2022). Coming out proud to erase the stigma of mental illness. *World Psychiatry, 21*(3), 388–389.

Coskun, M., & Ozturk, M. (2013). Sexual fetishism in adolescence: Report of two cases. *Journal of Psychiatry and Neurological Sciences, 26,* 199–205.

Costantino, G., Dana, R. H., & Malgady, R. G. (2007). *TEMAS (Tell-Me-A-Story) assessment in multicultural societies.* Mahwah, NJ: Lawrence Erlbaum Associates.

Costantino, G., Dana, R. H., & Malgady, R. G. (2020, August 26). *TEMAS (Tell-Me-A-Story) Assessment in multicultural societies.* New York: Routledge.

Costantino, G., Litman, L., Waxman, R., Dupertuis, D., Pais, E., Rosenzweig, C., . . . Canales, M. M. F. (2014). Tell-Me-A-Story (TEMAS) assessment for culturally diverse children and adolescents. *Rorschachiana, 35*(2),154–175.

Costantino, M. J., Boswell, J. F., & Coyne, A. E. (2021). Patient, therapist, and relational factors. In M. Barkham, W. Lutz, & L. G. Castonguay (Eds.). *Bergin and Garfield's handbook of psychotherapy and behavior change* (7th ed., Chap. 7). New York: Wiley.

Cottier, C. (2022, September 27). Serial killers have rapidly declined since the 1980s. *Discover.* Retrieved from https://www.discovermagazine.com/the-sciences/what-explains-the-decline-of-serial-killers.

Cottrell, D. B., & Williams, J. (2016). Eating disorders in men. *Nurse Practitioner, 41*(9), 49–55.

Coulter, A. W. (2022, October 3). 3 guided meditations to find balance during moments of panic. *Mindful.*

Cowan, R. G., & Cole, R. F. (2020). Understudied and underfunded: Potential causes of mass shootings and implications for counseling research. *Journal of Social Change, 12,* 124–133.

Cox, D. A. (2021, June 8). The state of American friendship: Change, challenges, and loss. *Survey Center on American Life.* Retrieved from https://www.americansurveycenter.org/research.

Cox, J. (2022, March 29). Body shaming: Uncovering it and understanding it. *PsychCentral.* Retrieved from https://psychcentral.com/health/body-shaming.

Coy, T., Brinza, E., DeLozier, S., Gornik, H. L., Webel, A. R., Longenecker, C. T., & White Solaru, K. T. (2023). Black men's awareness of peripheral artery disease and acceptability of screening in barbershops: A qualitative analysis. *BMC Public Health, 23,* 46.

Coyne, S. M., Hurst, J. L., Dyer, W. J., Hunt, Q., Schvanaveldt, E., Brown, S., & Jones, G. (2021). Suicide risk in emerging adulthood: Associations with screen time over 10 years. *Journal of Youth and Adolescence, 50,* 2324–2338.

CR (Choose Responsibility). (2020). Statistics on student athletes. *Choose Responsibility.* Retrieved from http://www.chooseresponsibility.org.

Crabtree, S. (2011). *U.S. seniors maintain happiness highs with less social time* (Gallup Poll #151457). *Gallup.* Retrieved from http://www.gallup.com/poll/151457.

Craighead, W. E. (2022). Cognitive and behavior therapies for depressive disorders. In C. B. Nemeroff, A. F. Schatzberg, N. Rasgon, & S. M. Strakowski (Eds.). *The American Psychiatric Association Publishing textbook of mood disorders* (2nd ed., Chap. 23). Washington, DC: American Psychiatric Association Publishing.

Cramer, H., Hall, H., Leach, M., Frawley, J., Zhang, Y., Leung, B., . . . Lauche, R. (2016, July 7). Prevalence, patterns, and predictors of meditation use among U.S. adults: A nationally representative survey. *Nature.*

Crandall, C. S., Preisler, J. J., & Aussprung, J. (1992). Measuring life event stress in the lives of college students: The Undergraduate Stress Questionnaire (USQ). *Journal of Behavioral Medicine, 15*(6), 627–662.

Crane, M. E., Norris, L. A., Frank, H. E., Klugman, J., Ginsburg, G. S., Keeton, C., . . . Kendall, P. C. (2021). Impact of treatment improvement on long-term anxiety: Results from CAMS and CAMELS. *Journal of Consulting and Clinical Psychology, 89*(2), 126–133.

Craske, M. (2022, September 27). Psychotherapy for panic disorder with or without agoraphobia in adults. *UpToDate*. Retrieved from https://www.uptodate.com.

Craske, M. (2023, September 15). Generalized anxiety disorder in adults: Cognitive-behavioral therapy and other psychotherapies. *UpToDate*. Retrieved from https://www.uptodate.com.

Craske, M., & Bystritsky, A. (2023, July 5). Generalized anxiety disorder in adults: Management. *UpToDate*. Retrieved from https://www.uptodate.com.

Crawford, P., & Go, K. V. (2022). Schizophrenia. *American Family Physician, 106*(4), 388–396.

CRC (Cyberbullying Research Center). (2023). *Bullying laws across America*. Retrieved from https://cyberbullying.org/bullying-laws.

Creese, B., Arathimos, R., Aarsland, D., Ballard, C., Brooker, H., Hampshire, A., . . . Ismail, Z. (2023). Late-life onset psychotic symptoms and incident cognitive impairment in people without dementia: Modification by genetic risk for Alzheimer's disease. *Alzheimer's & Dementia, 9*(2), e12386.

Crisan, S., Stoia, M., Predescu, E., Miu, A. C., & Szentagotai-Tatar, A. (2023, May 2). The association between adverse childhood events and cluster C personality disorders: A meta-analysis. *Clinical Psychology and Psychotherapy*. doi:10.1002/cpp.2856. [Online ahead of print]

Crisp, H., & Gabbard, G. O. (2020). Principles of psychodynamic treatment for patients with narcissistic personality disorder. *Journal of Personality Disorders, 34*(Suppl.), 143–158.

Crits-Christoph, P., & Gibbons, M. B. C. (2021). Psychotherapy process–outcome research: Advances in understanding casual connections. In M. Barkham, W. Lutz, & L. G. Castonguay (Eds.). *Bergin and Garfield's handbook of psychotherapy and behavior change* (7th ed., Chap. 8). New York: Wiley.

Crow, S. J. (2023, March 19). Bulimia nervosa in adults: Pharmacotherapy. *UpToDate*. Retrieved from http://www.uptodate.com.

Crowdis, M., Leslie, S. W., & Nazir, S. (2023, May 30). Premature ejaculation. *StatPearls*.

Crupain, M. (2017, January 5). The ultimate towel test—Separating fact from fiction. *Oz Experts*. Retrieved from https://aquashield.net/the-ultimate-towel-test-dr-oz.

CSAF (Chapman University Survey of American Fears). (2023). *The top 10 fears in America 2022*. Retrieved from https://blogs.chapman.edu/wilkinson.

CSP (COVID States Project). (2022, April). *COVID-19 deaths and depression*. Retrieved from https://www.covidstates.org/reports.

Cuijpers, P. (2022, July 12). Universal prevention of depression at schools: Dead end or challenging crossroads? *Evidence-Based Mental Health, 25*, 96–98.

Cuijpers, P., Reijnders, M., & Huibers, M. J. H. (2019). The role of common factors in psychotherapy outcomes. *Annual Review of Clinical Psychology, 15*(1), 207–231.

Cuncic, A. (2020, December 21). How do different cultures experience social anxiety disorder? *Verywellmind*. Retrieved from https://www.verywellmind.com.

Cuncic, A. (2020, May 15). What is avoidant personality disorder? *Verywellmind*. Retrieved from https://www.verywellmind.com.

Cuncic, A. (2021, April 9). Comorbidities in mental health. *Verywellmind*. Retrieved from https://www.verywellmind.com/what-is-comorbidity-3024480.

Cuncic, A. (2023, August 29). An overview of social skills training. *Verywellmind*. Retrieved from https://www.verywellmind.com/social-skills-4157216.

Cundari, M., Vestberg, S., Gustafsson, P., Gorcenco, S., & Rasmussen, A. (2023). Neurocognitive and cerebellar function in ADHD, autism and spinocerebellar ataxia. *Frontiers in Systems Neuroscience, 17*, 1168666.

Curtis, S. E., Hoffmann, S., & O'Leary Sloan, M. (2023). Prescriptive authority for psychologists: The next step. *Psychological Services, 20*(2), 363–381.

Cusack, C. (2018). Self-murder, sin, and crime: Religion and suicide in the Middle Ages. *Journal of Religion and Violence, 6*(2), 206–224.

CWLA (Child Welfare League of America). (2023). *Increased suicide rates among children aged 5 to 11 years in the U.S.* Washington, DC: Author.

Czaja, S. J. (2024, September). Health psychology interventions for older adults to promote health and independence. In N. Schneiderman (Ed.). *APA handbook of health psychology: Vol. 3. Health psychology and public health* (Chap. 23). Washington, DC: American Psychological Association.

D'Antonio, P. (2023). *History of psychiatric hospitals*. Penn Nursing. University of Pennsylvania. Retrieved from https://www.nursing.upenn.edu/nhhc/nurses-institutions-caring.

D'Souza, R. S., & Hooten, W. M. (2023, July 31). Extrapyramidal symptoms (EPS). *StatPearls*.

da Silva, A. P., Valente, A., Chaves, C., Matos, A., Gil, A., Santos, A. C., . . . Bicho, M. (2018, March 13). Characterization of Portuguese centenarian eating habits, nutritional biomarkers, and cardiovascular risk: A case control study. *Oxidative Medicine and Cellular Longevity, 2018*, 5296168.

da Silva, B. S., Grevet, E. H., Silva, L. C. F., Ramos, J. K. N., Rovaris, D. L., & Bau, C. H. D. (2023). An overview on neurobiology and therapeutics of attention-deficit/hyperactivity disorder. *Discover Mental Health, 3*(1), 2.

Daalman, K., Boks, M. P., Diederen, K. M., de Weijer, A. D., Blom, J. D., Kahn, R. S., & Sommer, I. E. (2011). The same or different? A phenomenological comparison of auditory verbal hallucinations in healthy and psychotic individuals. *Journal of Clinical Psychiatry, 72*(3), 320–325.

Dabiri, M., Firouzabadi, F. D., Yang, K., Barker, P. B., Lee, R. R., & Yousem, D. M. (2022). Neuroimaging in schizophrenia: A review article. *Frontiers in Neuroscience, 16*, 1042814.

Daddah, D., Ahanhanzo, Y. G., Kpozehouen, A., Dos Santos, B. H., Ouendo, E.-M., & Leveque, A. (2022). Prevalence and risk factors of post-traumatic stress disorder in survivors of a cohort of road accident victims in Benin: Results of a 12-month cross-sectional study. *Journal of Multidisciplinary Healthcare, 15*, 719–731.

Daderman, A. M., & Ragnestal-Impola, C. (2019). Workplace bullies, not their victims, score high on the dark triad and extraversion, and low on agreeableness and honesty-humility. *Heliyon, 5*(10), e02609.

Dahill, L. M., Hay, P., Morrison, N. M. V., Touyz, S., Mitchison, D., Bussey, K., & Mannan, H. (2023). Associations between parents' body weights/shape comments and disordered eating amongst adolescents over time: A longitudinal study. *Nutrients, 15*(6), 1419.

Dahill, L. M., Touyz, S., Morrison, N. M. V., & Hay, P. (2021). Parental appearance teasing in adolescence and associations with eating problems: A systematic review. *BMC Public Health, 21*(1), 450.

Dahling, J. J., Whitaker, B. G., & Levy, P. E. (2008). The development and validation of a new Machiavellianism scale. *Journal of Management, 35*, 219–257.

Dai, Y. G., Thomas, R. P., Brennan, L., Helt, M. S., Barton, M. L., Dumont-Mathieu, T., & Fein, D. A. (2021). Development and acceptability of a new program for caregivers of children with autism spectrum disorder: Online parent training in early behavioral intervention. *Journal of Autism and Developmental Disorders, 51*(11), 4166–4185.

Dakic, T., Jevdjovic, T., Vujovic, P., & Mladenovic, A. (2022). The less we eat, the longer we live: Can a caloric restriction help us become centenarians? *International Journal of Molecular Sciences, 23*(12), 6546.

Daliri, D. B., Afaya, A., Koomson, W. H. F., & Akatibo, E. (2022). Recurrent episodes of dissociative fugue with comorbid severe depression and alcohol dependence syndrome. *Case Reports in Psychiatry, 2022*, 7362823.

Dalle Grave, R., & Pike, K. M. (2023). Cognitive behavioral therapy and eating disorders. In P. Robinson, T. Wade, B. Herpertz-Dahlann, F. Fernandez-Aranda, J. Treasure, & S. Wonderlich (Eds.). *Eating disorders*. Edinburgh: Springer.

Dana, R. H. (Ed.). (2015). *Handbook of cross-cultural and multicultural personality assessment*. New York: Routledge.

Dane, F. C., & Carhart, E. (2022). *Evaluating research: Methodology for people who need to read research* (3rd ed.). Thousand Oaks, CA: Sage Publications.

Daniels, M., Van, H. L., van den Heuvel, B., Dekker, J. J. M., Peen, J., Bosmans, J., . . . Huibers, M. J. H. (2023). Individual psychotherapy for cluster-C personality disorders: Protocol of a pragmatic RCT comparing short-term psychodynamic supportive psychotherapy, affect phobia therapy and schema therapy (I-FORCE). *Trials, 24*(1), 260.

Danquah, M. N-A. (1998). *Willow weep for me: A black woman's journey through depression*. New York: W. W. Norton.

Darke, S., Duflou, J., Peacock, A., Chrzanaowska, A., Farrell, M., & Lappin, J. (2023). Rates, characteristics and toxicology of cocaine-related deaths in Australia, 2000–2021. *Addiction, 118*(2), 297–306.

Dash, G. F., Karalunas, S. L., Kenyon, E. A., Carter, E. K., Mooney, M. A., Nigg, J. T., & Feldstein Ewing, S. W. (2023). Gene-by-environment interaction effects of social adversity on externalizing behavior in ABCD youth. *Journal of Family Medicine and Primary Care, 53,* 219–231.

Dattilio, F. M., Shapiro, D. I., & Greenaway, D. S. (2023). *Cognitive-behavioral strategies in crisis intervention* (4th ed.). New York: Guilford Press.

Davis, B. A. (2020, February 25). Discrimination: A social determinant of health inequities. *Health Affairs.*

Davis, D. W., Jawad, K., Feygin, Y., Creel, L., Kong, M., Sun, J., . . . Pasquenza, N. (2021). Disparities in ADHD diagnosis and treatment by race/ethnicity in youth receiving Kentucky Medicaid in 2017. *Ethnicity & Disease, 31*(1), 67–76.

Davis, L., Pilkinton, P., & Aikens, G. (2023). Pharmacotherapy for PTSD. In M. J. Friedman, P. P. Schnurr, & T. M. Keane (Eds.). *Handbook of PTSD: Science and practice* (3rd ed., Chap. 23). New York: Guilford Press.

Davis, M., & Matthies, R. (2021). *The youth mental health crisis: States invest in suicide prevention, intervention, and postvention strategies.* Arlington, VA: Association of State and Territorial Health Officials.

Dawson, J. (2023). Compulsory community treatment: Is it the least restrictive alternative? In B. D. Kelly & M. Donnelly (Eds.). *Routledge handbook of mental health law* (Chap. 19). New York: Routledge.

DBSA (Depression and Bipolar Support Alliance). (2022). *Depression and diabetes.* Chicago: Author.

DCCESV (DC Coalition to End Sexual Violence). (2022). *Sexual Assault Awareness Month 2022: Community-specific facts and statistics.* Washington, DC: Author.

de Belen, R. A., Pincham, H., Hodge, A., Silove, N., Sowmya, A., Bednarz, T., & Eapen, V. (2023). Eye-tracking correlates of response to joint attention in preschool children with autism spectrum disorder. *BMC Psychiatry, 23,* 211.

De Cara, N. H., Maggio, V., Davis, O. S. P., & Haworth, C. M. A. (2023). Methodologies for monitoring mental health on Twitter: Systematic review. *Journal of Medical Internet Research, 25,* e42734.

De Jesus, O., Fogwe, D. T., Mesfin, F. B., & Das, J. M. (2023, August 28). Neuromodulation surgery for psychiatric disorders. *StatPearls.*

de Jongh, A., ten Broeke, E., Farrell, D., & Maxfield, L. (2022). EMDR therapy. In J. G. Beck & D. M. Sloan (Eds.). *The Oxford handbook of traumatic stress disorders* (Chap. 32). New York: Oxford University Press.

De Leo, D. (2022, January 20). Late-life suicide in an aging world. *Nature Aging, 2,* 7–12.

De Los Reyes, A., & Asmundson, G. J. G. (2022). Reimagining context within exposure-based treatments for adolescent social anxiety disorder: It all begins with optimizing the context-sensitivity of our clinical assessments. *Journal of Anxiety Disorders, 87,* 102545.

De Los Reyes, A., Epkins, C. C., Asmundson, G. J. G., Augenstein, T. M., Becker, K. D., Becker, S. P., . . . Youngstrom, E. A. (2023). Editorial statement about *JCCAP's* 2023 special issue on informant discrepancies in youth mental health assessments: Observations, guidelines, and future directions grounded in 60 years of research. *Journal of Clinical Child and Adolescent Psychology, 52*(1), 147–158. https://doi.org/10.1080/15374416.2022.2158842.

De Neve, J. E., & Ward, G. (2017). Happiness at work. In J. Helliwell, R. Layard, & J. Sacks (Eds.). *World happiness report 2017.* New York: Sustainable Development Solutions Network.

De Oliveira, J. M., Dueñas, J.-M., Morales-Vives, F., & Gallardo-Nieto, E. (2023). Educational agents and institutions called into action in suicide prevention, intervention, and postvention. *Frontiers in Psychology, 14,* 1213751.

De Rose, A. F., Chierigo, F., Ambrosini, F., Mantica, G., Borghesi, M., Suardi, N., & Terrone, C. (2021, January 5). Sexuality during COVID lockdown: A cross-sectional Italian study among hospital workers and their relatives. *International Journal of Impotence Research, 33*(1), 131–136.

De Visé, D. (2023, May 18). More women attempt suicide. More men die by suicide. *The Hill.*

De Wit-De Visser, B., Rijckmans, M., Vermunt, J. K., & van Dam, A. (2023). Pathways to antisocial behavior: A framework to improve diagnostics and tailor therapeutic interventions. *Frontiers in Psychology, 14,* 9933090.

DeAngelis, T. (2022, July 26). Treating trauma in the aftermath of the Uvalde school shooting. *Monitor on Psychology, 53*(6), 26.

deBettencourt, M. T., Bainbridge, W. A., & Rosenberg, M. D. (2023). Functional neuroimaging. In H. Cooper, M. N. Coutanche, L. M. McMullen, A. T. Panter, D. Rindskopf, & K. J. Sher (Eds.). *APA handbook of research methods in psychology: Foundations, planning, measures, and psychometrics* (pp. 631–653). Washington, DC: American Psychological Association.

Decker, B. W. (2020, August 18). *Daily mindfulness: 365 exercises to deepen your practice and find peace.* Emeryville, CA: Rockridge Press.

Deik, A. (2022, May 26). Tardive dyskinesia: Etiology, risk factors, clinical features, and diagnosis. *UpToDate.* Retrieved from https://www.uptodate.com.

Dela Cruz, G., Johnstone, S., Kim, S. K., & Castle, D. J. (2023). Review of third-wave therapies for substance use disorders in people of color and collectivist cultures: Current evidence and future directions. *Psychology of Addictive Behaviors, 37*(5), 681–694.

Delhey, J., Hess, S., Boehnke, K., Deutsch, F., Eichhorn, J., Kühnen, U., & Welzel, C. (2023). Life satisfaction during the COVID-19 pandemic: The role of human, economic, social, and psychological capital. *Journal of Happiness Studies, 24,* 2201–2222.

DeLisi, L. E. (2021). A commentary revisiting the viral hypothesis of schizophrenia: Onset of a schizophreniform disorder subsequent to SARS CoV-2 infection. *Psychiatry Research, 295,* 113573.

Dell, P. F. (2022). Clarifying the etiology of the dissociative disorders: It's not all about trauma. In M. J. Dorahy, S. N. Gold, & J. A. O'Neil (Eds.). *Dissociation and the dissociative disorders: Past, present, future* (Chap. 14). New York: Routledge.

Delrieu, J., Andrieu, S., & Vellas, B. (2024). Dementia research in 2023: The year of anti-amyloid immunotherapy. *Lancet Neurology, 23*(1), 13–15.

DeLuca, J. S., Novacek, D. M., Adery, L. H., Herrera, S. N., Landa, Y., Corcoran, C. M., & Walker, E. F. (2022). Equity in mental health services for youth at clinical high risk for psychosis: Considering marginalized identities and stressors. *Evidence-Based Practice in Child and Adolescent Mental Health, 7*(2), 176–197.

Demke, E. (2022). The vulnerability-stress-model—Holding up the construct of the faulty individual in the light of challenges to the medical model of mental distress. *Frontiers in Sociology, 7,* 833987.

Demory-Luce, D. (2023, October 18). Adolescent eating habits. *UpToDate.* Retrieved from https://www.uptodate.com.

Dempsey, C. L., Benedek, D. M., Zuromski, K. L., Riggs-Donovan, C., Ng, T. H. H., Nock, M. K., . . . Ursano, R. J. (2019). Association of firearm ownership, use, accessibility, and storage practices with suicide risk among US Army soldiers. *JAMA Network Open, 2,* e195383.

Denecke, K., Schmid, N., & Nüssli, S. (2022). Implementation of cognitive behavioral therapy in e-mental health apps: Literature review. *Journal of Medical Internet Research, 24*(3), e27791.

Denning, D. M., Newlands, R. T., Gonzales, A., & Benuto, L. T. (2022). Borderline personality disorder symptoms in a community sample of sexually and gender diverse adults. *Journal of Personality Disorders, 36*(6), 701–716.

Denno, D. W. (2017). Andrea Yates: A continuing story about insanity. In M. D. White (Ed.). *The insanity defense: Multidisciplinary views on its history, trends, and controversies* (Chap. 12). Westport, CT: Praeger Publishers.

DePrince, A. P., Dorahy, M. J., Lanius, R., & Schiavone, F. L. (2023). Trauma-induced dissociation. In M. J. Friedman, P. P. Schnurr, & T. M. Keane (Eds.). *Handbook of PTSD: Science and practice* (3rd ed., Chap. 8). New York: Guilford Press.

Derevensky, J., Marchica, L., Gilbeau, L., & Richard, J. (2022). Behavioral addictions in children: A focus on gambling, gaming, internet addiction, and excessive smartphone use. In V. B. Patel & V. R. Preedy (Eds.). *Handbook of substance misuse and addictions: From biology to public health* (pp. 2941–2964). New York: Springer.

Derosa, S., Misztak, P., Mingardi, J., Mazzini, G., Müllwe, H. K., & Musazzi, L. (2024). Changes in neurotrophic signaling pathways in brain areas of the chronic mild stress rat model of depression as a signature of ketamine fast antidepressant response/non-response. *Progressive Neuropsychopharmacological Biological Psychiatry, 128,* 110871.

Des Marais, N. S. (2023, February 18). Remembering the incarceration of Japanese Americans, and a look at the lasting health effects. *GoodRx Health.* Retrieved from https://www.goodrx.com/health-topic/aanhpi/internment-japanese-americans.

Desrochers, S. S., Spring, M. G., & Nautiyal, K. M. (2022). A role for serotonin in modulating opposing drive and brake circuits of impulsivity. *Frontiers in Behavioral Neuroscience, 16,* 791749.

Dev, D. K., Wardell, V., Checknita, K. J., Te, A. A., Petrucci, A. S., Le, M. L., . . . Palombo, D. J. (2022). Negative emotion enhances memory for the sequential unfolding of a naturalistic experience. *Journal of Applied Research in Memory and Cognition, 11*(4), 510–521.

DeVille, D. C., Whalen, D., Breslin, F. J., Morris, A. S., Khalsa, S. S., Paulus, M. P., & Barch, D. M. (2020). Prevalence and family-related factors associated with suicidal ideation, suicide attempts, and self-injury in children aged 9 to 10 years. *JAMA Network Open, 3*(2), e1920956.

DF (DrFirst). (2020). *DrFirst survey: 44% of Americans have used telehealth services during coronavirus pandemic but some admit not paying attention.* Rockville, MD: Author.

di Giacomo, E., Andreini, E., Lorusso, O., & Clerici, M. (2023). The dark side of empathy in narcissistic personality disorder. *Frontiers in Psychiatry, 14,* 1074558.

Di Vincenzo, M. (2023). New research on validity and clinical utility of ICD-11 vs. ICD-10 and DSM-5 diagnostic categories. *World Psychiatry, 22*(1), 171–172.

Dick, A. S., Silva, K., Gonzalez, R., Sutherland, M., Laird, A., Gurwitch, . . . & Comer, J. S. (2021). Neural vulnerability and hurricane-based media are associated with posttraumatic stress in youth. *Nature Human Behavior, 5,* 1578–1589.

Dick, D. M., Balcke, E., McCutcheon, V., Francis, M., Kuo, S., Salvatore, J., . . . Bucholz, K. (2023). The collaborative study on the genetics of alcoholism: Sample and clinical data. *Genes, Brain and Behavior, 22*(5), e12860.

Dickerman, A. L., & Jiménez, X. F. (2023). Psychosocial and psychodynamic considerations informing factitious disorder. *Psychodynamic Psychiatry, 51*(1), 98–113.

Dickey, L. M., & Puckett, J. A. (2022, August 30). *Affirmative counseling for transgender and gender diverse clients.* Boston: Hogrefe.

Diener, E., Seligman, M. E. P., Choi, H., & Oishi, S. (2018). Happiest people revisited. *Perspectives on Psychological Science, 13*(2), 176–184.

Difede, J., Rothbaum, B. O., Rizzo, A. A., Wyka, K., Spielman, L., Reist, C., . . . Lee, F. S. (2022). Enhancing exposure therapy for posttraumatic stress disorder (PTSD): A randomized clinical trial of virtual reality and imaginal exposure with a cognitive enhancer. *Translational Psychiatry, 12*(1), 299.

DiGuiseppi, G. T., Davis, J. P., Meisel, M. K., Clark, M. A., Roberson, M. L., Ott, M. Q., & Barnett, N. P. (2020). The influence of peer and parental norms on first-generation college students' binge drinking trajectories. *Addictive Behaviors, 103,* 106227.

Dill, L. J., Gousse, Y., Huggins, K., Fraser, M., Browne, R. C., Stewart, . . . & Wilson, T. E. (2020). Adjournment in community HIV prevention: Exploring transitions in community–academic partnerships. *Health Promotion Practice, 21*(4), 544–551.

Diller, S. J., Czibor, A., Szabó, Z. P., Restás, P., Jonas, E., & Frey, D. (2021). The positive connection between dark triad traits and leadership levels in self- and other-ratings. *Leadership, Education, Personality: An Interdisciplinary Journal, 3,* 117–131.

Dilmen, O. K., Meco, B. C., Evered, L. A., & Radtke, F. M. (2024). Postoperative neurocognitive disorders: A clinical guide. *Journal of Clinical Anesthesia, 92,* 111320.

Dimidjian, S. (2022, October 13). Behavioral activation therapy for treating unipolar major depression. *UpToDate.* Retrieved from https://www.uptodate.com.

Dimsdale, J. E. (2022, September). Factitious disorder imposed on another. *MSD Manual.* Retrieved from https://www.msdmanuals.com/professional/psychiatric-disorders/somatic-symptom-and-related-disorders.

Dishman, R. K., McDowell, C. P., & Herring, M. P. (2021). Customary physical activity and odds of depression: A systematic review and meta-analysis of 111 prospective cohort studies. *British Journal of Sports Medicine, 55*(16), 926–934.

Dlugacz, H., Wimmer, C., & Nettesheim, S. (2022). Mental health, autonomy, and the law. *ScienceDirect.* https://doi.org/10.1016/B978-0-323-91497-0.00045-X.

Dobson, K. S. (2024, April). *Clinical depression: An individualized, biopsychosocial approach to assessment and treatment.* Washington, DC: American Psychological Association.

Doctor, R. M., & Neff, B. (2001). Sexual disorders. In H. S. Friedman (Ed.). *Specialty articles from the encyclopedia of mental health* (Chap. 32). San Diego, CA: Academic Press.

Dodd, D. R., Wonderlich, S. A., & Peterson, C. B. (2023). Integrative cognitive-affective therapy (ICAT) and eating disorders. In P. Robinson, T. Wade, B. Herpertz-Dahlann, F. Fernandez-Aranda, J. Treasure, & S. Wonderlich (Eds.). *Eating disorders.* Edinburgh: Springer.

Doffer, D. P. A., Dekkers, T. J., Hornstra, R., van der Oord, S., Luman, M., Leijten, P., . . . Groenman, A. P. (2023). Sustained improvements by behavioural parent training for children with attention-deficit/hyperactivity disorder: A meta-analytic review of longer-term child and parental outcomes. *JCPP Advances, 3*(3), e12196.

Doherty, J. L., Cunningham, A. C., Crawner, S. J. R. A., Moss, H. M., Dima, D. C., Linden, D. E. J., . . . Singh, K. D. (2024). Atypical cortical networks in children at high-genetic risk of psychiatric and neurodevelopmental disorders. *Neuropsychopharmacology, 49*(2), 368–376.

Dohrmann, R. J., & Laskin, D. M. (1978). An evaluation of electromyographic feedback in the treatment of myofascial pain-dysfunction syndrome. *Journal of the American Medical Association, 96,* 656–666.

DOJ (Department of Justice). (2023). *Statistical briefing book: Law enforcement and juvenile crime: Juvenile arrest rate trends.* Retrieved from https://www.ojjdp.gov/ojstatbb/crime/JAR.

Dole, V. P., & Nyswander, M. (1965). A medical treatment for heroin addiction. *Journal of the American Medical Association, 193,* 646–650.

Dole, V. P., & Nyswander, M. (1967). Heroin addiction, a metabolic disease. *Archives of Internal Medicine, 120,* 19–24.

Dolotina, B., & Turban, J. L. (2022). A multipronged, evidence-based approach to improving mental health among transgender and gender-diverse youth. *JAMA Network Open, 5*(2), e220926.

Dominguez, O., & Carugno, P. (2023, March 19). Learning disability. *StatPearls.*

Domino, F. J. (2023, April 15). Overview of gambling disorder. *UpToDate.* Retrieved from http://www.uptodate.com.

Donahue, R. (2020, January 20). For me and other creatives with mental health issues, medication can be a light in the dark. *Allure.*

Doty, B., Bass, J., Ryan, T., Zhiang, A., & Wilcox, H. (2022). Systematic review of suicide prevention studies with data on youth and young adults living in low-income and middle-income countries. *BMJ Open, 12,* e055000.

Dowling, N. A., Merkouris, S., Youssef, G. J., Lubman, D. I., Bagot, K. L., Hawker, C. O., . . . Rodda, S. N. (2022). A gambling just-in-time adaptive intervention (GamblingLess: In-the-Moment): Protocol for a microrandomized trial. *JMIR Research Protocols, 11*(8), e38958.

Downey, C. A., & Chang, E. C. (2024). *Substance use disorders in underserved ethnic and racial groups: Using diversity to help individuals thrive.* Washington, DC: American Psychological Association.

Doyle, K. A., Hickey, M., & DiGiuseppe, R. (2022). Supervision and training in rational emotive behavior therapy. In E. A. Storch, J. S. Abramowitz, & D. McKay (Eds.). *Training and supervision in specialized cognitive behavior therapy: Methods, settings, and populations* (Chap. 3). Washington, DC: American Psychological Association.

Dozois, D. J. A., & Dobson, K. S. (Eds.). (2023). *Treatment of psychosocial risk factors in depression.* Washington, DC: American Psychological Association.

Dragioti, E., Radua, J., Solmi, M., Gosling, C. J., Oliver, D., Lascialfari, F., . . . Fusar-Poli, P. (2023). Impact of mental disorders on clinical outcomes of physical diseases: An umbrella review assessing population attributable fraction and generalized impact fraction. *World Psychiatry, 22*(1), 86–104.

Draps, M., Adamus, S., Wierzba, M., & Gola, M. (2022). Functional connectivity in compulsive sexual behavior disorder: Systematic review of literature and study on heterosexual males. *Journal of Sexual Medicine, 19*(9), 1463–1471.

DTL (Ditch the Label). (2019). *The Annual Bullying Survey 2019.* Los Angeles: Author.

DTL (Ditch the Label). (2023). *The Annual Bullying Survey 2020.* Los Angeles: Author.

Du, X., Wei, X., Ding, H., Yu, Y., Xie, Y., Ji, Y., . . . Qin, W. (2023). Unraveling schizophrenia replicable functional connectivity disruption patterns across sites. *Human Brain Mapping, 44*(1), 156–169.

Duenwald, M. (2003, March 18). "Oldest old" still show alertness. *New York Times.* Retrieved from https://www.nytimes.com/2003/03/18/health.

Duffy, K. E. M., Simmonds-Buckley, M., Haake, R., Delgadillo, J., & Barkham, M. (2023, June 14). The efficacy of individual humanistic-experiential therapies for the treatment of depression: A systematic review and meta-analysis of randomized controlled trials. *Psychotherapy Research.* doi:10.1080/10503307.2023.2227757. [Online ahead of print]

Duncan, P. M. (2020). *Substance use disorders: A biopsychosocial perspective.* New York: Cambridge University Press.

Duncan, R. S., Riordan, S. M., Gernon, M. C., & Koulen, P. (2024). Cannabinoids and endocannabinoids as therapeutics for nervous system disorders: Preclinical models and clinical studies. *Neural Regeneration Research, 19*(4), 788–796.

Dunkley, C. R., & Robichaud, M. (2022). Cognitive behavioral therapy for generalized anxiety disorder: Targeting intolerance of uncertainty. In G. Todd (Ed.). *Evidence-based treatment for anxiety disorders and depression: A cognitive behavioral therapy compendium* (Chap. 9). Cambridge: Cambridge University Press.

Duran, E. P., Hemmany, C., Vieira, R., Nascimento, O., Machado, L., de Oliveira, I. R., & DeMarzo, M. (2022). A randomized clinical trial to assess the efficacy of online-treatment with trial-based cognitive therapy, mindfulness-based health promotion and positive psychotherapy for post-traumatic stress disorder during the COVID-19 pandemic: A study protocol. *International Journal of Environmental Research and Public Health, 19*(2), 819.

Durkheim, E. (1897). *Suicide.* New York: Free Press. (Work reprinted in 1951.)

Dwyer, P. (2022). The neurodiversity approach(es): What are they and what do they mean for researchers? *Human Development, 66*(2), 73–92.

Dy, K. (2021, November 13). Animals that eat psychedelics and enjoy the trip. *Psychedelic Spotlight.* https://psychedelicspotlight.com/animals-that-eat-psychedelics-trip.

East, A. (2018, March 27). Four common mental illnesses in the elderly: Learn the risk factors and symptoms to watch for. *Caring People.* Retrieved from https://www.careingpeopleinc.com.

Eaton, C., Tarver, J., Shirazi, A., Pearson, E., Walker, L., Bird, M., . . . Waite, J. (2021). A systematic review of the behaviours associated with depression in people with severe-profound intellectual disability. *Journal of Intellectual Disability Research, 65*(3), 211–229.

Eberhaut, S., Schmidt, A. F., Banse, R., & Eher, R. (2022). Child abuse myths are pedophilic myths: Cognitive distortions are stronger in individuals convicted of sexual offenses diagnosed with pedophilia compared to those without such diagnosis. *Deviant Behavior, 44*(7), 1013–1025.

EBSCO. (2023). *Mental measurements yearbook with tests in print internacional.* Ipswich, MA: EBSCO. Retrieved from https://www.ebsco.com/products/research-databases.

Echeverria, S. E., & Stein, G. L. (2024, September). Physical activity and mental health. In N. Schneiderman (Ed.). *APA handbook of health psychology: Vol. 2. Clinical interventions and disease management in health psychology* (Chap. 16). Washington, DC: American Psychological Association.

Economist, The. (2010, December 16). Age and happiness: The U-bend of life. *The Economist.* Retrieved from http://www.economist.com/node/17722567.

Edelson, S. M. (2022). Understanding challenging behaviors in autism spectrum disorder: A multi-component, interdisciplinary model. *Journal of Personalized Medicine, 12*(7), 1127.

Edwards, C. J., Owrid, O., Miller, L., Jafari, H., Emsley, R., Rus-Calafell, M., . . . Ward, T. (2023). The voice characterisation checklist: Psychometric properties of a brief clinical assessment of voices as social agents. *Frontiers in Psychiatry, 14,* 192655.

Edwards, K. A., & Vowles, K. E. (2022). Acceptance and commitment therapy for chronic pain. In M. P. Twohig, M. E. Levin, & J. M. Petersen (Eds.). *The Oxford handbook of acceptance and commitment therapy* (Chap. 20). New York: Oxford University Press.

Eells, T. D. (2022). *Handbook of psychotherapy case formulation* (3rd ed.). New York: Guilford Press.

Egan, B. M. (2023, April 19). The prevalence and control of hypertension in adults. *UpToDate.* Retrieved from http://www.uptodate.com.

Egge, M. K. (2023). Medical child abuse: A review by subspecialty. *Advances in Pediatrics, 70*(1), 59–80.

Ehlers, A., Ehring, T., Wittekind, C. E., & Kleim, B. (2022). Information processing in posttraumatic stress disorder. In J. G. Beck & D. M. Sloan (Eds.). *The Oxford handbook of traumatic stress disorders* (Chap. 15). New York: Oxford University Press.

Ehmke, R. (2022). Signs a child might be suicidal: What to watch out for and how to help. *Child Mind Institute.* Retrieved from https://childmind.org/article/signs-a-child-might-be-suicidal.

Ehnvall, A., Parker, G., Hadzi, P. D., & Malhi, G. (2008). Perception of rejecting and neglectful parenting in childhood relates to lifetime suicide attempts for females—but not for males. *Acta Psychiatrica Scandinavica, 117*(1), 50–56.

Ehrenfeld, J. (2019, April 15). Are creative people crazier? *Psychology Today.* https://www.psychologytoday.com/us/blog/open-gently/201904/are-creative-people-crazier.

EIE (Enough Is Enough). (2017). *Cyberbullying statistics.* Retrieved from http://enough.org/stats_cyberbullying.

Ekern, J. (2020). *Anorexia nervosa: Causes, symptoms, signs and treatment help.* Retrieved from https://www.eatingdisorderhope.com/information.

Elam, K. K., Bountress, K. E., Ha, T., Shaw, D. S., Wilson, M. N., Aliev, F., . . . Lemery-Chalfant, K. (2022, August 19). Developmental genetic effects on externalizing behavior and alcohol use: Examination across two longitudinal samples. *Development and Psychopathology.* doi:10.1017/S0954579422000980. [Online ahead of print]

Elia, J. (2023, May). Conduct disorder. *Merck Manual Professional Version.* Retrieved from https://www.merckmanuals/com/professional/pediatrics/psychiatric-disorders-in-children-and-adolescents.

Elia, J. (2023). Suicidal behavior in children and adolescents. *Merck Manual Professional Version.* Retrieved from https://www.merckmanuals.com/professional/pediatrics.

Ellenberger, H. F. (1972). The story of "Anna O.": A critical review with new data. *Journal of the History of the Behavioral Sciences, 8,* 267–279.

Elliot, R., Watson, J., Timulak, L., & Sharbance, J. (2021). Research on humanistic–experimental psychotherapies: Updated review. In M. Barkham, W. Lutz, & L. Castonguay (Eds.). *Bergin and Garfield's handbook of psychotherapy and behavior change* (Chap. 13, pp. 421–468). New York: Wiley.

Ellis, A. (1962). *Reason and emotion in psychotherapy.* Secaucus, NJ: Lyle Stuart.

Ellwood, B. (2022, January 26). The more money people earn the happier they are—even at incomes beyond $75,000 a year. *PsyPost.*

Emanuel, E. J., Onwuteaka-Philipsen, B. D., Urwin, J. W., & Cohen, J. (2016). Attitudes and practices of euthanasia and physician-assisted suicide in the United States, Canada, and Europe, *JAMA, 316*(1), 79.

Eng, A. G., Bansal, P. S., Goh, P. K., Nirjar, U., Petersen, M. K., & Martel, M. M. (2024). Evidence-based assessment for attention-deficit/hyperactivity disorder. *Assessment, 31*(1), 42–52.

Engel, G. L. (1968). A life setting conducive to illness: The giving-up-given-up complex. *Annals of Internal Medicine, 69,* 293.

Engel, G. L. (1971). Sudden and rapid death during psychological stress: Folklore or folk wisdom? *Annals of Internal Medicine, 74,* 771–774.

Engel, S., Laufer, S., Klusmann, H., Schulze, L., Schumacher, S., & Knaevelsrud, C. (2023). Cortisol response to traumatic stress to predict PTSD symptom development: A systematic review and meta-analysis of experimental studies. *European Journal of Psychotraumatology, 14*(2), 2225153.

Engel, S., Steffen, K., & Mitchell, J. E. (2023, March 28). Bulimia nervosa in adults: Clinical features, course of illness, assessment, and diagnosis. *UpToDate.* Retrieved from http://www.uptodate.com.

Engelbrektsson, J., Salomonsson, S., Högström, J., Sorjonen, K., Sundell, K., & Forster, M. (2023, February 28). Parent training via internet or in group for disruptive behaviors: A randomized clinical noninferiority trial. *Journal of the American Academy of Child and Adolescent Psychiatry, 62*(9), 987–997.

Engin, E. (2023). GABAA receptor subtypes and benzodiazepine use, misuse, and abuse. *Frontiers in Psychiatry, 13,* 1060949.

EO (Elder Options). (2023). *Interesting facts about older adults.* Retrieved from https://agingresources.org.

EPR (European Pharmaceutical Review). (2020, March 27). Over 90 percent of medical marijuana in US contains high levels of THC, study finds. *European Pharmaceutical Review.* Retrieved from https://www.europeanpharmaceuticalreview.com/news.

Er, S. T., Demir, E., & Sari, E. (2023). Suicide and economic uncertainty: New findings in a global setting. *SSM Population Health, 22,* 101387.

Erdelyi, M. (2022, December 16). *The interpretation of dreams and of jokes: The art and the science.* New York: Routledge.

Eriksen, C. U., Konradsen, F., & Vildekilde, T. (2021). Searching online for methods of suicide. *Crisis, 42*(2), 136–143.

Ernst, M., Niederer, D., Werner, A. M., Czaja, S. J., Mikton, C., Ong, A. D., . . . Beutel, M. E. (2022). Loneliness before and during the COVID-19 pandemic: A systematic review with meta-analysis. *American Psychologist, 77*(5), 660–677.

Espinoza, R. T., & Unützer, J. (2023, October 4). Diagnosis and management of late-life unipolar depression. *UpToDate.* Retrieved from http://www.uptodate.com.

Esteban, L., Navas, P., Verdugo, M. A., Iriarte, E. G., & Arias, V. B. (2023). A community living experience: Views of people with intellectual disability with extensive support needs, families, and professionals. *Research in Developmental Disabilities, 137,* 104503.

Estévez, A., Macía, L., Momeñe, J., & Etxaburu, N. (2022). Attachment and behavioral addictions. In V. B. Patel & V. R. Preedy (Eds.). *Handbook of substance misuse and addictions: From biology to public health* (pp. 123–143). New York: Springer.

Evans, M. M., Kim, J., Abel, T., Nicki-Jockschat, T., & Stevens, H. E. (2024). Developmental disruptions of the dorsal striatum in autism spectrum disorder. *Biological Psychiatry, 95*(2), 102–111.

Evans, S. C., de la Peña, F. R., Matthys, W., & Lochman, J. E. (2024). Disruptive behaviour or dissocial disorders and attention deficit hyperactivity disorder. In G. M. Reed, P. L.-J. Ritchie, & A. Maercker (Eds.). *A psychological approach to diagnosis: Using the ICD-11 as a framework* (Chap. 14). Washington, DC: American Psychological Association.

Evans, S. C., Roberts, M. C., Keeley, J. W., Rebello, T. J., de la Pena, F., Lochman, J. E., . . . Reed, G. M. (2021). Diagnostic classification of irritability and oppositionality in youth: A global field study comparing ICD-11 with ICD-10 and DSM-5. *Journal of Child Psychology and Psychiatry, 62*(3), 303–312.

Evans, S. W., Owens, J. S., & Power, T. J. (2021). Attention-deficit/hyperactivity disorder. In M. J. Prinstein, E. A. Youngstrom, E. J. Mash, & R. A. Barkley (Eds.). *Treatment of disorders in childhood and adolescence* (4th ed.). New York: Guilford Press.

Everly, G. S., Jr., & Lating, J. M. (2022). *The Johns Hopkins guide to psychological first aid* (2nd ed.). Baltimore: Johns Hopkins University Press.

Everyday Health. (2018). *Special report: United States of Stress everyday health.* New York: Author.

Everyday Health. (2022). *Special reports.* New York: Author.

Facts.net. (2023, September 23). 50 fascinating Sigmund Freud facts to boggle your mind. Retrieved from https://facts.net/sigmund-freud-facts.

Fagan, A. (2022, November 1). 7 qualities of a great therapist. *Psychology Today.*

Fairbank, R. (2023, March 1). An ADHD diagnosis in adulthood comes with challenges and benefits. *APA Monitor on Psychology, 54*(2), 52.

Fairburn, C., & Murphy, R. (2020). The eating disorders. In J. R. Geddes, N. C. Andreason, & G. M. Goodwin (Eds.). *New Oxford textbook of psychiatry* (3rd ed., Chap. 101). New York: Oxford University Press.

Fakuda, A. M., Kavanaugh, B. C., Yuan, S., & Carpenter, L. L. (2022). Transcranial magnetic stimulation. In C. B. Nemeroff, A. F. Schatzberg, N. Rasgon, & S. M. Strakowski (Eds.). *The American Psychiatric Association Publishing textbook of mood disorders* (2nd ed., Chap. 19). Washington, DC: American Psychiatric Association Publishing.

Fang, L., Jiao, B., Liu, X., Wang, Z., Yuan, P., Zhou, H., . . . Shen, L. (2024). Specific serum autoantibodies predict the development and progression of Alzheimer's disease with high accuracy. *Brain, Behavior, and Immunity, 115,* 543–554.

Farber, B., Manevich, I., Metzger, J., & Saypol, E. (2005). Choosing psychotherapy as a career: Why did we cross that road? *Journal of Clinical Psychology, 61*(8), 1009–1031.

Farber, B. A., Suzuki, J. Y., & Lynch, D. A. (2019). Positive regard and affirmation. In J. C. Norcross & M. J. Lambert (Eds.). *Psychotherapy relationships that work: Vol. 1. Evidence-based therapist contributions* (Chap. 8, pp. 288–323). New York: Oxford University Press.

Farber, B. A., Suzuki, J. Y., & Ort, D. (2022, July 26). *Understanding and enhancing positive regard in psychotherapy: Carl Rogers and beyond.* Washington, DC: American Psychological Association.

Farberow, N. L., & Litman, R. E. (1970). *A comprehensive suicide prevention program* (Unpublished final report). Los Angeles: Suicide Prevention Center of Los Angeles.

Fariba, K. A., & Gupta, V. (2023, April 24). Involuntary commitment. *StatPearls.*

Fariba, K. A., Gupta, V., & Kass, E. (2023, April 17). Personality disorder. *StatPearls.*

Fariba, K. A., & Sapra, A. (2023, April 24). Avoidant personality disorder. *StatPearls.*

Fariba, K. A., Madhanagopal, N., & Gupta, V. (2022, June 9). Schizoid personality disorder. *StatPearls.*

Farkas, B. F., Takacs, Z. K., Kollárovics, & Balázs, J. (2023, July 24). The prevalence of self-injury in adolescence: A systematic review and meta-analysis. *European Child & Adolescent Psychiatry.* doi:10.1007/s00787-023-02264-y. [Open access]

Farnsworth, C. (2022, December 21). What is gestalt therapy? *Medical News Today.*

Farreras, I. G. (2023). History of mental illness. In R. Biswas-Diener & E. Diener (Eds.). *Noba textbook series: Psychology.* Champaign, IL: DEF Publishers.

Faul, L., & LaBar, K. S. (2022). Mood-congruent memory revisited. *Psychological Review.* doi:10.1037/rev0000394. [Online ahead of print]

Faulhaber, M. E., Lee, J. E., & Gentile, D. A. (2023). The effect of self-monitoring limited social media use on psychological well-being. *Technology, Mind, and Behavior, 4*(2). doi:10.1037/tmb0000111.

Faverio, M. (2022). *Share of those 65 and older who are tech users has grown in the past decade.* Washington, DC: Pew Research Center.

Fazeli, P. L., Hopkins, C., Vance, D. E., Vadley, V., Li, P., Turan, B., . . . Clay, O. J. (2024). Cognitive prescriptions for reducing dementia risk factors among Black/African Americans: Feasibility, acceptability, and preliminary efficacy. *Ethnicity & Health, 29*(1), 1–24.

FBI (Federal Bureau of Investigation). (2020). *Active shooter resources.* Washington, DC: Author.

FBI (Federal Bureau of Investigation). (2020). *2019 Preliminary semiannual uniform crime report, January–June.* Washington, DC: Author.

FBI (Federal Bureau of Investigation). (2022, May). *Active shooter incidents in the United States in 2021.* Washington, DC: Author.

FBI (Federal Bureau of Investigation). (2023). *Serial murder: Multi-disciplinary perspectives for investigators.* Washington, DC: Author.

FDA (U.S. Food and Drug Administration). (2020, August 19). *Regulations: Good clinical practice and clinical trials.* Retrieved from https://www.fda.gov/science-research/clinical-trials-and-human-subject- protection.

FDA (U.S. Food and Drug Administration). (2022). *Want to quit smoking? FDA-approved and FDA-cleared cessation products can help.* Retrieved from https://www.fda.gov/consumers/consumer-updates.

FDA (U.S. Food and Drug Administration). (2023). *Results from the Annual National Youth Tobacco Survey.* Silver Spring, MD: Author.

Fedoroff, J. P. (2020). *The paraphilias: Changing suits in the evolution of sexual interest paradigms.* New York: Oxford University Press.

Feeny, N. C., Klein, A. B., & Benhamou, K. S. (2022). Classification of posttraumatic stress disorder. In J. G. Beck & D. M. Sloan (Eds.). *The Oxford handbook of traumatic stress disorders* (Chap. 4). New York: Oxford University Press.

Feinstein, B. A., Katz, B. W., Benjamin, I., Macaulay, T., Dyar, C., & Morgana, E. (2023). Disparities in depression and anxiety related to sexual orientation and gender identity among older adults: The role of age discrimination. *Stigma and Health*. https://doi.org/10.1037/sah0000462. [Online ahead of print]

Fenaughty, J., Tan, K., Ker, A., Veale, J., Saxton, P., & Alansari, M. (2023). Sexual orientation and gender identity change efforts for young people in New Zealand: Demographics, types of suggesters, and associations with mental health. *Journal of Youth and Adolescence, 52*(1), 149–164.

Feriante, J., Torrico, T. J., & Bernstein, B. (2023, February 26). Separation anxiety disorder. *StatPearls*.

Ferleger, D. (2023). *The evolution of disability rights litigation (and some stories)*. Retrieved from https://mn.gov/mnddc/disability-litigation/right-to-treatment.

Fernandez, J., García-Pérez, M., & Orozco-Aleman, S. (2023). Unraveling the Hispanic health paradox. *Journal of Economic Perspectives, 37*(1), 145–168.

Fernando, S. C., Beblo, T., Lamera, A., Schlosser, N., Woermann, F. G., Driessen, M., & Toepper, M. (2023). Neural correlates of emotion acceptance and suppression in borderline personality disorder. *Frontiers in Psychiatry, 13*, 1066218.

Ferrando, C. (2023, August 30). Gender-affirming surgery: Male to female. *UpToDate*. Retrieved from https://www.uptodate.com.

Ferrando, C., Zhao, L. C., & Nikolavsky, D. (2024, January 2). Gender-affirming surgery: Female to male. *UpToDate*. https://www.uptodate.com/contents/gender-affirming-surgery-female-to-male#!.

Ferron, J. M., Kirby, M., & Lipien, L. (2023). Single-case experimental design. In H. Cooper, M. N. Coutanche, L. M. McMullen, A. T. Panter, D. Rindskopf, & K. J. Sher (Eds.). *APA handbook of research methods in psychology: Vol. 2. Research designs: Quantitative, qualitative, neuropsychological, and biological* (2nd ed., Chap. 33). Washington, DC: American Psychological Association.

Fielding, L. (2021). *Trans sex: Clinical approaches to trans sexualities and erotic embodiments*. New York: Routledge.

Figee, M., Riva-Posse, P., Choi, K. S., Bederson, L., Mayberg, H. S., & Kopell, B. H. (2022, July). Deep brain stimulation for depression. *Journal of the American Society for Experimental Neurotherapeutics, 19*(4), 1229–1245.

Figurasin, R., & Maguire, N. J. (2023, September 4). 3,4-methylenedioxy-methamphetamine toxicity. *StatPearls*.

Filipponi, C., Visentini, C., Filippini, T., Cutino, A., Ferri, P., Rovesti, S., . . . Di Lorenzo, R. (2022). The follow-up of eating disorders from adolescence to early adulthood: A systematic review. *International Journal of Environmental Research and Public Health, 19*(23), 16237.

Findling, R. L., Zhou, X., George, P., & Chapell, P. B. (2022). Diagnostic trends and prescription patterns in disruptive mood dysregulation disorder and bipolar disorder. *Journal of the American Academy of Child and Adolescent Psychiatry, 61*(3), 434–445.

Fink, S., & Risen, J. (2017, June 21). Psychologists open a window on brutal C.I.A. interrogations. *New York Times*. https://www.nytimes.com/interactive/2017/06/20/us/cia-torture.html.

Finkelstein, S. A., Carson, A., Edwards, M. J., Kozlowska, K., Lidstone, S. C., Perez, D. L., . . . Aybek, S. (2023). Setting up functional neurological disorder treatment services: Questions and answers. *Neurologic Clinics, 41*(4), 729–743.

Finkelstein, S. A., & Popkirov, S. (2023). Functional neurological disorder: Diagnostic pitfalls and differential diagnostic considerations. *Neurologic Clinics, 41*(4), 665–679.

First, M. B., Yousif, L. H., Clarke, D. E., Wang, P. S., Gogtay, N., & Appelbaum, P. S. (2022). DSM-5-TR: Overview of what's new and what's changed. *World Psychiatry, 21*(2), 218–219.

Firth, J., Solmi, M., Wootton, R. E., Vancampfort, D., Schuch, F. B., Hoare, E., . . . Stubbs, B. (2020). A meta-review of "lifestyle psychiatry": The role of exercise, smoking, diet and sleep in the prevention and treatment of mental disorders. *World Psychiatry, 19*(3), 360–380.

Fischer, A. E., Venter, W. D. F., Collins, S., Carman, M., & Lalla-Edward, S. T. (2021, February). The readability of informed consent forms for research studies conducted in South Africa. *South African Medical Journal, 111*(2), 180–183.

Fischer, B. A. (2012). Maltreatment of people with serious mental illness in the early 20th century: A focus on Nazi Germany and eugenics in America. *Journal of Nervous and Mental Disease, 200*(12), 1096–1100.

Fischer, B. A., & Buchanan, R. W. (2023, July 5). Schizophrenia in adults: Clinical features, course, assessment, and diagnosis. *UpToDate*. Retrieved from http://www.uptodate.com.

Fischer, B. A., & Buchanan, R. W. (2023, October 20). Schizophrenia in adults: Epidemiology and pathogenesis. *UpToDate*. Retrieved from http://www.uptodate.com.

Fischer, H. (2022, Summer). Dancing with spiders: Tarantellas and tarantism. *Hektoen International*.

Fischer, J. M., Kandil, F.-I., Kessler, C. S., Nayeri, L., Zager, L. S., Hennhöfer, T. R., . . . Jeitler, M. (2022). Stress reduction by yoga versus mindfulness training in adults suffering from distress: A three-armed randomized controlled trial including qualitative interviews (RELAX Study). *Journal of Clinical Medicine, 11*(19), 5680.

Fischer, M. A., & Corsetti, M. (2024). Geriatric psychiatric emergencies. *Emergency Medicine Clinics of North America, 42*(1), 135–149.

Fisher, E. B., Barreiro-Rosado, J. A., Carpenter, C., Evans, M. S., Luu, S. L., Qian, Y., . . . Yang, P. Y. (2024). Social isolation and loneliness. In N. Schneiderman, (Ed.). *APA handbook of health psychology: Vol. 3. Health psychology and public health* (Part III, Chap. 17). Washington, DC: American Psychological Association.

Fisher, K. A., & Hany, M. (2023, May 8). Antisocial personality disorder. *StatPearls*.

Fisher, K. A., & Marwaha, R. (2023, March 6). Paraphilia. *StatPearls*.

Fitzsimmons-Craft, E., & Pike, K. (2022, February 17). Anorexia nervosa in adults: Cognitive-behavioral therapy (CBT). *UpToDate*. Retrieved from http://www.uptodate.com.

Fletcher, J. M., & Miciak, J. (2024). Assessment of specific learning disabilities and intellectual disabilities. *Assessment, 31*(1), 53–74.

Floyd, A. E., & Gupta, V. (2023, April 24). Minnesota Multiphasic Personality Inventory. *StatPearls*.

Foa, E., Hembree, E., & Rothbaum, B. O. (2007). *Prolonged exposure therapy for PTSD: Emotional processing of traumatic experiences (treatments that work)*. New York: Oxford University Press.

Foitzick, M. F., Medina, N. B., Iglesias García, L. C., & Gravielle, M. C. (2020). Benzodiazepine exposure induces transcriptional down-regulation of GABAA receptor 1 subunit gene via L-type voltage-gated calcium channel activation in rat cerebrocortical neurons. *Neuroscience Letters, 721*, 134801.

Foldvary-Schaefer, N. (2023, September 7). Disorders of arousal from non-rapid eye movement sleep in adults. *UpToDate*. Retrieved from https://www.uptodate.com.

Fonagy, P. (2021). Emergence of antisocial behavior in middle childhood. In A. Venta, C. Sharp, P. Fonagy, & J. M. Fletcher (Eds.). *Developmental psychopathology* (Chap. 7, pp. 157–181). New York: Wiley-Blackwell.

Fonagy, P., Campbell, C., & Luyten, P. (2023). Alliance rupture and repair in mentalization-based therapy. In C. F. Eubanks, L. E. Samstag, & J. C. Muran (Eds.). *Rupture and repair in psychotherapy: A critical process for change* (pp. 253–276). Washington, DC: American Psychological Association.

Fonagy, P., Campbell, C., & Luyten, P. (2023). Attachment, mentalizing and trauma: Then (1992) and now (2022). *Brain Sciences, 13*(3), 459.

Foote, B. (2022, March 1). Dissociative identity disorder: Epidemiology, pathogenesis, clinical manifestations, course, assessment, and diagnosis. *UpToDate*. Retrieved from https://www.uptodate.com.

Ford, T. (2000). The influence of womanist identity on the development of eating disorders and depression in African American female college students. *Dissertation Abstracts International: Section A: Humanities and Social Sciences, 61*, 2194.

Forde, R., Peters, S., & Wittkowski, A. (2020). Recovery from postpartum psychosis: A systematic review and metasynthesis of women's and families' experiences. *Archives of Women's Mental Health, 23*, 597–612.

Forrester, E. A. (2022). CBT for OCD: Evidence-based treatment for contamination and checking. In G. Todd (Ed.). *Evidence-based treatment for anxiety disorders and depression: A cognitive behavioral therapy compendium* (Chap. 12). Cambridge: Cambridge University Press.

Fosslien, L., & Duffy, M. W. (2022, April 22). How to manage your anger at work. *Harvard Business Review*. Retrieved from https://hbr.org/2022/04.

Foster, J. D., Campbell, W. K., & Twenge, J. M. (2003). Individual differences in narcissism: Inflated self-views across the lifespan and around the world. *Journal of Research in Personality, 37,* 469–486.

Fountoulakis, K. N., Apostolidou, M. K., Atsiova, M. B., Filippidou, A. K., Florou, A. K., Gousiou, D. S., . . . Chrousos, G. P. (2021). Self-reported changes in anxiety, depression and suicidality during the COVID-19 lockdown in Greece. *Journal of Affective Disorders, 279,* 624–629.

Fox, J. A., Levin, J., & Fridel, E. E. (2018). *Extreme killing: Understanding serial and mass murder* (4th ed.). Thousand Oaks, CA: Sage Publications.

Fox, J. A., Levin, J., & Fridel, E. E. (2023). *Extreme killing: Understanding serial and mass murder* (5th ed.). Thousand Oaks, CA: Sage Publications.

Fox, M. H., Seto, M. C., Refaie, N., Lavrinsek, S., Hall, V., Curry, S.,. . . Lalumiere, M. L. (2022). The relation between the paraphilias and anxiety in men: A case-control study. *Archives of Sexual Behavior, 51*(8), 4063–4084.

Fox, N. A., Zeytinoglu, S., Valadez, E. A., Buzzell, G. A., Morales, S., & Henderson, H. A. (2022, September 19). Annual research review: Developmental pathways linking early behavioral inhibition to later anxiety. *Journal of Child Psychology and Psychiatry.* [Online ahead of print]

FP (Forensic Psychology Education). (2024). *Forensic psychologists as trial consultants.* Retrieved from https://www.forensicpsychologyedu.org.

FP (Forensic Psychology Education). (2024). *Forensic psychologists in determining insanity and competency to stand trial.* Retrieved from https://www.forensicpsychologyedu.org.

FP (Forensic Psychology Education). (2024). *Forensic psychologists in violent risk assessment.* Retrieved from https://www.forensicpsychologyedu.org.

FPS (Facial Plastic Surgery). (2020, February 17). *New stats: AAFPRS annual survey reveals face of plastic surgery goes younger.* Retrieved from https://www.aafprs.org.

FPS (Facial Plastic Surgery). (2022, February 10). *AAFPRS announces annual survey results: Demand for facial plastic surgery skyrockets as pandemic drags on.* Retrieved from https://www.aafprs.org/media/press_releases.

FPS (Facial Plastic Surgery). (2023). *AAFPRS press releases.* Alexandria, VA: Author.

FPS (Facial Plastic Surgery). (2023). *As Americans return to the office, AAFPRS unveils aesthetic trends from Annual Facial Plastic Surgery survey.* Alexandria, VA: Author.

Fraiman, E., Goldblatt, C., Loria, M., Mishra, K., & Pope, R. (2023). One survey fits all? Evaluating the relevance of sexual function measures designed for cis women in trans women postvaginoplasty. *Journal of Sexual Medicine, 20,* 1133–1138.

Francis, J., Jr., & Young, G. B. (2022, July 18). Diagnosis of delirium and confusional states. *UpToDate.* Retrieved from http://www.uptodate.com.

Francis, J., & Young, G. B. (2023, August 9). Patient education: Delirium (beyond the basics). *UpToDate.* Retrieved from http://www.uptodate.com.

Frank, G. K. W., Shott, M. E., Pryor, T., Swindle, S., Nguyen, T., & Stoddard, J. (2023). Trait anxiety is associated with amygdala expectation and caloric taste receipt response across eating disorders. *Neuropsychopharmacology, 48,* 380–390.

Frank, J. D. (1973). *Persuasion and healing* (Rev. ed.). Baltimore: Johns Hopkins University Press.

Freitag, G. F., Coxe, S., Cardinale, E. M., Furr, J. M., Herrera, A., & Comer, J. S. (2024). Irritability patterns and associations with family accommodation among youth with selective mutism: A latent profile analysis. *Research on Child and Adolescent Psychopathology.* https://doi.org/10.1007/s10802-023-01161-x. [Online ahead of print]

Freitag, G. F., Grassie, H. L., Mallidi, A., Jeong, A., Comer, J. S., Ehrenreich-May, J., & Brotman, M. A. (2023). Measuring emotion dysregulation in children and adolescents: A systematic review of existing questionnaires. *Journal of the American Academy of Child and Adolescent Psychiatry, 62*(7), 728–763.

Freitag, G. F., Salem, H., Conroy, K., Busto, C., Adrian, M., Borba, C. P. C., . . . Comer, J. S. (2023). The Patient-Reported Outcomes Measurement Information System (PROMIS) pediatric and parent-proxy short forms for anxiety: Psychometric properties in the Kids FACE FEARS sample. *Journal of Anxiety Disorders, 94,* 102677. https://doi.org/10.1016/j.janxdis.2023.102677.

Freitag, G. F., Urcuyo, A., & Comer, J. S. (2022). Moving beyond the clinic: Leveraging telehealth strategies to address youth mental health challenges. *Advances in Psychiatry and Behavioral Health.* https://doi.org/10.1016/j.ypsc.2022.06.004.

French, J. H., & Hameed, S. (2023, July 16). Illness anxiety disorder. *StatPearls.*

French, J. H., & Shrestha, S. (2022, September 26). Histrionic personality disorder. *StatPearls.*

Freud, S. (1894). The neuropsychoses of defense. In J. Strachey (Ed.). *The standard edition of the complete psychological works of Sigmund Freud* (Vol. 3). London: Hogarth Press. [Work reprinted in 1962.]

Freud, S. (1914). On narcissism. In *Complete psychological works* (Vol. 14). London: Hogarth Press. (Work reprinted in 1957)

Freud, S. (1915). A case of paranoia counter to psychoanalytic theory. In *Complete psychological works* (Vol. 14). London: Hogarth Press. (Work reprinted in 1957)

Freud, S. (1917). *A general introduction to psychoanalysis* (J. Riviere, Trans.). New York: Liveright. [Work reprinted in 1963.]

Freud, S. (1917). Mourning and melancholia. In *Collected papers* (Vol. 4, pp. 152–172). London: Hogarth Press and the Institute of Psychoanalysis. [Work republished 1950.]

Freud, S. (1924). The loss of reality in neurosis and psychosis. In *Sigmund Freud's collected papers* (Vol. 2, pp. 272–282). London: Hogarth Press.

Freud, S. (1933). *New introductory lectures on psychoanalysis.* New York: W. W. Norton.

Freudenreich, O., & McEvoy, J. (2023, January 4). Guidelines for prescribing clozapine in schizophrenia. *UpToDate.* Retrieved from https://www.uptodate.com.

Frey, B. (Ed.). (2022). *The SAGE encyclopedia of research design.* Thousand Oaks, CA: Sage Publications.

Frey, W. H. (2018, March 14). The U.S. will become "minority white" in 2045, Census projects. *Brookings.* Retrieved from https://www.brookings.edu/blog/the-avenue.

Frey, W. H. (2021, June 23). All recent U.S. population growth comes from people of color, new census estimates show. *Brookings.* Retrieved from https://www.brookings.edu/research.

Frey, W. H. (2023, August 1). New 2020 census data shows an aging America and wide racial gaps between generations. *Brookings.* Retrieved from https://brookings.edu/articles.

Frick, P. J. (2023). A commentary on Perlstein et al. (2023): The past and future of treating youth with limited prosocial emotions. *Journal of Child Psychology and Psychiatry, 64*(9), 1393–1395.

Frick, P. J., Barry, C. T., & Kamphaus, R. W. (2020). *Clinical assessment of child and adolescent personality and behavior* (4th ed.). New York: Springer.

Fried, A. L., & Jansen, K. L. (2023). Frameworks for causal inference in psychological science. In H. Cooper, M. N. Coutanche, L. M. McMullen, A. T. Panter, D. Rindskopf, & K. J. Sher (Eds.). *APA handbook of research methods in psychology: Vol. 1. Foundations, planning, measures, and psychometrics* (2nd ed., Chap. 3). Washington, DC: American Psychological Association.

Friederich, H. C., Zipfel, D., & Wild, B. (2023). Psychodynamic therapies and eating disorders. In P. Robinson, T. Wade, B. Herpertz-Dahlann, F. Fernandez-Aranda, J. Treasure, & S. Wonderlich (Eds.). *Eating disorders.* Edinburgh: Springer.

Friedman, M., & Rosenman, R. (1959). Association of specific overt behavior pattern with blood and cardiovascular findings. *Journal of the American Medical Association, 169,* 1286.

Friedman, S. H., Reed, E., & Ross, N. E. (2023, January 13). Postpartum psychosis. *Current Psychiatry Reports, 25,* 65–72. https://doi.org/10.1007/s11920-022-01406-4.

Frierson, R. L., & Joshi, K. G. (2023). Mental health criminal defenses in persons with neuropsychiatric disorders. *Behavioral Sciences & the Law.* doi:10.1002/bsl.2635. [Online ahead of print]

Frimpong, J. A., Shiu-Yee, K., Tross, S., D'Aunno, T., Perlman, D. C., Strauss, S. M., . . . Metsch, L. R. (2020). Bundling rapid human immunodeficiency virus and hepatitis C virus testing to increase receipt of test results: A randomized trial. *Medical Care, 58*(5), 445–452.

Fromm-Reichmann, F. (1948). Notes on the development of treatment of schizophrenia by psychoanalytic psychotherapy. *Psychiatry, 11,* 263–273.

Fu, X., Zhang, X., Jiang, T., Huang, Y., Cheng, P., Tang, D., . . . Du, J. (2020, June). Association between lifelong premature ejaculation and polymorphism of tryptophan hydroxylase 2 gene in the Han population. *Sexual Medicine, 8*(2), 223–229.

Fung, H. W., Wong, E. N. M., Lam, S. K. K., Chien, W. T., Hung, S. L., Ross, C. A., & Cloitre, M. (2023). Prevalence and sociocultural correlates of post-traumatic stress disorder and complex PTSD among Chinese community health service users in Hong Kong. *International Journal of Social Psychiatry, 69*(4), 895–905.

Furr, J. M., Sanchez, A. L., Hong, N., & Comer, J. S. (2020). Exposure therapy for childhood selective mutism: Principles, practices, and procedures. In T. Peris, E. Storch, & J. McGuire (Eds.). *Exposure therapy for children with anxiety and OCD: Clinician's guide to integrated treatment* (Chap. 6). New York: Elsevier.

Gabbard, G. O. (2022). Psychoanalytic and psychodynamic psychotherapy for depressive disorders. In C. B. Nemeroff, A. F. Schatzberg, N. Rasgon, & S. M. Strakowski (Eds.). *The American Psychiatric Association Publishing textbook of mood disorders* (2nd ed., Chap. 25). Washington, DC: American Psychiatric Association Publishing.

Gabbard, G., & DeJean, V. (2023, January 31). Unipolar depression in adults: Psychodynamic psychotherapy. *UpToDate*. Retrieved from https://www.uptodate.com.

Gagliardini, G., Gullo, S., Teti, A., & Colli, A. (2023). *Journal of Clinical Psychology, 79*(2), 514–530.

Gaines, J. M., Macdonald, E. J., Smith, A. J., Diefenbach, M. A., & Paduch, D. A. (2022). Race and ethnicity have a significant effect on the disclosure of erectile function: An analysis of NHANES response patterns. *Urology, 167,* 138–143.

Gallegos, M. I., Zaring-Hinkle, B., Wang, N., & Bray, J. H. (2021). Detachment, peer pressure, and age of first substance use as gateways to later substance use. *Drug and Alcohol Dependence, 218,* 108352.

Gallup News. (2020, January 6). Nurses continue to rate highest in honesty, ethics. *Gallup News.* Retrieved from https://news.gallup.com/poll/274673.

Gallup News. (2023, January 10). Nurses retain top ethics rating in U.S., but below 2020 high. *Gallup News.* Retrieved from https://news.gallup.com/poll/46780.

Gallup Poll. (2013, May 29). *U.S. support for euthanasia hinges on how it's described* (Poll 162815). Gallup. Retrieved from https://www.gallup.com/poll/1162815.

Gallup Poll. (2017, June 12). *Majority of Americans remain supportive of euthanasia.* Gallup. Retrieved from https://www.gallup.com/poll/211928.

Gallup Poll. (2018). *Americans' strong support for euthanasia persists.* Gallup. Retrieved from https://news.gallup.com/poll/2325145.

Galovski, T. E., McLean, C. P., Davis, C. A., & Wachen, J. S. (2023). Psychosocial treatments for adults with PTSD. In M. J. Friedman, P. P. Schnurr, & T. M. Keane (Eds.). *Handbook of PTSD: Science and practice* (3rd ed., Chap. 19). New York: Guilford Press.

Galovski, T. E., Norman, S. B., & Hamblen, J. L. (2023). *Cognitive processing therapy for PTSD.* Washington, DC: National Center for PTSD.

Gamwell, L., & Tomes, N. (1995). *Madness in America: Cultural and medical perceptions of mental illness before 1914.* Ithaca, NY: Cornell University Press.

Ganipisetti, V. M., & Bollimunta, P. (2023, April 25). Obesity and set-point theory. *StatPearls.*

Gant, J. (2022, August 22). When should I meditate? And how should I begin? *Mindful.*

GAO (Government Accounting Office). (2021, May 18). *Prescription drugs: Medicare spending on drugs with direct-to-consumer advertising.* Washington, DC: Author.

GAO (Government Accounting Office). (2023, September 8). *Medical advertising: Federal oversight of devices.* Washington, DC: Author.

Gao, H., Chen, J., Huang, Y., & Zhao, R. (2024). Advances in targeted tracking and detection of soluble amyloid-beta aggregates as a biomarker of Alzheimer's disease. *Talanta, 267*(Part 1), 125311.

Gao, X. (2022). Research on expressive writing in psychology: A forty-year bibliometric analysis and visualization of current status and research trends. *Frontiers in Psychology, 13,* 825626.

Gao, Y., Bagheri, N., & Furuya-Kanamori, L. (2022). Has the COVID-19 pandemic lockdown worsened eating disorders symptoms among patients with eating disorders? A systematic review. *Zeitschrift fur Gesundheitswissenschaften, 30*(11), 2743–2752.

Garcia-Lee, B., Strnadova, I., & Dowse, L. (2024). Researching belonging in the context of research with people with intellectual disabilities: A systematic review of inclusive approaches. *Journal of Applied Research in Intellectual Disabilities, 37*(1), 13178.

Gardiner, J. D., & Lawson, J. (2022). Depending on the Dark Triad: Exploring relationships between malign personality traits, substance and process addictions. *Journal of Substance Use, 28*(2), 243–248.

Garety, P., Edwards, C. J., Ward, T., Emsley, R., Huckvale, M., McCrone, P., . . . Craig, T. (2021). Optimising AVATAR therapy for people who hear distressing voices: Study protocol for the AVATAR2 multi-centre randomised controlled trial. *Trials, 22*(1), 366.

Garland, A. (2022). CBT for persistent depressive disorder. In G. Todd & R. Branch (Eds.). *Evidence-based treatment for anxiety disorders and depression: A cognitive behavioral therapy compendium* (pp. 383–401). Cambridge: Cambridge University Press.

Garner, D. M. (2005). *Eating Disorder Inventory TM-3 (EDI TM-3).* Lutz, FL: Psychological Assessment Resources.

Garner, D. M., Olmsted, M. P., & Polivy, J. (1984). *The EDI.* Odessa, FL: Psychological Assessment Resources.

Garner, D. M., Olmsted, M. P., & Polivy, J. (1991). *The EDI-2.* Odessa, FL: Psychological Assessment Resources.

Garner, D. M., Olmsted, M. P., & Polivy, J. (2004). *The EDI-3.* Odessa, FL: Psychological Assessment Resources.

Garrett, B. L., Crozier, W. E., Modjadidi, K., Liu, A. J., Kafadar, K., Yaffe. J., & Dodson, C. S. (2023). Sensitizing jurors to eyewitness confidence using "reason-based" judicial instructions. *Journal of Applied Research in Memory and Cognition, 12*(1), 141–157.

Garson, J. (2022, July 11). No, schizophrenia isn't caused by bad parenting. *Psychology Today.*

Gassó, A. M., Forero, C. G., Piqueras, J., & Gómez-Durán, E. (2022). Psychopathological aspects of sexting and IBSA perpetrators: A brief research report. *Frontiers in Psychiatry, 13,* 983881.

Gassó, A. M., Klettke, B., Agustina, J. R., & Montiel, I. (2019). Sexting, mental health, and victimization among adolescents: A literature review. *International Journal of Environmental Research and Public Health, 6*(13), 1–14.

Gassó, A. M., Mueller-Johnson, K., & Gómez-Durán, E. L. (2021). Victimization as a result of non-consensual dissemination of sexting and psychopathology correlates: An exploratory analysis. *International Journal of Environmental Research and Public Health, 18*(12), 6564.

Gaudiano, B. A., & Ellenberg, S. (2022). ACT for the treatment of psychosis and schizophrenia-spectrum disorders. In M. P. Twohig, M. E. Levin, & J. M. Petersen (Eds.). *The Oxford handbook of acceptance and commitment therapy* (Chap. 24). New York: Oxford University Press.

Gavurova, A., Ivankova, V., & Rigelsky, M. (2022). Linking stress, depression, and alcohol use. In V. B. Patel & V. R. Preedy (Eds.). *Handbook of substance misuse and addictions: From biology to public health* (pp. 1007–1032). New York: Springer.

Gay, P. (1999, March 29). Psychoanalyst Sigmund Freud. *Time*, pp. 66–69.

Gay, P. (2006). *Freud: A life for our time.* New York: W. W. Norton.

Gebhard, P. H. (1965). Situational factors affecting human sexual behavior. In F. Beach (Ed.). *Sex and behavior* (pp. 483–495). New York: Wiley.

Gecaite-Stonciene, J., Williams, T., Lochner, C., Hoffman, J., & Stein, D. J. (2022). Efficacy and tolerability of pharmacotherapy for obsessive-compulsive personality disorder: A systematic review of randomized controlled trials. *Expert Opinion on Pharmacotherapy, 23*(11), 1351–1358.

Gega, L., & Wright, B. J. (2022). CBT for specific phobia. In G. Todd (Ed.). *Evidence-based treatment for anxiety disorders and depression: A cognitive behavioral therapy compendium* (Chap. 3). Cambridge: Cambridge University Press.

Gelbar, N. W. (2023, August). Down syndrome. In M. Perfect, C. Riccio, & M. Bray (Eds.). *Health-related disorders in children and adolescents: A guidebook for educators and service providers* (2nd ed., Chap. 18). Washington, DC: American Psychological Association.

Gencarella, S. (2018). *Wicked weird & wily Yankees: A celebration of New England's eccentrics and misfits.* New York: Globe Pequot.

George, D. R. (2022, March 14). The link between lead poisoning and Alzheimer's disease. *Psychology Today.*

Georgiadis, C., Furr, J. M., & Comer, J.S. (2024). Intensive treatment of childhood selective mutism. In T. Davis & E. Storch (Eds.). *Brief CBT and science-based tailoring for children, adolescents, and young adults.* Berlin: Springer Nature.

Geppert, C. M. A. (2022, March 10). St. Dymphna: Patroness of psychiatry and mental illness. *Psychiatric Times.*

Geradt, M., Jahnke, S., Heinz, J., & Hoyer, J. (2018). Is contact with children related to legitimizing beliefs toward sex with children among men with pedophilia? *Archives of Sexual Behavior, 47*(2), 375–387.

Gerlach, J. (2023, October 9). How we may be letting kids with behavioral diagnoses down: Oppositional defiant disorder—or misunderstood? *Psychology Today.*

Gerrard, Y. (2020, March 9). TikTok has a pro-anorexia problem. *Wired.* Retrieved from https://www.wired.com/story/opinion-tiktok-has-a-pro-anorexia-problem.

Gerszberg, C. O. (2022, October 13). A mindful guide to navigating difficult emotions. *Mindful.*

Geurts, D. E. M., Van den Heuvel, T. J., Huys, Q. J. M., Verkes, R. J., & Cools, R. (2022). Amygdala response predicts clinical symptom reduction in patients with borderline personality disorder: A pilot fMRI study. *Frontiers in Behavioral Neuroscience, 16,* 938403.

Gharat, R., Dixit, G., Khambete, M., & Prabhu, A. (2024). Targets, trials and tribulations in Alzheimer therapeutics. *European Journal of Pharmacology, 962,* 176230.

Ghiasi, N., Azhar, Y., & Singh, J. (2023, March 30). Psychiatric illness and criminality. *StatPearls.*

Ghosh, D., Bhattacharya, S., Raj, S., Singh, T., Verma, S. K., & Arya, Y. K. (2023). Application of mindfulness-based cognitive therapy on suicidal behavior: A case study. In C. R. Martin, V. B. Patel, & V. R. Preedy (Eds.). *Handbook of cognitive behavioral therapy by disorder* (Chap. 45, pp. 491–497). New York: Academic Press.

Giacomini, J. L., Sadeghian, K., & Baldo, B. A. (2022). Eating driven by the gustatory insula: Contrasting regulation by infralimbic vs. prelimbic cortices. *Neuropsychopharmacology, 47*(7), 1358–1366.

Giangrande, E. J., Weber, R. S., & Turkheimer, E. (2022). What do we know about the genetic architecture of psychopathology? *Annual Review of Clinical Psychology, 18,* 19–42.

Giardina, E.-G. (2023, August 7). Cardiovascular effects of caffeine and caffeinated beverages. *UpToDate.* Retrieved from http://www.uptodate.com.

Gillespie, C. F. (2022). Neurochemistry of mood disorders. In C. B. Nemeroff, A. F. Schatzberg, N. Rasgon, & S. M. Strakowski (Eds.). *The American Psychiatric Association Publishing textbook of mood disorders* (2nd ed., Chap. 5). Washington, DC: American Psychiatric Association Publishing.

Gillespie, C., Murphy, M., & Joyce, M. (2022). Dialectical behavior therapy for individuals with borderline personality disorder: A systematic review of outcomes after one year of follow-up. *Journal of Personality Disorders, 36*(4), 431–454.

Gillette, H. (2022, February 15). Do people with bipolar disorder think more often about suicide? *PsychCentral.* Retrieved from https://psychcentral.com/bipolar/suicide-in-bipolar-disorder.

Gillson, S. (2023, February 2). Causes and risk factors of peptic ulcer disease. *Verywell Health.* Retrieved from https://www.verywellhealth.com.

Gindt, M., Fernandez, A., Battista, M., & Askenazy, F. (2021). [Psychiatric consequences of Covid 19 pandemic in the pediatric population]. *Neuropsychiatrie de l'Enfance et de l'Adolescence, 69*(3), 115–120.

Girgis, R. R., Rogers, R. T., Hesson, H., Lieberman, J. A., Appelbaum, P. S., & Brucato, G. (2023). Mass murders involving firearms and other methods in school, college, and university settings: Findings from the Columbia Mass Murder Database. *Journal of Forensic Sciences, 68*(1), 207–211.

Gjerdalen, O. S., Lystad, J. U., Bull, H., Ringen, P. A., Rossberg, J. I., Martinsen, E. W., . . . Evensen, S. (2023). Vocational rehabilitation augmented with cognitive behavioral therapy or cognitive remediation for individuals with schizophrenia: A 5-year follow-up study. *Nordic Journal of Psychiatry, 77*(1), 223–30.

Glick, I. D., Cerfolio, N. E., Kamis, D., & Laurence, M. (2021). Domestic mass shooters: The association with unmedicated and untreated psychiatric illness. *Journal of Clinical Psychopharmacology, 41*(4), 366–369.

Glick, I. D., Zamora, D., Davis, J. M., Suryadevara, U., Goldenson, A., & Kamis, D. (2020). Are patients with schizophrenia better off with lifetime antipsychotic medication? Replication of a naturalistic, long-term, follow-up study of antipsychotic treatment. *Journal of Clinical Psychopharmacology, 40*(2), 145–148.

Glina, F., Carvalho, J., Barroso, R., & Cardoso, D. (2022). Lay people's myths regarding pedophilia and child sexual abuse: A systematic review. *Sexual Medicine Reviews, 10*(4), 596–619.

GlobeNewswire. (2022). *Overview of the $58 billion U.S. weight loss market 2022.* Retrieved from https://www.globenewswire.com.

Glynn, L. M., Davis, E. P., Luby, J. L., Baram, T. Z., & Sandman, C. A. (2021). A predictable home environment may protect child mental health during the COVID-19 pandemic. *Neurobiology of Stress, 14,* 100291.

Gmelin, J. H., De Vries, Y. A., Baams, L., Aguilar-Gaxiola, S., Alonso, J., Borges, G., . . . WHO World Mental Health Survey Collaborators (2022). Increased risks for mental disorders among LGB individuals: Cross-national evidence from the World Mental Health Surveys. *Social Psychiatry and Psychiatric Epidemiology, 57*(11), 2319–2332.

Godart, N., Dorard, G., Duclos, J., Curt, F., Kaganski, I., Minier, L., . . . Berthoz, S. (2022). Long-term follow-up of a randomized controlled trial comparing systemic family therapy (FT-S) added to treatment as usual (TAU) with TAU alone in adolescents with anorexia nervosa. *Journal of Child Psychology and Psychiatry, 63*(11), 1368–1380.

Godena, E. J., Perez, D. L., Crain, L. D., Fishel, A. K., Flaherty, A., Harley, R., & Cohen, J. N. (2021). Psychotherapy for functional neurological (conversion) disorder: A case bridging mind, brain, and body. *Journal of Clinical Psychiatry, 82*(6), 21ct14246.

Goetz, K., Kleine-Budde, K., Bramesfeld, A., & Stegbauer, C. (2018). Working atmosphere, job satisfaction and individual characteristics of community mental health professionals in integrated care. *Health & Social Care in the Community, 26*(2), 176–181.

Goff, D. C. (2020). Promising evidence of antipsychotic efficacy without dopamine D2-receptor binding. *New England Journal of Medicine, 382*(16), 1555–1556.

Goff, D. C. (2021). The pharmacologic treatment of schizophrenia—2021. *JAMA, 325*(2), 175–176.

Golberstein, E., Wen, H., & Miller, B. F. (2020). Coronavirus disease 2019 (COVID-19) and mental health for children and adolescents. *JAMA Pediatrics, 174*(9), 819–820.

Goldman, H. H. (2022). How phantom networks and other barriers impede progress on mental health insurance reform. *Health Affairs, 41*(7), 1023–1025.

Goldstein, J. (2022, December 2). How hospitals respond when mentally ill people come in from the streets. *New York Times.*

Goldstein, T. R., Merranko, J., Rode, N., Sylvester, R., Hotkowski, N., Fersch-Podrat, R., . . . Birmaher, B. (2024). Dialectical behavior therapy for adolescents with bipolar disorder: A randomized clinical trial. *JAMA Psychiatry, 81*(1), 15–24. https://doi.org/10.1001/jamapsychiatry.2023.3399.

Gomez Rincon, M., Leslie, S. W., & Lotfollahzadeh, S. (2023, June 26). Nocturnal enuresis. *StatPearls.*

Gonzalez, D., Mirabal, A. B., & McCall, J. D. (2023, July 4). Child abuse and neglect. *StatPearls.*

González, R., Carvacho, H., & Jiménez-Moya, G. (2022). Psychology and indigenous people. *Annual Review of Psychology, 73,* 431–459.

Gonzalez-Rodriguez, A., Seeman, M. V., Izquierdo, E., Natividad, M., Guardia, A., Roman, E., & Monreal, J. A. (2022). Delusional disorder in old age: A hypothesis-driven review of recent work focusing on epidemiology, clinical aspects, and outcomes. *International Journal of Environmental Research and Public Health, 19*(13), 7911.

Goodwin, G., Woodyatt, J., Salva, C., & Allen, D. (2024). Substance use and impulse control disorders. In M. W. Parsons & M. M. Braun (Eds.). *Clinical neuropsychology: A pocket handbook for assessment* (4th ed., Chap. 23). Washington, DC: American Psychological Association.

Gordon, A. M., & Mendes, W. B. (2021, July 29). A large-scale study of stress, emotions, and blood pressure in daily life using a digital platform. *PNAS, 118*(31), e2105573118.

Gordon, S. (2020, January 5). 8 motives behind why kids cyberbully. *Verywell Family.* Retrieved from https://www.verywellfamily.com.

Gordon, S. (2020, April 20). 6 things every teen needs to know about sexting. *Verywell Family.* Retrieved from https://www.verywellfamily.com.

Gorelick, D. A. (2022, October 7). Cannabis use disorder in adults. *UpToDate.* Retrieved from http://www.uptodate.com.

Gorelick, D. A. (2023, November 10). Cannabis use: Epidemiology, pharmacology, comorbidities, and adverse effects. *UpToDate.* Retrieved from http://www.uptodate.com.

Gorelick, D. A. (2023, October 23). Cannabis withdrawal. *UpToDate.* Retrieved from http://www.uptodate.com.

Gorenstein, D. (2013, May 17). *How much is the DSM-5 worth? Marketplace.org.*

Gorrell, S., Simic, M., & Le Grange, D. (2023). Toward the integration of family therapy and family-based treatment for eating disorders. In P. Robinson, T. Wade, B. Herpertz-Dahlann, F. Fernandez-Aranda, J. Treasure, & S. Wonderlich (Eds.). *Eating disorders.* Edinburgh: Springer.

Gorun, A. A., Scherban, B. A., & Auchincloss, E. L. (2022). Narcissistic personality disorder. In R. Feinstein (Ed.). *Personality disorders* (Chap. 21). New York: Oxford University Press.

Gosling, S. D., Sandy, C. J., & Potter, J. (2015, April 28). Personalities of self-identified "dog people" and "cat people." *Anthrozoös, 23*(3), 213–222.

Gotlib, I. H., Miller, J. G., Borchers, L. R., Coury, S. M., Costello, L. A., Garcia, J. M., & Ho, T. C. (2022, December 1). Effects of the COVID-19 pandemic on mental health and brain maturation in adolescents: Implications for analyzing longitudinal data. *Biological Psychiatry Global Open Science, 3*(4), 912–918.

Gottesman, I. I. (1991). *Schizophrenia genesis.* New York: Freeman.

Gottlieb, D. J., Shiner, B., Hoyt, J. E., Riblet, N. B., Peltzman, T., Teja, N., & Watts, B. V. (2023). A comparison of mortality rates for buprenorphine versus methadone treatments for opioid use disorder. *Acta Psychiatrica Scandinavica, 147*(1), 6–15.

Goulian, A., Jauffret-Roustide, M., Dambélé, S., Singh, R., & Fullilove, R. E., III. (2022). A cultural and political difference: Comparing the racial and social framing of population crack cocaine use between the United States and France. *Harm Reduction Journal, 19,* 44.

Gourinat, A., Mazeaud, C., Hubert, J., Eschwege, P., & Koscinski, I. (2023, January 14). Impact of paternal age on assisted reproductive technology outcomes and offspring health: A systematic review. *Andrology, 11*(6), 973–986.

Grabb, D. J., & Angelotta, C. (2023). Emerging forensic implications of the artificial intelligence revolution. *Journal of the American Academy of Psychiatry and the Law, 51*(4), 475–479.

Graham, C., & Bancroft, J. (2020). The sexual dysfunction and paraphilias. In J. R. Geddes, N. C. Andreason, & G. M. Goodwin (Eds.). *New Oxford textbook of psychiatry* (3rd ed., Chap. 115). New York: Oxford University Press.

Graham, J. (2023, March 10). Seniors with anxiety frequently don't get help. Here's why. *Kaiser Health News.* Retrieved from https://kffhealthnews.org/news/article/seniors-anxiety-disorder-screening-mental-health-navigating-aging.

Grant, J. E., & Chamberlain, S. R. (2020). OCPD and its relationship to impulsivity and impulse-control disorders. In J. E. Grant, A. Pinto, & S. R. Chamberlain (Eds.). *Obsessive-compulsive personality disorder* (Chap. 5, pp. 85–98). Washington, DC: American Psychiatric Association Publishing.

Grashow, R., Weisskopf, M. G., Baggish, A., Speizer, F. E., Whittington, A. J., Nadler, L., . . . Pascual-Leone, A. (2020). Premortem chronic traumatic encephalopathy diagnoses in professional football. *Annals of Neurology, 88*(1), 106–112.

Grasso, D. J. (2022). Adverse childhood experiences and traumatic stress disorders. In J. G. Beck & D. M. Sloan (Eds.). *The Oxford handbook of traumatic stress disorders* (Chap. 8). New York: Oxford University Press.

Gray, H. (1959). *Anatomy of the human body* (27th ed.). Philadelphia: Lea & Febiger.

Greenberg, D. B. (2016, January 27). Somatization, epidemiology, pathogenesis, clinical features, medical evaluation, and diagnosis. *UpToDate.* Retrieved from https://www.uptodate.com.

Greenburgh, A., & Raihani, N. J. (2022). Paranoia and conspiracy thinking. *Current Opinion in Psychology, 47,* 101362.

Greenwood, T. A. (2020, February 10). Creativity and bipolar disorder: A shared genetic vulnerability. *Annual Review of Clinical Psychology, 16*(12), 1–26.

Greer, M. (2022, March 29). Anxiety and depression are biggest concerns for patients with cancer, survivors, caregivers. *ONS Voice.* Retrieved from https://voice.ons.org/news-and-views.

Greer, T. L., & Small, H. (2022). Exercise. In S. M. McClintock & J. Choi (Eds.). *Neuropsychology of depression* (Chap. 19). New York: Guilford Press.

Grieco, S. F., Holmes, T. C., & Xu, X. (2023, March 23). Probing neural circuit mechanisms in Alzheimer's disease using novel technologies. *Molecular Psychiatry.* doi:10.1038/s41380-023-02018-x. [Online ahead of print]

Griffiths, C., da Silva, K. M., Leathlean, C., Jiang, H., Ang, C. S., & Searle, R. (2022, April). Investigation of physical activity, sleep, and mental health recovery in treatment resistant depression (TRD) patients receiving repetitive transcranial magnetic stimulation (rTMS) treatment. *Journal of Affective Disorders Reports, 8,* 100337.

Grifoni, A., Alonzi, T., Alter, G., Noonan, D. M., Landay, A. L., Albini, A., & Goletti, D. (2023). Impact of aging on immunity in the context of COVID-19, HIV, and tuberculosis. *Frontiers in Immunology, 14,* 1146704.

Grigg, J. R. (1988). Imitative suicides in an active duty military population. *Military Medicine, 153*(2), 79–81.

Grimm, D. (2021, January 12). How many mice and rats are used in U.S. labs? Controversial study says more than 100 million. *Science,* 2489116.

Grimm, K. J., & Widaman, K. F. (2023). Construct validity. In H. Cooper, M. N. Coutanche, L. M. McMullen, A. T. Panter, D. Rindskopf, & K. J. Sher (Eds.). *APA handbook of research methods in psychology: Foundations, planning, measures, and psychometrics* (pp. 769–791). Washington, DC: American Psychological Association.

Gringer, B. (2020). *The deadliest known natural disasters.* Savannah, GA: Titlemax.

Groenewoud, A. S., Atsma, F., Arvin, M., Westert, G. P., & Boer, T. A. (2021). Euthanasia in the Netherlands: A claims data cross-sectional study of geographical variation. *BMJ Supportive and Palliative Care.* doi:10.1136/bmjspcare-2020-002573. [Epub ahead of print]

Groopman, J. (2017, January 9). The voices in our heads. *The New Yorker.*

Grossberg, G., Urganus, A., Schein, J., Bunday, R., Cloutier, M., Gauthier-Loiselle, M., . . . Aggarwal, J. (2024). A real-world assessment of healthcare costs associated with agitation in Alzheimer's dementia. *Journal of Medical Economics, 27*(1), 99–108.

Grover, S. (2023, August 25). 3 signs you're eccentric, and 3 reasons that's a good thing. *Psychology Today.*

Guarda, A. (2023, May 13). Eating disorders: Overview of epidemiology, clinical features, and diagnosis. *UpToDate.* Retrieved from https://www.uptodate.com.

Guetterman, T. C., & Perez, A. (2023). Mixed methods research in psychology. In H. Cooper, M. N. Coutanche, L. M. McMullen, A. T. Panter, D. Rindskopf, & K. J. Sher (Eds.). *APA handbook of research methods in psychology: Vol. 2. Research designs: Quantitative, qualitative, neuropsychological, and biological* (2nd ed., Chap. 12). Washington, DC: American Psychological Association.

Guglielmo, R., & Hasler, G. (2022). The neuroprotective and neuroplastic potential of glutamatergic therapeutic drugs in bipolar disorder. *Neuroscience and Biobehavioral Review, 142,* 104906.

Guinart, D., & Correll, C. U. (2020). Antipsychotic polypharmacy in schizophrenia: Why not? *Journal of Clinical Psychiatry, 81*(3), 19ac13118.

Gulens, M. (2022, July 14). It matters why you meditate. *Mindful.*

Guttmacher Institute. (2023, February 1). *Substance use during pregnancy.* Retrieved from https://www.guttmacher.org/state-policy/explore.

HA (HealthInAging). (2020). *Nursing homes.* New York: Author.

HA (HealthInAging). (2023). *Nursing homes.* New York: Author.

Ha, T., Tadi, P., & Dubensky, L. (2023, July 3). Neurosyphilis. *StatPearls.*

Haft, S. L., O'Grady, S. M., Shaller, E. A. L., & Liu, N. H. (2022). Cultural adaptations of dialectical behavior therapy: A systematic review. *Journal of Consulting and Clinical Psychology, 90*(10), 787–801.

Hageman, G., Hageman, I., & Nihorn, J. (2024). Chronic traumatic encephalopathy in soccer players: Review of 14 cases. *Clinical Journal of Sport Medicine, 34*(1), 69–80.

Hahlweg, K., & Baucom, D. H. (2022, March 16). Family therapy for persons with schizophrenia: Neglected yet important. *European Archives of Psychiatry and Clinical Neuroscience, 273*(4), 819–824.

Hahn, P. (2020, January 10). The real myth of the schizophrenogenic mother. *Mad in America.* Retrieved from https://www.madinamerica.com.

Hajek, A., König, H.-H., Blessmann, M., & Grupp, K. (2023). Prevalence and determinants of depressive and anxiety symptoms among transgender people: Results of a survey. *Healthcare (Basel), 11*(5), 705.

Hakamata, Y., Suzuki, Y., Kobachikawa, H., & Hori, H. (2022). Neurobiology of early life adversity: A systematic review of meta-analyses towards an integrative account of its neurobiological trajectories to mental disorders. *Frontiers in Neuroendocrinology, 65,* 100994.

Hakulinen, C., Webb, R. T., Pedersen, C. B., Agerbo, E., & Mok, P. L. H. (2020). Association between parental income during childhood and risk of schizophrenia later in life. *JAMA Psychiatry, 77*(1), 17–24.

Halaris, A., & Cook, J. (2023). The glutamatergic system in treatment-resistant depression and comparative effectiveness of ketamine and esketamine: Role of inflammation? *Advances in Experimental Medicine and Biology, 1411,* 487–512.

Halcomb, M., Yoder, K., & Cyders, M. (2022). Linking the neural correlates of addiction and negative urgency. In V. B. Patel & V. R. Preedy (Eds.). *Handbook of substance misuse and addictions: From biology to public health* (pp. 513–536). New York: Springer.

Hall, L., & Cohn, L. (2010). *Bulimia: A guide to recovery.* Carlsbad, CA: Gurze Books.

Hallward, L., Nagata, J. M., Rodgers, R. F., & Ganson, K. T. (2022, December 9). Examination of eating disorder psychopathology across sexual and gender identities among a Canadian sample. *International Journal of Eating Disorders.* https://doi.org/10.1002/eat.23872. [Online ahead of print]

Hamilton, L. G., & Petty, S. (2023). Compassionate pedagogy for neurodiversity in higher education: A conceptual analysis. *Frontiers in Psychology, 14,* 1093290.

Hamilton, S. S. (2022, June 2). Developmental coordination disorder: Clinical features and diagnosis. *UpToDate.* Retrieved from https://www.uptodate.com.

Hamilton, S. S. (2023, August 30). Reading difficulty in children: Clinical features and evaluation. *UpToDate.* Retrieved from https://www.uptodate.com.

Hamilton, S. S. (2023, March 22). Reading difficult in children: Normal reading development and etiology of reading difficulty. *UpToDate.* Retrieved from https://www.uptodate.com.

Hammad, A. M., Bachu, R. D., Muskiewicz, D. E., Hall, F. S., & Tiwari, A. K. (2022). Alcohol and cocaine co-use. In V. B. Patel & V. R. Preedy (Eds.). *Handbook of substance misuse and addictions: From biology to public health* (pp. 2797–2815). New York: Springer.

Hammarberg, S. I., Finn, S. W., Rosendahl, I., Andréasson, S., Jayaram-Lindström, N., & Hammarberg, A. (2023, September 2). Behavioural self-control training versus motivational enhancement therapy for individuals with alcohol use disorder with a goal of controlled drinking: A randomized controlled trial. *Addiction, 119*(1), 86–101. doi:10.1111/add.16325. [Online ahead of print]

Hammen, C. (2016). Depression and stressful environments: Identifying gaps in conceptualization and measurement. *Anxiety, Stress & Coping, 29*(4), 335–351.

Hammen, C. (2018). Risk factors for depression: An autobiographical review. *Annual Review of Clinical Psychology, 14*(1), 1–28.

Hampton, T. (2022, January 4). Study holds warning on pandemic drinking. *Harvard Gazette.* Retrieved from https://news.harvard.edu/gazette/story/2022/01/covid-related-drinking-linked-to-rise-in-liver-disease.

Hamwey, M. K., Gargano, L. M., Friedman, L. G., Leon, L. F., Petrsoric, L. J., & Brackbill, R. M. (2020). Post-traumatic stress disorder among survivors of the September 11, 2001 World Trade Center attacks: A review of the literature. *International Journal of Environmental Research and Public Health, 17*(12), 4344.

Han, B., Einstein, E. B., Jones, C. M., Cotto, J., Compton, W. M., & Volkow, N. D. (2022). Racial and ethnic disparities in drug overdose deaths in the US during the COVID-19 pandemic. *JAMA Network Open, 5*(9), e2232314.

Handrick, L. (2020, April 21). *Mental health in the workplace: Stats & trends.* Choosing Therapy. https://www.choosingtherapy.com/mental-health-in-the-workplace.

Hangen, M. M., Romero, A. N., Norris, H. M., Gorycki, K. A., Roberts, B. R., & Neidert, P. L. (2023). An assessment of token value and effectiveness: A replication. *Journal of Applied Behavior Analysis, 56*(4), 898–913.

Hany, M., Rehman, B., Ashar, Y., & Chapman, J. (2023, March 20). Schizophrenia. *StatPearls.*

Hao, R., Zhang, M., Zuo, J., Qi, Y., & Hu, J. (2023). Contribution of coping style to the association between illness uncertainty and demoralisation in patients with breast cancer, a cross-sectional mediation analysis. *BMJ Open, 13*(3), e065796.

Harada, T., Aikawa, Y., Takahama, M., Yumoto, Y., Umeno, M., Hasegawa, Y., . . . Asukai, N. (2022). A 12-session relapse prevention program vs. psychoeducation in the treatment of Japanese alcoholic patients: A randomized controlled trial. *Neuropsychopharmacology Reports, 42*(2), 205–212.

Harb, F., Bird, C. M., Webb, E. K., Torres, L., deRoon-Cassini, T. A., & Larson, C. L. (2023). Experiencing racial discrimination increases vulnerability to PTSD after trauma via peritraumatic dissociation. *European Journal of Psychotraumatology, 14*(2), 2211486.

Hardy, K. V., & Turkington, D. (Eds.). (2024). *Decoding delusions: A clinician's guide to working with delusions and other extreme beliefs.* Washington, DC: American Psychiatric Association.

Hare, R. D. (1993). *Without conscience: The disturbing world of the psychopaths among us.* New York: Pocket Books.

Hare, S. M. (2021). Hallucinations: A functional network model of how sensory representations become selected for conscious awareness in schizophrenia. *Frontiers in Neuroscience, 13,* 733038.

Hare, S. M., Benzer, S., Knight, S. R., Rouhakhtar, P. R., Reeves, G. M., McDonald, K., & RachBeisel, J. (2024). Virtual civil commitment hearings: Convenience at the cost of compromised communication and safety assessments. *Psychiatric Services, 75*(1), 3–5.

Haris, E. M., Bryant, R. A., Williamson, T., & Korgaonkar, M. S. (2023, October 16). Functional connectivity of amygdala subnuclei in PTSD: A narrative review. *Molecular Psychiatry.* doi:10.1038/s41380-023-02291-w. [Open access]

Harkness, A., & Pachankis, J. E. (2022). Supervision and consultation in delivery of cognitive behavior therapy to LGBTQ individuals. In E. A. Storch, J. S. Abramowitz, & D. McKay (Eds.). *Training and supervision in specialized cognitive behavior therapy: Methods, settings, and populations* (Chap. 19). Washington, DC: American Psychological Association.

Harmon-Jones, E., Amodio, D. M., Gable, P. A., & Dikker, S. (2023). Electro- and magnetoencephalographic methods in psychology. In H. Cooper, M. N. Coutanche, L. M. McMullen, A. T. Panter, D. Rindskopf, & K. J. Sher (Eds.). *APA handbook of research methods in psychology: Foundations, planning, measures, and psychometrics* (pp. 581–604). Washington, DC: American Psychological Association.

Haroon, H., Wolfe, N., Feizi, S., & Barboriak, P. (2023). Assessing two decades of insanity acquittee release from the North Carolina forensic program. *Journal of the American Academy of Psychiatry and the Law, 51*(3), 342–352.

Harrell, L., & Nam-Sonenstein, B. (2023, June 8). Unhoused and under arrest: How Atlanta polices poverty. *Prison Policy Initiative.* Retrieved from https://www.prisonpolicy.org/blog.

Harris Poll. (2008, February 8). *Three in ten Americans with a tattoo say having one makes them feel sexier.* Harris Poll No. 15. New York: Harris Interactive.

Harris Poll. (2013, May 30). *Are you happy? It may depend on age, race/ethnicity and other factors* (Harris Poll #30). New York: Harris Interactive.

Harris Poll. (2015, June 3). *Older Americans, those who are religious, and even political party members are happier* (Harris Poll #30). New York: Harris Interactive.

Harris Poll. (2016, July 8). *Latest happiness index reveals American happiness at all-time low* (Harris Poll #50). New York: Harris Interactive.

Hash, K. M., & Hicks Patrick, J. (2024). Health disparities among older adults: An introduction to the special issue. *International Journal of Aging and Human Development, 98*(1), 3–9.

Hashemi, D., & Gray, K. (2023). Cannabis use disorder in adolescents. *Child and Adolescent Psychiatric Clinics of North America, 32*(1), 13–20.

Hasin, D. S., Sarvey, A. L., Meyers, J. L., Saha, T., Ruan, W. J., Stohl, M., & Grant, B. F. (2018). Epidemiology of adult DSM-5 major depressive disorder and its specifiers in the United States. *JAMA Psychiatry, 75*(4), 336–346.

Hassed, C. (2022, June 26). Mindfulness in medical education. *The Clinical Teacher.*

Hatoum, A. S., Colbert, S. M. C., Johnson, E. C., Huggett, S. B., Deak, J. D., Pathak, G. A., . . . Agrawal, A. (2023). *Nature Mental Health, 1,* 210–223.

Hausdorff, M. (2019). Understanding assistance in dying: Arguments in favor of the End of Life Option Act. *Culture, Society, and Praxis, 11*(2), 4.

Hawajri, O., Lindberg, J., & Suominen, S. (2023). Virtual reality exposure therapy as a treatment method against anxiety disorders and depression: A structured literature review. *Taylor & Francis Online, 44*(4), 245–269.

Hawes, D. J., & Allen, J. L. (2023, July 8). A developmental psychopathology perspective on adverse childhood experiences (ACEs): Introduction to the special issue. *Research on Child and Adolescent Psychopathology.* doi:10.1007/s10802-023-01100-w. [Online ahead of print]

Hawes, D. J., Gardner, F., Dadds, M. R., Frick, P. J., Kimonis, E. R., Burke, J. D., & Fairchild, G. (2023). Oppositional defiant disorder. *Nature Reviews Disease Primers, 9*(1), 31.

Hawker, C. O., Merkouris, S. S., Youssef, G. J., & Dowling, N. A. (2021). Exploring the associations between gambling cravings, self-efficacy, and gambling episodes: An ecological momentary assessment study. *Addictive Behaviors, 112,* 106574.

Hawton, K., Saunders, K. E. A., & Pitman, A. (2020). Prevention of suicide and treatment following self-harm. In J. R. Geddes, N. C. Andreason, & G. M. Goodwin (Eds.). *New Oxford textbook of psychiatry* (3rd ed., Chap. 128). New York: Oxford University Press.

Hayes, A., Herlinger, K., Paterson, L., & Lingford-Hughes, A. (2020). *The neurobiology of substance use and addiction: Evidence from neuroimaging and relevance to treatment.* New York: Cambridge University Press.

Hayes, S. C., Ciarrochi, J., Hofmann, S. G., Chin, F., & Sahdra, B. (2022). Evolving an idionomic approach to processes of change: Towards a unified personalized science of human improvement. *Behavioral Research and Therapy, 156,* 104155.

Hayes, S. C., & Hofmann, S. G. (2020, October 1). *Beyond the DSM: Toward a process-based alternative for diagnosis and mental health treatment.* Oakland, CA: Context Press.

Hayes, S. C., Hofmann, S. G., & Ciarrochi, J. (2023). The idionomic future of cognitive behavioral therapy: What stands out from criticisms of ACT development. *Behavior Therapy, 54*(6), 1036–1063.

Hazzard, V. M., Loth, K. A., Crosby, R. D., Wonderlich, S. A., Engel, S. G., Larson, N., & Newmark-Sztainer, D. (2023). Relative food abundance predicts greater binge-eating symptoms in subsequent hours among young adults experiencing food insecurity: Support for the "feast-or-famine" cycle hypothesis from an ecological momentary assessment study. *Appetite, 180,* 106316.

Hazzard, V. M., Loth, K. A., Hooper, L., & Becker, C. B. (2020). Food insecurity and eating disorders: A review of emerging evidence. *Current Psychiatry Reports, 22*(12), 74.

He, H., Cao, H., Huang, B., He, M., Ma, C., Yao, D., . . . Duan, M. (2021). Functional abnormalities of striatum are related to the season-specific effect on schizophrenia. *Brain Imaging and Behavior, 15*(5), 2347–2355.

Head, T. (2021). *Homeless, mentally ill and behind bars.* Governing.com. https://www.governing.com/now/homeless-mentally-ill-and-behind-bars.html

Healy, D, (2022). *Psychiatric drugs explained* (7th ed.). New York: Elsevier Health Sciences.

Heckers, S., Engstrom, E. J., & Kendler, K. S. (2022). "Manifestations of insanity": Kraepelin's final views on psychiatric nosology in their historical context. *Molecular Psychiatry, 27*(1), 328–334.

Hedya, S. A., Avula, A., & Swoboda, H. D. (2023, June 26). Lithium toxicity. *StatPearls.*

Heflin, M. T. (2023, October 20). Geriatric health maintenance. *UpToDate.* Retrieved from http://www.uptodate.com.

Heidenreich, T., Noyon, A., Worrell, M., & Menzies, R. (2021). Existential approaches and cognitive behavior therapy: Challenges and potential. *International Journal of Cognitive Therapy, 14,* 209–234.

Heilbrun, K., Giallella, C., Wright, H. J., DeMatteo, D., Griffin, P. A., Gowensmith, N., . . . Pietruszka, V. (2023). Appraising Jackson-based unrestorability to competence to stand trial: The demonstration model. *Psychological Services, 20*(3), 553–564.

Heiman, J. R. (2007). Orgasmic disorders in women. In S. R. Leiblum (Ed.). *Principles and practice of sex therapy* (4th ed., pp. 84–123). New York: Guilford Press.

Hellstrom, W. J. G., & DeLay, K. (2021, July 14). Male dyspareunia. *UpToDate.* Retrieved from http://www.uptodate.com.

Hendrickson, B., Girma, M., & Miller, L. (2020). Review of the clinical approach to the treatment of disruptive mood dysregulation disorder. *International Review of Psychiatry, 32*(3), 202–211.

Hennekens, C. H. (2022, August 25). Overview of primary prevention of cardiovascular disease. *UpToDate.* Retrieved from http://www.uptodate.com.

Henriksen, M. G., Nordgaard, J., & Jansson, L. B. (2017). Genetics of schizophrenia: Overview of methods, findings and limitations. *Frontiers in Human Neuroscience, 11,* 322.

Henry, P. (2023, September 22). Theoretical orientation means and counseling. *BetterHelp.*

Hensums, M., Overbeek, G., & Jorgensen, T. D. (2022). Not one sexual double standard but two? Adolescents' attitudes about appropriate sexual behavior. *Youth & Society, 54*(4), 23–42.

Herbenick, D., Fu, T.-C., Wasata, R., & Coleman, E. (2022, March 21). Masturbation prevalence, frequency, reasons, and associations with partnered sex in the midst of the COVID-19 pandemic: Findings from a U.S. nationally representative survey. *Archives of Sexual Behavior, 52*(3), 1317–1331.

Herbst, D. (2022, November 2). Schizophrenia in Black people: Racial disparities explained. *Psycom.* Retrieved from https://www.psycom.net.

Hereth, J. E., & Durand, B. (2022, July 31). Incorporating transgender-affirmative practice models into substance use treatment and prevention. *Journal of Social Work Practice in the Addictions.* https://doi.org/10.1080/1533256X.2022.2106736. [Online ahead of print]

Herian, M. (2022). Pharmacological action of LSD. In V. B. Patel & V. R. Preedy (Eds.). *Handbook of substance misuse and addictions: From biology to public health* (pp. 2457–2475). New York: Springer.

Herman, B. (2015, May 28). Fat-shaming and body-shaming, a history: Author talks thigh gaps, "Dad bods" and why we hate fat. *International Business Times.* Retrieved from https://www.ibtimes.com.

Hernandez, C. M., Moreno, O., Garcia-Rodriguez, I., Fuentes, L., & Nelson, T. (2022). The Hispanic paradox: A moderated mediation analysis of health conditions, self-rated health, and mental health among Mexicans and Mexican Americans. *Health Psychology and Behavioral Medicine, 10*(1), 180–198.

Herpertz, S. C., & Bertsch, K. (2022). Opportunities and challenges of new classification systems for personality disorders: Commentary on "clinical utility of the AMPD: A 10th year anniversary review." *Personality Disorders: Theory, Research, and Treatment, 13*(4), 380–382.

Herzog, P., Kube, T., & Fassbinder, E. (2022). How childhood maltreatment alters perception and cognition: The predictive processing account of borderline personality disorder. *Psychological Medicine, 52,* 2899–2916.

Heun-Johnson, H., Menchine, M., Axeen , S., Lung, K., Claudius, I., Wright, T., & Seabury, S. A. (2021). Association between race/ethnicity and disparities in health care use before first-episode psychosis among privately insured young patients. *JAMA Psychiatry, 78*(3), 311–319.

HHS (U.S. Department of Health and Human Services). (2021). *U.S. Surgeon General issues advisory on youth mental health crisis further exposed by COVID-19 pandemic.* Washington, DC: Author.

HHS (U.S. Department of Health and Human Services). (2023). *Contingency management for the treatment of substance use disorders: Enhancing access, quality, and program integrity for an evidence-based intervention.* Washington, DC: Author.

HHS (U.S. Department of Health and Human Services). (2023). *Informed consent FAQs.* Washington, DC: Author.

Higgins-Walsh, E. (2023, January 27). *What is augmentative and alternative communication and how can it benefit autistic people?* National Autistic Society. Retrieved from https://www.autism.org.uk/advice-and-guidance/professional-practice/aug-alt-comm.

Hildebrand, A. S., Roesmann, K., Planert, J., Machulska, A., Otto, E., & Klucken, T. (2022). Self-guided virtual reality therapy for social anxiety disorder: A study protocol for a randomized controlled trial. *Trials, 23*(1), 395.

Hill, C. E., Spiegel, S. B., Hoffman, M. A., Kivlighan, D. M., & Gelso, C. J. (2017, January 30). Therapist expertise in psychotherapy revisited. *The Counseling Psychologist, 45*(1), 99–112.

Hirsch, I. H. (2022, September). Erectile dysfunction. *Merckmanuals*. Retrieved from https://www.merckmanuals.com/professional/genitourinary-disorders.

Hirsch, I. H. (2023, June). Overview of male sexual function and dysfunction. *Merckmanuals*. Retrieved from https://www.merckmanuals.com/professional/genitourinary-disorders.

Hirsch, M., & Birnbaum, R. J. (2022, August 9). Sexual dysfunction caused by selective serotonin reuptake inhibitors (SSRIs): Management. *UpToDate*. Retrieved from http://www.uptodate.com.

Hirsch, M., & Birnbaum, R. J. (2023, July 31). Selective serotonin reuptake inhibitors: Pharmacology, administration, and side effects. *UpToDate*. Retrieved from https://www.uptodate.com.

Hoertel, N., Rotenberg, L., Blanco, C., Camus, V., Dubertret, C., Charlot, V., . . . CSA Study Group. (2021). A comprehensive model of predictors of quality of life in older adults with schizophrenia: Results from the CSA study. *Social Psychiatry and Psychiatric Epidemiology, 56*(8), 1411–1425.

Hoffmann, F., Linz, R., Steinbeis, N., Bauer, M., Dammering, F., Lazarides, C., . . . Heim, C. (2024). Children with maltreatment exposure exhibit rumination-like spontaneous thought patterns: Association with symptoms of depression, subcallosal cingulate cortex thickness, and cortisol levels. *Journal of Child Psychology and Psychiatry, 65*(1), 31–41.

Hoffman, R. J. (2023, October 12). MDMA (ecstasy) intoxication. *UpToDate*. Retrieved from http://www.uptodate.com.

Hofmann, S. G. (2023, September 15). Social anxiety disorder in adults: Psychotherapy. *UpToDate*. Retrieved from https://www.uptodate.com.

Hogan, R. A. (1968). The implosive technique. *Behavioral Research and Therapy, 6*, 423–431.

Hogarth, S., Manning, E., & van den Buuse, M. (2022). Chronic methamphetamine and psychosis pathways. In V. B. Patel & V. R. Preedy (Eds.). *Handbook of substance misuse and addictions: From biology to public health* (pp. 2121–2146). New York: Springer.

Hogrefe. (2023, January 25). *The dark triad of personality at work: Why do organizations need to know about it?* Retrieved from https://www.hogrefe.com/us/article/the-dark-triad-of-personality-at-work-why-do-organizations-need-to-know-about-it.

Hogue, A., Bobek, M., Porter, N., Dauber, S., Southam-Gerow, M. A., McLeod, B. D., & Henderson, C. E. (2021, September 14). Core elements of family therapy for adolescent behavioral health problems: Validity generalization in community settings. *Journal of Clinical Child & Adolescent Psychology*, https://doi.org/10.1080/15374416.2021.1969939.

Holbrook, H. M., & Hudziak, J. J. (2020). Risk factors that predict longitudinal patterns of substantiated and unsubstantiated maltreatment reports. *Child Abuse & Neglect, 99*, 104279.

Holden, L. R., & Tanenbaum, G. J. (2023). Modern assessments of intelligence must be fair and equitable. *Journal of Intelligence, 11*(6), 126.

Holm, M., Taipale, H., Tanskanen, A., Tiihonen, J., & Mitterdorfer-Rutz, E. (2021). Employment among people with schizophrenia or bipolar disorder: A population-based study using nationwide registers. *Acta Psychiatrica Scandinavica, 143*(1), 61–71.

Holmes, T. H., & Rahe, R. H. (1967). The Social Readjustment Rating Scale. *Journal of Psychosomatic Research, 11*, 213–218.

Holmes, T. H., & Rahe, R. H. (1989). The Social Readjustment Rating Scale. In T. H. Holmes & E. M. David (Eds.). *Life change, life events, and illness: Selected papers*. New York: Praeger.

Holt, S. R. (2023, November 14). Alcohol use disorder: Pharmacologic management. *UpToDate*. Retrieved from http://www.uptodate.com.

Holtzheimer, P. E. (2022, January 20). Unipolar depression in adults: Treatment with surgical approaches. *UpToDate*. Retrieved from http://www.uptodate.com.

Holtzheimer, P. E. (2023, February 15). Unipolar depression in adults: Indications, efficacy, and safety of transcranial magnetic stimulation (TMS). *UpToDate*. Retrieved from https://www.uptodate.com.

Holtzheimer, P. E. (2023, August 23). Unipolar depression in adults: Overview of neuromodulation procedures. *UpToDate*. Retrieved from https://www.uptodate.com.

Holze, F., Erne, L., Duthaler, U., & Liechti, M. E. (2023, August 18). Pharmacokinetics, pharmacodynamics and urinary recovery of oral lysergic acid diethylamide administration in healthy participants. *British Journal of Clinical Pharmacology*. doi:10.1111/bcp.15887. [Online ahead of print]

Holze, F., Ley, L., Müller, F., Becker, A. M., Straumann, I., Vizell, P., . . . Liechti, M. (2022). Direct comparison of the acute effects of lysergic acid diethylamide and psilocybin in a double-blind placebo-controlled study in healthy subjects. *Neuropsychopharmacology, 47*(6), 1180–1187.

Holze, F., Vizeli, P., Müller, F., Ley, L., Duerig, R., Varghese, N., . . . Liechti, M. E. (2020). Distinct acute effects of LSD, MDMA, and d-amphetamine in healthy subjects. *Neuropsychopharmacology, 45*(3), 462–471.

Hong, C., Hoskin, J., Berteau, L. K., Schamel, J. T., Wu, E. S. C., . . . Frew, P. M. (2023). Violence victimization, homelessness, and severe mental illness among people who use opioids in three U.S. cities. *Journal of Interpersonal Violence, 38*(19–20), 11165–11185.

Hong, J. S., Chen, J.-K., Wang, S.-C., Lee, J. M., Algood, C. L., & Voisin, D. R. (2021). What types of delinquent activities are bullies, victims, and bully/victims in urban neighborhoods most likely involved in? *Journal of Pediatric Nursing, 59*, 55–62.

Hong, J. S., Hyun, S. Y., Lee, J. H., & Sim, M. (2022). Mental health effects of the Gangwon wildfires. *BMC Public Health, 22*(1), 1183.

Hong, N., Herrera, A., Furr, J. M., Georgiadis, C., Cristello, J., Heymann, P., . . . Comer, J. S. (2023). Remote intensive group behavioral treatment for families of children with selective mutism. *Evidence-Based Practice in Child and Adolescent Mental Health, 8*(4), 439–458.

Hong, N., Sanchez, A., & Comer, J. S. (2020). Multi-media field test: Can users strike out OCD with the NOCD app? *Cognitive and Behavioral Practice, 27*(1), 93–99.

Hood, R. W., Jr. (2022). The history and current status of the psychology of religion and spirituality). In L. J. Miller (Ed.). *The Oxford handbook of psychology and spirituality* (2nd ed., Chap. 1). New York: Oxford University Press.

Horowitz, J. M., Brown, A., & Cox, K. (2019). *Race in America 2019*. Washington, DC: Pew Research Center.

Horton, A. P. (2020, March 6). How burnout affects mental health workers. *BBC Worklife*. https://www.bbc.com/worklife/article/20200305.

Howarth, J. (2024, January 2). 57+ incredible smartphone addiction statistics for 2024. *Exploding Topics*. https://explodingtopics.com/blog/smartphone-addiction-stats.

Howell, E. F. (2011). *Understanding and treating dissociative identity disorder: A rational approach*. New York: Routledge/Taylor & Francis Group.

Howell, E. (2020). *Trauma and dissociation informed psychotherapy: Relational healing and the therapeutic connection*. New York: W. W. Norton.

Howe-Martin, L., Knox-Rice, T., Denman, D., & Brown, E. S. (2022). Depression and comorbid medical illness. In S. M. McClintock & J. Choi (Eds.). *Neuropsychology of depression* (Chap. 5). New York: Guilford Press.

Howes, L. (2022, January 24). Many of our proteins remain hidden in the dark proteome. *Chemical & Engineering News, 100*(3).

HP (Healthy People). (2023). *Access to health services*. Retrieved from https://health.gov/healthypeople/priority-areas/social-determinants-health/literature-summaries/access-health-services.

HP (Healthy People). (2023). *Poverty*. Retrieved from https://health.gov/healthypeople/priority-areas-social-determinants-health/literature-summaries/poverty.

Hsu, C. (2022). *Study explores pandemic-related shifts in alcohol sales across 16 U.S. states*. Buffalo, NY: University at Buffalo.

Hsu, M., Martin, B., Ahmed, S., Torous, J., & Suzuki, J. (2022). Smartphone ownership, smartphone utilization, and interest in using mental health apps to address substance use disorders: Literature review and cross-sectional study across two sites. *JMIR Formative Research, 6*(7), e38684.

Hu, Y., Quizley, B. M., & Taylor, D. (2021). Human mobility data and machine learning reveal geographic differences in alcohol sales and alcohol outlet visits across U.S. states during COVID-19. *PLoS ONE, 16*(12), e0255757.

Huang, J. (2023, February). Alzheimer disease. *Merck Manual Professional Version*. Retrieved from https://www.merckmanuals.com/professional/neurologic-disorders/delirium-and-dementia.

Huang, J. (2023, February). Behavioral and psychologic symptoms of dementia. *Merck Manual Professional Version*. Retrieved from https://www.merckmanuals.com/professional/neurologic-disorders/delirium-and-dementia.

Huang, J. (2023, February). Chronic traumatic encephalopathy (CTE) (Dementia pugilistica). *Merck Manual Professional Version*. Retrieved from https://www.merckmanuals.com/professional/neurologic-disorders/delirium-and-dementia.

Huang, J. (2023, February). Delirium. *Merck Manual Professional Version*. Retrieved from https://www.merckmanuals.com/professional/neurologic-disorders.

Huang, J. (2023, February). Dementia with Lewy bodies and Parkinson disease dementia. *Merck Manual Professional Version*. Retrieved from https://www.merckmanuals.com/professional/neurologic-disorders/delirium-and-dementia.

Huang, J. (2023, February). Frontotemporal dementia (FTD). *Merck Manual Professional Version*. Retrieved from https://www.merckmanuals.com/professional/neurologic-disorders/delirium-and-dementia.

Huang, J. (2023, February). HIV-associated dementia. *Merck Manual Professional Version*. Retrieved from https://www.merckmanuals.com/professional/neurologic-disorders/delirium-and-dementia.

Huang, J. (2023, February). Vascular cognitive impairment and dementia. *Merck Manual Professional Version*. Retrieved from https://www.merckmanuals.com/professional/neurologic-disorders/delirium-and-dementia.

Huang, Y., Kotov, R., de Girolamo, G., Preti, A., Angermeyer, M., Benjet, C., . . . Kessler, R. C. (2009). DSM-IV personality disorders in the WHO World Mental Health Surveys. *British Journal of Psychiatry, 195*(1), 46–53.

Hudson, C. G. (2021). Benchmarks for needed psychiatric beds for the United States: A test of a predictive analytics model. *International Journal of Environmental Research and Public Health, 18*(22), 12205.

Hughes, R. C. (2023). Cost sharing in managed care and the ethical question of business purpose. *Journal of Managed Care & Specialty Pharmacy, 29*(8), 965–969.

Hughto, J. M. W., Varma, H., Babbs, G., Yee, K., Alpert, A., Hughes, L., . . . Shireman, T. I. (2023). Disparities in health condition diagnoses among aging transgender and cisgender Medicare beneficiaries, 2008–2017. *Frontiers in Endocrinology, 14*, 1102348.

Huibers, M. J. H., Van Bronswijk, S. C., Peeters, F. P. M. L., & Lemmens, L. H. J. M. (2022, April 20). Does psychological process change during psychotherapy predict long-term depression outcomes after successful cognitive therapy or interpersonal psychotherapy? Secondary analysis of a randomized trial. *Psychotherapy Research*, 32(8), 1047–1063.

Hunt, C., Exline, J. J., Fletcher, T. L., & Teng, E. J. (2022). Intolerance of uncertainty prospectively predicts the transdiagnostic severity of emotional psychopathology: Evidence from a Veteran sample. *Journal of Anxiety Disorders, 86*, 102530.

Hwang, K. A. J., & Saadabadi, A. (2023, July 10). Lysergic acid diethylamide (LSD). *StatPearls*.

Hybholt, L., Higgins, A., Buus, N., Berring, L. L., Connolly, T., Erlandsen, A., & Morrissey, J. (2022). The spaces of peer-led support groups for suicide bereaved in Denmark and the Republic of Ireland: A focus group study. *International Journal of Environmental Research and Public Health, 19*(16), 9898.

Hyde, J. S. (1990). *Understanding human sexuality* (4th ed.). New York: McGraw-Hill.

Hyde, J. S., & Mezulis, A. H. (2020). Gender differences in depression: Biological, affective, cognitive, and sociocultural factors. *Harvard Review of Psychiatry, 28*(1), 4–13.

Hyde, M. (2023, July 14). America's most common recurring dreams. *Amerisleep*.

Ide-Okochi, A., Samiso, T., Kanamori, Y., He, M., Sakaguchi, M., & Fujimura, K. (2022). Depression, insomnia, and probable post-traumatic stress disorder among survivors of the 2016 Kumamoto earthquake and related factors during the recovery period amidst the COVID-19 pandemic. *Journal of Environmental Research and Public Health, 19*(7), 4403.

Ikier, S., Donerkayali, C., Halici, O. S., Gulseren, Z. A. K., Goksal, H., & Akbas, B. (2024). When is memory more reliable? Scientific findings, theories, and myths. *Applied Neuropsychology: Adult, 31*(1), 77–94.

Iltis, A. S., Fortier, R., Ontjes, N., & McCall, W. V. (2023, March 1). Ethics considerations in laws restricting incapacitated patients' access to ECT. *Journal of the American Academy of Psychiatry and the Law, 51*(1), 47–55.

Ineson, K. M., Erlangsen, A., Nordentoft, M., Benros, M. E., & Madsen, T. (2022, April 11). Traumatic brain injury and risk of subsequent attempted suicide and violent crime. *Psychological Medicine*. doi:10.1017/S0033291722000769. [Online ahead of print]

Innes, B., & Doncaster, L. (2022, October 11). *Criminal profiling: How psychological profiles help solve crime*. London: Amber Books.

Innocence Project. (2024). *Eyewitness misidentification*. New York: Author.

Ioannidis, K., Hook, R. W., Grant, J. E., Czabanowska, K., Roman-Urrestarazu, A., & Chamberlain, S. R. (2021). Eating disorders with over-exercise: A cross-sectional analysis of the mediational role of problematic usage of the internet in young people. *Journal of Psychiatric Research, 132*, 215–222.

IPA (International Psychogeriatric Association). (2023). *Geropsychology workforce crisis: An international perspective*. Milwaukee, WI: Author.

Ipsos. (2018, February 13). Most Americans experience feeling dissatisfied with how their body looks from time to time, including nearly two in five who feel this way whenever they look in the mirror. *Ipsos*. Retrieved from https://www.ipsos.com/en-us/news-polls.

Ipsos. (2022, February 4). COVID's worrying impact on Americans' relationship with food and body image. *Ipsos*. Retrieved from https://www.ipsos.com.

Irwin, M. R., & Bursch, B. (2023, March 27). Factitious disorder imposed on self (Munchausen syndrome). *UpToDate*. Retrieved from http://www.uptodate.com.

Islam, F., Shohag, S., Akhter, S., Islam, M. R., Sultana, S., Mitra, S. . . . Cavalu, S. (2022). Exposure to metal toxicity in Alzheimer's disease: An extensive review. *Frontiers in Pharmacology, 13*, 903099.

Islam, M. S., Rashid, M. H., Islam, M. K., Rahman, M. M., Bashar, M. A., Alam, M. M., . . . Uddin, M. N. (2020). Childhood adversities as risk factors and persistence of suicidal behavior: A descriptive cross-sectional study. *Mymensingh Medical Journal, 29*(2), 392–398.

Isomaa, R., & Isomaa, A.-L. (2014). And then what happened? A 5-year follow-up of eating disorder patients. *Nordic Journal of Psychiatry, 68*(8), 567–572.

Issac, A., Nayak, S. G., Yesodharan, R., & Sequira, L. (2022). Needs, challenges, and coping strategies among primary caregivers of schizophrenia patient: A systematic review and meta-synthesis. *Archives of Psychiatric Nursing, 41*, 317–332.

Ivcevic, Z., Grossman, E., & Ranjan, A. (**2022**). Patterns of psychological vulnerabilities and resources in artists and nonartists. *Psychology of Aesthetics, Creativity, and the Arts, 16*(1), 3–15.

Ivusic, B. (2022, November 15). 8 reasons selfies are good for your self-expression. *MakeUseOf*. Retrieved from https://www.makeuseof.com.

Iwamasa, G. Y. (2023, January 19). *Culturally responsive cognitive behavioral therapy for anxiety and depression*. Washington, DC: American Psychological Association. [Online course/Video on-demand]

Jacobs, J. R., & Bovasso, G. B. (2009). Re-examining the long-term effects of experiencing parental death in childhood on adult psychopathology. *Journal of Nervous and Mental Disease, 197*(1), 24–27.

Jacobs, P., Watchman, K., Wilkinson, H., Hoyle, L., & McGenily, L. (2023). Experiences of people with intellectual disability and dementia: A systematic review. *Journal of Applied Research in Intellectual Disabilities, 36*(2), 241–258.

Jafari-Sabet, M., Amiri, S., Aghamiri, H., & Fatahi, N. (2022). Cross state-dependent memory retrieval between cannabinoid CB1 and serotonergic 5-HT1A receptor agonists in the mouse dorsal hippocampus. *Neurobiology of Learning and Memory, 192*, 107638.

Jahandideh, M., Ebrahimi, E., Farzaei, M. H., & Barzegari, E. (2023). The effect of chronic lithium treatment on hippocampal progenitor cells: Transcriptomic analysis and systems pharmacology. *Brain and Behavior, 13*(10), e3215.

Jameel, S., Munivenkatappa, M., Arumugham, S. S., & Thennarasu, K. (2022, March 31). Cultural adaptation of cognitive behaviour therapy for depression: A qualitative study exploring views of patients and practitioners from India. *Cognitive Behaviour Therapist, 15*, e16.

Jamison, K. R. (1995). *An unquiet mind.* New York: Vintage Books.

Jamison, K. R. (1995, February). Manic-depressive illness and creativity. *Scientific American,* pp. 63–67.

Janackovski, A., Deane, F. P., Kelly, P. J., & Hains, A. (2022). Temporal exploration of the interpersonal theory of suicide among adolescents during treatment. *Journal of Consulting and Clinical Psychology, 90*(9), 682–695.

Jang, S., Ekyalongo, Y., & Kim, H. (2021). Systematic review of displacement and health impact from natural disasters in Southeast Asia. *Disaster Medicine and Public Health Preparedness, 15*(1), 105–114.

Janiri, D., Di Luzio, M., Montanari, S., Hitsch, D., Simonetti, A., Moccia, L., . . . Sani, G. (2024). Childhood trauma and self-harm in youths with bipolar disorders. *Current Neuropharmacology, 22*(1), 152–158.

Jansson, L. M. (2023, July 24). Prenatal substance exposure and neonatal abstinence syndrome (NAS): Management and outcomes. *UpToDate.* Retrieved from https://www.uptodate.com.

Janus, S. S., & Janus, C. L. (1993). *The Janus report on sexual behavior.* New York: Wiley.

Jarrett, R. B., & Vittengl, J. (2022, September 15). Unipolar depression in adults: Continuation and maintenance treatment. *UpToDate.* Retrieved from https://www.uptodate.com.

Jauk, E., & Dieterich, R. (2019). Addiction and the dark triad of personality. *Frontiers in Psychiatry, 10,* 662.

Javitt, D. C. (2023). Cognitive impairment associated with schizophrenia: From pathophysiology to treatment. *Annual Review of Pharmacology and Toxicology, 63,* 119–141.

JDRF (Juvenile Diabetes Research Foundation). (2022). *Type 1 diabetes and depression.* New York: Author.

Jegarl, A. M., Jegede, O., Isom, J., Ciarleglio, N., & Black, C. (2023). Psychotic misdiagnosis of racially minoritized patients: A case-based ethics, equity, and educational exploration. *Harvard Review of Psychiatry, 31*(1), 28–36.

Jellett, R., & Flower, R. L. (2023, January 13). How can psychologists meet the needs of autistic adults? *Autism.* https://doi.org/10.1177/13623613221147346. [Online ahead of print]

Jenkins, S. R. (2023). Thematic Apperception Test (TAT) and other narrative assessments of bipolar spectrum disorders. In J. H. Kleiger & I. D. Weiner (Eds.). *Psychological assessment of bipolar spectrum disorders* (pp. 155–170). Washington, DC: American Psychological Association.

Jensen, G. M. (1998). The experience of injustice: Health consequences of the Japanese American internment. *Dissertation Abstracts International Section A: Humanities and Social Sciences, 58*(7-A), 2718.

Jha, A. (2021, October 25). Find your focus: Own your attention in 12 minutes a day. *Mindful.*

JHM (Johns Hopkins Medicine). (2022). *Depression and heart disease.* Baltimore: Author.

JHM (Johns Hopkins Medicine). (2023). *5 vaping facts you need to know.* Baltimore: Author. Retrieved from https://www.hopkinsmedicine.org/health.

Ji, E., Weickert, C. S., Purves-Tyson, T., White, C., Handelsman, D. J., Desai, R., . . . Weickert, T. W. (2021). Cortisol-dehydroepiandrosterone ratios are inversely associated with hippocampal and prefrontal brain volume in schizophrenia. *Psychoneuroendocrinology, 123,* 104916.

Ji, X.-Y., Peng, X.-Y., Tang, H.-L., Pan, H., Wang, W.-T., Wu, J., . . . Wei, N.-L. (2024). Alzheimer's disease phenotype based upon the carrier status of the apolipoprotein Ee4 allele. *Brain Pathology, 34*(1), e13208.

Jiang, J., Liu, T., Crawford, J. D., Kochan, N. A., Brodaty, H., Sachdev, P. S., & Wen, W. (2020). Stronger bilateral functional connectivity of the frontoparietal control network in near-centenarians and centenarians without dementia. *NeuroImage, 215,* 116855.

Jibson, M. D. (2023, May 9). First-generation antipsychotic medications: Pharmacology, administration, and comparative side effects. *UpToDate.* Retrieved from https://www.uptodate.com.

Jimenez, A. L., Cruz-Gonzalez, M., Calhoun, T. F., Cohen, L., & Alegria, M. (2022, February 3). Late life anxiety and depression symptoms, and suicidal behaviors in racial/ethnic minority older adults in community-based organizations and community clinics in the U.S. *Cultural Diversity and Ethnic Minority Psychology.* doi:10.1037/cdp0000524. [Online ahead of print]

Jimenez, X. F., Nkanginieme, N., Dhand, N., Karafa, M., & Salerno, K. (2020). Clinical, demographic, psychological, and behavioral features of factitious disorder: A retrospective analysis. *General Hospital Psychiatry, 62,* 93–95.

Jin, S. V., & Ryu, E. (2022). "A streetcar named Instagram Desire": Evolutionary psychological perspectives on the multifarious human desires that shape Instagram selfie-and-groupfie cultures. *Behavioral Science, 12*(10), 396.

Jobes, D. A. (2023). *Managing suicidal risk: A collaborative approach* (3rd ed.). New York: Guilford Press.

John-Henderson, N. A., Counts, C. J., Strong, N. C. B., Larsen, J. M., & Jeffs, M. (2024). Investigating the role of emotion regulation in the relationship between childhood trauma and alcohol problems in American Indian adults. *Journal of Affective Disorders Reports, 344,* 440–445.

Johns, L., Hayward, M., Strauss, C., & Morris, E. (2021). Mindfulness and acceptance based therapies for psychosis. In C. A. Tamminga, E. I. Ivleva, U. Reininghaus, & J. van Os (Eds.). *Psychotic disorders: Comprehensive conceptualization and treatments* (Chap. 61, pp. 547–554). New York: Oxford University Press.

Johnsen, I. B., Wichstrøm, L., & Dahllöf, G. (2024). Prevalence and stability of blood-injection-injury phobia in childhood: A prospective community study in Norway. *Acta Paediatrica, 113*(1), 105–112.

Johnson, A. B., & Sadiq, N. M. (2023, February 9). Pentobarbital. *StatPearls.*

Johnson, J. (2020, March 30). Edibles: How long do they last? *Medical News Today.*

Johnson, J. F., Belyk, M., Schwartze, M., Pinheiro, A. P., & Kotz, S. A. (2022). Hypersensitivity to passive voice hearing in hallucination proneness. *Frontiers in Human Neuroscience, 16,* 859731.

Johnson, M. S., Magnussen, S., Asmyhr, A. F., Heldeland, J. J., Jonassen, M. P., Lundal, E., . . . Widmark, L. F. (2023). Doctored photographs create false memories of spectacular childhood events. A replication of Wade et al. (2002) with a Scandinavian twist. *Memory, 31*(7), 1011–1018.

Johnson, S. (2022). In times of adversity: A neuroscience perspective on stress, health, and implications for society post-pandemic. *Yale Journal of Biological Medicine, 95*(1), 165–170.

Johnson, S. R. (2022, September 7). Study shows rising demand for mental health treatment during pandemic. *U.S. News & World Report.*

Johnson, T. D. (2011, December). Online-only: Report: Teens who often eat dinner with family less likely to drink, smoke, or use drugs. *The Nation's Health, 41*(9), E46.

Johnson-Davis, K. L., & Ly, D. (2024). Quantification of olanzapine by liquid chromatography-tandem mass spectrometry (LC-MS/MS). *Methods in Molecular Biology, 2737,* 347–357.

Johnston, J. N., Campbell, D., Caruncho, J. H., Henter, I. D., Ballard, E. D., & Zarate, C. A., Jr. (2022). Suicide biomarkers to predict risk, classify diagnostic subtypes, and identify novel therapeutic targets: 5 years of promising research. *International Journal of Neuropsychopharmacology, 25*(3), 197–214.

Johnston, L. D., Miech, R. A., O'Malley, P. M., Bachman, J. G., Schulenberg, J. E., & Patrick, M. E. (2022). *Monitoring the Future national survey results on drug use, 1975–2021: Overview, key findings on adolescent drug use.* Ann Arbor: University of Michigan, Institute for Social Research.

Joiner, T. E. (2005). *Why people die by suicide.* Cambridge, MA: Harvard University Press.

Joiner, T. E. (2009). The interpersonal-psychological theory of suicidal behavior: Current empirical status. *American Psychological Association.* Retrieved from http://www.apa.org/science/about/psa/2009/06/sci-brief.aspx.

Joiner, T. E., Buchman-Schmitt, J. M., Chu, C., & Horn, M. A. (2017). A sociobiological extension of the interpersonal theory of suicide. *Crisis, 38*(2), 69–72.

Joiner, T. E., Jeon, M. E., Lieberman, A., Janakiraman, R., Duffy, M. E., Gai, A. R., & Dougherty, S. P. (2021). On prediction, reputation, and explanatory reach: A consideration of the Interpersonal Theory of Suicidal Behavior. *Preventive Medicine, 152*(Part 1), 106453.

Jonas, L., Salazar de Pablo, G., Shum, M., Nosarti, C., Abbott, C., & Vaquerizo-Serrano, J. (2022). A systematic review and meta-analysis investigating the impact of childhood adversities on the mental health of LGBT+ youth. *Advances, 2*(2), e12079.

Jonason, P. K., Czerwinski, S. K., Tobaldo, F., Ramos-Diaz, J., Adamovic, M., Adams, B. G., . . . Sedikides, C. (2022). Milieu effects on the Dark Triad traits and their sex differences in 49 countries. *Personality and Individual Differences, 197,* 111796.

Jonason, P. K., Foster, J. D., Egorova, M. S., Parshikova, O., Csatho, A., & Gouveia, V. V. (2017). The dark triad traits from a life history perspective in six countries. *Frontiers in Psychology, 8,* 1476.

Jonason, P. K., Girgis, M., & Milne-Home, J. (2017). the exploitive mating strategy of the dark triad traits: Tests of rape-enabling attitudes. *Archives of Sexual Behavior, 46*(3), 697–706.

Jonason, P. K., Koehn, M. A., Bulyk, R. A., & Davis, M. D. (2020). Standing out and not fitting in: The dark triad traits and social values. *Journal of Social Psychology, 160*(2), 164–169.

Jonason, P. K., Li, N. P., & Buss, D. M. (2010). The costs and benefits of the dark triad: Implications for mate poaching and mate retention tactics. *Personality and Individual Differences, 48*(4), 373–378.

Jonason, P. K., Li, N. P., Webster, G. D., & Schmitt, D. P. (2009). The dark triad: Facilitating a short-term mating strategy in men. *European Journal of Personality, 23,* 5–18.

Jonason, P. K., Valentine, K. A., Li, N. P., & Harbeson, C. L. (2011). Mate-selection and the dark triad: Facilitating a short-term mating strategy and creating a volatile environment. *Personality and Individual Differences, 51,* 759–763.

Jones, A. (2020, January 13). What schizophrenia does to families. *Washington Post Magazine.* Retrieved from https://www.washingtonpost.com/magazine/2020/01/13.

Jones, A. L., Rafferty, J., Cochran, S. D., Abelson, J., Hanna, M. R., & Mays, V. M. (2022). Prevalence, severity and burden of post-traumatic stress disorder in Black men and women across the adult lifespan. *Journal of Aging and Health, 34*(3), 401–412.

Jones, C. M., Han, B., Seth, P., Baldwin, G., & Compton, W. M. (2023). Increases in methamphetamine injection among treatment admissions in the U.S. *Addictive Behaviors, 136,* 107492.

Jones, C. M., Olsen, E. O., O'Donnell, J., & Mustaquim, D. (2020). Resurgent methamphetamine use at treatment admission in the United States, 2008–2017. *American Journal of Public Health, 110,* 509–516.

Jones, D. W. (2017). Moral insanity and psychological disorder: The hybrid roots of psychiatry. *History of Psychiatry, 28,* 263–279.

Jones, E. E., Blandl, F., Kreutzer, K. A., Bryan, C. J., Allan, N. P., & Gorka, S. M. (2024). Childhood adversity and youth suicide risk: The mediating role of intolerance of uncertainty. *Personality and Individual Differences, 216,* 112405.

Jones, J. M., & Lloyd, C. (2021). *Black Americans' reports of mistreatment steady or higher* (Gallup Poll #352580). *Gallup.* Retrieved from https://news.gallup.com/poll/352580.

Jones, M. C. (1968). Personality correlates and antecedents of drinking patterns in males. *Journal of Consulting and Clinical Psychology, 32,* 2–12.

Jones, M. C. (1971). Personality antecedents and correlates of drinking patterns in women. *Journal of Consulting and Clinical Psychology, 36,* 61–69.

Jones, N., Marks, R., Ramirez, R., & Ríos-Vargas, M. (2021). 2020 Census illuminates racial and ethnic composition of the country. Retrieved from https://www.census.gov/library/stories/2021/08/improved-race-ethnicity-measures-reveal-united-states-population-much-more-multiracial.html.u

Jones, S. A., Tipsord, J., Nagel, B. J., & Nigg, J. T. (2023). A preliminary study of white matter correlates of a laboratory measure of attention and motor stability in attention-deficit/hyperactivity disorder. *Journal of Psychiatric Research, 160,* 110–116.

Joseph, V. A., Martínez-Alés, Olfson, M., Shaman, J., Gould, M. S., & Keyes, K. M. (2022). Temporal trends in suicide methods among adolescents in the US. *JAMA Network Open, 5*(10), e2236049.

Joshi, P., Duong, K. T., Trevisan, L.A., & Wilkins, K. M. (2021). Evaluation and management of alcohol use disorder among older adults. *Current Geriatric Reports, 10*(3), 82–90.

Joshi, T., & Ahuja, N. (2023, February 14). The prion basis of progressive neurodegenerative disorders. *Interdisciplinary Perspectives on Infectious Diseases,* 6687264. [Open access]

Judd, B. G., & Sateia, M. J. (2023, June 30). Classification of sleep disorders. *UpToDate.* Retrieved from http://www.uptodate.com.

Judd, S., & Parker, G. F. (2018). Court-ordered evaluations from a mental health court. *Journal of the American Academy of Psychiatry and the Law, 46*(1), 52–62.

Justia. (2023, October). *Insanity defense in criminal cases.* Retrieved from https://www.justia.com.

Juvonen, J., & Ho, A. Y. (2008). Social motives underlying antisocial behavior across middle school grades. *Journal of Youth and Adolescence, 37,* 747.

Kaeley. (2021, January 22). Eccentric behaviors of famous artists throughout history. *Artistic Fuel.*

Kahn, A. P., & Fawcett, J. (1993). *The encyclopedia of mental health.* New York: Facts on File.

Kalin, N. H. (2020). Early-life environmental factors impacting the development of psychopathology. *American Journal of Psychiatry, 177*(1), 1–3.

Kalman, J. L., Burkhardt, G., Samochowiec, J., Gebhard, C., Dom, G., John, M., . . . Falkai, P. (2023). Digitalising mental health care: Practical recommendations from the European Psychiatric Association. *European Psychiatry, 67*(1), e4.

Kaminsky, M. (2022, May 2). What's the deal with lie detectors? *Legalzoom.* Retrieved from https://www.legalzoom.com/articles.

Kammen, A., Cavaleri, J., Lam, J., Frank, A. C., Mason, X., Choi, W., . . . Lee, D. J. (2022). Neuromodulation of OCD: A review of invasive and non-invasive methods. *Frontiers in Neurology, 13,* 909264.

Kampman, K. (2021, July 6). Psychosocial interventions for stimulant use disorder in adults. *UpToDate.* Retrieved from http://www.uptodate.com.

Kampman, K. (2023, July 5). Stimulant use disorder: Treatment overview. *UpToDate.* Retrieved from https://www.uptodate.com.

Kang, Y., Zhang, Y., Huang, K., & Wang, Z. (2023). The genetic influence of the DRD3 rs6280 polymorphism (Ser9Gly) on functional connectivity and gray matter volume of the hippocampus in patients with first-episode, drug-näive schizophrenia. *Behavioral Brain Research, 437,* 114124.

Kanner, B. (1995). *Are you normal? Do you behave like everyone else?* New York: St. Martin's Press.

Kanner, B. (1998, February). Are you normal? Turning the other cheek. *American Demographics.*

Kanner, B. (2005). *Are you normal about sex, love, and relationships?* New York: St. Martin's Press.

Kanner, L. (1943). Autistic disturbances of affective contact. *Nervous Child, 2,* 217.

Kanner, L. (1954). To what extent is early infantile autism determined by constitutional inadequacies? *Research Publications—Association for Research in Nervous and Mental Disease, 33,* 378–385.

Kantor, E. D., Rehm, C. D., Haas, J. S., Chan, A. T., & Giovannucci, E. L. (2015). Trends in prescription drug use among adults in the United States from 1999–2012. *Journal of the American Medical Association, 314*(17), 1818–1831.

Kapadia, S. V. (2022). Adapting AVATAR therapy: Using available digital technology for people living with auditory verbal hallucinations in low- and middle-income countries. *Indian Journal of Psychological Medicine, 44*(4), 405–408.

Kapil, R. (2019, February 6). 5 surprising mental health statistics. *mentalhealthfirstaid.* Retrieved from http://www.mentalhealthfirstaid.org.

Kaplan, D. B. (2023, April). Effects of life transitions on older adults. *Merck Manual Professional Version.* Retrieved from https://www.merckmanuals.com/professional/geriatrics.

Kaplan, D. B. (2023, April). Family caregiving for older adults. *Merck Manual Professional Version.* Retrieved from https://www.merckmanuals.com/professional/geriatrics.

Kaplan, H. S. (1974). *The new sex therapy: Active treatment of sexual dysfunction.* New York: Brunner/Mazel.

Kaplan, R. M. (2023, January 20). Daniel M'Naghten: The man who changed the law on insanity. *Psychiatric Times, 40*(1). https://www.psychiatrictimes.com/view/daniel-m-naghten-the-man-who-changed-the-law-on-insanity.

Kar, S. K., & Singh, S. (2023, July 10). Anomic suicides on rise during recently emerging crises: Revisiting Durkheim's model. *CNS Spectrums.* doi:10.1017/S1092852923002341. [Online ahead of print]

Karakurt, H. U., & Pir, P. (2022, October 14). *In silico* analysis of metabolic effects of bipolar disorder on prefrontal cortex identified altered GABA, glutamate-glutamine cycle, energy metabolism and amino acid synthesis pathways. *Integrative Biology, 14*(6), 127–136.

Karim, H. T., Ly, M., Yu, G., Krafty, R., Tudorascu, D. L., Aizenstein, H. J., & Andreescu, C. (2021). Aging faster: Worry and rumination in late life are associated with greater brain age. *Neurobiology of Aging, 101,* 13–21.

Karimi Tari, P., Parsons, C. G., Collingridge, G. L., & Rammes, G. (2024). Memantine: Updating a rare success story in procognitive therapeutics. *Neuropharmacology, 244,* 109737.

Karras, M., Csillik, A., & Delhomme, P. (2022). Empathy, impulsiveness, and sensation seeking as mediators between primary psychopathic traits and driving behaviors in French driving offenders. *Journal of Clinical Psychology, 79*(3), 886–901.

Kaseweter, K. A., Browne, M. E., & Prkachin, K. M. (2022). Insensitivity to suffering: Psychopathic traits and perception of others' pain. *Journal of Personality Disorders, 36*(5), 583–605.

Katajala-Peltomaa, S. (2020). *Demonic possession and lived religion in later Medieval Europe (Oxford Studies in Medieval European History).* New York: Oxford University Press.

Kathuria, H. (2023, January 17). E-cigarette or vaping product use-associated lung injury (EVALI). *UpToDate.* Retrieved from https://www.uptodate.com.

Kaufmann, K. (2023). Don't blame it on the moon. *Issues in Mental Health Nursing, 44*(3), 176–179.

Kawada, T. (2023). Comorbidity of eating disorders and borderline personality disorder. *International Journal of Eating Disorders, 56*(2), 478–479.

Kaylor, L., & Jeglic, E. L. (2021). Non-contact paraphilic disorders and offending. In L. A. Craig & R. M. Bartels (Eds.). *Sexual deviance: Understanding and managing deviant sexual interest and paraphilic disorders* (Chap. 11). Hoboken, NJ: Wiley-Blackwell.

Kazda, L., Bell, K., Thomas, R., McGeechan, K., Sims, R., & Barratt, A. (2021). Overdiagnosis of attention-deficit/hyperactivity disorder in children and adolescents: A systematic scoping review. *JAMA Network Open, 4*(4), e215335.

Kazda, L., McGeechan, K., Bell, K., Thomas, R., & Barratt, A. (2023). Increased diagnosis of attention-deficit hyperactivity disorder despite stable hyperactive/inattentive behaviors: Evidence from two birth cohorts of Australian children. *Journal of Child Psychology and Psychiatry, 64*(8), 1140–1148.

Kazdin, A. E. (2021). *Research design in clinical psychology* (5th ed.). New York: Cambridge University Press.

Keane, T. M. (2021, February 26). *Posttraumatic stress disorder* (Advances in Psychotherapy Evidence-Based Practice Series). Boston: Hogrefe Publishing.

Kearney, C. A. (2016). *Casebook in child behavior disorders* (6th ed.). Independence, KY: Cengage Publications.

Keatley, D. A., Golightly, H., Shephard, R., Yaksic, E., & Reid, S. (2018, March 24). Using behavior sequence analysis to map serial killers' life histories. *Journal of Interpersonal Violence.* doi:10.1177/0886260518759655.

Keefe, J. R., Kim, T. T., DeRubeis, R. J., Streiner, D. L., Links, P. S., & McMain, S. F. (2021). Treatment selection in borderline personality disorder between dialectical behavior therapy and psychodynamic psychiatric management. *Psychological Medicine, 51*(11), 1829–1837.

Keene, C. D., Montine, T. J., & Kuller, L. H. (2022, August 23). Epidemiology, pathology, and pathogenesis of Alzheimer disease. *UpToDate.* Retrieved from http://www.uptodate.com.

Keitner, G. (2023, September 20). Unipolar depression in adults: Family and couples therapy. *UpToDate.* Retrieved from https://www.uptodate.com.

Kelleher, I. (2023, January 12). Psychosis prediction 2.0: Why child and adolescent mental health services should be a key focus for schizophrenia and bipolar disorder prevention research. *British Journal of Psychiatry, 222*(5), 185–187.

Keller, M. H., & Dance, G. J. X. (2019, September 29). The Internet is overrun with images of child sexual abuse. What went wrong? *New York Times.*

Kellner, C. (2021, September 13). Unipolar major depression in adults: Indications for and efficacy of electroconvulsive therapy (ECT). *UpToDate.* Retrieved from http://www.uptodate.com.

Kellner, C. (2022, August 10). Overview of electroconvulsive therapy (ECT) for adults. *UpToDate.* Retrieved from https://www.uptodate.com.

Kellner, C. (2022, September 23). Technique for performing electroconvulsive therapy (ECT) in adults. *UpToDate.* Retrieved from https://www.uptodate.com.

Kellner, C. (2022, September 13). Unipolar major depression in adults: Indications for and efficacy of electroconvulsive therapy (ECT). *UpToDate.* Retrieved from https://www.uptodate.com.

Kellner, C. (2023, March 28). Patient education: Electroconvulsive therapy (ECT) (beyond the basics). *UpToDate.* Retrieved from https://www.uptodate.com.

Kelly, J. (2023, September 29). Gen-Z faces financial challenges, stress, anxiety and an uncertain future. *Forbes.*

Kelty, E., Chrzanowska, A., & Preen, D. B. (2022). Fatalities in patients with opioid use disorders. In V. B. Patel & V. R. Preedy (Eds.). *Handbook of substance misuse and addictions: From biology to public health* (pp. 1851–1867). New York: Springer.

Kendall, K. M., Walters, J. T. R., & Donovan, M. C. O. (2020). Genetics of schizophrenia. In J. R. Geddes, N. C. Andreason, & G. M. Goodwin (Eds.). *New Oxford textbook of psychiatry* (3rd ed., Chap. 59). New York: Oxford University Press.

Kendall, P. C., Ney, J. S., Maxwell, C. A., Lehrbach, K. R., Jakubovic, R. J., McKnight, D. S., & Friedman, A. L. (2023). Adapting CBT for youth anxiety: Flexibility, within fidelity, in different settings. *Frontiers in Psychiatry, 14,* 1067047.

Kendler, K. S., Heath, A., & Martin, N. G. (1987). A genetic epidemiologic study of self-report suspiciousness. *Comprehensive Psychiatry, 28*(3), 187–196.

Kendler, K. S., Walters, E. E., Neale, M. C., Kessler, R. C., Heath, A. C., & Eaves, L. J. (1995). The structure of the genetic and environmental risk factors for six major psychiatric disorders in women: Phobia, generalized anxiety disorder, panic disorder, bulimia, major depression, and alcoholism. *Archives of General Psychiatry, 52*(5), 374–383.

Kennebeck, S., & Bonin, L. (2021, June 21). Suicidal behavior in children and adolescents: Epidemiology and risk factors. *UpToDate.* Retrieved from http://www.uptodate.com.

Kennebeck, S., & Bonin, L. (2023, February 10). Suicidal ideation and behavior in children and adolescents: Evaluation and management. *UpToDate.* Retrieved from https://www.uptodate.com.

Kennedy, C. H. (2023, March 18). Prescribing psychology poised for expansion. *Psychology Today.* Retrieved from https://www.psychologytoday.com.

Kent, J., & Pinkham, A. (2024). Cerebral and cerebellar correlates of social cognitive impairment in schizophrenia. *Progress in Neuro-Psychopharmacology and Biological Psychiatry, 128,* 110850.

Kernberg, O. F. (2018). *Treatment of severe personality disorders: Resolution of aggression and recovery of eroticism.* Washington, DC: American Psychiatric Association Publishing.

Kernberg, O. F. (2020). Therapeutic implications of transference structures in various personality pathologies. *Journal of the American Psychoanalytic Association, 67*(6), 951–986.

Kernberg, O. F. (2021). Challenges for the future of psychoanalysis. *American Journal of Psychoanalysis, 81*(3), 281–300.

Kernberg, O. F. (2022). *Hatred, emptiness, and hope: Transference-focused psychotherapy in personality disorders.* Washington, DC: American Psychiatric Association Publishing.

Kerr, W. C., Ye, Y., Martinez, P., Karriker-Jaffe, K. J., Patterson, D., Greenfield, T. K., & Mulia, N. (2022, June). Longitudinal assessment of drinking changes during the pandemic: The 2021 COVID-19 follow-up study to the 2019 to 2020 National Alcohol Survey. *Alcohol: Clinical and Experimental Research, 46*(6), 1050–1061.

Kersten, L. (2020, January 8). *Instagram isn't doing enough to tackle pro-eating disorder content.* Retrieved from https://i-d.vice.com/en/article/3kxxxv.

Kessing, L. V. (2020). Epidemiology of mood disorders. In J. R. Geddes, N. C. Andreasen, & G. M. Goodwin (Eds.). *New Oxford textbook of psychiatry* (3rd ed., Chap. 67). New York: Oxford University Press.

Kessler, R. C., Benjet, C., Bromet, E. J., & Rosellini, A. J. (2022). The epidemiology of PTSD among adults. In J. G. Beck & D. M. Sloan (Eds.). *The Oxford handbook of traumatic stress disorders* (Chap. 6). New York: Oxford University Press.

Kessler, R. C., Berglund, P., Demler, O., Jin, R., Merikangas, K. R., & Walters, E. E. (2005). Lifetime prevalence and age-of-onset distributions of DSM-IV disorders in the National Comorbidity Survey Replication. *Archives of General Psychiatry, 62,* 593–602.

Kessler, R. C., Gruber, M., Hettema, J. M., Hwang, I., Sampson, N., & Yonkers, K. A. (2010). Major depression and generalized anxiety disorder in the National Comorbidity Survey follow-up survey. In D. Goldberg, K. S. Kendler, P. J. Sirovatka, & D. A. Regier (Eds.).

Diagnostic issues in depression and generalized anxiety disorder: Refining the research agenda for DSM-V (pp. 139–170). Washington, DC: American Psychiatric Association.

Kessler, R. C., Petukhova, M., Sampson, N. A., Zaslavsky, A. M., & Wittchen, H. (2012). Twelve-month and lifetime prevalence and lifetime morbid risk of anxiety and mood disorders in the United States. *International Journal of Methods in Psychiatric Research, 21*(3), 169–184.

Keuroghlian, A. S. (2022, July 18). Psychiatric care considerations for sexually and gender diverse populations. *Journal of Clinical Psychiatry, 83*(4), 22com14579.

Keyes, K. M., Kreski, N. T., Ankrum, H., Cerdá, M., Chen, Q., Hasin, D. S., . . . Miech, R. (2022). Frequency of adolescent cannabis smoking and vaping in the United States: Trends, disparities and concurrent substance use, 2017–19. *Addiction, 117*(8), 2316–2324.

Keys, A., Brozek, J., Henschel, A., Mickelson, O., & Taylor, H. L. (1950). *The biology of human starvation.* Minneapolis: University of Minnesota Press.

KFF (Kaiser Family Foundation). (2020). *Poll: 7 in 10 Black Americans say they have experienced incidents of discrimination or police mistreatment in their lifetime, including nearly half who felt their lives were in danger.* San Francisco: Author.

KFF (Kaiser Family Foundation). (2022). *How does use of mental health care vary by demographics and health insurance coverage?* Retrieved from https://www.kff.org/health-reform.

KFF (Kaiser Family Foundation). (2023, March). *Key data on health and health care by race and ethnicity.* Kaiser Family Foundation. Retrieved from https://www.kff.org.

Khera, M. (2023, January 3). Treatment of male sexual dysfunction. *UpToDate.* Retrieved from http://www.uptodate.com.

Khokhar, B., Weathers, S., & Mattingly, T. J., II (2022). Direct-to-consumer advertising and the advancement of the quadruple aim: A narrative review. *Journal of the American College of Clinical Pharmacy, 5*(4), 459–466.

Khoury, B., Atallah, E., Arango-de Montis, I., & Parish, S. J. (2024, March). Sexual dysfunctions and sexual pain disorders. In G. M. Reed, P. L.-J. Ritchie, & A. Maercker (Eds.). *A psychological approach to diagnosis: Using the ICD-11 as a framework* (Chap. 19). Washington, DC: American Psychological Association.

Kiburi, S. K., Ngarachu, E., Tomita, A., Paruk, S., & Chiliza, B. (2023). Digital interventions for opioid use disorder treatment: A systematic review of randomized controlled trials. *Journal of Substance Abuse Treatment, 144,* 108926.

Kidd, J. D., Tettamanti, N. A., Kaczmarkiewicz, R., Corbeil, T. E., Dworkin, J. D., Jackman, K. B., . . . Meyer, I. H. (2023, August). Prevalence of substance use and mental health problems among transgender and cisgender U.S. adults: Results from a national probability sample. *Psychiatry Research, 326,* 115339.

Kidd, K. N., Prasad, D., Cunningham, J. E. A., de Azevedo Cardosa, T., & Frey, B. N. (2022). The relationship between parental bonding and mood, anxiety and related disorders in adulthood: A systematic review and meta-analysis. *Journal of Affective Disorders, 307,* 221–236.

Kidron, A., & Nguyen, H. (2023, May 23). Phenothiazine. *StatPearls.*

Kiecolt-Glaser, J. K., Garner, W., Speicher, C., Penn, G. M., Holliday, J., & Glaser, R. (1984). Psychosocial modifiers of immunocompetence in medical students. *Psychosomatic Medicine, 46,* 7–14.

Kim, H. T. (2020). Vocal feminization for transgender women: Current strategies and patient perspectives. *International Journal of General Medicine, 13,* 43–52.

Kim, H., & Newman, M. G. (2022). Avoidance of negative emotional contrast from worry and rumination: An application of the Contrast Avoidance Model. *Journal of Behavioral and Cognitive Therapy, 32*(1), 33–43.

Kim, Y., Krause, T. M., & Lane, S. D. (2023). Trends and seasonality of emergency department visits and hospitalizations for suicidality among children and adolescents in the US from 2016 to 2021. *JAMA Network Open, 6*(7), e2324183. https://doi.org/10.1001/jamanetworkopen.2023.24183.

Kime, P. (2022, September 19). VA says veteran suicides continue to fall, but outside researchers find rates may be much higher. *Military News.* https://www.military.com/daily-news/2022/09/19.

King, C. (2021). *Suicide risk assessment and formulation in children and adolescents: An evidence-based approach.* New York: Routledge.

King, L. (2002, March 19). Interview with Russell Yates. *Larry King Live.* CNN.

Kingsberg, S. A., Althof, S., Simon, J. A., Bradford, A., Bitzer, J., Carvalho, J., . . . Shifrin, J. L. (2017). Female sexual dysfunction—Medical and psychological treatments, Committee 14. *Journal of Sexual Medicine, 14*(12), 1463–1491.

Kingsberg, S., & Spadt, S. K. (2023, March 2). Female sexual pain: Evaluation. *UpToDate.* Retrieved from http://www.uptodate.com.

Kingsberg, S. A., Tkachenko, N., Lucas, J., Burbrink, A., Kreppner, W., & Dickstein, J. B. (2013). Characterization of orgasmic difficulties by women: Focus group evaluation. *Journal of Sexual Medicine, 10,* 2242–2250.

Kirkner, A., & Ullman, S. E. (2019). Sexual assault survivors' post-traumatic growth: Individual and community-level differences. *Violence Against Women, 26*(15–16). https://doi.org/10.1177/1077801219888019.

Kirmayer, L. J. (2001). Cultural variations in the clinical presentation of depression and anxiety: Implications for diagnosis and treatment. *Journal of Clinical Psychiatry, 62*(Suppl. 13), 22–28.

Kirmayer, L. J. (2002). The refugee's predicament. *Evolution Psychiatrique, 67*(4), 724–742.

Kirmayer, L. J. (2003). Failures of imagination: The refugee's narrative in psychiatry. *Anthropology and Medicine, 10*(2), 167–185.

Kirsch, I. (2014). Antidepressants and the placebo effect. *Zeitschrift für Psychologie, 222*(3), 128–134.

Kirsch, I. (2019). Placebo effect in the treatment of depression and anxiety. *Frontiers in Psychiatry, 10,* 407.

Kirzinger, A., Neuman, T., Cubanski, J., & Brodie, M. (2019, August 9). *Data note: Prescription drugs and older adults.* Kaiser Family Foundation. Retrieved from https://www.kff.org/health-reform.

Kisely, S., & Xiao, J. (2017, December 14). Cultural and linguistic diversity increases the likelihood of compulsory community treatment. *Schizophrenia Research, 197,* 104–108.

Kittle, C. F. (2020, Spring). Benjamin Rush—Heritage and hope. *Hektoen International.*

Kleiger, J. H., & Khadivi, A. (2023). Assessment if bipolar spectrum and schizophrenia. In J. H. Kleiger & I. B. Weiner (Eds.). *Psychological assessment of bipolar spectrum disorders* (Chap. 16). Washington, DC: American Psychological Association.

Klein, D., & Attia, E. (2023, April 15). Anorexia nervosa in adults: Clinical features, course of illness, assessment, and diagnosis. *UpToDate.* Retrieved from http://www.uptodate.com.

Klein, D. F., & Fink, M. (1962). Psychiatric reaction patterns to imipramine. *American Journal of Psychiatry, 119,* 432–438.

Kline, N. S. (1958). Clinical experience with iproniazid (Marsilid). *Journal of Clinical and Experimental Psychopathology, 19*(Suppl. 1), 72–78.

Kluft, R. P. (2022). Encountering the singularities of multiplicity: Meeting and treating the unique person. In M. J. Dorahy, S. N. Gold, & J. A. O'Neil (Eds.). *Dissociation and the dissociative disorders: Past, present, future* (Chap. 43). New York: Routledge.

Knappik, F., Bless, J. J., & Larøi, F. (2022). Confusions about "inner" and "outer" voices: Conceptual problems in the study of auditory verbal hallucinations. *Review of Philosophy and Psychology, 13,* 215–236.

Knight, R., Cary, M., Jenkinson, P., & Preston, C. (2022, July 11). The impact of sexual orientation on how men experience disordered eating and drive for muscularity. *Journal of Gay & Lesbian Mental Health. Retrieved from* https://doi.org/10.1080/19359705.2022.2118921.

Knight, S., Jarvis, G. E., Ryder, A. G., Lashley, M., & Rousseau, C. (2022). Ethnoracial differences in coercive referral and intervention among patients with first-episode psychosis. *Psychiatric Services, 73,* 732–738.

Knight, S., Jarvis, G. E., Ryder, A. G., Lashley, M., & Rousseau, C. (2023). "It just feels like an invasion": Black first-episode psychosis patients' experiences with coercive intervention and its influence on help-seeking behaviours. *Journal of Black Psychology, 49*(2), 200–235.

Knowthenet. (2013). *Nineteen-year-old males revealed as top trolling target.* Retrieved from http://www.knowthenet.org.uk/articles/nineteen-year-old-males.

Knudsen, C. B., Hemager, N., Greve, A. N., Lambek, R., Andreassen, A. K., Veddum, L., . . . Bliksted, V. F. (2022). Neurocognitive development in children at familial high risk of schizophrenia or bipolar disorder. *JAMA Psychiatry, 79*(6), 589–599.

Knudson, A. (2021, July 6). What are the chances of being attacked by a shark in the U.S.? *SILive*. Retrieved from https://www.silive.com/news/2021/07/what-are-the-chances-of-being-attacked-by-a-shark-in-the-us.html.

Koh, H. K., & Fiore, M. C. (2022, November 4). The tobacco industry and harm reduction. *JAMA, 328*(20), 2009–2010.

Kohut, H. (2014). *The restoration of the self* (Reprint ed.). Chicago: University of Chicago Press.

Kolla, N. J., Boileau, I., Karas, K., Watts, J. J., Rusjan, P., Houle, S., & Mizrahi, R. (2021). Lower amygdala fatty acid amide hydrolase in violent offenders with antisocial personality disorder: An [11C]CURB positron emission tomography study. *Translational Psychiatry, 11*(1), 57.

Kõlves, K., Crossin, R., & Witt, K. (2022). Alcohol consumption and suicidal behavior: Current research evidence and potential for prevention. In V. B. Patel & V. R. Preedy (Eds.). *Handbook of substance misuse and addictions: From biology to public health* (pp. 1151–1176). New York: Springer.

Komenda, S., Brunevskaya, N., Moritz, P., Landskron, S. J., Novakovic, Oberleiter, S., . . . Zeilinger, E. L. (2023). Concepts of good mental health and wellbeing in people with intellectual disability: Study protocol for a systematic review. *Frontiers in Psychiatry, 14*, 1148702.

Koppers, D., Van, H. L., Peen, J., & Dekker, J. J. M. (2023). Exploring the effect of group schema therapy and comorbidity on the treatment course of personality disorders. *Current Opinions in Psychiatry, 36*(1), 80–85.

Korn, M. (2018, October 31). *Minding what matters: Incorporating mindfulness training at work*. Washington, DC: Fisher Phillips.

Korte, K. J., Jiang, T., Koenen, K. C., Galea, S., & Gradus, J. L. (2023). Epidemiology of trauma and PTSD in adults. In M. J. Friedman, P. P. Schnurr, & T. M. Keane (Eds.). *Handbook of PTSD: Science and practice* (3rd ed., Chap. 4). New York: Guilford Press.

Koskela, M., Stahlberg, T., Yunus, W. M. A. W. M., & Sourander, A. (2023). Long-term outcomes of selective mutism: A systematic literature review. *BMC Psychiatry, 23*(1), 779.

Koskinen, M.-K., & Hovatta, I. (2023). Genetic insights into the neurobiology of anxiety. *Trends in Neurosciences, 46*(4), 318–331.

Köstlin, D., Siem, B., & Rohmann, A. (2023). Social support in online peer groups for celiac disease. *European Journal of Health Psychology, 30*(3), 138–143.

Kotov, R., Jonas, K. G., Carpenter, W. T., Dretsch, M. N., Eaton, N. R., Forbes, M. K., . . . & the HiTOP Utility Workgroup. (2020). Validity and utility of Hierarchical Taxonomy of Psychopathology (HiTOP): I. Psychosis superspectrum. *World Psychiatry, 19*(2), 151–172.

Kotov, R., Krueger, R. F., Watson, D., Cicero, D. C., Conway, C. C., DeYoung, C. G., . . . Wright, A. G. C. (2021). The hierarchical taxonomy of psychopathology (HiTOP): A quantitative nosology based on consensus of evidence. *Annual Review of Clinical Psychology, 17*, 83–108.

Kótyuk, E., Potenza, M. N., Blum, K., & Demetrovics, Z. (2022). The reward deficiency syndrome and links with addictive and related behaviors. In V. B. Patel & V. R. Preedy (Eds.). *Handbook of substance misuse and addictions: From biology to public health* (pp. 59–74). New York: Springer.

Kotzeva, A., Mittal, D., Desai, S., Judge, D., & Samanta, K. (2023). Socioeconomic burden of schizophrenia: A targeted literature review of types of costs and associated drivers across 10 countries. *Journal of Medical Economics, 26*(1), 70–83.

Kovács, I., Gál, B., Horváth, Z., Demeter, I., Rózsa, S., Janka, Z., . . . Andó, B. (2022, March 18). Externalizing personality characteristics define clinically relevant subgroups of alcohol use disorder. *PLoS One, 17*(3), e0265577.

Kovacs, M. (2023). *Treating childhood depression with contextual emotion regulation therapy*. New York: Guilford Press.

Kowalski, C. M., Rogoza, R., Saklofske, D. H., & Schermer, J. A. (2021). Dark triads, tetrads, tents, and cores: Why navigate (research) the jungle of dark personality models without a compass (criterion)? *Acta Psychologica, 221*, 103455.

Kozanian, O. O., Nedelescu, H., Kufahl, P. R., Mayford, M., & Weiss, F. (2022). Compulsive alcohol seeking and relapse: Central role of conditioning factors associated with alleviation of withdrawal states by alcohol. *British Journal of Pharmacology, 179*(17), 4330–4343.

Kramer, A. D. I., Guillory, J. E., & Hancock, J. T. (2014). Experimental evidence of massive-scale emotional contagion through social networks. *PNAS, 111*(24), 8788–8790.

Kramer, E. B., Gaeddert, L. A., Jackson, C. L., Harnke, B., & Nazem, S. (2020). Use of the acquired capability for suicide scale (ACSS) among United States military and veteran samples: A systematic review. *Journal of Affective Disorders, 267*, 229–242.

Kramer, U., Levy, K. N., & McMain, S. (2024, March). *Understanding mechanisms of change in psychotherapies for personality disorders*. Washington, DC: American Psychological Association.

Krause, L., & Askew, C. (2022, January). Preventing and reducing fear using positive modelling: A systematic review of experimental research with children. *Behaviour Research and Therapy, 148*, 103992.

Kredlow, M. A., Fenster, R. J., Laurent, E. S., Ressler, K. J., & Phelps, E. A. (2022). Prefrontal cortex, amygdala, and threat processing: Implications for PTSD. *Neuropsychopharmacology, 47*, 247–259.

Krempel, L., Stricker, J., & Martin, A. (2023, October 31). Heart rate variability, autonomic reactivity, and emotion regulation during sadness induction in somatic symptom disorder. *International Journal of Behavioral Medicine*. doi:10.1007/s12529-023-10238-2. [Online ahead of print]

Krishna, S. (2019, December 31). Sexting: The technological evolution of the sexual revolution. *Psychiatric Times, 36*(12), 24–25.

Krishnan, R. (2022, December 6). Unipolar depression in adults: Epidemiology. *UpToDate*. Retrieved from https://www.uptodate.com.

Krishnan, R. (2022, August 31). Unipolar depression: Neurobiology. *UpToDate*. Retrieved from https://www.uptodate.com.

Krishnan, R. (2022, September 13). Unipolar depression: Pathogenesis. *UpToDate*. Retrieved from https://www.uptodate.com.

Kroenke, K., & Hirschtritt, M. E. (2023). Walking the benzodiazepine high wire. *Psychiatric Services, 74*(1), 73–75.

Krüger, C. (2020). Culture, trauma and dissociation: A broadening perspective for our field. *Journal of Trauma & Dissociation, 21*(1), 1–13.

Kruger, T. H. C., & Kneer, J. (2021). Neurobiological basis of sexual deviance. In L. A. Craig & R. M. Bartels (Eds.). *Sexual deviance: Understanding and managing deviant sexual interest and paraphilic disorders* (Chap. 5). Hoboken, NJ: Wiley-Blackwell.

Krull, K. R., & Chan, E. (2023, March 9). Attention deficit hyperactivity disorder in children and adolescents: Clinical features and diagnosis. *UpToDate*. Retrieved from https://www.uptodate.com.

Kuehn, K. S., Dora, J., Harned, M. S., Foster, K. T., Song, F., Smith, M. R., & King, K. M. (2022). A meta-analysis on the affect regulation function of real-time self-injurious thoughts and behaviours. *Nature Human Behaviour, 6*, 964–974.

Kugler, M. (2021, November 9). Munchausen syndrome by proxy overview. *Verywell Health*. Retrieved from https://www.verywellhealth.com.

Kuhn, R. (1958). The treatment of depressive states with G-22355 (imipramine hydrochloride). *American Journal of Psychiatry, 115*, 459–464.

Kuhn, T. S. (1962). *The structure of scientific revolutions*. Chicago: University of Chicago Press.

Kumar, A., Sidhu, J., Goyal, A., & Tsao, J. W. (2022, June 5). Alzheimer disease. *StatPearls*.

Kussman, A., & Choo, H. J. (2024). Mental health and disordered eating in athletes. *Clinical Sports Medicine, 43*(1), 71–91.

Kwon, D. (2023). What is narcissism? Science confronts a widely misunderstood phenomenon. *Scientific American, 329*(2). Retrieved from https://www.scientificamerican.com/article/what-is-narcissism-science-confronts-a-widely-misunderstood-phenomenon1.

Kyriakoulis, P., & Kyrios, M. (2023). Biological and cognitive theories explaining panic disorder: A narrative review. *Frontiers in Psychiatry, 14*, 957515.

Kyzer, L. (2023, August 25). Inconsistent polygraph policies at DEA, argues IG. *Clearancejobs*. Retrieved from https://www.news.clearancejobs.com.

La Greca, A. M., Zimmerman, C. T., Herge, W. M., & Danzi, B. A. (2022). Traumatic stress disorders in children and adolescents. In J. G. Beck & D. M. Sloan (Eds.). *The Oxford handbook of traumatic stress disorders* (Chap. 7). New York: Oxford University Press.

Lafortune, D., Girard, M., Dussault, E., Philibert, M., Hébert, M., Boislard, M.-A., . . .Godbout, N. (2023). Who seeks sex therapy? Sexual dysfunction prevalence and correlates, and help-seeking among clinical and community samples. *PLoS One, 18*(3), e0282618.

Lai, C.-H. (2020). Task MRI-based functional brain network of anxiety. *Advances in Experimental Medicine and Biology, 1191,* 3–20.

Lai, S. (2022, February 24). *How do we solve social media's eating disorder problem?* Washington, DC: Brookings Institution.

Lake, T. (2022). 6 of the world's deadliest natural disasters. *Britannica*. Retrieved from https://www.britannica.com/list.

Lal, P. V. (2020, May 9). 120 years of psychoanalysis: On Freud's footsteps in Vienna. *Money Control*. Retrieved from https://www.moneycontrol.com/news/trends.

Lancet, The. (2010, February 2). Retraction—Ileal-lymphoid-nodular hyperplasia, non-specific colitis, and pervasive developmental disorder in children. *The Lancet, 375*(9713), 445.

Landgren, V., Hedman, E., Lindblad, I., Gillberg, C., & Fernell, E. (2024). Adult psychiatric and psychosocial outcomes of children with mild intellectual disability: A register follow-up of a population-based cohort. *Journal of Intellectual Disability Research, 68*(1), 34–44.

Landgren, V., Olsson, P., Briken, P., & Rahm, C. (2022). Effects of testosterone suppression on desire, hypersexuality, and sexual interest in children in men with pedophilic disorder. *World Journal of Biological Psychiatry, 23*(7), 560–571.

Landgren, V., Savard, J., Dhejne, C., Jokinen, J., Arver, S., Seto, M. C., & Rahm, C. (2022). Pharmacological treatment for pedophilic disorder and compulsive sexual behavior disorder: A review. *Drugs, 82*(6), 663–681.

Lane, S. P., Aslinger, E. N., & Shrout, P. E. (2023). Reliability. In H. Cooper, M. N. Coutanche, L. M. McMullen, A. T. Panter, D. Rindskopf, & K. J. Sher (Eds.). *APA handbook of research methods in psychology: Foundations, planning, measures, and psychometrics* (pp. 723–743). Washington, DC: American Psychological Association.

Lange-Vaidya, N. (2023, November 16). Asthma in adolescents and adults: Evaluation and diagnosis. *UpToDate*. Retrieved from http://www.uptodate.com.

Langmann, C. (2021, November): Suicide, firearms, and legislation: A review of the Canadian evidence. *ScienceDirect, 152*(1), 106471.

Långström, N., & Seto, M. C. (2006). Exhibitionist and voyeuristic behavior in a Swedish national population survey. *Archives of Sexual Behavior, 35,* 427–435.

Lanius, R., Frewen, P. A., & Brand, B. (2022, August 3). Dissociative aspects of posttraumatic stress disorder: Epidemiology, clinical manifestations, assessment, and diagnosis. *UpToDate*. Retrieved from https://www.uptodate.com.

Laposa, J. M., Katz, D. E., Lisi, D. M., Hawley, L. L., Quigley, L., & Rector, N. A. (2022). Longitudinal changes in intolerance of uncertainty and worry severity during CBT for generalized anxiety disorder. *Journal of Anxiety Disorders, 91,* 102623.

Large, M., Callaghan, S., & Ryan, C. J. (2023). Risk of harm and involuntary psychiatric treatment. In B. D. Kelly & M. Donnelly (Eds.). *Routledge handbook of mental health law* (Chap. 18). New York: Routledge.

Large, M., & Nielssen, O. (2020). Homicide. In J. R. Geddes, N. C. Andreason, & G. M. Goodwin (Eds.). *New Oxford textbook of psychiatry* (3rd ed., Chap. 146). New York: Oxford University Press.

Lauche, R., Anheyer, D., Uebelacker, L. A., Sibbritt, D., Adams, J., & Cramer, H. (2023). Do yoga and meditation moderate the relationship between negative life events and depressive symptoms: Analysis of a national cross-sectional survey of Australian women. *Frontiers in Psychology, 14,* 1218976.

Launer, J. (2021). Light and gravity: Can the full moon really make you go mad? *Postgraduate Medical Journal, 97*(1154), 831–832.

Law, R., Ravitz, P., Pain, C., & Fonagy, P. (2022). Interpersonal psychotherapy and mentalizing: Synergies in clinical practice. *American Journal of Psychotherapy, 75*(1), 44–50.

Lawrence, R. E., & Bernstein, A. (2024). Schizophrenia and emergency medicine. *Emergency Medicine Clinics of North America, 42*(1), 93–104.

Lazarov, O., Robinson, J., Tang, Y. P., Hairston, I. S., Korade-Mirnics, Z., Lee, V. M., . . . Sisodia, S. S. (2005). Environmental enrichment reduces A-beta levels and amyloid deposition in transgenic mice. *Cell, 120*(5), 572–574.

Lazarus, R. S., & Folkman, S. (1984). *Stress, appraisal, and coping.* New York: Springer Publishing.

Le, L. K.-D., Tan, E. J., & Wilksch, S. (2023). Prevention of eating disorders. In P. Robinson, T. Wade, B. Herpertz-Dahlann, F. Fernandez-Aranda, J. Treasure, & S. Wonderlich (Eds.). *Eating disorders*. Edinburgh: Springer.

Leahy, N. (2023, February). *Alcohol abuse amongst the elderly: A complete guide.* Retrieved from https://aging.com/alcohol-abuse-amongst-the-elderly-a-complete-guide.

Leahy, R. L. (2017). *Cognitive therapy techniques: A practitioner's guide* (2nd ed.). New York: Guilford Press.

Leahy, R. L. (2022). Cognitive therapy supervision. In E. A. Storch, J. S. Abramowitz, & D. McKay (Eds.). *Training and supervision in specialized cognitive behavior therapy: Methods, settings, and populations* (Chap. 2). Washington, DC: American Psychological Association.

Leavy, P. (2022, October 26). *Research design: Quantitative, mixed methods, arts-based, and community-based participatory research approaches* (2nd ed.). New York: Guilford Press.

Lebow, H. I. (2022, March 25). Exploring the meaning of (your) life with existential therapy. *Psych Central*. Retrieved from https://psychcentral.com/health/existential-therapy.

Lebow, J., Sim, L., Wonderlich, S., & Peterson, C. B. (2023). Adapting integrative cognitive-affective therapy for adolescents with full and subthreshold bulimia nervosa: A feasibility study. *European Eating Disorders Review, 31*(1), 178–187.

Lebow, J. L., & Snyder, D. K. (Eds.). (2022, July 27). *Clinical handbook of couple therapy* (6th ed.). New York: Guilford Press.

Lebrun-Harris, L. A., Ghandour, R. M., Kogan, M. D., & Warren, M. D. (2022). Five-Year Trends in US Children's Health and Well-being, 2016-2020. *JAMA pediatrics, 176*(7), e220056. https://doi.org/10.1001/jamapediatrics.2022.0056

Leckman, J. F. (2022). New insights into the genetic architecture of obsessive-compulsive disorder: Another step along the way. *American Journal of Psychiatry, 179*(3), 177–179.

Ledesma, J., Bertin, M., Scruggs, T., & Bahl-Milne, S. B. (2022, March 30). An at-home meditation retreat you can share with those you love. *Mindful*.

Lee, A., & Park, J. (2021, December 27). Diagnostic test accuracy of the Beck Depression Inventory for detecting major depression in adolescents: A systematic review and meta-analysis. *Clinical Nursing Research, 31*(8), 1481–1490.

Lee, H.-S., Torregrossa, L. J., Shenoy, S., & Park, S. (2022). Embodiment of emotion in schizophrenia in the context of culture. *Science Direct, 4*(4), 100072.

Lee, J. D., Terol, A. K., Yoon, C. D., & Meadan, H. (2023, January 1). Parent-to-parent support among parents of children with autism: A review of the literature. *Autism*. https://doi.org/10.1177/13623613221146444. [Online ahead of print]

Lee, J. K. (2024), Mapping the intrinsic structural connectivity landscape in autism. *Biological Psychiatry, 95*(2), 100–101.

Lee, K., Cascella, M., & Marwaha, R. (2023, June 4). Intellectual disability. *StatPearls*.

Lee, K. S., & Vaillancourt, T. (2023, August 27). Trajectories, comorbidity, and risk factors for adolescent disordered eating and borderline personality disorder features. *Development and Psychopathology*. doi:10.1017/S0954579423000792. [Online ahead of print]

Lee, L. O., Grimm, K. J., Spiro, A., III, & Kubzansky, L. D. (2022). Neuroticism, worry, and cardiometabolic risk trajectories Findings from a 40-year study of men. *Journal of the American Heart Association, 11*(3), e022006.

Lee, N., Ross, P., & Bothwell, S. (2022, July 25). Is there really such a thing as an "addictive personality"? *The Conversation*. Retrieved from https://theconversation.com.

Lee, S. (2017, June 14). 20 years after being raped, I still struggle with PTSD. *Wear Your Voice*. Retrieved from https://wyvarchive.com.

Lee, S. H., & Jung, E.-M. (2024). Adverse effects of early-life stress: Focus on the rodent neuroendocrine system. *Neural Regeneration Research, 19*(2), 336–341.

Leff, J., Williams, G., Huckvale, M., Arbuthnot, M., & Leff, A. (2013). Computer-assisted therapy for medication-resistant auditory hallucinations: Proof-of-concept study. *British Journal of Psychiatry, 202,* 428–433.

Leff, J., Williams, G., Huckvale, M., Arbuthnot, M., & Leff, A. P. (2014). Avatar therapy for persecutory auditory hallucinations: What is it and how does it work? *Psychosis, 6*(2), 166–176.

Lehman, S. (2016, March 8). Kids who skip lunch are missing out on essential nutrients. *Health News*. Retrieved from https://www.reuters.com/article/us-health-kids-lunch-idUSKCN0WA2HY.

Lehmiller, J. J., & Gormezano, A. M. (2023). Sexual fantasy research: A contemporary review. *Current Opinions in Psychiatry, 49,* 101496.

Leichsenring, F., Abbass, A., Heim, N., Keefe, J. R., Kisely, S., Luyten, P., . . . Steinert, C. (2023). The status of psychodynamic psychotherapy as an empirically supported treatment for common mental disorders: An umbrella review based on updated criteria. *World Psychiatry, 22*(2), 286–304.

Leichsenring, F., Heim, N., & Steinert, C. (2023). A review of anxiety disorders. *JAMA, 329*(15), 1315–1316.

Leisman, G., Melillo, R., & Melillo, T. (2023). Prefrontal functional connectivities in autism spectrum disorders: A connectopathic disorder affecting movement, interoception, and cognition. *Brain Research Bulletin, 198,* 65–76.

LeMasters, K., Behne, M. F., Lao, J., Peterson, M., & Brinkley-Rubenstein, L. (2023). Suicides in state prisons in the United States: Highlighting gaps in data. *PLoS One, 18*(5), e0285729.

Lemon, C. (2023). Commentary; Poverty and mental health. *International Journal of Social Psychiatry, 69*(4), 1055–1056.

Lenzenweger, M. F. (2022, May 24). Proximal processes, temperament, and pathological narcissism: An empirical exploration from the longitudinal study of personality disorders. *Psychopathology, 56*(1–2), 41–51.

Leonard, J. (2023, May 23). What is learned helplessness? *Medical News Today.*

Leong, F. T. L., Bernal, G., & Buchanan, N.-C. T. (Eds.). (2024, July). *Clinical psychology in communities of color.* Washington, DC: American Psychological Association.

Leong, F., Lui, P. P., & Kalibatseva, Z. (2020). Multicultural issues in clinical psychological assessment. In M. Sellbom & J. A. Suhr (Eds.). *The Cambridge handbook of clinical assessment and diagnosis* (Chap. 3). Cambridge: Cambridge University Press.

Lerario, M. P., Fusunyan, M., Stave, C. D., Roldán, V., Keuroghlian, A. S., Turban, J., . . . Rosendale, N. (2023). Functional neurological disorder and functional somatic syndromes among sexual and gender minority people: A scoping review. *Journal of Psychosomatic Research, 174,* 111491.

Leroux, E. J., Clow, K.-A., Motayne, G., & Seto, M. C. (2020, April 23). The association of childhood sexual abuse with non-paraphilic and paraphilic sexual behaviors among adolescents who have sexually offended. *Journal of Sex Research, 57*(9), 1189–1201.

Leroux, R.-A., Dissaux, N., Le Reste, J. Y., Bronsard, G., & Lavenne-Collot, N. (2023). Association between HPA axis functioning and mental health in maltreated children and adolescents: A systematic literature review. *Children (Basel), 10*(8), 1344.

Lesinskiene, S., Kinciniene, O., Sambaras, R., & Zilinskas, E. (2022). Analysis of attempted suicide in a pediatric setting: Extracted notes for clinical practice and complexity of help. *International Journal of Environmental Research and Public Health, 19,* 8604.

Leung, Y., Barzilai, N., Batko-Szwaczka, A., Bekar, N., Boerner, K., Brayne, C., . . . Sachdev, P. (2022, December 1). Cognition, function, and prevalent dementia in centenarians and near-centenarians: An individual participant data (IPD) meta-analysis of 18 studies. *Alzheimer's & Dementia Journal.* doi:10.1002/alz.12828. [Online ahead of print]

Levenson, J. L. (2022, August 29). Illness anxiety disorder: Epidemiology, clinical presentation, assessment, and diagnosis. *UpToDate.* Retrieved from http://www.uptodate.com.

Levenson, J. L. (2022, August 29). Illness anxiety disorder: Treatment and prognosis. *UpToDate.* Retrieved from http://www.uptodate.com.

Levenson, J. L. (2022, September 19). Psychological factors affecting other medical conditions: Clinical features, assessment, and diagnosis. *UpToDate.* Retrieved from http://www.uptodate.com.

Levenson, J. L. (2022, August 10). Somatic symptom disorder: Epidemiology and clinical presentation. *UpToDate.* Retrieved from http://www.uptodate.com.

Levenson, J. L. (2022, September 1). Somatic symptom disorder: Treatment. *UpToDate.* Retrieved from http://www.uptodate.com.

Levenson, R. W., Chen, K.-H., Levan, D. T., Chen, E. Y., Newton, S. L., Paul, D., . . . Wang, G. (2024). Evaluating in-home assistive technology for dementia caregivers. *Clinical Gerontologist, 47*(1), 78–89.

Levine, M. P. (2020). Prevention of eating disorders: 2019 in review. *Eating Disorders, 28*(1), 6–20.

Levine, P. (2022, February 11). *What is my probability of getting into a car accident?* Retrieved from https://pl-law.com/what-is-my-probability-of-getting-into-a-car-accident.

Lew, B., Lester, D., Mustapha, F. I., Yip, P., Chen, Y.-Y., Panirselvam, R., . . . Siau, C. S. (2022). Decriminalizing suicide attempt in the 21st century: An examination of suicide rates in countries that penalize suicide, a critical review. *BMC Psychiatry, 22,* 424.

LeWine, H. E. (2023, January 20). Borderline personality disorder. *Harvard Health.* Retrieved from https://www.health.harvard.edu/a_to_z.

Lewinsohn, P. M., Antonuccio, D. O., Steinmetz, J. L., & Teri, L. (1984). *The coping with depression course.* Eugene, OR: Castalia.

Lewinsohn, P. M., Clarke, G. N., Hops, H., & Andrews, J. (1990). Cognitive-behavioral treatment for depressed adolescents. *Behavior Therapist, 21,* 385–401.

Leyhausen, J., Schäfer, T., Gurr, C., Berg, L. M., Seelemeyer, H., Pretzsch, C. M., . . . Ecker, C. (2024). Differences in intrinsic gray matter connectivity and their genomic underpinnings in autism spectrum disorder. *Biological Psychiatry, 95*(2), 175–186.

Li, K., Niu, Z., Maei, S., & Griffiths, M. D. (2022). A network analysis approach to the relationship between fear of missing out (FoMO), smartphone addition, and social networking site use among a sample of Chinese university students. *Computers in Human Behavior, 127,* 107086.

Li, M., Yao, X., Sun, L., Zhao, L., Xu, W., Zhao, H., . . . Cui, R. (2020). Effects of electroconvulsive therapy on depression and its potential mechanism. *Frontiers in Psychology, 11,* 80.

Li, T., Huang, Y., Jiang, M., Ma, S., & Ma, Y. (2023). Childhood psychological abuse and relational aggression among adolescents: A moderated chain mediation model. *Frontiers in Psychology, 13,* 1082516.

Li, W., Li, G., Xin, C., Wang, Y., & Yang, S. (2020, April 22). Changes in sexual behaviors of young women and men during the coronavirus disease 2019 outbreak: A convenience sample from the epidemic area. *Journal of Sexual Medicine, 17*(7), 1225–1228.

Li, W., Zhou, H., Thygesen, J. H., Heydtmann, M., Smith, I., Degenhardt, F., . . . McQuillin, A. (2023). Genome-wide association study of antisocial personality disorder diagnostic criteria provides evidence for shared risk factors across disorders. *Psychiatric Genetics, 33*(6), 233–242.

Li, Y.-F., Byrne, S., Yan, W., & Ewoldt, K. B. (2023). Self-monitoring intervention for adolescents and adults with autism: A research review. *Behavioral Science, 13*(2), 138.

Li, Z., Kang, Z., Xia, X., Li, L., Wu, J., Dai, J., . . . Wei, Q. (2024). Associations of resilience, white matter topological organization, and cognitive functions in first-episode, drug-naive schizophrenia patients: A moderated mediation analysis. *Progressive Neuropsychopharmacological Biological Psychiatry, 128,* 110867.

Li, Z., Liu, Y., Wei, R., Yong, V. W., & Xue, M. (2022). The important role of zinc in neurological diseases. *Biomolecules, 13*(1), 28.

Liang, T.-W. (2023, June 12). Tardive dyskinesia: Prevention, treatment, and prognosis. *UpToDate.* Retrieved from https://www.uptodate.com.

Lieberman, A., & Schroeder, J. (2020). Two social lives: How differences between online and offline interaction influence social outcomes. *Current Opinion in Psychology, 31,* 16–21.

Lieberman, J. A. (2024 April 23). *Malady of the mind: Schizophrenia and the path to prevention.* New York: Scribner.

Lim, A., Hoek, H. W., Deen, M. L., & Blom, J. D. (2016). Prevalence and classification of hallucinations in multiple sensory modalities in schizophrenia spectrum disorders. *Schizophrenia Research, 176*(2–3), 493–499.

Lim, C. T., Caan, M. P., Kim, C. H., Chow, C. M., Leff, H. S., & Tepper, M. C. (2022). Care management for serious mental illness: A systematic review and meta-analysis. *Psychiatric Services, 73*(2), 180–187.

Lin, C. (2021, September 9). Looking for your dream job? These careers are the happiest in America. *Fast Company.*

Lin, C.-C., & Huang, T.-L. (2020). Brain-derived neurotrophic factor and mental disorders. *Biomedical Journal, 43*(2), 134–142.

Lin, J., Arnovitz, M., Kotbi, N., & Francois, D. (2023, June 5). Substance use disorders in the geriatric population: A review and synthesis of the literature of a growing problem in a growing population. *Current Treatment Options in Psychiatry.* doi:10.1007/s40501-023-00291-9. [Online ahead of print]

Lin, L., Assefa, M., & Stamm, K. (2023, April 1). Practitioners are overworked and burned out, and they need our support. *Monitor on Psychology, 54*(3).

Lin, L., Christidis, P., & Conroy, J. (2019). Most psychologists are satisfied with their jobs. *Datapoint, 50*(3), 19. https://www.apa.org/monitor/2019/03/datapoint.

Lin, X., Zhuo, C., Li, G., Li, J., Gao, X., Chen, C., & Jiang, D. (2019). Functional brain alterations in auditory hallucination subtypes in individuals with auditory hallucinations without the diagnosis of specific neurological diseases and mental disorders at the current stage. *Brain and Behavior, 10*(1), e01487.

Linardon, J., Susanto, L., Tepper, H., & Fuller-Tyszkiewicz, M. (2020). Self-compassion as a moderator of the relationships between shape and weight overvaluation and eating disorder psychopathology, psychosocial impairment, and psychological distress. *Body Image, 33,* 183–189.

Linde-Krieger, L. B., Yates, T. M., & Carlson, E. A. (2022). A developmental pathways model of dissociation. In M. J. Dorahy, S. N. Gold, & J. A. O'Neil (Eds.). *Dissociation and the dissociative disorders: Past, present, future* (Chap. 9). New York: Routledge.

Lindeque, K. (2022, February 15). Asylums, optimism, and moral treatment: Was Victorian mental health care as cruel as we believe? *New Histories,* Vol. 12. Retrieved from https://newhistories.sites.sheffield.ac.uk.

Lindhiem, O., & Birmaher, B. (2022, October 27). Treatment of oppositional defiant and conduct disorders. *UpToDate.* Retrieved from https://www.uptodate.com.

Lindsay, C. (2022, April 4). All about gestalt therapy. *Psych Central.* Retrieved from https://psychcentral.com/health/gestalt-therapy.

Lindsey, M. A., Sheftall, A. H., Xiao, Y., & Joe, S. (2019). Trends of suicidal behaviors among high school students in the United States: 1991–2017. *Pediatrics, 144*(5), e20191187.

Ling, H., Meng, F., Yan, Y., Feng, H., Zhang, J., Zhang, L., & Yuan, S. (2022). Why is maternal control harmful? The relation between maternal control, insecure attachment and antisocial personality disorder features in Chinese college students: A sequential mediation model. *Journal of Environmental Research and Public Health, 19*(17), 10900.

Lippard, E. T. C., & Nemeroff, C. B. (2020). The devastating clinical consequences of child abuse and neglect: Increased disease vulnerability and poor treatment response in mood disorders. *American Journal of Psychiatry, 177*(1), 20–36.

Lisbona, N. (2022, January 31). True story: Lie detection systems go high-tech. *BBC.* Retrieved from https://www.bbc.com/news.

Liscum, M., & Garcia, M. L. (2022). You can't keep a bad idea down: Dark history, death, and potential rebirth of eugenics. *Anatomical Record, 305*(4), 902–937.

Lissek, S., & Berg, H. (2022). Learning models of PTSD. In J. G. Beck & D. M. Sloan (Eds.). *The Oxford handbook of traumatic stress disorders* (Chap. 14). New York: Oxford University Press.

Litke, S. G., Resnikoff, A., Anil, A., Montgomery, M., Matta, R., Huh-Yoo, J., & Daly, B. P. (2023). Mobile technologies for supporting mental health in youths: Scoping review of effectiveness, limitations, and inclusivity. *JMIR Mental Health, 10,* e46949.

Littell, J. H., Pigott, T. D., Nilsen, K. H., Green, S. J., & Montgomery, O. L. K. (2021, October 8). Multisystemic therapy for social, emotional, and behavioral problems in youth age 10 to 17: An updated systematic review and meta-analysis. *Cochrane Database of Systematic Reviews.* https://doi.org/10.1002/14651858.CD004797.pub4.

Littlefield, A. K. (2023). Longitudinal data analysis. In H. Cooper, M. N. Coutanche, L. M. McMullen, A. T. Panter, D. Rindskopf, & K. J. Sher (Eds.). *APA handbook of research methods in psychology: Vol. 3. Data analysis and research publication* (2nd ed., Chap. 11). Washington, DC: American Psychological Association.

Liu, J., Avery, R. J., Kim, J. J., & Niederdeppe, J. (2022). Maintaining a fair balance? Narrative and non-narrative strategies in televised direct-to-consumer advertisements for prescription drugs aired in the United States, 2003–2016. *Journal of Health Communication, 27*(3), 183–191.

Liu, L., Hay, P., & Conti, J. (2022). Perspectives on barriers to treatment engagement of people with eating disorder symptoms who have not undergone treatment: A qualitative study. *BMC Psychiatry, 22*(1), 239.

Liu, L., Wang, Y., Zhao, J., & Wang, M. (2022). Parental reports of stress and anxiety in their migrant children in China: The mediating role of parental psychological aggression and corporal punishment. *Child Abuse and Neglect, 131,* 105695.

Liu, N., Zhang, F., Wei, C., Jia, Y., Shang, Z., Sun, L., . . . Liu, W. (2020). Prevalence and predictors of PTSS during COVID-19 outbreak in China hardest-hit areas: Gender differences matter. *Psychiatry Research, 287,* 112921.

Liu, Y.-C., Li, I.-L., & Hsiao, F.-H. (2021). Effectiveness of mindfulness-based intervention on psychotic symptoms for patients with schizophrenia: A meta-analysis of randomized controlled trials. *Journal of Advanced Nursing, 77*(6), 2565–2580.

Liu, Y., Xu, Y., Yang, X., Miao, G., Wu, Y., & Yang, S. (2023). The prevalence of anxiety and its key influencing factors among the elderly in China. *Frontiers in Psychiatry, 14,* 1038049.

Liu, Y., Zhu, J., & He, J. (2022). Can selfies trigger social anxiety? A study on the relationship between social media selfie behavior and social anxiety in Chinese youth groups. *Frontiers in Psychology, 13,* 1016538.

Livingston, N. A., Berke, D., Scholl, J., Ruben, M., & Shipherd, J. C. (2020, March 16). Addressing diversity in PTSD treatment: Clinical considerations and guidance for the treatment of PTSD in LGBTQ populations. *Current Treatment Options in Psychiatry, 7,* 53–69.

Livingston, N. A., Brief, D. J., Miller, M. W., & Keane, T. M. (2023). Assessment of PTSD and its comorbidities in adults. In M. J. Friedman, P. P. Schnurr, & T. M. Keane (Eds.). *Handbook of PTSD: Science and practice* (3rd ed., Chap. 16). New York: Guilford Press.

Livingston, N. A., Lynch, K. E., Hinds, Z., Gatsby, E., DuVall, S. L., & Shipherd, J. C. (2022). Identifying posttraumatic stress disorder and disparity among transgender veterans using nationwide Veterans Health Administration electronic health record data. *LGBT Health, 9*(2), 94–102.

LLALLI (Law Library American Law and Legal Information). (2023). *Insanity: Empirical data and myths.* Retrieved from https://law.jrank.org/pages/1136/Excuse-Insanity-Empirical-data-myths.html.

Llamas, M. (2021, June 29). Selling side effects: Big Pharma's marketing machine. *Drugwatch.*

Loades, M. E., Chatburn, E., Higson-Sweeney, N., Reynolds, S., Shafran, R., Brigden, A., . . . Crawley, E. (2020). Rapid systematic review: The impact of social isolation and loneliness on the mental health of children and adolescents in the context of Covid-19. *Journal of the American Academy of Child and Adolescent Psychiatry, 59*(11), 1218–1239.

Lobb, M., & Cavaleri, P. (2023, March 24). *Psychopathology of the situation in gestalt therapy* (The Gestalt Therapy Book Series, 1st ed.). New York: Routledge.

Lochman, J. E., Powell, N. P., & Jones, S. (2022). The Coping Power program for children with aggressive behavior problems. In P. C. Kendall (Ed.). *Flexibility within fidelity: Breathing life into a psychological treatment manual* (pp. 211–230). New York: Oxford University Press.

Lock, J., Whyte, A., Matheson, B., & Datta, N. (2024). *Family-based treatment for eating disorders piece by piece: A practical guide for parents.* New York: Routledge.

Lodge, W., Biello, K., Valente, P. K., & Mimiaga, M. J. (2022). Methamphetamine use among sexual minority men. In V. B. Patel & V. R. Preedy (Eds.). *Handbook of substance misuse and addictions: From biology to public health* (pp. 2097–2119). New York: Springer.

Loeb, S. (2022, September 12). *Calls to new 988 suicide prevention line rose 45% in one month.* VatorNews. Retrieved from https://vator.tv/n/54ce.

Loewenstein, R. J. (2022). Conceptual foundations for long-term psychotherapy of dissociative identity disorder. In M. J. Dorahy, S. N. Gold, & J. A. O'Neil (Eds.). *Dissociation and the dissociative disorders: Past, present, future* (Chap. 47). New York: Routledge.

Loftus, E. F., & Klemfuss, J. Z. (2023, May 20). Misinformation: Past, present, and future. *Psychology, Crime & Law.* doi:10.1080/1068316X.2023.2219813. [Online ahead of print]

Logan-Greene, P., Bishop, A. S., Kim, B.-K. E., & Nurius, P. S. (2023). Protective factors against aggression and antisocial attitudes among probation youth with childhood adversity histories. *Prevention Science, 24*(1), 161–172.

Lomas Mevers, J., Call, N. A., Gerencser, K. R., Scheithauer, M., Miller, S. J., Muething, C., . . . McElhanon, B. O. (2020). A pilot randomized clinical trial of a multidisciplinary intervention for encopresis in children with autism spectrum disorder. *Journal of Autism and Developmental Disorders, 50*(3), 757–765.

Lombardo, P. A. (2017). A child's right to be well born: Venereal disease and the eugenic marriage laws, 1913–1935. *Perspectives in Biology and Medicine, 60*(2), 211–232.

Longpre, N., & Guay, J.-P. (2022). The impact of childhood trauma, personality, and sexuality on the development of paraphilias. *Journal of Criminal Justice, 82,* 101981.

Longstreth, G. F., & Hesketh, P. J. (2023, July 12). Characteristics of antiemetic drugs. *UpToDate.* Retrieved from http://www.uptodate.com.

LoParco, C. R., Cui, Y., Bar-Zeev, Y., Levine, H., Duan, Z., Wang, Y., . . . Berg, C. J. (2024). Driving under the influence of cannabis versus alcohol: A mixed-methods study examining perceptions and related risk behaviors among US and Israeli adults. *Addictive Behaviors, 148,* 107843.

López, G., Orchowski, L. M., Reddy, M. K., Nargiso, J., & Johnson, J. E. (2021). A review of research-supported group treatments for drug use disorders. *Substance Abuse Treatment, Prevention, and Policy, 16*(1), 51.

Lopez-Castroman, J., Moulahi, B., Azé, J., Bringay, S., Deninotti, J., Guillaume, S., & Baca-Garcia, E. (2020). Mining social networks to improve suicide prevention: A scoping review. *Journal of Neuroscience Research, 98*(4), 616–625.

Lopez-Villatoro, J. M., Shimano, R., Prittwitz, C., De la Torre, A., Diaz-Marsá, M., & Carrasco, J. L. (2023). Predictive value of the feeling of emptiness in suicidal behaviour of emotionally unstable disorders. *Clinical Psychology and Psychotherapy, 30*(1), 112–118.

Lorand, S. (1968). Dynamics and therapy of depressive states. In W. Gaylin (Ed.). *The meaning of despair.* New York: Jason Aronson.

Loue, S. (2022). *Diversity, cultural humility, and the helping professions: Building bridges across difference.* Cham, Switzerland: Springer Nature.

Lovejoy, M. (2001). Disturbances in the social body: Differences in body image and eating problems among African-American and white women. *Gender and Society, 15*(2), 239–261.

Lu, L., Shen, H., Tan, L., Huang, Q., Chen, Q., Liang, M., . . . Zhou, Y. (2023). Prevalence and factors associated with anxiety and depression among community-dwelling older adults in Hunan, China: A cross-sectional study. *BMC Psychiatry, 23*(1), 107.

Lu, S.-C., Xu, M., Wang, M., Hardi, A., Cheng, A. L., Chang, S.-H., & Yen, P.-Y. (2022). Effectiveness and minimum effective dose of app-based mobile health interventions for anxiety and depression symptom reduction: Systematic review and meta-analysis. *JMIR Mental Health, 9*(9), e39454.

Lu, Z., Yu, D., Wang, L., & Fu, P. (2024). Association between depression status and hearing loss among older adults: The role of outdoor activity engagement. *Journal of Affective Disorders, 345,* 404–409.

Luborsky, L. (1973). Forgetting and remembering (momentary forgetting) during psychotherapy. In M. Mayman (Ed.). *Psychoanalytic research and psychological issues* (Monograph 30). New York: International Universities Press.

Luetke, M., Hensel, D., Herbenick, D., & Rosenberg, M. (2020). Romantic relationship conflict due to the COVID-19 pandemic and changes in intimate and sexual behaviors in a nationally representative sample of American adults. *Journal of Sex & Marital Therapy, 46*(8), 747–762.

Lunghi, C., Cailhol, L., Massamba, V., Sidi, E. A. L., Sirois, C., Rahme, E., . . . Lesage, A. (2023). Psychotropic medication use pre- and post-diagnosis of cluster B personality disorder: A Quebec's health services register cohort. *Frontiers in Psychiatry, 14,* 1243511.

Lunghi, C., Rochette, L., Massamba, V., Tardif, I., Ouali, A., & Sirois, C. (2023). Psychiatric and non-psychiatric polypharmacy among older adults with schizophrenia: Trends from a population-based study between 2000 and 2016. *Frontiers in Pharmacology, 14,* 1080073.

Luo, G., Zhang, J., Song, Z., Wang, Y., Wang, X., Wu, . . . Gao, F. (2023). Effectiveness of non-pharmacological therapies on cognitive function in patients with dementia: A network meta-analysis of randomized controlled trials. *Frontiers in Aging Neuroscience, 15,* 1131744.

Luta, X., Bagnoud, C., Lambiris, M., Decollogny, A., Eggli, Y., Le Pogam, M.-A., . . . Marti, J. (2020). Patterns of benzodiazepine prescription among older adults in Switzerland: A cross-sectional analysis of claims data. *BMJ Open, 10*(1), e031156.

Luxton, D. D., Nelson, E.-L., & Maheu, M. M. (2023). *A practitioner's guide to telemental health: How to conduct legal, ethical, and evidence-based telepractice* (2nd ed.). Washington, DC: American Psychological Association.

Luyten, P., & Fonagy, P. (2022). An integrative developmental psychopathology approach to depression. In J. P. Jiménez, A. Botto, & P. Fonagy (Eds.). *Etiopathogenic theories and models in depression* (pp. 245–263). Cham, Switzerland: Springer Nature.

Lycke, S. T., Airosa, F., & Lundh, L. (2022, May 16). Emergency department nurses' experiences of a mindfulness training intervention: A phenomenological exploration. *Journal of Holistic Nursing.* [Free article]

Lyness, J. M. (2022, September 26). Unipolar depression in adults: Assessment and diagnosis. *UpToDate.* Retrieved from https://www.uptodate.com.

Lyness, J. M. (2023, July 6). Unipolar minor depression in adults: Epidemiology, clinical presentation, and diagnosis. *UpToDate.* Retrieved from https://www.uptodate.com.

Lynn, K. (2019, January 10). Understanding musical ear syndrome. *Flagstaff Business & Online News.*

Lyons, B. H., Walters, M. L., Jack, S. P. D., Petrosky, E., Blair, J. M., & Ivey-Stephenson, A. .Z. (2019). Suicides among lesbian and gay male individuals: Findings from the National Violent Death Reporting System. *American Journal of Preventive Medicine, 56*(4), 512–521.

Lyons, M., Houghton, E., Brewer, G., & O'Brien, F. (2020). The dark triad and sexual assertiveness predict sexual coercion differently in men and women. *Journal of Interpersonal Violence, 37*(7–8), 4905–4930.

Lyubomirsky, S. (2008). *The how of happiness: A new approach to getting the life you want.* New York: Penguin Books.

Lyubomirsky, S. (2019). The road to happiness is paved with a little gold, a lot of reporters, many e-mails, thousands of frequent flyer miles, and 604 hours of writing. *Perspectives on Psychological Science, 14*(1), 26–28.

Macaluso, M. (2022). Tricyclics, tetracyclics, and monoamine. In C. B. Nemeroff, A. F. Schatzberg, N. Rasgon, & S. M. Strakowski (Eds.). *The American Psychiatric Association Publishing textbook of mood disorders* (2nd ed., Chap. 14). Washington, DC: American Psychiatric Association Publishing.

Macdonald-Gagnon, G., & Potenza, M. N. (2022). Gambling disorder as an addiction. In V. B. Patel & V. R. Preedy (Eds.). *Handbook of substance misuse and addictions: From biology to public health* (pp. 2885–2902). New York: Springer.

MacGill, M. (2023, January 11). What you need to know about delayed ejaculation. *Medical News Today.*

Machado, P. P. P., & Rodrigues, T. F. (2023). Eating disorders and pandemics. In P. Robinson, T. Wade, B. Herpertz-Dahlann, F. Fernandez-Aranda, J. Treasure, & S. Wonderlich (Eds.). *Eating disorders.* Edinburgh: Springer.

MacIntosh, H. B., & Ménard, A. D. (2021). Couple and parenting functioning of childhood sexual abuse survivors: A systematic review of the literature (2001–2018). *Journal of Child Sexual Abuse, 30*(3), 353–384.

MacIntyre, M. R., & Appel, J. M. (2020, June). Legal and ethics considerations in reporting sexual exploitation by previous providers. *Journal of the American Academy of Psychiatry Law, 48*(2), 166–175.

MacPherson, R. (2022). What is body shaming and how to stop it. *Verywell Fit.* Retrieved from https://www.verywellfit.com.

Madill, A. (2023). Interviews and interviewing techniques. In H. Cooper, M. N. Coutanche, L. M. McMullen, A. T. Panter, D. Rindskopf, & K. J. Sher (Eds.). *APA handbook of research methods in psychology: Foundations, planning, measures, and psychometrics* (pp. 297–325). Washington, DC: American Psychological Association.

Magid, M., & Fox, I. (2022). Histrionic personality disorder. In R. Feinstein (Ed.). *Personality disorders* (Chap. 20). New York: Oxford University Press.

Magliocca, S., Romano, D., Joiner, T. E., Madeddu, F., Calati, R., Zeppegno, P., & Gramaglia, C. (2023, October 24). The interpersonal psychological theory of suicide in Italian university students: Validation of the INQ-15 and the ACSS-FAD. *Assessment.* doi:10.1177/10731911231203971. [Online ahead of print]

Mainwaring, J. M., Lee, T. K., Wassersug, R. J., & Wibowo, E. (2023). Scales for assessing male sexual function are not entirely applicable to gay and bisexual men with prostate cancer. *Urologic Clinics of North America, 50*(4), 549–561.

Mair, J. L., Hayes, L. D., Campbell, A. K., Buchan, D. S., Easton, C., & Sculthorpe, N. (2022). A personalized smartphone-delivered Just-in-time Adaptive Intervention (JitaBug) to increase physical activity in older adults: Mixed methods feasibility study. *MJIR Formative Research, 6*(4), e34662.

Malhi, G. S. (2020). Primary prevention of mood disorders: Building a target for prevention strategies. In J. R. Geddes, N. C. Andreasen, & G. M. Goodwin (Eds.). *New Oxford textbook of psychiatry* (3rd ed., Chap. 68). New York: Oxford University Press.

Malhi, G. S., Jadidi, M., & Bell, E. (2023). The diagnosis of bipolar disorder in children and adolescents: Past, present and future. *Bipolar Disorders, 25*(6), 469–477.

Malhi, P., & Bharti, B. (2021). School bullying and association with somatic complaints in victimized children. *Indian Journal of Pediatrics, 88*(10), 962–967.

Mallon, G. P., & Perez, J. (2020). The experiences of transgender and gender expansive youth in juvenile justice systems. *Journal of Criminological Research, Policy, and Practice, 6*(3), 217–229.

Malloy, L. C., Dykstra, V. W., Steen, R., Filoso, D., Salem, H., Comer, J. S., . . . Evans, A. D. (2024). Avoidant parent-child communication about COVID-19: A longitudinal investigation of associations with youth adjustment across the first 6 months of the pandemic. *Research on Child and Adolescent Psychopathology, 52*(2), 253–266.

Malone, R. M., Stewart, M. R., Gary-Smith, M., & Wadley, J. C. (Eds.). (2021). *An intersectional approach to sex therapy: Centering the lives of indigenous, racialized, and people of color.* New York: Routledge.

Manaba, N. (2020, March 9). *Percentage of black youths arrested remains high, even as juvenile arrests decline in Alachua County.* WUFT News. Retrieved from https://www.wuft.org.

Mandal, A. (2014). Hallucination types. *News-Medical.*

Mandal, P. K., Gaur, S., Roy, R. G., Samkaria, A., Ingole, R., & Goel, A. (2022). Schizophrenia, bipolar and major depressive disorders: Overview of clinical features, neurotransmitter alterations, pharmacological interventions, and impact of oxidative stress in the disease process. *ACS Chemical Neuroscience, 13*(19), 2784–2802.

Manicavasagar, V., & Silove, D. (2022). The cognitive behavioral treatment of agoraphobia. In G. Todd (Ed.). *Evidence-based treatment for anxiety disorders and depression: A cognitive behavioral therapy compendium* (Chap. 5). Cambridge: Cambridge University Press.

Mann, J. J., & Currier, D. (2020). Biological aspects of suicidal behaviour. In J. R. Geddes, N. C. Andreason, & G. M. Goodwin (Eds.). *New Oxford textbook of psychiatry* (3rd ed., Chap. 127). New York: Oxford University Press.

Mansueto, C. S. (2022). Comprehensive behavioral treatment for trichotillomania (hair pulling disorder) and excoriation (skin picking) disorder. In G. Todd (Ed.). *Evidence-based treatment for anxiety disorders and depression: A cognitive behavioral therapy compendium* (Chap. 16). Cambridge: Cambridge University Press.

Manza, P., Tomasi, D., Shokri-Kojori, E., Zhang, R., Kroll, D., Feldman, D., . . . Volkow, N. D. (2023). Neural circuit selective for fast but not slow dopamine increases in drug reward. *Nature Communications, 14,* 6408.

Marbin, D., Gutwinski, S., Schreiter, S., & Heinz, A. (2022). Perspectives in poverty and mental health. *Frontiers in Public Health, 10,* 975482.

Marchese, S., & Huckins, L. M. (2023). Trauma matters: Integrating genetic and environmental components of PTSD. *Advanced Genetics, 4*(3), 2200017.

Marchi, M., Travascio, A., Uberti, D., De Micheli, E., Grenzi, P., Arcolin, E., . . . Galeazzi, G. M. (2023). Post-traumatic stress disorder among LGBTQ people: A systematic review and meta-analysis. *Epidemiology and Psychiatric Sciences, 23,* e44.

Marchili, M. R., Diamanti, A., Zanna, V., Spina, G., Mascolo, C., Roversi, M., . . . Villani, A. (2023). Early naso-gastric feeding and outcomes of anorexia nervosa patients. *Nutrients, 15*(3), 490.

Marco, S., Mayoral, M., & Hervas, G. (2023, June 2). Dialectical behavioral skills group therapy for parents of adolescents with borderline personality disorder: A pilot study. *Clinical Child Psychology and Psychiatry.* doi:10.1177/13591045231177329. [Online ahead of print]

Marder, S. (2022, April 14). Psychosis in adults: Epidemiology, clinical manifestations, and diagnostic evaluation. *UpToDate.* Retrieved from http://www.uptodate.com.

Marder, S. (2023, February 1). Psychosis in adults: Initial management. *UpToDate.* Retrieved from http://www.uptodate.com.

Margolis, S., & Lyubomirsky, S. (2019). Experimental manipulation of extraverted and introverted behavior and its effects on well-being. *Journal of Experimental Psychology: General, 149*(4), 719–731.

Markel, H. (2020, April 4). Dorothea Dix's tireless fight to end inhumane treatment for mental health patients. *PBS News Hour.* Retrieved from https://www.pbs.org//newshour/health.

Markfield, M. H. (2019, Spring). A more perfect union: Eugenics in America. *NAELA Journal.* Retrieved from https://www.naela.org/NewsJournalOnline/OnlineJournalArticles/OnlineApril2019/Eugenics.aspx.

Markowitz, J. C. (2022). Interpersonal psychotherapy for depressive disorders. In C. B. Nemeroff, A. F. Schatzberg, N. Rasgon, & S. M. Strakowski (Eds.). *The American Psychiatric Association Publishing textbook of mood disorders* (2nd ed., Chap. 24). Washington, DC: American Psychiatric Association Publishing.

Marks, I. M. (1977). Phobias and obsessions: Clinical phenomena in search of a laboratory model. In J. Maser & M. Seligman (Eds.). *Psychopathology: Experimental models.* San Francisco: Freeman.

Marks, I. M., & Gelder, M. G. (1967). Transvestism and fetishism: Clinical and psychological changes during faradic aversion. *British Journal of Psychiatry, 113*(500), 711–729. https://doi.org/10.1192/bjp.113.500.711.

Marshall, H. (2023, February 15). Viagra (Sildenafil). *Medical News Today.*

Marshall, L. (2022, May 10). *Multiple diagnoses are the norm with mental illness: New genetic study explains why.* Boulder: University of Colorado Boulder.

Marshall, W. L., Serran, G. A., Marshall, L. E., & O'Brien, M. D. (2008). Sexual deviation. In M. Hersen & J. Rosqvist (Eds.). *Handbook of psychological assessment, case conceptualization and treatment: Vol. 1. Adults.* Hoboken, NJ: Wiley.

Martin, D., & Le, J. K. (2023, July 31). Amphetamine. *StatPearls.*

Martin, S. F., & Levine, S. B. (2023, October 24). Fetishistic disorder. *UpToDate.* Retrieved from http://www.uptodate.com.

Martinez, B., & Peplow, P. V. (2024). MicroRNAs as potential biomarkers for diagnosis of schizophrenia and influence of antipsychotic treatment. *Neural Regeneration Research, 19*(7), 1523–1531.

Martínez, V., Jiménez-Molina, A., & Gerber, M. M. (2023). Social contagion, violence, and suicide among adolescents. *Current Opinions in Psychiatry, 36*(3), 237–242.

Martin-Gagnon, G., Normandin, L., Fonagy, P., & Ensink, K. (2023). Adolescent mentalizing and childhood emotional abuse: Implications for depression, anxiety, and borderline personality disorder features. *Frontiers in Psychology, 14,* 1237735.

Masa, R., Inoue, M., Prieto, L., Baruah, D., Nosrat, S., Mehak, S., & Operario, D. (2023, October 6). Mental health of older adults by sexual minority status: Evidence from the 2021 National Health Interview Survey. *Journal of Applied Gerontology.* doi:10.1177/07334648231203838. [Online ahead of print]

Mascolo, J. (2023). Civil commitment for sex offenders. *FindLaw.* Retrieved from https://www.findlaw.com/criminal/criminal-charges.

Maslej, M. M., Srikanth, N., Froentjes, L., & Andrews, P. W. (2020). Why does expressive writing affect emotion: Considering the impact of valence and cognitive processing. *Canadian Journal of Behavioural Science, 52*(2), 85–96.

Maslow, A. H. (1970). *Motivation and personality* (2nd ed.). New York: Harper & Row.

Mason, D. (2020, February 25). Dayna's dose: The benefits of selfies and healthy narcissism. *B-Town Blog.* Retrieved from https://b-town-blog.com.

Mason, X. L. (2023). Challenges to the diagnosis of functional neurological disorder: Feigning, intentionality, and responsibility. *Neuroethics, 16*(1), 2.

Masters, W. H., & Johnson, V. E. (1966). *Human sexual response.* Boston: Little, Brown.

Masters, W. H., & Johnson, V. E. (1970). *Human sexual inadequacy.* Boston: Little, Brown.

Matcham, F., Leightley, D., Siddi, S., Lasers, F., White, K. M., Annas, P., . . . RADAR-CNS Consortium. (2022). Remote Assessment of Disease and Relapse in Major Depressive Disorder (RADAR-MDD): Recruitment, retention, and data availability in a longitudinal remote measurement study. *BMC Psychiatry, 22*(1), 136.

Mather, M. (2016). *Fact sheet: Aging in the United States*. Washington, DC: PRB.org.

Mather, M., Scommegna, P., & Kilduff, L. (2019, July 15). *Fact sheet: Aging in the United States*. Washington, DC: PRB.org.

Mathijs, L., Mouton, B., Zimmermann, G., & Van Petegem, S. (2023, May 5). Overprotective parenting and social anxiety in adolescents: The role of emotion regulation. *Journal of Social and Personal Relationships*. [Online ahead of print]

Matthews, T. A., Sembajwe, G., vijb Känel, R., & Li, J. (2022). Associations of employment status with opioid misuse: Evidence from a nationally representative survey in the U.S. *Journal of Psychiatric Research, 151*, 30–33.

Mattison, M. (2023, November 16). Hospital management of older adults. *UpToDate*. Retrieved from http://www.uptodate.com.

Mattos, J. I. P., Mosqueiro, B. P., Stuart, S., Salum, G., de Lima Duzzo, R., de Souza, L. R., . . . de Almeida Fleck, M. P. (2022). Implementation of group interpersonal psychotherapy in primary care. *Revista de Saude Publica, 56*, 23.

Matz, S. (2023, March–April). What psychological targeting can do. *Harvard Business Review*.

Maul, S., Giegling, I., Fabbri, C., Corponi, F., Serretti, A., & Rujescu, D. (2020). Genetics of resilience: Implications from genome-wide association studies and candidate genes of the stress response system in posttraumatic stress disorder and depression. *American Journal of Medical Genetics. Part B, Neuropsychiatric Genetics, 183*(2), 77–94.

Mayberg, H. S., Lozano, A. M., Voon, V., McNeely, H. E., Seminowicz, D., Hamani, C., . . . Kennedy, S. H. (2005). Deep brain stimulation for treatment-resistant depression. *Neuron, 45*, 651–660.

Maye, C. E., Wojcik, K. D., Candelari, A. E., Goodman, W. K., & Storch, E. A. (2022). Obsessive compulsive disorder during the COVID-19 pandemic: A brief review of course, psychological assessment and treatment considerations. *Journal of Obsessive-Compulsive and Related Disorders, 33*, 100722.

Mayer, L., Corrigan, P. W., Eisheuer, D., Oexle, N., & Rüsch, N. (2022). Attitudes towards disclosing a mental illness: Impact on quality of life and recovery. *Social Psychiatry and Psychiatric Epidemiology, 57*(2), 363–374.

Maymone, M., Laughter, M., Anderson, J. B., Secemsky, E. A., & Vashi, N. A. (2020). Unattainable standards of beauty: Temporal trends of Victoria's Secret models from 1995 to 2018. *Aesthetic Surgery Journal, 40*(2), NP72–NP76.

MCASA (Maryland Coalition Against Sexual Assault). (2020, November). *Sexual violence against transgender communities*. Silver Spring, MD: Author.

MCASA (Maryland Coalition Against Sexual Assault). (2020). *Sexual violence and the transgender community*. Silver Spring, MD: Author.

MCASA (Maryland Coalition Against Sexual Assault) (2022). *Sexual violence and the transgender community*. Silver Spring, MD: Author.

McBain, R. K., Eberhart, N. K., Breslau, J., Frank, L., Burnam, A., Kareddy, V., & Simmons, M. M. (2021). *Transforming mental health care in the United States*. Santa Monica, CA: RAND Corporation.

McCabe, R. E., & Bui, E. (2023, July 10). Management of specific phobia in adults. *UpToDate*. Retrieved from https://www.uptodate.com.

McCabe, R. E., & Bui, E. (2023, July 26). Specific phobia in adults: Cognitive-behavioral therapy. *UpToDate*. Retrieved from https://www.uptodate.com.

McCain, A. (2023, March 20). 25 insightful nursing home statistics [2023]: Residents, locations, and long-term care. *Zippia*. Retrieved from https://www.zippia.com/advice/nursing-home-statistics.

McCall, M. (2023, June 25). Involuntary commitment: Patient and public rights. *FindLaw*. Retrieved from https://www.findlaw.com/healthcare/patient-rights.

McCambridge, M., & Stinson, M. J. (2020). Advances in chronic traumatic encephalopathy. *JAAPA, 33*(4), 39–42.

McCann, S. (2022, December 22). For decades, Los Angeles jailed people with mental health needs. Now, it's finally prioritizing treatment. *Vera*. Retrieved from https://www.vera.org/news.

McCarthy, M. (2022, June 13). *With declining managed care rates and baseless denials, providers ask, "Is it worth it?"* Marcum LLP. Retrieved from https://www.marcumllp.com/insights.

McClintock, S. M., & Choi, J. (Eds.). (2022). *Neuropsychology of depression*. New York: Guilford Press.

McComb, S. E., & Mills, J. S. (2022). The effect of physical appearance perfectionism and social comparison to thin-, slim-thick-, and fit-ideal Instagram imagery on young women's body image. *Body Image, 40*, 165–175.

McConaughy, S. H., & Whitcomb, S. A. (2022, January 20). *Clinical interviews for children and adolescents: Assessment to intervention (Guilford Practical Intervention in the Schools Series)* (3rd ed.). New York: Guilford Press.

McConnell, D., & Phelan, S. (2022). The devolution of eugenic practices: Sexual and reproductive health and oppression of people with intellectual disability. *Social Science & Medicine, 298*, 114877.

McCutcheon, R. A., Keefe, R. S. E., & McGuire, P. K. (2023, January 23). Cognitive impairment in schizophrenia: Aetiology, pathophysiology, and treatment. *Molecular Psychiatry, 28*(5), 1902–1918.

McDermott, R., & Hatemi, P. K. (2020). Ethics in field experimentation: A call to establish new standards to protect the public from unwanted manipulation and real harms. *Proceedings of the National Academy of Sciences, 117*(48), 30014–30021.

McDermott, T. (2020, January 31). Combative and defiant, CIA psychologist reignites torture debate at 9/11 hearings. *Los Angeles Times*.

McDonald, W. (2022). Electroconvulsive therapy. In C. B. Nemeroff, A. F. Schatzberg, N. Rasgon, & S. M. Strakowski (Eds.). *The American Psychiatric Association Publishing textbook of mood disorders* (2nd ed., Chap. 18). Washington, DC: American Psychiatric Association Publishing.

McDonnell, C. G., DeLucia, E. A., Hayden, E. P., Penner, M., Curcin, K., Anagnostou, E., . . . Stevenson, R. A. (2021). Sex differences in age of diagnosis and first concern among children with autism spectrum disorder. *Journal of Clinical Child and Adolescent Psychology, 50*(5), 645–655.

McDuff, D. R., Garvin, M., Chang, J., & Thompson, D. (2024). Substance misuse in elite athletes: Early detection, brief intervention and referral to treatment. *Clinical Sports Medicine, 43*(1), 127–144.

McElroy, S. L., Guerdjikova, A. I., Mori, N., Houser, P. L., & Keck, P. E., Jr. (2020). Management and treatment of feeding and eating disorders. In J. R. Geddes, N. C. Andreason, & G. M. Goodwin (Eds.). *New Oxford textbook of psychiatry* (3rd ed., Chap. 106). New York: Oxford University Press.

McFarlane, S. J., Occa, A., Peng, W., Awonuga, O., & Morgan, S. E. (2022). Community-based participatory research (CBPR) to enhance participation of racial/ethnic minorities in clinical trials: A 10-year systematic review. *Health Communication, 37*(9), 1075–1092.

McGrath, J. L., & Reynolds, M. S. (2024). Recognizing and responding to patients with personality disorders. *Emergency Medicine Clinics of North America, 42*(1), 125–134.

McGrath, R. E., Twibell, A., & Carroll, E. J. (2023). The current status of "projective" "tests." In H. Cooper, M. N. Coutanche, L. M. McMullen, A. T. Panter, D. Rindskopf, & K. J. Sher (Eds.). *APA handbook of research methods in psychology: Foundations, planning, measures, and psychometrics* (pp. 433–450). Washington, DC: American Psychological Association.

McGuire, J. (2022). Psychosocial treatment of antisocial personality disorder. In D. W. Black & N. J. Kolla (Eds.). *Textbook of antisocial personality disorder* (Chap. 17). Washington, DC: American Psychiatric Association Publishing.

McIntosh, J. (2022, December 23). Everything you need to know about orgasms. *Medical News Today*.

McKay, D., & Jensen-Doss, A. (2021). Harmful treatments in psychotherapy. *Clinical Psychology: Science and Practice, 28*(1), 2.

McKay, J. R. (2022, July 25). Psychotherapies for substance use disorders. *UpToDate*. Retrieved from http://www.uptodate.com.

McKenzie, K., Gregory, J., & Hogg, L. (2022). Mental health workers' attitudes towards individuals with a diagnosis of borderline personality disorder: A systematic literature review. *Journal of Personality Disorders, 36*(1), 70–98.

McKenzie, K., Tanfield, Y., Murray, G., & Sandhu, R. (2024). Facilitating the identification of intellectual disability in schools: A qualitative study of stakeholder views. *Journal of Applied Research in Intellectual Disabilities, 37*(1), e13175.

McKeon, R. (2021). *Suicidal behavior, a volume in the Advances in Psychotherapy: Evidence-Based Practice series* (Rev. ed.). Cambridge, MA: Hogrefe Publishing.

McLaughlin, K. (2023, September 14). Posttraumatic stress disorder in children and adolescents: Epidemiology, pathogenesis, clinical manifestations, course, assessment, and diagnosis. *UpToDate*. Retrieved from https://www.uptodate.com.

McLean, C. L., Cummings, M. H., & Litz, B. T. (2022). Individual approaches to prevention and early intervention. In J. G. Beck & D. M. Sloan (Eds.). *The Oxford handbook of traumatic stress disorders* (Chap. 25). New York: Oxford University Press.

McLeod, B. D., Jensen-Doss, A., Lyon, A. R., Douglas, S., & Beidas, R. S. (2022). To utility and beyond! Specifying and advancing the utility of measurement-based care for youth. *Journal of Clinical Child and Adolescent Psychology, 51*(4), 375–388. https://doi.org/10.1080/15374416.2022.2042698.

Mcleod, S. (2023, June 14). *Cognitive behavioral therapy (CBT): Types, techniques, uses.* Retrieved from https://www.simplypsychology.org/cognitive-therapy.

McMahon, R. J., & Frick, P. J. (2021). Conduct and oppositional disorders. In M. J. Prinstein, E. A. Youngstrom, E. J. Mash, & R. A. Barkley (Eds.). *Treatment of disorders in childhood and adolescence* (4th ed., Chap. 5). New York: Guilford Press.

McNabney, S. M., Weseman, C. E., Hevesi, K., & Rowland, D. L. (2022). Are the criteria for the diagnosis of premature ejaculation applicable to gay men or sexual activities other than penile-vaginal intercourse? *ScienceDirect, 10*(3), 100516.

McNally, R. J. (2023). The return of repression: Evidence from cognitive psychology. *Topics in Cognitive Science*. https://doi.org/10.1111/tops.12638. [Online ahead of print]

McNamara, I. A., King, S. E., Corbin, W. R., & Fromme, K. (2022). A longitudinal examination of relations between competitive athletic participation, drinking norms, impulsivity, and sensation seeking and binge drinking throughout college. *Psychology of Addictive Behaviors, 36*(7), 837–848.

McNeil, E. B. (1967). *The quiet furies.* Englewood Cliffs, NJ: Prentice Hall.

McPherson, S. M., Parent, S., Miguel, A., McDonell, M., & Roll, J. M. (2022). Contingency management is a powerful clinical tool for treating substance use research evidence and new practice guidelines for use. *Psychiatric Times, 39*(9), 9–11.

McQuade, J. D., Dixon-Gordon, K. L., Breaux, R., & Babinski, D. E. (2022). Interactive effects of parent emotion socialization and child physiological reactivity in predicting adolescent borderline personality disorder features. *Research on Child and Adolescent Psychopathology, 50*(1), 89–100.

McQuillan, S. (2022, October 17). Avoidant personality disorder treatment. *Psycom*. Retrieved from https://www.psycom.net.

Meana, M., & Binik, Y. M. (2022). The biopsychosocial puzzle of painful sex. *Annual Review of Clinical Psychology, 18*, 471–495.

Meana, M., & Hall, K. (2023). Sexual dysfunctions. In F. T. L. Leong, J. L. Callahan, J. Zimmerman, M. J. Constantino, & C. F. Eubanks (Eds.). *APA handbook of psychotherapy: Vol. 1. Theory-driven practice and disorder-driven practice* (Chap. 27). Washington, DC: American Psychological Association.

Mechem, C. C. (2021, November 3). Pulmonary complications of cocaine use. *UpToDate*. Retrieved from http://www.uptodate.com.

Meehan, S., O'Connor, J., & Keogh, K. (2022). Beauty and the beast: A psychoanalytically oriented qualitative study detailing mothers' experience of perinatal obsessive-compulsive disorder. *International Journal of Applied Psychoanalytic Studies, 19*(1), 158–176.

Meesters, P. D. (2023). New horizons in schizophrenia in older people. *Age and Aging, 52*(9), afad161.

Mehler, P. (2022, August 3). Anorexia nervosa in adults: Evaluation for medical complications and criteria for hospitalization to manage these complications. *UpToDate*. Retrieved from http://www.uptodate.com.

Mehler, P. (2022, July 29). Anorexia nervosa in adults and adolescents: Medical complications and their management. *UpToDate*. Retrieved from http://www.uptodate.com.

Meichenbaum, D. H. (1975). A self-instructional approach to stress management: A proposal for stress inoculation training. In I. Sarason & C. D. Spielberger (Eds.). *Stress and anxiety* (Vol. 2). New York: Wiley.

Meichenbaum, D. H. (1993). Stress inoculation training: A 20-year update. In P. M. Lehrer & R. L. Woolfolk (Eds.). *Principles and practice of stress management* (2nd ed., pp. 373–406). New York: Guilford Press.

Meichenbaum, D. H. (2017). *The evolution of CBT: A personal and professional journey with Don Meichenbaum.* New York: Routledge.

Meichsner, F., O'Connor, M., Skritskaya, N., & Shear, M. K. (2020). Grief before and after bereavement in the elderly: An approach to care. *American Journal of Geriatric Psychiatry, 28*(5), 560–569.

Meier, K., van Hoeken, D., & Hoek, H. W. (2022). Review of the unprecedented impact of the COVID-19 pandemic on the occurrence of eating disorders. *Current Opinions on Psychiatry, 335*, 353–361.

Melechi, A. (2016, September 29). Bodies of evidence: Psychologists and the CIA torture scandal. *Times Higher Education.*

Melhem, N. M., Zhong, Y., Miller, J. M., Zanderigo, F., Ogden, R. T., Sublette, M. E., . . . Mann, J. J. (2022). Brain 5-HT1A receptor PET binding, cortisol responses to stress, and the familial transmission of suicidal behavior. *International Journal of Neuropsychopharmacology, 25*(1), 36–45.

Melli, G., Caccico, L., Micheli, E., Bulli, F., & Doron, G. (2024). Pathological narcissism and relationship obsessive-compulsive disorder (ROCD) symptoms: Exploring the role of vulnerable narcissism. *Journal of Clinical Psychology, 80*(1), 144–157.

Mello, M. F., Locali, R. F., Araujo, R. M., Reis, J. N., Salovici, S., Mello, L. F., & Rocha, F. E. T. (2023). A prospective and randomized study comparing the use of alarms, desmopressin and imipramine in the treatment of monosymptomatic nocturnal enuresis. *Journal of Pediatric Urology, 19*(3), 241–246.

Melmer, M. N., & Gutovitz, S. (2023, August 28). Child sexual abuse and neglect. *StatPearls.*

Melore, C. (2021, October 26). Paranormal nation: Nearly two-thirds of Americans believe in ghosts or aliens. *Study Finds*. Retrieved from https://studyfinds.org/americans-believe-ghosts-aliens-paranormal.

Melton, G., Petrila, J., Poythress, N., & Slobogin, C. (2020). Psychological evaluations for the courts. In S. Slobogin, T. L. Hafemeister, & D. Mossman (Eds.). *Law and the mental health system: Civil and criminal aspects* (7th ed., p. 1135). St. Paul, MN: West Academic Publishing.

Melton, G. B., Petrila, J., Poythress, N. G., Slobogin, C., Otto, R. K., Mossman, D., & Condie, L. O. (2017). *Psychological evaluations for the courts: A handbook for mental health professionals and lawyers* (4th ed.). New York: Guilford Press.

Mendel, R. (2023, March 1). *Why youth incarceration fails: An updated review of the evidence.* The Sentencing Project. https://www.sentencingproject.org/reports/why-youth-incarceration-fails-an-updated-review-of-the-evidence.

Mentis, A.-F. A., Dardiotis, E., Katsouni, E., & Chrousos, G. P. (2021). From warrior genes to translational solutions: Novel insights into monoamine oxidases (MAOs) and aggression. *Translational Psychiatry, 11*, 130.

Mento, C., Silvestri, M. C., Muscatello, M. R. A., Rizzo, A., Celebre, L., Praticò, M., . . . Bruno, A. (2021). Psychological impact of pro-anorexia and pro-eating disorder websites on adolescent females: A systematic review. *International Journal of Environmental Research and Public Health, 18*(4), 2186.

Merenstein, J. L., & Bennett, I. J. (2022). Bridging patterns of neurocognitive aging across the older adult lifespan. *Neuroscience and Biobehavioral Reviews, 135*, 104594.

Merschel, M. (2022, June 16). *The promise of meditation for the heart and mind.* Dallas, TX: American Heart Association.

Mesholam-Gately, R. I., Johnston, D., & Kechavan, M. S. (2023). What's in the name "schizophrenia"? A clinical, research and lived experience perspective. *World Psychiatry, 22*(1), 156–157.

Meston, C., & Stanton, A. M. (2020). *Delayed ejaculation.* Austin: Meston Lab, University of Texas. Retrieved from https://labs.la.utexas.edu.

Metzl, J. M., Piemonte, J., & McKay, T. (2021). Mental illness, mass shootings, and the future of psychiatric research into American gun violence. *Harvard Review of Psychiatry, 29*(1), 81–89.

Meyer, A., Wisniewski, H., & Torous, J. (2022). Coaching to support mental health apps: Exploratory narrative review. *JMIR Human Factors, 9*(1), e28301.

Meyer, D. M., Kilian, H. M., & Schlaepfer, T. E. (2022). Vagus nerve stimulation and deep brain stimulation. In C. B. Nemeroff, A. F. Schatzberg, N. Rasgon, & S. M. Strakowski (Eds.). *The American Psychiatric Association Publishing textbook of mood disorders* (2nd ed., Chap. 20). Washington, DC: American Psychiatric Association Publishing.

Meyer, T. D., Perich, T., Jones, S. H., & Lee, T. M. C. (2024). Bipolar disorders. In G. M. Reed, P. L.-J. Ritchie, & A. Maercker (Eds.). *A psychological approach to diagnosis: Using the ICD-11 as a framework* (Chap. 7). Washington, DC: American Psychological Association.

Meyers, R. S. (2023). Chronic pain: Psychologically-based treatments. In F. T. L. Leong, J. L. Callahan, J. Zimmerman, M. J. Constantino, & C. F. Eubanks (Eds.). *APA handbook of psychotherapy: Vol. 1. Theory-driven practice and disorder-driven practice* (Chap. 26). Washington, DC: American Psychological Association.

Meyersohn, L. H. (2023, March 8). The fight for mental health parity. *The American Prospect.*

MGH (Massachusetts General Hospital). (2023). *Post-traumatic stress disorder research laboratory.* Boston: Author.

MH (Mind Help). (2023). Histrionic personality disorder. *Mind.help.* Retrieved from https://mind.help/topic/histrionic-personality-disorder.

MHA (Mental Health America). (2023). *Adult data 2022.* Alexandria, VA: Author.

MHA (Mental Health America). (2023). *Black and African American communities and mental health.* Alexandria, VA: Author.

MHA (Mental Health America). (2023). *Depression in women.* Alexandria, VA: Author.

MHA (Mental Health America). (2023). *Electroconvulsive therapy (ECT).* Alexandria, VA: Author.

MHA (Mental Health America). (2023). *Housing.* Alexandria, VA: Author.

MHA (Mental Health America). (2023). *How race matters: What we can learn from Mental Health America's screening in 2020.* Alexandria, VA: Author.

MHA (Mental Health America). (2023). *Latinx/Hispanic communities and mental health.* Alexandria, VA: Author.

MHA (Mental Health America). (2023). *Position Statement 15: Parity in health insurance.* Alexandria, VA: Author.

MHA (Mental Health America). (2023). *The future of mental health starts with prevention.* Alexandria, VA: Author.

MHA (Mental Health America). (2024). *Position Statement 15: Parity in health insurance.* Alexandria, VA: Author.

MHA (Mental Health America). (2024). *Position Statement 55: Confining sexual predators in the mental health system.* Alexandria, VA: Author.

MHA (Mental Health America). (2024). *Position Statement 56: Mental Health treatment in correctional facilities.* Alexandria, VA: Author.

MHA (Mental Health America). (2024). *Position Statement 57: In support of the insanity defense.* Alexandria, VA: Author.

MHA (Mental Health America). (2024). *Position Statement 21: Rights of people with mental health and substance use conditions.* Alexandria, VA: Author.

MHA (Mental Health America). (2024). *Position Statement 22: Involuntary mental health treatment.* Alexandria, VA: Author.

MHF (Mental Health Foundation). (2023). *Uncertain times: Anxiety in the UK and how to tackle it.* London: Author.

MHN (Mental Help Network). (2023). *The choice of educational settings: The pros and cons of mainstreaming children with intellectual disabilities.* San Rafael, CA: Author.

MHN (Mental Help Network). (2023). Causes of eating disorders—Family influences. *MentalHealth.net.* Retrieved from https://www.mentalhelp.net/eating-disorders.

MHN (Mental Help Network). (2023). Classical conditioning and addiction. *MentalHealth.net.* Retrieved from https://www.mentalhelp.net.

MHN (Mental Help Network). (2023). Cognitive theory of depression: Aaron Beck. *MHN.* Retrieved from https://www.mentalhelp.net.

MHN (Mental Help Network). (2023). Paraphilias causes and treatments. *MHN.* Retrieved from https://www.mentalhelp.net.

MHN (Mental Help Network). (2023). *Schizophrenia symptoms, patterns and statistics and patterns.* Retrieved from https://www.mentalhelp.net/schizophrenia/statistics.

MHN (Mental Help Network). (2023). *Sociology of depression: Effects of culture.* Retrieved from https://www.mentalhelp.net/depression/sociology-and-effects-of-culture.

MHN (Mental Help Network). (2023). What happens to children of alcoholic parents? *MentalHealth.net.* Retrieved from https://www.mentalhelp.net.

Michal, M. (2022). Depersonalization/derealization disorder. In M. J. Dorahy, S. N. Gold, & J. A. O'Neil (Eds.). *Dissociation and the dissociative disorders: Past, present, future* (Chap. 23). New York: Routledge.

Miech, R. A., Johnston, L. D., Patrick, M. E., O'Malley, P. M., Bachman, J. G., & Schulenberg, J. E. (2023). *Monitoring the Future national survey results on drug use, 1975–2022: Secondary school students.* Ann Arbor: University of Michigan, Institute for Social Research.

Miglin, R., Rodriguez, S., Bounoua, N., & Sadeh, N. (2022). A multidimensional examination of psychopathy traits and gray matter volume in adults. *Social Cognitive and Affective Neuroscience, 17*(7), 662–672.

Mihura, J. L., Jowers, C. E., Dumitrascu, N., van den Hurk, A. W. V., & Keddy, P. J. (2022). The specific uses of the Rorschach in clinical practice: Preliminary results from an international survey. *Rorschachiana, 43*(1), 25–41.

Milburn, N. G., Rice, E., & Petry, L. (2024). Understanding homelessness among young people to improve outcomes. *Annual Review of Clinical Psychology, 20,* 1.

Mileva, B., Goshev, M., Alexandrov, A., & Gitto, L. (2022). The shame of truth: Death due to accidental autoerotic asphyxia. *Medico-Legal Journal, 90*(4), 189–194.

Miller, A. (2017, July 5). *Examples of why you want to be a counselor.* Career Trend. Retrieved from https://careertrend.com.

Miller, H. L., Licari, M. K., Bhat, A., Aziz-Zadeh, L. S., Van Damme, T., Fears, N. E., . . . Tamplain, P. M. (2024). Motor problems in autism: Co-occurrence or feature? *Developmental Medicine & Child Neurology, 66*(1), 16–22

Miller, J. N., & Black, D. W. (2020). Bipolar disorder and suicide: A review. *Current Psychiatry Reports, 22*(2), 6.

Miller, K. (2016, January 3). The shocking results of Yahoo Health's body-positivity survey. *Yahoo.com.*

Miller, N. S. (2022, May 18). Racial disparities in mental health care: An explainer and research roundup. *The Journalist's Resource.*

Miller, N. S. (2023, July 5). Mental health disparities in older LGBTQ+ populations: A research roundup. *The Journalist's Resource.*

Miller, P. M., Ingham, J. G., & Davidson, S. (1976). Life events, symptoms, and social support. *Journal of Psychiatric Research, 20*(6), 514–522.

Miller, W. R., & Rollnick, S. (2023). *Motivational interviewing* (4th ed.). New York: Guilford Press.

Mindlis, L., & Federman, A. D. (2024, September). Multimorbidity in the aging population. In N. Schneiderman (Ed.). *APA handbook of health psychology: Vol. 2. Clinical interventions and disease management in health psychology* (Chap. 19). Washington, DC: American Psychological Association.

Mineo, L. (2022, June 29). "Shadow pandemic" of domestic violence. *Harvard Gazette.*

Miner, M. H., & Munns, R. (2021). Psychological treatments for paraphilias and compulsive sexual behavior. In L. A. Craig & R. M. Bartels (Eds.). *Sexual deviance: Understanding and managing deviant sexual interest and paraphilic disorders* (Chap. 16). Hoboken, NJ: Wiley-Blackwell.

Minuchin, S. (2020, October 11). *Families and family therapy.* New York: Routledge.

MIPO (Mental Illness Policy Organization). (2022). *About Mental Illness Policy Org.* Retrieved from https://mentalillnesspolicy.org/about.

MIPO (Mental Illness Policy Organization). (2022). *Homeless mentally ill facts and figures.* Retrieved from https://mentalillnesspolicy.org/consequences/homeless-mentally-ill.

MIPO (Mental Illness Policy Organization). (2022). *250,000 mentally ill are homeless: 140,000 seriously mentally ill are homeless.* Retrieved from https://mentalillnesspolicy.org.consequences.

Mirabito, G., & Verhaeghen, P. (2022, September 23). The effects of mindfulness interventions on older adults' cognition: A meta-analysis. *Journal of Gerontology, B: Psychological Science and Social Science.* [Online ahead of print]

Mirandola, C., Lanciano, T., Battista, F., Otgaar, H., & Curci, A. (2023). Psychopathic personality traits are linked to reduced false memories for negative events. *British Journal of Psychology, 114*(1), 176–193.

Mishara, B. L., Tran, A. T., Chondo, L., Demmer, A., Harris-Lane, L., Harper, S., . . . Wilson, T. (2023). Evaluation of a community suicide prevention project (Roots of Hope): Protocol for an implementation science study. *JMIR Research Protocols, 12,* e39978.

Misurell, J. R., Zocca, J. M., & Anderson, L. (2023, August 18). Child sexual and physical abuse. In F. M. Dattillo, D. I. Shapiro, & D. S. Greenaway (Eds.). *Cognitive-behavioral strategies in crisis intervention* (4th ed., Chap. 11). New York: Guilford Press.

Mitchell, J. E. (2023, June 6). Bulimia nervosa in adults: Cognitive-behavioral therapy (CBT). *UpToDate.* Retrieved from http://www.uptodate.com.

Mitchell, J. E., & Peterson, C. B. (2020). Anorexia nervosa. *New England Journal of Medicine, 382*(14), 1343–1351.

Mitchell, J. E., & Zunker, C. (2022, August 29). Bulimia nervosa and binge eating disorder in adults: Medical complications and their management. *UpToDate.* Retrieved from https://www.uptodate.com.

Mitchell, R. H. B., Toulany, A., Chung, H., Cohen, E., Fu, L., Strauss, R., . . . Saunders, N. R. (2023). Self-harm among youth during the first 28 months of the COVID-19 pandemic in Ontario, Canada: A population-based study. *Canadian Medical Association Journal, 195*(36), e1210–e1220.

Mitchell, R. J., Wijekulasuriya, S., de Preez, J., Lystad, R., Chauhan, A., Harrison, R., . . . Braithwaite, J. (2024). Population-level quality indicators of end-of-life-care in an aged care setting: Rapid systematic review. *Archives of Gerontology and Geriatrics, 116,* 105130.

Mitchell, S. A. (2023). *Relationality: From attachment to intersubjectivity* (Relational Perspectives Book Series). New York: Routledge.

Mitchison, D., Broderstad, A. R., Burt, A., & Kvaløy, K. (2023). Eating disorders in indigenous peoples. In P. Robinson, T. Wade, B. Herpertz-Dahlann, F. Fernandez-Aranda, J. Treasure, & S. Wonderlich (Eds.). *Eating disorders.* Edinburgh: Springer.

Mitra, P., & Fluyau, D. (2023, March 13). Narcissistic personality disorder. *StatPearls.*

Mitra, P., & Jain, A. (2023, May 16). Dissociative identity disorder. *StatPearls.*

MLP (MedlinePlus). (2023). *Orgasmic dysfunction in women.* Retrieved from https://medlineplus.gov/ency/article/001953.htm.

Mobley, K., & Taasoobshirazi, G. (2022). Predicting suicide in counties: Creating a quantitative measure of suicide risk. *International Journal of Environmental Research and Public Health, 19*(13), 8173.

Moceri-Brooks, J., Garand, L., Sekula, L. K., & Joiner, T. E. (2023, March 1). Exploring the use of the interpersonal needs questionnaire to examine suicidal thoughts and behavior among post-9/11 U.S. combat veterans: An integrative review. *Military Psychology.* https://doi.org/10.1080/08995605.2023.2178223. [Online ahead of print]

Modesti, M. N., Rapisarda, L., Capriotti, G., & Del Casale, A. (2022). Functional neuroimaging in dissociative disorders: A systematic review. *Journal of Personalized Medicine, 12,* 1405.

Modinos, G., Allen, P., Zugman, A., Dima, D., Azis, M., Samson, C., . . . McGuire, P. (2020). Neural circuitry of novelty salience processing in psychosis risk: Association with clinical outcome. *Schizophrenia Bulletin, 46*(3), 670–679.

Mohan, L., Yilanli, M., & Ray, S. (2023, March 13). Conduct disorder. *StatPearls.*

Mohan, R. (2021). What is a case study? [+6 types of case studies]. *Venngage.* Retrieved from https://venngage.com/blog.

Mohler, H., & Okada, T. (1977). Benzodiazepine receptor: Demonstration in the central nervous system. *Science, 198*(4319), 849–851.

Moir, C.-L., Tzani, C., Ioannou, M., Lester, D., Synnott, J., & Williams, T. J. V. (2023, July 17). Cybersuicide: Online-assisted suicide. *Journal of Police and Criminal Psychology.* https://link.springer.com/article/10.1007/s11896-023-09602-5. [Open access]

Mokros, A., Wessels, J., Hofmann, M., & Nitschke, J. (2019). Coercive sexual sadism: A systematic qualitative review. *Current Psychiatry Reports, 21*(12), 135.

Molad, M., Gover, A., Marai, Z., Lavie-Nevo, K., Kessel, I., Shermer-Meiri, L., & Soloveichik, M. (2023). Neurodevelopmental outcome of very low birth weight infants in the northern district of Israel: A cross-sectional study. *Children (Basel), 10*(8), 1320.

Molen, L. V., Ronis, S. T., & Benoit, A. A. (2022, June 14). Paraphilic interests versus behaviors: Factors that distinguish individuals who act on paraphilic interests from individuals who refrain. *Sexual Abuse.* doi:10.1177/10790632221108949. [Online ahead of print]

Molkara, T., Motavasselian, M., Akhlaghi, F., Ramezani, M. A., Naghedi Baghdar, H., Ghazanfari, S. M., & Salari, R. (2021). The effects of herbal medicines on women sexual dysfunction: A systematic review. *Current Drug Discovery Technologies, 18*(6), e130921186972.

Monacis, L., Griffiths, M. D., Limone, P., Sinatra, M., & Servidio, R. (2020). Selfitis behavior: Assessing the Italian version of the selfitis behavior scale and its mediating role in the relationship of dark traits with social media addiction. *International Journal of Environmental Research and Public Health, 17*(16), 5738.

Monaghan, C., & Bizumic, B. (2023, February 3). Dimensional models of personality disorders: Challenges and opportunities. *Frontiers in Psychiatry, 14.* doi:10.3389/fpsyt.2023.1098452. [Online ahead of print]

Moncrieff, J., Cooper, R. E., Stockman, T., Amendola, S., Hengartner, M. P., & Horowitz, M. A. (2022). The serotonin theory of depression: A systematic umbrella review of the evidence. *Molecular Psychiatry.* doi:10.1038/s41380-022-01661-0. [Online ahead of print]

Moncrieff, J., Crellin, N., Stansfeld, J., Cooper, R., Marston, L., Freemantle, N., . . . Priebe, S. (2023). Antipsychotic dose reduction and discontinuation versus maintenance treatment in people with schizophrenia and other recurrent psychotic disorders in England (the RADAR trial): An open, parallel-group, randomised controlled trial. *Lancet Psychiatry, 10,* 848–859.

Monroe, S. M., & Harkness, K. L. (2022). Major depression and its recurrences: Life course matters. *Annual Review of Clinical Psychology, 18,* 329–357.

Monson, C. M., & Shnaider, P. (2014). *Treating PTSD with cognitive-behavioral therapies: Interventions that work.* Washington, DC: American Psychological Association.

Monson, C. M., Fredman, S. J., Dekel, R., Ennis, N., & Macdonald, A. (2022). Family models of posttraumatic stress disorder. In J. G. Beck & D. M. Sloan (Eds.). *The Oxford handbook of traumatic stress disorders* (Chap. 16). New York: Oxford University Press.

Monson, C. M., Macdonald, A., Fredman, S. J., Schumm, J. A., & Taft, C. (2023). Empirically supported couple and family therapies for PTSD. In M. J. Friedman, P. P. Schnurr, & T. M. Keane (Eds.). *Handbook of PTSD: Science and practice* (3rd ed., Chap. 21). New York: Guilford Press.

Monson, H., Gonzalez, E., Nister-Taroto, L., & Mandelcorn, M. (2018, November 11). When blindness induces hallucinations. *Retina Specialist.* Retrieved from https://www.retina-specialist.com.

Montejo, A. L. (2023). New challenges in sexuality and sexual dysfunction. *Journal of Clinical Medicine, 12*(1), 203.

Monteleone, A. M., Pellegrino, F., Croatto, G., Carfagno, M., Hilbert, A., Treasure, J., . . . Solmi, M. (2022). Treatment of eating disorders: A systematic meta-review of meta-analyses and network meta-analyses. *Neuroscience and Biobehavioral Reviews, 142,* 104857.

Moore, M. (2023, March 13). How to identify and reduce social anxiety. *Psych Central.*

Moore, M. (2023, September 22). Understanding delayed ejaculation. *Psych Central.*

Morales-Brown, L. (2023, May 18). What are the benefits of family counseling? *Medical News Today.*

Morandini, J. S., Kelly, A., de Graaf, N. M., Malouf, P., Guerin, E., Dar-Nimrod, I., & Carmichael, P. (2023). Is social gender transition associated with mental health status in children and adolescents with gender dysphoria? *Archives of Sexual Behavior, 52,* 1045–1060.

Moreland, C. S., & Bonin, L. (2022, August 31). Effect of antidepressants on suicide risk in children and adolescents. *UpToDate.* Retrieved from https://www.uptodate.com.

Moreno, M., Gutiérrez-Rojas, L., & Porras-Segovia, A. (2022). Implicit cognition tests for the assessment of suicide risk: A systematic review. *Current Psychiatry Reports, 24,* 141–159.

Moretti, G., Flutti, E., Colanino, M., Ferlito, D., Amoresano, L., & Travaini, G. (2024). Recidivism risk in male adult sex offenders with psychopathic traits assessed by PCL-R: A systematic review. *Medicine, Science and the Law, 64*(1), 41–51.

Morey, M. C. (2022, September 8). Physical activity and exercise in older adults. *UpToDate.* Retrieved from http://www.uptodate.com.

Morgan, P. L., & Hu, E. H. (2023). Sociodemographic disparities in ADHD diagnosis and treatment among U.S. elementary schoolchildren. *Psychiatry Research, 327,* 115393.

Morganstein, J. C., Herberman, H. B., Vance, M. C., Fullerton, C. S., & Ursano, R. J. (2023). Public mental health interventions following disasters. In M. J. Friedman, P. P. Schnurr, & T. M. Keane (Eds.). *Handbook of PTSD: Science and practice* (3rd ed., Chap. 31). New York: Guilford Press.

Mori, C., Cooke, J. E., Temple, J. R., Ly, A., Anderson, N., Rash, C., & Madigan, S. (2020, May). The prevalence of sexting behaviors among emerging adults: A meta-analysis. *Archives of Sexual Behavior, 49*(4), 1103–1119.

Mori, C., Park, J., Temple, J. R., & Madigan, S. (2022). Are youth sexting rates still on the rise? A meta-analytic update. *Journal of Adolescent Health, 70*(4), 531–539.

Morin, A. (2020, February 13). Common characteristics of a bully. *Verywell Family.* Retrieved from https://www.verywellfamily.com.

Morissette, S. B., Blessing, A., Russell, P., & Hale, W. (2023). Cannabis use disorder uniquely predicts educational impairment in college students over and above other mental health disorders. *Journal of American College Health.* doi:10.1080/07448481.2022.2155058. [Online ahead of print]

Morken, I. S., Viddal, K. R., von Soest, T., & Wichstrom, L. (2023). Explaining the female preponderance in adolescent depression: A four-wave cohort study. *Research on Child and Adolescent Psychopathology, 51,* 859–869.

Morland, J., Bretteville-Jensen, A. L., & Bramness, J. G. (2023). On the duration of cannabis effects and the presence of THC in the body. *Addiction, 118*(2), 390–391.

Morris, N. P., McNiel, D. E., & Binder, R. L. (2021, December). Estimating annual numbers of competency to stand trial evaluations across the United States. *Journal of the American Academy of Psychiatry and the Law, 49*(4), 530–539.

Morris, S. E., Sanislow, C. A., Pacheco, J., Vaidyanathan, U., Gordon, J. A., & Cuthbert, B. N. (2022). Revisiting the seven pillars of RDoC. *BMC Medicine, 20*(1), 220.

Morrison, J. (2023). *Diagnosis made easier: Principles and techniques for mental health clinicians* (3rd ed.). New York: Guilford Press.

Morrison, J. (2023). *DSM-5-TR made easy: The clinician's guide to diagnosis.* New York: Guilford Press.

Morrow, C. B. (2024). Geriatric psychiatry and the future of dementia care: Diagnosing TDP-43 neurodegenerative disease. *American Journal of Geriatric Psychiatry, 32*(1), 114–116.

Mortell, S. (2022). The alleged epidemic of social narcissism: Implications for nurse leaders. *Nursing Administration Quarterly, 46*(1), 45–51.

Mosconi, L., Berti, V., Glodzik, L., Pupi, A., De Santi, S., & de Leon, M. J. (2010). Pre-clinical detection of Alzheimer's disease using FDG-PET, with or without amyloid imaging. *Journal of Alzheimer's Disease, 20*(3), 843–854.

Mosconi, L., De Santi, S., Li, J., Tsui, W. H., Li, Y., Boppana, M., . . . de Leon, M. J. (2008). Hippocampal hypometabolism predicts cognitive decline from normal aging. *Neurobiology of Aging, 29*(5), 676–692.

Mosconi, L., Murray, J., Davies, M., Williams, S., Pirraglia, E., Spector, N., . . . de Leon, M. J. (2014). Nutrient intake and brain biomarkers of Alzheimer's disease in at-risk cognitively normal individuals: A cross-sectional neuroimaging pilot study. *BMJ Open, 4*(6), E004850.

Mosconi, L., Walters, M., Sterling, J., Quinn, C., McHugh, P., Andrews, R. E., . . . Convit, A. (2018). Lifestyle and vascular risk effects on MRI-based biomarkers of Alzheimer's disease: A cross-sectional study of middle-aged adults from the broader New York City area. *BMJ Open, 8*(3), e019362.

Moscovici, M., & Jones, R. M. (2022). Pharmacological treatment of antisocial personality disorder. In D. W. Black & N. J. Kolla (Eds.). *Textbook of antisocial personality disorder* (Chap. 18). Washington, DC: American Psychiatric Association Publishing.

Moskowitz, A., Nijenhuis, E., Moreira-Almeida, A., & Lewis-Fernández, R. (2024). Dissociative disorders. In G. M. Reed, P. L.-J. Ritchie, & A. Maercker (Eds.). *A psychological approach to diagnosis: Using the ICD-11 as a framework* (Chap. 11). Washington, DC: American Psychological Association.

Mosolov, S. N., & Yaltonskaya, P. A. (2022). Primary and secondary negative symptoms in schizophrenia. *Frontiers in Psychiatry, 12,* 766692.

Moss, G., & Wylde, K. (2020, May 13). How many active serial killers are there right now? *Bustle.* Retrieved from https://www.bustle.com/articles/112070.

Mowrer, O. H., & Mowrer, W. M. (1938). Enuresis: A method for its study and treatment. *American Journal of Orthopsychiatry, 8,* 436–459.

MP (Medical Xpress). (2020, February 20). Euthanasia's legal status in Europe. *Medical Xpress.*

Mrejen, M., Rosa, L., Rosa, D., & Hone, T. (2023, May 24). Gender inequalities in violence victimization and depression in Brazil: Results from the 2019 national health survey. *International Journal for Equity in Health, 22,* 100.

Mueller, A. S., Abrutyn, S., Pescosolido, B., & Diefendorf, S. (2021, March 31). The social roots of suicide: Theorizing how the external social world matters to suicide and suicide prevention. *Frontiers in Psychology, 12,* 621569.

Mueser, K. T. (2022, December 20). Assertive community treatment for patients with severe mental illness. *UpToDate.* Retrieved from https://www.uptodate.com.

Muhlheim, L. (2020, January 28). Relapses in bulimia recovery. *Verywellmind.* Retrieved from https://www.verywellmind.com.

Mukamal, K. J. (2023, June 7). Overview of the risks and benefits of alcohol consumption. *UpToDate.* Retrieved from https://www.uptodate.com.

Mullen, J. M., Richards, J. R., & Crawford, A. T. (2023, June 8). Amphetamine-related psychiatric disorders. *StatPearls.*

Müller, K. W., Dreier, M., & Wölfling, K. (2023). Personality traits and their role as risk modifiers in gaming disorder and internet use disorders. *Current Opinions in Psychiatry, 36*(1), 75–79.

Müller-Vahl, K. R., Pisarenko, A., Jakubovski, E., & Fremer, C. (2022). Stop that! It's not Tourette's but a new type of mass sociogenic illness. *Brain, 145*(2), 476–480.

Munakomi, S., & Puckett, Y. (2023, February 12). Repetitive head injury syndrome. *StatPearls.*

Munn-Chernoff, M. A., Johnson, E. C., Chou, Y.-L., Coleman, J. R. I., Thornton, L. M., Walters, R. K., . . . Agrawal, A. (2021). Shared genetic risk between eating disorder- and substance-use-related phenotypes: Evidence from genome-wide association studies. *Addiction Biology, 26*(1), e12880.

Munson, K. A., Janney, C. A., Goodwin, K., & Nagalla, M. (2022). Cultural representations of borderline personality disorder. *Frontiers in Sociology, 7,* 832497.

Murphy, C., & Hameed, S. (2023, July 31). Chronic headaches. *StatPearls.*

Murphy, M. P., Buzinova, V. A., & Johnson, C. E. (2024). The amyloid-beta peptide: Guilty as charged? *Biochimica et Biophysica Acta: Molecular Basis of Disease, 1870*(2), 166945.

Murphy, R. J. (2023). Depersonalization/derealization disorder and neural correlates of trauma-related pathology: A critical review. *Innovations in Clinical Neuroscience, 20*(1–3), 53–59.

Murphy-Oikonen, J., McQueen, K., Miller, A., Chambers, L., & Hiebert, A. (2022). Unfounded sexual assault: Women's experiences of not being believed by the police. *Journal of Interpersonal Violence, 37*(11–12), NP8916–NP8940.

Murray, B. P., & Kiernan, E. A. (2024). Physiologic effects of substance use. *Emergency Medicine Clinics of North America, 42*(1), 69–91.

Murray, S., & Kaye, W. H. (2023). Brain neurotransmitters and eating disorders. In P. Robinson, T. Wade, B. Herpertz-Dahlann, F. Fernandez-Aranda, J. Treasure, & S. Wonderlich (Eds.). *Eating disorders.* Edinburgh: Springer.

Mutschler, C., Junaid, S., Tellez, C., Franco, G., Gryspeerdt, C., & Busche, J. (2022). Community-based residential treatment for alcohol and substance use problems: A realist review. *Health and Social Care in the Community, 30*(2), e287–e304.

Mutwalli, H., Lewis, Y. D., Conti, C., Treasure, J., & Himmerich, H. (2023). Pharmacological treatment and eating disorders. In P. Robinson, T. Wade, B. Herpertz-Dahlann, F. Fernandez-Aranda, J. Treasure, & S. Wonderlich (Eds.). *Eating disorders.* Edinburgh: Springer.

Myllyaho, T., Siira, V., Wahlberg, K.-E., Hakko, H., Tikkanen, V., Läksy, K., . . . Räsänen, S. (2022). Dysfunctional family functioning in high socioeconomic status families as a risk factor for the development of psychiatric disorders in adoptees: The Finnish Adoptive Family Study of Schizophrenia. *Social Psychiatry and Psychiatric Epidemiology, 57*(7), 1367–1377.

Na, P. J., Bommersbach, T., Pietrzak, R. H., & Rhee, T. G. (2022). Durkheim's theory of social integration and suicide revisited: Is it diversity of social networks or perceived strengths of social support that matters? *Journal of Clinical Psychiatry, 84*(1), 22m14477.

Na, P. J., Fischer, I. C., Shear, K. M., & Pietrzak, R. H. (2023). Prevalence, correlates, and psychiatric burden of prolonged grief disorder in U.S. military veterans: Results from a nationally representative study. *American Journal of Geriatric Psychiatry, 31*(7), 543–548.

NAA (National Autism Association). (2023). *Autism fact sheet.* Portsmouth, RI: Author.

Nadal, K. L. Y. (2023, March). *Dismantling everyday discrimination: Microaggressions toward LGBTQ people* (2nd ed.). Washington, DC: American Psychological Association.

Nadison, M., Flamm, L. J., Roberts, A., Staton, T., Wiener, L., Locke, J., . . . & Horberg, M. A. (2022). Kaiser Permanente's Good Health & Great Hair Program: Partnering with barbershops and beauty salons to advance health equity in West Baltimore, Maryland. *Journal of Public Health Management Practice, 28*(2), E369–E379.

Nakamura, N., Dispenza, F., Abreu, R. L., Ollen, E. W., Pantalone, D. W., Canillas, G., . . . Vencill, J. A. (2022). The APA Guidelines for Psychological Practice with Sexual Minority Persons: An executive summary of the 2021 revision. *American Psychologist, 77*(8), 953–962. https://doi.org/10.1037/amp0000939.

NAMI (National Alliance on Mental Illness). (2023). *About NAMI.* Arlington, VA: Author. https://www.nami.org/about-nami.

NAMI (National Alliance on Mental Illness). (2023). *Criminal justice system.* Arlington, VA: Author.

NAMI (National Alliance on Mental Illness). (2023). *Criminalization of people with mental illness.* Arlington, VA: Author.

NAMI (National Alliance on Mental Illness). (2023). *Finding stable housing.* Retrieved from https://www.nami.org/Your-Journey/Individuals-with-Mental-Illness.

NAMI (National Alliance on Mental Illness). (2023). *Getting treatment during a crisis.* Retrieved from https://www.nami.org/Learn-More/Treatment.

NAMI (National Alliance on Mental Illness). (2023). *Mental health by the numbers.* Arlington, VA: Author.

NAMI (National Alliance on Mental Illness). (2023). *Psychotherapy.* Arlington, VA: Author.

NAMI-M (National Alliance on Mental Illness Michigan). (2022). *DID Fact Sheet: What is dissociative identity disorder (DID)?* Retrieved from https://namimi.org/mental-illness/dissociative-disorder/didfactsheet.

Nath, M., & Gupta, V. (2023, April 24). Mood stabilizers. *StatPearls.*

Nathan, D. (2011). *Sybil exposed: The extraordinary story behind the famous multiple personality case.* New York: Free Press.

Nayak, V., Patra, S., Rout, S., Jena, A. B., Sharma, R., Pattanaik, K. P., . . . Kerry, R. G. (2024). Regulation of neuroinflammation in Alzheimer's disease via nanoparticle-loaded phytocompounds with anti-inflammatory and autophagy-inducing properties. *Phytomedicine, 122,* 155150.

NB (No Bullying). (2017, April 10). *Bullying statistics: The ultimate guide!* Retrieved from https://nobullying.com.

NBPC (National Bullying Prevention Center). (2020, May). *Bullying statistics.* Bloomington, MN: Pacer Org.

NBPC (National Bullying Prevention Center). (2020, May). *Cyberbullying.* Minneapolis: PACER's National Bullying Prevention Center.

NBPC (National Bullying Prevention Center). (2023). *Information.* Minneapolis: PACER's National Bullying Prevention Center.

NCAC (National Council for Aging Care). (2020). *Alcohol abuse amongst the elderly: A complete guide.* Washington, DC: Author. Retrieved from https://www.aging.com.

NCBH (National Council for Behavioral Health). (2015, August 31). *Is the problem cultural incompetence or racism?* Washington, DC: Author.

NCCIH (National Center for Complementary and Integrative Health). (2022, June). *Meditation and mindfulness: What you need to know.* Washington, DC: Author.

NCD (National Council on Disability). (2023). Deinstitutionalization: Unfinished business (companion paper to Policy Toolkit). https://beta.ncd.gov/report/deinstitutionalization-unfinished-business-companion-paper-to-policy-toolkit.

NCDAS (National Center for Drug Abuse Statistics). (2023). *Drug overdose death rates.* Washington, DC: Author.

NCHS (National Center for Health Statistics). (2020). *Index.* Retrieved from https://www.cdc.gov/nchs/index.

NCOA (National Council on Aging). (2023, March 13). *Get the facts on healthy aging.* Retrieved from https://www.ncoa.org/article.

NCOA (National Council on Aging). (2023). *The top 10 most common chronic conditions in older adults.* Arlington, VA: Author.

NCPTSD (National Center for PTSD). (2023). *Peer support groups.* Washington, DC: Author.

NCPTSD (National Center for PTSD). (2023). *PTSD basics.* Washington, DC: Author.

NCSC (National Center for State Courts). (2023). *Assisted outpatient treatment (AOT), community-based civil commitment.* Williamsburg, VA: Author.

NCSC (National Center for State Courts). (2023). *Implementation of the National Judicial Task Force to examine state courts' response too mental illness: Report and recommendations.* Williamsburg, VA: Author.

NCSC (National Center for State Courts). (2023). *The task force made a number of important findings, with corresponding recommendations.* Williamsburg, VA: Author.

NCTE (National Center for Transgender Equality). (2022). *Additional help.* Washington, DC: Author.

NCVS (National Crime Victimization Survey). (2014). *Rape trauma syndrome.* Washington, DC: Bureau of Justice Statistics.

NCVS (National Crime Victimization Survey). (2017). *Data collection.* Retrieved from https://bjs.ocp.usdoj.gov/index.

NEDA (National Eating Disorders Association). (2022). *Eating disorders in LGBTQ+ populations.* Plano, TX: Author.

NEDA (National Eating Disorders Association). (2022). *Statistics and research on eating disorders.* New York: Author.

NEJM (New England Journal of Medicine). (2022, May 4). *Is depression undertreated following stroke?* Waltham, MA: Author. Retrieved from https://www.jwatch.org/na54854.

Nelemans, S. A., Keijsers, L., Colpin, H., van Leeuwen, K., Bijttebier, P., Verschueren, K., & Goossens, L. (2020). Transactional links between social anxiety symptoms and parenting across adolescence: Between- and within-person associations. *Child Development, 91*(3), 814–828.

Nelemans, S. A., Mastrotheodoros, S., Çiftçi, L., Meeus, W., & Branje, S. (2023). Do you see what I see? Longitudinal associations between mothers' and adolescents' perceptions of their relationship and adolescent internalizing symptoms. *Research on Child and Adolescent Psychopathology, 51*(2), 177–192.

Nelson, C. (2023, March 21). Serotonin-norepinephrine reuptake inhibitors: Pharmacology, administration, and side effects. *UpToDate.* Retrieved from https://www.uptodate.com.

Nelson, C. (2023, January 19). Unipolar depression in adults: Treatment with second-generation antipsychotics. *UpToDate.* Retrieved from https://www.uptodate.com.

Nelson, K. J. (2021, July 21). Pharmacotherapy for personality disorders. *UpToDate.* Retrieved from http://www.uptodate.com.

Nelson, L. S., & Odujebe, O. (2023, October 13). Cocaine: Acute intoxication. *UpToDate.* Retrieved from http://www.uptodate.com.

Nelson, T. D., & Olson, M. A. (2023). *The psychology of prejudice* (3rd ed.). New York: Guilford Press.

Nemani, K., Li, C., Olfson, M., Blessing, E. M., Razavian, N., Chen, J., . . . Goff, D. C. (2021). Association of psychiatric disorders with mortality among patients with COVID-19. *JAMA Psychiatry, 78*(4), 380–386.

Neumark-Sztainer, D. R., Wall, M. M., Haines, J. I., Story, M. T., Sherwood, N. E., & van den Berg, P. A. (2007). Shared risk and protective factors for overweight and disordered eating in adolescents. *American Journal of Preventive Medicine, 33*(5), 359–369.

Newman, M. G., Basterfield, C., Erickson, T. M., Caulley, E., Przeworski, A., & Llera, S. (2022, September 15). Psychotherapeutic treatments for generalized anxiety disorder: Cognitive and behavioral therapies, enhancement strategies, and emerging efforts. *Expert Review of Neurotherapeutics, 22*(9), 751–770.

NFER (National Foundation for Educational Research). (2010). *Tellus4 national report* (DCSF Research Report 218). Retrieved from http://www.nfer.ac.uk/publications/TEL01/.

NHF (National Headache Foundation). (2022). *National Headache Foundation position statement on the treatment of migraine.* Chicago: Author.

NHF (National Headache Foundation). (2023). *Headache fact sheets.* Chicago: Author.

NHS (National Health Service, UK). (2023, January 3). Treatment: Bipolar disorder. Retrieved from https://www.nhs.uk/mental-health/conditions.

NHSE (NHS England). (2023, December 7). *The offender personality disorder pathway: A joint strategy for 2023 to 2028—Annexes A to E.* NHSE. Retrieved from https://www.england.nhs.uk/long-read.

NHTSA (National Highway Traffic Safety Administration). (2022). *Alcohol-impaired driving.* Washington, DC: Author.

NHTSA (National Highway Traffic Safety Administration). (2022). *Early estimate of motor vehicle traffic fatalities in 2021.* Washington, DC: Author.

NIA (National Institute on Aging). (2022). *Facts about aging and alcohol.* Gaithersburg, MD: Author.

NIAAA (National Institute on Alcohol Abuse and Alcoholism). (2022). *Deaths involving alcohol increased during the COVID-19 pandemic.* Bethesda, MD: Author. Retrieved from https://www.niaaa.nih.gov/news-events/research-update.

NIAAA (National Institute on Alcohol Abuse and Alcoholism). (2023). *Alcohol facts and statistics.* Retrieved from https://www.niaaa.nih.gov/publications/brochures-and-fact-sheets.

NIAAA (National Institute on Alcohol Abuse and Alcoholism). (2023). *Alcohol-related deaths, which increased during the first year of the COVID-19 pandemic, continued to rise in 2021.* Bethesda, MD: Author.

NIAAA (National Institute on Alcohol Abuse and Alcoholism). (2023). *Alcohol-related emergencies and deaths in the United States.* Bethesda, MD: Author.

NIAAA (National Institute on Alcohol Abuse and Alcoholism). (2023). *College drinking.* Retrieved from https://www.niaaa.nih.gov/publications/brochures-and-fact-sheets.

NIAAA (National Institute on Alcohol Abuse and Alcoholism). (2024). *Alcohol's effects on health: Older adults.* Retrieved from https://www.niaaa.nih.gov/alcohols-effects-health.

Nicdao, E., Huh, D., Parker, M., Duran, B. M., Simoni, J. M., Solomon, C. C., & Walters, K. L. (2023). Prevalence of mental health disorders and treatment utilization among urban lesbian, gay, bisexual, and transgender American Indians and Alaska Natives. *American Indian and Alaska Native Mental Health Research, 30*(1), 35–52.

Nicula, M., Pellegrini, D., Grennan, L., Bhatnagar, N., McVey, G., & Couturier, J. (2022). Help-seeking attitudes and behaviours among youth with eating disorders: a scoping review. *Journal of Eating Disorders, 10*(1), 21.

NIDA (National Institute on Drug Abuse). (2019). *Genetics and epigenetics of addiction.* Bethesda, MD: Author. Retrieved from https://www.drugabuse.gov/publications.

NIDA (National Institute on Drug Abuse). (2020). *Genetics and epigenetics of addiction.* Bethesda, MD: Author. Retrieved from https://nida.nih.gov/publications/drugfacts.

NIDA (National Institute on Drug Abuse). (2022). *Overdose death rates.* Bethesda, MD: Author. Retrieved from https://nida.nih.gov/research-topics/trends-statistics.

NIDA (National Institute on Drug Abuse). (2023). *Drug control programs.* Bethesda, MD: Author.

NIDA (National Institute on Drug Abuse). (2023). *Drug overdose death rates.* Bethesda, MD: Author.

NIDA (National Institute on Drug Abuse). (2023). *Methamphetamine.* Bethesda, MD: Author.

NIDA (National Institute on Drug Abuse). (2023). *NIDA Center for Genetic Studies: Providing data and biomaterials for research on the genetics of addiction.* Bethesda, MD: Author.

NIDA (National Institute on Drug Abuse). (2023). *Trends and statistics.* Bethesda, MD: Author.

Nielsen, K. D., Hovmand, O. R., Jorgensen, M. S., Meisner, M., & Arnfred, S. M. (2023, September 7). Psychotherapy for patients with schizotypal personality disorder: A scoping review. *Clinical Psychology and Psychotherapy.* doi:10.1002/cpp.2901. [Online ahead of print]

Nietzel, M. T. (2021, May 24). Almost half of Americans don't seek professional help for mental disorders. *Forbes.* https://www.forbes.com/sites/michaeltnietzel/2021/05/24/why-so-many-americans-do-not-seek-professional-help-for-mental-disorders/?sh=1d0fc5d73de7.

Nigg, J. T. (2016). Attention and impulsivity. In D. Cicchetti (Ed.). *Developmental psychology: Vol. 3. Maladaptation and psychopathology* (3rd ed., Chap. 14). New York: Wiley.

Nigg, J. T. (2017). Annual research review: On the relations among self-regulation, self-control, executive functioning, effortful control, cognitive control, impulsivity, risk-taking, and inhibition for developmental psychopathology. *Journal of Child Psychology and Psychiatry, 58*(4), 361–383.

Nigg, J. T., Karalunas, S. L., Feczko, E., & Fair, D. A. (2020, February 24). Toward a revised nosology for attention-deficit/hyperactivity disorder heterogeneity. *Biological Psychiatry, Cognitive Neuroscience and Neuroimaging, 5*(8), 726–737.

Nigg, J. T., Karalunas, S. L., Mooney, M. A., Wilmot, B., Nikolas, M. A., Martel, M. M., . . . Fair, D. A. (2023). The Oregon ADHD-1000, A new longitudinal data resource enriched for clinical cases and multiple levels of analysis. *Developmental Cognitive Neuroscience, 60*, 101222.

Nijhof, A. D. (2023). Recent neural advantages in studies on theory of mind and autism. *Social Neuroscience, 18*(4), 205–206.

Nimbi, F. M., Tripodi, F., Rossi, R., Navarro-Cremades, F., & Simonelli, C. (2020). Male sexual desire: An overview of biological, psychological, sexual, relational, and cultural factors influencing desire. *Sexual Medicine Reviews, 8*(1), 59–91.

Nimbi, F. M., Tripodi, F., Rossi, R., & Simonelli, C. (2018). Expanding the analysis of psychosocial factors of sexual desire in men. *Journal of Sexual Medicine, 15*(2), 230–244.

NIMH (National Institute of Mental Health). (2017). *Agoraphobia among adults.* Bethesda, MD: Author.

NIMH (National Institute of Mental Health). (2017). *Obsessive-compulsive disorder (OCD).* Bethesda, MD: Author.

NIMH (National Institute of Mental Health). (2017). *Panic disorder among adults.* Bethesda, MD: Author.

NIMH (National Institute of Mental Health). (2017). *Schizophrenia.* Bethesda, MD: Author.

NIMH (National Institute of Mental Health). (2017). *Social anxiety disorder.* Bethesda, MD: Author.

NIMH (National Institute of Mental Health). (2022). *Recovery after an initial schizophrenia episode (RAISE).* Bethesda, MD: Author.

NIMH (National Institute of Mental Health). (2022). Suicide. Retrieved from https://www.nimh.nih.gov.

NIMH (National Institute of Mental Health). (2022). *Suicide.* Bethesda, MD: Author.

NIMH (National Institute of Mental Health). (2023). *Agoraphobia.* Bethesda, MD: Author.

NIMH (National Institute of Mental Health). (2023). *Any anxiety disorder.* Bethesda, MD: Author.

NIMH (National Institute of Mental Health). (2023). *Bipolar disorder.* Bethesda, MD: Author.

NIMH (National Institute of Mental Health). (2023). *Eating disorders.* Bethesda, MD: Author.

NIMH (National Institute of Mental Health). (2023). *Generalized anxiety disorder.* Bethesda, MD: Author.

NIMH (National Institute of Mental Health). (2023). *Major depression.* Bethesda, MD: Author.

NIMH (National Institute of Mental Health). (2023). *Messages About Research Domain Criteria (RDoC).* Bethesda, MD: Author.

NIMH (National Institute of Mental Health). (2023). *Obsessive-compulsive disorder (OCD).* Bethesda, MD: Author.

NIMH (National Institute of Mental Health). (2023). *Panic disorder.* Bethesda, MD: Author.

NIMH (National Institute of Mental Health). (2023). *Persistent depressive disorder (dysthymic disorder).* Bethesda, MD: Author.

NIMH (National Institute of Mental Health). (2023). *Schizophrenia.* Bethesda, MD: Author.

NIMH (National Institute of Mental Health). (2023). *Social anxiety disorder.* Bethesda, MD: Author.

NIMH (National Institute of Mental Health). (2023). *Specific phobia.* Bethesda, MD: Author.

NIMH (National Institute of Mental Health). (2023). *Suicide.* Bethesda, MD: Author.

NIOSH (National Institute for Occupational Safety and Health). (2022). *Suicide and occupation.* Washington, DC: Author. Retrieved from https://www.cdc.gov/niosh.

Nissim, H. S. B., Dill, J., Douglas, R., Johnson, O., & Folino, C. (2022, May). *The Ruderman White Paper Update on mental health and suicide of first responders.* Retrieved from https://www.officer.com/command-hq/press-release/21272378.

Nittle, N. (2023, February 20). The link between depression and creativity. *Verywellmind.* Retrieved from https://www.verywellmind.com.

NITV (National Institute for Truth Verification). (2022). *Does the polygraph "lie detector" work?* West Palm Beach, FL: Author. Retrieved from https://www.cvsa1.com.

NLIHC (National Low Income Housing Coalition). (2022, November 14). *Study finds supportive housing helps reduce arrests of people without homes by police for minor offenses.* Washington, DC: Author.

NMVVRC (National Mass Violence Victimization Resource Center). (2022). *Effects of mass violence incidents on communities: Findings from Parkland, El Paso, and Pittsburgh needs assessment surveys.* Charleston, SC: Author.

Nook, E. C., Jaroszewski, A. C., Finch, E. F., & Choi-Kain, L. W. (2022). A cognitive-behavioral formulation of narcissistic self-esteem dysregulation. *Focus, 20*(4), 378–388.

NORC (National Opinion Research Center). (2020). *COVID impact survey.* NORC at the University of Chicago. Retrieved from https://www.norc.org/Research/Projects.

NORC (National Opinion Research Center). (2022). *COVID impact survey.* NORC at the University of Chicago. Retrieved from https://www.norc.org/research/projects.

NORC (National Opinion Research Center). (2023). *COVID impact survey.* NORC at the University of Chicago. Retrieved from https://www.norc.org/projects/covid-impact-survey.aspx.

Norcross, J. C., Bike, D. H., & Evans, K. L. (2009). The therapist's therapist: A replication and extension 20 years later. *Psychotherapy Theory, Research, Practice, Training, 46*(1), 32–41.

Norcross, J. C., & Farber, B. A. (2005). Choosing psychotherapy as a career: Beyond "I want to help people." *Journal of Clinical Psychology, 61*(8), 939–943.

Norcross, J. C., Karpiak, C. P., & Santoro, S. O. (2005). Clinical psychologists across the years: The division of clinical psychology from 1960 to 2003. *Journal of Clinical Psychology, 61*(12), 1467–1483.

Norcross, J. C., & Lambert, M. J. (2011). Psychotherapy relationships that work II. *Psychotherapy, 48*(1), 4–8.

Norcross, J. C., Pfund, R. A., & Cook, D. M. (2022). The predicted future of psychotherapy: A decennial e-Delphi poll. *Professional Psychology: Research and Practice, 53*(2), 109–115.

Nordentoft, M., Madsen, T., & Erlangsen, A. (2020). Epidemiology and causes of suicide. In J. R. Geddes, N. C. Andreason, & G. M. Goodwin (Eds.). *New Oxford textbook of psychiatry* (3rd ed., Chap. 125). New York: Oxford University Press.

Nordhal, H., & Wells, A. (2022). CBT for social anxiety disorder. In G. Todd (Ed.). *Evidence-based treatment for anxiety disorders and depression: A cognitive behavioral therapy compendium* (Chap. 7). Cambridge: Cambridge University Press.

Normandin, L., Weiner, A., & Ensink, K. (2023, January 25). An integrated developmental approach to personality disorders in adolescence: Expanding Kernberg's object relations theory. *American Journal of Psychotherapy, 76*(1), 9–14.

NPOHA (National Poll on Healthy Aging). (2021). *Alcohol use among older adults.* Ann Arbor: University of Michigan, Institute for Healthcare Policy and Innovation. Retrieved from https://deepblue.lib.umich.edu/bitstream/handle/2027.42/167901/0236_NPHA-Alcohol-report-FINAL-06082021.pdf.

NSF (National Sleep Foundation). (2020). *Sleep in America Poll 2020.* Arlington, VA: Author.

NSF (National Sleep Foundation). (2022). *Sleep in America Poll 2022.* Arlington, VA: Author.

NSOPW (National Sex Offender Public Website). (2020). *About NSOPW (National Sex Offender Public Website).* Retrieved from https://www.nsopw.gov.

NSOPW (National Sex Offender Public Website). (2023). *Questions and answers about sexual assault and sexual offending.* Retrieved from https://www.nsopw.gov/en/SafetyAndEducation/QuestionsAndAnswers.

NSVRC (National Sexual Violence Resource Center). (2019). *Sexual violence and transgender/non-binary communities.* Harrisburg, PA: Author.

NSVRC (National Sexual Violence Resource Center). (2021, November 19). *Resources and support for transgender survivors.* Harrisburg, PA: Author. Retrieved from https://www.nsvrc.org/blogs.

NTAC (National Threat Assessment Center). (2023). *Mass attacks in public spaces: 2016–2020.* Retrieved from https://www.secretservice.gov/newsroom/reports/threat-assessments.

Nunes, J. C., Carroll, M. K., Mahaffey, K. W., Califf, R. M., Doraiswamy, P. M., Short, S., . . . Hong, D. S. (2022). General Anxiety Disorder-7 Questionnaire as a marker of low socioeconomic status and inequity. *Journal of Affective Disorders, 317,* 287–297.

Nwosu, S., Boardman, S., Husain, M. M., & Doraiswamp, P. M. (2022). Digital therapeutics for mental health: Is attrition the Achilles heel? *Frontiers in Psychiatry, 13,* 900615.

NWS (National Weather Service). (2023). *How dangerous is lightning?* Retrieved from https://www.weather.gov/safety/lightning-odds.

NYC. (2023). *9/11 health: Mental health.* New York: Author. Retrieved from https://www.nyc.gov/site/911health.

NYP (New York Presbyterian). (2023). *Understanding BPD.* Retrieved from https://www.nyp.org/bpdresourcecenter.

NYTEB (NY Times Editorial Board). (2022, October 4). The solution to America's mental health crisis already exists. *New York Times.* Retrieved from https://www.nytimes.com/2022/10/04/opinion/us-mental-health-community-centers.html.

O'Brien, J., Taylor, J. P., Ballard, C., Barker, R. A., Bradley, C., Burns, A., . . . Ffytche, D. (2020). Visual hallucinations in neurological and ophthalmological disease: Pathophysiology and management. *Journal of Neurology, Neurosurgery, and Psychiatry, 91,* 512–519.

O'Donnell, R., Chan, J. C. K., Foster, J. L., & Garry, M. (2023). Experimental and meta-analytic evidence that source variability of misinformation does not increase eyewitness suggestibility independently of repetition of misinformation. *Frontiers in Psychology, 14,* 1201674.

O'Higgins, M., Benito, A., Real-Lopez, M., Gil-Miravet, I., Ochoa, R., & Haro, G. (2022). Relationship of DRD5 and MAO-B VNTR polymorphisms with paranoid and antisocial personality disorders in polydrug users. *Personality and Mental Health, 17*(1), 77–86.

O'Mara, M., Greene, D., Watson, H., Shafran, R., Kenworthy, I., Cresswell, C., & Egan, S. J. (2023). The efficacy of randomised controlled trials of guided and unguided self-help interventions for the prevention and treatment of eating disorders in young people: A systematic review and preliminary meta-analysis. *Journal of Behavioral Therapy and Experimental Psychiatry, 78,* 101777.

O'Neil, J. A. (2022). Dissociative multiplicity and psychoanalysis. In M. J. Dorahy, S. N. Gold, & J. A. O'Neil (Eds.). *Dissociation and the dissociative disorders: Past, present, future* (Chap. 8). New York: Routledge.

O'Reilly, L. M., Pettersson, E., Quinn, P. D., Klonsky, E. D., Baldwin, J. R., Lundström, S., . . . D'Onofrio, B. M. (2021). A co-twin control study of the association between bullying victimization and self-harm and suicide attempt in adolescence. *Journal of Adolescent Health, 69*(2), 272–279.

O'Reilly, R., Allison, S., & Bastiampiallai, T. (2019). Observed outcomes: An approach to calculate the optimum number of psychiatric beds. *Administration and Policy in Mental Health and Mental Health Services Research, 46*(4), 507–517.

O'Shea, B. A., Glenn, J. J., Millner, A. J., Teachman, B. A., & Nock, M. K. (2022). Decomposing implicit associations about life and death improves our understanding of suicidal behavior. *Suicide and Life-Threatening Behavior, 50*(5), 1065–1074.

O'Sullivan, L., Sukumar, P., Crowley, R., McAuliffe, E., & Doran, P. (2020). Readability and understandability of clinical research patient information leaflets and consent forms in Ireland and the UK: A retrospective quantitative analysis. *British Medical Journal, 10*(9), e037994.

Obbels, J., Gijsbregts, E., Verwijk, E., Verspecht, S., Lambrichts, S., Vansteelandt, K., & Sienaert, P. (2022, December). ECT-related anxiety during maintenance ECT: A prospective study. *Acta Psychiatrica Scandinavica, 146*(6), 604–612.

OCF (Oral Cancer Foundation). (2023). *Tobacco and addiction.* Newport Beach, CA: Author.

Ochieng, N., Rae, M., Biniek, J. F., & Newman, T. (2022, May 12). *Most office-based physicians accept new patients, including patients with Medicare and private insurance.* Retrieved from https://www.kff.org.

OCP (Online Counseling Programs). (2020, April). *25 rewarding reasons why you should become a counselor.* Retrieved from https://onlinecounselingprograms.com.

Ogbru, A. (2022, August 4). The comprehensive list of antidepressant medications. *RxList.* Retrieved from https://www.rxlist.com.

OHA (Oregon Health Authority). (2022). *Oregon Death with Dignity Act.* Salem, OR: Author.

OJJDP (Office of Juvenile Justice and Delinquency Prevention). (2024). *Working for youth justice and safety.* Washington, DC: Author.

Okan, C., Bilson, L., Zhong, D., Weidemann, G., & Bailey, P. E. (2022, September 2). Validating the interpersonal theory of suicide among older adults pre- and peri-COVID-19 pandemic. *Aging and Mental Health, 27*(8), 1552–1558. https://doi.org/10.1080/13607863.2022.2116402.

Okawa, J. B., & Hauss, R. B. (2007). The trauma of politically motivated torture. In E. K. Carll (Ed.). *Trauma psychology: Issues in violence, disaster, health, and illness: Vol. 1. Violence and disaster.* Westport, CT: Praeger.

Okazaki, D. (2020, March 15). Japan university offers seniors cognition training exercises to prevent dementia. *The Mainichi.*

Olano, F. J. A., & Rosenbaum, B. (2022). Short-term psychodynamic psychotherapy. [Article in Danish]. *Ugeskr Laeger, 184*(27), V03220168.

Olfson, M., Cosgrove, C. M., Altekruse, S. F., Wall, M. M., & Blanco, C. (2022). Living alone and suicide risk in the United States, 2008–2019. *American Journal of Public Health, 112*(12), 1774–1782.

OMH (Office of Mental Health). (2024). *Electroconvulsive therapy review guidelines in New York State.* New York: Author. Retrieved from https://www.omh.ny.gov.

OMH (Office of Mental Health). (2024). *Rights of inpatients in New York State Office of Mental Health psychiatric centers*. New York: Author. Retrieved from https://omh.ny.gov.

OMH (Office of Minority Health). (2021). *Mental and behavioral health: African Americans*. Rockville, MD: Author.

OMH (Office of Minority Health). (2021). *Mental and behavioral health: American Indians/Alaska Natives*. Rockville, MD: Author.

OMH (Office of Minority Health). (2023). *Asthma and African Americans*. U.S. Department of Health and Human Services. Retrieved from https://minorityhealth.hhs.gov.

OMH (Office of Minority Health). (2023). *Diabetes and African Americans*. U.S. Department of Health and Human Services. Retrieved from https://minorityhealth.hhs.gov.

OMH (Office of Minority Health). (2023). *Heart disease and African Americans*. U.S. Department of Health and Human Services. Retrieved from https://minorityhealth.hhs.gov.

OMH (Office of Minority Health). (2023). *Heart disease and Hispanic Americans*. U.S. Department of Health and Human Services. Retrieved from https://minorityhealth.hhs.gov.

OMH (Office of Minority Health). (2023). *Mental and behavioral health: American Indians/Alaska Natives*. Rockville, MD: Author. Retrieved from https://minorityhealth.hhs.gov.

OMH (Office of Minority Health). (2023). *Mental and behavioral health: African Americans*. Rockville, MD: Author. Retrieved from https://minorityhealth.hhs.gov.

ONS (Office for National Statistics). (2019, May 15). *Personal and economic well-being: What matters most to our life satisfaction?* Retrieved from https://www.ons.gov.uk/peoplepopulationandcommunity/wellbeing/articles.

Opotow, S. (2022). Subverting an ethical code: American Psychological Association and the post-9/11 war on terror. *Qualitative Psychology, 9*(3), 344–358.

Öri, D., Szocsics, P., Molnár, T., Motlova, L. B., Kazakova, O., Mörkl, S., . . . Rozsa, S. (2023). Attitudes of psychiatrists towards people with mental illness: A cross-sectional, multicentre study of stigma in 32 European countries. *eClinicalMedicine, 66,* 102342.

Ormseth, C. H., LaHue, S. C., Oldham, M. A., Josephson, S. A., Whitaker, E., & Douglas, V. C. (2023). Predisposing and precipitating factors associated with delirium: A systematic review. *JAMA Network Open, 6*(1), e2249950.

Ornstein, N., & Leifman, S. (2022, May 30). Locking people up is no way to treat mental illness. *The Atlantic*. Retrieved from https://www.theatlantic.com/ideas/archive/2022/05.funding-incarceration/643115.

Orr, N., Wahl, K., Joannou, A., Hartmann, D., Valle, L., Yong, P., . . . Renzelli-Cain, R. I. (2020). Deep dyspareunia: Review of pathophysiology and proposed future research priorities. *Sexual Medicine Reviews, 8*(1), 3–17.

Orsolini, L., Pompili, S., & Volpe, U. (2022). Schizophrenia: A narrative review of etiopathogenetic, diagnostic and treatment aspects. *Journal of Clinical Medicine, 11,* 5040.

Ortega, M. A., Pekarek, T., Fraile-Martinez, O., Garcia-Montero, C., Pekarek, L., Rodriguez-Martin, S., . . . Alvarez-Mon, M. A. (2023). A review: Integrative perspectives on the features and clinical management of psychotic episodes in pregnancy. *Journal of Clinical Medicine, 12,* 656.

Oshri, A., Cui, Z., Carvalho, C., & Liu, S. (2022, August). Is perceived stress linked to enhanced cognitive functioning and reduced risk for psychopathology: Testing the hormesis hypothesis. *Psychiatry Research, 314,* 114644.

Ostermaier, K. K. (2022, June 6). Down syndrome: Clinical features and diagnosis. *UpToDate*. Retrieved from https://www.uptodate.com.

Otgaar, H., Dodier, O., Garry, M., Howe, M. L., Loftus, E. F., Lynn, S. J., . . . Patihis, L. (2022, October 13). Oversimplifications and misrepresentations in the repressed memory debate: A reply to Ross. *Journal of Child Sexual Abuse*. doi:10.1080/10538712.2022.2133043. [Online ahead of print]

Ouafik, M., Henrard, G., Belche, J.-L., & Giet, D. (2023). Functional disorders in primary care. [Article in French]. *Revue Medicale de Liege, 78*(5–6), 255–260.

Ouellet-Courtois, C., Aardema, F., & O'Connor, K. (2021). Reality check: An experimental manipulation of inferential confusion in eating disorders. *Journal of Behavior Therapy and Experimental Psychiatry, 70,* 101614.

Overton, D. (1964). State-dependent or "dissociated" learning produced with pentobarbital. *Journal of Comparative Physiology and Psychology, 57,* 3–12.

Overton, D. (1966). State-dependent learning produced by depressant and atropine-like drugs. *Psychopharmacologia, 10,* 6–31.

Özkan, E., Celik, S. B., Yaran, M., & Bumin, G. (2023). Joint attention-based occupational therapy intervention in preschoolers with autism spectrum disorder: A randomized controlled trial. *American Journal of Occupational Therapy, 77*(2), 7702205090.

Pachankis, J. E., McConocha, E. M., Clark, K. A., Wang, K., Behari, K., Fetzner, B. K., . . . Lehavot, K. (2020). A transdiagnostic minority stress intervention for gender diverse sexual minority women's depression, anxiety, and unhealthy alcohol use: A randomized controlled trial. *Journal of Consulting and Clinical Psychology, 88*(7), 613–630.

Pachankis, J. E., Soulliard, Z. A., Morris, F., & Seager van Dyk, I. (2022). A model for adapting evidence-based interventions to be LGBQ-affirmative: Putting minority stress principles and case conceptualization into clinical research and practice. *Cognitive and Behavioral Practice, 30*(1). https://doi.org/10.1016/j.cbpra.2021.11.005.

Pachankis, J. E., Soulliard, Z. A., Morris, F., & van Dyk, I. S. (2022). A model for adapting evidence-based interventions to be LGBQ-affirmative: Putting minority stress principles and case conceptualization into clinical research and practice. *Cognitive and Behavioral Practice*. https://doi.org/10.1016/j.cbpra.2021.11.005

Padilla-Valdez, M. M., Diaz-Iniguez, M. I., Ortuno-Sahagun, D., & Rojas-Mayorquin, A. E. (2024). Neuroinflammation in fetal alcohol spectrum disorders and related novel therapeutic approaches. *Biochimica et Biophysica Acta: Molecular Basis of Disease, 1870*(1), 166854.

Paganini, S., Meier, E., Terhorst, Y., Wurst, R., Hohberg, V., Schultchen, D, . . . Messner, E.-M. (2023). Stress management apps: Systematic search and multidimensional assessment of quality and characteristics. *JMIR mHealth and uHealth, 11,* e42415.

Pahwa, R., Goyal, A., & Jialal, I. (2023, August 7). Chronic inflammation. *StatPearls*.

Palmer, K. N. B., Rivers, P. S., Melton, F. L., McClelland, D. J., Hatcher, J., Marrero, D. G., . . . & Garcia, D. O. (2021). Health promotion interventions for African Americans delivered in U.S. barbershops and hair salons—A systematic review. *BMC Public Health, 21*(1), 1553.

Pan, S., Ali, K., Kahathuduwa, C., Baronia, R., & Ibrahim, Y. (2022). Meta-analysis of positive psychology interventions on the treatment of depression. *Cureus, 14*(2), e21933.

Panayi, A. (2020, April 3). COVID-19 is likely to lead to an increase in suicides. *Scientific American Observations*. Retrieved from https://blogs.scientificamerican.com/observations.

Pape, S. E., al Janabi, T., Ashton, N. J., Hye, A., Sheehan, R., Gallagher, P., . . . Strydom, A. (2021, June 29). The reliability and validity of DSM 5 diagnostic criteria for neurocognitive disorder and relationship with plasma neurofilament light in a Down syndrome population. *Scientific Reports, 11,* 13438.

Pappas, S. (2023, July 1). More than 20% of teens have seriously considered suicide: Psychologists and communities can help tackle the problem. *American Psychological Association Monitor, 54*(5), 54.

Pappas, S., & Means, T. (2022, March 3). 10 of the deadliest natural disasters in history. *Live Science*. Retrieved from https://www.livescience.com/33316-top-10-deadliest-natural-disasters.html.

Paris, J. (2018). Childhood adversities and personality disorders. In W. J. Livesley & R. Larstone (Eds.). *Handbook of personality disorders: Theory, research, and treatment* (2nd ed., Chap. 17). New York: Guilford Press.

Paris, J. (2020). *Social factors in the personality disorders: Finding a niche* (2nd ed.). New York: Cambridge University Press.

Paris, J. (2022). *Nature and nurture in personality and psychopathology*. New York: Routledge.

Parise, L. F., Parise, E. M., Sial, O. K., & Bolaños-Guzmán, C. A. (2022). Social buffering is dependent on mutual experience in adolescent male mice exposed to social defeat stress. *Chronic Stress, 6*. https//doi.org/10.1177/24705470221111094; PMID: **35874910**; PMCID: PMC 9305802. [Free PMC article]

Park, A.-L., Rinaldi, M., Brichmann, B., Killackey, E., Aars, N. A. P., Mykletun, A., & McDaid, D. (2022). Economic analyses for supported employment programmes for people with mental health conditions: A systematic review. *European Psychiatry, 65*(1), e51.

Park, B.-Y., Kebets, V., Larivière, S., Hettwer, M. D., Paquola, C., van Rooij, D., . . . Bernhardt, B. C. (2022). Multiscale neural gradients reflect transdiagnostic effects of major psychiatric conditions on cortical morphology. *Communications Biology, 5*(1), 1024.

Park, C. L., Kaiser, A. P., Finkelstein-Fox, L., Spiro, A., III, & Wachen, J. S. (2022). Risk and resilience factors for traumatic stress disorders. In J. G. Beck & D. M. Sloan (Eds.). *The Oxford handbook of traumatic stress disorders* (Chap. 23). New York: Oxford University Press.

Park, C. L., & Slattery, J. M. (2024, September). Religiousness and spirituality in health psychology. In N. Schneiderman (Ed.). *APA handbook of health psychology: Vol. 1. Foundations and context of health psychology; Vol. 2. Clinical interventions and disease management in health psychology; Vol. 3. Health psychology and public health* (Chap. 26). Washington, DC: American Psychological Association.

Park, K. K.-H., & Koo, J. (2023, July 27). Skin picking (excoriation) disorder and related disorders. *UpToDate*. Retrieved from https://www.uptodate.com.

Park, S.-E., Jeon, Y.-J., & Baek, H.-M. (2023). Functional and structural brain abnormalities and clinical characteristics of male patients with alcohol dependence. *Brain Sciences, 13*(6), 942.

Park, T. W. (2022, July 5). Benzodiazepine use disorder. *UpToDate*. Retrieved from http://www.uptodate.com.

Parker, L., & Harriger, J. A. (2020). Eating disorders and disordered eating behaviors in the LGBT population: A review of the literature. *Journal of Eating Disorders, 8,* 51.

Parker, M. N., Clark, K. E., & Juarascio, A. S. (2023). An exploration of homework completion in cognitive behavioral treatments for bulimia-spectrum eating disorders. *Eating Disorders, 31*(1), 21–32.

Parmigiani, G., Mandarelli, G., Meynen, G., & Ferracuti, S. (2023). Structured instruments for insanity defense evaluations: Opportunities and limitations. *Behavioral Sciences & the Law, 41*(5), 432–444.

Parnas, J., Sandsten, K. E., Vestergaard, C. H., & Nordgaard, J. (2019). Schizophrenia and bipolar illness in the relatives of university scientists: An epidemiological report on the creativity-psychopathology relationship. *Frontiers in Psychiatry, 10,* 175.

Parogni, I. (2022, June 29). What were the worst hurricanes in history? *New York Times*. https://www.nytimes.com/2022/06/29/climate/what-hurricanes-ever.html.

Parra, K., Vandenbosch, L., & Mas-Manchón, L. (2023). Social media as risk factor for eating disorders. In P. Robinson, T. Wade, B. Herpertz-Dahlann, F. Fernandez-Aranda, J. Treasure, & S. Wonderlich (Eds.). *Eating disorders*. Edinburgh: Springer.

Parsons, M. W., & Braun, M. M. (2024, January). *Clinical neuropsychology: A pocket handbook for assessment* (4th ed.). Washington, DC: American Psychological Association.

Passer, M. (2021). *Research methods: Concepts and connections* (3rd ed.). Fort Worth, TX: Worth Publishers.

Patel, M., & Chalder, T. (2024, September). Treatment of somatic symptom disorders. In N. Schneiderman (Ed.). *APA handbook of health psychology: Vol. 1. Foundations and context of health psychology; Vol. 2. Clinical interventions and disease management in health psychology; Vol. 3. Health psychology and public health* (Chap. 19). Washington, DC: American Psychological Association.

Patel, N. A., & Elkin, G. D. (2015). Professionalism and conflicting interests: The American Psychological Association's involvement in torture. *AMA Journal of Ethics, 17*(1), 924–930.

Patel, S. R., Comer, J. S., & Simpson, H. B. (2021). Innovations in the delivery of exposure and response prevention for obsessive-compulsive disorder. In N. A. Fineberg & T. W. Robbins (Eds.). *The neurobiology and treatment of OCD: Accelerating progress*. New York: Springer.

Patihis, D. (2023, January 5). *Trauma, memory, and law, 2nd ed.: Lectures on repressed memories, memory distortions, and trauma*. Independently published.

Patihis, L., & Pendergrast, M. H. (2018). Report of recovered memories of abuse in therapy in a large age-representative U.S. national sample: Therapy type and decade comparisons. *Clinical Psychological Science, 7*(1), 3–21.

Patihis, L., Wood, R. S., Pendergrast, M. H., & Herrera, M. E. (2022). Reports of recovered memories in therapy in undergraduate students. *Psychological Reports, 125*(1), 129–147.

Patil, O., & Kaple, M. (2023). Sensory processing differences in individuals with autism spectrum disorder: A narrative review of underlying mechanisms and sensory-based interventions. *Cureus, 15*(10), e48020.

Patrick, M. E., Peterson, S. J., Terry-McElrath, Y. M., Rogan, S. E. B., & Solberg, M. A. (2024). Trends in coping reasons for marijuana use among U.S. adolescents from 2016 to 2022. *Addictive Behaviors, 148,* 107845.

Pattakos, A. (2022, February 13). Find meaning, and boost your immunity. *Psychology Today*. Retrieved from https://www.psychologytoday.com/us/blog/the-meaningful-life/202202.

Paul, G. L. (1967). The strategy of outcome research in psychotherapy. *Journal of Counseling Psychology, 31,* 109–118.

Paul, S. (2023, February 21). *Mental health in older adults: Common conditions and how to treat them*. Retrieved from https://www.forbes.com/health/senior-living.

Paulhus, D. L., & Williams, K. M. (2002). The dark triad of personality: Narcissism, Machiavellianism and psychopathy. *Journal of Research in Personality, 36,* 556–563.

Paulus, M. (2023, August 28). Methamphetamine use disorder: Epidemiology, clinical features, and diagnosis. *UpToDate*. Retrieved from http://www.uptodate.com.

Payne, A. F. (1928). *Sentence completion*. New York: New York Guidance Clinics.

Payne, J. (2021, July 23). Postpartum psychosis: Epidemiology, pathogenesis, clinical manifestations, course, assessment, and diagnosis. *UpToDate*. Retrieved from http://www.uptodate.com.

Payne, J. (2022, December 13). Treatment of postpartum psychosis. *UpToDate*. Retrieved from http://www.uptodate.com.

PCAA (Prevent Child Abuse America). (2024). *What we do*. Chicago: Author.

Pear, R. (2013, December 11). Fewer psychiatrists seen taking health insurance. *New York Times*. https://www.nytimes.com/2013/12/12/us/politics/psychiatrists-less-likely-to-accept-insurance-study-finds.html.

Pearce, J. M. S. (2020, Spring). The beginnings of humane psychiatry: Pinel and the Tukes. *Hektoen International*.

Pearlman, A. T., Schvey, N. A., Higgins Neyland, M. K., Solomon, S., Hennigan, K., Schindler, R., . . . Tanofsky-Kraff, M. (2020). Associations between family weight-based teasing, eating pathology, and psychosocial functioning among adolescent military dependents. *International Journal of Environmental Research and Public Health, 17*(1), 24.

Peavy, K. M. (2023, October 24). Opioid use disorder: Psychosocial management. *UpToDate*. Retrieved from https://www.uptodate.com.

Peay, J. (2023). Mental illness and criminal law: Irreconcilable bedfellows? In B. D. Kelly & M. Donnelly (Eds.). *Routledge handbook of mental health law* (Chap. 13). New York: Routledge.

Pedersen, M. L., Gildberg, F. A., Baker, J., & Tingleff, E. B. (2023). A systematic review of interventions to reduce mechanical restraint in adult mental health inpatient settings. *International Journal of Mental Health Nursing*. doi:10.1111/inm.13267. [Online ahead of print]

Pedersen, T. (2022, June 15). Avoidant personality disorder vs. social anxiety: What's the difference? *Psych Central*. Retrieved from https://psychcentral.com.

Peeling, J. L., & Muzio, M. R. (2023, May 8). Conversion disorder. *StatPearls*.

Pelak, V. S. (2019, March 29). Approach to the patient with visual hallucinations. *UpToDate*. Retrieved from http://www.uptodate.com.

Pelak, V. S. (2021, August 31). Visual release hallucinations (Charles Bonnet syndrome). *UpToDate*. Retrieved from http://www.uptodate.com.

Pelham, W. E., III, Altszuler, A. R., Merrill, B. M., Raiker, J. S., Macphee, F. L., Ramos, M., . . . Pelham, W. E., Jr. (2022). The effect of stimulant medication on the learning of academic curricula in children with ADHD: A randomized crossover study. *Journal of Consulting and Clinical Psychology, 909*(5), 367–380.

Pelham, W. E., West, S. G., Lemery-Chalfant, K., Goodman, S. H., Wilson, M. N., Dishion, T. J., & Shaw, D. S. (2021). Depression in mothers and the externalizing and internalizing behavior of children: An attempt to go beyond association. *Journal of Abnormal Psychology, 130*(1), 60–77.

Pellicane, M. J., & Ciesla, J. A. (2022). Associations between minority stress, depression, and suicidal ideation and attempts in transgender and gender diverse (TGD) individuals: Systematic review and meta-analysis. *Clinical Psychology Review, 91,* 102113.

Pennebaker, J. W., & Smyth, J. M. (2016). *Opening up by writing it down: How expressive writing improves health and eases emotional pain* (3rd ed.). New York: Guilford Press.

Penninx, B. W., Pine, D. S., Holmes, E. A., & Reif, A. (2021). Anxiety disorders. *Lancet, 397*(10277), 914–927.

Pennoyer, T. (2017, May 5). Quoted in T. Wayne, Social insecurity? Internet turns boomers into twits. *New York Times*.

Perera, R. M., & Diliberti, M. K. (2023, September 21). What does the research say about how to reduce student misbehavior in schools? *Brookings*. Retrieved from https://www.brookings.edu/articles.

Perez, D., & Finkelstein, S. A. (2023). *Functional neurological disorder, an issue of neurologic clinics*. New York: Elsevier.

Perez-Curiel, P., Vicente, E., Morán, M. L., & Gómez, L. E. (2023). The right to sexuality, reproductive health, and found a family for people with intellectual disability: A systematic review. *International Journal of Environmental Research and Public Health, 20*(2), 1587.

Perkins, A. M., Meiser-Stedman, R., Spaul, S. W., Bowers, G., Perkins, A. G., & Pass, L. (2023). The effectiveness of third wave cognitive behavioural therapies for children and adolescents: A systematic review and meta-analysis. *British Journal of Clinical Psychology, 62*(1), 209227.

Perlin, M. L. (2021). *Advanced introduction to mental health law*. Northampton, MA: Elgar Publishing.

Perls, T. (2023, February 21). Successful aging and its subtypes in centenarians: The Chinese experience. *Journal of the American Geriatrics Society*. [Free access]

Perlstein, S., Fair, M., Hong, E., & Waller, R. (2023). Treatment of childhood disruptive behavior disorders and callous-unemotional traits: A systematic review and two multilevel meta-analyses. *Journal of Child Psychology and Psychiatry, 64*(9), 1372–1387.

Perreault, L., & Laferrère, B. (2023, June 27). Overweight and obesity in adults: Health consequences. *UpToDate*. Retrieved from http://www.uptodate.com.

Pester, B. D., Tankha, H., Caña, A., Yong, S., Grekin, E., Bruinsma, J., . . . Lumley, M. A. (2022). Facing pain together: A randomized controlled trial of the effects of Facebook support groups on adults with chronic pain. *Journal of Pain, 23*(12), 2121–1234.

Pesut, B., Thorne, S., Greig, M., Fulton, A., Janke, R., & Vis-Dunbar, M. (2019). Ethical, policy, and practice implications of nurses' experiences with assisted death: A synthesis. *Advances in Nursing Science, 42*(3), 216–230.

Peters, A. L., Saunders, W. J., & Jackson, M. L. (2022, October 13). Mindfulness-based strategies for improving sleep in people with psychiatric disorders. *Current Psychiatry Reports*. [Online ahead of print]

Peters, J. (2020, March 4). Reddit to launch new suicide prevention tools. *The Verge*. Retrieved from https://www.theverge.com/2020/3/4/21164687.

Petersen, A. (2021, October 5). Why it's so hard to find a therapist who takes insurance. *Wall Street Journal*. Retrieved from https://www.wsj.com/articles/why-its-so-hard-to-find-a-therapist-who-takes-insurance-11633442400.

Petrov, C. (2020). Cyberbullying statistics 2020. *Techjury*. Retrieved from https://www.techjury.net.

Petti, E., Klaunig, M. J., Smith, M. E., Bridgwater, M. A., Roemer, C., Andorko, N. D., . . . Rouhakhtar, R. (2021, November 22). Mental health care utilization in individuals with high levels of psychosis-like experiences: Associations with race and potentially traumatic events. *Cultural Diversity and Ethnic Minority Psychology, 29*(3), 302–315.

Pettypiece, S. (2015, April 10). How psychiatrists are failing the patients who need them most. *Bloomberg.com*.

Pew Research Center. (2015, October 5). California legalizes assisted suicide amid growing support for such laws. *Pew Research*. Retrieved from https://www.pewresearch.org/fact-tank/2015/10/05.

Pew Research Center. (2017, July 11). *Online harassment 2017*. Retrieved from https://www.pewresearch.org.

Pew Research Center. (2019). *Race in America 2019*. Retrieved from https://www.pewresearch.org/social-trends/2019/04/09.

Pew Research Center. (2020). *Polling shows signs of public trust in institutions aid the pandemic*. Washington, DC: Author.

Pew Research Center. (2022). *Race and ethnicity*. Pew Research Center. Retrieved from https://www.pewresearch.org.

Pew Research Center. (2023, August 15). *32% of Americans have a tattoo, including 22% who have more than one*. Retrieved from https://www.pewresearch.org/short-reads/2023/08/15/32-of-americans-have-a-tattoo-including-22-who-have-more-than-one.

Pfeffer, C. R. (2003). Assessing suicidal behavior in children and adolescents. In R. A. King & A. Apter (Eds.). *Suicide in children and adolescents* (pp. 211–226). Cambridge: Cambridge University Press.

Pfiffner, L. J., Dvorsky, M. R., Friedman, L. M., Haack, L. M., Chung, S., Charalel, J. M., . . . Spiess, M. (2023). Development of a web-based training platform for school clinicians in evidence-based practices for ADHD. *School Mental Health, 15*, 49–66.

Phillips, K. A. (2022, November 28). Body dysmorphic disorder: Clinical features. *UpToDate*. Retrieved from https://www.uptodate.com.

Phillips, K. A. (2023, April 10). Body dysmorphic disorder: Choosing treatment and prognosis. *UpToDate*. Retrieved from https://www.uptodate.com.

Phillips, K. A. (2023, June 6). Frequently asked questions about treatment for body dysmorphic disorder (BDD). *International OCD Foundation*. Retrieved from https://bdd.iocdf.org/blog/2023/06/06/frequently-asked-questions-about-treatment-for-body-dysmorphic-disorder-bdd.

Phillips, M. L. (2022). Using social media in your research. *American Psychological Association*. Retrieved from https://www.apa.org/gradpsych/2011/11/social-media.

Phillips, M. L., & Drevets, W. C. (2020). Neuroimaging of bipolar disorder. In J. R. Geddes, N. C. Andreasen, & G. M. Goodwin (Eds.). *New Oxford textbook of psychiatry* (3rd ed., Chap. 71). New York: Oxford University Press.

Pichot, P., & Goodwin. G. M. (2020). The history of psychiatry as a medical specialty. In J. R. Geddes, N. C. Andreasen, & G. M. Goodwin (Eds.). *New Oxford textbook of psychiatry* (3rd ed., Chap. 4). New York: Oxford University Press.

Pierrat, V., Marchand-Martin, L., Marret, S., Arnaud, C., Benhammou, V., Cambonie, G., . . . EPIPAGE-2 Writing Group. (2021). Neurodevelopmental outcomes at age 5 among children born preterm: EPIPAGE-2 cohort study. *British Medical Journal, 373*, n741.

Pilch, I. (2020). As cold as a fish? Relationships between the dark triad personality traits and affective experience during the day: A day reconstruction study. *PLoS One, 15*(2), e0229625.

Pinals, D. A., Packer, I., Fisher, B., & Roy, K. (2004). Relationship between race and ethnicity and forensic clinical triage dispositions. *Psychiatric Services, 55*, 873–878.

Pinciotti, C. M., Wadsworth, L. P., Miron, L. R., Riemann, B. C., & Leonard, R. C. (2022). Transgender and gender diverse patients in intensive mood disorder treatment: A comparative examination of clinical presentation and treatment outcomes. *ScienceDirect, 53*(5), 1062–1076.

Pinna, F., Paribello, P., Somaini, G., Corona, A., Ventriglio, A., Corrias, C., . . . Carpiniello, B. (2022). Mental health in transgender individuals: A systematic review. *International Review of Psychiatry, 34*(3–4), 292–359.

Pinto, A. (2020). Psychotherapy for OCPD. In J. E. Grant, A. Pinto, & S. R. Chamberlain (Eds.). *Obsessive-compulsive personality disorder* (Chap. 9, pp. 143–178). American Psychiatric Association Publishing.

Pirkis, J., Gunnell, D., Shin, S., Del Pozo-Banos, M., Arya, V., Aguilar, P. A., . . . Spittal, M. J. (2022). Suicide numbers during the first 9–15 months of the COVID-19 pandemic compared with pre-existing trends: An interrupted time series analysis in 33 countries. *eClinicalMedicine, 51*, 101573. https://doi.org/10.1016/j.eclinm.2022.101573.

Pishghadam, R., Faribi, M., Ahari, M. K., Shadloo, F. Z., Gholami, M. J., & Shayesteh, S. (2022). Intelligence, emotional intelligence, and emo-sensory intelligence: Which one is a better predictor of university students' academic success? *Frontiers in Psychology, 13*, 995988.

Pivalizza, P. (2022, January 4). Intellectual disability (ID) in children: Management, outcomes, and prevention. *UpToDate*. Retrieved from https://www.uptodate.com.

Pivalizza, P., & Lalani, S. R. (2023, January 10). Intellectual disability in children: Evaluation for a cause. *UpToDate*. Retrieved from https://www.uptodate.com.

Plante, T. G. (2022). Spirituality, religion, health, and professional psychology. In L. J. Miller (Ed.). *The Oxford handbook of psychology and spirituality* (2nd ed., Chap. 23). New York: Oxford University Press.

Plateau, C. R., & Arcelus, J. (2023). Sport and exercise as risk factors for eating disorders. In P. Robinson, T. Wade, B. Herpertz-Dahlann, F. Fernandez-Aranda, J. Treasure, & S. Wonderlich (Eds.). *Eating disorders.* Edinburgh: Springer.

Plomin, R., & Viding, E. (2022). Commentary: Will genomics revolutionise research on gene-environment interplay? *Journal of Child Psychology and Psychiatry, 63*(10), 1214–1218.

Pollard, C., Bucci, S., & Berry, K. (2023, February 12). A systematic review of measures of adult disorganized attachment. *British Journal of Clinical Psychology, 62*(2), 329–355.

Poller, W. C., Downey, J., Mooslechner, A. A., Khan, N., Li, L., Chan, C. T., . . . Swirski, F. K. (2022). Brain motor and fear circuits regulate leukocytes during acute stress. *Nature, 607*(7919), 578–584.

Pontzen, N., Schomerus, G., & Steinberg, H. (2022). The practice of medicinal alcohol withdrawal in the psychiatry of the GDR: The methods of aversion and disulfiram treatment. *Psychiatrische Praxis, 49*(7), 375–381.

Popat, A., & Tarrant, C. (2022). Exploring adolescents' perspectives on social media and mental health and well-being: A qualitative literature review. *Clinical Child Psychology and Psychiatry, 28*(1), 323–337.

Pope, K. S. (1988). How clients are harmed by sexual contact with mental health professionals. *Journal of Counseling and Development, 67,* 222–226.

Pope, K. S. (1994). *Sexual involvement with therapists: Patient assessment, subsequent therapy, forensics.* Washington, DC: American Psychological Association.

Pope, K. S., Chavez-Dueñas, N. Y., Adames, H. Y., Sonne, J. L., & Greene, B. A. (2023). *Speaking the unspoken: Breaking the silence, myths, and taboos that hurt therapists and patients.* Washington, DC: American Psychological Association.

Pope, K. S., & Tabachnick, B. G. (1993). Therapists' anger, hate, fear, and sexual feelings: National survey of therapists' responses, client characteristics, critical events, formal complaints and training. *Professional Psychology: Research and Practice, 24,* 142–152.

Pope, K. S., Tabachnick, B. G., & Keith-Spiegel, P. (1987). Ethics of practice: The beliefs and behaviors of psychologists as therapists. *American Psychologist, 42,* 993–1006.

Pope, K. S., & Vasquez, M. J. T. (2016). *Ethics in psychotherapy and counseling: A practical guide* (5th ed., Hoboken, NJ: Wiley.

Pope, K. S., Vasquez, M. J. T., Chavez-Duenas, N., & Adames, H. Y. (2021). *Ethics in psychotherapy and counseling: A practical guide* (6th ed.). Hoboken, NJ: Wiley.

Pope, K. S., & Wedding, D. (2019). Contemporary challenges and controversies. In D. Wedding & R. J. Corsini (Eds.). *Current psychotherapies* (11th ed., Chap. 16). Independence, KY: Cengage Publications.

Post, R. M. (2023, April 19). Bipolar disorder in adults: Choosing maintenance treatment. *UpToDate.* Retrieved from https://www.uptodate.com.

Powell-Hamilton, N. N. (2023, October). Down syndrome (trisomy 21). *Merck Manual Professional Version.* Retrieved from https://www.merckmanuals/com/professional/pediatrics/chromosome-and-gene-abnormalities.

Powell-Hamilton, N. N. (2023, October). Fragile X syndrome. *Merck Manual Professional Version.* Retrieved from https://www.merckmanuals/com/professional/pediatrics/chromosome-and-gene-abnormalities.

Pozza, A., Starcevic, V., Ferretti, F., Pedani, C., Crispino, R., Governi, G., . . . Coluccia, A. (2021). Obsessive-compulsive personality disorder co-occurring in individuals with obsessive-compulsive disorder: A systematic review and meta-analysis. *Harvard Review of Psychiatry, 29*(2), 95–107.

PRB (Population Reference Bureau). (2019). Fact sheet: Aging in the United States. *PRB, 70*(2). Retrieved from https://www.prb.org.

PRB (Population Reference Bureau). (2023). *Aging.* Retrieved from https://www.prb.org/what-we-do/focus-areas/aging.

Press, D. (2022, April 7). Management of neuropsychiatric symptoms of dementia. *UpToDate.* Retrieved from http://www.uptodate.com.

Press, D., & Buss, S. S. (2021, September 30). Treatment of Alzheimer disease. *UpToDate.* Retrieved from http://www.uptodate.com.

Price, R. K., & Tastet, H. H. (2023). Epidemiology. In H. Cooper, M. N. Coutanche, L. M. McMullen, A. T. Panter, D. Rindskopf, & K. J. Sher (Eds.). *APA handbook of research methods in psychology: Vol. 2. Research designs: Quantitative, qualitative, neuropsychological, and biological* (2nd ed., Chap. 17). Washington, DC: American Psychological Association.

Prochaska, J. O., & Norcross, J. C. (2018). *Systems of psychotherapy: A transtheoretical analysis* (9th ed.). New York: Oxford University Press.

Prochazkova, P., Roubalova, R., & Papezova, H. (2023). Central modulators of appetite in eating disorders. In P. Robinson, T. Wade, B. Herpertz-Dahlann, F. Fernandez-Aranda, J. Treasure, & S. Wonderlich (Eds.). *Eating disorders.* Edinburgh: Springer.

ProCon. (2022). Euthanasia & physician-assisted suicide (PAS) around the world. ProCon. Retrieved from https://euthanasia.procon.org.

ProCon. (2022). *Is social media good for our society?* Chicago: Author.

Pruccoli, J., De Rosa, M., Chiasso, L., Perronoe, A., & Parmeggiani, A. (2022). The use of TikTok among children and adolescents with eating disorders: Experience in a third-level public Italian center during the SARS-CoV-2 pandemic. *Italian Journal of Pediatrics, 48,* 138.

PT (*Psychology Today*). (2016, June 9). *Celebrity meltdown.* Retrieved from https://www.psychologytoday.com/intl/articles/199911/celebrity-meltdown.

PT (*Psychology Today*). (2022, March 23). Fetishistic disorder. *Psychology Today.*

PT (*Psychology Today*). (2023). Shyness. *Psychology Today.* Retrieved from https://www.psychologytoday.com/us/basics/shyness.

Puckett, J. A., Dyer, C., Maroney, M. R., Mustanski, B., & Newcomb, M. E. (2023). Daily experiences of minority stress and mental health in transgender and gender-diverse individuals. *Journal of Psychopathology and Clinical Science, 132*(3), 340–350.

Puckett, J. A., Wilklund, L. O., Louis, C., Gallik, C., Brown-Wren, L., Chu, H., . . . Strong, E. (2023). Clinical practice with transgender and gender diverse clients: Setting up an inclusive practice and training considerations. *Practice Innovations, 8*(4), 265-276. https://doi.org/10.1037/pri0000209.

Pulgar, C. A., Shaikh, A. N., Shannonhouse, L., & Davis, D. (2022). The role of religious coping in understanding the suicide risk of older adults during COVID-19. *Religions, 13,* 731.

Purple.com. (2022, February 24). *Side sleepers: Dr. tips & recommendations.* Retrieved from https://purple.com/the-side-sleepers-guide-to-sleeping.

PUSA (Poverty USA). (2022). *The population of Poverty USA.* Washington, DC: Author.

Putnam, F. W. (1984). The psychophysiologic investigation of multiple personality disorder. *Psychiatric Clinics of North America, 7,* 31–40.

Putnam, F. W., Zahn, T. P., & Post, R. M. (1990). Differential autonomic nervous system activity in multiple personality disorder. *Journal of Psychiatric Research, 31*(3), 251–260.

Qaswal, A. B. (2020). Lithium stabilizes the mood of bipolar patients by depolarizing the neuronal membrane via quantum tunneling through the sodium channels. *Clinical Psychopharmacology and Neuroscience, 18*(2), 214–218.

Quadflieg, N., Voderholzer, U., & Fichter, M. M. (2023). Outcome of bulimia nervosa. In P. Robinson, T. Wade, B. Herpertz-Dahlann, F. Fernandez-Aranda, J. Treasure, & S. Wonderlich (Eds.). *Eating disorders.* Edinburgh: Springer.

Quayle, E. (2021). Online sexual deviance and pedophilia. In L. A. Craig & R. M. Bartels (Eds.). *Sexual deviance: Understanding and managing deviant sexual interest and paraphilic disorders* (Chap. 14). Hoboken, NJ: Wiley-Blackwell.

Quigley-McBride, A., & Wells, G. L. (2023). Eyewitness confidence and decision time reflect identification accuracy in actual police lineups. *Law and Human Behavior, 47*(2), 333–347.

Quiñones, M. (2022). Adverse childhood experiences and dissociative disorders: A causal pathway based on the disruptive impacts of cumulative childhood adversity and distress-related dissociation. In M. J. Dorahy, S. N. Gold, & J. A. O'Neil (Eds.). *Dissociation and the dissociative disorders: Past, present, future* (Chap. 12). New York: Routledge.

Rabayda, C. C., & Hoover, S. (2023). Youth eating disorders soared during COVID-19: Schools can help. *Journal of School Health, 93*(1), 88–91.

Rachman, S. (1966). Sexual fetishism: An experimental analog. *Psychological Record, 16*(3), 293–296

Radez, J., Reardon, T., Creswell, C., Orchard, F., & Waite, P. (2021). Adolescents' perceived barriers and facilitators to seeking and accessing professional help for anxiety and depressive disorders: A qualitative interview study. *European Child & Adolescent Psychiatry, 31*(6), 891–907.

Radin, R. A., Dileo, R., Lustig, R. H., & Epel, E. S. (2024). Biology of appetite, weight, and overeating: Metabolic, psychological, and behavioral influences and clinical directions. In N. Schneiderman (Ed.). *APA handbook of health psychology: Vol. 1. Foundations and context of health psychology* (Chap. 17). Washington, DC: American Psychological Association.

Rahaman, T. (2023). Empowering patients one app at a time: An introduction to digital therapeutics. *Medical Reference Services Quarterly, 42*(3), 301–307.

Rahim, Z. (2017, March 20). Norway is happiest country in the world. What's the secret? *Time.com.*

Rahme, C., El Kadri, N., Haddad, C., Fekih-Romdhane, F., Obeid, S., & Hallit, S. (2023). Exploring the association between lifetime traumatic experiences and positive and psychotic symptoms in a group of long-stay patients with schizophrenia: The mediating effect of depression, anxiety, and distress. *BMC Psychiatry, 23*(1), 29.

RAINN (Rape, Abuse & Incest National Network). (2022). *What is child sexual abuse material (CSAM).* Washington, DC: Author. Retrieved from https://www.rainn.org/news.

RAINN (Rape, Abuse & Incest National Network). (2023). *Campus sexual violence: Statistics.* Washington, DC: Author. Retrieved from https://www.rainn.org/statistics/campus-sexual-violence.

RAINN (Rape, Abuse & Incest National Network). (2023). *Perpetrators of sexual violence: Statistics.* Washington, DC: Author. Retrieved from https://www.rainn.org/statistics/perpetrators-sexual-violence.

RAINN (Rape, Abuse & Incest National Network). (2023). *Scope of the problem: Statistics.* Washington, DC: Author. Retrieved from https://www.rainn.org/statistics/scope-problem.

RAINN (Rape, Abuse & Incest National Network). (2023). *The criminal justice system: Statistics.* Washington, DC: Author. Retrieved from https://www.rainn.org/statistics/criminal-justice-system.

RAINN (Rape, Abuse & Incest National Network). (2023). *Victims of sexual violence: Statistics.* Washington, DC: Author. Retrieved from https://www.rainn.org/statistics/victims-sexual-violence.

Raise-Abdullahi, P., Meamar, M., Vafaei, A. A., Alizadeh, M., Dadkhah, M., Shafia, S., . . . Rashidy-Pour, A. (2023). Hypothalamus and post-traumatic stress disorder: A review. *Brain Science, 13*(7), 1010.

Ramchand, R., Gordon, J. A., & Pearson, J. L. (2021). Trends in suicide rates by race and ethnicity in the United States. *JAMA Network Open, 4*(5), e2111563.

Ramchand, R., Schuler, M. S., Schoenbaum, M., Colpe, L., & Ayer, L. (2022, November 8). Suicidality among sexual minority adults: Gender, age, and race/ethnicity differences. *American Journal of Preventive Medicine, 2,* 193–202.

Ramey, C. T., & Ramey, S. L. (2004). Early learning and school readiness: Can early intervention make a difference? *Merrill-Palmer Quarterly, 50*(4), 471–491.

Ramey, C. T., & Ramey, S. L. (2007). Early learning and school readiness: Can early intervention make a difference? In G. W. Ladd (Ed.). *Appraising the human developmental sciences: Essays in honor of Merrill-Palmer Quarterly* (pp. 329–350). Detroit: Wayne State University Press.

Ramirez Echeverría, M. de L., Schoo, C., & Paul, M. (2023, November 19). Delirium. *StatPearls.*

Ranasinghe, P. D., Zhang, X., Hwang, J., Ranasinghe, P. M., Karunathilake, I. M., & Everly, G. S. (2023). PTSD and depression 8 years after the 2004 tsunami in Sri Lanka. *Disaster Medicine and Public Health Preparedness, 17*(4), e183.

Randall, A. B., van der Star, A., Pennesi, J. L., Siegel, J. A., & Blashill, A. J. (2023). Gender identity-based disparities in self-injurious thoughts and behaviors among pre-teens in the United States. *Suicide and Life-Threatening Behavior, 53*(2), 241–249.

Randall, K. N., Bernard, G., & Durah, L. (2023). Association between employment status and quality of life for individuals with intellectual or developmental disability. *Journal of Applied Research in Intellectual Disabilities, 36*(2), 270–280.

Ransome, Y. (2020). Religion, spirituality, and health: New considerations for epidemiology. *American Journal of Epidemiology, 189*(8), 755–758.

Rasgado-Toledo, J., Duvvada, S. S., Shah, A., Ingalhalikar, M., Alluri, V., & Garza-Villarreal, E. A. (2024). Structural and functional pathology in cocaine use disorder with polysubstance use: A multimodal fusion approach structural-functional pathology in cocaine use disorder. *Progressive Neuropsychopharmacological Biological Psychiatry, 128,* 110862.

Rashid, M. H., Zahid, M. F., Zain, S., Kabir, A., & Hassan, S. U. (2020). The neuroprotective effects of exercise on cognitive decline: A preventive approach to Alzheimer disease. *Cureus, 12*(2), e6958.

Rasmusson, A. M., Kim, B. K., Lago, T. R., Brown, K., Ridgewell, C., & Shalev, A. Y. (2023). Neurochemistry, neuroendocrinology, and neuroimmunology of PTSD. In M. J. Friedman, P. P. Schnurr, & T. M. Keane (Eds.). *Handbook of PTSD: Science and practice* (3rd ed., Chap. 10). New York: Guilford Press.

Rauscher, L., & Wilson, B. D. (2017). Super heroes and lucky duckies: Racialized stressors among teachers. *Cultural Diversity & Ethnic Minority Psychology, 23*(2), 220–229.

Ravan, M., Noroozi, A., Sanchez, M. M., Borden, L., Alam, N., Flor-Henry, P., . . . Hasey, G. (2024). Diagnostic deep learning algorithms that use resting EEG to distinguish major depressive disorder, bipolar disorder, and schizophrenia from each other and from healthy volunteers. *Journal of Affective Disorders, 346,* 285–298.

Raviv, S. (2010). *Being Ana.* Bloomington, IN: iUniverse.

Reale, K. S., Chopin, J., Gauthier, A., & Beauregard, E. (2022, November 15). Sadistic sexual crimes against children: Comparing the manifestation of sexual sadism and crime-commission process. *International Journal of Offender Therapy and Comparative Criminology.* doi:10.1177/0306624X221132225. [Open access]

Reddy, Y. C. R. (2020). Diagnosis and clinical features of OCPD. In J. E. Grant, A. Pinto, & S. R. Chamberlain (Eds.). *Obsessive-compulsive personality disorder* (Chap. 2, pp. 27–48). Washington, DC: American Psychiatric Association Publishing.

Reed, G. M., Ritchie, P. L.-J., & Maercker, A. (2024, March). *A psychological approach to diagnosis: Using the ICD-11 as a framework.* Washington, DC: American Psychological Association.

Reininger, K. M., Biel, H. M., Hennig, T., Zitzmann, S., Weigel, A., Spitzer, C., . . . Löwe, B. (2023). Beliefs about emotions predict psychological stress related to somatic symptoms. *British Journal of Clinical Psychology, 62*(4), 699–716.

Ren, R., & Yan, B. (2022). Personal network protects, social media harms: Evidence from two surveys during the COVID-19 pandemic. *Frontiers in Psychology, 13,* 964994.

Renn, B. N., Hoeft, T. J., Lee, H. S., Bauer, A. M., & Areán, P. A. (2019). Preference for in-person psychotherapy versus digital psychotherapy options for depression: Survey of adults in the U.S. *NPJ Digital Medicine, 2*(1), 6.

Rennoch, G., Schlomann, A., & Zank, S. (2024). Internet use in very old age: The role of the social context and individual characteristics. *Journal of Applied Gerontology, 43*(1), 78–88.

Ressler, K. J. (2020). Translating across circuits and genetics toward progress in fear- and anxiety-related disorders. *American Journal of Psychiatry, 177*(3), 214–222.

Restar, A., Dusic, E. J., Garrison-Desany, H., Lett, E., Everhart, A., Baker, K. E., . . . Hughto, J. M. W. (2022). Gender affirming hormone therapy dosing behaviors among transgender and nonbinary adults. *Humanities and Social Sciences Communications, 9*(1), 304.

Rettew, D. C. (2019, November 12). Avoidant personality disorder. *Medscape.*

Reuman, L., & Abramowitz, J. S. (2022). CBT for somatic symptom disorder and illness anxiety disorder. In G. Todd & R. Branch (Eds.). *Evidence-based treatment for anxiety disorders and depression* (Chap. 8, pp. 136–151). Cambridge: Cambridge University Press.

Reynolds, C. R., Altmann, R. A., & Allen, D. N. (2020). *Mastering modern psychological testing: Theory and methods* (2nd ed.). New York: Springer.

Reynolds, E. (2020, March 12). Taking selfies is probably fine for your self-esteem, editing them might not be. *Research Digest.* British Psychological Society. Retrieved from https://www.bps.org.uk/research-digest/taking-selfies-probably-fine-your-self-esteem-editing-them-might-not-be.

Reynolds, J. B. (2023). The value of conditional release for insanity acquittees. *Journal of the American Academy of Psychiatry and the Law, 51*(3), 353–356.

Rice, S. C. (2020, March 24). Inhibited sexual desire. *Healthline*. Retrieved from https://www.healthline.com.

Richards, J. R., & Le, J. K. (2023, June 8). Cocaine toxicity. *StatPearls*.

Richards, P. S., Allen, G. E. K., & Judd, D. (Eds.). (2022, November 15). *Handbook of spiritually integrated psychotherapies*. Washington, DC: American Psychological Association.

Riddle, M. C., & Safer, J. D. (2022). Medical considerations in the care of transgender and gender diverse patients with eating disorders. *Journal of Eating Disorders, 10*, 178.

Rieber, R. W. (1999, March). Hypnosis, false memory, and multiple personality: A trinity of affinity. *History of Psychiatry, 10*(37), 3–11.

Rieber, R. W. (2002). The duality of the brain and the multiplicity of minds: Can you have it both ways? *History of Psychiatry, 13*(49, Pt. 1), 3–17.

Rigotti, N. A., & Reddy, K. P. (2023, October 4). Vaping and e-cigarettes. *UpToDate*. Retrieved from https://www.uptodate.com.

Riley, R. (2022, August 25). *Relaxation techniques for high blood pressure*. Madison, WI: Preventive Cardiovascular Nurses Association.

Riley, S., & LaMarre, A. (2023). Developments in qualitative inquiry. In H. Cooper, M. N. Coutanche, L. M. McMullen, A. T. Panter, D. Rindskopf, & K. J. Sher (Eds.). *APA handbook of research methods in psychology: Vol. 2. Research designs: Quantitative, qualitative, neuropsychological, and biological* (2nd ed., Chap. 1). Washington, DC: American Psychological Association.

Ringwald, W. R., Forbes, M. K., & Wright, A. G. C. (2023). Meta-analysis of structural evidence for the Hierarchical Taxonomy of Psychopathology (HiTOP) model. *Psychological Medicine, 53*(2), 533–546.

Ritchie, H., Roser, M., & Ortiz-Ospina, E. (2022). Suicide. *Our World in Data*. Retrieved from https://ourworldindata.org/suicide.

Rizvi, A., & Torrico, T. J. (2023, October 28). Obsessive-compulsive personality disorder. *StatPearls*.

Rizvi, S. L., Bitran, A., Oshin, L. A., Yin, Q., & Ruork, A. K. (2024). The state of the science: Dialectical behavior therapy. *Behavior Therapy*.

Rizzo, F. R., Bruno, A., Federici, M., & Mercuri, N. B. (2022). 3,4-methylenedioxymethamphetamine (MDMA) and synaptic dopamine. In V. B. Patel & V. R. Preedy (Eds.). *Handbook of substance misuse and addictions: From biology to public health* (pp. 2195–2213). New York: Springer.

Roberge, E. M., Liefker, F. R., Baker, S. N., Rozek, D. C., & Bryan, C. J. (2022). Suicide following trauma. In J. G. Beck & D. M. Sloan (Eds.). *The Oxford handbook of traumatic stress disorders* (Chap. 11). New York: Oxford University Press.

Roberts, B. L., & Karatsoreos, I. N. (2021). Brain-body responses to chronic stress: A brief review. *Faculty Reviews, 10*, 83. https://doi.org/10.12703/r/10-83.

Roberts, L. (2021, March 23). Pros and cons of direct-to-consumer advertising in the pharma industry. *Orientation Marketing*. Retrieved from https://www.orientation.agency/insights.

Robinson, M., Udupa, N. S., Rice, T. B., Wilson-Lemoine, E., Joiner, T. E., & Rogers, M. L. (2024). The interpersonal theory of suicide: State of the science. *Behavior Therapy*.

Robles, R., Fresán, A., & Ayuso-Mateos, J. (2024). Depressive disorders. In G. M. Reed, P. L.-J. Ritchie, & A. Maercker (Eds.). *A psychological approach to diagnosis: Using the ICD-11 as a framework* (Chap. 6). Washington, DC: American Psychological Association.

Roche, T. (2002, January 20). The Yates odyssey. *TIME.com*. Retrieved from https://content.time.com/time/subscriber/article/0,33009,1001706,00.html.

Rochon, P. A. (2023, September 12). Drug prescribing for older adults. *UpToDate*. Retrieved from http://www.uptodate.com.

Rodgers, M., Simmonds, M., Marshall, D., Hodgson, R., Stewart, L. A., Rai, D., . . . Couteur, A. L. (2021). Intensive behavioural interventions based on applied behaviour analysis for young children with autism: An international collaborative individual participant data meta-analysis. *Autism: The International Journal of Research and Practice, 25*(4), 1137–1153.

Rodolico, A., Bighelli, I., Avanzato, C., Concerto, C., Cutrufelli, P., Mineo, L., . . . Leucht, S. (2022). Family interventions for relapse prevention in schizophrenia: A systematic review and network meta-analysis. *Lancet Psychiatry, 9*(3), 211–221.

Rodriguez, C. (2019, March 17). Euthanasia tourism: Is the E.U. encouraging its growth? *Forbes*.

Rodriguez-Seijas, C., Morgan, T. A., Zimmerman, M. (2021). Is there a bias in the diagnosis of borderline personality disorder among lesbian, gay, and bisexual patients? *Assessment, 28*, 724–738.

Rodway, C., Tham, S.-G., Turnbull, P., Kapur, N., & Appleby, L. (2020). Suicide in children and young people: Can it happen without warning? *Journal of Affective Disorders, 275*, 307–310.

Roesch, R. (1991). *The encyclopedia of depression*. New York: Facts on File.

Roesler, T. A., & Jenny, C. (2022, June 22). Medical child abuse (Munchausen syndrome by proxy). *UpToDate*. Retrieved from http://www.uptodate.com.

Rogers, C. R. (1951). *Client-centered therapy*. Boston: Houghton Mifflin.

Rogers, C. R. (1987). Rogers, Kohut, and Erickson: A personal perspective on some similarities and differences. In J. K. Zeig (Ed.). *The evolution of psychotherapy* (Chap. 3, pp. 179–187). New York: Brunner/Mazel.

Rogers, C. R., Rogers, T. N., Matthews, P., Le Duc, M., Zickmund, S., Powell, W., . . . & Griffith, D. M. (2022). Psychosocial determinants of colorectal cancer screening uptake among African-American men: understanding the role of masculine role norms, medical mistrust, and normative support. *Ethnicity & Health, 27*(5), 1103–1122.

Rogers, J. (2023). A shared pathway connects schizophrenia and bipolar disorder. *Nature Reviews Neuroscience, 24*(1), 2.

Rogiers, R., Van Parys, H., Baeken, C., Van den Abbeele, D., Remue, J., De Raedt, R., & Lemmens, G. M. D. (2022). Treatment experiences during a cognitive behaviour therapy group intervention targeting repetitive negative thinking: A qualitative study. *Psychology and Psychotherapy: Theory: Research and Practice, 95*(2), 447–466.

Roncato Barcelos, T., Fransceschini, S., & Lara, L. (2022). The sexual function of transgender people. *International Continence Society, S25*, abstract 414.

Ronningstam, E., Weinberg, I., & Maltsberger, J. T. (2021). Psychoanalytic theories of suicide: Historical overview, empirical evidence, and clinical applications. In D. Wasserman (Ed.). *Oxford textbook of suicidology and suicide prevention* (2nd ed., Chap. 20). Oxford: Oxford University Press.

Roper Center for Public Opinion. (2017). *Public attitudes about mental health*. Ithaca, NY: Author.

Roper Center for Public Opinion. (2022). *Public attitudes about mental health*. Retrieved from https://ropercenter.cornell.edu/public-attitudes-about-mental-health.

Rösch, S. A., & Hilbert, A. (2023). Outcome: Binge-eating disorder. In P. Robinson, T. Wade, B. Herpertz-Dahlann, F. Fernandez-Aranda, J. Treasure, & S. Wonderlich (Eds.). *Eating disorders*. Edinburgh: Springer.

Ros-DeMarize, R., Klein, J., & Carpenter, L. A. (2023). Behavioral parent teaching engagement among young children with autism spectrum disorder. *Behavior Therapy, 54*(5), 892–901.

Rosell, D. R. (2023, September 15). Approach to treating schizotypal personality disorder. *UpToDate*. Retrieved from http://www.uptodate.com.

Rosell, D. R. (2023, October 24). Psychotherapy for schizotypal personality disorder. *UpToDate*. Retrieved from http://www.uptodate.com.

Rosell, D. R. (2023, September 15). Schizotypal personality disorder: Epidemiology, pathogenesis, clinical manifestations, course, and diagnosis. *UpToDate*. Retrieved from http://www.uptodate.com.

Rosell, D. R., Slifstein, M., Thompson, J., Xu, X., Perez-Rodriguez, M. M., McClure, M. M., . . . Koenigsberg, H. W. (2023). Serotonin transporter availability in physically aggressive personality disordered patients: Associations with trait and state aggression, and response to fluoxetine. *Psychopharmacology, 240*(2), 361–371.

Rosen, R. C., & Khera, M. (2022, August 25). Epidemiology and etiologies of male sexual dysfunction. *UpToDate*. Retrieved from http://www.uptodate.com.

Rosenberg, D. (2022, February 28). Obsessive-compulsive disorder in children and adolescents: Epidemiology, pathogenesis, clinical manifestations, course, assessment, and diagnosis. *UpToDate*. Retrieved from https://www.uptodate.com.

Rosenberg, D. (2022, October 12). Treatment of obsessive-compulsive disorder in children and adolescents. *UpToDate*. Retrieved from https://www.uptodate.com.

Rosenberg, J. B., Jepsen, J. R. M., Mohammadzadeh, P., Sevelstad, A., Vinding, R., Sørensen, M. E., . . . Ebdrup, B. H. (2024). Maternal inflammation during pregnancy is associated with risk of ADHD in children at age 10. *Brain, Behavior, and Immunity, 115*, 450–457.

Rosenhan, D. L. (1973). On being sane in insane places. *Science, 179*(4070), 250–258.

Rosenthal, R. (1966). *Experimenter effects in behavioral research*. New York: Appleton-Century-Crofts.

Ross, C. (2018). *Treatment of dissociative identity disorder: Techniques and strategies for stabilization*. Richardson, TX: Manitou Communications.

Ross, C. A. (2022). Dissociative amnesia and dissociative fugue. In M. J. Dorahy, S. N. Gold, & J. A. O'Neil (Eds.). *Dissociation and the dissociative disorders: Past, present, future* (Chap. 22). New York: Routledge.

Ross, C. (2022). False memory researchers misunderstand repression, dissociation and Freud. *Journal of Child Sexual Abuse, 31*(4), 488–502.

Rossmo, D. K. (2023, October 17). Behavioral profiling in the Golden State Killer investigation: A comparative analysis. *Homicide Studies*. https://doi.org/10.1177/10887679231201801. [Open access]

Rosso, A. M., & Camoirano, A. (2022, July). The effect of administration skills on Rorschach protocols. *Acta Psychologica, 227*, 103607.

Roth, A. (2020). *Insane: America's criminal treatment of mental illness*. New York: Basic Books.

Rothbaum, B. O., Foa, E. B., Riggs, D. S., Murdock, T., & Walsh, W. (1992). A prospective examination of posttraumatic stress disorder in rape victims. *Journal of Traumatic Stress, 5*(3), 455–475.

Rothenberg, A. (2015, March 8). Creativity and mental illness: Creativity is highly 2nd adaptive and the actual processes involved are all healthy. *Psychology Today*.

Rothenberg, A. (2022, September 27). Creativity and mental illness. *Psychology Today*.

Rothschild, A. J. (2023, January 3). Unipolar major depression with psychotic features: Maintenance treatment and course of illness. *UpToDate*. Retrieved from https://www.uptodate.com.

Roy, A. K., & Comer, J. S. (2020). Advances in the conceptualization, assessment, and treatment of pediatric irritability. *Behavior Therapy, 51*, 207–210.

Roy-Byrne, P. P. (2022, February 9). Panic disorder in adults: Epidemiology, clinical manifestations, and diagnosis. *UpToDate*. Retrieved from https://www.uptodate.com.

Roy-Byrne, P. P., & Craske, M. (2022, August 11). Management of panic disorder with or without agoraphobia in adults. *UpToDate*. Retrieved from https://www.uptodate.com.

Rozel, J. S., Toohey, T., & Amin, P. (2023). Legal considerations in emergency psychiatry. *Focus, 21*(1), 3–7.

Ruch, D. A., Heck, K. M., Sheftall, A. H., Fontanella, C. A., Stevens, J., Zhu, M., . . . Bridge, J. A. (2021). Characteristics and precipitating circumstances of suicide among children aged 5 to 11 years in the United States, 2013–2017. *JAMA Network Open, 4*(7), e2115683.

Ruchika, F., Shah, S., Neupane, D., Vijay, R., Mehkri, Y., & Lucke-Wold, B. (2023). Understanding the molecular progression of chronic traumatic encephalopathy in traumatic brain injury, aging and neurodegenerative disease. *International Journal of Molecular Sciences, 24*(3), 1847.

Rudy, L. J. (2023, August 21). Autism inclusion in recreation. *Verywellhealth*. Retrieved from https://www.verywellhealth.com.

Rudy, L. J. (2023, May 4). 8 types of schools for autistic kids. *Verywellhealth*. Retrieved from https://www.verywellhealth.com.

Ruiz, J. M., O'Neill, R. M., Juster, R.-P., & Irgens, M. S. (2024, September). Dimensions of diversity and influences on health disparities. In N. Schneiderman (Ed.). *APA handbook of health psychology: Vol. 1. Foundations and context of health psychology; Vol. 2. Clinical interventions and disease management in health psychology; Vol. 3. Health psychology and public health* (Chap. 3). Washington, DC: American Psychological Association.

Rukundo, G. Z., Ogbolu, R. E., & Mugisha, J. (2023). Editorial: Hopelessness and suicide among children and adolescents in low and middle income countries. *Frontiers in Sociology, 8*, 1215073.

Rupert, P. A., Miller, A. O., Tuminello Hartman, E. R., & Bryant, F. B. (2012). Predictors of career satisfaction among practicing psychologists. *Professional Psychology: Research and Practice, 43*(5), 495–502.

Ruppert, R., Kattari, S. K., & Sussman, S. (2021). Review: Prevalence of addictions among transgender and gender diverse subgroups. *International Journal of Environmental Research and Public Health, 18*, 8843.

Ruppert, R., Sussman, S., & Kattari, S. K. (2020). Prevalence and co-occurrence of addictions among sexual minority subgroups. *Annals of LGBTQ Public and Population Health, 1*, 210–248.

Rus-Calafell, M. R., Ehrbar, N., Ward, T., Edwards, C., Huckvale, M., Walke, J., . . . Craig, T. (2022). Participants' experiences of AVATAR therapy for distressing voices: A thematic qualitative evaluation. *BMC Psychiatry, 22*(1), 356.

Rush, A. J. (2023, September 12). Unipolar depression in adults and initial treatment: General principles and prognosis. *UpToDate*. Retrieved from https://www.uptodate.com.

Rush, A. J. (2023, May 17). Unipolar depression in adults: Treatment with antidepressant combinations. *UpToDate*. Retrieved from https://www.uptodate.com.

Rush, A. J. (2023, October 17). Unipolar major depression in adults: Choosing initial treatment. *UpToDate*. Retrieved from https://www.uptodate.com.

Russell, L., Abbass, A., & Allder, S. (2022). A review of the treatment of functional neurological disorder with intensive short-term dynamic psychotherapy. *Epilepsy & Behavior, 130*, 108657.

Rustamov, E., Musayeva, T., Xalilova, X., Ismayilova, G., & Nahmatova, U. (2023). Exploring the relationship between social connectedness and mental wellbeing: The mediating role of psychological resilience among adults in Azerbaijan. *Discover Psychology*. Retrieved from https://link.springer.com/article/10.1007/s44202-023-00080-8.

Rutledge, P. (2013, October 20). Positively media: How we connect and thrive through emerging technologies. *Psychology Today*. Retrieved from https://www.psychologytoday.com/us/blog/positively-media.

Rutledge, P. (2017, April 12). *Interview: Positive psychology of selfies: Empowerment not narcissism*. Retrieved from https://www.pamelarutledge.com.

Rutledge, P. (2023). Positively media. *Psychology Today*. Retrieved from https://www.psychologytoday.com/us/blog/positively-media.

Ruzek, J. I. (2023). Technology-based interventions for PTSD. In M. J. Friedman, P. P. Schnurr, & T. M. Keane (Eds.). *Handbook of PTSD: Science and practice* (3rd ed., Chap. 28). New York: Guilford Press.

Ruzek, J. I., Yalch, M. M., & Burkman, K. M. (2023). *Group approaches to treating traumatic stress: A clinical handbook*. New York: Guilford Press.

Ryff, C. D. (2022, March 17). Positive psychology: Looking back and looking forward. *Frontiers in Psychology, 13*, 840062.

SA (Sleep Advisor). (2020, January). *54 shocking sleep statistics and trends for 2020*. Retrieved from https://sleepadvisor.org.

SA (Sleep Advisor). (2022, August). *54 shocking sleep statistics and trends for 2022*. Retrieved from https://sleepadvisor.org.

Saadedine, M., Faubion, S., Kingsberg, S., Enders, F., Kuhle, C., Kling, J. M., . . . Kapoor, E. (2023). Adverse childhood experiences and sexual dysfunction in midlife women: Is there a link? *Journal of Sexual Medicine, 20*(6), 792–799.

Sabaroedin, K., Tiego, J., & Fornito, A. (2023). Circuit-based approaches to understanding corticostriatothalamic dysfunction across the psychosis continuum. *Biological Psychiatry, 93*(2), 113–124.

Sabihi, S., Goodpaster, C., Maurer, S., & Leuner, B. (2021). GABA in the medial prefrontal cortex regulates anxiety-like behavior during the postpartum period. *Behavioural Brain Research, 398*, 112967.

Sacks, O. (2012). *Hallucinations*. New York: Vintage Books.

Sacks, O. (2017). *The river of consciousness*. New York: Knopf.

Saeed, S. A., & Gargano, S. P. (2022). Natural disasters and mental health. *International Review of Psychiatry, 34*(1), 16–25.

Sáez-Clarke, E., Comer, J. S., Evans, A., Karlovich, A. M., Malloy, L., Peris, T. S., . . . Ehrenreich-May, J. (2022). Development and validation of the Fear of Illness & Virus Evaluation (FIVE) COVID-19 scales for children—Parent/caregiver report development and validation. *Journal of Anxiety Disorders, 89*, 102586.

Sagiv, L., & Schwartz, S. H. (2022). Personal values across cultures. *Annual Review of Psychology, 73*, 517–546.

SAHM (Society for Adolescent Health and Medicine). (2022). Medical management of restrictive eating disorders in adolescents and young adults. *Journal of Adolescent Health, 71*(5), 648–654.

Sajatovic, M., & Chen, P. (2023, November 23). Geriatric bipolar disorder: Epidemiology, clinical features, assessment, and diagnosis. *UpToDate*. Retrieved from http://www.uptodate.com.

Sajatovic, M., & Chen, P. (2023, December 22). Geriatric bipolar disorder: Treatment of mania and major depression. *UpToDate*. Retrieved from http://www.uptodate.com.

Sakata, M., Toyomoto, R., Yoshida, K., Luo, Y., Nakagami, Y., Uwatoko, T., . . . Furukawa, T. A. (2022, May 16). Components of smartphone cognitive-behavioural therapy for subthreshold depression among 1093 university students: A factorial trial. *Evidence-Based Mental Health*, 25(e1), e18–e25.

Salari, N., Hasheminezhad, R., Almasi, A., Hemmati, M., Shohaimi, S., Akbari, H., & Mohammadi, M. (2023). The risk of sexual dysfunction associated with alcohol consumption in women: A systematic review and meta-analysis. *BMC Women's Health, 23*, 213.

Salmon, M., Sibeoni, J., Harf, A., Moro, M. R., & Ludot-Grégoire, M. (2022). Systematic review on somatization in a transcultural context among teenagers and young adults: Focus on the nosography blur. *Frontiers in Psychiatry, 13*, 897002.

Saloner, B., Krawczyk, N., Solomon, K., Allen, S. T., Morris, M., Haney, K., & Sherman, S. G. (2022). Experiences with substance use disorder treatment during the COVID-19 pandemic: Findings from a multistate survey. *International Journal of Drug Policy, 101*, 103537.

Salters-Pedneault, K. (2019, July 19). Is venting your anger a good idea? *Verywellmind*. Retrieved from https://www.verywellmind.com.

SAMHSA (Substance Abuse and Mental Health Services Administration). (2014). *Projections of national expenditures for treatment of mental and substance use disorders, 2010–2020* (HHS Publication No. SMA-14-4883). Rockville, MD: Author.

SAMHSA (Substance Abuse and Mental Health Services Administration). (2017). *Suicide clusters within American Indian and Alaska Native communities: A review of the literature and recommendations* (Publ. SMA28-5050). Rockville, MD: Author.

SAMHSA (Substance Abuse and Mental Health Services Administration). (2020, April 20). *SAMHSA moves quickly to begin releasing $110 million in emergency grant funding to provide Americans with substance use treatment and mental health services during the COVID-19 pandemic* [Press release]. Rockville, MD: Author. https://www.samhsa.gov/newsroom/press-announcements/202004200430.

SAMHSA (Substance Abuse and Mental Health Services Administration). (2021). *Facts on college student drinking*. Rockville, MD: Author.

SAMHSA (Substance Abuse and Mental Health Services Administration). (2022). *HHS's new mental health and substance use disorder benefit resources will help people seeking care to better understand their rights* [Press release]. Rockville, MD: Author. https://www.samhsa.gov/newsroom/press-announcements/20220427.

SAMHSA (Substance Abuse and Mental Health Services Administration). (2022). *U.S. transition to 988 suicide and crisis lifeline begins Saturday*. Rockville, MD: Author.

SAMHSA (Substance Abuse and Mental Health Services Administration). (2023). *Behavioral health services for people who are homeless*. Rockville, MD: Author.

SAMHSA (Substance Abuse and Mental Health Services Administration). (2023, April 24). *Community Mental Health Services Block Grant*. Rockville, MD: Author.

SAMHSA (Substance Abuse and Mental Health Services Administration). (2023). *Fiscal year 2023: Justification of estimates for appropriations committees*. Rockville, MD: Author.

SAMHSA (Substance Abuse and Mental Health Services Administration). (2023). *Mental health myths and facts*. Rockville, MD: Author.

SAMHSA (Substance Abuse and Mental Health Services Administration). (2023). *2021 National survey on Drug Use and Health detailed tables*. Rockville, MD: Author.

Samra, C. K., & Abdijadid, S. (2023, May 1). Specific phobia. *StatPearls*.

Sanacora, G., & Kitay, B. M. (2022). Ketamine and other investigational agents. In C. B. Nemeroff, A. F. Schatzberg, N. Rasgon, & S. M. Strakowski (Eds.). *The American Psychiatric Association Publishing textbook of mood disorders* (2nd ed., Chap. 22). Washington, DC: American Psychiatric Association Publishing.

Sanborn, M., Ali, M. M., & Creedon, T. B. (2023, July). National trends in psychotropic medication prescribing before and during the COVID-19 pandemic. *Psychiatry Research, 325*, 115248.

Sanchez, A. L., Javadi, N., & Comer, J. S. (2023). Family engagement in a behavioral parenting intervention: A randomized comparison of telehealth versus office-based treatment formats. *Journal of Consulting and Clinical Psychology*. doi:10.1001/jamapediatrics.2022.5204. [Online ahead of print]

Sanchez A. L., Jent, J., Aggarwal, N. K., Chavira, D., Coxe, S., Garcia, D., . . . Comer, J. S. (2022). Person-centered cultural assessment can improve child mental health service engagement and outcomes. *Journal of Clinical Child and Adolescent Psychology, 51*(1), 1–22. https://doi.org/10.1080/15374416.2021.1981340.

Sánchez-Manso, J. C., Gujarathi, R., & Varacallo, M. (2023, August 4). Autonomic dysfunction. *StatPearls*.

Sanders, M. J., & Bursch, B. (2020). Psychological treatment of factitious disorder imposed on another/Munchausen by proxy abuse. *Journal of Clinical Psychology in Medical Settings, 27*(1), 139–149.

Sansone, R. A., & Sansone, L. A. (2011, April 29). Personality disorders: A nation-based perspective on prevalence. *Innovations in Clinical Neuroscience, 8*(4), 13–18.

Sardesai, A., Muneschwar, K. N., Bhardwaj, M., & Goel, D. B. (2023). The importance of early diagnosis of somatic symptom disorder: A case report. *Cureus, 15*(9), e44554.

Sareen, J. (2022, September 15). Posttraumatic stress disorder in adults: Epidemiology, pathophysiology, clinical manifestations, course, assessment, and diagnosis. *UpToDate*. Retrieved from https://www.uptodate.com.

Satariano, A. (2022, October 1). British ruling pins blame on social media for teenager's suicide. *New York Times*. Retrieved from https://www.nytimes.com/2022/10/01/business/instagram-suicide-ruling-britain.html.

Sauer, M., & Walsh, K. (2022, April 13). 13 benefits of sex that can improve your mental and physical health. *Business Insider*. Retrieved from https://www.businessinsider.com/guides/health/mental-health/benefits-of-sex.

Sauer, W. H., & Kimmel, S. E. (2022, June 7). Sexual activity in patients with cardiovascular disease. *UpToDate*. Retrieved from http://www.uptodate.com.

Saunders, H., Guth, M., & Eckart, G. (2023, January 10). *A look at strategies to address behavioral health workforce shortages: Findings from a survey of state Medicaid programs*. Retrieved from https://www.kff.org.

SAVE (Suicide Awareness Voices of Education). (2022). *Suicide statistics*. SAVE.org. Retrieved from https://save.org/about-suicide/suicide-statistics.

SAVE (Suicide Awareness Voices of Education). (2023). *Suicide statistics: 2021 USA general statistics*. Bloomington, MN: Author.

Saviano, A. (2022). Cannabis and organ damage: A focus on pancreatitis (to include different scenarios). In V. B. Patel & V. R. Preedy (Eds.). *Handbook of substance misuse and addictions: From biology to public health* (pp. 1343–1352). New York: Springer.

Savino, A. C., & Fordtran, J. S. (2006). Factitious disease: Clinical lessons from case studies at Baylor University Medical Center. *Proceedings (Baylor University Medical Center), 19*(3), 195–208.

Saxon, A. J. (2022, April 19). Alcohol use disorder: Psychosocial treatment. *UpToDate*. Retrieved from http://www.uptodate.com.

Sayer, M. A., Ostrowski-Delahanty, S., Pacella-LaBarbara, M. L., & Delhanty, D. L. (2022). Classification of acute stress disorder. In J. G. Beck & D. M. Sloan (Eds.). *The Oxford handbook of traumatic stress disorders* (Chap. 3). New York: Oxford University Press.

SB (StopBullying.gov). (2019, June 10). *Facts about bullying*. Washington, DC: Author.

SB (StopBullying.gov). (2021, September 9). *Facts about bullying*. Washington, DC: Author.

SC (Sure Call). (2018). *The attachment problem: Cellphone use in America*. Retrieved from https://www.surecall.com.

Schattke, K., & Marion-Jetten, A. S. (2021). Distinguishing the explicit power motives: Relations with dark personality traits, work behavior, and leadership styles. *Zeitschrift für Psychologie, 230*(4), 290–299.

Schatzberg, A. F., & Nemeroff, C. B. (Eds.). (2024). *The American Psychiatric Association Publishing textbook of psychopharmacology* (6th ed.). Washington, DC: American Psychiatric Association Publishing.

Schechter, M., Goldblatt, M. J., Ronningstam, E., & Herbstman, B. (2022). The Psychoanalytic Study of Suicide, Part II: An integration of theory, research, and clinical practice. *Journal of the American Psychoanalytical Association, 70*(1), 139–166.

Scherer, K. R. (2022, November 2). Learned helplessness revisited: Biased evaluation of goals and action potential are major risk factors for emotional disturbance. *Cognition and Emotion, 36*(6), 1021–1026.

Scheunemann, J., Kühn, S., Biedermann, S. V., Lipp, M., Peth, J., Gallinat, J., & Selinek, L. (2023). Implicit cognitions on self-injurious and suicidal behavior in borderline personality disorder. *Journal of Behavior Therapy and Experimental Psychiatry, 79,* 101836.

Schildkraut, J. J. (1965). The catecholamine hypothesis of affective disorders: A review of supporting evidence. *American Journal of Psychiatry, 122*(5), 509–522.

Schirmer, M. D., Arichi, T., & Chung, A. W. (Eds.). (2023, April 15). *Connectome Analysis: Characterization, methods, and analysis.* New York: Academic Press.

Schlensog-Schuster, F., Keil, J., Von Klitzing, K., Gniewosz, G., Schulz, C. C., Schlesier-Michel, A., . . . White, L. O. (2024). From maltreatment to psychiatric disorders in childhood and adolescence: The relevance of emotional maltreatment. *Child Maltreatment, 29*(1), 142–154.

Schlichthorst, M., Reifels, L., Spittal, M., Clapperton, A., Scurrah, K., Kolves, K., . . . Krysinska, K. (2023). Evaluating the effectiveness of components of national suicide prevention strategies: An interrupted time series analysis. *Crisis: The Journal of Crisis Intervention and Suicide Prevention, 44*(4), 318–328.

Schlosser, R. W., & Koul, R. (2023, March 30). Advances in augmentative and alternative communication research for individuals with autism spectrum disorder: Moving research and practice forward. *Augmentative and Alternative Communication, 39*(1), 2–6.

Schmidt, J., & Gilboy, J. (2020). "Voluntary" hospitalization of the mentally ill. In S. Slobogin, T. L. Hafemeister, & D. Mossman (Eds.). *Law and the mental health system: Civil and criminal aspects* (7th ed., p. 975). St. Paul, MN: West Academic Publishing.

Schmidt, K., Barac-Dammeyer, D., Kowalski, A., Teigelack, P., Pfeiffer, C., Robitzsch, A., . . . Teufel, M. (2023). Implementing biofeedback treatment in a psychosomatic-psychotherapeutic inpatient unit: A mixed methods evaluation of acceptance, satisfaction, and feasibility. *Frontiers in Psychiatry, 14,* 1140880.

Schnackenberg, N., & Petro, S. (2016). *Reflections on body dysmorphic disorder: Stories of courage, determination, and hope.* London: Body Dysmorphic Disorder Foundation.

Schneider, J., Pegram, G., Gibson, B., Talamonti, D., Tinoco, A., Craddock, N., . . . Forshaw, M. (2023). A mixed-studies systematic review of the experiences of body image, disordered eating, and eating disorders during the COVID-19 pandemic. *International Journal of Eating Disorders, 56*(1), 26–67.

Schneider, K. J. (2007). The experiential liberation strategy of the existential-integrative model of therapy. *Journal of Contemporary Psychotherapy, 37,* 33–39.

Schneiderman, N. (Ed.). (2024). *APA handbook of health psychology: Vol. 1. Foundations and context of health psychology; Vol. 2. Clinical interventions and disease management in health psychology; Vol. 3. Health psychology and public health.* Washington, DC: American Psychological Association.

Schneier, F. R. (2023, September 14). Social anxiety disorder in adults: Epidemiology, clinical features, assessment, and diagnosis. *UpToDate.* Retrieved from https://www.uptodate.com.

Schölin, L., Tucker, Z., Chopra, A., Borschmann, R., & McKay, C. (2024). Detention of children and adolescents under mental health legislation: A scoping review of prevalence, risk factors, and legal frameworks. *BMC Pediatrics, 24*(1), 12.

Schreiber, F. R. (1973). *Sybil.* Chicago: Regnery.

Schreiber, J., & Culpepper, L. (2023, June 28). Suicidal ideation and behavior in adults. *UpToDate.* Retrieved from https://www.uptodate.com.

Schuckit, M. A., Smith, T. L., Danko, G., Bucholz, K. K., Hesselbrock, V., Hesselbrock, M., . . . Porjesz, B. (2023). Do personality characteristics predict future alcohol problems after considering current demography, substance use, and alcohol response? *Alcoholism: Clinical and Experimental Research, 47*(6), 1179–1190.

Schumacher, L. M., Martinelli, M. K., Convertino, A. D., Forman, E. M., & Butryn, M. L. (2021). Weight-related information avoidance prospectively predicts poorer self-monitoring and engagement in a behavioral weight loss intervention. *Annals of Behavioral Medicine, 55*(2), 103–111.

Schwartz, C. E., Louie, R. J., Toutain, A., Skinner, C., Friez, M. J., & Stevenson, R. E. (2023). X-linked intellectual disability update 2022. *American Journal of Medical Genetics, 191*(1), 144–159.

Schwarzinger, D. (2023). *The dark triad of personality selection.* Boston: Hogrefe.

Schyns, B., Braun, S., & Neves, P. (2022). Connecting dark personality research with workplace issues. *Zeitschrift für Psychologie, 230*(4), 280–289.

Scott, J. R. (2023, May 4). The differences between binge eating and overeating. *Verywellmind.* Retrieved from https://www.verywellmind.com.

SCP (Society of Clinical Psychology). (2023). *Social learning/token economy programs for schizophrenia.* Atlanta, GA: Author.

SD (Science Daily). (2022, May 19). Major uptick reported in cannabis vaping for all adolescents. *Science Daily.* Retrieved from https://www.sciencedaily.com/releases/2022/05/220519115311.htm.

Sebastian, R. S., Goldman, J. D., & Enns, C. W. (2010, October). *Snacking patterns of U.S. adolescents (Dietary Data Brief No. 2).* Beltsville, MD: Food Surveys Research Group, USDA. Retrieved from https://www.ars.usda.gov/ARSUserFiles/80400530.

Seeman, M. V. (2020). Portrait of an exhibitionist. *The Psychiatric Quarterly, 91*(4), 1249–1263.

Seery, M. D., Holman, E. A., & Silver, R. C. (2010). Whatever does not kill us: Cumulative lifetime adversity, vulnerability, and resilience. *Journal of Personality and Social Psychology, 99,* 1025–1041.

Segal, S. P., Rimes, L., & Badran, L. (2023). Crime and victimization outcomes following civil rights limits to the u se of compulsory treatment. *Psychiatry Research, 327,* 115377.

Segal, Z. (2023, August 21). Unipolar major depression: Treatment with mindfulness-based cognitive therapy. *UpToDate.* Retrieved from https://www.uptodate.com.

Sekhon, S., Patel, J., & Sapra, A. (2023, June 27). Late onset depression. *StatPearls.*

Seligman, M. E. P. (1975). *Helplessness.* San Francisco: Freeman.

Seligman, M. E. P. (2002). *Authentic happiness: Using the new positive psychology to realize your potential for lasting fulfillment.* New York: Free Press.

Seligman, M. E. P. (2012). *Flourish: A visionary new understanding of happiness and well-being.* New York: Atria Books.

Seligman, M. E. P. (2018). *The hope circuit: A psychologist's journey from helplessness to optimism.* Lebanon, IN: PublicAffairs/Hachette Book Group.

Seligman, N. S., Cleary, B. J., & Berghella, V. (2023, January 3). Methadone and buprenorphine pharmacotherapy of opioid use disorder during pregnancy. *UpToDate.* Retrieved from http://www.uptodate.com.

Seligman, N. S., Rosenthal, E., & Berghella, V. (2023). Opioid use disorder: Overview of treatment during pregnancy. *UpToDate.* Retrieved from https://www.uptodate.com.

Selkie, E., Adkins, V., Masters, E., Bajpai, A., & Shumer, D. (2020). Transgender adolescents' uses of social media for social support. *Journal of Adolescent Health, 66*(3), 275–280.

Selkoe, D. J. (1992). Alzheimer's disease: New insights into an emerging epidemic. *Journal of Geriatric Psychiatry, 25*(2), 211–227.

Selkoe, D. J. (2011). Alzheimer's disease. *Cold Spring Harbor Perspectives in Biology, 3*(7), a004457.

Selling, L. S. (1940). *Men against madness.* New York: Greenberg.

Serafini, G., Nasrallah, H. A., & Amore, M. (2022). The use of modern dopamine partial agonists in bipolar depression: Is the evidence sound? *Current Medical Research and Opinion, 38*(5), 773–775.

Serretti, A. (2023). Anhedonia and depressive disorders. *Clinical Psychopharmacology and Neuroscience, 21*(3), 401–409.

Sevarino, K. A. (2023, October 23). Opioid withdrawal: Clinical manifestations, course, assessment, and diagnosis. *UpToDate.* Retrieved from http://www.uptodate.com.

Severe, J., Tang, R., Horbatch, F., Onishchenko, R., Naini, V., & Blazek, M. C. (2020, November 3). Factors influencing patients' initial decisions regarding telepsychiatry participation during the COVID-19 pandemic: Telephone-based survey. *JMIR Formative Research, 4*(12), e25469.

Severino, K. A. (2023, October 23). Opioid withdrawal: Medically supervised opioid withdrawal during treatment for opioid use disorder *UpToDate*. Retrieved from http://www.uptodate.com.

SF (Sleep Foundation). (2020). *Healthy sleep tips.* Retrieved from https://www.sleepfoundation.org.

SF (Sleep Foundation). (2022). *Healthy sleep tips.* Retrieved from https://www.sleepfoundation.org.

Sforzini, L., Nettis, M. A., Weston, F., & Pariante, C. M. (2022). Psychoneuroendocrinology of mood disorders. In C. B. Nemeroff, A. F. Schatzberg, N. Rasgon, & S. M. Strakowski (Eds.). *The American Psychiatric Association Publishing textbook of mood disorders* (2nd ed., Chap. 6). Washington, DC: American Psychiatric Association Publishing.

Shah, P., Thornton, I., Turrin, D., & Hipskind, J. E. (2023, June 5). Informed consent. *StatPearls.*

Shahar, G. (2023). *Complex depression: The role of personality dynamics and social ecology.* Washington, DC: American Psychological Association.

Shandrow, M. (2023). *Protestants churchgoers' perspectives on alcohol consumption.* Costa Mesa, CA: Asana Recovery.

Shang, Z.-X., Fang, C.-Q., Lang, X.-E., & Zhang, X.Y. (2024). Gender difference in association between clinical symptoms and alexithymia in chronic schizophrenia: A large sample study based on Chinese Han population. *Journal of Affective Disorders, 344,* 519–527.

Shapira, B., & Neumark, Y. (2022). Substance use disorder treatment in the age of COVID-19: Challenges, responses, and lessons for the future. In V. B. Patel & V. R. Preedy (Eds.). *Handbook of substance misuse and addictions: From biology to public health* (pp. 305–326). New York: Springer.

Sharma, N. P., & Spiro, P. M. (2023, August 2). Psychoanalytic therapy. *StatPearls.*

Sharma, V., Singh, T. G., Kaur, A., Mannan, A., & Dhiman, S. (2022, October 29). Brain-derived neurotrophic factor: A novel dynamically regulated therapeutic modulator in neurological disorders. *Neurochemical Research, 48*(2), 317–339.

Shaw, A. M., Hare, M. M., Conroy, K., Kehrer, S. M., Cummings, L. R., Ramos, M. C., & Comer, J. S. (2024). Telehealth-delivered dialectical behavior therapy for adolescents: A pilot study of treatment engagement and preliminary efficacy. *Psychological Services.*

Shaw, D. S. (2023, September 6). The premise, promise, and challenges of intensive assessment and dynamic quantitative methods for child and adolescent externalizing problems. *Research on Child and Adolescent Psychopathology.* doi:10.1007/s10802-023-01120-6. [Online ahead of print]

Shaw, K. (2004). *Oddballs and eccentrics.* Edison, NJ: Castle Books.

Shawcroft, J., Gale, M., Coyne, S. M., Twenge, J. M., Carroll, J. S., Wilcox, W. B., & James, S. (2022). Teens, screens and quarantine: The relationship between adolescent media use and mental health prior to and during COVID-19. *Heliyon, 8*(7), e09898.

Shea, T., Dotson, S., Tyree, G., Ogbu-Nwobodo, L., Beck, S., & Shtasel, D. (2022). Racial and ethnic inequities in inpatient psychiatric civil commitment. *Psychiatric Services, 73*(12), 1322–1329.

Sheidow, A. J., McCart, M. R., & Drazdowski, T. K. (2022). Family-based treatments for disruptive behavior problems in children and adolescents: An updated review of rigorous studies (2015–April 2020). *Journal of Marital and Family Therapy, 48*(1), 56–82.

Sheikh, K. (2017, August 10). Do you hear what I hear? Auditory hallucinations yield clues to perception. *Scientific American.*

Shelton, R. C. (2022). Selective serotonin reuptake inhibitors and related antidepressants. In C. B. Nemeroff, A. F. Schatzberg, N. Rasgon, & S. M. Strakowski (Eds.). *The American Psychiatric Association Publishing textbook of mood disorders* (2nd ed., Chap. 15). Washington, DC: American Psychiatric Association Publishing.

Shen, K. J., Colloff, M. F., Vul, E., Wilson, B. M., & Wixted, J. T. (2023). Modeling face similarity in police lineups. *Psychological Review, 130*(2), 432–461.

Shenk, D. (2001). *The forgetting: Alzheimer's: Portrait of an epidemic.* New York: Doubleday.

Shepherd, B. F., Brochu, P. M., & Rodriguez-Seijas, C. (2022). A critical examination of disparities in eating disorder symptoms by sexual orientation among US adults in the NESARC-III. *International Journal of Eating Disorders, 55*(6), 790–800.

Sher, L. (2020, April 19). The 2003 SARS outbreak and suicide among older adults. *Internet and Psychiatry.* Retrieved from https://www.internetandpsychiatry.com/wp.

Shergill, S. S., Brammer, M. J., Williams, S. R., Murray, R. M., & McGuire, P. K. (2000). Mapping auditory hallucinations in schizophrenia using functional magnetic resonance imaging. *Archives of General Psychiatry, 57*(11), 1033–1038.

Sherva, R., & Kowall, N. W. (2022, May 19). Genetics of Alzheimer disease. *UpToDate.* Retrieved from http://www.uptodate.com.

Shetty, K. V., Math, S, B., Marimuthu, P., & Rawat, V. S. (2023). Family intervention for expressed emotion in schizophrenia: Indian context. *Indian Journal of Psychiatry, 65*(4), 453–459.

Shifren, J. L. (2022, May 4). Overview of sexual dysfunction in females: Epidemiology, risk factors, and evaluation. *UpToDate.* Retrieved from http://www.uptodate.com.

Shifren, J. L. (2023, February 1). Overview of sexual dysfunction in females: Management. *UpToDate.* Retrieved from http://www.uptodate.com.

SHN (Sharp Health News). (2022, March 22). Suicide rates rise among Black youth and young adults. Sharp Health News. Retrieved from https://www.sharp.com/health-news.

Shneidman, E. S. (1963). Orientations toward death: Subintentioned death and indirect suicide. In R. W. White (Ed.). *The study of lives.* New York: Atherton.

Shneidman, E. S. (1981). Suicide. *Suicide and Life-Threatening Behavior, 11*(4), 198–220.

Shneidman, E. S. (1985). *Definition of suicide.* New York: Wiley.

Shneidman, E. S. (1987, March). At the point of no return. *Psychology Today.*

Shneidman, E. S. (1993). *Suicide as psychache: A clinical approach to self-destructive behavior.* Northvale, NJ: Jason Aronson.

Shneidman, E. S. (2001). *Comprehending suicide: Landmarks in 20th-century suicidology.* Washington, DC: American Psychological Association.

Shneidman, E. S. (2005). Anodyne psychotherapy for suicide: A psychological view of suicide. *Clinical Neuropsychiatry, 2*(1), 7–12.

Shobassy, A. (2021). Elderly bipolar disorder. *Current Psychiatry Reports, 23*(2), 5.

Shoib, S., Chandradasa, M., Nahidi, M., Amanda, T. W., Khan, S., Saeed, F., . . . DeBerardis, D. (2022). Facebook and suicidal behaviour: User experiences of suicide notes, live-streaming, grieving and preventive strategies: A scoping review. *International Journal of Environmental Research and Public Health, 19*(20), 13001.

Shor, S. (2022). *Which professions are the happiest at work?* Retrieved from https://resume.io/blog.

Silbersweig, D. A., Stern, E., Frith, C., Cahill, C., Holmes, A., Grootoonk, S., . . . Frackowiak, R. S. J. (1995). A functional neuroanatomy of hallucinations in schizophrenia. *Nature, 378,* 176–179.

Silva, J. R., Capellan, J. A., Schmuhl, M. A., & Mills, C. E. (2021, January 20). Gender-based mass shootings: An examination of attacks motivated by grievances against women. *Violence Against Women, 27*(12–13), 2163–2186.

Simão, A. Y., Antunes, M., Marques, H., Rosado, T., Soares, S., Goncalves, J., . . . & Gallardo, E. (2022). Amphetamine in biological specimens: Impact and implications for public health. In V. B. Patel & V. R. Preedy (Eds.). *Handbook of substance misuse and addictions: From biology to public health* (pp. 2003–2027). New York: Springer.

Simeon, D. (2022, September 29). Depersonalization/derealization disorder: Epidemiology, pathogenesis, clinical manifestations, course, and diagnosis. *UpToDate.* Retrieved from https://www.uptodate.com.

Simeon, D. (2022, September 16). Psychotherapy of depersonalization/derealization disorder. *UpToDate.* Retrieved from https://www.uptodate.com.

Simon, M., Yang, J., Gigas, J., Earley, E. J., Hillpot, E., Zhang, L., . . . Gorbunova, V. (2023). A rare human centenarian variant of SIRT6 enhances genome stability and interaction with Lamin A. *EMBO Journal, 42*(3), e113326.

Simonazzi, C., Natali, L., Valmaggia, L., Rowlands, K., Meregalli, V., Rabarbari, E., . . . Cardi, V. (2023). Food-related aversion in a female sample of people with anorexia nervosa: Cognitive-behavioural correlates, somatic and subjective anxiety, and early experiences. *Appetite, 180,* 106366.

Simone, M., Hazzard, V. M., Askew, A. J., Tebbe, E. A., Lipson, S. K., & Pisetsky, E. M. (2022). Variability in eating disorder risk and diagnosis in transgender and gender diverse college students. *Annals of Epidemiology, 70,* 53–60.

Simons, E. I., Noteboom, F., & van Furth, E. F. (2023, October 31). Pro-anorexia coaches prey on individuals with eating disorders. *International Journal of Eating Disorders.* doi:10.1002/eat.24074. [Online ahead of print]

Simpson, H. B. (2023, May 5). Obsessive-compulsive disorder in adults: Epidemiology, pathogenesis, clinical manifestations, course, and diagnosis. *UpToDate.* Retrieved from https://www.uptodate.com.

Simpson, H. B., van den Heuvel, O. A., Miguel, E. C., Reddy, Y. C. J., Stein, D. J., Lewis-Fernández, . . . Wall, M. (2020). Toward identifying reproducible brain signatures of obsessive-compulsive profiles: Rationale and methods for a new global initiative. *BMC Psychiatry, 20*(1), 68.

Sinclair, B. (2017). *Eccentricity: Society's secret sauce: The value of being eccentric.* Dearborn, MI: Alpha Academic Press.

Singh, A. K., Malviya, R., Prakash, A., & Verma, S. (2024). Neuropsychiatric manifestations in Alzheimer's disease patients: Genetics and treatment options. *CNS & Neurological Disorders–Drug Target, 23*(1), 39–54.

Singh, J., Singh, S., Gupta, S., & Chavan, B. S. (2023). Cognitive remediation and schizophrenia: Effects on brain complexity. *Neuroscience Letters, 808,* 137268.

Singh, P. (2022, August 5). Top meditation app statistics to know in 2022. *Appinventiv.* Retrieved from https://appinventiv.com/blog.

Singh, S., & Sagar, R. (2022). Time to have effective regulation of the mental health apps market: Maximize gains and minimize harms. *Indian Journal of Psychological Medicine, 44*(4), 399–404.

Sinyor, M., Tran, U. S., Garcia, D., Till, B., Voracek, M., & Niederkrotenthaler, T. (2021). Suicide mortality in the United States following the suicides of Kate Spade and Anthony Bourdain. *Australian and New Zealand Journal of Psychiatry, 55*(6), 613–619.

Sioutis, S., Zikopoulos, A., Karampikas, V., Mitsiokapa, E., Tsatsaragkou, A., Katsanos, S., . . . Magrogenis, A. F. (2024). Hip fractures in patients with dementia: An emerging orthopedic concern. *Journal of Long-Term Effects of Medical Implants, 34*(1), 85–93.

SIRC (Social Issues Research Centre). (2023). *Totally in control.* Oxford: Author.

Siris, S. G., & Braga, R. J. (2023, July 25). Anxiety in schizophrenia. *UpToDate.* Retrieved from http://www.uptodate.com.

Siris, S. G., & Braga, R. J. (2023, August 4). Depression in schizophrenia. *UpToDate.* Retrieved from http://www.uptodate.com.

Sistani, F., de Bittner, M. R., & Shaya, F. T. (2022, July 11). COVID-19 pandemic and telemental health policy reforms. *Current Medical Research and Opinion, 38*(12), 2123–2126.

Sizemore, C. C. (1991). *A mind of my own: The woman who was known as "Eve" tells the story of her triumph over multiple personality disorder.* New York: William Morrow.

Sizemore, C. C., & Pittillo, E. S. (1977). *I'm Eve.* Garden City, NY: Doubleday.

Skinner, B. F. (1957). *Verbal behavior.* Englewood Cliffs, NJ: Prentice Hall.

Skinner, B. F. (1958). Diagramming schedules of reinforcement. *Journal of the Experimental Analysis of Behavior, 1,* 67–68.

Skodol, A. (2022, June 2). Borderline personality disorder: Epidemiology, pathogenesis, clinical features, course, assessment, and diagnosis. *UpToDate.* Retrieved from http://www.uptodate.com.

Skodol, A., & Bender, D. (2022, October 28). Approaches to the therapeutic relationship in patients with personality disorders. *UpToDate.* Retrieved from http://www.uptodate.com.

Skrba, A. (2020, May 2). *Cyberbullying statistics, facts, and trends (2020).* FirstSiteGuide.com. Retrieved from https://firstsiteguide.com/cyberbullying-stats.

Slade, S., & Sergent, S. R. (2023, April 24). Interview techniques. *StatPearls.*

Sleek, S. (2023, June 30). The bad-behavior blend: Scientists explore the interplay of genes, environment, and antisocial behavior. *Association for Psychological Science,* July/August. Retrieved from https://www.psychologicalscience.org/observer.

Sletved, K. S. O., Coello, K., Stanislaus, S., Kjaerstad, H. L., Melbye, S. A., Faurholt-Jepsen, M., . . . Kessing, L. V. (2022). Socio-economic status and functioning in patients newly diagnosed with bipolar disorder and their unaffected siblings: Results from a cross-sectional clinical study. *Journal of Affective Disorders, 310,* 404–411.

Sloan, D. M., Marx, B. P., Acierno, R., Messina, M., Muzzy, Gallagher, M. W., . . . Sloan, C. (2023, August 23). Written exposure therapy vs. prolonged exposure therapy in the treatment of posttraumatic stress disorder: A randomized clinical trial. *JAMA Psychiatry.* doi:10.1001/jamapsychiatry.2023.2810. [Online ahead of print]

Sloan, D., Marx, B. P., Resick, P. A., Young-McCaughan, S., Dondanville, K. A., Straud, C. L., . . . Peterson, A. L. (2022). Effect of written exposure therapy vs cognitive processing therapy on increasing treatment efficiency among military service members with posttraumatic stress disorder: A randomized noninferiority trial. *JAMA Network Open, 5*(1), e2140911.

Slobogin, C., Hafemeister, T. L., & Mossman, D. (2020). *Law and the mental health system: Civil and criminal aspects* (7th ed.). St. Paul, MN: West Academic Publishing.

SMCH (Stanford Medicine Children's Health). (2023). *A child's concept of death.* Stanford, CA: Author.

Smietana, B. (2016, December 6). Most Americans say assisted suicide is morally acceptable. *Lifeway Research.*

Smith, B. M., Smith, G. S., & Bluett, E. J. (2022). ACT for anxiety and trauma-related disorders. In M. P. Twohig, M. E. Levin, & J. M. Petersen (Eds.). *The Oxford handbook of acceptance and commitment therapy.* New York: Oxford University Press.

Smith, B. W., deCruz-Dixon, N., Erickson, K., Guzman, A., Phan, A., & Schodt, K. (2023). The effects of an online positive psychology course on happiness, health, and well-being. *Journal of Happiness Studies, 24*(3), 1145–1167.

Smith, K. (2022, November 3). Heart disease and depression. *Psychom.net.* Retrieved from https://www.psycom.net.

Smith, K. E., Graf, E., Faig, K. E., Dimitroff, S. J., Rockwood, F., Hernandez, M. W., & Norman, G. J. (2023, August 10). Perceived control, loneliness, early-life stress, and parents' perceptions of stress. *Scientific Reports.* https://doi.org/10.1038/s41598-023-39572-x. [Online ahead of print]

Smith, L. (2022, July 21). *Meditation statistics: How many people meditate?* Retrieved from https://www.thegoodbody.com.

Smith, L. (2022, February 18). What you need to know about vaginismus. *Medical News Today.*

Smith, M. L., & Glass, G. V. (1977). Meta-analysis of psychotherapy outcome studies. *American Psychologist, 32*(9), 752–760.

Smith, M. L., Glass, G. V., & Miller, T. I. (1980). *The benefits of psychotherapy.* Baltimore: Johns Hopkins University Press.

Smith, M. M., McCabe, G. A., & Widiger, T. A. (2022, July 11). Experimental manipulation of the BFI-2, IPIP-NEO-120, and the IPC-5. *Assessment.* doi:10.1177/10731911221107622. [Online ahead of print]

Smith, M., & Segal, J. (2022, November 2). Recovering from rape and sexual trauma. *Helpguide.org.* Retrieved from https://www.helpguide.org/articles/ptsd-trauma.

Smith, T. E., Pangilinan, M., Rodgers, I., Li, X., Claverie, G., & Katagiri, J. (2022). Mental health service utilization review patterns in a Medicaid managed care program. *American Journal of Managed Care, 28*(2), 81–84.

Smith-Apeldoorn, S. Y., Vischjager, M., Veraart, J. K., Kamphuis, J., Rot, M. A. H., & Schoevers, R. A. (2022). The antidepressant effect and safety of non-intranasal esketamine: A systematic review. *Journal of Psychopharmacology, 36*(5), 531–544.

Snook, J. (2018, May 21). The real civil commitment crisis and how to solve it. *Health Affairs Blog.* Retrieved from https://www.healthaffairs.org.

Snowden, L. R., Cordell, J. K., & Bui, J. (2022, September 6). Racial and ethnic disparities in health status and community functioning among persons with untreated mental illness. *Journal of Racial and Ethnic Health Disparities.* doi:10.1007/s40615-022-01397-1. [Online ahead of print]

Snyder, C. R., Lopez, S. J., Edwards, L. M., & Marques, S. C. (2021, January 14). *The Oxford handbook of positive psychology* (Oxford Library of Psychology, 3rd ed.). New York: Oxford University Press.

Snyder, P. J., & Rosen, R. C. (2020, January 11). Overview of male sexual dysfunction. *UpToDate.* Retrieved from https://www.uptodate.com.

SO (Special Olympics). (2023). *What is intellectual disability?* Retrieved from https://www.specialolympics.org.

So, B. K., & Kim, P. Y. (2022). Understanding prescription drug advertising. *StatPearls.*

Soberay, K. A., Cerel, J., Brown, M. M., & Maple, M. (2022). An examination of suicide exposure and fearlessness about death on suicide risk among active duty service members, veterans, and civilians. *Archives of Suicide Research, 26*(3), 1198–1218.

Sockol, L. E. (2022). Cognitive behavioral therapy for perinatal depression. In G. Todd & R. Branch (Eds.). *Evidence-based treatment for anxiety disorders and depression: A cognitive behavioral therapy compendium* (pp. 418–458). Cambridge: Cambridge University Press.

Solan, M. (2023). *Overcoming resistant hypertension.* Cambridge, MA: Harvard University Press.

Solanto, M. V. (2023, October 10). Attention deficit hyperactivity disorder (ADHD) in adults: Psychotherapy. *UpToDate.* Retrieved from https://www.uptodate.com.

Soldati, L., Recordon, N., Clemen, M., Köhl, J., & Perroud, N. (2022, October). Gender dysphoria and dissociative identity disorder: A case report and review of literature. *ScienceDirect, 10*(5), 100553.

Somma, A., Borroni, S., Sellbom, M., Markon, K. E., Krueger, R. F., & Fossati, S. (2020). Assessing dark triad dimensions from the perspective of moral disengagement and DSM-5 alternative model of personality disorder traits. *Personality Disorders: Theory, Research, and Treatment, 11*(2), 100–107.

Sommers-Flanagan, J., & Sommers-Flanagan, R. (2018). *Counseling and psychotherapy theories in context and practice: Skills, strategies, and techniques* (3rd ed.). New York: Wiley.

Song, K., Kim, H. K., & Lee, M. (2022). Effectiveness of therapeutic community program on resilience and change in lifestyle in people with alcohol use disorder. *Journal of Addictions Nursing, 33*(4), 255–263.

Song, L.-L., Tang, Y.-P., & Law, B. Y. K. (2024). Targeting calcium signaling in Alzheimer's disease: Challenges and promising therapeutic avenues. *Neural Regeneration Research, 19*(3), 501–502.

Sood, M. R. (2022, June 6). Functional fecal incontinence in infants and children: Definition, clinical manifestations, and evaluation. *UpToDate.* Retrieved from https://www.uptodate.com.

Sood, M. R. (2023, February 1). Chronic functional constipation and fecal incontinence in infants, children, and adolescents: Treatment. *UpToDate.* Retrieved from https://www.uptodate.com.

Sorensen, J. B., Tayebi, S., Brokhattingen, A., & Gyawali, B. (2022). Alcohol consumption in low- and middle-income settings. In V. B. Patel & V. R. Preedy (Eds.). *Handbook of substance misuse and addictions: From biology to public health* (pp. 1111–1129). New York: Springer.

Spadoni, A. D., Vinograd, M., Cuccurazzu, B., Torres, K., Glynn, L. M., Davis, E. P., . . . Risbrough, V. B. (2022, July 14). Contribution of early-life unpredictability to neuropsychiatric symptom patterns in adulthood. *Depression and Anxiety, 39*(10–11), 706–717. https://doi.org/10.1002/da.23277.

Sperry, L. (2022). Spiritually sensitive psychotherapy: An impending paradigm shift in theory and practice. In L. J. Miller (Ed.). *The Oxford handbook of psychology and spirituality* (2nd ed., Chap. 13). New York: Oxford University Press.

Sperry, L., & Casteleiro, G. (2022). Avoidant personality disorder. In R. Feinstein (Ed.). *Personality disorders* (Chap. 22). New York: Oxford University Press.

Spiegel, D. (2023, May). Depersonalization/derealization disorder. *Merck Manual, Professional Version.* https://www.merckmanuals.com/professional/psychiatric-disorders/dissociative-disorders/depersonalization-derealization-disorder.

Spiegel, D. (2023, May). Dissociative amnesia. *Merck Manual.* Retrieved from https://www.merckmanuals.com/home/mental-health-disorders/dissociative-disorders/dissociative-amnesia.

Spiegel, D. (2023, May). Dissociative identity disorder. *Merck Manual.* Retrieved from https://www.merckmanuals.com/home/mental-health-disorders/dissociative-disorders.

Spilde, I. (2020). The placebo effect: From mystical magnetism to using our bodies' inherent powers. *Science Norway.* Retrieved from https://sciencenorway.no/history-of-medicine-medical-methods-placebos/1650983.

Spilde, I., & Jakobsen, S. E. (2023, September 14). *Why are there 500 different types of psychotherapy?* Retrieved from https://sciencenorway.no/health-psychology.

Spores, J. (2022, June 9). *Psychological assessment and testing: A clinician's guide* (2nd ed.). New York: Routledge.

Spratt, T. J. E. (2023). Understanding "fat shaming" in a neoliberal era: Performativity, healthism and the UK's "obesity epidemic." *Feminist Theory, 24*(1), 86–101.

SPRC (Suicide Prevention Resource Center). (2023). *Older adults.* Waltham, MA: Author. Retrieved from https://sprc.org/populations.

SPRC (Suicide Prevention Resource Center). (2023). Racial and ethnic disparities. Oklahoma City, OK: Author.

SR (Speaking of Research). (2022). *Animal rights extremism.* Retrieved from https://speakingofresearch.com/extremism-undone.

SR (Speaking of Research). (2022). *FAQ about animal research.* Retrieved from https://speakingofresearch.com/facts.

SR (Speaking of Research). (2022). *US animal research statistics.* Retrieved from https://speakingofresearch.com/facts.

SSA (Social Security Administration). (2023). *Actuarial life table.* Retrieved from https://www.ssa.gov/oact/STATS.

Stacey, D. (2021, October 11). What is Munchausen syndrome (factitious disorder imposed on self)? *Verywellmind.* Retrieved from https://www.verywellmind.com.

Stackpole, R., Greene, D., Bills, E., & Egan, S. J. (2023). The association between eating disorders and perfectionism in adults: A systematic review and meta-analysis. *Eating Behaviors, 50,* 101769.

Stahl, B. (2022, May 6). A mindful inquiry: Calming the rush of panic. *Mindful.*

Stamatis, C. A., Roddy, M. K., & Timpano, K. R. (2022). Cognitive-behavioral therapy for hoarding disorder. In G. Todd (Ed.). *Evidence-based treatment for anxiety disorders and depression: A cognitive behavioral therapy compendium* (Chap. 17). Cambridge: Cambridge University Press.

Staples, J. M., & Fuller, C. C. (2021). Adult sexual assault severity among transgender people of color: The impact of double marginalization. *Journal of Aggression, Maltreatment, & Trauma, 5,* 694–706.

Starvaggi, I., Dierckman, C., & Lorenzo-Luaces, L. (2023). Mental health misinformation on social media: Review and future directions. *Current Opinions in Psychology, 56,* 101738.

Statista. (2023). *Alcoholic drinks: United States.* Retrieved from https://www.statista.com/outlook/cmo/alcoholic-drinks/united-states.

Statista. (2023). *Impact of the COVID-19 pandemic on older adults in the U.S.: Statistics and facts.* Retrieved from https://www.statista.com/topics/8276.

Statista. (2023). *Number of centenarians in the U.S. 2016–2060.* Retrieved from https://www.statista.com/statistics/996619.

Statista. (2023). *Reported forcible rape rate in the United States from 1990 to 2021.* Retrieved from https://www.statista.com/statistics/191226.

Statista. (2023). *Share of U.S. adults who have taken a selfie 2018, by age group.* Retrieved from https://www.statista.com/statistics/304861.

Statista. (2023). *Total U.S. expenditure for mental health services 1986–2020.* Retrieved from https://www.statista.com/statistics/252393.

Statista. (2024). *Share of adults in the United States who use the internet in 2021, by age group.* Retrieved from https://www.statista.com/statistics/266587.

Statista. (2024). *Total U.S. expenditure for mental health services, 1986–2020.* Retrieved from https://www.statista.com/statistics/252393.

Stavem, K., Heir, T., Dammen, T., Bronstad, E., Lerum, T. V., Durheim, M. T., . . . & Einvik, G. E. (2022). The course and determinants of post-traumatic stress over 12 months after hospitalization for COVID-19. *Frontiers in Psychiatry, 13,* 931349.

Stavrinaki, M., Kelly, M. M., & Karekla, M. (2022). Acceptance and commitment therapy (ACT) for substance use. In M. P. Twohig, M. E. Levin, & J. M. Petersen (Eds.). *The Oxford handbook of acceptance and commitment therapy* (Chap. 22). New York: Oxford University Press.

Steadman, H. J., Monahan, J., Robbins, P. C., Appelbaum, P., Grisso, T., Klassen, D., . . . Roth, L. (1993). From dangerousness to risk assessment: Implications for appropriate research strategies. In S. Hodgins (Ed.). *Mental disorder and crime.* Newbury Park, CA: Sage Publications.

Steel, C. M. S., Newman, E., O'Rourke, S., & Quayle, E. (2023). Lawless space theory for online child sexual exploitation material offending. *Aggression and Violent Behavior, 68,* 101809.

Stein, A. T., Carl, E., Cuijpers, P., Karyotaki, E., & Smits, J. A. J. (2020). Looking beyond depression: A meta-analysis of the effect of behavioral activation on depression, anxiety, and activation. *Psychological Medicine, 51*(9), 1491–1504.

Stein, M. B. (2022, June 6). Pharmacotherapy for social anxiety disorder in adults. *UpToDate*. Retrieved from https://www.uptodate.com.

Stein, M. B. (2023, October 2). Posttraumatic stress disorder in adults: Treatment overview. *UpToDate*. Retrieved from http://www.uptodate.com.

Stein, M. B., & Norman, S. (2023, September 13). Posttraumatic stress disorder in adults: Psychotherapy and psychosocial interventions. *UpToDate*. Retrieved from http://www.uptodate.com.

Stein, M. B., & Taylor, C. T. (2022, June 7). Approach to treating social anxiety disorder in adults. *UpToDate*. Retrieved from https://www.uptodate.com.

Steinberg, D., Perry, T., Freestone, D., Bohon, C., & Baker, J. H. (2023). Effectiveness of delivering evidence-based eating disorder treatment via telemedicine for children, adolescents, and youth. *Eating Disorders, 31*(1), 85–101.

Steiner, P. M., Shadish, W. R., & Sullivan, K. J. (2023). Frameworks for causal inference in psychological science. In H. Cooper, M. N. Coutanche, L. M. McMullen, A. T. Panter, D. Rindskopf, & K. J. Sher (Eds.). *APA handbook of research methods in psychology: Vol. 1. Foundations, planning, measures, and psychometrics* (2nd ed., Chap. 2). Washington, DC: American Psychological Association.

Steinglass, J. (2023, April 28). Anorexia nervosa in adults and adolescents: Nutritional rehabilitation (nutritional support). *UpToDate*. Retrieved from http://www.uptodate.com.

Stentz, L. A., & Cougle, J. R. (2022). Effects of safety behavior fading on social anxiety and emotional disclosure. *Behavioral Research and Therapy, 157*, 104165.

Stern, A. M. (2016). Eugenics, sterilization, and historical memory in the United States. *História, Ciências, Saúde-Manguinhos, 23*(Suppl. 1), 195–212.

Stern, D. B. (2022). Dissociation and unformulated experience: A psychoanalytic model of mind. In M. J. Dorahy, S. N. Gold, & J. A. O'Neil (Eds.). *Dissociation and the dissociative disorders: Past, present, future* (Chap. 20). New York: Routledge.

Stern, R. S., King, A. A., & Diamond, G. (2022, June 25). Repairing attachment in families with depressed adolescents: A task analysis. *Journal of Clinical Psychology, 79*(1), 201–209.

Stewart, C. S., Baudinet, J., Munuve, A., Bell, A., Konstantellou, A., Eisler, I., & Simic, M. (2022). From efficiency to effectiveness: Child and adolescent eating disorder treatments in the real world (Part 2): 7-year follow-up. *Journal of Eating Disorders, 10*(1), 14.

Stice, E., Johnson, S., & Turgon, R. (2019). Eating disorder prevention. *Psychiatric Clinics of North America, 42*(2), 309–318.

Stice, E., Onipede, A., Shaw, H., Rohde, P., & Gau, J. M. (2021). Effectiveness of the Body Project eating disorder prevention program for different racial and ethnic groups and an evaluation of the potential benefits of ethnic matching. *Journal of Consulting and Clinical Psychology, 89*(12), 1007–1019.

Stice, E., Rohde, P., Gau, J. M., Butryn, M. L., Shaw, H., Cloud, K., & D'Adamo, L. (2021). Enhancing efficacy of a dissonance-based obesity and eating disorder prevention program: Experimental therapeutics. *Journal of Consulting and Clinical Psychology, 89*(10), 793–804.

Stice, E., Rohde, P., Shaw, H., & Gau, J. M. (2020). Clinician-led, peer-led, and internet-delivered dissonance-based eating disorder prevention programs: Effectiveness of these delivery modalities through 4-year follow-up. *Journal of Consulting and Clinical Psychology, 88*(5), 481–494.

Stice, E., Yokum, S., Rohde, P., Shaw, H., Gau, J. M., Johnson, S., & Johns, A. (2019). Randomized trial of a dissonance-based transdiagnostic group treatment for eating disorders: An evaluation of target engagement. *Journal of Consulting and Clinical Psychology, 87*(9), 772–786.

Stojek, M. M., Sherrill, A. M., Stevens, T., & Rothbaum, B. O. (2022). Promising psychological treatments for posttraumatic stress disorder. In J. G. Beck & D. M. Sloan (Eds.). *The Oxford handbook of traumatic stress disorders* (Chap. 33). New York: Oxford University Press.

Stolbach, A., & Hoffman, R. S. (2023, August 17). Acute opioid intoxication in adults. *UpToDate*. Retrieved from http://www.uptodate.com.

Stoll, J., Müller, J. A., & Trachsel, M. (2020, February 11). Ethical issues in online psychotherapy: A narrative review. *Frontiers in Psychiatry, 10*, 993.

Stone, D., Trinh, E., Zhou, H., Welder, L., End of Horn, P., Fowler, K. & Ivey-Stephenson, A. (2022, September 16). Suicides among American Indian or Alaska Native persons: National Violent Death Reporting System, United States, 2015–2020. *Morbidity and Mortality Weekly Report, 71*(37), 1161–1168.

Stone, J., & Sharpe, M. (2023, August 1). Functional neurological symptom disorder (conversion disorder) in adults: Epidemiology, pathogenesis, and prognosis. *UpToDate*. Retrieved from http://www.uptodate.com.

Stone, J., & Sharpe, M. (2023, August 1). Functional neurological symptom disorder (conversion disorder) in adults: Terminology, diagnosis, and differential diagnosis. *UpToDate*. Retrieved from http://www.uptodate.com.

Stovall, J. (2022, July 29). Bipolar mania and hypomania in adults: Choosing pharmacotherapy. *UpToDate*. Retrieved from https://www.uptodate.com.

Stovall, J. (2023, May 31). Bipolar disorder in adults: Epidemiology and pathogenesis. *UpToDate*. Retrieved from https://www.uptodate.com.

Strada, E. A.,. & Portenoy, R. K. (2022, December 23). Rehabilitative and integrative therapies for pain in patients with cancer. *UpToDate*. Retrieved from http://www.uptodate.com.

Strain, E. (2022, July 7). Opioid use disorder: Epidemiology, pharmacology, clinical manifestations, course, screening, assessment, and diagnosis. *UpToDate*. Retrieved from http://www.uptodate.com.

Strain, E. (2023, November 14). Opioid use disorder: Pharmacologic management. *UpToDate*. Retrieved from https://www.uptodate.com.

Stratton, K. L. (2022, January 1). Delayed ejaculation: Symptoms, doctors, treatments, advances and more. *MediFind*. Retrieved from https://www.medifind.com/conditions/delayed-ejaculation/5739.

Strawn, J. R., Lu, L., Peris, T. S., Levine, A., & Walkup, J. T. (2020). Research review: Pediatric anxiety disorders—What have we learnt in the last 10 years? *Journal of Child Psychology and Psychiatry, 62*(2), 114–139.

Strawn, J. R., Mills, J. A., Surech, B., Peris, T. S., Walkup, J. T., & Croarkin, P. E. (2022). Combining selective serotonin reuptake inhibitors and cognitive behavioral therapy in youth with depression and anxiety. *Journal of Affective Disorders, 298*(Part A), 292–300.

Stroup, T. C., & Marder, S. (2023, November 14). Schizophrenia in adults: Maintenance therapy and side effect management. *UpToDate*. Retrieved from https://www.uptodate.com.

Struble, C. A., Borodovsky, J. T., Habib, M. I., Livne, O., Walsh, C. A., Aharonovich, E., . . . Budney, A. J. (2024). Evaluating age-related disparities in cannabis-related problems among LGBT+ versus non-LGBT+ adults. *Addictive Behaviors, 148*, 107861.

Stunkard, A. J. (1959). Eating patterns and obesity. *Psychiatric Quarterly, 33*, 284–295.

Subramanyam, A., Somaiya, M., Shankar, S., Nasirabadi, M., Shah, H., Paul, I., & Ghildiyal, R. (2020). Psychological interventions for dissociative disorders. *Indian Journal of Psychiatry, 62*(8), 280.

Sue, D. W., Sue, D., Neville, H. A., & Smith, L. (2022). *Counseling the culturally diverse: Theory and practice* (9th ed.). New York: Wiley.

Suekane, A., Takayama, W., Hashimoto, R., Morishita, K., & Otomo, Y. (2024). Risk factors for recurrence of suicide attempt via overdone: A prospective observational study. *American Journal of Emergency Medicine, 75*, 1–6.

Sullivan, H. W., Aikin, K. J., Berktold, J., Stein, K. L., & Hoverman, V. J. (2020). Direct-to-consumer prescription drug advertising and patient–provider interactions. *Journal of the American Board of Family Medicine: JABFM, 33*(2), 279–283.

Sultan, R. S., Liu, S.-M., Hacker, K. A., & Olfson, M. (2021). Adolescents with attention-deficit/hyperactivity disorder: Adverse behaviors and comorbidity. *Journal of Adolescent Health, 68*(2), 284–291.

Summer, J. (2022, June 24). *Hypnopompic hallucinations*. Seattle, WA: Sleep Foundation.

Summer, J. (2023, January 12). *Hypnagogic hallucinations*. Seattle, WA: Sleep Foundation.

Summer, J., & Rehman, A. (2023, September 22). How to interpret your dreams. *Sleep Foundation*.

Summers, R. F., Barber, J. P., & Zilcha-Mano, S. (2024). *Psychodynamic therapy: A guide to evidence-based practice* (2nd ed.). New York: Guilford Press.

Sun, W., Ueno, D., & Narumoto, J. (2022). Brain neural underpinnings of interoception and decision-making in Alzheimer's disease: A narrative review. *Frontiers in Neuroscience, 16*, 946136.

Sündermann, O., & Veale, D. (2022). Cognitive-behavioral approach to body dysmorphic disorder: Assessment, treatment, and new developments. In G. Todd (Ed.). *Evidence-based treatment for anxiety disorders and depression: A cognitive behavioral therapy compendium* (Chap. 15). Cambridge: Cambridge University Press.

Sündermann, O., & Veale, D. (2022). Obsessive-compulsive disorder: An updated cognitive behavioral approach. In G. Todd (Ed.). *Evidence-based treatment for anxiety disorders and depression: A cognitive behavioral therapy compendium* (Chap. 11). Cambridge: Cambridge University Press.

Suni, E. (2022, November 3). *Insomnia*. Seattle, WA: Sleep Foundation. Retrieved from https://www.sleepfoundation.org.

Suppes, B. C. (2022). *Family systems theory simplified: Applying and understanding systemic therapy models*. New York: Routledge.

Suppes, T. (2022, October 27). Bipolar disorder in adults: Assessment and diagnosis. *UpToDate*. Retrieved from https://www.uptodate.com.

Suppes, T. (2022, October 28). Bipolar disorder in adults: Clinical features. *UpToDate*. Retrieved from https://www.uptodate.com.

Surjan, J., Grossi, J. D., Del Porto, J. A., Delfino, R. S., de Oliveira Cerqueira, R., Lucchese, A. C., . . . Lacerda, A. L. T. (2022). Efficacy and safety of subcutaneous esketamine in the treatment of suicidality in major depressive disorder and bipolar depression. *Clinical Drug Investigation, 42*(10), 865–873.

Sverak, T., Linhartova, P., Gajdos, M., Kuhn, M., Latalova, A., Lamos, M., . . . Kasparek, T. (2022). Brain connectivity and symptom changes after transcranial magnetic stimulation in patients with borderline personality disorder. *Frontiers in Psychiatry, 12,* 770353.

Swaim, E. (2022, April 1). The real differences between psychopaths and sociopaths and why you can't be officially diagnosed as either. *Business Insider India*. Retrieved from https://www.businessinsider.in/science/health/news.

Swanson, J., Swartz, M., Van Dorn, R. A., Monahan, J., McGuire, T. G., Steadman, H. J., & Robbins, P. C. (2009). Racial disparities in involuntary outpatient commitment: Are they real? *Health Affairs, 28*(3), 816–826.

Swanson, S. A., & Colman, I. (2013). Association between exposure to suicide and suicidality outcomes in youth. *Canadian Medical Association Journal, 185*(10), 870–877.

Swartz, H. A. (2023, November 3). Interpersonal psychotherapy (IPT) for depressed adults: Indications, theoretical foundation, general concepts, and efficacy. *UpToDate*. Retrieved from https://www.uptodate.com.

Swartz, H. A., Bylsma, L. M., Fournier, J. C., Girard, J. M., Spotts, C., Cohn, J. F., & Morency, L.-P. (2023). Randomized trial of brief interpersonal psychotherapy and cognitive behavioral therapy for depression delivered both in-person and by telehealth. *Journal of Affective Disorders, 333,* 543–552.

Swartz, M. S., & Swanson, J. W. (2019). Mandated community treatment in services for persons with mental illness. In H. H. Goldman, R. G. Frank, & J. P. Morrissey (Eds.). *The Palgrave handbook of American mental health policy* (pp. 171–196). New York: Palgrave Macmillan.

Swee, M. B., Wilmer, M. T., & Heimberg, R. G. (2022). Cognitive behavioral therapy for social anxiety disorder. In G. Todd (Ed.). *Evidence-based treatment for anxiety disorders and depression: A cognitive behavioral therapy compendium* (Chap. 6). Cambridge: Cambridge University Press.

Swierkosz-Linart, K., Dos Santos, J. F. A., Elowe, J., Clair, A.-H., Bally, J. F., Riquier, F., . . . Mallet, L. (2023). Therapies for obsessive-compulsive disorder: Current state of the art and perspectives for approaching treatment-resistant patients. *Frontiers in Psychiatry, 14,* 1065812.

Swimmer, K. R., & Sandelich, S. (2024). Substance use disorder. *Emergency Medicine Clinics of North America, 42*(1), 53–67.

Sysko, R., & Devlin, M. (2022, August 29). Binge eating disorder in adults: Overview of treatment. *UpToDate*. Retrieved from http://www.uptodate.com.

Sysko, R., & Devlin, M. (2023, April 15). Binge eating disorder: Cognitive-behavioral therapy (CBT). *UpToDate*. Retrieved from http://www.uptodate.com.

Szasz, T. S. (1960). The myth of mental illness. *American Psychologist, 15,* 113–118.

Szasz, T. S. (1963). *The manufacture of madness*. New York: Harper & Row.

Szasz, T. S. (2011). The myth of mental illness: 50 years later. *The Psychiatrist, 35*(5), 179–182.

TAC (Treatment Advocacy Center). (2022, January). *Schizophrenia: Fact sheet*. Arlington, VA: Author.

Takeda, A. (2015, April 13). Zoe Kravitz gets real about past struggles with eating disorders: New film *The Road Within* "triggered some old stuff." *Us Weekly*.

Takeuchi, H., & Remington, G. (2020). Immediate versus wait-and-gradual discontinuation in antipsychotic switching: A meta-analysis. *Journal of Psychopharmacology, 34*(8), 914–919.

Tallis, F. (2014, January 23). *How to stop worrying: New edition (Overcoming common problems)*. London: Sheldon Press.

Tallis, F. (2015, October 22). *The Sheldon short guide to worry and anxiety*. London: Sheldon Press. [Kindle Edition]

Tallis, F. (2019). *How to stop worrying (overcoming common problems)*. London: Sheldon Press.

Tallis, F., Davey, G., & Capuzzo, N. (1994). The phenomenology of non-pathological worry: A preliminary investigation. In G. Davey & F. Tallis (Eds.). *Worrying: Perspectives on theory, assessment and treatment* (pp. 61–89). Chichester: John Wiley.

Tampellini, D. (2024). Activity-dependent mechanisms of neuroprotection: Promising avenues against dementia. *Neural Regeneration Research, 19*(7), 1409–1410.

Tan, E., Zeytinoglu, S., Morales, S., Buzzell, G. A., Almas, A. N., Degnan, K. A., . . . Fox, N. A. (2024). Social versus non-social behavioral inhibition: Differential prediction from early childhood of long-term psychosocial outcomes. *Developmental Science, 27*(1), e13427.

Tangpricha, V., & Safer, J. D. (2023, June 30). Transgender men: Evaluation and management. *UpToDate*. Retrieved from https://www.uptodate.com.

Tangpricha, V., & Safer, J. D. (2023, October 12). Transgender women: Evaluation and management. *UpToDate*. Retrieved from https://www.uptodate.com.

Tappenden, P., Pratchett, L., & Yehuda, R. (2022). Biological contributions to PTSD: Predictors of long-term symptoms. In J. G. Beck & D. M. Sloan (Eds.). *The Oxford handbook of traumatic stress disorders* (Chap. 13). New York: Oxford University Press.

Tasca, G. (2020). What clinicians want from psychotherapy research. *Society for the Advancement of Psychotherapy*. Retrieved from https://www.societyforpsychotherapy.org.

Tassinary, L. G., Hess, U., Carcoba, L. M., & Orr, J. M. (2023). The perimetric physiological measurement of psychological constructs. In H. Cooper, M. N. Coutanche, L. M. McMullen, A. T. Panter, D. Rindskopf, & K. J. Sher (Eds.). *APA handbook of research methods in psychology: Foundations, planning, measures, and psychometrics* (pp. 531–564). Washington, DC: American Psychological Association.

Taylor, C. T., Campbell-Sills, L., Kessler, R. C., Sun, X., Nock, M. K., Ursano, R. J., . . . Stein, M. B. (2023). Social network size and personality traits independently and prospectively predict distress disorders and suicidal behavior in U.S. Army soldiers. *Psychological Medicine, 53*(11), 5081–5090.

Taylor, S. (2022). The psychology of pandemics. *Annual Review of Clinical Psychology, 18,* 581–609.

Tayyeb, M., & Gupta, V. (2023, June 5). Dyspareunia. *StatPearls*.

TD (Trauma Dissociation). (2023). *Posttraumatic stress disorder (PTSD)*. Retrieved from http://traumadissociation.com/ptsd.html.

Tebbe, E. A., & Budge, S. L. (2022). Factors that drive mental health disparities and promote well-being in transgender and nonbinary people. *Nature Reviews Psychology, 1,* 694–707.

Teles, R. V. (2020). Hermann Rorschach: From klecksography to psychiatry. *Dementia & Neuropsychologia, 14*(1), 80–82.

Terjesen, M. D., Doyle, K. A., DiGiuseppe, R. A., Vaz, A., & Rousmaniere, T. (2023, May). *Deliberate practice in rational emotive behavior therapy*. Washington, DC: American Psychological Association.

Tesli, M., Nasvag, R., Haukvik, U. K., Gustavson, K., Tesli, N., Friestad, C., . . . Ystrom, E. (2023). Common genetic and environmental risk for personality disorders and psychotic-like experiences in young adult twins. *Acta Psychiatrica Scandinavica, 148*(6), 561–569.

Tessier, A., Roger, K., Gregoire, A., Desnavailles, P., & Misdrahi, D. (2023). Family psychoeducation to improve outcome in caregivers and patients with schizophrenia: A randomized clinical trial. *Frontiers in Psychiatry, 14,* 1171661.

Thackray, A. E., Deighton, K., King, J. A., & Stensel, D. J. (2016, September 21). Exercise, appetite and weight control: Are there differences between men and women? *Nutrients, 8*(9), 583.

Thakur, T., & Gupta, V. (2023, February 13). Auditory hallucinations. *StatPearls*.

Thapliyal, M., & Ahuja, N. J. (2023). Underpinning implications of instructional strategies on assistive technology for learning disability: A meta-synthesis review. *Disability and Rehabilitation. Assistive Technology, 18*(4), 423–431.

Thase, M., & Connolly, K. R. (2023, August 24). Ketamine and esketamine for treating unipolar depression in adults: Administration, efficacy, and adverse effects. *UpToDate*. Retrieved from https://www.uptodate.com.

Thase, M., & Connolly, K. R. (2023, October 19). Unipolar depression in adults: Choosing treatment for resistant depression. *UpToDate*. Retrieved from https://www.uptodate.com.

The Trevor Project. (2021). *2021 National survey on LGBTQ youth mental health*. West Hollywood, CA: Author.

The Trevor Project. (2022). *2022 National Survey on LGBTQ youth mental health*. Retrieved from https://thetrevorproject.org.

The Trevor Project. (2023). *2023 U.S. national survey on the mental health of LGBTQ young people*. West Hollywood, CA: Author.

Thigpen, C. H., & Cleckley, H. M. (1957). *The three faces of Eve*. New York: McGraw-Hill.

Thodis, A., Dang, T.-H., Antoniades, J., Gilbert, A. S., Nguyen, T., Hlis, D., . . . Brijnath, B. (2023). Improving the lives of ethnically diverse family carers and people living with dementia using digital media resources: Protocol for the Draw-Care randomised controlled trial. *Digital Health, 9,* 20552076231205733.

Thomas, J. (2014, January/February). Most psychologists misinformed on "duty to warn." *The National Psychologist,* pp. 3–4.

Thomas, N., & Juckel, J. (2022). Gender and drug policy. In V. B. Patel & V. R. Preedy (Eds.). *Handbook of substance misuse and addictions: From biology to public health* (pp. 289–303). New York: Springer.

Tietze, K. J., & Fuchs, B. (2022, November 2). Sedative-analgesic medications in critically ill adults: Properties, dose regimens, and adverse effects. *UpToDate*. Retrieved from http://www.uptodate.com.

Tillory, C. (2021, October 20). *Why labels can be harmful when you have mental illness*. Retrieved from https://www.nami.org/Blogs/NAMI-Blog.

Timberlake, A. F. V., & Fesel, D. (2023). The development of narrative identity in the psychodynamic treatment of avoidant personality disorder: A case study. *Frontiers in Psychiatry, 14,* 1141768.

Timmons, A. C., Duong, J. B., Fiallo, N. S., Lee, T., Vo, P. Q., Ahle, M. W., . . . Chaspari, T. (2023). A call to action on assessing and mitigating bias in artificial intelligence applications in clinical psychology. *Perspectives on Psychological Science*. https://doi.org/10.1177/17456916221134490. [Online ahead of print]

Tirel, M. (2023, January 29). *Are counseling psychologists happy themselves?* Retrieved from https://www.trackinghappiness.com/are-counseling-psychologists-happy-themselves.

Titus, C. E., & DeShong, H. L. (2020). Thought control strategies as predictors of borderline personality disorder and suicide risk. *Journal of Affective Disorders, 266,* 349–355.

Todd, G., & Branch, R. (2022). *Evidence-based treatment for anxiety and depression: A cognitive behavioral therapy compendium*. Cambridge: Cambridge University Press.

Todzia-Kornas, A., Szczegielniak, A., & Gondek, T. M. (2024). Suicidality and non-suicidal self-injury in females diagnosed with attention-deficit hyperactivity disorder: A narrative review. *Current Opinions in Psychiatry, 37*(1), 38–42.

Tofler, G. H. (2022, March 7). Psychosocial factors in acute coronary syndrome. *UpToDate*. Retrieved from http://www.uptodate.com.

Tofler, G. H. (2023, January 9). Psychosocial factors in coronary and cerebral vascular disease. *UpToDate*. Retrieved from http://www.uptodate.com.

Tofler, G. H. (2023, February 28). Psychosocial factors in sudden cardiac arrest. *UpToDate*. Retrieved from http://www.uptodate.com.

Tooley, U. A., Bassett, D. S., & Mackey, A. P. (2021). Environmental influences on the pace of brain development. *Nature, 22,* 372.

Tordoff, D. M., Wanta, J. W., Collin, A., Stepney, C., Inwards-Breland, D. J., & Ahrens, K. (2022). Mental health outcomes in transgender and nonbinary youths receiving gender-affirming care. *JAMA Network Open, 5*(2), e220978.

Torrey, E. F. (2001). *Surviving schizophrenia: A manual for families, consumers, and providers* (4th ed.). New York: HarperCollins.

Torrey, E. F. (2019, March 26). *Surviving schizophrenia: A family manual* (7th ed.). New York: Harper Perennial.

Torrey, T. (2020, February 15). Arguments in favor of right-to-die legislation. *Verywell*. Retrieved from https://www.verywell.com.

Toups, M., & Nemeroff, C. B. (2022). Role of the immune system in mood disorders. In C. B. Nemeroff, A. F. Schatzberg, N. Rasgon, & S. M. Strakowski (Eds.). *The American Psychiatric Association Publishing textbook of mood disorders* (2nd ed., Chap. 7). Washington, DC: American Psychiatric Association Publishing.

Trägårdh, K., Karlén, M. H., Andiné, P., & Nilsson, T. (2023). Lethal and severe violence: Characterizing Swedish female offenders with and without a severe mental disorder. *Frontiers in Psychiatry, 14,* 1143936.

Trane, K., Aasbrenn, K., Renningen, M., Odden, S., Lexén, A., & Landheim, A. S. (2022). Flexible assertive community treatment in rural and remote areas: A qualitative study of the challenges and adaptations of the model. *Frontiers in Public Health, 10,* 913159.

Trestman, R. L., Rahmani, E., & Bhatia, N. (2022). Criminal justice system and antisocial personality disorder. In D. W. Black & N. J. Kolla (Eds.). *Textbook of antisocial personality disorder* (Chap. 20). Washington, DC: American Psychiatric Association Publishing.

Troy, A. S., Willroth, E. C., Shallcross, A. J., Giuliani, N. R., Gross, J. J., & Mauss, I. B. (2023). Psychological resilience: An affect-regulation framework. *Annual Review of Psychology, 74,* 547–576.

Trucco, E. M., Fallah-Sohy, N., Hartmann, S. A., Cristello, J. V., Comer, J. S., & Sutherland, M. T. (2022). The impact of COVID-19 experiences on adolescent mental health problems and substance use among a predominantly Latinx sample. *Journal Youth and Adolescence, 51*(5), 821–831.

Truong, T. T., Li, B., Shorter, D., Moukaddam, N., & Kosten, T. R. (2024). *Pharmacotherapy for complex substance use disorders*. Washington, DC: American Psychiatric Association.

Tsehay, M., Necho, M., & Mekonnen, W. (2020). The role of adverse childhood experience on depression symptom, prevalence, and severity among school going adolescents. *Depression Research and Treatment, 2020,* 5951792.

Tseng, H.-W., Chou, F.-H., Chen, C.-H., & Chang, Y.-P. (2023). Effects of mindfulness-based cognitive therapy on major depressive disorder with multiple episodes: A systematic review and meta-analysis. *International Journal of Environmental Research and Public Health, 20*(2), 1555.

Tu, N. D., & Baskin, L. S. (2022, June 2). Nocturnal enuresis in children: Management. *UpToDate*. Retrieved from https://www.uptodate.com.

Tu, N. D., Baskin, L. S., & Arnhym, A. M. (2022, November 21). Nocturnal enuresis in children: Etiology and evaluation. *UpToDate*. Retrieved from https://www.uptodate.com.

Tull, M. (2022, April 14). How to cope with a sense of foreshortened future. *Verywellmind*. Retrieved from https://www.verywellmind.com.

Tunheim, K., Dammen, T., Baardstu, S., Moum, T., Munkhaugen, J., & Papageorgiou, C. (2022). Relationships between depression, anxiety, type D personality, and worry and rumination in patients with coronary heart disease. *Frontiers in Psychology, 13,* 929410.

Turkat, I. D., Keane, S. P., & Thompson-Pope, S. K. (1990). Social processing errors among paranoid personalities. *Journal of Psychopathology and Behavioral Assessment, 12*(3), 263–269.

Turkle, S. (2013, October 10). "We need to talk": Missed connections with hyperconnectivity. *NPR*. Retrieved from https://www.npr.org/2013/02/10/171490660.

Turkle, S. (2015). *Reclaiming conversation: The power of talk in a digital age*. New York: Penguin Press.

Turkle, S. (2017). *Alone together: Why we expect more from technology and less from each other* (Rev. ed.). New York: Basic Books.

Turkle, S. (2021). *The empathy diaries: A memoir.* New York: Penguin Press.

Turner, B. E., Steinberg, J. R., Weeks, B. T., Rodriguez, F., & Cullen, M. R. (2022). Race/ethnicity reporting and representation in US clinical trials: A cohort study. *Lancet Regional Health Americas, 11,* 100252.

Turner, E. H., Alavi, S., Cipriani, A., Furukawa, T., Ivlev, I., McKenna, R., & Ogawa, Y. (2020). An update on reporting bias in the antidepressant literature: An FDA-controlled examination of drug efficacy. *Peer Review Congress*. Retrieved from https://peerreviewcongress.org.

Turner, E. H., Cipriani, A., Furukawa, T. A., Salanti, G., & de Vries, Y. A. (2022). Selective publication of antidepressant trials and its influence on apparent efficacy: Updated comparisons and meta-analyses of newer versus older trials. *PLoS Medicine, 19*(1), e1003886.

Turner, E. H., Matthews, A. M., Linardatos, E., Tell, R. A., & Rosenthal, R. (2008). Selective publication of antidepressant trials and its influence on apparent efficacy. *New England Journal of Medicine, 358*, 252–260.

Twenge, J. M. (2019). The sad state of happiness in the United States and the role of digital media. In J. Helliwell, R. Layard, & J. Sachs (Eds.). *World happiness report 2019* (Chap. 5). New York: Sustainable Development Solutions Network.

Twenge, J. M. (2023). *Generations: The real differences between Gen Z, millennials, Gen X, boomers, and silents—and what they mean for America's future.* New York: Atria Publishing.

Twenge, J. M., & Cooper, A. B. (2022). The expanding class divide in happiness in the United States, 1972–2016. *Emotion, 22*(4), 701–713.

Twenge, J. M., & Foster, J. D. (2008). Mapping the scale of the narcissism epidemic: Increases in narcissism 2002–2007 within ethnic groups. *Journal of Research in Personality, 42*, 1619–1622.

Twenge, J. M., & Hamilton, J. L. (2022). Linear correlation is insufficient as the sole measure of associations: The case of technology use and mental health. *Acta Psychologica, 229*, 103696.

Twohig, M. P., Levin, M. E., & Petersen, J. M. (2022). *The Oxford handbook of acceptance and commitment therapy* (Oxford Library of Psychology Series). New York: Oxford University Press.

Tyrer, P., & Mulder, R. (2022). Cultural perspectives: Epidemiology of personality disorders. In *Personality disorder: From evidence to understanding* (pp. 39–51). Cambridge: Cambridge University Press.

Uchino, B., Ong, A., & Sbarra, D. (2024, September). Relationships, social support, and health. In N. Schneiderman (Ed.). *APA handbook of health psychology: Vol. 1. Foundations and context of health psychology; Vol. 2. Clinical interventions and disease management in health psychology; Vol. 3. Health psychology and public health* (Chap. 27). Washington, DC: American Psychological Association.

Uittenhove, K., Jopp, D. S., Lampraki, C., & Boerner, K. (2023, February 25). Coping patterns in advanced old age: Findings from the Fordham Centenarian Study. *Gerontology*. doi:10.1159/000529896. [Online ahead of print]

United Nations. (2019). *World population aging 2019: Highlights*. New York: Author.

United Nations. (2020). *Aging*. Retrieved from https://www.un.org/en/sections/issues-depth/ageing.

United Nations. (2022). *World population prospects 2022: Summary of results*. New York: Author.

United Nations. (2023). *Leaving no one behind in an ageing world: World social report 2023*. New York: Author.

United Nations. (2023). *Sustainable development goals*. New York: Author.

Upchurch, D. M., & Johnson, P. J. (2019). Gender differences in prevalence, patterns, purposes, and perceived benefits of meditation practices in the United States. *Journal of Women's Health, 28*(2), 135–142.

Urcuyo, A. E., Conroy, K., Sanchez, A. L., Silva, K., Furr, J. M., Bagner, D. M., & Comer, J. S. (2023). Psychometric evaluation of the Abbreviated Multidimensional Acculturation Scale (AMAS) in a treatment-seeking sample of first-generation immigrant caregivers. *Child Psychiatry and Human Development*. https://doi.org/10.1007/s10578-023-01525-w. [Online ahead of print]

U.S. Census Bureau. (2018). *The population 65 years and older in the United States: 2016*. Washington, DC: Author.

U.S. Census Bureau. (2019). *The graying of America: More older adults than kids by 2035*. Washington, DC: Author.

U.S. Census Bureau. (2020). *Older population and aging*. Washington, DC: Author.

U.S. Census Bureau. (2020). *U.S. Census Bureau releases 2019 population estimates by demographic characteristics*. Washington, DC: Author.

U.S. Census Bureau. (2022). *National poverty in America Awareness Month: January 2022*. Washington, DC: Author.

U.S. Census Bureau. (2023, September 12). *Health insurance coverage in the United States: 2022*. Retrieved from https://www.census.gov.

U.S. Census Bureau. (2023). *National Poverty in America Awareness Month: January 2023*. Washington, DC: Author.

U.S. Census Bureau. (2023, March 21). *National Single Parent Day: March 21, 2023*. Washington, DC: Author.

U.S. Census Bureau. (2023). *Older population and aging*. Washington, DC: Author.

USAFacts. (2023). Our changing population: United States. Retrieved from https://usafacts.org/data/topics/people-society.

USAgov. (2023). *Find help for substance abuse*. Retrieved from https://www.usa.gov/ssubstance-abuse.

USDOE (U.S. Department of Education). (2023). *A history of the Individuals with Disabilities Education Act*. Washington, DC: Author.

USDVA (U.S. Department of Veteran Affairs). (2022). *Overview of VA research on posttraumatic stress disorder (PTSD)*. Retrieved from https://www.research.va.gov/topics.

USDVA (U.S. Department of Veteran Affairs). (2023, February 3). *How common is PTSD in veterans?* Retrieved from https://www.ptsd.va.gov/understand/common.

USDVA (U.S. Department of Veterans Affairs). (2023, March 14). *Mindfulness practice in the treatment of traumatic stress*. Washington, DC: Author.

USDVA (U.S. Department of Veterans Affairs). (2023, May 11). *What to expect in the wake of mass violence*. Washington, DC: Author.

Uwagbai, O., & Kalish, V. B. (2023, January 14). Vascular dementia. *StatPearls*.

Vakil, N. B. (2022, July 19). Peptic ulcer disease: Clinical manifestations and diagnosis. *UpToDate*. Retrieved from http://www.uptodate.com.

Vakil, N. B. (2022, July 20). Peptic ulcer disease: Epidemiology, etiology, and pathogenesis. *UpToDate*. Retrieved from http://www.uptodate.com.

Vaknin, S. (2015, June 30). *Malignant self-love: Narcissism revisited* (10th ed.). Amazon Digital Services.

Vaknin, S. (2016). The borderline patient: A case study. *HealthyPlace*. Retrieved from https://www.healthyplace.com/personality-disorders.

Valentine, J. C., Pigott, T. D., & Morris, J. (2023). Meta-analysis. In H. Cooper, M. N. Coutanche, L. M., McMullen, A. T. Panter, D. Rindskopf, & K. J. Sher (Eds.). *APA handbook of research methods in psychology: Data analysis and research publication* (pp. 539–559). Washington, DC: American Psychological Association.

Valentine, S. E., Livingston, N. A., Salomaa, A. C., & Shipherd, J. C. (2022). *Trauma, discrimination and PTSD among LGBTQ+ people*. Retrieved from https://www.ptsd.va.gov/professional/treat/specific.

Valero-Bover, D., Fradera, M., Carot-Sans, G., Parra, I., Piera, J., Pontes, C., & Palao, D. (2022). Impact of COVID-19 pandemic on the incidence of suicidal behaviors: A retrospective analysis of integrated electronic health records in a 7.5-million population. *International Journal of Environmental Research and Public Health, 19*(21), 134364.

Vall, E., & Wade, T. D. (2015). Predictors of treatment outcome in individuals with eating disorders: A systematic review and meta-analysis. *International Journal of Eating Disorders, 48*(7), 946–971.

Van Ameringen, M. (2022, July 22). Comorbid anxiety and depression in adults: Epidemiology, clinical manifestations, and diagnosis. *UpToDate*. Retrieved from https://www.uptodate.com.

van Aswegen, T., Samartzi, E., Morris, L., van der Spek, N., de Vries, R., Seedat, S., & van-Straten, A. (2023). Effectiveness of family-based therapy for depressive symptoms in children and adolescents: A systematic review and meta-analysis. *International Journal of Psychology, 58*(6), 499–511.

Van Bogart, K., Engeland, C. G., Sliwinski, M. J., Harrington, K. D., Knight, Zhaoyang, R., . . . Graham-Engeland, J. E. (2022). The association between loneliness and inflammation: Findings from an older adult sample. *Frontiers in Behavioral Neuroscience, 15*, 801746.

van der Weele, S., Bredewold, F., Leget, C., & Tonkens, E. (2021). The group home as moral laboratory: Tracing the ethic of autonomy in Dutch intellectual disability care. *Medicine, Health Care, and Philosophy, 24*(1), 113–125.

Van Green, T. (2022, November 22). *Americans overwhelmingly say marijuana should be legal for medical or recreational use.* Pew Research Center. Retrieved from https://www.pewresearch.org/fact-tank/2022/11/22.

Van Huysse, J., & Luzier, J. (2023). Eating disorders. In F. T. L. Leong, J. L. Callahan, J. Zimmerman, M. J. Constantino, & C. F. Eubanks (Eds.). *APA handbook of psychotherapy: Vol. 1. Theory-driven practice and disorder-driven practice* (Chap. 23). Washington, DC: American Psychological Association.

Van Malderen, E., De Coen, J., Taquet, J., & Goossens, L. (2023). The role of family factors in eating disorders. In P. Robinson, T. Wade, B. Herpertz-Dahlann, F. Fernandez-Aranda, J. Treasure, & S. Wonderlich (Eds.). *Eating disorders.* Edinburgh: Springer.

van Ommen, M. M., van Laar, T., Cornelissen, F. W., & Bruggeman, R. (2019). Visual hallucinations in psychosis. *Psychiatry Research, 280,* 112517.

Vancheri, F., Longo, G., Vancheri, E., & Henein, M. Y. (2022). Mental stress and cardiovascular health: Part I. *Journal of Clinical Medicine, 11*(12), 3353.

Vasquez, M. J. T., & Johnson, J. D. (2022). *Multicultural therapy: A practical imperative* (Theories of Psychotherapy Series). Washington, DC: American Psychological Association.

VAWnet (Violence Against Women Network). (2020). *Violence against trans and non-binary people.* Retrieved from https://vawnet.org/sc/serving-trans-and-non-binary-survivors-domestic-and-sexual-violence.

Vayisoglu, S. (2023). Symptoms of exhibitionism that regress with bupropion: A case report. *Frontiers in Psychiatry, 13,* 1079863.

Vece, G. (2020, February 10). The failed mental health system: How did we get here? *Medpage Today.* Retrieved from https://www.medpagetoday.com/psychiatry/generalpsychiatry/84796.

Vedel, A., & Thomsen, D. K. (2017). The dark triad across academic majors. *Personality and Individual Differences, 116,* 86–91.

Velez, G., & Adam, B. (2023, September 26). Maui's wildfires carry immeasurable MH toll. *Psychiatric News.*

Vella, A. (2022, May 6). Factitious hypoglycemia. *UpToDate.* Retrieved from http://www.uptodate.com.

Vella, C., Berry, C., Easterbrook, M. J., Michelson, D., Bogen-Johnston, L., & Fowler, D. (2023). The mediating role of social connectedness and hope in the relationship between group membership continuity and mental health problems in vulnerable young people. *British Journal of Psychiatry, 9*(4), e130.

Velligan, D., & Rao, S. (2023). Schizophrenia: Salient symptoms and pathophysiology. *Journal of Clinical Psychiatry, 84*(1), MS21078COM7.

Velligan, D., & Rao, S. (2023). The epidemiology and global burden of schizophrenia. *Journal of Clinical Psychiatry, 84*(1), 45094.

Vertessen, K., Luman, M., Oosterlaan, J. (2024). ADHD medication adherence: The importance of adequate prescribing. *Lancet Psychiatry, 11*(1), 2–3.

Vesentini, L., Van Overmeire, R., Matthys, F., De Wachter, D., Van Puyenbroeck, H., & Bilsen, J. (2022). Intimacy in psychotherapy: An exploratory survey among therapists. *Archives of Sexual Behavior, 51*(1), 453–463.

Vesentini, L., Van Puyenbroeck, H., De Wachter, D., Matthys, F., & Bilsen, J. (2023). Managing romantic and sexual feelings towards clients in the psychotherapy room in Flanders (Belgium). *Sex Abuse, 35*(3), 263–287.

Vetter, H. J. (1969). *Language behavior and psychopathology.* Chicago: Rand McNally.

Vieta, E., & Colom, F. (2022, September 6). Bipolar disorder in adults: Managing poor adherence to maintenance pharmacotherapy. *UpToDate.* Retrieved from https://www.uptodate.com.

Vieta, E., & Colom, F. (2023, April 16). Bipolar disorder in adults: Psychoeducation and other adjunctive maintenance psychotherapies. *UpToDate.* Retrieved from https://www.uptodate.com.

Vignaud, P., Lavalle, L., Brunelin, J., & Prieto, N. (2022). Are psychological debriefing groups after a potential traumatic event suitable to prevent the symptoms of PTSD? *Psychiatry Research, 311,* 114503.

Villarosa, L. (2022, June 12). The long shadow of eugenics in America. *New York Times Magazine,* p. 30.

Villines, Z. (2019, November 15). What to know about hallucinations. *Medical News Today.*

Vimefall, E., Sahrblom, F., & Nordlöf, K. (2022). Costs and benefits of an early intervention for juvenile offenders: The "Treatment Foster Care Oregon Program." *Children and Youth Services Review, 142,* 1106452.

Vink, V., Carlsson, J., Poulsen, S., & Vindbjerg, E. (2022). Comparing Western symptoms of depression with Arabic idioms of distress: A qualitative study. *Current Psychology, 41*(12), 2985–2997.

Vinney, C. (2022, September 8). What is suicide contagion? (And how to prevent it). *Verywellmind.* Retrieved from https://www.verywellmind.com.

Vissia, E. M., Lawrence, A. J., Chalavi, S., Giesen, M. E., Draijer, N., Nijenhuis, E. R. S., . . . Reinders, A. A. T. S. (2022). Dissociative identity state-dependent working memory in dissociative identity disorder: A controlled functional magnetic resonance imaging study. *BJPsych Open, 8*(3), e82.

Vojinovic, I. (2023, April 7). Heart-breaking cyberbullying statistics for 2023. *DataProt.* Retrieved from https://dataprot.net/statistics/cyberbullying-statistics.

Volkert, J., Schulz, H., Härter, M., Wlodarczyk, O., & Andreas, S. (2013). The prevalence of mental disorders in older people in Western countries: A meta-analysis. *Ageing Research Reviews, 12,* 339–353.

Volkow, N. D. (2021). Addiction should be treated, not penalized. *Neuropsychopharmacology, 46,* 2048–2050.

Volkow, N. D., & Blanco, C. (2023). Substance use disorders: A comprehensive update of classification, epidemiology, neurobiology, clinical aspects, treatment and prevention. *World Psychiatry, 22*(2), 203–229.

Volpe, K. D. (2022, April 7). A perfect storm: Rise in eating disorders among teens during COVID-19. *Clinical Advisor.*

von Hahn, L. E. (2023, March 7). Specific learning disorders in children: Clinical features. *UpToDate.* Retrieved from https://www.uptodate.com.

von Hahn, L. E. (2023, February 17). Specific learning disorders in children: Educational management. *UpToDate.* Retrieved from https://www.uptodate.com.

Vromen, E. M., de Boer, S. C. M., Teunissen, C. E., Rosemuller, A., Bjerke, M., . . . Tijms, B. M. (2023). Biomarket A+T-: Is this Alzheimer's disease or not: A combined CSF and pathology study. *Brain, 146*(3), 1166–1174.

WA (World Atlas). (2023). *How many serial killers are on the loose today?* Retrieved from https://www.worldatlas.com/articles.

Wagner, C., & Cáceres-Melillo, R. (2023). Mindfulness-based cognitive therapy (MBCT) and mindfulness-based stress reduction (MBSR) in the treatment of post-traumatic stress disorder (PTSD): A literature review. *Salud Mental, 46,* 35–42.

Waite, E. E., DeFontes, C., Weiss, N. H., Karnedy, C., Woods, S. E., Haliczer, L. A., & Dixon-Gordon, K. L. (2024). Borderline personality disorder and multidimensional impulsivity: The roles of positive and negative emotion dysregulation. *Journal of Affective Disorders, 344,* 635–643.

Wakefield, A. J., Murch, S. H., Anthony, A., Linnell, J., Casson, D. M., Malik, M., . . . Walker-Smith, J. A. (1998). Retracted: Ileal-lymphoid-nodular hyperplasia, non-specific colitis, and pervasive developmental disorder in children. *The Lancet, 351*(9103), 637–641.

Wakeman, S. Y., Pennington, R., Cerrato, B., Saunders, A., & Ahlgrim-Delzell, L. (2021). Parent perceptions regarding literacy instruction for students with intellectual disability. *Journal of Intellectual Disability Research, 65*(1), 86–98.

Wald, A. (2023, January 3). Factitious diarrhea: Clinical manifestations, diagnosis, and management. *UpToDate.* Retrieved from http://www.uptodate.com.

Walker, E. F., Ryan, A. T., Bridgman Goines, K. C., Novacek, D. M., Goulding, S. M., Brasfield, J. L., . . . Trotman, H. D. (2016). Multilevel approaches to schizophrenia and other psychotic disorders: The biobehavioral interface. In D. Cicchetti (Ed.). *Developmental psychopathology: Vol. 3. Maladaptation and psychopathology* (Chap. 22, pp. 997–1038). Hoboken, NJ: Wiley.

Walker, V. G., & Harrison, T. C. (2023, October 31). Life course perspectives of aging with schizophrenia spectrum disorders in psychiatric and long-term care facilities. *Frontiers in Pharmacology.* doi:10.1093/geront/gnad149. [Online ahead of print]

Walsh, E. H., Herring, M. P., & McMahon, J. (2023). A systematic review of school-based suicide prevention interventions for adolescents, and intervention and contextual factors in prevention. *Prevention Science, 24,* 365–381. https://doi.org/10.1007/s11121-022-01449-2.

Walter, K. (2022). What is migraine? *JAMA, 327*(1), 93.

Walters, S. (2022, November 22). These 5 animals trip on psychedelic and psychoactive drugs, too. *Discover.* https://www.discovermagazine.com/planet-earth/these-5-animals-like-to-take-psychedelic-trips-themselves.

Wampold, B. E., & Owen, J. (2021). Methods, magnitude, and characteristics of effective therapists. In M. Barkham, W. Lutz, & L. G. Castonguay (Eds.). *Bergin and Garfield's handbook of psychotherapy and behavior change* (7th ed., Chap. 9). New York: Wiley.

Wang, C., Pan, R., Wan, X., Tan, Y., Xu, L., Ho, C. S., & Ho, R. C. (2020). Immediate psychological responses and associated factors during the initial stage of the 2019 coronavirus disease (COVID-19) epidemic among the general population in China. *International Journal of Environmental Research and Public Health, 17*(5), 1729.

Wang, G. S. (2023, October 27). Cannabis (marijuana): Acute intoxication. *UpToDate.* Retrieved from http://www.uptodate.com.

Wang, J., Ren, F., Gao, B., & Yu, X. (2022, March 7). Mindfulness-based cognitive therapy in recurrent MDD patients with residual symptoms: Alterations in resting-state theta oscillation dynamics associated with changes in depression and rumination. *Frontiers in Psychiatry.* [Online ahead of print]

Wang, P. S., Lane, M., Olfson, M., Pincus, H. A., Wells, K. B., & Kessler, R. C. (2005). Twelve-month use of mental health services in the United States. *Archives of General Psychiatry, 62,* 629–640.

Wang, S., Xu, H., Zhang, S., Yang, R., Li, D., Sun, Y., Wan, Y., & Tao, F. (2022). Linking childhood maltreatment and psychological symptoms: The role of social support, cooping styles, and self-esteem in adolescents. *Journal of Interpersonal Violence, 37*(1–2), NP620–NP650.

Wang, Y. (2023). Gender differences and possible improvement in histrionic personality disorders. *Lecture Notes in Education Psychology and Public Media, 3,* 390–397.

Wang, Y., Hung, K. S. Y., Deng, M. Y., Lui, S. S. Y., Lee, J. C. Y., Mak, H. K. F., . . . Chan, R. C. K. (2017). Altered resting-state functional connectivity of striatum in first-episode schizophrenia. *Schizophrenia Bulletin, 43*(Suppl. 1), S197–S198.

Wang, Y., Liu, G., Zhao, Z., Li, L., Yin, S., Sun, X., . . . Yang, Y. (2022). The relationship between Type D personality with atherosclerotic plaque and cardiovascular events: The mediation effect of inflammation and kynurenine/tryptophan metabolism. *Frontiers in Cardiovascular Medicine, 9,* 986712.

Wang, Y.-H., Wang, X.-F., Shi, L.-D., Xu, X.-M., Wei, L.-N., Li, S.-S., . . . Wang, K.-Q. (2023). Retrospective case-control study of facial emotion recognition in male veterans with chronic schizophrenia and its correlation with interpersonal communication. *BMC Psychiatry, 23*(1), 47.

Wang, Z.-J., Liu, C.-Y., Wang, Y.-M., & Wang, Y. (2024). Childhood psychological maltreatment and adolescent depressive symptoms: Exploring the role of social anxiety and maladaptive emotion regulation strategies. *Journal of Affective Disorders, 344,* 365–372.

Wang, Z., Zhu, X., Ni, X., Wen, Y., & Shang, D. (2022). Knowledge atlas of the involvement of glutamate and GABA in alcohol use disorder: A bibliometric and scientometric analysis. *Frontiers in Psychiatry, 13,* 965142.

Waraan, L., Siqveland, J., Hanssen-Bauer, K., Czjakowski, N. O., Axelsdottir, B., Mehlum, L., & Aalberg, M. (2023). Family therapy for adolescents with depression and suicidal ideation: A systematic review and meta-analysis. *Clinical Child Psychology and Psychiatry, 28*(2), 831–849.

Ward, T., Rus-Calafell, M., Ramadhan, Z., Soumelidou, O., Fornells-Ambrojo, M., Garety, P., & Craig, T. K. J. (2020). Avatar therapy for distressing voices: A comprehensive account of therapeutic targets. *Schizophrenia Bulletin, 46,* 1038–1044.

Ware, J., McIvor, L., & Fernandez, Y. M. (2021). Behavioral control models in managing sexual deviance. In L. A. Craig & R. M. Bartels (Eds.). *Sexual deviance: Understanding and managing deviant sexual interest and paraphilic disorders* (Chap. 20). Hoboken, NJ: Wiley-Blackwell.

Warren, C. S., & Akoury, L. M. (2020). Emphasizing the "cultural" in sociocultural: A systematic review of research on thin-ideal internalization, acculturation, and eating pathology in US ethnic minorities. *Psychology Research and Behavior Management, 13,* 319–330.

Washington, N., & Scaccia, A. (2022, September 22). How to recognize and treat the symptoms of a nervous breakdown. *Healthline.*

Waters, B. (2015, June 24). 23 mental health professionals interviewed about their jobs. *Psychology Today.*

Watkins, E. R. (2022). Rumination-focused cognitive behavioral therapy. In G. Todd & R. Branch (Eds.). *Evidence-based treatment for anxiety disorders and depression: A cognitive behavioral therapy compendium* (pp. 402–417). Cambridge: Cambridge University Press.

Watson, D., Levin-Aspenson, H.F., Waszczuk, M.A., Conway, C.C., Dalgleish, T., Dretsch, M.N., . . . & the HiTOP Utility Workgroup. (2022). Validity and utility of Hierarchical Taxonomy of Psychopathology (HiTOP): III. Emotional dysfunction superspectrum. *World Psychiatry, 21*(1), 26–54.

Watson, H. J., Davies, H. L., & Palmos, A. B. (2023). Genetics of eating disorders. In P. Robinson, T. Wade, B. Herpertz-Dahlann, F. Fernandez-Aranda, J. Treasure, & S. Wonderlich (Eds.). *Eating disorders.* Edinburgh: Springer.

Watson, J. B., & Rayner, R. (1920). Conditioned emotional reaction. *Journal of Experimental Psychology, 3,* 1–14.

Watson, P. J., Canetti, D., & Hobfoll, S. E. (2023). Terrorism. In F. M. Dattillo, D. I. Shapiro, & D. S. Greenaway (Eds.). *Cognitive-behavioral strategies in crisis intervention* (4th ed., Chap. 18). New York: Guilford Press.

Watts, D., de Azevedo Cardoso, T., Librenza-Garcia, D., Ballester, P., Passos, I. V., Kessler, F. H. P., . . . Kapczinski, F. (2022). Predicting criminal and violent outcomes in psychiatry: A meta-analysis of diagnostic accuracy. *Translational Psychiatry, 12,* 470.

Waugh, E., Ivanich, J., O'Keefe, V., Usher, J., Haroz, E., Goklish, N., . . . Cwik, M. (2023). Understanding opioid use within a Southwestern American Indian Reservation community: A qualitative study. *Journal of Rural Health, 39*(1), 179–185.

Way, B. M., & Uchino, B. (2024, September). Physiological pathways mediating between psychological stress and health. In N. Schneiderman (Ed.). *APA handbook of health psychology: Vol. 1. Foundations and context of health psychology; Vol. 2. Clinical interventions and disease management in health psychology; Vol. 3. Health psychology and public health* (Chap. 14). Washington, DC: American Psychological Association.

WC (The World Counts). (2022). Social connections and happiness. *The World Counts.*

WCSAP (Washington Coalition of Sexual Assault Programs). (2022). *Sexual assault: How often does it happen?* Pasco, WA: Author.

Wdowik, M. (2017, November 6). The long, strange history of dieting fads. *The Conversation.* Retrieved from https://theconversation.com/the-long-strange-history-of-dieting-fads-82294.

Weaver, D. F. (2023). Alzheimer's disease as an innate autoimmune disease (AD^2): A new molecular paradigm. *Alzheimer's & Dementia Journal, 19*(3), 1086–1098.

Webb, L. M., & Chen, C. Y. (2022). The COVID-19 pandemic's impact on older adults' mental health: Contributing factors, coping strategies, and opportunities for improvement. *International Journal of Geriatric Psychiatry, 37*(1), 10.

Weber, B. (2016, August 6). Chris Costner Sizemore, patient behind "The Three Faces of Eve," dies at 89. *New York Times.*

Webster, H. (2023, August 30). What to know about existential theory and therapy. *Medical News Today.*

Weeks, D. J. (2015). *The gifts of eccentrics: Imagination in reality.* Scotts Valley, CA: CreateSpace.

Weeks, D., & James, J. (1995). *Eccentrics: A study of sanity and strangeness.* New York: Villard.

Weems, C. F., Russell, J. D., Herringa, R. J., & Carrion, V. G. (2021). Translating the neuroscience of adverse childhood experiences to inform policy and foster population level resilience. *American Psychologist, 76*(2), 188–202.

Weimer, M. (2022, September 30). Mind wandering. *Faculty Focus.*

Weinberger, L. E., & Markowitz, E. (2022). Mental institutions: Legal issues and commitments. *ScienceDirect.* https://www.sciencedirect.com/topics/medicine-and-dentistry/mental-hospital.

Weiner, R. (2014, September 13). Colleges ramp up efforts to prevent sexual assaults. *USA Today.*

Weinstein, A. M. (2023). Reward, motivation and brain imaging in human healthy participants: A narrative review. *Frontiers in Behavioral Neuroscience, 17,* 1123733.

Weishaar, M. E., & Beck, A. T. (2006). Cognitive theory of personality and personality disorders. In S. Strack (Ed.). *Differentiating normal and abnormal personality* (2nd ed., pp. 113–135). New York: Springer Publishing.

Weiss, D. C. (2020, December 17). Serial killings are waning, leading to speculation about the cause. *ABA Journal.*

Weissman, L. (2021, October 27). Autism spectrum disorder in children and adolescents: Pharmacologic interventions. *UpToDate.* Retrieved from https://www.uptodate.com.

Weissman, L. (2023, December 4). Autism spectrum disorder in children and adolescents: Behavioral and educational interventions. *UpToDate.* Retrieved from https://www.uptodate.com.

Weitzman, C., & Rojmahamongkol, P. (2022, March 7). Fetal alcohol spectrum disorder: Clinical features and diagnosis. *UpToDate.* Retrieved from https://www.uptodate.com.

Weitzman, C., & Rojmahamongkol, P. (2022, March 23). Fetal alcohol spectrum disorder: Management and prognosis. *UpToDate.* Retrieved from https://www.uptodate.com.

Wells, A. (2005). The metacognitive model of GAD: Assessment of meta-worry and relationship with DSM-IV generalized anxiety disorder. *Cognitive Therapy and Research, 29*(1), 107–121.

Wells, A. (2019). Breaking the cybernetic code: Understanding and treating the human metacognitive control system to enhance mental health. *Frontiers in Psychology, 10,* 2621.

Wells, A. (2021, April 5). *Cognitive therapy of anxiety disorders: A practical guide* (2nd ed.). Hoboken, NJ: Wiley-Blackwell.

Wells, A., Reeves, D., Heal, C., Fisher, P., Doherty, P., Davies, L., . . . Capobianco, L. (2023). Metacognitive therapy home-based self-help for anxiety and depression in cardiovascular disease patients in the UK: A single-blind randomised controlled trial. *PLoS Medicine, 20*(1), e1004161.

Weme, A. V., Sorensen, K. D., & Binder, P.-E. (2023). Agency in avoidant personality disorder: A narrative review. *Frontiers in Psychology, 14,* 1248617.

Wen, J., Trost, B., Engchuan, W., Halvorsen, M., Pallotto, L. M., Mitina, A., . . . Szatkiewicz, J. P. (2023). Rare tandem repeat expansions associate with genes involved in synaptic and neuronal signaling functions in schizophrenia. *Molecular Psychiatry, 28,* 475–482.

Wentz, E. (2023). Outcomes of anorexia nervosa. In P. Robinson, T. Wade, B. Herpertz-Dahlann, F. Fernandez-Aranda, J. Treasure, & S. Wonderlich (Eds.). *Eating disorders.* Edinburgh: Springer.

Wenzel, S. (2023, July 17). Treatment of severe asthma in adolescents and adults. *UpToDate.* Retrieved from http://www.uptodate.com.

Wertheimer, A. (2001). *A special scar: The experiences of people bereaved by suicide* (2nd ed.). East Sussex: Brunner-Routledge.

West, J. C., Benedek, D., & Wynn, G. H. (2022). Pharmacotherapy for PTSD. In J. G. Beck & D. M. Sloan (Eds.). *The Oxford handbook of traumatic stress disorders* (Chap. 37). New York: Oxford University Press.

Westermeyer, J. (1993). Substance use disorders among young minority refugees: Common themes in a clinical sample. *NIDA Research Monograph, 130,* 308–320.

Westermeyer, J. (2001). Alcoholism and co-morbid psychiatric disorders among American Indians. *American Indian and Alaska Native Mental Health Research, 10,* 27–51.

Westermeyer, J. (2004). Acculturation: Advances in theory, measurement, and applied research. *Journal of Nervous and Mental Disease, 192*(5), 391–392.

Weston-Green, K. (2022). Antipsychotic drug development: From historical evidence to fresh perspectives. *Frontiers in Psychiatry, 13,* 903156.

Wharton, M. (2023). *Self-injury and choking: Destructive behaviors in children and teenagers.* Washington, DC: National Center for Health Research. Retrieved from https://www.center4research.org.

Wheelwright, T. (2022, January 24). *2022 cell phone usage statistics: How obsessed are we?* Retrieved from https://www.reviews.org/mobile/cell-phone-addiction.

Whisman, M. A., Beach, S. R. H., & Davila, J. (2022). Couple therapy for depression or anxiety. In J. L. Lebow & D. K. Snyder (Eds.). *Clinical handbook of couple therapy* (6th ed., Chap. 26). New York: Guilford Press.

Whisman, M. A., Sbarra, D. A., & Beach, S. R. H. (2021). Intimate relationships and depression: Searching for causation in the sea of association. *Annual Review of Clinical Psychology, 17,* 233–258.

Whitaker, R. (2002). *Mad in America: Bad science, bad medicine, and the enduring mistreatment of the mentally ill.* Cambridge, MA: Perseus.

Whitaker, R. (2010). *Anatomy of an epidemic: Magic bullets, psychiatric drugs, and the astonishing rise of mental illness in America.* Norwalk, CT: Crown House Publishing.

White, A. I. R. (2022, February 5). Xenophobia, prejudice, and blame in pandemic times. *The Lancet, 399*(10324), 512–513.

Whitney, N., Samuel, A., Douglass, L., Strand, N. K., & Jahromi, A. H. (2022). Avoiding assumptions: Sexual function in transgender and non-binary individuals. *Journal of Sexual Medicine, 19*(6), 1032–1034.

WHO (World Health Organization). (2020). *Direct-to-consumer advertising under fire.* Retrieved from https://www.who.int/bulletin/volumes/87/8/09-040809/en.

WHO (World Health Organization). (2022, October 1). *Ageing and health.* Retrieved from https://www.who.int/news-room/fact-sheets/detail.

WHO (World Health Organization). (2022, September 19). *Child maltreatment* [Fact sheet]. Retrieved from https://www.who.int/news-room/fact-sheets.

WHO (World Health Organization). (2022). *Mental disorders.* Retrieved from https://www.who.int/news-room/fact-sheets/detail.

WHO (World Health Organization). (2022, January 10). *Schizophrenia.* Retrieved from https://www.who.int/news-room/fact-sheets/detail.

WHO (World Health Organization). (2022). *Tobacco.* Retrieved from https://www.who.int/health-0topics/tobacco.

WHO (World Health Organization). (2022). *World Suicide Prevention Day 2022.* Retrieved from https://www.who.int/campaigns.

WHO (World Health Organization). (2023, February 6). *Artificial intelligence in mental health research: new WHO study on applications and challenges* [Press release]. Retrieved from https://www.who.int/europe/news/item/06-02-2023.

WHO (World Health Organization). (2023, March 15). *Dementia.* Retrieved from https://www.who.int/news-room/fact-sheets/detail/dementia.

WHO (World Health Organization). (2023, March 31). *Depressive disorder (depression).* Retrieved from https://www.who.int/news-room/fact-sheets.

WHO (World Health Organization). (2023, February 23). *New WHO guidelines on parenting aim to help prevent child maltreatment and enhance parent-child relationships.* Retrieved from https://www.who.int/news/item/23-02-20233.

WHO (World Health Organization). (2023). *Tobacco.* Retrieved from https://www.who.int/health-0topics/tobacco.

Widiger, T. A., & Gore, W. L. (2016). Histrionic personality disorder. In H. S. Friedman (Ed.). *Encyclopedia of mental health* (2nd ed., pp. 270–277). New York: Elsevier.

Widiger, T. A., & Hines, A. (2022). The Diagnostic and Statistical Manual of Mental Disorders, Fifth Edition alternative model of personality disorder. *Personality Disorders: Theory, Research, and Treatment, 13*(4), 347–355.

Widiger, T. A., Hines, A., & Crego, C. (2024). Evidence-based assessment of personality disorder. *Assessment, 31*(1), 191–198.

Wieder, L., Brown, R., Thompson, T., & Terhune, D. (2020). Suggestibility in functional neurological disorder: A meta-analysis. *Journal of Neurology, Neurosurgery & Psychiatry, 92*(2), 150–157.

Wiegelmann, H., Speller, S., Verhaert, L.-M., Schirra-Weirich, L., & Wolf-Ostermann, K. (2021). Psychosocial interventions to support the mental health of informal caregivers of persons living with dementia: A systematic literature review. *BMC Geriatrics, 21*(1), 94.

Wilcoxson, R., & Turley, E. (2023, March 7). Lie detection tests have worked the same way for 3,000 years, and they're still hopelessly inaccurate, say researchers. *Phys Org.* Retrieved from https://phys.org/news.

Wilhelm, S., Weingarden, H., Greenberg, J. L., McCoy, T. H., Ladis, I., & Summers, B. J. (2022). Development and pilot testing of a cognitive-behavioral therapy digital service for body dysmorphic disorder. *Behavior Therapy, 51*(1), 15–26.

Williams, J., & Nieuwsma, J. (2022, February 23). Screening for depression in adults. *UpToDate.* Retrieved from https://www.uptodate.com.

Williams, M. T., & La Torre, J. (2022). Clinical supervision in delivering cognitive behavior therapy across race, ethnicity, and culture. In E. A. Storch, J. S. Abramowitz, & D. McKay (Eds.). *Training and supervision in specialized cognitive behavior therapy: Methods, settings, and populations* (Chap. 18). Washington, DC: American Psychological Association.

Williams, P. G., & Carlson, S. E. (2024, September). Personality and emotional adjustments in health risk and resilience. In N. Schneiderman (Ed.). *APA handbook of health psychology: Vol. 1. Foundations and context of health psychology; Vol. 2. Clinical interventions and disease management in health psychology; Vol. 3. Health psychology and public health* (Chap. 20). Washington, DC: American Psychological Association.

Williams, R. M., Day, M. A., Ehde, D. M., Turner, A. P., Ciol, M. A, Gertz, K. J., . . . Jensen, M. P. (2022). Effects of hypnosis vs mindfulness meditation vs education on chronic pain intensity and secondary outcomes in veterans: A randomized clinical trial. *Pain, 163*(10), 1905–1918.

Williams, T. M. (2008). *Black pain: It just looks like we're not hurting*. New York: Scribner.

Willis, B. M., Kersh, P. P., Buchanan, C. M., & Cole, V. T. (2022). Internalizing and externalizing pathways to high-risk substance use and geographic location in Australian adolescents. *Frontiers in Psychology, 13,* 933488.

Wilson, D. K., Sweeney, A. M., & Zarrett, N. (2024, September). Behavioral risk and protective factors: Evidence, models, and interventions. In N. Schneiderman (Ed.). *APA handbook of health psychology: Vol. 1. Foundations and context of health psychology; Vol. 2. Clinical interventions and disease management in health psychology; Vol. 3. Health psychology and public health* (Chap. 18). Washington, DC: American Psychological Association.

Wilson, S., & Olino, T. M. (2021). A developmental perspective on personality and psychopathology across the life span. *Journal of Personality, 89*(5), 915–932.

Winick, B. (2020). The side effects of incompetency labeling and the implications for mental health law. In S. Slobogin, T. L. Hafemeister, & D. Mossman (Eds.). *Law and the mental health system: Civil and criminal aspects* (7th ed., p. 1053). St. Paul, MN: West Academic Publishing.

Winkelman, J. W. (2023, February 7). Overview of the treatment of insomnia in adults. *UpToDate*. Retrieved from http://www.uptodate.com.

Winslade, W.J., & Ross, J. W. (1983). *The insanity plea*. New York: Scribner.

Wipond, R. (2023, January 24). *Your consent is not required: The rise in psychiatric detentions, forced treatment, and abusive guardianships*. Dallas, TX: BenBella Books.

Wise, E. H. (2018, January/February). Torture scandal prompts broader look at ethics. *The National Psychologist*, p. 21.

Wittgens, C., Fischer, M. M., Buspavanich, P., Theobald, S., Schweizer, K., & Trautmann, S. (2022). Mental health in people with minority sexual orientations: A meta-analysis of population-based studies. *Acta Psychiatrica Scandinavica, 145*(4), 357–372.

Wittlin, N. M., Kuper, K. E., & Olson, K. R. (2023, December 20). Mental health of transgender and gender diverse youth. *Annual Review of Clinical Psychology, 19,* 207–232.

WMD (WebMD). (2021). *Quit-smoking aids: Know your options*. Retrieved from https://webmd.com.

WMD (WebMD). (2023). *The 5 most addictive drugs, and how you can get help*. Retrieved from https://webmd.com.

Wolberg, L. R. (1967). *The technique of psychotherapy*. New York: Grune & Stratton.

Wolberg, L. R. (2005). *The technique of psychotherapy*. Lanham, MD: Jason Aronson.

Wolpe, J. (1969). *The practice of behavior therapy*. Oxford: Pergamon Press.

Wolpe, J. (1987). The promotion of scientific psychotherapy: A long voyage. In J. K. Zeig (Ed.). *The evolution of psychotherapy*. New York: Brunner/Mazel.

Wong, Q. (2021, October 1). Suicide and self-harm content is scarily easy to find on social media. *CNET*. Retrieved from https://www.cnet.com/health/personal-care.

Woo, E (2023, May 11). The link between creativity and mental illness. *Getty News*.

Wooldridge, T. (2022, August 193). *Eating disorders*. New York: Routledge.

Woolston, C. (2020, January 1). Aging and stress. *HealthDay*. Retrieved from https://consumer/healthday.com.

WPB (World Prison Brief). (2023). *United States of America*. London: Author.

WPR (World Population Review). (2022). *Suicide rate by country 2022*. Retrieved from https://worldpopulationreview.com/country-rankings.

WPR (World Population Review). (2023). *Recreational weed states: States that have legalized weed 2023*. Walnut, CA: Author.

WPR (World Population Review). (2023). *States with medical marijuana 2023*. Walnut, CA: Author.

WPR (World Population Review). (2023). *Suicide rate by country 2023*. Retrieved from https://worldpopulationreview.com/country-rankings.

WPR (World Population Review). (2024). *Involuntary commitment laws by state 2024*. Retrieved from https://www.worldpopulationreview.com/state-rankings.

WPR (World Population Review). (2024). *Serial killers by state 2024*. Retrieved from https://worldpopulationreview.com/state-rankings.

WPR (World Population Review). (2024). *Suicide rate by country 2023*. Retrieved from https://www.worldpopulationreview.com/country-rankings.

Wu, B., Zhou, L., Deng, Y., Zhao, J., & Liu, M. (2022). Online disinhibition and online trolling among Chinese college students: The mediation of the dark triad and the moderation of gender. *Cyberpsychology, Behavior, and Social Networking, 25*(11), 744–751.

Wu, C.-C., Liao, M.-H., Su, C.-H., Poly, T. N., & Lin, M.-C. (2023). Benzodiazepine use and the risk of dementia in the elderly population: An umbrella review of meta-analyses. *Journal of Personalized Medicine, 13*(10), 1485.

Wu, D., Yu, L., Yang, T., Cottrell, R., Peng, S., Guo, W., & Jiang, S. (2020). The impacts of uncertainty stress on mental disorders of Chinese college students: Evidence from a nationwide study. *Frontiers in Psychology, 11,* 243.

Wu, H., Lu, L., Qian, Y., Jin, X-H., Yu, H-R., Du, L., . . . Chen, H-L. (2022). The significance of cognitive-behavioral therapy on suicide: An umbrella review. *Journal of Affective Disorders, 317,* 142–148.

Wu, H., Manglike, A., Chen, Y., Liu, Z., Fritzsche, K., & Lu, Z. (2023). Scoping review update on somatic symptom disorder that includes additional Chinese data. *General Psychiatry, 36*(3), e100942.

Wu, K. (2022, August 21). Selfie-taking: Why it's okay for us, but not for others. *Psychology Today*. Retrieved from https://www.psychologytoday.com/us/blog/the-modern-heart/202208.

Wu, T., Hu, J., Davydow, D., Huang, H., Spottswood, M., & Huang, H. (2022). Demystifying borderline personality disorder in primary care. *Frontiers in Medicine, 9,* 1024022.

Wu, Z., Liu, P., Huang, B., Deng, S., Song, Z., Huang, X., . . . Cheng, S. (2023). A novel Alzheimer's disease prognostic signature: Identification and analysis of glutamine metabolism genes in immunogenicity and immunotherapy efficacy. *Scientific Reports, 13*(1), 6895.

Wuyts, E., & Morrens, M. (2022). The biology of BDSM: A systematic review. *Journal of Sexual Medicine, 19*(1), 144–157.

Wyant, K. J., & Chou, K. L. (2023, May 31). Drug-induced parkinsonism. *UpToDate*. Retrieved from https://www.uptodate.com.

Xiao, Q., Song, X., Huang, L., Hou, D., & Huang, X. (2022). Global prevalence and characteristics of non-suicidal self-injury between 2010 and 2021 among a non-clinical sample of adolescents: A meta-analysis. *Frontiers in Psychiatry, 13,* 912441.

Xiao, Q., Yi, X., Fu, Y., Jiang, F., Zhang, Z., Huang, Q., . . . Chen, B. T. (2023). Altered brain activity and childhood trauma in Chinese adolescents with borderline personality disorder. *Journal of Affective Disorders, 323,* 435–443.

Xiao, Y., Yip, P. S. F., Pathak, J., & Mann, J. J. (2022). Association of social determinants of health and vaccinations with child mental health during the COVID-19 pandemic in the U.S. *JAMA Psychiatry, 79*(6), 610–621.

Xiao, Z., Obsuth, I., Meinck, F., & Murray, A. L. (2024). Relations between childhood psychological maltreatment and mental health dimensions within a higher-order model. *International Journal of Clinical and Health Psychology, 24*(1), 100416.

Xu, C., Wang, S., Su, B. B., Ozuna, K., Mao, C.-X., Dai, Z., & Wang, K. (2024). Associations of adolescent substance use and depressive symptoms with adult major depressive disorder in the United States: NSDUH 2016–2019. *Journal of Affective Disorders Reports, 344,* 397–406.

Xu, L., Tao, X., Lou, Y., & Engström, M. (2024). Sleep quality, frailty and overall health among community-dwelling older people: A longitudinal study. *Journal of Advanced Nursing, 8*(1), 328–338.

Yager, J. (2022, September 21). Eating disorders: Overview of epidemiology, clinical features, and diagnosis. *UpToDate*. Retrieved from http://www.uptodate.com.

Yager, J. (2022, October 26). Eating disorders: Overview of prevention and treatment. *UpToDate*. Retrieved from http://www.uptodate.com.

Yalch, M. M., Ceroni, D. B., & Dehart, R. M. (2023). Influence of child abuse and neglect on histrionic personality pathology. *Journal of Trauma and Dissociation, 24*(1), 111–124.

Yang, F., Jin, Z., He, J., Han, B., Huang, Chen, K., & Wang, J. (2022). Aggressive behaviors and associated factors in Chinese left-behind adolescents: A cross-sectional study. *BMC Pediatrics, 22,* 677.

Yang, H., Wang, M., Wu, F., Li, Q., Zheng, Y., & Qin, P. (2020). Diminished self-monitoring in hallucinations: Aberrant anterior insula connectivity differentiates auditory hallucinations in schizophrenia from subjective tinnitus. *Asian Journal of Psychiatry, 52,* 102056.

Yang, J., Hellerstein, D. J., Chen, Y., McGrath, P. J., Stewart, J. W., Peterson, B. S., & Wang, Z. (2022, April 15). Serotonin-norepinephrine reuptake inhibitor antidepressant effects on regional connectivity of the thalamus in persistent depressive disorder: Evidence from two randomized, double-blind, placebo-controlled clinical trials. *Brain Communications, 4*(3), fcac100.

Yang, Y., Dongdong, Y., & Yu, H. (2021). Comparative study on relationship between inconsistent online-offline social performance and self-efficacy of university students based on types of social activity. *Frontiers in Psychology, 12,* 603971.

Yao, L., & Kabir, R. (2023, February 9). Person-centered therapy (Rogerian therapy). *StatPearls.*

Yasaei, R., & Saadabadi, A. (2023, May 1). Methamphetamine. *StatPearls.*

Yasgur, B. S. (2019, January 11). Challenging stigma: Should psychiatrists disclose their own mental illness? *Psychiatry Advisor.* Retrieved from http://www.psychiatryadvisor.com/home/topics/mood- disorders/depressive-disorder.

Ye, J., Wan, H., Chen, S., & Liu, G.-P. (2024). Targeting tau in Alzheimer's disease: From mechanisms to clinical therapy. *Neural Regeneration Research, 19*(7), 1489–1498.

Yehuda, R. (2022, July 1). How parents' trauma leaves biological traces in children. *Scientific American.*

Yi, H., Li, L., Wang, Y., Tao, H., Yu, X., Yu, B., . . . Lin, P. (2022). The potential mediating effects of inflammation on the association between Type D personality and coronary plaque vulnerability in patients with coronary artery disease: An optical coherence tomography study. *Psychosomatic Medicine, 84*(4), 468–477.

You, X.-R., Gong, X.-R., Guo, M.-R., & Ma, B .-X. (2024). Cognitive behavioural therapy to improve social skills in children and adolescents with autism spectrum disorder: A meta-analysis of randomised controlled trials. *Journal of Affective Disorders, 344,* 8–17.

You, Z., Wang, C., Lan, X., Li, W., Shang, D., Zhang, F., . . . Ning, Y. (2024). The contribution of polyamine pathway to determinations of diagnosis for treatment-resistant depression: A metabolomic analysis. *Progressive Neuro-psychopharmacological Biological Psychiatry, 128,* 110849.

Yu, Y., Ozonoff, S., & Miller, M. (2024). Assessment of autism spectrum disorder. *Assessment, 31*(1), 24–41.

Yuan, Y., Lee, H., Eack, S. M., & Newhill, C. E. (2023). A systematic review of the association between early childhood trauma and borderline personality disorder. *Journal of Personality Disorders, 37*(1), 16–35.

Yuen, J., Goyal, A., Rusheen, A. E., Kouzani, A. Z., Berk, M., Kim, J. H., . . . Oh, Y. (2023). High frequency deep brain stimulation can mitigate the acute effects of cocaine administration on tonic dopamine levels in the rat nucleus accumbens. *Frontiers in Neuroscience, 17,* 1061578.

Yung, A. R., Wood, S. J., Malla, A., Nelson, B., McGorry, P., & Shah, J. (2021). The reality of at risk mental state services: A response to recent criticisms. *Psychological Medicine, 51*(2), 212–218.

Zabidi, A. S., Hastings, R. P., & Totsika, V. (2023). Spending leisure time together: Parent child relationship in families of children with an intellectual disability. *Research in Developmental Disabilities, 133,* 104398.

Zablotsky, B., & Alford, J. M. (2020, March). Racial and ethnic differences in the prevalence of attention-deficit/hyperactivity disorder and learning disabilities among U.S. children aged 3–17 years. *NCHS Data Brief, 358,* 1–8.

Zachar, P., First, M. B., & Kendler, K. S. (2023). Prolonged grief disorder and the DSM: A history. *Journal of Nervous and Mental Disease, 211*(5), 386–392.

Zaejian, J. (2014, February 18). Current research on outpatient commitment laws ("Laura's Law" in California). *Mad in America*. Retrieved from https://www.madinamerica.com.

Zagaria, T., Antonucci, G., Buono, S., Recupero, M., & Zoccolotti, P. (2021). Executive functions and attention processes in adolescents and young adults with intellectual disability. *Brain Sciences, 11*(1), 42.

Zahid, A., & Best, M. W. (2023, April 24). Examining cognitive biases uniquely associated with schizotypy. *Psychopathology.* doi:10.1159/000529742. [Online ahead of print]

Zahid, U., Onwordi, E. C., Hedges, E. P., Wall, M. B., Modinos, G., Murray, R. M., & Egerton, A. (2023). Neurofunctional correlates of glutamate and GABA imbalance in psychosis: A systematic review. *Neuroscience and Biobehavioral Reviews, 144,* 105010.

Zahn-Waxler, C. (2023). Afterword: A reminiscence on origins of prosociality and antisociality. In T. Malti & M. Davidov (Eds.). *The Cambridge handbook of prosociality: Development, mechanisms, promotion* (pp. 614–630). New York: Cambridge University Press.

Zamarripa, C. A., Spindle, T. R., Surujunarain, R., Weerts, E. M., Bansal, S., Unadkat, J. D., . . . Vandrey, R. (2023). Assessment of orally administered 9-tetrahydrocannabinol when coadministered with cannabidiol on 9-tetrahydrocannabinol pharmacokinetics and pharmacodynamics in healthy adults: A randomized clinical trial. *JAMA Network Open, 6*(2), e2254752.

Zanella, E., & Lee, E. (2022). Integrative review on psychological and social risk and prevention factors of eating disorders including anorexia nervosa and bulimia nervosa: Seven major theories. *Heliyon, 8*(11), e11422.

Zeljic, K., Xiang, Q., Wang, Z., Pan, Y., Shi, Y., Zhou, Z., . . . Liu, D. (2021). Heightened perception of illusory motion is associated with symptom severity in schizophrenia patients. *Progress in Neuro-Psychopharmacology & Biological Psychiatry, 104,* 110055.

Zemel, R. (2022, May 18). A COVID-19 call to action: Psychological first aid training for medical professionals and trainees. *Academic Psychiatry, 46*(6), 769–773.

Zemestani, M., Heshmati, R., Comer, J. S., & Kendall, P. C. (2022). Intolerance of uncertainty as a transdiagnostic vulnerability to anxiety disorders in youth. *Current Psychology.* https://doi.org/10.1007/s12144-022-03645-3.

Zerwas, S., Lund, B. C., Von Holle, A., Thornton, L. M., Berrettini, W. H., Brandt, H., . . . Bulik. C. M. (2013). Factors associated with recovery from anorexia nervosa. *Journal of Psychiatric Research, 47*(7), 972–979.

Zhang, M., Liang, C., Chen, X., Cai, Y., & Cui, L. (2024). Interplay between microglia and environmental risk factors in Alzheimer's disease. *Neural Regeneration Research, 19*(8), 1718–1727.

Zhang, Y., Tao, S., Coid, J., Wei, W., Wang, Q., Yue, W., . . . Li, T. (2024). The role of total white blood cell count in antipsychotic treatment for patients with schizophrenia. *Current Neuropharmacology, 22*(1), 159–167.

Zhang, Y., Zhang, G. Y., Zhu, X. B., Zhang, Z. E., Gan, J., & Liu, Z. G. (2022). Clinical characteristics of minor hallucinations in Chinese Parkinson's disease patients. *Frontiers in Aging Neuroscience, 13,* 723405.

Zhang, Z.-Y., Harischandra, D. S., Wang, R., Ghaisas, S., Zhao, J. Y., McMonagle, T. P., . . . Yang, X. (2023). TRIM11 protects against taupathies and is down-regulated in Alzheimer's disease. *Science, 381*(6656), eadd6696.

Zhao, G., Cheng, Q., Dong, X., & Xie, L. (2021). Mass hysteria attack rates in children and adolescents: A meta-analysis. *Journal of International Medical Research, 49*(12). doi:10.1177/03000605211039812.

Zhong, R., Moreno, A., & Wasser, T. (2023). A proposal for the capacity to stipulate to civil commitment and a 50-state review of statutes. *Journal of the American Academy of Psychiatry and the Law, 51*(1), 93–102.

Zhou, A., McDaniel, M., Hong, X., Mattin, M., Wang, X., & Shih, C.-H. (2023). Emotion dysregulation mediates the association between acute sleep disturbance and later posttraumatic stress symptoms in trauma exposed adults. *European Journal of Psychotraumatology, 14*(2), 2202056.

Zhou, B., Wang, G., Hong, Y., Xu, S., Wang, J., Yu, H., . . . Yu, L. (2020). Mindfulness interventions for rheumatoid arthritis: A systematic review and meta-analysis. *Complementary Therapies in Clinical Practice, 39,* 101088.

Zhou, S.-J., Zhang, L.-G., Wang, L.-L., Guo, Z.-C., Wang, J.-Q., Chen, J.-C., . . . Chen, J.-X. (2020). Prevalence and socio-demographic correlates of psychological health problems in Chinese adolescents during the outbreak of COVID-19. *European Child & Adolescent Psychiatry, 29*(6), 749–758.

Zhu, X., Fan, H., Fan, F., Zhao, Y., Tan, Y., Yang, F., . . . Tan, S. (2020). Improving social functioning in community-dwelling patients with schizophrenia: A randomized controlled computer cognitive remediation therapy trial with six months follow-up. *Psychiatry Research, 287,* 112913.

Zhu, X., Huang, J., Zhou, Y., Tong, J., Zhang, P., Luo, X., . . . Tan, Y. (2022). Abnormal cortisol profile during psychosocial stress among patients with schizophrenia in a Chinese population. *Scientific Reports, 12,* 18591.

Zide, J. (2022, September 12). The kids aren't alright: What is behind an epidemic of child and teen suicide? *Manistee News.* Retrieved from https://www.manisteenews.com/news/article.

Zimbardo, P. (1976). Rational paths to madness. Presentation at Princeton University, Princeton, NJ.

Zimmerman, M. (2023). Antisocial personality disorder (ASPD). *Merck Manual, Professional Version.*

Zimmerman, M. (2023). Avoidant personality disorder (AVPD). *Merck Manual, Professional Version.*

Zimmerman, M. (2023). Borderline personality disorder (BPD). *Merck Manual, Consumer Version.*

Zimmerman, M. (2023). Dependent personality disorder (DPD). *Merck Manual, Professional Version.*

Zimmerman, M. (2023). Histrionic personality disorder (HPD). *Merck Manual, Professional Version.*

Zimmerman, M. (2023). Narcissistic personality disorder (NPD). *Merck Manual, Professional Version.*

Zimmerman, M. (2023). Overview of personality disorders. *Merck Manual, Professional Version.*

Zimmerman, M. (2023). Paranoid personality disorder (PPD). *Merck Manual, Professional Version.*

Zimmerman, M. (2023). Schizoid personality disorder (ScPD). *Merck Manual, Professional Version.*

Zimmerman, M. (2023). Schizotypal personality disorder (STPD). *Merck Manual, Professional Version.*

Zippia. (2022, April 18). *Counselor demographics and statistics in the U.S.* Retrieved from https://www.zippia.com/counselor-jobs/demographics.

Zippia. (2022, April 18). *Psychiatrist demographics and statistics in the U.S.* Retrieved from https://www.zippia.com/psychiatrist-jobs/demographics.

Zippia. (2022, April 18). *Psychologist demographics and statistics in the U.S.* Retrieved from https://www.zippia.com/psychiatrist-jobs/demographics.

Zippia. (2022, April 18). *Social worker demographics and statistics in the U.S.* Retrieved from https://www.zippia.com/social-worker-jobs/demographics.

Zouraraki, C., Kyriklaki, A., Economou, E., & Giakoumaki, S. G. (2023). The moderating role of early traumatic experiences on the association of schizotypal traits with visual perception. *Scandinavian Journal of Psychology, 64*(1), 10–20.

Zsedel, K. (2019). The "price" of creativity? Predictive and protective factors in the suicide of Sylvia Plath [in Hungarian]. *Psychiatria Hungarica, 34*(2), 172–182.

Zubair, U. (2021). Prevalence and correlates of depression among trans-genders of Pakistan. *European Psychiatry, 64*(51), S597–S598.

Zuccon, M., Topino, E., Musetti, A., & Gori, A. (2023). Psychodynamic therapies for the treatment of substance addictions: A PRISMA meta-analysis. *Journal of Personalized Medicine, 13*(10), 1469.

Zürcher, S. J., Zürcher, M., Burkhalter, M., & Richter, D. (2023). Job retention and reintegration in people with mental health problems: A descriptive evaluation of supported employment routine programs. *Administration and Policy in Mental Health, 50*(1), 128–136.

Credits

Chapter 2

Page 52: Wolberg, L. R. (1967). *The technique of psychotherapy.* WB Saunders Co. Elsevier Health Science Books. (p. 662). **Page 63:** Schneider, K. J. (2007). The experiential liberation strategy of the existential-integrative model of therapy. *Journal of Contemporary Psychotherapy,* 37(1), 33–39. Copyright © 2007 Springer Nature. Reproduced with permission of SNCSC. **Page 65:** Excerpt from "Does Labeling Mental Illness Do More Harm Than Good?" by Jeannette Cooperman, published April 6, 2022, in *The Common Reader,* Washington University's journal of the essay. Used with permission. https://commonreader.wustl.edu/does-labeling-mental-illness-do-more-harm-than-good/ **Page 69:** Sommers-Flanagan, J., & Sommers-Flanagan, R. (2018). *Counseling and psychotherapy theories in context and practice: Skills, strategies, and techniques* (3rd ed.). Copyright © 2018 John Wiley & Sons, Inc. Reproduced with permission of the Licensor through PLSclear. **Page 73**: Pachankis, J. E., Soulliard, Z. A., Morris, F., & van Dyk, I. S., Excerpt from "A model for adapting evidence-based interventions to be LGBQ-affirmative: Putting minority stress principles and case conceptualization into clinical research and practice," *Cognitive and Behavioral Practice,* 30(1), 1–17. © 2023 Association for Behavioral and Cognitive therapist behaviors Therapies. Published by Elsevier Ltd; permissions conveyed through Copyright Clearance Center, Inc. **Page 76:** Excerpt from "Does Labeling Mental Illness Do More Harm Than Good?" by Jeannette Cooperman, published April 6, 2022, in *The Common Reader,* Washington University's journal of the essay. Used with permission. https://commonreader.wustl.edu/does-labeling-mental-illness-do-more-harm-than-good/

Chapter 4

Page 124: Hogan, R. A. (1968). The implosive technique. *Behaviour Research and Therapy,* 6, 423–31. Copyright © 1968. Republished with permission of Elsevier Science and Technology Journals; permission conveyed through Copyright Clearance Center, Inc. **Pages 135–136:** AIPC (Australian Institute of Professional Counsellors). (2013, June 7). Case study: Obsessive-compulsive disorder. Retrieved from https://www.aipc.net.au/articles/case-study-obsessive-compulsive-disorder. Copyright © Mental Health Academy. Used by permission. **Page 140:** From *Reflections on Body Dysmorphic Disorder: Stories of Courage, Determination and Hope,* edited by Nicole Schnackenberg and Sergio Petro. Copyright © 2016 by The Body Dysmorphic Disorder Foundation. Reprinted by permission.

Chapter 5

Page 154: Lee, S. (2017, June 14). 20 years after being raped, I still struggle with PTSD. *Wear Your Voice.* Retrieved from https://wearyourvoicemag.com/20-years-raped-still-struggle-ptsd/. Copyright © 2017. Reprinted with permission.

Chapter 6

Page 181: Danquah, M. N.-A. (1998). From WILLOW WEEP FOR ME: A BLACK WOMAN'S JOURNEY THROUGH DEPRESSION by Meri Nana-Ama Danquah. Copyright © 1998 by Meri Nana-Ama Danquah. Used by permission of W. W. Norton & Company, Inc. Copyright Meri Nana-Ama Danquah and reprinted by permission of McKinnon Literary. All rights reserved. **Page 195:** Lorand, S. (1937). Dynamics and therapy of depressive states. *The Psychoanalytic Review,* 24, 337–349. Copyright © 1937 Guilford Press. Used with permission of Guilford Publications; permission conveyed through Copyright Clearance Center, Inc. **Page 201:** Leahy, R. L. (2017). *Cognitive therapy techniques: A practitioner's guide* (2nd ed.). Copyright © 2017 Guilford Press. Republished with permission of Guilford Publications; permission conveyed through Copyright Clearance Center, Inc. **Page 210:** Anonymous. (2006, September 1). On madness: a personal account of rapid cycling bipolar disorder. *British Journal of General Practice,* 56(530), 726–728. Reprinted by permission of the Royal College of General Practitioners.

Chapter 8

Page 251: Savino, A. C., & Fordtran, J. S. (2006, July). Factitious disease: Clinical lessons from case studies at Baylor University Medical Center. Baylor University Medical Center Proceedings, 19(3). Copyright © 2006 Baylor University Medical Center. Reprinted by permission. **Page 269:** Crandall, C. S., Preisler, J. J., & Aussprung, J. (1992). Measuring life event stress in the lives of college students: The Undergraduate Stress Questionnaire (USQ). *Journal of Behavioral Medicine,* 15(6), 627–662. Copyright © 1992 Springer Nature B V. Used with permission of Springer Nature B V; permission conveyed through Copyright Clearance Center, Inc.

Chapter 9

Page: 279: Raviv, S. (2010). Being Ana: A memoir of anorexia nervosa. iUniverse. Reprinted by permission. **Pages 283, 285:** Hall, L., with Cohn, L. (1980). "Eat without fear." Gürze. Reprinted with permission.

Chapter 11

Page 376: Coskun, M., & Ozturk, M. (2013). Sexual Fetishism in Adolescence: Report of Two Cases. *Düsünen Adam: The Journal of Psychiatry and Neurological Sciences,* 26(2), 199–205. Copyright © 2013. Reprinted by permission. **Pages 381–382:** Janus, S. S., & Janus, C. L. (1993). *The Janus report on sexual behavior.* Wiley. Reprinted with permission of the Janus estate.

Chapter 12

Page 394: Anonymous. (1996). Used with permission of Oxford University Press, from First person account: Social, economic, and medical effects of schizophrenia, *Schizophrenia Bulletin,* 22(1), 183–85, 1996; permission conveyed through Copyright Clearance Center, Inc. **Page 409:** Whitaker, R. "Anecdotal Thoughts" from ANATOMY OF AN EPIDEMIC: MAGIC BULLETS, PSYCHIATRIC DRUGS, AND THE ASTONISHING RISE OF MENTAL ILLNESS IN AMERICA by Robert Whitaker, copyright © 2010 by Robert Whitaker. Used by permission of Crown Books, an imprint of Random House, a division of Penguin Random House LLC. All rights reserved.

Chapter 13

Pages 438–439: Hare, R. D. (1993). *Without conscience: The disturbing world of the psychopaths among us.* Pocket Books. Copyright © 1993 by Robert D. Hare, PhD. Republished with the permission of Guilford Publications; permission conveyed through Copyright Clearance Center, Inc. **Page 443:** Vaknin, S. (2015). *Malignant self-love: Narcissism revisited.* Narcissus Publications. Copyright © 1999–2013 by Lidija Rangelovska. Reprinted by permission.

Chapter 14

Pages 471–472, 484, 495–496: Kearney, C. A. (2016). *Casebook in child behavior disorders* (6th ed.). Copyright © 2017, 2013 Cengage Learning, Inc. Reproduced by permission. www.cengage.com/permissions.

Chapter 15

Pages 528–529: Shenk, D. (2001). Excerpt(s) from THE FORGETTING: ALZHEIMER'S: PORTRAIT OF AN EPIDEMIC; Copyright © 2001, 2002 by David Shenk. Used by permission of Doubleday, an imprint of the Knopf Doubleday Publishing Group, a division of Penguin Random House LLC. All rights reserved.

Chapter 16

Pages 548–549: Coleman, L. (1984). *The reign of error: Psychiatry, authority, and law.* Beacon Press. Copyright © 1984 by Lee Coleman. Used by permission.

Name Index

Subject Index

Note: Page numbers followed by f and t indicate figures and tables, respectively